THE ENGLISH
HISTORICAL REVIEW

EDITED BY

REGINALD L. POOLE, M.A., LL.D.

KEEPER OF THE ARCHIVES OF THE UNIVERSITY OF OXFORD
AND FELLOW OF MAGDALEN COLLEGE AND OF THE BRITISH ACADEMY

VOLUME XXVII.

1912

LONGMANS, GREEN AND CO.
39 PATERNOSTER ROW, LONDON
NEW YORK, BOMBAY AND CALCUTTA
1912

DA
20
.E58

CONTENTS OF VOL. XXVII.

	PAGE
THE RESTORATION OF THE CROSS AT JERUSALEM. By *Norman H. Baynes*	287
THE TRIBAL HIDAGE. By *J. Brownbill*	625
THE DANES AT THORNEY ISLAND IN 893. By *Professor F. M. Stenton*	512
BURGUNDIAN NOTES. II. CISALPINUS AND CONSTANTINUS. By *Reginald L. Poole, LL.D.*	299
YORKSHIRE SURVEYS AND OTHER ELEVENTH-CENTURY DOCUMENTS IN THE YORK GOSPELS. By *W. H. Stevenson*	1
WILLIAM THE CONQUEROR'S MARCH TO LONDON IN 1066. By *G. J. Turner*	209
THE MAKING OF THE NEW FOREST. By the *Hon. F. H. Baring*	513
A REPORT ON THE PENENDEN TRIAL. By *Dr. W. Levison*	717
THE EXETER DOMESDAY. By the *Hon. F. H. Baring*	309
THE FOREST LAWS AND THE DEATH OF WILLIAM RUFUS. By the late *F. H. M. Parker*	26
THE REIGNING PRINCES OF GALILEE. By *H. Pirie-Gordon*	445
EZELO'S LIFE OF HUGH OF CLUNY. By *Miss L. M. Smith*	96
THE ABACUS AND THE KING'S CURIA. By *Professor C. H. Haskins*	101
NORMANDY UNDER GEOFFREY PLANTAGENET. By *Professor Haskins*	417
KING PHILIP AUGUSTUS AND THE ARCHBISHOP OF ROUEN. By *Professor Powicke*	106
THE BATTLE OF SANDWICH AND EUSTACE THE MONK. By *Henry Lewin Cannon*	649
STUDIES IN MAGNA CARTA. I. WAYNAGIUM AND CONTENEMENTUM. By *Professor James Tait*	720
CHANCELLOR AND KEEPER OF THE SEAL UNDER HENRY III. By *Miss L. B. Dibben*	39
A PAPAL VISITATION OF BURY ST. EDMUNDS AND WESTMINSTER IN 1234. By *Miss Rose Graham*	728
HENRY SYMEONIS. By *Reginald L. Poole, LL.D.*	515
THE MISSING PART OF ROGER BACON'S 'OPUS TERTIUM'. By *A. G. Little*	318

CONTENTS OF THE TWENTY-SEVENTH VOLUME

	PAGE
THE POWERS OF JUSTICES OF THE PEACE. By C. G. Crump and C. Johnson	226
THE FIRST VERSION OF HARDYNG'S CHRONICLE. By C. L. Kingsford	462, 740
SIR JOHN FORTESCUE IN FEBRUARY 1461. By *Miss Cora L. Scofield*	321
GERMAN OPINION OF THE DIVORCE OF HENRY VIII. By *Preserved Smith*	671
COPYHOLD TENURE AT FELSTED, ESSEX. By the *Rev. Andrew Clark, LL.D.*	517
AN ENGLISH SETTLEMENT IN MADAGASCAR IN 1645-6. By *W. Foster*	239
CLARENDON AND THE PRIVY COUNCIL, 1660-7. By *E. I. Carlyle*	251
INNER AND OUTER CABINET AND PRIVY COUNCIL, 1679-1783. By *H. W. V. Temperley*	682
THE TREATY OF CHARLOTTENBURG. By *J. F. Chance*	52
NORTHERN AFFAIRS IN 1724. By *J. F. Chance*	483
STRUENSEE AND THE FALL OF BERNSTORFF. By *W. F. Reddaway*	274
BURKE, WINDHAM, AND PITT. By *J. Holland Rose, Litt.D.* Part I	700
DOCUMENTS RELATING TO THE RUPTURE WITH FRANCE IN 1793. By *J. Holland Rose, Litt.D.*	117, 324
THE ANGLO-FRENCH PEACE NEGOTIATIONS OF 1806. By *Colonel E. M. Lloyd, R.E.*	753
CASTLEREAGH AND THE SPANISH COLONIES, 1815-18. By *C. K. Webster*	78
FRANCE AND THE BALEARIC ISLANDS IN 1840. By *Charles N. Scott*	330
THE NAMES OF ZERMATT. By the *Rev. W. A. B. Coolidge, Ph.D.*	522
REVIEWS OF BOOKS	124, 336, 531, 755
SHORT NOTICES	181, 390, 591, 801
INDEX	834

The English Historical Review

NO. CV.—JANUARY 1912

Yorkshire Surveys and other Eleventh-Century Documents in the York Gospels.

IN 1859 the late Canon Raine, of York—a meritorious and learned antiquary—first drew from its obscurity a valuable manuscript belonging to the dean and chapter of York. In language that cannot be accused of erring on the side of enthusiasm he described it as

a manuscript of the Gospels in the custody of the Chapter clerk. The book itself is written in a fine bold hand, circa 900, and is of the quarto size. Prefixed is the canon, on eight leaves, arranged in compartments in which a good deal of architectural skill is manifested. At the end of the volume are several charters and Saxon documents, which have been hitherto unnoticed, including a list of the relics belonging to the Minster, and some very early deeds connected with land and its measures. At the beginning, on the fly-leaves, are several forms of oaths to be administered to the canons and other officers of the church. In fact, I should say that this is the very copy of the Evangelists upon which every new officer of the church took his oath from the year 900 downwards.[1]

The reference to the 'very early deeds connected with land and its measures' attracted my attention many years ago, but as it is not stated that these deeds were older than the Norman Conquest, I did not follow up the trail. Recently a young German scholar, Otto Homburger, of Karlsruhe, was good enough to send me photographs of part of the manuscript, which he examined

---

[1] *The Fabric Rolls of York Minster*, p. 142, Surtees Society, vol. xxxv, 1859. It is to all appearances the volume described in a fifteenth-century inventory as 'unus textus ornatus cum argento, non bene deaurato, super quem iuramenta decani et aliarum dignitatum ac canonicorum in principio inseruntur' (Raine, *Memorials of York*, Rolls Series, iii. 387). In the passage quoted in the text Raine has ascribed too early a date to the manuscript.

VOL. XXVII.—NO. CV.   * All rights reserved.   B

in connexion with his studies of Old English palaeography and illuminations of the tenth and eleventh centuries, a subject upon which he is working with an energy and enthusiasm worthy of his master, the great Traube. From these photographs I was pleased to find that the deeds referred to by Raine are in early eleventh-century hands, and that they are of very great interest for the history of land-owning in the Danish districts of England, a subject that lies shrouded in almost complete darkness outside the range of the glimmering and uncertain light reflected upon it by the Domesday Survey. Upon my recognizing the importance of these documents, Mr. Homburger consented in the most generous way to my publishing what is really his discovery.[2]

I have since had an opportunity, thanks to the kindness of the chapter clerk (Dr. J. Ramsay), of inspecting this manuscript at York. It is a parchment volume bound in smooth calf some two centuries or so ago, when the leaves appear to have been cut down in the execrable manner of the old binders, but the binder's knife has not impinged upon the text. The leaves at present measure about 10¾ by 8 inches. The Latin gospels, which form the greater part of the volume, are written in Caroline minuscules of an English character in a very early eleventh-century hand. The preface of St. Jerome is written in a different but contemporary hand of the same description, in which the Hiberno-Saxon form of r occurs. At the beginning are bound up several pages of parchment, upon which are written copies of deeds, charters, forms of oaths, and the like in hands of the thirteenth to the fifteenth century. In the same way there are bound up at the end of the volume several pages of parchment containing the eleventh-century entries, followed on a fresh page by a contemporary copy of the proceedings in *Quo Warranto* concerning the archbishop's privileges in the great eyre of William Herle in 1330.[3] This is followed by a list of the relics in St. Peter's Minster, York, written about the middle of the thirteenth century.[4]

The publication of the Old English documents in this volume has proceeded slowly. Raine commenced it in 1859 by printing the Sherburn inventory (No. IV, below). Bishop Stubbs gave a translation of the charter of Cnut (No. III) in his *Select Charters*, 1870, and in 1873[5] printed the text and translation under the title 'A Charter of Canute from the York Gospels. In usum amicorum. W. S.,' without date, comment, or preface. In 1875

---

[2] Since writing this I find that Professor Napier copied the whole of the documents in question some thirty years ago.

[3] *Placita de Quo Warranto*, Record Commission, 1818, ii. 197, 221.

[4] Printed by Raine, *Fabric Rolls*, p. 150 *seqq.*

[5] According to W. A. Shaw, *Bibliography of the Historical Works of Dr. Creighton, Dr. Stubbs, Dr. S. R. Gardiner, and the late Lord Acton*, p. 19 (1903).

Dean Henderson published the Bidding Prayer (No. V). The list of Ælfric's 'festermen' (No. VI) was published by the eccentric George Stephens in 1881, from a photograph sent to him by Canon Simmons. The three homilies (No. II) were edited by Professor Napier in 1883.

With the exception of Cnut's charter and the homilies the printed texts of these documents are either inaccurate or inaccessible, and I therefore give a new text based directly upon the manuscript, as these texts have an important bearing upon the question of date of the whole of the entries in Old English hands. The contents occur in the following order :

I

(fo. 149 verso, 150.) Three documents, to which I have given the name of surveys, of the archbishop's estates at Sherburn-in-Elmet, Otley, and Ripon, all in Yorkshire. The texts of these surveys form the staple of this article, and will be given below. It is important to notice that they commence upon the verso of the last leaf of the gospel of St. John, a position that precludes any suggestion that these documents have been brought into connexion with the gospel by later binding or by any other accident.

II

(fo. 150 recto and verso.) Three homilies of Lupus, that is Wulfstan, archbishop of York, 1003–23. These so-called homilies, which have been edited by Professor Napier,[6] are mainly concerned with the exposition of ecclesiastical and civil laws, and it is doubtful whether they are the works of Wulfstan, although these copies are almost contemporary with him.

III

(fo. 152 recto and verso.) Cnut's charter of liberties, addressed to his archbishops, bishops, Earl Thorcyl, and all his people, clerical and lay, in England. This mention of Thorkel, the gigantic Norwegian, 'the tallest of all men,'[7] and a famous figure in history and saga, fixes the date as earlier than 1021, when he was exiled from England, and as later than Cnut's return from Denmark in 1020.[8] It has been published from Stubbs's privately printed text by Pauli in 1874,[9] and is now accessible in Liebermann's text, by whom also it is assigned to 1020.[10] No other

[6] Wulfstan, *Sammlung der ihm zugeschriebenen Homilien*, nos. 59, 60, 61 (pp. 307–11), Berlin, 1883.
[7] Olafs Saga Tryggvasonar, c. 133 (*Flateyjarbók*, i. 168).
[8] Stubbs, *Select Charters*, 8th edition, p. 75.
[9] *Forschungen zur deutschen Geschichte*, xiv. 390.
[10] *Die Gesetze der Angelsachsen*, i. 273, Berlin, 1898–1903.

text of this charter is known, and its preservation in the York Gospels would be alone sufficient to confer upon that manuscript a very high rank in English historical sources. Historically and diplomatically it is the most important document contained in the manuscript. It is, in substance and in form, the direct lineal ancestor of the Anglo-Norman charters of liberties and, in consequence, of Magna Charta. For in form these documents are developments of the Anglo-Norman writ-charter, and that in its turn is, as I maintained fifteen years ago,[11] merely the Anglo-Saxon writ translated into Latin. At that time I was able only

[11] *Ante*, xi. 735. The opinion of Giry, *Manuel de Diplomatique*, p. 795, there cited, that the charters of William the Conqueror do not differ from those of the dukes of Normandy except by the addition of the title *Rex Anglorum*, is an illustration of the pitfalls that beset the path of the compiler of manuals, however learned he may be. This statement, which is probably an extension of that of the authors of the *Nouveau Traité de Diplomatique*, v. 760, Paris, 1762, overlooks the most important difference between the two, the use in the Anglo-Norman charters of the pendent double-faced great seal instead of the seal *plaqué*, a single-faced seal affixed to the surface of the document, that was characteristic of French royal charters until the time of Louis VI (1008–1137), when the pendent great seal was, according to Giry himself (p. 640), introduced into the French chancery. In the imperial chancery it did not come into use until a much later time (Bresslau, *Handbuch der Urkundenlehre*, i. 942). Thus Edward the Confessor's use of the double-faced seal was not derived from the Normans, the usual facile conclusion based upon the ascription to the Normans of a more highly organized administration than was known in England (as to which the wise remarks of Stubbs, *Constitutional History*, fifth edition, i. 235, may be recommended). It is noteworthy in this connexion that the double-faced seal, which was in use in Lower Italy from the end of the ninth century, disappeared under the Norman domination (Bresslau, i. 942). The charters of the dukes of Normandy before the conquest of England of which we have record are few in number, and are mostly derived from later copies. They are, like those of the other great feudatories, imitations of the Capetian royal charters, and are validated by crosses, frequently autograph (*Nouveau Traité*, v. 760; iv. 227; Giry, p. 795). They omit the reference to the seal, which was *plaqué* in the royal charters. If the seal was used on a Norman charter it should accordingly appear in this shape, not as a pendent double seal. An original charter of Robert Curthose in 1106, in the possession of the town of Bayeux, which is drawn up on continental Norman lines, has the seal so fixed (*Bibliothèque de l'École des Chartes*, xlviii. 176[1887]). It was not until the eleventh century that the use of seals began to spread from the royal chancery to the great feudatories, although Arnulf I, count of Flanders, the grandson of King Alfred, used one in the early part of the preceding century (*Nouveau Traité*, iv. 219 seqq., 423; Giry, p. 637). The original charter of Duke Richard II of Normandy, *ante* 1024, of which a facsimile is given in the *Musée des Archives départementales*, Paris, 1878, plate 15, no. 21, has no seal or seal-clause. But the authors of the *Nouveau Traité*, v. 226, give an engraving of a seal of this duke affixed to a charter made by him to Dudo of St. Quintin, the first Norman historian. They and Giry, 641, accept the authenticity of this charter (which is also printed in *Gallia Christiana*, xi, instrum. col. 284), about which one would like to know more. The seal seems to have been suspended by two cords, which is suspicious at so early a date. This appears to be the only seal, whether genuine or not, of a Norman duke prior to 1066 of which we have any notice in modern times. In 1304 Philip V recited in a *Vidimus* a *carta non sigillata* of Duke Robert I, dated 1035, which contained, despite this description, the royal clause *confirmamus et annuli nostri impressione roboramus* (*Gallia Christiana*, xi, instrum. col. 327). In 1035 William is said in a later document to confirm a grant by his seal (*ibid*. col. 229 = Round, *Calendar of Documents preserved in France*, p. 341, where this clause does not appear).

to cite an early copy of a writ of Cnut's investing a bishop with the rights of his see, a form of writ that continued in use, sometimes in Old English with a Latin version, but generally in Latin only, until the time of John. The form of the present writ-charter is an interesting anticipation of what became the form of the compellation of the royal charter when, at the end of the twelfth century, the writ was differentiated into charters, letters patent, letters close, and the ordinary judicial writs. The Anglo-Saxon writ was in its origin a letter from the king to a shire-moot, and this characteristic clung closely to the Anglo-Norman writ-charter of the twelfth century. Gradually it ousted entirely the formal charter or diploma, of which we can still trace some use in Norman times. The writ or epistolary charter had the great merit of adaptability to all purposes, and thus its great progeny in the later middle ages is intelligible. It is clearly older than Cnut's time, for we hear of Alfred delivering his 'hondseten' as testimony of his confirmation of a private grant, and this document is described as an 'insegel' or seal.[12] In a contemporary record of 990-4 King Æthelred sends his 'insegel' to a shire-moot, greeting all the witan there assembled.[13] In 995-1005 the same king sends his 'gewrit and his insegel' to the archbishop and thanes in Kent, bidding them to bring to agreement the parties in a suit.[14] This has been already adduced by Dugdale as a proof of the antiquity of the judicial writ.[15] In manuscript E of the Chronicle under 1048 ' gewrit and insegel ' is the description applied to the king's writ of investiture of a bishop.[16] As this must imply a seal, since we have several original writs with pendent great seal of Edward the Confessor, and ' breve et sigillum ' is a term frequently used in Domesday to describe the writs of Edward and William in connexion with land transfers, we are driven to conclude that the earlier ' gewrit and insegel '

---

[12] *Cart. Saxonicum*, ii. 237; Ordnance Survey *Facsimiles of Anglo-Saxon Charters*, i, plate 13. It is a letter of a contemporary of King Alfred to the king (Edward the Elder), and is in a curious rough hand of the tenth century, hardly, I think, from the linguistic evidence that of a contemporary of Alfred's.

[13] *Codex Diplomaticus*, iii. 292; Thorpe, *Diplomatarium Anglicum*, 288; British Museum *Facsimiles of Ancient Charters*, iii, plate 37. Hickes, *Dissertatio Epistolaris*, p. 5, n. u, proposed to render *insegel* (which is derived from *sigillum*) by monogram, on the analogy of the imperial signatures. This, it need hardly be said, is quite inadmissible, for we could hardly have failed to have a record of such monograms had they been used by the Anglo-Saxon kings.

[14] *Codex Diplomaticus*, iv. 266; Thorpe, *Diplomatarium Anglicum*, 302. This is derived from the trustworthy Textus Roffensis.

[15] *Origines Iuridiciales*, 1671, 34.

[16] The writ of Æthelred to the shire-moot of Hampshire, derived from the twelfth-century Codex Wintoniensis, a cartulary containing numerous forgeries, is the earliest writ of which we have the text (*Cod. Diplom.* iii. 293). Even if the recapitulation of the estates is an addition due to the copyist of the charter, the text is still open to suspicion as it relates to the reduction of hidage of a hundred hides to one, a claim of the monks that necessitated a long series of twelfth-century forgeries.

also bore a seal. No example, however, of the use of a seal by the kings before Edward the Confessor is known.[17] But the use of seals by the Anglo-Saxons is proved by the existence of the matrices of several seals.[18] Among these is one of Cenwulf,

[17] Thomas Elmham, writing in the early years of the fifteenth century, states that he had met with no seals of English kings in the archives of St. Augustine's, Canterbury, earlier than the Norman Conquest, with the exception of a *carta* of Cnut, 'qui fuit alienigena et conquestor' (*Historia Mon. S. Augustini*, p. 118, Rolls Series). Like Hickes (*Praefatio*, p. ix), I cannot accept this testimony as conclusive, although on different grounds to his. Walter Mapes's story of Earl Godwine's breaking Cnut's seal and substituting another message, a remarkable parallel to Saxo's story of Hamlet, need not detain us (*De Nugis Curialium*, p. 208, Camden Society). It is a very remarkable circumstance that the Saga of St. Olaf ascribes to Cnut a seal (*Flateyjarbók*, c. 191, ii. 253). In the older form of this saga in Fagrskinna, c. 113, p. 91 (cf. *Flateyjarbók*, c. 210, ii. 278), there is a story that Queen Emma got hold of Cnut's seal and caused a letter to be sealed with it ordering the Danes to make her son Harthacnut king of Denmark. We are told how Jarl Ulf (the brother-in-law of Earl Godwin) caused this letter, which was addressed, in the manner of the Old English writ, to all the greatest chiefs of Denmark ('á þessu bréfi váru nefndir allir hinir stoerstu hǫfðingjar í Danmǫrku'), to be read by his chaplain before the 'thing' at Viborg. The Crowland story of a confirmation under King Edgar's seal of a grant to that abbey (Ordericus Vitalis, iv. 16, ed. Le Prevost, ii. 282) must be rejected. The text of the charter of this king that has come down to us, an obvious and late forgery (*Cart. Sax.* iii. 437), does not agree with Orderic's description. See Liebermann, *Ueber Ostenglische Geschichtsquellen*, Berlin, 1892, p. 26 (*Neues Archiv*, xviii. 250). The Ramsey historians state that seals were not in use in the time of King Edgar (*Chronicon Abbatiae Ramesiensis*, p. 65). Hickes, *Dissertatio Epistolaris*, 71, describes the great Pershore charter of Edgar, dated 972 (British Museum *Facsimiles*, iii, pl. 30; *Cart. Sax.* iii. 583), as having attached to it in his time a letter of Godfrey, archdeacon of Worcester, 1148–67, to the pope describing it as being validated by the seals of King Edgar, Dunstan, and Ealdorman Ælfhere. He doubts the identity of the charter with that described by Godfrey, although it was accepted by Selden, Stillingfleet, and, I may add, Dugdale, *Origines Iuridiciales*, 33, because it has five (really six) horizontal seal slits at the bottom. He thinks these were added by the monks to deceive the Normans, a suggestion that excited the rage of the authors of the *Nouveau Traité*, iv. 202. This charter is the oldest example of the continental *pancharta*, in which all the estates of a monastery were confirmed, and is alien to Old English diplomatics. The hand appears to me to be about the middle of the eleventh century. Doubt is cast upon the charter by the fact that it belongs to a suspicious group of charters drawn up in the same words (*Cart. Sax.* iii. 253, 257, 450, 593—there were two exemplars of this at Worcester in 1643, Wanley, *Catalogus*, in Hickes, *Thesaurus*, iii. 299; *Cod. Dipl.* iii. 264; Brit. Museum *Facsimiles*, iii, pl. 36, eleventh century).

[18] Those of Bishop Ethilwald of Dunwich, 830–70, now in the British Museum (*Archaeologia*, xx. 479); Godwin minister with that of Godgyth monacha on the back (*Proceedings of the Society of Antiquaries*, series ii, vol. viii. 468); Eadgyth, Regalis Adelpha (St. Edith of Wilton, daughter of King Edgar), which was used as the seal of Wilton priory as late as the fourteenth century (*Archaeologia*, xviii. 40). Similarly the monks of Durham used a seal that is said to be a tenth-century production (*ibid.* xxiv. 360). The seal of Ælfric, identified by Sir Francis Palgrave with the Ealdorman of Mercia of that name, 983–1007, now in the British Museum, bears a diademed figure with a sword, showing a remarkable approximation to the 'seal of majesty', the great seal of later times (*ibid.* xxiv. 359). The small leaden bulla of Archdeacon Boniface in the Whitby Museum, ascribed by Canon Raine to St. Wilfrid's teacher (*Historians of York*, i. 8, n. 3), is no doubt Italian and not English. As the seals of Offa and Edgar in the St. Denis muniments still figure as genuine in the new edition of the *Encyclopaedia Britannica*, despite my exposure of the spurious nature of the charters to which they are attached (*ante*, vi. 736 *seqq.*), I may state

king of Mercia 796–819, which it is interesting to note, in view of the development of the double-seal from the bulla, is a leaden bulla.[19] The writs of Edward the Confessor have pendent seals affixed to a tongue of the parchment, just as the early Anglo-Norman seals were before cords were introduced. This tongue was very liable to tear away from the body of the deed owing to the weight of the seal, and this may account for the absence of any examples of the seals earlier than Edward the Confessor. In this connexion I may mention that a number of Anglo-Saxon charters, both writs and diplomas, have, in the facsimiles, irregular corners at the edge of the left side at the foot of the document strongly resembling Anglo-Norman writ-charters from which the seals have become detached.

This method of fixing the seal, called by the French 'sceau pendant sur simple queue', which is illustrated by Giry, *Manuel de Diplomatique*, p. 628, fig. 29, is difficult to describe succinctly. It consisted in making a cut half an inch, more or less, from the bottom of the parchment running parallel with the bottom from the righthand side of the parchment to within an inch or two of the left-hand side. This had the effect of producing a tongue or tag of parchment attached to the body of the charter by the unsevered portion where the cut had stopped short. When the heavy seal was attached to the loose end of this tongue, the weight of the seal was very liable to tear off the tongue. The course of the tear varied according to the direction of the pressure applied to produce it. In some instances the tear is simply a horizontal continuation of the cut: in these cases there is hardly anything left to suggest that the document once had a seal attached to it. This may be most easily realized by examining the original writs of Edward the Confessor in the British Museum *Facsimiles of Ancient Charters*, iv, plates 29, 40, 41. Sometimes the tear pursued an upward course, removing the left corner of the parchment, as may be seen in the two facsimiles of charters of Henry I given by Mr. Salter in this *Review*, xxvi. 488. If the tear proceeded downwards from the end of the cut to the bottom of the parchment, a sort of step of parchment was left projecting at the left-hand side of the bottom of the charter. This again may be clearly seen in the writs of Edward the

that photographs of these charters, presented to me some years ago by Professor A. W. Kirkaldy, amply prove that they are forgeries by continental monks. They are in what is evidently a feigned hand, in which the Old English characters are written in a way unknown to native scribes, with exaggerated features. The Offa charter could not have been written in his time either in England or on the continent. The Frankish form of *g* is used in Edgar's charter, the insular in that of Offa. Both use the continental *d*, with the upright descending below the line, instead of the curved insular form. Both betray late eleventh- or early twelfth-century features in the writing. They were accepted as genuine by the somewhat credulous authors of the *Nouveau Traité*, iv. 204. The interesting seal of Thor Longus at Durham, attached to a letter to Edgar, king of Scotland (Lawrie, *Early Scottish Charters*, 1905, no. 33), and engraved in the *Archaeological Journal*, xiv. 48, is probably to be ascribed to English and not Norman usage.

[19] *Archaeologia*, xxxii. 449. It has an inscription on the obverse and reverse. It was found in Italy, and was therefore probably attached to a letter.

Confessor in the British Museum *Facsimiles*, iv, plates 36, 39 ; Ordnance Survey *Facsimiles of Anglo-Saxon Charters*, ii, Westminster, plates 10, 11. Turning to earlier documents, an undoubted seal-tag is still adhering to the charter of Ealhhere, 860–6, which is confirmed by King Æthelberht, the brother of King Alfred,[20] who must be the ' Ælfred, filius regis ', who witnesses it. The charter is in genuine early formulas, and linguistically may well be contemporary. But the palaeographical evidence is not so clear. Mr. Birch describes it as a twelfth-century copy, which seems to me far too late a date. The hand is a very curious one, and if it is a later copy, it reproduces very accurately early features, such as the insular compendium for *autem*, subscript *i*, and the abbreviation *Arhī epīc* for *archiepiscopi*, and it relates to such a small parcel of land that its reproduction or forgery in later times does not seem likely. In the same volume the letter referred to in note 12 above has what may be a ' step '. In the will of Æthelric, 997,[21] the ' step ' is clear, and a very small one is discernible in the will of Æthelstan Ætheling, 1015.[22] In the second volume of this collection, Westminster, plate 1, 693, *Cart. Sax.* i. 116, has a ' step ', but the charter is in a much later hand than its ostensible date, and the charter of Edgar, Westminster, plate 4, *Cart. Sax.* iii. 260, is not in a contemporary hand.[23] Three contemporary royal charters with ' steps ' may be seen in this same volume : Eadwig, 957, Winchester, plate 2, *Cart. Sax.* iii. 202 ; Edgar, 965, Ilchester, plate 1, *Cart. Sax.* iii. 418, and Cnut, 1024, Ilchester, plate 2, *Cod. Dipl.* iv. 29. In the third volume another charter of Cnut, 1035, has a ' step ', Ashburnham, plate 42. In addition to these there are many charters that have lower corners, sometimes the right one, torn off, and there are others with irregular edges at the bottom, but some of these may be due to accidents of another nature than that of the tearing away of the seal tongue, and some may be due to the irregular shape of the parchment used to write the text upon.

We may find confirmation of Cnut's use of the writ in the fact that the Anglo-Saxon writ obviously was the model upon which the early Scandinavian kings formed their charters,[24] since they are not likely to have borrowed the use from the Anglo-Norman kings. On the other hand it was probably from the latter that the use spread into the royal chancery of Scotland, although even here a direct borrowing from the English before the Norman Conquest is possible. The writ-charter is therefore, as Professor Bresslau has pointed out to me, the greatest English contribution to diplomatics. It occupies accordingly a position in reference to continental diplomatics curiously resembling that of English law in comparison with the continental developments from Roman law.

[20] Ordnance Survey *Facsimiles*, i, plate 9 ; *Cart. Sax.* ii. 128.
[21] Plate 16 ; *Cod. Dipl.* iii. 304.
[22] Plate 18 ; *Cod. Dipl.* iii. 361.　　　[23] *Crawford Charters*, p. 90.
[24] Cf. L. M. Larson, *The King's Household in England before the Norman Conquest*, Madison, Wisconsin (*Bulletin of the University of Wisconsin*), 1904, p. 198, where it is pointed out that the Norwegians used the word *insigli*, representing the Old English *insigel, insegel*, for the seal.

IV

(fo. 153 recto.) Inventory of church goods at Sherburn (in Elmet), co. York. Printed by Raine in 1859[25] and from his text by Mr. Birch.[26]

[27] Þis syndon þa cyrican madmas on Scirburnan : þæt synd twa Cristes bec, *ond* ii. rodan, *ond* i. ' aspiciens,'[28] *ond* i. ' ad te levavi,'[29] *ond* ii. pistol-bec, *ond* i. mæsse-boc, *ond* i. ymener, *ond* i. salter, *ond* i. calic, *ond* i. disc, *ond* twa mæsse-reaf, *ond* iii. mæsse-hakelan, *ond* ii. weoved sceatas, *ond* ii. overbrædels, *ond* iiii. handbellan, *ond* vi. hangende bellan.

V

(fo. 153 verso.) Bidding prayer, over which is written in a hand of the latter part of the sixteenth century 'Bidding of prayer', the older sense of bid meaning 'pray' having been forgotten at the Reformation. It has been twice printed.[30] This is the earliest known form of bidding prayer in English. The only clue to the date, apart from the palaeographical evidence, is afforded by the direction to pray for Thorferth's soul and, what has not yet been noticed, for that of Mælmære (genitive singular feminine), possibly his wife. Unfortunately the scanty tenth- and eleventh-century northern records have preserved no record of the Norse-named Thorferth or of Mælmære, who bears an Irish or Gaelic name.[31]

[25] *Fabric Rolls of York Minster*, p. 142.   [26] *Cart. Sax.* iii. 660.
[27] *Translation*: 'These are treasures of the church at Sherburn : that is to say two Christ's books, and two roods, and one "aspiciens", and one "ad te levavi", and two books of epistles, and one mass-book, and one hymnal, and one psalter, and one chalice, and one dish, and two mass-vestments, and three mass-copes (?), and two altar sheets (frontals ?), and two coverings (altarcloths ?), and four handbells, and six hanging bells.' Raine has mistranslated *weoved-sceatas* by 'woven sheets'; the first word is merely a late form of *weofod* 'altar'.
[28] *Aspiciens* appears in the Breviary as the response to the first lesson in the first nocturn of the first Sunday in Advent.
[29] In the inventory of the gifts of Bishop Leofric to Exeter there is entered 'i. ad te levavi', which Canon Warren explains 'as probably an antiphonary, so called from the opening words of the introit for the first Sunday in Advent' (*The Leofric Missal*, Oxford, 1883, p. xxii, n. 4).
[30] By Dean Henderson, *York Manual*, p. 220* (Surtees Society, vol. lxiii, 1875). and by Canon Simmons, *Lay Folks Mass Book*, Early English Text Society, 1879, pp. 62, 321.
[31] Maelmuire, masc. (literally, the 'shaved servant of Mary'), appears in the Orkneyinga Saga as Melmare (W. A. Craigie, 'Gaelic Words and Names in the Icelandic Sagas,' in *Zeitschrift für keltische Philologie*, i. 449). Melmor (from whom Melmerby, Cumberland, probably derives its name) is mentioned as a former tenant in that county in the curious Old English writ of Gospatric, dating apparently about the time of the Norman Conquest, of which a corrupt thirteenth-century facsimile was discovered some few years ago, printed in the *Scottish Historical Review*, i. 62–9, and with facsimile, by Liebermann, *Archiv für das Studium der neueren Sprachen*, Berlin, 1903, cxi. 275 *seqq.*, who assigns it to *c*. 1056–67. It is possible that the name may be masculine in the Bidding Prayer, and that it is uninflected, but it would be difficult to find a parallel for this. If masculine, the York benefactor might be identical with the Melmer of Gospatric's writ. But the name occurs in Irish also as a woman's name, e. g. Malmaire, daughter of Kenneth Macalpin, whose death is recorded in the Ulster Annals under 913.

It is a likely guess that she is the person of this name who is recorded in the village-name Melmerby, near Ripon, or Melmerby, in the parish of Coverham.

[32] Wutan we gebiddan God ealmihtine, heofena heah cyning, and Sancta Marian, and ealle Godes halgan þæt we moton Godes ælmihtiges willan gewyrcan þa hwil þe we on þyssan lænan life wunian þæt hy ús gehealdan and gescyldan wið ealra feonda costnunga, gesenelicra and ungesenelicra, Pater noster.

Wutan we gebiddan for urne papan on Róme, and for urne cyning, and for ⟨ur⟩ne arcebiscop and for ⟨ur⟩ne [33] ealdorman, and for ealle þa þe us gehealdað frið and freondscype on feower healfe into þysse halgan stowe, and for ealle þa ċe ús fore gebiddað binnan Angelcynne and butan Angelcynne, Pater noster.

Wutan we gebiddan for ure godsybbas and for ure cumæðran,[34] and for ure gildan and gildsweostra, and ealles þæs folces gebed þe þas halgan stowe mid ælmesan seceð, mid lihte and mid tigeðinge, and for ealle ða þe we æfre heora ælmessan befonde wæron, ær life and æfter life, Pater ⟨noster⟩.

Bidde we ⟨rest of line blank.⟩

⟨Blank line.⟩

For þor⟨f⟩erþes saule bidde we Pater noster, and for Mælmære saule, and for ealle þa saula þe fulluht under-fengan and on Crist gelyfdan fram Adames dæge to þisum dæge, Pater noster.

[32] *Translation*: 'Let us pray God Almighty, the high king of heaven, and Saint Mary, and all God's saints that we may work God's will so long as we dwell in this transitory life, that he may preserve and protect us from all the temptations of enemies, seen and unseen, Pater Noster.

'Let us pray for our pope in Rome, and for our king, and for our archbishop, and for our ealdorman, and for all those who observe peace and friendship towards us on four sides (i.e. in all quarters) to this holy place, and for all those who pray for us within England and without England, Pater Noster.

'Let us pray for our sponsors (at christening) and for our godfathers, and for our gild-brethren and gild-sisters, and pray for all the folk who " seek " (pertain legally to) this holy place with alms, with light, and with tithing, and for all those from whom we at any time received alms during life and after life, Pater Noster.

'Pray we ⟨*line unfinished.*⟩

⟨*Blank line.*⟩

'For Thorferth's soul pray we Pater Noster, and for Mælmære's soul, and for all the souls that have received baptism and that have believed in Christ from the days of Adam to this day, Pater Noster.'

A hole in the parchment caused by damp has engulfed the *f* and part of the preceding *r* of þorferþes. The curious expression *ǣr life ond ǣfter life*, literally 'before life and after life,' occurs in the synonymous *ǣr dæge ond æfter* in an interesting agreement regarding land made during the episcopacy of Æthelstan, bishop of Hereford 1012-56 (*Cod. Dipl.* iv. 235, 17; British Museum *Facsimiles*, iv, pl. 14). Canon Simmons reads the impossible *micel mere* for *Mælmere* and translates it equally impossibly as 'many more (souls)'.

[33] It is curious that the scribe should have twice made the mistake of jumping from the *r* of *for* to that of *urne*, but there can, I think, be no doubt that this is what he did.

[34] The word *cumæðran*, a *vox nihili*, seems to be a mistake for *compeðran*, if, indeed, that word be not the one really written. The confusion has arisen from omitting the down stroke of the *p* and writing the *e* so that it touches the loop of the consonant, thus producing something very like the ligature *œ*.

VI

(*Ibid.*) List of Ælfric's 'festermen' (sureties). The first to refer to this list in print was Bishop Stubbs, whose knowledge of the manuscript was probably due to his friendship and long connexion with Canon Raine. He states that 'an unpublished list of the "festermen" of Archbishop Elfric exists on a fly-leaf of the York Gospels Book', and argues that priests were required in the same way as laymen to find security for the observance of the peace (the well-known institution of the 'frith-borh') on the evidence of this list and of the provision in the Northumbrian Priests' Law.[35] But there is some confusion here. The Northumbrian Priests' Law, in the passage quoted by him,[36] requires every priest to find twelve 'festermen' that he will rightfully observe the priests' law (*preost-lagu*); there is no reference to the lay 'frith-borh'. The provision seems to relate to the ordination of priests, and there is no statement that prelates upon their consecration were required to find 'festermen', On the strength of Stubbs's identification Stephens dated the list 1023,[37] the year of Ælfric's consecration as archbishop of York. There is, it may be noted, no statement that Ælfric was the archbishop, but it is natural to connect the list with him, for the most important landowners in Northumbria appear in it. Finally, we have the fact that the list is entered in a book containing important records of about the time of Archbishop Ælfric (1023–51). But the hand in which this list is written is considerably later than this date, and has the appearance of a twelfth-century one. If it belongs to the eleventh century at all, it must be assigned to a late period of that century. The philological evidence also points to some such date.[38] Palaeo-

---

[35] *Constitutional History of England*, 1st edition, i, p. 244 (1874).

[36] Section 2 (ed. Liebermann, by whom it is assigned to 1028–60), i, p. 380.

[37] *Blandinger udgivne af Universitets-Jubilæets Danske Samfund*, Copenhagen, 1881, pp. 60–6 (reprinted in the *Transactions of the Yorkshire Dialect Society*, pt. vii, pp. 44–9, 1906). Stephens's text is inaccurate, and suffers in addition from his extending the final mark of suspension as *er* in every case. The list has since been printed with a facsimile by Dr. Jón Stefansson in the *Saga Book of the Viking Club*, iv. 296–307, under the title of 'The Oldest known List of Scandinavian Names', which is based upon Stephens's ascription of the list to 1023. Many of the names in this list have been explained by Professor Erik Björkmann of Gothenburg, in *Nordische Personennamen in England in alt- und frühmittel-englischer Zeit*, Halle, 1910 (in Morsbach's *Studien zur englischen Philologie*, Heft 37).

[38] The confusion of *a* and *e*, due to the obscurity of pronunciation of the unstressed vowels, such as the genitives *Elfricas, Unbainas, Asbeornas, Sœfugelas*, and in the names *Ebastan, Forna, Rauan*, is common in late eleventh-century and twelfth-century deeds, and is possibly due to Norman influence. The representation of Old Norse *ei* by *ai*, as against the Old English *ege, eg, ei*, is also late enough to be due to Norman spellings. The constant use of *u* for Old English *f*, which occurs sporadically early in the eleventh century, eventually driving out *f* altogether by the Middle English period, is in marked contrast to the correct use of *f* in the other texts in this collection.

graphically it is noticeable for the invariable use of ꝥ to mark abbreviations by suspension. This mark is met with occasionally in English manuscripts written in Latin of about Ælfric's time, mostly with its original value of *m*. It is hardly ever found in manuscripts written in English, which are always very sparing in the use of abbreviations. In the early twelfth century this mark became all but universal. Some of the men named in the list can be identified with men living shortly after Ælfric's death. Merleswain, of whose identity there can be little doubt, figures in Northumbrian history in 1067 and 1069; Ligulf was the name of a great Northumbrian thane, who has claims to be considered as the ancestor of the great Neville family, and was murdered in 1080. Domesday Book mentions as tenants in Yorkshire in the time of Edward the Confessor, that is in 1066, several men bearing names that occur among the 'festermen', but here, from the absence of surnames or of other distinguishing features, it is not possible to be sure of the identity of the 'festermen' and the Domesday tenants.[39] It is difficult to understand why this list should have been copied at a later date. Yet I feel that it is a copy, partly modernized in orthography by the copyist, who seems to have been unable to read the whole of the text before him, and consequently leaves spaces blank and appends his mark of suspension to words that he could not fully read. We may perhaps guess that it was copied from an end-leaf at the beginning or end of the volume that had become torn or illegible, and that it was thus copied for no other reason than that the original list had been entered in this official Gospel Book. The list, which is of great interest, is subjoined.

[40] Ðis sindan þa festermen Elfricas: Ulfcetel, cyninges réue, *ond* Merleswuain, Wulstain, Ulf, Ligolf, Barað, Farðain greua, *ond* Ascetel,[41] Ósulf *ond* Wulfheh, Folcric *ond* Elfre⟨d⟩, Wegga *ond* Áldsceorl, Gamal pres⟨byter⟩, Grim *ond* Grimcetel, Asmund rosꝥ,[42] Grimcetel in Barnabi,[43] Godwina, Folcꝥ,[44] Berhðor, Bretecol *ond* Árðolf, *ond* Forna, Menning

[39] In the case of very common names, such as *Grimcetel, Gamal, Grim*, and the like, it is impossible to establish identity. But in the case of rare names, such as *Baraδ, Farδain, Wegga, Blih*, the identity with the Domesday tenants may be assumed.

[40] In the manuscript a point (representing, as usual in Old English manuscripts, a comma) occurs after every name before 'presbyter' and the like, so that it is difficult to decide in some cases whether a name is a nickname or the name of another man. The extension of several of the abbreviations is doubtful, and it is even uncertain whether or not they are nicknames, descriptions, official or local names. The error, corrected by erasure, of writing *G* for *C* seems to show that the list is copied from some older manuscript, and that the scribe was not well acquainted with the personal names thus wrongly copied. Capitals are not always used in the manuscript at the commencement of personal or local names, a fact that adds another element of uncertainty to the list.

[41] *ond Ascetel* interlined. [42] For Roscetel or a nickname of Asmund (?).

[43] Barnby, probably Barnby Dun, co. York.

[44] For Folcwine, Folchere, or some other compound name in Folc-, or a nickname of Godwine (?).

ond Wulger, Þór in Ca᛬ [45] ond Arcetel, Siuerð, Rauan,[46] Arn᛬,[47] Colbrand [48] ce᛬,[49] Blíh, Elfwine vel [50] Snel, Godwine, Lef᛬,[51] Eðastan, Ulf᛬, Elnod fre᛬,[52] Roscetel ond Edric, Grimcetel Háw᛬,[53] Ascetel, Grím in Cir᛬,[54] Cetel pres⟨byter⟩, Gunner, Alfcetel [55] in Há᛬,[56] Ioluarð in Burhtun, Ulfcetel pres⟨byter⟩, Alfcetel ond Asmund, Leofnoð in Broðortun, Þorcetel Unbainas⟨una⟩,[57] Ulf pres⟨byter⟩, Þirne beorn, ond Áilaf in Braiþatun,[58] Wúlfric ond Iustan, Rót in Hillum, . . orfana [59] ond Gr⟨im⟩cetel [60] hís mah, Raganald Asbeornnas suna, Órd ru [61]
. . . proh [62] in Bærnabi, Hálwærð Sæfugalasuna, ond Arþor,[63]
. . . ldolf [64] pres⟨byter⟩, Auðcetel pres⟨byter.⟩

This list cannot be cited to prove that the documents that precede it were written down prior to 1023 or even 1051. It is, however, to the episcopate of Ælfric that they can be referred with the greatest probability. A *terminus post quem* is supplied by Cnut's charter, which cannot be later than 1021. It is to be presumed that so important a document would be entered into this register within a few years of its promulgation. The issue of this charter of liberties after the wars and disturbances that preceded Cnut's accession to the throne might well induce the archbishop of York to overhaul his estates,

[45] No doubt Ca⟨wuda⟩ is meant.   [46] The second a of *Rauan* has faded.
[47] For Arngrim, Arnolf, or some other compound of Arn.
[48] Colbrand, the initial is altered by erasure from G.
[49] The meaning is doubtful.
[50] The usual abbreviation *uł* for *vel*. There is no point before it in manuscript, but there is one following, which suggests that it is not intended for the Latin conjunction.
[51] It is doubtful whether this represents Old Norse *Leifr*, as held by Björkmann, since there is a mark of abbreviation after the *f*.
[52] For a compound name in Freo- (?).
[53] For Há⟨warð⟩ (= Old Norse *Hávarðr*, whence the surnames Howard, Haworth, Howorth) (?).
[54] For Cir⟨cebi⟩ (?).   [55] The *t* of this name is faded.
[56] Ha⟨rawude⟩, Harewood (?).   [57] The *s* of *Unbainas* is somewhat faded.
[58] Brayton, near Selby, co. York.
[59] Part of the initial has disappeared with the margin of the page. The remainder looks like part of the þ or p, but the latter letter does not occur as a capital in the text, and once only (in Mærleswuain) as a small letter. The r is not quite certain, but the *f* is clearly discernible. There is a mark over the *a* that appears in a photograph as an acute accent, but in the manuscript seems to be a later, accidental mark. The initial is much larger than any capital þ in the text.
[60] The *im* of this name have disappeared owing to wear or decay of the parchment.
[61] A space equal to five or six letters follows this word, but there is no trace of writing or erasure in the manuscript, and the space seems therefore to have been intentionally left blank, perhaps because the scribe could not read his original. At the beginning of the next line the parchment has disappeared for a space equal to that of fifteen or sixteen letters.
[62] The second existing letter may be the upper part of an *f* or *r*.
[63] A space similar to that after *ru* (n. 61) is left at the end of the line.
[64] The commencement of the line has disappeared and also part of the foot of the page. The piece torn off represents the space of about twenty-three letters. The bottom of the *l* and of the *d* have been torn off.

which must have been slowly recovering from the ravages of the prolonged struggle. There is an earlier instance of a great archbishop, St. Oswald, placing upon record in the early days of King Ethelred the estates that had been taken away from Otley, Ripon, and Sherburn, the three great sokes dealt with in the present surveys, and also adding a list of estates in Northumbria that had been acquired by his predecessor Oscytel (958–71), some of which had been taken away from the see unjustly.[65] It is noticeable that the surveys are entered before the text of Cnut's charter and before the so-called homilies of Lupus. The ascription of these works to Lupus is probably later than his death, which occurred in 1023. The surveys are obviously earlier than 1069, when William ravaged Yorkshire with such severity and thoroughness that the effects are still discernible in the Domesday entries relating to these three great sokes of the archbishop of York. A comparison between the surveys and the Domesday entries shows that much more land was cultivated in the former than in the latter, and the ominous *wasta est* supplies the cause. For the rest little light upon the surveys can be derived from Domesday, partly for this reason, and partly because Domesday groups the members of the sokes somewhat differently, omitting some estates and including others that do not appear in the surveys.

The palaeographical evidence supports the date thus assigned. The writing of the surveys and of Cnut's charter and the homilies present features to be met with in southern manuscripts of the first half of the eleventh century. Whether one or more scribes were employed upon the transcription is doubtful. There are certain differences to be noted, such as the use of the long and the short forms of *e, s,* and the use of ligatures. But as these variations are sometimes found in one and the same text, it is possible that they may be caused by the scribe sometimes using his own forms and at others copying those in the manuscript before him. Dr. Liebermann assigns the hand of Cnut's charter to about 1030, and that is a probable date for the surveys and homilies. The Bidding Prayer is written in a different hand, more regular, upright, thicker, and less compressed, but little, if at all, later in date. The list of treasures at Sherburn is in yet another hand, a rounder, more regular, and larger hand, which may be slightly later.

The language agrees with the date thus assigned. The charter of Cnut and the homilies are naturally in West Saxon, which

[65] Harl. MS. 55, f. 4', written in an early eleventh-century hand. It is printed, somewhat inaccurately, by Birch, *Cart. Sax.* iii. 577, 578. It is addressed to some king, described in the usual form as ' my lord ' (*min hláford*), later than Edgar, who is mentioned by name. It must therefore be dated between 975, the date of Edgar's death, and 992, when Oswald died.

1912 DOCUMENTS OF THE ELEVENTH CENTURY 15

had obtained by this time the position not only of a chancery language but also that of the literary language. In this development England preceded the nations of western Europe by some centuries. It is a remarkable proof of the position thus obtained by West Saxon that these Yorkshire surveys were drawn up in it. The author has preserved a trace of his Northumbrian origin in the use of $d\bar{æ}l$ as a neuter instead of masculine, the only gender recorded in West Saxon.[66]

1. [67] Ðis is seo socn into Scyre-burna,[68] mid folc-rihte : twa dæl of Cauda [69]; *ond* Wicstow [70] eal ; *ond* ufer Seleby [71] eal ; *ond* twa oxna gang on Fleaxlege [72] ; *ond* healf Bernlege [73]; *ond* eal Breiče-tun,[74] butan healf ploges land ; *ond* eall Byrne [75]; *ond* eall Burhtun,[76] butan healf ploges

---

Translation : 1. 'This is the soke (pertaining) to Sherburn, with "folk-right" : two parts of Cawood ; and all Wistow ; and all upper Selby ; and two oxgangs in Flaxley ; and half Barlow ; and all Brayton, except half a ploughland ; and all Burn ; and all Burton, except half a ploughland ; and all Gateforth ; and all (the)

---

[66] *Sal-lege* seems also to be Northumbrian, if it is a compound of *salh*, West Saxon *sealh*, 'willow' (preserved in 'sallow-willow'). *Lege* may also be Northumbrian, but is more probably only a late West Saxon form ; the regular West Saxon *lǽge* occurs more frequently. The early Northumbrian form *lǽh* (recorded in Beda's Pægna-laech) became *leh* by the tenth century. These forms necessitate in the dative sing. *lǽge*, *lege* respectively. But in compound local names it seems clear that *lǽh* and *lǽge* underwent the usual shortening and so escaped the Anglian 'smoothing' to *leh* and *lege*. Hence Domesday represents the nom. by *lac* and the dative by *lage, lai, laia* (Latinized), *leie*, &c. The nom. has persisted in *Skirlaugh*, which occurs in Domesday in the dat. *Schire(s)lai* ; and in *Healaugh*, near Tadcaster, *Hailaga, Helaga* in Domesday Book ; and in *Healaugh*, in the parish of Grinton, *Hale* in Domesday Book, *Helach* in 1280 (*Calendar of Inquisitions post Mortem*, ii. 222). Healy (with Sutton) appears in the *Nomina Villarum*, 1316, as *Helagh*. There can be little doubt that all three names represent a Northumbrian *Hēa-lǽh, 'high-leigh' (*hēa* being the weak nom. sing. feminine). The Healaugh near Tadcaster has been connected with Beda's Heiu, the earliest Northumbrian nun known to him, on the strength of an identification of an inscription on a stone found there with her name by the uncritical D. H. Haigh. The drawing of the stone in Hübner, *Inscriptiones Britanniae Christianae*, no. 174, shows that the reading adopted by Hübner is obtained by joining three letters in the first line on to a *v* in the second, although a great portion of the side of the stone is broken away. The use of this Old Northumbrian *-lǽh* and Norman spelling is responsible for the appearance of the name of Helmsley in the strange but easily explained form of Hamlake in the baronial title of Roos of Hamlake. Laughton (Domesday Book *Lastone*, with usual Norman *s* for the Old English velar spirant) shows *Lǽh* (shortened) as the first part of the compound.

[67] In printing the texts of the surveys I have extended the sign for the conjunction as *ond* in italics, and have used capitals where necessary instead of the small letters of the original. Words that are really compounded although written as two I have linked together by hyphens.

[68] Sherburn in Elmet. *Scireburne*, D. B. i. 302 b, 1.

[69] *Cawuda*, below. Cawood. Not mentioned in D. B.

[70] Wistow. Not mentioned in D. B.   [71] Selby. Not mentioned in D. B.

[72] Flaxley (Lodge), parish of Selby. Not in D. B.

[73] Barlow, parish of Drayton. *Berlai*, D. B. i. 325 b, 2, Paganel. This is another instance of the interchange of Northumbrian *-lǽh* (here producing *low*) and *-lǽge* (see n. 66).

[74] Brayton. Not in D. B.

[75] Burn, in the parish of Brayton. See n. 83, below. Not in D. B.

[76] Burton (Hall), Gateforth, parish of Brayton.

land ; *ond* eall Gǽite-ford [77] ; *ond* eall twegen Þorpas [78] ; *ond* twa Hyrst eal [79] ; *ond* twa Haðel-sǽ [80] eall ; *ond* fif oxna gang on þriddan Haðel-sǽ ; *ond* healf Byrcene [81] ; *ond* eall Suðtun [82] ; *ond* eall Byrnum [83] ; *ond* Breiðe-tun eal [84] ; *ond* Froðer-tun [85] eall ; *ond* eall Faren-burne,[86] butan healf þridde ploges land ; *ond* twa ploges land on Ledes-ham [87] ; *ond* án on Niwan-þorp,[88] *ond* eall Micla-feld [89]; *ond* eall Hyllum [90] ; *ond* eall Fristun [91]; *ond* eall Lundby [92] ; *ond* eall Styfe-tun [93] ; *ond* eall Myleford [94] ; *ond* eall Fenntún,[95] butan healf ploges land ; *ond* twa ploges land *ond* fif oxna gang on Barces-tune [96] ; *ond* eall Lutering-tun [97] ; *ond* eal Hehferðe-hegðe [98] ; eall Hudeles-tun.[99]

On Scireburnan toecan þam inlande syndan iiii. hida weorc-landes; *ond* on Luteringa-tune iii. hida, *ond* on Barces-tune i. hid *ond* fif oxna gang, *ond* of Styfing-tune tune [100] ⟨*sic*⟩ þreora oxna gang.

Ond on Wic-stowe twegea oxnagang, *ond* on Cawuda twa dǽl þæs landes is agen land into Scireburnan, *ond* Fentun is lǽn oðer healf ploges land.[101]

2. [Fo. 150 recto.] Into Ottanleage [102] iiii. ploga land ; *ond* on Bǽgel-

two Thorpes; and all ⟨the⟩ two Hirsts; and all ⟨the⟩ two Haddleseys; and five oxgangs in ⟨the⟩ third Haddlesey ; and half Birkin ; and all Sutton ; and all Burn ; and all Brayton ; and all Brotherton ; and all Fairburn, except two and a half plough-lands; and two ploughlands in Ledsham ; and one in Newthorpe ; and all Micklefield ; and all Hillam ; and all Fryston ; and all Lumby ; and all Steeton ; and all Milford ; and all Fenton, except half a ploughland ; and two ploughlands and five oxgangs in Barkston ; and all Lotherton, and all " Hehferthe(s) Hegthe " ; and all Huddleston.

' In Sherburn there are in addition to the " inland " four hides of " workland " ; and in Lotherton three hides; and in Barkstone one hide and five oxgangs; and of Steeton three oxgangs.

' And in Wistow two oxgangs ; and in Cawood two parts of the land is "own land" into Sherburn ; and Fenton is " loan-land ", one and a half ploughlands.

2. ' To Otley ⟨pertain⟩ four ploughlands ; and in Baildon two ; and in Hawks-

---

[77] Gateforth, parish of Brayton. Not in D. B.
[78] The ' two thorpes ' are, no doubt, Thorpe Willoughby, parish of Brayton and Thorpe (Hall), parish of Selby.
[79] Temple Hirst and Hirst Courtney, both in the parish of Haddlesey. Not in D. B.
[80] Haddlesey includes West Haddlesey, East Haddlesey, and Chapel Haddlesey. Not in D. B.   [81] Birkin. *Berchine*, D. B. i. 373 b, 1, land of Ulf.
[82] Sutton, parish of Brotherton. Not in D. B.
[83] This seems to be a repetition of Byrne. See n. 75.
[84] Brayton, also a repetition. See n. 74.   [85] Brotherton. Not in D. B.
[86] Fairburn, parish of Ledsham. *Fareburne*, D. B. i. 315 b, 1, De Lacy.
[87] Ledsham. *Ledesham*, D. B. i. 315 b, 1, De Lacy.
[88] Newthorpe, parish of Sherburn. Not in D. B.
[89] (Old and New) Micklefield, a modern parish, formerly a chapelry of Sherburn. Not in D. B.   [90] Hillam, parish of Monk Fryston. Not in D. B.
[91] Monk Fryston. Not in D. B.   [92] Lumby, parish of Sherburn. Not in D. B.
[93] Steeton (Hall), in South Milford, parish of Sherburn. Not in D. B.
[94] South Milford, a modern parish formed from parts of the parishes of Sherburn and Monk Fryston. Not in D. B.
[95] Church (older Kirk) Fenton. *Fentun*, D. B. i. 315 b, 1, De Lacy.
[96] Barkston (Ash), parish of Sherburn. *Barchestun*, D. B. i. 315 b, 1, De Lacy.
[97] Lotherton, parish of Sherburn. Not in D. B.   [98] Unknown.
[99] Huddleston (cum Lumby), parish of Sherburn.   [100] Steeton. See n. 93.
[101] About half a page is left blank here in the manuscript.
[102] Otley. *Othelai*, D. B. i. 303 b, 1.

tune [103] ii.; on Hafeces-weorðe [104] ii.; on oðeran Hafeces-weorðe [105] ii.; on Dentune [106] ii.; on Timbel [107] oðer healf ploges land; on Ectune [108] healf ploges land, þis is unbesacen agenland. *Ond* þærto eacan hyrað þas socn-lande [109] into Ottanleage; on Ottan-leage ii. ploh; *ond* on Bældune [110] ii.; *ond* on Hafeces-weorðe ii.; *ond* on oðeran Hafeces-weorðe ii.; on Scefinge [111] i.; on Mensingtune [112] iii.; on Burhleage [113] vi.; on Meðeltune [114] iii.; on Yllic-leage [115] syx oxna gang; on Dentune ii. ploh; on Cliftune [116] i.; on Biceratune [117] iii. [118]; on Fearnleage iiii. [119]; on Ectune oðer healf; on Pofle [120] iii.; on Linde-leage [121] iii. [122]

---

worth two; in the second Hawksworth two; in Denton two; in Timble one and a half ploughlands; in "Ectun" half a ploughland, this is unquestionably "own land". And thereto in addition belongs the soke-lands (pertaining) to Otley: in Otley two ploughlands; and in Baildon two; and in Hawksworth two; and in the second Hawksworth two; in Chevin one; in Menston three; in Burley six; in Middleton three; in Ilkley six oxgangs; in Denton two ploughs; in Clifton one; in "Biceratun" three (?); in Farnley four; in Ecton one and a half; in Poole three; in Lindley three.

---

[103] This seems to correspond to *Bældun*. See n. 110.

[104] Hawksworth, parish of Otley. *Henochesuurde* (error for *Heuoch-*), *alia Henochesuurde*, D. B. i. 303 b, 1.

[105] See previous note. This second Hawksworth has disappeared.

[106] Denton, parish of Otley. *Dentune*, D. B. i. 303 b, 1.

[107] Little Timble, parish of Otley (detached). *Timbe*, D. B. i. 303 b, 1. *Timmel* (printed *Tunnel*) in St. Oswald's certificate (see n. 61).

[108] Unknown. *Ectone*, D. B. i. 303 b, 1. [109] So in manuscript.

[110] Baildon, parish of Otley. See n. 103. *Beldone*, D. B. i. 303 b, 1.

[111] The Chevin, hill-range at Otley (?). Not in D. B.

[112] Menstone, parish of Otley.

[113] Burley in Wharfedale, parish of Otley. *Burghelai*, D. B. i. 303 b, 1.

[114] Middleton, parish of Ilkley. *Middeltune*, D. B. i. 303 b, 1. The Old English *middel* seems to occur in D. B., the corresponding Old Norse *meðal* in the survey.

[115] Ilkley. *Ilecliue*, D. B. i. 303 b, 1. There is an *Illicleia*, i. 321 b, 1, among the lands of William Percy, which is identified with Ilkley by Skaife, *Domesday Book for Yorkshire* in the *Yorkshire Archaeological Journal*, 1896. Ilkley appears in Archbishop Oswald's certificate (see n. 61) as *Hyllicleg*. The united testimony of these forms seems to prove that the double *ll* of the name is correct. If this is so, it puts out of court the derivation of the first part of the name from *Olicana*, the name of the Roman station (accepted by Alois Pogatscher, *Zur Lautlehre der griechischen, lateinischen und romanischen Lehnworte im Altenglischen*, Strassburg, 1888, § 225). The Roman station is probably recorded in the *burh* of Burley, and a second commemoration of it by its Roman name so near at hand is improbable. Oswald writes *Gislicleh* for the old name of Guisely, which occurs in D. B. as *Gisele*. This seems to be a case of the reduction of the possessive suffix *ing* through *inc* to *ic*, and it is possible that this is what has happened in the case of Ilkley, which in that case could be compared with Illingworth in Yorkshire and Illington in Norfolk, *Illinketuna*, D. B. ii. 164 b = Old English *Yllingatun*. The first part of *Gislicleh* can hardly be anything else than the Old Norse man's name *Gisl* or *Gisli*. Similarly Patrington appears in Domesday Book as *Patrictone*.

[116] Clifton, parish of Otley. *Cliftun*, D. B. i. 303 b, 1.

[117] Unknown. *Bichertun*, D. B. i. 303 b, 1.

[118] In the manuscript this is written *iii* with a bottom loop connecting the two first numerals, so that it may be an alteration of *iii* to *ui* = *vi*.

[119] Farnley, parish of Otley. *Fernelai*, D. B. i. 303 b, 1.

[120] Poole, parish of Otley. *Pouele*, D. B. i. 303 b, 1.

[121] Lindley, parish of Otley. Not in D. B.

[122] In the manuscript a space equal to about three lines is left blank here.

3. Æt Rypum [123] ærest mile gemet on ælce healfe; *ond* Biscoptun [124] is in on þam ii. hida; *ond* Carle-wic [125] v. hida; *ond* healf Muneca-tun [126] his agen land feorðe healf hide; *ond* healf Mercinga-tun [127] þridde healf hide; on Hereles-ho [128] healf hid; on Stodlege [129] iii. hida; on Suðtune [130] oþer healf hide; on Nunne-wic [131] iii. hida; on Þorntune [132] ii. hida.[133]

Ond þys synd weste land: An is Sal-lege [134]; oðer is Grante-lege [135]; þridde is Efes-tun [136]; *ond* feorðe is Wifeles-healh [137]; *ond* v. is healf Cnearres-weorð.[138]

Þon' syndan þis preosta land: on West-wic [139] iiii. hida [140] on Norð

---

3. 'At Ripon first the space of one mile on each side; and Bishopton is within that two hides; and "Carlewic" five hides; and half Monkton is "own land" three and a half hides; and half of Markington two and a half hides; in "Hereles-hoh" half a hide; in Studley three hides; on Sutton one and a half hides; in Nunwick three hides; in Thornton two hides.

'And these are waste lands: one is Sawley; the second is Grantley; the third is Eavestone; and the fourth is Wilshill (?); and the fifth is half ⟨of⟩ "Cnearres-weorth".

'Then these are the priests' lands: in Westwick four hides; in North Stainley

---

[123] Ripon. *Ripum*, D. B. i. 303 b, 2.
[124] Bishopton, parish of Ripon. Not in D. B. Probably the two carucates held in demesne by the archbishop in Ripon of D. B. 303 b, 2. [125] Unknown.
[126] Bishop's Monkton, parish of Ripon. *Monucheton*, D. B. i. 303 b, 2.
[127] Markington, parish of Ripon. *Merchintone*, D. B. i. 303 b, 2.
[128] *Erlesholt*, D. B. i. 303 b, 2. This is probably the land occupied by Herelles ('þæs oþre land þe Herelles onstandaþ') of St. Oswald's certificate (see n. 65). It occurs as *Herleso*, 1132, and *Herleshowia*, 1147-53, in original charters in Walbran, *Memorials of Fountains Abbey*, Surtees Society, 1863, xlii. 156, 157, and c. 1200 as *villa de Herleshou* in the fifteenth-century 'Narratio de Fundatione Fontania Monasterii', *ibid.* i. 54, where it is described by the editor as 'a lost village by How Hill by Fountains Abbey'. In 1346 it is called *Michaell Howe alias Harlesshawe* (*ibid.* i. 201).
[129] Studley, parish of Ripon. *Estollai* (Norman spelling of Studlai), D. B. i. 303 b, 2.
[130] Sutton Grenge, parish of Ripon. *Sudton*, D. B. i. 303 b, 2.
[131] Nunwick, parishes of Ripon and Kirklington. *Nonnewic*, D. B. i. 303 b, 1.
[132] Bishop Thornton, parish of Ripon. *Torentune*, D. B. i. 303 b, 2.
[133] In the manuscript a space equal to a line is left blank.
[134] Sawley, parish of Ripon. *Sallaia*, D. B. i. 303 b, 2.
[135] High and Low Grantley, parish of Ripon. *Grentelaia*, D. B. i. 303 b, 2.
[136] Eavestone, parish of Ripon. *Euestone*, D. B. i. 303 b, 2.
[137] Wilsil, parish of Ripon (?). *Wifleshale*, D. B. i. 303 b, 2.
[138] Probably near the *Kenaresforde* of D. B. i. 303 b, 2. In 1328 in Archbishop Melton's register there is mention of 'Skeldon, quae quondam vocabatur Knarford' (Skaife, *Kirkby's Quest for Yorkshire*, Surtees Society, 1867, vol. xlix. 417). Skeldon was in the parish of Ripon; it is to be distinguished from Skelton, which was also in Ripon, and which occurs in D. B. i. 303 b, 2, as *Scheldone*. The confusion of 'ford' and 'worth' is not uncommon in later times, but does not seem to have occurred so early as this. *Cnearres*, which is familiar in *Knaresborough*, is borrowed from Old Norse *knǫrr*, gen. *knarrar*, 'a merchant-ship,' and is evidently an English genitive of *Knǫrr*, used as a nickname and then in true Scandinavian fashion as a real name. It is recorded as a man's name in late times in Iceland, Sweden, and Norway (E. H. Lind, *Norsk-Isländska Dopnamn och fingerade Namn från Medeltiden*, Uppsala, 1905, &c., col. 699). In the manuscript a space equal to one line is left blank after *Cnearres-weorð*.
[139] Westwick, parish of Ripon. *Westuic*, D. B. i. 303 b, 2.
[140] The *a* has been apparently altered from *æ*.

Stanlege [141] iiii.; on Gyðing-dale [142] i. hide; on Mercing-tune þreo oxna gang; on Muneca-tune þreo oxna gang; on Hotune [143] ii. oxna gang.

4. Ðis syndan socn-land into Rypum: on Gyþinga deal (*sic*) viii. hida; *ond* ofer eall Muneca-tun vii. hida; *ond* on East-wic [144] ii. hida; on Mercinga-tune þridde healfe hide; *ond* on Hereles-ho þridde healf hide; *ond* on Suðtune oðer healf hide; on Nyrran Stanlege [145] v. hida; *ond* on Norð Stanlege i. hide; *ond* on Nunne-wic i. hide; *ond* on Heawic [146] v. hida; *ond* on Sleaninga forda [147] ii. hida.

---

four; in Givendale one hide; in Markington three oxgangs; in Monkton three oxgangs; in Hutton two oxgangs.

4. 'These are the soke-lands (pertaining) to Ripon: in Givendale eight hides; and over all Monkton seven hides; and in Eastwick two hides; in Markington two and a half hides; and in "Hereles-hoh" two and a half hides; and in Sutton one and a half hides; in the Nearer Stainley five hides; and in North Stainley one hide; and in Nunwick one hide; and in Hewick five hides; and in Sleningford two hides.'

The estates mentioned were ancient possessions of the archbishop of York. Eddi records that King Alchfrith granted to Wilfrid, about 660, 'terram decem tributariorum Æt Stanforda, et post paululum coenobium in Hrypis, cum terra triginta mansionum,' [148] which is reproduced by Beda.[149] This is the Ripon estate, in which are included possibly some later acquisitions. King Athelstan is said to have granted to Ripon one mile 'in circuitu'; [150] the survey is the earliest documentary evidence of this *Leuga Sancti Wilfridi*, as it is called in Domesday. Sherburn is recorded to have been granted by King Edgar to Archbishop Oscytel in 963.[151] This is the date of Edgar's grant of twenty hides at Sherburn to Eslac, the text of which is preserved in the York Liber Albus.[152] Of the acquisition of Otley nothing is known.

[141] North Stainley, parish of Ripon. *Estanlai, Stanlai*, and *Nordstanlai*, D. B. i. 303 b, 2.
[142] Givendale, parish of Ripon. *Gherindale*, D. B. i. 303 b, 2 (misreading of O. E. ʒ = f as p = r ?).   [143] Hutton Conyers. *Hottone*, D. B. i. 303 b, 2.
[144] 'Eastwick' (D. B. i. 303 b, 2, *Estuinc*, by common error for *-uuic*) has disappeared, but Westwick, parish of Ripon, still survives.
[145] 'Nyrran' is a late West Saxon form of *nearran*, dat. sing. of the comparative *nearra* of *neah*, 'nigh.' It is probably absorbed in North Stainley, which is mentioned next.
[146] Copt Hewick and Bridge Hewick, parish of Ripon. *Havvinc* (for *-uuic*), *Hadewic*, D. B. i. 303 b, 2.
[147] Sleningford, parish of Ripon. *Scleneforde*, D. B. i. 303 b, 2.
[148] *Vita Wilfridi Episcopi*, c. 8 (ed. Raine, *Historians of York*, i. 12).
[149] *Hist. Eccl.* lib. v, c. 19. There is great doubt as to the situation of the former place, which is usually, but improbably, identified with Stamford in Lincolnshire. Smith suggested Stamford Bridge, near York. The name 'Stoneford' must have been a fairly common one. As Beda, iii. c. 25, states that the gift at Ripon was 'xl. familiarum', it would seem that he regarded Stanford as merged in the grant of land at Ripon. According to D. B. i. 303 b, 2, there were in the 'leuga S. Wilfridi' forty-three carucates *ad geldum*, the three carucates presumably representing acquisitions or improved cultivation after Wilfrid's time.   [150] *Memorials of Ripon*, i. 33.
[151] 'Chronicles of the Archbishops of York,' in *Historians of York*, ii. 340 n.
[152] *Cart. Sax.* iii. 345, 695.

But it is noteworthy that Simeon of Durham states that after the Danish conquest of Yorkshire in 867 the archbishop retired to Hatyngham,[153] that is Addingham, which appears in Oswald's certificate as part of the estate at Otley.[154]

The surveys of these estates are the oldest detailed accounts of lands in Yorkshire or the north generally that have come down to us. On these grounds alone they would challenge the interest of scholars. They have many other points of interest. They contain the earliest account of any of the great sokes so characteristic of the Danish parts of England, and they afford the earliest clear instance of the use of 'socn' as a descriptive name for the district in which *sōcn* (in its abstract and more original sense) was exercised. The sokes are older than the date of these surveys, for the certificate of Oswald speaks of thirteen *tunas* or parts of *tunas* that had been taken away (illegally) from Otley, and of six similar losses at Ripon, and of some at Sherburn, where mention is made of the loss of half the *sōcn* (evidently used in the abstract sense) that pertained to that place. Another important contribution to economic history is the proof of the use of 'hide' in Yorkshire as late as the early part of the eleventh century. I drew attention to traces of the use of this word in the north in the pages of this Review twenty years ago.[155] Professor Vinogradoff admits that, 'although the documents in which they occur are open to suspicion, it is by no means improbable that the ancient reckoning according to hides was still in use [in the north] in the tenth century'.[156] The hide is the general southern English measurement in early charters and in Domesday, and its occurrence in the north, where Domesday

---

[153] In his account of the archbishops of York in *Historians of York*, ii. 255. The medieval historians of York know nothing of any grant by King Athelstan of Otley to the archbishop of York. The statement to this effect in Gough's Camden seems to be the figment of some antiquary, like the 'King Athelstan's Palace' at Sherburn on the new ordnance map. The statement is repeated without qualification by T. Arnold in his unsatisfactory edition of Simeon of Durham, ii. 58 n., where he suggests that the monastery 'Ætlæto', where Archbishop Eanbald died in 796, is Otley. But it is obvious that the first syllable is merely the preposition *æt*, merged as usual in Simeon's text with the local name governed by it, which appears here correctly as a dative singular. The place meant may be Leake, near Northallerton, written *Leche* in the early years of the twelfth century (*Liber Vitae Dunelmensis*, Surtees Soc., vol. xiii. 77), since *c* frequently appears as *t* in Simeon's printed texts.

[154] See n. 65.

[155] v. 143. The reference to hides by the Humber in *Cod. Dipl.* vi. 144 should be struck out, as the Humber appears to be the old name of a brook at Haseley, co. Oxford, to which place the charter relates.

[156] *English Society in the Eleventh Century*, 147. I can see no reason for looking with suspicion upon St. Oswald's certificate (see n. 65), which Dr. Vinogradoff adds to the instances given by me, or upon the will of Wulfric Spott, despite the lateness of the manuscript authority. Hides are mentioned at Sherburn and its dependent villages in the charter of 963 (*Cart. Sax.* iii. 346, 695), where the manuscript is certainly very late.

and later documents know only of carucates or ploughlands, can only be explained as a survival of an older system of nomenclature, and therefore proof of its use in the eleventh century carries with it proof of its employment in the tenth. The statement of St. Oswald in his certificate that Archbishop Oscytel bought three hides 'æt Bracenan'[157] of King Edgar might be got round by arguing that the word 'hide' merely represents the chancery equivalent of 'ploughland', or that it is a familiar West Saxon translation of the Latin word, whatever it was, used in the king's charter. Neither of these objections lies against the York surveys, for they were obviously written down by a Northumbrian in Yorkshire, probably at Sherburn. It is noticeable that the components of the hide are not the regular 'yards' or 'yardlands', more familiar to us as 'virgates', but 'oxgangs'. From the mention upon two occasions of 'five oxgangs' it seems clear that the hide contained eight oxgangs instead of the regular four virgates. There is here clear evidence of the encroachment of the ploughland and oxgang upon the hide and virgate system. The mention of oxgangs as the constituents of the hide dissipates any lingering possibility that the latter word may be due to the use of West Saxon instead of Northumbrian, for it is only in the Danish districts that the oxgang is met with.

It has been generally assumed that the ploughland and oxgang are due to Danish influence. The word 'plough' has been found once only in Old English documents in the alliterative legal formula 'ne plot ne plōh',[158] while the compound 'ploughland' has not been met with. These surveys afford plenty of instances of this compound, in the form 'plōgs-land', which corresponds exactly to the Old Norse *plōgs-land*, which is said to mean an acre,[159] that is, the traditional area ploughed in one

---

[157] *Cart. Sax.* iii. 578. This should be Bracken, parish of Kilnwick, a possession in later times of the archbishops of York, and is, if correct, probably an Old English form of the northern word 'bracken'. The initial in the manuscript is much rubbed, but it seems to be *b*. It appears as a small *d* in the copy in the hand of Junius (Harl. MS. 6841, p. 129'), which has considerably influenced Birch's text, notably in the reading 'ten' hides instead of 'one' (*an*) hide at Stanleh (Stainley).

[158] The curious formula beginning 'Hit becwæð ond becwæl' in Thorpe, *Ancient Laws and Institutes*, p. 76, Schmid, 408, Anhang xi, Liebermann, i. 400, who denotes it by its first verb as 'Becwæð'. He assigns it to c. 1020–60. *Plōh*, *tōft*, and the ἅπαξ λεγόμενον *ne lǣðes ne landes* (cf. Old Norse *lað ok land*) suggest a Danish element in this formula, although it is evidently outside the wapentake district and within that of the hundreds. I am not certain that *plōh* in this case means plough.

[159] By Cleasby and Vigfusson, no doubt on later Danish evidence (cf. 'plogsgang' in O. Kalkar, *Dansk Ordbog*). But the only reference given by them and by Fritzner, *Ordbog over det gamle norske Sprog*, 2nd edition, is to the Orkneyinga Saga, c. 80 (Rolls Series, i. 132, translated in iii. 137), where we are told that Rǫgnvald, earl of Orkney, exacted from every owner of *óðal* (or family) land a mark for every 'plōgs-land', not as a relief but as a redemption of his feudal claims. In the tenth century

day, while the 'ploughland' is that ploughed in a season *plus* the fallow. In view of the paucity of the Scandinavian evidence special weight must be given to the evidence of these surveys. The composition of *plōgs-land* with the genitive singular is a proof of its Old Norse origin, the Old English dialects adhering to the older (Indo-Germanic) and more proper stem-composition. The mention in the surveys of two or more *plōgs-land* shows that this word was a compound; otherwise we should have the genitive plural *plōga land*, which does occur under Otley. The mention under this soke of *ii. plōh* shows that 'plough' was neuter, and not masculine as in Old Norse. This is an early instance of the use of 'plough' uncompounded in the sense of 'ploughland'.

The evidence of the use of the ploughland in the Scandinavian north is very imperfect, owing to the lateness of the records and to the fact that these records obviously disclose an artificial method of denominating land-areas, based upon the amount of money paid by them or the quantity of seed required to sow them. Steenstrup has maintained that the original unit in Denmark was the ploughland, and the same suggestion has been made in regard to Sweden.[160] A trace of such a system has been found in the *krokland* of Finland, which derived its name from *krok*, a Swedish dialectal name for a primitive plough[161] (from Old Norse *krōkr*, the origin of our 'crook').

the Scandinavian mark was worth half an English pound. But it cannot have depreciated so much by 1136, the date of this transaction, as to have been leviable upon an acre of land. It is probable, therefore, that the Orkney *plōgsland* corresponded in meaning with the Anglo-Danish ploughland. In the Egils Saga King Æthelstan is made to offer to Olaf before the great battle of Vinheithr a silver shilling from every plough in his realm (c. 52, § 22), which looks like a remembrance of the levying of the Danegeld. It is unfortunate that the history of the Old Norse word *plōgr* should be so obscure. It was an improved (probably a wheeled) plough as distinguished from the earlier form, which bore in Old Norse the name *arðr* (the cognate of *aratrum*, ἄροτρον), which is still represented in the Scandinavian dialects. See L. B. Falkmann, *Om Mått och Vigt i Sverige*, Stockholm, 1884, i. 140; Guthmundsson's excellent article on early Scandinavian agriculture in Hoops, *Reallexikon der germanischen Altertumskunde*, i. 34; Hans Hildebrand, *Sveriges Medeltid*, Stockholm, 1879, &c., i. 184. Yet the word 'plough' is not restricted in England and Scotland to the wheeled variety. Pliny describes this latter as a recent invention of the Rhaetians, and gives *plaumoratum* as their name for it, a word that is as great a crux as 'plough'. The supersession of *aratrum* by *carruca* among the Gauls is clearly due to the introduction of wheeled ploughs, since *carruca* undoubtedly meant primarily a wagon. The all-conquering progress of 'plough' throughout the Germanic dialects is probably to be explained in the same way. As the Old English *sulh*, which is cognate with Latin *sulcus*, continued in use throughout the middle ages in the south, and still exists in dialects as *sull*, it is hardly possible that this term should have meant in Old English solely the wheelless plough, and it is unlikely, if it had this restricted meaning and if *plōh* was a native Old English term for the wheeled plough, that the latter should not have found some record in Old English better than the alliterative formula mentioned above.

[160] Falkmann, i. 136.
[161] *Ibid.* 132; Hildebrand, *Sveriges Medeltid*, i. 184, 276 n. 3, 745.

Some countenance for the theory that the ploughland was introduced into this country by the Northmen may perhaps be found in the fact that the Normans used this system of land-measurement. The ploughland is found translated into Latin as *terra unius aratri* or *terra unius carrucae* in Norman charters before and after the conquest of England.[162] It generally contained sixty Norman *acres*.[163] The Norman *acre* contains 81 *ares* 72 *centiares* against the 40 *ares* 46 *centiares* of the English statute acre.[164] As the Norman acre contains a little more than two English acres, the Norman ploughland roughly corresponded in contents to the English hide or ploughland. The Normans accordingly had no difficulty in recognizing the identity of these denominations with their own,[165] although they usually restricted *carrucata*, the latinization of the Romance word that they adopted as the designation of the *terra unius aratri*, to the ploughland of the Danish districts of England. They were also acquainted in Normandy with the oxgang, which is similarly translated into Latin as *terra ad unum bovem* and *bovata*.[166] It was easy to latinize ploughland and bovate, but when they came to the acre there was no obvious way of converting this Germanic measure into Latin or French. Hence the word retained its Germanic form. It is impossible to derive the Norman word from the Latin *ager* owing to Romance sound-changes, and for the same reason it is difficult to assign it to the Saxons of Bayeux, who have, according to Meitzen,[167] left so enduring a mark upon the map of Normandy. The word can hardly be borrowed from the English, as is assumed in the latest French etymological dictionary,[168] and nothing remains but the conclusion that it is Scandinavian. For the same reasons that render the tracing of ploughlands in the north difficult it is not easy to prove that the Northmen used acre as

[162] See Ordericus Vitalis, ii. 31 (the text of this charter is printed in v. 174), 33, 36 (text in v. 177), 37 (text in v. 177), 110, 133, 413, 425, 441, 443 ; iv. 66 ; *Gallia Christiana*, xi. instrum. coll. 12, 59, 107, 126, 153, 203, 226 (facsimile of original in *Musée des Archives départementales*, plate 18). See also Léopold Delisle, *Études sur la Condition de la Classe agricole et l'État de l'Agriculture en Normandie au moyen âge*, Évreux, 1851, pp. 298, 538. [163] Delisle, p. 538.
[164] Henry Moisy, *Dictionnaire de Patois Normand*, Caen, 1887, s.v. ' acre.'
[165] Ordericus Vitalis, iii. 311, ' omnes carrucatas, quas Angli hidas vocant.'
[166] Charter of William the Conqueror to Coutance, 1061, in Léchaudé d'Anisy's *Cartulaire de la Basse-Normandie*, i. 131 (Public Record Office, Transcripts, 140 B), *Terra ad tres bovatas* (omitted in *Gallia Christiana*, xi. instrum. col. 229, Round, *Calendar*, p. 341). See also Guérard, *Cartulaire de l'Abbaye de Saint-Père de Chartres*, p. clxx, § 159.
[167] *Siedelung und Agrarwesen*, iii. 237.
[168] Hatzfeld and Darmesteter, *Dictionnaire général de la langue française*, who state in the *Traité*, p. 19, that acre is confined to Normandy. Mackel, *Die germanischen Elemente in der französischen und provenzalischen Sprache*, Heilbronn, 1887, 63, ascribes the word to a late borrowing from German, which is excluded by its appearance in Latinized forms in the eleventh century.

a measure.[169] The Norman acre, like the English, was divided into four parts called *vergées*, which correspond in meaning with the English rood, each *vergée* consisting, again like our English equivalent, of forty square *perches* or perches (the Norman form is *perque*).[170] The *acre*, *vergée*, and *perque* are still used in Normandy in setting out land, despite the legal prohibition of the ancient customary measures.[171] In Latin deeds the Norman acre appears as *acra, ager*, or *accrus*,[172] the latter preserving the Germanic gender. The Normans must also have been acquainted with the furlong (which consists of forty square rods), since they rendered it in Domesday Book and in our English legal Latinity by *quarentena*.[173]

The word *inland*, which occurs in the Sherburn survey, has been explained since the days of Lambarde as equivalent to demesne. It is, however, a word of widely varying meaning, and is sometimes mentioned as something distinct from the demesne, and is sometimes applied to land belonging to a manor that lay in another village, sometimes at a considerable distance. In Nunwick, one of the places mentioned in the Ripon survey, there were in the time of the Domesday survey three carucates of inland *ad geldum*, and therefore presumably not demesne. In this case the inland is contrasted with the sokeland, and it is possible that the like contrast is intended in the Sherburn survey.[174] It is remarkable that in the grant of Sherburn in 963 the boundaries speak of the whole of the twenty hides as *inland*, and then specify lands in nine villages, which occur in the survey among the sokelands. The demesne appears to be represented in the surveys

---

[169] There are some indications of its existence in the fact that in the thirteenth century and in modern times twenty-four furrows ('lands' or ridges ?) make an acre (*ager*) in Falkmann, i. 136, 145, though this may correspond to the English 'furlong', a division of the open field consisting of parallel 'lands', which was known in the Danish districts of England as a 'wong', a word that I have been unable to trace with this meaning in Scandinavia. The Norman-Latin word for the furlong or wong was *cultura*.

[170] Moisy, *ut supra*; Delisle, p. 535; Guérard, *ut supra*, p. clxix, § 158.

[171] Moisy, *ut supra* and in his *Glossaire comparatif anglo-normand*, Caen, 1889, s. v. 'perque'.

[172] *Gallia Christiana*, xi. instrum. coll. 12, 59, 64, 153, 203.

[173] In Godefroy's *Dictionnaire de l'ancienne langue française*, x. 454, it is stated that the *quarantaine* contained forty perches, but the definition seems to be taken from the English evidence in Ducange. Another interesting Norman word in Moisy, *Dict. de Patois*, is *forière*, 'headland of a ploughed field.' This is the source of the *forera* of our medieval Latin deeds. Side by side with it we meet with *forerda, forertha, forerdum*, which are latinizations of the Old English *for(e)-yrð*, a word that has been omitted from the dictionaries, although amply recorded. See my article in the *Transactions of the Philological Society*, 1898, 530. The Old English word is a compound of *fore*, 'before,' and *ierð*, 'ploughing,' connected with the verb *erian*, 'plough,' which has a cognate in the Swedish *ärja*.

[174] Cf. Vinogradoff, p. 366. The contrast between inland and sokeland may mean that inland is the land, demesne, and otherwise, actually owned by the lord of the soke, and that the sokeland is that over which he had rights of jurisdiction and little else.

by *āgen-land*, literally ' own-land ', a new word in Old English land tenure.[175] In Ectun in the Otley survey land is said to be ' indisputably *āgen-land* ', which raises a doubt as to the equivalence of this term and demesne. But it is difficult to suggest any other meaning for it, for the surveys are concerned with the lands of the archbishop, and hence it is not necessary to distinguish any land as his from that assigned to the chapter. This latter is described as ' priests' land ' in the Ripon survey. *Lǣnland*, or land let out on *lǣn* (the English cognate of German *lehn*) or in fee, is already known. But *weorc-land* in the Sherburn survey, where it seems to mean the non-demesne land, is an addition to the Old English agricultural terminology. Here the work would seem to be the services rendered to the lord by the tenants ; if this is correct, the ' works ' must have been something more than the *opera* or boon-works of the tenants in thirteenth-century and later customals and surveys. The waste lands mentioned under Ripon recall the familiar Domesday entry *terra wasta est*.

The soke, it will be noticed, is said to be *mid folcrihte* ' with folk-right '. This phrase occurs as *mid fullan folc-rihte* in the formula relating to land claims quoted above, perhaps as a definition of full ownership, much like the *in dominio suo ut de feodo* of later times.[176] It is rendered by Schmid *nach vollem Volksrecht* and by Liebermann *nach vollem Landsrecht*, but it is difficult to find parallel instances of such a use of the preposition. Grammatically it would be more satisfactory if we could take it in the sense of *geriht*, ' rights, dues,' and regard the phrase as meaning that the *sōcn* carries with it all the secular dues of the folk within it. But for this I can find no proof. It is not easy to see how a special exempt jurisdiction such as a soke could be said to be ' in accordance with the ancient folk-law '.

W. H. STEVENSON.

[175] Vinogradoff, p. 353, states that the Old English name for demesne was *hīred*. But the passage quoted by him from a late Old English will, in which the testator emancipates all his men ' on hirede and on tune ', does not prove this. It is surely more reasonable to take this as a reference to the serfs living in the house (*hīred*) and those engaged in farm labour on the manor-farm (*tūn*).

[176] In *Cart. Sax.* ii. 134 we have a Kentish reference to a *folcriht* requiring the leaving of space for the evesdrip, where *folcriht* would seem to mean a by-law of Canterbury.

The Forest Laws and the Death of William Rufus[1]

THOUGH the verdict of history has condemned William I for his forest policy, and in particular for the creation of the New Forest, the evidence on which that verdict was based has been greatly discredited. The earlier chroniclers, writing in strains of indignant denunciation, relate that William drove out a flourishing community from a tract of land thirty miles in extent in order to make a hunting-ground, and threw down churches wholesale, so committing an offence against both man and God, which in days to come was visited on his children. On the other hand, the Hampshire antiquaries assert that modern investigation does not confirm this story, but rather shows that the prosperity which William I is said to have so ruthlessly swept away never existed in that district. This conflict of opinion involves not a mere archaeological discussion about the state of a corner of Hampshire eight hundred years ago, but a much wider issue; for the traditional account of William's wanton cruelty has affected every estimate of Norman rule, the position of the forest laws in constitutional history, and perhaps popular feeling towards the game laws in later years.

Having regard to the amount of study already devoted to the subject, and to the limited sources of information—the statements of the monastic historians, the evidence of archaeological research, and the facts of the Domesday Survey—it is unlikely that much further progress can be made by the use of them alone. The search must be continued outside. And, as Domesday Book and the antiquaries deal in facts which can be tested, it is upon the accusations made by the old annalists that doubt falls where there is a contradiction. Hence we get a clue in the search: to ascertain whether there was anything which would lead them to tamper with the truth. It is not pretended

[1] This article was in the press at the time of the author's sudden and lamented death on 25 November. It has been necessary, therefore, that I should assume the responsibility for its revision, and I have decided to make some small omissions of matter, about which I had hoped to be able to communicate with Mr. Parker.—ED. *E.H.R.*

that the district occupied by the New Forest was not affected during William's reign; but it is maintained that the data of modern archaeologists, together with the silence of the Saxon Chronicle on the subject, justify a belief that the creation of the New Forest involved no consequences worth recording in history, and that the statements of the old writers are, either through error or design, untrue. What is now required is to discover the cause of the error or the object of the misrepresentation, and the means by which the story obtained its extraordinary hold on the public mind.

Let us first examine the story of the New Forest as set down by Florence of Worcester. He says:

Then, on the second day of August ... William the younger, king of England, while hunting in the New Forest, was struck by an arrow aimed carelessly by a certain Norman, Walter Tirell, and died. ... Doubtless, as common report has it, this was verily the righteous vengeance of God. For in the days of old, that is, in the days of King Edward and other kings of England before him, that land flourished plentifully with country-folk, with worshippers of God and with churches; but at the bidding of King William the elder, men were driven away, their houses thrown down, their churches destroyed, and the land kept as an abiding-place for beasts of the chase: and thence, it is believed, was the cause of the mischance.[1]

This passage contains a point which arrests the attention of the student of forest law. The term *forest*, as then understood, had a technical meaning which renders unnecessary the idea of devastation on which Florence lays such stress. In modern use we should take it to mean an area covered with timber. Freeman notes that the word meant a wilderness rather than a forest.[3] If by this sentence he means that the creation of a forest involved making a wilderness of land which was occupied before—*solitudinem faciunt, forestam appellant*—it is incorrect. Such land would as a rule correspond to a modern deer forest, waste land which could not easily be adapted to tillage—*foris*, outside the cultivated area. The term *forest*, moreover, conveyed an abstract idea, for in later times it was customary to speak of the justice of the forest, not of the forests, north or south of Trent. A forest became such by a stroke of the pen, not by any physical change; the difference was that after the land was afforested certain rules were enforced within it for the preservation of the vert, that is, the trees and shrubs, and the venison, which included the deer and wild boars. To waste a district and ruin the inhabitants was unnecessary to the making of a forest, and is only alleged in this one case; and it is doubtful whether William

[1] *Chron.*, ed. Thorpe, ii. 44–5.
[3] *History of the Norman Conquest*, iv. (2nd ed., 1876) 609; v. (1876) 456.

would have countenanced cruelty of so useless a kind as this, or whether he was a man to commit gross acts of sacrilege. We may admit that he wasted the country during the campaign of Hastings, and that he afterwards wasted the north ; but in each of these cases he had a definite purpose, in the first strategic, in the second political.

These considerations are sufficient to arouse suspicion. Now Florence says that William I found a flourishing countryside here, and left nothing but ruins. To this the antiquary replies that he finds no trace of early or pre-English villages, except the settlements of charcoal burners or potters, and these only at the northern part of the forest. Records of cultivation, sale, and apportionment before the Norman invasion, though numerous in other parts of the country, hardly exist in this area. Practical agriculturists could see no sign of cultivation on the heaths round about, and the evidence of geology makes early development highly improbable. Finally, there are no remains, such as kitchen middens, which would be expected on the sites of the villages which are said to have existed.

Mr. F. H. Baring, in his investigations on the subject of the New Forest,[4] endeavours to ascertain what was done, not how or why. He contends that a large number of families were evicted from a part of the district. Now a body of men might be transplanted without causing distress, and he does not suggest that a crime was committed which might call for the vengeance of heaven, as do the chroniclers. He says with perfect justice that we cannot infer from the absence of remains of houses that there were none, as they would certainly have been of wood. But if the absence of remains does not prove that there never were houses, it does not prove that there were any. When Mr. Baring says that too much stress has been laid on the silence of the Saxon Chronicle, we readily agree that this silence is no answer to his views about the evictions ; but we hold that it is strong evidence that what was done was nothing to invite indignation, and that the outcry which arose later was due to extraneous causes of which the origin should be explored. To the inferences which may be drawn from Mr. Baring's analysis we shall revert later.

Let us pass from the New Forest, which is said to have been created at the cost of so much suffering, to the general economy of the forests, which are said to have led to so much needless inconvenience. These were, in fact, land not chosen for the purpose, but relinquished to it because, though breeding deer, it was uncultivated for want of men. In many of these tracts modern science has worked great changes, but similar districts exist, especially

[4] *Domesday Tables* (1909), pp. 194 seq. ; *ante*, xvi (1901), p. 427.

in Scotland, to this day. In this connexion we may notice a recent paper dealing with the subject from the sheep-farmers' point of view, in which the author expressed the opinion, formed as the result of his researches into the history of the breed,

that the early ovine inhabitants of the Highlands more resembled deer than the sheep of the present time. They were of little value for the production of either mutton or wool; the inference being that most of the mountains and glens could only carry sheep stock of this worthless description. This opinion was confirmed by another extensive sheepfarmer who, while lamenting the substitution of deer for sheep, admitted that the land which would not grow lambs to a fair size, might be better employed in raising deer.[5]

Similarly, to use these areas as deer preserves was probably the best use to which the Normans could have put them, for salted venison was a valuable asset in those days when meat was less plentiful. Thus the Pipe Roll for 18 Henry III records a payment for killing and salting no less than 235 deer in Cumberland, while in the 35th and 36th 200 harts and 200 hinds were killed, salted, and removed.[6] There are other entries about this time dealing with the taking of venison in the same county, probably representing similar amounts, though only the sum paid is recorded. It is manifestly incorrect to say that the forests were devoted to amusement, for in these cases the wages of the huntsmen are mentioned, it is stated that they were sent to take venison, and the destination of the salted carcasses is given; so that it is clear that they were killed for use and not for sport.

This more useful function of the forests might have been noticed had it been observed that the timber was also protected; indeed, that the forests, apart from the deer, were carefully managed as estates. The grazing lands (*laundae*) within the forest were agisted or leased; dead and fallen wood was sold; honey found in the king's demesne woods was accounted for. Timber must not be taken without leave; but where it was plentiful there existed generous customary rights, as was the case in Inglewood. Gifts of oaks were frequently made by the king's writ for the erection of religious houses, churches, and similar public works. In a word, the guiding principle of the management of the forests was sound economy. But the system did not

---

[5] Leading article in *The Field*, 18 February 1911.
[6] *The Pipe Rolls of Cumberland and Westmorland*, 1222-60, ed. F. H. M. Parker. The Forest of Cumberland is not chosen as an illustration with a special object, but because the present writer is acquainted with it and its records, while its size makes its history representative. It was of immense extent, even after being stripped of additions made by Henry II, including Inglewood, running from Carlisle to the Westmorland border, and flanked by Allerdale, the two bailiwicks reaching from the Eden on the east to the sea at Maryport. In Inglewood Edward I killed 400 red deer in a day (Forest Proceedings, Exchequer, Lord Treasurer's Remembrancer, 5. 35 d).

go on without change. From the time of John we have records of grants of small holdings, clearings, or encroachments made ; as time went on larger grants are mentioned, then the grass-lands, instead of being agisted, were leased, first for short terms, then for a life or lives, and finally conveyed in fee simple or tail.[7] It is quite true that the records from which these facts are drawn are at least a century later than the first complaints against the New Forest, and that there was plenty of time for usages to be ameliorated ; but even making every allowance for improvement, it is impossible to reconcile the sound, business-like management shown in these documents with the wasteful tyranny attributed to William I in the New Forest.

Next we may notice the feeling raised against the forest laws by stories of harsh or cruel punishments. The Charter of the Forest, in 1217, enacted that no one should thereafter suffer in life or in limb for a trespass in the forest. Presumably we may infer from this that both death and mutilation had been employed as penalties, though it is agreed that the forest laws of William are not to be found in the shape of any genuine ordinance : their nature has to be made out from later notices and from the rhetorical complaint of the national chronicler. But even if this assumption is right, a similar severity did not evoke a like protest in other cases. Concerning the false moneyers Freeman writes :

> In all these cases, bodily mutilation was the doom of the offender: and it may be noticed that, in this generation, we never meet with any feeling against punishments of this kind, if only the sufferers were believed really to be guilty.[8]

We frequently find the old complaint supported by the catch phrase that the life of a deer was worth more than the life of a man ; yet the same thing may be said with even more force of the life of a sheep, for the death penalty for forest offences—assuming that it had been previously inflicted—was obsolete in 1217, and sheep-stealing remained a capital offence till 1832.

At the period for which trustworthy records exist, the punishment was nothing more barbarous than a fine : occasionally the culprit was detained in order to make certain of his appearance for sentence, if he could not find sureties ; but where this occurred, the justices were advised of it, and special consideration was shown.[9] And if the procedure was free from cruelty, the practice was reasonable, if strict, the justices looking to the

---

[7] The Pipe Rolls for Cumberland in the fifteenth century contain numerous instances of these leases.

[8] *Norman Conquest*, v. 159 *seq.*

[9] The procedure is fully described by Mr. G. J. Turner, *Select Pleas of the Forest*, Selden Society, xiii.

spirit rather than to the letter of the law. For example, a case is given where a man was charged because his mastiff had killed a stag. It was then shown that the stag had tried to cross Colemire, a marsh near the Solway, during a frost: the poor brute fell on the ice and broke its leg, and the mastiff, seeing its struggles, went and throttled it. It was further reported that no complaint had been made previously against either the dog or his master, and the case was very properly dismissed, though a conviction on the facts would have been perfectly good.[10] On another occasion two men were charged together: one was fined forty pence to the other's twenty shillings, for no apparent reason except that he had broken his leg in the meantime, and therefore deserved compassion.[11] These aspects of the forest law have been mentioned in order to show that it is as easy, with the help of trustworthy materials, to describe it as a useful and fair scheme, as to hold it up as a system of meaningless cruelty. But picturesque fiction is much easier to write and to read than a careful estimate of facts; and it is doubly hard to doubt the sixty churches, which Orderic says were destroyed to make the New Forest, when Palgrave graphically describes the ruins.

Our next task is, therefore, to ascertain how a gravely erroneous report came into existence, why the merits of the forest system were suppressed, its true objects misrepresented, and its defects emphasized. The quest is not a long one, for the two great events in the history of the forest, its foundation and the death of William Rufus within it, are connected by the monastic writers, who suggest that one was a crime the other its punishment. But if we do not accept the story of the creation of the New Forest, to what must we ascribe the death of William Rufus? Nothing is so incriminating as the attempt to hide something. To drag in supernatural intervention to account for an accident which might have occurred to any one, suggests a deliberate scheme to introduce the judgement of God to hide the unlawful act of man.

Beyond doubt William Rufus possessed many enemies, and had made himself specially obnoxious to the church. Possibly through mistrust of the clergy, he was a free thinker; and it cannot be denied that in his spoken opinions on religion he was tactless and brutal in a way that put a weapon into their hands. Thus, where certain accused persons came unscathed from the ordeal, he cursed any one who should in future believe that God was a just judge, and directed that such matters should henceforth be tried in his court,[12] meaning

[10] Forest Proceedings, Exchequer, Lord Treasurer's Remembrancer, 5. 8d.
[11] Ibid. 10d.   [12] Eadmer, Hist. Nov., p. 102.

probably only that he believed the prisoners were guilty and had escaped by jugglery. Strong in mind and body, he was impatient of anything which could not be explained on materialistic grounds; he would not suffer his sovereignty either to be overruled or undermined. It needs no daring flight of fancy to imagine a plot against the life of such a man.

And there are many signs which go to indicate, not merely that William Rufus was slain of malice, but that there existed a powerful and elaborately organized conspiracy to compass his death. Among them the most remarkable is contained in a sermon delivered on the feast of St. Peter ad Vincula (1 August), the day before the king's death. This was preached by Fulchered, abbot of Shrewsbury, in the church of St. Peter at Gloucester. Speaking in terms of the strongest denunciation, he cried that the bow of the heavenly wrath was bent against the evildoers: suddenly and soon shall it smite.[13] The authenticity of the statement has been taken for granted; even if this is a mistake, the fabrication has much the same significance. Orderic clearly intends the words to be treated as prophetic; but it is at least as easy to suppose that they were spoken with guilty knowledge in order to safeguard the conspirators. Then, on the very morning of his death, the king received a warning letter from Serlo, abbot of Gloucester, in whose church Fulchered's remarkable utterances were made. Can we reasonably be asked to believe that both these things were due to chance alone? Probably Serlo was implicated, and was playing a move like that of Themistocles before Salamis, sending the king a message which would not compromise the plot, but if it failed might afford himself protection, perhaps promotion, when the king set about punishing the would-be regicides. Serlo's warning is said to have been based on the dream of one of his monks: but some such fiction was needed to account for his knowledge without admitting guilt; and the identity of the seer is concealed under the description of 'quidam monachus bonae famae sed melioris vitae'.

It seems, too, that when William Rufus fell, there was a certain preparedness, a certain readiness to make the best of the situation, that reads strangely. Henry, it is said, was hunting in the New Forest at the time, and on being informed of his brother's death left the body to the good offices of a rustic, and rode post-haste to Winchester to seize the royal treasury. The corpse, when it arrived—the crazy vehicle which conveyed it is said to have broken down on the road—was interred with malignant irreverence. The decisive action Henry took suggests that he knew his part and was ready to play it. The conduct

[13] Ordericus Vitalis, x. 12.

of the ecclesiastics, in burying William without the rites or even the decencies of Christian burial, seems needlessly offensive unless they had their cue; and it is odd that, if he was so vile a being as he was then represented, his biographers need afterwards have accounted for his death by reference to a sin of his father. In both these cases the effect is overstrained.

But the most interesting speculations connected with the story are those which centre round Walter Tirell, who is usually, though not always, said to have shot the fatal arrow by which the king fell. Mr. Round, writing about Tirell's family associations, has a passage which is probably the most suggestive contribution to this topic :

Returning to the parentage of Walter's wife, we find that it raises a curious question by the family circle to which it introduces us. For we now learn that Gilbert and Roger de Clare, who were present at Brockenhurst when the King was killed, were brothers-in-law of Walter Tirel, while Richard, another brother-in-law, was promptly selected to be Abbot of Ely by Henry I, who further gave the see of Winchester, as his first act, to William Giffard, another member of the same powerful family circle. Moreover, the members of the house of Clare were in constant attendance at Henry's court, and ' Eudo Dapifer ', whose wife was a Clare, was one of his favourites. I do not say that all this points to some secret conspiracy, to which Henry was privy, but it shows at least that he was on excellent terms with Walter Tirel's relatives.[14]

In the light of these sentences, Tirell's movements at the time of William Rufus's death gain a new significance. He is commonly said to have been present, and to have slain the king; he immediately fled to the coast and made his escape to his native Picardy, and never returned. This suggests guilt: but Suger, abbot of St. Denis, records that Tirell most solemnly affirmed, when he had no longer any motive for doing so, that he did not see the king that day, and was not hunting in that part of the forest. As he did this when he had nothing to fear or to gain he is entitled to credence.

These facts strengthen the suspicion that a conspiracy existed. As Tirell's name is associated with the king's death, it is probable that he was in some way implicated; but we have his denial that he killed him. Why then should he take to flight ? Having regard to Mr. Round's testimony, he cannot have had much to fear from Henry, and in spite of Orderic, it is not likely that any of the dead king's friends would trouble him;[15] otherwise he might have been afraid that some one, perhaps the far-seeing Serlo, might denounce him. The simplest explanation is that

[14] *Feudal England*, p. 472.
[15] The indignation shown against Tirell at Winchester by the baser sort, described by Orderic, may be intended merely to discredit William.

his part was to divert suspicion from the real criminal by his hasty departure to his home, to which he may have been desirous to return. We may notice that, notwithstanding his flight, he is not accused of having wilfully killed the king, and that his lands in England were not forfeited. An equivocal position such as his would then be, would prompt a man to make a solemn denial of any hand in the murder, in order to right himself with generations to come.

There is also a tradition, a survival from that memorable day, which fits in curiously with the story. It is related in detail by Palgrave,[16] who tells us that about the hour that Rufus died Henry, having recently parted from his brother, was hunting in another and distant part of the Jettenwold.[17] His arbalist sprung. While he was repairing it beside a hovel, an old crone hobbled forth, and inquired of an attendant the stranger's name. 'It is Henry, brother of our Lord the King.' 'Nay, nay,' murmured she, 'say Henry the King; unless my spells are false, before an hour passes, Henry gains the Royal Crown.' Henry rode on, and presently heard of his brother's death, and by prompt action anticipated all opposition. This anecdote suggests not merely that the old woman knew of the existence of a plot, as Sharon Turner thought,[18] but that Henry, innocently seated by her door with his crossbow out of action, had more to do with his brother's death than any historian has hinted, and was manufacturing an alibi till he could make a natural appearance on the scene and learn the news.

Seeing that Mr. Round, with the evidence at his disposal, will not infer that Henry was a party to a conspiracy against his brother—even though the idea of a conspiracy is more or less openly introduced by Sharon Turner, Palgrave,[19] and Freeman[20]—we will not venture to suggest that Henry took his life. But, supposing that he did it, or was believed to have done so, there would be a specially strong motive for fabricating a story that the founding of the New Forest was a crime to be visited on the head of William Rufus, for attempting to find a scapegoat, and for traducing the dead monarch's character in such a way as would discourage sympathetic inquiry into his last moments.[21]

---

[16] *Normandy and England*, iv. 732.

[17] 'The Eotena-wald, the Giants' Weald, where curses hovered under every shade:' *ibid.* iv. 644.

[18] *Hist. of Engl.* i. 148 note.

[19] iv. 676, where the anticipation of the king's death is mentioned.

[20] *William Rufus*, ii. 325. Theodore Wilks, the Hampshire historian, also frankly sums up the evidence: 'On the whole it seems most probable that William II was shot by design': Woodward, Wilks, and Lockhart, *Hampshire*, iii. 38.

[21] Thus Eadmer deprecates such debates as unprofitable, 'seeing that it is enough that he fell by the just judgment of God': p. 116.

Thus we have evidence consistent with the belief in a plot: motive before, and apparently attempts to divert suspicion afterwards.

But, if we maintain that the popular account of the origin of the New Forest is untrue, some reason must be given for the origin of the story, for it is impossible to think that it was purely a fabrication. The narrative is probably based on an incident referred to in the Saxon Chronicle under the year 1085:

> Men had great affliction this year; and the king caused the land about the sea to be laid waste, that if his foes should land, they might not have whereon they might so readily seize.[22]

The locality is not indicated; we will show why the wasted coastline should be identified with the New Forest area. In the first place, that district is vulnerable from a strategist's point of view, and one which William might naturally strengthen. Secondly, though the Saxon Chronicle is silent on the point, later writers assume that it is intended, and may do so on the strength of a persistent tradition that the object of the operations was military. It is noteworthy that the authors cited below, though vague and inconsistent as to details, all preserve the idea of a military object. Then again this hypothesis would account for, and is the only way of accounting for, the depopulation which Mr. Baring describes, and so clears up the one point which modern antiquaries have not made good, and which has caused their hesitancy to reject the evidence of the chroniclers. For if a strip of land adjacent to an existing forest was first depopulated for military purposes, and afterwards, as a separate enterprise, added to the forest, we understand why Mr. Baring finds so much depreciation, while the Saxon Chronicle does not denounce the creation of the New Forest. Moreover, if the so-called wasting had been for the object of national defence, though it might involve distress, it would not have caused the indignation which would have been felt if it had been done to make a hunting-ground. On the other hand, a very simple process would cause it to be believed, first that the strip, then that the whole district, had been cleared in order to form a forest. Indeed, there are strong indications that the traditional account passed through these stages of evolution. In later times Henry Knyghton, after stating that it was William Rufus who destroyed the churches, records that he did not hunt there for seven years, so that the forest might be stocked with deer.[23] This suggests that there had been an interval between the clearance and the afforestation. Two hundred years earlier the story took another form, namely, that William I destroyed many villages

[22] Thorpe's translation, Rolls Series, ii. 185.   [23] *Chron.*, ed. Lumby, i. 110 f.

to *enlarge* the forest.[24] This is greatly in favour of the view that William only created a part of the New Forest.

The accepted story obtained a footing with extraordinary rapidity. Florence, whose account has been noticed, appends it to the death of William Rufus; William of Malmesbury introduces it into an excursus to the life of William I, describing his character and children. Next it becomes an integral part of his biography. Even then the details are remarkably inconsistent. Orderic alleges that the enormous number of sixty parishes—including presumably as many churches—were destroyed. Walter Map gives thirty-six as the figure;[25] Henry Knyghton gives as alternatives twenty-two and fifty-two. As for Orderic, it is hard to deny that he has allowed his feelings to override his judgement. His statement about the churches aroused some forcible comments from William Cobbett, who remarked that, if they were true, 'this country must, at the time of the Norman Conquest, have literally swarmed with people'.[26] Moreover, Orderic gives a graphic explanation of the name of the forest. After mentioning the death of Richard, son of Robert, and grandson of William the Conqueror, he says,

Observe, reader, why the wood in which this youth died is called New. In ancient times the district there was well peopled, rich in villages well fitted for the dwellings of mankind . . . but William the First, because he was a lover of the woods, wilfully destroyed more than sixty parishes, drove the country-folk to other parts, and put beasts of the woods there instead of men, in order to have the pleasure of the chase.

This does not follow. The average community calls a new cluster of houses Newton or Newtown, if no more distinctive name occurs, because it is a new town. 'New Forest' need mean no more than land newly afforested, an idea which involves no idea of destruction. To say that 'New' implies in this case land artificially reconverted from cultivation to a wilderness is straining the sense to get a desired meaning. It may be, however, that Orderic here, like the continuator of William of Jumièges or Knyghton elsewhere, is blundering very near the truth; for it is conceivable that a portion cleared for defensive purposes, if afterwards afforested, might get the name of the New Forest, and the name afterwards be generally applied.

It was left for a French writer to be the first to cast a doubt upon the traditional story of the New Forest. In 1753 Voltaire published his *Abrégé de l'Histoire universelle*, in which occurs this passage:

On lui reproche encore d'avoir détruit tous les Villages qui se trouvoient dans un circuit de quinze lieues, pour en faire une Forêt, dans laquelle il

[24] Contin. of William of Jumièges, *Hist. Norm.* viii. 9.
[25] *De Nugis Curialium*, v. 6, p. 222.   [26] *Rural Rides* (1830), pp. 623-30.

pût goûter le plaisir de la chasse. Une telle action est trop insensée pour être vraisemblable. Les Historiens ne font pas attention qu'il faut au moins vingt années pour qu'un nouveau plan d'arbres devienne une Forêt propre à la chasse. On lui fait semer cette Forêt en 1080, il avoit alors 63 ans. Quelle apparence y a-t-il qu'un homme raisonnable ait à cet age détruit les Villages pour semer quinze lieues en bois dans l'espérance d'y chasser un jour ?[27]

The blow told. It struck a cherished belief of six centuries and jarred the whole superstructure built upon it. True, there is a weak point in Voltaire's argument, because he assumes that a 'forest' must be timbered; still, it set people thinking. Gough, re-editing Camden in 1789, takes up an uneasy defensive position on the subject, suggestive of one who has been surprised by an insignificant opponent; but on the whole he adopts the old attitude. Two of his sentences read curiously in view of later work:

In this age, which will have probabilities instead of facts, Mr. Voltaire has first raised a doubt on this occasion.... One cannot reasonably suppose that so many writers of the greatest authority should have published a story the falsehood of which must have been notorious to all England, especially about a matter in which religion nor party had any concern.[28]

The last few words, it is submitted, involve an error, for both religion and party were concerned in the matter.

Warner, in 1795, investigated the question with care and summed it up with fairness:

Though he [William I] certainly either enlarged the limits of an ancient forest by adding a considerable tract of land to its former dimensions or formed a new one altogether ... yet that act was not attended by those circumstances of outrage and violation which the monkish writers have so minutely described.[29]

Here at last the old chroniclers are fairly met, and later local historians, Mudie, Messrs. Woodward, Wilks, and Lockhart, and John R. Wise also side against them. In 1846 the matter was commented upon by the Rev. Edward Duke, an antiquary of original and independent views:

It is astonishing in the early ages how readily a fiction promulgated by one was eagerly seized on and adopted by successive writers until at last it surreptitiously took its place among established truths ... To the recorded fact that William the First dispeopled the country for 30 miles round and destroyed 30 churches to make a new forest I attach very slight faith: but I believe that he afforested merely that which was native woodland; that he rendered then a large tract of country subject to the forest laws.[30]

[27] i. 280.   [28] i. 127.   [29] *Hampshire*, i. § 2, p. 37.
[30] *Druidical Temples of the County of Wilts*, 116.

Palgrave, however, not only adheres tenaciously to the old faith, but develops it in language prejudiced and pictorial. He accepts the sixty ruined churches;[31] he accepts the legend of Purkiss the charcoal-burner; he quotes St. Jerome to show that though persons of divers callings have been canonized no hunter was among them. His description is reminiscent of Pope's lines on Windsor Forest.[32] The views he expresses cannot be regarded as a logical judgement, but as he has unquestioningly sided with the chroniclers his authority is a force to be reckoned with. Much more weight is carried by Freeman's decision in favour of the traditional story. But even here, in assessing the value of his considered opinion, we must bear in mind the difficulty of deciding against the vast bulk of written evidence: there was no explanation to account for its inaccuracy, there was merely contradiction.

If the circumstances of William Rufus's death led to the circulation of an untrue version of the origin of the New Forest, may not the same process have caused the whole system of the forest law to be viewed with unmerited censure as an evil tree which could not bring forth good fruit, have ignored its uses, and emphasized its defects to point a moral?

F. H. M. PARKER.

[31] *Normandy and England*, iv. 9, 646.

[32] Lines 43 *seqq.* give a paraphrase of the accounts of William I and the New Forest, overstated in a manner which even poetic licence cannot justify.

Chancellor and Keeper of the Seal under Henry III

ALTHOUGH so much has been done towards writing the history of Henry III's reign from the records, the history of the chancellors, except those of Henry III's minority, rests where it did when it was written chiefly from the chronicles. The views of Matthew Paris have the field almost to themselves, as regards the chancery of the period covered by his chronicle, and colour the existing accounts even of later chancellors, for whose work the record evidence was better known. Matthew Paris was conscious that the chancery had undergone great changes in his time. He describes the transference of the seal from one holder to another, but is unwilling to give the name of chancellor to any of the holders of the seal. According to him the holder of the seal, from the time that Ralph Neville resigned it down to 1258, is *custos sigilli, baiulus sigilli,* or *vices agens cancellarii,* not chancellor outright. The language of Matthew Paris and the analogy of contemporary France account for the widely received opinion that there was no chancellor from Ralph Neville to some date after the Provisions of Oxford. For instance, Stubbs, in his list of Henry's chancellors in the *Select Charters,* makes Walter of Merton in 1261 the next successor to Ralph Neville.[1] Most of the writers in the *Dictionary of National Biography* went nearly as far.[2] This view, however, would have been modified had the works in question been written after the publication of the calendars of patent and close rolls of the reign. It is true that in Hardy's *Catalogue of Lords Chancellors* the great majority of the memoranda in the chancery rolls about the custody of the seal have long been summarized;[3] but Hardy's list is not absolutely complete, and even as a work of reference its usefulness is limited, because it seldom goes beyond the memoranda or formal notices

[1] p. 316. Compare the *Const. Hist.* ii. 51 and note 1, which shows that Stubbs here followed Foss.
[2] The article in the *Dictionary of National Biography* on Simon of Cantilupe goes to the other extreme, and states that he was chancellor in 1238.
[3] *A Catalogue of Lords Chancellors, Keepers of the Great Seal, Masters of the Rolls, and Principal Officers of the High Court of Chancery,* London, 1843.

of the custody of the seal.[4] From these alone it would often be impossible to know whether the holder of the seal was the head of the chancery, or whether he was taking the place of a chancellor who was employed elsewhere. I have therefore made some investigations in order to ascertain who was chancellor at definite dates. Such information as I have been able to collect points to the conclusion that the distinction between the ' properly constituted chancellors ' before 1238 and after 1258, and the ' keepers of the seal ' of the intervening period, has been exaggerated. The chancellor's position was indeed much changed after 1238, but the change was a permanent one.

There is no need to say anything about the chancery of Henry III's minority,[5] or of the succeeding ten years. Difficulties begin with the disgrace of Ralph Neville in 1238. From that date until Neville's death in 1244 there was a succession of keepers acting for short periods. From 1244 to 1250 the seal was held in turn by Silvester of Everdon, John Mansel, and John Lexinton, but whether any or all of these were chancellors it is by no means easy to decide. From 1253 William of Kilkenny, and from 1255 Henry Wengham, are called chancellors so definitely in the records that there seems to be little doubt that they really held the office. With Wengham's successor, Nicholas of Ely, in 1260, begins the payment of a chancellor's fee, which makes it comparatively easy to trace the tenure of office by the remaining chancellors of the reign.

The chancellor of Henry III's early years was still very much what he had been under John. The government of the papal legate had introduced foreign forms into the chancery for the time being, but the chancellor's position was untouched. This is very clearly brought out by the charters of 12 February 1227 and 14 June 1232, granting to Ralph Neville the chancery and the custody of the king's seal for life. He was to have the chancery ' with the issues, liberties, and privileges thereof ', as enjoyed by the chancellors of previous kings of England, and the custody of the king's seal ' with all the liberties and customs thereto belonging '.[6] Things remain exactly where they were when Walter de Gray received a similar grant of the chancery in 1205. The chancellor is still a powerful ecclesiastic, who is allowed to make what he can out of the issues of the king's seal. It might

[4] Frequently under Henry III the only record of a change is a minute note in the margin of the roll, as *Hic recepit I. de Lexinton sigillum regis*; but towards the end of the reign the form which is usual in the fourteenth century, *Memorandum quod*, &c., with precise indication of time and place, becomes commoner, and is written in large letters across the membrane.

[5] See Professor Powicke's article on ' The Chancery during the Minority of Henry III ', *ante*, vol. xxiii. 220–35, 1908.

[6] *Cal. of Charter Rolls*, i. 9, 156.

be expected that the king would have profited by his experience of his first chancellor, Richard Marsh, who left all the work of the chancery to the vice-chancellor, Ralph Neville. He was tenacious of his position as chancellor, but it is hard to see what practical use he was to king or country. Yet Henry III appointed Ralph Neville for life, thus burdening himself with another chancellor who could not be removed; and what is more, he deliberately contemplated that Neville would delegate his work to somebody else. He is either to keep the seal in his own proper person, or to appoint a sufficient person 'who shall make oath to the king that he will faithfully keep the seal, before he receives the custody of it'. Moreover, if this person dies, or receives promotion, or is removed by the king or the chancellor, or resigns, the chancellor may appoint somebody else. However, Neville does not seem to have availed himself of this permission. From 1227 to the day when he gave up the seal in August 1238 charters are given by his hand with the utmost regularity. The very few given by the king's hand are so given for a special reason, generally because they were in favour of Neville or the see of Chichester.[7] The only time when we hear of a vice-chancellor is in 1230, during the king's absence abroad. Then charters were given by the hand of N. Neville as the chancellor's representative.[8]

Down to 1238, then, we are still far from the 'constitutional' chancellors of the end of the reign. Owing to 'the accident of Henry III's minority', however, Neville's formal appointment was made in the parliament of 1227, and it was possible to look back in later years and say that he was appointed with the assent of the council; but in view of the terms of his appointment,[9] too much importance must not be attached to this claim. His real right to continue in office after his quarrel with the king in 1238 was not that he could only be removed with the consent of the barons, but that he had been appointed, like Walter de Grey, for life. It must be remembered that in other ways the chancery was from 1227 to 1238 still very much in the same primitive condition as under John. The staff still consisted of the clerks and serjeants of the king's chapel. The chancellor still received an irregular income from the profits of the seal, without accounting to the king for any part of it. It was only after Neville's disgrace that the chancery staff became clearly differentiated from that of the chapel, and that on the one hand the issues of the seal began to be accounted for by an officer who developed into the keeper of the hanaper, while on the other,

---

[7] e. g. the grant of the chancery to Neville.
[8] Charter Roll, 14 Henry III, pt. 2, schedule of charters *dat. per manum N. de Neuill. gerentis vices venerabilis patris R. Cicestrensis episcopi, cancellarii nostri.*
[9] Cf. Stubbs, *Const. Hist.* ii. 41.

the chancellor, no longer allowed to farm the issues of the seal, was compensated by the payment of a reasonable stipend from the exchequer.

When the king received the seal from Neville in August 1238 [10] he could not appoint a new chancellor, and it is probable that he was not very anxious to do so. He had by this time learnt a lesson about the inconvenience of life chancellors. For some weeks writs were made in the wardrobe.[11] The charters of the next few years, given by the king's hand, are attested by an ever-changing group of household officers and clerks; but the records give us no definite information about the custody of the seal until 1240. The chroniclers have a good deal to say about this period. The Annals of Tewkesbury tell us that the seal was held by William of Cantilupe the younger, Brother Geoffrey of the Temple, and others;[12] Matthew Paris, that it was held by Brother Geoffrey and John Lexinton.[13] This is likely enough, for during the time that the seal was in the wardrobe it would probably be in the charge of Brother Geoffrey, then keeper of the wardrobe. In later years, too, when the seal was left in the wardrobe during the chancellor's absence from court, a lay officer of the household was often associated with the keeper of the wardrobe in its custody. William of Cantilupe, as steward of the household,[14] was likely enough to be chosen for this duty. The next statements of Matthew Paris are less easy to believe. On 7 April 1239 William of Cantilupe, the steward's father, died, and next week Henry III tried in vain to recall Ralph Neville to office.[15] If the younger Cantilupe were in charge of the seal, it is credible enough that he would wish to resign it after his father's death. It is likely, too, that Ralph Neville, having secured the profits of the seal, would refuse to undertake the work again. As yet, however, I have not found any evidence in the records for or against the story. About the 15th of August 1239 the count of Flanders visited England, and received a grant of 500 marks a year from the exchequer.[16] The following Easter, Paris tells us, Master Simon the Norman, who had had the custody of the seal for some time, was compelled to give it up, and banished from the king's court and council, because he refused to sign the grant of a toll of fourpence a sack on wool taken from England to Flanders. Brother Geoffrey was disgraced at the same time, because he also would not agree to it, and the abbot of Evesham

---

[10] *Cal. of Charter Rolls*, l. 235; *Cal. of Pat. Rolls*, 1232–47, p. 231; *Close Rolls*, 1237–42, p. 95.

[11] *Cal. of Pat. Rolls*, 1232–47, p. 232.

[12] *Annales Monastici*, i. 110.   [13] *Chron. Mai.* iii. 495.

[14] Charter Roll, 23 Hen. III, 30 October, &c. A writ of 13 October 1338 was to be sealed in his presence by Henry of Bath: *Close Rolls*, 1237–42, p. 148.

[15] *Chron. Mai.* iii. 529, 530.   [16] *Ibid.* p. 617.

received the seal.[17] It is certain that Brother Geoffrey was succeeded by Peter of Aigueblanche as keeper of the wardrobe in February 1240,[18] and that in April 1240 Richard Crassus, abbot of Evesham, received the seal.[19] The grant of 500 marks a year to the count of Flanders is well authenticated,[20] but the story of Simon's custody of the seal and disgrace remains obscure.

In 1242, when the king went abroad, the records introduce the names of the men who in turn held the seal for nearly ten years to come. The seal used in England was held by Silvester of Everdon under the direction of the bishop of Chichester, then restored to favour.[21] The king's seal abroad was held in succession by the abbot of Evesham, John Lexinton, and John Mansel.[22] During the few months which intervened between the king's return from Gascony in September 1243 and Neville's death in February 1244, Neville seems to have continued to act as chancellor. A charter of 6 December and two later ones are given by his hand.[23] On 18 January 1244 the sheriffs were ordered to compel all who owed fees to the chancellor for writs to pay their debts.[24]

Ralph Neville's death left the king free to appoint a chancellor. The problem is whether he did so. There is evidence that some changes in the working of the chancery at once took place. A memorandum on the Fine Roll of 1244-5 tells us that fines were taken into the king's hands in that year.[25] It seems probable that the system of chancery organization which prevailed until the end of the middle ages was introduced almost at once, for a certain Wibert de Kancia accounted for the issues of the chancery from the time that the king took it into his own hands to Michaelmas 1246,[26] and before very long this Wibert is described as keeper of the hanaper.[27] For the rest of the reign there are frequent references to the keeper of the hanaper, and the surviving accounts of Wibert's successor, John Fauconer, show that Henry's keeper of the hanaper received the fees for writs and charters, bought wax and parchment, and paid the wages of his

---

[17] *Ibid.* iii. 629; iv. 63; v. 91.   [18] *Ante* vol. xxiv, p. 439, 1909.
[19] *Cal. of Charter Rolls*, i. 251.
[20] Memorandum that the count of Flanders received 500 marks *de annuo feodo suo* from 24-40 Hen. III, Close Roll, 51 Hen. III, m. 8.
[21] *Cal. of Pat. Rolls*, 1232-47, p. 290; *Foedera*, i. 244.
[22] *Close Rolls*, 1237-42, pp. 502, 514, 517, 519; *Rôles Gascons*, i. 29, 97, 115, 127, 519, 674, 1120; *Cal. of Pat. Rolls*, 1232-47, p. 390.
[23] Charter Roll, 28 Hen. III, m. 4.
[24] Close Roll, 28 Hen. III, m. 16 d: *Rex vicecomiti Wigornie. Precipimus tibi quod omnes illos de comitatu tuo qui tenentur in debito venerabili patri R. Cycestrensi episcopo, cancellario nostro, distringas ad debita illa ei soluenda. Ita quod ei soluantur antea clausum Pasche.* A list of charters follows.
[25] Fine Roll, 29 Hen. III, m. 12 d.   [26] Liberate Roll, 30 Hen. III, m. 3.
[27] Liberate Roll, 43 Hen. III, m. 7.

underlings, just in the same way as his successors in the fourteenth century.

In November 1244 Silvester of Everdon received the seal,[28] and held it until he was promoted to the see of Carlisle at the end of 1246.[29] The Waverley and Tewkesbury annals describe him as the king's chancellor; Matthew Paris, however, is careful to say that he was acting in the place of a chancellor.

He was succeeded by one of the most puzzling of Henry's seal-bearers, John Mansel. Mansel held the seal for nearly a year from November 1246 to August 1247,[30] and again for about a year from August 1248 to September 1249.[31] Throughout his long career Mansel assumed a position of authority in the chancery which is not easy to account for. Did he in later years tear up writs, pass letters with his approval, and order them to be enrolled, because he was a trusted counsellor of the king, or because he had once been his chancellor? It has been stated that before 1240 he had acted as the king's chancellor.[32] As Neville was still alive in 1240 Mansel could not, of course, be chancellor of England. But there seems to be some ground for surmising that Henry wished him to succeed to Neville's office. If the office in the exchequer to which he was appointed in 1234 was that of chancellor of the exchequer,[33] he was in direct line of succession to the chancellorship of England, for several times in this reign the chancellor of the exchequer was chosen for the higher office. In January 1240 John Mansel received 20 marks towards a sum of £25 which he claimed for the wages of a clerk, *qui sedit ad scaccarium loco ipsius Iohannis, a festo Sancti Michaelis anno regni nostri xxii°* (1238) *vsque ad Natale anno regni nostri xxiiij°* (1239), *ut dicitur*.[34] Now in May 1238 John Mansel was sent abroad on the king's business.[35] So it is possible that the clerk in question simply took Mansel's place at the exchequer while he was engaged elsewhere. On the other hand, the phrase is exactly that used of the clerk who sat at the exchequer in the place of the king's chancellor. It is just possible that Mansel soon returned from his mission in 1238, and was in time to assume the custody of the seal in September 1238, after the few weeks of irregular custody in the wardrobe which followed Neville's disgrace in August 1238. In May 1240 Mansel was sent on

[28] Close Roll, 29 Hen. III, m. 20.
[29] Everdon received the seal again from the wardrobe on 18 March 1246: *Cal. of Charter Rolls*, i. 291.
[30] *Cal. of Pat. Rolls*, 1232–47, p. 508.
[31] Close Roll, 32 Hen. III, m. 5; *Cal. of Pat. Rolls*, 1247–58, p. 47.
[32] Gasquet, *Henry III and the English Church*, pp. 196–8.
[33] Close Roll, 18 Hen. III, m. 16, printed by Madox, *Hist. of the Exch.*, p. 580, note *r* (ed. 1711).
[34] Liberate Roll, 24 Hen. III, m. 20.
[35] *Cal. of Pat. Rolls*, 1232–47, pp. 219 and 220.

another embassy,[36] and this may account for the seal being given to the abbot of Evesham in April. In 1242 Mansel held the seal for a short time while the king was abroad, but his chief occupation in 1242 and 1243 was the government of Gascony.[37] A curious little memorandum sewn on to the Close Roll of 1243–4 seems to show that John Mansel enjoyed peculiar advantages of access to the king and obtaining writs. Mansel is to be asked on behalf of the justiciary of Ireland to speak to the king about having the custody of the land which belonged to John le Poer. He is also to be asked to speak to the king about having royal letters directed to the justiciary performing what the king promised at Waltham in the presence of Earl Richard his brother, Peter of Savoy, and the archbishop of York.[38]

It is a remarkable fact that a layman, John Lexinton, the *miles literatus* of Matthew Paris, should have had the custody of the seal for such long periods. He held the seal longer than anybody else while the king was abroad in 1242 and 1243. He had it again for a year from 1247 to 1248,[39] and for more than a year from 1249 to 1250.[40] It seems pretty clear, however, that he was not a premature instance of a lay chancellor, for he is distinctly described as the steward while he held the seal.[41] If there was any chancellor at this time, it was more probably the absent John Mansel.

The report of the parliaments of 1244 and 1248 given by Matthew Paris[42] affords some hints about the position of the chancellorship at that time. The parliament of 1244 sums up very forcibly the lessons to be learnt from the last years of Ralph Neville. A justiciar and a chancellor are to be elected, and they ought to be constantly with the king. If for any reason the king removes the seal from the chancellor, whatever is signed in the interval is to be null and void. The seal must be restored to the chancellor, and no new justiciar or chancellor can be appointed without the solemn assembly and assent of all. This is, of course, a condemnation of the removal of the seal from Ralph Neville, and of the succession of courtier keepers. Still less do the magnates wish to see the chancellorship in abeyance altogether. The year of Neville's death, when no successor had been appointed,

[36] Liberate Roll, 24 Hen. III, m. 12.
[37] *Cal. of Pat. Rolls*, 1232–47, pp. 345, 361, 399.
[38] Close Roll, 28 Hen. III, m. 17 d.
[39] Fine Roll, 31 Hen. III, m. 2: *Hic suscepit Iohannes de Lexinton custodiam sigilli* (after writ of 15 September). Close Roll, 32 Hen. III, m. 9: *Memorandum quod I. de Lessinton recessit a curia die Lune decimo die Maij, de Wallingeford, postquam sigillauerat, & rediit ad curiam apud Wodestok die Iouis proximo ante sigillacionem.*
[40] Close Roll, 33 Hen. III, m. 2; *ibid.* 34 Hen. III, mm. 15, 13, and 12.
[41] *Cal. of Pat. Rolls*, 1247–58, p. 3 (10 December 1247); Fine Roll, 32 Hen. III, mm. 12 and 13 (5 January and 15 March 1248).
[42] *Chron. Maj.* iv. 367; v. 7, 20.

was a favourable one in which to urge that there should again be a powerful justiciar and a powerful chancellor, chosen by the magnates and removable only by them. In 1248 the grievance is a very different one. The magnates do not complain that the great offices of state are not filled, but that they are filled by unworthy, self-seeking men, who consult, not the public welfare, but the king's arbitrary will, and, incidentally, try to line their own pockets. The king answers that he will not *remove* his justiciar, chancellor, or treasurer, or appoint others in their places. This account is not easily reconciled with the theory of a vacant chancellorship.

William of Kilkenny's tenure of the seal is typical of the close connexion of the chancery with the king's household in the middle period of the reign. John Lexinton was thrice absent from court in 1250. On two of these occasions the seal was committed to the care of Peter of Rivaux, the keeper of the wardrobe, and of Master William of Kilkenny, then controller.[43] As controller of the wardrobe, probably, he had been ordered in December 1249 to provide Christmas robes for the clerks of the chancery.[44] When Kilkenny's sole charge of the seal began the records do not make clear. Matthew Paris makes it 1250.[45] At any rate, in 1251 he is officially described as *portitor sigilli*.[46] Kilkenny held the seal until he was succeeded in January 1255 by Henry Wengham;[47] but in what capacity he held it contemporary opinion was not agreed. At the end of his time of office he was exempted 'from all reckonings and demands for the time that he was keeper of the seal in England ',[48] and I have only been able to discover one passage in the chancery rolls in which he was officially called chancellor.[49] A charter of Peter of Savoy, of 18 April 1253, was attested by 'William of Kilkenny, the chancellor', as well as by John Mansel, Henry Wengham, and others.[50] That Kilkenny should be so described in a formal document enrolled on the Patent Roll might be enough to prove that he was officially regarded as chancellor, at any rate by 1253. Several letters address him as chancellor,[51] but too much reliance cannot be placed on these. Ralph Neville, for instance, was frequently called chancellor by his correspondents

[43] Close Roll, 34 Hen. III, mm. 15 and 12.
[44] Close Roll, 34 Hen. III, m. 18. [45] *Chron. Mai.* v. 130.
[46] Close Roll, 35 Hen. III, m. 9, 1 July. On 16 May 1253, when Kilkenny was ill, Lexinton and Peter Chaceporc received the seal; Fine Roll, 37 Hen. III, m. 9.
[47] Close Roll, 39 Hen. III, m. 19; *Cal. of Charter Rolls*, i. 438; *Cal. of Pat. Rolls*, 1247–58, p. 393. [48] *Ibid.* p. 393.
[49] The other instance given in the article on Kilkenny in the *Dictionary of National Biography* is from *Placitorum Abbreviatio*, p. 133.
[50] *Cal. of Pat. Rolls*, 1247–58, p. 188; *Foedera*, i. 288.
[51] Ancient Correspondence, vi. 172, 173, printed in *Royal Letters*, ed. Shirley, ii. 98, 100; cf. *Cal. of Papal Registers, Letters*, i. 302.

during the chancellorship of Richard Marsh, when Neville was only vice-chancellor. It was natural that petitioners for some favour should magnify the office of their patron. The Winchester and Burton annals call Kilkenny the king's chancellor.[52] Paris is uncertain how to describe him. He says that Kilkenny was appointed to the custody of the seal in 1250. Later he says that Kilkenny filled the office of chancellor, and was called chancellor, and describes him as *domini regis cancellarius, vel vices agens cancellarii*.[53] On the whole, Paris seems to think that Kilkenny did the work of a chancellor, but is not quite sure whether he was entitled to the name, which the world in general gave him.

Henry Wengham, Kilkenny's successor, presents fewer difficulties. We are definitely told that he received the seal on 5 January 1255, the day that Kilkenny gave it up. He is described as chancellor when he witnesses important deeds, just as Kilkenny was, but more instances of this survive; for instance, a quit-claim of July 1255, and a bond to the Italian merchants in June 1257.[54] From time to time the records note that certain things were done in the chancery in the presence, or by the orders, of Wengham, the chancellor. On 10 June 1256 the proceeds of chancery fines were handed to the treasurer in the presence of Henry Wengham, the chancellor.[55] A bond of 25 July 1256 was enrolled by licence of Henry Wengham, the chancellor.[56] On 14 March 1257, Henry Wengham, the chancellor, handed the letters of the countess of Provence to Peter of Winchester, clerk of the wardrobe.[57] A charter was sealed by Henry Wengham, the chancellor, on Tuesday in Whitsun week, 1258.[58] In November 1259, Henry Wengham, the chancellor, was present together with the marshal and justiciary of England at a council in the queen's chapel at Westminster.[59] He is described as chancellor when the royal assent was given to his election as bishop of London on 29 June 1259.[60] It is perhaps hardly necessary to recall these facts, for Henry Wengham has been generally recognized as a chancellor. Stubbs refers to him as the royal chancellor in 1258,[61] though he does not include him in his list of 'properly constituted chancellors' in the *Select Charters*. Wengham has obtained recognition, however, principally because he was allowed

[52] *Annales Monastici*, ii. 94, i. 318.
[53] *Ipsis diebus supplevit officium cancellarii magister Willelmus de Kilkenni . . . qui et cancellarius appellatus est*: *Chron. Mai.* v. 464.
[54] *Cal. of Pat. Rolls*, 1247–58, pp. 440, 563.
[55] Close Roll, 40 Hen. III, m. 10 d; cf. *Cal. of Charter Rolls*, 1257–1300, p. 3, a notarial instrument of 15 Kal. Ian. 1257.
[56] *Cal. of Pat. Rolls*, 1247–58, p. 521; cf. remission of fees on certain charters by the chancellor in September 1260; *Cal. of Charter Rolls*, ii. 28 and 29.
[57] Close Roll, 41 Hen. III, m. 10 d.   [58] *Cal. of Charter Rolls*, ii. 27.
[59] *Cal. of Pat. Rolls*, 1258–66, p. 61.   [60] *Ibid.* p. 29.
[61] *Const. Hist.* ii. 655 (3rd ed.).

to continue in office after the Provisions of Oxford. But it should be noted that in the official record of his oath to the barons in July 1258 he is not called chancellor; we are simply told that *Henricus de Wengham prestitit sacramentum coram baronibus Anglie de custodia sigilli regis.*[62] It is hardly safe, therefore, to lay too much stress on the fact that Kilkenny is simply called *custos sigilli nostri* in his quittance in 1255. Henry Wengham stands on the line of transition to the later type of chancellor. He was undoubtedly a chancellor, and yet at the same time he was appointed in the first instance by the king, and not by the council, and he did not receive the income of four or five hundred marks from the exchequer which all the later chancellors of the reign enjoyed.

The careers of the later chancellors are well known, but it has not always been noticed how among the violent alternations between baronial and royalist chancellors the position of chancellor acquired certain permanent characteristics. On 28 November 1260 Henry ordered the exchequer to pay 100 marks to Master Nicholas, archdeacon of Ely, the chancellor, for the support of himself and the clerks of the chancery.[63] The roll continues:

et sciendum quod per regem & magnates predictos (de consilio nostro) prouise sunt quadringente marce ad sustentacionem cancellarii & clericorum predictorum percipiende per annum ad quatuor terminos, videlicet in festo Sancti Martini C marce, in festo Sancti Hillarii C marce, in quindena Pasche C marce, in quindena Natiuitatis Sancti Iohannis Baptiste C marce, per regem & consilium.

Now this grant, devised for the benefit of the baronial chancellor in 1260, continued without intermission to the end of the reign. For Thomas of Cantilupe it was raised from 400 to 500 marks; but after the battle of Evesham, when Cantilupe was summarily replaced by Walter Giffard, the grant continued, and at the same rate, 500 marks. It was not until the beginning of Edward I's reign that the chancellor's fee was allowed to fall into abeyance, and then in the middle of the reign it was revived, and continued to be the normal remuneration for the chancellor for considerably more than a century to come.

Henceforth the writs for payment of the chancellor's fee make it pretty clear who held the seal, and also that the keepers of the seal were fully recognized chancellors. Nevertheless the rapid changes, and the way in which the same men held office twice over, have caused some confusion. Walter of Merton, chancellor from 12 July 1261[64] to 1263, was naturally called upon

---

[62] Close Roll, 42 Hen. III, m. 6 d.   [63] Liberate Roll, 45 Hen. III, m. 16.
[64] Liberate Roll, 45 Hen. III, m. 6; Close Roll, 45 Hen. III, mm. 8 and 10 d; *Cal. of Pat. Rolls,* 1258–66, p. 165; *Cal. of Charter Rolls,* ii. 37. Merton had frequently

to take office between the death of Henry III and the return of Edward I from abroad. Nicholas, archdeacon of Ely, was chancellor from 18 October 1260 [65] to July 1261, and again from 19 July to December 1263.[66] John Chishull was chancellor from December 1263 [67] to February 1265, and from 30 October 1268 [68] to July 1269. Chishull has met with hard treatment. Hardy omits his first chancellorship altogether, and *The Dictionary of National Biography* says that he received the seal on the first occasion 'only apparently as an official responsible for its safe keeping', and that 'he is never definitely spoken of as chancellor'. But as early as 24 December 1263 we hear that Chishull, *cancellarius noster*, had received 20 marks *ad sustentacionem suam & clericorum cancellarie nostre*,[69] and Chishull is twice called chancellor, during his second brief tenure of office, on the Liberate Roll of 53 Henry III, and four times at least on the Patent Roll.[70] The other chancellors have fared better; but even in the case of men like Nicholas of Ely and Walter of Merton, whose constitutional importance drew attention to the chancery memoranda about their custody of the seal, some vague statements have passed current.[71]

The evidence of the Charter Rolls is against the view that there is a great gulf between Wengham and the later chancellors. It is stated in the introduction to the first volume of the *Calendar* of them [72] that a charter 'was originally stated to be given

held the seal when Wengham was ill, or absent from court: Close Roll, 42 Hen. III, m. 8; *Cal. of Pat. Rolls*, 1247–58, pp. 628, 629 (7 May 1258); Close Roll, 43 Hen. III, m. 15; Liberate Roll, 43 Hen. III, m. 8 (15 to about 25 November 1258); *Cal. of Pat. Rolls*, 1258–66, p. 29; Close Roll, 43 Hen. III, m. 8; Liberate Roll, 43 Hen. III, m. 4 (5 June and 6 July 1259).

[65] Close Roll, 44 Hen. III, mm. 2 and 3 d; Liberate Roll, 44 Hen. III, m. 1; *Cal. of Pat. Rolls*, 1258–66, p. 97.

[66] Close Roll, 47 Hen. III, m. 6; *Cal. of Pat. Rolls*, 1258–66, p. 281.

[67] Chishull obtained the seal after the king left Windsor (*Cal. of Pat. Rolls*, 1258–66, p. 305), and held it while the king was abroad, from 23 December (Close Roll, 48 Hen. III, m. 7; Liberate Roll, 48 Hen. III, m. 5).

[68] Close Roll, 53 Hen. III, m. 13; Pat. Roll, 53 Hen. III, m. 30.

[69] Liberate Roll, 48 Hen. III, m. 7. There is an order for another instalment in similar terms on 4 February 1264: *ibid.* m. 5.

[70] Liberate Roll, 53 Hen. III, mm. 10 (24 February 1269) and 6 (20 May 1269); Patent Roll, 53 Hen. III, mm. 23, 22, 20, and 14. Ancient Correspondence, vol. viii, nos. 2–6, are addressed to him as chancellor.

[71] Stubbs and the *Dictionary of National Biography* make Merton succeed Ely 'probably' in April 1261, but the records are quite precise about July 12. Godfrey Giffard ceased to be chancellor 'before 1270' (*Dictionary of National Biography*), though Chishull certainly succeeded him on 30 October 1268. Hardy, usually so accurate, makes Richard of Middleton chancellor on 14 January 1269, but 29 July is the real date (Close Roll, 53 Hen. III, m. 3; Liberate Roll, 53 Hen. III, m. 3; *Cal. of Charter Rolls*, ii. 124). Sir James Ramsay in *The Dawn of the Constitution* has a full list of chancellors from Merton to Middleton, but under keepers of the seal he mentions only Kilkenny, Wengham, and John of Caux. In connexion with the last named he makes a curious slip. In the parliament of October 1260 'John of Caux, abbot of Peterborough, became keeper of the seal, and Nicholas, archdeacon of Ely, treasurer'. [72] p. v.

by the hand of the chancellor or his deputy; but from the year 1227, when King Henry III took the seal into his own hands, the final clause has normally run, *Data per manum nostram apud &c., die, &c.*' Now this, though true no doubt as a wide generalization covering a considerable period of time, is misleading as a summary of the facts. It is misleading to say that Henry took the seal into his own hands in 1227, since the one use he made of his complete majority in this connexion was to issue a charter granting the chancery to Neville with very full powers. Secondly, from 1227 to 1238 charters are, with very few exceptions, granted *per manum Radulfi de Neville, cancellarii nostri*. But from the time when Henry took the seal into his own hands in 1238 very few charters are given by the hand of the chancellor, and it is even rare for the chancellor to be mentioned amongst the witnesses. Nicholas of Ely only appears as chancellor amongst the witnesses in two charters of 1260–1, 5 and 28 February.[73] His name is not mentioned at all after that, until in June there is a group of charters given, in the old fashion, by the hand of the chancellor, on 1, 14, 18, and two on 25 June. It would be unsafe, however, to assume that because in Nicholas of Ely's time we have a recurrence to the old formula, there is something wrong about the omission of reference to a chancellor in the time of Wengham and Kilkenny. Merton is seldom a witness, and then is not called chancellor. Chishull is not mentioned at all. In the Charter Rolls the next appearance of the chancellor in an official position is on 14 March 1265. Charters of 14, 20, 29, and 1 March are *dat. per manum magistri Thome de Cantilupo, cancellarii nostri*. Walter Giffard, though he appears at the head of witnesses to charters immediately after Evesham, is not there described as chancellor. His successor, Godfrey Giffard, hardly ever appears amongst the witnesses in the Charter Rolls of 51 & 52 Henry III, until he heads the witnesses as *cancellarius noster* on 22 February 1268. From that time he appears frequently among the witnesses, but is not always described as chancellor. He is quite as often simply ' G. elect of Worcester '. John Chishull witnesses as chancellor pretty constantly in the roll of 53 Henry III, but his successor, Middleton, only appears once in this roll. So the old formula, ' by the hand of the chancellor,' is only used for two short periods, by the two most baronial chancellors, Nicholas of Ely and Cantilupe. It is quite common for the chancellor's name to be omitted altogether from the list of witnesses, or to be mentioned without the name of his office, even down to the end of the reign of Henry III.

Despite the wish of the reforming oligarchy to get back to

[73] Charter Roll, 45 Hen. III, charters in favour of Imbert of Montferraunt and Philip Basset.

the good old days of Henry's ancestors, the chancellors of the period after 1259 have more in common with the chancellors or keepers of 1238-59 than with those of an earlier period. The constant changes in personnel were of course actually brought about by changes of fortune between the contending parties. Yet the barons in 1258 declared for an annual as well as for an elective chancellor. If their programme had been carried out there would have been a succession of 'constitutional' chancellors even more short-lived, powerless, and unlike the Ralph Neville type than Everdon, Mansel, Lexinton, and Kilkenny. The chancellor's fee was devised by king and council for the benefit of Nicholas of Ely, yet it was adopted by Henry for his own chancellors because it accorded with the policy he had already formulated for himself. The hanaper system was worked out between 1244 and 1255, when the king had the chancery in his own hands.

With regard to the status of the seal bearer from 1244 to 1260, we must remember that there was not much need to define the position of Mansel and the rest in the records. The old habit of describing the office of each witness to a charter was falling into desuetude. For nearly ten years after 1227 the stewards, for instance, are carefully distinguished in a list of witnesses, but after that only a rare and unusually formal list would mention their office. On the other hand, the Patent and Close Rolls, still in their early days, are on the whole meagre in their information, compared even with those of the end of the reign. Even after 1258, when memoranda about the seal are fuller and more frequent, it is quite common to mention the transference of the seal from one holder to another without mentioning whether either was chancellor. Our best source of information about later chancellors is the order for the payment of their fee. Had the chancellor's fee been devised by 1244, it seems not improbable that John Mansel at least would have lived to receive it.

To turn to wider and more important issues, it seems clear that king and barons both took their share in substituting a salaried officer of limited powers and term of office for the old type of irresponsible magnate. Save in times of exceptionally strained relations, the barons allowed Henry's charters to be 'given by his own hand'. But if the chancellor no longer loomed so large in charters, the actual custody of the seal was held to be of greater importance than ever before. It was too important for the chancellor to delegate it to anybody else, except for a short time. Even for a few days the chancellor's absence is recorded. If the chancellor had lost some of his dignity as a magnate, he had become more important as the keeper of the seal.

L. B. DIBBEN.

The Treaty of Charlottenburg

THE treaty signed by Great Britain and Prussia at Charlottenburg on 10 October 1723 seems to have been concluded at short notice. There is no hint of any preliminary negotiation either in the dispatches of James Scott from Berlin [1] or in those of the Prussian envoy to George I, Baron von Wallenrodt.[2] Townshend's letter of 8 September, cited below, shows that it was in contemplation then, and the full powers used by him and Carteret are dated the previous day.[3] But they were for concluding treaties with any of the king's German neighbours, not with Prussia specifically, and those given to the Prussian ministers bore even date with the treaty. Certainly both the British government and Frederick William I were anxious to draw the existing bonds of alliance closer, but on the other hand George I was cool in the matter, and Bernstorff and his following in the Hanoverian ministry were not less jealous of Prussia than of old. Before speculating on the particular conjunction which produced the treaty, it will be well to examine the position of Prussia, and secondarily of Sweden and Denmark, in this year 1723, and particularly in their relations with George I and Peter the Great. Notice also must be taken of the alarm excited by the cruise of the Russian fleet. I have shown in a previous article [4] how the efforts of France, after the peace of Nystad, to make alliance with Russia were thwarted by the insistence of George I that he must be included as a principal party.

Since George had forced upon Frederick William the treaties of 1719 with Great Britain and Hanover,[5] a reasonable accord between them had been maintained by their joint contentions with Austria and by their common interest in defending protestant liberties in Germany. But there was still a lack of harmony on other questions. With the great issue of the time, the settlement of southern Europe on the terms of the quadruple alliance, Frederick William would not concern himself ; and, in spite of all

---
[1] Record Office, Prussia 17.
[2] Königliches Geheimes Staatsarchiv, Berlin.
[3] The original, Staatsarchiv, Berlin ; a copy in the king of Prussia's ratification, Record Office, Treaties 411.   [4] *Ante*, xxvi. 278.
[5] See the author's *George I and the Northern War*, ch. xxiii.

that George could do, he steadily refused to be involved in any action against Peter the Great. On the other side Hanoverian jealousy obtruded itself constantly, and Robert Walpole in England, resolute against expensive entanglements abroad, withheld Great Britain from giving support on German and Polish questions to the extent that Frederick William desired. Thus, when in 1722 proposals were made for the formation of a defensive protestant league, James Scott at Berlin was informed that, although there was 'no doubt to be made of the views of the Papists', there were 'no solid hopes of success', for such a league would be encountered 'by a strict Confederacy on the part of the Catholicks, and would naturally produce a warr, where the zeal and forwardness of England would scarce be better supported than we have been in other engagements'. Care must be taken, it was said, that Great Britain should not be drawn 'into such hazardous and burthensome projects. . . . Your Court might set an example by exerting itself, where they see their representations may be of use, but I cannot help doubting of their courage and steddiness in this matter.'[6] In another dispatch it was stated that the king would not share in the expense of raising opposition to the candidature of the electoral prince of Saxony for the Polish throne : 'those who are nearest will take their own measures as to the bestowing of their money,' just as the king had had to bear the whole charge 'when dangers have threatened us nearer home'.[7] And when conferences at Berlin were proposed to concert measures for the defence of the protestants in Poland, Scott was authorized to attend them indeed, but only to listen and report, the king suspecting that their real object was to further Prussian interests in Poland.[8]

Indeed, reminders of backwardness on the part of Prussia to assist George I on occasion, while ever ready to seek his aid in schemes of advantage to herself, were frequent. Thus Townshend in the second dispatch cited :

I cannot conclude without making this one observation as to the Court of Prussia, they are perpetually upon all, even the most remote occasions, teazing the King to join hand, heart, and purse wherever their interest is concerned, and in return whenever His Majesty proposes to them any thing relating to his service and security, he is sure to meet with nothing but cold assurances of there being no danger, no need of any precautions ; these joined to some trifling objections to what His Majesty proposes are to serve as a full answer for their not joining with the King our Master. . . . Keeping up a good correspondence with them, you may, however, take proper opportunities of letting them see that they ought to be as earnest in the King's interest, as they expect He should be in theirs.

[6] Townshend to Scott, 24 July (o.s.) 1722, Record Office, Foreign Entry Book 53.
[7] The same, 7 September (o.s.). [8] The same, 6 November (o.s.).

And in February 1723, it being recalled how in 1719 the treaty of Vienna had been rendered ineffectual by Prussian opposition, and how in 1721 the proposed defensive league with Hesse and Denmark had been refused,[9] Scott was again ordered to do nothing but listen and report, and 'keep them from pursuing wrong and dangerous projects'. Experience, he was told, had shown that it was very difficult to gain the Prussian court to any scheme which did not promise it extravagant advantages, a late instance of which was the coolness shown towards the plan for removing the duke of Holstein-Gottorp from St. Petersburg,[10] so soon as it appeared that the king of Prussia was expected to contribute to his support. The proposal to remove that negotiation to Stockholm had seemed to show a desire to throw the whole burden and expense upon his majesty.[11]

With George's particular enemy, Peter the Great, the dangerous neighbour and the desirable ally Frederick William insisted on maintaining the best terms. The Russian ambassador at Berlin, Alexis Golovkin, received all possible assurances both in regard to the duke of Holstein-Gottorp and on other matters, and he on

[9] *George I and the Northern War*, pp. 468-70. An alliance with Denmark without Prussia was not considered sufficient. Townshend wrote to Whitworth on 6 October (o.s.) 1721 : 'As to what you say about an allyance with Denmark, I easily conceive the advantages of it; but at the same time considering the personal weakness of that King, with the poverty and low circumstances of his Kingdome, we shall run too great a risk of being drawn into excessive expences by engaging with him alone. If Prussia could be brought to joyn in such an allyance with Denmark and us I should then think it would put the King's affairs into a much better situation both with regard to the North and to the South, and such a treaty would be desirable above any other thing. But I believe there is little hopes of prevailing with the Court of Prussia to enter into any engagement of that kind ; they being for the most part carried away with by-views, and narrow selfish notions, besides that althô they are masters of so great a number of troops, they are not remarkable for courage or resolution. So that the little bargains they may have made with the Duke of Holstein, and the fear of the Czar, will be invincible obstacles to any concert of the nature I have mentioned.' (British Museum, Add. MS. 37386). Whitworth agreed (to Tilson and to Bothmer, 21 October, *ibid.*). The 'little bargains' referred to a reported agreement with the duke of Holstein-Gottorp that if with the help of Prussia he should obtain the crown of Sweden, he should give up to her the remainder of Swedish Pomerania. Wallenrodt actually informed the British government of the desire of the king of Prussia to have Stralsund and Rügen, saying, however, that he would not proceed in the matter without King George's approval. The latter, on being informed, said that he would not oppose the project, but foresaw the difficulties of its realization (Tilson to Whitworth, 13 October (o.s.) 1721, *ibid.*). Whitworth, replying, favoured the proposal, but Count Bothmer shortly informed him that Wallenrodt said that in the present circumstances it must be postponed (28 November, *ibid.*).

[10] *Ante*, xxvi. 296.

[11] Townshend to Scott, 1 February (o.s.) 1723, *loc. cit.* There was some truth in this accusation, for Frederick William stated plainly in 1724: 'Es ist bey Uns bishehr eine beständige maxime gewesen, bey der Wir auch ferner bleiben werden, in dergleichen Neue Tractate Uns nicht zu engagiren, wann Wir nicht dabey ein considerables avantage finden.... Ohne acquirirung eines solchen avantage, glauben Wir, dass es besser vor Uns sey, freye Hände zu behalten' (to Mardefeld at St. Petersburg, 26 September 1724, Staatsarchiv, Berlin).

his part made corresponding professions, promising accomplishment of the much-desired Brandenburg-Courland marriage—the tsar, he said, held to the treaty for it concluded in 1718, though he hesitated to proceed in the matter at present for fear of rousing jealousies in Poland—and stating that the Russian ambassador to the king of Poland was ordered to act in unison with the Prussian envoy.[12] After the break-up of the Polish diet of 1722, adverting to conciliatory advances from Vienna, which he thought might be designed to involve him in measures prejudicial to the tsar or to France, Frederick William declared, I hold to the Russian emperor, not to the Roman.[13]

It was desired indeed at Berlin, as at Paris, to effect a reconciliation between George I and Peter the Great, and from the same motives of self-interest. But when Frederick William made a formal offer in London of his good offices to that end, it was met with suspicion as due to a desire to forestall the mediation undertaken by France and to substitute Prussia for that power in the alliance to be made with Russia and Great Britain. One of Wallenrodt's chief arguments, Townshend wrote, was 'the necessity of our coming into measures with the Czar in order to prevent him putting himself intirely into the hands of France'. He was answered politely, if falsely, that the king having no quarrel with the tsar, no reconciliation was necessary; had it been, the good offices of the king of Prussia would have been preferred to those of any other prince.[14]

But at the end of 1722 a change in Prussian feeling towards Russia began to manifest itself, a change which Whitworth had foretold a year before.[15] Thus Scott on 16 January 1723 :[16] ' Par

[12] Golovkin asked for money for the tsar's use in Poland, and Frederick William agreed to supply some, but asked that it might be repaid soon, as General Schwerin (his envoy) wanted it for bribery himself.

[13] Solov'ev, *Istoria Rossey*, book xviii, ch. 2. Whitworth wrote on 6 December 1721 : ' If the Emperor thinks to mortify the K. of Prussia by an alliance with the Czar, He will find himself extreamly mistaken in the event; for the Czar makes his court to the K. of Prussia more than ever, and will probably prefer his friendship always to that of the Emp^r, as more convenient for his views about Poland, his aims at having a share and authority in the business of the Empire, and the plan which the court of France is laying with him for that end ' (to Townshend, British Museum, Add. MS. 37387). The scheme secondly referred to, for incorporating Livonia in the empire and so obtaining for the tsar a seat and vote in the diet, was started, says Whitworth, by Urbich, the Russian envoy at Vienna, soon after the battle of Poltava.

[14] Townshend to Whitworth, 6 October (o.s.) 1721, British Museum, Add. MS. 37386.

[15] ' Autant que je puis juger, le plan de cette Cour à présent est, de n'entrer dans aucun engagement touchant les affaires du Nord, de part ou d'autre; mais quand Elle aura veu ses espérances du côté du Czar remplies, ou frustrées, car l'une ou l'autre aura à peu près le même effet, Elle pourra peut-être changer de sentiment, surtout si l'on Luy puisse montrer un plan solide' (to Bernstorff, 27 January 1722, British Museum, Add. MS. 37387).

[16] Record Office, Prussia 17.

toutes les conversations que j'ay eues depuis peu avec M^r le Baron d'Ilgen, et son gendre,[17] je dois juger que ces deux Messieurs sont contraires aux vues des Russes, et qu'ils font aussi tout ce qu'ils peuvent pour y rendre contraire le Roy leur Maître.' Principal causes which he noted were jealousy of the Franco-Russian alliance believed to be making and anger at the tsar's failure to carry out the Courland marriage-contract.[18] He concluded that the Prussians were not so inclined to be closely allied with the tsar, as had been supposed. In these deductions Scott was correct, as is shown by a definite statement of the king of Prussia's intentions sent to Wallenrodt. After reference to the danger threatening from the Russo-French negotiations, and particularly to the reported proposal to hand over Bremen and Verden to the duke of Holstein-Gottorp in compensation for his share of Sleswick, the rescript declared explicitly that in all matters arising in the north the king would stand firmly by the king of England for the maintenance of their conquests, and would resist with him any attempt, under any pretext whatsoever, against Hanover or other state of the Empire, in the same manner as though it were made against Prussia. The assurances to this effect contained in a letter to the king of England Wallenrodt was ordered, when presenting it, to emphasize out of his own mouth.[19] Later, commenting on the bad condition of the tsar's affairs, Scott wrote :

Ce qui me persuade plus que toute autre chose que les affaires des Russes vont en déclinant c'est la manière dont on en parle icy. Votre Excellence sçait jusques à quel point cette Cour a poussé la complaisance pour les Moscovites, lorsqu'on les a cru dans la prospérité. Présentement on entend dire que ce sont des gens qui n'ont ni foy ni loy, et qui ne méritent nullement les regards qu'on a témoigné pour eux. . . . Enfin, My Lord, autant que je suis capable de juger on est peu content icy des Russes.[20]

[17] Scott's opinion of Ilgen and his son-in-law Cnyphausen may be noted. The former ' is of long experience in affairs, and is very laborious, but is thought to be naturally of a fearful temper, and easily cast down and discouraged. . . . Monsieur Kniphausen in my oppinion hath the best parts, and a head the most turned for business of any I have known here ; he is generally thought to be indolent, and lazy ; but I doubt these qualitys in him are more affected, than natural. He knows his Master perfectly well. . . . I have always found him and also his father-in-law well inclined towards us, and no great friends of the Russ, but the truth is, there can be no great stress laid upon these their inclinations in a place where more reguard is often had to the advices and oppinions of military men, even of the lowest rank, than to those of a first Minister' (6 July 1723, ibid.).

[18] As a further cause Scott mentioned the tsar's omission to send the king of Prussia certain tall recruits promised in exchange for eighty Prussian sailors sent to Riga, at the rate of one giant for two sailors (17 April, ibid.). Frederick William, as is well known, took offences on this head more to heart than others of greater importance ; there are many instances of this in the dispatches.

[19] Rescript to Wallenrodt, 5 January 1723, Staatsarchiv, Berlin.

[20] Scott, 17 April 1723, Record Office, Prussia 17.

Peter the Great, however, was desirous of maintaining good relations. Chancellor Golovkin having come to Berlin in May, Mardefeld at St. Petersburg was informed that he had given assurance that the sincerity of the tsar's intentions was absolute, and would be proved by the proposals which he would make on his (Golovkin's) return.[21]

In her relations with Austria, Prussia was not very far removed from war. George I in his disputes with the court of Vienna had the German ministers there more or less on his side, but, in the case of Prussia, to the influence of those who were promoting measures against the protestants was added the particular hatred of Prince Eugene. Diplomatic intercourse was broken off in October 1721, when the Prussian resident was expelled from Austria in consequence of the firm stand taken by Frederick William in regard to his reprisals upon his catholic subjects, and for two years all efforts to heal the breach failed, whether by the British envoy, General de St. Saphorin, to whom Prussian interests were confided,[22] or by the Russian resident Lanchinsky,[23] or by the king of Poland, desirous of reconstituting against the tsar the Vienna alliance of 1719 with inclusion of Prussia.

On this matter also views at Berlin were now open to change. Although Frederick William always cordially detested Augustus II, in 1723 he began to give some attention to his overtures. As late as January in that year Scott, advocating a league between the emperor and the kings of Poland and Prussia as a 'contre-batterie' against Peter the Great, received from Ilgen the reply that his court would have nothing to do with that of Poland, as it was not to be trusted.[24] And Frederick William warned the Russian court of what was on foot.[25] But somewhat later renewed advances by Augustus had better success, and early in April General Seckendorff, formerly in the Prussian and now in the Austrian service, and also in the Saxon as governor of Leipzig,[26] came to Berlin. Personally agreeable to the king of Prussia, he was well received, and when he visited Berlin a second time in May in the company of

---

[21] Rescript to Mardefeld, 25 May, Staatsarchiv, Berlin.

[22] 'Je ne sçay rien de plus difficile ioy, où toutes les choses le sont beaucoup, sinon de réunir la Cour Impériale avec celle de Prusse, et d'y établir une confidence réciproque' (St. Saphorin, 21 October 1721, Record Office, Germany, Empire, 44). And such is the burden of his further dispatches, which include direct correspondence with the king of Prussia.

[23] Who was ordered in the autumn of 1722 to proffer the tsar's good offices, though cautiously, and without exhibiting undue zeal. The reply which he received was polite but reserved (Solov'ev, loc. cit.).

[24] Scott, 16 January 1723, Record Office, Prussia 17. He thought, however, that a combination, in which George I should take the place of Augustus II, might be favourably considered.

[25] Through Mardefeld (rescript to him of 2 February, Staatsarchiv, Berlin).

[26] St. Saphorin, 10 April 1723, Record Office, Germany, Empire, 49.

Count Flemming, the king of Poland's first minister, their arguments procured the signature of a 'punctation' of six articles designed to serve as the basis of a future treaty.[27] Scott, after Flemming left on 4 June, wrote that a foundation seemed to be laid for a good understanding, which 'may very much conduce to the keeping of the imperial and czarish courts within bounds'.[28] But Frederick William instructed his ministers at London, St. Petersburg, and Warsaw to let it be known that he was ignorant of the king of Poland's intentions, and would enter into no new relations with the Polish court. The discussions, he protested, had been limited to certain differences respecting trade and boundaries.[29] Little came of the agreement beyond a restoration of diplomatic intercourse between Austria and Prussia. When Seckendorff and Flemming arrived at Prague, where Charles VI was spending the summer for his Bohemian coronation, they found small disposition to enter into their plans. Flemming, St. Saphorin wrote on 19 September, was leaving completely disabused of his hopes of success.[30] But the affair gave Frederick William an opportunity to testify his sincerity towards George I. Immediately on the signature of the agreement he communicated it to him in a personal letter, saying that nothing was yet concluded, and that, if he would let his sentiments on the subject be known, they would be conformed to entirely.[31]

Towards the end of June the British court removed to Hanover. George I was accompanied by both his secretaries of state, Lords Townshend and Carteret, their duties in England being taken over for the time by Robert Walpole and Thomas Pelham-Holles, duke of Newcastle. His arrival was immediately followed by that of Frederick William of Prussia, who was returning home from a visit of inspection to Cleves and Wesel. He stayed five days, and so had full time to discuss the European situation in all its bearings. As soon as he had departed the court adjourned to Pyrmont for the waters, returning to Hanover on 22 July. Then all minds were occupied with the news of a great armament which

[27] Copies in French and German, Record Office, Prussia 17. The preamble stated that the articles were intended to re-establish harmony between the kings of Poland and Prussia as electors. It was agreed (1) to adjust differences as to frontiers, commerce and cartel in accordance with the laws of the empire, (2) to promote a reconciliation between the king of Prussia and the emperor, (3) to work thereafter for a reconciliation between the king of England and the tsar, (4) to preserve the constitutions and liberty of Poland, especially in regard to a future election, (5) the king of Poland to do what he could to promote an accommodation between Prussia and the republic of Poland, and (6) to arrange a time for a conference to conclude a formal treaty, which other powers might be invited to join.

[28] 5 June, *ibid.*

[29] Rescript of 25 May, Staatsarchiv, Berlin.

[30] Record Office, Germany, Empire, 50.

[31] 1 June, Record Office, Prussia 17, the French version of the agreement therewith, the German with Scott's of 10 July.

Peter the Great was preparing at Cronslot and Reval,[32] whose destination no man knew, though its probable objective, many thought, was to place the duke of Holstein-Gottorp on the throne of Sweden. There was no hint of such a thing, Townshend wrote, in the dispatches of William Finch from Stockholm, but the Hanoverian minister there, Colonel Bassewitz, had sent word that the Russian and Holstein ministers were about to leave the country, 'which confirms His Majesty in the opinion that the affair is concerted there, and will soon break out.'[33]

The state of affairs in Sweden was briefly as follows.[34] The Hessian king, Frederick I, had lost almost all credit. Not only had he to bear the chief blame for the peace of Nystad—it was held that from fear of his rival, the duke of Holstein-Gottorp, he had agreed to terms even worse than was necessary—but he was accused of courting in his progresses of 1722 popularity among the peasants with the view of recovering what he could of the royal prerogatives abolished in 1719.[35] To the active opposition, therefore, of the Holstein party was added that of all those who would maintain the present democratic constitution; practically the whole of the upper classes.[36] And the stoppage of English

[32] The news, exaggerated as usual, came from the Prussian and Danish ministers at St. Petersburg, and was forwarded by Scott on 20 July and by Lord Glenorchy from Copenhagen on the 27th (Record Office, Prussia 17, Denmark 46). A list of the fleet assembled at Reval, forwarded by Finch from Stockholm on 17 July (o.s.), showed twenty-four of the line, six of them of eighty-eight guns or more, and seven frigates, with eight admirals and 14,000 men. But resident Jackson wrote four days later, on the authority of one who had seen the fleet, 'in all respects it falls far short of what the list makes it' (Record Office, Sweden 32, 33). Of the Russian fleet in 1722 an eyewitness wrote (Record Office, Russia 9): 'No English sailors below a Boatswain in yᵉ Service & the Rushian sailors are fainthearted & unskilfull & there is not men enoufgh for 30 ships, & yᵉ Shipps doe not last above 8 years before they are rebuilt because the Timber is bad, & many of the Shipps are rotten & now repairing. Also all yᵉ ships of yᵉ English names are so rotten that they doe not goe to sea. They have no method in victualling their ships for they know not how to pickle any meat, but only dry salt it, & their meat is grass fed of 3 months in the summer which will stink in a months time as I have known.'

[33] Townshend to Robert Walpole, 30 July, private, Record Office, Regencies 4.

[34] For particulars see the dispatches, Record Office, Sweden 30 to 33; Bestuzhev's reports in Solov'ev; Stavenow, *Sveriges historia intill tjugonde seklet*, vii. 53 ff.

[35] Complaints of the senate's delays, says resident Jackson, and expressions of desire for restoration of the king's authority were general among the peasantry. He instances petitions presented and returned with the observation that 'the King was very desirous to redress their grievances but had no power to do it', an insinuation disliked even by those most devoted to him. (See Jackson, January and February 1722, and secretary Richard Poley, 17 January and 12 September (o.s.), Record Office, Sweden 30, 31).

[36] Thus Finch on 5 August (o.s.) 1723: 'The Act which has passed the Diet in favour of the Duke of Holstein was carry'd thro' rather by those who pique themselves upon being true Patriots and firm to the Form of Government than by the Holstein party, and was consented to as a point which might counterballance any design of settling the succession in the King's Family, and might show His Majesty, that every step made for raising the first would but raise the second' (Record Office, Sweden 32).

and French subsidies deprived Frederick of that means of influence. When the riksdag assembled in January 1723 the three higher estates and their grand secret committee [37] were found to be all but unanimous in the resolve to resist any extension of the royal authority; when, indeed, the peasants' estate presented a resolution in favour thereof it was summarily rejected and its authors were thrown into prison.

Moved by this principle of restraining the king, the riksdag forced upon him measures in favour of the duke of Holstein-Gottorp, and in particular the grant of the title of royal highness, implying his right of succession to the throne. Michael Bestuzhev, who had come in February 1722 as minister from the tsar, and was openly courted by the Holstein party, had already presented a request for this, as well as for recognition of the tsar's imperial title, and the demand was pressed by the duke's privy councillor Bassewitz, who arrived soon after the meeting of the riksdag and to whom Frederick was compelled, against his declared will, to grant an audience.[38] Although, in spite of warnings from Campredon at Moscow,[39] he strenuously resisted [40]—and Queen Ulrica was even more recalcitrant—he was forced to give way and to send letters to the tsar and to the duke conceding the required titles.[41] In fact, the result of the proceedings of the riksdag was to reduce the royal authority almost to a cipher. It was ordained that, if the king refused to sign the conclusions of his council, the council might sign in his name, and that all dispatches from ministers abroad should be sent to the president of the chancery for consideration by a secret committee.[42] After the close of the riksdag Frederick practically ceased to interest himself in political affairs.

All this by no means implied submission to the tsar. He was still the enemy to be feared, and the man to whom the Swedes looked for protection against him was still George I. The only notable exception was Count Vellingk, who of old had governed

---

[37] Composed of 100 nobles, 50 clergy, and 50 burghers. Its function was to examine in strictest secrecy into the conduct of affairs generally, and especially of foreign.

[38] He had informed Campredon at Moscow that he would not receive Bassewitz, unless he came before the meeting of the riksdag (extract from his letter of 24 September (o.s.) 1722 with Finch's of 6 February (o.s.) 1723, Record Office, Sweden 32). And it was said that he had sent orders to Finland to have him arrested on his way, but that Bestuzhev had found means for their evasion.

[39] Who wrote: 'Je vois avec peine que ce prince rejette la proposition de tout accommodement avec le duc de Holstein. . . . J'ai pris la liberté de faire là-dessus les plus justes représentations, qu'il m'a été possible, au roi de Suède. S'il ne veut pas en profiter et que les suites ne soient pas heureuses, il ne pourra s'en prendre qu'à lui' (26 December 1722, *Sbornik* xl. 416).

[40] He told Finch that he would not grant the title nor any other such 'inlet' into Sweden (Finch, 17 April (o.s.) 1723).

[41] Translations with Jackson's of 21 July and 5 August (o.s.), Record Office, Sweden 33.   [42] Stavenow, p. 57.

the lost province of Bremen. He was for a complete accord with Russia and an inquiry into the negotiation of the treaties of 1719-20 with Hanover and Prussia, producing a list of the bribes which had been given to the senators responsible. But he made little impression, says Finch, for the other members of the senate were jealous of or interested against him; and the chancellor, Count Horn, the most powerful man in Sweden, gave assurance that nothing disagreeable to the king of England would be brought forward in the riksdag.[43] And Frederick, in spite of George's continued refusal to assist him financially—in answer to a pressing appeal in January 1723 the latter pleaded the heavy indebtedness of the nation and the expenses incurred in connexion with the 'Atterbury plot'[44]—still expressed his intention of maintaining a constant attachment.[45] On the other side Finch was ordered to say that George I in no way concerned himself with the interests of the duke of Holstein-Gottorp;[46] this in consequence of declarations to the opposite effect made by Bassewitz. The latter thereupon complained to Townshend, recalling a memorandum delivered to the duke at Hanover in July 1719, which stated that George would willingly see him accepted as successor to the Swedish throne and would use his best offices to that end, though he could not then treat him as the heir, and must refer the question of the restitution of Sleswick to the negotiations for peace. Townshend replied with a polite letter of excuse, explaining why the king could not and would not interfere in the domestic affairs of Sweden.[47] And in June Finch reaffirmed to King Frederick his orders in the matter.[48]

The other power which had to fear a Russian attack was Denmark. When, in March 1722, news came of the tsar's naval preparations, everything was made ready at Copenhagen for defence, and Westphalen was sent back to St. Petersburg, principally with the object of discovering the tsar's intentions. He was instructed to ask, in return for recognition of the imperial title, withdrawal of the request for exemption from the Sound tolls and a guarantee of Sleswick. Further, approaches were made to Sweden for a defensive alliance, and the old proposals for treaties with Great Britain and Hanover[49] were renewed. The former met with scant welcome; the Danes were too much hated in Sweden,

---

[43] Finch and Jackson, 2 January (o.s.) 1723 and later dispatches, Record Office, Sweden 32, 33. For the bribery, see *George I and the Northern War*, p. 356.
[44] Copies of Frederick's letter of 28 December 1722 (o.s.) and of George's reply and dispatch to Finch of 12 February (o.s.) 1723, Record Office, Foreign Entry Book 155. [45] Finch, 13 March (o.s.).
[46] Townshend to him, 19 March (o.s.), Record Office, Foreign Entry Book 155.
[47] Copies of Bassewitz's letter of 12 May, with the memorandum of 22 July 1719, and of Townshend's reply of 29 June, *ibid.* 248. [48] Finch, 29 May (o.s.).
[49] See *George I and the Northern War*, pp. 190-1, 259, 272-4, 303-4.

and the Russians too much feared; it was held that no alliance could be less useful than that of Denmark, and that it was to the interest of Sweden for the duke of Holstein-Gottorp to have Sleswick back.[50] But in the latter case ear was given to the Danish proposals, for it was the time of the 'Atterbury plot', and ships and soldiers were wanted from abroad in case of need. Drafts for treaties with Great Britain and Hanover were sent to Copenhagen and communicated also to St. Saphorin at Vienna, he having expressed the opinion that the Vienna alliance of 1719 might be reconstituted with inclusion of Denmark.[51] But dissension on certain points—in particular the questions of wrecks on the Danish coasts and of trade with Norway, and the refusal of the Danes to furnish naval succour outside the Baltic—could not be composed, and the fear of a Jacobite rebellion died out.[52] Moreover, the making of the treaties was not well looked upon at Paris, Dubois opining that they would both prejudice Campredon's work in Russia and be insufficient to stay the tsar from infringing the Swedish treaties, if he meditated doing so. Better, he thought, to hold them back as an inducement to him to be tractable, though he agreed that, if Denmark were attacked, it would be necessary to defend and protect her.[53] Accordingly Frederick IV, always ready to transfer his confidence from one minister to another, now gave heed to the counsels of his minister of war and marine, Admiral Gabel, a declared opponent of alliance with George I, and the Russian minister at Copenhagen, Alexis Bestuzhev, reported him willing to come to terms with the tsar. Bestuzhev attributed the hostility hitherto displayed towards Russia to the two Holsteins [54] and the Hanoverian envoy, General Bothmer, and recommended a firm attitude, continued patronage of the duke of Holstein-Gottorp, renewal of the demand for exemption from the Sound tolls and for recognition of the imperial title, and bribery,[55] the foundation, he alleged, of Bothmer's influence. In March 1723 Gabel brought him to see the king privately. Frederick IV, he reported, pro-

[50] See E. Holm, *Danmark-Norges Historie i Frederik IV's sidste ti Regeringsaar*, pp. 68–73.

[51] St. Saphorin, 11 and 14 March 1722, Record Office, Germany, Empire, 46; Townshend to him, 23 March (o.s.), *ibid.* 42. See also (Prussia 105) a draft for a dispatch to Lord Whitworth at Berlin, not sent, entering fully into the question of communicating the scheme to the court of Prussia.

[52] For particulars of the above see Record Office, Treaty Papers 4, extracts of General Bothmer's dispatches from Copenhagen of April to August 1722. Also Holm, pp. 98, 99.

[53] Schaub, 20 and 27 May 1722, British Museum, Add. MS. 22522; Carteret to him, 12 May (o.s.), *ibid.* 22517.

[54] The grand chancellor, Ulrich Adolphus, Count Holsteinborg, and privy councillor John George Holstein.

[55] To the grand chancellor 10,000 ducats, to the other Holstein 6,000, to privy councillor Lente 6,000, and to councillor of state Hagen 3,000.

mised that, if the tsar would guarantee to him Sleswick and the duke definitely resign his claim thereto, then he would allow the latter the title of royal highness and help him to obtain the Swedish crown; and if the tsar should endeavour to deprive Hanover of Bremen and Verden in favour of the duke, or should invade Mecklenburg, he would not only not oppose him but help him, giving his fleet the use of the Danish harbours. But if, in spite of these offers, the tsar should reject his friendship, then he must not be surprised if he made alliance with King George. He would recognize the tsar's imperial title, and remit the Sound tolls on receiving free of cost a supply of hemp, pitch, and tar to serve as an excuse for the remission at other courts. A present of 3,000 ducats should at once be sent to Gabel.[56]

But all this came to nothing. Peter the Great, Solov'ev comments, was not ready to deprive the duke of Holstein-Gottorp of all hope of recovering Sleswick, only in order to secure the neutrality of Denmark in a possible war with George I. There was nothing for the Danes to do in 1723 but to prepare again for defence, and they prepared.[57] And the proposals for alliance with Sweden were brought forward once more. Finch had wind in April of a discussion on the subject in the secret committee of the riksdag, and forwarded a copy of a letter from the king of Denmark accepting with pleasure definite proposals made in one from the king of Sweden of 8 March (o.s.).[58] But nothing had resulted when the news of the sailing of the Russian fleet intervened. Immediately on receipt of it at Copenhagen anxiety for the treaties with George I revived. Lord Glenorchy reported:

This Court begins now to be sensible of their danger and have none to depend on for assistance but England, wherefore the Ministers desired me to propose to His Majesty to enter into an alliance for the common good and to send fourteen or fifteen ships into the Baltick, which joined with the fleet here will put a stop to the progress of the Czar.

To his reference to former backwardness on their part they had replied, he said, that they were now sincere, and hoped that a fleet would be sent, if not at once, then in good time in the ensuing spring.[59] But Townshend was of opinion that neither Denmark nor ' this side of the Empire ' were in danger.

His Danish Maj^{ty} has too great a force by sea and too many troops at command to give room to such a very wary prince as the Czar to make

---

[56] Solov'ev, *loc. cit.*, and Holm, pp. 78–80.   [57] Holm, pp. 81, 82.
[58] Finch, 3 and 10 April (o.s.) 1723, Record Office, Sweden 32.
[59] Glenorchy to Robert Walpole, 27 July 1723, in cipher, Record Office, Denmark 46. Walpole wrote to Newcastle: 'There was another letter came ye Post before from Ld Glenorchy wth offers from ye King of Denmark to enter into an im'ediate Treaty wth His Majesty, the effect of their great fright, but that I have refer'd to Hanover (2 August (o.s.) British Museum, Add. MS. 32686).

any attempt that must certainly prove unsuccessful, and the making any impression on these parts of the Empire will be attended by so many ill consequences, that his Ma^{ty} cannot conceive how any practicable enterprize on these coasts can be formed. That there has not been such an alliance, as they may now seem to wish for, was entirely their own fault.

If however, contrary to reason and expectation, the tsar should think of disturbing the king of Denmark, the latter knew that the king of England would always be ready to do what could in reason be expected for his preservation, so that he 'need not abandon himself to counsels unworthy of his honour and dignity'. If the Danes were so much alarmed and really desirous of a defensive alliance, they had better send some one to Hanover to treat.[60]

Campredon's opinion was in consonance. The Russian fleet, he had lately written, could not stand against that of Denmark, especially if it were true that an English squadron were to join it, nor did a descent on Mecklenburg appear more practicable, opposed as it would be by the emperor and the whole empire, and the tsar having lost most of his cavalry on his Caspian campaign. He might, perhaps, be intending to attack Dantzig, having cause to do so, but his finances were exhausted, and he had sent 18,000 men under General Matyushkin to the Caspian. It was more likely that the king of Sweden's conduct had given him the occasion, which perhaps he sought, to establish the duke of Holstein-Gottorp on the throne of Sweden immediately.[61]

In accordance with Townshend's suggestion the Danish general Lövenörn, now envoy at Berlin, was sent to Hanover to try, as Lord Glenorchy expressed it, 'how his Majesty is disposed to enter into measures for the common good and security of the Baltick.'[62] But he had no success, and of his unfavourable report secretary Hermann wrote: 'On s'inquiète ici [at Copenhagen], et le Ministre de Russie s'en rit.'[63] Frederick William of Prussia also had recourse to Hanover. While doubting that the Russian expedition meant anything, he instructed Wallenrodt to ascertain exactly the king of England's sentiments, in order that he might conform to them.[64] It was replied that it was thought best to wait, because the blow would have fallen before measures could be taken to prevent it. Ministers, Wallenrodt said, thought that the Swedes themselves might have invited a Russian intervention, and that it depended on the Swedish army whether a revolution took place

---

[60] Townshend, 30 July and 3 August, and further similarly 10 August, Record Office, Foreign Entry Book 5.
[61] Campredon, 5 July, *Sbornik* xlix. 352.
[62] 17 August, Record Office, Denmark 46. Lövenörn stayed at Hanover during September.   [63] 27 November, Record Office, *ibid.*
[64] 'Allermass Wir auch in allen Unseren übrigen Consiliis und Actionen zu thun aufrichtig gemeinet sind' (rescript of 24 July).

or not; nor were they entirely satisfied with the king of Sweden's conduct.[65] Later he wrote that Bernstorff had twice submitted a letter to the king to sign, inviting the king of Prussia to consult upon measures to be undertaken against Russia, but he had refused, Townshend opposing from the opinion that evil might result, if the answer should not be what was expected.[66]

But it was thought necessary at Hanover to take measures of precaution against the Russian danger, and in the first place to have in hand a sum of British money for use as occasion might require. The plea employed by Townshend in setting forth the proposal to Robert Walpole was that a conquest of Sweden would give the tsar the control of its ports,

and we might in a little time see Swedish and Muscovite squadrons in conjunction at Gothenburg, able to terrify and distress all the coasts of Great Britain. . . . The King, tho' mighty tender and unwilling to make any proposal, that should seem to burthen his Kingdoms; yet seeing in this exigency . . . that nothing but a good summ of money . . . can be of service to help us, has ordered me with the utmost secrecy [67] to open this affair to you. . . . You will please therefore to cast about in your thoughts how you may have at command, with the least noise possible, one or two hundred thousand pounds, if necessary, to be disposed of to prevent the kingdom of Sweden's falling under the disposal of the Czar.

The plan was, if the present king of Sweden should be overthrown at once, then, in the interests of Great Britain, to be as well with the new monarch as might be, but on the other hand, if he should be able to make a stand,

then to have a summ of money ready to assist the king of Denmark and other princes, who would be exceeding jealous of such an exorbitant accession of power to the Czar, to stand by his Swedish Majesty, and to oppose the efforts of the Muscovites, and the Swedish faction.

The king being bound by his last treaty to succour the king of Sweden in such a case, parliament would undoubtedly sanction such a disposal of money for the good of the kingdom. To think of equipping a squadron would be folly; even if the lateness of the season allowed it, the cost would exceed the sum now asked for.[68]

[65] Wallenrodt, 28 and 31 July.

[66] The same, 11 August. Bernstorff, he says, was also opposed by the Hanoverian privy councillors Eltz, Busch, and Alvensleben, as also by Court-Marshal Hardenberg, who was beginning to gain credit. The first three, we learn elsewhere, had stood in opposition to Bernstorff for some time past (Plessen to Robert Walpole from Pyrmont, 7 July 1723, Record Office, Regencies 4).

[67] 'Because the matter, 'if it should take the least air in England, might do great hurt to publick credit, and consequently to our other domestick affairs.'

[68] Townshend to Walpole, 27 July, very secret and to be confided only to the duke of Newcastle, Record Office, Regencies 4 (original); printed by Coxe, *Memoirs of Sir Robert Walpole*, ii. 253, but dated in the old style.

Carteret, inheritor of Stanhope's forward views in foreign policy, and himself the enthusiastic partisan of Sweden when ambassador at Stockholm in the last years of the war, strongly supported the proposal, as also did the Hanoverian ministers. But Walpole, intent upon restoring the financial credit of England, objected. Humouring the king's views in his official reply to Townshend, in a private letter to him he expressed dissent as strongly as he dared.[69] And he wrote to the duke of Newcastle :[70]

The other letter wch I wrote to Ld Townshend, being to be seen both by the King and Ld Carterett was so calculated accordingly, and I hope I was so good a Courtier as both to please His Majesty, and to defy Ld Carterett from being able to impute to me either want of zeal or readiness to serve His Majesty in any thing that He had at heart.[71]

The substance of that letter was that I could answer for £150,000 betwixt Mich. and Christmas, in case His Majesty came over time enough for ye Parliament to pass the Land-Tax before Christmas.[72] I did not forgett to make such a state of ye Revenue, as show'd the service I was to undertake neither easy nor insignificant, but treated the occasion, if necessary, in such a manner as I thought would not be disagreeable to the King, and that our friend [73] can take no advantage of.

I had not indeed time to take a copy of that letter, or else y^r Grace should have seen it.

But notwithstanding what I wrote in publick, I must own my apprehensions are great upon this occasion, & if an emulation or endeavour to outvye one another should transport us into any rash engagements, I dread ye consequences, wch made me write in ye manner I did, and if I had not been afraid of displeasing L^d. Townshend at this distance in a point where I do not know his way of thinking, I should have inlarged a great deal more upon ye topick of caution.

The duke of Newcastle was not helpful. He shared with Townshend the apprehension of a Russian invasion and with Walpole the fear of discontents at home.[74] After discussing the circumstances, he stated the dilemma to be that if the tsar became too strong he might ' at once overset us ', while, ' if an opposition be made by sending a fleet, or granting a subsidy, that may create ill humour amongst our friends.' He relied on Walpole's great

[69] 23 July (o.s.), printed by Coxe, ii. 263 ; an unsigned draft, Record Office, Regencies 4.

[70] 25 July (o.s.) British Museum, Add. MS. 32686.

[71] Carteret was already the enemy, and the discreditable intrigue, which was to deprive him of his office of secretary of state, was in conception. (The original correspondence thereon, Record Office, Regencies 5. Ballantyne in his *Lord Carteret* writes from it with truth ; Coxe's account is biased.)

[72] In his private letter to Townshend Walpole said that the £150,000 could be raised out of the provision made for the king's staying abroad over Christmas, if he returned sooner, but not otherwise. [73] Carteret.

[74] The demand would ' certainly give new life to the Jacobites, and may possibly occasion a breach among our friends '.

ability and on the zeal of parliament to find an expedient, and thought that while Townshend, being on the spot, must be a better judge of the gravity of the affair than they at home, yet Walpole's hint of caution to him could certainly do no harm.[75] Later Townshend wrote that the king was entirely satisfied with what Walpole proposed, hoped that the money would not be wanted, and would only ask for it in case of necessity. Bernstorff and Carteret, he said, had laboured to keep up the scare, but the king was steady, and most complimentary to Walpole's capacity for business.[76]

Another demand was from the king of Sweden for £10,000. The grant of this Townshend bitterly opposed, finding that the money was to be employed, not for defence against the tsar, but to influence the riksdag. Bernstorff, he told Walpole, had pressed not only for it but for the dispatch of six or eight British men-of-war to act with the Danish fleet; but 'His Ma^ty is firmly resolved not to assist Sweden with a farthing of money till the case of the treaty shall actually exist' and some effectual measure be proposed to avert the common danger.[77] Accordingly Finch at Stockholm was instructed that the advance could not be proposed to parliament, as it did not come under the treaty with Sweden. The king's father, the landgrave of Hesse-Cassel, Townshend observed, was more nearly concerned and would doubtless find the money;[78] if he would not, how could it be required of the king of England? If it appeared that the tsar would use his forces to create disturbance in Sweden, and threatened its coasts, then the king would punctually perform his engagements; and though it was too late in the season to send men-of-war, 'would take all others the best and most effectual measures he can to support the King of Sweden against any hostile attack whatsoever.'[79] Finch replied that people of the best sense were of opinion that the tsar was only making a demonstration. He had waited, he said, upon the king and communicated his master's assurances. There was general satisfaction thereat, and the secret committee of the riksdag had pronounced the offer to be 'the most generous and the most à propos that could be', and it had been unanimously resolved, if the tsar came near the coast, to break up the riksdag

---

[75] Newcastle to Walpole, 26 July (o.s.), the original, Record Office, Regencies 4; a copy, British Museum, Add. MS. 32686.

[76] To Walpole, 10 and 11 August, Record Office, Regencies 4.

[77] 6 August, private, Record Office, Regencies 4; printed by Coxe, ii. 258, but without a date. Townshend went on to advocate afresh the larger proposal, and to assure Walpole of the confidence which the king showed in them as against Carteret and Bernstorff.

[78] 'The Landgrave has large territorys, and cannot fail of getting a greater summ than that when he will at a moderate interest.'

[79] Townshend to Finch, 2 August, Record Office, Foreign Entry Book 155, Regencies 4.

F 2

and rescind the acts passed at his desire. 'People here are very jealous of the Czar's meddling with the domestick affairs.'[80]

One ground on which Walpole objected to any help being given to Sweden was that in Russia it might be made 'a pretence to prevent a reconciliation betwixt the King and the Czar, wch I taste very much, and my politicks are in a narrow compasse, if we keep perfectly well wth France and the Czar, I am under no apprehensions of foreign disturbances, wch alone can confound us here '.[81] But when he wrote this, apprehensions had been laid aside, for news had come first that no Russian galleys had sailed from Cronslot,[82] and later that Peter the Great had left the fleet suddenly and returned to St. Petersburg, on advices, it was said, that the Turks had occupied Georgia and were threatening Derbent.[83]

The supposition that Peter the Great designed to subjugate Sweden with a view to an attack upon Great Britain seems to us absurd, but it shows, at least, in what estimation his power was held. Perhaps he wished to intimidate the Swedes into accepting the proposal made by Bestuzhev to King Frederick privately at the end of 1722 for an offensive and defensive alliance, including conditions for the nomination of the duke of Holstein-Gottorp as successor to the throne and joint efforts for the recovery of Sleswick for him. Bestuzhev was then answered that such a treaty could only be considered if the king of England were made a principal party to it.[84] But after the business of the titles had been carried through he reintroduced the subject formally, and the Swedish ministers then told those of George I that they did not think fit to reject the proposal, provided that the condition above stated was allowed. They suggested that the king of England's requirements in regard to the treaty of Nystad might thus be satisfied and his differences with the tsar be accommodated.[85] Townshend in reply to Finch's report of this stated that an indispensable preliminary to any such negotiation would be a declaration on the part of the tsar that he was ready to enter into a perfect friendship with the king of England and to forget the past, when the latter would be ready to join the alliance proposed as a principal party. It was believed,

---

[80] Finch 5 August (o.s.).

[81] To Newcastle, 31 August (o.s.), British Museum, Add. MS. 32686.

[82] Townshend, 10 to 17 August, Record Office, Regencies 4. On 20 August he wrote decisively, 'the Czar has not the least thought of disturbing Sweden.'

[83] Glenorchy and secretary Hermann from Copenhagen, 31 August and 7 September, Record Office, Denmark 46. On 10 September advice, dated 25 July, was received from Abraham Stanyan at Constantinople to the effect that the pasha of Erzerum, appointed seraskier, had taken Tiflis and the whole province of Georgia without opposition (Record Office, Turkey 24). Carteret's reply to this of 22 September, British Museum, Add. MS. 22519.

[84] Finch, 19 December (o.s.) 1722, Record Office, Sweden 30.

[85] Finch, 31 July (o.s.) 1723, *ibid.* 32 and Regencies 4.

he said, that the only matter requiring accommodation was the expulsion of the tsar's minister from London; but in that it was to the king, if to any one, that satisfaction ought to be given, and so far as he was concerned, the incident might be forgotten.[86]

Full particulars of the negotiations which ensued are to be found in the correspondence of Townshend and Finch,[87] but they do not concern us now. Briefly, the Swedes offered their mediation between George I and Peter the Great, and, when it was refused by the former, turned to make alliance with the latter. George's position in the meantime was greatly strengthened by the signature of the treaty of Charlottenburg, and to that we may now proceed.

It is probable that the queen of Prussia, George's daughter, had some share in the inception of the treaty. She came to Hanover on 23 July, immediately upon the return of the court from Pyrmont. In her hurry to be there she arrived three days before she was expected,[88] and she stayed till 10 August. She had many private conversations with her father, but, unfortunately, she carefully excludes any reference to what passed from the affectionate letters which she wrote to her husband daily.[89] She says that, while she has much to report, she will wait to do so by word of mouth on her return home. The single thing which she reveals, apart from mention of the affection exhibited by her father and of her expectation of success in all her 'petits articles', is that, immediately upon her arrival, she pressed him to pay a visit to Berlin. There seems to be no reason to doubt the statement of the margravine of Baireuth, then the Princess Wilhelmine of Prussia and one of the persons concerned,[90] that the principal subject of discussion was the double marriage between the two royal houses, which the queen had so much at heart and had urged so long. She has it also that George was wanted at Berlin in order that he might see for himself that certain reports of her unfitness to be Prince Frederick's bride were untrue.[91] And this is corroborated by what Wallenrodt wrote on the queen's departure. Having been informed

[86] Townshend to Finch, 26 August 1723, Record Office, Foreign Entry Book 155, Regencies 4.
[87] Record Office, Foreign Entry Book 155, Sweden 32.
[88] The excuse devised by Wallenrodt was that she had not seen her father for seven years, and on her last two journeys had had the ill fortune to arrive too late (25 July, Staatsarchiv, Berlin).
[89] Königliches Hausarchiv, Charlottenburg.   [90] See her Memoirs.
[91] As, in Wallenrodt's phrase, 'kränklicher Constitution und particularen humeur.' The reports were ascribed to Wilhelmine's discarded governess, M{dlle} Leti ('par dépit ihres Abschiedes'), who was now at Hanover under the protection of the countess of Darlington, the duchess of Kendal's rival. How M{dlle} Pöllnitz ('ein vergiffteter Drache') and other Hanoverian ladies came to Berlin to make a close inspection of the princess is related in her Memoirs.

of the reports, he says, at Pyrmont by the duchess of Kendal[92] and Townshend, he had resolved to lay them before the queen immediately on her arrival, and also to inform her of the state of parties at the Hanoverian court. She determined to try at once to persuade her father to go to Berlin, in order that he might be disabused of this and of other insinuations. And she managed so prudently as to gain the duchess of Kendal's confidence, without offending the opposing party. He doubted whether the queen would have written anything on these matters, as such was not her habit, but suggested that a positive invitation should be sent; everything, however, to himself should be put in cipher, in order that Bernstorff might not be informed, for he was so curious, and so alarmed at the queen's private interviews with her father, that he would certainly have the dispatches opened.[93]

But the marriage cannot have been the only subject of the conversations, and it may well be supposed that the queen suggested, at least, a closer political union between Great Britain and Prussia. This, we know, was favoured by her husband, and strongly advocated by the British ministers. And they must have had a much more important thing in view in bringing George I to Berlin, the impression, namely, which the visit would make upon the courts of Europe. It was natural for him to call at Hanover on his way back from Westphalia, and natural for his queen to travel to see her father, but a special journey of the king of England to Berlin was calculated to inform Europe that the two powers intended to act in foreign politics in unison. Frederick William instructed Wallenrodt to cultivate the friendship of the duchess of Kendal and Townshend, as they seemed to be the best inclined to Prussia, and to find out what King George really meant and what might be expected from him. It was not known, the rescript said, what further deference could be shown, or what potentate of Europe's friendship could be more convenient and useful to him. A letter was being sent inviting him to Berlin, and requesting him to signify his positive resolve.[94] Wallenrodt was shortly informed by the duchess of Kendal that the king had characterized the letter as a very obliging one, and he expressed confidence that the visit would take place; when, however, was uncertain, but probably on the king's way to his hunting at the Göhrde.[95] George, on his side, through his envoy Scott, intimated the most sincere assurances of his desire to be well with the king of Prussia, both on account of their near relationship and of the

[92] Now definitely associated with the Walpole-Townshend party in the British ministry.
[93] Wallenrodt, 11 August, Staatsarchiv, Berlin.
[94] Rescript of 17 August, *ibid.*
[95] Wallenrodt, 21 August, *ibid.*

necessity of defending protestant interests in Germany.[96] And Townshend wrote on 8 September :

The King of Prussia has made all imaginable court to the King our Master, and has used all possible endeavours to gett him over to Berlin. His Maty has certainly very little inclination for this journey, and has not hitherto declared his resolution upon it; but I live in hopes that he will conquer his aversion, and not refuse so trifling a compliance, which may open the way to a better understanding between the two Crowns. A neighbouring Prince so nearly related, so well affected to the Protestant cause, who has a standing force of 80m men and such an extent of dominions as the King of Prussia, is certainly worth gaining even upon much harder terms ; and I am satisfied nothing would contribute more to bring the Czar to reason and to facilitate our treaty with him, than the renewing our antient alliances with Prussia, which I shall therefore labour all I can.[97]

But still George could not be persuaded to give a decision. The duchess of Kendal, pressing him on the subject, was answered that he was too greatly overcome by affairs to be able to resolve.[98] He was anxious, besides, to get as soon as possible to the Göhrde, and, as Wallenrodt testifies, he was not in good health; indeed, when he came to Charlottenburg, a seizure at his first supper nearly made an end of him.[99] However, after an audience on 25 September, Wallenrodt flattered himself that his arguments had made a serious impression, and that the journey would be undertaken,[100] and at length, on the evening of 8 October, he arrived. The visit lasted five days and passed off excellently.[101]

To conclude a treaty in two days was rapid work, but the settlement of the terms need not have been difficult, for it was, in form, only a renewal of those of 1661 and 1690,[102] with alterations suited to the present circumstances. The first clause, after reciting this, established a faithful, firm, and perpetual friendship,

[96] Scott to Ilgen, 30 August, and the reply in suitable terms, 4 September, *ibid.*
[97] To Robert Walpole, Record Office, Regencies 4 ; printed by Coxe, ii. 266.
[98] Wallenrodt, 19 September. 'Die grossen Intriguen der Weiber,' he wrote, 'halten den König ab von einer fermen resolution darüber.' Previously he had written (15 August), 'Je mehr man selbigen zu einer Sache pressirt, je mehr man Ihn difficiler macht.'
[99] Of which the margravine of Baireuth gives a graphic account. Townshend says that, arriving late after travelling more than 100 miles that day without eating or drinking, as was his custom, he ate too heartily in a hot and crowded room, and fainted (to Walpole, 9 October, Record Office, Regencies 5).
[100] Wallenrodt, 26 September.
[101] A printed account, with a poem, with Scott's of 16 October, Record Office, Prussia 17. Another in the *Lettres historiques,* lxiv. 532. More interesting is that of the margravine, who remarks on the coldness of George's manner and relates how he examined her closely from top to toe by the light of a candle.
[102] Hence, presumably, the curious mention of Cleves and Juliers in the secret article, Cleves having long been Prussian. The duchies, the succession to which was now in question, were those of Juliers and Berg.

alliance, and confederation by land and sea, and went on: 'On s'évertuera à avancer les intérêts mutuels, et à maintenir l'un l'autre réciproquement dans les royaumes, provinces, états, droits, commerce, immunités et prérogatives quelconques dont ils se trouvent maintenant en possession soit dedans ou dehors de l'Empire, sans exceptions, et à se secourir mutuellement en cas de trouble ou d'attaque.' Clause 2, reciting the fact that the treaty of 1690 was partly offensive against France, stated that it was renewed only so far as it was defensive, and not otherwise. Under clause 3 the mutual succour was fixed at 8,000 infantry or their equivalent in money at the rate of 10,000 Dutch florins per 1,000 men per month, or, in the case of aid to the king of Prussia, a strong squadron of the line, if he so desired. Were he called upon to send troops to England, he was to furnish their ordinary pay, and King George was to raise it to the English scale. But if the troops of either party were called out elsewhere, then he who was succoured should not be called upon to provide anything but bread and forage. By clause 4 the king of Prussia undertook to provide, on notice given, an additional force of 8,000 foot and 2,000 cavalry of his own or of hired troops on the same conditions as his father had supplied them for the war in Flanders, to be paid by the king of England at the same rate as the most favoured Prussian corps had been paid in that war. If by this action he incurred the resentment of any power, King George undertook to take his part ' hautement ', and not to allow him to suffer harm, but to repair to him any damage done ; employing for this purpose, on demand, as many troops and men-of-war as should be necessary. The last two clauses provided for exchange of ratifications within six weeks and for counterpart copies.

There were two separate articles. The first expressly declared that, Charles II having been possessed only of dominions appertaining to the crown of Great Britain, the present treaty extended to all the states, rights, dignities, and prerogatives of the king of England within the empire. The second bound the latter to do his best to obtain the inclusion of the king of Prussia's principality of Neuchâtel, comprising the counties of Neuchâtel and Vallengin, in the treaty about to be made by France with the Swiss Confederation as a member thereof ; so that should war break out between France and the empire, and the king of Prussia be obliged to furnish his contingent of troops for the service of the latter, the principality should be exempt from attack. A secret article renewed the obligation of the treaties of 1661 and 1690 that, if there should be no heir to the house of Neuburg, the king of England should support the Prussian claim to Cleves [103] and

[103] See last note.

Juliers; an agreement which, when it leaked out, supplied fresh fuel to the jealousy of the court of Vienna.[104]

From Berlin George travelled straight to the Göhrde, and Townshend signified him to be 'extremely pleased with his noble and affectionate entertainment', and added his warmest thanks for the civilities shown to himself, especially by Ilgen and Cnyphausen.[105] Wallenrodt, too, reported that the king had received him most graciously and expressed his contentment with his visit, and that the duchess of Kendal, who had worked so hard for it, was charmed at its good effect. He himself, he said, was offered a lodging at the Göhrde, to the jealousy of the other foreign ministers, who had to put up at Danneberg. He could not sufficiently express what a change he found: 'alle Leuthe nach des Königs Exempel voritzo wollen Preussisch seyn;' whether they were so in heart, events would show, 'wenigstens müssen sie sich voritzo sehr contregniren.'[106]

It remains to surmise, in default of direct evidence, why the treaty was made. The general intention of the British government is clearly expressed in private letters of Townshend to the two Walpoles. While, he wrote, no further engagements were taken on the British side than 'the renewal and confirmation of our old Treatys', yet, in his private thoughts, he greatly appreciated the value of what was done, since the military support lost by the sinking of the Dutch republic would be replaced by the fine army of Prussia. The king, he said, would now be able 'to act more independently from the houses of Austria and Bourbon, and preserve the peace of Europe with less submission to the terms of either'. The treaty would endure, would sound well in England, and so on.[107] And again:

We fix the King of Prussia in our friendship, which was a most necessary point to be sure of in this juncture. As the present situation in Holland is extremely weak, and under such disorder and confusion, we could not doe a better thing, than to cover ourselves with this alliance, which must inspire more respect towards the King, both in the Emperour and the Czar, since His Majesty is now at the head of a mighty force by land, as well as Master of the most powerfull fleet in Europe. And it was time to strike in, and prevent the effect of Count Flemming's designs and negotiations by securing the King of Prussia to England in our own way.

He went on to remark how agreeable the treaty must be to France, how an impression was already noticed upon the imperial and

---

[104] The treaty, Record Office, Treaties 411; copies and papers in connexion, Treaty Papers 59 and British Museum, Add. MS. 22519.
[105] To Scott and to Wallenrodt, 15 October, Record Office, Foreign Entry Book 222.
[106] 27 October, Staatsarchiv, Berlin.
[107] To Robert Walpole, 18 October, Record Office, Regencies 5.

Saxon ministers, how it was approved in Holland, and what an advantage it was to have 18,000 to 20,000 auxiliaries at call, whether for support of guarantees or for defence.[108]

But, apart from these general views, there must have been some special reason to account for the suddenness of the conclusion. It can hardly have been the scare of the Russian Baltic expedition, for that was past, as has been said, by the end of August. Nor was there any marked increase of acuteness yet in relations with Austria; the negotiations connected with the Congress of Cambray, though making little progress, were still not without promise of success. Of what was uppermost in Frederick William's mind we have knowledge from the papers at Berlin—an alliance between France and Russia, intended, in his phrase, to bridle Germany.[109] This has been noticed above, and the fear was particularly evident at the beginning of 1723, when, in a memorandum addressed to their master, Ilgen and Cnyphausen spoke of advices both from St. Petersburg and Paris of the advanced state of the negotiations. They pointed out its menace to Prussia, and recalled the fact that the treaty of Amsterdam of August 1717 entitled Prussia to be included in any fresh treaty between Russia and France. No doubt, they said, France wanted to play the pipes in the north;[110] and they suggested that the king of England, who had so great influence with the Regent, could best work to bring the project to naught, a better plan than for Prussia to be included in the treaty, for that would make great noise and rouse great jealousy in Europe. God, they concluded, had given his majesty so much strength and power, that he would be welcomed as an ally on any side.[111] Frederick William approved of this, and noted upon it that it would be well to excite the fears of George I in regard to Bremen and Verden; hence the reference to this cited above. And when Wallenrodt reported that the king of England consented to act as desired, satisfaction was expressed, and it was promised that all possible information should be sent to him privately.[112]

[108] To Horatio Walpole, now at Paris, 25 October, British Museum, Add. MS. 22519. And similarly to St. Saphorin (27 October, Staatsarchiv, Hanover): 'Nous avons conclu un Traitté, . . . et nous avons par là renoué et reserré plus étroitement l'amitié intime entre le Roy notre maître et celuy de Prusse, que tous les bons Serviteurs de sa Ma.té jugeront sans doute être un Ouvrage très à propos, très utile, et des plus salutaires.'

[109] To Mardefeld, 2 January 1723, printed in *Sbornik* xv. 213.

[110] To which Frederick William noted, 'Ist wahr.'

[111] 2 January 1723, Staatsarchiv, Berlin.

[112] Rescript of 2 February, *ibid*. From those of 5 and 19 January may be quoted the following sentences: 'Weilen die neue Alliantz zwischen Frankreich und Moscken Uns so wenig, als dem Könige in Engelland etwas gutes ominirt, so werden die dortigen Minister hoffentlich ihr bestes anwenden solche Alliantz annoch, wo möglich, zu verhindern.' And, 'Werden Wir auch Unseres Orts alles, was Uns möglich, thun, damit diese Alliantz zu keiner Consistenz kommen möge.'

In February, indeed, Mardefeld was informed that the apprehensions entertained were unfounded, though he must keep carefully on the watch; but in August fresh warnings were sent him of a likely alliance between Russia, France, and Sweden.[113] And still, after the treaty of Charlottenburg was signed, fears were maintained.[114] When that of February 1724 between Russia and Sweden became known, the belief was expressed that France had had a leading hand in it, in order to form a northern league which, when the occasion arose, might hold in check the forces of Prussia and Hanover in the empire.[115]

Such, then, was Frederick William's principal fear, and it happened that, in August and September 1723, the court at Hanover lay under a like apprehension. Chavigny had come from Paris with the proposal that, instead of a triple alliance between France, Russia, and Great Britain, the two former powers should make a separate treaty first, to which Great Britain might accede subsequently. George I would not listen to this. And at the same time came the news of the death of Cardinal Dubois, on whom hitherto the maintenance of the accord between Great Britain and France had chiefly depended. The new secretary for foreign affairs, the Comte de Morville, was found to favour seriously the policy of a separate treaty, which Dubois had only, in the last moments of his life, suggested.[116] Seeing that, on the communication of the treaty of Charlottenburg to France, the new idea was definitely laid aside, it seems probable that the main object of that treaty was so to impress the French court as to produce this very result. To quote Carteret, who anticipated the most intimate union henceforth between Great Britain and Prussia,

Ce Traitté nous fournira un argument très solide, pour faire revenir la Cour de France de tout empressement à se lier avec le Czar, si ce n'est en signant conjointement avec le Roy le Traitté avec Sa Maj^{té} Czarienne.[117]

And similarly Chambrier, the Prussian resident at Paris:

Le Traité ... fait icy un très grand bien aux Anglois, puisque le Comte de Morville n'osera plus continuer à leur insçu ses négociations en Moscovie, et que cela l'obligera désormais à s'attacher à eux totalement, dans la crainte de se perdre s'il continueroit la route qu'il avait enfilée depuis quelque temps. Ainsi selon toutes les apparences les Anglois vont avoir icy plus de crédit que jamais, à quoy Votre Majesté contribue beaucoup.[118]

[113] Rescripts to Mardefeld, 9 February and 21 August, *ibid.*
[114] To the same, 16 November, and to him and to Wallenrodt in January and February 1724, *ibid.*
[115] To Wallenrodt, 11 April 1724, *ibid.*
[116] See on this *ante*, xxvi. 303–7.
[117] To Schaub at Paris, 24 October (o.s.), British Museum, Add. MS. 22519.
[118] 6 November, Staatsarchiv, Berlin.

Frederick William readily agreed to the communication of the treaty to France; indeed he wanted to inform Michel, the French secretary at Berlin, and Chambrier at once. Scott, however, objected that its ratification must be waited for.[119] Chambrier, therefore, was only instructed that it was agreed to inform the duke of Orleans of it privately, and that he must see Schaub and learn what orders he had received.[120] Later he was told, in reply to his dispatch above cited,

Vous aurez soing aussy de trouver adroitement, et faire valoir cette nouvelle Alliance d'une telle façon, que si sa conclusion donne du plaisir au Duc d'Orléans, elle tienne à moy, aussy bien qu'à l'Angleterre, lieu de mérite auprès de la France, et que, par là, cette Couronne soit engagée d'avoir pour moy d'autant plus de considération.[121]

When the communication had been made, Morville, says Chambrier, showed sensible pleasure, saying that nothing could be more agreeable to France than to see Great Britain and Prussia more closely united, and that he himself had done his best to procure a good intelligence between them.[122]

In November Frederick William paid a ten-days' return visit to George at the Göhrde. Scott reported him on his return 'mighty well pleased' with his reception, but said that Ilgen still complained of Bernstorff's behaviour, and he would do what he could 'towards the hindering of their particular squabbles'.[123] That Frederick William was resolved to maintain the best relations with his father-in-law was shown by his frank conduct in December, when a report spread that he was renewing his alliance with Peter the Great. In a long letter to George I he explained that the treaty in question was only for the marriage of the duchess of Courland to Prince Charles of Brandenburg;[124] and he sent to England as evidence the counterpart of the treaty delivered by Golovkin together with Peter the Great's original letter, and asked that if George entertained the smallest further doubt he would please to express it, when all further explanation necessary should be given. George replied with assurances of perfect confidence

---

[119] Scott, 30 October, Record Office, Prussia 17.
[120] Rescript of 30 October, Staatsarchiv, Berlin.
[121] The same, 20 November.
[122] Dispatch of 7 December, *ibid.*; and similarly Schaub and Horatio Walpole, *ante*, xxvi. 306.
[123] 23 November, Record Office, Prussia 17. Frederick William, however, had one cause for dissatisfaction, in that he was obliged to go hunting instead of shooting, as he wished, being ashamed to cry off when George, twice his age, he said, preferred it. 'Man schweitzet Horrible,' he wrote, but found himself extremely well after the exercise (*Briefe . . . an den Fürsten Leopold zu Anhalt-Dessau*, p. 236).
[124] Substituted for the candidate of 1718, the margrave of Brandenburg-Schwedt. Droysen considers this treaty to have been an effect of that of Charlottenburg (*Geschichte der preussischen Politik*, IV. ii. 356).

and sympathy, saying, however, 'J'étois bien aise de remarquer que Votre Majesté connoit si bien les desseins et les manières du Czar, que de ne pas prendre des nouveaux engagemens avec Luy, se contentant seulement de tirer de Luy l'exécution de ceux qu'il avoit pris cy-devant.'[125] In answer Frederick William wrote in the following warm terms :

Monsieur mon Frère

L'on ne sçauroit estre saisi d'une plus vive reconnoissance que je l'ay été à la lecture de la Lettre que Vôtre Majesté m'a fait l'honneur de m'écrire ce 17 de Janvier, et par la quelle Elle m'a asseuré avec un vray excès de bonté de ce que je souhaite le plus dans ce monde, à sçavoir de l'amitié et de l'affection véritablement paternelle qu'Elle a pour moy.

Je prie Vôtre Majesté d'être persuadé qu'il n'y aura jamais rien d'assés impossible que je ne vueille tascher de faire, pour me conserver un si grand bien.

La confidence que j'ay cru Luy devoir faire des affaires de Courlande, et dont Vôtre Majesté me tesmoigne estre si satisfaite, sera toujours la moindre des preuves que je mettray en usage pour Luy faire voir que je n'ay rien de réserve pour Elle, et qu'il n'y aura jamais quoy que ce soit, que je ne Luy sacrifie avec plaisir lors qu'il sera question de Luy marquer mon attachement à Sa Personne Sacrée, à Ses intérêts et à Son service, car on ne peut estre ny avec plus de devouëment ny avec plus de vénération, que je le suis et le seray sans cesse

de Vostre Majesté
le très devoues Fils
F. GUILLAUME R.[126]

J. F. CHANCE.

[125] These documents, Record Office, Royal Letters 46, King's Letters 52. Frederick William's letter (original) is of date 21 December ; Peter the Great's (in Russian) of 1 October (o.s.); George's reply (draft), 17 January (o.s.) 1724.
[126] 12 February 1724, Record Office, Royal Letters 46, original.

Castlereagh and the Spanish Colonies.
I. 1815–1818

LORD CASTLEREAGH'S character and career have recently received more favourable treatment at the hands of historians, and the mists of the legend which Canning constructed have begun to clear away. But as yet little attempt has been made to investigate the facts of his diplomacy, and in none of the great transactions in which he played a part have his services been more neglected than in the question of the emancipation of the Spanish colonies. On this point historians have been attracted by the dramatic actions of his successor; they have neglected the cautious but successful diplomacy which alone made these later events possible. Such a result was perhaps natural, for while much of Canning's work was done in the open and was explained and defended with all the resources of a brilliant oratory, Castlereagh's actions were only known to the inner circle of European statesmen, and can only be appreciated in the light of subsequent research. During the whole of Castlereagh's tenure of power this problem was in the very forefront of his policy. Even during the struggle with Napoleon it had occupied much of the attention of British ministers. As soon as the great war was over it became the first charge on the exertions of our foreign office. Its enormous possibilities were indeed recognized by all European statesmen. Whenever they could take their anxious gaze from French politics it was across the ocean that they turned their eyes, and many of the minor points that seemed to occupy their attention were but skirmishes before this all-important battle.

The factors in the situation were many. Spain, free but impoverished, and governed rather by a secret committee of the king's favourites than by her fitful succession of foreign ministers, still sought, though half knowing it was in vain, for a complete recognition of her old supremacy. Meanwhile British commerce had taken advantage of the situation. Ever since the Assiento treaty, merchants had looked with envious eyes on the rich treasures of the Spanish provinces, and the first real trade war had been fought on their behalf. The French Revolution and the conquests of Napoleon had at last provided the opportunity so long awaited, and Pitt's successors had even thought of conquest and annexation. The alliance with Spain had caused this absurd idea to be abandoned, but the revolt of the colonies from their mother country had resulted in a rapid extension of British commerce. The goods shut out from the old world found a ready market in the new, and when peace came in Europe this country was determined not to lose the advantages she had gained. Whatever the solution of the problem was to be, Great Britain was not going to lose some of her best customers. Spain herself was in no condition to thwart our policy, but it was not Spanish interests that alone were concerned. Both in the old world and the new there were powerful rivals to be met.

In Europe on this question, as on others, Britain was opposed by France and Russia. French statesmen were keenly alive to the necessity of not allowing their ancient rival a monopoly of the new commerce. But the traditions of the eighteenth century were still strong, and they looked to a settlement rather in alliance with Spain than in rivalry with her.[1] In 1815, too, France lay conquered and impoverished in the grasp of the allied armies, and she could not act by herself. But already a rift could be seen in the great alliance, and it was to Alexander, whose restless mind never shrank from contemplating any project, that both France and Spain turned, not altogether without effect, and soon all the chanceries were buzzing with the suspected designs of these three powers. Meanwhile, in the new world, the United States was hoping to increase both her influence and her commerce by the establishment of sister republics in southern America according to the prophecies of her founders. Hers was the best position of all. For only a united Europe could frustrate her hopes, and it was not likely that the other powers, and least of all Spain, would accept the only conditions on which England was prepared to act with them. One of Castlereagh's first duties at the foreign office had been to define the British position. The cortes had tried to win British assistance by the offer of special privileges for her commerce. The reply had been definite. The offer of mediation had been accepted, but certain conditions had been laid down as an indispensable preliminary to negotiation. All secret advantages were rejected; the mediation was to apply to all the colonies; and (most important of all) force was not to be used. As perhaps might have been expected, this offer was not accepted, and, though Castlereagh showed every disposition to press the negotiation, Wellesley from

[1] Richelieu's instructions to the Marquis d'Osmond of 31 December 1815, cited by M. Schefer, *La France moderne et le Problème colonial*, p. 230; see also Hyde de Neuville, *Memoirs*, ii. 326, and M. Escoffier, 'La Restauration, l'Angleterre et les Colonies,' *Revue d'Histoire diplomatique*, 1907.

the first had little hope of a successful conclusion. The only result was a clause in the treaty of alliance of 1814, by which Spain promised that if the colonial trade was thrown open to any power, Great Britain should be admitted to a full share, this country in her turn promising not to assist the insurgents. To this policy, then so emphatically enunciated, Castlereagh adhered during the whole of the subsequent negotiations until the time came for him to write his instructions for the congress of Verona.[2]

After the peace it was Spain who made the first move. Overtures for assistance were made to Vaughan, the English chargé d'affaires in Wellesley's absence, and the bribe of special privileges was again offered. Vaughan's stubborn refusal to depart from the conditions of 1812 caused a change of tone, and there appeared to be some prospect of a guarantee of complete freedom of commerce between the colonies and the rest of the world. Vaughan had discovered, too, that other powers, and especially France, were offering their services, and so he brought the subject before his government. His dispatch was as follows:

Mr. Cevallos has repeatedly manifested to me the desire of the Spanish Government to avail itself of the mediation of Great Britain for the re-establishment of His Catholic Majesty's authority in his American colonies. . . . He has entreated me to state to the British Government as a basis of the negotiations that Spain will concede to Great Britain a participation in the trade with America, upon such terms as should ensure only a due preference to Spanish subjects, provided the British Government can succeed by any means in its power, in reuniting the Spanish American Colonies with the Mother Country. In explanation of this proposal Mr. Cevallos informed me that it was absolutely necessary that the grant from the Spanish Government of a participation in the trade with Spanish America, should be the reward of some special service, in order to prevent the claims of other states to a similar privilege, under the stipulations of the Treaty of Utrecht. . . . As I positively refused to be the channel of communication to the British Government of proposals which could tend in any shape to involve Great Britain in the hostilities carrying on in Spanish America, Mr. Cevallos desisted from that point, and has since given me every assurance that the Spanish Government is disposed to leave His Royal Highness the Prince Regent at liberty to interpose his good offices for the reconciliation of the Colonies in any manner that it may be thought advisable, Spain engaging on her part, whenever the Colonies return to their allegiance to the Mother Country through the mediation of His Royal Highness, to open the trade exclusively to Great Britain.

[2] Council of regency to Wellesley, 29 January 1811; reply of Wellesley, 1 July; Castlereagh to Wellesley, 1 April 1812, Foreign Office, Spain 204; Castlereagh to Wellesley, 29 August 1812 (private), Foreign Office, Spain 128; *Castlereagh Correspondence*, viii. 247, 267 ff., 282, 342; *British and Foreign State Papers*, i. 275, 293.

Vaughan criticized the conduct of the Spanish government during the last negotiations and asked for straightforward dealing, and Cevallos said the question was now changed. A report of the council of the Indies of 12 July 1815, which Vaughan had seen, confirmed this view. The dispatch continues :

> The most interesting part of the report of the Council of the Indies is that which seems to confirm the sentiments of the Spanish Government with regard to the mediation of His Royal Highness the Prince Regent. The Council expressed the deepest concern that His Royal Highness' offer should have been rejected by the Spanish Government, and earnestly recommends it to His Catholic Majesty to preside in the Council of his Ministers and to call upon them to examine the state of the relations between Spain and Great Britain, and to lose no time in conciliating the interests of the latter by an adjustment of all differences, and a fair treaty of commerce, as unless the trade to Spanish America is opened to Great Britain, the colonies cannot be preserved to Spain:—that every effort should be made to obtain the powerful influence of England for a reconciliation of the Colonies, which Spain cannot hope to bring about by her own means....'
> The Report of the Council of the Indies and the conferences which I have had with Mr. Cevallos will serve to show your Lordship that a material change in the disposition of the Spanish Government has taken place since the question of mediation was last under discussion. The opening of the trade is no longer so repugnant to the Spaniards, and they begin to feel the impossibility of subduing their colonies to allegiance by force.
> I conceive that it is of great importance that the subject of the mediation of His Royal Highness the Prince Regent with the Spanish Colonies should be brought without delay under the consideration of His Majesty's Government, as the re-establishment of the tranquillity of Europe leaves it open to the insurgents to negotiate for the security of their independence with other European powers; and I am assured by Mr. Cevallos, that Spain has already received proposals from France for assisting her in restoring His Catholic Majesty's authority in America.... Spain appeals to England in preference to any other state, to assist her in recovering her colonies, and though little hope can be entertained of a successful issue to the best exertions of the British Government, it appears to me imprudent to reject the appeal of the Spanish Government, as a sincere endeavour to aid Spain, whatever may be the issue, will improve the cordiality of the alliance subsisting between the two countries, and cause the suspension for some time of overtures to any other state.[3]

Castlereagh's reply was to repeat the conditions laid down in 1812. He wrote to Vaughan :

> His Royal Highness would willingly encounter the difficulties of a mediation if, by any pacific efforts in his power to employ, he could hope to bring it to a satisfactory result, but in the present distracted state to which these possessions were reduced, the misfortune is that all his exertions may be unavailing, and only serve to bring upon the British Government

[3] Vaughan to Castlereagh, 16 November 1815, Foreign Office, Spain 177.

in an increased degree the urgent reproaches of both the contending parties.

The only chance of averting this evil and consequently of inducing the Prince Regent to engage in the undertaking would be the receiving of some undoubted proofs, that the Government of Spain were sincere in their purpose of conciliating the people of South America, and were prepared to adopt liberal principles as the basis of their future supremacy over this great country. . . . I can venture to assure you that to the principles disclosed in your dispatch the British Government would for the sake of both countries feel objection ; to command success the views of both nations ought to be liberal to the people of South America and not invidious to other nations. A system of exclusive commercial advantage to the Mediating Power would render her interposition odious and destroy all her just influence : you will perceive that the Prince Regent has never sought for any exclusive advantages. He has always recommended the commerce of South America to be open to all nations upon moderate duties with a reasonable preference to Spain herself as the best means of settling that country in connection with Spain, and from this opinion His Royal Highness sees no reason to depart.[4]

The Spanish government was not ready to accept these conditions, and turned to other powers for assistance. But the diplomacy is complicated by three subordinate questions. Spain was being pressed by Great Britain to abolish the slave trade, a measure which English public opinion rendered indispensable as a preliminary to any action on our part. She was also in heated dispute with Portugal, who had occupied a portion of the Spanish provinces in the Plata as a precautionary measure against the insurgents. War had only been averted by the interference of the alliance and the strong action of England, who, while she did not altogether defend the position of her old ally, was nevertheless determined not to allow Spain to compensate herself for her losses in South America by seizing the Portuguese dominions in Europe. Eventually the dispute was referred to the committee of ambassadors at Paris, where, as will be seen, it was to serve for the introduction of the Russo-Spanish schemes.[5] Spain was, too, negotiating with the United States over the question of the Floridas, and this also had a bearing on the larger question of the colonies, since it helped to prevent the recognition of the insurgents by the United States, and was used by Spain to try and foment discord between the United States and Great Britain.[6]

---

[4] Castlereagh to Vaughan, 20 December, 1815, Foreign Office, Spain 177, autograph draft.

[5] *Infra*, p. 85.

[6] 'Mr. Onis proposes that the Spanish Government should cede to England the Floridas, that the former may be placed as a barrier against the encroachments of the U.S.' : Vaughan's dispatch quoted above.

These complications caused a suspension of the negotiations, and it was not until 17 October 1816 that Fernan-Nuñez, the Spanish ambassador in England, again sounded Castlereagh on the subject, still refusing all the conditions which had been laid down as a necessary preliminary to English assistance.

It is difficult therefore [wrote Castlereagh to Wellesley], to conceive a rational motive for doing so, unless the Court of Madrid wishes to drive the British Government into a peremptory negative, and upon that refusal to found some change either in the system of its political relations in Europe with a view of procuring support against their revolted colonies, or in their South American policy, finding the other hopeless in point of success.

Under these circumstances no official answer was given to Fernan-Nuñez's request, but he was made to understand that English principles had not changed.[7] Spain was, indeed, looking elsewhere for help. The Russian plans were not yet matured, nor could even the camarilla be ignorant that England was the only power that possessed the means to assist them. Thus at the beginning of 1817 the Spanish ambassador was again instructed to sound Castlereagh, and a liberal policy promised in return for armed mediation. Castlereagh's answer was to reaffirm the cardinal points of English policy, the abolition of the colonial system and an utter refusal to employ force against the colonies.

I represented to Count Fernan-Nuñez that we had invariably declined interposing by force of arms between the King of Spain and his subjects, that we had sufficiently experienced in our own American colonies the difficulty of such a contest, and that we could not embark for a foreign state in an undertaking from which we had been obliged, in our own case, to desist ; that we had recommended a change of system to Spain, because we were satisfied that she never could re-establish her authority, or tranquillize that great continent upon the principles of her ancient colonial policy ; and that we had, on various occasions, evinced our disposition to support His Catholic Majesty's pretensions by every exertion of influence and good offices, provided his system towards his subjects in the New World was such as would enable the British Government to become its publick advocate, consistently with what it owed to its own character ; that a long perseverance on the part of Spain in false notions of imposing by force a restrictive and exclusive system upon that country had already alienated the minds of the people from her rule, but that the only chance she had of success was to lose no time, for her own sake, and not for ours, to put her system there upon a national footing. In short I told him plainly, that armed assistance was out of the question, and that if the

---

[7] Fernan-Nuñez to Castlereagh, 17 October 1816, Foreign Office, Spain 191 ; Castlereagh to Wellesley, 20 December 1816, *ibid.* 184. The new move was partly due to the accession of a new foreign minister, Pizarro, to office ; and Castlereagh had already been warned by his ambassador at Paris of French interest in the change : Sir Charles Stuart to Castlereagh, 14 November 1816, Foreign Office, France 139.

Spanish Government looked to any other description of assistance in the nature of mediation, it must be upon a change of system on her part, for which Monsʳ Pizarro's recent appointment, and the known sentiments of the Council of the Indies, and what Spain was about to do upon the slave trade, appeared to have prepared the way....'[8]

There were men in Spain ready to listen to this advice, and even Pizarro himself seemed to be in favour of accepting English mediation. But the camarilla was committed to another policy, and the foreign minister was held back by the court. Wellesley, however, encouraged negotiation, for he hoped to use the colonial question as a lever to secure the long-promised slave trade treaty, and in April he declared formally that England was prepared to offer peaceful mediation if her terms were accepted.[9]

Meanwhile the plans of the other powers, or at least of their ambassadors, were maturing. General Pozzo di Borgo, the Russian ambassador at Paris, had been plying his court with indignant remonstrances against the overbearing policy of England,[10] and he was in constant communication with his colleague at Madrid, Count Tatistcheff. The latter, a man of considerable ability and boundléss ambition, had seized the opportunity which Spanish jealousy of Great Britain had afforded. He had succeeded in establishing a dominant position in the councils of the camarilla, and his energetic and mysterious actions had aroused the attention of all Europe. At the end of 1815 Vaughan had reported an intrigue to marry the king of Spain to a Russian princess, which, however, came to nothing. More serious were Tatistcheff's attempts to stir up Spanish jealousy against the British South American policy, and his projects of reviving the Bourbon alliance under Russian protection.[11] Castlereagh, true to his policy of never openly encouraging suspicions against Russia, discredited this information, and ordered Vaughan to make his language conform with the spirit of the alliance.[12] But at the end of 1816 the complaints broke out

[8] Castlereagh to Wellesley (private), 10 January 1817, Foreign Office, Spain 196.
[9] Wellesley to Castlereagh, 14, 15 January 1817, Foreign Office, Spain 197 Wellesley to Pizarro, 12 April 1817, Foreign Office, Spain 198.
[10] *Imperial Russian Historical Society*, vol. cxix, *passim*. Pozzo's correspondence with his court to the end of 1820 are printed *in extenso* in volumes cxii, cxix, and cxxvii of this series, and give a most valuable *contrôle* for this period.
[11] Vaughan to Castlereagh, 26 November 1815 : '... The most confidential intercourse subsists between Mr. Tatischeff and the French Ambassador, and I am persuaded that the proposals of the latter for the renewal of the ancient alliance between the branches of the House of Bourbon ... will be renewed with success.' Cf. dispatch of 10 December 1815, Foreign Office, Spain 177.
[12] Castlereagh to Vaughan, 20 December 1815 : '... It is necessary to caution you upon the alarms which Mr. Tatischeff's conduct has lately given rise. The habits of the individual, and his feelings towards this country render it by no means improbable that he may excite and engage in intrigues which he may hope will be received by

again. Tatistcheff's conduct, Vaughan hinted, must be supported by his court, since he had lately been made an ambassador, and he suggested that Russia was promising naval assistance in South America in return for the cession of Minorca.[13]

For the next six months rumours of the treaty poured in from every court in Europe. The English representatives at Berlin and Naples had heard of it, and Metternich spoke of it as a *fait accompli*.[14] Even Castlereagh was compelled to give more credence to the report and inquiries were set on foot at St. Petersburg. There it was categorically denied by both Nesselrode and the emperor, though, according to the Austrian ambassador, Capo d'Istria used less conciliating language. Whatever had been planned, the eventual result was no more than the sale of some old Russian boats to Spain, and their subsequent unseaworthiness added a touch of comedy to Alexander's attempt to rival British sea power.[15] Pozzo, however, had other schemes which were now rapidly maturing. On 2 July Fernan-Nuñez (now transferred to Paris) presented a note to the ambassadorial committee, which was attempting to settle on behalf of the great powers the Spanish-Portuguese dispute. In this document the dangerous effects of the revolutionary movements in the New World upon the legitimate governments of Europe were pointed out, and the great powers were urged to assist Spain in her efforts to suppress the disorders. Pozzo succeeded in persuading both the Austrian and Prussian ambassadors to join him in returning a friendly reply, but Sir Charles Stuart, the English ambassador, refused to act with his colleagues until he should hear from his government, and, according to Pozzo, though the fact is not stated in his own

his Court as proofs of zeal; but I am happy to inform you that His Majesty's Government have no reason to suppose that such views are countenanced by the Emperor of Russia. . . . A feeble government, uneasy at being excluded from what it holds to be its due share of influence in the greater politics of Europe, is not unlikely to endeavour to ferment disunion amongst the powers whose existing connection diminishes its influence. . . .', Foreign Office, Spain 177.

[13] Vaughan to Castlereagh, 24 July, 28 November 1816, Foreign Office, Spain 187, 188.

[14] A'Court to Castlereagh, 10 February 1817, Foreign Office, Sicily 80; Rose to Castlereagh, 6 April 1817, Foreign Office, Prussia 107; Lord Stewart to Castlereagh, 29 January, 19 February 1817, Foreign Office, Austria 135. Cf. Gentz, *Dépêches inédites*, i. 290, 296.

[15] Cathcart to Castlereagh, 1 March, 22 March 1817, Foreign Office, Russia 108; Lebzeltern to Metternich, 23 February 1817; Stewart to Castlereagh, 15 March, 6, 19, 30 April 1817, Foreign Office, Austria 136. This curious intrigue has not been entirely solved by historians, who have mainly relied on Gentz's evidence; see, however, Stern, i. 215. Castlereagh was of the opinion that Tatistcheff signed the treaty, but that his court refused to ratify it, Castlereagh to Cathcart, 16 May 1817. He carefully concealed all anger from his own ambassadors, but he seems to have spoken strongly to Lieven on the subject; cf. F. Martens, *Recueil des Traités*, xi. 268. The Russian court could indeed have no doubt as to the attitude of Europe. Even Pozzo urged moderation, and recounted the indignant alarm of Wellington.

dispatches, claimed the question as a purely British one. It was in vain that Fernan-Nuñez renewed the attack in successive notes. By this time the suspicions of Stuart were fully awakened; Wellington pressed on Richelieu the English point of view, and the ambassadors had perforce to wait for the decision of their cabinets.[16]

It was time for Castlereagh to declare the English policy to the powers. His alliance with Austria assured him of the support of Metternich, and Vincent, the Austrian ambassador at Paris, was soon ordered to act in accordance with Stuart; meanwhile Castlereagh administered an emphatic rebuke to the presumptuous Pozzo.[17] But something more was necessary, and the views of the British government were conveyed to the powers of the alliance in a confidential memorandum of 28 August.[18] In this document the policy that Castlereagh had laid down in 1812 was enunciated to the allies. As the first open declaration of British policy it was of great importance, and merits more consideration than historians have given to it. After alluding to the events at Paris which made the memorandum necessary, it continues :

Although the Prince Regent has felt it his duty to observe a strict neutrality throughout the contest which has agitated the South American Provinces, His Royal Highness has never ceased to entertain an anxious desire that that great continent might be restored to tranquillity under the ancient sovereignties of the Crowns of Spain and Portugal. The Prince Regent has looked to this object with the more earnestness from the regret with which His Royal Highness has seen ancient authorities subverted— from the peculiar interest which He feels in whatever may concern the dignity and welfare of the illustrious families whose possessions are thereby endangered, and from a firm persuasion that the continent of

[16] Stuart to Castlereagh, 10, 21 July, 4, 17 August 1817, Foreign Office, France 160, 161. For Pozzo's account see *Imperial Russian Historical Society*, cxix. 276. Wellington seems to have believed in the honesty of the French Government, and that the whole affair was planned between Pozzo and the Spanish ambassador there seems little doubt ; cf. *Wellington Supplementary Dispatches*, xi. 735 ; xii. 3. Stuart's attitude towards French policy may be illustrated from the following quotation from one of his dispatches : 'The irritation manifested by the King and his ministers at the time they ascertained the nature and extent of the stipulations respecting the family compact contained in the Treaty signed last year at Madrid has long since convinced me that the re-establishment of the political connection between the different branches of the family of Bourbon is the only measure of foreign policy which is seriously contemplated by the French Government,' Stuart to Castlereagh, 17 June 1816, Foreign Office, France 133.

[17] Castlereagh to Stuart, 21 August 1817 : ' I cannot too strongly represent to you the importance of making the Spanish and all other Governments feel that the allied ministers are limited in their functions to the execution of the late treaties and to such special duties as their courts may think fit to impose upon them, but that it neither appertains to them to originate discussions on other subjects, nor to become a channel of general reference to their courts upon subjects foreign to their immediate duties,' Foreign Office, France 151.   [18] Foreign Office, Spain 204.

South America must long remain a prey to its own internal convulsions, before it can assume any separate form of regular government capable of providing for the happiness of its own inhabitants or of adequately maintaining relations of peace and amity with other states. It is, however, the opinion of the Prince Regent that this desirable object can alone be obtained by a speedy settlement of all existing differences, and by the restoration of a perfect understanding between the Crowns of their Catholick and Most Faithful Majesties, and further by each determining to adopt a system of government within their respective dominions favourable to the interest and congenial to the feelings of the natives of these countries; it being obvious that whatever may have been the original policy of the Colonial System of either Crown, it has become in the progress of time, inapplicable to countries of such extent and population.

This observation is more particularly true of the Crown of Spain, as Brazil has followed a wiser policy.

Wellesley's instructions of 1812 were then alluded to as showing the British conditions of mediation, and the increase of disorder during the interval was lamented, though some hope was still held out that the colonies might return to their allegiance. This result, however, could only be brought about if Spain conceded all the British conditions and came to a frank understanding with her and the other powers. These conditions were again enumerated, viz. (1) that Spain should have signed a satisfactory treaty to Great Britain on the slave trade; (2) that a general amnesty and armistice shall be proclaimed to the insurgents; (3) that the South Americans should be placed on an equal legal footing with other Spanish subjects; and (4) 'that the people of South America shall have secured to them free commercial intercourse with all nations, Spain enjoying, as the parent state, a fair preference in the intercourse with this portion of her dominions'. Then followed a solemn warning which was made not only to Spain but to Europe:

There is another branch of this question of great importance, and upon which the Prince Regent is desirous to be most distinctly understood:— namely that H.R.H. cannot consent that His mediation shall under any circumstances assume an armed character; that while He is ready to employ, with the utmost zeal and sincerity, His best exertions to re-establish tranquillity, and restore harmony between the Crown of Spain and its South American subjects, He can, under no circumstances, be induced to be a party, to any attempt to dictate by force of arms the terms of such a reconciliation; nor can H.R.H. become the guarantee of any settlements that may be effectuated, to the extent of undertaking the obligation of enforcing its observance by acts of hostility against either of the parties. His intervention must throughout be understood to be confined within the bounds of good offices, and the employment of that just influence which must belong to any great power when labouring only to promote the welfare of an allied sovereign and his people.

H.R.H. deems it proper to be more explicit upon this branch of the question, as he is persuaded that the party in Spain, which still unfortunately clings to the ancient colonial system of that country, and which has hitherto had influence enough to prevent any effectual attempt at reconciliation will continue to obstruct any such attempt, so long as they are permitted to indulge a hope of involving other powers in the contest, and thereby of availing themselves of foreign arms, for the subjugation of the Spanish Colonies.

The uniformity and consistency of British policy was demonstrated by the enclosure of some of the dispatches to Wellesley. Spain and the powers were invited to communicate their views, and in the event of the acceptance of the British terms, Paris or London were named as places where a conference as to further proceedings might take place.

The importance of this document can scarcely be overestimated. No doubt could be left in the minds of the allies that Great Britain would allow no European interference except on such terms as she chose to dictate. The schemes of Pozzo were entirely ruined. He was furious at his defeat, though he tried to claim credit at his court for having made Great Britain declare her views. He was especially annoyed at the idea of the matter being referred to a London conference, and he regarded mediation without force as equivalent to no mediation at all. He could only entreat his court to insist on Paris as the place of conference and give no opinion on the English conditions.[19] But the ineptitude of the Spanish government prevented any effective reply. Spain did, indeed, conclude the slave-trade treaty, but Fernan-Nuñez handed in a reply to the memorandum which was made directly insulting to Great Britain by a copy not being given to Stuart, and the Spanish government refused all the British conditions and asked that the mediation conference should sit at Madrid. Indeed, it probably preferred no terms at all to those that Great Britain offered, and still clung to a vain hope that Russia and France would do something for it.[20] But both these powers avoided a conflict. Richelieu practically conceded the British case to Stuart. The Russian answer, though it was evidently inspired by Pozzo, was vague and without force. It attempted to link the colonial mediation with that between Spain and Portugal, thus making Paris the seat of the conferences ; it laid down the duty of the powers : ' de faire participer les vastes contrées du nouveau monde aux avantages

[19] *Imperial Russian Historical Society*, cxix. 359, 392 ; *Castlereagh Correspondence*, xi. 368.

[20] Castlereagh to Stuart, 4 November 1817, Foreign Office, France 152 ; Wellesley to Castlereagh, 5 October 1817, Foreign Office, Spain 200 ; *Wellington Supplementary Dispatches*, xii. 114.

dont jouit l'Europe sous les auspices des stipulations de Vienne et de Paris de l'année 1815 ;' it suggested the use not of force but of some measure of commercial coercion, and it avoided all acceptance of the British terms.[21] It had, however, no result except to expose the strength of the British position. Metternich placed his vote entirely at the disposal of the British government, and of course Prussia followed the Austrian lead.[22] Castlereagh did not even reply to the Russian memoir by another formal document. He had no wish to emphasize differences in the alliance provided he got his own way. But he spoke his mind to Lieven in no uncertain manner:

> Sur quel principe de droit ou de moralité (he said to the Russian ambassador) l'Angleterre se fondrait-elle pour se légitimer de prendre part au moindre acte de contrainte qu'on voudrait exercer contre ces peuples ? De quel droit forcerait-elle une population devenue libre, parce que l'autorité qui la gouvernait était oppressive, à se replacer sous la domination de ce même gouvernement ?[23]

And he wound up the discussion in a later dispatch to Cathcart with the remark:

> The Emperor will not wonder that the Prince Regent's Government should rest upon their oars, till they see some course open to them, which looks like a sincere purpose on the part of Spain to prosecute the mediation *in the sense of a mediation*: as yet they perceive nothing but a disposition to compromise other states in their controversies and to do nothing effectual themselves.[24]

Thus closed the first attempt of England's rivals on the continent to embark on the thorny question of the Spanish colonies. Castlereagh had seized the opportunity to make his policy clear to Europe, and his alliance with Metternich had left Alexander completely isolated. (It may be doubted whether Castlereagh sincerely desired a mediation on the terms he laid down.) He must have known how little chance it had of success. But he saw the advantages of not acting in isolation as matters stood then, both in the new world and the old. He wished to check the intrigues that had been so long going on at the court of Madrid, and he did not wish to split the great alliance

---

[21] Russian Memorandum, 29 November 1817. It is quoted in full in *Wellington Supplementary Dispatches*, xii. 125, and *Imperial Russian Historical Society*, cxix. 474. Cf. Cathcart to Castlereagh, 3 December 1817: 'I stated that I did not know whether to accept or transmit this memorial as an answer to the communications I had been commanded by the P. R. to make to the Emperor, those communications being scarcely named in the Memoir,' Foreign Office, Russia 109.

[22] Gordon to Castlereagh, 2 October 1817; Metternich to Esterhazy, 8 October 1817, Foreign Office, Austria 133, 138.

[23] F. Martens, *Recueil*, xi. 269.

[24] Castlereagh to Cathcart, 27 March 1818, Foreign Office, Russia 112.

which he thought was so necessary to the peace of Europe.[25] But he had also another powerful motive to keep alive the idea of mediation under the auspices of Europe. He was aware of the danger from the United States, and he had no desire to see that power win credit and influence in South America by recognition of the claims of the colonies. (All his policy, therefore, was directed to keeping her back from any decisive step until England should be ready to act, either for mediation or for recognition.)

From the first moment after the peace of 1814 Castlereagh had set himself to the task of winning the confidence of the American government. He was well aware of the difficulty of the task, but helped by the conciliatory policy of Bagot, the British minister at Washington,[26] he at least succeeded in establishing relations sufficiently friendly to enable him to convey the impression he wished the United States to have of British policy towards South America. In his conversations with Adams, before that minister left to become secretary of state to Monroe, he was always careful to insinuate that Europe might yet act against the colonies, though he took care to promise the United States equal commercial privileges with the European powers.' He seized the opportunity of offering a mediation between the United States and Spain to cause Bagot to renew these assurances.[27] It will be noticed that the English memorandum was not yet communicated, though it was already sent to the courts of Europe. Castlereagh had no wish to tell the United States more than he could help of the rivalries of the European powers. The effect on the American cabinet was what he had expected, and fear of a European intervention was one of the main reasons which made Adams delay recognition for so long.[28]

Meanwhile the Spanish government was in no condition to take advantage of the respite. There was a considerable party at the Spanish court which regarded the colonial question as

[25] See his letter to Wellington in *Wellington Supplementary Dispatches*, xii. 51.

[26] 'We were certainly never on such good terms (I believe never before on any terms at all) with the Government of the United States as we have been since he (Bagot) was appointed minister:' Captain Bagot, *George Canning and his Friends*, ii. 68.

[27] Castlereagh to Bagot, 10 November 1817 (private and confidential) : '... I took occasion to explain to Mr. Adams the course we had uniformly pursued in the dispute between Spain and her South American colonies, and our determination in the event of any amicable mediation being undertaken for terminating these differences, either by the Govt. singly, or in conjunction with other states, that it should be founded on liberal principles towards the people of S. America, and that so far from seeking any exclusive advantages in point of commerce, he might rest assured we should support a system which should favour the reception of all foreign flags, including that of the U. S., upon equal terms, in the ports of Spanish America. As discussions are now pending in Europe on this subject you may safely assure Mr. Adams that this just and liberal principle will be held steadily in view,' Foreign Office, America 120; cf. Adams, *Memoirs*, iii. 551. [28] *Infra*, p. 94.

hopeless and looked for compensation to Portugal, where they had some supporters.[29] The council of the Indies was strongly in favour of English mediation, and Pizarro himself was not unfriendly.[30] But the camarilla still pursued its fitful policy of intrigue with the Russian ambassador, and Pozzo was still weaving schemes at Paris. All Europe was now becoming seriously alarmed lest the United States should recognize the insurgent colonies. The American ambassadors had been instructed to drop hints that recognition was imminent, and caused great perturbation in the European chanceries. Metternich suggested tentatively that an American representative should be asked to sit in the Paris conference.[31] Pozzo hoped to use English jealousy of the United States to drive England into an effective mediation.[32] The Spanish government was so much moved that it addressed representations to England urging her to prevent the dreaded event.[33] Castlereagh was in a difficult position. He could only point out that the best way for Spain to save her colonies was to accede to his terms, that the delay already gained was largely due to his efforts, and that these could only continue to be successful if Spain showed some signs of accepting peaceful mediation. His private letter to Wellesley confessed that the danger was real, though not imminent, and evinced but little hope that the Spanish court would adopt a more sensible policy.[34]

His prophecy proved true. The whole attention of the courts was now turning to the coming conference at Aix-la-Chapelle. Spain knew that the allies must here consider her position, and she claimed representation at the conference. France and Russia encouraged her in this scheme, for they hoped by its means to overcome the victorious opposition which the English-Austrian

[29] Cf. *Wellington Supplementary Dispatches*, xii. 197.
[30] Wellesley to Castlereagh, 16 February 1818, Foreign Office, Spain 210.
[31] Stuart to Castlereagh, 18 December 1817, Foreign Office, France 165.
[32] *Imperial Russian Historical Society*, cxix. 593.
[33] Wellesley to Castlereagh, 2 March 1818, Foreign Office, Spain 210.
[34] Castlereagh to Wellesley, 27 March 1818 : ' With respect to addressing to the Govt. of the United States any representation against the apprehended recognition of any of the local governments in South America, your Excellency will make Mr. Pizarro feel the great delicacy of any direct interference in the policy of an independent state on such a subject. Your Excy. has already been informed of the spontaneous endeavour which under the Prince Regent's orders I made, in conversation with Mr. Adams on the eve of his departure for America, to avert such a circumstance by confidentially apprizing him of the probability of a mediation being undertaken by the European powers upon principles so liberal and fair in themselves as to leave the U. S. no reason to apprehend in such an event any system of exclusion to the prejudice of their national interests ; on a subsequent occasion, to obviate the inconvenience of delay, I directed Mr. Bagot to renew these representations, but your Excy. will at once see, that to return again on the same subject would be only to weaken impressions and to provoke inquiries which must lead to the admission, that since the month of April no effective progress has been made in the proposed mediation,' Foreign Office, Spain 209.

alliance had everywhere opposed to their schemes. With this move the question of the Spanish colonies was intimately connected, for every one knew that it would be one of the subjects of the conference. Before the uncompromising opposition of Castlereagh, however, Alexander recoiled. France had not yet shown sufficient stability of government to make her a weapon strong enough to fight the other members of the alliance; Spain had showed too often her incompetence and pride; the schemes which Pozzo and Capodistrias had evolved were regarded by the emperor as too visionary, and the attempt to use a Bourbon alliance as the instrument of Russian policy was postponed, if not abandoned.[25]

The effect of these attempts to force the portals of the alliance was to leave Spain divided and distracted in her counsels. At one moment she seemed inclined to turn to England for aid, at another to risk all in a desperate attempt to gain the help of France and Russia. The unseaworthiness of the Russian fleet (which had been received with much pomp and ceremony, as a force which would 'defend the faithful subjects who in the colonial dominions are victims of anarchy and disorder') for a time caused Tatistcheff to lose some of his influence.[26] Pizarro was trying to break his power and consequently approached nearer to England. On 17 June a note was sent to the powers which went much further towards accepting the English terms than all previous documents. It offered an amnesty, accession to public offices, and some sort of commercial freedom to the insurgents, and accepted London or Paris as a place of mediation.[27] It was too late, however, for the negotiation to proceed. Castlereagh was already preparing to go to the conference. He seized the opportunity, however, to urge Spain to an explicit declaration of policy, and offered if that was done to see that its interests were considered at Aix-la-Chapelle.[38] At Madrid, however, Pizarro had

[25] I cannot give here the details of these transactions, which cover a large part of the correspondence of 1818. Metternich at first showed some desire to admit Spain to the conference, but he eventually submitted to the wishes of England. The letter in which Capodistrias informs Pozzo that his schemes are abandoned is given in *Imperial Russian Historical Society*, cxix. 772. The connexion with the Spanish colonies may be seen in the following extract from a letter of Castlereagh's to Wellington of 21 August 1818: 'I had a visit from d'Osmond in which he made a strong attack as he said by the Duke of Richelieu's orders to induce us to concur in bringing the King of Spain to Aix.... The avowed motive was the critical state of S. American affairs. ... I strongly advised the Duke de Richelieu not to stir the question which could lead to no other result than unsettling the views of the Spanish Govt.,' Foreign Office, Cont. 33.

[26] Wellesley to Castlereagh, 12 April 1818, Foreign Office, Spain 211.

[27] Spanish note to the powers, 17 June 1818, *British and Foreign State Papers*, v. 1217.

[38] Castlereagh to Wellesley, 14 August 1818: '... The Court of Madrid, to procure itself any advantage from their mediation, must therefore speak out, and make itself

been compelled to give up his appeal to England. Spain was still hoping that Russia would force the other powers to include her in the conference. New information reached London that the Spanish government were still intriguing for an armed mediation, and Castlereagh set out for the conference with no very pleasant feelings towards either Spain or Russia.[39] But before he set out he made an attempt, not altogether unsuccessfully, to stop premature action on the part of the United States. He was not without hope that he could manage to win the co-operation of that power. In March he had written to Wellesley:

From the general tenor of Mr. Bagot's report as well as Mr. Adams' language before he left England, my impression is that the Cabinet of Washington has not yet made up its mind to play a revolutionary game in South America and that by good management, it might be yet kept within the limits which ought in good sense and sound principle to guide the principal powers of Europe in any intervention they may undertake in these concerns. There is no doubt a formidable party in the United States which will endeavour to propel the Government in the revolutionary direction, but my persuasion is, that were Spain placed on good grounds, and were the mediation taken up by the European states upon liberal and conciliatory principles, that the United States might not only be prevented from breaking loose upon this question, but that the interest and influence of that state might gradually be brought to operate powerfully in repressing disorder in that quarter.[40]

This rather optimistic opinion was confirmed by reports from Bagot which reached him at the beginning of June, reporting the discussions which had recently taken place in the house of representatives on the subject of the Spanish colonies.[41] Bagot

intelligible, not merely to the confiding but to the most jealous and distrustful of their South American population; this was always the line of conduct which the Prince Regent recommended, but after the delays that have unfortunately attended the whole course of their policy since the negotiations of 1812, ... to pursue any other course at this day ... will be to sacrifice the best chance that remains of re-establishing the Dominions of Spain in that quarter of the Globe,' Foreign Office, Spain 209.

[39] Castlereagh to Wellesley, 1 September 1818: '... It almost looks as if they [Spain] meant to take Aix by storm. If you can see any movement of this nature you will represent the very awkward position in which either the King or an accredited minister from Spain would stand, were they to arrive there not only uninvited, but in defiance of the declared opinion of all the Allied Powers.... It is quite obvious that Spain is intriguing in all quarters and in all directions, and there are feelings connected with the old Family Alliance which gives her too easy an access to certain of the powers. Whilst Russia gives in to it to a certain degree, the Emperor seems half to avow to Lord Cathcart that something sinister is contemplated,' Foreign Office, Spain 209.

[40] Castlereagh to Wellesley (private and confidential), 27 March 1818, Foreign Office, Spain 209.

[41] Bagot to Castlereagh, 7 April 1818: '... It appears evident that it is not the intention of the Government, nor, I think, the disposition of the country in general, to take at present any step which can be considered as a direct acknowledgement of

had, however, rather overstated the case. It was true that the United States government, and least of all Adams, did not contemplate any immediate recognition of the Spanish colonies, but they were hoping that recognition would ultimately be possible. For the moment their own negotiations with Spain no less than their uncertainty as to the attitude of the European powers made an active policy impracticable. Adams especially was eager to prevent inopportune precipitancy; but he feared and distrusted the policy of England. On the 13th of May the question came before the American cabinet, and it was decided not to attempt to act with England. Meanwhile instructions were sent to the United States' ambassadors which definitely, though cautiously, foreshadowed recognition in order to test the feelings of the powers, and Castlereagh thus learnt from reports in Europe of a change in the American tone.[42] Before proceeding to Aix he took further steps to secure at least their neutrality. In July he informed Rush that the Spanish colonies would be discussed at Aix-la-Chapelle, and spoke in sanguine tones of their prospects of success.[43] In August he sent Bagot the confidential memorandum of 28 August 1817, together with the last note from Spain, which seemed to show that Spain would accept English conditions, and the dispatch of Wellesley of August last quoted above.[44] These were also shown to Rush, whom he sounded on the attitude of his government. The American ambassador assured him that 'the United States would decline taking part, if they took part at all, in any plan of pacification, except on the basis of the independence of the Colonies', a remark

the independence of these colonies.' Enclosed in the dispatch was a cutting from the New York *Evening Post*, which Bagot believed represented the views of the administration, and which while professing sympathy with colonial independence, contained this statement: 'It is scarcely to be doubted that the foreign governments have been sounded, and their policy as respects the war between Spain and the Colonies seems to be impartial and neutral. If the United States pursue a different course, may not the powers which have charged themselves with the high police of Europe, instead of confining their cares to the old world, be disposed to take into consideration the affairs of the new?' And as to the consequences of recognition, it confessed that it would be an unfriendly act which would bring the United States into collision with Spain; then 'This collision could have but one result—some persons see nothing discouraging in a war with Spain, and a war with Spain alone would not be formidable, but we cannot be certain, nay, we can hardly expect, in the extraordinary condition of Europe, that other powers may not be drawn in to take a part in a war having for its object the separation of the Spanish Colonies,' Foreign Office, America 131. See also in *Castlereagh Correspondence*, xi. 405, a letter of Bagot's of 8 February 1818, which was received at the same time as the above dispatch, a storm having delayed the packet (Adams, *Memoirs*, iv. 84).

[42] Adams, *Memoirs*, iv. 91; Gallatin, *Writings*, ii. 73; cf. F. L. Paxson, *The Independence of the South American Republics*, pp. 147 ff.

[43] Rush, *Residence at Court of London*, 1st series, p. 228.

[44] Castlereagh to Bagot, 8 August 1818, Foreign Office, America 129; Adams, *Memoirs*, iv. 136 ff.

at which Castlereagh appeared to be disappointed.[45] He had thus found it necessary to avow England's declaration to Europe that force was not to be used. But at the same time he had conveyed an impression that a European mediation was probable, and rendered it impossible for the United States to take immediate action.

The effect produced on the American cabinet was what he had expected. Adams told Bagot that the mediation must fail, though he admitted that it was only fair to Spain to make the attempt.[46] It produced, however, a considerable effect on his mind. At the cabinet meeting to consider the president's message to congress he strongly opposed too premature an allusion to an intention to recognize the Spanish colonies. The reports of the commissioners sent out to investigate the conditions of the colonies gave, he said, ample reason against immediate recognition.

Another reason [he added] equally decisive for that postponement was the mediation undertaken by the European allies between Spain and South America, which is now in operation, and which we know must fail, because it goes upon the principle of restoring the colonies to the subjugation of Spain and yet utterly disclaims the application of force in any event. It is our true policy to let this experiment have its full effect, without attempting to disturb it, which might unnecessarily give offence to the allies; and after it shall have failed, as fail it must, and as England certainly must know it will, we shall then be at perfect liberty to recognize any of the South American Governments without coming into collision with the allies.[47]

It was, indeed, dangerous for the United States to interfere actively in South America as long as there was a chance of Europe uniting against her. It was not until the rupture between England and her rivals was displayed to the world that a Monroe doctrine was possible.   C. K. WEBSTER.

[45] Rush, p. 354 ff.
[46] Adams, *Memoirs*, iv. 136 ff.
[47] Adams, *Memoirs*, iv. 164 ff. Henry Clay, Adams's great opponent, did not of course fail to taunt him with his dependence on England. ' If Lord Castlereagh says we may recognize, we do; if not, we do not. A single expression of the British minister to the present secretary of state, then our minister abroad, I am ashamed to say, has moulded the policy of our government towards South America:' quoted in Mr. Latané's *The Diplomatic Relations of the United States and Spanish America*, p. 59.

Notes and Documents

Ezelo's Life of Hugh of Cluny

THE manuscript here printed is to be found in the British Museum, in the Harleian MS. 3036, fo. 3. The first two leaves contain extracts from Alcuin, fo. 3 the life here given, and the rest of the volume the homilies of Pope Gregory the Great. There is no heading or prologue to the life of Hugh, which may account for its having been overlooked, the more so as the volume is marked on the back ' seculum x '.[1] The writing of the homilies is, however, rather of the eleventh century, and of the life, early twelfth.

Of the lives of Hugh of Cluny six [2] have already been published, and it was further known that another life had been written by a certain Ezelo. For Hildebert in his prologue excuses himself for writing after Ezelo and Gilo : ' veniam confiteor postulandam quod post amplioris litteraturae viros Ezelonem loquor atque Gilonem qui de beatissimo Hugone illo vigilanter scripsisse leguntur ; '[3] and in a later passage cuts short an account of distinguished Cluniacs because Ezelo and Gilo were said to have written about them : ' de quibus loqui plura supersedemus . . . quod ante nos de eis Ezelo atque Gilo clarissimi scilicet viri vigilantius scripsisse traduntur.'[4] Hildebert's life being regarded as a more polished and elaborate piece of work than the two above mentioned, they were allowed to fall out of notice, so that when Papebroch[5] published the lives of Hugh both were unknown to him. A copy of the prologue of Gilo's life, however, was discovered and printed in 1717 ;[6] while Dom L'Huillier later found two copies of the life itself in the Bibliothèque Nationale.[7] But discussion as to whether there had ever been a separate life by

---

[1] Hugh died in 1109.

[2] These are by Gilo, Hildebert, Rainald, Hugh, Anonymus I, Anonymus II, and also a book *Miracula beati Hugonis*. The lives by Hildebert, Hugh, and Anonymus I were first printed in the *Bibliotheca Cluniacensis*, 1614.

[3] Migne, 159, p. 859.

[4] *Ibid.* sect. 42. As R. Lehmann pointed out, Hildebert suggests here that he personally did not know the lives. The discovery of the life by Gilo shows, however, that Hildebert wished to mislead the reader, for in many passages he follows Gilo almost verbatim.   [5] Bolland. *Acta SS. Apr.* iii.

[6] Martène et Durand, *Thes. nov. Anecd.* iii. 322.

[7] L'Huillier, *Vie de St. Hugues*, 1888.

Ezelo arose with the Bollandist publication of the lives in 1675, when Papebroch argued that there had been but one life written by the two authors in collaboration : *vitam primi scripserunt Gilo et Ezelo, uti testatur Hildebertus.*[8] Papebroch did not know whether this life existed, but he had a certain *Compendium ex MS. cenobii Bodecensi anno* 1040 *erutum a P. Ioanne Gamans*, which he published as *Epitome Vitae., ab Ezelone atque Gilone. scriptae., per Anonymum excerpta*,[9] basing his conclusion on the similarity between the extracts and Hildebert's life,[10] and passing over without remark Hildebert's suggestion that he did not know the work of the two earlier authors.

Mabillon was the next to examine the lives, and though he said nothing about Papebroch's theory, it is clear that he did not agree with it. For after giving an account of the two writers, he added : ' Gilonis libellum habemus, non Ezelonis, nisi is sit liber de miraculis sancti Hugonis ; '[11] a suggestion shown to be inadmissible, as the book of miracles was written after Hildebert's life.[12] Then came the discovery of Gilo's prologue in 1717, which destroyed[13] a misconception that had made Papebroch's theory tenable, namely, that two monks were not likely to have been writing in the same monastery, on the same subject, and about the same time ; a difficulty removed by Gilo's statement that he wrote at Rome. The next writer, and the first to make a detailed and critical study of the lives, was Lehmann. He attacked Papebroch for having formulated a theory without any evidence in support of it and without any thorough examination of the subject.[14] A life by Ezelo, he contended, had certainly existed.[15]

The matter rested there till Dom L'Huillier again took it up in his *Vie de St. Hugues*, when he adopted Papebroch's theory with enthusiasm, and attacked Lehmann in not very happy terms. Had a separate life by Ezelo existed, some trace of its influence would, he argued, have been visible in Hildebert's life, ' car enfin Hildebert avait l'une et l'autre sous les yeux et il

---

[8] *Acta SS., Apr.*, iii. 641.   [9] *Ibid.* p. 663.
[10] Lehmann, *Forschungen zur Geschichte des Abtes Hugo I von Cluny*, 1869, p. 45. Judging strictly from Hildebert's words this similarity was rather an argument against than for Papebroch's conclusion, and Lehmann wrote: 'Jedenfalls hat Papebroch, da die von Ezelo und Gilo verfassten Lebensbeschreibungen ihm so unbekannt waren wie sie mir es sind . . . kein Recht, wegen der Verwandtschaft mit Hildebert diesen Anonymus als einen Epitomator Ezelos und Gilos zu bezeichnen.'
[11] Mabillon, *Ann.* v. 529, 1713.
[12] Lehmann, p. 8.
[13] *Histoire littéraire*, 1756, x. 65.   [14] Lehmann, p. 8.
[15] A year after, R. Neumann, in his dissertation *de sancto Hugone*, though not studying the relation between the lives, mentions that he agreed with Papebroch : ' de ratione viro doctissimo (Lehmann) assentire non possum, sed Papebrochi sententiam retinendam puto.' Pignot, *Histoire de Cluny*, ii. 345, also followed Papebroch.

déclare qu'il se règle sur elles.' This Hildebert never did, and Dom L'Huillier can only arrive at his conclusion by mistranslating the phrase on which his evidence rests.[16] Further to support his theory and answer the objection that there is no mention of Ezelo's name in Gilo's life, he has to suppose that ' Ezelon a bien pu collaborer avec son confrère en lui laissant le soin de donner la forme définitive à l'œuvre que Gilon allait terminer à Rome '. Molinier accepted this theory : ' Hildebert cite l'ouvrage sous les noms d'Hezelon et de Gilon : il (Ezelo) a dû collaborer à l'ouvrage de Gilon.' [17]

The dispute seems to the present writer to be settled by the discovery of the life here printed.[18] The name of the author, it is true, is not given, for the prologue—if ever there was one—is missing. The external evidence, however, would point to Ezelo as author, the writing of the manuscript being of the early twelfth century.[19] The style, too, in its greater simplicity and directness differs from that of Gilo. The character of the life would explain why it had been allowed to fall out of notice, for, as Dom L'Huillier pointed out, should such a life exist, ' aujourd'hui considérée comme perdue, elle n'eut pas grande influence, aucun des biographes ne s'en est inspiré.' It is such, indeed, as might have been written at Cluny immediately after Hugh's death, as a memorandum of his early life, and superseded by Gilo's longer work. Yet its very brevity and lack of historical interest are important for comparison with the other lives which, lengthy though they are, contain little more of fact or historical interest ; being written for edification, for the glorification of the monkish virtues, and recounting tedious tales and trivial miracles. Of all the biographies of the early abbots of Cluny those of Hugh are the most disappointing—the more when we consider that he lived when the monastery was at the height of its prosperity, and that his rule lasted sixty years, during which the struggle between church and empire had convulsed Europe.

Before leaving the life, the account of Gregory VII's vision may be noted : ' Gregorius affirmabat Dominum Iesum Christum in capitulo docenti patri nostro assedisse.' In Hildebert, who followed Gilo, this is given as 'Hildebrandus . . . directus in Gallias, Cluniacense capitulum intravit. Ubi cum aliquandiu sedisset, collateratum B. Hugoni Christum vidit monastici regulas ordinis

---

[16] L'Huillier, p. 566. He quotes Hildebert's words (p. 2) as 'nous ne parlerons pas davantage de cela, parce qu'Ezelon et Gilon en ont parlé avant nous dans les meilleurs termes', thus altering the sense by leaving out the important word *traduntur*.

[17] *Sources de l'Histoire de France*, I. ii. 242.

[18] The only copy the writer has found after going through the catalogues of the Bibliothèque Nationale at Paris, the Royal Library at Brussels, the Bodleian, and the Vatican ; the handwriting of the manuscript is earlier than that of the other lives.

[19] Hildebert probably wrote about 1121 ; Gilo about 1115.

ac decreta suggerentem'.[20] At one time this was taken as evidence that Hildebrand was a monk at Cluny, and since that theory was discredited the passage has been cited in proof that he was a monk, for none but a monk could be present *in capitulo*. In a second and less important instance Hildebert, following Gilo, again embellishes the Ezelo account, namely in the story of the priest's vision. In Ezelo this runs: 'dum studiose missam rogatam decantaret, et in contemplatione fixus permaneret, pueri nascentis imaginem vidit;' in Gilo: 'qui dum missarum solemnia attentius peroraret et in contemplatione suspensus super se semet extolleret, vidisse fertur in calice cui ardentius incumbebat speciem infantilem supra humanum modum mirifice radiantem.' Hildebert writes: 'deinde sacrum celebranti mysterium, velut cuiusdam pueri species in calice apparuit inestimabilem preferens claritatem;'[21] and Lehmann takes this story as an instance of how stories of visions and miracles grew up, whereas all the priest saw in the chalice was his own face diminished in reflexion.

It is characteristic also of Ezelo to have put briefly in verse some of the many miracles attributed to Hugh. A detailed account of these is to be found in the other biographies.[22]   L. M. SMITH.

Harl. MS. 3036.

Beatissimus[1] et vere sapientissimus, Deoque et hominibus dilectissimus, pater noster sanctissimus atque piissimus, nullique tempore suo secundus, domnus et abba Hugo Augustidunensi ortus territorio castro Sine muro, patre Dalmatio, matre progenitus Arenburga, de nobilium stirpe clarissima, adeo ut nobilior vir non[2] inveniatur in Europa. A patre quoque prudentissimo commendatus est ad erudiendum Hugoni Authisiodorensis urbis episcopo sollertissimo. Ubi dum liberalibus litterarum studiis erudiretur, et[3] etiam secundum posse suum in lege Domini meditaretur, cepit dicta consiliaque sapientum ad animi recondere firmamentum. Inpiorum vero consilia, actus, vel testimonia vitabat ut mortifera. Hanc sibi ingenitam religionem Deus demonstravit ante illius nativitatem per huiusmodi revelationem. Cum mater illius fide plena, adhuc in utero portaret eum paritura, quendam sanctum rogavit presbiterum, ut orando suum protegeret partum. Qui dum studiose missam rogatam decantaret, et in contemplatione fixus permaneret, pueri nascentis imaginem vidit. Iam significabat Dei gratia quanta vir iste foret exornandus gloria. Denique, quia serpentis antiqui astucia prothoplaustus Adam deiectus a paradisi gloria totum genus humanum morti subdidit, gule intemperantia naturaque viciata imago Dei in hominibus est corrupta, Verbum caro

---

[20] *Vita Hugonis*, cap. ii. 9 (Migne, clix. 866). In Gilo this ran: 'Hic (Gregory) positus in Cluniacensi capitulo ipsum mundi Iudicem parhibuit se vidisse sancto Hugoni collateralem....'   [21] *Ibid.* cap. i.

[22] [There is some corruption in lines 8, 9. It was Theoderic (line 10) who used water in which the saint had washed his hands, and the leper who was the wretched man in a hovel; and line 8 cannot be translated.—ED. *E. H. R.*]

[1] The initial is not filled in.   [2] *non* omitted.   [3] *et* omitted.

factum est de Virgine inviolata et per calicis salutaris antidotum a cordibus humanis expulit mortale venenum. Et ideo sanctum virum per calicis imaginem voluit demonstrare, ut per eum alii discerent de imagine Dei in se ipsis recuperanda non desperare. Et quia multi qui ad imaginem Dei facti erant, sed eandem imaginem male vivendo corruperant, ab eo cum adiutorio Dei spiritaliter de morte anime resuscitandi erant, hoc significabat imago illa in calice salutari tam evidenter exposita, quod vir tantus ac talis in locum illius esset substituendus, qui *signaculum similitudinis, plenus sapientia, perfectus decore, in deliciis paradisi Dei*[4] a propheta dicitur fuisse, quamvis inde per superbiam cognoscatur corruisse. Hic enim vir beatus ab ineunte etate castitatis imitator, et perpetue virginitatis perseverans et humilis custos, Deum studebat ardenti desiderio obsecrare,[5] ut ad Eum posset per obedientiam redire, a quo genus humanum per inobedientiam probatum exorbitare. Huius rei gratia ad ordinem monasticum cepit totis precordiis[6] et medullis cordis fortiter suspirare. Sed pater, quasi alterius Martini, bono proposito invidens ad terrenam militiam volebat eum pertrahere, celestem parvipendens. Quod dum bone indolis adolescens comperisset, timebat ne anime sue detrimentum faceret, si non honores fugitivaque gaudia seculi fugiens Illum imitatus fuisset qui pro nobis *pauper factus est cum dives esset*.[7] Et quanto magis pater terrenus, prudentiam animi eius intelligens, omnibus fratribus etiam natu[8] maioribus volebat eum preponere, honoribusque temporalibus pre omnibus sublimare, tanto magis ipse celestis Patris exempla preponens et seculi contemptum in mente sua disponens patrocinia sanctorum implorabat. Christum cotidianis vel assiduis precibus exorabat, ut Ille qui omnia nosset et sine quo nichil boni quis facere posset, daret sibi adinplere bonum quod vellet. Nec mora quin Deus ipse petitionibus eius annueret et bona quecumque desideraret inplere concederet. Relicta itaque domo sive parentibus et transitorie felicitatis[*] delectationibus clam fugiens Cluniacum habitum monachi diu suscepit desideratum. Sic igitur Cluniacensis gubernator postmodum futurus de mundi naufragio evasit nudus. Quod cum pater eius audisset, et, ut carnalis homo, immenso dolore perculsus fuisset, cepit insequi vestigia eius, ut, si fieri posset, retro post Satanan revocaret animum eius. Ea tempestate regebat Cluniacense cenobium sanctus Odilo, monachorum decus egregium. Huius sanctissimi viri magisterio beatus Hugo, cunctis mundi huius spretis oblectacionibus, Christi se iugo subiciens, documentis sanctis suum prebuit auditum. Post cuius obitum Cluniacensis ecclesie gubernator effectus, apostolum imitabatur qui ait, *Castigo corpus meum, et in servitutem redigo*,[9] ne aliis predicans ipse reprobatus officeretur, ita ut subtus ad carnem lorica gravissima suum adtereret corpus. Et quanto magis adtendebat ne iusticiam suam faceret coram hominibus ut videretur ab eis,[10] tanto magis Ille sibi aderat cuius preceptis obediens erat. Testati sunt hoc non parve auctoritatis homines, inter quos Gregorius Romane urbis papa septimus, affirmabat Dominum nostrum Iesum Christum in capitulo docenti patri nostro assedisse, et quasi proprio ore testimonium ei prebuisse his verbis, *Qui vos audit me audit, et qui vos spernit me spernit*.[11]

[4] Ezech. xxviii. 12, 13. [5] MS. *obsetrare*. [6] MS. *precordiis*. [7] 2 Cor. viii. 9.
[8] MS. *natum*.   [*] MS. *felicitalibus*.   [9] 1 Cor. ix. 37.   [10] Matt. vi. 1.
[11] Luc. x. 16.

Quid dignum memorem vel quanta laude perorem,
Quantos conversos zabuli de fauce reversos
Ad Dominum traxit, secli de morte retraxit ?
Te, Ponci frater, captabat spi.itus ater,
Ni male te fictum iam solveret ille relictum;
Se petit absolvi quem contigit ante resolvi
Quam male celatum sateretur forte reatum ;
Per quoque mundati leprosi [12] veste beati
Abluit unde manus, febrosus fit cito sanus.
Teodorice, pedem deflens, miserabilis edem
Intrans, tinxisti [13] nec postea sic doluisti;
Fit quoque quod mandat Petro Pauloque remandat,
Atque famem pellunt, mala denique cuncta repellunt ;
Maior ut aptetur ecclesia sanctificetur,
Nuncius est Gunzo, fit sanus denique Gunzo ;
Iam quoque Durannum Tolosanum commemoremus ;
Hunc quoque sanatum post mortem significemus ;
Quid modo dicemus si finem iam titulemus ?
Materiem dolor ipse gravat nimis extenuatam ;
Finis consequitur naturam iam viciatam.
Festi Pascalis tunc gaudia mundus habebat,
Quando patri iam continuum festum veniebat:
Quinta dies Pasche sollempnis tunc veniebat;
Nox quoque precedens nos mestos morte tenebat.
Sancte pater, iam iamque tuo [14] tu namque relinquens
Corpore ditatum Cluniacum, sicque relinquens
Nos miseros flentes, Christum iam mente tenebas
Cui nos commendes fratres quos iure docebas,
Ipso prestante qui vivit et regnat per omnia secula seculorum. Amen.

The Abacus and the King's Curia

A QUESTION of special obscurity respecting the early history of the exchequer is the origin and introduction of its distinctive system of reckoning, *secundum consuetum cursum scaccarii non legibus arismeticis*.[1] Inasmuch as the exchequer table was merely a peculiar form of the abacus,[2] some light on the problem may be expected from an examination of treatises upon this method of computation, particularly such as can be connected in any way with England and with the king's court. One compend of this sort, written by a royal clerk named Thurkil, is preserved in a manuscript of the twelfth century in the library

---

[12] MS. *lepei*.   [13] MS. *tinc sisti*.   [14] MS. *tua*.

[1] *Dialogus*, i. 5 (ed. Oxford, 1902, p. 75). On this phase of the origin of the exchequer, see Round, *Commune of London*, p. 74 f. ; the Oxford edition of the *Dialogus*, p. 42 f. ; and Petit-Dutaillis' edition of Stubbs, i. 806–8.

[2] It is worth noting that, whereas the analogy of the chessboard is the only argument hitherto adduced for the existence of transverse lines on the exchequer table, such lines are regularly found in the abacus as described in the medieval treatises.

of the Vatican, and although it has been in print since 1882,[3] it has not, so far as I am aware, been studied from this point of view. It begins :

Socio suo Simoni de ROTOL' TURchillus compotista salutem. In his regunculis quas dilectioni tue, venerande amice, super abacum scripsi et obtuli, licet quid quod tibi displiceat forte reperias, non me tamen, more quorundam quibus nulla inest bonitatis soliditas, iniquo dente livoris mordeas, sed si adhuc solite discretionis es, mee impericie pie ignoscas et, si alicubi necesse est, sic et de meo demas et de tuo addas ut eas sapienter corrigas. Non enim usque adeo perverse mei amator sum ut quod ego inveni pro perfecto defendam, cum in humanis inventionibus, ut ait Priscianus, nichil sit perfectum. Et si quid in huius inventionis scintillula utilitati tue dilectissime conducibile inveneris, nec mihi nec tibi, cuius gratia hoc specialiter edidi, verum venerabili magistro nostro Guillelmo R. [et [4]], quem universis calculatoribus hodie viventibus preferre non timeo, ascribas queso. Vale.[5]

The date of the treatise can be approximately fixed by the following sentence :

Ducentę marce sunt inter .iid^d hidas dividende, que sunt hide totius Eisexie, ut ait Hugo Bocholaudie.[6]

Two men of this name are known in the twelfth century, one of them sheriff of eight counties under Henry I,[7] the other a tenant in Berkshire in 1166 and sheriff of the same county a few years later.[8] There is, however, nothing to connect the younger Hugh de Bocland with Essex, which is in other hands throughout the Pipe Rolls of Henry II, whereas the elder Hugh can be traced as sheriff of Essex in 1101 and the years immediately following.[9] He is found in charters as late as 1114,[1] but by 1117 his lands are in other hands [11] and in 1119 he has been succeeded in his

---

[3] Vat. MS. Lat. 3123, ff. 55–63ʳ, edited by Narducci, in the *Bullettino di Bibliografia e di Storia delle Scienze Matematiche*, xv. 111–54. Cf. Eneström, in *Bibliotheca Mathematica*, 3rd series, viii. 78 f., 415 ; and on the Vatican MS. see also Bethmann, in Pertz's *Archiv*, xii. 233–5.

[4] The manuscript here has a sign which is apparently meant for &, but which is probably a corruption of an original ℞, the ℞ now in the text having been inserted later above the line.

[5] p. 135 of the edition. The edition is for the most part careful, but I have made an occasional correction from the manuscript.

[6] p. 153. Narducci noted the mention of Hugh de Bocland, but (pp. 128–30) was misled into placing the treatise in the second half of the century by identifying the author with a Thurkil of Essex mentioned in a vision of 1206.

[7] *Chronicon Monasterii de Abingdon*, ii. 117 *et passim* ; Ordericus Vitalis, iv. 164 ; *ante*, xxvi. 490.

[8] *Red Book*, i. 306 f. ; Eyton, *Itinerary of Henry II*, pp. 313, 337.

[9] Round, *Geoffrey de Mandeville*, p. 328 ; *Monasticon*, i. 164 ; vi. 105 ; *Cartularium S. Iohannis de Colecestria*, i. 22, 24, 27.

[10] He is addressed in two charters of Reginald, who became abbot of Ramsey in 1114 : *Cartularium Monasterii de Ramseia*, i. 130, 133.

[11] J. Armitage Robinson, *Gilbert Crispin*, p. 154 f.

principal office, the shrievalty of Berks.[12] Our treatise is thus anterior to 1117 and may even go back to the reign of William Rufus, under whom Hugh de Bocland can be traced as witness to the king's charters [13] and as sheriff of Berkshire [14] and Hertfordshire,[15] the latter of which was regularly held with Essex.

Neither Thurkil nor his colleague Simon 'of the rolls',[16] who must likewise have been an expert with the abacus, has been identified, but both were evidently members of the royal *curia*, since Thurkil says, speaking of ordinary division and division by differences:

Si quis tamen cur de utroque divisionum genere, cum ut nunc dictum est ad unum utreque redeant, scripsi quesierit, propterea inquam quod ille ad quoslibet, iste vero non nisi ad curiales tantum pertinet.[17]

Their master, 'Guillelmus R.,' who is mentioned in two other passages,[18] has been sought in vain among the abacists of this period. He was plainly no common teacher or computer, for he has invented a special sign for the *semuncideunx* and is authority for the statement that the conventional figures of the abacus came from the Pythagoreans but their names from the Arabs. The titles *donnus* and *venerabilis vir* would seem to indicate that he was a bishop or an abbot, but I have found no contemporary prelate of this name who would justify Thurkil's characterization, unless it be William, bishop of Syracuse, *c.* 1104–15, who is said to have been of Norman origin and whom Adelard of Bath addresses as *omnium mathematicarum artium eruditissime*.[19]

Like other abacists, Thurkil confines himself to multiplication,

[12] *Chron. Abingdon*, ii. 160.
[13] *Monasticon*, vi. 156; viii. 1272. [14] *Chron. Abingdon*, ii. 43.
[15] The Hertfordshire text of Henry's coronation charter is addressed to him: *Transactions of the Royal Historical Society*, new series, viii. 33, 40; Liebermann, *Gesetze*, i. 521. He is also addressed by William II in a charter concerning Middlesex (Robinson, *Gilbert Crispin*, p. 138, no. 12) and appears as a royal officer in Sussex in the following writ: '.W. rex anglorum Rannulfo episcopo Dunelmensi et H. dapifero et Ursoni de Abetot salutem. Precipio vobis ut faciatis habere Sancte Trinitati de Fiscanno et abbati et monachis eius omnes rectitudines suas et consuetudines de castello de Estanigis et de Bedingis et parrochiam suam vivos et mortuos et oblationem et decimam, siouti hec omnia dirratiotinaverunt in curia patris mei et in mea contra. monachos S. Florencii de Salmur et contra Philippum filium Willelmi de Braiosa. Et facite eis reddi quicquid predicti monachi inde acceperunt. Et mittite Hugonem de Bochelanda ad hanc iusticiam faciendam. Et videte ne inde clamorem audiam pro penuria recti. Teste comite de Mellend apud Lindebonam.' Original, 13 × 5 centimetres, with *simple queue* gone, in the archives of the Seine-Inférieure at Rouen. The royal initial is lacking in the Fécamp cartulary, and Mr. Round, whose treatment of the charters of Fécamp leaves much to be desired, was inclined to attribute this writ to Henry I (*Calendar of Documents preserved in France*, no. 119).

[16] Narducci (p. 121) extends 'Rotolandia', which seems to me much less likely than 'rotolis'.
[17] p. 148 [where for *contra* we should perhaps read *cur*.—ED. *E. H. R.*]
[18] pp. 136, 150. [19] *De eodem et diverso*, ed. Willner, p. 3. See *ante*, xxvi. 492.

division, and fractions, and so throws no light upon the procedure at the exchequer table, which consisted merely of addition and subtraction. The king's clerks had, however, frequent occasion to multiply and divide, and Thurkil's illustrations are obviously drawn from familar subject-matter, as in his brief account, dedicated to a certain Gilbert, of the conversion of marks into pounds and vice versa.[20] What is the product when twenty-three knights owe you six marks each ? Divide £800,137 among 1,009 knights. The most interesting example is the one relating to Essex, which is printed above. A payment of two hundred marks is assessed against a shire and the amount due from each hide is to be determined—just such a case as would arise in levying the *assisa communis* described in the *Dialogus*, and just the amount which Essex pays as *donum* in the early years of Henry II.[21] This coincidence can hardly be accidental, but indicates rather that the *assisa communis*, as a supplement to Danegeld and a corrective to its unequal assessment, goes back to the reign of Henry I, in which case it should probably be identified with the *novo geldo propter hidagium* mentioned between 1100 and 1107 in a charter for Westminster.[22] The hidation which is taken as the dividend, 2,500, has already shrunk from the Domesday quota of 2,650 [23] but has not yet reached 2,364, which is the number of geldant hides in the Pipe Roll of 1130.[24] Moreover, it is reported on the authority of Hugh de Bocland, who as sheriff would know the actual number of hides liable in such a case. A meagre illustration of this sort is especially irritating when we think of what Thurkil might have told us. It may be argued that his failure to mention so interesting a form of the abacus as the exchequer table is an indication that it was not yet in existence ; but the answer is that there is no place for this in his treatise,[25] nor should we expect an account of its relatively simple operations in a work which had to explain the ' iron process ' of division by means of differences. The evidence that royal clerks were familiar with the abacus at the beginning of the twelfth century implies rather that it was already in use for balancing the royal accounts.

[20] Printed by Narducci, *loc. cit.*, p. 127 f. In the manuscript (f. 64ᵛ) this is followed without a break by a chapter ' De collectione diei qui dicitur saltus lune ', the beginning of which indicates that it is a continuation of the treatise of Thurkil : ' Item si scire volueris quot momenta ex unius diei momentis. . . .'

[21] *Dialogus*, i, 8, 11 (ed. Oxford, 1902, pp. 95, 103) ; *Pipe Roll*, 2–4 Henry II, pp. 18, 133. Cf. Maitland, *Domesday Book and Beyond*, pp. 473–5.

[22] Robinson, *Gilbert Crispin*, p. 141, no. 19.

[23] This is the number given by Maitland, p. 400. Rickwood argues for 2,800 : *Transactions of the Essex Archaeological Society*, new series, xi. 249.

[24] p. 59 f.

[25] ' In multiplicacione et divisione constat hec scientia,' p. 137.

Two of Thurkil's contemporaries mention the abacus in a way that brings it into connexion with the *curia regis* at a still earlier date. Robert, who became bishop of Hereford in 1079, is described by William of Malmesbury as *omnium liberalium artium peritissimus, abacum precipue et lunarem compotum et celestium cursum astrorum rimatus*.[26] At his death in 1095 the prior of Winchester, Geoffrey, wrote of him :

Non tua te mathesis, presul Rodberte, tuetur,
Non annos aliter dinumerans abacus.[27]

It is not certain that Robert's writings included a treatise on the abacus,[28] but the passages just cited are conclusive as to his special familiarity with this method of reckoning and the fame it brought him in England. Now Robert was a royal chaplain before his elevation to the bishopric,[29] and heard pleas in the Red King's court only a few months before his death.[30] Moreover, he was a native of Lorraine,[31] which in the eleventh century was the chief centre for the study of the abacus and produced such eminent mathematicians as Heriger of Lobbes, Adelbold of Utrecht, Reginbald of Cologne, and Ralph and Franco of Liège ;[32] and his zeal for the introduction of Lotharingian culture into England is seen in his importation of the chronicle of Marianus Scotus and his use of Charlemagne's church at Aachen as the model for his own cathedral.[33] Robert was, of course, not the only connecting link with the lands beyond the Scheldt in this period, for Lotharingian influence had been strong at the court of Edward the Confessor,[34] and among the prelates of his own

---

[26] *Gesta Pontificum*, p. 300.

[27] Hardy, *Descriptive Catalogue*, ii. 76 ; Wright, *Anglo-Latin Satirists and Epigrammatists*, ii. 154. It may be observed, in connexion with what is said later, that Geoffrey was a native of Cambrai : *Gesta Pontificum*, p. 172.

[28] The mathematical tables ascribed to him by Bale (edition of 1557, ii. 125) may be simply an inference from the phrases of the chroniclers, but the commentary on Marianus Scotus is evidence of his attainments in chronological computation.

[29] Annals of Winchester, in *Annales Monastici*, ii. 32.

[30] *Gesta Pontificum*, p. 302 ; *Vita Wulstani*, in *Anglia Sacra*, ii. 268.

[31] *Gesta Pontificum*, p. 300.

[32] 'Cogis enim et crebris pulsas precibus ut tibi multiformes abaci rationes persequar diligenter. . . . Quod si tibi tedium non esset harum fervore Lotharienses expetere, quos in his ut cum maxime expertus sum florere. . . .', Bernelinus, in Olleris, *Œuvres de Gerbert*, p. 357 ; and Bubnov, *Gerberti Opera Mathematica*, p. 383. See further the passages cited in Bubnov, p. 205 ; Tannery and Clerval, *Une Correspondance d'Écolâtres au XIe siècle*, in *Notices et Extraits des MSS.*, xxxvi. 487–541 ; Cantor, *Vorlesungen über Geschichte der Mathematik*, edition of 1907, i. 872–8, 880–90 ; Kurth, *Notger de Liège* (Paris, 1905), c. 14, especially pp. 282–6 ; Dute, *Die Schulen im Bistum Lüttich im 11. Jahrhundert* (Marburg Programm, 1882).

[33] *Gesta Pontificum*, p. 300 f. For the chronological tract in which Robert elaborated the introduction of Marianus, see W. H. Stevenson, *ante*, xxii. 72 ff.

[34] Freeman, *Norman Conquest*, 3rd edition, ii. 81, 455 f., 598–601, 693–8 ; Steindorff,

time Walcher of Durham had been a clerk of Liège and Thomas of York and Samson of Worcester had apparently been at school there;[35] but his knowledge of the abacus was evidently considered something new and exceptional in England, and had doubtless been brought from his Lotharingian home. We can at least be sure that the abacus was known to members of the *curia* under William Rufus and, since Robert's promotion dates from 1079, even under the Conqueror, and for light upon its introduction we may well look in the direction of Lorraine. C. H. HASKINS.

King Philip Augustus and the Archbishop of Rouen (1196)

IN the troubled rule of Walter of Coutances as archbishop of Rouen, the years 1193 to 1197 were probably fullest of anxieties. The vigorous and excitable Cornishman[1] had first to deal with a quarrel between the citizens and the cathedral chapter in Rouen; then the war between the kings of England and France made havoc of the property of the Norman church, especially on the frontier;[2] then the conclusion of peace in December 1195 and January 1196 revealed a curious understanding between the two kings which threatened the ecclesiastical authority of the archbishop. It seems worth while to unravel this last incident, a tangled little episode in Norman history; for its details, never fully explained by the biographers of Walter, have sometimes been confused with those of the later quarrel between the archbishop and King Richard concerning Andeli. The facts are of interest to the general student of the relations between church and state.

We will begin with a brief extract from Roger of Howden. After speaking of the terms of the peace made at Louviers in January 1196, the chronicler continues:

et ut haec omnia rata haberentur, statuerunt inter se poenam xv millia marcarum argenti, ita quod ille, qui hanc pacem frangeret, daret alteri xv millia marcarum argenti, et super hoc invenerunt sibi ad invicem fideiussores.

Praeterea rex Franciae petiit ad opus suum Andeli, manerium Rothomagensis archiepiscopi. Quod cum nulla ratione fieri posset, rex Franciae postulavit sibi fieri fidelitatem a Waltero Rothomagensi archiepiscopi de illa parte archiepiscopatus quae est in regno Franciae, scilicet de Vogesin

---

Heinrich III, ii. 67 f.; Pauli, in *Nachrichten* of the Göttingen Gesellschaft der Wissenschaften, 1879, pp. 324–30; Round, *Commune of London*, pp. 36–8.

[35] Simeon of Durham, i. 9, 105; ii. 195; Ordericus, iii. 265 f.

[1] Girald. Cambr., *Opera*, iv. 408, &c. See Delisle, Introduction to *Actes de Henri II*, and *Dict. of Nat. Biogr.* s.v. Coutances.

[2] Letter to Ralph de Diceto (Rad. Dic. ii. 144).

le Francais. Videns igitur Rothomagensis archiepiscopus hoc sibi grave et ignominiosum esse, appellavit ad dominum papam pro statu ecclesiae suae, et abiit, timens ne dominus suus rex Angliae ipsum ad hoc faciendum propter favorem regis Franciae cogeret.[3]

It should be noted that Roger of Howden is referring to negotiations which preceded the final agreement. There are four points : first, the clause with regard to sureties ; secondly, Philip's attempt to have Andeli added to his gains during the war ; thirdly, the allusion to the French Vexin ; lastly, the fear of the archbishop that King Richard would support Philip in the demand for his fealty. We will put aside for the moment consideration of the two first points. The writer has not got the fourth point correctly ; as we shall see, the archbishop feared royal collusion on a different issue. Whether or not Philip demanded the archbishop's oath of fealty for the lands in the French Vexin is hard to say ; certainly the king of England did not press him on the matter, and there are no references to it in the archbishop's letters. But the French Vexin played a part in the ensuing quarrel, and it will be desirable to deal with this point first.

Of the six archdeaconries into which the diocese of Rouen was divided the French Vexin[4] accounted for one, which in its turn contained two small archdeaconries of feudal origin. Pontoise and Chaumont. Originally and till the end of the eleventh century the Vexin, Norman and French, formed one archdeaconry ; but the division is clear by 1143.[5] It appears, from a well-known charter of Philip I of France (1091),[6] that the lands possessed by the archbishops of Rouen in the Vexin were early distinguished into those held of the king of France (*de fedio meo*) and those which pertained to the archbishopric. The former were to be held of the king by certain services, the latter of the duke or count of Normandy, *cuius est archiepiscopus*. After granting in fee to the archbishop the abbey of Saint Melon of Pontoise, the charter proceeds :

Preter hec etiam concedo et confirmo redditionem illam qua Gualterius comes, filius Drogonis comitis, reddidit Maurilio, Rotomagensi archiepiscopo, et omnibus successoribus suis totum illud quod pertinet ad archidiaconatum de Vilcassino sive in castello de Ponte Isare sive extra, et quodcunque ipse antehac in manu sua detinebat vel aliquis per eum

[3] Rog. Howden, iv. 3, 4.
[4] The French Vexin, after a troubled history, was attached to France in 1076–7 : see Flach, *Les Origines de l'ancienne France*, iii. 525 *seqq*. For the archdeaconries of the diocese of Rouen see Longnon, *Pouillés de la province de Rouen* (1903), pp. xi, xii.
[5] Longnon, pp. x–xiii ; *Gallia Christiana*, xi. instrum. 22.
[6] *Actes de Philippe I*, ed. Prou, pp. 321–3, no. cxxvii. M. Prou has vindicated the genuineness of this charter in his introduction, p. lviii note, and ascribes it to the year 1091, not, as in the text, to 1092.

habebat et possidebat, similiter et in Calvomonte et reliquis sive burgis sive villis. Hanc, inquam, redditionem tali racione confirmo ut, si est de fedio meo, de me illud habeat Rotomagensis archiepiscopus, si vero est de archiepiscopatu, de comite Normannorum teneat, cuius est archiepiscopus. Hoc autem erit servicium quod pro prefato fedio faciet mihi Rotomagensis archiepiscopus : per singulos annos veniet ad unam ex curiis meis, sive Belvacum, sive Parisius, sive Silvanectum, si fecero eum convenienter submoneri, nisi ipse legitimam excusationem habuerit, etc.

It is clear from the terms of this charter that the archbishops of Rouen, although vassals of the kings of France for certain lands in the Vexin, could hardly be expected to swear fealty for all that part of his archbishopric which lay outside the borders of Normandy. The charter seems, indeed, to have been of transitory effect, and the lands held of the king were not really controlled by the archbishop. Yet as, in the course of time, the territorial distinction between France and Normandy became increasingly important, more than one delicate question may easily have been raised. We may remember that as late as the first half of the twelfth century the bishop of Bayeux still had to find ten of his best knights for the service of the king of the Franks for forty days.[7] As the conflict between France and Normandy became acute the problem of double service for those who held lands in both France and Normandy must have become acute also. Moreover, Walter of Coutances was inclined to regard the interests and the possessions of his church as things above the inconvenient quarrels of princes ; he was quick to use the weapon of excommunication and the interdict ; and it would not be surprising if Philip Augustus protested against the division between the secular and spiritual systems of the Vexin. Even after the union of France and Normandy the position was difficult ; part of the diocese of Rouen was influenced by the custom of Normandy and looked to the Norman Exchequer, and part was subject to the Parlement of Paris. What was, for example, the status of the layman of the Vexin in an ecclesiastical suit ? It was to solve problems of this kind that St. Louis arranged for the creation of the grand vicariate of Pontoise, an ecclesiastical jurisdiction of first instance in matters other than heresy and perjury for those lands which acknowledged the Parlement of Paris.[8]

We may note that King Philip seized the opportunity of a reconciliation with Walter of Coutances in June 1196 to make a special arrangement for the future of Saint Martin of Pontoise.[9]

[7] *Red Book of the Exchequer*, ii. 646–7.

[8] Longnon, p. xiii. The right of presentation to the 'archdeaconry' of Pontoise was surrendered by the king to the archbishop, who was, in his turn, to see that an ecclesiastical judge sat at Pontoise.

[9] Delisle, *Cartulaire Normand*, p. 279, no. 1061 'Actum apud Compendium anno ab Incarnatione Domini M°C° nonagesimo sexto', &c. Since Philip was at Compiègne

The monastery had decayed, and was in the meantime to be subjected to the care of the great abbey of Saint Denis. Philip states that he does this ' ex consensu et voluntate Galteri Rothomagensis archiepiscopi et dilecti nostri magistri Helluini, abbatis sancti Martini Pontisarensis', and in the next phrase ('concedimus ut prefatum *eorum* monasterium ') explicitly refers to the ecclesiastical supremacy of the archbishop.

We may now return to the passage in Howden which refers to Andeli. It is very likely that, during the negotiations, King Philip had tried to forestall Richard by putting in a claim for Andeli. The strategic value of the great rock which rises above the Seine in this old archiepiscopal manor was now obvious to all. The surrender of Gisors and of most of the fortresses on the Epte had opened the route to Rouen ; the strong castle of Vaudreuil was on the wrong side of the Seine, and could not control the road on the right bank. The final wording of the treaty seems to imply that there had been a good deal of discussion between the kings upon the future of Andeli.

De Andeliaco sic erit, quod nec dominus noster rex Francie nec nos in eo clamamus feodum sive dominium. Et si contigerit quod archiepiscopus Rothomagensis in terram regis Francie aut suorum sentenciam interdicti vel excommunicationis miserit, dominus rex Francie poterit assignare ad Andeliacum et ad ea que archiepiscopus ibi habet et ad eius pertinentias, usque dum duo diaconi vel presbiteri, quos rex Francie per sacramentum suum bona fide ad hoc elegerit, et duo diaconi vel presbiteri, quos nos per sacramentum nostrum bona fide ad hoc elegerimus, decreverint utrum interdictum vel excommunicatio iuste latum fuerit an iniuste. Si decreverint quod iuste, rex Francie predicto archiepiscopo reddet Andeliacum et ea que interim exinde levaverit, et ad verbum dictatorum faciet emendari. Si vero decreverint quod iniuste positum fuerit, ea que rex Francie de Andeliaco et de pertinentiis eius levaverit, in deperdito erunt archiepiscopi, et archiepiscopus interdictum vel excommunicationem solvet. Similiter erit de nobis. Si aliquis predictorum dictatorum moreretur hinc vel inde, per sacramentum alterius nostrum alter loco mortui similiter supponetur. Quando archiepiscopum mori contigerit, redditus de Andeliaco et de pertinentiis erunt in manu capituli beati Marie Rothomagensis, donec alius succedat archiepiscopus : nec nos aliquod malum faciemus predictis dictatoribus propter a bitrium ipsorum. Andeliacum non poterit inforciari.[10]

The last four words have usually been quoted alone, but it will be seen that they form the conclusion of a long arrangement about the future possession of Andeli. The plan is remarkable.

in June, and the archbishop was in France from April to the end of June, I date this charter in June. St. Martin of Pontoise had disputes with Walter both before and after this reform, concerning the archiepiscopal right to share in the election of the abbot: *Gall. Christ.* xi. 256–7.

[10] From the text of the treaty in *Cartulaire Normand*, pp. 276–7.

The manor [11] was taken, so to speak, out of Normandy and was to be neutral territory, subject during a vacancy to the chapter of Rouen. The great feudal lords agreed to establish a little sovereign state. Yet, on the other hand, the revenues of Andeli are to be the pledge of good behaviour on the part of the archbishop. We know that this provision was actually enforced by Philip when Archbishop Walter laid an interdict upon his lands. Ralph de Diceto has preserved a letter from King Philip to Walter which commences as follows :

Memores sumus quod dilectos et fideles nostros Ansellum decanum Turonensem et Vrsonem camerarium ad vos transmisimus, per quos vobis nostra voluntas innotuit, videlicet quod in nostro eratis amore et gratia, *et quod vobis Andeleium*, et aliam terram vestram, et alia quae ad vos pertinebant, *libere reddideramus*.[12]

The elaborate precautions against an interdict upon the French part of the province of Rouen seem to imply that this form of warfare was not a novelty ; and, indeed, there is evidence which goes to show that in 1195 Archbishop Walter had resorted to the interdict on account of the damage done to ecclesiastical property. On St. Martin's day (11 November) 1194 King Richard had appropriately restored the property of the clergy of Tours, which he had confiscated,[13] and in return the archbishop of Rouen attempted, with the papal legate, to secure a similar restitution from the king of France of Norman property.[14] In this he succeeded. It is clear, however, from a letter of Philip's that relations had been much strained. I am inclined to connect with this attempt the letter which King Richard wrote to the archbishop from Saumur. The letter is dated 10 February, and is assigned by Mr. Round and Dr. Cartellieri to 1196.[15] Richard thanks the archbishop for removing the interdict from the lands of the king of France so promptly, and begs him to quit-claim Philip by his letters patent of the cause of the same ; for the earl of Leicester, who has suffered much for his loyalty, is still detained in captivity, because the archbishop has not yet quit-claimed the king of France. There are obvious reasons for assigning this letter to the year 1196. In the first place, the

[11] For the manor of Andeli see the remarks in Miss Norgate, *Angevin Kings*, ii. 376 and notes. It is significant that the deanery of Andeli was one of the 'ecclesiae extravagantes' of the diocese. It contained eleven parishes : Longnon, *Pouillés*, p. xiv.

[12] Rad. Dic. ii. 139. It appears from the letters in which the archbishop raised the interdict that Philip had previously attacked Andeli ; see below, p. 115. So far as it goes this fact lends weight to the view that the kings had had experience of the interdict before 1196.

[13] Rad. Dic. ii. 122.   [14] See the letters in Rad. Dic. ii. 122.

[15] Round, *Calendar of Documents preserved in France*, p. 95, no. 279 ; Cartellieri, *Philipp II August*, iii. 222, no. 244. Cartellieri also dates in 1196 the letter from Richard to the bishop of Salzburg, from Chinon, 25 Jan. (*Chron. Magni Reichersperg., Monum. Germ. Hist.*, Scriptt. xvii. 523), although 1195 is more probable.

earl of Leicester was actually released early in 1196, and secondly, the archbishop laid the lands of Philip under an interdict in this year. On the other hand, quite apart from the friendly tone of Richard's letter, unnatural in February 1196, it is clear, according to the archbishop's own letters, that the lands of Philip were still under an interdict in the middle of the year;[16] and, moreover, the earl of Leicester was apparently released at the time of the treaty in January.[17] He had been taken prisoner in 1194, and Roger of Howden speaks of his prolonged captivity owing to the non-observance of the truce of July 1194, and in spite of his willingness to surrender the castle of Paci.[18] Finally, King Richard was in the north-west of his dominions in March 1195.[19] Still, the argument is not conclusive. It is possible that Walter laid an interdict twice in the spring of 1196, and that the earl of Leicester was not immediately released.

However this may be, in January 1196 both kings desired to avoid an interdict, and their elaborate plan for controlling the thunder of the archbishop brings us to the real cause of the quarrel between Walter and the kings. The cause was neither Andeli nor the French Vexin, although, as we have seen, both Andeli and the Vexin had their share in the later troubles. It was, rather, the proposal to set up a joint committee of four deacons or priests; and it was heightened by the attempt of Richard to make the archbishop a surety for what he regarded as a scandalous attack upon his ecclesiastical rights. The archbishop tells the story in the first of a series of long letters to the dean of St. Paul's. He had been at the conference between the two kings; from morn till eve Richard had urged him, through various channels, to become his surety for the observance of the treaty:

ut nos et capitulum nostrum fideiuberemus pro eo, quod nisi scilicet praecise et integre singula capitula, sicut in autentico inter ipsum et regem Francorum confecto continentur. observaret, ad solutionem ij milium marcarum regi Francorum faciendam teneremur, super sponsione etiam facta litteras sigillis nostris impressas praeberemus.[20]

The archbishop naturally insisted upon a perusal of the document before he agreed, and found to his horror the passage already

[16] Rad. Dic. ii. 145.
[17] The order of events in Howden's narrative is certainly, so far as it is worth anything, in favour of the view that the earl was not released in January (iv. 5). On the other hand, the various transactions of January 1196 presume that the earl was to be immediately released, nor do we hear of any infringement of the treaty in this respect. Thus, 'his omnibus peractis, comes Lecestrie et omnes prisones et ostagii prisonum, prout divisum est, hinc inde liberabuntur;' and compare the act of surety of the same date, given by Simon, count of Montfort (Cart. Norm., pp. 278-9).
[18] Rog. Howden, iii. 278. [19] See the acts in Cartellieri, iii. 221.
[20] Rad. Dic. ii. 136. The date was 11-13 January 1196.

quoted, which he gives in his own words. Instead of acquiescing in Richard's proposal, he forthwith excommunicated all who had had any share in the compilation of the treaty ('omnes inventores et fautores illius execrabilis auctentici') except the two kings. On the second day he proposed a compromise. Would Philip allow him to act as surety 'salva integritate ordinis nostri, et iuris, et potestatis ecclesiae Rothomagensis'? The king of France very naturally refused to allow an arrangement which would have been worthless. The archbishop on the third day begged leave of absence through the bishop of Évreux and other ecclesiastics. But in the night (it was Saturday) [21] two knights came from the king with a summons to appear before him in the morning. The archbishop preferred flight, and accompanied by a clerk and a servant took refuge in Cambrai.[22]

In a later letter he again explains the cause of the quarrel:

> Nec contentus est malignus spiritus nobis in exterioribus adversari, sed et in caput nostrum ille adversarius, cui nulla sufficit iniquitas, calcaneum erexit, et reges nostros adeo veneticae suggestionis artificio reddidit insensatos, ut catholicae professionis immemores quatuor nobis vellent superponere primates, et nostrae iurisdictionis potentiam sub eorum ministerio sepelire.[23]

The plan of appointing *dictatores* was not new. It had been employed, probably with the support of the archbishop himself, in the truce of 1194;[24] it was to become a favourite solution of constitutional difficulties in the next century; but applied to the supervision of a primate of the church in the exercise of his supreme ecclesiastical privilege it was a bold proposal. Yet it illustrates in its great disregard of ecclesiastical custom and its careless artifice an attitude towards the church which is too much overlooked. Richard was certainly decided, as the following letter patent shows:

> Richardus, Dei gratia, rex Anglie, dux Normannie, Aquitanie, comes Andegavie, omnibus ad quos littere presentes pervenerint, salutem in Domino. Noveritis nos concessisse et promisisse domino nostro Philippo, regi Francie, quod, si archiepiscopus Rothomagensis vel alius fideiussorum, clericus vel laicus, quos daturi eramus fideiussores eidem Philippo, regi Francie, pro pace inter nos servanda fideiubere nollet, nos illum de terra nostra eiciemus nec de redditibus suis quos in terra nostra habuerit eum aliquid habere permittemus, nec ipse archiepiscopus in terram nostram redire poterit, nisi ipse pro duobus milibus marcis argenti fide-

---

[21] Rad. Dic. ii. 137, *nocte Sabbati*.

[22] It was in this year that the chapters of Rouen and Cambrai formed a *societas* for mutual protection and shelter, which was to last so long as the sons of men set themselves to accomplish the ruin of God's church. The act of union is in Martène, *Thesaurus*, i. 663–4. [23] Rad. Dic. ii. 144.

[24] The archbishop had arrived in Normandy shortly before (Rad. Dic. ii. 115).

iusserit domino regi Francie pro nobis, aut per regem Francie, nec aliis, nisi fideiussione facta, vel nisi per regem Francie. Idem erit de successore archiepiscopi et de successoribus ecclesiarum et de heredibus baronum. Actum inter Gallionem et Vallem Rodotii anno Incarnati Verbi M⁰ C⁰ nonagesimo quinto.[25]

It is not known when the archbishop laid the interdict on the lands of the king of France, but it is clear, from his letters and from the act in which he announces that he has raised it, that an interdict was laid. The struggle lasted until June, and became confused (1) with the relations between King Richard and the ecclesiastics whom King Philip had put forward as his sureties, and (2) with the demand for indemnification put forward by the archbishop on behalf of the lesser clergy of his province.

The first step seems to have been taken by Philip. After all, an interdict was terrible enough to bring a king to his knees. He restored Andeli, which he had evidently seized,[26] and sent safe conducts and friendly letters to the archbishop.[27] In another letter to the dean of St. Paul's the archbishop describes how Philip received him with kindness and submission at Pontoise (17 April) and Paris (30 April). If Richard would do the same by the French sureties Philip promised to absolve the Norman sureties from any obligation. The archbishop thus summarizes the king's words :

> Noveritis, dilecte archiepiscope et sacerdos Christi, etiam cum contradictione satraparum et consiliariorum nostrorum [28] nos intuitu Dei et personae nostrae non tantum preces vestras velle exaudire, sed et illis hoc conditionaliter superaddere, videlicet non solum nos, sed et episcopos et abbates, omnes conventus et ecclesias diocesis vestrae, qui fideiusserunt pro rege Angliae, absolvi a plegio et fideiussione qua nobis obligati sunt, si episcopos, abbates, conventus, et ecclesias, qui pro nobis erga eum (i.e. Richard) fideiusserunt, voluerit et concesserit absolvi.[29]

It is to the following weeks in May and June that we should assign the letters of Richard which are given on an earlier page of the dean's chronicle. The king of England had also begun to approach Walter. It would never do to allow the king of France to make terms with the Norman archbishop. He promised to absolve the archbishop of Tours, who was apparently the chief surety for Philip, if Philip would absolve the archbishop of Rouen. In a letter to the bishop of Evreux he explains how Philip agreed.[30] After this peace was soon secured. The archbishop was free to return to his own church, and leaving

---

[25] *Cart. Norm.*, p. 278, no. 1058.
[26] Above, p. 110.
[27] Rad. Dic. ii. 139, 140.
[28] This is an interesting constitutional point.
[29] Rad. Dic. ii. 142.
[30] Rad. Dic. ii. 139–40. Stubbs's marginal note that Philip changed his mind is misleading. He acquiesced in a proposal of King Richard's.

French territory,[31] reached Rouen on the third Sunday after Trinity (7 July).[32] Before he left France he raised the interdict.[33]

During the negotiations which preceded his departure three points were settled, besides the release of the sureties from all obligation. In the first place, the church of Rouen was secured in an annual grant of £500 as an indemnity. The archbishop refers to this grant as the result of an agreement between the kings (*sicut lex compositionis inter ipsos initae diffinivit*). There is no mention of such a compensation in the treaty of January. In that treaty the kings agreed to pay no compensation, but to forbear from attacks upon ecclesiastical property in the future.[34] Unless some later agreement, now lost, was arrived at, I assume that the archbishop referred to negotiations of 1195, for in that year King Richard issued a charter at Rouen to the church of Rouen, by which in recompense for the losses and damages caused to the archbishop and canons by the king of France, he granted 300 *muids* of wine annually out of the wine-due of Rouen.[35] In 1198 this grant was worth £583 10s.,[36] although in 1195 the contemplated value was 20s. a *muid*. Secondly, the archbishop refers to the fortunes of certain abbots:

> Abbates vero, pro quorum dampnis nos opponebamus, nobis litteris suis patentibus ediderunt, quod dominus rex Angliae eos securos reddiderat, quod eis satisfaceret competenter.[37]

It should be noted that, as the archbishop did not reach Rouen before 7 July, the final arrangements were not reached before the end of June; and that by this time hostilities had already broken out again between Philip and Richard.[38] It is, therefore, just possible that the abbots to whom Archbishop Walter refers were the abbots whose goods Richard seized after he heard of Philip's attack upon Aumâle. Roger of Howden is our authority:

---

[31] He had been staying 'in partibus Galliae iurisdictioni nostrae subiectae' (Rad. Dic. ii. 142). This shows that the word *Gallia*, like *Francia*, was commonly used in a limited sense. [32] Rad. Dic. ii. 145. [33] *Ibid.*

[34] 'Nos domino nostro regi Francie faciemus quitari omnia illa que cepit de rebus ecclesiarum terre nostre, que sunt in terra sua, et idem rex Francie similiter nobis; neque nos neque rex Francie de cetero, propter aliquam guerram que evenire possit, aliquod capiemus vel supercapiemus de rebus ecclesiarum alter de terra alterius': *Cart. Norm.*, p. 277.

[35] Round, *Calendar of Documents preserved in France*, p. 18, no. 67. The date is probably about 3 September, since Richard refers to his anniversary; he was crowned on 3 September, 1189. Stapleton assigns the charter to December (*Observations*, ii, p. xxi), but overlooks the fact that the king was not at Rouen during that month; he spent Christmas at Poitiers (Howden, iii. 308).

[36] 'Eidem Archiepiscopo et canonicis Sancte Marie de Rothomago d. li. quater xx li. lxx. so. hoc anno pro ccc. modiis vini per cartam Regis': Rot. Scacc. ii.

[37] Rad. Dic. ii. 145.

[38] Probably in middle of June (cf. Delaborde's edition of Rigord, i. 135), though Gervase of Canterbury (i. 532) says that peace lasted till the feast of St. John the Baptist (24 June).

Procedente itaque tempore, poenituit regem Franciae se talem fecisse cum rege Angliae conventionem; et magnum congregavit exercitum, et obsedit Albemarliam: quo facto, rex Angliae praecepit saisiri in manu sua, in omni loco dominationis suae citra mare et ultra, omnes res et possessiones abbatum de Maiurmuster, et de Cluinni, et de Sancto Dionisio, et de la Charite. *Erant enim praedicti abbates fideiussores erga regem Angliae*, quod rex Franciae supradictam pacem servaret; et nisi fecerit, darent regi Angliae xv. milia marcarum argenti.[39]

By the terms of the recent arrangement Richard was not justified in this act of spoliation; and it is not improbable that the archbishop of Rouen found it his interest, no less than his duty, to protest and secure the financial safety of these great ecclesiastics. In the third place, the archbishop obtained Richard's promise to compensate the lesser clergy for their losses. Only when this promise had reached him did he raise the interdict on the land of the French king.

The letters of relaxation, with the seals of the archbishop and his chapter, still exist, and have been printed by M. Teulet.[40] They show that the interdict had only been laid upon the French Vexin,[41] and that, in consequence of Richard's promise of compensation, the archbishop surrenders all claim for the losses inflicted upon ecclesiastical property in Normandy previously to 5 December 1195, a few days before the truce between the kings at Issoudun which ripened into the treaty of the following month.

Noverit excellentia vestra satisfactum esse nobis[42] et canonicis nostris et ceteris ecclesiasticis personis omnibus de provintia nostra, plenarie, ad honorem Dei et ecclesie nostre et nostrum, super universis dampnis per vos et vestros, et eos qui ad vos pertinent, nobis illatis, et quod nos et predicte persone omnes, tam Andelitii quam omnium reddituum et aliarum rerum nostrarum, plenam habemus restitutionem, et ideo interdictum, sub quo terram vestram in provintia nostra concluseramus, relaxavimus, et quietamus in perpetuum vos et vestros, et universos qui ad vos pertinent, de universis rebus illis, quas de rebus nostris et ecclesiarum de terra domini regis Anglie in provintia nostra cepistis ante vigiliam sancti Nicholai anni Dominice incarnationis MCXC quinti, etc.

The renewal of war, and Richard's seizure of Andeli, nullified the elaborate clauses of the treaty. The archbishop was plunged into fresh controversy, and apparently suffered no more from

---

[39] iv. 4 f.

[40] Teulet, *Layettes du Trésor des Chartes*, i. 187, no. 442. The editor wrongly ascribes the letters to the months of January to March, instead of to the end of June or beginning of July, 1196.

[41] Unless authorized by the pope, an archbishop could not lay an interdict on lands outside his own province. Krehbiel, *The Interdict*, p. 21, limits archiepiscopal powers to the diocese; but Walter certainly laid the whole of Normandy under an interdict at the end of the year. Cf. Howden, iv. 14, 16.

[42] The grammar of this passage bears out the suggestion in the archbishop's letter (Rad. Dic., ii. 145) that it was Richard, not Philip, who paid compensation.

the bargain between the two kings. Yet, ephemeral though the struggle between the kings and himself was, its history is not without interest. It is rarely that we are able to test the casual and incomplete narrative of a chronicler by the correspondence of the chief actors. Without the letters of Archbishop Walter to the dean of St. Paul's we should not know that the terms of the treaty of Louviers had met with such resistance, or if we suspected it from a charter of King Richard, we should be in complete ignorance of the details of the controversy.[43]

The documents preserved by Ralph de Diceto present some features of diplomatic interest. Besides the correspondence, we have letters patent and close of King Richard's, and references to the letters patent of various ecclesiastics. It may be of interest, in conclusion, to give side by side a safe conduct of Philip Augustus and letters of King John ; Philip's letter was concerned with the subject of this paper.

Safe conduct of Philip Augustus for the archbishop of Rouen (1196).[44]	Safe conduct of King John for William, king of Scotland (1207).[45]	Letter of protection of King John for the abbot of Fécamp (1202).[46]
Philippus Dei gratia rex Francorum universis praepositis et bailivis ad quos litterae praesentes pervenerint, salutem. Noveritis quoniam fidelis noster Rothomagensis archiepiscopus et omnes qui cum eo sunt per nostram terram in nostro sunt conducto, unde vobis praecipimus quod ipsum et suos per terram nostram salvo conducatis.	... Sciatis quod salvum et securum conductum praestamus dilecto consanguineo nostro illustri Regi Scottie Willelmo in veniendo ad nos ad loquendum nobis cum pro negotiis inter nos tractatis et in redeundo in partes suas. . . .	Iohannes, Dei gracia rex Anglie, dominus Hibernie, dux Normannie, Aquitanie, comes Andegavie, omnibus castellanis et baillivis suis Normannie salutem. Mandamus vobis quod manuteneatis et defendatis omnes terras, homines, res, redditus et possessiones dilecti nostri abbatis Fiscannensis, nec inferatis ei nec ab aliquo inferri permittatis molestiam aut gravamen, et si quid ei in aliquo forisfecerit, id ei sine dilacione faciatis emendari. Teste me ipso apud Rothomagum xxvii die Iulii.

[43] Other letters have been lost : see the archbishop's reference to his letters to the archbishop of Canterbury (Rad. Dic. ii. 141). It should be noted that Howden, in the passage quoted at the beginning of this paper, refers to an appeal to the pope. The accuracy of this statement is proved by the fact that Innocent III, two years later, wrote to the archbishop of Rouen about the proposal made in the treaty of January 1196 to place four clerks ' super caput tuum ', and urges resistance (*Patrologia Latina*, ccxiv. 219). The papal chancery moved slowly.

[44] Rad. Dic. ii. 138 ; also a safe conduct addressed to the archbishop, p. 140.

[45] Rot. Pat. p. 69b.

[46] *Bibliothèque de l'École des Chartes*, vol. lxv (1904), p. 396. The original in the Musée of the distillery at Fécamp.

In the collection from which M. Delisle printed the letters of protection for the abbot of Fécamp there is a letter of Philip's which, though entirely irrelevant to this paper, has a suggestive date: '_apud Gaillart,' March 1204.[47] The rock of Andeli, of which so much was heard in 1196 and the following years, is intended. During the siege of 1203 Philip dated some of his letters 'ante Gallardum'.[48] The nickname with which King Richard saluted his castle, though used by William the Breton, was, according to M. Deville, not to be found in official documents before 1261.[49] These charters show that it was occasionally employed more than fifty years earlier.   F. M. POWICKE.

Documents relating to the Rupture with France in 1793

PART I

THIS paper and a subsequent one consist mainly of new documents which throw light on the Anglo-French negotiations of November 1792—February 1793. The course of that dispute having been described somewhat fully in my work, *William Pitt and the Great War* (ch. iii, iv), it is unnecessary to do more than present further documents bearing on the question. The first is fairly well known, but deserves quotation as tending to refute the later assertions of Lebrun, French minister of foreign affairs after the revolution of 10 August 1792, that the attitude of the Pitt ministry to France was always unfriendly. On the contrary, in his report to the legislative assembly, dated 23 August 1792, there occurred these sentences :

. . . Il reste à parler d'Angleterre et de la Hollande. Ces deux Puissances annoncent toujours le désir de rester dans les termes de stricte neutralité. L'ambassadeur britannique [Earl Gower], en s'éloignant momentanément de la France, nous laisse à cet égard un témoignage satisfaisant des sentimens de sa cour. . . . L'Angleterre n'a équipé cette année qu'une foible escadre, et cette escadre est même déjà rentrée dans le port ; mais il ne paroît pas qu'on s'apprête à la désarmer, malgré que la saison des évolutions soit passée. Enfin on ne remarque depuis un mois aucun mouvement extraordinaire dans les ports de la Grande Bretagne. Mais l'on sait que sa marine est dans tous les tems si bien ordonnée qu'en moins de six semaines elle peut avoir en mer une flotte considérable.

The reasons for the withdrawal of Earl Gower from Paris were that the government of Louis XVI, to which he was accredited,

---

[47] *Ibid.*, p. 390.   [48] *Cartulaire Normand*, no. 67 and note.
[49] Deville, *Château-Gaillard*, p. 40; Miss Norgate, *Angevin Kings*, ii. 380 note. William the Breton says in his prose Chronicle § 111 : 'totamque munitionem illam vocavit Gaillardium ' (ed. Delaborde, i. 209).

ceased to exist on 10 August, and that the presence of a noble in that city was thereafter attended with some danger. No signs of tension became manifest between the two governments until after the French victory at Jemappes (6 November 1792), which laid the Austrian Netherlands at the feet of the invaders. Any such event had always been resisted by Great Britain, as must have been known by the British Jacobinical clubs, several of which then sent messages of congratulation and offers of money and boots to the French government. To the weeks after Jemappes I am inclined to assign these two undated drafts, which directed some person, not named, to proceed from London to Paris for the following purpose :[1]

Sir,
It having been judged adviseable by the King's servants that you should proceed to Paris with a view to the opening such a communication and to the obtaining such explanations as appear highly important in the present moment for the general advantage of Europe, as well as for the mutual interests of this country and of France, I have thought it right to intrust you with this letter which you may show as your authority for entering into all such conferences and discussions as may be necessary for these purposes.

Sir,
In addition to the objects which I have stated to you in my other letter of this date, I think it right to recommend to your very particular attention the procuring the best possible information respecting the real state of France in all the important particulars which are connected with the occasion of your mission. The state of the interior of the Provinces (*sic*), that of Paris, the degree of stability which the republican form of government may appear to have acquired from the late successes, the disposition, character, and weight of the persons who conduct the public measures in the Council and in the Convention, the state and amount of their naval preparations, and their prospects in point of finance, are all points which it would be highly interesting to ascertain. It is a matter of a more delicate nature, but it would be of great utility if you could establish any channels of secret information by which it would be possible for us to receive intelligence, even in the event of a war, respecting the transactions at the different ports, or respecting the plans of the Government.

I have found no proof that this mission was ever fulfilled, and obviously it was regarded less as a means of establishing official negotiations than of gaining news. The dispute entered on a serious phase when the French convention passed the decree of 16 November 1792, throwing open the navigation of the Scheldt estuary, which the Dutch had kept closed since 1648, and that of three days later offering armed help to malcontents who desired to throw off the yoke of their governments. The

[1] Foreign Office, France 40.

former decree contravened the Anglo-Dutch treaty of defensive alliance of the year 1788. The dispatches that passed between Lord Grenville, foreign minister at Whitehall, and Lord Auckland, British ambassador at The Hague, are therefore important, as will be seen by the following, taken from Foreign Office, Holland 41, 42, which may be supplemented by others in volume ii of the *Dropmore Papers* (Hist. MSS. Commission). On 13 November 1792 Grenville informs Auckland of the concern felt at the news of the departure of Austrian officials from Brussels on the approach of the victorious army of Dumouriez. He continues :

In this situation H[is] M[ajesty] could not but feel that the only probable means of averting the danger is to meet it with firmness. And, deeply as the King would lament on every account the necessity of giving any interruption to that state of external tranquillity from which his subjects derive so many advantages, H. M.'s regard to his engagements, as well as his sense of the real and permanent interest of his people would leave him no hesitation as to the propriety of his assisting the Dutch Republic as circumstances might require against any attempt made on the part of any other Power to invade its dominions or to disturb its government. Feeling the necessity of taking this determination, if the case should arise, H. M.'s servants have thought that it might in many views be highly advantageous, that the King's intentions should be early and publicly notified, both to give encouragement to the Dutch Government and the well disposed persons in the Provinces, and to apprize those who may have hostile intentions, of all the extent of those consequences which must arise from the execution of their plans.

Your Excellency is therefore instructed to deliver without delay the enclosed Note to be laid before Their High Mightinesses in the usual form ; and this, without waiting for any application on the part of the States General to H. M. ; as the impression to be produced by this step will probably be greater if it is known to originate from the King's solicitude for the interests of Allies than if it is considered only as an act of compliance with a request on their part. Your Excellency will of course observe that it is not the King's wish that this Declaration should remain secret, but that, on the contrary, part of the effect to be expected from it must depend on its being known as early as possible both at Paris and at the Head Quarters of the French army ; and this may probably be effected without difficulty thro' the ordinary channels of communication. . . .[2]

Lord Auckland to Lord Grenville

The Hague, 16 Nov. 1792.

[Auckland has just received Grenville's dispatch of Nov. 13, and has requested separate conferences with the Grand Pensionary, the Greffier, the Prince Stadholder, the Princess of Orange, the President of the week, and afterwards the States General. He adds—] It is impossible to

[2] The British declaration (for which see *Annual Register*, 1792) stated that as the French troops were nearing Holland, the king renewed the assurances of his steadfast friendship and of his resolve to support the republic at all points.

convey to your Lordship an adequate sense of the impression made by this voluntary Declaration of H. M.'s sentiments and intentions respecting the Republic on the occasion of the present crisis. The generosity of this measure, which in a few hours was generally known, and which to-morrow will be circulated over the Continent in the newspapers of the Republic, is acknowledged by everyone. Justice must at the same time be rendered to the confidence which the Dutch Ministers had reposed in H. M.'s good faith, and which had prevented them from soliciting the assurances now given by H. M. and made known to all Europe. In a more essential point of view the measure has a tendency to prevent evils with which we are menaced, and at the worst to prepare both this Country and Great Britain to meet those evils with advantage if they cannot be avoided.

I inclose the answer from Their High Mightinesses to H. M.'s Declaration. It was brought to me this evening by the Greffier Fagel, and is expressed in terms which I hope H. M. will approve. [He then names a report that Dumouriez had said he would dine at The Hague on Jan. 1, 1793. The Grand Pensionary had no fear, but others had.]

Thus the British declaration of a resolve to defend all the rights of the Dutch republic was published on 16 November, the very day on which the French convention passed the decree throwing open the estuary of the Scheldt. A few days later French gun-vessels sailed up the Scheldt, despite the opposition of the Dutch guardship at the mouth. The following dispatch refers to the resulting crisis which the British government regarded as certain to lead to war unless the French retracted their decree and withdrew their vessels:

Lord Grenville to Lord Auckland

Whitehall, Nov. 26, 1792.

Your Excellency's despatches of the 23rd inst. were received here this morning. As the point respecting the line to be adopted towards the French boats in the Scheldt must by this time have been decided, it seems unnecessary to say anything further upon it than to express the full reliance of H. M.'s servants on the prudence and wisdom of the Dutch Gov^t in these critical circumstances. If the French are determined to force us to a rupture, it seems of little moment what is the particular occasion that is to be taken for it, except with a view to the benefit of standing on the most advantageous ground with respect to the public opinion in the two Countries. But it is a much more material question to determine to what degree it would be more or less advantageous to us, or the French, in point of our respective state of preparation, that things should come to their crisis now or a short time hence, supposing that such a crisis cannot ultimately be avoided.

Such preparatory steps as were judged advisable, and not likely to attract too much notice, have already been taken with a view to enabling us to proceed with more expedition in case of any sudden necessity for augmenting our naval force; and one of the principal objections to such a demonstration as it is proposed to us to make at Flushing or in the

Downs is that it would impede the measures to which I have alluded. The season of the year affords another strong objection to this step, and may be ostensibly used as a reason for our declining what is asked of us in this respect. . . .

PS. Since this dispatch was written, I have been informed of the decree of the [French] Executive Council relative to the opening of the navigation of the Scheldt. I shall be extremely impatient to know how far this decree has been followed up on the part of M. Dumourier; and in that case, what is the opinion of the Dutch Ministers with a view to the situation of the Republic; whether it would be more advantageous that this point should immediately be brought to its issue; or that by representations time should be given for further preparations. With respect to this question, much must of course depend on the manner in which this business is brought forward by M. Dumourier. If the circumstances are such as to afford room for negotiation, without committing the dignity of the Republic, and of its allies, it should seem that much advantage might result from gaining time. But it is impossible not to feel that the transaction may assume such a shape as to make this impossible.

I shall of course write to Your Excellency again upon this subject as soon as I am apprized of any further particulars respecting it, or am enabled to communicate to you a more precise opinion.

No. 25.
The Same to the Same

Whitehall, Nov. 27, 1792.

My Lord,
I received this morning Your Excellency's dispatches to No. 57 inclusive, which I acknowledge by this mail merely for the purpose of expressing the satisfaction with which the King's servants have seen the resolution of Their High Mightinesses on the application of the States of Zealand.

We must now wait to see the result of this important business, which, in its consequences may bring on that necessity which both H. M. and the States General have so long been desirous to avoid. It would be highly interesting to us in the present moment, to be informed as nearly as possible of the exact state of the Dutch forces, naval and military, and of the situation in which it is supposed they could be placed by any sudden exertions. Your Excellency will see that precise details on this subject become more important in proportion as the probability of our being forced into a state of hostility against France increases.

No. 27.
The Same to the Same

Whitehall, Dec. 4, 1792.

[News had arrived that the French troops had demanded to pass through Maestricht. H. M. waited anxiously to hear of the state of the Dutch armaments.]—The Conduct of the French in all their late proceedings appears to H. M.'s Servants to indicate a fixed and settled design of hostility against this Country and the Republic. [The writer then recapitulates their aggressions and states that military preparations were now being made. The King trusts that the Dutch will prevent the passage of the French through any part of their land.]

No. 31.
The Same to the Same

Whitehall, Dec. 28, 1792.

[Woronzow, the Russian ambassador, had made an overture from the Empress Catherine for a concert with Great Britain on the subject of French affairs.] H. M. has expressed his willingness to enter into such a concert, confining it to the object of opposing a barrier to the danger which threatens the tranquillity of all other countries and the political interests of Europe from the intrigues and ambitious plans pursued by France, without directing his views to any interference in the interior government of that Country. The time does not admit of my entering further into the detail of this subject at present, but I am persuaded that the line adopted by the King will be found by the Dutch Ministers to be entirely conformable to the principles settled between the two Governments. . . .

Meanwhile, the Anglo-French negotiations proceeding at London were only of a semi-official character, the British government refusing to recognize in an official capacity the *ci-devant* Marquis de Chauvelin after the fall of the government of Louis XVI which had deputed him. There being no British ambassador at Paris, the question was therefore treated in an unsatisfactory manner. Chauvelin's vanity and ambition led him to resent as a personal slight the refusal to treat with him officially, and Lebrun and the Conseil Exécutif at Paris sought by all possible means to bring the British government to an official recognition of him, which it consistently refused. Into these questions it is needless to enter except in so far as they explain certain passages in the following paper. It is endorsed by Lord Grenville 'Minutes of a Conference with M. Chauvelin, on 29 November 1792' (Foreign Office, France 40):

M. Chauvelin told me in substance that circumstances changed so rapidly in France, that he could only say now, that, at the time when he wrote the Note to desire to see me, he was authorized to contradict the reports, which he observed to prevail in London, of an intention on the part of the French to attack Holland; that, on the contrary he could have renewed the assurances which he had before given, of their disposition to respect the Neutral Powers: that since this, he had seen the note delivered by Lord Auckland to the States General, and had yesterday heard that there was an account of two French ships having been fired at by the Dutch in the Scheldt; that he could not say what alteration such an aggression (as he called it) on the part of the Dutch might produce; but that the most earnest wish of all the French was to cultivate peace and friendship with England. He spoke always of the opening of the Scheldt as of a thing determined upon, saying that it was a natural right, which the French acquired by the conquest of Brabant, and he showed himself very desirous to obtain an admission, expressed or implied, that this was the case ; and that our Treaty with Holland did not extend to this point. He stated that, in his answer to my letter, he had particularly mentioned that it was a *conversation particulière* that he wished, in order to mark that it was not his wish that any point of form should stand in the way of friendly communications between the two countries; and that the Conseil Exécutif had thought this was the best mode of proceeding ; and that it ought to be left to England to judge at what time she might think proper to re-establish the correspondence between the two countries by formal and official intercourse. In the conversation he intimated that France had thought she saw in the note presented by Lord Robert Fitzgerald at Geneva, a proof of ill disposition on the part of this country.

My answer was in substance, that, as he confined himself to what he might have said some days since, I could only say in reply that we should have received with satisfaction any full and sufficient assurances of the disposition of France with respect to the rights of this country and its Allies. That if such communication had been made, I should have been able from the terms of it to judge whether it went as far as we wished and to have regulated my answer accordingly. That I had desired to see him chiefly for the purpose of showing that, on our part, we were not desirous to suffer mere points of form and etiquette to stand in the way of essential objects ; it being always understood that, by avoiding to dwell on such points, as obstacles in the beginning, we did not engage ourselves further. That with respect to Lord Robert Fitzgerald's note [3] and the point of the opening of the Scheld (*sic*), I thought the first sufficiently explained itself ; and as to the second, I was not authorized to discuss it at all with him or to say anything upon it to him. In answer to an offer of his to convey any assurances of our friendly disposition, I said that I did not feel that we were in the case of sending any such assurances, especially as he had confined what he had said to the assurances which he should have been enabled to give some days ago. That if there was, as he had said, any coolness or distance between the two countries, this Government had certainly nothing to reproach itself with on that head ; and that if, as he had also said, consequences afflicting to Humanity might follow from it, it would not be the fault of England. At the end of the conversation I told him that it did not appear to me that under the circumstances of what he had said I had anything more to add. That he had seen what had been the system which the King had uniformly followed with respect to French affairs, but that it was a part of that system that the King was resolved to maintain inviolate all the rights of this country and those of its allies.

He ended by saying that, if he heard more, he should be desirous to communicate it to me *dans la même forme* ; and I told him that in that way I should be ready to see him.

J. HOLLAND ROSE.

[3] This referred to the disputes between France and the Genevese Republic. Our envoy Fitzgerald set forth the rights of Geneva as a neutral state (*Ann. Reg.*, 1792, p. 194).

Reviews of Books

Geschichte der neüeren Historiographie. Von EDUARD FUETER. (München: Oldenbourg, 1911.)

THE development of modern historiography has hitherto had to be laboriously tracked through a number of books which, whether separately or in combination, fail to give the student what he requires. It is only treated incidentally in the excellent handbooks of Bernheim and Gustav Wolf. Even the more detailed review in Langlois' *Manuel de Bibliographie historique* is little more than a skeleton. Flint and Molinier deal with France alone; Wegele confines himself to Germany, and halts on the threshold of the nineteenth century. With the appearance of Dr. Fueter's work we are at last in possession of a comprehensive survey of historical writing from the early Renaissance to our own day. The preface explains the limits which the writer has imposed upon himself. He omits the philosophy of history, and only deals casually with historical method and the science of research. His aim is to study works of narration. Yet even this territory is too vast to be completely mapped in a single volume. Many admirable historians, he laments, are excluded in order to make room for a fuller treatment of the founders of schools and original thinkers. He is more concerned to describe all the important tendencies than all the important writers. Historians of law, literature, and religion are in almost every case excluded, and living scholars are omitted. Even with these limitations Dr. Fueter fills 600 large pages in which there is not a superfluous word.

The first of the six books into which the volume is divided is devoted to Italian Humanism, the treatment of which forms perhaps the most original feature of the work. Modern historiography, declares Dr. Fueter, like other literary *genres*, starts from humanism, and the earliest masters of the new learning, Petrarch and Boccaccio, were its creators. They were, however, only amateurs, and the finished model was provided by the Florentine Bruni (1369–1444), ' the first modern historian who on principle employs criticism.' Soon every Italian state and city had its Bruni. Aiming at the closest possible reproduction of the classics, the humanists condemned themselves to sterile imitation; but they took the step without which real progress was impossible. ' They completely secularized history. They wholly eliminated the conception that a Divine Providence determines either the march of the world or the sequence of particular events.' The first generations of humanists regarded history as a literary exercise. A further stage was reached when Machiavelli and Guicciardini, while retaining the forms of humanism, turned history into politics.

Caring nothing for literature and much for practical needs, the great Florentines sought lessons in the art of government. History ceased to be a record of a dead past and became the master-key to the problems of the present. Dr. Fueter is not prone to enthusiasm; but he is warm in his expressions of admiration for the services of the two great realists who lifted historiography out of literature and related it to the life of states.

The second book traces the spread of humanist historiography over Europe. Dr. Fueter repeatedly insists that the influence of Italian models was far wider and more permanent than is usually realized; and in the light of this discovery he contests the originality and challenges the importance of such famous writers as Aventinus, Zurita, and Mariana. The severity of his verdict on the German humanists will come as a surprise to those who have been taught to find in the circle of the Emperor Maximilian the prophets of a new age. ' In no land did Humanist historiography free itself so imperfectly from theological presuppositions as in Germany. In no other land did historical criticism remain at such a low level.' Their works, indeed, were scarcely even imitations of Italian models, and belong rather to the expiring *genre* of medieval chronicles. Humanistic historiography, invented and perfected in Italy, remained the dominant type till the *Aufklärung* of the eighteenth century; but it did not cover the whole ground. The controversies of the Reformation led to the foundation of church history, which in the hands of Flacius and Baronius, Sarpi and Bossuet, proved a formidable weapon in the long struggles of confessionalism. In the next place the seventeenth century witnessed the birth of a school of disinterested research, adorned by the great names of Mabillon and Tillemont, Leibnitz and Muratori, to whom we owe not only vast accumulations of precious material, but also the foundation of the critical use of documents. It is with these two schools that book iii is mainly concerned.

Book iv deals with the historiography of the *Aufklärung*, the merits and defects of which are indicated with great lucidity. The historians of the new school, like their predecessors, failed to realize the differences in atmosphere and outlook between different ages, and were too prone to make their writings the instruments of political and philosophic propaganda; but despite their glaring faults their work marks a real advance. They put an end to the era of mere compilation; they widened the scope of history from a record of political and ecclesiastical events into a survey of civilization; they attempted to introduce critical standards and sociological principles. To Voltaire, the founder of the school, Dr. Fueter gives sympathetic and even generous recognition. He pronounces the *Siècle de Louis XIV* ' the first modern historical work', the first book in which the whole life of the state is portrayed; while the *Essai sur les Mœurs*, though written with a slender equipment of knowledge and disfigured by incessant polemic, is the first real history of mankind. The ripest fruits of the historiography of the *Aufklärung*, writes Dr. Fueter, were gathered in England, for it was there that the school was least propagandist. The judgements of Robertson and Hume are fair and adequate; but the verdict on Gibbon is amazing. After devoting two pages to Robertson, the critic dismisses the author of the *Decline and*

Fall in two pages filled with acrid sentences. 'He possessed neither the manifold interests nor the historic vision of his Scotch contemporary. If he has won greater fame, the inference must not be drawn that he was a greater historian. The contrary is rather the case.' He derived advantage from his clever choice of subject and from providing the first systematic account of the rise of Christianity; but in his historical views he made no advance beyond Voltaire, and his style was deplorable. It is curious to find such a judgement in a work so judicial. It can scarcely be anything but an oversight that no mention is made of Professor Bury's classical edition. The survey of the *Aufklärung* in Germany naturally includes not only Schlözer and Spittler, the disciples of Voltaire, but Schiller, Johannes Müller, and Schlosser, the children of Rousseau. But the greatest historian of the age was not only independent of, but actually hostile to, the main tenets of the dominant school. The pages devoted to Justus Möser, the founder of social history, are among the most valuable in the book, and the praise of that lonely pioneer is in no way excessive.

Book v deals with the romantic and liberal schools which dominated the first half of the nineteenth century. The French Revolution had discredited theory. The wisdom of tradition, the worth of unconscious development, proclaimed by Burke, was adopted by Savigny; cosmopolitanism yielded to nationalism, and the middle ages rose into favour. Dr. Fueter has a very low opinion of the romantics who wrote in the spirit of Chateaubriand and Walter Scott, and denounces them for their devotion to the trappings of history. Indeed, he is distinctly unfair to the greatest of them, Thierry, whom he pronounces to lack charm, style, and the power to make his characters live. He does not mention that Thierry grew in stature, and that his sketch of the growth of the *Tiers État* is a very much more solid performance than the *Conquête d'Angleterre*. Nor will he carry all his readers with him in his judgements of the two supreme masters of the picturesque school. Carlyle he allows to be neither an historian nor a biographer; and he roundly declares that his portraits aim not at truth but at edification. Again, while recognizing the genius of Michelet, he does less than justice to the volumes on the middle ages, which he considers inferior to the *French Revolution*. The latter work, he declares, suited his ideas better. But the Michelet of the thirties was a different man from the Michelet of the forties; and the first was as fit to deal with St. Louis and Joan of Arc as the second to portray Danton and Robespierre. The greatest figure in book v is Ranke, who combined the better elements of romanticism with the critical treatment of sources which Niebuhr introduced. From Wilhelm von Humboldt he took the conception of ruling ideas which formed the kernel of his philosophy. The treatment of the greatest of all historians is full and adequate, and forms one of the most admirable parts of the book. Dr. Fueter points out his neglect of the economic factors of history, his tendency to survey events too much from the windows of the council-chamber, his excessive confidence in the Venetian relations, his inability to utilize certain classes of material. On the other hand he warmly recognizes his great qualities, and categorically declares that no one has approached so close to the ideal of the historian. The treatment of some other writers is less convincing. He underrates the fruitful activity of Otfried Müller, and fails to mention some of his most important works. His references to Waitz and Stubbs are grudging and inadequate, and he conveys a misleading impression of the value of Giesebrecht's contribution to the critical study of medieval sources.

The sixth and final book bears the title of 'The Realistic Reaction against Romanticism and the Influence of the Social Movement'. This label covers both the increased emphasis on the rôle of the state and the growing attention to social and economic developments. The 'Prussian School', which is the most striking representative of 'realism', is carefully analysed; but it is unfortunate that Droysen, its founder, should be discussed in book v, and Sybel and Treitschke in book vi. In dealing with the influence of the social movement, the author rightly lays stress on the reverberation of the events of 1848, the rise of the fourth estate suggesting to historians more detailed study of the historic life of the working classes. The first and most important work of this school was Tocqueville's *Ancien Régime*, described by the author as 'the first truly philosophic book in political history'. It is, by the way, a curious mistake in such an admirer of Tocqueville to attribute to him the *Histoire philosophique du règne de Louis XV*, published in 1846 by his father. The verdict on Fustel de Coulanges is equally favourable, many readers will think too favourable. He has also pleasant things to say of Green and Maitland.

In view of the vast complexity of modern studies no survey of historiography can be otherwise than amorphous and incomplete; but it is none the less surprising to find the famous Ultramontane Janssen travelling in the same compartment with Riehl and Gustav Freytag. It is unfair to Lecky that he appears merely as a disciple of Buckle and that his chief work passes without notice. Again, if Leslie Stephen is brought on the stage, do not many other historians of thought of equal merit deserve mention? Why should Brunetière, who was a literary critic and moralist, be entitled to a page and Sorel be dismissed in a few lines? And it might have been possible to find space for some mention of writers so important as Arneth and Seeley. But these minor criticisms are of no real importance. Dr. Fueter's work is marked by profound erudition and sound judgement. It will become the friend and companion of every working historian who desires to know more of the great masters of his craft. It is also a contribution to the history of European thought, which is mirrored not less in historiography than in every other branch of intellectual activity.
G. P. GOOCH.

Caesar's Conquest of Gaul. By T. RICE HOLMES. Second edition. (Oxford: Clarendon Press, 1911.)

THE first edition of Mr. Holmes's work, which may be said to have become a classic of research, was exhausted in 1899: and its revision, as the author tells us, 'required the almost incessant labour of two years.' Those who know the intensity of effort which Mr. Holmes puts into his work will appreciate what this means; and, in fact, the book has not merely been materially increased in bulk, but very largely rewritten. Mr. Holmes has, it is true, found it possible to throw overboard some of the heavy ballast of the first edition : it is no longer necessary for him to demonstrate at length that the site of Bibracte is to be found at Mont Beuvray, nor to deal with the anthropological arguments of the late Mr. Isaac Taylor in favour of the identification of the Basque language with that of the Ligurians. But the space thus gained has proved all too small for the discussion of the topics of controversy about which so much ink has been spilt in the last decade. The three volumes of the *Histoire de la Gaule* of Camille Jullian (to whom Mr. Holmes pays a warm tribute in his preface) and the two volumes of Déchelette's *Manuel d'archéologie préhistorique* are among the more important works of French scholars which have to be reckoned with ; and although the attack upon the credibility of Caesar's narrative has somewhat slackened, Ferrero (a host in himself) has plunged into the fray, only to meet his match, and more, in Mr. Holmes. We rejoice, therefore, to see this invaluable work brought up to date, and to hear Mr. Holmes's views on the latest vagaries of the specialists, to whom he is as merciless as ever : but we are sorry to be told that in its present form the book ' may be regarded as final ' ; for it is very certain that in another ten years' time some scholar—whether (as we devoutly pray) Mr. Holmes or another—will be summoned to do battle with yet another swarm of sciolists. Moreover, though it may be true to say that of Caesar's conquest, which is the main subject of the book, we are unlikely ever to know much more than we do now, it is not so clear that the researches of ethnologists may not lead to more definite results than they have hitherto attained. Who can be sure, for example, that the *Monumenta Linguae Ibericae* will always remain a sealed book ?

It is to the section on the ethnology of Gaul (pp. 257–343) that the reader who is familiar with Mr. Holmes's work will naturally turn. ' The main interest of these studies,' he says, ' is the *certaminis gaudium* ' (p. 337), and the joy of battle is dear to his heart : though he assures us that ' the warfare of the specialists is entertaining to the onlooker ' (p. 292), he not infrequently steps into the arena and deals some shrewd blows. Yet we cannot but feel that his genius is critical rather than constructive, and that though the presumptuous dogmatist may fare ill at his hands, the upshot of his labours has not been to advance our knowledge greatly. There are even places where the *labor limae* which we associate with Mr. Holmes's work has been lacking. At the very beginning of the section on the Ligurians he tells us that ' in the time of *Hesiod* the islands of Hyères were called Λιγυστίδες ', and supports the statement by a quotation from the *Argonautica*—of *Apollonius Rhodius*. On the next page ' Herodotus ' is doubtless a mere misprint for ' Herodorus ' ; but if this author (whose son, Bryson the Sophist, was a contemporary of Plato) spoke of the Iberian territory as extending to the Rhone, the fact has a more important bearing on the date of the invasion of southern Gaul from the Spanish peninsula than Mr. Holmes seems to allow.

There is one remarkable omission in Mr. Holmes's review of the theories which have been broached with regard to the Ligurian race. He is evidently acquainted with Professor Ridgeway's tract, *Who were the Romans ?*—indeed, he cites it in order to refute the doctrine that conquering peoples adopt the speech of those whom they subdue—but the startling theory which makes the aboriginal element in the population of Rome Ligurian, and Latin the language of this stock, is passed over in silence. We would gladly have sacrificed some of the pages in which it is shown that the attempt to explain the Iberian inscriptions by the Basque language has hitherto failed for a candid examination of an hypothesis which, if verified, must be considered of the highest ethnological value. Perhaps Mr. Holmes may yet give us such a criticism ἐν παρέργῳ. There is yet another ethnological hypothesis which readers of this Review might expect to find subjected to examination in this book, namely, that of Sir Henry Howorth on the ' Germans of Caesar '.

Many will probably turn at once to the pages in which the *Portus Itius*, comes up for discussion. Readers of this Review will not need to be reminded how in 1899 Mr. Holmes was confident that the identity of the Itian harbour with Wissant would ' sooner or later be generally accepted as morally certain ' ; how, in 1907, he wrote, ' it is not possible to prove that the Portus Itius was at Wissant: it is possible to prove that it was not,' whilst in the following year he treated either view as possible.[1] Mr. Holmes now reprints from the *Classical Review* his 'last words on Portus Itius'. 'Last words ' they are no longer ; for in a final summary Mr. Holmes expresses the view that Caesar's words suggest that the port from which he sailed on his second expedition was not that which he had used in the previous year, adding that this impression is not removed by the words of *B. G.* v. 2 *omnes ad Itium portum convenire iubet, quo ex portu commodissimum in Britanniam traiectum esse cognoverat*. He is thus in agreement with the view taken by the present writer in his notice of *Ancient Britain and the Invasions of Julius Caesar* ; and by accepting it he has made himself free to allow the nautical considerations which determine his view their full weight. But he has learnt how unsafe it is to claim finality for his conclusions, and begins the final paragraph of his discussion with the words, ' my only aim has been to show that the case for Boulogne cannot be regarded as absolutely proved '. What he *has* shown is that the case for Wissant is the more probable.

One or two archaeological points remain to be noted. The famous bust in the British Museum, whether a portrait of Caesar or not, is not a work of Caesar's time : the plastic rendering of the iris and pupil shows this. There is, no doubt, a good deal to be said for the view that the bust is a portrait of Caesar the surface of which has been worked over in modern times ; but at any rate it cannot be regarded as a contemporary presentation of the dictator in its original state. Probably the most faithful ancient portrait of Caesar is that in the Campo Santo at Pisa. On p. 583 Mr. Holmes quotes Sir R. Payne-Gallwey's work on the *Projectile-throwing Engines of the Ancients*. He should have noticed that of Colonel Schramm, whose models are to be seen in the museum of the Saalburg ; and if he had compared Sir R. Payne-Gallwey's account of ancient artillery with that of Schramm in the *Jahrbuch für lothringische Geschichte und Altertumskunde*, he would probably have found something to say about the relation of the two. In discussing the defensive armour of the Roman soldier

[1] *Ante*, vol. xxiv, 1909, pp. 115 f., 604.

(p. 584) Mr. Holmes should have noticed that the coat of chain-mail (ἀλυσιδωτὸς θώραξ, i. e. *lorica hamata*) mentioned by Polybius is found on the well-known relief in the Louvre representing the *Suovetaurilia*, the date of which is almost certainly about 35 B.C.

H. STUART JONES.

Catalogue of the Coins of the Vandals, Ostrogoths, and Lombards, and of the Empires of Thessalonica, Nicaea, and Trebizond, in the British Museum. By WARWICK WROTH. (London: printed by order of the Trustees, 1911.)

THIS volume is a supplement to the *Catalogue of Byzantine Coins* which appeared in 1908 by the same author, whose early death will be mourned by all who are interested in numismatics, and contains the coins of Byzantine type struck by the barbarian rulers of Italy and Africa, as well as a few Italian coins of the imperial restoration and some which are described as quasi-autonomous coins of Rome and Ravenna, and the coins of the Byzantine sovereigns who ruled during the Latin occupation of Constantinople. In some points, however, it is something more than a supplement, for, whereas the Byzantine catalogue begins with Anastasius, the present work begins with Gaiseric, sixty years earlier; and, as the early Vandal kings struck coins in the names of western emperors, their coinage cannot be described as in any sense Byzantine. Moreover, it includes the coins of the dukes and princes of Beneventum down to the union with Capua, and these rulers from the time of Charles the Great, as well as the later Lombard kings, put no eastern emperor's head upon their coins. The combination of the western coinage with the coins of the eastern dynasties of the thirteenth century is peculiar and inconvenient, especially as the latter part of the title is not put on the cover, and no one would therefore imagine from the outside that any eastern coins were described in the book. The rather illogical separation of the Nicene from the Constantinopolitan coins has, however, this advantage, that the author has been able to correct his previous catalogue, twenty-one coins there ascribed to John Comnenus being now given on apparently good grounds to John Ducas Vatatzes. It is not necessary to praise Mr. Wroth's work as a numismatist, nor the excellence of the printing and arrangement of the volume, which are the same as in the Byzantine catalogue;[1] and, as some coins not in the British Museum are included for the sake of completeness, the catalogue should take the place of the works of Mr. Keary and Sabatier as a handbook of the coinages with which it deals.

The historical introduction is concise and accurate, only a few points, mostly of small importance, needing correction. The chronological argument as to the coinage of Odovacar loses some of its force from the fact that the reign of Basiliscus is wrongly dated. The date November 475, which depends upon the Code of Justinian, has certainly been maintained, but would hardly now be defended. John of Antioch definitely places Zeno's flight on 9 January 475, and with this all other authorities except the Code, in which the dates are often wrong, agree.[2] Mr. Wroth also commits the strange mistake of making Theodahad marry Amala-

[1] See *ante*, xxiv. 116.   [2] See *ante*, viii. 217.

suntha, though we know from Cassiodorus (*Var.* x. 21, 24) and Procopius (*B. G.* i. 6) that he had another wife. Another marriage, that of Grimoald III of Beneventum with a niece of Constantine VI, should not have been stated without a caution. No brother or sister of Constantine is known, and, even if his wife's niece is meant, there is a chronological difficulty. Erchempert does not name the emperor, and perhaps refers to a niece of Irene (the emperor being Leo IV); but Wantia has little resemblance to a Byzantine name. Of less importance is it that Ildibad is called son, instead of nephew, of Theudis (p. xxxvii). The statement on p. lxviii that Radelchis employed Saracens and Siconolf Moors surely conveys nothing. These allies are described as coming from Africa ('Agarenos Libicos') and Spain ('Hismaelitas Hispanos'); but this difference is not expressed by the words 'Saracens' and 'Moors'. On p. xxxvii, l. 4 from the bottom, '5th' should apparently be '6th', and there must be some error on p. lxxiii, where, though the proclamation of Michael as joint-emperor is placed in January 1260, the reign of John is said to have ended in 1259.

In connexion with the Lombard coinage an interesting historical point arises. The substitution of the king's name for the emperor's begins in the time of Perctarit, and about the same time the dukes of Beneventum began to strike coins of their own, on which, however, they put the emperor's head. Now the restoration of Perctarit brought with it a complete breach between the kingdom and the duchy, and it is a very likely conjecture that the duke acknowledged the imperial supremacy, and the king retaliated by ceasing to coin in the emperor's name; and we then naturally think of the statement of Theophanes that in 678 the ῥῆγες ἔξαρχοί τε καὶ κάσταλδοι sent presents to the emperor and made peace.   E. W. BROOKS.

A History of Wales from the earliest times to the Edwardian Conquest. In two volumes. By JOHN EDWARD LLOYD, M.A., Professor of History in the University College of North Wales, Bangor. (London: Longmans, 1911.)

EVER since the revival of the serious study of medieval Welsh history there has been felt an ever-increasing need of a sound and scientific textbook which would set forth fully, clearly, and impartially the facts generally accepted by scholars who have busied themselves with this subject. This want has at last been well supplied by Professor Lloyd's two handsome volumes. His book shows exactly the right qualities required in such a work of synthesis. He has carefully traversed the whole ground, and is well acquainted both with the original sources and with the writings of the best modern scholars. He has worked himself on large parts of the field in such detail that he is able to understand the difficulties which other workers have met with, besides being able to contribute something original of his own to the common stock. He has an admirable eye for proportion, a judgement which is always sane and cool, a sympathy which is hardly ever lacking, and a precision and clarity of statement which never leaves us at a loss for his meaning. Though he seldom loses space in unnecessary words, and resolutely puts aside details which would have swelled his volumes to an unmanageable size, he works on a sufficiently large canvas to give him room to describe all, or nearly all, that is essential to his purpose. It is hard to imagine a book better adapted as a textbook to the increasing number of students who, in the Welsh university and elsewhere, are devoting themselves to the advanced study of early Welsh history. It is not enough to say that it will supersede all other books on the subject. A book on such lines, or of such a type, has never previously been written.

It is not easy to make early Welsh history an attractive and popular subject. In the earlier ages no fact can be regarded as substantiated without elaborate discussion, and in later times the over-abundance of trivial political and military details obscures the working of any general principles, and soon exhausts the attention even of the attentive student. It is no small praise to Mr. Lloyd that he has made the stubborn material with which he has perforce to deal so intelligible, so coherent, and so consecutive. Part of this success is due to the skill with which he has mastered and grouped his material; part to the keen interest in the past of his own land, which makes his whole subject a living reality to him; and part to the pleasant and flowing literary style which carries the reader along to the successful conclusion of the two volumes. Above all, however, Mr. Lloyd is to be congratulated on having made his subject so wide a one that it includes a great deal more than the annalistic and political history of the old school. Such annalistic narrative always tends to be dull and unattractive. In Welsh history it becomes absolutely repulsive, because the details of Welsh political history are not only singularly dry but singularly unimportant. In few parts of his book has Mr. Lloyd forgotten such aspects of his theme as social and economic life, culture and civilization, the history of religion, the legal basis of society, and that minute investigation of local topography without which the history of a land so devoid of all centralization as medieval Wales becomes absolutely unintelligible. Of equally vital importance is the fact that Mr. Lloyd does not treat Welsh history as something standing by itself. He is well acquainted with the corresponding periods of English history, and with the general course of European history. Much more than the majority of his predecessors he puts Welsh history in its proper setting as part of a general process of development.

A work that ranges from palaeolithic man to the end of the thirteenth century requires for its composition knowledge and aptitude of a very varied order. Substantially the book breaks itself up into three great divisions. The first division, covering nearly two hundred pages, can hardly be regarded as specifically Welsh history at all. It is rather the general history of southern Britain from palaeolithic man to the end of the sixth century, when the substantial settlement of the boundary between the Britons and the English invaders enables the local history of Wales to be treated in isolation. It is true that Mr. Lloyd regards his subject from the point of view of what is now called Wales, but in some parts of his subject, notably in dealing with Roman Wales, it is extremely difficult to separate the facts relevant to this particular district from those common to the Roman occupation in all the less assimilated regions in the north and west of the province. Sometimes, too, there is just a trace of a suggestion that, because Wales afterwards became a racial and political entity, it was so at an earlier stage than history warrants. Otherwise it is hard to see why so good a scholar as Mr. Lloyd should have accepted the doctrine of Professor Hugh Williams, which regards Wales as substantially heathen until the beginning of the fifth century, and makes the Celtic church, at least in Britain, something which arose afresh after the so-called departure of the Romans. This view was not too severely characterized by Professor Haverfield in these pages when he said that it is 'doubtful whether it ought to have been put forward'.[1] If, as is now generally believed, St. Patrick found Ireland largely a Christian country, it is incredible that Christianity should have made no way among the subjects of Rome in the western part of her British provinces. It is, perhaps, the same unconscious bias that leads Mr. Lloyd to doubt whether the Britons, driven from their home in the south-east by the English invaders, found a refuge in large numbers in Wales. For him the 'Brythonic conquest of Wales' is completely explained by the legendary migrations of Cunedda and his sons. It is characteristic, perhaps, of this point of view that he tells us next to nothing of the Brythonic emigration to Armorica, though this is substantiated alike by the indefinite thing called 'genuine Welsh tradition', the legends of innumerable saints, and the still abiding facts of Breton history. Neither here nor later do Celtic Brittany, Ireland, and Highland Scotland furnish to Mr. Lloyd quite as much illustration of his theme as might perhaps have been drawn from them.

The second half of the first volume takes Welsh history from the end of the sixth century to the eve of the Norman Conquest. Though critical, Mr. Lloyd is an even more whole-hearted follower of Sir John Rhŷs than in the part dealing with Roman Wales he has been of Professor Haverfield. The ogham inscriptions, for instance, are regarded as the work of an indigenous Goidelic population, and not of pirates or settlers from Ireland. Each point is brought out with admirable clearness, and with becoming reservations, though the symmetry of the structure may sometimes make us tend towards forgetting the insecurity of the foundations. All through this section the annalistic portion is skilfully minimized. By far the most interesting chapters are those on the tribal divisions of Wales and on early Welsh institutions. The former, which is based largely on the author's own personal work, is the most careful and elaborate survey that has as yet been written of the puzzling problems of early Welsh topography. If the result still leaves us in doubt as to whether the cantref or the commote was the more 'active' administrative division, it suggests also the likely solution that cantref and commote may have been more fundamental in different districts, or at different periods, and makes it clear that the commote did not stand to the cantref in the relation similar to that of the hundred to the shire. In both these chapters, however, the lateness of the mass of the material used compels the author to take us out of the period to which they are attached into the time subsequent to the Norman Conquest.

Mr. Lloyd's survey of Welsh ecclesiastical institutions is not always quite

[1] *Ante*, xi. 429.

complete. There is an interesting account of the 'clas', but the process by which the four bishoprics of later history came into being is not indicated. It is perhaps doubtful whether Mr. Lloyd does not underrate the hold of diocesan episcopacy on the early Welsh church. There is no evidence of the swarm of bishops in Wales that there was in Ireland or in Celtic Scotland, and it is hard not to believe that the reason for this was the continuity of the Roman tradition in lands which had once been Roman provinces. In this relation we must be permitted to doubt whether the 'saith esgopty Dyfed' of the Dimetian code are really, as Mr. Lloyd thinks, evidence of the existence at a former age of seven episcopal sees within the small district roughly corresponding with the modern Pembrokeshire and western Carmarthenshire; and in the same way we remain unconvinced by the argument that Asser was bishop of St. David's when he agreed to spend part of his time at the court of King Alfred.

The arguments advanced by Mr. Lloyd that the determination of the border between the Welsh states and Mercia was brought about in the age of Penda and Wulfhere, and not, as is generally thought, in the age of Offa, demands very serious consideration. The evidence from place-names is perhaps of varying value, but that from ecclesiastical foundations is convincing. One circumstance only inclines us to a suspension of judgement. One of the recognized facts of Penda's reign is his long alliance with the Welsh kings. How could Penda be at the same time the ally of the Welsh against Northumbria and the conqueror of the Severn valley at their expense? Mr. Lloyd holds that the silence of Bede and the fact that the dialect of Cheshire is Mercian, not Northumbrian, dispose of the view that the battle of Chester was followed by the occupation of the plain round that city by Æthelfrith and his Northumbrians (p. 180). If that be so, does not this argument also 'dispose of the view', advocated on p. 183, that, after the conquest of Elmet a few years later, Edwin 'must have effected that breach between the Cymry of the north and those of Wales which the battle of Chester foreshadowed but did not actually bring about'? Here, again, it seems easier to set down the Mercian conquest of Cheshire as having been effected from the Northumbrians a generation or two later. Anyhow, it is hard to limit Mercian influence to the regions south of the Mersey.

The second volume of Professor Lloyd's book begins with the preliminaries of the Norman Conquest. It is more detailed, more annalistic, but at the same time more original than the mass of the first volume. Never before have the last two centuries of what is loosely called Welsh independence been studied so fully, so carefully, so consecutively, so accurately, and in such close relation to the broader movements of Anglo-Norman history, of which both the Norman conquest of Wales and the largely successful Welsh reaction from it form integral parts. Mr. Lloyd is here necessarily concerned with details, but he has been successful in making the big facts stand out with a reasonable amount of clearness. In particular, the history of the national revival in the twelfth and thirteenth centuries is exceedingly well done. Owain Gwynedd, Rhys ap Gruffydd, and the two Llywelyns appear, not only as taking definite shares in undoing the work of the Norman conquerors, but as human beings with characters of their own which differentiate them from the normal Welsh warrior leader. Our only complaint here is that Mr. Lloyd is, perhaps, a little over-eager to accentuate the existence of Welsh national feeling, which in any self-conscious condition can hardly be said to have existed even after the two Llywelyns had done so much to put themselves at the head of a general Welsh movement. Occasionally, also, phrases like 'the three realms of Wales', on p. 650, show that Mr. Lloyd has not quite shaken off the influence of traditional categories, though his detailed narrative, of course, shows that there never were three realms of Wales in the period now under review. We may regret that a description of the marcher states from the marchers' own point of view did not enter into his scheme, that the formative side of the Normans' work is ignored, that he tells us next to nothing as to the archaeology of the early castles in Wales, that he does not do much to advance our knowledge of the Welsh twelfth-century laws, and that his descriptions of Welsh society and monastic life and the literary revival are shorter and more meagre than we should have wished. Faithful to his leading idea of writing from the Welsh point of view, he cuts very short his narrative of the concluding stages of Llywelyn ap Gruffydd's reign, and excludes altogether any account of the Edwardian settlement. All, however, that he has undertaken to do Mr. Lloyd has done with admirable accuracy and care. It is only on a very few points, which are much more matters of opinion and inference than fact, that we have the least wish to join issue with him. It is hard, however, to agree to reject with him the positive and repeated testimony of Orderic that Gruffydd ap Cynan was the leader of the Welsh band that brought about the death of Robert of Rhuddlan. We are disposed also to accept the evidence of the annals of Margam that Cardiff was built in the reign of William the Conqueror. Cordial praise should be bestowed on the luminous pointing out of the important effects of the withdrawal of the most truculent of the Welsh marchers to the conquest of Ireland on the progress of the power of the Lord Rhys in south Wales, and on the clear emphasis laid upon the position of Hubert de Burgh, and Peter de Rivaux after him, on the southern march.

There is an admirably full and accurate index, and the map fully warrants the claim made for it that it will be of general service to those who may use the book. It is to be regretted, however, that we have not the advantage of Mr. Lloyd's remarkable topographical knowledge of Wales being embodied in a series of maps illustrating, however roughly, the actual facts of Welsh history and geography at various periods. There are also some very useful genealogies, and a fairly elaborate bibliography.

T. F. TOUT.

Geschichte Italiens im Mittelalter, iii. 2: *Die Anarchie.* Von L. M. HART-MANN. (Gotha: F. A. Perthes, 1911.)

IT would be difficult to exaggerate the misery of Italy, a fate shared by the other lands of the Carolingian empire, during the eighty years succeeding the death of the Emperor Lewis II in 875, which form the subject of the latest instalment of Dr. L. M. Hartmann's authoritative history. So tangled and fragmentary are the events, so purposeless and confused are the lines of political development, that the period seems given over to a mere annalistic treatment. But Dr. Hartmann's thorough knowledge of the facts, and his insight into their meaning and sense of their relative proportion, have enabled him to give a continuous and vertebrate narrative, bringing out the connexion of cause and effect. The central power of the state, to use the author's expression (p. 183), had become bankrupt, partly owing to the internal development of West European society, partly owing to the novel stress of the attacks from outside. While the royal authority, based on a combination of Germanic tribal cohesion and Roman state-tradition, was ever more ineffective to control the great local land-owning magnates whose strength was founded on actual material conditions, the plundering races around the empire, Normans, Saracens, and Magyars, devastated province after province and showed that the existing state-structure was incapable even of the simplest self-defence.

Thus the ills, caused by weakness, increased trebly the weakness to which they owed their origin. And in the wreck of law and order and security there appeared the moral degeneration born of social despair; we are in the age of the scandalous monasteries and of Theodora and Marozia. The primitive instincts at least remained. Yet what is more striking than this social degeneration is the permanence in spite of all and through all of civilized ideas and of the fabric of civilized organization. In political matters two refuges remained for these in Italy, the empire and the papacy, the state and the church. It was the second of the two which presented the purer and also the less adaptable medium. For the emperor, such as Lewis II, was bound to rest largely on military power, i.e. on the support of his *fideles*, on the feudal and land-owning element in short, while the papacy, with its spiritual function, remained by the nature of the case bureaucratic and Byzantine in its organization. Feudalism could only be a temporary perversion in its history. The contrast comes out strongly on the death of Lewis II, which left the papacy free under the statesman-pope John VIII. That skilful diplomatist, attractive if only for his clear vision and definite purpose amid the elementary cunning and eddying passions of his day, set himself to free the papacy and the papal territory from imperial control, and even to dominate Italy and the emperor's Italian policy by virtue of the ceremony of coronation. The pope, he argued, who made the emperor by crowning him, must also be understood to confer the dignity. But the escape from imperial control meant the loss of imperial protection. A political influence in Italy entailed the political use of his spiritual powers. John VIII, with his bureaucracy, could not even govern the over-feudalized papal state. His schemes to expel the devastating heathen broke down, and the pope, almost now a petty secular prince, was murdered in a palace-revolt in 882.

The foundation of states, that were to be national in the future, on the break-up of Charles III's empire produced one special phenomenon in Italy, the local empire, due to the papal right of crowning the emperor, one of the many by-products in fact of that epoch-making accident. Under Lambert, the most successful of the warring, fleeting Italian kings, the title of emperor is robbed of all real meaning and implies little more than a protectorate of the papal state; conversely, Hugh of Provence, who never became emperor, was debarred from the rule of Rome, if not of Ravenna, by Alberic, Marozia's son. Under the latter the Roman landowning class at last won a complete victory over the bureaucratic curia and subdued the papacy to its will. Rome became a small mid-Italian state: the popes were in secular leading-strings. Alberic's independence, and Hugh's anxiety to avoid external interference, both had the further result of leaving undisturbed the East Roman hegemony in south Italy, won over a generation back. It was the Greeks who took up the defence of that half of the peninsula on Lewis II's death; and, in spite of the hatred they gained from their subjects by financial oppression and corruption, and from the Lombards of Benevento by their schemes of conquest, the superiority of their more civilized organization gave them success. Their action was decisive in the destruction of the Saracens on the Garigliano in 915. By 934 Saracenic marauding there might be in plenty, but no further attempts at conquest on the mainland, for all that the island of Sicily was by that time almost a Saracen stronghold. Yet the Greeks were never strong enough to unify the south, and this fact left a means of intervention open there to the next Germanic conqueror.

Alberic made a political mistake when he arranged for his successor Octavian to be pope also as John XII. The office, however unexpectedly and oddly, conquered the man, and John was soon appealing as pope for a foreign ruler's intervention against his local secular foes. Thus Otto the Great was enabled to complete his policy of uniting Italy to Germany and to revive the empire in something like the Carolingian sense. From another point of view his imperial coronation in 962 was the complement of the ruin of the Magyar army on the Lechfeld. The protector of central Europe must needs be its ruler. From the time of Otto's victory and the disappearance of the separate kings of Italy, the restoration of order and reconstruction of society could steadily advance. But in the work the sovereign could be at best one partner. There were two other overt factors and one embryonic element which was to rule the future. First there were the great vassals. Headed by the marquesses, who each ruled in person or by deputy over several counties, they exercised the purely local functions of the state, and strong in their wide lands and immunities they could turn these functions into a kind of feudal landlordism and depress the status of the ordinary freeman and small owner into vassalage. The most important, like those of Tuscany, played the part of king-makers, preferring indeed that there should be two rival monarchs to act as a check on one another; and even the long-reigning Hugh of Provence could only change the *personnel* of the feudal office-holders, he could not diminish their overgrown power. Change of *personnel*, however, was frequent in the long civil wars—more frequent, perhaps, than readily appears from Dr. Hartmann's narrative—and it was partly due to the short roots the great families had time to put out, that the kings, feeble as they were, could specially favour the second factor, the bishops. Besides the missatic power which was entrusted to them by Charles the Bald, the charters of the period tended to give the prelates the exercise of all public functions over their lands and their inhabitants. Along with these concessions were granted to the bishops some of the royal prerogatives in their cities, such as toll and market rights or control of the city fortifications. And finally on a few favoured sees the entire comital jurisdiction over the cathedral city and a radius round was conferred, the count being shut out altogether. Obviously, on the one hand these grants imply the decadence of the comital power in some districts—it is significant that in the territories of the great marquesses they scarcely occur—and on the other the weakness of the kingship, which was yielding up its most valuable rights and duties, toll of trade and national defence.

It should not be forgotten, however, that a quite restricted number of bishops as yet obtained the privilege of jurisdiction over their city. Only under the Ottos did it become large, and then because the bishops were serviceable champions of the German monarchy. Under the Italian kings such grants perhaps mostly legalized an existing situation. It had fallen to the bishop to take the lead of his unorganized citizens, whose number was being rapidly increased by refugees from the country-side. And in the privileges and special jurisdiction thus obtained we may see the first beginnings of the later commune, of which another glimpse—more perhaps than *interessante* (p. 265, n. 9)—is furnished by Berengar II's privilege, not to bishop or noble, but to the inhabitants of Genoa. C. W. PREVITÉ ORTON.

Le Duc de Normandie et sa Cour (912–1204); *Étude d'Histoire juridique.* Par LUCIEN VALIN. (Paris : Larose & Tenin, 1910.)

THIS book, the work of an *avoué* of Rouen who has shown commendable interest in matters of local history, should be welcomed as the first attempt at a systematic study of the ducal power and the ducal *curia* in Normandy. Though presented as a thesis for the doctorate in law, it is distinctly superior to the average of such treatises, especially because of the use which its author has made of the principal unpublished cartularies of the province and of certain portions of the departmental archives, from which thirty-three documents are printed, though not in every case for the first time, in the appendix. Fair acquaintance is shown with modern works in French and with such English authorities as Stubbs and the *History of English Law*, but no German authorities are mentioned, a serious defect in a field upon which so much light has been thrown by Professor Brunner.

The first part, dealing with the ducal power, is sketchy, and betrays insufficient knowledge of recent discussions of the questions involved, such as are to be found in M. Lot's *Fidèles et Vasseaux*, M. Guilhiermoz' *Origine de la Noblesse*, and especially in Professor Böhmer's *Kirche und Staat in England und in der Normandie*. The second part, which treats of the organization and functions of the duke's court, is fuller and more substantial, and at certain points adds to our knowledge of Norman institutions. M. Valin traces the growth of permanence and definiteness in the *curia* and its differentiation under Henry II into the court of the itinerant justices, the court of the seneschal, and the exchequer, the last-named being, according to his view, not a regular civil jurisdiction, but a fiscal body which sat twice a year at Caen and was wholly different from the tribunal which bears its name in the thirteenth century. Moreover, finding no trace of the Norman exchequer before 1176, he maintains that it was first organized as a part of the reforms instituted in that year by the bishop of Winchester; and against the specific mention of the *scaccarium* under Henry I, in the plea published by Mr. Round (*ante*, xiv. 426), he urges that this document is not a charter but a notice into which English terminology was introduced by the canons of Merton who drew it up. This explanation is not impossible, but the word *scaccarium* also occurs in the surviving fragment of the Norman inquest of 1171 (*ante*, xxvi. 326–8) in a passage which shows, what I have sought to establish from other evidence, that there is entire continuity between the exchequer arrangements of Henry II and those of Henry I and, probably, of William I. So long as we know the nature of the fiscal system, the first appearance of the name is a matter of secondary importance. In connexion with the membership of the *curia* M. Valin treats briefly of the household officers, the justiciars, seneschal, and treasurer, and the *hautshommes*. The court is considered as a council, as an assembly of the barons and an assembly of the church, and as a judicial body, most space being naturally given to its competence and procedure as a court of law, a field where the writer's legal training is of considerable assistance. The treatment of recognitions is intelligent, and makes use of a certain amount of fresh material, but it needs elaboration on the basis of a wider study of the sources. Curiously enough, nothing is said of the existence of a system of written records of judicial decisions, although the author reprints (appendix, no. 25) the charter cited on this point half a century ago by Delisle. A more serious defect is the absence of any historical account of the subject of ecclesiastical jurisdiction.

Having traversed considerable portions of the same ground in a series of articles published between 1903 and 1909, I find it somewhat embarrassing to review M. Valin's book, for he has made no use of these articles, nor of many of the documents they contain, and our conclusions, being based upon different bodies of evidence, are often incommensurable. I am, however, glad to find that we have sometimes reached the same results by different routes, and feel confident that an examination of the same materials would have led to still further agreement. Thus, with regard to the judicial supremacy of the duke and the *haute justice* of the barons, M. Valin would have fortified his position, which in general is also mine, by an examination of the *Consuetudines et iusticie* of the Conqueror[1] and a more thorough study of the early charters. Similarly, the account of the establishment of the system of recognitions errs fundamentally by ignoring the demonstration,[2] since accepted by the editor of the cartulary, that the Bayeux documents which first mention the duke's assize were issued by Geoffrey and not by Henry II. For the reign of Henry I there is evidence on the judicial and financial administration[3] which would have amplified M. Valin's meagre pages on this period, while for

[1] *Ante*, xxiii. 502–8. [2] *American Historical Review*, viii. 613–40.
[3] *Ante*, xxiv. 209–31.

the following half-century it is particularly unfortunate that Delisle's great work on the documents of Henry II was published too late to be used. It is to be hoped that a new edition may utilize more thoroughly the available material, and that M. Valin may extend his researches into the private charters which, especially in the twelfth century, have still so much to teach us concerning Norman law.

CHARLES H. HASKINS.

Den Kaiser macht das Heer. Von EDMUND E. STENGEL. (Weimar: Bohlau, 1910.)

Two alternatives were open to those medieval publicists who denied that the pope could dispose of the imperial office. They could base the emperor's title upon popular election, or they could argue that might is right. Either theory required careful handling. The first could be supported by an imposing array of texts; but according to the more precise of these it was the *populus Romanus* who ought to elect the emperor, and it was difficult to rebut the presumption, intolerable to a self-respecting candidate, that *populus Romanus* meant the mob of the Eternal City. On the other hand the second theory, when stated in abstract terms, was repugnant to many who accepted the judicial combat as a reasonable institution and were prepared to let the sword decide the differences of secular powers and parties. For it appeared impious to assert that the church, a society founded upon law and reason, should bow before the might embodied in the person of a lay ruler. That might was right was seldom argued by imperialists, never by those who held a responsible position. Yet it is possible that this doctrine exercised some influence on the minds of many who shrank from a direct appeal to it. Dr. Stengel thinks that the chronicler Widukind turns history upside down to prove that Otto I obtained the empire by the will of his army, and as a consequence of the victory of the Lechfeld; it is the case that Widukind appears to ignore the Roman coronation as an irrelevant and superfluous ceremony. Noteworthy, again, is the boast, which Otto of Freising puts into the mouth of Frederick Barbarossa, that his predecessors had won the empire by force of arms and he would hold it by the same title. Finally—and this is the main point of the essay—we find, in and after the thirteenth century, frequent appeals to the maxim, *exercitus facit imperatorem*.

This maxim rested on very slight authority. St. Jerome, who is usually cited as vouching for it, does nothing of the kind. In one of his letters, which happens to be quoted in the *Decretum*, he says that the bishops of the primitive church were elected by the presbyters, *quomodo si exercitus faciat imperatorem*. It is extraordinary that so well-known a passage should have been so grossly perverted; still more extraordinary that papalist writers should have neglected to expose the fraud. Perhaps the authenticity of the doctrine would have been more critically examined if those who used it had given it a bolder interpretation. But, as a rule, it was used either with the negative object of proving that it is not the pope who makes the emperor, or as a subsidiary proof of the doctrine of election. Lewis the Bavarian uses it negatively in the proclamation

Fidem Catholicam (1338); William of Ockham explains that the *exercitus* elected emperors in virtue of a commission from the Roman people, and that the commission has now been transferred to the German electors. A bolder interpretation is only to be found in minor and unauthoritative writers, such as Johann von Buch, the commentator on the Sachsenspiegel. He argues that, while a king of the German nation is elected, the empire is acquired by the strong hand; it is the right of every German king to appropriate, if he is able, the imperial title and prerogative.

This essay is reprinted, with some alterations, from a *Festschrift* presented to Karl Zeumer; it is full of learning, and the interest is by no means confined to the main subject of discussion. Dr. Stengel has collected many passages which illustrate the popular attitude towards the empire and the effect of classical tradition upon medieval political theory. He also discusses at considerable length the authenticity of a charter, purporting to be granted by Archbishop Robert of Trier within a month after the battle of the Lechfeld, in which Otto I is styled *gloriosus rex et imperator*. If genuine, this charter confirms in a striking manner the statement of Widukind, that Otto was acclaimed *pater patriae imperatorque* immediately after his victory. Dümmler and Giesebrecht declined to admit the evidence of the charter, which is known to us only through a single copy. Dr. Stengel thinks their conclusion too positive, and reviews the evidence with some ingenuity; but in the end he is forced to conclude that, at the best, the case against the charter can only be regarded as not proven.

H. W. C. DAVIS.

Gilbert Crispin, Abbot of Westminster, a study of the Abbey under Norman Rule. By J. ARMITAGE ROBINSON, D.D., Dean of Westminster. (Cambridge: University Press, 1911.)

WHAT Westminster loses in Dr. Robinson's transference to a more restricted sphere of influence at Wells is a loss also to the country as a whole, if we except the diocese to which he has returned. His parting gift, however, to the great abbey which he has left proves that the troubles of health which have led him to seek this removal had neither abated his desire for work nor deteriorated the quality of his achievement. The third volume of *Westminster Notes and Documents* contains work like that of the first two, and equally good, and it contains also work of a rather different, in some ways more difficult, kind. Gilbert Crispin has three titles to fame. He was one of the chain of notable men in the generation or two succeeding the Norman conquest by whom the highest traditions of monastic life were transplanted from Bec into several of the greater monasteries of southern England. He was for over thirty years a capable administrator of the abbey of Westminster. He was also a theologian of high reputation in his day. In each of these aspects Dr. Robinson has been able both to collect and to add to our information about him. Gilbert, apart from his own direct influence, as a Canterbury monk and as abbot of Westminster, in introducing Bec manners and customs into those monasteries, sought to teach the world at large what the nature of those customs was by his Life of Herluin, the founder of Bec, which is indeed one of the principal authorities by which we judge in what consisted the influence of Lanfranc, Anselm, Gundulph, and their fellows. But the Life of Herluin has never been printed in a complete form. The shape in which it occurs in D'Achery's edition of Lanfranc's works is not only incomplete but calculated to mislead. Dr. Robinson has now printed it in full. Of the theological works, one, 'De simoniacis,' is also now printed for the first time, and a useful analysis is given of the others, including the popular 'Disputatio Iudaei cum Christiano', which is the only one of which many copies have come down to us. If after reading these we are still rather surprised at the opinion of a contemporary who, in putting forward Crispin's opinion on a difficult point in opposition to that of St. Bernard, spoke of him as a scholar superior both to Anselm of Laon and to Gilbert the Universal, it is not so much because Crispin's works are lacking in any qualities necessary for a scholar, as because their most noticeable merits in our eyes are a moderation and tolerance which we are apt to conceive of as less appreciated in his day than in our own.

Excellently well as all this is done, the portion of the book which must have cost the dean the greatest trouble, and perhaps also that which will serve most to lighten the trouble of others, is the selection of charters printed and analysed at the end. The dean modestly excuses his inexperience, and speaks of himself as 'prepared to find that my ignorance has led me into serious blunders', but his methods are so sound that, though no doubt an exhaustive search of the evidences will eventually alter some of his conclusions, serious errors are not likely to be many. The Westminster charters catalogued number forty-three, and range in date from William I to Henry I. Six at most are originals (one being perhaps a forgery); the rest are collected from various Westminster cartularies, a laborious task for which much gratitude is due; and full reasons are given for the dating. An appendix deals with the curious history of the charters of St. John's Abbey, Colchester, the spurious character of which Dr. Round had already pointed out. The evidence adduced by the dean goes far to show, what is apparently the exception rather than the rule in these cases, that the fabrication was a fraudulent one in the sense that it gave the abbey property which rightfully belonged to another foundation. A second appendix is devoted to the boundaries of Westminster property at Tyburn and Charing as given by the charter of Ethelred. We have noticed but one misprint: the date 1184 on p. 31 should be 1124. J. P. GILSON.

Annals of the Reigns of Malcolm and William, Kings of Scotland, A.D. 1153–1214. Collected, with Notes and an Index, by Sir ARCHIBALD CAMPBELL LAWRIE, LL.D. (Glasgow: MacLehose, 1910.)

SIR ARCHIBALD LAWRIE has followed up his useful and suggestive volume of *Early Scottish Charters* by a scarcely less valuable work, which contains the chief sources of the political history of Scotland, from the death of David I to the death of William the Lion, his two volumes thus serving to illustrate Scottish history down to the beginning of the thirteenth century. His selections are drawn chiefly from English chroniclers; the historian of Scotland has always a special grievance against Edward I of England for the loss and destruction of the records before the War of Independence, and except for the slight chronicles of Melrose and Holyrood, some scraps of legal information, and a few relevant charters, Sir Archibald Lawrie has to depend upon English sources. His book thus traverses, to some extent, ground already covered by Mr. A. D. Anderson in his *Scottish Annals from English Chronicles*, but he treats a much shorter period on a much larger scale, and he quotes his Latin authorities in the original.

The reign of Malcolm the Maiden (1153–65) saw the last, or almost the last, efforts of the Scots to overthrow the anglicized dynasty of Malcolm Canmore. The new king was a boy of twelve when he succeeded his grandfather, David I, and the men of Moray, in conjunction with Somerled of the Isles, took the opportunity of rebelling. The few references which Sir Archibald Lawrie can give us for this rebellion are sufficient evidence of our ignorance of the struggle, which began in Moray and ended in the capture of the northern leader, Malcolm MacHeth, as far away from Moray as Whithorn. King Malcolm's revenge on the men of Moray, as recorded much later by Fordun, took the form of a settlement which Fordun compares to the dispersion of the Jews by Nabugodonosor : not one native of the land remained, he says. Fordun's authority is worthless except as preserving a tradition ; there is no reason to doubt that the rebels were punished by the forfeiture of their estates, but the colonization of Moray has been taken too seriously by many writers. Malcolm accompanied Henry II of England on the expedition to Toulouse, and the contemporary Melrose writer attributes another rebellion to indignation at this journey, a statement interesting as showing the tendency of Scottish feeling. The Melrose writer speaks of the revolt as led by six earls who were incensed against Malcolm because he had gone to Toulouse ; the fifteenth-century chroniclers expand this into indignation because he 'was over friendly with the King of England'. The rising of the six earls was followed by a rebellion in Galloway, which Malcolm subdued in three campaigns. Fergus, the lord of Galloway, became a canon of Holyrood, and gave the abbey lands in his own country, a step towards the anglicization of the Galwegians.

The fifty years' reign of William the Lion abounds in problems for the Scottish historian, alike in constitutional and in ecclesiastical history, and in the relations between England and Scotland. The Scotichronicon for 1211 contains a well-known passage about a great council held by William at Stirling, at which 'there were present his optimates, who gave him ten thousand marks besides six thousand marks promised by the burgesses', a passage on which Lord Hailes and Gilbert Stuart founded their theory of the presence of burgesses in the great council in the beginning of the thirteenth century. Cosmo Innes pointed out that the 'words here used would seem rather to indicate that the burgesses did not vote or deliberate in the same assembly with the optimates', and the existence of conventions of burghs and of separate negotiations between individual towns and the king seems to us to remove anything suspicious in the statement. Sir Archibald Lawrie remarks that it does not appear in Fordun nor in Wyntoun, and that it is unsupported by any other record, and adds :

'It seems to me that it is an invention of Bower.' The absence of any other evidence is not remarkable in view of the poverty of Scottish records, and an explanation which involves an unnecessary and meaningless invention by a chronicler is really more difficult than an acceptance of the view that he had some authority for his statement.

The influence of England upon Scotland can be traced in fragments of laws made by or attributed to William the Lion, which are borrowed from the legislation of Henry II. The Assize of Clarendon was the model for Scottish police regulations, the severity of which sometimes went beyond their English exemplar. There is not much that is new to say about either the treaty of Falaise or the bargain between William and Richard I which annulled that treaty, and left the question of the overlordship precisely where it was before; but the relations between William and John are very puzzling. The meetings of the two kings at York in 1206 and 1207 are known to us only from safe-conducts in the Patent Rolls (although Fordun knew of the 1206 conference). The means by which war was narrowly averted in 1209 are similarly obscure, as are also the reasons for the treaty of Norham when William gave two daughters as hostages and promised to pay 15,000 marks to John. The arrangement was *contra voluntatem Scottorum*, says the chronicle of Melrose, and it may be connected with the rising of Guthred in 1211, a rebellion which, according to Walter of Coventry and the Annals of St. Edmund's, was suppressed with English help. Sir Archibald Lawrie shows, from the itinerary of King John, that it is improbable that he led an army into Scotland in person, and English records do not confirm the statements of the chroniclers, but it is difficult to regard the story as in itself unlikely. William had just granted John the right of choosing a wife for his heir, Alexander, and the old Lion's insistence upon his claims to English territory seems to have led him into agreements which went far to compromise the independence of Scotland. Sir Archibald Lawrie does not attempt to deal with more than a few of the problems which occur to the reader of these materials for a history of Scotland under Malcolm and William the Lion; to do so would have increased his book to an inconvenient size, and changed its character; but what he does say is useful and apposite. Alike for the student of charters and for the student of political and constitutional history, he has produced a careful and competent work of reference. We hope he will follow it up by a collection of the charters of the period.

ROBERT S. RAIT.

Ireland under the Normans, 1169–1216. By G. H. ORPEN. 2 vols. (Oxford: Clarendon Press, 1911.)

THE smoke of political controversy is so apt to blind us to the real meaning of the critical events which took place in Ireland during the second half of the twelfth century, that a comprehensive history of the Anglo-Norman conquest and settlement entirely free from passion and prejudice deserves the gratitude of the historical student. Mr. Orpen had already shown his fitness for the task by his edition of the *Song of Dermot* and his many articles on various aspects of the settlement contributed to this

Review and other periodicals. In particular the demonstration by Mrs. Armitage and others of the Norman origin of the motte and bailey type of castle in England and Wales led him to devote much attention to the identification of such pre-stone castles in Ireland as evidence of the area occupied by the Anglo-Norman conquerors within half a century of their coming. These investigations are utilized in the chapters on the subinfeudation of the various districts and in a most useful map appended to the second volume. This map brings out the fact that, while the newcomers were most thickly entrenched in Leinster and Meath, they had spread more widely beyond these districts in the limited period under review than is always appreciated. A few mottes are found as far west as Kerry, and the only regions that are free from them are Connaught (practically) and Ulster west of the river Bann. In his text Mr. Orpen sometimes notes the traces of later stone buildings on mottes, but rarely states whether the mounds in these cases are artificial or natural. His doubts, expressed in a note (ii. 141), whether cylindrical keeps like that at Dundrum had been introduced so early as 1205 are hardly justified if the generally accepted date (late twelfth century) of that at Conisborough in Yorkshire be unassailable.

Not only was Anglo-Norman domination in Ireland more complete in the thirteenth century than has been generally realized, it was also, on the evidence adduced by Mr. Orpen, more beneficial. This has too often been obscured by an over-flattering estimate of Irish civilization before the arrival of the Normans on the one hand, and on the other by carrying back the crippled condition of the colony after Edward Bruce's harrying into the preceding century. In his introductory chapters the author goes to the Irish Annals and Brehon Law Tracts for an unimpeachable picture of the political and social conditions of the country before the advent of the invaders, and an impartial reader will feel that it justifies the heading of 'Anarchic Ireland'. More rose-coloured views are seldom thought worthy of direct refutation, but a delicious exposure of the kind of argument by which they are too often supported will be found in a note on the bridge of Athlone (ii. 281). Positive evidence of the state of Ireland in the thirteenth century is none too abundant, but such as it is—returns of customs dues, municipal charters, and so forth—it all goes to strengthen the conclusion drawn from less direct indications, such as the cessation of interprovincial wars, that for a considerable period the English settlement gave the greater part of Ireland a growing measure of peace and prosperity. We have little fault to find with the way in which Mr. Orpen develops his contention, except that he might perhaps have provided a more distinct picture of the ecclesiastical condition of Ireland just before the conquest, and that his judgement on King John does not err on the side of leniency. He is inclined to give all the credit for the reduction of feudal franchises and the beginning of shire administration which, though not so thoroughgoing as has long been believed, was an outstanding feature of his reign, to the justiciar John de Gray. Yet the reforms of Gray's governorship (1210-13) did but carry out the policy which John had formulated years before, and with which, in the absence of evidence to the contrary, he must be credited.

Although the author's method is, we believe, sound, his main conclusions well established, and his book therefore a valuable addition to historical literature, it is not without some obvious flaws. The difficulties of arranging his narrative naturally become serious when the guidance of Giraldus is lost, but they hardly justify the amount of repetition that is found in the second volume. There are also some errors and omissions. A hybrid title like *earl* of Mortain and the confusion of a personal with a territorial designation as in earl *of* Ferrers are not indeed vital matters, but a nice historical scholarship avoids them. More serious is Mr. Orpen's apparent belief that there could be friars in Ireland in the first years of the thirteenth century (ii. 21, 229). Such mistakes are generally the result of too specific an interpretation of *fratres*, but this does not account for the conversion of the prior and brethren of the hospital of St. John the Baptist at Downpatrick into Crouched Friars in 1202, for which of course there is no authority in the reference given in the note. The post-dating of the young Henry's coronation by a year (i. 281) is probably a mere slip. Of omissions we notice the absence of any reference to Mr. Round's article on the *Geste* of John de Courcy in his *Peerage and Pedigree*, and, which is more surprising, a complete unconsciousness of the fruitful investigations of the late Miss Bateson on the municipal customs known as the Laws of Breteuil, though they were published in this Review ten years ago and had by this time, one supposed, become the common property of all historians. Mr. Orpen does indeed recognize the influence of Breteuil in John's charters to Drogheda (Bridge) and Dungarvan (ii. 315–16), with their Anglo-French forms, Bretoill and Breteill—which, however, are extended here as if they represented oblique cases of Bretoillium and Breteillium. But nothing is known, we are told, of the exact nature of these customs, though 'they were probably not dissimilar from those granted to Bristol in 1188', and no suspicion crosses the author's mind that the *legem Bristolli* of the Trim and Kells charters, which are next mentioned, may be a mere misreading of *legem Britoli*. The grant of the privileges of Bristol to Dublin, Cork, and a few other Irish boroughs made this confusion almost inevitable, but Miss Bateson showed that in no case of clear affiliation to Bristol is the phrase 'law of Bristol' used, its privileges being granted 'as the citizens of Bristol have them', or in some similar form. The Lacy family, who granted the charters to Trim and Kells as well as to other boroughs in Meath, had already bestowed the customs of Breteuil on the burgesses of Ludlow, and were closely connected with William Fitz-Osbern, lord of Breteuil, who originally introduced them into England. Mr. Orpen has missed an opportunity by not paying more attention to the municipal aspect of the Anglo-Norman settlement.

A perusal of Miss Bateson's articles would have added at least three to his list of borough charters granted before 1216, in one case certainly and in the others probably conceding the customs of Breteuil, one by Bishop Herlwin to Old Leighlin, and two by Walter de Lacy to Duleek and Drogheda respectively. Owing to ignorance of Walter's interesting charter to Drogheda of 1194, conferring with other privileges the 'liberam *legem Britoli*', Mr. Orpen has given a rather unsatisfactory account of the early history of that town. The charter mentions the castle, but in the chapter on the subinfeudation of Meath (ii. 79) we read that ' the castle here does not appear to be mentioned before 1203, when John gave to Nicholas de Verdun, the custody of the [castle of the] bridge of Drogheda . . . as Nicholas's father [Bertram de Verdun] held it '. In his comment on this passage the author seems justly enough to feel some surprise at finding the lord of Dundalk on the Louth side of the Boyne in possession of what should have been a Lacy castle as early as 1192, when Bertram de Verdun died, but has no explanation to offer save a royal sequestration which, we find later (ii. 261), did not take place until 1210. The truth is that the grant of 1203 has nothing to do with the castle on the Meath bank of the Boyne which Mr. Orpen quite gratuitously reads into it, but only with the northern *tête-de-pont* in Louth which was known as Bridge of Drogheda. This was a borough as early as 1213, when John, as we have seen, gave it the law of Breteuil, but Mr. Orpen, failing to grasp its separate existence, treats this as the first grant to Drogheda *in Meath* of the privileges which it had in point of fact enjoyed for nearly twenty years. These things may, however, be set right in the future work in which the author promises to trace the full development of the new prosperity and order which the Anglo-Norman settlement had introduced into Ireland, and to examine the causes of the ultimate failure of this fair prospect. JAMES TAIT.

Coutumes et Privilèges du Rouergue. Par ÉMILE BAILLAUD et P. A. VERLAGUET. 2 vols. (Bibliothèque Méridionale, 2ᵉ série, ix, x.) (Toulouse: Privat, 1910.)

MM. BAILLAUD and Verlaguet are bringing out a work which will be of the greatest assistance to students of local history in France. Only two volumes are at present published of the *Coutumes et Privilèges du Rouergue*; these are to be followed by one if not two others, and the most important part as far as criticism is concerned—the introduction, index, and notes— is yet to come. A very substantial piece of work has, however, been already done. In the first volume we have, most carefully collected and edited, the principal communal charters of Rodez itself, the chief town of the district, and the second volume contains similar documents concerning eleven other places belonging to the old province of Rouergue. A few of these charters have previously been printed in the *Ordonnances des Rois de France*, and in Gaujal's *Études historiques sur le Rouergue*; but the newer work has corrected many of the mistakes which occur in the earlier and less careful copies; and whilst Gaujal contented himself in some instances with an epitome of the manuscripts, they are here reproduced in full, and are arranged, annotated, and headed with the greatest clearness and care. There are various additions which occur to one as necessary to enable the reader to make full use of the documents —some account of the changes in the seigneurial families, some explanation of the historic setting of a few of the charters, and perhaps a glossary of some of the more difficult words in the local dialect—but these gaps will doubtless be filled in the volume which is to follow, and it is impossible to criticize an unfinished work with any fairness. It is to be hoped, however, that the introductory volume will give a clear sketch of the history of Rouergue during the years covered by the collection of documents, since such a work is much needed. The history of Bonal,[1] an old book, is confusing, and principally concerned with ecclesiastical history; and the *Études* of Gaujal, though full of learning and information, are not very clearly arranged, and require considerable study before their value can really be turned to account.

The documents of this collection do not begin until the thirteenth century, at which time the town of Rodez was no longer under the same suzerain as the county of Rouergue. In the ninth century Rouergue had been united to the county of Toulouse, and with it became a direct possession of the crown of France in 1271. The peace of Brétigny made it, for a short time, part of the principality of Edward the Black Prince, but it was the first of his territories to revolt from him in 1368. Rodez was separated from Rouergue early in the twelfth century, when it came into the hands of the Vicomtes de Carlat, who added to this title that of Comtes de Rodez, and they were still in possession when the records published in this collection begin. In the fourteenth century it was brought by marriage into the hands of the family of Armagnac, and it was Jean d'Armagnac who appealed to the French king in 1368, when the *fouage* levied by the Black Prince had roused his indignation. Confiscated for a short time by Louis XI, in consequence of the treason of its count, Rodez passed through the hands of the dukes of Alençon into the possession of the Albret family, and with the accession of Henri IV became definitely united to the royal estates. The documents mark these vicissitudes, although they give no actual details of political history. Their chief interest is the light which they throw on the social and economic condition of the town and its development to communal life and to a certain degree of self-government.

Rodez, like so many French towns, was composed of a *cité* and a *bourg*, and this volume gives a valuable illustration of the course of development often pursued in such cases. The *cité* was under the bishop, the *bourg* under the count; and though the bishop and his town were on very good terms and privileges were constantly granted apparently with no struggle, it was the *bourg* which led the way towards independence. The earliest charter still preserved for the *bourg* is dated 1201, but this confirms older privileges and speaks of the commune and of the seal *curie communis*. The first appearance of consuls in the *cité* is uncertain. They are mentioned in 1275, at which date their existence is taken for granted, without any hint of concession or new creation; but the earliest charter of privileges to the *cité* in 1244 speaks only of knights and *prudhommes*, and the seal appears for the first time in 1302. The *bourg* again had its *cloche communale* in 1304; the *cité* not till 1356. Both parts of the town, however, had consular government in the thirteenth century, and both made their privileges as secure as possible by formal recognition; the *cité* by every new bishop, the *bourg* by every new count. Disputes between the two seigneurs seem to have led to the establishment of a *cour de paréage*, but it was not till 1666 that the town was united under one municipal body, managed by the same four consuls. Rodez, not being a really independent

[1] *Comté et Comtes de Rodez*, 1843.

commune, but only a privileged town, with some self-government granted by a seigneur who was king of France from the sixteenth century, retained its privileges when more advanced towns were falling into subjection and having their rights curtailed or annulled.

Perhaps this first volume of the *Coutumes du Rouergue* is, in one way, the more interesting of the two, because it gives so full a picture of one place, which the sparser documents for the smaller towns are scarcely able to do. There is, however, plenty of valuable information in the second volume also, and information which has been rather less generally sifted and studied than the history of communal growth in the larger towns. Some of these towns of Rouergue are centres of considerable seigneuries, comprising villages, hamlets, and isolated houses, united by common customs and a common government. They are all rural in character, and the documents consist largely of rules concerning the supervision of common woods and pasture, the holding of markets, the sale of rural produce, and the like. The inhabitants of these places can go and come, buy and sell, inherit property, and do other things impossible to unfree cultivators, and forced labour only survives for such things as wall-work and repair of common ovens, &c., those who do such work being always provided with food. Consular government is the normal condition in all these rural towns. The consuls are elected, not always by the inhabitants unless it is the first time, but as a rule by the outgoing officers; and over these consuls preside the seneschals and bailiffs of the seigneur. High justice is never given to the town, and the usual consular jurisdiction is little more than police regulation. Financial matters are, however, nearly always in the hands of the consuls, and they have the choice of rural surveyors and other town officials. Like Rodez, these smaller places seem to have possessed a limited but useful and durable form of self-government, under the control and protection of a friendly seigneur.

The documents concerning Saint-Geniez-d'Olt are of especial interest, but all are valuable, and it would take too long to enumerate the many subjects of importance which they illustrate. Amongst other things there is much information concerning the *commun de la paix*. The whole of Rouergue owed this contribution, and some elaborate tables are published here fixing its amount in different places. Long after its original purpose of providing for special town defence was over it seems to have continued as a sort of poll-tax, and due on animals, which must have brought in considerable sums of money. There is one curious entry amongst the privileges of Villeneuve d'Aveyron, recording a promise 'ut nunquam teneamini sequi comunias pacis', which the editors say that they prefer to translate as *association de la paix*, but without explaining their reasons. It would be interesting to have fuller information as to this, and also as to any possible connexion between it and the *paix de Dieu*; but possibly this explanation will come later in the greatly needed third volume. The documents abound in illustrations of tolls, dues, market rights, common property, police regulations, and many other points of rural government. The important part played by common property of all sorts, whether actual possession or merely rights of usage, in helping to draw the inhabitants into a community and giving them a bond of connexion, is shown in numerous instances; as also the share taken by the inhabitants themselves in obtaining and carrying on their consular administration. In Rouergue advance appears to be made gradually and peacefully. The lords grant or confirm, at request of the inhabitants, a modified form of self-government, and the inhabitants in their turn submit with apparent content to the supreme control and supervision of the seigneurial officials.

Enough has been said to show that this collection of Rouergue documents is of the greatest interest and value, especially to the student of social and economic history. It is undoubtedly edited with extreme care and thoroughness; but much might still be done in the introductory volume to render the book of more general interest by explaining and pointing out the importance of the material which it contains.

ELEANOR C. LODGE.

Fratris Rogeri Bacon Compendium Studii Theologiae. Edited by H. RASH-DALL. With an Appendix *De Operibus Rogeri Bacon*, edited by A. G. LITTLE. (Aberdeen: University Press, 1911.)

THIS treatise, which Bacon composed in 1292, appears as volume iii of the British Society of Franciscan Studies. Dr. Rashdall bases his text on a manuscript now in the British Museum (Royal MS. 7 F. vii), with some assistance from another manuscript, in the possession of University College, Oxford. The relation of the work to other surviving fragments of Bacon he does not attempt to determine. In a case of this kind, where, as we are told, the principal manuscript is hard to read, and where the scribe did not fully understand what he was writing, the question of the correct reading must often depend upon the interpretation of Bacon's meaning; and for this reason Dr. Rashdall appears to get into difficulties in his treatment of part ii, chapter i, where Bacon propounds his doctrine of *signa*. A *signum*, he says, is either *naturale* or *datum ab anima*. Under the former head are two cases: (*a*) when the relation of *signatum* to *signum* is one of *concomitancia, consequentia naturalis*, &c.; (*b*) when the relation is one of *configuratio* or *conformatio*, in which connexion Bacon observes that *omnia artificialia representant artem in mente artificis*. Under the latter head are also two cases, namely: (*a*) *quod dicitur naturaliter significare*, e.g. the barking of dogs; (β) the *signum ad placitum*, e.g. the meaning deliberately assigned to words. Now, properly speaking, Bacon is not here making a logical division on a single basis, but considering two distinct questions, of which the first is preliminary to the second, while the whole argument culminates in the distinction between a mere *vox* and a *nomen*. He is, however, anxious to show that he is not guilty of a cross-division or confusion, and therefore he points out, first, that the sense of *natura* implied in *signum naturale* is not the sense implied in *naturaliter significans*, secondly, that the *signa ad placitum* are not in the same position as *artificialia*. In other words, he assures us that he is not confusing (*a*) with (α) nor (*b*) with (β). To illustrate his second sense of *natura* Bacon refers to Aristotle in these words, *Aristoteles dividit agens in naturam et intellectum agentem ex proposito et deliberacione*, and here Dr. Rashdall, by a strange freak of imagination, discovers an allusion to the technical sense of *intellectus agens*, as meaning God. Having done this, he finds in *ars* allusions to the Great Artificer, decides that, in the phrase *configuratur arti*, *arti* is ' of course ' ablative, and in two places, therefore, alters the manuscript *ei* into *arti*. But there is no allusion to any such exalted matters. The phrase *intellectus agens ex proposito* refers simply to deliberate human action, and wherever Bacon introduces *ars* he is merely alluding to the relation between *signatum* and *signum* expressed in the words *omnia artificialia representant artem in mente artificis*. The *species*, or whatever we please to call it, is in the mind of the artist, who forthwith expresses it in some such form as a statue; and then arises the relation of *configuratio* between the *signum* (here the statue) and the *signatum*. Obviously this relation of resemblance will be expressed by the dative case, not by the ablative; and the ablative would even suggest the relation of cause and effect, which Bacon implores us not to confuse with the relation of *signatum* and *signum*. *Arti* being dative, the manuscript *ei* can stand in both places where Dr. Rashdall would alter it. On p. 39 it refers to *signatum*, on p. 42 to *species*, though on p. 39 *figurata* is probably a slip for *configurata*.

As to the value of Bacon's work for historians of philosophy, the statements relating to the obscure Ricardus Cornubensis are of some interest, but Bacon's account of the condition of Aristotelian studies is preposterous. It proves, in fact, nothing except that Bacon was full of spite against the Dominicans. With regard to the particular statement, *Parisius excommunicabantur ante annum Domini* 1237, Dr. Rashdall suggests that 1237, if not a mistake for 1231, may be the date at which the excommunication of Aristotle's works was rescinded. But how then can we account for the fact[1] that in January 1263 Urban IV assumes that the prohibition is still in force ? More probably there never was any formal repeal, and the popes adopted the common policy of leaving *factum* and *ius* to take care of each other. Mr. Little's appendix will be greatly valued by scholars, though, as Mr. Little himself is the first to admit, a complete bibliography of Roger Bacon is almost an impossibility. W. H. V. READE.

Six Town Chronicles of England. Edited by RALPH FLENLEY, M.A., B.Litt. (Oxford: Clarendon Press, 1911.)

MR. FLENLEY has in this volume edited with praiseworthy care portions of six chronicles, of which all but one belong to London, the exception being a Lynn chronicle which affords an interesting example of the records (generally of late date) kept in many provincial towns. The series of London chronicles contain so much in common that Mr. Flenley has wisely confined his attention to those portions which afford matter of fresh interest. Taken as a whole the new matter is not very large in quantity nor important in quality; the text occupies little over a hundred pages. Apart, however, from their contents, these chronicles are of value

[1] Cf. *Chart. Univ. Paris.*, i, p. 427.

for their evidence on the growth and composition of records of this class; they do not, however, disturb the main conclusions at which I arrived in the Introduction to my *Chronicles of London*. The established position of the version compiled in 1440 is illustrated by the fact that the Latin chronicle in Rawlinson B. 355, and the English chronicle of Robert Bale, both become independent in that year. The Rawlinson chronicle, and the English chronicle from Gough MS., London 10, throw some valuable light on the composition of the main city chronicle, which formed the originals both of the Vitellius chronicle and of Robert Fabyan. From 1440 to 1452 the Rawlinson chronicle appears to be based on a better but briefer version of the original made use of in Vitellius. It is free from the confusion of chronology, and contains a little fresh matter in which it resembles Fabyan. In its latter portion (it ends in 1459) it sometimes resembles one and sometimes the other of the later versions. Its early date accounts for the reference to the establishment of the mayor's water-procession in 1453 as having destroyed 'the honourable riding of the citizens of London', and for the omission of the reference to the invention of printing. The Gough chronicle carries the history somewhat further; from 1450 onwards it has a close affinity to Vitellius, the two copies presenting frequent verbal similarities, which prove clearly their derivation from a common source. Though Vitellius is generally the fuller Gough occasionally supplies some additional detail. The main chronicle breaks off abruptly in 1470, and was probably written in the latter part of the reign of Edward IV. A fragment for 1494-5, which has a general resemblance to the corresponding passage in Vitellius, seems to be the work of another hand. Unlike Rawlinson (and *Caxton's Chronicles*) Gough has no marked parallels to Fabyan's chronicle. It seems probable that Fabyan used an older version than that followed in Gough and Vitellius.

For its contents Robert Bale's chronicle is the best in this volume; it is for the most part independent, and though it contains little of distinct novelty supplies many small details which are valuable as a presentment of contemporary opinion and as illustrating the disordered state of the country at the close of the reign of Henry VI. Of the other chronicles the Longleat copy furnishes only a few variations of no great moment from Julius B. II. Tanner MS. 2 supplies a Latin chronicle which comes down to 1524-5, but contains little of original value except in its later years. The interest of the Lynn chronicle 'lies primarily in the fact that it is an early example of a town chronicle written outside London'; the references to local affairs are of little importance, and most of those to general history are borrowed from the 1542 edition of Fabyan. The provincial town chronicles now extant are compilations of the sixteenth and seventeenth centuries, and like the Lynn chronicle, a Dublin chronicle described by Mr. Flenley in his introduction, and Adams's chronicle of Bristol, took their principal facts from Fabyan.

Mr. Flenley has edited his texts well, and has added a number of useful footnotes. But the interest of the volume is much increased by the lengthy and excellent introduction, in which he has brought together much material on the history of the chronicles of London and of some other towns. Incidentally he describes many such chronicles in addition to the six of which he has printed portions. His review begins with the earliest chronicles of London, and is carried down to the close of the sixteenth century. It is a sound and careful piece of work, and together with the critical introductions to his printed texts forms a most valuable contribution to the study of English historical sources. There is a useful list of chronicles of London, both manuscript and printed. The index alone leaves something to be desired, and might with advantage have been made more complete. C. L. KINGSFORD.

Chroniken der Stadt Bamberg. II: *Chroniken zur Geschichte des Bauernkrieges und der Markgrafenfehde in Bamberg.* Edited by ANTON CHROUST. (Leipzig: Meyer, 1910.)

THIS substantial volume of seven hundred pages contains some interesting and admirably edited materials for the sixteenth-century history of Germany. They do not provide sources for the continuous history of Bamberg, but relate exclusively to two episodes, the Peasants' War, and the great private war waged by the margrave Albrecht Alcibiades in 1552–4. The narratives and documents relating to the first of these episodes enable us to distinguish various stages in the movement and to appreciate the attitude towards it of different sections in the Bamberg community, though its manifestations were mild compared with those in other parts of Germany. There was no parallel to the massacre of Weinsberg, and no revenge comparable with that exacted by the margrave Casimir; although according to Herr Chroust the religious element was throughout subordinate to the social and economic.

The first of the narratives is ascribed by the editor to one Marx Halbritter, a member of the Bamberg council, largely on the ground that its main object appears to be to magnify Halbritter's share in the transactions. Its date of composition is assigned to 1525; but the original manuscript is not extant, and this date, as well as the theory of Halbritter's authorship, requires the assumption that the existing text incorporates some later glosses. Herr Chroust, however, gives good reasons for accepting his conclusion rather than that of a former commentator, W. Stolze, who assigns the manuscript to Jerome Cammermeister (not to be confused with the better-known Joachim Cammermeister or Camerarius). The second narrative is attributed to the bishop of Bamberg's secretary, Martin Müllner, who appears to have been the mouthpiece of some member of the chapter, and naturally represents a different point of view from Halbritter's; the comparison between the two is instructive, not merely as checking their statements of fact but as illustrating the relations between church and state in Bamberg. Müllner's original manuscript is extant, and dates from 1529. Then follow a brief diary which Herr Chroust attributes to Cammermeister, a letter from a nun of the Klarissenkloster in Bamberg, two others from the abbess written to the famous Charitas Pirckheimer, two ballads by the bishop's secretary Pankras Mayer and 120 pages of documents from the Bamberg archives.

The sources for the margrave's war are not less interesting. The most important is a diary written apparently by Hans Zeitlos, deputy burgomaster (*Bürgermeisteramtsverwalter*) of Bamberg, who took a leading part in the negotiations with the margrave, and had to follow him about as hostage for the ransom which Albrecht exacted from the city. Again, the motive of the author seems to have been self-glorification; but Zeitlos is more modest than Halbritter, and successive redactions of the original manuscript by his own or by another hand further reduced the egotism of the narrative. It is a businesslike story, drawn almost entirely from personal experience, with just a reference to Sleidan's *Commentaries* thrown in at the end. The second narrative is written by a nun of the Klarissenkloster, who shows a feminine disrespect for chronology and arithmetic, a touching faith in the emperor's ability to overcome all his enemies, a loyalty which enables her to believe any evil of his foes (she thinks Moritz of Saxony wanted to kill Charles V), a great belief in portents, and a horror of cruelty which leads her to magnify the margrave's misdeeds and multiply his victims. Her outlook is very different from that of Zeitlos; but there is no question of antagonism between clergy and laity, because the outrageous conduct of the margrave had, for the time, obscured the religious issue. Still, the narrative yields many interesting illustrations of what the world looked like from the inside of a German nunnery in the middle of the sixteenth century. The volume is well produced, and does credit to the Gesellschaft für fränkische Geschichte. A. F. POLLARD.

Lettres de Catherine de Médicis. Publiées par M. Le Comte BAGUENAULT DE PUCHESSE. Tome X. Supplément, 1537–87. (Collection de Documents Inédits sur l'Histoire de France.) (Paris: Imprimerie Nationale, 1909.)

THIS concluding volume contains the gleanings from a wide acreage of years. Of the 887 letters printed, however, only 42 belong to the years which precede 1560, and 52 to those which follow the close of 1579. The periods of the twenty intervening years which receive most illustration are those which extend from the peace of Amboise to that of Saint-Germain, and from the siege of La Rochelle in 1573 to the Estates of Blois in 1576. This somewhat haphazard collection is a fair epitome of Catherine's correspondence, by far the greater part of which was addressed to the trustworthy diplomatists who represented France abroad, or the loyal soldiers upon whom she relied for the government of the more difficult provinces. Among the former Bellièvre, who was accredited first to the Grisons and then to the Swiss, received no less than 170 letters, while after him come Saint-Sulpice and Fourquevaulx, ambassadors at the court of Spain, the bishop of Dax, envoy at Constantinople, and the Baron de Férals, resident first at Rome and then in the Netherlands. Chief among the military correspondents are Mandelot, governor of Lyons, Du Lude, lieutenant-governor in Poitou, Maugiron, lieutenant-general in Dauphiné, and Matignon, governor of Normandy. This volume supports its fellows in refuting the slander that Catherine ruled France through an Italian clique: the men upon whom she mainly leant were the nation's truest servants. The letters to Saint-Sulpice and Bellièvre illustrate the queen-mother's increasing fear and jealousy of Spain. After the first civil war she believed that Philip's ambassador Chantonnay was intriguing to break the peace—*tels instruments*, she wrote on 14 November 1563, *ne sont que pour troubler une bonne feste*. She ultimately plucked up courage to demand his recall. Early in 1564 we find her hotly protesting to her daughter Elisabeth against the pope's attempted interference with the queen of Navarre: her son will not suffer pope or inquisition to do the queen harm or give her kingdom for a prey. A curious letter of March 1573 severely handles a proposal reported by the papal nuncio for the marriage of her son with a sister or daughter of Philip II and a joint conquest of England, while Don John should marry Mary Stuart and receive the Netherlands as his share. England, she wrote, was not to be conquered in a day, and she would not have the bastard put on a level with her son, whereas the difference between them was clear. In the summer of 1576 she stoutly refuses to give John Casimir or even Condé the governorship of the Three Bishoprics, but she is prepared to subsidize them in secret for an attack upon the Netherlands, as she had done three years before. This is one of the clearest references to her activity in the Low Countries.

Catherine's ambassadors were useful in executing small commissions. Saint-Sulpice was asked to send her half a dozen skins of black morocco, and the best Portuguese sealing-wax of all colours. Gilles de Noailles was expected to forward from Constantinople a supply of white calamite (chalk), a good and sovereign remedy for colic, together with detailed instructions as to how to use it, for nobody knew in France. Her kindness of heart is shown in a letter which begs the duchess of Bourbon to pardon a man for killing a stag, because a wife and six children depended on him, but on condition that he should receive exemplary punishment if he repeated the offence. In the birth and upbringing of children she always took an expert's interest. After a letter to her daughter Elisabeth full of detailed recommendations as to a coming event, she informs the prince of Eboli that she is dispatching a *sage-femme* and an experienced nurse; the only fault of the latter was that she was always chattering, but this had amused her husband, and therefore might entertain Philip: both women were not only catholics *mais bigottes*. Of some real interest is a letter advising her sister-in-law, Margaret of Savoy, who remained somewhat of an old maid, not to coddle the infant Charles Emmanuel. The advice was not taken, and the child, owing to his mother's fussiness, remained puny and delicate till her death, when his father adopted the hardening process which converted him into the most indefatigable of princes. A passage of the letter may be worth quoting: 'I entreat you to take care of the boy, to give the boy a good nurse, to recommend him to God, and not to be always with him, for you could not help fashing yourself over the least thing that happens; never did a child grow up without plenty of little illnesses, and yours must have them like the rest. If I had always been with mine, I should have been dead, and killed them too, while meaning to do them good, but I have relied on the good servants in whose charge I placed them, and, thank God, they are all well.' In conclusion may be noticed a charming letter written in the very troublous year

1584 to Catherine's grandchild, the Infanta Isabella, whom she had never seen.

Among the documents in the appendix are Catherine's marriage settlement, and a useful schedule of her household from 1 July 1547 to 1585. Very valuable also is the itinerary which the editor has compiled, and which shows that Catherine visited 314 different places, a creditable record for a queen even in the most modern days. E. ARMSTRONG.

Philipp Marnix von St. Aldegonde. Von ALBERT ELKAN. Teil I. *Die Jugend Johanns und Philipps von Marnix.* (Leipzig: Dyk, 1910.)

No man of letters has surely left so little information about his youth as St. Aldegonde. The story of his life from his birth in 1539 until the troubles of 1566 is but a series of possibilities or probabilities. And it is Dr. Elkan's merit that he has not been tempted to make his critical and well-written biography the more attractive by converting these into facts. The present section of the work comprises also all that is known of the life of Philip's elder brother John, lord of Toulouse, who was, indeed, until his untimely death, the more prominent of the two. This death, however, made the scantiness of records in his case the less surprising. Dr. Elkan has at all events corrected the errors concerning the dates of the brothers' birth. It seems certain that John was born in 1538 and Philip early in 1539. An ingenious argument also makes it highly probable that Philip received the lesser orders and a canonry of the see of Terouenne, the Belgian canons of which church were, after the destruction of Terouenne in 1553, transferred to Saint Omer. The first notice of this is found in the second edition of the *Flandria illustrata* of Antonius Sanderus (1735), but it has never until now received any confirmation. The date of Philip's admission is placed between 14 March 1558 and 29 June 1559, while he must have resigned at the end of 1562 at latest. It is indeed strange that neither Marnix, nor his friends, nor his enemies should ever have mentioned this important incident. Both brothers matriculated at Louvain in October 1553, and probably they were members of the Collège des Trois Langues. Philip stayed till at least August 1555, and then possibly went to Paris. The next definite date is 1557, when both went to the university of Dôle, where Jean was elected rector, an office which was terminated by his father's death. At Dôle Jean studied civil law, Philip, probably, theology. It is not known whither Philip went from Dôle, perhaps to Poitiers, perhaps to Paris. In 1558 Jean was a law student at Padua ; Philip joined him in Italy, and visited Pavia, Venice, and possibly Rome. Dr. Elkan does not believe in the theory that the brothers went from Italy to Spain. A most important fact in the career of Jean and Philip was their matriculation in the new university of Geneva, where they were among the first Netherland students. The story that they lived in Calvin's house is untrue ; they lodged with the Sieur d'Agnon, a noble French ex-canon. They are supposed to have been intimate with Calvin and Bèze, but there is little information on the subject. In 1561 they left Geneva for home, and soon afterwards married. Until the outbreak of the troubles they must have lived a comparatively quiet life, and at all events escaped the notice of the inquisition. The author presumes from Philip's later writings that they were inspired by the growing hatred for Granvelle, and that they were brought into connexion with the later liberal leaders, acting as intermediaries between the higher nobility and the middle classes; but of this there is no proof.

The same uncertainty exists with regard to Philip's religious development. It is unlikely that he became infected with Calvinism at the orthodox university of Dôle, though eminent Calvinists of later days were there, noticeably Paul Buys. He may, however, have been brought into contact with Calvinism during either of his visits to France, or again in Italy. It is improbable that the brothers would have gone to Geneva unless they had had strong Calvinist leanings, and they must pretty certainly have been confirmed in them there. Yet Philip is strangely silent on the subject, and the first evidence of Calvinism is his elegy to the notorious Calvinist humanist, Olympia Fulvia Morata, published in 1562 by a Calvinist professor of Basel. The author thinks that Philip perhaps learnt his political attachment to France during his first supposed visit, but for a century or more it had been no uncommon feature in the Hainault nobility. The Italian tour must have contributed to his humanistic tastes. He stood first among the very few learned nobles in the Netherlands, being well versed in the Greek and Latin classics, in catholic theology, in medieval history, and political theory. Erasmus was his model, and he was familiar with Rabelais and Machiavelli. He knew Hebrew, Greek, and Latin, Flemish, Spanish, and Italian, and later English and German. He collected pictures, and was fond of music, and yet was first in all knightly exercises. These accomplishments are at least undoubted. In strong contrast with the biographical uncertainties is the mass of information which the author has collected on the property and connexions of the Marnix family. To the original Savoyard possessions Philip's grandfather added domains in Franche-Comté and in Brabant, while his father added to these latter and received from his wife Sainte Aldegonde and Boulant in Hainault, which fell to Philip on his father's death. The elder brother received the Savoyard and Burgundian lands, and took his title from Toulouse, which lies in the neighbourhood of Dôle. E. ARMSTRONG.

Rapport sur une Mission scientifique aux Archives d'Autriche et d'Espagne. Par M. G. CONSTANT. (Nouvelles Archives des Missions scientifiques, tome XVIII.) (Paris: Imprimerie Nationale, 1910.)

M. CONSTANT is to be congratulated on the achievement of an arduous and excellent piece of historical exploration. The sub-title describes his volume as ' étude et catalogue critiques de documents sur le Concile de Trent '; by council of Trent are here meant its later sessions during the pontificate of Pius IV; and M. Constant's documents are limited to the years 1559-65. But they number between four and five thousand dispatches, and M. Constant's catalogue comes to nearly three hundred pages, the rest of his volume being devoted to critical accounts of the various ambassadors and their diplomatic work. It is to be hoped that the Comité des Travaux Historiques will soon be able to carry out the intention indicated on p. 363, and publish the materials M. Constant has catalogued in the *Collection de documents inédits*. Primarily, of course, the duty of M. Constant and of the Comité has been to illustrate the history of France; but the council of Trent belongs to the history of the world; and apart from the indirect bearing of all its proceedings upon English history, there are in the archives explored by M. Constant a number of *Zeitungen, avvisi*, or 'news-letters' giving direct information about English affairs, which lie off the beaten track of English archivists and have not been published in any calendar of state papers or other collection of documents. M. Constant's materials are arranged under various heads. First come the dispatches to the Emperor Ferdinand of his ambassadors at Rome, Franz von Thurm and Prospero d'Arco. Ferdinand's son Maximilian, however, also maintained an independent correspondence with Rome; and the letters of his agents Ippolito Pallavicini and Galeazzo Cusano are often fuller than the emperor's. Cusano was especially informing because he concealed the nature of his employment from the papal curia. Then follows the 'correspondance conciliaire', which is not as complete as might be wished. Ferdinand experienced great difficulty in finding suitable representatives at Trent; and when he had constrained Siegmund von Thun and Brus, archbishop of Prague, to accept his offers, their presence at the council was very intermittent, the proximity of Thun's estates frequently inducing him to prefer the society of his family to that of the fathers at Trent. But fragmentary as it is, this correspondence is practically virgin soil.

From Vienna M. Constant passed to Simancas, on the archives of which he has already written in the *Revue Historique* (t. xcvi), and the great mass of his Spanish documents come from this source. There are a few interesting documents in the Biblioteca Nacional at Madrid; but M. Constant's researches among provincial libraries, even when assisted by 'bibliothécaires habitués à ne voir aucun visiteur' (p. 180), yielded practically nothing, and the muniments of noble houses in Spain remain closed to historical inquirers. M. Constant begins his Spanish documents with the official correspondence of Philip II's ambassadors at Rome, Vargas and Requesens. The personal enmity between Pius IV and Vargas, and the publication of some of Vargas's letters, which had been secured by the English agent, William Trumbull, at Brussels, had the curious result, as Burnet's readers know, of converting one of the bitterest enemies of heresy into a favourite Protestant witness in seventeenth-century controversy; but his letters at Simancas are, like so many others, ignored in the *Spanish Calendar*. He was succeeded by Requesens, whose pacific character had more effect upon Pius IV than it had later upon the Netherlands. There are also some letters from Gurone Bertano, about whose earlier diplomatic activity in England M. Constant will find many details in the last volume of the *Letters and Papers of Henry VIII*. Philip II's correspondence with the council of Trent was maintained by Pescara and Luna, some of whose dispatches have been published by Döllinger and Don José Rayón. M. Constant has been able to trace a large number which should not have escaped Don José Rayón. He has also occasion to reflect upon the idiosyncrasies of Thomas Gonzalez, who was charged by Ferdinand VII with the duty of reorganizing the archives at Simancas, and whose meagre notes are all that survive of some of the most important documents committed to his care. A brief appendix refers cursorily to the correspondence of Spanish ambassadors in France, Germany, and England, who deal but incidentally with the council of Trent. We could wish that a mission as scientific as M. Constant's were appointed to deal with the Spanish sources for English history. A. F. POLLARD.

England und die katholische Kirche unter Elisabeth und den Stuarts. Von ARNOLD OSKAR MEYER. Erster Band. (Rome : Loescher, 1911.)

DR. MEYER, who is now Professor of History at Rostock, is already known to students of English history through his excellent little book on *Die englische Diplomatie in Deutschland zur Zeit Eduards VI und Mariens*. He has followed it up by the first volume of an ambitious work on the relations between the English government and Roman catholicism, both domestic and foreign. It is the fruit of several years' labour at the Prussian school in Rome and of several prolonged visits to England ; and both at Rome and in England Dr. Meyer has profited by the advice and assistance of archivists of all denominations and of dignitaries of the Roman catholic church, a co-operation that is all the more welcome in that Dr. Meyer's own point of view is not Roman catholic. Dr. Meyer is admirably equipped for the task he has undertaken ; he possesses a thorough knowledge of Latin, Italian, French, and English, in addition to his native tongue ; he has been well trained in historical technique ; and friendly intercourse with scholars of all persuasions helps him to deal with a difficult subject in a singularly dispassionate and open-minded manner.

As a foreigner he enjoys some special advantages in writing English ecclesiastical history. One relates to his terminology ; a German can without offence and without being misunderstood use the term ' protestant ' of all Englishmen who rejected the papal jurisdiction ; an English historian dare not, and is driven to seek some term to designate those who rejected the papal jurisdiction but never called themselves protestants or subscribed to any of the formularies of the distinctively protestant churches. This difficulty induces, perhaps, a keener appreciation of the impossibility of describing, with any approach to exactness, the numerical distribution of religious parties in 1559. Dr. Meyer declines to accept Dom Birt's exaggerated estimate of the number of Roman catholic clergy who lost their livings as a consequence of the Acts of Supremacy and Uniformity, while he properly admits that the number given by Camden and universally accepted by Anglican and Protestant historians must be modified. But the problem is qualitative quite as much as it is quantitative ; Roman catholics and avowed protestants were certainly both in a minority, perhaps together they were a minority of the nation ; but how are we to describe the majority ? Dr. Meyer writes (p. 48) : ' In der Geschichte des englischen Katholicismus ist die Frage noch unbeantwortet, in welche Zeit die Umwandlung der grossen katholischen Masse in eine kleine Minderheit fällt, und in welcher Form der Übertritt dieser Massen zum Protestantismus sich vollzog.' Before a really satisfying answer is possible, one would have to determine in what sense this majority was catholic before the change and protestant after it. One can hardly talk of 'conversion' in any religious sense; the process seems rather to have been one by which loyalty to the queen or national state gradually outweighed in the mind of the majority loyalty to the pope or [Roman] catholic church.

Pius V's bull of excommunication and deposition was probably the most effective factor in this change. It compelled those who were hesitating between two forms of loyalty to make their choice under circumstances in which all the material advantages lay in choosing loyalty to the queen. Indeed, the catholic mission was required mainly to counteract the fatal effects of the bull; and partial success in this was the principal achievement of the missionaries. They had no great success in reconverting protestants; they merely established in their faith some of the waverers; and Dr. Meyer produces interesting statistics to show that the proportion of Roman catholics to the whole population has remained almost constant ever since. The mission saved the Roman catholics in England from sinking to the numbers and position of the protestants in Spain. It is doubtful whether this would have been possible, but for the technical invalidity of Pius V's bull which gave English Romanists a loophole of escape from their dilemma, and for the temporary dispensation to be loyal with which Gregory XIII provided the missioners in 1580-1.

The persecution which attended this mission is examined by Dr. Meyer with judicial impartiality. We think he has established his point that the missioners were not in thought or deed political agents or conspirators (with the exception of Parsons, whose political activity at this time is passed over rather lightly), and that such phrases as Dr. Meyer quotes from J. R. Green—' fresh and more vigorous missionaries egged on the English catholics to revolt '—and from Froude—' the Jesuit mission of 1580 was the commencement of a new series of conspiracies '—should disappear from English histories. But there is one point in the judicial proceedings against them which seems to have escaped Dr. Meyer. Camden tells us that Campion and his associates were ' accusati ex lege Maiestatis xxv Edwardi III Reginae Regnoque perniciem struxisse, Pontifici Romano Reginae hosti adhaesisse '. The papal invasion of Ireland in 1579 gave point to the question addressed to the missioners, whether in case of an invasion they would adhere to the queen or the pope. Dr. Meyer condemns this question as savouring of the methods of the Inquisition, which the government professed, and were anxious, to avoid; and he does not seem quite to appreciate the advantage which Edward III's law gave to the government in dealing with ' adherents ' of the queen's enemies. We quite concur, however, in his objections to the corroborative details about impossible conspiracies by which the government sought either, as Dr. Meyer thinks, to avoid inquisitorial methods, or perhaps to prejudice juries. His conclusion appears sound: ' soweit die Gerichte in den Priestern Verschwörer und Attentäter sahen, waren die Verurteilten mit wenigen Ausnahmen Opfer von Justizmorden. Soweit aber das Wirken der Priester, auch derer, die ganz unpolitisch sein wollten, als staats gefährlich angesehen wurde, soweit waren die Urteile eine politische Notwendigkeit, ein Gebot der staatlichen Selbsterhaltung.' Elizabeth would not long have continued to reign over a people converted by Campion; the innocence of his intentions would not have made the results of his action less fatal to the security of the realm.

We should like to follow Dr. Meyer's interesting discussions of similar points further; but we can only indicate one or two of his original contributions to our positive knowledge. He exposes Green's assertion that 'no layman was brought to the bar or the block' by showing that the proportion of catholic laymen executed to catholic priests was 60 to 130. He clears up the old story that Sixtus V re-excommunicated and deposed Elizabeth by proving that Sixtus V's brief (not a bull) merely revoked the temporary licence to be loyal granted by Gregory XIII; and he prints an unpublished letter from the cardinal of Como to the nuncio Sega at Madrid, which practically clinches the evidence in support of Gregory XIII's approval of plots to assassinate Elizabeth. The slips we have noticed are so trifling that they need not be mentioned, but it is hardly fair to cite T. G. Law as 'ein katholischer Historiker' (pp. 76, 88). We hope that the further remarks which Dr. Meyer promises on Gregorio Leti (p. 295) will include a thorough examination of that writer's historical romances; and he will find a few fresh references in M. Constant's recent report on his survey of the Vienna and Simancas archives. Dr. Meyer's book is admirable from so many points of view that we hope it will find an English translator and publisher.   A. F. POLLARD.

Acts and Ordinances of the Interregnum, 1642–60. Collected and edited by C. H. FIRTH and R. S. RAIT for the Statute Law Committee. Three volumes. (London: H.M. Stationery Office, 1911.)

THE statute law committee have earned the gratitude of historians for publishing this much-needed collection of the acts and ordinances passed during the civil war and the interregnum. The legislation of this period naturally finds no place in the statute book, and up to the present the student has been obliged to go to a variety of sources for the text of individual enactments. The collections, published either officially or unofficially at the time, contain no doubt the more important documents, but the most exhaustive of them, Henry Scobell's, was compiled by a lawyer for lawyers, and many acts or ordinances of historical interest were omitted and remained more or less inaccessible. The first two volumes of the present work are devoted to the text of the acts and ordinances issued between 1642 and 1660, and the third contains an introduction by Professor Firth, a table giving the dates and titles of the acts printed in the preceding volumes, as well as of others which, for one reason or another, have been omitted, an index of subjects and an index of names, places, and things. The collection is 'primarily intended for the historian', and although ordinances of little or no permanent interest—those, for example, dealing with individual cases of sequestration—have been omitted for reasons of space, the editors have approached the task of selection with a broad mind, and practically everything of general or local importance has been printed.

The acts and ordinances now brought together for the first time are necessarily of varied character. The successive changes in the constitution of the governing power serve to mark the main divisions and to classify the legislation of the period, but the salient date is, of course, the year 1649. Before that date the ordinances issued by the two houses sitting at Westminster were, as far as the institutions in church and state were concerned, chiefly destructive: after 1649, upon the ground thus effectively cleared, begins a series of experiments in the making of a constitution. Both the earlier and the later periods have their distinctive interest as illustrating on the one hand an attempt to modify an existing order, and on the other a venture in the direction of something entirely new. The distinguishing characteristic of the more important constitutional changes in these years is that they form part, not of a consistent course of policy undertaken deliberately and with set purpose, but of one to a great extent adopted to suit the exigencies of the moment and as the result of a struggle the real nature of which neither party fully appreciated and with the outcome of which the victors were unprepared to deal. But even so, the effect of this period of unconstitutional legislation was far from being merely transitory. Though the measures passed between the sixteenth year of Charles I's reign and the '12th year of Charles II's' were at the Restoration naturally regarded as invalid, the principle of some was embodied in later acts. The Navigation Act and the act abolishing the courts of wards and liveries are cases in point. The union with Scotland, though longer delayed, was nevertheless a return to the protector's policy, and even when they did not foreshadow the future course of legislation the experiments made during the interregnum in such matters as religious toleration mark an important stage in the development of thought.

Professor Firth's introduction contains much valuable information on the legislation of the period. He describes at some length the various sources from which the collection is drawn, and then proceeds to an account of the manner by which the power of legislating by way of ordinance, without the royal assent, was first assumed by the parliament. He brings out the fact that this unconstitutional procedure occasioned comparatively little comment until it was employed in matters of far-reaching importance. Ultimately the question of how far the parliamentary ordinances were to hold good became one of the chief points at issue in the negotiations between the contending parties. The overthrow of the monarchy in 1649 settled the question for the moment, but with the subsequent changes in the supreme authority the question was raised again in another form, and reached its most acute stage in the controversy between the restored Long Parliament and the officers of the army in 1659. The issue here was the confirmation of the enactments made during the Protectorate and, in this connexion, Professor Firth thinks that the act of 11 October 'against the Raising of Money upon the People without their consent in Parliament' has hardly been given its due importance. In answer to the demand that the acts in question should be deemed valid until actually repealed, the parliament by this measure definitely treated them as invalid until renewed or confirmed. Professor Firth concludes with a review of the acts the principles of which survived the Restoration, and of the orders of the Restoration parliament with regard to the records of the Interregnum.

There are one or two misprints in the introduction. '1659' on p. vi,

l. 26, should be '1649'; 'with' on p. xiii, l. 29, should be 'without'; and a word seems to have been omitted on p. xvii, l. 9. In the table of acts no reference is given to the text of the ordinance of 30 March 1644, which is printed in the Lords' Journals. As the collection is certain to become the standard work of reference for the legislation of the years 1642-60, it is perhaps to be regretted that acts, mentioned in the table, but not printed in the collection, are not to be found in the index; but the point is a very small one, and otherwise the index appears to be excellent.

G. B. TATHAM.

Calendar of Treasury Books. Edited by W. A. SHAW. Vols. II–V: 1667–79. (London: H.M. Stationery Office, 1905-11.)

THESE volumes are an addition of very great value to the authorities for the history of the seventeenth century, and the calendar is one of the best of the long series issued under the authority of the master of the rolls. In the first volume of the calendar Dr. Shaw dealt with papers anterior to March 1667—a somewhat miscellaneous and defective collection of records. The real history of the treasury as an independently organized department of state begins in 1667, with Dr. Shaw's second volume. After the death of the earl of Southampton the treasury was put into commission (24 May 1667), and its organization was reformed by Sir George Downing, the secretary to the commissioners. 'My heart is very glad of it,' wrote Pepys, 'for I do expect they will do much good, and it is the happiest thing that hath appeared to me for the good of the nation since the King came in.' Downing seemed to him 'as fit a man as any in the world' for the office he held. At the moment the government was in the greatest possible straits for money. This was not due merely to the cost of the war with Holland and France. Ever since his restoration Charles II had been in difficulties. Parliament had promised him a revenue of £1,200,000 a year, but the taxes they voted for that purpose never brought in more than eight or nine hundred thousand per annum. Consequently he began the war with the Dutch with a debt of over a million caused by these annual deficits. Parliament voted considerable sums for the support of the war: a royal aid of £2,477,500, an additional aid of £1,250,000, and a three months' tax which amounted to £210,000. But it provided nothing to meet the old debt, and the war taxes, which should have brought in nearly £5,000,000, produced only £4,355,000. Hence the sailors had to be paid in tickets instead of money, the fleet could not be sent out in the spring of 1667, and De Ruyter's burning of the ships at Chatham was made possible. Parliament attributed this disaster and the financial distress in general not to its own insufficient grants, but to the mismanagement of the government. Hence the appointment in December 1667 of a committee of nine persons to examine into the accounts. Dr. Shaw traces in detail the history of this committee, and shows that the king and his ministers were very unfairly censured.

On 8 April 1669 a new treasury commission was appointed, which was superseded on 28 November 1672 by the appointment of Lord Clifford as lord treasurer, a post which he held about seven months. During

M 2

the years 1669–72 parliament voted additional grants to the extent of £660,000, but the sum was not sufficient to cover the deficit in the ordinary revenue, much less to defray the debt resulting from the war. By 1672 the government was in debt to the extent of between two and two and a quarter millions: it owed about a million to the bankers and had anticipated one year's revenue. Hence came the 'Stop of the Exchequer' (January 1672), a declaration of insolvency on the part of the government. It thereby postponed the payment of the orders on the treasury held by bankers from whom it had borrowed. The general effect of the stop was to enable the king to receive his revenue as and when it came in, and to employ it in paying the various services instead of being ear-marked for the liquidation of debt. It did not put him in the immediate possession of funds. It merely enabled him as his revenue came in to employ it unhampered for the navy and other branches of national expenditure (*Calendar*, 1669–73, p. xlvi). In the years 1677–9 Charles made provision for the permanent payment of interest to the bankers by granting letters patent for the payment of annuities to those concerned. The interest due for the period during which payment had been suspended was calculated at the rate of 6 per cent. per annum, and added to the capital sum of the debt. This created a fixed charge in the revenue amounting to about £77,000 per annum.

While the bankruptcy of 1672 thus increased the expenditure it also led to the diminution of the receipts. To pay his debts—or rather the debts of the state—the king sold between 1672 and 1679 fee-farms to the annual value of about £52,000. So many of these rents were thrown on the market that their price fell from 18 years' purchase to 16 (vol. iv, pp. viii–xv). The combined result of the provision made for the payment of the bankers and the sale of the fee-farms was to diminish the king's income by between £120,000 and £130,000 per annum. The subsidies of Louis XIV may have been intended to make the king independent of parliament, but they hardly covered the reduction in income made by the two transactions mentioned. According to Dr. Shaw, Charles received from Louis in the six years 1672–7 a total of £741,985, that is, an average of £123,664 per annum (vol. iii, p. lxvi).

If the management of the king's revenue had remained in the reckless and incapable hands of Clifford the restoration of financial order would have been impossible. Fortunately Danby succeeded him as lord treasurer on 19 June 1673, and 'within an incredibly short space of time Charles's finances took on another aspect'. 'Danby,' says Dr. Shaw, 'was a statesman consistently sound, clear-headed, and business-like.' With the second Dutch war on his hands, towards which the parliament had granted an inadequate supply, he still

succeeded in restoring credit so far as to be able to borrow money at 8 per cent., whereas previously 10 per cent. had been paid for the loans to the government. He not merely paid the seamen in ready money, whereas previously for years they had been paid only in tickets, or part tickets and part money, but he also furnished the stores with cash to enable them to make purchases at cash value instead of at 40 per cent. enhanced prices for deferred payment. Finally, he never rested till he had made a completely honest, even a generous, provision for the interest due to the bankers (vol. iv, p. xvii).

Danby could never have done this if he had not been favoured by the revival of trade. The customs, which had yielded £162,000 in 1670-1, yielded over £400,000 in 1674 and over £700,000 in 1675. The excise, which had hitherto produced £250,000 to £300,000 per annum, produced over £750,000 in 1674 and about £500,000 in 1675. The result was that Charles's settled or hereditary revenue, which had been fixed in 1660 at £1,200,000, but which had never before 1672 amounted to more than £900,000, rose in 1674 and 1675 to over £1,400,000 (without counting his subsidies from Louis). Though the receipts fell again in 1676, 1677, and 1678 the king's average income for three years was a little under £1,200,000. The fall in the revenue was met by an attempt to cut down the expenditure. 'The scheme of his Majesty's yearly expense,' drawn up on 28 January 1676, is a very interesting estimate (vol. v, p. 117), and should be compared with the financial statement given by Macaulay in his third chapter.

During Danby's administration there were also certain special grants made by parliament to meet extraordinary expenditure. A special aid was granted the king for the second Dutch war. It consisted of an eighteen months' assessment estimated to bring in £1,123,000 and actually producing £1,116,000. This grant was quite inadequate for its purpose, as the war involved a total addition of not less than a million and a half to the normal cost of military and naval armaments during the period for which it lasted. An Act passed in April 1677 imposed an assessment lasting for seventeen months, for raising money to build thirty new ships. It was estimated that the assessment would yield about £585,000, but the ships cost not less than £654,000. In March 1678 a poll tax was imposed by parliament in order to raise an army for a war against the French king. It was expected that this would bring in a million, and an army of over 27,000 men was raised by Charles on the strength of it. But the actual receipts for the tax were much less than this sum, and the money came in so slowly that loans had to be raised by the king to maintain the soldiers in this interim. Parliament then changed its mind, and voted in June 1678 that the newly raised soldiers should be disbanded. For their payment and disbandment, and other purposes, it imposed an eighteen months' assessment estimated to produce about £620,000. The history of the disbandment, however, and the financial transactions of the last five years of the king's reign, belong to a future volume.

Dr. Shaw's general conclusion is that the pecuniary difficulties of Charles II's government were not caused by his own extravagance, or by his misappropriation of the supplies granted by parliament, but that the ordinary revenue of the crown was from the first insufficient for the ordinary expenses of government, and the extraordinary grants insufficient for the military and naval expenditure they were designed to meet. This view is not a new one. It was set forth with great vigour by Thomas Carte in 1742, in his 'Full Answer to the Letter from a By-stander to a Member of Parliament', and in his 'Vindication of the Full Answer'. In the controversy Carte got much the better of his antagonist, Corbyn Morris, but he had, for the most part, only the insufficient evidence contained in the Journals of Parliament at his disposal. Dr. Shaw, with the fuller and more detailed evidence afforded by the papers he has calendared, succeeds in proving his case conclusively. But when he goes further, writes as if Charles was entirely blameless, and undertakes a thoroughgoing defence of his foreign policy (vol. v, pp. lxiii–lxxxiii), it becomes impossible to follow him. However, historians will be so grateful to Dr. Shaw for the careful tables of revenue and expenditure he has compiled, for the skill with which he has made financial operations plain, and for the accuracy and conciseness with which he has summarized a great mass of miscellaneous papers, that they will pardon these digressions.

The method in which the calendar is arranged is new, and should be specially mentioned, since it affords an example which may be followed with advantage in future collections of departmental papers. The treasury minute-book forms the text of the calendar. All the other series of treasury records are put in the form of a table, following the text of the minute-book, and printed in smaller type. For instance, the minute-book of 1667 fills 158 pages, and pp. 159–215 consist of letters, warrants, commissions, and other papers. There are difficulties in carrying out this system caused by the imperfections of the records preserved. The minute-book for the period from 17 August 1670 to 2 October 1671 is missing, and its place has to be supplied by memoranda books kept by Sir George Downing containing rough minutes and agenda (vol. iii, p. 323). The volume of the minute-book beginning with October 1671 and ending in November 1672 exists still in the Record Office, but those extending from 1672 to 1689 are missing from the series preserved there. Consequently Dr. Shaw had to search outside the Record Office for the most important part of his materials. The minute-book for Clifford's administration (November 1672—June 1673) could not be discovered anywhere; but a very imperfect substitute was found in the shape of an 'appointment-book', which provided some indications of the business transacted at different meetings of the board. For Danby's administration, June 1673 to March 1679, Dr. Shaw discovered three minute-books covering the whole period, one in the possession of the British Museum, two in the possession of the duke of Leeds, besides other treasury papers of the time. These had been taken away by Danby when he left office, and while part had been sold by his family, part remained in their hands. One can only hope that Dr. Shaw will succeed in tracing the missing minute-books of 1679–89. The history of this calendar shows the necessity of more often suspending the rule which limits the editors of Record Office calendars to papers contained in the office. In consequence of the dispersion of the official papers of the sixteenth and seventeenth centuries there are great gaps in the various series on the shelves of the Record Office. When state papers in private hands come into the market the Record Office cannot fill its gaps by purchasing them, since no money is granted it for that purpose. They are sold to other private collectors or at best bought by the British Museum. It is absurd that when a part of a set of public records are bought with public money they should not be placed in the repository where the rest of the series of records in question are preserved.

C. H. FIRTH.

La Diplomatie secrète au XVIIIe Siècle; ses Débuts. III. *Le Secret de Dubois.* Par ÉMILE BOURGEOIS. (Paris: Colin, *s. a.*)

THIS is the third of a trilogy of secrets, the two former being those of the regent and the Farnesi. It is a somewhat lengthy method of telling secrets, which had indeed much in common, and which were not very closely kept. M. Bourgeois makes the secret of Dubois to consist in sacrificing the national interests to the dynastic ambitions of the regent and his own insatiate love of authority. France after the death of Louis XIV needed peace, and this every one admits. While professing to give her peace, the regent, under the guidance of Dubois, plunged her into active hostilities in the war against Spain, while he defrayed the expenses of war in the Baltic. The Quadruple Alliance in the Mediterranean had its counterpart in the Triple Alliance of England, France, and Sweden in the Baltic, and both were for the benefit of England and to the detriment of France. France, it is urged, should have been the mediator, the angel of peace; instead of this Dubois provoked the war with Spain, a nation and dynasty naturally allied to France, while in the Baltic, after conniving at the dismemberment of Sweden, the ally of the past, he alienated Russia, a most promising ally for the future. It is shown that Dubois's method was indeed directed towards peace, but it consisted in siding with the stronger power in order to enforce it. This principle is ingeniously extended to the religious quarrel in France, for the author points out that Dubois threw his weight upon the side of the papacy and the constitutionalists to overpower the national party and the Jansenists.

This, after all, was the system considered by Machiavelli as essential to a weak state, for which he regarded neutrality as ruinous. Now France during the early days of the regency was a relatively weak state, just as England was a relatively strong one. It is improbable that the benevolent and impartial neutrality of France would have been accepted, and she would then have been forced to support the weaker combatant. France, moreover, is a highly sensitive nation, and at the moment when she has suffered humiliation is the most eager to reassert herself. The policy of Dubois, therefore, in so far as it was militant, was in accord with the temperament and traditions of the nation; nor does the author deny that the regent made a considerable figure in European politics, though he paid too dearly for it. It may be admitted that in Spain the policy of France, as that of England, was precipitate and brutal. In the Baltic she did not engage in actual hostilities, but she subsidized the Swedish fleet, and bought off the Danish attack on Sweden, and all this to secure Bremen and Verden for her Hanoverian ally. Yet, if she had not intervened, Sweden would have been irretrievably lost. The power of Russia was in *posse* rather than in *esse*, and Peter, and still less his successor, could not be regarded as a friend to be trusted. The naturalness of a Franco-Russian alliance is antedated; it is doubtful whether the aggrandizement of Russia was to the interest of France, when Prussia was as yet France's probable counterpoise to the Habsburgs. Again, it may be doubted whether Spain and France were kindred spirits. The Spaniards had much devotion for Philip, who had stood to his post when Louis XIV decided on withdrawal;

but there was no friendly feeling at all for the French nation, the secular enemy of Spain, and, if Philip had deserted his throne for that of France, loyalty would have given place to passionate indignation. The insistence of Dubois on the Orleanist claim is regarded as a crime, but it was a recognized fact in the law of Europe, and its abrogation must have been followed by a revival of the War of the Spanish Succession. The action of Dubois tided the danger over; every year that he could fight off Philip's claim was a year gained for the strength and growth of the delicate boy king.

M. Bourgeois divides Dubois's policy sharply into two halves, the alliance with England and the alliance with Spain, the treaty of Hanover and the treaty of Madrid. He skilfully converts a chapter on Law into a hinge between the two halves. Dubois's attack on the System is, indeed, represented as being engineered by Stanhope, who throughout plays the Mephistopheles to Dubois's Faust, whilst to France falls the part of Marguerite. The fall of Law suited England, but Dubois, to avert a powerful combination against himself, had to make his peace with the royal bastards and the old court, and, for this end, to throw himself into the arms ostensibly of Spain, but really into those of the Farnesi. Dubois, it may be said, surrendered to the duke of Parma, that is, to the principle of war against the emperor in Italy. But he showed his skill by accepting the principle, but indefinitely postponing the fact. The reconciliation between Philip V and Orleans, purchased at the expense of France by the surrender of Pensacola, was followed by the accession of England to the treaty of Madrid. This is explained as being due to her weakness, caused by the split in her government and the ruinous results of the South Sea Bubble. The force of this change of policy is perhaps exaggerated. Both England and France were all along not so much opposed to the claims of the Farnesi as to their methods, and England's change of front was due less to weakness than to determination that France should not monopolize Spanish commercial favour. The alliance between the Spanish and French courts was cemented by the Orleans-Spanish marriages. It was indeed a triumph for Orleans that one daughter should sit on the throne of Spain and another on that of a considerable state to be formed in Italy. France unquestionably paid a heavy price in the betrothal of the growing king to the child infanta, and the postponement of his marriage opened new chances for the Orleanist succession. Nevertheless, France did avert grave internal and external dangers by the reconciliation with Philip and his voluntary abandonment of his claim.

The last act of Dubois was to prepare for a possible war with the Habsburgs by the reconciliation of the tsar with England and Sweden. Here again Orleanist interests were in the forefront, for a marriage was being negotiated between the Duc de Chartres and Peter's daughter Elisabeth, with the prospect of the reversion of the crown of Poland. Too much weight must, perhaps, not be attributed to this scheme, for the beautiful young girl was tossed at the heads of many princes, at that of Louis XV among others.

In spite of the author's invective against Dubois's foreign policy, he is fair to his personal character. After close examination he concludes that, while corrupting others, he was himself incorruptible. Having given an excellent account of the skill with which Dubois shouldered out every enemy or rival, he admits his fruitful labours for the efficiency of the army, and for a sounder system of taxation, finance, and commerce. The chief indictment is his initiation of the evil practice of secret, unofficial agents such as Lafiteau, Destouches, Chavigny, and Mornay, from whose correspondence he derives his newest and most interesting matter. It is true that Dubois carried this system to an unprecedented length, but the history of the treaty of Utrecht alone would prove that it was nothing new, and Alberoni is a striking personal example.

The volume is a little over long, but the mechanism is skilful, and the arguments are forcibly thrust home. Italian geography is not the author's *forte*. He makes the Spaniards at Palermo issue from the lava beds of Etna to attack the Austrians. Parma and Tuscany are described as occupying *tout le centre de l'Italie du Tibre au Pô*, and separating *en deux tronçons les domaines de l'Empire*. He forgets that Modena was thrust in as a wedge between Parma and Tuscany, that the latter only touched the uppermost Tiber at a single point, and that the Austrians had a straight run from Mantua through Papal Ferrara and Bologna to the great southern highroad, without touching the intended Farnesi state.   E. ARMSTRONG.

J. P. BRISSOT, *Mémoires (1754–93) publiés avec Étude critique et Notes*. Par C. PERROUD. (Paris: Picard, s. a.)

THE memoirs of Brissot, edited by F. de Montrol, were first published in the years 1830–2. Neither then nor at any later time was the original manuscript forthcoming, and, from the first, doubts were expressed as to the authenticity of the memoirs. Some years afterwards Quérard stated positively that part of the third and the whole of the fourth volume were the work of Lhéritier, a literary hack, who had succeeded Montrol as editor. Montrol himself had hinted at certain liberties taken with the text by himself and by Lhéritier. He also used expressions implying that there was no one complete manuscript of the memoirs, but a number of fragmentary manuscripts hastily thrown together by Brissot and therefore marked by a confusion and an incoherence which would tempt an editor to complete and to harmonize. All these circumstances suggested the need of a careful investigation. This M. Perroud undertook, and the results are set forth in his critical introduction. They illustrate what critics know so well, the unsatisfactory character of ' contemporary memoirs ' as sources of history.

That Brissot did write memoirs, and that the original editors worked upon manuscripts from his pen, M. Perroud thinks certain. But these manuscripts not being enough to furnish out a full biography, the editors supplemented them in various ways. The edition of 1830–2 was in four volumes containing about 1,300 pages of text. Close examination showed M. Perroud that about 600 pages had been transferred by them from the published writings of Brissot, especially from the newspaper edited by him during the revolution, the *Patriote Français*. About 100 more were made up of letters written by or to Brissot which the editors had found in different places and inserted in the text, modifying it so far as was necessary to make them fit neatly. Worse still, they incorporated with the memoirs certain compositions of other men. So far we are on solid ground, for these borrowings, or more correctly thefts, can be verified by comparison with their originals. But there remain many pages of doubtful origin. Long before the Revolution Brissot was a journalist, and some of his fugitive writings are now probably lost. Various portions of the published memoirs which break the narrative and look suspicious may have been taken from these missing articles. They may have been purloined from other authors who cannot be identified, or may in some cases have been the composition of the editors or of friends whom the editors wished to oblige by letting them speak through Brissot. Thus out of 1,300 pages there remain, according to M. Perroud, about 500 which we may regard as authentic and about 100 more which are doubtful.

The 500 authentic pages fall into two masses. First, we have a more or less continuous autobiography down to the year 1787. Secondly, we have certain documents with belong to the very close of Brissot's career; an account of his flight from Paris and of his arrest at Moulins, a reply to the report in which St. Just attacked the Girondins and the text of Brissot's defence before the revolutionary tribunal. Thus for the earlier years of the revolution, when Brissot was most actively engaged in politics and became the leader of a party, the years which should have furnished the most valuable part of the memoirs, we have little or nothing which we can treat as fully authentic. During that period Brissot probably lacked the time, even if he felt the wish, to write memoirs. The original editors filled the gap with materials such as we have described above. These pages are singularly barren of information concerning Brissot and the Girondins. They consist chiefly of rambling disquisitions on the *Société des Amis des Noirs*, on Barnave, on Lafayette, and on other politicians of the time. In the present edition the 600 pages of the original issue which can be traced with certainty to the published writings of Brissot or of other men have been omitted, with certain exceptions specified in the notes. The letters inserted by the first editors are likewise omitted, as M. Perroud means to include them in an edition of Brissot's correspondence. The suspect pages have been retained, but are printed in smaller type. In dealing with that part of the original issue which covered the years from 1787 to 1793, M. Perroud, if we understand him aright, has been more lenient than elsewhere, keeping much that his predecessors had stolen from the *Patriote Français* and other sources. To this he was no doubt prompted by the dislike of too great a breach in the continuity of the memoirs. But in the notes he has stated his suspicions and reservations with sufficient clearness to save the student from being misled.

F. C. MONTAGUE.

Paris pendant la Terreur; Rapports des Agents secrets du Ministre de l'Intérieur, publiés pour la Société d'Histoire Contemporaine. Par PIERRE CARON. Tome I. (Paris: Picard, 1910.)

THIS is the first volume of a collection of reports sent in to the minister of the interior by his secret agents during the reign of terror. The secret agents were appointed in pursuance of a suggestion made in May 1793 by Garat, then minister, to the provisional executive council. The system was to cover all France as well as Paris, although the peculiar importance of the capital demanded an exceptional number of agents. The functions of these agents were various, but the most essential was to report daily upon the state of public feeling and opinion. They continued at work until Robespierre and St. Just had gained a complete ascendancy. Thinking, or professing to think, that the system of secret information had been the instrument of their rivals, particularly of Danton, these rulers suppressed it in Germinal, Year II, after a duration of eleven months. M. Caron has concerned himself only with the reports of the agents for Paris. Although many have been lost, enough remain to form a large mass of manuscript. Those for the period ending with July 1793 have already been published by Schmidt in his well-known *Tableaux de la Révolution Française*, and therefore have not been reprinted here. For the ensuing months there are extant no less than 1,463 originals, together with official extracts from others which have perished. A few of these had been published either by Schmidt or by Dauban in his *La Démagogie en 1793 à Paris*, and *Paris en 1794 et 1795*. Nevertheless M. Caron has thought well to publish them all in the present collection. The volume before us covers the period from August to Christmas 1793. The editor appears to have done his work with extreme care, his introduction and notes affording all the help that a student can desire.

The reports contain a medley of interesting and sometimes amusing information. They are naturally most copious on the subject which caused most anxiety to the rulers of Paris, the supply of necessaries, especially of bread and fuel. We read of bakers who put ashes in the bread to make it heavier and to disgust people with the government, and of grocers who sold lamp oil for olive oil, a still more effective expedient. There are occasional references to engrossers. We have, what is more surprising, bold criticisms of the Maximum. Some agents assert that, since the enactment of the law, the markets have been worse and worse furnished, that Paris is in danger of famine, that the peasants will not send in supplies, that all circulation is arrested, that some amendment is imperative. The reports also contain many notices of public sentiment on religious matters and of the attendance at places of worship. One reporter urges that the principle of tolerance professed by the convention should be enforced, and all attacks on worshippers strictly punished. Another says that the people, when assembled, march with giant steps towards the abolition of religious prejudices, but doubts 'whether they preserve their *aplomb* in the bosom of their families'. A third remarks that the ancient festivals are still respected, and that the markets were generally deserted on Christmas Day.

Women sometimes attracted the attention of these reporters. They note the disturbances caused by an order of the commune that no woman without the tricolor cockade should be admitted to public buildings or gardens. It is singular that under the reign of terror the fishwives should sometimes have presumed to flog such persons of their sex as obeyed this order. Certain of the disaffected sought to persuade women that they had as much right as men to a share in the government and to all civil and military employments. Women, often with babies in arms, crowded the courts of justice, so that the din of cries and conversation made it hard even for the judges to hear what was going on. Women also delighted to attend the sittings of the convention, of the Jacobin club, and of the popular assemblies, where, as one of the reporters rudely remarks, they often ' fill the place of a citizen who might·be useful to the Republic by his reflections'. Much is said about public amusements. We read of one Sunday in September 1793 that the park at St. Cloud was full of parties dancing and picnicking, and that this frank and keen enjoyment could be the portion of none but a free people. Gaming-houses are said to have multiplied lately and to be shelters for aristocrats. The theatres naturally attracted the observation of the secret agents. Some deplore the licentious character of the ordinary play. Others concern themselves with the political influence of the stage. The play of *Mutius Scaevola* glows with the love of liberty and the hatred of tyrants, but it unhappily depicts Porsenna as extorting by his virtue the esteem of the Romans. And what proves the danger of the piece—' As I went out, I heard somebody say, " This Porsenna might very well be the duke of York." ' The *Père de famille* of Diderot, ' the work of a severe philosopher,' is undoubtedly one of the best dramas which have come down from the monarchical period, but it represents the old order of society in too favourable a light. Such themes are demoralizing. ' Somebody will say, " Must we always have Brutus ? " Yes, always Brutus, and woe to him who shall tire of listening to the proud language of freedom.' F. C. MONTAGUE.

1809; Campagne de Pologne. Vol. I. Par WLADYSLAW DE FEDOROWICZ. (Paris : Plon, 1911.)

THAT detachments should be avoided or only made when there is some very special need is one of the most elementary of strategical maxims, but it is among the commonplaces of military history that Napoleon's hardly-won victory of Wagram might have been a disastrous defeat had the Austrians seen fit to call in to that battlefield some of the many corps which they were at that time employing in other quarters. One of these absent detachments was the force of 30,000 men under the Archduke Ferdinand, who were operating in Galicia and Poland, and had enjoyed the barren triumph of driving Poniatowski's Poles out of Warsaw. The elucidation of this somewhat unfamiliar episode in the campaign has been undertaken by M. Wladyslaw de Fedorowicz, and volume i of his *1809, Campagne de Pologne*, contains his collection of documents in the French language bearing on the subject. Other volumes will be devoted to the documents in other languages. When these volumes are published the student of the campaign of 1809 will know where to look for evidence on this part of his subject, but the present volume is naturally somewhat incomplete. M. de Fedorowicz has not as yet attempted to set forth the results of his researches. However, there is a good deal to be learnt from the perusal of this portion of the evidence. One has plenty of proof that Austria was expecting support from the other German states, not merely from Prussia and from the north-west of Germany, where the population was certainly already hostile to Napoleon, but also from the south parts of Germany which remained faithful to the emperor until late in 1813. Thus one report (p. 149) represents Bavaria as likely to assist the Austrians should they take the offensive against Napoleon, and the districts which had formerly been under Austrian rule are reported as being extremely keen to rise (p. 18). More importance perhaps attaches to the projects for Anglo-Austrian co-operation, Italy and north Germany being the districts indicated as those in which England might best assist her ally. Indeed one object put before the Austrian troops in Poland is the securing of Dantzic to facilitate a descent by an English force (p. 320). The Austrian government does certainly seem to have grasped the possibilities of utilizing our command of the sea to affect the military situation in Europe, and the various documents dealing with the topic only make it clearer than ever that if England had been sufficiently well organized and prepared to profit by her chances on the continent in 1809, Napoleon's defeat might have been anticipated by several years. As this correspondence makes clear, Prussia was quite near to joining in as it was, and if Russia did go so far towards keeping her pledges to Napoleon as to send troops into Galicia the invasion was a mere form (p. 320), and was treated as such by the Austrians. C. T. ATKINSON.

Garibaldi and the Making of Italy. By GEORGE MACAULAY TREVELYAN. (London : Longmans, 1911.)

Cavour. Von WALTER FRIEDENSBURG. Band I. (Gotha: F. A. Perthes, 1911.)

MR. TREVELYAN has concluded with this volume his Garibaldian trilogy, for he announces that he does not propose to write of Aspromonte, Mentana, Dijon, and the appearance of his hero in parliament at Rome. From the artistic point of view he is right—and he is certainly a great literary artist ; but it could have been wished that so sympathetic and yet so sensible a critic had seen his way to describe for us in detail the results of the Garibaldian epic. The present volume, occupied exclusively with the latter half of that *longus et unus annus*, 1860, is based, like its predecessors, upon personal knowledge of the ground, upon first-hand study of documents (in which the author has had the aid of Sir Rennell Rodd and Mr. Nelson Gay, the two Anglo-Saxons in Rome who know most about the *Risorgimento*), and upon conversations with the dwindling band of surviving Garibaldians. For specialists the most important pages of the book are those which contain Victor Emmanuel II's two secret letters to Garibaldi in Sicily (pp. 102, 116), and those which describe Sir J. Lacaita's visit to Lord John Russell, whereby Great Britain was induced to reject the French proposal to prevent Garibaldi's crossing to Calabria (pp. 105-8). These three incidents form the clue to all that followed.

Mr. Trevelyan, however, does not write for specialists alone, but also for the general public, which, fifty years after these events, has rather a hazy idea of ' the making of Italy '. For that large class of reader the book may be warmly recommended ; for, although its author makes no concealment of his strongly liberal sentiments, he can see the faults of the Garibaldians and admit the bravery of those adherents of a lost cause who rallied round their king at Gaeta. He lets us see clearly what Neapolitans tell us now, that the open referendum at Naples on the question of union did not express the real feelings of a not inconsiderable minority, while he quotes the prescient remark of Sir James Hudson, that the junction of the Neapolitans with northern Italy would not improve the tone of Italian public life. Crispi, to whom Mr. Trevelyan scarcely does justice, was adverse to the hasty *plébiscite* at Naples and in favour of autonomy for Sicily; and Italian politicians to-day, except in after-dinner speeches, seem to agree that uniformity of legislation for all parts of a country of such different traditions and of such various planes of civilization and education is a mistake, further accentuated by the fact that, for economic reasons, while the civil service is mainly composed of southerners, the solid commercial interests are chiefly in the north. Thus, the south makes public, and especially foreign, policy and the north pays for it. Mr. Trevelyan says little about the British legion, of whose deeds much was heard in Rome last summer from the mouths of the nine chosen survivors, who were then the guests of the municipality. He criticizes the ingratitude of Victor Emmanuel II to the Garibaldians, who had won him a kingdom (p. 278); but harder still was the lot of the combatants at Mentana, who had to wait thirty-eight years for their pension.

Excellent scholar as he is, Mr. Trevelyan makes one or two slips in translation. Thus (p. 134), *pescare* does not mean to 'give a ducking'; it is the very common Italian vulgarism for *trovare*. 'Mongibello,' the local name for Etna, is not 'the fair mountain', but is composed of both the Italian and the Arabic words for 'mountain'; such bilingual combinations, e.g. 'Linguaglossa,' are found in the south of Italy. Similarly, we believe that 'Aspromonte' is not 'the rugged mountain', but 'the white mountain'—a name half Greek, half Latin. Nor is it ethnographically correct to say that 'no alien race dwells beside the Italian within the boundaries of the Peninsula'. Italy contains 100,000 Albanians, a Slav colony near Cividale, not a few Greeks in Calabria, Saracen blood in Sicily, an Aragonese settlement, still speaking Catalan, at Alghero in Sardinia. When Mr. Trevelyan wrote, it was true to say that Italian nationalism had not been directed to conquest abroad. But that was before Tripoli.

Much has been written about Cavour, and the two recent anniversaries—the centenary of his birth and the jubilee of his death—have added considerably to the literature. There seems accordingly to be no special reason why Dr. Friedensburg's work should have been published; and its author, who has lived long in Italy, might have more usefully employed his knowledge of the Italian character to the elucidation of that neglected period of Italian history—the last four decades. His only unpublished source is the correspondence of the Prussian legation at Turin; and, if he writes agreeably, he adds little to our information about a statesman so well known as Cavour. Not a single reference is given to the authorities for the statements made in the text. This first volume deals with the life of Cavour before he became a minister in 1850. His farming operations at Leri and his brief experience of journalism in connexion with the moderate liberal *Risorgimento* are of no particular interest, for the future statesman was an average farmer and an indifferent journalist, not quite sure of the language in which he wrote. Of far greater importance for his political development were his two visits to England in 1835 and 1843, which deeply impressed him, though here the author's unfamiliarity with the Inns of Court has led him to make some strange solecisms in his description of his hero's legal investigations (p. 96). Cavour returned from England a strenuous opponent of the Repeal of the Union and a convinced free-trader; but his confident forecast of the speedy triumph of the latter principle has been signally falsified in the case of his own country, whose 508 deputies are, with, at the most, two exceptions, ardent protectionists—for Italy. Cavour's three unsuccessful attempts to enter parliament in April 1848 are described, and his failure attributed to his aristocratic birth—even to-day a disadvantage to an Italian candidate. His subsequent defeat in January 1849 was due to the suspicion that he was a reactionary. At the present moment, when the reform of the Italian senate has been recently under discussion, his opinion in favour of an elective upper house is worth citing (p. 274). WILLIAM MILLER.

The Progress of Japan, 1853–71. By J. H. GUBBINS, C.M.G. (Oxford: Clarendon Press, 1911.)

IN this volume Mr. Gubbins gives the best account extant in any western language of the constitutional history of Japan from the visit of Commodore Perry in 1853 to the abandonment of its peculiar feudalism in 1871. The course of events is described from an inside rather than from an outside point of view, and the story is based mainly upon Japanese documents: hence of western diplomacy, as of western commerce as well as of military matters, scarcely any notice is taken; even so prominent a person as Sir Harry Parkes is barely mentioned. This neglect is pushed somewhat too far; Mr. Gubbins might urge in defence considerations of space, and perhaps the policy of the Foreign Office that still withholds from students the greater and most interesting portion of the diplomatic correspondence of the period. The omission, however, is to be regretted as it somewhat adds to the difficulty of understanding the policy of Japan during the transition from the Bakufu to the Meiji system of government.

Now that we know more about it that transition is shorn of most of its mystery. Through a brief sketch of old Japanese history and polity Mr. Gubbins leads up to a picture of the Japanese state at the close of the Tokugawa era. The Mikado at Kiōto was a mere shadow even *de iure*; the Kubo or Shōgun was, not seldom, not much more than a shadow *de facto* at Yedo. The country was divided into some two hundred and sixty daimiates of Shōgunal creation, possessed of almost unlimited home rule yet held together by a feeling of *chiushin* or loyalty or submission that was extremely strong in old Japan, and that was exhibited towards the Shōgun in conjunction with a vaguely dominant reverence for the Mikado, both loyalty and reverence being shown rather to the office than the person of Mikado or Shōgun. Such a polity was one of unstable equilibrium, and was maintained by various regulations which restricted the independence of the daimios, prevented their combination, and kept the Kiōto court in tutelage. The downfall of the whole system was, and could not but be, rapid when it came, and was only in part due to the advent of the foreigner. The Tokugawa administration bore within it the seeds of its own ruin ; as the memory of its founder faded the prestige of the Kubo diminished, and the visit of Commodore Perry, in all probability, merely hastened the fall of an already loosened structure. The first evident symptom of its approaching ruin was the weakness shown by the Yedo government in 1853 and again in 1858, when it submitted the question of the treaties to the approval of the court at Kiōto. There was no need for this reference, for, as Mr. Gubbins shows, the supremacy of the Shōgun, in all administrative matters, was clearly laid down in article 2 of the Kiōto Arrangement of 7 September 1615, made no doubt at the instance of Iyeyasu himself, who died in 1616. Again, even the Tokugawa house was divided against itself. Tokugawa Nariaki, the ex-prince of Mito, was a strong supporter of the *Jō-i* or court party, which took advantage of the conduct of the Yedo government in 1853 and 1858 to manipulate the feeling against foreigners—an adventitious, not a natural or originally national feeling, as the history of the Christian century and the treaty with James I agreed to by Iyeyasu, the founder of the Tokugawa system, show—so as to serve the hostility of the south and west, which had never come so completely under Tokugawa influences as the rest of the country. Keiki, the last of the Shōguns, originally nominated as guardian of the young Taikun by Nariaki, was himself rather a *Jō-i* partisan than a defender of the Yedo (his own) government. The famous Ii Kamon no Kami was the protagonist on the other side, but was assassinated by Mito outlaws in 1860, and he had no successor. Hence in the struggle with the western clans, which lasted through the sixties, the Tokugawa party was bound to succumb in the end, and with the fall of the Shōgun in 1868 the whole system crumbled away.

The immediate cause was the ultimate defeat of the Shōgun's forces in the war of 1866 with Chōshiu, which was the renewal not easily explained of a more successful but still inconclusive struggle in 1865. How it came about that the Shōgun's party was defeated in spite of its superior position and advantages in connexion with foreign trade is not quite clear—the result has been ascribed to the inferiority of the rank and file of the eastern army. The story is very briefly told by Mr. Gubbins, and further elucidation seems necessary. Even before the victory of the Kiōto party was assured the *Jō-i* policy was practically abandoned, the very policy for not carrying out which the whole opposition of the victors had been sustained from 1853 to the abolition of the Shōgunate. Here again elucidation is desirable, but the time has not yet come, if it ever will or indeed can, for a complete history of the years 1860–68. Very probably no real elucidation is possible ; Japanese parties found themselves in a totally new position, there were no precedents to help them, and they were divided among themselves upon the question of foreign intercourse, to which, in reality, the opposition was in the main that merely of *omne ignotum pro terribili*. As already stated, and as is very sufficiently shown by Mr. Gubbins, after the fall of the Shōgunate that of feudalism became a necessity. Its rapidity is not astonishing when the peculiar constitution of the clans, well set forth in the present volume, is considered: it was in fact no one's interest to maintain the system, and the *samurai* profited more than any other class by the abolition of a many-graded tyranny which cramped their energies and kept them in poverty and obscurity ill-compensated by a profitless and tedious dignity of position.

There are many interesting pages in Mr. Gubbins's work. He gives an excellent account of the system of delegation of power in old Japan, whose motto might have been *agere per alium*, which coupled with the practice of abdication, public and private, and adoption, combined, after a curious fashion, a certain stability of state and family with great party and individual uncertainty. The story of the negotiation of the various treaties and of the first emergences of Japan from its isolation of centuries is well narrated, and full allowance is made for the difficulties she had to overcome. Justice again is done to the character of the people, of whom Dr. Ainslie, sent to Japan by Sir Stamford Raffles in 1813, spoke in high terms, as the missionaries had done in the sixteenth century. The race is indeed a happy mixture of various elements that once achieved has been permitted to develop in a healthy segregation from untoward influences. The book is no mere compilation, it is the fruit of very considerable research based upon Japanese as well as foreign authorities. In the appendices will be found the principal treaties, including the Russian treaty, not previously, I believe, published in any English work; and among other interesting Japanese documents the extremely curious and valuable 'Statement of Reasons for the Shōgun's Resignation', presented by the Japanese minister to the foreign representatives in November 1867, is in itself a summary of the history of the transition. F. VICTOR DICKINS.

A History of Perugia. By WILLIAM HEYWOOD. (London : Methuen, 1910.)

MR. HEYWOOD'S *History of Perugia* is the best account of medieval Perugia in English. The author expressly states that he has limited his inquiry to printed sources. This is not to say that the resulting product does not thoroughly deserve the epithet of 'original', for these sources have never yet been consistently worked; and within the limits imposed the author has been most diligent. His strongest point lies in the methodical setting out of the annals of the Commune during its great formative period down to the Sienese war (1358). But the book does not satisfactorily fulfil the promise of its title. It compares unfavourably with the *History of Siena* of Mr. Langton Douglas, not merely in the quality of readableness, but in its grasp of the entire spirit and life of the people of the city-state. As he reaches the sixteenth century the author's ecclesiastical bias so ostentatiously paraded diminishes confidence in the validity of his judgements. The main defect of his work as a history of the Umbrian city is that Mr. Heywood has little or no interest in his subject beyond the close of the medieval period. It may be that the administration and civic life of Perugia subsequent to 1500 are not specially attractive, but the reader may well desire an opportunity of deciding that for himself:

Mr. Heywood allows four pages, mostly of polemic. Admitting that the city was in a peculiar sense ground under the heel of papal despotism—which may well be disputed—there is all the better reason for illustrating from such harsh experience the methods of papal rule, and the causes of its inevitable limitations and defects. In any case a sincere attempt to understand and to exhibit the lot of Perugia and its citizens, its administration, its economy, its learning and art, during the three centuries which divide Paul III from Victor Emanuel is essential to a complete history of the state. There is ample material for such an inquiry, and an adequate account of the organization of papal rule outside of Rome during the seventeenth and eighteenth centuries is much needed. In this connexion the editors would be well advised in urging the excision of certain exaggerations which disfigure pp. 331-5. It is questionable whether historians should encourage the lax use of the term ' feudal ' which, for example, marks Mr. Heywood's argument upon the relation of Perugia to its *contado* and to its conquered subject communes. Are we to regard the church as 'feudal' over-lord to its vicariates, such as Urbino or Rimini? It will not be long before the king of England is described as ' the feudal superior' of the Khedive. The importance of the period of Gianpaolo Baglioni is scarcely realized by Mr. Heywood. The Borgia adventures in Umbria paved the way directly for the work of the Farnese pope. The co-operation of the lord of Perugia with Vitellozzo in the attack on Arezzo in 1502 brought Machiavelli on to the scene of Borgia politics; it led to the determination of Cesare to stamp out the pestiferous brood of the Condottieri, to the defensible executions of Sinigaglia, and indirectly, with other causes, to a profound revolution in Italian military organization.

A bibliographical list of all works quoted is essential to such a book as the present. The maps and plans are scarcely adequate. When will Italian geographers give us an authoritative historical atlas of their country in necessary detail? W. H. WOODWARD.

Geschiedenis eener Hollandsche Stad. Eene hollandsche Stad in de Middeleeuwen. Door P. J. BLOK. ('s Gravenhage : Nijhoff, 1910.)

THIS is a new and entirely revised edition of Professor Blok's history of Leyden in the middle ages, which first appeared in 1888. The book in its earlier form had been undertaken at the suggestion and under the inspiration of the writer's master and predecessor in the field of Dutch history, Robert Fruin, and was based on a thorough study both of the municipal and national archives. But great progress has been achieved since then in the study of civic origins in general, and important contributions have been recently made to the history of Leyden, so that Professor Blok had an adequate motive, as he had happily adequate energy, for a thorough revision of his earlier work. Though it embodies a great mass of new material the original plan of the book has been preserved. After a first chapter dealing with origins (little is known of Leyden before the thirteenth century), a second discussing the charters of the city, and a third surveying the topography in the fourteenth century, the remainder of the book is distributed under subject headings—the *burggraf*, the *landsheer*, the civic constitution, the *poorters*, gilds and crafts, markets and trade, law, finance, charitable and religious institutions. This method has obvious disadvantages. It breaks up chronological sequence and renders difficult anything like artistic unity. But it secures serious scientific consideration for what are now recognized as the specific problems of medieval municipal history. Thus the valuable account of the functions of the *burggraf*, and of the persistence of the office in the hands of the van Kuik and van Wassenar families until the loss of its more effectual powers in 1421, not only serves to supplement the recent exhaustive researches of Dr. Rietschel in respect to the episcopal cities of Germany, but might help to cast a light on the position of Geoffrey de Mandeville and the claims of Robert FitzWalter in regard to London. So, too, the careful study of civic finance in its several aspects, i.e. the constitutional relations with the *landsheer*, the distribution of the burden of taxation, the transition from direct taxes (*schot*) to the indirect excise, and the development of a system of loans and annuities, whilst it clearly owes much to the recent researches of Bücher, Pirenne, Kuske and others, would provide the student of English municipal finance with a helpful supplement to Miss Bateson's *Records of Leicester*.

The history of Leyden and of other Dutch towns before the Reformation has more in common than that of the Flemish and Rhenish cities with the history of the larger English towns during the same period. In both cases the constitution generally exhibits a continuance of the older magisterial forms—court leet or portmanmoot corresponding to *schout* and *schepen*—unbroken by any such 'gild-revolution' as occurred in Cologne, in Ghent, and in London during the fourteenth century. But the municipal oligarchy of Leyden was narrower and more feudally dependent than was usual in English towns of the same size. The functions of the *schout* and *schepen*, whose offices were not secured from alienation by the lord to outsiders till the charter of 1434 and which till 1421 were subject to the hereditary control of the *burggraf*, were supplemented by a curiously restricted *raad* of four *burgemeesters* or *poortmeesters* chosen one from each ward by the *vroedschap*, who numbered some sixty persons at the end of the fourteenth century and who correspond roughly to the 'Forty-eight' of English boroughs. This body formed the base of the civic oligarchy, and was composed of those who had held office and might hold it again. According to Professor Blok, the gilds, whether of merchants or craftsmen, played an entirely subordinate and almost negligible part in the constitutional development of Leyden. This would differentiate Leyden widely from the English parallels. In the more typical English boroughs the apparent continuity of the older legal forms was only secured by conceding the substance of power to the gild, which, as it had been mainly instrumental in procuring civic independence, either continued as a private association to supply the social force that worked the constitution (e.g. at Coventry), or remained alongside the portmote as a co-ordinate institution, in some cases gradually displacing it (e.g. at Southampton), in others being itself gradually absorbed (e.g. at Leicester), but in all cases contributing largely to the development of the constitution.

The highly interesting account given by Professor Blok of the gilds of Leyden, whilst it certainly seems to show that the principal merchant gild had no directly formative influence on the constitution, does not preclude the possibility of its having exercised, as elsewhere, a large informal power. The comparative lateness of its authorization in 1393 does not tell against this possibility any more than in the exactly contemporary cases of the greater London companies. The fact of the gild being dedicated to St. Nicholas tells strongly in favour of it (since St. Nicholas was the favourite patron saint of market churches and merchant gilds founded in the twelfth and thirteenth centuries), and so does the designation of its members as ' Calissenobels ', i.e. those who traded to Calais for wool. Such a class may be presumed to have played the same leading part in the early government of Leyden as the *Englandfahrer* did in that of Cologne and the members of the Hanse of London in that of Bruges.

English readers will be interested in an account (p. 204) of a treaty with England in 1428, when Leyden regained its share of the wool-supply through Calais by timely concession in the mercantile law of debt. The regulation of the important textile industry, the development of a system of civic poor relief, the struggle of Leyden with Dort as to staple rights, and the beginnings of civic mercantilism, as described in the later chapters (where the recent researches of Drs. Posthumus and Ligtenberg have been available) furnish admirable materials for the comparative study of municipal history. Two excellent maps are added, and a number of illustrative documents including a series of civic budgets.

GEORGE UNWIN.

Short Notices

IN *La Synthèse en Histoire, Essai Critique et Théorique* (Paris: Alcan, 1911), M. Henri Berr, the learned editor of the *Revue de Synthèse Historique*, has undertaken to survey the more recent controversies which have been waged, in his own journal and elsewhere, over the fundamental problems of historical method. The survey is admittedly incomplete, since German theories are reserved for discussion in a later volume, and English theories receive little or no attention. It is a shock to discover that the late Dr. Reich is regarded, on the other side of the Channel, as the leading exponent of British historical method. The work of Professor Flint, though in form only an exposition of continental theories, deserved better treatment than a passing reference in a footnote. The inaugural lecture of Professor Bury is a plea for scientific method at least as cogent as any of those which M. Berr has analysed; and it is singular that he should altogether ignore the name and the views of Lord Acton. *Le pragmatisme anglo-saxon* is duly reviewed in a footnote; but more pains should have been taken to discover and explain the views of English historians. We have no doubt that the promised account of the German literature will be laborious and exhaustive. But we cannot imagine a more arbitrary *principium divisionis*, in a work of this character, than that of language or nationality. Historical schools of thought are no longer to be defined by geographical frontiers. The truth is that M. Berr has the defects of his qualities; there is too much of mere erudition, too little of logical synthesis, in this elaborate essay. We are grateful for the bibliographical information which can be collected from his pages. But we cannot help feeling that he would have done more to advance the discussion with which he is concerned, if he had been less meticulous in his attention to second-rate and third-rate dissertations. For, as one reads, it becomes apparent that the serious debates on historical method are at present confined to a small number of issues. It seems that the future of historical method depends upon the issue of a struggle for existence between two schools of thought which are not primarily historical. On the one hand there are the intuitionists, led by Croce and Bergson, who would have the historian adopt the methods of aesthetic. On the other hand the sociologists of Durkheim's following emphasize the dependence of the individual upon the social consciousness, and maintain that history, if it is to be a fruitful study, should investigate the institutions and the phenomena of social life, with the ultimate object of exploring and describing the 'collective mind'. Of intuitional philosophy we have heard a good deal in England, where M. Bergson is at present more discussed than any other metaphysician. The central idea of Durkheim is more familiar to us than the writings of his school, since in a somewhat obscure and confused form it has inspired not only Green's *Short History of the English*

People but also the profounder studies of our constitutional historians, from Stubbs downwards. But on English soil the idea has languished from want of scientific development, and from the fact that it has been applied to a relatively narrow field of historical research. It appears to us that Durkheim has at least sketched the outlines of a working method ; and that the intuitionists, with all their criticisms, have only indicated some limitations of his theory. It is not adequate to explain all social phenomena, and it is a dangerous instrument if used without intelligence. It is properly applicable only to the conventions, the traditional ideas, the established usages of society. But every historian will admit that the study of these subjects is always important for his purpose and is sometimes all-important.

H. W. C. D.

In the second part of his *Recherches sur l'Histoire et la Civilisation de l'ancienne Égypte* (Leipzig : Hinrichs, 1911) the late Professor J. Lieblein carried on his researches from the eighteenth dynasty to the end of the twenty-fifth, interspersing the historical sketch with ingenious notes and excursuses in order to combat errors which have crept into standard works. A section identifying the *anti* tree (found by Queen Hatshepsut in Punt) with the *Boswellia* which produces frankincense is especially useful for the good illustrations. At the end is a tabular view of the kings from the nineteenth to the twenty-sixth dynasties, along with contemporary high priests of Ammon, Apis bulls, and various genealogical material : it shows at a glance Lieblein's peculiar arrangement of the dynasties, essential to his chronology, and impossible to disprove. It is curious, however, that the ' divine wives ' of Ammon are here still counted as regular queens, the consorts of the king and the carnal mothers of their adopted ' daughters '. The religious-political system of adoption inaugurated by the Ethiopians for securing the influence and the vast estates of the Theban Ammon to the reigning family has become sufficiently clear in the last few years, and monuments have been found naming the real mother as well as the religious or adoptive mother ; but all this is ignored by Lieblein. Notwithstanding, there is much that demands respectful attention in the views of the lamented Egyptologist.

F. Ll. G.

Signor Corrado Barbagallo's work on *Lo Stato e l'Istruzione pubblica nell'Impero Romano* (Catania : Battiati, 1911) was undertaken, as the author tells us in his introduction, because there was no monograph on the subject in the Italian language, and none at all covering exactly the same ground. His object has been to trace, from Augustus to Justinian (including both reigns), the relations of the Roman state to teachers, students, educational and literary institutions, the preservation of monuments, physical and musical training and competitions, and all else that comes under the head of instruction or culture. The arrangement of the chapters is chronological, so that the educational policy of dynasties or of epoch-making emperors can be traced and compared, and an excellent analytical table of contents enables the reader to refer to the discussions of the various topics treated, such as the kinds of immunities conferred on teachers or professors ; the great schools, especially the University of Athens, the Athenaeum of Rome, the Museum of Alexandria ; the institutions for young men (the Collegia Juvenum, Pueri Alimentarii), &c. Among the facts emphasized are the omission of the primary teachers in the grants of privileges to professors of the more advanced subjects; the tendency, as time went on, for the emperors to intervene more actively in educational affairs (a process marked by Julian's edict on the choice of professors, Valentinian's disciplinary rules for the Athenaeum in Rome, and Justinian's official syllabus for the four-years' curriculum for law students); and in spite of this tendency, the extensive freedom generally allowed to teachers and scholars in the unexamined colleges of the Empire, in which pecuniary aid was given without constituting the recipients public officials. The sources of which the author has availed himself are numerous and extensive: inscriptions, contemporary literature, modern investigations. It is to his honour that although he makes no secret of his own sympathies and antipathies, he is careful to bring out the strong points in policies which he disapproves. Not till near the end does he indulge in somewhat pessimistic remarks as to the nullity of all efforts, in ancient or modern times, to produce first-rate scientific or artistic work by governmental patronage or organization. Officialism is his bugbear, yet he treats with toleration and respect the statesmen whose regulations both fostered and hampered the intellectual life and culture of the Later Empire.

A. G.

In respect of Mr. John Ward's *Roman Era in Britain* and *Romano-British Buildings and Earthworks* (London: Methuen, 1911) it is only necessary to say here that historians will find little or nothing in either work which will assist or even concern them. Despite the title of the first-named book, both are archaeological or antiquarian. What sort of candle-sticks, keys, and seal-boxes were used in Roman Britain, what carvings adorned Roman altars, what classes of *fibulae* are represented in which museums, what arrangements were made for staircases, doors, windows in Roman villas—such are the problems to which Mr. Ward seems principally to call his readers' attention. To the historical evidence deducible from archaeological remains and to history generally he gives little space, and, so far as we can judge, what he says on these points is of little moment and by no means always up to date—witness, for example, his remarks on the Romans in Scotland. Of the real character of the 'Roman Era in Britain', of the civilization and culture of the province, he says next to nothing. The value of his archaeological and antiquarian work is not a matter with which this Review can properly deal. We will venture only one criticism. If the dishes called *mortaria*, round shallow basins clearly intended for trituration of food-products, were used as Mr. Ward describes and figures on p. 177 of the *Roman Era*, they must have been constantly getting broken. T.

In commemoration of the Italian jubilee, the indefatigable Professor N. Jorga has written a *Breve Storia dei Rumeni* (Bucarest: 'Lega di Cultura,' 1911). This summary possesses far greater merit than similar publications, because its author is a man of great erudition, who has written many treatises on Rumanian history. The special feature of his last work is to emphasize the relations between Italy and the Rumans.

Trajan's column and the monument at Adamklissi, the Genoese colonies at Chilia and Akkerman, the Italian doctors of the Moldavian prince Stephen the Great, the Tuscan auxiliaries of Michael the Brave, the Moldavian exiles who came to Venice at the end of the sixteenth century, are all links in the chain, now become weaker, between the two Latin countries. Those who have visited the Rumanian section of the archaeological exhibition in the Baths of Diocletian may be recommended to read this brief compendium, which will, however, occasionally surprise Italian readers by the strangeness of its diction, while the last chapter gives a particularly clear account of the Rumanian resurrection. It is worthy of note, that the author cites inscriptions to prove that the colonists planted by Trajan on the lower Danube came mostly from the provinces of the empire and not from Italy itself.

In another jubilee treatise, *Les Éléments originaux de l'ancienne Civilisation roumaine* (Jassy: Ştefăniu & Cie, 1911), Professor Jorga has celebrated the festival of the university of Jassy by a concise account of art and architecture in Rumania. After premising that 'all that concerns the elements of culture and of art is neither Latin nor Slav', he shows how the famous cathedral of Curtea-de-Argeş is a mixture of both eastern and western styles, how the convent of Tismana is Serbo-Byzantine, the church of Baїa and the many ecclesiastical foundations of Stephen the Great of Moldavia are Gothic, and the church of Dealu Venetian. W. M.

In the *Byzantinische Zeitschrift*, xix. 3, 4, we note papers by T. Preger on the topography of Constantinople (the walls of Constantine); by A. Semenov on the origin and meaning of the logothetae in Byzantium; by F. Görres on the Byzantine origin of the Visigothic kings Erwich and Witiza, and the relations of the emperor Maurice to the Germanic world; and by J. R. Asmus on Isidore's Life of Damascius, showing that its chief sources are Suidas and Photius. In xx. 1, 2 E. Weigand discusses the date of the Peregrinatio Aetheriae (the pilgrimage was made in 395), and P. Garabed Der Sahaghian prints an Armenian document on the genealogy of Basil I. U.

Mr. C. D. Cobham, the leading authority on the medieval history of Cyprus, has published a valuable summary of Gedeón's Πατριαρχικοὶ Πίνακες (*The Patriarchs of Constantinople*. Cambridge: University Press, 1911). Mr. Cobham disclaims original research, but has printed from the Greek writer chronological and alphabetical lists of the patriarchs, with a prefatory note, to which the Rev. Adrian Fortescue and the Rev. H. T. F. Duckworth have added two brief essays on the patriarchate. The violent deaths of many patriarchs, their constant resignations and reappointments, the connexion of their office with the secular importance of Constantinople, the date and meaning of their present epithet of 'Œcumenical', their gain of power by the Turkish conquest and their loss of it by the secession of the Russian church, by the creation of an autocephalous establishment in the kingdom of Greece, and by the erection of the Bulgarian exarchate—are all emphasized. One or two small errors merit correction. Greek books frequently distinguish 'homonymous Patriarchs by numbers' (p. 10); the church of Trnovo was not 'Roumanian' but Bulgarian, nor did it continue to be independent 'to the time of the capture of Constantinople', but only till 1394 (pp. 32, 65); the cession of the Ionian Isles was not in 1866 but in 1864 (p. 33); and Ipek is the usual form of 'Pekion' (p. 65). W. M.

Les Chrétientés Celtiques, by Dom Louis Gougaud (Paris: Lecoffre, 1911), is a summary of facts well worthy of a place in the same series with Dom Leclercq's *L'Afrique Chrétienne*. The author's wide knowledge, which is shown in an admirable bibliography, raises the work above the level of a compilation. He is cautious, and inspired rather by the spirit of Dottin than of Sir John Rhŷs. It is significant of his temper that Glastonbury is unmentioned in his pages; but if we admire the absence of credulity, we regret that his sense of probability has led him to suppress much of the grotesque side of Old Celtic life and belief. This deprives his picture of some of its value; but it is rarely that we miss actual facts of history. He ought, however, to have told us of those three Irish pilgrims who reached Cornwall in 891, after a seven days' voyage without oar or sail. There is no reason to suppose that this suicidal impulse was a solitary case, and it casts a light upon the Celtic type of Christianity. The same tendency has been found by others in the sudden death of Ethne and Fedelm immediately after their baptism, an incident which Dom Gougaud relates without comment. Perhaps it would not be unfair to suspect a little partiality, especially as our author is rather too fond of winning easy and superfluous victories over protestant controversial statements. But if he sometimes sees only the better side, he is very independent in his criticisms. Legends of saints receive no mercy, the traditions of Armagh are decisively rejected, and he is disposed to regard the bull *Laudabiliter* as authentic. The chapters on Brittany and on Irish art and scholarship are perhaps the most interesting, but the whole work is excellent, and well proportioned, though something more should have been said at the end about the disappearance of the Culdees. The printing is remarkably accurate, and the whole is worthy of Benedictine scholarship. E. W. W.

A thesis by Dr. Otto Goldhardt on *Die Gerichtsbarkeit in den Dörfern des mittelalterlichen Hennegaus*, published in the *Leipziger historische Abhandlungen* (1910), will be found full of suggestion to the English student of manorial and leet jurisdiction. The local seignoral courts of Hainault in the twelfth and thirteenth centuries covered the whole ground of the later 'low', 'middle', and 'high' justice. The *Grundgericht* or manorial court had the same competence as the *basse justice* of the seventeenth century, with the addition of a small jurisdiction *de catallis* which passed later into the domain of 'middle justice'; whilst the *Mittelgericht* of the seventeenth century corresponded to the *Dorfgericht* of the thirteenth without the fines for bloodshed. Where, then, resided the high justice of the earlier period ? According to Dr. Goldhardt this also fell to the *Meyer* and *Schöffen* of the *Dorfgericht* as far as process was concerned, the execution only being reserved to the Vogt of the Graf, to whom also there was an appeal in case of default. Dr. Goldhardt shows that the *allgemeine Dinge* held thrice yearly by the Vogt were not in the twelfth century of greater but rather of lesser competence than the *Dorfgericht*, and he argues against the assumption that this restricted jurisdiction was a mere remnant of the Vogt's earlier powers. In a final section of much interest the origin of the *Dorfgericht* as an immunity jurisdiction is discussed, and its connexion with the development of the status of the freeman into that of the *miles* is elucidated. G. U.

The pupils of Professor Hampe are at present usefully employed in sifting the materials for the history of the last Hohenstaufen and their adherents. Like Dr. Stieve, the biographer of Ezzelin da Romano, Miss Zippora Schiffer in *Markgraf Hubert Pallavicini* (Leipzig : Quelle & Mayer, 1910), and Dr. Oskar Canz in *Philipp Fontana, Erzbischof von Ravenna* (Leipzig : Quelle & Mayer, 1910), have taken north Italy for their special field. Their researches are supplementary to those of their fellow student, and are presented in a similar form. They have no new materials to present, but they have made an exhaustive survey of the printed sources; both might have studied with advantage the literary style of their distinguished master. In these essays there is a lamentable want of perspective. Dr. Canz, moreover, has neglected the elementary duty of giving the dates which are essential to an intelligent study of his narrative. On the other hand, each has at least one idea of interest. Miss Schiffer has turned to good account some hints of Schütter (*Der Apenninenpass des Monte Bardone und die deutschen Kaiser* [1901]) on the strategic importance of the various posts occupied by Pallavicini in his character of an imperial lieutenant. Dr. Canz remarks that Fontana, who was employed by the church to check the spread of despotism, was himself the stuff of which despots were made : the egotism of the tyrant was to be found among Guelfs no less than Ghibellines ; it was the spirit of the age, not of one particular class or party. Miss Schiffer is the more fortunate in her hero. Pallavicini was no genius ; and, owing to the paucity of details about his private life, his personality is something of an enigma. He exemplified in a remarkable fashion the dictum of Thucydides that it is commonly the plain man who goes furthest in times of revolution. Pallavicini habitually pursued a policy of short views and sharp measures ; and by doing so he earned the glory of outwitting Ezzelin, who was infinitely his superior in foresight and finesse. Ezzelin apparently supposed that his rival would never be so foolish as to help the church in the reduction of a fellow tyrant. Pallavicini committed the folly and reaped a passing success at the cost of ultimate ruin. But he outlived Ezzelin, and came nearer to establishing a solid principality. Had both men committed a fundamental miscalculation in ranging themselves on the side of the empire ? We are naturally inclined to think so. But the life of Philip of Fontana suggests a different conclusion. Philip was for some years (1250–8) the right-hand man of the papacy in north Italy, as important among the Guelfs as were Ezzelin and Hubert Pallavicini among the Ghibellines. But Philip never received an adequate reward for his services. After the death of Alexander IV he found himself relegated to the background, lost all influence with the curia, and was not even allowed to extend his power in the Romagna. The most controversial matter in either essay is Miss Schiffer's defence of the charters, in favour of Hubert Pallavicini, which bear the names of Frederick II and Conrad.

Their authenticity has been impugned by no less a critic than Ficker. Miss Schiffer deals with the question far too lightly, not touching on the form of these documents but contenting herself with the proof that the tenor of the charters is consistent with the general lines of Hohenstaufen policy.
H. W. C. D.

In *Acta Imperii, Angliae et Franciae ab A. 1267 ad A. 1313, Dokumente vornehmlich zur Geschichte der auswärtigen Beziehungen Deutschlands* (Tübingen: Mohr, 1911), Dr. Fritz Kern has produced a collection of documents illustrative of international relations in the thirteenth and fourteenth centuries, but limiting himself to the period from the downfall of the Hohenstaufen to the death of Henry VII. In spite of the material brought together by Dr. H. Finke in his *Acta Aragonensia*, the subject is one which has hitherto received very meagre consideration, and the materials contained in printed collections are imperfect. His task, therefore, involved a prolonged search in the archives of Germany, France, England, and Italy. As a result we have an invaluable collection of over three hundred documents. Many of them are of course slight in themselves, and consist of little more than formal instructions and commissions to envoys. But the collection as a whole is one of wide interest, by no means confined to diplomacy, but throwing light on German constitutional history and on social and economic questions. Numerous documents are derived from the volumes of Ancient Correspondence in the Record Office, and it is a matter of just reproach that so rich a source has been so little explored by English scholars. Pauli and Stubbs have sketched the diplomatic relations of England and Germany during the reign of Edward I, but their complete history has still to be studied in the light of the documents here brought together. Another topic of special interest to English students is afforded by the war of 1294 to 1297; there are many documents bearing on the relations of England and the Low Countries during these years, and on the course of the negotiations with France. Not the least interesting of the letters from English sources are the reports from the king's agents and representatives in Italy on events in that country (nos. 2, 48, 52; the first of these, on 10 August 1273, mentions that Edward had sent for Francesco Accursi ' meliore legista de mundo ' to assist him in his negotiations with the French king). The documents from French sources are of special interest for the relations of France and Germany with the borderlands of Lorraine and Burgundy. The English and French interest decreases in the latter part of the collection, when we come to a large number of papers relating to the expedition of Henry VII to Italy in 1310–13. The history of these years is further illustrated by four Italian chronicles, which Dr. Kern prints in the third section of his volume. These are a Pisan chronicle of contemporary date from the archives at Lucca, which the editor describes as ' an historical source of high rank ', with a conclusion of Luccan origin in a hand of the sixteenth century; a longer ' Chronicon Parmense ', the greater part of which belongs to 1312–13; and a very brief fragment of a Siena chronicle. The whole volume is excellently edited, with a full chronological table of its contents, a copious index of persons and places, and a list of noteworthy expressions.
C. L. K.

In *Four Thirteenth Century Law Tracts* (New Haven: Yale University Press, 1910) Mr. George E. Woodbine gives a critical text of four law-tracts which from internal evidence appear to have been composed between 1267 and 1307; the latest of them is probably not of much later date than the Second Statute of Westminster (1285). They are here printed in chronological order under the titles Fet Asaver, Iudicium Essoniorum, Modus Componendi Brevia, Exceptiones ad Cassandum Brevia. A part of Fet Asaver was printed at the end of the first (1647) and second (1685) editions of Fleta; but the remaining three treatises have hitherto been known only to the students of manuscripts. All four are severely technical in matter and treatment. They deal with points of procedure—with writs, essoins, and exceptions. They give little information that is new, and are valuable chiefly as samples of the textbooks which were fashionable among lawyers of the early fourteenth century. Fet Asaver and the Exceptiones are written in Norman French, the other two in Latin. In an excellent introduction Mr. Woodbine establishes from internal evidence the approximate dates of the four, and proves that the tract Exceptiones is merely the second part of Modus Componendi Brevia, though written in a different language. He argues with much plausibility that we owe Fet Asaver and Iudicium Essoniorum to the industry of Ralph Hengham. The proof rests chiefly on a comparison of Hengham's Magna Summa with these tracts; but in the case of Fet Asaver the attribution is confirmed by the authority of two manuscripts; and Tanner mentions a manuscript in which Hengham is named as the author of Iudicium Essoniorum. Mr. Woodbine's work is marred, both in the introduction and in the text of the treatises, by a number of slight but irritating misprints. *Deullo* (p. 117) should be *duello*; *carcuata* (p. 120) should be *carucata*. *Illuis* (p. 125) is a misprint for *illius*; *siesina* (p. 133) for *seisina*; *distinguenden* (p. 135) for *distinguendum*; *iudico* (p. 143) for *iudicio*; *dominco* (p. 152) for *dominico*. H. W. C. D.

In the *Calendar of the Fine Rolls*, vol. i, Edward I, 1272–1307 (H. M. Stationery Office, 1911), the deputy keeper continues, after a long interval, the work begun by the Record Commission, when it published in 1835–6 the Fine Rolls of John and excerpts from the Fine Rolls of Henry III. As is natural, this new undertaking assumes the form of a calendar in English, and the inclusion of all the Fine Rolls of Edward I in a single volume suggests that this new series will not be a very long one. Of the execution of this calendar it is superfluous to speak. The tradition of how such work is to be done is fortunately becoming well established in the Record Office, and Mr. Bland, the compiler, has produced a calendar well worthy of the company of its predecessors. The index represents a higher standard than that set in some of the earlier volumes. The identification of place-names has been successful, Welsh names in particular presenting few terrors to Mr. Bland, who is responsible for index as well as text. Perhaps one's only complaint of the index is some deficiency in it as regards subjects. Some institutions and officers, for example chancery and chancellor, exchequer and treasurer, are duly indexed, and there is a useful list of abbeys and castles named in the text. Yet other branches of the administration and their official chiefs are entirely ignored. For example, there are no index references to the wardrobe, the great wardrobe, or the prince of Wales's wardrobe. Neither is there any collective reference to the officers at the head of these institutions, though those functionaries mentioned in the text generally have their offices recorded under their names in the index It is worth noting, however, that Roger de Insula is called ' keeper of the wardrobe ' on p. 652. He was, as the text records on p. 373, ' keeper of the great wardrobe.' Similarly, the king's lay officers are not collected in the index under their titles, as for example, the steward. Had the ' king's stewards ' been put together under that head in the index, the interesting fact would have been brought out that more than one officer seems to have held this title at the same time. Of these, Thomas de Normanville is definitely called ' steward of the king's castles and demesnes beyond Trent' and Richard of Holebrok had his sphere limited to the midlands, though both are often simply described as the 'king's steward'. Ralph Sandwich, however, who is indexed as ' steward of the king's demesnes', is, in more than sixty cases, described simply as the ' king's steward', and in one case (p. 64) as ' keeper of the king's demesnes', but never, so far as I can discover within the limits of this volume, as ' steward of the king's demesnes'. T. F. T.

Dr. David Schaff has completed the *History of the Christian Church* by his father, the late Dr. Philip Schaff, by a volume (v, pt. 2) on *The Middle Ages from Boniface VIII, 1294, to the Protestant Reformation, 1517* (New York: Scribner, 1910). The book is the fruit of wide reading over a somewhat lengthy period, and is apparently founded upon lectures to theological students. If the reading and citation would seem sometimes a little indiscriminate and the passing and less conscious judgements occasionally naïve, Dr. Schaff is always learned, cautious, and scrupulously conscientious, while his more deliberate and reasoned judgements are measured and thoughtful. Dr. Schaff has neglected little that he should have seen, but in one of the English chapters one finds Gascoigne cited through Mr. Gairdner; and surely the executions of the fifteenth and sixteenth centuries in England were, with a very small number of exceptions between the years 1401 and 1414, carried out, not under the famous statute *de haeretico comburendo* of the former year, but under the less well-known one of the latter. Dr. Schaff has not chosen his portrait of Wycliffe happily, nor would many modern writers perhaps agree with him when he contrasts Luther with Wycliffe as being ' fully a man of the new age ', but Luther falls beyond the scope of the book. Of some of the side issues of his subject Dr. Schaff seems to have made a special study, as, for instance, of magic and witchcraft, and this in a number of the sixteenth and seventeenth-century writers as well as in the more modern. Nor has he neglected the *montes pietatis*, that most interesting form of fifteenth-century charity. Probably the use of the phrase ' medieval age ' in the preface is a slip, as may be also that of ' archdeanery of Canterbury ' on p. 311, but they should be corrected in later editions. A. M. C.

The *Registrum Iohannis de Trillek* (London: Canterbury and York Society, 1911) is full of interest. Trillek's episcopate, 1343 to 1360, coincided with some of the most memorable years of Edward III's reign, and such events as the Black Death and the French campaigns are duly reflected in the pages of his register. Even more illuminating, however, than these local illustrations of national crises is the plain record of Trillek's diocesan work. His ecclesiastical career had begun at a very early age, thanks to the good offices of his uncle, Adam of Oriton, to whom he continued to act as secretary and chaplain even after he had received the cure of souls. However, the man who had owed his promotion to nepotism and been guilty of pluralism and non-residence became an excellent and hardworking bishop, who could rarely be persuaded to leave his diocese or take any share in external affairs. His register, accordingly, as the record of twenty years' labour, is a valuable illustration of the characteristics of the church of his day, quite apart from its strong local interest. There are few aspects of episcopal difficulties of which examples cannot be found in its entries. Many of these, such as the diminution in the numbers of the clergy after the plague, the contest between lay and spiritual courts both as to ecclesiastical causes and ecclesiastical persons, the visitation of monasteries, assaults on clerks and frays in churches, are brought out in the admirable introduction. In connexion with the benefit of clergy, two entries call for special attention. The first (p. 56) concerns a certain John Pyrie, who 'tunc infans sive infancie proximus' had received the first tonsure as a boy at school at Gloucester, though 'quod faciebat penitus ignorabat'. The other (p. 181) relates how William Corbet broke into the bishop's prison at Hereford, abstracted both the keys and the jailer, and threw the latter into the town prison. This seems to suggest that there was some ground for the assertion which enemies to clerical privilege liked to make, that a bishop's prison was not always a safe place of keeping. The editor, in referring to the foundation of Flanesford priory in 1346, remarks that this event was 'the more notable because the flow of benefactions to the monastic orders had perceptibly decreased, though only the beginnings of the decay of the system were visible'. Flanesford, however, a house of Austin canons, was the type of foundation which bridged the gulf between clerk and monk. Active monasticism of this kind was still very much alive, though contemplative monasticism of the Benedictine or Cistercian type was no longer so popular. Another illustration of this is given by the constant references in the register to the work of the Dominicans. H. J.

Herr Emil Göller has completed his study of the papal penitentiary to the date of its reformation (*Die Päpstliche Pönitentiarie*, ii, 1, 2. Rome : Loescher, 1911), the first part of which has already been noticed in this Review (xxiii. 554). The present section includes the period from Eugenius IV to Pius V, by whom the bulk of the business as regards the issuing of letters was transferred to the papal chancery. The scheme of this volume is substantially that of the preceding. The section dealing with materials naturally drops out, as the same sources are used for both volumes, and a section is devoted to that favourite battle-ground of theologians, the 'taxes' of the penitentiary. Herr Göller has no difficulty in showing that the old charge of simony is untenable, unless the English law-courts can rightfully be accused of 'selling justice', as the payments are simply the fees for the issue of the necessary letters. This, however, was a point on which no serious historian could be in doubt. The special mention in these lists of *Hibernici* as the typical examples of poor pilgrims entitled to lower fees is interesting, but hardly unexpected. It is amusing to find that the proposal to print the tariff was opposed at quite an early date on the ground of the handle it might give to the attacks of heretics. As before, the book concludes with a section on the bull *In Coena Domini*, which often included the names of quite undistinguished persons. Thus in 1466 we find Henry Crichton, the deposed abbot of Paisley, excommunicated by name for endeavouring to regain possession of his monastery by force of arms. As to the history of the staff and practice of the department, it is the usual tale of increasing centralization and of unavailing attempts at reform, blocked, until the great change introduced by Pius V, by the purchase of offices—which that pope abolished. There are a number of corrections of the previous volume, the most important of which is the statement that the register of the penitentiary was not, as had been supposed, carried off by Napoleon, but is in perfect preservation at Rome. Herr Göller has also supplied the much-needed index, but this is somewhat disappointing, as it does not refer to the illustrative documents in either volume, and even as applied to the text is only concerned with persons and places and is not absolutely perfect. C. J.

In a couple of articles, reprinted from the *Revue de Hongrie* under the title of *Le traité de paix de Szeged avec les Turcs (1444)*, Professor D. Angyal seeks to fix the date of that treaty between 26 July and 1 August, and ascribes its denunciation, so terribly avenged at Varna, to the conflict of rival Polish parties around the young king Wladislas I. W. M.

The third volume of the *Registres du Conseil de Genève* (Geneva: Kündig, 1911), an important collection of documents, the former volumes of which (published respectively in 1900 and 1906) have been already noticed in these pages (xix. 399, and xxii. 791), give the text (in Latin, of course) of the registers of the Conseil of the city of Geneva for the period running from 1477 to 1487, but the year 1478 in these registers is imperfect and 1479 is entirely wanting. This period was of considerable importance for the little city on the Rhone, still in the hands of the house of Savoy. Several texts refer to the financial embarrassments caused by the fine imposed on the city by the Swiss after their victories over the duke of Burgundy, whose ally was Savoy. Later on, in 1477, the bishop himself, with the consent of the citizens, concluded with Berne and Fribourg, for the space of his life, a treaty of alliance, the first link in the long series which was much later, in 1815, to lead to the entrance of Geneva into the Swiss confederation. Still later, internal struggles resulted in the great increase of the episcopal authority in the city. It is hard nowadays to think of Geneva as Savoyard and non-Calvinist, but this well-edited volume depicts in a lively fashion what were nearly the last phases of the Savoyard dominion in Geneva. A very full and clearly arranged index of 100 pages closes this volume, the publication of which does great honour to the Société d'Histoire et d'Archéologie de Genève. W. A. B. C.

Five English Consorts of Foreign Princes, by Miss Ida Woodward (London: Methuen, 1911), is a collection of biographical sketches dealing with the following ladies: Mary and Margaret Tudor, queens of France and Scotland respectively, Elizabeth, queen of Bohemia, Mary Stuart, princess of Orange, and Henrietta, duchess of Orleans. A certain amount of popular historical exposition is attempted in the way of describing the political conditions of the countries with which they became connected by marriage. C. E. M.

In *Early Spanish Voyages to the Strait of Magellan* (London: Hakluyt Society, 1911) Sir Clements Markham has published slightly abridged translations of the accounts of several expeditions to those parts. The voyage of Sayavedra from Mexico to 'Maluco' (pp. 109–32) has no connexion whatever with the strait, but was evidently included on account of the light it throws on Loaysa's expedition. The translations are free, but in consequence read well. The maps and index are also good. It is a pity, however, that no indication is given, even in a note, of the whereabouts of the originals. Who, for instance, would ever surmise that the 'Description of the Strait of Magellan by the Pilot Martin de Uriarte' (pp. 90–101) is an excerpt from Fernando de la Torre's 'Derrotero' in Navarrete's *Colección*, v. 259–68 ? Similarly, though pp. 111 to 168 have been translated from volume v of the *Colección de Documentos inéditos relativos al Descubrimiento etc. de las antiguas Posesiones españolas*, this is nowhere stated. One or two slips may be pointed out: 'God was served' (pp. 215 and 216) is a clumsy rendering of the original, as is also 'he had awoken' (p. 223). Before writing the note on Gomez (p. 13) the editor would have done well to consult Medina's little book on that navigator. V.

The Rationale of Ceremonial, 1540–3, with Notes and Appendices, and an Essay on the Regulation of Ceremonial during the reign of King Henry VIII, by Mr. Cyril S. Cobb (London: Longmans, 1910), is a careful edition of the Lambeth MS. of *The Book of Ceremonies* or *Rationale* as it has become the custom to call it. The British Museum MS. (edited both by Strype and Collier) has been collated, and the results suggested by a comparison of the two manuscripts is given (p. lxv ff.). Careful and full notes—with much information upon liturgic and ritual matters—are added. Sufficient study has not hitherto been given generally to the ecclesiastical documents of the reign of Henry VIII, but they throw great light upon the tendencies and purposes of the day. A discussion of the date of composition will be found on p. li n.; 1538 and 1547 are clearly inferior and superior limits; Mr. Cobb rejects Mr. Brightman's late date (1545–7) in favour of Mr. Dixon's earlier (and much more probable) date of 1540. While the work itself and the notes are of the greatest value, some of the generalizations in the introduction are less convincing. That the English reformation was throughout 'national' while the German was 'individual' cannot be affirmed without large reservations. The *centum gravamina* of Germany—with their long preparatory history, and their connexion with Maximilian's plan of a German national church—can hardly be called essentially 'individual'. Even Luther's primary works, if on one side they insist upon individual freedom, on the other side show strong national feeling. Nor is it quite correct to describe the foreign reformers as primarily concerned with doctrine, while the English were mainly ecclesiastical and constitutional. Nor can we agree (p. xix) that in England, under Henry VIII, 'there was no great social upheaval pending as in Germany, and no temptation to use religious reform as a lever to promote a social revolution'. It is very easy to formulate generalizations and stretch them too far ; the interests of history are served far better by the patient presentment of contemporary evidence and the accurate study of details which we have in the rest of the book. There is a useful index, but two references, 'reception of the Eucharist once frequent, 42', and 'reconciling churches and yards, 5', have got mingled. The book is a sound contribution to the excellent work of the Alcuin Society, and we note that the author derived much help from the late Bishop Collins, whose loss is in this field peculiarly great. J. P. W.

Social France in the Seventeenth Century, by Miss Cécile Hugon (London : Methuen, 1911), purports 'to represent the general aspect of the century in a few rough strokes'. It is a collection of essays upon a variety of desultory topics, ranging from 'Housekeeping' to 'Culture', in which the *mémoires* of the period have been extensively utilized. Miss Hugon writes well and maintains interest, but she does not attempt to add to knowledge, and her style is at times open to criticism. W.

Dr. H. G. de Boer's pamphlet on *De Armada van 1639* (Groningen : Noordhoff, 1911) puts this expedition for the first time in a proper light as in most respects a worthy rival of the famous one of 1588. Although it contained only about half the number of ships, its strength, due to its greater units, was even more formidable according to the progress of naval warfare (cp. p. 22 with Froude, xii. 377 ff.), and besides transporting troops to the Dutch theatre of war, its aim was no less to fight at sea any enemy that might encounter it (pp. 26, 36–42). As in 1588 England, so now Holland alone of all protestant powers had to stand the whole attack, and that under the greatest difficulties. Tromp had to organize his fleet almost in the face of the Spaniards, and his command was hampered by the jealousy of Witte de Witt. The French navy, under the valiant bishop of Bordeaux, was stationed far away in the Atlantic. And the attitude of England was worse than the inactivity with which Elizabeth had reproached the States. The helplessness of Charles I just before the rebellion is here illustrated from a specially deplorable side. The dignity of this nation was as much impaired by the impudent higgling of his government when asked to grant protection and ammunition to the enemy of the protestant cause as by the inability of the navy and the Cinque Ports (p. 51) to keep up the declared neutrality of the Downs, where the Spanish admiral De Oquendo was at last defeated by Tromp. Dr. de Boer's pamphlet is adorned with some contemporary prints reproduced from Muller's *Gouden Eeuw*. There are not a few misprints in the quotations from English and Spanish sources. In the complicated chronological statements of the author it is well to note that 'Augustus', on p. 29, l. 10 from bottom, must be a mistake for 'September'. C. B.

The financial organization of the clergy of France and the amount of their contribution in the time of Louis XIV are the objects of two learned and exhaustive monographs of M. Albert Cans (*L'Organisation financière du Clergé de France à l'époque de Louis XIV* and *La Contribution du Clergé de France à l'Impôt pendant la seconde moitié du règne de Louis XIV, 1689–1715*. Paris: Picard, 1910). To both volumes the author has prefixed a careful and accurate account of his sources; and in the text references are given to the original documents. M. Cans shows both a wide knowledge of the literature of his subject and, what is more valuable, a power of criticizing and handling it. His account of ecclesiastical immunity is lucid, and his description of the central power in the organization of the clergy is excellent. In the technical chapters dealing with the subsidies furnished to Louis XIV, their distribution among the different dioceses, and their incidence, the author never loses sight of principles in his analysis of details. It is obvious that the centralizing policy of the monarchy was severely felt by the clergy, and all attempts at independence, even by such a prelate as Nicolas Pavillon of Alet, were crushed out. In the second book named M. Cans deals with the amounts paid for the war of the League of Augsburg and the war of the Spanish Succession. He gives some startling totals. Between 1690 and 1715 the total sum was no less than 143,500,000 livres, and even the thirty years preceding 1690 yield a fairly large amount. From 1660 to 1690 the author calculates that the clergy paid 11 per cent. of their revenue in taxation, and that from 1690 to 1715 it was increased to 58 per cent. M. Cans unravels the tangled detail with great adroitness.   R. H. M.

The second volume of the *Briefwisseling tusschen de Gebroeders van der Goes* (1659–73), edited by C. J. Gonnet in the *Werken uitgegeven door het Historisch Genootschap gevestigd te Utrecht* (Derde Serie, No. 11. Amsterdam: Müller, 1909), contains a genealogy of the family and an index of names and places to the whole edition; the rest of the editorial work is limited to short paragraphs at the head of each letter, a few brief notes, and the short biographical introduction published with the first volume in 1899. The well-known importance of letter-writing as a supplement to the news press in the infancy of journalism gives to the private correspondences of the time almost, and in a sense even more than, the interest of a public periodical. And the person and residence of the two brothers Van der Goes, Adriaen the barrister at the supreme court of Holland and Willem the honoured exile at Vienna, seem to guarantee the value of the information with which they used to supply each other twice a month for about six years (Willem does not come in as a regular correspondent until 1667), while the fact that they were Roman catholics helped to increase the breadth and impartiality of their insight into international politics. On the relations of England to the continent, and particularly to the two countries which the brothers inhabited, many useful sidelights are thrown. It was in the retinue of the Archduchess Claudia Felicitas, proposed as bride to the duke of York, that Willem hoped to re-establish himself in Holland, and at last he was legally pardoned through the mediation of the prince of Orange for the manslaughter he had committed in a duel twenty years before.   C. B.

Mr. G. B. Tatham, in his essay *Dr. John Walker and the Sufferings of the Clergy* (Cambridge: University Press, 1911), gives an excellent appreciation of the value of Walker's work, and has appended a calendar of the Walker MSS. which shows how he collected his materials, and will be of great service if a critical edition of it should ever be undertaken. He lays due stress on the controversial character of the book. Begun as a reply to Calamy's *Abridgment*, which was first published in 1702, and, after long preparation and various delays, produced hurriedly in 1714, the year after the appearance of the second edition of the *Abridgment*, it answered a challenge: the nonconformists complained of harsh treatment, and specially of the ejection of 2,000 nonconforming ministers in 1662; Walker replied by exhibiting in his part i the ruin which in the day of their power they had brought upon the church as an institution, and in his part ii by recording the sufferings they had inflicted on a large number of individuals among the loyal clergy, as a proof that, if all was known, the sequestered clergy would be found far to exceed in number those ejected on St. Bartholomew's day. While the first part is superseded by the works of more modern historians, with greater facilities for gaining information, a less ponderous style, and more idea of narrative arrangement, it treats some matters, in later times generally passed lightly by, with a vigour and copiousness that give them their proper weight, and it lacks neither picturesqueness nor force of expression. The progress of the author's undertaking, the difficulties he encountered, and the character of each class of his authorities, whether printed or in manuscript, are fully described, and a chapter is devoted to the contemporary criticism evoked by his book. As regards the use which Walker made of such authorities as he had, Mr. Tatham finds that he is generally accurate, and that he cannot fairly be accused of wilful suppression—indeed, he more than once notes facts or reports which tell against his contention—but that his printed authorities were too exclusively taken from those on the royalist side, and that his party bias led him to accept their statements too unreservedly. He understood the value of original documents, but for them he was often forced to rely on extracts and copies, and though he warns his readers when he is doubtful as to their trustworthiness, he did not compare them with their originals, either from inability to do so or from the haste with which his book was at last produced. The biographical notices in part ii were chiefly derived from letters from the families of the sequestered clergy or from their successors in office, a matter which receives illustration from Mr. Tatham's calendar. Walker acknowledges the unsatisfactory nature of such evidence, and having done so, uses it without reserve, unless there was special reason to the contrary. Many of these letters came in answer to requests published through the archdeacons; from some dioceses they came in plenty, from others, where there is reason to believe that the sequestrations were as many, he received few. In all, however, he notices, we are told, about 2,300 parochial sequestrations. Mr. Tatham observes that there are 'singularly few cases' about which he has been found to have been mistaken; and he calculates that if the additions made by documents to which he had not access are taken into consideration, it is reasonable to suppose that the parochial sequestrations amounted roughly to 3,500. His scholarly treatise shows that in spite of the effects which Walker's partisanship had upon his work, he deserves more honour than has generally been accorded to him. W. H.

Mr. A. C. A. Brett's *Charles II and his Court* (London: Methuen, 1910) is based upon wide reading, and the writer has consulted the important authorities. There are, however, some strange omissions. Thus he does not include Ranke's *History of England*, nor W. P. Christie's *Life of Shaftesbury*; and he often omits to give the dates of publication of the editions he uses; the indexes, however, are excellent, and there are valuable illustrations. In the account of the life of Charles II at Jersey the writer might have used with advantage the article written by Lord Acton on the secret history of this reign. The chapter on the second exile, 1651-60, and that on London are well done. On the court Mr. Brett has only a chapter, and for this we are not altogether sorry.

R. H. M.

The aim of Dr. E. Kimball in *The Public Life of Joseph Dudley* (New York: Longmans, 1911) is to examine the Stuart colonial policy, and to set forth the practical political problems connected with its application. He makes careful use of the authorities, and it is not his fault that the subject of Dudley's career has been dealt with in some of the most impressive pages of Hutchinson's history. Mr. Kimball's treatment, however, of the subject is on a more elaborate scale, of special excellence being his use of the 'Dudley Records' in the chapter on Dudley's presidency of the Massachusetts council. The volume is distinguished by extreme fairness and impartiality; indeed, the action of the home government in appointing as governor of Massachusetts a strong partisan, who was very unpopular with the body of the people, is treated with more favour than perhaps it deserves. It seems an exaggeration to say that Bellomont 'died, worn out by disappointment and mortification, conscious of failure in America'; and though he complained of lack of support from England, the trouble, in great measure, arose from the delay in receiving replies to his dispatches. It is strange to compare Bellomont with Phips, and to say that their characters were not such as to promise success. This addition to the Harvard Historical Series is perhaps of less permanent importance than were some of its predecessors. Still, it is an excellent monograph on a subject of interest to all students of British colonial policy. H. E. E.

The *Biography of Thomas Deacon the Manchester Non-juror*, by Mr. Henry Broxap (Manchester: University Press, 1911), forms an appropriate subject for a volume in the Historical Series published by the university of Manchester. Deacon (1697-1753) was a bishop, not only of the non-jurors, but of that sect within a sect which insisted on the restoration of the 'usages' of the primitive church, and called itself 'The Orthodox British Catholic Church'. Nevertheless, he practised the medical profession in Manchester, and the chief interest of this book, apart from such light as it throws on the history of the non-jurors, consists in the account of Jacobite circles there towards the middle of the eighteenth century. The failure of the rebellion of 1745 (in which 'Dr.' Deacon lost three of his sons) was a great blow to that world, but it will surprise many people to learn that as late as 1804 there was still a non-juring congregation in Manchester. What is known about Deacon really comes to very little, but the book has been carefully compiled. A good deal of the background is provided by the *Remains of John Byrom*, published by the Chetham Society.   G. McN. R.

Miss Mary Maxwell Moffat's wide reading, as evidenced by her useful bibliography, entitles her *Maria Theresa* (London: Methuen, 1911) to a high place among popular biographies. The numerous memoirs and collections of letters that have been at her service have enabled her to write a very full personal study without being drawn into the larger problems of Austrian or European history. Miss Moffat's style is not distinguished, but, with the help of some excellent illustrations, she has written a readable book containing a mass of information, previously not easily available to the English reader.   G. B. H.

In consequence of Mr. Grant's appointment as professor of colonial history at the Queen's University, Kingston, the fourth volume of the *Acts of the Privy Council of England, Colonial Series* (London: H.M. Stationery Office, 1911), which includes the years 1745-66, has been edited by Mr. J. Munro alone. It shows every appearance of the same care and thoroughness as the earlier volumes. The entries differ little in character from those in the preceding volume. There is a full introduction with a lucid analysis of the principal contents. A small improvement has been made by giving references in the index to pages instead of the number of the entry. The references in the introduction are generally made to the numbers, and not to pages. It would have been, therefore, a further convenience if the number of the entries had been repeated at the top of the page, e. g. no. 525 extends from p. 580 to p. 609 ; a long entry of this kind makes the entries on either side of it difficult to find quickly.   H. L.

A missing link in the complete history of the American revolution is supplied by Dr. F. Edler, who, in *The Dutch Republic and the American Revolution* (Johns Hopkins University Studies in History and Political Science, xxix. 2), traces the successive steps by which the United Provinces, from a position of friendly neutrality towards the Americans, were drawn into active participation in the war with Great Britain. Excellent use has been made of the diplomatic correspondence mainly contained in the Sparks and Bancroft MSS. The monograph is written with a strong bias against Great Britain ; but this by no means detracts from its value.   H. E. E.

Mr. Arthur Hassall's *Life of Napoleon* (London: Methuen, 1911) summarizes in some three hundred pages the additions that recent research has made to the conventional picture of Napoleon. Although the necessity of yet one more volume on this subject is questionable at first sight, the utility of Mr. Hassall's handsome and well-illustrated book impresses itself on the reader. His style is plain and direct. A sound bibliography, accompanied by genealogical trees and lists of dates, will be helpful to students, and if the tendency to enumerate causes and results with the aid of numerals in brackets is more suggestive of the lecturer than the historian, we cannot but appreciate the skill with which Mr. Hassall marshals great multitudes of facts without losing his sense of proportion or sacrificing the effectiveness of his portraiture.　　　　　　　　　　　　　　　G. B. H.

Mr. G. A. C. Sandeman's *Metternich* (London : Methuen, 1911) may be of some use in correcting the views of those to whom Metternich is only a name or a bogy, and who, for instance, are quite unaware that the great conservative minister was in his home policy by no means devoid of liberal tendencies, to which he was partly too timid, partly too much wanting in initiative, to try to give effect. But its execution as a whole is so careless that it cannot be recommended as a handbook to serious students. The assertion in the preface that 'as an authority Metternich's *Autobiography* must be used upon the principle that when it conflicts with other authorities the latter are probably correct' is only quite incidentally illustrated in the course of the volume ; but it cannot be taken on trust from a writer who in the same preface informs the reader that Demelitsch's most important book (of which unfortunately only a single volume has been or is ever likely to be published) 'examines every phase of Austrian policy during Metternich's period in the minutest detail'. The looseness of Mr. Sandeman's own manner is by no means confined to a disregard for *minutiae*. We suppose his printer should be made accountable for misprints such as ' Foster ' for Forster (Georg), ' Iphigénie in Taurus,' ' Catalini ' for Catalani, and ' Jacobitism ' for Jacobinism in an oddly translated sentence of Metternich's. In the same way, perhaps, Frederick William II is paired with Queen Louise, and the congress of Rastatt is once called the 'Council'. To describe the Wartburg as 'the Grand Duke's castle at Weimar' is a less venial slip ; and we pass into the region of perplexity on reading that of Metternich's ancestors two served the catholic cause in the Thirty Years' War—one as the companion of ' John of *Worth* ', while the other was ' employed by the *Saxon* Court as Ambassador to Count Tilly when that general was ordered to lay down his arms '. This inaccuracy, together with a certain flippancy of style, lands him, in spite of his familiarity with parts of his theme, in a quite inadequate treatment of it as a whole. In corroboration of this criticism we may refer to the 'Conclusion', summarizing Metternich's career and character, and to the budget of facile but fallacious paradoxes which it spreads before the reader.　　　　　　　　　　　　　　　　　A. W. W.

The *Bibliothèque de la Révolution et de l'Empire*, judging from the first two volumes which have appeared—*Lettres de 1812* and *Lettres de 1815*, edited by M. Arthur Chuquet (Paris : Champion, 1911)—promises to be an admirable series. Here are volumes of a handy size, plainly and pleasantly printed, and full of relevant information upon two of the most dramatic episodes in modern European history, Napoleon's Russian campaign and Napoleon's return from Elba. The name of the editor is a sufficient guarantee of discretion in the selection, and of knowledge in the commentary, of the pieces here printed for the first time or reprinted from rare or inaccessible books and newspapers. Most of these pieces are private letters, but though the title-page speaks of letters only, M. Chuquet does not confine himself to this type of authority, but wisely prints any document or fragment of a document, such for instance as the evidence given at a trial, which may throw light upon his theme. Thus not the least interesting portion of the 1815 volume is the series of depositions put in at the trial of Marshal Ney. Still, in the main, M. Chuquet prints a collection of letters, and very striking they often are. For instance, there are two brief letters from Kutusov dictated in November 1812, and full of temperament, in which the old general describes the horrors of the retreat and his own emotions at the extraordinary character of his success. 'Je ne suis pas gai comme à l'ordinaire. . . . On ne saurait être gai quand on est ému.' And these are followed by a conversation between Kutusov and a French prisoner (previously printed in Puibusque's *Lettres sur la Guerre de Russie*) in which the old man shrewdly remarks that Napoleon was too much accustomed to short campaigns to employ two years in conquering a single power, and that consequently the design of spreading the Russian campaign over two years can never have been seriously entertained by him. H. A. L. F.

The Life and Letters of Sir John Hall, M.D., by Mr. S. M. Mitra (London : Longmans, 1911), is a noteworthy book, if only by reason of its authorship. That an Englishman whose most important public service was performed in South Africa and in the Crimea should find his biographer in a Hindu man of letters is an astonishing proof of the fusion of east and west under the British flag. Mr. Mitra appears to have made himself master of the circumstances with which he has to deal, especially of the complications of the medical department in the Crimean War, and there is no trace of foreign idiom in his style. All that is told us of Hall himself is to his credit as a man. He started life without interest to back him, and made his way by the conscientious thoroughness with which he performed his duties as a military doctor. He was perhaps a little *dour*, but there are many evidences of his kindness of heart. The *Life* does not reveal a specially interesting personality, nor does it provide anything in the way of good stories or sketches of character. What value it possesses lies in some notes of tours in Spain made by Dr. Hall in 1838 and 1839, in his letters and diaries describing the Kafir Wars of 1847-8 and 1850-1, and the Boer rising under Pretorius of 1848, and in the very full account of the medical organization during the Crimean War, when Dr. Hall was principal medical officer of the British army. Dr. Hall received this appointment on the ground of his rank when he was in Bombay, and he proceeded direct to the seat of war without any consultation with the authorities at home. This was perhaps itself of bad omen. But Mr. Mitra makes out a strong case that the sufferings of our soldiers during the winter of 1854–5 were to be ascribed not to Dr. Hall's incompetence, but to the chaos of authorities, the red tape and want of forethought in the administration at home. Whether or not Dr. Hall was in any way at fault, the presentation of his case based on his own memoranda must contribute to a final judgement in which justice is done to all parties.

Mr. Mitra speaks in his preface of the difficulties of his work: 'Illegible proper names, too, had to be verified by reference to other works.' In his South African chapters, at least, it would have been better if Mr. Mitra had done this rather more thoroughly. Thus on p. 96 'Hinga' should probably be 'Hinza' ('Hintza'), on p. 135 'Utenhagr' and on p. 207 'Utenlage' should be 'Uitenhage', on p. 138 'Niral' should probably be 'Nicol' ('Nicholls') (see Theal's *History of South Africa, 1834-54*, p. 285), on p. 142 'Wansnam' should be 'Woosnam' (*ibid.* p. 295), on p. 171 ' T'Slambic ' should be ' T'Slambie ', on p. 195 'Fount' should perhaps be 'Faunt', on p. 203 'Jukosé' should be 'Inkosé', and on pp. 215, 239, 'Jukosé Jukulu' should be 'Inkosé Inkulu'. Some passages in Dr. Hall's letters of mere tittle-tattle about private individuals (as on pp. 121, 223) could well have been omitted. The inclusion in the book of portraits of some of Sir John Hall's living descendants is in doubtful taste.
G. C. M. S.

Unless the industrial history of Belgium is to be conceived of as commencing with the treaty of Paris, the title of *L'Évolution industrielle de la Belgique*, by J. S. Lewinski (Bruxelles: Misch & Thron, 1911), is rather too comprehensive. Of the two sections into which the book is divided, the second provides a detailed contrast between the industrial conditions of 1846 and those of 1896 as revealed in the census enumerations of both periods, and in the reports of numerous commissions of inquiry. Here, again, the scope of the work is limited to one aspect—doubtless the most important aspect—of Belgian industrial development, i.e. the relative decadence of the *métier* and of the *industrie à domicile*, and their displacement by more integrated and capitalized forms of organization. M. Lewinski has appropriated in a wise eclectic spirit the results of German scholarship, and acknowledges special indebtedness to Bücher and Sombart. Indeed, this part of the book may be regarded as an application to Belgium of the methods used in reference to Germany by Sombart in *Der moderne Kapitalismus*. This work was well worth doing, and is excellently done. It will provide English students with a useful supplement to Mr. Rowntree's recent study of Belgian industrial conditions. Perhaps M. Lewinski is a little too eager to celebrate the irresistible advance of the big battalions of capital, and does not fully realize what a variety of effectual cover the small man can still find for himself. The first half of the book is more ambitious and less adequate. It is an attempt, with special reference to Belgian history, to define the causes of the industrial revolution. Incidentally, M. Lewinski throws much new light on the beginnings of industrial capitalism in Belgium; but the development was not indigenous, and the Belgian facts are not adequate to an explanation. The industrial revolution is a very complex social result—a late birth of time with a long and wide pedigree of causes. M. Lewinski is inclined to select increase of population as the *vera causa* and to turn all other factors into secondary conditions. But this view requires stronger support than a reference to the proofs afforded by Meitzen and Lamprecht in respect to the progress of prehistoric agriculture. An admirable bibliography of some eighty pages is added.
G. U.

Dr. Victor Fleury's *Le Poète Georges Herwegh* (Paris: Cornély, 1911) appears to be the earliest of the volumes composing the series 'La Révolution de 1848', issued by the historical society of that name, which deals with a writer or theme other than French. It would almost seem as if Dr. Fleury had felt called upon to pay a debt of honour on the part of his own country to a poet who declared that 'France is a religion' and a politician whose sympathies in the great war of 1870 were with the conquered rather than the conquered cause. If so, he has paid it with interest; for a more searching analysis of the life and writings of a modern man of letters has rarely been given to the world. Whether there is matter enough in the poetry of Herwegh, 'tendentious' as it is from first to last, and whether there is real originality enough in its singularly brilliant form to warrant such treatment, must be decided by other critics. As a politician, he was, in a phrase of his own, an 'audacious enthusiast' who was disillusioned by every great movement, whether liberal or national, through which he had lived—beginning with that of 1848, the only one in which he played an active part. He was, no doubt, much misunderstood in his day; his share in the Baden insurrection was far from being really discreditable to him, while his earlier interview with Frederick William IV furnished no proof either of servility or of insolence. But he was impracticable with an impracticability far surpassing that of the 'professors' for whom (though it seems as if he would at one time have himself accepted a chair in distant Naples) he expressed, and no doubt felt, so thorough a contempt. Extraordinarily acute in the judgement of men, and master of a style which, whether in prose or in verse, never failed to attract by its grace, wit, and fire, he rendered no material service to any cause to which he gave his sympathy, unless as a journalist to the party of Mazzini, and as a song-writer to the followers of Lassalle. Yet in neither case was he able to subordinate his own opinions, and to the last he claimed the right of absolute intellectual independence. Thus what he said as the poet, though he thought it inapplicable to the publicist, really held good of his entire activity as a writer. He found out much that was wrong, but it was not his task to find out remedies. At least, he could specify none except the sword, and of this, too, he came to despair. For all that, he held by his faith, and the commentary furnished by his life on an evolution which he abhorred will not be wholly useless to historians. As a record of refugee literature and journalism from 1840 onwards it has special value. A. W. W.

An interesting phase of Prussian history is treated by Dr. Walter Schmidt in his account of the liberal-conservative faction which during the lean years 1850 to 1858 played a conspicuous though not determining part in the affairs of the monarchy (*Die Partei Bethmann-Hollweg und die Reaktion in Preussen, 1850–1858*. Berlin: A. Duncker, 1910). Notwithstanding some repetition, and an often rather involved style, this essay is worth attention, both as a contribution to the history of the reaction of those years and as a careful analysis of the origin, principles, and conduct of the Bethmann-Hollweg party, which sought to modify that movement and helped to prepare the nation for the endeavours of the so-called 'new era'. As for the reaction, the spirit of it, when at once most consistent and most high-minded, stands fully revealed to us in the memoirs of its true leader, Ludwig von Gerlach, of whom and of whose associates Dr. Schmidt says with truth, that their policy was one of principles, not of interests. He is equally ready to render justice to the chief instrument of the reaction, the publication of whose own memoirs has helped to bring about a reconsideration of the contemptuous judgement with which Manteuffel was visited by a generation that reaped the fruits of his patience and self-abnegation. But the main theme of this essay is to be found in the efforts of the men who, while at heart both royalists and conservatives, yet recognized that the future of Prussia could not lie with a patriarchal absolutism, born from the ideas of Haller and fed by the fancies of King Frederick William IV and his *camarilla*. Bethmann-Hollweg, a Frankfort patrician of great legal learning and strong religious sympathies, and the diplomatists and lawyers who were the chief members of his party, would at first have been contented to act with Manteuffel, who, not only in connexion with the eastern question, showed himself more or less amenable to the influence of their notions. But by the spring of 1854 the plan of a fusion, on which the king had seemed to smile, had broken down, and the *Kreuzzeitung* had triumphed over the *Wochenblatt*, the liberal-conservative organ (1851–61). The dismissal of Count Albert Pourtalès, followed by the fall of Bunsen, implied the hopelessness of a conservative reunion; and henceforth the eyes of the Bethmann-Hollweg faction were turned rather to the possibilities of a remoter future than to any thoughts of a present share in the government of the state. To what extent the leaders of the party were consoled, and to what disappointed, on the advent to power of the prince of Prussia in the autumn of 1858—when Bethmann-Hollweg, as minister of *Cultus*, and some of his associates were included in the ministry of Prince Hohenzollern, whom they had long designated for the presidency—may be read in the later pages of Dr. Schmidt's essay. In his earlier chapters he has traced very clearly the policy of the party, while in opposition and nicknamed 'the Malcontents' by their adversaries, in both home and foreign affairs; their loyalty to the new constitution (of January 1850) and resistance to the reversal of its principles as to both legislation and administration; their leaning to England and to English constitutional ideas; their endeavours for the separation of church and state. Throughout he has kept in view and illustrated with much acumen the affinity between their political conceptions and the interests and ideas of the western half of the Prussian monarchy, in contrast to those of the so-called 'old' or eastern provinces. Less convincing, perhaps, is the section dealing with the German policy of the party; at least, we cannot feel quite satisfied with the explanation of Bethmann-Hollweg's advice to Frederick William IV to accept the imperial crown, viz. a fear on his part that a refusal would be followed by a revolt of the Rhenish provinces. A. W. W.

Two volumes in the Columbia University *Studies in History, Economics, and Public Law*, xxxix. 2, and xl. 2, by Dr. S. D. Brumner and Dr. G. H. Porter, deal with the *Political History of New York State during the Period of the Civil War*, and with *Ohio Politics during the Civil War Period.* Both writers make good use of newspaper material, and the general contrast between the condition of things in New York and in Ohio makes more striking the similarity of the position of those in either state who, though nominally in favour of the union, disliked the abolitionists more than they disliked the confederates, and who had serious doubts both as to the power and as to the right of the north to prevent secession. H. E. E.

It would be futile to bring a charge of cruelty against Dr. Kurt Dorien on account of the process which he has instituted against the *Bericht des Herzogs Ernst II von Koburg über den Frankfurter Fürstentag 1863* (*Historische Bibliothek*, vol. xxi. Munich: Oldenbourg, 1910). For the earlier volumes of the duke's memoirs have been before the world something like a quarter of a century; and with their writer have passed away most of the men of light and learning who helped him in their production—notably Ottokar Lorenz, whose correspondence with the duke on the subject seems, in part at least, to have, perhaps with sufficient reason, remained unpreserved in the Coburg archives. The memoirs themselves, which cannot be said to be particularly good reading or equal in style to what might have been expected from the Maecenas of so many eminent literary men, still, as even Dr. Dorien condescends to admit, have their use; though this use is limited by the well-known character of Ernest II and by its influence upon his ways as a historian of his own time. He was neither quite so important a personage as he believed, nor quite so dangerous as Bismarck pretended to think him when he proposed to King William to spirit him away by means of a regiment of hussars. But, as even his present critic allows, ' when everything in Germany favoured a dark reaction, he alone protected liberal ideas and was impervious to the attacks of his princely colleagues.' As for his memoirs, they can be made to yield the truth by means of an ' application of the historic method '; and this method Dr. Dorien has here applied, with the utmost thoroughness, to the episode, in which Duke Ernest played a prominent part, of the Frankfort *Fürstentag* of 1863. His general estimate of the character of the memoirs is given in an introduction, and his judgement of the duke himself in one of the longest and least genial postscripts ever attached to an essay of this description. The *Fürstentag* itself is now well understood to have been a false move. Dr. Dorien is at great pains to expose the discrepancy between the duke's apologetic attempt to represent himself as throughout a friend to the claims of Prussia (consistently advocated by Baden) and the emperor of Austria as showing a just appreciation of these claims, and the actual state of the case. It is certainly surprising, not that the action of Austria should have for a time at least taken captive the imagination of the sanguine duke, and that he should have believed the Emperor Francis Joseph to have been personally willing to concede to Prussia the place due to her in the reformed confederation, but that so many others, including, as Dr. Dorien fails to mention, foreign diplomatists of insight, should have shared in the delusion that the *Fürstentag* would prove anything but an addled egg. No doubt, the most interesting passages of this essay are those which throw serious doubt on the wish of the emperor and his government to come to an understanding with Prussia beforehand, or to avoid as a final result that isolation of her which the absence of the king from the congress—really more important than anything which happened at it—betokened. A. W. W.

Though the contents of Mr. Hawkling L. Yen's *Survey of Constitutional Development in China* (Columbia University *Studies in History, Economics, and Public Law*, no. 104, 1911) are not all of equal value, still much of the information in it about ancient China will be both new and interesting to the European student. It is not on that account, however, that we give it a hearty welcome. At the present moment China is struggling, amid difficulties, towards constitutional government, and is in sore need of competent advisers. She may best hope to find such persons, not among Europeans, but among those of her own sons who, like Mr. Yen, not only have studied the history of their own country, but are well acquainted with the political institutions of western nations. T. L. B.

The rule which forbids the discussion in this Review of subjects of current politics allows us only to record the appearance of an important contribution to recent history in *The Life of Spencer Compton, eighth Duke of Devonshire* (London: Longmans, 1911), which Mr. Bernard Holland has written in two volumes with much skill and with intimate knowledge. We may, however, say that the materials which it contains form a valuable supplement to the Lives of Mr. Gladstone and Lord Granville by Lord Morley of Blackburn and Lord Fitzmaurice. X.

A large part of Mr. R. W. Seton-Watson's treatise on *The Southern Slav Question and the Habsburg Monarchy* (London: Constable, 1911) is devoted to political questions outside the scope of this Review. But it also has chapters, which contain useful summaries of Croatian and Servian history and literature, based upon the best authorities and showing much research. One or two mistakes may be detected, such as the statements that Stephen Uroš V 'was murdered in 1367 by Vukašin' (whose death in 1371 he survived by two months), and that the Bosnian queen, whose monument still exists in Ara Coeli, was the 'mother' (instead of the stepmother) of Stephen Tomasević (pp. 38, 40, n. 46). Much interest attaches to the correspondence between Gladstone and Bishop Strossmayer, published in an appendix, and an excellent account of that remarkable ecclesiastical statesman's services to Slav scholarship is given. Mr. Seton-Watson's ideal is not a Great Servia under the auspices of Belgrade or Cetinje, but Serbo-Croatian unity under Habsburg sway, supplemented by a customs' union and a military convention between the thus reconstructed triune monarchy and the two independent Servian kingdoms. A full bibliography completes a valuable book, of which the defects are a lack of proportion in dealing with some recent events, and a rather obvious, but scarcely avoidable, partisanship. W. M.

Sir William R. Anson has published a revised reissue of the fourth edition of the first volume of his *Law and Custom of the Constitution* (Oxford: Clarendon Press, 1911), in which he has done his best to incorporate the changes made by the Parliament Act of last session, and has introduced a couple of paragraphs on the payment of members. The matter which has been removed to make room for these insertions leaves a distinct historical value to the unrevised fourth edition of 1909. Y.

The Flintshire Historical Society has made a good start by printing the address given last January by Professor T. F. Tout on *Flintshire, its History and its Records* (1911), in which he dealt with the formation of the modern county and the sources from which its history may be built up. Coming from an authority so experienced, the lecture is sure to give a lead as well as a stimulus to much valuable local research. Mr. Tout treats his subject with much frankness. The history of the district before it became an administrative unit at a comparatively late period is so obscure that the need of forming a society for special investigation was amply justified. The lecturer did not conceal from the members the difficulties in front of them, nor did he attempt to clear up disputed points: his object was rather to indicate the obscurities which awaited explanation, and the hints thrown out, as to methods of work and the most productive sources for the recovery of materials, will prove of great assistance in solving the geographical and fiscal problems which lie at the root of Flintshire history. In the department of ecclesiastical history, of which Mr. Tout has said little, a suggestion has been made to account for the peculiar type of architecture found in Flintshire churches which deserves the consideration of ecclesiologists. It is not only new and original, but seems entirely happy and conclusive. Church architecture in the vale of Clwyd is distinguished by a double nave of equal dimensions, which is exceedingly rare in Britain. It is suggested that the type was Dominican, as may be seen in the great church at Toulouse, erected as the church of the mother house of the Order, and in other Dominican churches in that region. In support of the conjecture good reasons have been advanced to show that Dominican influence was preponderant in Flintshire when churches were rebuilt after the devastations of the Welsh wars in the latter half of the thirteenth century. One can scarcely conceive a better manual for the guidance of the new society than Mr. Tout's paper. If a similar production could be put into the hands of members of local archaeological societies in England, covering the area of their respective operations, a great service to history would be achieved. J. W.

The first thing that strikes one in the *Historical Collections of Staffordshire*, 1911 (William Salt Archaeological Society), is the extraordinary energy of the honorary secretary, Mr. J. C. Wedgwood, M.P., who, not content with having brought about a great increase of members, has directly, or indirectly, edited a great part of this volume, and has written all the reviews in it himself. The contents are slightly miscellaneous, but all deal with periods earlier than the reign of Edward III. They include a summary of the Liberate Rolls of Henry III so far as they affect Staffordshire, and, with a similar limitation, the Final Concords of Edward I and Edward II, and the Post-mortem Inquests of Henry III, Edward I, and Edward II. This third item, which occupies more than half of the book, usefully supplements the new printed calendar by giving the Staffordshire inquests in full. A study of the Staffordshire 'Testa de Nevill' and other local feodaries, and an instalment of a Staffordshire cartulary, 1200–1327, complete the volume. The William Salt Society is lucky in being able to work from the immense mass of transcripts preserved in its library at Stafford, but would it not be better, when these transcripts are printed, for them to be compared with the original records ? In the last part Mr. Wedgwood prints and comments on some little-known deeds in various custodies. His observations are acute and helpful, but is he not going rather too far in saying ' prior to the reign of Edward II charters very rarely have a dating clause ' ? T. F. T.

Mr. Walter H. Godfrey's *History of Architecture in London* (London : Batsford, 1911) is likely to be a useful book as well as a popular one. It is by far the best existing guide-book to old London buildings, and it will make an admirable introduction to the study of ancient architecture for those who live in London. It is generously illustrated with nearly 250 figures, and it has excellent lists of buildings with clear key-maps showing their position. It must take its place as an indispensable ' London book ', and it would be well if such an account of the monuments of every county were in existence; the sentiment of local regard for our old buildings needs to be brought out. History best begins at home. The text of the present volume is written from the point of view of making London buildings illustrate a general history of architecture ; the figures in the text should lead to a direct study of the buildings themselves. It should be said that no full and critical account of the large number of buildings referred to is to be found in this work : it is a remarkably full schedule of London buildings with a descriptive text which points out their place in architectural history, while the illustrations provide a convenient and valuable record of works which now exist. It certainly does ' reveal the architectural riches of London '. W. R. L.

The last volumes that have reached us of the Dublin Parish Register Society are perhaps not likely to prove so generally attractive as those which preceded them, but they are equally with them of value to the local historian and genealogist. To take them in order, the *Registers of St. Catherine, Dublin, 1636–1715* (1908), though containing few names of mark, deserve notice owing to the close connexion with the parish of the Brabazon family, as the lords of Thomas Court. Of the ancestor of the earls of Meath, Sir William Brabazon, whose body was interred here and a memorial slab to him erected by his son Edward, while his heart was placed in Eastwell Church, Leicestershire, there is no notice. Indeed, except for certain extracts contained in a manuscript in Trinity College, it is only in 1679 that the register properly begins. The parish was always a poor one, and perhaps the wealthiest householder in it at that time was Captain Samuel Molyneux, at whose house in New Row his two sons, William, the author of the famous tract on Ireland being bound by laws made in England, and Dr., afterwards Sir Thomas, were born ; but none of the family are buried in the church. Like the Molyneux, the Desmineers were of Dutch origin, though the latter in the first instance apparently came from Rouen. In 1637 Daniel Desmineer, the founder of the family, was assessed at £4 as his share of the first subsidy voted in that year by parliament, which does not show great wealth. With the parish of St. Catherine we are still in the city of Dublin, with that of the union of *Monkstown, 1669-1786* (1908) we pass into the county. According to the editor, Mr. H. S. Guiness, the union of Monkstown included from 1670 the parishes of Monkstown, Kill o' the Grange, Dalkey, Killiney, Tully, Stillorgan, and Kilmacud, in fact the entire district bounded by the suburban parish of Donnybrook on the north, the parish of Bray on the south, on the east by the sea, and the Dublin mountains on the west. It appears from a list of persons residing in the union, returned in 1766, that while the protestants, to the number of 448, were liberally provided for as regards churches, the catholics, who numbered 1,273, had no place of public worship.

More interesting as well as historically more important than either of these two volumes is that containing the *Registers of Derry Cathedral, 1642-1703* (1910), to which Canon Hayes has prefixed a short but sufficient introduction. With the exception of that of Lisburn, the Derry Cathedral Register is the oldest outside Dublin, and from a note at the beginning it is apparent that one book at least preceding that beginning in May 1642 was once in existence. Its loss is greatly to be deplored as a record of the names of the first settlers in that part of Ireland. As noticed by Canon Hayes, there are considerable gaps in the register. The war of 1641-52 accounts for one; the siege in 1689 for another; but what caused the gap in the marriage list between 1668 and 1678 is a mystery. The evidence that Derry was a garrison town is plainly written in the number of soldiers married and buried in the parish. But perhaps for most students the most interesting part of the volume is that falling between 1653 and 1660. In stating that from 1647 to the Restoration the city was under the command of Sir Charles Coote, Canon Hayes is not quite accurate. Coote's authority ended with the appointment of the commissioners of revenue for Ulster in 1651; and there is less than justice in his remark that during the whole period ' probably either officers from the army or itinerants from Dublin were alone permitted to preach within the city'. Derry had its own minister in the person of the Rev. George Holland. R. D.

It is an interesting task to compare the organization of the German ' Grundherrschaft' with that of an English manor: such comparisons throw light on the essential traits of both institutions, and on the conditions of their economic development. Dr. C. Brinkmann has just published an interesting monograph on *Wustrau, Wirtschafts- und Verfassungsgeschichte eines brandenburgischen Ritterguts* (Leipzig: Duncker & Humblot, 1911), which is likely to recall to mind the results of Miss Davenport's book on Forncett and of Mr. A. Ballard's paper on Woodstock in the *Vierteljahrsschrift für Social- und Wirtschaftsgeschichte*, 1909. Wustrau is an estate near Ruppin in Brandenburg belonging to Count von Zieten-Schwerin. It grew out of a fee granted to the Zietens, a family of knights of possibly Slavonic origin, on conquered Slavonic soil. The name of the place is the Slavonic designation of *island*. A register of 1491 shows the intermixture of rights and scattering of plots under which the Zieten possessions were held. The gradual concentration of the estate and the progress of its farming are described by Dr. Brinkmann at some length. The most interesting document in the history of the estate is an award of 1771, and a terrier connected with it (pp. 100 ff.), which show how the lord succeeded in extricating his land from the fetters of the open-field system. It would be out of the question to follow the author in his patient investigation of manorial rights, rents, services, and technical points of agriculture, but, of course, it is just this thoroughness of treatment and wealth of concrete facts that make such monographs interesting and suggestive. P. V.

Philip's New Historical Atlas for Students, by Professor Ramsay Muir (London, 1911), is an enlarged edition of the author's *New School Atlas of Modern History*, which appeared early last year. It contains 197 maps, plans, and diagrams, as compared with 149 in the former issue; and the plates are folded and mounted on guards, so that the book takes the convenient form of an octavo instead of a quarto volume. We do not know of any English historical atlas to compare with it as a work for general reference published at a low price; Professor Muir would be the first to disclaim its adequacy for detailed study of an advanced kind. But within its scope it deserves hearty recommendation. The maps are well drawn and excellently produced; the scale of each is clearly marked; the names inserted are, as a rule, well chosen and are not too numerous. Physical features are, wherever possible, indicated, and there are some maps constructed on a strictly physical basis. There is a very interesting series of plates showing side by side the advance of geographical knowledge and the progress of colonial expansion. It would have been a good thing if the editor had mentioned more specifically the authorities which he has followed in planning his maps. The arrangement of the maps, while it shows much ingenuity, is sometimes a little confusing; but any difficulty arising from this cause will be met by consulting the classified table of contents. An index of names adds to the merits of a thoroughly useful book. Z.

CORRECTIONS IN THE OCTOBER NUMBER

P. 727. We are asked by Mr. Round to express his regret that he inadvertently quoted a misrendering of 'pesage' from the *Calendar of Inquisitions post Mortem*, ii. 277, where it is in fact given correctly. It is only in the index (p. 704) that the word is given as 'passage'.

P. 805. The publisher of M. Mathiez's *Rome et le Clergé français* is not, as stated, M. Félix Alcan, but M. Armand Colin.

THE ENGLISH HISTORICAL REVIEW

NO. CVI.—APRIL 1912 *

William the Conqueror's March to London in 1066

IT has been generally agreed that William the Conqueror, on approaching London after the battle of Senlac, made no attempt to cross the Thames, but marched along its right bank and found a crossing at Wallingford nearly fifty miles above the city. A suggestion has recently been proposed that his movements were governed by military considerations, as ' a long sweep about a hostile city was favourite strategy of William's '.[1] In this essay I am chiefly concerned to show that William crossed the Thames at Kew, and to explain the reasons for his subsequent march to Wallingford.

Our direct sources of information about his movements are few and poor. First, there is the chronicle [2] of William of Poitiers, his chaplain, whose statements must be accepted as valuable on account of his official position, but used cautiously as coming from a man of foreign birth who probably knew little of English geography. No convincing reason has ever been cited for supposing that he was with the Conqueror at Senlac, or even shortly after the battle. He omits the names of the leaders of the army; he gives no description of the submission of any town of importance, except Dover, Canterbury, and London, and he records no incident which betrays curiosity or even personal observation. We have instead a meagre and colourless narrative, which reads as though it were based on what had been told him either by his master the Conqueror or by some of his master's servants.

Next we may notice the Latin song [3] written soon after the

---

[1] G. B. Adams, *The Political History of England, 1066–1216*, p. 6.
[2] Printed in Migne's *Patrologiae Cursus Completus*, tom. cxlix.
[3] *De Bello Hastingensi Carmen*, printed by Henry Petrie and John Sharpe in the *Monumenta Historica Britannica*.

VOL. XXVII.—NO. CVI.　　　　　　　　　　　　　　　　　　　P

* All rights reserved.

Conquest and ascribed to Guy, bishop of Amiens. It has the appearance of being in substance a truthful narrative, though statements in a song are more likely to be untrustworthy in point of detail than those in a prose chronicle. Guy has much to say on matters which the other chroniclers pass by in silence, such, for instance, as the preparations for the siege of London. These have been treated by modern critics as purely imaginary events on the ground that they are inconsistent with what William of Poitiers has said. Nevertheless, instead of rejecting Guy's statements, we ought to seek explanations by which they can be reconciled with those of other authorities.

The chronicle of Florence of Worcester, who died in or about 1118, and the version of the Saxon Chronicle, sometimes designated by the letter D and often called the Worcester chronicle, contain very brief accounts of the events which occurred between the battle of Senlac and the coronation of William. Florence gives the fuller narrative, but he says nothing which contradicts the statements in the Worcester chronicle. These authorities are valuable in that they supply some information about the doings of the English, which, coming from an English source, is at least presumptively trustworthy. William, the monk of Malmesbury, who died about 1142, gives an even briefer account than Florence's; and it is somewhat different. If we accept Florence of Worcester's account rather than William of Malmesbury's, it is partly because Florence has the better reputation for accuracy, and partly because his account is more consistent with what may be learnt from the other authorities.

Some indirect evidence was published by Mr. F. H. Baring in this Review in January 1898.[4] He found from Domesday Book that certain manors in the counties round London were of considerably less value at the date when the Domesday tenant received them, than they had been in the reign of the Confessor, and were afterwards at the time of the survey. He assumed that they had been wasted by the Conqueror before his coronation, and he so constructed from Domesday an itinerary of the invaders. But it is unlikely that the main army laid waste the country wherever it marched. Its advance was rapid and almost certainly along good roads. Small forces sent to obtain supplies and secure the submission of the county towns are more likely to have burnt farms than the main army. We can believe that the Kentish peasantry allowed the victorious William to pass unmolested, and yet attacked small detachments of his army and so provoked reprisals. Again, many of the low valuations on which Mr. Baring relies might be explained otherwise. Famine, for instance, has her own tale of woe to tell, and often she wanders

[4] *Ante*, xiii. 17–25.

far from the stricken field of battle. We know, too, that before Harold left London it had been proposed to lay waste the country between the city and the channel, so as to impede the march of the invaders.[5] It is likely enough that many acts of wanton destruction were perpetrated by the English soldiers in their flight from Senlac. Moreover, if military considerations compelled William to burn some manors, prudence must have counselled him to leave others intact. In all probability his instructions were brief and general. His men were to encourage submission and punish resistance. Domesday is no easy document to interpret. The dates when the tenants received their lands varied; the three separate valuations are not always recorded; and there are other difficulties which make it impossible to construct from it the actual itinerary of the Conqueror and his army. Nevertheless, we may gather from Mr. Baring's interesting paper some useful information.

William's first move after the battle at Senlac was to Hastings, where, according to Guy of Amiens, he stayed five days.[6] He then marched to Dover, stopping on his way at Romney to avenge the slaughter of some of his men who had landed there in error.[7] This done, he took possession of the town and castle of Dover without fighting, and remained there eight days, which he occupied in strengthening the fortifications.[8] On his withdrawal the citizens of Canterbury came to meet him, swore fealty to him, and gave him hostages.[9] The next day he arrived at the Broken Tower, where he pitched his camp.[10] Where was this Broken Tower, or *Turris Fracta*? There is no town or village in Kent bearing a name which could be correctly so rendered in Latin. Either the name is a blunder, or it must be used of some small stronghold which ceased to exist soon after the Conquest. The chronicler is most emphatic in stating that his master pitched his camp the next day at the Broken Tower and then fell ill. But the Conqueror is not likely to have marched from Dover to some obscure and insignificant place for his next halt. Wherever the Broken Tower may have been, it was at or near some town capable of supporting an army for a short time. I believe that *Turris Fracta* is either a blunder, which cannot now be explained, for Sandwich, or else some small fortress in or adjoining

---

[5] Wace, *Le Roman de Rou*, ed. Frédéric Pluquet, ii. 166.

[6] 'Hastinge portus castris tunc quinque diebus mansit,' l. 597.

[7] 'poenam exigit pro clade suorum, quos illuc errore appulsos:' William of Poitiers, p. 1257.

[8] 'Recepto castro, que minus erant per dies octo addidit firmamenta:' *ibid.* p. 1257.

[9] 'Occurrunt ultro Cantuarii haud procul a Douera, iurant fidelitatem, dant obsides:' *ibid.* p. 1258.

[10] 'Veniens postero die ad Fractam Turrim castra metatus est, quo in loco grauissima sui corporis ualetudine animos familiarium pari conturbauit aegritudine:' *ibid.*

that town.[11] The Conqueror was already in possession of Pevensey, Hastings, Romney, and Dover. Moreover, as Winchelsea and Rye lie between Hastings and Romney, and Hythe between Romney and Dover, we may regard it as certain that he seized these three towns on his march. Only the occupation of Sandwich was needed for him to be in possession of the eight chief seaports of east Sussex and Kent. He was bound to seize these ports promptly in order to prevent their inhabitants from equipping fleets with which to intercept reinforcements. The ships which had brought the Norman army to England were now needed to bring yet more soldiers from Normandy, and the invaders, we must assume, having for a while no navy at their disposal, were compelled to seize the seaports from the land.[12] It is highly probable that at this time a detachment of the army was also sent to seize Seaford, Shoreham, and Bosham, the three chief seaports of Sussex which lay to the west of Pevensey.

From Sandwich the Conqueror marched to Canterbury, where, according to Guy of Amiens, he stayed a month.[13] Too much stress must not be laid on Guy's precise words, for he wrote in Latin elegiacs, and it possibly suited his metre to speak of a month's stay when the true period was really less. If the Conqueror's subsequent movements be considered he can scarcely have stayed at Canterbury more than three weeks, and probably left there about 21 November.

While William was at Canterbury he sent to Winchester and demanded tribute from its citizens. Edith, the widow of the Confessor, who held the city in dower, after taking counsel of her chief men, decided to comply with the demand.

> Guincestram misit, mandat primatibus urbis,
> Vt faciunt alii, ferre tributa sibi.
> Hanc regina tenet . . .
> Solum uectigal postulat, atque fidem.
> Vna primates reginae consuluerunt
> Illaque concedens ferre petita iubet.[14]

If we may trust Guy of Amiens the tribute was paid before the Conqueror left Canterbury, for he says,

> Rex sic pacatus tentoria fixa resoluit.[15]

It is probable that William made arrangements for the occupation of the city by a Norman garrison, and we may suspect

[11] Possibly the Conqueror lodged at Richborough. W. Boys, in his *History of Sandwich*, p. 835, gives Ruppecester as one of the variant names of Richborough. A blundering writer might render Ruppecester or some similar form by *Turris Fracta*.

[12] Reinforcements actually came, but where they landed is not known. See below, p. 221.

[13] 'Per spatium mensis cum gente perendinat illic :' l. 623.

[14] *Ibid.* ll. 625-32.   [15] *Ibid.* l. 635.

that he gave directions that reinforcements from Normandy should disembark at Bosham or one of the neighbouring ports and proceed without delay to Winchester.

From Canterbury the Conqueror advanced towards London. Mr. Baring contends that he marched through various small towns and villages, leaving Rochester and even Maidstone on his right. As his advance was rapid, it is much more likely that he kept to the old Roman road through Rochester, a place of strategic importance. Neither William of Poitiers nor Guy of Amiens has recorded any resistance at Rochester, and probably none was offered. A battle or siege after the ready submission of Dover and Canterbury would have been noteworthy, whereas the surrender of another city would scarcely have appeared worth recording. Indeed, it may be that Rochester had already surrendered before William left Canterbury, for Guy of Amiens states that after the surrender of that city other towns and boroughs offered him gifts, and that from all sides men came to bend their knees and kiss the Conqueror's feet.[16] But whether Rochester had already surrendered or not, the Conqueror is not likely to have left the city in the possession of the English before he marched onwards to London.

Meanwhile the great men of the realm were busy in the metropolis. Aldred, archbishop of York, the earls Edwin and Morkere, and the citizens and the butsecarls wished to elect Edgar Atheling, the grandson of Edmund Ironside, as their king, and promised that they would fight for him; but when all warlike preparations had been made, the earls withdrew their support and went home with their army. This is Florence of Worcester's account;[17] that of the monk of Malmesbury reads a little differently. He tells us that when news of the death of Harold reached London the two earls tried to arrange that one or other of them should be made king, but that when they found that their efforts were in vain they withdrew to Northumbria in the belief that the Conqueror would never visit that part of the island.[18] Then the monk goes on to say that the rest of the magnates would have chosen Edgar as their king if they had had the bishops as their supporters. It looks very much as if, while the magnates were in the midst of their preparations for the coronation, messengers came from the pope forbidding the bishops to take part in the ceremony, and ordering them to submit to the Conqueror.[19]

Perhaps the most significant feature of these accounts is that

[16] *Ibid.* ll. 611–22.
[17] Ed. B. Thorpe, i. 228.
[18] ii. 307, ed. W. Stubbs.
[19] It will be remembered that the pope had sent William a consecrated banner: William of Poitiers, p. 1246.

they say nothing of Stigand, the archbishop of Canterbury; and yet we may gather from William of Poitiers that if Stigand was not among the English magnates in London, he was at least in correspondence [20] with Edwin and Morkere about this time. Yet, as Mr. Baring has observed, in the general devastation of the manors in the south of Kent Stigand's remained conspicuously intact. We may perhaps infer from this that he surrendered by letter or deputy when the Conqueror first entered Kent. May it not be that the men who surrendered at Canterbury were eagerly following the example of Stigand, chief among the Kentish magnates? [21] The submission of Winchester, a see which he held with his archbishopric, would have induced him, if further inducement were needed, to adhere to his new lord. If he was, as I think, among the first of the magnates to submit, the Conqueror may have seen in him a useful ally. The bishops as a body may have mistrusted their metropolitan as a heretic, but he was in a position to secure the support of a large part of the clergy in the important dioceses of Canterbury and Winchester; and his brother Ethelmar was bishop of the important diocese of Elmham. Stigand's early submission would explain his name not appearing in the English chronicles as one of the magnates who wished to have Edgar Atheling as their king. But if Edgar had been chosen it would in the ordinary course of events have fallen to the lot of Stigand to crown him; and if the pope's messengers had, as I have suggested, forbidden the bishops to take part in the coronation, the magnates would naturally have begged the heretic Stigand, in spite of his surrender, to perform the ceremony. There was a chance of his deserting his new lord, and an archbishop who had received his pall from an anti-pope might be expected to pay little attention to the orders and prohibitions of the true pope. Many a strong man in Stigand's place would have vacillated, and we may well believe that Stigand vacillated. In Matthew Paris's *Gesta Abbatum* [22] we read of the archbishop, ' Ipse similis arundini uentis agitate nunc regi nunc Anglis uidebatur inclinari.' It is likely enough that when the Conqueror reached the south bank of the Thames he learnt that Stigand was in friendly communication with the earls Edwin and Morkere, and forthwith determined to lay waste such of his manors as were then near at hand.

A body of citizens was sent across London bridge to attack William as he drew near to the city.[23] They were driven back

[20] See the passage quoted on p. 215 below.
[21] It is possible that Stigand was himself responsible for the submission.
[22] i. 45, Rolls Series.
[23] ' Praemissi illo equites Northmanni quingenti, egressam contra se aciem refugere intra moenia impigre compellunt, terga cedentes:' William of Poitiers, p. 1258. The continuation is quoted in the text below, p. 216.

with much slaughter by an advance-guard of five hundred Norman knights, who then burnt all the houses they could find on the south side of the Thames. It was probably then that Edwin and Morkere withdrew 'with their army' to the north. Perhaps as soldiers of experience with an army at their disposal they had their own ideas of the best method of resisting the invaders. If the Londoners declined to follow their advice they are likely to have refused all further assistance. Some such quarrel between them and the intimates of the Atheling might explain the discrepancy between the accounts of what happened in London given by Florence of Worcester and William of Malmesbury respectively. A claim to exercise military authority might easily have been misrepresented as a claim to the throne. But the simpler explanation of the earls' conduct may be the true one, that they saw the impossibility of maintaining the claims of the Atheling, and were already willing to surrender on the most favourable terms they could obtain. It is not clear where the two earls went on leaving London. Florence of Worcester says that they went home,[24] William of Malmesbury that they departed for Northumbria.[25] There can be no doubt that they went northward, and, having regard to the fact that immediately after the battle at Senlac they had sent their sister Ealdgyth to Chester, it is likely enough that they marched towards that city along Watling Street.[26]

Here we may pause to consider what William of Poitiers [27] says of Stigand and the proposed coronation of Edgar.

Interea Stigandus Cantuariensis archipraesul, qui sicut excellebat opibus atque dignitate, ita consultis plurimum apud Anglos poterat, cum filiis Algardi aliisque praepotentibus praelium minatur. Regem statuerunt Edgarum Adelinum ex Edwardi nobilitate annis puerum.

The word *interea* refers to the period between the Conqueror's departure from Canterbury and the defeat of the Londoners near Southwark. We may without difficulty suppose that when the Conqueror reached the banks of the Thames and moved westwards he came to Stigand's manor of Mortlake, and there learned that the archbishop had been making plans with the earls Edwin and Morkere for resisting the invaders. It is significant that though the archbishop's manors in the south of Kent appear to have been spared in the general devastation of that part of the county, the Domesday Book suggests that his manor of

[24] 'Cum suo exercitu domum redierunt :' p. 228.
[25] 'Northanhimbriam discesserant ex suo coniectantes ingenio nunquam illuc Willelmum esse uenturum :' ii. 307.
[26] 'Et sororem suam Aldgitham reginam sumptam ad ciuitatem Legionum misere :' Florence of Worcester, p. 228.
[27] p. 1258.

Mortlake on Thames was wasted by the invaders.[28] But whether the Conqueror first learnt of Stigand's duplicity when he reached Mortlake or some time earlier, we have in William of Poitiers's account evidence that the archbishop was at this time the political associate of the earls Edwin and Morkere. This is a fact which throws some light on subsequent events.

According to the received opinion the Conqueror, after burning Southwark, marched to Wallingford without crossing the Thames. The only authority which has been cited in its support is a passage in the chronicle [29] of William of Poitiers, which appears to me to have been seriously misinterpreted.

Multae stragi addunt incendium, cremantes quidquid aedificiorum citra flumen inuenere ut malo duplici superba ferocia contundatur. Dux progrediens dein quoque uersus placuit transmeato flumine Tamesi uado simul atque ponte ad oppidum Guarenfort peruenit.

The chronicler here states distinctly that William reached Wallingford after he had crossed the river. As the town is on the Berkshire side of the Thames, the received opinion supposes that the chronicler's account is inaccurate, but it fails entirely to explain the inaccuracy. It is, however, quite easy to believe that William crossed the river twice before he reached Wallingford, the first time from south to north (as I hold, at Kew), the second time in the reverse direction. The second crossing being further from London would have been less worthy of notice than the first, where the river was broader. There is, therefore, nothing remarkable in William of Poitiers mentioning one crossing only, and in that crossing being the one nearer London; more especially if the first crossing was difficult and the second easy.

The Conqueror was now master of Dover, the chief port of the kingdom, Canterbury, its ecclesiastical capital, and Winchester, its second city in political importance. He had repulsed the men whom the citizens of London had sent to oppose him, and he was now, so we are told, free to go where he would. Without doubt his next object was to secure the submission of London with as little delay as possible. To do this he had no need to march some fifty miles to the west of the city. There were several fords much nearer London than Wallingford, by which he could have crossed the river, had he chosen to do so. There was no strategic advantage in occupying Wallingford rather than several other towns on the banks of the Thames.

The nearest ford to London was between Lambeth and Westminster, where in ancient times Watling Street crossed the Thames. The Conqueror almost certainly made no serious

[28] 'Totum manerium T.R.E. ualebat xxxii lib. et post x lib. Modo xxxviii lib.:' D.B. f. 31ʳ.   [29] p. 1258.

attempt to cross here. There is some reason for thinking that the ford was no longer used; but if it were in use, no prudent general would have ventured to pass through a ford more than a quarter of a mile long, and not two miles distant from a strong and populous city like London. If the Conqueror had crossed here, William of Poitiers would have given some account of his successful landing at Westminster, which would have been a military exploit well worth recording.

The next ford [30] of military importance up the river was between Kew and Brentford. Just fifty years earlier Edmund Ironside had led an army across the Thames at Brentford.[31] The story of that exploit, then still lingering in the neighbourhood, would have reached the Conqueror's ears, who was likely to have attempted what Edmund had achieved. Kew is situate on the south bank of the Thames at a distance of nearly nine miles from London Bridge and five miles from Kingston, at this time a place of no military importance, but perhaps, after Southwark and Guildford, politically the chief town in Surrey. Kingston seems to have surrendered without a fight; at any rate the chroniclers say nothing of a siege, and Domesday [32] suggests that it had suffered no waste when it came into the king's hands. The Conqueror might have been content to send a detachment of his troops to accept the surrender of Kingston, while he busied himself with the ford at Kew; and if there was a bridge at Kingston at this date the detachment may have been directed to cross the river by the bridge and then proceed to Brentford. This at first sight might be taken to be the explanation of the words 'transmeato flumine Tamesi uado simul atque ponte'. A part of the army crossed at Kingston by bridge, the rest by ford at Kew. This is not the best explanation. The existence of the bridge at Kingston is very doubtful, and the distance of Kew from Kingston is too great for the words *simul atque* to refer to such a double crossing. We may therefore turn to what is, I contend, the true explanation of the words of William of Poitiers.

In the middle ages Old Brentford was a small town consisting of one long street lying along the north bank of the Thames. Not being of sufficient importance to form a parish of itself, it was ecclesiastically a part of Ealing. A chain of three islands called 'aits', or 'eyots', nearer Brentford than Kew, lies in the bed of the river, stretching almost from one end of the town

---

[30] There were ferries at Chelsea and Fulham in the middle ages. Perhaps at the time of the Norman Conquest fords were in use in these places, but there is no reason for supposing that they were considered important from a military point of view.

[31] *Two Saxon Chronicles*, ed. C. Plummer, i. 150.

[32] 'T.R.E. et post et modo ualuit xxx libre:' D.B. f. 30ᵛ.

to the other.[33] To-day when the channel lies on the Surrey side of the aits, the other passage is at low tide choked with mud. In former days it was not so : there was a narrow but navigable channel between the aits and Brentford, and the Surrey passage was broad and shallow.[34] So much importance was attached to the maintenance of the ancient channel that when, in 1757, one Robert Tunstall obtained an act of parliament [35] for constructing a bridge across the river, a section was inserted prohibiting gravel, sand, or mud from being taken from the river bed between Kew and the aits ; the intention, no doubt, being that nothing should be done by which the ancient channel might be diverted from the Brentford side of the aits to the Surrey side.

The situation of the ford across the Thames can be identified without difficulty. From the main street of Brentford a steep lane, now called Smith Hill, running southwards to the water's edge, serves as the chief approach from the street to the river. If the lane were continued southwards it would pass over the topmost ait before reaching the Surrey bank. Continued northwards it crosses the main street at right angles and leads to Ealing, in which parish, as already mentioned, Old Brentford formerly lay. Next to the main street this lane, which is still called Ealing Lane, was until recently the most important road in Old Brentford.[36] But if Smith Hill were continued across the river, passing over the topmost ait, it would reach the Surrey bank at a place where another lane formerly ran into the river. This lane, which, in 1748, was called Love Lane and then separated Kew Gardens from Richmond Gardens, led to Sheen.[37] There can be no reasonable doubt that the ancient ford connected

[33] The two lower aits almost join one another, and they probably once formed a single island which was called Brentford Ait. On the official map sold at Kew Gardens these two aits are called Kew Aits ; and the upper ait is called Lot's Ait.

[34] The aits, though nearer Brentford than Kew, were in the county of Surrey. (T. Faulkner, *Brentford, Ealing, and Chiswick*, p. 163.) In the earliest ordnance maps the channel is represented as lying between Lot's Ait and the Brentford Aits, and between the Brentford Aits and Brentford. At an earlier date, however, the channel probably lay between Lot's Ait and the Brentford shore. Possibly it was diverted when the Grand Junction Canal, which joins the Thames just above Lot's Ait, was constructed.

[35] 30 Geo. II, c. 63.

[36] Even now an omnibus plies between Ealing and Old Brentford along this road.

[37] This lane is called Love Lane on the two plans of Richmond Gardens by John Roque, which are dated 1734 and 1748 respectively, and are now in Museum iii at Kew. It will also be found clearly marked on a manuscript map at the British Museum, by Thomas Richardson, made in 1771 ; but it is there called Kew Foot-lane. This map is described as 'The Royal Gardens of Richmond and Kew. ... Taken under the direction of Peter Burrell Esq. ... by Thomas Richardson'. In Museum iii there is another map by Peter Burrell, also dated 1771, of the Manor of Richmond, which includes Kew. In this map Lot's Ait is marked as lying outside the manor ; but it should not on that account be assumed that this ait was then in Middlesex, and not in Surrey.

Smith Hill and Love Lane. It was along this line of connexion that Robert Tunstall proposed to construct the bridge for which he obtained the act of parliament already mentioned. It was to begin at Smith Hill in Brentford and pass over the topmost ait.

In these geographical facts we may see the best explanation of the words of William of Poitiers, 'transmeato flumine Tamesi uado simul atque ponte.' The invaders crossed the broad and shallow passage from Kew to the island by the ford, and the narrow and deeper channel from the island to Old Brentford by a bridge. If the river were swollen, as is likely, by the winter floods, it would have been difficult, perhaps impossible, to pass through the deeper channel by the ford, and a bridge of boats or some other military bridge would have been a necessity. The crossing would have been especially difficult at neap tides, which occurred in the last days of November.[38]

Let us now assume that the Conqueror crossed the Thames at Kew. Having marched up Smith Hill he found himself in the principal street of Old Brentford, which was then part of the main road from London to Winchester. His first business was to make preparations for the siege of London. If we may believe Guy of Amiens this was precisely the course which the Conqueror adopted.

> Paruit extemplo, celeri uelocius aura
>   Agmen belligerum castra locare sibi:
> Densatis castris a laeua moenia cinxit,
>   Et bellis hostes esse dedit uigiles.
>
> . . . .
>
> Aedificat moles, ueruecis cornua ferro,
>   Fabricat et talpas, urbis et excidium.[39]

Guy's statements have been doubted; but it is most improbable that, writing very soon after the Conquest, he would give a detailed account of what never happened merely for the sake, as has been suggested, of glorifying his master. If his story were a string of falsehoods it would have deceived nobody, and it is much more likely that he wrote what was substantially the truth. His account, too, is quite consistent with that given by William of Poitiers. Guy tells the story as he heard it from one who took part in the siege, while William bases his narrative on the statements of the Conqueror or some of his companions on the march, who took no part in the siege.

The whole of the Norman army was not needed for the siege, and as William of Poitiers says nothing of the preparations, we may suppose that the Conqueror marched with the remainder

---

[38] I assume that the ford could only have been crossed when the tide was low.
[39] ll. 661–73.

along the road to Winchester. It was important to secure the submission of the country between the two cities. It may be that the reinforcements which had come from 'over the sea'[40], or some of them, were at Winchester, and that with these the Conqueror wished to strengthen his well-worn troops. In any case it was almost a political necessity that he should lose no time in personally visiting the second, and in some respects the first, city of the island. This is an explanation which seems to me to be consistent both with the account of the siege of London given by Guy of Amiens and with the statement of William of Poitiers, which we must next consider. From the time, however, when William reached Brentford the narrative is necessarily in a large measure conjectural.

There seems to have been no direct road from London to Winchester during the Roman occupation. There was a straight road westwards to Silchester passing through Brentford and crossing the Thames, probably by a bridge, at Staines; and there was another almost straight road southwards from Silchester to Winchester which passed through Worting, a village adjoining Basingstoke on its west side. If the Roman road were still in use as far as Silchester, the Conqueror probably marched along it to that town. In modern times, however, the main road has deviated from the Roman road near what is now Virginia Water to pass through Bagshot, Hartford Bridge, and Basingstoke. If, then, the Conqueror marched along this newer road (which may have existed in his day) he found himself on reaching Basingstoke just off the ancient road from Winchester to Silchester which led northwards to Pangbourne on Thames,[41] whence another road led to Wallingford, the chief military centre of Berkshire, and the town to which William of Poitiers says that the Conqueror marched after leaving the neighbourhood of Southwark. The chronicler, however, gives no information either of the route or the object of the march to Wallingford. I suggest, and nothing but suggestion is possible, that on his arrival at Silchester or Basingstoke the Conqueror received a message from Stigand not only offering to surrender but also to mediate with the English magnates. As William of Poitiers is the only chronicler who speaks of the Conqueror being at Wallingford, his words[42] should be carefully noted: 'Adueniens eodem Stigandus pontifex metropolitanus manibus ei sese dedit, fidem sacramento confirmauit, abrogans Adelinum quem leuiter elegerat.' Stigand, as bishop of Winchester, held the manor of Harwell, situate

---

[40] See p. 221 below.
[41] At this date, however, there may have been a more direct road connecting Winchester and Wallingford.
[42] p. 1258.

scarcely eight miles from Wallingford, and also several 'haws' in the borough itself.[43] His presence at Wallingford therefore needs no special explanation.

For long periods during the middle ages Oxfordshire and Berkshire had a sheriff in common; and in the eleventh and twelfth centuries Wallingford was as important a place as any in these counties. It is likely enough that when Stigand decided to surrender at the great Berkshire stronghold the magnates of both these counties met and resolved to follow his example. The mere fact that, after the defeat of the Londoners, Stigand's surrender is the only incident of the march (except the crossing of the Thames) which William of Poitiers mentions, suggests its supreme importance. But his surrender is suggestive of something more than this. In an earlier passage the same chronicler especially mentions Stigand as acting in concert with Edwin and Morkere; so that we may perhaps see in the impending surrender of the two earls one of the causes of the Conqueror turning away from Winchester and marching from Basingstoke or Silchester northwards to Wallingford. With his new allies the surrender of London might well seem imminent, and an immediate visit to Winchester be considered as of secondary importance. And here we should remember that from a military point of view these two Mercian earls were still the chief obstacles to the Conqueror's success. Of royal birth, their names counted for much in that large part of England which lay beyond the boundaries of Wessex, and though they had been defeated at Fulford Gate, scarcely three months before, they still commanded the soldiery of Northumbria and of many of the counties of Mercia which had taken no part in the disastrous battle at Senlac. If the Conqueror's army had been reinforced from Normandy, it must also have been weakened by detachments assigned for special duties in the southern counties. Edwin and Morkere were still foes whose submission was to be desired.

We next hear of the Conqueror at Berkhamsted. Our authority is the Worcester chronicle,[44] which says, after describing the battle of 14 October:

And Count William went afterwards again to Hastings, and there awaited whether the nation would submit to him; but when he perceived that they would not come to him, he went up with all his army which was left to him, and what had afterwards come over sea to him, and harried all that part which he passed over, until he came to Berkhamsted. And there came to meet him archbishop Ealdred, and Eadgar child, and earl Eadwine, and earl Morkere, and all the best men of London.

[43] 'Walchelinus episcopus habet xxvii hagas de xxv solidis, et sunt appreciatae in Bricsteuuelle manerio eius:' D.B. i. 56ʳ. 'In Walingeford iii hagae de xv denariis:' D.B i. 58ʳ.

[44] *Anglo-Saxon Chronicle*, ii. 168, Rolls Series.

Some scholars have in recent years held that the place here mentioned was not Great Berkhamsted, but Little Berkhamsted, a small village, never of any importance, in the south-east of Hertfordshire. But where the names of two places are distinguished from one another by the addition of the adjectives Great and Little, the place-name, when standing by itself without an adjective, must obviously refer to the greater place. The identification of Berkhamsted with Little Berkhamsted rests solely on the itinerary compiled by Mr. Baring, which ought not, for the reasons already stated, to be accepted as established.

If the Conqueror on receiving the submission of Stigand had intended to march forthwith on London, he would almost certainly have chosen some route other than the one by which he had come. He would have preferred that his army should be provisioned by districts which had not already suffered in this way. He would also have welcomed the opportunity of establishing his authority in other parts of the country. Actually the distance from Wallingford to London through Tring, Berkhamsted, and Stanmore was rather shorter than through Pangbourne, Silchester, and along the Roman road eastwards to the city, and it was considerably shorter than through Pangbourne, Basingstoke, Staines, and Brentford. If, then, the Conqueror was expecting the surrender of Edwin and Morkere, it is not surprising that he decided to meet them at Berkhamsted on his way to London, rather than to wait for them at Wallingford and so waste valuable time. To reach Berkhamsted he would have marched along the Upper Icknield Way [45] in a north-easterly direction as far as Tring, when he would have turned to the right and found Berkhamsted four miles to the south-east on the direct road from Tring to London. But if Edwin and Morkere had, as is not unlikely, retired to Chester, and on Stigand's recommendation had decided to come and surrender to the Conqueror at Wallingford, they would have journeyed towards London along Watling Street as far as Dunstable and then have turned to the right along the Upper Icknield Way. Thus, if time was important to the Conqueror, Berkhamsted, just four miles off the road between Wallingford and Dunstable, was an excellent place of meeting. It is also likely to have been a stronghold which the Conqueror would have been glad to occupy.

On the way from Wallingford to Berkhamsted the Norman army passed through the village of Monk's Risborough. The manor there belonged to one Esegar the staller, who held it of Christ Church, Canterbury, so that Esegar had done homage,

[45] The Icknield Way actually crosses the Thames a little below Wallingford, but it lay within easy reach of that town.

if not to Stigand, at least to the prior of Christ Church.[46] These are most significant facts, for Guy of Amiens states that one Ansgar, who is no doubt the same person as Esegar, not only directed the military operations of the citizens during the siege of London, but also received messengers from the Conqueror about the surrender of the city.[47] Now Esegar, as one of the Christ Church knights, would at any time have found it well to pay special attention to the archbishop's wishes, but if the latter ever counselled him to surrender, Esegar would never have been less unwilling to oblige him than just when the Conqueror was marching with fire and sword towards his manor of Monk's Risborough.

Florence of Worcester's story [48] of the march on London is in substantial agreement with the Worcester chronicle :

Meanwhile Count William devastated Sussex, Kent, Hampshire, Surrey, Middlesex, Hertfordshire, and never ceased burning towns and slaying men until he came to the town which is called Beorcham ; and there Aldred the archbishop, Wulstan, bishop of Worcester, and Walter, bishop of Hereford, Edgar child, the earls Edwin and Morcar and all the most noble men from London with many others came to him ; and when they had given hostages they surrendered to him and swore fealty to him.

Apart from the fact that one account is fuller than the other, the only point on which they disagree is that the town, which in the Worcester chronicle is described as Berkhamsted, Florence describes as 'the town which is called Beorcham'. Having regard to the ancient spelling, we can have little doubt that Great Berkhamsted is the town Florence intended to designate. For the rest his account is noteworthy because it mentions some of the counties through which the Conqueror passed on his way to London. They are obviously not written in the correct order, and Berkshire, Oxfordshire, and Buckinghamshire are omitted entirely. It is not unlikely that he marched rapidly through these three counties, and that, owing to the influence of Stigand, their inhabitants offered no resistance. Domesday Book suggests that they suffered little from burning and slaughter, and this may perhaps be taken as a sufficient explanation of the omission of these counties from Florence of Worcester's list.

[46] ' Hoc manerium tenuit Asgarus Stalre de ecclesia Cristi Cantuarie ita quod non poterat separari ab ecclesia T.R.E. : ' D.B. i. 143ᵛ.
[47]   ' Omnibus ille tamen primatibus imperat urbis,
     Eius et auxilio publica res agitur.
    Huic per legatum clam rex potiora reuelat
     Secreti, poscens quatinus his faueat : ' ll. 685–8.
[48] ii. 228.

We may now return to William of Poitiers, who writes thus :

> Hinc procedenti, statim ut Lundonia conspectui patebat, obuiam exeunt principes ciuitatis, sese cunctamque ciuitatem in obsequium illius, quemadmodum ante Cantuarii tradunt, obsides quos et quot imperat adducunt.[49]

Now if the words 'statim ut Lundonia conspectui patebat' are taken literally, the place where the chief men of London surrendered to the Conqueror can scarcely be Berkhamsted, which is some twenty-seven miles distant from that city. But if, as I think, William of Poitiers was not with the Norman army, we may take it that the words mean little more than 'when he was drawing near to London'. Vague words such as these certainly offer no sufficient ground for doubting the precise statement of the Worcester chronicle that the surrender took place at Berkhamsted. A later passage,[50] which reads thus :

> Praemisit ergo Lundoniam qui munitionem in ipsa construerent urbe et pleraque competentia regia magnificentia praepararent, moraturus interim per uicina. Aduersitas omnis procul fuit, adeo ut uenatui et auium ludo, si forte libuit, secure uacaret,

certainly suggests that William of Poitiers thought that the place of surrender was at some distance from London.

A more serious difficulty is to be found in a still later passage.[51] After describing the coronation William of Poitiers proceeds thus :

> Egressus e Lundonia, dies aliquot in propinquo loco morabatur Bercingis, dum firmamenta quaedam in urbe contra mobilitatem ingentis ac feri populi perficerentur. Uidit enim in primis necessarium magnopere Lundonienses coerceri. Ibi ueniunt ad obsequium eius Eduinus et Morcardus, maximi fere omnium Anglorum genere ac potentia Algardi illius nominatissimi filii, deprecantur ueniam, si qua in se contra eum senserant, tradunt se cunctaque sua eius clementiae; item alii complures nobiles et opibus ampli.

Here we have statements which directly contradict Florence of Worcester and the Worcester chronicle. Edwin and Morkere are here represented as having surrendered not before but after the coronation, and not at Berkhamsted in Hertfordshire but at Barking in Essex, just seven miles from the city of London. The statements of the English chroniclers seem to me to be almost certainly correct. They agree better with the rest of the story, and the foreign writer is more likely to have blundered through the similarity of the names Berkhamsted and Barking than the Worcester chronicler. Indeed, it is quite possible that the Conqueror never stayed at Barking at all. It was an insignificant place in the middle ages, remarkable only for its convent of

[49] p. 1258.   [50] p. 1259.   [51] p. 1262.

Benedictine nuns, whom it is difficult to picture as the hostesses of the newly crowned king. Freeman said that William of Poitiers was capable of any disregard of chronology, but without concurring in this hostile judgement we may believe that the chronicler has repeated the substance of an earlier paragraph, which is printed above, and inserted it out of chronological order. In that case the few days which the Conqueror spent ' at Barking while certain fortifications were being completed in the city ' were the same days as those which he spent at Berkhamsted after he had sent men to construct a fortress in the city and make preparations for the coronation. But even if the Conqueror really stayed for a few days at Barking after the coronation. the similarity of the names Barking and Berkhamsted would be quite sufficient to account for William of Poitiers attributing the surrender of the earls Edwin and Morkere to the former place instead of the latter. It will be remembered that Florence of Worcester, an Englishman, speaks of the surrender having taken place at Beorcham (by which Berkhamsted is no doubt meant), and William of Poitiers, a man of foreign birth, might easily confuse Berkhamsted with Barking, more especially if (as I think) he was not one of the companions of the Conqueror on his march from Senlac to London.

G. J. TURNER.

The Powers of Justices of the Peace

IN the following paper we have endeavoured to trace the history of the doctrine that by the act of 34 Edward III, cap. i, justices of the peace were given power to bind over persons not of good fame to be of good behaviour. In the course of our inquiry we have considered the text of the act itself, the nature and cause of the discrepancy between the early translations and the authentic words of the act, and the effect of the translation in use upon the language of the textbooks. No attempt has been made to deal with the case-law of the subject; only a trained lawyer can safely attempt the delicate task of interpreting the language of legal decisions and estimating their effect upon the law. But this omission is not likely to affect our main argument. The history of the commissions issued to the justices of the peace are dealt with in some detail, and especially the very remarkable changes in form which took place at the date when the act became law, and part of the argument will be found to rest upon this evidence.

We print below (no. I) a specimen of the form of commission issued to justices of the peace before the passing of the statute in question; and we here give an abstract of the powers thereby conferred. The justices are to cause the statutes of Winchester and Northampton to be observed, and to see that the men of the county are properly armed according to their rank; and may compel the men of the county to aid them in the discharge of their office. They are to inquire into offenders against the currency and the customs, and into any sums of money extorted by sheriffs and other officials from workmen or servants; they have general powers of inquiring into felonies, trespasses, conspiracies, and a long list of other offences, and of hearing and determining the same at the king's suit only, so that this jurisdiction is purely criminal. There is also power to conclude all proceedings begun under the preceding commission; and the remainder of the commission deals with the fixing of the place and time of their sessions. It will be noted that no power of binding over to keep the peace is given to them. The date of the commission is 19 March, 31 Edward III (1357); and there is no reason to believe that any change was made in the commission before the statute of 34 Edward III.

It is not necessary for our present purpose to deal with the whole of this enactment. But we must point out that the passing of this act follows closely upon the conclusion of the treaty of Brétigny ; and that it is in part an emergency law intended to deal with discharged soldiers returned from the wars and indisposed to settle down as peaceful citizens. We have printed the text of the part of the statute in question below (no. II), and we give here a translation of it:

These are the things which our Lord the King, prelates, lords, and the commons have ordained in this present parliament held at Westminster the Sunday next before the feast of the Conversion of St. Paul to be kept and published openly throughout the realm, that is to say :—

First that in every county of England there be assigned for the keeping of the peace one lord and with him three or four of the best chosen of the county together with some persons learned in the law, and that they have power to distrain the evil-doers, rioters, and all other barrators, and to pursue, arrest, take, and chastise them according to their trespass or misprision, and to cause them to be imprisoned and duly punished according to the law and customs of the realm, and according to what in their discretion and good counsel shall seem best to them ;

And also to inform themselves and to inquire touching all those who have been plunderers and robbers beyond the sea and are now returned and go wandering and will not work as they were used to do before this time, and to take and arrest all those whom they are able to find by indictment or by suspicion, and to put them in prison, and to take of all those who are of good fame, where they shall be found, sufficient security and mainprise for their good bearing towards the king and his people, and the others duly to punish, to the end that the people be not by such rioters troubled or damaged, nor the peace broken, nor merchants or others passing on the high roads of the realm disturbed or put in fear of the peril which may arise from such evil-doers.

In this translation we have broken the text into paragraphs on the assumption that the words *And also* (or in the French *Et auxint*) mark the beginning of a new clause, a method of construction which is warranted by a comparison of the language of contemporary statutes. The first clause adds nothing to the powers already possessed by the justices ; but the following clause is entirely new. It may be as well to point out here that the text from which we have made our translation is the contemporary version enrolled on the statute roll, and that another, though less authoritative contemporary manuscript, confirms the reading of the statute roll in every particular.

In the second clause the justices are to inquire concerning any persons who have been plunderers in France, and have returned thence and are living in idleness ; if they find any, they are to arrest them ; those who are of good report in the neighbourhood are to give security to continue in good behaviour ; those against whom anything is alleged are to be properly punished ; and any brigandage is in this way to be put down.[1] The havoc wrought in France by disbanded soldiers is well known ; and there can be no doubt that the same cause produced much disorder in England. The story told in the extract from the Patent Roll of 37 Edward III, which is printed below (no. V), furnishes one instance of the kind. The writ is addressed to Warin del Isle. The counties of Wiltshire, Berkshire, and Hampshire had informed the king that a body of returned soldiers had joined with other criminals to form an armed troop, and were riding in warlike array with swords drawn through the towns of those counties, and were robbing the inhabitants, killing and maiming some and putting others to ransom. The king complains that Warin del Isle was doing nothing to oppose such violence, and orders him to join the keepers of the peace with all his power in putting down any disturbance of the kind.

There can be no doubt that legislation was needed, and the terms of the commissions issued almost immediately after the passing of the new act are even more stringent than its clauses quoted above seem to justify. The text of one of these commissions will be found below (no. III), and it may be noted that the writ to Warin del Isle has to some extent followed its phraseology. It is a long and complicated document, bearing traces of temper and alarm, and recites at length the inconvenience arising from the return of large numbers of evil-doers from abroad who lived by highway robbery and blackmail, and grants the justices the following powers. They are to keep the peace, and to enforce especially the clauses of the statutes of Winchester, Northampton, and Westminster relating thereto ; to arrest, chastise, and punish all persons found armed contrary to the statute of Northampton, or offending or suspected of offending against any of the statutes named ; to compel all men returning from foreign parts who are suspected of evil-doing, as well as any persons who may have threatened bodily injury or arson, to give sufficient security for their good behaviour, and to punish at their discretion those who refuse to do so. They are to inquire into all felonies and trespasses, and to hear and determine them at the king's suit only ; to inquire into and correct all false weights and measures and punish the users of them ; to conclude all cases left over from previous commissions ; and to punish all workmen and

[1] These persons were thus treated as though they were convicted persons holding charters of pardon (Stat. 10 Edw. III. cap. 3).

others offending against the statute made in the last parliament, that is to say, the statute of labourers.

Commissions of the peace for the counties of Stafford, Cambridge, and Norfolk in the same terms were issued on 3 July 1362. The terms of the commission should be carefully noted ; the power to take security for good behaviour is more extensive than that given by the statute. The statute only refers to persons who have been plunderers and robbers beyond the sea ; the commission mentions also persons who may threaten [2] any of the king's subjects with bodily hurt or the burning of their houses : the statute limits its scope to persons who are of good report ; the commission has no such limitation. It is possible that the justices of the peace were not willing to exercise the powers so given them, or that some doubts arose as to the legality of this commission. In any case, in the next commissions of the peace issued on 20 November 1362 (below, no. IV) all allusion to evil-doers from beyond the sea has entirely disappeared ; the justices are only empowered to take sufficient surety for good behaviour from those who threaten bodily harm or arson, and to imprison those who refuse to give it ; and this is the form which persisted during the fifteenth century and even down to modern times. So far as the form of the commission can prove anything, it would seem that the second clause of the statute must have fallen into disuse within a very few years. We have now to trace the curious history of its revival in a new and improved form.

Among the miscellaneous books of the king's remembrancer of the exchequer [3] there is a volume containing copies of the statutes. In this the first statute is that of 1 Edward III, and the last in the hand of the first scribe is that of 23 Henry VI : the remainder of the volume contains the statutes from 25 to 39 Henry VI ; it is in a later hand, and the table at the beginning of the volume does not refer to this portion. The handwriting and the ornaments used by the first scribe are of the fifteenth century ; and it is probable that the first part was completed about the 24th year of Henry VI (1445-6). In itself the volume is of no authority ; its importance lies in the fact that it is seemingly the source from which the early printed copies of the statutes and the early translations were derived. It was more accessible than the statute roll, it was from its shape easier to consult, and it was either the parent or the close relative of other manuscript collections of statutes. We print at the end of this article (no. VI) the version given by it of our statute ; but we do not insert here a translation of our own, because we are wholly

[2] This portion of the commission extends to the justices of the peace the power exercised by the chancellor under the writ *de minis*. There is no statutory authority for it. [3] Exch. K.R., Misc. Books, vol. 10.

unable to attach any meaning to part of the versions given ; and we have therefore fallen back on the translation printed in the *Great Book of the Statutes*, apparently issued between 1524 and 1533, and printed by Redman and Berthelet. We omit the preamble and a portion of the first clause :

they shall have power to restreyne the offenders ryotours and all other baratours and to pursue arrest take and chastyse them accordynge to theyr trespas and offens. And do to be imprisoned and duely punysshed accordynge to the lawe and customs of the realme, and accordynge to that that to them shall seame best to do by theyr discrecyons and good avisement, and also to enfourme them and to enquyre of all those that hathe ben pyllours and robbers in the partyes beyonde the see and be nowe come agayne, and goeth wandrynge and wyll not laboure as they were wont in tymes past, and to take and arrest all those that they may find by endytement or by suspeccion and to put them in prison, and to take of all them that be not of good fame where they shall be found sufficyent suertye and maynprise of theyr good bearynge towardes the kyng and his people, and the other duely to punysshe to the intent that the people be not by such ryotours or rebelles troubled nor endamaged nor the peace bleamysshed nor marchauntes nor other passyng by the hyghe wayes of the realme distourbed nor put in peryll whiche may happen of suche offenders. And also, &c.

It will be seen that the main difference introduced by the exchequer scribe is the insertion of the word ' not ' before ' of good fame '. He apparently hesitated to set down that a person who *was* of good fame could be called upon to find sureties, and inserted the fatal ' not ' in the hope of making sense of the passage. How he proposed to interpret ' the others ', who were to be duly punished, it is impossible to guess ; and indeed, subsequent editors of this statute have been driven to strange devices in their endeavours to evade the crux provided for them. Some of the expedients adopted we shall deal with below ; but our present concern is with the legal consequences of this instance of legislation by a stroke of the pen.

The first victim we have discovered is one William Barnard, clerk, a Norfolk man, who seems to have been in trouble about 1515. We find him obtaining a *supersedeas* ; the justices of the peace for Norfolk had committed him to prison as a person not of good bearing or reputation, but an evil-doer, rioter, barrator, disturber of the peace, and oppressor by virtue of the statute 34 Edward III. The writ (below, no. VII) sets out that he has proved that he *is* of good bearing and fame, and not as above described ; he has also found four sureties in £20 and his own recognizances in 40 marks, and in consequence the chancery orders the committal to prison to be quashed. The professional bail was not unknown at this date, and these sureties were probably of that order; it is clear that William Barnard had not found sureties in Norfolk, or the *supersedeas* would have quashed his recognizances instead of his committal. But the main point to be noticed is that the courts at this date believed that the justices of the peace had statutory power to take security from those who were *not* of good fame.

We may now turn to the writers of textbooks. It is clear from the case of William Barnard that there was matter for their ingenuity to work upon, nor was their ingenuity lacking for the task. The first writer who deals with the matter at length is William Lambarde, a learned antiquary and an active justice of the peace, who wrote at the end of the sixteenth century. He begins by pointing out that there is very little difference between surety of the peace and surety of good behaviour, and that good behaviour consists in refraining from actions directly contemplating a breach of the peace, even if no breach actually occurs, and he quotes the language of the judges in the case of Sir Richard Crofts and Sir Richard Corbet.[4] Unfortunately the zeal of his office carries him away, and he proceeds to consider how he can amplify his jurisdiction in the following words:

But all this notwithstanding, me thinketh that a man may reasonably affirme, that the *Suretie of good abearing*, should not be restrained to so narrow bounds.

For first, the Statute (34. *E. 3. Cap.* 1) enableth the *Wardens* of the Peace, to take of all them that *be not of good fame (where they shall be found) sufficient suretie & mainprise of their good Abearing towards the king & his people*. So that, if a man be defamed, he may by vertue hereof be bound to his good *behauiour*, at the discretion of the *Wardens* and *Justices* of the peace. And I once received a speciall *writ* out of the Chancerie, directed *Custodibus pacis ac vicecomiti : & eorum cuilibet*, and grounded upon the same statute, for the binding of a man with *Sureties, quod ipse boni gestus & famæ de cætero erit, & quod nihil in contrarium statuti prædicti quouismodo attemptabit &c.* wherein I proceeded as a *Minister* only. But the doubt resteth in this, to understand concerning what matters this defamation must be: and that (as I think) may be partly gathered out of the said statute also. For, after it hath first given power to the *Wardens* of the peace, *to arrest and chastice* offendors (S. against the *Peace, Riottors, and Barretors*) then it willeth them *to enquire of such as hauing bin robbers beyond the sea, were come ouer hither, and would not labour as they were wont*: & Lastly, it authorized them, *to take suretie of the good behauiour of such as be defamed* namely (as I thinke) *for any of those former offences*: for so it standeth well together, that they shall both punish such as have alreadie so offended, and shall also provide, that others shall not likewise offend. And even so doe they of the *Chancery* understand it, as by their speciall *Supersedeas*, which I afterward received from them upon that *writ* (whereof I spake even now) I did well perceive.[5]

[4] Year Book, 2 Henry VII, 2.   [5] *Eirenarcha*, p. 117.

The same doctrine was maintained by subsequent writers; in the list of authorities given in Burn's *Justice of the Peace* (1845 edition) we find Pulton, Dalton, Hawkins, and Crompton all agreed that any person who is not of good fame may be called upon to find security to be of good behaviour under the statute 34 Edward III. Dalton gives us no less than twenty methods whereby a man may so defame himself as to bring himself within the statute, and Hawkins and Crompton add four more. Burn, indeed, casts doubt upon the legality of this monstrous extension, and suggests that the power should be used with great caution, but of the existence of the power for some purposes he has no doubt; nor are we aware of any modern writer who has disputed it.

As a matter of fact few legal writers seem to have looked at the statute itself; they have relied upon the translation. Reeves, the historian of English law, whose work in its original form expresses the mind of the pure lawyer of his day, has some suggestive remarks upon the authority of the early translation of the statutes. In his preface on page viii he says:

The text of our old statutes was translated in the time of Henry VIII. The ear of a lawyer by long use and frequent quotation has been so familiarized to the language of this translation that it has obtained in some measure the credit of an original. Conformably with the general deference paid to this translation I have mostly followed the words of it, except where I found it deviated from the text.

If we refer to vol. ii, p. 473 (ed. 1787), we shall find that in this case he either was using a bad text or was quite unaware that the translation deviated from it. But this attitude of uncritical belief in the early printed translations as authoritative seems to have affected the minds of other lawyers. Even in the only critical edition of the statutes, that issued by the Record Commission in 1811 under the care of Luders, Tomlins, France, and Taunton, the editors seem always influenced in their suggestion of variant readings in the text by a desire to make it correspond with the translation.[6] *The Statutes Revised* (1870) have simply reprinted the *Statutes of the Realm*, without attempting to deal with the difficulty of the reading in any way whatever.

English law is an experimental science, and it would be presumptuous to suppose that the considerations adduced above need necessarily affect its development. All we claim to have

[6] For instance, in the present case they print Cay's translation (1751), which runs, 'them that be [not²] of good fame', and the note 2 points out ' All the translations read thus'. The text is as follows: ' ceux [qi sònt¹] de bone fame,' with a note, ' l. qi ne sont. Lib. Scacc. Westm. 9 ... and the old printed copies.' The impression left on the mind is that the editors thought the translation right and the Statute Roll wrong; and so they probably did.

established is that the undoubted power possessed by justices of the peace to bind over persons not of good fame to be of good behaviour was conferred upon them, not by the wisdom of the high court of parliament at Westminster assembled in the thirty-fourth year of King Edward III, but by an unknown exchequer clerk who made a blunder in his transcript some time in the fifteenth century. C. G. CRUMP.
C. JOHNSON.

I

Patent Roll, 31 Edward III, pt. 1, m. 17 d.

Rex dilectis et fidelibus suis Galfrido de Say [*et ceteris*] salutem. Sciatis quod assignavimus vos coniunctim et divisim ad pacem nostram necnon ad statuta apud Wyntoniam et Norhamptoniam pro conservatione pacis eiusdem edita in omnibus suis articulis in comitatu Kantie tam infra libertates quam extra custodienda et custodiri facienda, et ad omnes illos quos contra formam statutorum predictorum delinquentes inveneritis castigandos et puniendos, prout secundum formam statutorum predictorum fuerit faciendum, et ad ordinandum, supervidendum, et faciendum quod omnes et singuli homines in comitatu predicto infra libertates et extra iuxta eorum status et facultates armis competentibus muniantur, arraientur, et parentur, et de intendendo [1] et auxiliando vobis et cuilibet vestrum in hiis que pacis et statutorum predictorum conservationem concernunt ipsos compellendos, prout melius videbitur expedire; assignavimus etiam vos, tres et duos vestrum, iustitiarios nostros ad inquirendum per sacramentum proborum et legalium hominum de comitatu predicto tam infra libertates quam extra, per quos rei veritas melius sciri poterit, qui malefactores et pacis nostre perturbatores falsam monetam bone monete nostre auri et argenti in comitatu predicto contrafecerunt et huiusmodi falsam monetam a partibus exteris in comitatum predictum duxerunt et solutiones deceptivas scienter inde fecerunt, et lanas, pelles lanutas, et alias res custumabiles non custumatas nec cokettatas a comitatu predicto extra regnum nostrum Anglie ad partes exteras, contra proclamationem et defensionem nostram inde factas et contra formam ordinationis per nos et concilium nostrum inde facte, duxerunt, ac etiam de quibuscunque summis de operariis, artificibus, et servitoribus per vicecomites senescallos, ballivos, et ministros nostros et aliorum, contra formam ordinationis et statuti inde factorum, perceptis, necnon de quibuscunque aliis feloniis, transgressionibus, conspirationibus, confederationibus, oppressionibus, extorsionibus, cambipartiis ambidextriis, alleganciis iniustis, falsitatibus, forstallariis, dampnis, gravaminibus, et excessibus nobis et populo nostro in comitatu predicto infra libertatem et extra per quoscunque et qualitercunque factis, et de premissis omnibus et singulis et aliis articulis et circumstantiis premissa qualitercunque contingentibus plenius veritatem, et premissa omnia et singula ad sectam nostram tantum audienda et terminanda secundum legem et consuetudinem regni nostri Anglie. Assignavimus etiam vos, tres et duos vestrum, iustitiarios nostros ad omnia indictamenta coram Bartholomeo de Burgherssh qui iam mortuus est et vobis prefatis W. et W. et aliis sociis vestris nuper custodibus pacis nostre et iustitiariis nostris

[1] MS. *incedendo*.

ad huiusmodi felonias, transgressiones, et alia in literis nostris patentibus inde confectis contenta in comitatu predicto audienda et terminanda assignatis, facta ac processus inde inchoatos ac nondum terminata que coram vobis sub pede sigilli nostri mittemus inspicienda et debito fine terminanda secundum legem et consuetudinem supradictas. Et ideo vobis mandamus quod ad certos dies et loca quos vos, tres vel duo vestrum, ad hoc provideritis, inquisitiones super premissis faciatis, et premissa omnia et singula audiatis et terminetis in forma predicta, facturi inde quod ad iustitiam pertinet secundum legem et consuetudinem regni nostri Anglie, salvis nobis amerciamentis et aliis ad nos inde spectantibus. Mandavimus enim vicecomiti nostro comitatus predicti quod ad certos dies et loca quos vos, tres vel duo vestrum, ei sciri faciatis, venire faciat coram vobis, tribus vel duobus vestrum, tot et tales probos et legales homines de balliva tam infra libertates quam extra per quos rei veritas in premissis melius sciri poterit et inquiri. In cuius &c. Teste Rege apud Westmonasterium xix die Marcii. *per consilium.*

II

P.R.O. Statute Roll (Chancery), no. 1, m. 10.

Statutum factum in parliamento tento apud Westmonasterium anno xxxiiij[to] — Ces sont les choses queles nostre Seignur le Ro Prelatz Seignours et la commune ont ordinez en ceste present parlement tenuz a Westmustier le dymenge preschein devant la feste de la Conversion de Seint Poul a tenir et publier overtement parmy le Roialme. Cestassavoir. Primerement que en chescun Countee Dengleterre soient assignez pur la garde de la pees un Seignur et ovesque lui trois ou quatre des meultz vauez du Countee ensemblement ove ascuns sages de la ley, et eient poer de restreindre les meffesours, riotours, et touz auters barettours et de les pursuir, arester, prendre, chastier selonc leur trespas ou mesprision et de faire emprisoner et duement punir selonc la ley et custumes du roialme et selonc ce qils verront mieltz affaire par lour discrescions et bon avisement, et auxint de eux enformer et denquere de touz ceux qi ont este pilours et robeours es parties de dela, et sont ore revenuz et vont vagantz et ne voillent travailler come ils soleient avant ces hours, et de prendre et arester touz ceux qils purront trover par enditement ou par suspecion et les mettre en prisone, et de prendre de touz ceux qi sont de bone fame ou ils serront trovez souffisant seurete et meinprise de lour bon port devers le Roi et son poeple, et les auters duement punir au fin que le poeple ne soit par tieux riotours troble nendamage ne la pees enblemy ne marchantz nauters passantz par les hautes chemyns du roialme destourbez ne abaiez du peril que purra avenir de ticux meffesours. et auxint etc.

III

Patent Roll, 35 Edward III, pt. 2, m. 33 d.

De pace conservanda

Rex dilectis et fidelibus suis Roberto Herle *et ceteris* salutem. Quia ex clamosa informacione communitatis regni nostri accepimus quod quamplures vagabundi, aggregata sibi ingenti multitudine malefactorum et pacis nostre perturbatorum, tam de illis qui in partibus exteris de pilagio et latrocinio ibidem vixerunt quam aliis, in diversis confederacionibus et conventiculis in diversis comitatibus regni nostri infra libertates et extra congregati, armati et modo guerrino arraiati hominibus in passibus mercatis et alibi in comitatibus predictis infra libertates et extra insidiantes, quosdam ex eis verberantes, vulnerantes, et male tractantes, et quosdam ex eis membris mutilantes, quosdam de bonis et rebus suis depredantes, et quosdam nequiter interficientes, et quosdam capientes, et in prisona secum quousque fines et redempciones cum eis ad voluntatem suam fecerint detinentes, et alia rapinas, incendia, felonias, et malefacta facientes vagantur et discurrunt in nostri contemptum et preiudicium, et populi nostri terrorem et commocionem manifestam, et contra pacem nostram. Nos dictam pacem nostram illesam observari et malefactores huiusmodi puniri volentes, ut est iustum, assignavimus vos coniunctim et divisim ad dictam pacem nostram, necnon ad statuta apud Wyntoniam, Norhamptoniam, et Westmonasterium edita in hiis que dicte pacis nostre conservacionem concernunt in comitatu Kancie infra libertates et extra custodienda et custodiri facienda, et ad omnes illos quos armatos contra formam predicti statuti Norhamptonie vel in aliquo contra formam eiusdem statuti et statutorum predictorum delinquentes inveneritis, et alios quoscumque de quibus suspicio maleficiorum huiusmodi haberi poterit arestandos et capiendos, et habito respectu ad quantitatem delictorum suorum iuxta discreciones vestras castigandos et puniendos, prout de iure et secundum legem et consuetudinem regni nostri ac formam statutorum predictorum fuerit faciendum, et ad omnes illos qui a dictis partibus exteris in regnum nostrum venerunt, vel quos ex nunc ab inde in Comitatum predictum venire contigerit, de quorum gestu sinistra suspicio haberi poterit, et eciam alios qui aliquibus de populo nostro de corporibus suis vel incendio domorum suarum minas fecerint, viis et modis quibus melius poteritis ad sufficientem securitatem de bono gestu suo erga nos et populum nostrum inveniendam compellendos, et eos quos contrarios vel rebelles in hac parte inveneritis iuxta dictas discreciones vestras castigandos, et puniendos prout de iure et secundum legem et consuetudinem predictas fuerit faciendum. Assignavimus eciam vos septem, sex, quinque, quatuor, et tres vestrum iusticiarios nostros ad inquirendum per sacramentum proborum et legalium hominum de Comitatu predicto tam infra libertates quam extra, per quos rei veritas melius sciri poterit de quibuscumque feloniis et transgressionibus in Comitatu predicto, qualitercumque et per quoscumque factis et que exnunc ibidem fieri contigerit, et de eorundem malefactorum et felonum manutentoribus et fautoribus ac aliis articulis et circumstanciis premissa tangentibus plenius veritatem, et eciam de hiis qui mensuris et ponderibus in eodem Comitatu infra libertates vel extra contra formam statutorum et ordinacionum inde editorum utebantur vel iam utuntur. Et ad easdem felonias et transgressiones ad sectam nostram tantum audiendas et terminandas secundum legem et consuetudinem predictas, necnon ad debitam correccionem fieri faciendam de ponderibus et mensuris predictis et condignam punicionem illis quos de abusu ponderum et mensurarum predictarum culpabiles inveneritis iuxta iuris exigenciam et formam statutorum et ordinacionum predictorum imponendam. Et eciam ad omnia indictamenta coram quibuscumque Iusticiariis nostris ad felonias et transgressiones in Comitatu predicto temporibus preteritis audiendas et terminandas assignatis facta, unde processus nondum sunt terminati, inspicienda, et ea debito fine terminanda secundum legem et consuetudinem supradictas, et ad omnes artifices, servitores, et operarios quos contra formam ordinacionis in iam ultimo parliamento nostro facte delinquentes per debitum processum coram vobis invenire contigerit castigandos et puniendos, prout secundum formam ordinacionis predicte fuerit faciendum. Et ideo vobis mandamus quod ad certos dies et loca quos, &c., ad hoc provideritis inquisiciones super premissis faciatis, et felonias et transgressiones predictas audiatis et terminetis, et premissa omnia et singula faciatis et expleatis in forma predicta facturi &c. Salvis, &c. Mandavimus enim vicecomiti Comitatus predicti quod ad certos, &c., quos, &c. ei scire faciatis, venire faciat coram vobis, &c., tot, &c., tam infra libertates quam extra per quos, &c., et inquiri. Et quod ordinaciones in dicto iam ultimo parliamento nostro apud Westmonasterium tento, ut predicitur, factas vobis liberet execucioni demandandas. In cuius, &c. Teste Rege apud Westmonasterium xx. die Marcii. *per consilium.*

IV

Patent Roll, 36 Edward III, pt. 2, m. 7 d.

et ad omnes illos qui aliquibus de populo nostro de corporibus suis vel incendio domorum suarum minas fecerint per sufficientem securitatem de bono gestu suo erga nos et populum nostrum inveniendam compellendos et si huiusmodi securitatem facere recusaverint tunc eos in prisonis nostris quousque huiusmodi securitatem fecerint salvo custodiri faciendos. Assignavimus &c. Teste Rege apud Westmonasterium 20 Nov.

Per ipsum regem et totum parliamentum.

V

Patent Roll, 37 Edward III, pt. 2, m. 8 d.

De malefactoribus arestandis

Rex dilecto et fideli suo Warino del Isle, salutem. Quia ex horribili querimonia communitatis Wiltescire, Berkescire, et Suthantescire accepimus quod quamplures malefactores et pacis nostre perturbatores qui nuper de pilagio et latrocinio in partibus exteris vixerunt, aggregatis sibi aliis malefactoribus more guerrino arraiati per villas tam mercatorias quam alias armis discoopertis armati tam de die quam de nocte equitarunt et equitant, quamplures eorundem Comitatuum de bonis et rebus suis depredantes et quosdam interficientes, quosdamque mahemiantes, et quosdam capientes et secum quousque fines et redempciones cum eis ad voluntatem suam fecerint detinentes, et alia mala et dampna innumera populo nostro ibidem facientes, vagantur notorie et discurrunt, et licet vos sicut ceteri pares vestri potentes aliorum Comitatuum regni nostri pro repulsione malicie huiusmodi notoriorum malefactorum et salvacione populi nostri iuxta ligeancie vestre debitum laborare teneamini ; vos tamen hucusque quicquam inde facere non curastis per quod dicti malefactores audaciores efficiuntur consimilia mala in hac parte perpetrandi in nostri contemptum et preiudicium et populi nostri parcium illarum terrorem et commocionem manifestam, de quo conturbamur quam plurimum et movemur; vobis mandamus in fide et ligeancia quibus nobis tenemini et sub periculo quod incumbit quod absque alicuius excusacionis obstaculo, quociens de huiusmodi malefactoribus imineat in Comitatibus predictis vel partibus vicinis iminere poterit periculum aliquale, cum posse vestro una cum Custodibus pacis nostre in partibus illis et eorum quolibet vel aliis quibuscumque de eisdem partibus, vel vos cum propria familia et retinencia vestris, circa capcionem et destruccionem eorundem malefactorum diligenter intendatis. Ita quod in vestri defectum seu tepiditatem dampnum decetero populo nostro in hac parte non eveniat, per quod ad vos materiam habeamus tanquam ad fautorem malefactorum predictorum capiendi. In cuius, &c. Teste Rege apud Westmonasterium xiiij die Decembris.

VI

Exch. K.R., Misc. Books, vol. 10.

[1] ¶ INCIPIT STATUTUM APUD WESTMONASTERIUM EDITUM ANNO XXXIIIJ^{to}

[2] Ces sont les choses queux nostre seigneur le Roy prelats seignours et la commune ount ordeignez en ceste present parlement tenuz a Westmoustier le dymenge proschein devaunt le fest de la Convercion de seint Paule lan du regne le Roy tierce apres le conquest xxxiiij^{to} a tenir et publier overtement parmy le roialme. [3] ¶ [4] ¶ ca^m. PRIMIEREMENT que chascun counte dengleterre soit assigne pur la sauf garde de la pees un seignour et ovesque luy quatre ou treys des meultz vauees du countee ensemblement ove ascuns sages de la ley et eient poair de destreindre les meffesours, riotours, et totz autres barettours et de les pursuir et arrester, prendre, et chastier solonque lour trans [5] ou mesprisions, et de les faire emprisoner et duement punir solonque la ley et custume de roialme et solonque ceo quils verront meultz affaire par lour discrecion et bon avisement, et auxint deux enfourmer et denquere de totz ceux quount este pilours et robbours es parties de dela et sount ore revenuz et vount vagarantz et ne voillent travailler come ils soloient avaunt ces heurez, et de prendre et arester touts ceux quils pourront trover par enditement ou per suspecion et les mettre en prison, et de prendre de totz ceux qui ne sont de bone fame ou qils seront trouez sufficiante seurte et mainpris de lour bon port devers le Roy et son poeple et les autres duement punir, au fyn que le poeple ne soit par tielx riotours trouble nendamage ne la peas emblemy ne merchantz nautres passantz par les hautes chimyns de roialme destourbez nabbeyez de perill que purra avenir de tielx meffaisours, et auxint [&c.].[6]

[1] In red.
[2] In blue.
[3] Gilt initial letter covering five lines inset.
[4] In red. In the original on the right-hand margin.
[5] Sic.
[6] The book is a collection of statutes beginning 1 Edward III. Down to 23 Henry VI it is all in one hand and the style of ornament is uniform. The rest of the volume is 25-39 Henry VI and is in a different style of ornament and in another hand, of the same class of writing. The initial table only applies to the first part.

VII

Writ of Supersedeas, 7 Henry [VIII].

Rex custodibus pacis sue in Comitatu Norfolcie ac vicecomiti eiusdem comitatus et eorum cuilibet, salutem. Cum vos, ex quodam relatu nuper accipientes Walterum Barnard, clericum, non boni gestus et fame sed malefactorem, riotorem, barrectatorem, pacis perturbatorem, et oppressorem esse, eundem Walterum, vigore cuiusdam statuti in parliamento domini E. nuper Regis Anglie tercii progenitoris nostri apud Westmonasterium anno regni sui tricesimo quarto contra huiusmodi malefactores, riotores, barrectatores, pacis perturbatores, oppressores, ac personas non boni gestus et fame editi, proxime prisone nostre mancipari iussistis. Et quia ex testimonio satis fide digno informamur quod prefatus Walterus boni gestus et fame est nec huiusmodi condicionis prout superius versus eum suspicatur, ac pro eo quod Willelmus Bexley de Villa Westmonasterii in Comitatu Middelsexie yoman, Simon Harvy de eadem villa yoman, Willelmus Harvy de eadem villa yoman, et Thomas Grenewey de eadem villa yoman coram nobis in Cancellaria nostra personaliter constituti manu ceperunt videlicet quilibet eorum sub pena viginti librarum pro prefato Waltero, ac idem Walterus assumpsit pro se ipso sub pena quadraginta marcarum quod ipse decetero boni gestus, &c., quam quidem summam, &c., si ipse boni gestus, &c., tunc cuicumque aresto versus ipsum Walterum racione premissorum faciendo supersedeatis omnino. Et si ipsum, &c. Teste Rege apud Westmonasterium xvij die Augusti. Anno regni nostri septimo.

Throkmerton.

An English Settlement in Madagascar in 1645-6

THAT the reign of Charles I was marked by a great outburst of colonizing activity, directed especially towards the Atlantic seaboard of America and certain of the West Indian islands, is of course familiar. But it is not equally well known that among the movements thus started was one for settlements in more distant regions, and that in 1645-6 an attempt was actually made to compete with the French in colonizing the tropical island of Madagascar. This interesting experiment we now propose to examine, in the light of the contemporary records.

Madagascar—or the island of St. Lawrence, as it was frequently called, from the name bestowed upon it by its Portuguese discoverer—was from an early date known to the East India Company's seamen, who regularly used St. Augustine's Bay, on its south-western coast, as a place of call, both outwards and homewards. Here they filled their water-casks, cut billets for firewood, and bartered brass wire, beads, or calicoes with the natives for oxen and fresh provisions. There was, however, no thought of permanent settlement, for to any such idea the leading members of the Company were entirely opposed. They disliked all expenditure not productive of profit, either immediate or in the near future, and they were always urging their servants to spend as little as possible on fortifications or buildings of any sort. Their rivals, the Hollanders, might send out large numbers of soldiers, maintain squadrons of fighting-ships, erect strong castles, encourage European settlers, and aim steadily at building up an empire in the far east ; but the English merchants desired nothing more than peaceful commerce, with as little expenditure as possible on what they termed 'dead stock'. As John Fryer observes, the policy of the Dutch was

> grounded on a different principle from our East India Company, who are for the present profit, not future emolument. These, as they gain ground, secure it by vast expences, raising forts and maintaining souldiers : ours are for raising auctions and retrenching charges ; bidding the next age grow rich, as they have done, but not affording them the means.[1]

[1] *New Account of East India*, 1698, p. 46.

But while this procedure commended itself to the Company as the wisest, if not the only possible course, it was viewed with some impatience by others, who saw in it a mere selfish pursuit of immediate gain, in which the higher interests of the nation were systematically disregarded. These critics pointed to the admitted success of the Dutch, and argued that the only chance of rivalling their achievements lay in adopting their methods—methods, too, which at an earlier date had been largely instrumental in establishing the supremacy of the Portuguese in the east. To the excuse that the Company was hampered by want of funds and could not afford, even if it wished, to embark upon the larger policy, answer was made that this state of affairs was largely due to want of enterprise, and that, if its resources were so limited, it ought not to be allowed to monopolize English trade with so large a slice of the earth's surface : if it could not effectively carry out the bolder policy, it should make room for those who both could and would.

Arguments like these were doubtless used to secure the royal assent in 1635 to the establishment of the rival Company generally known as Courteen's Association,[2] a busy promoter of which was Endymion Porter, who was an especial favourite at court. In the royal commission granted for the first venture of the new body, it is expressly alleged that the existing Company had neglected to plant and settle trade in the East Indies, and had made no fortifications to encourage any in future times to adventure thither, contrary to the practice of the Dutch and the Portuguese ; while a writer of the time [3] declares that the intention of the new association was 'to settle factories and plant collonies after the Dutch manner'. As a matter of fact, however, no attempt at colonization was made by the Association during the first few years of its existence, its whole attention and all the money it could command being needed for the outfit of the annual trading fleets.

But although Courteen and his partners made no attempt in this direction, the idea of a 'plantation' in the east was not lost sight of ; and before long we hear of a scheme for establishing one in Madagascar. The names of Lord Arundel and Endymion Porter were mentioned in connexion with the project ; and no less a person than the king's nephew, Prince Rupert, then a lad of seventeen, was fixed upon as the leader of the enterprise. Facts (and fictions) were collected from seamen and others who had visited the island, and who spoke enthusiastically of its

---

[2] From the name of its leading member, Sir William Courteen. He died in 1636, when the management of the concern fell into the hands of his son, also named William, who was commonly termed Squire Courteen, to distinguish him from his father.

[3] Darell, *Strange News*, p. 4.

fertility and its great natural resources. Spices were believed to be indigenous there; cotton had been found; and the soil was thought to be suitable for indigo. The natives were known to possess some silver, and hence the existence of valuable minerals was confidently assumed; while coral, pearls, and ambergris were counted upon as well. The climate was declared to be healthy: the inhabitants simple and tractable. Further—though this was whispered rather than openly spoken of—slaves were procurable at a small cost, and were a valuable article of merchandise in all parts of the east. Finally, in addition to the scope it afforded for commercial operations, the island was to be a place of arms, dominating the traffic between Asia and Europe. As Sir William Davenant put it, in a turgid poem foretelling the prosperity of Madagascar under Rupert's rule, it was

> An isle so seated for predominance,
> Where navall strength its power can so advance,
> That it may tribute take of what the East
> Shall ever send in traffique to the West.[4]

However, the youthful prince was destined for quite a different career from that thus prognosticated. His mother poured ridicule on the whole scheme. In a letter to Sir Thomas Roe she laughed at the idea of her son setting forth on such a mad expedition, with Porter playing Sancho Panza to his Don Quixote, and begged her correspondent's assistance in putting 'such windmills out of Rupert's head'. But the prince himself seems to have thought seriously of the matter, for in the spring of 1637 an attempt was made, with the king's approval, to collect funds sufficient to dispatch a vessel to the island under Captain John Bond, the prince proposing to follow in the autumn. The East India Company was invited to join in the venture, but respectfully excused itself, on the ground of want of means to do more than carry on its ordinary trade. In the end the necessary money was not forthcoming and the project fell through. In May 1637, Roe, in a letter to the queen of Bohemia, wrote: 'The dream of Madagascar, I think, is vanished, and the squire must conquer his own island;' and in the following month Rupert embarked for the continent to join the army of the Stadtholder.

Two years later the proposal was revived, apparently under the auspices of Lord Arundel. On 29 March 1639 a royal warrant was issued to Bond, authorizing him to proceed to Madagascar as captain-general of the intended expedition; but want of money or some other difficulty again brought about a postponement. Later in the year, however, Lord Arundel announced his intention of proceeding to the island in person, and King Charles

[4] *Madagascar, with other Poems*, by W. Davenant, Kt., London, 1648.

promised to assist by lending a vessel from the royal navy. Shares were offered to all who were willing to subscribe to the venture, and would-be colonists were invited to set down their names. Any one paying in £20 was to be given a free passage and enrolled as a freeman-adventurer; while those who were willing to go, but could not afford to contribute, the earl promised to entertain in his service for four years and then make them adventurers and freemen. Arundel at the same time proposed to the East India Company that it should freight his ships, after their arrival at the island, to carry home goods from its own factories in the east. To this the Company returned a civil refusal; and a further request from his lordship, that fifty of his men should be carried out to Madagascar in the Company's fleet, was similarly declined. In addition, the court of committees protested strongly to the privy council that schemes of this character were likely to do the Company much prejudice, especially as the adventurers were already so discouraged that the abandonment of the East India trade was being seriously discussed. As a result the king put a stop both to Arundel's intended voyage and to a similar scheme for Mauritius, for which Lord Southampton was responsible.[5]

The threatening aspect of home politics soon drove out of Arundel's head any idea of quitting the country; and the scheme of a plantation in Madagascar slumbered until towards the close of 1642, when Captain Bond announced to the Company his intention of proceeding to the island with a body of nearly three hundred settlers. Thereupon an appeal was made to parliament to stop such an infraction of the Company's charter. The matter was referred to the committee for trade, on whose report (February 1643) it was resolved that Bond should be allowed to proceed on his voyage, provided he gave security before starting that he would do nothing to injure the Company's interests. From some cause or other, however, the project was dropped for that year. It was renewed a little later, and this time with more success. To rouse public interest in the scheme a book was published, with a dedication to Bond, entitled *Madagascar, the Richest and most Fruitfull Island in the World* (London, 1643). The author, Walter Hammond, had been a surgeon in the employ of the East India Company, and had on one occasion spent three months in the island. In 1640 he had published a pamphlet praising its excellence and declaring that its inhabitants were the happiest people in the world; and this panegyric he now amplified in the interests of the proposed expedition. Soon after, we may here note, Richard Boothby, a discharged servant of the Company, published *A Briefe Discovery or Description of . . . Madagascar,*

[5] *Court Minutes of the East India Company,* 1640–3, p. 296.

in which he likewise set forth the many advantages offered by the island both for colonization and commerce.

The project had now been taken up in earnest by the younger Courteen and his associates, whose competition with the East India Company under the grant obtained in 1635, while inflicting considerable loss upon the older body, had not produced much profit to the promoters. Through his wife, Lady Katherine, daughter of the first earl of Bridgewater, Courteen had found considerable support among the members of King Charles's court; and this may have been his reason for taking up the Madagascar scheme, though all his resources were really needed to carry on his operations in India itself. Preparations were pushed on vigorously; settlers were collected, to the number of 140 men, women, and children; and these were embarked in the *Sun*, *Hester*, and *James*, three of Courteen's outgoing fleet, which left the Downs in August 1644. Bond had evidently given up all idea of taking part in the enterprise, and the colonists had been placed under the command of John Smart, a relative of Courteen's partner, Kynaston.

Our chief authority for the history of the subsequent proceedings is a manuscript volume in the British Museum (Additional MS. 14037), which contains a record of the consultations held and letters written by Smart and his assistants. In addition, there are many references in the contemporary records of the East India Company (now at the India Office), particularly the series known as the Original Correspondence. The ships touched at the Canaries in September, to procure water and a supply of wine, and then made their way to the Cape, where they anchored in January 1645. There had been little sickness on board, and only one death, that of the physician engaged for the colony. On the other hand, Smart wrote: 'Wee are increased in our number by the birth of foure brave boyes, besides expectacion of others: which makes us conclude God goes along with us.' After a short stay, the voyage was resumed, and early in March the three ships reached St. Augustine's Bay, in Madagascar. Here, on the south side, a settlement was formed; houses were built; corn was sown; and an attempt was made to open up friendly relations with the natives, who, however, were indisposed to trade except for a kind of Indian bead, called *vacca*, with which the colonists were unprovided.

Smart's first care was to dispatch the *Sun*, in pursuance of his instructions, on a voyage of exploration round the southern end and up the eastern side of the island. The merchants in charge were ordered to call at Santa Lucia Bay, and, if possible, obtain from the natives a grant of land for the establishment of another colony, together with an exclusive concession of trade for a term of years. They were next to go on to Antongil Bay for similar purposes; and then possibly to Mauritius, to search for the remains of a ship of Courteen's that had been wrecked there. At all the places visited inquiry was to be made for minerals and trade products, while slaves and foodstuffs were to be purchased. The *Sun* sailed on 15 May; and on the same date the *Hester* also departed, in obedience to a secret commission from Courteen, the contents of which had not been communicated to Smart.

In July arrived three ships belonging to the East India Company, outward bound. These only stayed eight days, during which their officers kept rather aloof from the settlers, though they supplied them with some bread and beer in exchange for fresh provisions. While these vessels were still in the road the *Sun* returned from the east coast, with intelligence that there were 'little hopes of any trade or settling of a plantation on that side the island'. Santa Lucia had been reached, but only to find the French strongly established there, with posts 'at Tallengara, Mattatana, and more notherly at St. Maries Island: at all which places they are fortefied, besides a vessell of 300 tons in port of great strength'. The new-comers were met with a formal protest against their intrusion, coupled with a threat of hostile action should any attempt be made to traffic with the natives; and in any case there seemed little likelihood of profitable commerce, for the French ship had been lying in the port for over a year and yet was only a third full. The prolongation of the voyage was discouraged by news that the Dutch were already 'settled and fortefied at Antongill'; and so it was decided to return to St. Augustine's.

Meanwhile Smart had prepared the *James* for a longer voyage. She was first to proceed along the coast to the northward and visit 'Messelage' and 'Assada',[a] for the purpose of buying slaves and procuring rice and timber. With a cargo thus made up she was to proceed in turn to Muskat, Gombroon (Bandar Abbas), and certain Indian ports, to dispose of her lading, and to bring back calicoes, foodstuffs, silkworms' eggs, and seeds for the use of the plantation. Should this voyage prove impracticable, owing to the lateness of the season, the ship was to go instead to the East African ports. If Assada looked suitable for plantation, a concession of ground, with promise of sole trade, was to be sought. On this errand the vessel departed, 8 August 1645. Eight days later the *Sun* also put to sea. It had been in contem-

---

[a] 'Old' Messelage was the modern Majambo Bay; while 'New' Messelage was Mojanga, a little to the south of the former. 'Assada' is now the island of Nossi-bé, on the north-west coast. A few years later it was the scene of a further attempt at colonization, which ended as disastrously as that narrated in the text.

plation to send her to Brazil with a cargo of slaves, timber, &c., and thence to England with a lading of sugar ; but this intention had been frustrated by the failure of her previous expedition. To keep her idle in the road was out of the question, and so it was now determined to dispatch her to India and Persia, to seek a lading for England ; failing that, she was to return to the colony with supplies, which it was hoped she would obtain from Courteen's factors in India.

The outlook for the settlers was far from promising, and it must have been with heavy hearts that they saw the last of their three ships depart. In the same month, however, they were somewhat cheered by the arrival from India of one of Courteen's ships, the *William*, homeward bound. From her Smart obtained a boat, some fishing-tackle, and a quantity of brass wire to be used in barter for cattle. By this vessel he sent Courteen a report which painted the situation in gloomy colours. The district round the settlement was for miles a barren waste ; the crops the colonists had sown had failed entirely ; and there was not even enough grass to pasture the cattle which they had bought from the natives. The latter had been found to be ' of soe base and falce a condition that they have not their fellowes in the whole world ', and they were always stealing the cattle on which the settlers depended for subsistence. No trace had been discovered of minerals or of the other valuable products they had been led to expect. They themselves had suffered every sort of privation. The expedition had been badly fitted out in the first instance, and many necessaries had been forgotten ; and the supplies they had brought were now nearly expended. Illness had been rife ; ague and dysentery had carried off many, with the result that only forty men were left fit to bear arms, the rest being ' old, ignorant, weake fellowes '. As for the women, Smart said, they were of ' no other use but to distroy victuals ', and he wished he could be rid of such ' she-cattle '. He earnestly begged an early supply of stores of all sorts, without which disaster seemed inevitable. As it was, the settlers had decided that, if the *James* on her return brought an encouraging account of Assada, they would remove thither in her ; and apparently they would have made the experiment, in such boats as they possessed, without waiting for her arrival, had not the year been too far spent to leave them any hopes of establishing themselves in their new quarters before the rains set in.

A couple of months after the departure of the *William*, two vessels, the *Rebecca* and the *Friendship*, came in from England, bringing a few more colonists, including a gardener with a quantity of vines and roses, most of which, however, had perished on the way. The ships arrived almost destitute of provisions, and they had brought no brass wire, which was now the chief means of obtaining supplies. In this extremity an offer was received from a native chief to supply the English with cattle, if they would come and fight for him against a hostile tribe that was threatening him with invasion. It appears that similar aid had previously been afforded to this chief, whose name was 'Dian Brindah', but he had ungratefully omitted on that occasion to pay his allies the stipulated reward; and, moreover, his followers were accused of having participated in the thefts of cattle from which the colonists had suffered. Smart now resolved to punish the chief and at the same time procure the beef of which both the settlers and the sailors were so much in need. To lull suspicion he agreed to lend the desired assistance; and early in November he landed with forty men, well armed, at 'Metorees towne, twenty leagues to the northward of this baie'. The natives showed great pleasure at their arrival, and the following day the chief, with three of his sons, came unsuspectingly into the camp. There he was plied with liquor until he subsided into a drunken sleep, when he and his children were seized and hurried into the boats, which at once put to sea on their return voyage. His followers, who had been too surprised for the moment to attempt a rescue, collected a drove of oxen and followed along the coast to the English settlement, where, after some negotiation, Brindah and his sons were ransomed for two hundred head of cattle. Smart declared that a complete reconciliation ensued, the natives confessing that the English 'had done nothing but what was just and reasonable'; but the relations between the two parties were certainly not improved by the incident, and the many subsequent acts of 'treachery' on the part of the natives, of which he so naïvely complains, found at least some excuse in the example he had unwisely set them.

For a time, however, Smart was inclined to plume himself on the success of his manœuvre. The cattle thus obtained not only relieved the colonists from the fear of starvation, but enabled the *Rebecca* to be provisioned and dispatched on her voyage to Achin, where Courteen's Association had established a factory. She sailed in the middle of December, and about the same time the *Thomas and John*, another of Courteen's vessels, anchored in St. Augustine's Bay on her way home from India. After a brief stay she resumed her voyage, having been able to spare the settlers nothing but a little wine. The situation now rapidly grew critical. The settlers had no bread or corn—in fact no food of any sort save a few half-starved cattle; while for drink they were dependent upon a mineral spring, with a slender allowance of wine. The rains had come; and as a consequence fever was spreading and the number of invalids increased daily. Their stock of medicines was by this time exhausted, and their only doctor was 'the most unworthy that ever came amongst men'. Their one hope lay in the fact that they still had at their disposal the *Friendship*; and Smart now resolved to go in her to Assada, to seek supplies and arrange, if possible, for the transfer of the settlement to that island. He hoped also to procure there a number of slaves which he could send to Achin for sale in the *Friendship*. He set sail accordingly on 28 December 1645, leaving Samuel Levett in charge of the colony during his absence.

The voyage proved an entire failure. Smart wished to keep along the shore, examining the coastline as he went; but the vessel was only a hired one, and the master refused to risk shipwreck on a little-known and dangerous coast, and so he put well out to sea. It was then decided to call at the Comoro Islands, in hopes of learning there what success the *James* had had at Assada. After vainly attempting to reach Johanna (the island most visited by European ships), the *Friendship* anchored off Mayotta, another member of the group. Some of the party landed, and were much struck by the fertility of the island; but little was obtained in the nature of supplies, and it was only with great difficulty, owing to a storm, that the ship was regained. Smart now gave orders to make for Assada. Soon, however, the *Friendship* struck a reef, though fortunately without doing herself much damage; and the terrified master thereupon absolutely refused to persevere with the voyage. The others on board were inclined to side with him, especially as provisions were running short; and Smart found himself obliged to acquiesce in the return of the ship to St. Augustine's Bay. Even this was only accomplished with great difficulty, and it was 12 March 1646 before the exhausted voyagers saw once again the royal colours that waved over their forlorn little settlement.

Things had gone badly during Smart's absence. Most of the settlers' cattle had been entrusted to natives to pasture at a distance, owing to the barrenness of the country immediately round the plantation. Soon after the departure of the *Friendship* two Englishmen were dispatched to bring away some of the oxen and buy others; but on the way home they were attacked by the natives and killed. In revenge the settlers 'executed' two prisoners that they had taken, and determined to put to death all others that fell into their hands. It was not long before two more Englishmen were waylaid and murdered; and the natives next cut adrift one of the English boats and burnt another, besides setting fire to the smith's forge. Finally, one of the settlers, who had strayed into the woods to gather water-melons, was found with his throat cut. Smart had left at his departure a hundred settlers, including the women and the children;

at his return only sixty-three were alive, and of these the able-bodied men numbered but twenty.

To make up theire misery compleat, they were sore hunger bitten, haveing but 4 lb. salt beefe for a mess [i. e. four persons] for a day, and nothing elce in the world to subsist with; which made them fall to eating of hydes that were saved, being fresh, which kept them alive; cutting and spoyling more then they did eate.

The resulting discontent showed itself in a general disregard of discipline, and the men ' became insolent and unruly, saying what they thought fitt themselves, noe man daring to controle them '.

In this deplorable estate [says Smart] I found them at my returne, as not haveing above four dayes provisions left. So had it not pleased Almighty God to send us hither so oportunely as He did, wee had perished at sea for want of victualls, and they in little better case ashoare.

The settlers had still a small stock of beads, and Smart, who seems to have kept his health throughout, at once made a voyage to the northwards and purchased sufficient cattle to meet immediate requirements. It was now generally agreed that the settlement must be abandoned, and the necessary preparations were made with all speed. Two more expeditions along the coast resulted in the collection of a quantity of grain, goats, and oxen. The latter were salted down for ship's provisions, the colonists living meanwhile on the offal and hides—' very good meat,' said Smart cheerfully, ' if well drest.' The ordnance brought out for defence was with some difficulty got on board. The settlers' houses, ' many and well built,' were burnt to prevent the natives enjoying them, though one, which was provided with ovens and chimneys, was spared, as likely to be useful to the crew of any ship that might touch there. Letters explaining the desertion of the settlement and the future plans of the survivors were buried in a suitable spot, and over them the king's colours were left floating as an indication of their whereabouts. Then, full of joy at leaving ' this most accursed place ', the disillusioned colonists departed on 19 May 1646, in the *Friendship* and an attendant shallop. Their number had been reduced to sixty in all, of whom half were men.

Their immediate intention was to make for Mayotta, ' being a fruitfull place and where wee conceave wee may be more secure and live cheaper with our small remainder of people '; and their resources consisted of about £40 in money and a stock of iron for sale. Among the letters left behind was one addressed to Courteen's agent in India, imploring him to send a vessel to their assistance ; ' otherwise in all likelyhood wee have no other hopes but to perrish and die miserably.' Mayotta was sighted after a week's voyaging. Though the mate of the *Friendship* had been at the island twice before, he failed to find the harbour, and the ship was forced to anchor on the coast in an exposed position. Smart landed with a large party and went to the king's town, where he was well received and supplied with provisions. The king declared that 'his desire was to be sonn and subject to the King of England', and he showed an eager desire to propitiate the new-comers and induce them to remain. A native pilot was sent out to bring the *Friendship* into the port; but meanwhile a storm had forced her to sea. News soon came that she had reached Johanna in safety; whereupon Smart determined to follow her thither. So, leaving two of his party with the king, he embarked with the rest on 16 June and reached his destination two days later. It was not, however, his intention to remain there; and a few days later he sent orders to those of the colonists who had landed, commanding them to re-embark in the *Friendship* for the purpose of proceeding to Achin. Most of the men, however, and all the women, absolutely refused to obey. They were sick of braving the perils of the sea in a crazy, ill-provisioned vessel. At Johanna they had at least a chance of getting back to England in some homeward-bound ship, or at the worst of being carried to some settlement in India from whence they might hope to be helped home. No such opportunity was likely to present itself at Achin; and meanwhile they were more comfortable in their present quarters than they were likely to be in the deadly climate of a Sumatran port. To Smart's summons, therefore, they replied that 'they would rather be hanged then come aboard the ship againe'. He protested, but without avail; and all he could do was to dismiss the recalcitrants from the service of Courteen—a punishment which, in the circumstances, was not likely to disturb them greatly.

Our story now hastes to a conclusion. Smart sailed away to Achin, carrying with him only twenty-three out of the hundred and forty settlers he had brought from England. He reached his destination on 3 August 1646, and found the factory there in an impoverished and distracted condition. Manfully he strove to put things straight and to dispose of his scanty stock of merchandise to the benefit of his employer. It was, however, an uphill task, and at last his sorely tried strength gave way. In a letter of 26 January 1647 he said that he was very weak from dysentery, and, feeling that his end was near, he commended to Courteen's care the wife he had left behind him in England. He died on the 3rd of the following month.

Meanwhile, the letters left at St. Augustine's Bay had been found by two of Courteen's ships, the *Loyalty* and the *Lioness*. Both, however, were bound for England, and their commanders did not feel justified in turning back to the Comoros in order to fetch away the settlers ; they therefore reburied the letters, with others of their own, commending the task of rescue to some outgoing vessel. The chances of this were rather remote ; and in fact the duty was discharged by a ship that was already in those seas, namely, the *Ruth*, under Edward Thompson. He took off the survivors and carried them to Rajapur, on the west coast of India, where they arrived on 8 September 1646. Some of them made their way from thence to Goa, to seek their fortunes among the Portuguese. Others induced the commander of one of the East India Company's ships, the *Dolphin*, to take them to Surat, where their immediate necessities were relieved by the charity of the English factors. Two married couples and two widows, having some means left, were able to engage passages to England in a vessel that sailed from Rajapur ; while a few more were sent home from Surat in 1647 and 1648. One young man was taken into the Company's service at the latter place ; and finally it is recorded that Mrs. Dabbs, the widow of a carpenter, was married to Bartholomew Austin, the Company's carpenter at Surat, by the chaplain there. In all, we are told, not a dozen of the adventurers returned to their native country.

This last item we owe to Paul Waldegrave, a merchant who had shared in all the misfortunes of the expedition, had accompanied Smart to Achin, and had proceeded thence to Masulipatam in the *Rebecca*. There he and his associates were forced to sell their ship for want of means, and he owed to the charity of the East India Company's servants first a passage to Surat and then another to England. After his arrival in London he published (1649) an answer to Boothby's and Hammond's panegyrics on Madagascar, in which he indignantly traversed the glowing accounts given by those writers of the riches of the island, and defended the Company from the many aspersions that had been cast upon it in connexion with the scheme of colonization. Thus ends the story of Smart's settlement at St. Augustine's Bay.

W. FOSTER.

Clarendon and the Privy Council, 1660–1667

I. Clarendon's Theory of Administration

THE restoration of Stuart monarchy in England was accompanied by the re-establishment of the administrative system of early Stuart times. The innovations of the Commonwealth and Protectorate were swept away, and, in appearance at least, the executive was restored to the form and practice of the time before the civil war. The presiding genius of this reconstitution was Sir Edward Hyde, created in 1661 earl of Clarendon, by which title it will be convenient to designate him. Clarendon embodied the principles and beliefs of the older constitutional royalists. During the exile he had constantly striven against the arbitrary ideas of those more advanced royalists who inclined to despotism, as well as against the tendency of the queen mother's party to alienate national feeling by seeking aid at the hands of foreigners. In ecclesiastical matters he, like Charles I, was a staunch supporter of the church of England, while in civil government he had unbounded confidence in the efficacy of entrusting the administration to a sworn privy council, strong enough on the one hand to restrain the encroachments of parliament, while respecting its privileges, and on the other to check the undue influence of unofficial favourites, while adding weight and dignity to the royal authority.

> The members of that board [he said] had been always those great officers of state, and other officers, who in respect of the places they held had a title to sit there, and of such few others who, having great titles and fortunes and interest in the kingdom, were an ornament to the table.[1]

He held the highest estimate of its rights and duties.

> For by the constitution of the kingdom, and the very laws and customs of the nation, as the privy-council and every member of it is of the king's sole choice and election of him to that trust, (for the greatest office in the state, though conferred likewise by the king himself, doth not qualify the officers to be of the privy-council, or to be present in it, before by a new assignation that honour is bestowed on him, and that he is sworn of the council;) so the body of it is the most sacred, and hath the greatest authority in the government next the person of the king himself, to whom

[1] *Continuation of the Life of Edward, Earl of Clarendon*, Oxford, 1857, § 733.

all other powers are equally subject : and no king of England can so well secure his own just prerogative, or preserve it from violation, as by a strict defending and supporting the dignity of his privy-council.[2]

The privy council and the administration generally, according to Clarendon's conception of them, had no other head than the king. The modern notion of an English prime minister had not yet appeared, while the older French conception of an adviser, dependent on the king for his authority, while relieving him of the burden of administration, was opposed to Clarendon's views. He himself, during the short period when he enjoyed the monopoly of the royal favour, was solicited to assume such a position, but declined on the ground that it was foreign to the English constitution.

Some time subsequent to March 1661 Ormonde proposed to him that, in order to shield the king from the evil influences to which he was exposed, he should give up his office of lord chancellor, and betake

himself wholly to wait upon the person of the king. . . . By this means he would find frequent opportunities to inform the king of the true state of affairs, and the danger he incurred, by not thoroughly understanding them. . . . That the king from the long knowledge of his fidelity, and the esteem he had of his virtue, received any advertisements and animadversions, and even suffered reprehensions, from him, better than from any other man ; therefore he would be able to do much good, and to deserve more than ever he had done from the whole kingdom.[3]

In fact it was suggested that instead of filling a great office of state he should take a position which the example of the French ministers, Richelieu and Mazarin, to say nothing of the great favourite of the last reign, the duke of Buckingham, had rendered familiar to English politicians. Clarendon, however, was not to be tempted. In his reply he asserted ' that England would not bear a favourite, nor any one man, who should out of his ambition engross to himself the disposal of the public affairs '. Referring to the term ' first minister ', he characterized it as ' a title so newly translated out of French into English, that it was not enough understood to be liked, and every man would detest it for the burden it was attended with '. He added that

the king himself, who was not by nature immoderately inclined to give, would be quickly weary of so chargeable an officer, and be very willing to be freed from the reproach of being governed by any . . . at the price and charge of the man who had been raised by him to that inconvenient height above other men.[4]

Clarendon's own conception of the functions of the privy council was singularly lucid. In his mind, as clearly as later in that

[2] *Contin. of Life,* § 912.   [3] *Ibid.* § 85.   [4] *Ibid.* §§ 86–90.

of Locke, existed the conception of the separation of legislature and executive. The legislative functions were to be committed to the king in parliament, while the whole superintendence of the executive was to be entrusted to the king in council. By the presence of the great officers of state, the chancellor, the treasurer, the general, the lord high admiral, the two secretaries of state, and the chancellor of the exchequer, as also of several lesser officials and several officers of the household, the council would be in touch with all the great departments and would bind them into a single administrative system. Through the treasury it would control the assignment and expenditure of the entire revenue of the crown;[5] through the secretaries it would have cognizance of the foreign relations of the state. The general and the admiral were the heads of military and naval affairs, while the chancellor was at once the representative of the judicial body and the official president of the house of lords. Every important executive measure would be submitted to its judgement, and even in legislative matters the initiative of the crown was to be placed at its disposal.

Clarendon believed that his conception of the privy council was in accordance with the traditional practice of the state. It was in fact ideal, and never had had an historical existence. His privy council differed largely from the privy council of Henry VIII and Elizabeth, dependent on the personal will of the monarch and in great matters rather a consultative than an executive body. It differed no less from the council of the earlier Stuarts overshadowed by the influence of unofficial favourites, who, being naturally rivals of the great servants of the crown, continually strove to restrict the king's confidence to an inner ring of their own friends and dependants. Clarendon's conception of the position of the privy council was that which he and other constitutional royalists had endeavoured to establish during the period of their parliamentary opposition to the predominance of Buckingham and Strafford, and which they had endeavoured later to oppose to the encroachments of the Long Parliament on the independence of the executive.

II. THE ORGANIZATION OF THE PRIVY COUNCIL

The complexity of the administration was already so great at the Restoration that it was necessary to organize the council somewhat elaborately to meet it. The greater part of the work was transacted in committees, and of these three distinct kinds may be distinguished. There were in the first place a considerable

[5] This control was not exercised by the treasury itself as at the present day. For a clear statement of the position of the treasurer see Dr. W. A. Shaw's preface to the *Calendar of Treasury Books*, 1660–7, pp. xxxv–xxxvii.

number of temporary committees to put business into shape for the council. There were also in the second place two committees of a more permanent character to deal with naval affairs and with matters relating to the colonies. And there was, lastly, the foreign committee, which was in fact an inner council dealing with affairs of special moment.

(a) *The Temporary Committees*

Whenever a question involving detail came before the council it was usual to relegate its consideration to a small committee, which investigated it and reported to the council. About fifty such committees were appointed between 8 August 1660 and 2 January 1666–7.[6] Many of them are concerned with points of foreign policy, others with domestic matters, and others again with trade. Their duration varied. Usually they were dissolved or fell into abeyance as soon as council had accepted their reports. Sometimes, however, if the nature of their business required it, they continued in existence longer, and council, when it deemed it necessary, ordered them to meet.

(b) *The Standing Committees and the Councils for Trade and Foreign Plantations*

The standing committees were two in number, the committee for naval affairs, which will be dealt with in a later part of this article, and the committee for plantations. Colonial matters are so closely connected with trade that it is convenient to take them together. There were precedents for referring either subject to a specially constituted body.[7] In Charles I's reign a commission for trade had been appointed in 1625, which did not include any privy councillors and which was described as a subcommittee under the grand council,[8] and in 1630 a committee for trade had been formed within the privy council. On 28 April 1635 a separate committee for foreign plantations which dealt with the internal affairs of the American colonies had been appointed[9]. During the Protectorate and Commonwealth the administrative methods were considerably varied, but the usage had been to entrust trade and colonial business to independent bodies of commissioners. This

---

[6] See two partial lists of them in the Record Office, State Papers, Domestic, Charles II, vol. 7, no. 40; vol. 104, no. 76; and a complete list in vol. 276, no. 251.

[7] This subject has been carefully treated by Professor Charles M. Andrews in his 'British Committees, Commissions, and Councils of Trade and Plantations, 1622–75', published in 1908 in the *Johns Hopkins University Studies in Historical and Political Science*, series xxvi, nos. 1–3.

[8] *Ante*, xxi. 678 (1906); Andrews, p. 12.

[9] Register of the Privy Council, Charles I, vol. x; State Papers, Colonial, Charles I, vol. 8, no. 12.

was part of a general tendency to develop departmental government to which Clarendon was strongly opposed. In consequence the Restoration saw a change of system.

Clarendon's plan was to submit questions of trade and commerce to the full council, while sending colonial matters to a committee. On 4 July 1660 a committee of plantations was established, consisting of ten privy councillors.[10] They were appointed to consider ' petitions, propositions, memorials, or other addresses . . . concerning the Plantations, as well in the Continent as islands of America ', and to make reports from time to time to the council. Clarendon intended to restrict trade and colonial matters to bodies composed solely of privy councillors. But the advantages of the recent practice of the Protectorate were too evident, and although his committee of plantations continued in permanence until after his fall, he was obliged before the close of 1660 to permit the constitution of two more representative bodies composed of persons interested in trade. The powers and functions of these bodies were defined in accordance with the suggestions of Thomas Povey, and were modelled on those of the corresponding bodies under the Protectorate although they were more restricted.

On 7 November 1660 the king issued a commission constituting a numerous body, including Clarendon, commissioners for managing and improving trade. This body included members of the privy council, country gentlemen, customers, merchants, traders, officers of the navy, gentlemen versed in affairs, and doctors of civil law, as well as persons nominated by the merchant companies.[11] According to its instructions it was to deliberate on any injuries arising to English trade from non-observance of treaties with foreign powers, and on any decay or corruption with regard to home manufactures, and to suggest redress ; it was also to consider the best means to improve native commodities, to regulate the fisheries, the balance of exports and imports, and matters relating to navigation, bullion, foreign plantations, and other kindred topics.[12] The functions of the council of trade were deliberative and not administrative. They were intended to direct the attention of the privy council to matters requiring regulation, and at most to suggest methods of proceeding. The privy council

[10] Register of the Privy Council, 4 July and 5 September 1660, 5 and 10 September 1662 ; State Papers, Domestic, Charles II, vol. 7, no. 40 ; vol. 276, no. 251 ; State Papers, Colonial, vol. xiv, no. 15.

[11] State Papers, Domestic, Charles II, vol. 19, nos. 21–5, vol. 21, no. 26 ; Register of the Privy Council, 17 August, 19 September, 10 October 1660. The companies requested to nominate members were the Turkey Merchants, Merchant Adventurers, the East India, Greenland, and Eastland, as well as the traders with Spain, France, Portugal, Italy, and the West India Plantations.

[12] State Papers, Domestic, Charles II, vol. 21, no. 27, printed in Cunningham's *Growth of Engl. Industry and Commerce*, ed. 1907, II. ii. 913–15.

still dealt directly with the trading companies,[13] and until the failure in Skinner's case it might be considered to control them.[14] It exercised the power of partially suspending the act of navigation and of granting and revoking licences to dispense with it.[15] But although the establishment of the council of trade apparently left the influence of the privy council unimpaired, it failed to meet with Clarendon's approval. It did not form part of his general scheme, and he condemned it as useless. The committee, he said, 'produced little other effect than the opportunity of men's speaking together, which possibly disposed them to think more, and to consult more effectually in private, than they could in such a crowd of commissioners.'[16]

On 1 December 1660 a second council, consisting of thirty-five members, was constituted for the management of the foreign plantations.[17] The two councils were distinct, but were in communication with each other. The council of trade was to consider the general state of the navigation and trade of the foreign plantations, so far as they affected the rest of the king's dominions, and was to take advice, as occasion required, with the council of foreign plantations.[18] The latter council was to collect information on the state of foreign plantations, the constitution of their laws and government, to report to the king complaints from the colonies, to use 'prudential means' for bringing the colonies into a more uniform way of government, to inquire into the execution of the navigation acts and consider matters relating to emigration and transportation, and the propagation of the gospel in the colonies. The council of foreign plantations was possessed of considerably greater powers within its sphere of action than the council for trade.[19] Besides being charged to inform themselves of the state and condition of all foreign plantations,[20] the members were directed to order and settle a continual correspondence, so as to be able, as often as required, to give to the king an account of the government of each colony

---

[13] *Calendar of State Papers, Domestic*, 1660–1, p. 607; 1663–4, pp. 434, 469, 632.

[14] *Ibid.* 1663–4, p. 673; for Skinner's case see *The Grand Question concerning the Judicature of the House of Peers, stated and argued*, 1669; Cobbett's *State Trials*, vi. 709–70. The orders concerning Skinner were erased from the council books, State Papers, Domestic, Charles II, vol. 273, no. 92.

[15] Cf. *Calendar of State Papers, Domestic*, 1661–2, pp. 19, 421; 1663–4, p. 252; 1664–5, p. 267.

[16] *Contin. of Life*, § 442.

[17] State Papers, Domestic, Charles II, vol. 19, nos. 45, 46; Andrews, *British Committees*, p. 67; F. S. Thomas, *Notes of Materials for a Hist. of the Public Departments*, 1846, p. 77; Preface to *Calendar of Colonial State Papers, America and West Indies*, 1661–8, p. viii. [18] Cunningham, ii. 915.

[19] The articles of instruction are in State Papers, Colonial, vol. 14, no. 59. Most of them are printed by Professor Andrews (pp. 69–70), and they are summarised in Thomas, *Notes of Materials*, p. 77, and the *Calendar of Colonial State Papers, America and West Indies*, 1574–1660, pp. 492–3. [20] Art. i.

and of their complaints;[21] and they were 'to use prudential means ... for bringing the several Colonies and Plantations, within themselves, into a more certain, civil, and uniform method of government', applying, if expedient, the methods of administration employed by other European states towards their colonies.[22] It must not, however, be supposed that the authority of the council of plantations was antagonistic to that of the privy council. It rather stood to it in the same relation as did the council of the north, or the council of the marches in Wales, before the act of 1641 for regulating the privy council and abolishing the Star Chamber was passed. In important matters the approbation of the privy council was usually sought.[23]

The outbreak of the Dutch war proved fatal to the activity of these councils. The records of the council of plantations come to an end on 24 August 1664, but the council was still in existence as late as 24 February 1664/5.[24] When it ceased to act its business was conducted by the privy council's committee for foreign plantations, which was revived on 15 December 1666.[25] The council of trade has no records later than July 1664, and though its commission was not revoked, its business was transferred to the privy council.[26]

(c) *The Foreign Committee*

When the privy council was reconstituted in 1660 it was drawn from two hostile parties who had only united in a temporary alliance in order to place Charles II on the throne. Immediately on Charles's landing at Dover, before the reconstitution of the council, Monck presented him with a list of some seventy persons whom he recommended to be made privy councillors. With one or two exceptions they were presbyterians or parliament men, and though Monck afterwards assured Charles that the list was a mere formality to fulfil promises which he had made,[27] yet the king found himself obliged by the political requirements of the situation to include in his council men of all parties.[28] By September 1660, in addition to the king's brothers, who were unsworn, the council consisted of twenty-seven members. Of these, nine—Clarendon, Ormonde, Norwich, St. Albans, Nicholas, Carteret, Cornwallis, Wentworth the younger, and Sir Charles Berkeley—had shared the king's exile; seven—Southampton,

---

[21] *Ibid.* Art. 4.
[22] *Ibid.* Arts. 5 and 6.
[23] See, for instance, *Calendar of State Papers, Domestic,* 1664–5, p. 4.
[24] *Calendar of State Papers, Colonial,* 1661–8, nos. 790, 833; Andrews, *British Committees,* pp. 78–9.
[25] Register of the Privy Council, 7, 12 December 1666; Andrews, p. 80.
[26] Andrews, pp. 86–7.
[27] *Contin. of Life,* §§ 11–12.
[28] Cf. *ibid.* § 41.

Somerset, Leicester, Berkshire, Seymour, Lindsey, and Dorchester—were royalists, who had remained in England; seven —Morice, Northumberland, Annesley, Manchester, Saye and Sele, Holles, and Robartes—were presbyterians or parliament men; and four—Albemarle, Cooper, Howard, and Sandwich— had taken part in the government under Cromwell. Although several of these councillors, including Lindsey and Manchester, took no share in the administration, the number was increased in the succeeding three years to between thirty and forty.[29] So heterogeneous an assembly was unfitted for confidential deliberations, because, as Charles said in 1679, the great number of the council prevented the secrecy and dispatch necessary in many great affairs, and also because it soon became obvious that the presbyterians, while strong in council, were unable to hold their own in parliament and the country. In consequence, on the suggestion of Clarendon, a secret committee was formed on 13 June 1660 for the conduct of foreign affairs.[30]

The preliminary discussion of foreign affairs by a committee of council was not a novelty. But this committee soon undertook the consideration of many other important matters besides foreign affairs, and that was a new departure. I have shown in a former article [31] that the foreign committees of Charles I's reign in all probability were strictly limited to foreign affairs, that the wider junto described by Clarendon as existing in the earlier months of 1640 was not identical with the standing committee for foreign affairs, but with a committee for Scottish affairs, which had been created in October 1639; and also that it is likely that Clarendon, who was then in opposition, misapprehended its character and ascribed to it the characteristics of his own foreign committee of 1660. There was, however, a junto of six, of whom he was one, formed in 1643, which dealt generally with affairs; but this was in time of war, and it was rather a substitute for privy council than a committee of that body.

The committee for foreign affairs under Charles II was very informal. Its members were varied at the discretion of the king. At the outset it was composed of Clarendon, Southampton, Ormonde, Albemarle, and the secretaries of state, Nicholas and Morice.[32] At a slightly later date, when the sale of Dunkirk was under discussion, Ormonde was omitted, and three naval authorities

---

[29] Register of the Privy Council. The list for June 1660 in Masson's *Life of Milton*, vi. 17–19, is not quite correct for that month; it includes Dorchester, who was not sworn until 27 August.

[30] State Papers, Domestic, Charles II, vol. 23, no. 94; Lister, *Life of Clarendon*, 1838, ii. 6.

[31] *Ante*, xxi. 673.

[32] *Contin. of Life*, § 46; but cf. State Papers, Domestic, Charles II, vol. 23, no. 94, which includes also Colepeper, who died on 11 July 1660.

—the duke of York, Sandwich, and Carteret—were added.[33] When Charles consulted it with regard to the arrangements concerning his marriage, only Clarendon, Southampton, Ormonde, Manchester, and secretary Nicholas were included.[34] When early in 1663 he submitted the preliminary draft of an act declaratory of the nature of the royal dispensing power, Lord Robartes and Lord Ashley, who afterwards introduced the bill in parliament, were present in addition to the ordinary members.[35] The functions of the committee were mainly deliberative. It discussed proposals which were afterwards laid before the full council.[36] In the case of foreign negotiations, however, the privy council was sometimes not acquainted with them until a late stage, though Charles did not, during Clarendon's period of office, actually conclude treaties without its sanction. On the occasion of the sale of Dunkirk the negotiations with the French envoy, D'Estrades, were conducted chiefly by Clarendon, with the cognizance of the secret committee. When they had proceeded for some time the matter was broached by the king at a close council, that is at one from which the clerk was ordered to withdraw and at which no minutes were taken. It was not finally considered in open council until 17 October 1662,[37] when the terms had been settled and the treaty was ready to be signed.[38] In dealing with foreign powers, therefore, this committee had considerable discretionary powers.

The committee for foreign affairs dealt only with matters of foreign policy of particular moment. Temporary committees were frequently appointed to negotiate with foreign ambassadors, and these were different in composition from the foreign committee. Thus the committee appointed on 6 September 1661 to treat with the French ambassador consisted of Robartes, Manchester, Leicester, Anglesey, Ashley, Carteret, and the secretaries.[39]

III. OPPOSITION TO CLARENDON'S SYSTEM

Such was the arrangement of the business of the privy council under Clarendon's administration. Almost from the outset, however, the complete realization of his ideas was rendered impossible by the hostility of other members of the government, and in the end his whole scheme of rule was overthrown by independent assaults from parliament and the king.

---

[33] *Contin. of Life*, § 456.   [34] *Ibid.* § 154.   [35] *Ibid.* § 584.
[36] *Ibid.* § 1197. Some notes of the proceedings of the foreign committee by Secretary Nicholas are in State Papers, Domestic, Charles II, vol. 23, nos. 93–104.
[37] Register of the Privy Council, 17 October 1662.
[38] See *Notes which passed at the Meetings of the Privy Council between Charles II and Clarendon*, Roxburghe Society, 1896, p. 73 ; *Contin. of Life*, § 462.
[39] Register of the Privy Council, 6 September 1661. For other temporary committees dealing with foreign affairs see State Papers, Domestic, vol. 276, no 251.

(a) *Opposition from Parliament*

The demand that had been made before the civil war that council should be composed of persons approved by parliament was of course abandoned after the Restoration, but it was necessary to establish an understanding between the two bodies with regard to large measures of policy. Clarendon was chiefly concerned with influencing parliament, but he found eventually that the influence of parliament on the council was more important.

At first Charles II entrusted the conduct of affairs in parliament to Clarendon and Southampton. These ministers

> had every day conference with some select persons of the house of commons, who had always served the king, and upon that account had great interest in that assembly, and in regard of the experience they had and their good parts were hearkened to with reverence. And with those they consulted in what method to proceed in disposing the house, sometimes to propose, sometimes to consent to what should be most necessary to the public; and by them to assign parts to other men, whom they found disposed and willing to concur in what was to be desired : and all this without any noise, or bringing many together to design, which ever was and ever will be ingrateful to parliaments, and, however it may succeed for a little time will in the end be attended with prejudice.[40]

This method, however, did not suit some of the younger royalists, who desired to form a definite party in the commons to act in the king's interests. Prominent among these, according to Clarendon, were Sir William Coventry, who was private secretary to the duke of York, Sir Henry Bennet, keeper of the privy purse, Thomas Clifford, whose advances, according to Burnet,[41] Clarendon had rejected, and Winston Churchill, father of the first duke of Marlborough. The influence of this party was enhanced on the retirement of Sir Edward Nicholas from the office of secretary of state on 15 October 1662 by the succession of Sir Henry Bennet to his office, and by the appointment of several new privy councillors, including the duke of Buckingham, who had already been sworn at Breda during the exile. 'From this time,' says Clarendon, 'they who stood at any near distance could not but discern that the chancellor's interest and credit with the king manifestly declined.'[42] When parliament reassembled in February 1662–3, Bennet and Coventry communicated to the king their idea of forming a party in the commons. To their proposals Clarendon objected 'that great and notorious meetings and cabals in parliament had been always odious in parliament', and that they had almost always ended unluckily.[43]

---
[40] *Contin. of Life*, § 395. [41] *Own Time*, i. 225. [42] *Contin. of Life*, § 439.
[43] *Ibid.* § 409. Here we have that dislike of the party system inherited by the earl of Chatham.

The matter was compromised for the moment by including Bennet, Clifford, and Churchill in the parliamentary committee, but their presence is considered by Clarendon to have impaired the efficiency of these conferences by producing divisions among those present.[44] In fact we find that the persons who eventually succeeded Clarendon in the direction of the administration first made their influence felt in the commons, that they then gained access to the parliamentary committee, and that they were thus enabled to weaken Clarendon's general control of the government in spite of the fact that his influence was still preponderant in the privy council. The increased power of parliament rendered it necessary to submit to the parliamentary committee for discussion many topics which formerly would have been reserved for the council alone. Thus it was possible for Clarendon's opponents in this committee to make his unpopularity with parliament an effective weapon against him and to represent him as out of touch with public opinion. Bennet and Coventry, for instance, used their position, according to Clarendon, to force on the war with the Dutch in 1665 by assuring the king 'that he could not ask more money of the parliament than they would readily give him, if he would engage in this war which the whole kingdom so much desired'.[45]

In consequence of the necessity of humouring parliament persons were made members of the privy council whom Clarendon did not consider suitable. He held that the council should be composed exclusively of great officials and magnates. Taking this view he particularly objected to the proposal to make William Coventry, the duke of York's secretary, a privy councillor, both on the ground that a servant of the king's brother was not a suitable person and that no servant of the prince of Wales had ever been a privy councillor, with the exception of the earl of Newcastle, the present king's governor, and also because ' there were at present too many already, and the number lessened the dignity of the relation '.[46] In spite of these objections Coventry was knighted and called to the privy council on 26 May 1665, and was soon after admitted to the foreign committee,[47] where Clarendon complains that his influence was employed to diminish his own credit with the king.

In another direction parliament struck directly at the independence of the council. The control of finance was the weapon which it had formerly used against the crown. Clarendon's views on this subject were clear. The right of granting supplies belonged unquestionably to parliament, but the appropriation and control of expenditure was exclusively the function of the

[44] *Contin. of Life*, §§ 412-14.
[45] *Ibid.* § 733.
[46] *Ibid.* § 534.
[47] *Ibid.* § 739.

council. The constant waste and misapplication of supplies which marked the king's government [48] made parliament little inclined to acquiesce in Clarendon's opinion. During the Dutch war dissatisfaction became acute, and Sir George Downing urged, says Clarendon, that

the root of all miscarriage was the unlimited power of the lord treasurer, that no money could issue without his particular direction, and all money was paid upon [no] other rules than his order ; so that, let the king want as much as was possible, no money could be paid by his, without the treasurer's warrant.[49]

Downing meant to insinuate that the treasurer could not prevent the king diverting supplies from the public service, and to remedy this he proposed to add a provision to the subsidy bill of 1665 (17 Charles II, cap. i), appropriating the entire grant exclusively to the purpose of carrying on the Dutch war. The assent of the king was obtained, and the provision was introduced when the subsidy bill was in committee. It was regarded by the constitutional royalists as 'introductive to a commonwealth and not fit for monarchy'. It was also observed that the appropriation of supplies in the Long Parliament was the prelude to rebellion, and that Cromwell had never permitted such clauses.[50] It was opposed by the solicitor-general, Sir Heneage Finch, and others, and Clarendon thinks that it would have been thrown out but for the intervention of the king, who ordered Finch to abandon his opposition. The king was mainly influenced by the consideration that the new clause, by reassuring the public, would enable him to borrow the money from the bankers on easier terms.

In consequence of the reluctance of the constitutional royalists a meeting to discuss the bill privately was held in Clarendon's bedchamber. Those present were the king, the duke of York, Clarendon, Southampton, Ashley, Arlington, Sir Geoffrey Palmer the attorney-general, Finch the solicitor-general, Coventry, and Downing. Clarendon reproached Downing with initiating so important a proposal without acquainting his superiors in the exchequer, and told him

that it was impossible for the king to be well served, whilst fellows of his condition were admitted to speak as much as they had a mind to ; and that in the best times such presumptions had been punished with imprisonment by the lords of the council without the king's taking notice of it.[51]

Clarendon was irritated because Downing had not submitted his proposal to the treasurer, who would in due course have brought

---

[48] See Pepys's *Diary*, 30 June 1663, 29 February 1663–4.
[49] *Contin. of Life*, § 780.   [50] *Ibid.* § 787.   [51] *Ibid.* § 804.

it before council for discussion before proposing it to parliament. Charles, however, did not share his feelings, and afterwards reprimanded him severely for his attack on Downing.[52]

But although Charles was willing to allow parliament to appropriate extraordinary grants to the war he did not intend to observe the conditions with any strictness: sums continued to be expended on other objects, and council was quite unable to check him even if it desired to do so. Moreover, at the close of 1664 he had created a fund upon which he was able to draw without being subject to any control whatever. In December he appointed Lord Ashley treasurer for the sums received by the crown from prizes made during the war, and directed that he was to make payments in obedience to the king's warrant under his sign manual without accounting into the exchequer.[53] Clarendon opposed this measure in vain,[54] and Charles subsequently made large grants out of this fund for various purposes unconnected with the war.[55]

The freedom with which the king diverted supplies, and the general corruption of the officials, gave rise to grave dissatisfaction. When parliament met on 21 September 1666 it found that the previous supplies had not sufficed to meet the expenses of the war. It was much discontented, and the commons resolved to make the appropriation a reality by investigating the accounts of the navy, ordnance, and stores.[56] In spite of the opposition of the court party they appointed on 26 September a select committee for the inspection of all the accounts of money voted and spent for the war. On 8 October they ordered the accounts of prize goods, which, it will be remembered, were under a distinct treasurer, to be brought to the committee.[57] Owing to the fact, however, that the committee had not power to take evidence on oath, it was impossible to obtain satisfactory results. Further steps were therefore resolved on. On 9 November 1666, the question being put in the commons that a bill be brought in enabling certain persons to take an account of the disbursements of the public monies upon oath, it passed in the negative by 118 to 107, and a resolution was substituted

that his Majesty having been graciously pleased to command his officers to bring into the House of Commons their accompts of the Receipts and Disbursements of the publick monies raised to maintain this present war, that the Lords be desired to name a committee of their House to join with

---

[52] *Ibid.* §§ 805–6.
[53] The warrant for his commission is dated 24 December 1664, *Calendar of State Papers, Domestic*, 1664–5, p. 122.
[54] *Contin. of Life*, §§ 575–81; cf. Christie's *Life of Shaftesbury*, 1871, i. 279–82.
[55] *Calendar of State Papers, Domestic*, 1664–5, pp. 339, 344, 363, 388, 452; 1665–6, pp. 48, 50, 102; 1666–7, p. 412; 1667, p. 99.
[56] *Journals of the House of Commons*, 21, 26, 28 September 1666.
[57] *Ibid.* 8, 11 October 1666.

a committee of this House to the end the same accompts may be examined and taken upon oath.[58]

The lords, however, did not approve of this procedure by means of a joint committee, considering that there was no precedent for a committee of lords and commons having power given them to examine by oath;[59] and no arrangement being arrived at, the commons proceeded on 6 December to attach an additional clause in committee to a bill for raising a part of the supplies by means of a poll-tax, in which it was ordered that an account of the public monies given and spent for the war should be taken upon oath.[60] This provision was carried by thirty or forty voices in spite of the efforts of the court party.[61]

The king and his ministers were considerably disturbed. The treasurer of the navy, Sir George Carteret, and Lord Ashley, the treasurer of the prize money, were reluctant to face the threatened scrutiny, and Charles knew that both treasurers had issued sums on warrants from him which he could not wish to be produced. In consequence he called 'that committee of the privy-council with which he used to advise', and complained to them of the unwonted procedure of the commons.[62] The committee appeared unanimous in the opinion that these proceedings must be stopped, and Clarendon, while acknowledging the necessity of respecting parliamentary privilege, was emphatic on the urgency of restraining the houses from extending their jurisdiction to cases with which they had no concern.[63]

Measures were therefore taken to prevent the passage of the objectionable clause. The ministerial supporters in the house of commons had sufficient influence to separate the clause from the poll-tax bill. On 11 December it was converted into a distinct bill and read for the second time. In the lords it was read for a second time on 19 December, and referred to a committee of the whole house. Then, with a view to shelving it, it was resolved to petition the king to issue a commission under the great seal to take account of the public monies.[64] On 29 December the king, in answer to this petition, appointed a commission under the great seal to examine the war accounts.[65] On this being communicated to the commons on 3 January 1666-7 they resolved

that this proceeding of the Lords in going by petition to the King, for a commission for taking the publick accompts, there being a bill sent up from

[58] *Journals of the House of Commons*, 9 November 1666; *Journals of the House of Lords*, 9 November 1666.
[59] *Journals of the House of Lords*, 12, 16, 22, 23 November 1666.
[60] *Journals of the House of Commons*, 7, 10, 11 December 1666.
[61] Pepys's *Diary*, 8 December 1666.
[62] *Contin. of Life*, § 947-8. [63] *Ibid.* § 949.
[64] *Journals of the House of Lords*, 19, 20, 22 December 1666; State Papers, Domestic, vol. 182, nos. 94, 95. [65] *Journals of the House of Lords*, 29 December 1666.

this House, and depending before them, for taking the accompts in another way, is unparliamentary and of dangerous consequence.[66]

In consequence of this remonstrance the lords resumed the consideration of the bill, and on 24 January sent it down to the commons amended. There it was still under discussion when parliament was prorogued on 8 February 1666/7.[67]

But the commons were resolved not to abandon the principle for which they were contending. When parliament reassembled after Clarendon's fall, a committee was appointed on 15 October 1667 to prepare a bill, which was introduced on 26 October.[68] It named a commission of nine with power to examine upon oath all persons connected with the expenditure of the previous war grants.[69] Their powers were limited to the next three years. The bill was sent to the lords on 17 December, passed on the 19th, and received the royal assent on the same day. The commissioners made two statements to the house of commons on 14 March 1667/8 and 14 April 1668, and presented a report to both houses on 25 October 1669.[70] In consequence of the statement made on 14 April 1668, Admiral Sir William Penn was suspended from sitting in the commons on 21 April[71] and impeached on 24 April.[72] The impeachment came to an end on the adjournment of parliament in May 1668 and the subsequent prorogation. After the presentation of the report both houses proceeded to investigate the conduct of Sir George Carteret, who had been treasurer of the navy from 1661 to 1667. A committee appointed by the house of lords reported favourably to Carteret, but the house of commons voted him guilty of misdemeanour on several of the charges,[73] and suspended him from sitting on 10 December 1669.[74] On the other hand the report exonerated Ashley. His accounts were completely in order, but it appeared from them that the king had used the prize money for other purposes than the war, though not to the extent that had been reported. Pepys in fact asserts, on the authority of Sir Hugh Cholmley, that £400,000 had gone into the privy purse since the beginning of the war.[75] This statement need not refer to Ashley's fund exclusively; but possibly

---

[66] *Journals of the House of Commons*, 3 January 1666/7; *Journals of the House of Lords*, 12 January, 1666–7; see also Grey's *Debates*, 1769, i. 3–5.
[67] *Journals of the House of Lords*, 24 January 1666/7; *Journals of the House of Commons*, 7, 8 February 1666/7.
[68] *Ibid.* 15, 26 October 1667; Grey's *Debates*, i. 3.
[69] *Statutes of the Realm*, 19 & 20 Car. II, cap. i.
[70] Grey's *Debates*, i. 116, 133–9, 157–9, 163–8, 169–74, 178–82, 202–4, 213–15; the report is printed in *Hist. MSS. Comm.*, 8th Report, app. i. 128–33.
[71] Grey's *Debates*, i. 141–3.
[72] *Ibid.* i. 145; Cobbett, *State Trials*, 1810, vi. 869–78; G. Penn, *Memorials of Sir W. Penn*, 1833, ii. 464 *seq.*; Pepys's *Diary*, 16, 20, 21, 24, 27, 29 April 1668.
[73] Grey's *Debates*, i. 174, 179, 182. [74] *Ibid.* i. 215.
[75] Pepys's *Diary*, 12 December 1666.

Cholmley reckoned the whole of Ashley's receipts as going into the privy purse. According to the report Ashley received nearly £437,500. His payments included over £26,000 'for secret services', and over £46,000 'for his Majesty's more particular use'. Of the expenditure of the latter sum further details were given.[76] Although it appeared that the bulk of the money had been properly spent, this part of the report, which showed how Charles had encroached on receipts which ought to have been sacred to the war, cannot have been gratifying to the king. It was even more serious from his point of view that the way was prepared for the assumption by parliament of that control of expenditure which Clarendon desired to entrust to the privy council, and for that control of the working executive which was its inevitable concomitant.

(b) *Opposition from the King*

Charles disliked and distrusted the aristocratic and bureaucratic control over state affairs which Clarendon intended council to exercise. The king, he says,

> thought that those officers who immediately depended upon himself and only upon himself were more at his devotion than they who were obliged to give an account to any other superior. And from the time that he first came into France he had not been accustomed to any discourse more than to the undervaluing the privy-council, as if it shadowed the king too much, and usurped too much of his authority and too often superseded his own commands. And the queen his mother had, upon these discourses, always some instances of the authority which in such a case the council had assumed against the king's judgment; the exception to which, according to the relation which nobody could question, seemed to be very reasonable. This kind of discourse, being the subject of every day, made so great impression that it could never be defaced, and made the election and nomination of counsellors less considered, since they were to be no more advised with afterwards than before.[77]

This remarkable passage, written after Clarendon's impeachment, and tinged with the passion of an exile who saw the work of his lifetime shattered, sets forth with extraordinary clearness the points of difference between Charles II and Clarendon, which continued to increase until the catastrophe of 1667. Clarendon, imbued with the constitutional traditions of the past, found himself in constant opposition to Charles II, who was fascinated

---

[76] *Hist. MSS. Comm.*, 8th Report, app. i. 129. The details of the expenditure may be found in the Public Record Office in the warrant entry books, and particularly in Entry Book 22.

[77] *Contin. of Life*, § 564; see also §§ 77, 163, 193, 470, 912.

by French principles of government, and designed by emancipating the various departments of state from the control of the council and by isolating them from each other to bring them all under his personal sway. During Clarendon's administration Charles took steps in this direction with regard to both the treasury and the navy.

(i) *The Treasury*

At the Restoration Clarendon's particular friend, the earl of Southampton, was lord treasurer. As he sympathized with the chancellor's views on administration the business of the treasury was carried on in subordination to the council,[78] and important payments were sanctioned by an order in council. The king disliked this method of procedure. It placed restraints upon his expenditure, which he endured with impatience. But he was influenced mainly by the shortcomings of the administration. The privy council was not a suitable board of financial control. While itself inefficient, it hindered any changes in system within the treasury also. The shortcomings of the treasury, its antiquated and cumbrous methods, were constantly pointed out to the king by men of the younger generation, notably by Downing and Cooper. Under the influence of these advisers, Charles, as has been shown, attempted to form a separate fund during the Dutch war under Cooper's management. Parliament, however, showed disquiet at this device, and as the treasury itself could not be reformed while Southampton was at its head, Charles desired to remove Southampton and to place it in commission. In order to understand how this would affect the chancellor's system it is necessary to remember that he considered that council should be composed of great officials with a few magnates. The administration was in fact to be carried on by the heads of the departments of state. Each of these, individually, from the importance of his office, would have great weight in the council. But if the great offices were put in commission, not only would the individual importance of the official councillors be lost, but the king might, by introducing members of various opinions into the same commission, altogether destroy the political influence of the department, while those members of the commission who were not privy councillors would have a natural preference for independent departmental action.

According to Clarendon, Downing's proposal in 1665 to request parliament to appropriate supplies for the war was made partly in the hope that the affront might drive Southampton to resign. Finding this attempt fruitless the king, shortly afterwards, directly proposed to Clarendon that he should induce the treasurer

[78] Shaw, preface to *Calendar of Treasury Books*, 1660–7, xxxv–xxxvii.

to withdraw on account of ill health, and that the office should be put in commission, as it had been in Cromwell's time. In reply Clarendon said ' that he was very sorry to find his majesty so much inclined to commissioners, who were indeed fittest to execute all offices according to the model of a commonwealth, but not at all agreeable to monarchy '. Cromwell, he said, had had an army of one hundred thousand men, which made him have no need of the authority and reputation of a treasurer.[79] He succeeded, with the assistance of the duke of York, in dissuading the king from the change for the time, but on the death of Southampton in May 1667 Charles revived the idea. On this occasion, finding his objections to placing the office in commission disregarded, the chancellor proposed to follow the ' old course ' and to compose the commission of the keeper of the great seal (at this time the lord chancellor),[80] the two secretaries of state,[81] two other principal persons of the council, and the chancellor of the exchequer.[82] He found that Charles had already determined on his commissioners. The king would not hear of the chancellor or the secretaries, nor would he restrict himself to privy councillors, remarking that he would choose ' rough and ill-natured men, not to be moved with civilities or importunities in the payment of money ; but apply it all to his present necessities '. He proposed Sir John Duncombe and two privy councillors, Sir Thomas Clifford and Sir William Coventry. Clarendon induced him to add Albemarle and the chancellor of the exchequer, Lord Ashley,[83] and to make Duncombe a privy councillor in order to obviate the inconvenience of having an unsworn commissioner.[84] But this was all that he could accomplish, and his failure to hinder the placing of the treasury in commission was a presage of his approaching disgrace. The change, however, was of great benefit to the treasury. Downing was made secretary to the commissioners, and ' from 1667 onwards ', says Dr. Shaw, ' under Downing's inspiration, the routine of Treasury business and Treasury bookkeeping was systematised and regulated in a remarkably thorough and regular manner.'[85] Resolutions, which in Southampton's time took the form of an order scribbled on the face or dorse of a petition or case, were after consideration before the board drawn up into a formal minute.[86] From the date of this commission begins the history of the treasury as an independently organized department of state.

[79] *Contin. of Life*, §§ 811-17.
[80] Clarendon.
[81] Morice and Arlington.
[82] Lord Ashley.
[83] With regard to the reasons for the king's reluctance to make Ashley a commissioner see Christie, *Life of Shaftesbury*, i. 307.
[84] *Contin. of Life*, §§ 1082-88.
[85] Preface to *Calendar of Treasury Books*, 1660-7, p. xliii.
[86] *Ibid.* pp. xliv-xlv.

(ii) *The Admiralty*

On 6 June 1660 the office of lord high admiral was bestowed on the duke of York.[87] As the king's brother he was too high a person to be easily controlled, and he was encouraged by his secretary, William Coventry, to regard himself as responsible to none but the king, and to keep the nomination of officers in his own hands. The duke, Clarendon says, considered that 'being high admiral he was to render account to none but the king, nor suffer anybody else to interpose in any thing relating to' the navy or the admiralty.

Whereas in truth there is no officer of the crown more subject to the council-board than the admiral of England, who is to give an account of all his actions and of every branch of his office constantly to the board, and to receive their orders: nor hath he the nomination of the captains of the ships, till upon the presentation of their names he receives their approbation, which is never denied. Nor was there any counsellor who had ever sat at the board in the last king's time, to whom this was not as much known as any order of the table.

But there was no retrieving this authority, not only from the influence Mr. Coventry, and they of the family who adhered to him, had upon the duke, but from the king's own inclination, who thought that those officers who immediately depended upon himself and only upon himself were more at his devotion than they who were obliged to give an account to any other superior.[88]

In consequence the whole of the offices at the disposal of the admiral were filled up, without any reference to the privy council, by Coventry, who took advantage of his position, Clarendon asserts, to obtain large sums of money,[89] and for this consideration retained in their posts the men who had served under Cromwell. The result of this loss of authority on the part of the privy council Clarendon considers to be an immense growth of corruption, embezzlement, and, consequently, of inefficiency in the admiralty and navy; but his opinion is not borne out by the evidence.

Within a few weeks a further important resolution was arrived at. At the date of the Restoration the administration of the navy was controlled by twenty-eight commissioners, who had been appointed by parliament in December 1659.[90] This commission

---

[87] *Pepys's Diary*, 16 May 1660, and note in Wheatley's edition. The original appointment was made shortly before September 1649. See Register of the Privy Council, 31 August 1649.

[88] *Contin. of Life*, §§ 563, 564.

[89] Pepys corroborates the statement that he sold places: *Diary*, 28 October 1667.

[90] See Dr. J. R. Tanner's preface to *Catalogue of Pepysian MSS.*, in the Publications of the Navy Records Soc. xxvi. 6.

was temporarily continued until 2 July.[91] Clarendon was anxious to prevent the continuation of the arrangement, which would give the lord high admiral the services of an administrative body independent of the privy council. The natural established council of the lord high admiral, he says, is the three superior officers of the navy.[92] It was customary for them to attend him once a week.[93] Coventry, however, was hostile to them, and especially to Sir George Carteret, who, besides being treasurer of the navy, was vice-chamberlain of the king's household and therefore a privy councillor. He proposed to the duke

that in regard of the multiplicity of business in the navy, much more than in former times, and the setting out greater fleets than had been accustomed in that age when those officers and that model for the government of the navy had been established, his royal highness would propose to the king to make an addition by commissioners, of some other persons always to sit with the other officers with equal authority, and to sign all bills with them.[94] It is very true [Clarendon adds] there have frequently been commissioners for the navy; but it hath been in the [place] of the admiral and to perform his office: but in the time of an admiral commissioners have not been heard of.

The duke proposed this innovation at the council board, where it passed without opposition; and after it had been considered by a committee, seven persons were appointed commissioners on 4 July 1660.[95] These were the three chief officers of the navy, the treasurer Sir George Carteret, the future comptroller,[96] the surveyor Sir William Batten, Lord Berkeley, Sir William Penn, Peter Pett, and Samuel Pepys;[97] Coventry was added on 12 May 1662.[98] Early in 1664 their authority was extended by an act of parliament giving them for two years summary jurisdiction with regard to unruly sailors, and so investing them with some of the powers of justices of the peace.[99]

[91] Register of the Privy Council, 31 May, 2 June 1660, printed in G. Penn's *Memorials of Sir W. Penn*, ii. 241.
[92] The treasurer, comptroller, and surveyor. See also the statement of the duke of York in State Papers, Domestic, Charles II, vol. 213, no. 65, dated 12 August 1667.
[93] Cf. Pepys's *Diary*, 8 September 1662.
[94] *Contin. of Life*, § 569.
[95] Register of the Privy Council, 27 June, 4 July 1660. The order in council is inserted before the minutes for 4 July, and is printed in G. Penn's *Memorials of Sir W. Penn*, ii. 241-3. Cf. preface to *Catalogue of Pepysian MSS.* i. 6-7. Dr. Tanner is mistaken in dating the order 2 July, if the copy in the Register of the Privy Council be correct. See also Pepys's *Diary*, 2, 3 July 1660.
[96] Colonel Robert Slingsby was appointed in August.
[97] Register of the Privy Council, 4 July 1660; Sir G. Jackson's *Naval Commissioners*, 1889.
[98] *Calendar of State Papers, Domestic*, 1661-2, p. 368.
[99] 16 Car. II, cap. 5; cf. *Calendar of State Papers, Domestic*, 1663-4, p. 82; *Journals of the House of Commons*, 24, 27 July 1664; preface to *Catalogue of Pepysian MSS.*, i. 185-8.

The council thus lost the power of appointing naval officers and much of the administrative control. But it still retained considerable authority. On 9 November 1660 a committee for naval affairs was appointed consisting of the duke of York, Southampton, Albemarle, and seven other privy councillors.[100] To its consideration were referred the requirements of the ensuing year in men, shipping, and provisions, and it was entrusted with the duty of making contracts for the supplies required.[101] At the time of the first Dutch war this committee received unrestricted powers to deal with any emergencies that might arise.[102] It had been strengthened by the addition of Prince Rupert, Berkeley, and Bennet on 11 November 1663, and subsequently Lauderdale, Buckingham, and Ormonde were added.[103]

IV. CLARENDON'S FALL

Clarendon's fall was due largely to the difference between him and Charles with regard to principles of administration. The king was not in agreement with him as to the constitutional position of the privy council. Charles, says Clarendon, 'rather esteemed some particular members of it, than was inclined to believe that the body of it ought to receive a reverence from the people, or be looked upon as a vital part of the government.'[104] The principal cause of his fall was not the personal feelings of the king and the duke of York, though he himself believed it was. Charles was assured of Clarendon's devotion to his service,[105] and felt that he owed his restoration largely to Clarendon's counsels. Until he became acutely dissatisfied with the conduct of affairs he did not wish to break with him. But he found the position of the crown weakened by the defective working of the administration. The heads of the departments had such weight in council that they prevented proper supervision and control.

To this general cause must be added Clarendon's political blunders, which formed one of the reasons for the dissatisfaction of parliament and for the resolve to institute an inquiry into the conduct of the Dutch war. In writing to the duchess of Orleans Charles says, ' the truth is the ill conduct of my Lord Clarendon in my affairs has forced me to permit many enquiries to be made, which otherwise I would not have suffered the Parliament to have done.'[106] Clarendon's position was weakened by the disasters of the Dutch war. He disliked the war, and was incapable of con-

---

[100] Register of the Privy Council, 9 November 1660, 11 November 1663.
[101] Ibid. 14 November 1660; 8, 15 February 1660-1.
[102] Ibid. 11 November 1664.
[103] Ibid. 11 November 1663; 16, 25, 30 November 1664.
[104] Contin. of Life, § 912.   [105] Ibid. § 899.
[106] Miss Julia Cartwright (Mrs. Ady), Madame, 1900, p. 248.

ducting it. ' As I did from my soul,' he says, ' abhor the entering into this war, so I never presumed to give any advice or counsel by way of managing it, but by opposing many propositions which seemed to the late lord treasurer and myself to be unreasonable.' [107] This was an impossible attitude for a man in his position to take up, and he ought at least to have anticipated the co-operation of Louis XIV with the Dutch. But, as Burnet says, ' he had not a right notion of foreign matters.' [108] The country generally attributed all the disasters of the war to him.

While his loss of reputation in the eyes of the king and nation was due partly to his political prepossessions and partly to blunders in practical politics, the final catastrophe was made inevitable by his blindness to the real power and position of parliament. After the Dutch attack on Sheerness, in June 1667, he opposed the immediate reassembling of parliament on the ground that as it had been prorogued to October it would be unconstitutional to recall it sooner.[109] He suggested the impracticable course of dissolving parliament and resorting to a general election at a time when the country was in a state of alarm and of intense irritation, and he proposed until supplies could be obtained from the new parliament to place the forces raised to resist the Dutch at free quarters.[110] He was himself conscious later that this proposal had injured him,[111] and in fact it aroused the dread of military government inherited from the time of the Commonwealth. Parliament came up unmanageable on 15 July and was immediately prorogued, but not before it had demanded the disbanding of the forces raised. Charles foresaw that when it met again it would demand the punishment of Clarendon, and he was determined not to enter into a contest with it in defence of the minister. New men were needed who understood the meaning of what had passed between 1640 and 1660.

About the middle of August the king sent the duke of York to Clarendon to urge him to resign the great seal, because the commons were certain to impeach him.[112] Clarendon had an interview with Charles on 26 August in which he declared himself determined not to deliver up the seal unless he were deprived of it. He showed his failure to gauge the situation by beseeching the king ' not to suffer his spirits to fall, nor himself to be dejected, with the appearance of the formidable power of the Parliament, which was more, or less, or nothing, as he pleased to make it '.[113] Such advice at the close of a mismanaged war, when the king was unable to raise money to carry on the administration

[107] *Contin. of Life*, § 1197.
[108] Miss Foxcroft's *Supplement to Burnet's History of My Own Time*, 1902, p. 55.
[109] *Contin. of Life*, §§ 1099–1101.   [110] *Ibid.* § 1104.
[111] *Ibid.* § 1105; cf. Pepys's *Diary*, 13 October 1667.
[112] *Contin. of Life*, § 1134.   [113] *Ibid.* § 1142.

and was therefore compelled to throw himself on parliament, seriously detracts from Clarendon's ability as a statesman. His next words, 'it was yet in his power to govern them, but if they found it was in their power to govern him, nobody knew what the end would be,' are interpreted by Lister as a warning to the king in regard to his private and political conduct, and, if they were thus intended, they are singularly unhappy in the mouth of a minister against whom the nation was crying out. He further prejudiced his case by an attack on Lady Castlemaine.

This interview is particularly worthy of attention because it is so illuminating as to Clarendon's view of the position. He persisted in ascribing his decline in Charles's regard to the personal influence of Buckingham and Lady Castlemaine,[114] and refused to recognize that the failure of his administration had shaken Charles's confidence in his ability, while his unpopularity made the risk of supporting him enormous. Charles showed a truer appreciation of the situation when he replied to those who interceded for Clarendon, that 'he had made himself odious to parliament, and so was no more capable to do him service'.[115] 'There can be nothing advanced in the Parl:' wrote Charles to his sister, 'until this matter of my Lord Clarendon be over, but after that I shall be able to take my measures to with them, as you will see the good effects of it;'[116] and in March 1668 he added, 'most of the vexation and trouble I have at present in my affairs I owe to him.'[117] That closer relations with parliament were Charles's aim appears from his speech to the body on 10 October, when he said, with reference to the prorogation in July, 'I have given myself time to do some things I have since done, which I hope will not be unwelcome to you, but a foundation for a greater confidence between us for the future.'[118] In reply the commons expressly thanked the king for depriving the chancellor of office.[119] Charles summed up the position in a letter to Ormonde:

The truth is, his behaviour and humour was grown so unsupportable to myself, and to all the world else, that I could no longer endure it, and it was impossible for me to live with it and do those things with the Parliament that must be done or the Government will be lost. When I have a better opportunity for it, you shall know many particulars that have inclined me to this resolution, which already seems to be well liked in the world, and to have given a real and visible amendment to my affairs.[120]

E. I. CARLYLE.

[114] Evelyn's *Diary*, 27 August 1667.
[115] *Contin. of Life*, § 1144; but cf. Burnet, i. 251.
[116] Miss Cartwright's *Madame*, p. 249.   [117] *Ibid.* p. 260.
[118] *Journals of the House of Lords*, 10 October 1667.
[119] *Journals of the House of Commons*, 14 October 1667; Pepys's *Diary*, 12, 14 October 1667. On the other hand, Povey and others thought that Clarendon's removal had softened the feeling against him: Pepys's *Diary*, 10, 11 September 1667.
[120] Charles II to Ormonde, 15 September 1667, Ellis, *Original Letters*, 2nd series, iv. 39.

Struensee and the Fall of Bernstorff

FOUR generations after his death, the mystery of Struensee is still unsolved. It is well known that in the years 1770 and 1771 a young German doctor wielded an immense influence over the king and queen of Denmark, and used that influence to create the most conspicuous and unrestrained benevolent despotism in Europe. Within some eighteen months, indeed, the council of ministers who ruled Denmark by favour of Russia having first been paralysed, he remodelled countless institutions in accordance with the new enlightenment, called forth from Altona to Trondhjem a universal curse, confessed that he had seduced the queen, and died, a Christian penitent, upon the scaffold. But, in spite of verdicts not a few, the ability and character of the man who thus amazed Europe have perhaps never yet been adequately appraised. At his fall, as was natural, the Danes were unanimous in injustice. Even the chief jurists reported to the king :

> Neither we nor any of your Majesty's faithful subjects can think without sorrow and the utmost horror upon the kind of attachment that Struensee had for your Majesty, the kind of care that he took for your life and personal happiness.[1]

In 1824, when Professor Höst published the first methodical history of Struensee and his ministry, he had become the man of the people, 'who created a new spirit in government and nation which, if maintained, would have borne the most notable fruit; he established laws and institutions which have stood the test of half a century.'[2] An equal interval elapsed before the brilliant Jena professor, Karl Wittich, surveying a widened field of research, found Struensee a talented man of rich nature, although without genius : 'no hero, no philosopher, and not cast in tragic mould ; he was shattered on the contradiction between his high task and his inadequate personality.'[3] In the twentieth century the learned and lucid history[4] of Professor Edward

---

[1] J. K. Höst, *Struensee og hans Ministerium*, iii. 219.   [2] *Ibid.* i. 79.
[3] K. Wittich, *Struensee* (Leipzig, 1879), p. 156. His biography of Struensee in the *Allgemeine Deutsche Biographie*, xxxvi. (1893), is only slightly more favourable.
[4] *Danmark-Norges Historie under Christian VII* (1766–1808), t. i, ii. 1, 2 (Copenhagen, 1902).

Holm, supported by a far richer store of documents, portrays Struensee too unfavourably not to challenge inquiry. It would be astounding, indeed, if even under a weak autocrat with a consort imperious yet frail, a lowly new-comer to the Danish court could have achieved so much had he been merely a shallow materialist, mediocre in ability and education, and untruthful.

Struensee's alleged untruthfulness, since it raises a question rather of fact than of opinion, may perhaps be more easily proved or disproved than the other qualities named. And here his apologist must give way if his own Defence,[5] which was written in prison and dated 14 April 1772, be successfully impugned. There, if anywhere, he told the truth, and—except for deliberate silence with regard to the insanity of the king[6] and the adultery of the queen—the whole truth. The Defence was composed without counsellors and without documents. Its author professed to have renounced all hope of life, and, in the fervour of his new-found faith, almost all desire to live. His one aim, so far as can be judged, was to repair the mischief which he had done. Both at the time of writing the Defence and, a few weeks later, on the very verge of death, he assured his confessor of its truthfulness. He now stands acquitted of the only charge, that of falsifying the accounts, regarding which the confessor found it hard to accept the assurance. According to Professor Holm, however, Struensee's Defence 'showed that he still believed that he could deal with the matter purely in the fashion of an advocate, so that on various points he by no means kept to the truth. To this extent, his conversion to Christianity could not be said to have stood the test to which it was put.'[7] The following pages form an attempt to determine whether this charge is valid.

A substantial and weighty part of the Defence deals with the memorable journey of Christian VII through Holstein in 1770, a journey marked by the recall to court, first, of Struensee's friend Brandt, and next, of his patron Count Rantzau; and, finally, by the dismissal of Count Holck, long the bosom friend of the king. This last took place on 27 July. A month later the court returned to Copenhagen. In the middle of September Count Bernstorff was dismissed, and the old régime of the ministers came to an end. In the eyes of Europe Bernstorff was Denmark, while to the Danes he represented the crown. His fall was held

[5] *Verantwortung des Grafen von Struensee an die Königliche Commission*, printed in Höst, iii. 108-39.
[6] Compare Struensee's 'Relation' (regarding the king's health), translated by N. Lassen, *Den Struensee'ske Proces*, in *Tidsskrift for Retsvidenskab*, 1891, p. 246. This helps to repulse the bitter but unconvincing attack of C. Molbech upon the Defence, *Nyt historisk Tidsskrift*, IV. ii. 637.
[7] L. ii. 2. 418.

to portend a revolution in home and foreign policy alike, and from it the historian dates the autocracy of Struensee.

With regard to the journey of 1770, Struensee makes four clear assertions in his Defence. He asserts, first, that Holck, who had been losing the king's favour, proposed the journey 'in order, as I believe, to maintain his position' (*sich zu souteniren*); secondly, that the queen (by this time admittedly his own paramour) was determined to remove Holck from court; thirdly, that to this end, after vainly endeavouring to allay her hostility, he suggested the recall of Brandt and Rantzau; and, fourthly, that down to the time of their recall no plan existed for the alterations in the ministry. This narrative is expressly discredited by Professor Holm. How, he asks (I. i. 220), could the journey serve Holck ? It was far more probably Struensee and the queen who wished for it. Again (240, 241), 'the development of his [Struensee's] own conduct in the time which followed is quite inexplicable' if his own account be accepted. 'Nothing could be more foolish than his desire to make the world believe that the battle in which Rantzau was to assist was directed against the insignificant Holck, not against the ministers and the whole ruling system.'

At first sight it appears somewhat difficult to attribute a well-planned and far-reaching political design to an adventurer whose career is portrayed as a series of short-sighted steps dictated by no plan or principle. The dictum of Dean L. Koch[8] seems distinctly more plausible. He says of Struensee, that

when he became the Queen's lover, he scarcely regarded this as a means of gaining greater and greater power: but he very speedily discovered that he had come into so dangerous a situation that it was impossible for him to suffer any superior, if he would not hazard being crushed: care for his own safety drove him further and further forward, and higher and higher up.

It is significant, moreover, that no conclusive corroboration of the charge of having formed far-reaching political designs appears to have resulted from the seizure, early in 1772, of Struensee's papers and of the correspondence between some of his alleged accomplices. Rantzau's letters to General Gähler during the summer of 1770 demonstrate the existence of a royalist party, Struensee's membership of that party, its expectation of a campaign, and the possibility that 'the Beast' Holck might be overthrown. They are far from suggesting that Struensee rather than Gähler was the leader of the party, or that its members were conscious of possessing, from whatever source it might have come, a definite plan of action. Only

[8] *Historisk Tidsskrift*, vi. 5, i. 90.

late in July, and when beside himself with rage and disappointment at Bernstorff's refusal to countenance his recall to court, does Rantzau bluster to his friend General Gähler that that 'most reverend Mufti, surnamed the Sheep', 'may even himself lose his place' if he does not yield. In his Defence Struensee states that he suggested Rantzau's recall as that of a man 'personally agreeable to the King', and 'fitted to balance the reputation of the then Ministry which, the Queen feared, would re-establish the credit of Count Holck by removing those who stood in his way'. This theory suggests an entirely adequate reason for the vapourings of his fantastic and egotistical ally at the time. Holck, it is true, neither possessed nor desired to possess any pretensions to statesmanship. But his high place in the court, and his remarkable intimacy with the autocratic head of the state, had made him in the past a distinct factor in policy. This was well known to George III before his Danish guests reached England in 1768, it terrified his representative at Copenhagen, it was admitted and turned to their own uses by Bernstorff and his colleagues.[9] So long as the Danes owed allegiance to a monarch who found his keenest pleasure in cashiering, but who, unaided, was unequal to any decisive act, the favourite must be a political factor of high importance.

In this connexion the English dispatches [10] are not without interest. Gunning, our resident at Copenhagen, had learned in four years that 'the politics of Denmark seem incapable of any other production than that of intrigue'. For this, and particularly for interference by France, he had a watchful eye, and in 1769, while recording successive proofs of Holck's continued importance, he notes the rising influence of young Warnstedt, the king's former page, whom he names, and of Struensee, whose name he carefully omits. From February to April 1770 he pays each month a tribute to the power of Holck. First, the king passes some hours every day with him, and thereby has dangerous opportunities of intercourse with his guest the Spanish ambassador. Next, he receives a share in the control of the privy purse. Finally, the king exhorts the fiery Russian minister to live at peace with him. Then, on 1 May, Gunning reports that 'the Court have taken a sudden resolution of going into Holstein. Orders are actually given to have everything in readiness by the beginning of next month for that journey; it is not known by whom this Project has been planned.' Why, it may well be asked, should not the plan have been that of Holck? A former royal journey, that memorable tour of 1768 in England and France on which Struensee first accompanied the king, had

[9] A. Friis, *Bernstorffsche Papiere*, ii. 203; State Papers, *passim*.
[10] State Papers, Foreign, Denmark 122 123, *passim*.

brought Holck's fortune to its zenith. It was of Holck that Bernstorff wrote from Brussels in August 1768: 'So he has become His Excellency: not bad progress in six or eight months. . . . He is prodigiously in favour. The King treats him absolutely as a brother, sometimes as a superior.'[11] And in spite of the notorious fickleness of Christian VII the impression then made had remained uneffaced at least down to the first months of 1770. Might Holck not now hope for its renewal? A pleasure-tour might well give scope for the social powers of the court marshal and revive his waning lustre. He would possess many allies in the court, while the presence of the queen, his enemy, was contrary to precedent. The Saxon ambassador, indeed, mentioned on 1 May the rumour that on this occasion she had 'declared that she would follow His Majesty, even if he journeyed to the Antipodes',[12] but hitherto she had been conspicuously thwarted and neglected.

The honest Swiss philosopher, Reverdil, the very type of a dispassionate contemporary historian, to whom all the actors in the Struensee tragedy were well known, declares that it was by Holck that the ministers had been reconciled to the former journey, and by Holck that the plan of this one was devised.[13] The execution of the plan, it must not be forgotten, was postponed for some time by the illness and death of a queen dowager, who was buried with hardly decent haste on 14 June. In the remarkable series of confidential letters to Gähler which Rantzau wrote from his exile in Holstein, and which are preserved in the Danish archives, the idea of a royal visit is canvassed as early as 23 February and is reported on 9 March to have taken definite shape. Its inception dated back to the time prior to Struensee's successful inoculation of the crown prince, to the time when the Danish fashionable world was only beginning to watch with excitement and alarm the signs that he and his friend Warnstedt were threatening the hitherto unchallenged primacy of Holck.

Whenever Danish correspondence contemporary with the journey is published, we may expect evidence that at the outset Holck was regarded as a force to be reckoned with, that the queen hated him, that public opinion ran in his favour, and that the capital hoped that the journey would restore him to power. Thus that censorious court lady Fru Louise Gramm wrote in March 1770 of the zealous efforts then being made to depose Holck; in April, of the current but vain desire that the ministers

---

[11] Friis, *Bernstorffsche Papiere*, i. 522.
[12] Printed in C. Blangstrup's translation of Wittich, *Struensee* (Copenhagen, 1887), p. 164.
[13] *Mémoires*, ed. Roger (Paris, 1858), pp. 133, 154.

should take action against 'those who had such an evil influence upon the Queen'; early in May, that a great mine had been sprung at court, for Holck had been within an ace of dismissal by the queen and her party; and at the end of the same month, that the court was the abode of vice and shamelessness, adding, 'I await something good from the journey to Holstein, but all my hope is confined to that.'[14] Another lady, Fru Pauli, writing to Duke Frederick of Glücksburg on 12 June, states that Count Holck is still in a measure holding his own. A week later she reports that at the departure of the court all was well with him once more, and the public earnestly wishes that it may so continue. 'It is said that a few days earlier the Council, together with many others, endeavoured to remove Councillor of Conference Struensee, but in vain.'[15] At the end of June Rantzau, pouring out his counsels in a most secret dispatch to Gähler, suggests that the net result of all the convulsions hitherto has been to make 'H. tout ce qu'il est'. At least as late as the middle of July, Copenhagen, nervous yet hopeful, gave credit to rumours of Struensee's loss of influence and even of his approaching fall.[16] In these the wish was father to the thought. So late as 10 July, however, the surface of the court seemed unruffled, and Holck, although excluded from the tiny circle which surrounded the king, was treated by him 'with affection and with the ordinary distinctions'.[17]

In the absence of any evidence to disprove Holck's authorship of the scheme, it is perhaps unnecessary to demonstrate further that on this head the Defence is not merely credible but entitled to credit. We may, however, pertinently inquire why, if it were false, Struensee should have made the assertion and why Holck should not have contradicted it. The alleged origination of the journey forms one of a number of consecutive statements with regard to Holck and his position at court, several of which the most good-natured man could not have read of himself without resentment. The Defence was published immediately and widely diffused. Yet Holck lived until 1800 without, so far as is known, giving Struensee the lie in any particular. The inference is that the statements regarding him were true, and this inference is strengthened by reflection on the futility, at that juncture, of untruth. Whether the Defence were written for the judges or for posterity, a demonstrable falsehood could do Struensee nothing save harm.

A weightier question, however, is that of the origin of the fall of Bernstorff. Is the Defence to be accepted, or was the recall of Rantzau one step in a far-reaching political design

[14] Cited by Aage Friis in *Tilskueren*, October 1900, pp. 793 ff.
[15] Cited by L. Bobé in Charlotte Dorothea Biehl's *Breve* (Copenhagen, 1901), p. 174.
[16] Friis, *Bernstorffsche Papiere*, i. 600, 602, 612.   [17] Ibid. p. 608.

which Struensee had already formed ? On this, as on the other points at issue, we possess an admirable guide in the correspondence of Bernstorff himself. His letters to and from his nephew, in particular, are the written intercourse of two statesmen who are tender friends. While the younger impressed his contemporaries as a man ' raised high above the envy which marks small souls and bad hearts ', the elder at this period justified daily Professor Holm's fine tribute to him as ' a man with whom it is ethically strengthening to have to do '. No fewer than thirty-six letters, which passed between them during the ten weeks 19 June to 25 August 1770, are printed by Dr. Friis in the first volume of his *Bernstorff Papers*. Within the limits of the discretion imposed by the insecurity of the post, and still more by conscientious loyalty to the king, these form a narrative equally frank, full, authoritative, and precise.

The elder Bernstorff left the capital in mid-June and journeyed towards Holstein in the train of the king and queen. Not for the first time did this veteran diplomatist, the soul of everything virtuous and liberal, find himself strangely isolated amid the immoral rabble which commended itself to the royal taste. He was ready, however, to endure every discomfort, and to protract his daily labours until past midnight, if only he could advance the treaty of exchange with Russia, which would make his master undisputed lord of Holstein. From the court life of 1770, indeed, he might well prefer to be excluded. For, although he had seen and heard too much of courts to feel surprise that kings, or even queens, should have their ' favourites ', and although he would not entirely refuse to make these favourites, by honest means, subserve his honest policy, he beheld the king's choice of intimates with sadness; the queen's, with feelings too deep for written words.

Bernstorff, like others of the council, felt some anxiety with regard to the changes, favourable or the reverse, which every one expected the journey to bring about. While he had good reason for believing himself indispensable, he knew that the king was in theory an autocrat; in practice, a weathercock. In the background, or banished from the court, were men who, like Marshal St. Germain and Count Rantzau, looked to a military monarchy with perhaps the alliance of France for the redemption of Denmark. Within the court and outside was doubt and danger, and Bernstorff's early letters are marked by strong reserve. Struensee, whom his nephew designates 'the Favourite ',[15] is never mentioned by him. On 27 June, however, writing from

---

[15] Struensee's friend, General von Falkenskjold, asserts in his *Memoirs* (Danish transl., Copenhagen, 1847, p. 37) not only that he advised Struensee, when in power, to recall Bernstorff, but that Struensee did not scout the idea ' since he [Bernstorff]

Schleswig, he notes the return of Brandt, 'received well enough, although without any excessive demonstration,' and his reinstatement in the king's service which, 'I confess, appears to me to be just.' Rantzau is expected in the small circle at Traventhal, where the king had hoped to be by the end of the month. 'Nothing is better than his words, and it is only to be regretted that his actions do not correspond with them.' The veteran statesman looks on 'some change' as possible, and if so, as imminent, but not as probable. Three days later he writes, under seal of secrecy, 'I have passed few days in my life as important and as agitated as these last, but for some hours I have been calmer. God has once more taken pity upon us, and showed us a way to avert the evils which we had to fear.' What had happened ? The reply of the nephew indicated that he did not know. But the treatment by the uncle of his items of news, read in the light of his later letters, gives a hint. The queen was ill. Holck was becoming almost a stranger to the king, but Bernstorff begins to believe that he would not be driven from office unless he chose to resign. The harmless Brandt, to Bernstorff's delight, was to go to Traventhal. 'He seems to gain favour, less as yet with the master than with those who approach him.' No irreparable step had yet been taken, but portents were many. 'The elder Warnstedt has been sent to Rantzau and has returned to-day. It is more than probable that they think of placing him (Rantzau) at Copenhagen, but this I shall oppose to the utmost.'

On 4 July the situation is unchanged, save that the king and queen more than ever limit their intercourse to that with Struensee, Warnstedt, and two court ladies. The nephew, with his accustomed sagacity, replies in effect that he is not reassured with regard to the danger of changes. Old servants at a distance from their master and without access to him must be in peril. *Ennui* will be averted by schemes of change. The public dislikes the return of Brandt, and strongly supports Holck. The post is believed to be unsafe, and rumours of a rupture between Bernstorff and 'one of the first favourites' are rife. On 10 July, from Traventhal, the elder Bernstorff promises that he will some day explain his anxieties, which have in great part returned. We may infer from Rantzau's letters that they were due to the inquiry pressed by Struensee, 'May Count Rantzau accept the King's summons to Court, and if not, who forbids him ? ' Bernstorff declares himself determined to bring matters to a head in a few days. Alluding apparently to his nephew's remark 'the public assigns to Brandt the Directorship of Entertainments', he says : 'keep to what I tell you, my dear

was of a cheerful disposition, and moreover accustomed to acquiesce in the power of Favourites'.

nephew, and do not believe public rumours. In less than ten days you will know what there is to fear or hope.' The danger is not imminent.

A week later, while the capital was enjoying reports that Struensee was in weak health,[19] and that he was succumbing before Brandt, who had ' chosen the good part of following the men of goodwill ', Bernstorff penned to his nephew the first of three bulletins from what had become the scene of battle. He notes that Holck had lost the post of superintendent of pleasures, continuing, with probably not accidental juxtaposition, ' The improvement in the Queen's health is maintained. I have never seen her so radiant.' Then, in effect,

Rantzau arrived yesterday. He has required much entreaty : Struensee and Brandt have made several journeys to decide him to come. The King and Queen received him graciously, but without specially distinguishing him in public. After dinner he had an audience of the King. His début has been worthy in all respects. He paid me a long visit and we spoke our minds freely. I have told him that I shall be obliged to explain to the King the drawbacks to his coming. He demurred, but I did not disguise from him that my duty compelled me to do it. So the battle is about to begin. I purpose to go to the King to-morrow. May God give me the needful wisdom and skill. However, His will be done ! It will be a grim struggle.

Three days later, on 20 July, he resumes. He has denounced the recall of Rantzau to the king with all the force which he possesses, and has supported his appeal with a written memorial. The king has received his representations graciously.

I know that the Favourite is embarrassed, and as I have several times spoken, and made others speak, to him, I perceive that he is struck by my arguments and by the danger to which he is exposing himself, but despite all this, I am under no illusion ; I shall lose the day ; the King, a province which it rested with him only to gain ; and the State, its happiness. The Favourite, who however acts in this affair only as the subaltern of a superior hatred (this, which tells you everything, is for yourself alone and in the deepest confidence), and who therefore is unable to retrace or retard his steps, will carry the day, being the only person consulted and listened to.

Bernstorff has left no decent and lawful method untried, but he regards ' the battle as lost and the work of twenty years annihilated '. He renders justice to the worthiness of Rantzau in speech and action, records that the queen has never appeared better in health or spirits, and adds that the king has just ordered a number of courtiers, including Holck's sister, to return to Copenhagen. ' I do not divine the cause and the object of this order, unless it be to get rid of Holck, and perhaps his sister.'

[19] Rantzau to Gähler, 14 July 1770. (Rigsarkiv.)

To this the nephew replies that the troubles are caused 'by motives which I almost blush to fathom. Often I am as much surprised as pained. . . . Is it possible that there are people so wretched as to forget for long all that religion, duty, and common sense can demand from them?' Such words as these, and an allusion to 'wounded consciences which shun the light of day', form the only references to the great scandal of the court which these loyal servants permit themselves.

On 24 July Bernstorff announces his defeat and that of 'the good cause'. The king had thrice read his memorial, was visibly agitated, and seemed for an instant about to yield, but the opposition had been too strong. Despite the grave peril to the treaty of exchange, Rantzau was to enter the war office as third deputy. The nephew had expressed surprise that Struensee and Brandt should introduce into the king's circle a man sometimes so brilliant. 'If they needed this support,' he argued, 'I could understand it; as it is, I count it one of those mistakes and contradictions which often occur in the conduct of men who act rather by impulse than by system.' 'I emphatically do not believe that he will be allowed to attain intimacy or high favour,' replies the uncle, 'mais il servira secondairement aux vues que l'on a.' 'The principles of Marshal St. Germain are going to be reborn, but it is another question whether they can be carried out.' Holck is imperilling himself by 'inconceivable frivolity and mismanagement'. In his own position Bernstorff marks no difference. The victorious party is neither bitter nor cold towards him.

Three days later (27 July) he records 'a *coup* which has probably been the chief end to which all the other operations have been aimed. Poor little Holck is dismissed from all his charges (these are the very words of the order)' with a pension which to him is nothing. Reventlow, the harsh governor of the king's boyhood, is politely dismissed from the control of the privy purse, fortunately for one 'who after the fall of Holck could no longer support this business'. This letter possesses high importance for our judgement of Struensee's Defence. It shows that 'the oracle of Denmark', while perceiving with agony that his life's work might be shattered by the recall of Rantzau, and while familiar with the idea that the influence which secured the recall of Rantzau might bring about the dismissal of himself and his friends, believed that the king had been carried to the confines of his dominions, many of his train sent home, public opinion disregarded, Rantzau implored to come to court, and Struensee compelled to hazard his future—all this in order that Holck might be overthrown. And in all this he believed Struensee was only the involuntary agent of 'a superior hatred'—the hatred of a sister of George III who believed that her husband had been corrupted, her foster-mother banished, and her married life ruined—by Holck. Further, Bernstorff believed that, despite all the influence of the queen and her party, Holck would have maintained himself but for his own imprudence. The letters abound in indications that his dictum in his dispatch of 7 August to St. Petersburg represents his unreserved opinion. 'He could have maintained his position if he had been willing and sufficiently intelligent to follow the advice of those who wished him well, but he is incapable of direction.'[20]

In the letters immediately succeeding, both Bernstorffs throw further light on Holck's unique position. The elder records on 31 July : 'Yesterday the king said only a single word about poor Holck : "He would have it so." I leave you to comment on these words as you think fit.' The commentary which seems most warrantable is that the queen's party may have thought it necessary to their purpose that the king should hear of the loose vows of resignation which Holck is known to have made. And, a week later, the younger reports that the former favourite was cherishing a growing expectation of recall. Holck's position, it must be repeated, had been unique. His fall was diagnosed by some acute contemporaries as due to the machinations of foreign courts ; by others, eighteen months later, as due to Struensee's deep-laid design. 'All this,' declared Struensee himself in his Defence, 'aimed at security at court, without views or plan in respect of the subsequent alterations in the Ministry.' The contemporary official statement of the chief minister runs as follows :[20]

Poor Holck's successors are shut up in their own circles, attentive only to what passes there, and, I vouch for it, have to the present moment no sort of connexion with the ministers of the opposing courts.[21] They will not disturb our work, if we do not attack them, and their safety will bind them to respect us, if we do not drive them to extremity.

Bernstorff's correspondence during the month of August, though full of interest, merely gives a general confirmation to the conclusions which may be drawn from what precedes. More sanguine, as well as better informed, than his nephew and Count A. G. Moltke, he holds that all may yet be well—that his own incessant exertions may prevent Russia from taking umbrage, and that the victorious party may carry change no further. To safeguard the progress of his work, he takes a step to lessen

[20] P. Vedel, *Correspondance ministérielle du comte J. H. E. Bernstorff*, 1751-70, ii. 478.

[21] France and Sweden. In France it had in fact been surmised that England might be ' directing all the threads of these intrigues '. D'Aiguillon to Blosset, 12 July 1770, in Barthélemy, *Hist. des relations de la France et du Danemarck*, 1751-70, p. 322.

the number of its enemies, which he regards as justifiable only by necessity, and the nature of which his nephew cannot divine. It has been conjectured that he stooped to obtain from Struensee an assurance that the queen would not oppose him. It is certain that he remonstrated successfully against the seclusion of the king. As time went on fears and rumours grew, and the dreaded recall of St. Germain seemed less and less remote. Other names, that of Struensee among them, began to be mentioned in Copenhagen as those of his possible colleagues in the service of the king.

Towards the end of August uncle and nephew enjoyed that meeting for which both had yearned. Correspondence between them of course became superfluous until, some six weeks later, the elder quitted his adopted country and the wreck of her old administration. In the interval the humiliating failure of the Danish bombardment of Algiers had entered as a new factor into the political situation. A commission of inquiry had received orders to interrogate Bernstorff, and two memorable ordinances of necessary reform had been drawn up without the aid or approbation of the council. Then, on 15 September, as the man who had steered the Danish state for nearly two decades did not voluntarily cease to toil for her, he received a note of dismissal phrased with the wonted hypocritical graciousness of the king. The way was thus prepared for government from the royal cabinet, which in the following year became government by Struensee.

What was the share of Struensee in the final overthrow of Bernstorff—the statesman whom the best men in Denmark regarded as 'the stay of the laws, of virtue, and of government'? His Defence supplies his own answer, which is tolerably clear and full. He frankly admits that, 'without having personal dislike or ill-will for any of the Ministers,' he had long been an opponent of their administration. He states his reasons, and asserts that his subsequent experience has convinced him that they were valid. He had aimed, he declares, at enabling the king to form an independent opinion, and

therefore I believed it necessary that the King should have other persons of contrary opinion to the then Ministers. If subsequently alterations and decisions to this end followed more quickly, this came rather from the King's personal notions and from casual circumstances than from a determined resolve and plan, at least on my part.

He admits that he did not seek to diminish the unfavourable impression which the king had formed of the ministers, and which was deepened by a series of offences culminating in the Algerine fiasco.

In this frame of mind the King returned from Holstein, and it may easily be imagined that those who then were most listened to did nothing to change it. Their attention was chiefly directed to the effects which the presence of Count Rantzau would produce. With regard to this, Count Bernstorff had given the King a memorial at Traventhal. Count Rantzau had answered it

giving assurances for the security of the negotiations with Russia.

In an unfortunate fashion Count Bernstorff spoke in his addresses and on other occasions of the enemies of the Russian alliance. This occasioned his departure and the consequent alterations. I cannot call to mind that special steps were planned to bring these about.

Struensee's statement, then, is that the king had long disapproved of his ministers; that he and his friends had also, from their own point of view, disapproved of them; that they gained the ear of the king; and that out of this situation, acted upon by the Algerine fiasco and Bernstorff's indiscretion, came Bernstorff's dismissal. Under the circumstances, this account of his conduct is rather a confession than an apology.

When Professor Holm observes (I. i. 271) that 'Struensee has forgotten to tell how much he himself laboured to nourish the King's exasperation against the Ministers which was roused by the mishap at Algiers', he seems either to ignore the obvious interpretation of Struensee's words or to imply that Struensee was already omnipotent, while Rantzau and the others of the party were mere shadows. It is significant that well-informed contemporaries saw Rantzau's hand in the work; that Rantzau, who hinted on occasion that the ministers deserved to be hanged,[22] afterwards boasted of it; and that Bernstorff, less than a week before his fall, wrote of his opponents in terms which could not possibly apply to Struensee alone.[23]

To determine finally the basis of Struensee's character a far wider investigation is required. The vindication of a part of his Defence does not necessarily demonstrate the truth of the whole, and the vindication of the whole would by no means prove him to have been truthful before his conversion. His judges, in deciding the fate of his accomplices, drew a distinction between his statements made before and 'after the time when he had become completely convinced that there was life after this life, where there was punishment or reward to be expected'. But a scrutiny of the accessible contemporary evidence seems to uphold Struensee's own account of his share in the fall of Bernstorff against that of 'the latest and only critically purified portrayal of the Struensee period'.

W. F. REDDAWAY.

[22] Compare his letters to Gähler in 1770 *passim*, and in particular those of 30 June, 4; 13, 17 July (Rigsarkiv).

[23] Bernstorff to Scheel, 10 September 1770, summarized by Holm, I. i. 277.

Notes and Documents

The Restoration of the Cross at Jerusalem

IN an elaborate paper recently published Bolotov has studied the chronology of the years 628–30 of our era. In the present note I desire to show that the Russian scholar's suggested reconstruction is untenable and, further, to propose a different solution.[1] The crucial point in the discussion is the date of the restoration of the Cross, which had been captured by the Persians on the fall of Jerusalem in 614. Bolotov's reconstruction of the chronology [2] may be roughly outlined as follows : After the preliminary negotiations of Heraclius with Persia in the spring of 628, of which an account is given in the Paschal chronicle, Sheroe (or Kobad) sent the newly appointed Catholicos Ishoyab on an embassy to the emperor (August–September 628). The Persian king was mortally ill at the time, and was anxious that Heraclius should protect his infant son Ardeshir :[3] he would choose a Christian to influence a Christian, and the mission was the more

---

[1] See V. Bolotov, *K Istorii Imperatora Irakliya*, in *Vizantuiskii Vremmenik*, xiv (1907), St. Petersburg, 1908, pp. 68–124 ; E. A. W. Budge, *The Book of Governors, The Historia Monastica of Thomas Bishop of Marga* A.D. 840, 2 vols., London, 1893; J. Labourt, *Le Christianisme dans l'Empire perse sous la dynastie Sassanide*, in *Bibliothèque de l'Enseignement de l'Histoire Ecclésiastique*, 2ᵐᵉ édition, Paris, 1904 ; N. Marr, *Antiokh Stratig, Plyenenie Ierusalima Persami v 614 g.*, St. Petersburg, 1909 ; *Tekstui i Razuiskaniya po armyano-gruzinskoi Philologii, Kniga viii, Izdaniya Fakul'teta Vostochnuikh yazuikov imperatorskago S. Peterburgskago Universiteta* (if Marr's work should be inaccessible, see Archimandrit Kallistos, Ἀντίοχος Στρατήγιος, Ἅλωσις τῆς Ἰερουσαλὴμ ὑπὸ τῶν Περσῶν τῷ 614 Γεωργιανὸν κείμενον, &c., ἐν Ἱεροσολύμοις. τύποις Π. Τάφου 1910, reprinted from Νέα Σιὼν ΣΤ καὶ Ζ' ἔτους, which gives a *résumé* of Marr's work and a Greek translation of the Georgian text, and compare also F. C. Conybeare, *ante*, xxv. 502, 1910) ; Th. Nöldeke, *Geschichte der Perser und Araber zur Zeit der Sassaniden, aus der arabischen Chronik des Tabari*, &c., Leyden, 1879 (cited hereafter as *Geschichte*), and *Die von Guidi herausgegebene syrische Chronik*, in *Sitzungsberichte der kaiserl. Akad. der Wissenschaften in Wien*, cxxviii, Abh. ix, 1893 ; A. Pernice, *L'Imperatore Eraclio, Saggio di Storia Bizantina* (*Pubblicazioni del reale Istituto di Studi Superiori Pratici e di Perfezionamento in Firenze*, 1905) ; L. Sternbach, in *Rozprawy Akademii Umiejętności. Wydział Filologiczny*, Serya ii, tom. xv, Krakow, 1900, and *Georgii Pisidae Carmina Inedita* (*Wiener Studien*, xiii (1891), pp. 1–62 ; xiv (1892), pp. 51–68) ; W. A. Wigram, *An Introduction to the History of the Assyrian Church or the Church of the Sassanid Persian Empire*, London, 1910.

[2] *Op. cit.* pp. 77–94.

[3] Compare the confused notice in Nicephorus 20²¹, ed. de Boor.

likely to succeed if Ishoyab bore with him the Holy Cross. The delay in sending this may well have been due to the difficulty of discovering the sacred relic, which might have been placed, Bolotov suggests,[4] in one of the monasteries, either Nestorian or Monophysite, favoured at different times by Sirin, the Christian wife of Chosroes;[5] its precise location might have been thus uncertain.[6] The solemnity of the occasion and the fact that Ishoyab was unaccompanied by other Nestorian bishops serve to explain why the Catholicos ventured to attend a celebration of the eucharist in the emperor's presence, probably at Theodosiopolis.[7] Heraclius then held the synod of Karin (i. e. Theodosiopolis) and effected a union with the Armenian church (in the winter of 628–9), after which he distributed pieces of the true Cross among the notables of Armenia and thence proceeded to Caesarea.[8] From Caesarea, it would seem, Heraclius sent the true Cross to Constantinople,[9] and in June the Persians began to evacuate Roman territory, while in July 629 the emperor finally concluded terms of peace with Sahrbarâz at Arabissos Tripotamos.[10] He returned to Constantinople, probably in September 629, and in the spring of 630, in the month of March, bore the Cross to Jerusalem, where it was restored to the place from which it had been carried in 614. In this year Heraclius assisted Sahrbarâz in his successful attack on the Persian capital, where Ardashir had been reigning since October 629.[11] This reconstruction of the chronology has been accepted by Professor Marr,[12] who therefore

[4] *Op. Cit.* pp. 79–81.
[5] On her change from the Nestorian to the Monophysite allegiance compare Wigram, pp. 253, 259.
[6] This is in itself improbable: and further, compare the definite assertion (overlooked by Bolotov) of *Chron. Guidi*, ed. Nöldeke, p. 32, mentioning the Cross of Christ, 'das sie von Jerusalem gebracht hatten und das *im persischen Schatzhause niedergelegt war* '.
[7] That Ishoyab was dispatched by Sheroe on a mission to Heraclius unaccompanied by any metropolitans or bishops is purely conjectural. Thomas of Marga, who alone (Budge, ii, pp. 125 *seqq.*) places this embassy in the reign of Sheroe (though cf. Barhebraei, *Chronicon Ecclesiasticum*, ed. Abbeloos and Lamy, Paris, 1877, vol. iii, coll. 114–16—the patriarch a *rege* Persarum missus est legatus ad Graecorum imperatorem), states that there went with him the metropolitans of Nisibis and Adiabene and other influential bishops of the Nestorian church. For Bolotov's reasons for his conjectural reconstruction see *Viz. Vrem.*, *loc. cit.*, pp. 86 *seqq*. The mission of which Thomas of Marga speaks was almost certainly dispatched by Bôrân, who became queen in 630. Cf. Budge, *loc. cit.*, n. 2; *Chron. Guidi*, pp. 32–3; H. Gismondi, *Maris Amri et Slibae de Patriarchis Nestorianorum Commentaria*, pars i, Romae, 1899, p. 54; pars ii, Romae, 1896, p. 31; Nöldeke, *Geschichte*, p. 392, n. 1; Labourt, pp. 242–3; Wigram, pp. 300 *seqq*.
[8] John Mamikonian, *Fragmenta Historicorum Graecorum*, ed. Muller, v. ii. 380.
[9] Niceph. 22.
[10] *Corpus Scriptorum Christianorum Orientalium, Scriptores Syri*, Versio, Series tertia, tomus iv, *Chronica Minora*, pars secunda, Paris, 1904, pp. 108, 113, 114.
[11] This summary will serve our present purpose; the student will consult Bolotov's paper for the elaborate argumentation by which he seeks to support his conclusions.
[12] Marr, p. 5.

concludes that the Cross was restored to its place in Jerusalem on 21 March 630, adopting the date 21 March from Antiochus Strategos.

But Bolotov has not paid sufficient attention to the western authorities, and he has altogether neglected two important sources—the chronicle of Agapius of Hierapolis and the *Carmina Inedita* of George of Pisidia. We can best take these for the starting-point of our criticism.

(i) The text of that part of the chronicle of Agapius with which we are concerned is not yet published, but a Russian translation by Baron von Rosen appeared in 1884 in the *Journal of the Ministry of Public Enlightenment*. As this periodical is to be found in but few libraries in the west of Europe, I may be pardoned for giving an English rendering from the Russian of the two relevant passages.[13] (p. 72) After the accession of Sheroe—

> Then Heraclius departed on his way back and stopped at the village called Semanen. This is the same village where the ark stopped in the flood in the days of Noah: and he went up to the mountain called Al-Djûdi, and looked upon it at the place of the ark and gazed on all four sides. And then he went in the direction of Amid and there he spent the whole of that winter. And Sheroe the son of Kisre [Chosroes] sent ambassadors to Heraclius asking for peace. And Heraclius agreed thereto on condition that all the towns and villages which his father [i.e. Chosroes] had taken from the Greeks should be restored and that Heraclius should send into Persia all the Persians which were in his power. [Here follows a mention of certain philosophers of the time.] . . . Then Heraclius determined to depart for Mesopotamia and Syria, and he summoned to him his brother Theodore and ordered him to grant the Persians who were to be found in the whole of Mesopotamia and Syria permission to retire from his empire and to return into Persia. And Theodore started forth at the head of the advance-guard, and Heraclius began to go into each town one after another and to settle his representatives in them, until he had gone round them all, and then returned to his kingdom to Constantinople. [Then follows an account of Theodore's difficulties at Edessa and Heraclius' subsequent attempts to introduce orthodoxy there. Further, evidently from another source, on p. 64 we read: In the 18th year of Heraclius] Kesra [Chosroes] son of Hormizd emperor of the Persians was killed, after he had reigned 38 years. Then after him his son Kobad reigned, and concluded peace with the Greeks, and returned to them the towns which he and others had captured up to Dara which is above Nisibîn. [A comet appears.] Then Heraclius gave orders to the Greeks that they should leave the territory [of the Persians (e coniectura)] and should go to the territory of the Greeks in

---

[13] Baron von Rosen, *Zamyetki o Lyetopisi Agapiya Manbidzhskago*, in *Zhurnal Ministerstva Narodnago Prosbyeshcheniya*, pt. ccxxxi, February 1884, pp. 47–75; and for information on Agapius see A. Vasiliev, *Agapy, Manbidzhsky kristiansky arabsky Istorik X Vyeka*, in *Viz. Vrem.* xi (1904), pp. 574–87.

accordance with the terms of the peace which Greeks and Persians had concluded with each other. And Sahrbaz [Sahrbarâz] gave orders to all the Persians that they should return to their own land, each to his own town and family, and that they should not raise disturbances in the land, but they did not attend to his words. And in the end of the 20th year of Heraclius the Persians made an expedition to the Euphrates, and Shahrbaz [Sahrbarâz] took [into captivity] many warriors of the Greeks, and many of the Persian [read Greek] generals and their followers were killed.[14] And in the 21st year of Heraclius Shahrbaz [Sahrbarâz] died who had grasped at empire over the Persians, and Burân his daughter [the relationship is of course incorrect] reigned. And she concluded peace with the Greeks and then died.

From this we learn that Heraclius did retire into Armenia in 628, and thus we gain a confirmation of the account of John Mamikonian, who may be reasonably trusted at this point, as Bolotov has truly observed (p. 90), since he is here recording local traditions and copying from a local chronicle of the year 681. He writes as follows (I employ the translation of Emine as I am unfortunately unable to read the original Armenian) :[15] Heraclius after his victory over Persia

ramena la Sainte Croix avec les captifs. Il passa sans s'arrêter devant beaucoup de localités, distribua beaucoup de morceaux [de la Croix] dans le pays d'Arménie et aux grands seigneurs. Lorsqu'il se rendit à Eveznavan [16] le serviteur en coupa un grand morceau et voulut s'enfuir.[17] Mais quelqu'un, l'ayant su, en informa le roi qui lui reprit ce morceau, et lui trancha la tête. Étant ensuite allé à Césarée avec son armée, Héraclius remit ce fragment au patriarche de Césarée qui s'appelait Jean et lui-même gagna sa ville capitale de Constantinople.

Then follows the subsequent history of this piece of the Cross, which after many vicissitudes was treasured at Dzidzarn in Armenia.

But we gain from Agapius the further important fact that Heraclius spent the whole winter at Amida : this, apart from the further arguments adduced by Owsepian in his *Entstehungsgeschichte des Monothelitismus*,[18] disproves Bolotov's view that Heraclius remained at Theodosiopolis (Karin) and held the famous

---

[14] So Baron von Rosen : but this is a mistaken translation ; the authority which Agapius is transcribing is referring to the fact that Roman troops acted in concert with Sahrbarâz in his invasion of Persia ; cf. Sebeos, Macler's translation, Paris, 1904 *Chron. Guidi*, pp. 30 seqq. We should therefore, I doubt not, translate ' and Sahrbarâz took [as his allies] many warriors of the Greeks, and many of the Persian generals and their followers were killed '.

[15] *Fragmenta Historicorum Graecorum*, ed. Müller, v. ii. 380.

[16] Eveznavan is apparently only mentioned in this passage ; its precise position seems to be unknown : cf. H. Hübschmann, *Die altarmenischen Ortsnamen*, &c., in *Indogermanische Forschungen*, xvi (1904), p. 424.

[17] ' Relics are fair game—things that the most honourable and conscientious of men may blamelessly annex :' Wigram, p. 303.   [18] Leipzig, 1897

synod there during the winter of 628-9. The emperor's difficulties were in fact by no means surmounted : Sahrbarâz was still in Asia Minor with his army, and refused to recognize the authority of Ardeshir.[19] At Amida Heraclius occupied a strong position on the frontier from which he could best take effective action.

(ii) The cardinal confusion, however, in Bolotov's account arises from the fact that he, with Sternbach, places Heraclius's return to the capital before the restoration of the Cross in Jerusalem.[20] This is shown to be wrong by the carefully dated account of Nicephorus, p. 22, which we must shortly consider, and, as Pernice[21] has seen, by an important passage in the *Carmina Inedita* of George of Pisidia : in the poet's Αὐτοσχέδιοι πρὸς τὴν γενομένην ἀνάγνωσιν τῶν κελεύσεων[22] χάριν τῆς ἀποκαταστάσεως τῶν τιμίων ξύλων he begins :

ὦ Γολγοθᾶ σκίρτησον· ἡ κτίσις πάλιν
ὅλη σε τιμᾷ καὶ καλεῖ θεηδόχον·
ἐκ Περσίδος γὰρ ὁ βασιλεὺς ἀφιγμένος
τὸν σταυρὸν ἐν σοὶ δεικνύει πεπηγμένον.[23]

This is confirmed by the unedited chronicle[24] contained in Codex Matritensis Palat. 40, at f. 408. Heraclius τὰ τίμια ξύλα ἀπὸ Περσίδος ἀναλαβὼν καὶ εἰς Ἱερουσαλὴμ παραγενόμενος, κ.τ.λ., and by the whole series of chroniclers who are represented by Georgius Monachus.[25] There can, indeed, be no doubt on this point. The text of Theophanes[26] can be for the moment reserved for future discussion.[27]

(iii) But when was it that Heraclius made this journey to Jerusalem ? Pernice accepts the traditional date for the restoration of the Cross—14 September—but this is disproved by a hitherto unnoticed passage of George of Pisidia. In the *Carmina Inedita*, no. ii, vv. 104 *seqq.*,[28] we read

τούτων παρ' ἡμῖν τῶν ἀγαθῶν ἡγγελμένων
εἰς καιρὸν εὐπρόσδεκτον, εἰς νικηφόρον,
ὅτε προσελθὼν τοῖς τυράννοις τῶν τάφων
ὁ τὴν καθ' ἡμᾶς οὐσίαν ἀναπλάσας
ζωὴν ἐφῆκε τῷ νεκρῷ τοῦ Λαζάρου—

---

[19] Cf. Sebeos, pp. 86-7.
[20] Sternbach (*Rozprawy*, &c., p. 36) in 628, Bolotov in 629.
[21] Pernice, appendix iii, p. 317.
[22] Cf. Sternbach in *Wiener Studien*, xiii (1891), p. 29, n. 12. κέλευσις is the technical term for an imperial dispatch. Compare for the use of the word *Chron. Pasch.*, p. 728. 15, 729. 15, 730. 3, &c. ; Geo. Pisid., *De Bello Avarico*, 30.
[23] *Carmina Inedita*, ii, in *Wiener Studien*, xiii. 4-5.
[24] Falsely attributed to Cyril of Alexandria and George of Pisidia. On the manuscripts of this chronicle cf. Th. Preger, *Die angebliche Chronik des hl. Kyrillos und Georgios Pisides*, in *Byz. Zeitschr.* vii (1898), pp. 129-33.
[25] Ed. de Boor, Leipzig, 1904, ii. 672.
[26] Ed. de Boor, i. 327-8.
[27] Cf. *infra*, pp. 293 *seqq.*
[28] Sternbach, p. 8.

ἔδει γὰρ οἶμαι τῇ νεκρῶν ἀναστάσει
σταυροῦ γενέσθαι καὶ πάλιν μηνύματα.
ὅλη συνῆλθεν εἰς ἑαυτὴν ἡ πόλις (? ἑορτὴν or ἀνάκτορ',
e coni. Sternbach)
ὡς ψάμμος ὡς ῥοῦς ὡς ἄμετρα κύματα
ποιοῦντα πολλὰς σωματώδεις ἐκχύσεις·
σπουδὴν γὰρ εἶχον, οἷα δορκὰς ἐν θέρει
διψῶσα καὶ σφύζουσα, συντόμως φθάσαι
τῶν σῶν, κράτιστε, συλλαβὼν τὰς ἰκμάδας.

That is, the news of the triumphant restoration of the Cross reached the capital when the inhabitants were celebrating the festival of the resurrection of Lazarus. But, as Hoffmann has shown,[29] this festival was celebrated by the Greek church on the Saturday before Palm Sunday.[30] Therefore the generally received September date for the restoration of the Cross is untenable.[31] But Antiochus Strategos gives 21 March:[32] is this then 21 March of 629 or, as Bolotov and Marr maintain, March 630?[33] In 629 the 'Saturday of Lazarus'[34] fell on 9 April, but in 630 on 30 March. That the news of the restoration of the Cross should travel from Jerusalem to Constantinople in eight days is, considering the confused state of the empire after the protracted Persian war, surely impossible. We are compelled to adopt the year 629, and thus the contemporary poem of George agrees with and supports the dating of Antiochus Strategos.

(iv) From Jerusalem the emperor turned to recover the towns which had been captured by the Persians. We know from Thomas the Presbyter that Alexandria and the towns of Syria were evacuated in June 629, and in July 629 Heraclius, marching north, met Sahrbarâz at Arabissos, and concluded an agreement with him whereby the Euphrates was to be the boundary between the two realms.[35] Thence it would appear he marched to Caesarea.[36] We are now in a position to consider the evidence of Nicephorus. After describing the restoration of the Cross in Jerusalem, he continues:[37]

ὑψωθέντων δὲ αὐτῶν (i. e. τὰ ζωοποιὰ ξύλα) ἐκεῖσε εὐθὺς ἐς τὸ Βυζάντιον ὁ βασιλεὺς ἐξέπεμψεν. ἃ δὴ Σέργιος ὁ τοῦ Βυζαντίου ἱεράρχης ἐκ Βλαχερνῶν

[29] In a learned note in H. Feige, *Die Geschichte des Mâr 'Abhdîshô'*, Kiel, 1890, Nachträge zu Anmerkung 23, pp. 56–7.

[30] Cf. Nilles, *Calendarium utriusque Ecclesiae*, &c., ed. 2, Innsbruck, 1897, ii, pp. 195 seqq.

[31] Theophanes is in fact quite right when he states, 629: τούτῳ τῷ ἔτει ἀπάρας ὁ βασιλεὺς ἅμα ἔαρι ... ἐπὶ τὰ Ἱεροσόλυμα ἐπορεύετο ἀπαγαγὼν τὰ τίμια καὶ ζωοποιὰ ξύλα τοῦ ἀποδοῦναι τῷ θεῷ τὴν εὐχαριστίαν, 328,¹³⁻¹⁵; for a further proof cf. Geo. Pisid. *Carmina Inedita*, ii. 1. 7 νέους προευτρέπιζε φοινίκων κλάδους | πρὸς τὴν ἀναστὴν τοῦ νέου νικηφόρου: the fresh young shoots appear in *spring*, not in September.

[32] Cf. Conybeare, *ante*, xxv. 516.

[33] Cf. Labourt, p. 242, who dates the return of the cross after 27 April 630.

[34] Cf. Budge, i, p. xx.   [35] Cf. *supra*, p. 288.

[36] Cf. John Mamikonian, *supra*, p. 290.   [37] p. 22, ed. de Boor.

(ἱερὸν δὲ αἱ Βλαχέρναι τῆς θεομήτορος) λιτανεύων ὑπεδέξατο, καὶ πρὸς τὴν μεγίστην ἐκκλησίαν ἀγαγὼν ταῦτα ἀνύψωσε· δευτέρα δὲ ἦν ἰνδικτιὼν ἡνίκα ταῦτα ἐπράττοντο. μετ᾽ οὐ πολὺ δὲ καὶ Ἡράκλειος πρὸς τὸ Βυζάντιον ἐχώρει, ὑπὸ πολλῆς εὐφημίας καὶ δόξης ὑπερβαλλούσης παρὰ τῶν ἐκεῖσε δεχθείς.

The order of events is thus exaltation of the Cross in Jerusalem, then a similar exaltation in Constantinople, and after this the return of the emperor to his capital. But the Cross itself must have remained in Jerusalem :[38] the passage of John Mamikonian above quoted enables us to offer an explanation of the difficulty. Just as Heraclius had given fragments of the true Cross to Armenian nobles, and as another fragment was later given to the church in Caesarea, so doubtless he dispatched from Jerusalem a piece of the sacred relic to Constantinople.[39] This reached the capital during the second indiction, i.e. before 1 September 629, and soon after, i.e. directly he had concluded the peace with Sahrbarâz, the emperor himself made a triumphal progress to Constantinople (probably in August 629).

(v) There remains the extremely difficult problem of the text of Theophanes. The order of events as given by him is as follows : 628 : Theodore is dispatched to superintend the return of the Persians from Roman territory and from the cities of the empire. Heraclius enters the capital thus celebrating a μυστικὴ θεωρία : as God at creation had toiled for six days and then enjoyed the Sabbath of His rest, so Heraclius after six years of warfare was at length at peace. 629 : Heraclius leaves the capital in the spring for Jerusalem and restores the Cross. How are we to explain this error in the order of events ? We may at once notice that the material used by Theophanes contradicts his own chronology : the six years of warfare are 623 [40] to 628; the 'Sabbatic year' is therefore 629, and not as Theophanes gives, 628. The following paragraph is only offered tentatively as a contribution towards a possible solution.[41]

Emphasizing this qualification, I suggest that Theophanes had before him two sources, each of which was thoroughly well informed. He attempted to combine them and to fit them into his annalistic scheme, and the result has been confusion. One source (B) is represented for us by Georgius Monachus, Leo Grammaticus, Theodosius Melitenus, the unpublished Pseudo-Pisides, the unedited Constantinus Lascaris, and, apparently in a very abbreviated form by Michael Glycas ; further, in part

[38] Until the capture of the city by Saladin.
[39] Cf. Sergy, *Polnuy Myesyatseslov Vostoka*, 2nd ed., Vladimir (1901), II. ii. 375-6.
[40] That the second campaign of Heraclius began in 623 and not (as Gerland maintains) in 624 I have endeavoured to prove in a paper on 'The Date of the Avar Surprise' which will shortly appear in the *Byzantinische Zeitschrift*.
[41] For the unedited texts used by me for the following paragraph I am indebted to Sternbach, *Rozprawy*, &c., pp. 35 seqq.

by Theophanes, Cedrenus, and the unedited Codex Parisinus Gr. 1712. The other source (A) can only be reconstructed from Theophanes himself and from the shorter and slightly different version in Cedrenus. Some subsequent chronicler made a conflation of A and B, and this conflation is represented in different ways by the unedited Symeon Magister, by Ephraemius, and in an individual form by Zonaras.[42] Source A was probably of eastern origin, and was not concerned with the affairs of Constantinople and the west; it had close affinities with the authority used (probably mediately) by Agapius of Hierapolis (cited above). Source B would seem to have been written in the capital, and to have made use of some part of the *Heraclias* of George of Pisidia now lost to us.[43] Source A contained a full account of the restoration of the Cross to Jerusalem, carefully dating the event—and, as we have seen, rightly—to the spring of 629. Theophanes determined to follow source A for Heraclius's visit to the holy city. It has, however, long been recognized that Theophanes has confused his chronology by placing the accession of Sheroe and the conclusion of peace in 627. Kretschmann's attempt to follow the chronology of Theophanes at this point was foredoomed to failure.[44] Owing to this antedating of the accession of Sheroe, and the Cross being restored only in 629, Theophanes was in difficulties as to how to fill up the year 628— what was the emperor doing during these twelve months ? As he wrote, he had before him the western source (B), which after a summary mention of the setting up of the Cross in Jerusalem dealt at length with the return of Heraclius to Constantinople. He saw in this account an activity of the emperor which would provide material for the awkward hiatus in the chronological scheme which he had himself created by antedating events under the year 627. Clearly in 628, he argued, Heraclius returned to the capital. He accordingly adopted the western source (B) for his chronicle of the year 628, but having previously rightly determined to follow source A in placing the restoration of the Cross in the spring of 629, he naturally omitted the brief reference to that event which stood in source B before the account of the emperor's return to the capital. Thus when using source A for the year 629 he adapted it to his own composite scheme by

[42] The Synopsis Sathae (K. N. Sathas, Μεσαιωνικὴ Βιβλιοθήκη, τόμος ζ´ Venice, 1894, p. 108) stands alone, but has considerable resemblances to Theophanes.

[43] H. C. Rawlinson, ' The Site of the Atropatenian Ecbatana,' *Journal of the Royal Geographical Society*, x (1840), pp. 65-158, long ago showed that the *Heraclias*, as it has come down to us, extends only to the capture, not of Dastagero, but of Ganzaca (Takhti-Soleimán) in the first year of the second Persian campaign in 623. On the lost cantos of the *Heraclias* cf. Pernice, *op. cit.* xiii–xiv. I accept his arguments.

[44] Kretschmann, *Die Kämpfe zwischen Heraclius I und Chosroes II*, Teil i, Programm, Domschule zu Güstrow, 1875, Teil ii, 1876.

ádding the words ἀπὸ τῆς βασιλευούσης πόλεως (328¹²⁻¹⁴), thus making Heraclius depart for Jerusalem *from Constantinople*, in which he was, of course, in error.

Before tracing the two sources in our authorities it is only right to note a possible consequence of this hypothesis. As we have seen, source B states fully the theory of the μυστικὴ θεωρία. Those who have studied long and closely the style and thought of George of Pisidia must, I think, agree with Sternbach [45] that this whole conception can only have arisen in the pious fancy of the court poet, and, following Pernice's argument, almost as certainly must have appeared in the lost cantos of the *Heraclias*. If this were so, a source of Theophanes had already used the poems of George as material for a prose chronicle. We might thus be led to the conclusion that the account given by Theophanes of the Persian campaigns was derived by him only mediately from George of Pisidia, and that he was here transcribing the work of an earlier historian.

Traces of A and B in the Byzantine Historians

Source A. Its reconstruction for the purpose of this note (with which cf. Agapius, p. 72).

Theophanes, 327¹⁹, εἰρήνης (δὲ) γενομένης μεταξὺ Περσῶν καὶ Ῥωμαίων, ἀπέστειλαν ὁ βασιλεὺς Θεόδωρον τὸν ἑαυτοῦ ἀδελφὸν (τὸν ἀδελφὸν αὐτοῦ Cedr. I 735 Bonn) μετὰ γραμμάτων καὶ ἀνθρώπων Σιρόου, τοῦ βασιλέως Περσῶν (μετὰ γ. Σιρόη τῷ βασιλεῖ Περσῶν καὶ ἀνθρώπων αὐτοῦ Cedr.), ὅπως τοὺς ἐν Ἐδέσῃ καὶ Παλαιστίνῃ καὶ Ἱεροσολύμοις (κ. Ἱερ. om. Cedr.) καὶ ταῖς λοιπαῖς πόλεσι τῶν Ῥωμαίων (τ. Ῥω. om. Cedr.) Πέρσας μετὰ εἰρήνης (μετ' εἰρήνης Cedr.) ἀποστρέψωσιν ἐν Περσίδι καὶ ἀβλαβῶς παρέλθωσι τὴν τῶν Ῥωμαίων γῆν. (ἐν δὲ τῷ ἐννεακαιδεκάτῳ ἔτει τῆς βασιλείας αὐτοῦ) Theoph. 328¹³ ἀπάρας ὁ βασιλεὺς ἅμα ἔαρι [ἀπὸ τῆς βασιλευούσης πόλεως secludendum, cf. supra] ἐπὶ τὰ Ἱεροσόλυμα ἐπορεύετο ἀπαγαγὼν τὰ τίμια καὶ ζωοποιὰ ξύλα τοῦ ἀποδοῦναι τῷ θεῷ τὴν εὐχαριστίαν. ἐλθόντι δὲ αὐτῷ ἐν Τιβεριάδι, κ.τ.λ. usque ad 328,²²: [haec omnia semper ab inferioris aetatis scriptoribus omissa] εἰσελθὼν δὲ ὁ βασιλεὺς ἐν Ἱεροσολύμοις καὶ ἀποκαταστήσας Ζαχαρίαν τὸν πατριάρχην καὶ τὰ τίμια καὶ ζωοποιὰ ξύλα εἰς τὸν ἴδιον τόπον καὶ πολλὰ εὐχαριστήσας τῷ θεῷ ἀπήλασε τοὺς Ἑβραίους ἀπὸ τῆς ἁγίας πόλεως ... usque ad πλησιάζειν. καταλαβὼν δὲ τὴν Ἐδέσαν ἀπέδωκε τὴν ἐκκλησίαν τοῖς ὀρθοδόξοις, κ.τ.λ. Theoph. 328¹³ sqq. = Cedrenus τῷ ιθ' ἔτει ἅμα ἔαρι ἀπάρας ὁ βασιλεὺς τῆς βασιλίδος ἐπὶ τὰ Ἱεροσόλυμα ἐπορεύθη καὶ ἀπήγαγε τὰ τίμια καὶ ζωοποιὰ ξύλα καὶ ἀποδοὺς τῷ θεῷ τὴν εὐχαριστίαν ἀποκατέστησε τὸν πατριάρχην Ζαχαρίαν. [sequuntur Iudaeorum exclusio et Nestorianorum ex Edessa expulsio.].

Source A appears otherwise only to be found in a conflation with source B; cf. *infra*.

Source B. Its reconstruction for the purpose of this note.

A good representative of source B is Georgius Monachus: [46] there are

---

[45] *Rozprawy*, &c., pp. 35 seqq.
[46] Ed. De Boor, ii. 672.

only slight verbal differences between the text of Georgius Monachus and that of Leo Grammaticus[47] and Theodosius Melitenus.[48] I have, however, inserted in brackets ( ) the most important variations of the chronicle of Pseudo-Pisides, Codex Matritensis Palat. 40, f. 408 seqq.

(Heraclius) οὐκ ἐφείσατο κατασφάζων καὶ πυρπολῶν καὶ καταστρέφων πᾶσαν τὴν Περσίδα ἐν ἔτεσὶν ἕξ. τῷ δὲ ἑβδόμῳ ἔτει τὰ ζωοποιὰ ξύλα τοῦ πανσέπτου σταυροῦ ἀναλαβὼν εἰς Ἱερουσαλὴμ παραγενόμενος (τὰ τίμια ξύλα ἀπὸ Περσίδος ἀναλαβὼν καὶ εἰς Ἱερ. παραγ.) καὶ ταῦτα καθιψώσας μετὰ πολλῆς χαρᾶς καὶ εἰρήνης ἐπὶ τὴν Κωνσταντινούπολιν ὑπέστρεψε μυστικήν τινα θεωρίαν ἐν τούτῳ πληρώσας· ὥσπερ γὰρ ἐν ἡμέραις ἓξ ὁ θεὸς πᾶσαν τὴν κτίσιν δημιουργήσας τὴν ἑβδόμην ἀναπαύσεως ἡμέραν ἐκάλεσεν, οὕτω δὴ καὶ οὗτος ἐν τοῖς ἓξ χρόνοις πολλοὺς διανύσας πολέμους[49] καὶ κοπιάσας, ἐν τῷ ἑβδόμῳ ἔτει μετ' εἰρήνης ὑποστρέψας ἀνεπαύσατο. οἱ δὲ τῆς πόλεως τὴν ἔλευσιν αὐτοῦ γνόντες ἀκατασχέτῳ πόθῳ πάντες εἰς τὴν Ἱέρειαν ἐξῆλθον (ἐν τοῖς παλατίοις τῆς Ἡρίας ἐξῆλθον), σὺν τῷ πατριάρχῃ καὶ Κωνσταντίνῳ τῷ βασιλεῖ καὶ υἱῷ αὐτοῦ, βαστάζοντες κλάδους ἐλαιῶν καὶ λαμπάδας εὐφημοῦντες αὐτὸν μετὰ πολλῆς εὐφροσύνης. καὶ ὁ μὲν υἱὸς αὐτοῦ προσελθὼν ἔπεσεν εἰς τοὺς πόδας τοῦ πατρός, ὁ δὲ πατὴρ περιπλακεὶς τῷ υἱῷ κατέβρεξαν ἀμφότεροι τὴν γῆν τοῖς δάκρυσιν· ὅπερ θεασάμενος ὁ λαὸς εὐχαριστηρίους ὕμνους τῷ θεῷ σὺν δάκρυσιν ἀνέπεμπον καὶ οὕτω λαβόντες τὸν βασιλέα χαίροντες εὐφημοῦντες κροτοῦντες εἰσῆλθον ἐν τῇ πόλει (εἰσῆλθον εἰς τὸ παλάτιον).

Later traces of this hypothetical source (B).

Theophanes, 327[24], treats source B thus:

628: ὁ δὲ βασιλεὺς ἐν ἓξ ἔτεσι καταπολεμήσας τὴν Περσίδα τῷ ζ΄ ἔτει εἰρηνεύσας μετὰ χαρᾶς μεγάλης ἐπὶ Κωνσταντινούπολιν ὑπέστρεψε (omni crucis mentione omissa et restitutione crucis in annum 629 translata) μυστικήν τινα θεωρίαν ἐν τούτῳ πληρώσας. ἐν γὰρ ἓξ ἡμέραις πᾶσαν τὴν κτίσιν δημιουργήσας ὁ θεὸς τὴν ἑβδόμην ἀναπαύσεως ἡμέραν ἐκάλεσεν· οὕτω καὶ αὐτὸς ἐν τοῖς ἓξ χρόνοις πολλοὺς πόνους διανύσας[49] τῷ ἑβδόμῳ ἔτει μετ' εἰρήνης καὶ χαρᾶς ἐν τῇ πόλει ὑποστρέψας ἀνεπαύσατο. ὁ δὲ λαὸς τῆς πόλεως τὴν ἔλευσιν αὐτοῦ μαθόντες ἀκατασχέτῳ πόθῳ πάντες εἰς τὴν Ἱερείαν ἐξῆλθον εἰς συνάντησιν αὐτοῦ σὺν τῷ πατριάρχῃ καὶ Κωνσταντίνῳ τῷ βασιλεῖ καὶ υἱῷ αὐτοῦ, βαστάζοντες κλάδους ἐλαιῶν καὶ λαμπάδας, εὐφημοῦντες αὐτὸν μετὰ χαρᾶς καὶ δακρύων· προσελθὼν δὲ ὁ υἱὸς αὐτοῦ ἔπεσεν ἐπὶ τοὺς πόδας αὐτοῦ καὶ περιπλακεὶς αὐτῷ ἔβρεξαν ἀμφότεροι τὴν γῆν τοῖς δάκρυσιν. τοῦτο θεασάμενος ὁ λαὸς ἅπαντες εὐχαριστηρίους ὕμνους τῷ θεῷ ἀνέπεμπον. καὶ οὕτω λαβόντες τὸν βασιλέα σκιρτῶντες εἰσῆλθον ἐν τῇ πόλει.

Cedrenus, i. 735, represents an abbreviated form of Theophanes.

Following on καὶ ἀβλαβῶς παρελθοῦσι τὴν τῶν Ῥωμαίων γῆν of the hypothetical source (A) he proceeds μυστικὸν δέ τι ἐνταῦθα θεωρεῖται· τὴν γὰρ κτίσιν πᾶσαν ὁ θεὸς ἐν ἓξ ἡμέραις ἐποίησε καὶ τῇ ζ΄ ἀνεπαύσατο καὶ ὁ βασιλεὺς ἐν ἓξ ἔτεσι τὴν Περσίδα καταπολεμήσας τῷ ζ΄ εἰρήνευσε καὶ μετὰ χαρᾶς τὴν Κωνσταντινούπολιν καταλαμβάνει. ὁ δὲ λαὸς τῆς πόλεως μετὰ τοῦ βασιλέως Κων-

---

[47] Pp. 152 seqq. (Bonn).

[48] Ed. Tafel, in *Monumenta Saecularia*, published by the Königl. bayerische Akademie der Wissenschaften, Munich, 1859, pp. 105 seqq.

[49] Here Theophanes represents more nearly than Georgius Monachus the original text of B = George of Pisidia. αὐτός for the emperor is a peculiarity of the style of the poet, and George does not use πόλεμος save in one place, *Exp. Pers.* iii. 63, which Sternbach has emended; *Rozprawy*, &c., p. 18.

σταντίνου τοῦ υἱοῦ τοῦ Ἡρακλείου καὶ τοῦ πατριάρχου Σεργίου, μετὰ κλάδων ἐλαιῶν καὶ λαμπάδων τοῦτον ὑποδεξάμενος εὐχαριστοῦντες τῷ θεῷ εἰς τὰ βασίλεια εἰσήγαγον.

The text of the unpublished Codex Parisinus Gr. 1712, f. 180ᵛ seqq. is extremely instructive and deserves careful study. It represents the effort of an unskilful scribe to combine the text of Theophanes with the shorter version of Cedrenus. It is, I should imagine, but rarely that one has so good an opportunity of watching a conflation in the making. The manuscript is by Sternbach denoted Π, and I reproduce from him the actual text, of which he himself has not noted the full significance.

ὁ δὲ βασιλεὺς ἐν ἓξ ἔτεσι τὴν Περσίδα καταπολεμήσας τῷ ζ´ ἔτη εἰρηνεύσας μετὰ χαρᾶς μεγάλης ἔτι (sine accentu) Κωνσταντινουπόλεως ὑπέστρεψε μυστικήν τινὰ θεωρίαν ἐν τούτῳ πληρώσας· ἐν γὰρ ἓξ ἡμέραις πᾶσαν τὴν κτίσιν δημιουργήσας ὁ θεὸς τὴν ἑβδόμην ἀναπαύσεως ἡμέραν ἐκάλεσεν· οὕτω καὶ αὐτὸς ἐν τοῖς ἓξ (inc. f. 181ʳ.) χρόνοις πολλοὺς πόνους διανοίσας τῷ ἑβδόμῳ ἔτει μετ᾽ εἰρήνης καὶ χαρᾶς ἐν τῇ πόλει ὑποστρέψας ἀνεπαύσατο. ὁ δὲ λαὸς τῆς πόλεως μετὰ τοῦ βασιλέως Κωνσταντίνου τοῦ υἱοῦ Ἡρακλείου καὶ τοῦ πατριάρχου Σεργίου μαθόντες τὴν ἔλευσιν τοῦ βασιλέως ἐξῆλθεν εἰς συνάντισιν αὐτοῦ σὺν τῷ πατριάρχῃ καὶ Κωνσταντίνῳ τῷ βασιλεῖ καὶ υἱῷ αὐτοῦ βαστάζοντες κλάδους ἐλαιῶν καὶ λαμπάδων εὐφημοῦντες αὐτὸν μετὰ χαρᾶς. προσελθὼν δὲ ὁ υἱὸς αὐτοῦ ἔπεσεν ἐπὶ τοὺς πόδας αὐτοῦ καὶ περιπλακεὶς αὐτῷ ἔβρεξαν ἀμφότεροι τὴν γῆν τοῖς δάκρυσι. τοῦτο θεασάμενος ὁ λαὸς πάντες εὐχαριστηρίους ὕμνους τῷ Θεῷ ἀνέπεμπον καὶ οὕτω λαβόντες τὸν βασιλέα σκιρτῶντες εἰς τὰ βασίλεια εἰσήγαγον.

It is impossible, so far as I am aware, to follow further the hypothetical source (B) in the form which it took in the hands of Theophanes, Cedrenus, and the scribe of Π. But the unedited Constantinus Lascaris of Codex Matritensis, iv. 72 (f. 170ʳ) represents another and independent abbreviation of B. He writes:

καὶ ἓξ ἔτη τοὺς Πέρσας ἐδῄου· τῷ δὲ ἑβδόμῳ ἀναλαβὼν τὸ ζωοποιὸν ἅγιον ξύλον καὶ ἄλλα καὶ εἰς Ἰερουσαλὴμ παραγενόμενος ὕψωσε. καὶ μετὰ ταῦτα ἐπανῆκεν εἰς τὴν πόλιν ᾧ ὑπήντησαν πάντες περιχαρῶς μετὰ κλάδων ἐλαιῶν καὶ λαμπάδων δορυφορουμένῳ καὶ ὁ υἱὸς αὐτοῦ Κωνσταντῖνος.

It will be noted that the proper order of events as it stood in the original form of B before Theophanes operated upon it is here restored.

I am further inclined to think, though this might be disputed, that Michael Glycas[50] represents another independent, original, and highly abbreviated form of B (with reminiscences from other parts of B?):

ἐν ἓξ ἔτεσι πᾶσαν καθελὼν τὴν Περσίδα καὶ αὐτὸν τὸν Χοσρόην, ὃς ἑαυτὸν ἀπεθέωσε, πρὸς τούτοις δὲ καὶ τὸ τίμιον ξύλον ἐπανασώσας (ἔτυχε γὰρ ἀπὸ Ἱεροσολύμων σκυλευθῆναι) λαμπρῶς ἐπανέζευξε.

We have now reached the last stage of this inquiry. Some later authority attempted to combine sources A and B, and we have now to seek the traces of this conflation.

We find it in the unedited Symeon Magister of the Codex Escurialensis, Y. 1. 4, f. 62ᵛ.

Τὰ ζωοποιὰ ξύλα καὶ τὸν πατριάρχην Ζαχαρίαν ἐν Ἱεροσολύμοις ἀπεκατέστησε μεγαλοπρεπῶς ὑποστρέψας ἐν τῇ βασιλίδι τῶν πόλεων· ὃν ὁ πατριάρχης Σέργιος καὶ Κωνσταντῖνος ὁ [υἱὸς αὐτοῦ καὶ] βασιλεὺς καὶ υἱὸς αὐτοῦ σὺν παντὶ τῷ λαῷ μεθ᾽ ὅσης τῆς ἡδονῆς ὑπεδέξαντο, ἐλαίων (sic) κλάδους καὶ λαμπάδας κατέχοντες.

[50] p. 512. 12 (Bonn).

The unmistakable conjunction of the restoration of Cross and patriarch can only represent A, and the now familiar text of B reappears.

The same fusion, with alterations demanded by the exigencies of a metrical form, appears in Ephraemius, vv. 1395–1400 : [51]

ταῦτ' ἐν χρόνοις ἐξ Ἡράκλειος ἀνύσας
ξύλα τε σεπτὰ καὶ Σιὼν ἀρχιθύτην
Ἱερουσαλὴμ ἐγκαταστήσας πόλει
πρὸς βασιλίδα καθυποστρέφει πόλιν
ἐν ἑβδόμῳ κάλλιστα χαίρων τῷ χρόνῳ
ὑμνούμενος στόμασιν ἀστῶν μυρίων.

We have yet another representative of this class in Zonaras, xiv. 16. 22,[52] together with what is probably an addition by Zonaras himself :

ταῦτα ἐν ἓξ ἔτεσιν ἀνύσας Ἡράκλειος καὶ ἀποκαταστήσας τῇ Ἱερουσαλὴμ τὰ τίμια ξύλα καὶ τὸν πατριάρχην αὐτόν, τῷ ἑβδόμῳ ἐπανῆλθεν εἰς τὰ βασίλεια μετ' εὐφημίας καὶ κρότων δεχθεὶς καὶ λαμπρότητος παρά τε τῆς γερουσίας (a Zonara interpositum ?) καὶ τοῦ πλήθους τῆς πόλεως.

Notice that the true order of events is restored, and that therefore this fusion was not made through consulting the chronicle of Theophanes or Cedrenus.

(vi) With regard to the contradictions in the eastern authorities,[53] it should be borne in mind that the terms of the peace with Persia were (1) evacuation of Roman territory by the Persians and on each side the surrender of prisoners of war, and (2) the restoration of the Holy Cross. Thus as each successive ruler of Persia entered into treaty relations with Rome it was concluded that these were the terms agreed upon between the two empires, the chroniclers thus ignoring the fact that the Cross had reached the hands of Heraclius by the close of the year 628.[54] The negotiations were begun by Sheroe, the Cross itself was perhaps restored under Ardeshir (ascended the throne October 628), Sahrbarâz ultimately accepted (July 629) the condition that Roman territory should be evacuated, and when with the aid of Roman troops he had overthrown Ardeshir only to fall a victim to assassination after a forty-days' rule, his successor, the Queen Bôrân, felt it imperative to placate the emperor through an imposing embassy of Christian prelates.[55] The terms accepted in each case were apparently the same, and thus the restoration of the Cross has been attributed to each sovereign in turn,[56] although as a matter of fact neither Sahrbarâz nor Bôrân was concerned in the matter.

[51] p. 65 (Bonn).   [52] Vol. iii, pp. 211–12 (Bonn).
[53] Most of these are tabulated and classified by Bolotov in a note on p. 84.
[54] ' Die verschiedenen Unterhandlungen und Gesandtschaften der rasch wechselnden (persischen) Fürsten konnten schon von den Zeitgenossen leicht verwechselt werden,' Nöldeke, *Chron. Guidi*, p. 32, n. 1.   [55] Cf. *supra*, p. 288, n. 7.
[56] An interesting parallel to this confusion may be seen in Nicephorus, who although he knows that the Cross was restored in 629 yet attributes that restoration to Sahrbarâz, who only ascended the Persian throne in 630 ; cf. 21[13] with 22[14].

(vii) Lastly, there remains an unexplained difficulty. The eastern church had long observed a festival in honour of the invention of the Cross,[57] celebrated on 14 September,[58] and did not apparently introduce a new celebration to commemorate its restoration, but joined this to the older rite. This new celebration was, however, introduced in the west, and such a commemorative festival can be traced as early as c. 650.[59] This was observed on 3 May. Why was this date chosen ? Is it possible that the fragment of the true Cross sent by the emperor to Constantinople reached the capital on this date ?[60]

We are at the end of our discussion, and as a result it would appear that we may safely accept the date given by Antiochus Strategos for the solemn restoration of the Cross in Jerusalem, viz. 21 March, and further that this took place in the year 629.

NORMAN H. BAYNES.

Burgundian Notes

II. CISALPINUS AND CONSTANTINUS [1]

FLODOARD of Rheims is conspicuous among medieval annalists for his orderliness and precision. He relates facts as they came to his knowledge. He does not think it his business to examine the relations of cause and effect : he simply sets down the in-

[57] So rightly the pilgrim Theodosius about 530: P. Geyer, *Itinera Hierosolymitana Saeculi IIII–VIII*, Vindobonae, 1898 (*Corpus Scriptorum Eccles. Lat.* xxxix. 149). More usually the festival is known as the ὕψωσις τοῦ τιμίου καὶ ζῳοποιοῦ σταυροῦ or τῶν ἁγίων ξύλων; thence its western name Exaltatio Crucis : cf. Arculf in Adamnanus, *De locis Sanctis*, 3. 3 ; Geyer, *op. cit.*, pp. 286. 22, 287. 3 *seqq.*, 288. 11, 295. 21, 322. 14.

[58] This festival was only known in the west in the eighth century, and won its way to acceptance slowly and partially. It was received quite late in many churches, e. g. in Milan in 1035.

[59] Cf. K. A. Heinrich Kellner, *Heortology*, London, 1908, pp. 333–41 ; and for further information on the subject see von Maltzew, *Myesyatseslov pravoslavnoi Katholicheskoi Vostochnoi Tserkvi*, pt. i, pp. 81, 93, Berlin, 1900 ; G. Debol'sky, *Dni Bogosluzheniya prav. Kath. Vost. Tserkvi*, Kniga i, pp. 84, 91, St. Petersburg, 1846. It is interesting to notice that in the west the festival celebrated for the victory of Heraclius on 12 December 627 continued to be observed for a longer period than in the east, and was kept on the same day as the commemoration of the exaltation of the Cross. For the evidence of this compare S. A. Morcelli, Μηνολόγιον τῶν Εὐαγγελίων Ἑορταστικόν sive *Calendarium Ecclesiae Constantinopolitanae*, Rome, 1788, i. 266–7 ; and Sergy, *Polnuy Myesyatseslov Vostoka*, Moscow, 1876, II. i. 327 ; and Zamyetki, II. ii. 289 *seqq.*, 2nd ed., Vladimir, 1901, II. i. 383, II. ii. 374 *seqq.*

[60] I am unable to offer any suggestion why the Egyptian and Abyssinian Synaxaria give for 6 March a Manifestatio S. Crucis per Heraclium Imp.

[1] The first of these notes appeared last year (xxvi. 310–17). The present paper was in part written very long ago, but I have only recently had the opportunity of putting my materials into shape. I am again under great obligations to my friend the Rev. W. A. B. Coolidge, who has directed me to a good deal of evidence which would probably have otherwise eluded me ; but I have no reason to suppose that he shares the views which I here advocate.

formation he received in the order in which he received it. He has to speak of a number of persons, of whom not a few bear the same name; and he constantly guards against any possible confusion by carefully attaching to each distinctive epithets or descriptions. I propose in the light of these two characteristics to seek the identification of a person whom Flodoard describes as Hugo Cisalpinus, and to suggest an explanation of the epithet Constantinus which he applies to Charles, count of Vienne. But if the negative arguments which I present obtain acceptance, I am the first to admit that my positive inferences must remain in the present state of our knowledge hypothetical.

i. *Cisalpinus*

1. As for Hugh the Cisalpine, who is introduced in the Annals under 939, it is not necessary to go into the entire history of a very complicated year of warfare; we have only to try to ascertain how much of that history Flodoard knew. I begin by giving a summary of what he records.

Lewis IV of France paid a visit to Hugh, son of Richard [the duke of Burgundy, his only vassal on whose loyalty he could constantly depend]. The two returned from Burgundy together, and marched against Hugh, son of Robert [Hugh the Great, duke of the French], and William the Norman.... Hugh gave hostages to observe an armistice until 1 June.

The men of Lorraine rebelled against King Otto [of Germany] and came to Lewis, who deferred receiving them on account of the amity which had been arranged between them [the two kings].

Count Arnulf [of Flanders] captured Montreuil, the castle of Erluin, and sent his wife and children oversea to King Athelstan. Soon afterwards Erluin, with the help of the Normans, recovered Montreuil.

The nobles of Lorraine, headed by their duke, came again to King Lewis and commended themselves to him; but the bishops for a time held aloof.

King Otto crossed the Rhine and plundered Lorraine. An English fleet was sent by Athelstan to the assistance of Lewis, but it did nothing more than ravage parts of the French coast.

King Otto had a meeting with Hugh [the Great], Herbert [count of Vermandois], Arnulf, and William the Norman; and they all took oaths to a treaty with him: then he returned beyond the Rhine.

These detached notices may be presumed to be written down in chronological order. In order to fix the dates we have to turn to the German evidence. It is known that Otto the Great marched against the rebels led by his brother Henry and Gilbert, duke of Lorraine, and defeated them at Birten, near Xanten; but it is unlikely that he then crossed the Rhine.[2] He was recalled to

---

[2] Wilhelm von Giesebrecht (*Gesch. der Deutschen Kaiserzeit*, i, 5th ed., 1881, p. 263) thought that Otto made a short pursuit into Lorraine, but was recalled by the news

Saxony by a rising in its eastern regions, and he besieged Merseburg for nearly two months.[3] A document proves that he was at Magdeburg on 7 June.[4] It was after this that Otto set himself to put down the rebellion in Lorraine. He crossed the Rhine and besieged his brother and Duke Gilbert at Chèvremont, near Liège. This seems to be the only possible time in the year in which he could have had the meeting with the four French feudatories mentioned by Flodoard; and that meeting must have taken place between 7 June and 11 September, when he is found again in Saxony, at Werla, near Dortmund.[5]

At this point, after the mention of Otto's recrossing the Rhine, occurs the critical passage in Flodoard :

Rex interea Ludowicus Virdunensem pagum petit, ubi quidam regni Lothariensis episcopi sui efficiuntur. Indeque in pagum proficiscitur Elisatium, locutusque cum Hugone Cisalpino, et quibusdam ad se venientibus receptis Lothariensibus, nonnullis quoque Othonis regis fidelibus trans Rhenum fugatis, Laudunum revertitur.

Now we have seen that, according to Flodoard, Hugh the Great engaged to observe an armistice until 1 June. After that two separate embassies from the Lorrainers are recorded, and then the fact that Hugh made treaty with Otto, who did not leave Saxony until after 7 June. 'Meanwhile' Lewis moved in a south-easterly direction through the country of Verdun into Alsace; he had a meeting with Hugh the Cisalpine and then returned to Laon. This Hugh is believed by almost all modern scholars to be Hugh the Black, duke of Burgundy. Lewis's route, however, would not approach at any point the border of the duchy, but Alsace would lead him directly to the kingdom of Burgundy, in the upper valley of the Doubs. It is true that at a somewhat later date Hugh the Black is found exercising authority in these parts;[6] but I conclude from Flodoard's use of names that if he had meant him he would not have described him as Hugh the Cisalpine.

Two charters tell us something of King Lewis's movements

from the east. There is, however, no evidence for this. Adalbert, the continuator of Regino's Chronicle, alone mentions such a movement: but he relates the siege of Chèvremont as the immediate sequel of the battle of Birten, and was unaware of the events which followed in the east of Saxony.

[3] Widukind, *Res gestae Saxonicae*, ii. 19.

[4] *Diplomata Ottonis I*, no. 21 (*Monum. Germ. Hist.*, 1879); Böhmer, *Regesta Imperii*, ii (ed. Ottenthal, 1893), no. 77.

[5] *Dipl. Otton.* no. 22; Böhmer, no. 78.

[6] See H. Bresslau, *Jahrbücher des Deutschen Reichs unter Konrad II* (1884), ii. 34 f.; R. Poupardin, *Le Royaume de Bourgogne* (1907), pp. 208 ff. At a much earlier date, 914, Charles the Simple granted to Hugh certain property which he possessed 'in comitatu Warasco, ex suo videlicet comitatu' (*Recueil des Hist. de France*, ix. 521); but there is no evidence to show that he retained it. He is not found again in this neighbourhood until 951.

in the summer. On 20 June he was just within the frontier of Lorraine, *in Querceto iuxta Dotiacum villa*, near Douzy, on the Chiers, not far from Sedan, and there he granted a charter to the abbey of Cluny at the petition of *quidam fidelis noster Hugo filius Richardi, vir illustrissimus et marchio*,[7] that is to say, Hugh the Black. The second charter proves that the king was back at Laon on 2 August. It is difficult to fit in these dates with Lewis's march into Alsace, which cannot well have begun until July at the earliest, and it is more natural to consider his visit to Douzy to have taken place in connexion with the negotiations with the Lorrainers already mentioned and before Otto was in the west at all. In this case he would not have set out for Alsace until after 2 August. That such was the order of events was clearly pointed out by Dümmler, who held that on each occasion the king's interview was with Hugh the Black.[8] M. Philippe Lauer, on the other hand, who also identifies Hugh the Cisalpine with Hugh the Black, thinks that there was only one interview, namely, that at Douzy ; and in order to prove that there was no meeting with Hugh (the Cisalpine) in the course of Lewis's expedition to Alsace, he adopts the bold device of suppressing the words *locutusque cum Hugone Cisalpino*, without any indication of the omission, in his quotation of the passage from Flodoard which I have given above, and blames Richer for making substantially the same statement as Flodoard.[9] It was in fact, to all appearance, the alliance which was formed between King Otto and the four great French princes, about July, that led King Lewis to make a plundering raid into Lorraine and Alsace, and while there to seek the assistance of Hugh the Cisalpine. On the news of his movement Otto broke up the siege of Chèvremont and turned to meet him. Some misunderstanding has been caused by the perfectly correct statement that he went first to Saxony, and was at Werla, near Dortmund, on 11 September. But this was only just within the border of Saxony. He had to make a détour in order to avoid the parts of Lorraine which had been raised against him, and probably also to get reinforcements : so he crossed the Rhine and then hastened southwards, recrossing the river so as to attack Lewis. On his advance towards him Lewis ' returned to Laon '. So says Flodoard, who knows nothing of Otto's doings all this time. Adalbert speaks more plainly :

Interim Ludowicus, rex Galliae Romanae, . . . Alsatiam petit ; ubi, quaeque poterat, plus hostiliter quam regaliter gessit. Quod rex Otto

[7] *Chartes de l'Abbaye de Cluny*, i. (1876) 483 ff., no. 499.
[8] Köpke and Dümmler, *Kaiser Otto der Grosse* (1876), pp. 86, 88.
[9] *Le Règne de Louis IV* (1900), p. 43, n. 6 ; cf. n. 3.

patienter non ferens Caprimontem obsidione absolvit, et Alsatiam petens Ludowicum regem expulit.[10]

I lay stress upon this Alsatian campaign, which seemed to Otto important enough to cause his abandonment of his operations in the north-west, because it may help us to find out who Hugh the Cisalpine was. He was a man who was to be approached by way of Alsace and whose support Lewis desired to gain. The young Conrad, king of Burgundy, had been carried off by Otto not long before, when Hugh of Italy attempted to annex his kingdom, and was now living under the German king's protection: Otto would have every reason for wishing to frustrate any negotiations which might bring the Burgundian kingdom into alliance with France.

2. Flodoard is invariably careful to distinguish between different rulers of the same name, and where necessary between the different territories over which they ruled. The following are, I believe, all the instances which bear upon the question before us. I group them under the territories and add the year under which the notice is given.

Duke of the French: Hugo filius Rotberti (or Rotberti filius) 922, 923, 924 twice, 925 thrice, 926, 927 twice, 928 twice, 936, 939; Hugo comes 923, 924, 929 twice, 934, 936, 948, 949 thrice, 952; Hugo princeps 937, 942, 945, 946 twice, 947 thrice, 948 four times, 949, 950, 951 twice, 953, 954 twice, 955, 956; Hugo princeps filius Rotberti 938, 940; Hugo Albus 939, 941 twice; Hugo dux Francorum 943, 944, 946; Hugo dux 943 five times, 944 thrice, 945 four times, 946; Hugo Transsequani (v.l. trans Sequanam) dux 960.

Duke of Burgundy: Rodulfus filius Richardi 922, 923; Hugo frater regis Rodulfi 936, 938; Hugo filius Richardi 922, 936, 939; Hugo Niger 940 twice, 941, 950.[11]

King of Burgundy: Rodulfus Cisalpinae Galliae rex (or Cisalpinae rex Galliae) 922, 923, 924, 926; Rodulfus Iurensis et Cisalpinae Galliae rex 937; Rodulfus rex Iurensis 935, 940; Conradus Cisalpinae Galliae rex 946; Conradus rex Iurensis 951.

Count of Vienne and king of Italy: Hugo de Vienna 924; Hugo Viennensis 924; Hugo filius Bertae 926; (Wido frater Hugonis regis 928;) Hugo rex Italiae 933, 936, 942, 945, 946 twice.

Nothing can be more plain than that Flodoard intends to distinguish between Hugh the White, son of Robert, whom we call Hugh the Great, duke of the French, and Hugh the Black, son of Richard, who is never in terms described as duke[12] of Bur-

[10] *Contin. Regin.* a 939. This is not a contradiction of Flodoard, as M. Lauer says (*ibid.* n. 6), but an addition to what he records.

[11] Under 946 'Hugo Nneigro filio Richardi' is anomalous both in grammar and spelling.

[12] His usual style is *comes* or *comes et marchio*, but *dux* is also found in charters: see Poupardin, *Le Royaume de Bourgogne*, p. 207.

gundy, though he is always mentioned in connexion with the Burgundian duchy. In like manner Hugh the Black's brother, Rodulf, who for a time was king of France, is distinguished as son of Richard, while Rodulf, king of Burgundy, is styled king of Cisalpine Gaul. Moreover, in the Annals, Cisalpine Gaul is used definitely to mean the kingdom of Upper Burgundy; it is not used of the kingdom of Provence. Were it not that once in the History of the Church of Rheims Flodoard speaks of the Carolingian Charles, king of Provence, as *Cisalpinae Galliae regis*,[13] we might conclude that Flodoard designedly reserved the epithet Cisalpine for the Upper kingdom. But in no case can it be understood of any region outside the kingdom of Burgundy. Arguing from this evidence Freeman,[14] who was followed by Carl von Kalckstein,[15] maintained that Hugo Cisalpinus must be Hugh of Vienne, better known as Hugh of Arles, marquess of Provence and king of Italy; but this opinion can hardly be reconciled with the ascertained facts of Hugh's history and is now universally abandoned.[16] We have then to seek for another Hugh holding an influential position in the Burgundian kingdom to whom Flodoard may refer.

3. It is necessary first to inquire by whom the government of the kingdom of Burgundy was administered in the time following the death of Rodulf II in July 937. The historians give us very little information on the subject. Liutprand says that Hugh of Italy forthwith married his widow Bertha, and affianced his son to her daughter Adelaide.[17] This no doubt implies a visit to Burgundy. Flodoard on his side tells us that Rodulf's young son, Conrad, was carried off by Otto of Germany and kept in his charge.[18] We have to fill in the date by means of two charters, in which Hugh made a wedding gift to Queen Bertha.[19] They

[13] *Hist. Rem. Eccl.* iii. 26; Migne, cxxxv. 239 B.
[14] *Hist. of the Norman Conquest*, i. (3rd edition) 229, n. 3.
[15] *Gesch. des Französischen Königthums unter den ersten Capetingern*, i. 218, n. 4, 1877.
[16] See, e.g., Köpke and Dümmler, *Otto der Grosse*, p. 88, n. 3; Lauer, p. 43, n. 3.
[17] *Antapodosis*, iv. 13.
[18] 'Quem iam dudum dolo captum sibique adductum retinebat:' *Ann.* a. 940.
[19] See Dümmler, in the *Forschungen zur Deutschen Geschichte*, x. (1870), 305-7, and *Codex diplomaticus Langobardiae* (*Monumenta Historiae Patriae*, xiii., 1873), 942-5. The charters bear date 12 December 938, *anno regni Hugonis* XII, *Lotharii* VII [M. Poupardin, p. 67 n. 2, accidentally says VIII], *Indictione* XI. The regnal years indicate 937, which agrees with the eleventh Indiction of September and the year reckoned in the Pisan style from the 25th March preceding what we call the current year. The usage in Hugh's chancery was irregular; but the September Indiction appears in his first year (*Cod. dipl. Langob.* p. 890), and the *calculus Pisanus* is found three times in 936 and 937 (*ibid.* pp. 933, 938; and Dümmler, *ubi supra*, p. 302). On the other hand the Indiction of Christmas occurs in 931 (*ibid.*, p. 301); and in two documents of the same year (pp. 299, 301) and in one of 941 (p. 310) the Pisan style is not adopted. Some of these differences may be due to scriptural errors, as a document of 932 is dated 931 (*Cod. dipl. Langob.* p. 929), and the Indiction is wrong in 926 and 943 (pp. 887, 977).

were granted *in Burgundia in corte quę Columbaris dicitur*, that is at Colombier, north of Morges, on the right bank of the lake of Geneva, on 12 December 937. There is no reason to doubt that Hugh took his bride and her daughter back to Italy,[20] where he is found in the following July.[21] On the other hand, it is extremely unlikely that Otto himself appeared on the scene,[22] and there is some probability in Giesebrecht's conjecture[23] that a party among the Burgundian nobles secured Conrad and sent him off to Germany to save him from falling into Hugh's hands.

The question then must be repeated: now that the queen-mother and her daughter were withdrawn into Italy and the young king into Germany, who had sufficient authority in Burgundy to set up and maintain some sort of government? Was it established in the interests of Conrad or in those of Hugh? Long ago it was asserted by Frédéric de Gingins-la-Sarra, in his interesting but uncritical memoirs on the history of the kingdom of Burgundy, that during Conrad's detention in Germany his dominions were administered by Queen Bertha, his mother, assisted by his uncle Hugh, the count palatine, younger son of King Rodulf II.[24] But the only evidence furnished for this Hugh's relationship is contained in the charter subjecting Romainmotier to Cluny by Adelaide, widow of Richard the Justiciar, duke of Burgundy in 928,[25] in which she speaks of her sons, King Rodulf [of France[26]] and Hugh [the Black].[27] There is no mention here of any Hugh, count palatine.

But Hugh, the count palatine, really existed. In a suit heard before King Rodulf II of Burgundy 'in Cartris villa',[28] on 18 January 926, he is associated with Turimbert, count [in Vaud], and Anselm, count of the *pagus Equestricus* (Nyon), for the

---

[20] Cf. Liutprand, *Antapod.* iv. 14.
[21] *Cod. dipl. Langob.* pp. 939 f.
[22] Widukind alone states this (ii. 35), in a later connexion, after a notice relating to the year 943.
[23] *Gesch. der Deutschen Kaiserzeit*, i. 314.
[24] *Archiv für Schweizerische Geschichte*, viii (1851), 87. This Hugh—'von dem man sonst nichts weiss,' as Professor Bresslau truly remarks (*Jahrbücher des Deutschen Reichs unter Konrad II*, ii. 35 n.)—has been evolved from a confusion of notices relative to Hugh the Black.
[25] The regnal year given in this charter indicates 928, the Indiction 929.
[26] This identification is certain: see Bresslau, l. c.
[27] *Chartes de l'Abbaye de Cluny*, i. 358–61, no. 379. Among the subscriptions is that 'Ugonis incliti comitis et frateri S. [*sic*, for 'fratris'] augusti Rodulfi regis'. The text is taken from a copy in a chartulary. In a later paper (*Archiv*, ix. 188 f., 1853) Gingins suggested that Herman, duke of Suabia, took charge of the Burgundian kingdom during Conrad's minority; but the only authority he cited (Liutprand, *Antapod.* v. 1, 10) mentions Herman only in connexion with his own duchy.
[28] M. Poupardin, *Le Royaume de Bourgogne*, p. 270, explains this as 'Saint-Gervais près de Genève'.

hearing of a petition [29] ; and in 927 or 928 [30] he was one of the witnesses to the election of Libo, bishop of Lausanne :

Hugo marchio similiter consensit. Hugo comes palatinus similiter.[31]

Hugh the marquess is Hugh the Black, duke of Burgundy, who was an important personage in the Burgundian kingdom as well, though it is perhaps impossible on the existing evidence to define the territories in it over which he held autbority as distinguished from those in which he possessed lands. Hugh, the count palatine, would on all analogy be the king's representative for judicial administration.[32] Who was this Hugh who held the office ?

In 1896 it appeared to me possible that two grants to Montiéramey, in the country of Troyes, which were described by M. Giry in the *Études d'Histoire du Moyen-Âge dédiées à Gabriel Monod*,[33] might supply the required clue. The first of these was made in 927 by *Hugo comes* and his wife Wila, and the second more than forty years later by the widow. Their special value consisted in the precise enumeration of the grantors' children. But, like M. Giry, I hesitated to pursue the identification, and it was not until the publication of M. Georges de Manteyer's brilliant essay on *Les Origines de la Maison de Savoie en Bourgogne* in 1899[34] that I became convinced that the clue could be successfully worked out. M. de Manteyer possesses the double advantage of a minute topographical knowledge and of a quite exceptional gift of genealogical combination. If in some directions he may be thought to have pushed his faculty of divination too far, these hypotheses do not affect the particular question before us. His results on this point may be briefly summarized as follows.

The Hugh mentioned in the Montiéramey charter was the son of Warner, viscount of Sens and count (probably of Troyes), who died fighting against the Normans in 925.[35] Warner married Theutberga, the sister of Hugh of Vienne, count of Arles and afterwards king of Italy, and had by her three sons, Hugh, Richard, and Manasses.[36] Doubtless through the influence of the powerful uncle, Manasses was made archbishop of Arles as early as 920 : [37] how he followed him into Italy and possessed himself of three other

[29] *Chartes de Cluny*, i. 247-9, no. 256. The subscription is ' S. Ugoni comte palatii' [*sic*].

[30] Both dates are given in two texts of the *Annales Lausannenses, Monum. Germ. Hist.* xxiv. 780.

[31] Contin. of Cono, *Gesta Episc. Lausann., ibid.* p. 805.

[32] See Poupardin, p. 189 f. [33] pp. 135, 136, nos. 27 and 31.

[34] In the *Mélanges d'Archéologie et d'Histoire* of the École Française de Rome, xix, fasc. v.

[35] Manteyer, pp. 451-4. [36] *Ibid.*, pp. 440 f., 446.

[37] *Cartulaire de Saint-André-le-Bas*, ed. U. Chevalier, 1869, p. 88, no. 124 ; Manteyer, pp. 439, 445.

bishoprics as well is notorious from the narrative of Liutprand.[38] After Warner's death his widow, Theutberga, married Engelbert, viscount of Vienne,[39] the brother of Sobo, who became archbishop of Vienne about 927. In consequence of this double connexion the centre of interest in Count Warner's family became transplanted from the north of the Burgundian duchy to the west of the Burgundian kingdom. Hugh, the eldest son, seems to have lost whatever position he held in the former, when the whole northern part of the duchy was annexed by Hugh the Great, duke of the French, in 936 [40]; but he retained his landed estates there. In the same year, 936, he was granted a large property of 700 manses in the Viennois by his uncle Hugh, king of Italy.[41] A year later King Rodulf II died, and his old rival, King Hugh, laid claim to the succession. A count palatine named Hugh is then found in office in the region north of the lake of Geneva. It is natural to suppose that King Hugh appointed his nephew to this post. The difficulty is that, so far, Hugh, son of Warner, has not been traced in the Burgundian kingdom outside the Viennois. Could we prove that the Warner, nephew of Hugh, who was granted lands in the district of Nyon in 910 [42] was his father, the hypothesis would gain in probability; but Warner was not an uncommon name, and the charter cited does not lead to a positive conclusion.

The case therefore stands thus. Hugh was the nephew of Hugh of Vienne, king of Italy, who had been the most powerful man in the Viennois; he was nephew also of Boso, the brother-in-law of King Rodulf II; and Rodulf's widowed mother and later on his own widow were successively the wives of Hugh of Vienne.[43] These connexions mark Hugh, the son of Warner, as a man to whom high office was likely to be confided; and as his younger brother, Manasses, was made archbishop of Arles, so it would be in the natural order of events that he should be given some high civil post. During his absence in Italy King Hugh needed some officer who could represent him in various ways. It was most important that there should be some one, a count palatine, to preside over the judicature of the country; and whom would King Hugh be more likely to appoint to this office than his sister's son? This identification, however, remains, pending the discovery of new evidence, unproved; but if the conjecture

[38] *Antapod.* ii. 6, 7.   [39] Manteyer, p. 431.   [40] *Ibid.* pp. 454 f.
[41] *Cartul. de Saint-André-le-Bas*, pp. 232 f., app. no. 22; Manteyer, pp. 442–5. The charter is dated according to the *calculus Pisanus* in 937; but the Indiction and the regnal years fix the date to 936.
[42] *Recueil des Hist. de France*, ix. 693; Manteyer, p. 462.
[43] The former marriage, which took place about 912, is proved by a charter in which Hugh count and marquess speaks of 'uxoris mee nomine Ville regine': *Cartul. de Saint-André-le-Bas*, p. 223, app. no. 14; Manteyer, p. 464.

be accepted, I believe that we have found the Hugo Cisalpinus whom King Lewis of France went to meet in 939. The young Conrad was out of the way, and Hugh of Italy had asserted his authority in the kingdom of Burgundy. Lewis needed support from that kingdom, and he sought it in the man whom King Hugh had appointed as his count palatine. It may be added that one son of Hugh, whom I should like to identify with this count palatine, Theobald, became archbishop of Vienne, and another, Humbert, was the father of Humbert who is claimed to be the same person with Humbert, known to later writers as Humbert *aux Blanches Mains*, who was the founder of the House of Savoy.[44]

ii. *Constantinus*

Charles, the son of the Emperor Lewis III, is styled by Flodoard and by Richer, who follows him, *Constantinus*. In all the documents in which his name appears he is simply Charles the count or the count of Vienne. *Constantinus* is peculiar to Flodoard and his copyist. Now the use of two names in juxtaposition is, I believe, without example in Charles's time. If a man bore one name by birth and another by baptism, he would be described or would describe himself as ' Carolus qui et Constantinus '. But Charles never makes any addition to his name: the addition is Flodoard's. Now Flodoard, we have seen, is extraordinarily precise in his discrimination of persons bearing the same name. This is particularly clear in the case, on which I have commented, of the numerous men named Hugh whom he has occasion to mention. There is no instance to my knowledge in the works of Flodoard in which he speaks of any one with a double Christian name, or of any one with a Christian name and a surname. He often adds a descriptive adjective, but this is always of topographical import. If we pass by the countless instances in which he mentions bishops with the adjectives of their sees, the only attributes which I have noticed in his History of the Church of Rheims are Transrhenensis, Aquitanicus, Normannus, Flandrensis, and Transmarinus (meaning ' English '). All these speak for themselves. In the Annals we have only to add Cisalpinus, on which I have said enough, and perhaps Transsequanus.[45]

According to Flodoard's usage, then, it would appear that Constantinus must be a name derived from some place.[46] The adjective he takes from Constance in Suabia is Constanciacensis.[47]

[44] See Manteyer, *passim*, especially pp. 436 ff., 476–84 ; Poupardin, p. 262 f.
[45] See above, p. 303.
[46] After I had arrived at this conclusion I found that Freeman had suggested it as a possible alternative: i. 229 n. 7.
[47] *Ann.* a. 948.

Constantinus more naturally is the adjective of Coutances in Normandy, but there is no sort of link to connect Lewis III with that region. We can trace him from Arles, when he was king of Lower Burgundy (or Provence), into Italy, and after his troubles there back to Vienne.[48] I would suggest that Flodoard wished to indicate this Lower Burgundian connexion. There is a rare use of *Constantina urbs* for Arles. It occurs in a rescript of Honorius and Theodosius II of 418 ordering that synods should be held yearly *in Constantina urbe*. Sirmond, who first assigned this document to its proper authors, refers to Hincmar, epist. vi, in evidence [49]; but I have sought in vain for any mention of it in the works of Hincmar. Still, the rescript became famous from its inclusion in more than one canonical collection; it was well known at Cologne as it was at Arles:[50] and in this way—still more if it was cited by Hincmar—the passage may have become known to Flodoard. If this suggestion appear farfetched, I would adduce a parallel from Richer, in which a similar attempt is made to discover a Latin equivalent for Burgundy with a less successful result. Richer seems to have understood Burgundia in the limited sense of the duchy of Burgundy [51]: so when he had to speak of Conrad *rex Galliae Cisalpinae*, as Flodoard calls him, he boldly searched in Horace for an Alpine folk, and, regardless that the Genauni belonged to Rhaetia, described Conrad as *rex Genaunorum*.[52]

REGINALD L. POOLE.

The Exeter Domesday

WAS the Exchequer Domesday compiled, as to the southwestern counties, from the Exeter Domesday? Let us look at the evidence suggested by the collation of the two texts, for Devon by Mr. Reichel and for Somerset by Mr. Bates-Harbin, in the Victoria County Histories (vols. i, quoted as *D.* and *S.*). To keep the names distinct we will call the one manuscript Exon, the other D.B. Exon is a pretty full digest of the original returns for Somerset, nearly all Devon, and Cornwall, each fief of impor-

[48] Cf. Poupardin, *Le Royaume de Provence*, pp. 189 f., 1901.
[49] See his notes to Sidonius Apollinaris, p. 146 f., Paris, 1652. The rescript is also printed in G. Haenel's *Corpus Legum quae extra Constitutionum Codices supersunt* (1857), p. 238, and in the *Monum. Germ. Hist., Epist.* iii. (1892), 13 f.
[50] See an account of the manuscripts given by F. Maassen, *Gesch. der Quellen des canon. Rechts*, i. (1870) §§ 670, 786, and by W. Gundlach in the *Neues Archiv der Gesellsch. für ältere Deutsche Geschichtsk.*, xiv. (1889) 277–312.
[51] He once uses 'Cisalpini', *Hist.* ii. 42, for the inhabitants of the duchy. The word only occurs elsewhere, I think, in ii. 17, where he borrows 'Hugo Cisalpinus' from Flodoard. [52] *Hist.* ii. 53; cf. 98.

tance having a separate booklet or quire; also for nearly half Dorset and one manor in Wiltshire, the rest having, no doubt, been lost before the manuscript was bound together about 1400. That Exon did not always copy the returns in full will be proved later by the *terrae occupatae*. It includes live stock and some other items not found in D.B., but is arranged, like D.B., by fiefs, while the returns are arranged, like those of other counties, by hundreds, as is proved by Exon taking the hundreds in much the same order in different fiefs, and by the arrangement in hundreds of the list of *terrae occupatae* in Devon.[1]

Eyton and Mr. Reichel thought that for Somerset and Devon the two manuscripts were compiled independently from the original returns,[2] but examination seems to show that D.B. was compiled from Exon, and if so, no doubt it was also derived from Exon (then complete) for Cornwall, Dorset, and Wiltshire. We may probably infer that in many other counties, if not in all, a digest by fiefs, similar to Exon, was made from the original return arranged by hundreds, from which digests the great Domesday Book was afterwards compiled. Little Domesday, printed as volume ii of D.B., covering the eastern counties, which resembles Exon in size of folio and fullness of detail, looks like one of these digests.[3] The many socmen and the complicated details of Norfolk and Suffolk seem to have frightened the compilers of D.B. so much that they did not make an abstract of the eastern circuit, but left Norfolk, Suffolk, and Essex to be represented by the preliminary digest; the abbreviated digest of Great Domesday being never quite completed.

In a good many cases the figures and names of D.B. differ from those of Exon, but D.B. is often clearly wrong. Exon distributes the hidage between demesne and villeins, so as to confirm its total, at least within a fraction. Now in Devon, D.B. has 1 hide for Exon's $1\frac{1}{2}$ hide, detailed as $\frac{3}{4} + \frac{3}{4}$, at Bochelanda, f. 327 b; $1\frac{1}{2}$ hide for $1\frac{3}{4}$ ($\frac{1}{2} + 1\frac{1}{4}$) at Doducheswilla, f. 338 b; 1 virg. for $\frac{1}{2}$ virg. ($\frac{1}{4}+\frac{1}{4}$) at Wica, f. 481 (*D.* under these folios). D.B. is also plainly wrong in giving 'i teamland' for 'x' with $3 + 5$ teams at Liega, f. 179 b, and 4 teamlands with 8 villein teams at Sotebroca, where Exon, f. 215 b, has 8 and 4. In Somerset D.B. 87 has iii hides for iiii ($2 + 2$) at Martock (f. 113, *S.* 440); D.B. 89 has ii thegns for ix at Newton (ff. 149, 521 b);

---

[1] *Devon Association Transactions*, xxviii (1896), p. 457, 'Analysis of Exon'; *Victoria County History, Devon* (quoted below as *D*), i. 536–49.

[2] Eyton's *Somerset*, i. 6. *D.* 377–9; pace Mr. Reichel, Exon's Dorset, which gives live stock, cannot be taken from D.B., nor can the corrections in Exon, which extend to live stock, have been made 'to agree with D.B.' (*D.* 480, n. 5).

[3] Little Domesday, about $10\frac{1}{4} \times 6\frac{1}{2}$ to 7 inches, is a little larger than Exon (10×6), and the writing is rather larger and wider apart; for facsimiles see the Record Exon (D.B. iv) and plate 244 of the Palaeographical Society.

D.B. 96 b has iii hides for ii at Brewham (*S.* 428 n., 507); D.B. 92 has 1 hide for 1½ at Aisse (ff. 269, 514, *S.* 476). Also, as 'dim.' is easily missed and unlikely to be invented, D.B. is presumably wrong in a dozen other cases where it has 1 for 1½ or ½ (*S.* notes). The names of places can be tested by their names now, and in a score of them the modern name shows that D.B. is wrong.[4] Again, Exon, f. 165 b, has 'Alward holds ½ hide which Alestan held T.R.E.', but D.B. 90 a 2, l. 52, has 'Alestan holds ½ hide'. At Rode, D.B. 99 has wrongly *ipse tenuit* for the *ipse emit* of Exon, f. 464 (*S.* 526). At Wells, D.B. 89 gives to three under-tenants 17 villeins instead of Exon's 25 (10 + 8 + 7, f. 156), having missed Richard's 8. In Devon, D.B. overlooked and omitted the Sotrebroc on f. 459, and at Chiwarthewis D.B. 117 b omits Fulcher's under-tenant Helgot (f. 471). The mills at Taunton and Hatherleigh could hardly be misplaced by Exon, ff. 174 b, 178, but very easily by D.B. (87 b 1, l. 34; 103 b), and in a dozen other cases we can see that D.B. is certainly or probably wrong.

Clearly D.B. was no more always correct in the south-western counties than Mr. Round found it in Cambridgeshire. We cannot, therefore, infer that D.B. was independent of Exon from occasional differences in figures or personal names. They are mainly mistakes common in copying, iii for ii, or xv for xxv, or ii for ix; or mistakes of letters by the dictator or of sounds by the scribe, Leimar and Letmar, Aluiet and Almer, Aedmar and Almar, Siward and Sedward, Alestan for Alestilla, Godeman for Goderone, &c.[5] These differences can prove nothing, for D.B. is as likely to have miscopied Exon, as Exon to have miscopied the return. That D.B. was not very careful with names is shown by its place-names, and D.B. 95 is no doubt wrong at Burnham, where for the Reinewal of Exon, f. 354, it gives the Rademer of two previous entries (*S.* 449). The makers of D.B. were pretty clearly in pairs—a compiler, who dictated an abstract of the manuscript from which he worked, and a scribe who wrote from his dictation, so that there was a double chance of mistake; the compiler might misrepresent his original, or the scribe misrepre-

---

[4] The variations of D.B. are in italics:

S. 436 *Bei-* Betminstre (Bedminster)
436 *Brum-* Breuutona (Bruton)
456 *Littelaneia -lande* (Lytleinge)
460 *Und-* Vudewica (Woodwich)
464 *Coriscoma -tona* (Crossoombe)
481 *Babcari -can* (Babcary)
487 *Loptone* Lopena (Lopen)
507 *Novia* Nonin (Nunney)
507 *Eir-* Ciretona (Cheriton)
513 *Leding* Ledich (Dyche)
513 *Telwe* Telma (Elm) and several others.

D. 416 *Bed-* Bretricestan (Brichestone)
417 *Sov-* Stoverton (Staverton)
449 *Honechercha -rde* (Honeychurch)
451 *Ovel-* Dueltona (Dolton)
457 *Smi-* Esnideleia (Snedley)
479 *Tid-* Lidefort (Lydford)
493 *Cob-* Scobacoma (Shapcombe)
503 *Crin-* Incrintona (Ilkerton)
521 *Limor* Linor (Leonard)
539 *Cwr-* Citrametona (Chittlehampton).

[5] At Speccot the 'Ailaf (*Exch.* Goisbert)' of *D.* 507 is a slip, D.B. 115 has Eilaf.

sent the dictator. We must, therefore, test the relation of D.B. to Exon in other ways ; where necessary the entries to be quoted have been examined in the manuscript at Exeter.

The test is to see if D.B. repeats Exon's mistakes and variations. At Cercilla (*D.* 489) and Cilletone (*S.* 485), where Exon, ff. 366 b, 423, has wrongly 1 virg. (1 + 2 !) and 1 virg. (1¼ + ¼ !), D.B. 111, 93, has also in both cases 1 virg. At Netelcumbe, Exon, f. 104, reads '*reddit libras et* 12s.' The '1½ virgate' of demesne in this entry should be ' 1 hid. ½ virg.', so the scribe was sleepy, and no space is left before *libras*.[6] This and the '12s.' seem to show that the missing figure was omitted by a mere slip, and was given in the original return ; if the figure there had been absent or illegible attention would no doubt have been called to it and space left for it in Exon. Yet D.B. 86 b gives no figure, but '*reddit—libras et* 12s.' with a note '*require*' to look it up—apparently in the original return. Again, the Mameorda and Bolewis of Exon seem to be Wembworth and Moulish (*D.* 453, 480), Clutona is clearly Clapton, Ceptona probably Chilton, and Udecoma, Cutcombe (*S.* 449, 461, 402). Yet D.B. repeats all these wrong names. In many other cases the figures and omissions of Exon are very suspicious, e.g. a score of cases in Devon and Somerset where, though the villeins pay a fair share of the hidage, their teams are omitted [7]—every suspicious figure and omission is repeated in D.B. It may be said that these mistakes came from the returns ; but at Netelcumbe that seems unlikely.

The entries in D.B. follow the order of Exon, except where D.B. picks out some entry or entries to head the fief. Though in Devon D.B. sometimes groups together the lands of certain under-tenants or Saxon owners, in each group the order of Exon is preserved.[8] Now while the entries in Exon for each fief, being taken from returns arranged by hundreds, are as a rule grouped by hundreds and the order of hundreds is fairly regular, there are many entries, especially in Somerset, which interrupt the regular order—belated entries, apparently omitted in the proper place and afterwards made between the entries of other hundreds. All these irregularities are repeated in D.B. In Devon comparison is complicated by the D.B. grouping in large fiefs, so let us take

[6] The manuscript is well represented by the printed text of D.B. iv. 96. The total hidage was '2 hid. 3 virg.' of which the villeins had '1¼ hid. ½ virg.' leaving 1 hid. ½ virg. for the demesne.

[7] Dorset has other cases : Frome, f. 48 b, Canolla and Holna, f. 62.
    f. 38 b Ronescumbe : terra 6 car. ; dem. 2 teams ; 7 vill. 3½ hid. (no teams).
    f. 56 Wintreborne : terra 3 car. ; dem. 1 team ; 5 vill. 1¼ hid. (no teams).

[8] The one exception, in the lands of Walter de Clavil, proves to be really evidence that D.B. was *not* independent of Exon, for the entries misplaced in D.B. correspond exactly to ff. 388–91, one of the quires or booklets of which the Exon MS. is composed ; see *Devon Association Transactions*, xxxvii (1905), pp. 249, 266, ' The History of Exon,' by the late Rev. T. W. Whale. He also noticed various other points given here.

Somerset.[9] In Roger Arundel's fief four entries in North Petherton (Durston to Newton, f. 441) come first, as they should, but Sydenham in the same hundred comes in the middle, after Kittisford; so it does in D.B.[10] Independent compilers, even if they made the same omission, would not correct it after just the same interval. On ff. 142–3 are a dozen estates, Estona, &c., in Porbury hundred, but Wraxall and Winford in the same hundred on f. 145 are separated from them by Freshford, Langridge and [Bath]wick in Bath hundred; so they are in D.B. 88 b (*S.* 448–51). On f. 276 Carlingcot and Ekewick in Wellow hundred come in the middle of entries for Bruton cum Wincanton; so they do in D.B. 92 b (*S.* 481). In the fief of Turstin fitz Rolf (f. 383), Syndercome, in Willetone, the 7th hundred, comes in the middle of Bruton the 52nd; so it does in D.B. 97 b. There are also variations in the order of hundreds, probably due to exchange of rolls or quires between the clerks in the course of their work. Plintone hundred follows Walchetone on ff. 328–30, but precedes it on f. 417 (*D.* 475, 515); D.B. agrees. Carentone generally follows Willetone, but, ff. 358–62, we have eighteen entries in Carentone by one scribe (Aucoma, &c.) preceding fifteen in Willetone by another (Cantocheve, &c., *S.* 502–7);[11] again D.B. agrees. D.B.'s agreement with all these irregularities and others like them seems to show that D.B. was compiled from Exon. The alternative would be to suppose that D.B. was compiled independently, yet by help of some not quite regular index to the returns which was also used by Exon. But if D.B.'s compilers had Exon's index, surely they would have Exon's text, and would use it rather than repeat the troublesome process of rearranging the returns. Exon might have used D.B.'s index if Exon had been compiled *after* D.B., but that is most improbable. Nor would such an inversion as that of Carentone and Willetone hundreds be likely in an index, which would probably be made by one man working straight through the hundreds.

On one point we can check Exon's text. At the end, ff. 495–525, is a list, headed *terrae occupatae*, of the many changes in manors between 1065 and 1086 in Devon (f. 495, *D.* 536) and Somerset (ff. 508–25). Its commonest entries run like this: 'X. holds Blackton, to this has been added 1 hide which 1 thegn held T.R.E. worth 5s.' In the corresponding entries Exon uses three forms about equally: (*a*) is similar, 'X. holds Blackton,

---

[9] Analysis in Mr. Whale's *Principles of Somerset Domesday*; that for Devon is in *Devon Association Trans.* xxviii (1896), and in *D*'s footnotes.

[10] D.B. takes Halse, Huish, and 'Wyslagintone' to head the fief.

[11] One uses '&', the other writes generally '7' for 'et', but 'ten&' and often 'v. & m' and '& reddidit'. Again, in Devon the order of Dippeforde (Stanborough), Cadelintone (Colrige), and Allerige (Ermintone) hundreds varies similarly in Exon and D.B. (*D.* 442, 470, 490, 500, 516).

which G. held T.R.E. and it gelded for 3 hides worth 10*s*. . . . to this has been added 1 hide worth 5*s*., &c.; ' (*b*) joins the 1 hide to the 3 thus, 'Blackton which two thegns held T.R.E. and it gelded for 4 hides worth 15*s*.; ' (*c*) is just like (*b*), but adds 'G. held 3 hides and H. 1 hide'. As (*b*) and (*c*) do not distinguish the values added and (*b*) not even the hidage, the list in question, which does give them, must have been derived, not from Exon, but from the original return, and the return must have divided the values of the added lands from those of the holdings to which they were added, as it did in the cases for which Exon uses (*a*). It is clear that Exon does not always give a full copy of the original return. In some twenty cases in Devon and twenty-five in Somerset Exon uses form (*a*), which followed the original return; and so does D.B. with one or two exceptions, e.g. D.B. 92 uses (*b*) at Doniet and Hache. These exceptions do not show D.B.'s independence, for the compiler might summarize Exon as easily as the return. But Exon uses form (*b*) in a dozen cases in Devon,[12] and in Somerset (*b*) in thirty cases and (*c*) in nearly thirty others—all three forms may be conveniently found in the bishop of Coutances' fief, ff. 136–52. Now (*b*) and (*c*) do not distinguish the added values given in the return, yet in every case D.B., using as was natural the shorter form (*b*), agrees with Exon in rolling up the added value. The use of (*a*), (*b*), or (*c*) does not depend on size; small additions are often distinguished by (*a*) and larger ones rolled up in (*b*). It may be, no doubt, that there was something in the forms of the return which inclined Exon to use (*b*) or (*c*) instead of (*a*), for in some cases (*a*) runs according to the hundreds. But some hundreds have both (*a*) and (*b*) or (*c*),[13] and in all cases the return did distinguish, as Exon did not, the added values; if D.B. were compiled from the return, it would

[12] Engestecota, ff. 122 b, 496 b; Ailesvescota, 127 b, 500; Sidelham, 318, 495 b; Gatepada, 341 b, 502 b; Hagitona, 345, 498 b; Olurintona, 367, 501; Bochiwis, 407, 497; Pultimora, 469 b, 500; Chiwarthwis, 471, 500; Lewendona, 472 b, 502; and variations at Alra, 377 b, 499 b; Molacota, 469, 498 b. D.B. 101^2, 102^4, 108^4, 114^3, 111^4, 111^1, 115^3, 117^3, 117^2, and 116^2, 117^2.

[13] In Devon, Lifton, the 1st hundred (f. 495, *D.* 536), has (*a*) at Bratton, (*b*) at Sydenham; Witheridge (501, *D.* 543) also has both (*a*) and (*b*); in Somerset we have

Exon		*Bruton Hundred.*		*Exon*		*Milverton Hundred.*	
f. 519 b	2⅔ h.	Woolston, f. 275 b	(*b*)	f. 514	1½ h.	Ash (brittle), f. 269	(*a*)
520	3½	Keinton, 276 b	(*b*)	511 b	1½	Bathcalton, 362 b	(*c*)
520 b	½	Wincanton, 352	(*a*)	,,	1	Runington, 362 b	(*c*)
521	2¼	So. Cadbury, 383 b	(*a*)	,,	½	Poleshill, 362 b	(*a*)
		Carhampton Hundred.				*Canington Hundred.*	
511	⅓ h.	Bickham, 358	(*b*)	509	½ h.	Stoke Courcy, 369	(*a*)
,,	¼	Staunton, 359	(*a*)	,,	¼ ?	Stringston, 372	(*a*)
,,	¾	Luxborough, 360	(*c*)	509 b	⅓	Dudesham, 424	(*b*)
512	⅔	'Alra' (Porlock), 430 b	(*c*)	510	1/10	Blackmore in Canington, 426	(*a*)
,,	½	Golsoncot, 431	(*c*)				
510 b	1/16	Timberscombe, 442 b	(*a*)				

be strange that the divided values should not find their way into D.B. in some of these seventy cases.

Perhaps the best evidence of all comes from individual cases. Caffecoma is peculiar; to it were added according to f. 509 '3 *mansiones* worth 40s.'; Exon, joining up *one* of them by 'Caffecoma which 2 thegns held'', adds '*two*' worth '20s.', and with this odd mixture of (*a*) and (*b*) D.B. 87 b agrees. In ff. 495–525 we have over fifty cases in Devon and fifteen in Somerset of this kind: 'X. holds M., to this has been added another *mansio* N.' In over sixty of them Exon notes that N. was held of M., and so, with one exception,[14] does D.B. But in six cases in Devon and one in Somerset Exon omits N.'s connexion with M. [15]; so in every case does D.B., yet the connexion must have been given in the returns. On f. 499 Chefecoma is added to Chrietona, on f. 497 b four *mansiones* are added to Slapeforda, on f. 512 a ferling is lost at Hunecota, and on f. 516 b a ½ hide is added to Ceorlatona. They seem quite ordinary entries, but of these four items there is no mention in Exon, nor in D.B.[16] At Ywis f. 497 says '*Tetbald socer (Odonis) occupavit* 1 *ferding*'. Exon, 376 b, mentions the ferding, but says nothing of Tetbald; nor does D.B. 116 b. In Devon on f. 499 b there is added to Mollanda '¼ virgate called Nimet held by two sisters'; Exon, f. 95, noting the addition of Nimet, omits, contrary to its practice, the holders and the '¼ virgate'; so also, contrary to its practice, does D.B. 101. Again, at Wasforda D.B. 112 b, agrees with Exon, 392 b, in omitting the holder of a ferding (501) or else in a curiously framed entry. Here are fourteen cases, quite apart from form (*b*), where D.B. agrees with Exon's omission of items which were given in the return, and should, in the ordinary course, have appeared in both of them. What better evidence could we have that D.B. was compiled from Exon?

It may be added more as a matter of interest than of evidence, that we seem to get one other glimpse of the original returns. A chartulary of Bath abbey has a description of its manors in demesne which plainly belongs to the Domesday Survey.[17] Besides other differences and some items not found in Exon, it gives at Weston '*cc oves et iiii*', at Preston '*de nemore et pascua c agros xiii minus*', at Stanton '*homines ii hid. et dim.*', while Exon gives '*cc oves*' only, '80 *agros pascuae*,' and (wrongly)

---

[14] Anestige+Ringedone, Exon, ff. 300, 499 b, D.B. 107.
[15] Exon, f. 495 b, Leuya+Wadelscota (f. 289); f. 496, Tamerlanda+Pech (411–12); f. 496 b, Chiempabera+Radcliva (412); Braordina+Esestapla (335, 399); f. 498, Lollardestona+Dwelanda (390); f. 500 b, Bradeforda+Tornelous (317 ı); and f. 519 in Somerset Alduica+Ragiol (452). D.B. 106⁴, 114–15, 115¹, 114¹ (110²), 112², 108⁴; and 97–8.
[16] Exon, ff. 117, 109 b, 431, 443 b; D.B. 101⁴, 101², 94¹, 94⁴.
[17] *Somerset Record Soc.* vii. 67 (Corpus Christi College, Cambridge, MS. cxi, p. 128).

'*ii hid.*' only. D.B. agrees with Exon's 80 acres of pasture (the other items it omits)—but the Bath figures may have come, not from the return made by the commissioners, but from a draft of it, for the values given to Weston and Bathford are below those in Exon and D.B.

We have yet further evidence in D.B.'s wrong place-names, where some of the wider differences seem to correspond to slightly imperfect letters in the Exon MS., which are like the following sketches and which the D.B. compiler might easily misread.

In Exon's 'babakari' (Babcary) in Somerset on f. 277 b the twist in the *r* is slight, so that *ri* (1) is a little like *n*, and D.B. 92 b has Babac*han*, though on f. 99 b Babecari. In Devon the last *h* of Exon's Honechercha (Honeychurch, f. 292) has an imperfect hook, making the *ch* (2) look like *d*, and D.B. 106 has Honecher*de*. In Exon's Dueltona (Dolton, f. 295) the D is rounder than it should be, and D.B. 106 b has Oveltone. In Exon's Lidefort (Lidford, f. 335) the L (3) has a sort of cross-line at the top, due to a smudge or a mistake erased, and D.B. 114 has Tideford. On f. 394 b Exon has a strange initial (4) meant apparently for A(isa) [Ash Thomas, *D.* 499]; but to Mr. Barnes, who copied for the Record edition, it looked like D, and D.B. 112 b has Disa.[18] At Hatherley, f. 178, where D.B. has 'valuit £9' for Exon's £4+ 2, the 4 is in the manuscript a *vij* altered to *jjij*, which D.B. might read as *vij*. In two other cases, noticed below, where Mr. Barnes read a ii altered to v and a vi to ijj as 2 and 6, D.B. began by writing ii and vi, altering its figures forthwith to v and iii. Yet another case where D.B. corresponds to something in Exon has been given in note 8.

The cumulative evidence seems to prove beyond doubt that D.B. was derived from Exon. All Eyton's cases to the contrary in Somerset break down on examination. At Aissecota he has missed 'Waltona' in the line written above it in Exon, f. 164 b, while at Sanforda, Bochelanda and the like Exon's mistakes are such as any copyist could correct. Elsewhere the printed Exon has misled both him and Mr. Reichel. In the manuscript Exon, f. 375, has Loc*h*intona, not *d*, and at Ferenberga, f. 141, the *ii* and *ii* are altered to *v* and *v*. Also at Bochelanda, f. 490, '*vi virg.*' is altered to *ijj*.[19] In Devon, Lim, f. 161, has £3, and

[18] But here the omission of the name of this ½ hide on f. 502 b suggests that the original return may have been indistinct.

[19] Except for the detail these alterations might easily be taken to be from *v* to *ii* (they resemble a *y*) and *iii* to *vi*, and D.B., like Mr. Barnes, fell at first into both

Bernintona, f. 179, has 3 hides, not 4; at Boleham, f. 306, printed with '2¼ hid.' and 'viii car.', the '*et dim.*' and the last ii of viii are cancelled.[20] So also in doubtful letters Exon should no doubt be read on f. 134 as Talebri*i*a, not -bru*a*, f. 337 b, Han*c* not Han*e*,[21] f. 388, Alues*d*ef not -*cl*ef[22]; while I and L, much alike in manuscript, are exchanged in the printed text of both Exon and D.B. In all these cases D.B. and Exon do not really differ.

The differences in Saxon names have been already dealt with; they are not evidence either way, for D.B. might as easily miscopy Exon, as Exon miscopy the return. In giving Wiltone, Welland, Wedicheswelle for Pilton, Pilland, Pickwell (*D*. 421-2), D.B. 102 b is wrong (*pace*, *D*. 379), not Exon. The hard letters of Exon (*D*. 379), chiefly some thirty cases of -fort in Devon scattered among fifty of -forda, would be softened in D.B. by the mouth of a new dictator. Except several lost folios (*D*. 376) and items now illegible, no case has been found where an item omitted in Exon is supplied by D.B., nor any difference of D.B. from Exon which could not be due to mistake in copying or suggested by something in Exon itself. In Devon, at the end of the Albemarle fief Wida comes to the bottom of f. 421 b, and Witelie, which follows in D.B. (only), was no doubt on another folio since lost. The men of two Bochelande entries on f. 129 have been confused by D.B. 102 b; at Bera, f. 395 b, the last 'i' in 'iii' is doubtful in manuscript, and the 'ii virgates' of D.B. 98 b agree with the detail; on f. 309 Clist's '*valet xvs. . . . valebat xvs.*' is so awkward and unusual that D.B. 107 might well read or hazard '*olim xxs.*' In Somerset, at Sheligate, D.B. 94 b has '½ car.' for '1 car.' of villeins, but this seems a confusion with '*et dim. hid.*' interlined above '1 car.' in Exon, f. 442; if '1 car.' was wrong, surely it would have been corrected at the same time. For the correct 'Neuhalle' of D.B. 96 b, Exon, f. 464, reads 'uuiahalla', but D.B. might easily read 'n' for 'u', or guess it, as on 83 b 'ad Brigam' for Exon's 'Adbrigam' f. 57, and 100 b wrongly 'in Crintone' for Exon's 'Incrintona' (Ilkerton, f. 402); it is possible that Exon once had '*n*uiahalla', for there seems to be a slight speck or scratch in the parchment which might turn the 'n' into 'u'.

Sidbury, held by Alwin and Godwin T.R.E., is curious. D.B.

traps, for (88, 98 b) the manuscript has ii altered to v and apparently vi to iii; the ii to v is plain in the facsimile, but its heavy strokes do not show that in the iii at Bochelande on 98 b the first ii of the iii are in new ink over an erasure, nor show well their slight irregularity in the manuscript.

[20] *Devon (Association's) Domesday*, ii. 504; *et ipse vidi*.

[21] The scribe seems to have made the 'c' too short and added a higher top—the 'n' is also too short; the result is like (5) and quite unlike any 'e' near it.

[22] The 'd' (6) is open at bottom, but that does not suit 'cl' any better. He is spelt Alwatet on f. 109 (Alware, D.B. 101 b), so was apparently called Alwardheth— d and t standing constantly for dh and th.

102 gives it 5 hides, 30 teamlands, and 2 + 25 teams, while Exon, 118 b, has 3, 20, and 2 + 18. But in the manuscript Exon's figures prove to be alterations; new ink and erasures show that the items were originally those of D.B.[23] After Exon's original entry was made the 5 hides seem, for some special reason, to have been separated into two parts, 2 hides, perhaps Godwin's, being presumably entered on a slip since lost, for the joint value of £6 was left (see f. 506). Unless the alteration was a later one, D.B. joined the two parts together again as at Doniet. This mysterious alteration cannot upset the cumulative evidence that D.B. was derived from Exon.[24]

F. H. BARING.

The missing part of Roger Bacon's Opus Tertium

WHEN Professor Duhem published his important discovery of the latter part of Bacon's *Opus Tertium*,[1] he pointed out that there was still a lacuna between the end of the fragment published by Brewer and the beginning of the fragment discovered by himself—that we were still without Bacon's commentary on the last sections of part iv of the *Opus Maius*, those namely on geography and astrology (or, as Bacon puts it, on the value of mathematics in politics), which occupy in Bridge's edition pp. 286–403 of vol. i. It has been my good fortune to discover this missing fragment in manuscript 39 of Winchester College, to which my attention was drawn by Dr. M. R. James, and which the college authorities courteously sent to the British Museum at my request. I am preparing an edition of it for the British Society of Franciscan Studies; meanwhile a preliminary description of the newly discovered fragment will not be without interest.

The manuscript was presented to the college in 1543 by William Moryn, *quondam huius collegii alumnus*. It is on paper, written about the middle of the fifteenth century; the leaves measure $c.\ 12\frac{1}{2} \times 8$ in., and are not numbered. The contents are (1) *Tractatus de consideratione quinte essentie*, 'quem aliqui attribuunt magistro Roger Bachon, aliqui Iohanni de Rucepissa' (*sic*), as the colophon states. (2) An alchemical treatise without author's name or title, beginning, 'Quesivisti quis trium lapidum

---

[23] Italics mark new ink and (*oo*) erasures. Clearly 'possunt arrare .oxx. car.' was once '.xxx.', and in demesne 'i hidam et d*uas oo* carr.' was 'et dim et [ii] carr.', for the 'u' in 'd*uas*' is made up of an old 'i' and another old stroke (minim) joined at bottom by new ink. The total has no room for 'dim', so 'villani .*oii*. hid. *et xviii* .*ooo* carr.' was 'iii hid. et dim. et [xxv] carr.', the total '*iii* hid.' was 'v' ($1\frac{1}{2}+3\frac{1}{2}$).

[24] Mr. Reichel has very kindly discussed with me the 'internal evidence' of *D.* 379 for the independence of D.B. and all the points he raised are among the cases mentioned; he holds that the small differences in personal names are important.

[1] *Un Fragment inédit de l'Opus Tertium de Roger Bacon*, Quaracchi, 1909.

nobilior, breuior, et efficacior.' (3) *Tractatus magistri Rogeri Bacon de multiplicatione specierum*. (4) Roger Bacon's *Opus Maius* (without title), parts i–iv, ending abruptly in the middle of the word *Cili[ciam]*, Bridges, i. 350—*ciam* forming the catchword of the next (lost) quire. (5) The treatise here described. (6) *Opus tertium fratris Rogeri Bacon*, a fragment corresponding to Brewer's edition, pp. 3–38.

The fifth treatise begins without any title or other heading, but is called in the *explicit* ' 2[m] Opus fratris Rogeri Bacon '. It was clearly not regarded by the scribe or scribes as part of the *Opus Tertium*, which begins on the next leaf of the same quire. But that it was in reality part of the *Opus Tertium*, not of the *Opus Minus*, is proved by such expressions as ' in secundo Opere scripsi primo de Alkimia practica sub enigmatibus ', ' nunc in hoc Opere Tertio volo figuras protrahere ', &c. It contains in fact that part of the *Opus Tertium* printed by Duhem without the long digression *De motibus corporum celestium*, but with some additional matter at the beginning. This additional matter occupies five and a half pages (each page containing from forty-six to fifty-two lines), and is divided into four main sections or paragraphs.

The first begins:

> Post hec sequitur operatio mathematice ad rem publicam fidelium dirigendam. Et hec directio est in 2[abus] maximis rebus, scilicet in cognitione presentium, preteritorum, et futurorum secundum possibilitatem philosophie, et in operatione mirabilium pro vtilitate rei publice. Et iam data est via qualiter publice est conuenienter indicare : sed de operibus parum tactum est. Non est autem possibile hec duo adimpleri nisi sciamus complexiones rerum, quia secundum varietates rerum stat omne iudicium. Nam secundum quod complexiones variantur, tam hominum quam aliorum, variantur sanitates et infirmitates hominum, et scientie et artes et occupationes et negocia et lingue et mores, vt videmus in diuersis regionibus. Nam in omnibus his non solum remote regiones in eodem tempore sed propinque [variantur], vt omnibus notum est. Item res eiusdem regionis variantur multipliciter in eodem tempore. . . . Sed complexiones rerum istarum sciri non possunt nisi cause huiusmodi complexionum sciantur. Cause vero omnium istorum inferiorum sunt celestia que influant virtutes suas et faciant varias complexiones in diuersis.

The rest of the section is occupied with evidence of the truth of this principle.

The second section begins, ' Radices horum iudiciorum inueniuntur penes naturas stellarum.' It deals with the properties and influences of particular celestial bodies.

The third section begins :

> Hec igitur et huiusmodi consideranda sunt in celestibus quatenus sciamus complexiones et naturas rerum in hoc mundo inferiori. Sed

5tum (?) quod est hic sciendum et primo est vt sciamus distinguere partes habitabilis (*sic*) secundum situs suos et figuras, et hoc est vnum de maximis fundatis sapientie, tum propter diuina tum propter humana.

Bacon refers to his map, but adds nothing to the geographical facts given in the *Opus Maius*, his attention here being confined to pointing out the ' utilities ' of geographical knowledge. These he treats under the headings : (1) position and distances ; (2) climate ; (3) natural products ; (4) effects on human life ; (5) interpretation of scripture ; (6) conversion of the infidels ; (7) protection against invasions of barbarians and Antichrist.

The fourth section begins :

Posui ergo propter has causas loca mundi astronomice in scripto et figura et deinde copiosius omnes nationes secundum sanctos et naturales et eos qui propria experientia mundum peruagati sunt. Et hec omnia feci principaliter propter duo, scilicet propter cognitionem futurorum presentium et preteritorum tam in naturalibus quam in voluntariis secundum proprietatem cuiuslibet. . . . Aliud autem est principalius et vltimum quod potest fieri, vt loca cognita promoueantur et mala preuisa impediantur et contraria excludantur. Et hec sunt opera astronomie et geometrie et aliarum scientiarum [MS. duarum] diuersa. Nam astronomia habet proprias sapientie considerationes, primo vt rectificet omnia opera scientiarum aliarum, vt medicine alkimie et agriculture et huiusmodi omnium quarum opera electa tempora requirunt. Et non solum opera istarum scientiarum sed opera artificialia et moralia, quando scilicet (?) melius et perfectius et sine impedimento fiant, salva tamen in omnibus arbitrii libertate.

Then follows more about ' electa tempora ', which leads him to the subject of magic :

Et hec origo cognoscendi an virtutem aliquam habeant ymagines, caracteres, carmina, orationes, et deprecationes, et multa huiusmodi, que estimantur a vulgo esse magica sed a sapientibus in multis philosophica. Nam hec possunt fieri bene et male, et bona intentione et mala, et ad bonum vel malum, sicut per arma fiunt bona et mala.

There are two kinds of magicians properly so called : first, charlatans who do not understand the principles, and if they produce anything, do so only by accident and with the help of demons ; secondly, ' those who work according to truth, but contrary to the law of philosophy, like one who kills a man with a knife unjustly '. The study of these dangerous sciences should not be forbidden, but should be confined to those who receive papal licence.

Et tamen verum est quod iste scientie magnifice, per quas [MS. que] magna bona fieri possunt sicut et magna mala, non debent sciri nisi a certis personis et hoc auctoritate summi pontificis, qui subiecti et subditi pedibus ratione ecclesie debent pro vtilitate magna ad papale imperium operari, ita quod etiam possit in omnibus suis tribulationibus recurrere ad ista, vt tandem finaliter obuiaretur Antichristo et suis, vt, cum similia opera fierent per fideles, ostenderetur quod non esset Deus, et impediretur eius persecutio in multis et mitigaretur per huiusmodi opera perpetranda. Et ideo si ecclesia de studio ordinaret, possent homines boni et sancti laborare in huiusmodi scientiis magicis auctoritate summi pontificis speciali. Hec autem que iam de locis mundi et alterationibus locorum et rerum per celestia et de iudiciis et operibus secretis tetigi, non posui omnia in maiori opere, sed de locis tantum. Alia posui in minori opere, quando veni ad declarandam intentionem istius partis operis maioris. Non enim proposui tunc plura ibi in opere maiori tractare, volens festinare propter vestre sanctitatis mandatum.

Bacon then goes on to refer to wonderful mechanical contrivances which are in no sense magical, such as burning glasses, flying machines, ships and chariots propelled by mechanical means, in almost the same words which he uses in the *De mirabili potestate artis et naturae*, and with no further details. Finally, he points out the value of 'applied mathematics' (*operatio mathematice*) in war, especially in wars against the infidel.

Nam ista opera . . . possunt nunc fieri contra Tartaros, Saracenos, idolatras, et alios infideles; et certum est quod nunquam aliter reprimentur vt exigit vtilitas mundi ; quia bella sunt dubia, et ita male accidit Christianis sepe sicut infidelibus, vt patet in vltima inuasione Damiete per dominum regem Francie Lodowicum. Et si aliquando vincantur infideles, tamen redeuntibus Christianis ad propria, infideles suas recuperant regiones et semper multiplicantur vt parati sint bella dare, quandocunque velint, Christianis.

The next section begins ' Postquam manifestaui ' and forms the first chapter in Duhem's *Fragment inédit*.[2]

A. G. LITTLE.

Sir John Fortescue in February 1461

THE following entry from the Close Roll of the twentieth year of Edward IV, which seems to have escaped the researches both of Lord Clermont, the historian of the Fortescue family, and of Mr. Charles Plummer, the editor of Sir John Fortescue's treatise on *The Governance of England*, not only throws additional light on the question as to where Sir John's possessions in Middlesex and Hertfordshire were located, a point about which

---

[2] Winchester College possesses another (astrological) work ascribed to Roger Bacon ' qui experimentarius dicitur '. This is preserved in a late fifteenth-century manuscript (Y. 8), also apparently presented by William Moryn in 1543, is entitled *Tractatus subtilissime considerationis*, and begins, ' Scribo vobis qui vultis de mutabilibus pronosciorum elementorum que ab astris contingunt.'

there has been some uncertainty,[1] but helps us to make a decision as to the time at which the chief justice threw in his lot with Margaret of Anjou and her son. We have always known that Sir John was with them at the battle of Towton, but just how long before that event he joined them has never been satisfactorily determined.[2] Hardyng, it is true, mentions him among those who went north with Margaret after the second battle of St. Albans,[3] but as Hardyng's list includes the names of several persons who undoubtedly marched south with the queen as well as north with her, it proves little. Now, however, we learn that 'a little before or a little after the feast of Candlemas in the xxxix year of King Harry', about two weeks, that is to say, before Queen Margaret came south and the battle of St. Albans was fought, Fortescue was making provision for his wife, 'because of the trouble and jeopardy' that he 'was and stood in', out of his possessions at North Mimms (Hertfordshire) and South Mimms (Middlesex), and sending his steward to read a deed and make livery of seisin at the former place. It seems more than probable, therefore, that while Queen Margaret was on her way south from York, Fortescue, if not actually staying at North or South Mimms, was at least not far from them; and, if this was the case, it follows that he did not join the queen until the eve of the battle or immediately after her futile victory was won.

CORA L. SCOFIELD.

[Close Roll 20 Edward IV, m. 9 dorso.[4]]

To all to whom this present writyng herafter shall come Roberte Hande, Guy Bailly, and Hamond Parker sende gretyng. For asmoche as it hath be gevyn vs in knowledge that it hath be noysed that aboute the secunde feld of seynt Albones that sir John Fortescu, knyght, shuld haue made estate of all his maners, londes, and tenementes in the Shires of Hertford and Middlesex to diuers persones for terme of the lif of Dame Elizabeth, wif of the said sir John Fortescu, The remayndre therof to on Martyn the Son of the seid sir John Fortescu and to his heires for euermore, And how that we, the said Roberte Hande, Guy Baillye, and Hamonde Parker, shuld haue been at the said Estate makyng: We and euery of vs wyll, depose, and swere that we neither herde ner vnderstode of any estate or Remayndre that shuld be made to Martyn the sunne. But for asmoche as it is merytorie and necessary euery trouth to bě openyd and vnderstande, and also for the declaracion of vs and what we dede or vnderstande of any takyng of astate aboute the seid tyme of the last felde of Seynt Albones, we, the seyd Robert Hande, Guy Bailly, and Hamond

---

[1] Plummer, pp. 44, 50 notes. Lord Clermont (p. 235) found trace of the manor at North Mimms, but he seems to have known nothing of the lands and tenements at South Mimms.

[2] Plummer, pp. 54–5. [3] Hardyng's *Chronicle* (ed. 1812), p. 405.

[4] The membranes of this roll are numbered from both ends. The more usual method of numbering would make this m. 11 dorso.

Parker, by this our present writyng confesse and knoulege, as true men shuld, that a lytell before or a lytell after the fest of Candlemasse in the xxxix yere of kyng Herry, and before the last feld of seynt Albones, oon Thomas Pony, which was oone of the Clerkes of the seid sir John Fortescu, was with vs, and one John Knyghton then beyng present also, at the house of the seid Guy Bailly in Northemymmes in the Counte of Hertford, by the commaundment of the forsaid Sir John Fortescu, and went frome thens to the grounde that was at that tyme the seid Sir John Fortescu, and there was a dede redde by the seid John Knyghton, by the which the seide Sir John Fortescu made astate of all his londes and tenementes, rentes and seruices, that he hadde in the Shires of Hertford and Middlesex to one Thomas Yonge and the seid Thomas Pony, and other whose names we remembre not, and deliuere of season made to the seid Thomas Pony, as to one of the feoffes in the name of all the remenant, and the seid John Knyghton was in the lettre of attourney for to delyuere seasyn, the which dede was rede by the seyd John Knyghton, in which dede was comprised, as by the redyng we vnderstode, that the seyd Thomas Yonge, Thomas Pony, and the seid other Feffes shuld haue estate to theym for terme of the lif of the seid Dame Elizabeth. And like maner estate was made to theym in landes and tenementes that were in Suthmemmys in the Countie of Middlesex, For all manors, landes, tenementes that he had in the Countie of Middlesex. And by the same dede other maner of estate was not made nor taken at that tyme, and the consideracion of the makyng of the forseyde estate, as was rehersed atte that tyme, was this, that bicause that all the londes that the same Dame Elizabeth had for her Joyntour in the Countie of Deuenshire was made suer to Martyn Fortescu and his wif for her Joyntour, so that the same Dame Elizabeth was in no maner of suerte for her Joyntour till that the seid estate afore rehersed was made; and the cause of the haste for the makyng of the seid estate was bicause of the trouble and Joperde that the seide sir John Fortescu was and stode in, that she might be made sure of her ioyntour, as is affore rehersed, and other estate was not made, nor other entent nor cause rehersed atte that tyme, So help vs God, And as we all dare depose and swere as largely as Cristen men shuld atte all tymes. And furthermore herde the seyde John Knyghton declare for trouthe that he was the Stiward of the landes of the seid sir John Fortescu, the which vnderstode as muche as euer was done in as bi feffement in all the seid londes bifore the seid estate and sithyn, how that it was the [5] laste estate that euer was made byfore the mariage of John Fortescu, Squier, and other estate or feffement neuer vnderstode we of. In witnesse wherof we, the forsaid Roberte Hande, Guy Bailly, and Hamond Parker, in maner and fourme as is affore rehersyd, euery man for that is spokyn to his knoulege, haue set theire seales. Yeven vnder oure Seales the xx[ti] day of Februarii, the xix yere of the Reigne of kyng Edward the Fourth.

Et memorandum quod predicti Robertus & Hamo venerunt in Cancellariam Regis apud Westmonasterium decimo septimo die Marcii anno presenti & recognouerunt scriptum predictum & omnia contenta in eodem in forma predicta.

[5] MS. *he.*

Documents relating to the Rupture with France in 1793

PART II

HAVING described elsewhere the course of events at London and Paris in December 1792 and down to the middle of January 1793, I need not here refer to them or to the conference of Pitt with Maret at Downing Street on 2 December. My aim is to publish new documents bearing on the dispute with France, the early stages of which were described in the last number of this Review (pp. 117-23). Chauvelin, the French chargé d'affaires at London, being much disliked at Downing Street and Whitehall, efforts were made to substitute a friendly though unofficial communication with Maret, one of the head clerks at the French foreign office, who was in London at the time when the crisis became acute. W. A. Miles, who knew both Lebrun and Maret well, placed great hope in the latter, and sought to thrust himself into the position of go-between, as appears in his *Correspondence on the French Revolution*. Pitt had employed Miles in clandestine efforts at Paris to influence Mirabeau and others during the dispute with Spain respecting Nootka Sound in the summer and autumn of 1790.[1] Thereafter Miles pestered Pitt with requests for pecuniary assistance; and it is not surprising that the prime minister looked on him as a busybody and his pacific efforts as a dubious intrigue. This accounts for the tone of the following letter (Pitt MSS., 102, Public Record Office):

Downing Street, January 13, 1793.

Sir,

I have just received your two letters. I am at a loss to imagine how a paper which you term an official dispatch can have been addressed to you, but I can have no objection to seeing any information respecting the sentiments of persons in France. I therefore wish you either to bring or send to me immediately the paper to which you refer; but I think it right to apprise you beforehand that it will be impossible for me to have any communication with you respecting its contents.

I am, &c.

W. Miles, Esq.   W. PITT.

As will be seen by reference to Miles's *Correspondence*, he continued to hope that the French foreign minister, Lebrun, would listen to reason, and that Maret, who had left London for Paris on 19 December, would return in an official or semi-official capacity with offers or assurances which might ease the tension. There can be little doubt that Maret coveted Chauvelin's place, for, in describing his interview of 2 December with Pitt, he stated

[1] See my work on *William Pitt and National Revival*, pp. 578-81.

that the minister finally expressed the wish that he (Maret) should be the accredited envoy of the Republic at London. As Pitt in his equally full account made no mention of any such remark,[2] we may doubt its authenticity. Certain it is that the situation was complicated by the cabals which went on at the French embassy in Portman Square. For several reasons the position of Chauvelin at that embassy became very unpleasant, especially when he was stiffly informed by Lord Grenville that he (Chauvelin), having no official position, came within the scope of the Aliens Bill passed near the end of December 1792. The Conseil Exécutif therefore decided on or just before 24 January to recall him and to send Maret to look after the papers of the embassy. Talleyrand, then residing at Juniper Hall, between Leatherhead and Dorking, probably had a hand in the affair; certainly he knew of it; for on 28 January he wrote to Grenville that Maret would soon arrive charged with a plan of Dumouriez' for arriving at a general pacification.[3] The second journey of Maret to London having often been represented as an official mission, it is desirable to present the exact words in which Lebrun described it to Grenville :

Paris, 25 Janvier 1793.

M. le Comte,

Le citoyen Chauvelin, ministre plénipotentiaire de la République française, ayant reçu l'ordre de se rendre à Paris, j'ai l'honneur de prévenir Votre Excellence que le citoyen Maret, qui aura celui de lui remettre cette lettre, se rend à Londres pour veiller aux papiers de la Légation et de les mettre en ordre. Je prie V. E. de vouloir bien lui accorder son appui et sa bienveillance dans les circonstances où il croira nécessaire de les réclamer, et d'être persuadé de ma reconnaissance.

J'ai, etc.,

A Mylord Greenville (sic).   LE BRUN.

Maret did not arrive in London until 30 January; and the *Memoirs of Dumouriez* make it clear that he (Maret) proceeded thither merely in order to feel the way for a pacific though unofficial overture which Dumouriez hoped to make.[4] The following letters are significant. The first is from Maret to Grenville :

Portman Square, le 30 Janvier [1793].

Mylord,

J'ai l'honneur d'adresser à Votre Excellence une lettre du Ministre du Département des Affaires Étrangères en France.[5] Arrivé depuis quel-

[2] See my work on *William Pitt and the Great War*, pp. 80, 81.
[3] *Dropmore Papers*, ii. 375.
[4] *Mémoires de Dumouriez*, ii. 128–31 (edition of 1794).
[5] i. e. the letter previously quoted. It will be observed that Maret had no credentials whatever; and this fact surely explains why (to use Lecky's words, *Hist. of England*, vi. 126) 'he thought it advisable not to describe himself as *chargé d'affaires*'.

ques heures dans cette ville, j'ai cru qu'il étoit de mon devoir de ne pas tarder un instant à présenter à V. E. l'hommage du respect avec lequel j'ai l'honneur d'être, etc.,

Hugues Bernard Maret.

So far as I have been able to discover, Maret took no step towards opening a negotiation; and Miles, who hoped that this was about to take place, could not understand his friend's inaction. Meanwhile the arrival of Chauvelin at Paris, his report as to the discontent prevalent in England, and his account of his 'expulsion' by the British Government (though, as we have seen, he would have left in any case), produced a warlike feeling, which resulted in the unanimous vote of the French Convention on 1 February for a declaration of war against Great Britain and Holland. The following is Lebrun's dispatch to Grenville :

Paris, le 1er Février 1793.

Mylord,

Le citoyen Chauvelin à son retour de Londres m'a remis l'ordre qui lui a été signifié de la part de Sa Majesté Britannique de quitter l'Angleterre avant le premier Février. Quelqu'ait été le motif de cette mesure, qui ne peut être considérée que comme un commencement d'hostilités, les Représentans de la République française et son Conseil Exécutif n'ont rien à se reprocher. Pour maintenir la bonne harmonie entre les deux peuples ils ont épuisé tous les moyens qui pouvaient se concilier avec la dignité d'une grande nation.

Je ne puis cependant m'empêcher de vous exprimer mes regrets d'une mesure qui aura les suites les plus funestes pour l'humanité et pour le repos de l'Europe. Les guerres antérieures entre les deux nations n'ont été que des guerres de Gouvernement ; les peuples n'y prenaient part qu'autant que leur commerce et leur navigation y étaient intéressés. L'épuisement des finances mettait de part et d'autre un terme aux animosités ministérielles.

Une guerre vraiment nationale va succéder à ces luttes d'ambition. Une haine implacable pourra prendre la place des sentimens d'estime qui unissaient les deux nations. La ruine entière d'un des combattants sera peut-être l'unique terme de ce combat sanglant. Je ne vous dirai pas qui sera responsable de toutes les calamités qui en seront la suite : l'histoire et la postérité en jugeront.

Cette rupture paraissant aujourd'hui inévitable, il est du moins à désirer que pendant la guerre les communications entre les deux pays ne soient pas entièrement interrompues. Un nombre déterminé de paquebots, enregistrés dans les ports de Calais et de Douvres et autorisés, pourraient continuer à entretenir cette communication de la même manière qu'elle s'est faite dans la dernière guerre. Je vous prie de proposer cette mesure à S. M. B. et de me faire connaître ses intentions, pour que de notre côté nous puissions prendre des mesures analogues.

J'ai l'honneur, etc.,

Le Brun.

PS. (in Lebrun's handwriting) J'ai chargé votre concitoyen, David Williams,[6] de remettre cette lettre à V. E. Les conversations que j'ai eues avec lui m'avaient laissé pendant quelque tems l'espoir de maintenir la bonne harmonie entre les deux pays. Tous les vœux tendaient à ce but si désirable. Mais le Conseil Britannique en a décidé autrement. Puisse le philanthrope, David Williams, en vous entretenant des dispositions qu'il a dû observer dans le peuple françois, vous ramener à des sentiments plus pacifiques et plus convenables à l'intérêt des deux pays.

Endorsed 'rec^d 11th by Mr. Williams'.

It is curious that Lebrun sent this important letter, not to Maret at the French embassy, but by the hands of David Williams, to be given by him to Lord Grenville. Evidently Maret had not the position which his biographer Ernouf and subsequent writers have claimed for him. As will shortly appear, Grenville, on 3 February, charged Lord Auckland to respond to the overtures of Dumouriez made through the medium of de Maulde, French envoy at the Hague;[7] but, in view of the declaration of war by France, nothing could come of them. It is questionable whether Dumouriez did not use them as a means of gaining time before he delivered his blow at the Dutch republic. However that may be, acts of hostility took place at Calais on 1 February. On 2 February at 2.30 a.m. the postmaster at Dover informed the foreign office that ' an embargo took place yesterday at Calais and other ports of France on all French (?), English, Prussian, Dutch, and Russian vessels except the packets and bye-boats ', and he added that British vessels arriving at Calais would be refused permission to land. A packet left Calais on 1 February at 3 p.m. with this news.[8] These acts amounted practically to hostilities ; and the decision must have been formed at Paris before 1 February. As I have shown, the war-policy gained the upper hand in the Conseil Exécutif on 10 January.[9]

On 4 February Grenville warned Maret ' que dans les circonstances actuelles, il ne vous peut pas être permis de prolonger votre séjour ici, et que vous recevrez aujourd'hui la notification formelle de l'ordre de S. M. pour votre départ '. To this Maret replied on 4 February :

Mylord,
    Je n'ai point reçu l'ordre que Votre Excellence a pris la peine de m'annoncer, et je m'occupe déjà des dispositions nécessaires pour m'y conformer sans délai. Je prie V. E. de donner des ordres afin que je puisse transporter avec sûreté les papiers de la Légation, et qu'il me soit accordé des passeports pour moi et quatre personnes qui m'accompagnent.

[6] For David Williams see Mr. J. G. Alger's *Englishmen in the French Revolution*, pp. 84, 116–17.
[7] *Dropmore Papers*, ii. 377 ; Lecky, vi. 127.   [8] Foreign Office, France, 41.
[9] *William Pitt and the Great War*, p. 107.

On 5 February Maret sent to Grenville the following :

La République Française, inaccessible à la crainte, aussi incapable de manquer de confiance dans la puissance de ses moyens que dans la justice de sa cause, croyait cependant devoir à ses principes de faire encore de derniers efforts pour prévenir les malheurs d'une guerre dont elle ne saurait redouter l'issue. Le Gouvernement français en conséquence m'avait ordonné de me rendre à Londres. Il ignorait alors que le ministre plénipotentiaire de la République avait été obligé de quitter l'Angleterre. J'ai dû penser que cet évènement suspendait l'exercice de ma mission. J'ai demandé de nouveaux ordres au Pouvoir Exécutif de France, et je me croyais à la veille de les recevoir lorsque S. M. B. m'a fait notifier celui de sortir dans trois jours du Royaume.

Les Passeports que V. E. a donné ordres à M. Aust de m'envoyer me parviennent à l'instant ; et, sans me permettre aucune représentation je m'empresse d'en faire usage. Je désire que V. E. ne voye dans cet empressement qu'un témoignage de respect pour les autorités légales d'un pays où les circonstances m'avaient appelé. Si ce respect est un devoir pour tous les hommes il est plus particulièrement imposé à celui qui fut honoré de la confiance du gouvernement de sa patrie ; et à quelque point que puissent être compromis par sa retraite des intérêts chers à l'humanité, il doit l'effectuer sans délai lorsqu'elle est exigée au nom de la loi.

The declaration of war by France was not known in London until 8 February. Meanwhile, on the 4th, Grenville sent to Auckland at the Hague a dispatch, instructing him to confer with de Maulde or Dumouriez, in order to make one more effort for peace, though on the previous day he (Grenville) had expressed his belief that war must ensue. After declaring that no regular negotiation could take place with France until she removed the embargo on British vessels, he continued :

You will further acquaint him that . . . the inconvenience which arose from speculations in our public funds occasioned by the equivocal situation and conduct of M. Maret have determined H. M.'s Ministers to order that person and his secretary, M. Mourgue, to quit the Kingdom without delay. You will further add, that if there is a real intention on the part of M. Dumourier to proceed in a negotiation with you with candour and good faith, nothing but disadvantage can result from opening other channels of communication, and that for this reason, as well as for those above mentioned, no other person will be permitted under present circumstances to reside here as agent in any manner employed by the Executive Council. Subject to these conditions Y. E. may express that you are authorized to hear any suggestions which may be made to you by M. Dumourier for the maintenance of peace. [He then states that the grounds of negotiation are to be the revocation of the decrees of 19 November and 15 December. H. M. is concerting a Plan of pacification with the Powers. He adds :] The abandonment of the conquests made by France and of all measures tending to disturb the tranquillity of other countries must unquestionably form parts of such a plan. The security of Her

Most Christian Majesty [Marie Antoinette] and of her family is in all events a point on which . . . the Court of Vienna has a natural and just claim to insist. And it would certainly tend greatly to conciliation and promote at the same time the real interests of France under any form of Government, if the unjust and cruel decrees of confiscation, banishment, and death which have been pronounced against so many persons could be either wholly or in great part removed. [He states that H. M. has a right to expect that no French fleet will be sent out against any British colonies.] But if in this and other respects the conduct of France should be such as H. M. has a right to expect, the King on his part will not break through the existing neutrality, while such communications are pending, altho' every preparatory measure will be persisted in here.

In a 'private' letter to Auckland of 5 February (not 3 February as in the *Dropmore Papers*, ii. 377) Grenville stated why he lent an ear to Dumouriez' offer. The news of the French declaration of war cut short this negotiation. De Maulde was promptly recalled in disgrace, and Dumouriez received orders to invade Holland forthwith. The general informed Auckland of this, and expressed his deep regret, as did de Maulde. On 13 February Grenville informed Auckland that, if Dumouriez made any further overtures, Auckland was to transmit them to London without comment.

It may be well to include some of the dispatches which passed between Grenville and Sir James Murray, the British envoy at the head-quarters of the Prussian army campaigning against France :—

Sir James Murray to Lord Grenville

Frankfort, Jan. 19, 1793.

[Murray states that he arrived there on the 14th inst. and delivered his letters to the King of Prussia. He also saw the Prussian Minister, Lucchesini, with respect to the suggested joint declaration to France. No decision was possible at present. On the present situation he writes :] The indemnification [part of Poland] required by the King of Prussia happening to be first mentioned, however, I did not fail to express the impossibility which H. M. felt of adopting any such principle or concurring in such a plan as that which was held out. To this little reply was made ; but what I had said seemed to give M. de Lucchesini considerable uneasiness. Should this Project become hereafter a subject of argument and discussion, I apprehend that it will be attempted to disjoin it from the present war and to have it considered as a separate and distinct object. He proceeded to communicate that part of the system which relates to the exchange of Bavaria.[10] He did not show me the paper transmitted by the Court of Vienna, but only mentioned it in general terms. I have understood from another quarter that Lille and Valenciennes are proposed to be given as a barrier to the new dominion ; if so, it is probably stated as a part of the Plan. I am informed likewise that the compliance of the

[10] The exchange of the Belgic Netherlands for Bavaria was still desired by Austria.

Empress of Russia in regard to the encroachment upon Poland is to be purchased by a full permission to maintain the influence or dominion over the rest of that country, which she now possesses.

In regard to the affairs of France, I am inclined to believe that the zeal which has been shown for the re-establishment of monarchy is much abated, and that any material change in the government of that country is now looked upon either as a subordinate or unattainable object; and that therefore proposals for peace upon your Lordship's ideas might not be unlikely to meet with the approbation of the two Courts, if the Project now in agitation were to be laid aside. The Empress of Russia seems to adhere more rigidly to the principle of re-establishing the ancient Government or something resembling it. But in regard to that sovereign I ought to observe that, from language which has been lately held relative to dangers upon the side of Sweden and Turkey, she seems to be preparing grounds for a refusal to take an active part, with her troops at least, in the next campaign.

[He then adds that in the next campaign 70,000 Austrians would enter the Low Countries under the Prince of Coburg, who would soon arrive at Frankfort. These troops and also some of Clerfayt's were already on the march towards Cologne; 20,000 Prussians would assemble at Wesel under the Duke of Brunswick, who left Frankfort for Wesel two days ago; 4,000 Hanoverians would join them. 17,000 Austrians were marching upon Mannheim.]

Lord Grenville to Sir James Murray

Whitehall, 20 January, 1793.

[He expresses regret at seeing His Prussian Majesty's Declaration respecting Polish affairs.] I have it in command from the King to instruct you to hold the same language upon the subject, respecting the impolicy as well as the injustice of the King of Prussia's views of further aggrandisement on the side of Poland. [He adds that H. M. would in no case become] a party to a plan for obtaining a compensation for the expenses of the war by acquisitions wrested from a neutral and unoffending Power. . . . It will be a matter of sincere regret if this incident should be productive of coldness and distance between H. M. and those Powers who have a common interest with H. M. in the establishment of the most perfect concert and good understanding. [He concludes by stating that H. M. is bound by no engagement to Poland, but may find himself under the necessity of publishing his views on this subject.]

J. HOLLAND ROSE.

France and the Balearic Islands in 1840

How near, in 1840, was England to a war with France, a war that would not improbably have been disastrous to both countries, is not unknown. When the European powers combined to urge the withdrawal of Mehemet Ali from Syria, France after a while held back, and the convention of 15 July 1840 was signed only by Great Britain, Austria, Prussia, and Russia on the one part, and by the Porte on the other. Armed action was then taken and Acre was captured. Popular feeling in France was greatly excited, and it was believed that England desired to expel the pasha from Egypt as well.

At so critical a time, and with so energetic a foreign secretary as Lord Palmerston, nothing was more likely to be a *casus belli* than, had it not been baffled, the project of M. Thiers to seize by surprise the Balearic Islands, when the troubled condition of Spain offered him both a pretext and an urgent reason for so unjustifiable a proceeding. But, although this imminent danger to the peace of Europe cannot have failed to be more than suspected from what came out in a statement, rather hazarded, as will be seen, of Count Jaubert [1] in the French chamber, how it was tided over remained a secret until the publication, in 1870, of *The Life of Henry John Temple, Viscount Palmerston*, by the late Sir Henry L. Bulwer.[2] And, as this is called by the eminent diplomatist, who was the author of the work referred to, one of ' the Curiosities of Diplomacy ', I venture to offer a contribution thereto from the following correspondence between my father, the late Mr. Newton S. Scott,[3] and the late Lord Emly.[4]

Mr. Scott to Lord Emly

Biarritz, 21 Feb., 1886.

Dear Lord Emly,

You have been so kind as to listen to a narrative of certain political events which occurred in Spain in the year 1840, and in which, from the circumstances of my official position at the time at Madrid, I was called upon to take an active part. Our mutual friend, Mr. O'Brien, moreover assures me that you will be pleased to have an account of them in writing, and therefore with pleasure I avail myself of your permission to do so.

I will endeavour to spare your valuable time as much as possible, but I must in the first place quote from an interesting and much read work, *The Life of Viscount Palmerston*, by the late Sir Henry Lytton Bulwer (Lord Dalling), Vol. II, page 301, of the Tauchnitz edition :—

I quote an extract from a letter to Lord Granville of the 20th October, because it refers to a singular intention which betokened that restless desire to do something, when it cannot do the thing it wants, which has often characterized the French Government. Lord Palmerston writes to Lord Granville [5]: 'Can you find out by any means at your disposal what is the *coup d'éclat* for which the French squadron has been brought back to Toulon ? I conclude it is to be ready to meet and drive back

---

[1] Hippolyte-François, Comte Jaubert, minister of public works in the administration of March 1840.

[2] Afterwards Lord Dalling and Bulwer, and sometime ambassador at Constantinople.

[3] Paid attaché at Madrid, 1840–5, secretary of legation to Switzerland, 1845–6.

[4] William Monsell, Baron Emly, P.C., postmaster-general, 1853, lord-lieutenant of Limerick, 1871.

[5] Then British ambassador at Paris, with Bulwer for secretary of embassy.

the Russian squadron from the Baltic; but that squadron will not come out at present, though we now hear that it will winter at Revel, where it will be free to come out almost the whole of the winter.' Lord Granville asked me to obtain the information which Lord Palmerston was seeking. I did so. The French fleet was not collecting at Toulon, as Lord Palmerston supposed, for the purpose of driving back the Russian fleet should it make its appearance in the Mediterranean; another purpose was assigned to it. Queen Christina, as it is known, had just retired or been driven from Spain (Oct. 12), and the Government of General Espartero, then the Regent and supposed to be acting under English influence, was installed in the place of that of the Queen Mother. The notion of the French Cabinet was to seize the Balearic Islands, partly as a protest against English action or supposed action in the affairs of the Spanish peninsula, and partly because, if a war in the Mediterranean should eventually take place, it would be of great importance to France to have those islands, with reference to their connexion with Algeria, in their power. The seizure of islands belonging to Spain, because Mehemet Ali was driven out of Syria, seemed a proceeding so little in relation with its cause, that, although I was positively assured that such were the instructions given to Admiral Lalande, I could not feel confident that I was not misled; but at all events my information, such as it was, communicated to Lord Granville, and through him to Her Majesty's Government, reached Mr. Scott, then at Madrid (Mr. Aston[*] being absent), who warned the Spanish Government of the design contemplated.[7] M. Thiers, however, went out of office shortly after this. Nothing was done with respect to the Balearic Isles, and of course great doubt was entertained as to whether the plan revealed to me had really existed. All doubt, however, was soon dispelled, for M. Joubert, who had been in M. Thiers' Cabinet, being provoked by a question put in the course of discussion as to what the Government he had belonged to—the menacing language and attitude of which was not denied—had ever seriously contemplated, rose up from his seat, and said that if the Government to which allusion had been made had remained but a short time longer in office, the French flag would have floated on the Balearic Islands![8]

'If "The Curiosities of Diplomacy" are ever published, this anecdote may take a place amongst them.'

Your Lordship will remark that the concluding sentence about the curiosities of Diplomacy seems a challenge or at all events an invitation to me to narrate an anecdote illustrative of them. One thing is certain: if Bulwer, at that time Secretary of Embassy at Paris, had not, many years later, published an account of the historical event with which I am concerned, it would remain still unknown. I cannot however help regretting that he did not enter into the interesting details, which must have been known to him, which immediately touch me, and that he has confined himself to what concerned himself, and testified to the ability with which he succeeded in finding out an important secret of the French Government.

A short time previous to the 'Pronunciamiento' of September, 1840, the Queen-Regent Christina, accompanied by her daughter, Queen Isabella, started for Barcelona, contrary to the advice of the English Minister, but, as it was supposed, in accordance with that of the French Ambassador, M. de Rumigny, in the remote hope of gaining over General Espartero (who had just victoriously brought the Carlist war to an end) to espouse the obnoxious policy of the Government in the matter of the law relative

[*] British minister plenipotentiary to Spain, afterwards Sir Arthur Aston, G.C.B.
[7] In a footnote, Bulwer adds here :—' Mr. Scott was speaking to me not long since of his having received the information.'
[8] 'Après la chute du cabinet du 1ᵉʳ mars 1840, M. Jaubert vint s'asseoir sur les bancs de l'opposition, et, à quelque temps de là, on eut à lui reprocher une indiscrétion qui fit du bruit dans le monde parlementaire, relativement aux îles Baléares.'— *Nouvelle Biographie Générale*, tom. xxvi. 1858 (Firmin Didot).

to Municipalities ('Ley de Ayuntamientos'), which provoked a general insurrection in the country. Having failed in her purpose, Christina fled to Valencia, and, after a few days' residence, was forced to abdicate the Regency, and embarked for France. Mr. Aston, the English Minister, as well as the other chiefs of missions accredited to Her Majesty, accompanied her to Barcelona and to Valencia, and I, the senior Attaché, was left in charge of the Mission at Madrid, in which capacity I corresponded officially with Her Majesty's Secretary of State for foreign affairs.

At this juncture I received from the late Earl Granville, Her Majesty's Ambassador at Paris, a dispatch, which, very unusually and to my great dismay, was in cipher; for, in the hurry of his departure, Mr. Aston had forgotten to deliver the cipher to me.—My first act was a bold one, and, if I had not been on terms of intimate friendship with my chief, I should probably not have ventured to do it. With a crowbar I had to break open several of his private dispatch boxes, and was at length successful in getting at what I wanted, and in deciphering the following dispatch :—

Intelligence of Queen Christina's expulsion from Spain and her arrival at Port Vendres has reached this Government, and I learn from undoubted authority that Admiral Lalande, in command of the French fleet in the Mediterranean, has been instructed to proceed to the Balearic Islands, and, if possible, to take possession of Port-Mahon.

It struck me at once that it was of the greatest importance that some attempt should be made to prevent this, and I cannot say how deeply I regretted, at such a critical moment, the total absence of any suggestion from Lord Granville as to the steps to be taken in such an emergency. I had no instructions, and it was therefore not without much hesitation, from a natural fear of committing the error of showing ' trop de zèle ', that I made up my mind to take upon myself the responsibility of acting as follows.

First of all I ascertained from an employé of the Spanish Ministry of War that the garrison of Port-Mahon consisted only of a few soldiers under the command of a subaltern; and it would therefore be easy for Admiral Lalande to carry out his instructions; but, if a sufficient number of troops to repel an attack could be dispatched in time, the French Admiral would hesitate to occupy the place by force: such an attempt would have been tantamount to a declaration of war, and one which England would not have tolerated. I therefore determined to lose no time in addressing a letter to General Espartero, who, I learnt that day, was on his march at the head of the Army to Madrid, and who, at that time, could alone dispose of the Spanish troops. I confided my letter, written in Spanish, to Captain Lynn, R.E.,[9] Military Attaché to the Mission, on whose discretion and intelligence I could rely, and who carefully concealed it about his person. I supplied him with the best horse I had and with sufficient funds, and I accompanied him some miles, ostensibly on a sporting excursion.

All this seems very much like a chapter from one of A. Dumas' novels, but you must bear in mind that no railways or telegraphic wires existed in those days, and that it took thirteen days to get an answer from England.

[9] Then Lieutenant James Lynn, Captain, 1843, Lieut.-Colonel, 1854.

As I was not at that time personally acquainted with General Espartero, and it was not likely that he knew of my existence, I had in the first instance to explain what my official position at Madrid was, the truth of which my messenger would confirm; and, having stated the important intelligence received from Paris, I ventured further and suggested to him the advisability of sending back to Valencia or any other nearest port to Mahon a portion of the troops under his command, in order that they might be embarked for that fortress, in the hope of their arriving in time to resist a coup de main (or 'coup d'éclat', as Lord Palmerston writes) on the part of the French.

The result of my letter was, I may say, marvellously successful. Captain Lynn fell in with Espartero at Albacete, on the line of his march from Valencia to Madrid, in the middle of the night. The General rose from his bed to receive him, and without hesitation gave orders to carry out the measure which I had ventured to suggest.

I may here remark that, but for the great activity displayed by all the parties concerned, the result would not have proved so satisfactory. The time occupied by me from the moment I received Lord Granville's ciphered communication to Captain Lynn's departure did not exceed four hours; and the whole thing was done with the utmost secrecy and discretion.

The considerable reinforcement of Spanish troops did arrive in time (some forty-eight hours before the Toulon fleet), and Admiral Lalande did not think proper, in consequence probably of the unexpected strength of the garrison, to land troops, and make an attempt, under the plea of watering, to seize the place, from which he sailed back to Toulon.

The correctness of Lord Granville's information was proved, as your Lordship will see by referring to the above-quoted extract from *The Life of Viscount Palmerston*.

If this French plan had succeeded, another civil war would probably have been the consequence, to say nothing of the complication of affairs in Europe, especially with regard to English interests, at a time when the irritation caused by Lord Palmerston's policy in signing the treaty of July 1840, on the Syrian question, was nigh producing a rupture with France.

The rules of the Diplomatic service precluded me from accepting at the time from the Spanish Government the offer it made me of a distinctive mark of its gratitude for the service it was my good fortune to render to Spain,[10] but Captain Lynn was promoted to the rank of commander of the order of Charles III.

I was honoured and gratified however by the approbation of my chief, as well as by that of Lord Palmerston, whose flattering dispatch must be in the archives of the Foreign Office.

* * * * * * * *

---

[10] Some years, however, after his retirement, owing to serious ill-health at the time, from the diplomatic service, my father was agreeably surprised (Narvaez, who had upset Espartero in 1843, being then in power) by being made Commander *de numero extraordinario* of the order of Charles III, by royal decree of 6 January 1857. But I believe that he neglected to ask for authorization to wear the star and badge, presented to him, in his own country.

Before I conclude this long letter, I would point out three inaccuracies in Bulwer's narrative. In the first place, Espartero had not yet been elected Regent : this took place several days later[11] and after his arrival at Madrid. Secondly, the communication in cipher was not made to me by the Foreign Office, but by Earl Granville, H.M. Ambassador at Paris. Thirdly, it was Count Jaubert, and not Monsieur Joubert, the ex-minister who defended M. Thiers' policy in the French Chamber.[12]

* * * * * * * *

Lord Emly to Mr. Scott

London, March 14, 1886.

My dear Mr. Scott,

I am very much obliged to you for your letter. It was kind indeed of you to take the trouble of writing it. It puts me in possession of an authentic record of one of the most romantic and important incidents I ever heard of. I hope that we may always have diplomatists as courageous and clear-sighted as you proved yourself.

I am
very sincerely yours
EMLY.

In a subsequent letter to Lord Emly, my father remarks on his obligation of silence until the veil of secrecy had been lifted by Sir Henry Bulwer's *Life of Lord Palmerston*.

CHARLES N. SCOTT.

---

[11] Rather some months after. I have also found that Mr. Aston did not leave Madrid, at any rate in September, to be near the Queen-Regent at Barcelona, but must have gone straight to Valencia, whatever may have been the case with other chiefs of missions. These little slips of memory of things *not directly concerning himself* were to be expected in a man of my father's advanced age, nearly half a century after the occurrences.

[12] These slight inaccuracies are reproduced in *The Life of Henry John Temple, Viscount Palmerston*, by the Hon. Evelyn Ashley.

Reviews of Books

Die Indogermanen im Alten Orient; mythologisch-historische Funde und Fragen. By MARTIN GEMOLL. (Leipzig: Hinrichs, 1911.)

IN this book Herr Gemoll, following on the lines of his *Grundsteine zur Geschichte Israels*, produces abundant evidence which, in his opinion, allows us to associate Semitic, Indo-European, and especially Celtic myths and traditions with each other. For example, the old British Arthur is equated with the Iranian Ahura and with the Semitic Abram and Aššur; Gebal is Cybele; Attis is connected with Khatti (the Hittites) and the Celtic Aedd(on); Lot with Lud; Gideon with Wodan, Odin, and the Celtic Gwydian; and Gilead, as we are now prepared to discover, obviously with Galahad. The many ingenious comparisons in this treatise are supported by a wealth of evidence taken from ancient and modern sources, and all in all Herr Gemoll's book is one which it is difficult to review with perfect fairness. It is well known that in recent years a new school of 'comparative' research has come to the front in Germany: a school that does not hesitate to find astonishing examples of the underlying oneness of all pre-Copernican thought and mythology. To this class the book evidently belongs, and in a recrudescence of solar, lunar, deluge, and other myths we appear to move once more in that atmosphere which some of us thought had been relegated to the past. The fact is that the modern discovery of ancient civilizations and spheres of influence, together with the rapid accumulation of material, permits the most promiscuous and most hazardous correlations on the 'comparative' system. With a little good will one can find support for any view—one recalls Renan's remark about the prolific Arabic lexicon; the amount of knowledge has increased enormously without a corresponding advance in the method of handling data.

There is no *a priori* reason why similar features of myth and story should not be found in fields far apart, but the school to which Herr Gemoll belongs is vitiated by its readiness to pursue inquiries over a wide area without any preliminary investigation of similar features in a less restricted area where the factors are less intricate. Not to waste space upon his philological equations, it is enough to say that he relies too much upon possibilities, and by equally unscientific methods it would be as easy to find Semitic connexions with the natives of central Australia. Moreover, he does not take into account all that goes to shape local or national tradition, the difference between objective and subjective history, and the extent to which relatively late writers have been consciously or unconsciously influenced by extant material (e.g. the Bible). Any preliminary study of mythology would surely have shown the difference between common elements, irrelevant for historical purposes, and the more distinctive features of local or national origin. In like manner the sort of factors that have to be taken into consideration would have been obvious had there been some attention paid to the development of traditions in a single field. There is much in Herr Gemoll's book that is interesting and valuable; he has cast his net over a wide area and has brought up not a few pearls. But he must be read with caution, and indeed with such discrimination that like all extremists he runs the risk of being ignored. This would be a pity. If, on the other hand, the captivating simplicity with which the numerous data are brought together and unified seems to offer an easy 'key' to the *mythologisch-historisch* student, the result will scarcely be conducive to the real progress of either mythology or history. One feels that the book is unfortunately in line with some characteristic features of the thought of to-day, in so far that alert and receptive minds in their anxiety to establish some synthesis or some reconstruction impatiently avoid the necessary rigorous and stringent analysis of the relevant data. The world of scholarship, too, has its present-day anarchical tendencies. S. A. COOK.

The Stone and Bronze Ages in Italy. By T. E. PEET. (Oxford: Clarendon Press, 1909.)

WE regret that an unavoidable cause has delayed our notice of this book. On all hands it has been recognized that Mr. Peet has done a sound and solid piece of work, and he deserves general thanks for his clear presentation of the facts, and congratulations on the balance and sanity of most of his judgements. His estimate (p. 45) of the evidence from the Balzi Rossi caves and his reference to a Balkan origin (pp. 415-16) for the incised pottery of the bronze age found in South Italy seem entirely convincing, and he need not have put out this hypothesis so tentatively (p. 427). And there are throughout the work many shrewd observations, e.g. that the presence of obsidian in the Ligurian and Tuscan neolithic caves shows that even then there were trade connexions between these districts and Sardinia or the Lipari Islands or some other obsidian-bearing island (p. 62); that the Moustérien in Italy at least was not a phase through which Chelléen civilization passed afterwards, and that the Solutréen was in Italy an outcome of the Chelléen, or at least was developed among the same people (pp. 73-4); and his distrust of Chierici's argument that the inhabitants of the neolithic huts at Campeggine were agricultural (p. 94). His confidence (p. 278) that there was continuity of race through the neolithic and eneolithic periods has since been confirmed by Professor Tagliaferro's discoveries near Mkabba.

A good example of his solid judgement may be seen (pp. 109-10) in his summing up of the character of the neolithic hut-villagers, and of the conclusions to be drawn from the neolithic burial rites (pp. 117 ff.), or in his conclusions as to the original home of the neolithic inhabitants of Italy and the routes by which they entered Italy (pp. 174 ff.). But the work abounds in mature judgements built on a broad survey and firm grasp of a vast multitude of facts. On the other hand, the discussion of the relation between the Stentinello and Villafrati wares is unconvincing, a fact betrayed by the repetition of the insinuating ' surely ' (pp. 138–43). This is the more to be regretted, since (pp. 480–90) his treatment of the literary evidence as to the early migrations which affected Sicily leaves much to be desired. Our authorities do not imply an absolute ethnological difference between Sicani and Siculi, and every year confirms the substantial value of traditions similar to those the author discards. Professor Burrows's Cretan studies and Mr. King's Babylonian show that the old scepticism is ill-advised. The probabilities are against such scepticism in Sicilian history only, and ethnology cannot distinguish between closely related peoples. It is interesting to notice that Mr. Peet's reluctance in most cases to assume the immigration of a new race (p. 140), and his conception of the relations certain to subsist between neighbours of different races (p. 252), lend no countenance to Professor Ridgeway's theory as to the conditions under which the Homeric civilization existed (cf. too p. 369). It would of course be absurd in such a work to ask for a lively and interesting style ; but it must be confessed that the expression is occasionally displeasing : ' reliable ' and ' unreliable ' (*passim* at first), ' different to ' (p. 320), ' how explain ' (p. 462)—a telegraphic note—and the bizarre archaism ' whoso wishes ' (p. 514). In a few places the author's reasoning overlooks some possibility. The neolithic axes of nephrite (but not those of other materials) may be fairly used to show whence their users originally came (p. 153), and this evidence is in harmony with that from the pearl oyster valve found at Rivaltella and the *Mitra oleacea* found in the Ligurian caves (p. 168). Again, in discussing the eneolithic cave of La Tana della Mussina (p. 197) Mr. Peet suggests that cremation may have been copied from the men of the *terremare*, although in many other places it is the strength of his argument to insist that burial customs are tenaciously preserved, and a change in them is strong evidence of a change in race (pp. 276, 280, 323, 510). If vases of Mycenaean type were found on Torcello, it does not necessarily follow that Mycenaean trade actually reached ' the top of the Adriatic ' (pp. 512, 515). That trade might reach only a centre, which was reached also from the Adriatic.

One or two suggestions, prompted by a study of the evidence adduced by Mr. Peet, may perhaps be recorded here with advantage. Colini thinks the eneolithic daggers of Italy came from some centre in the western Mediterranean (p. 261). Spain may be suggested ; Orsi (p. 282) has nearly said as much. The ornamental sticks or sceptres of the *terremare* (p. 356) may be interpreted by the practice in Homer of the heralds handing a σκῆπτρον to a speaker—it is so also in the account of Achilles' shield. The superstition, too, that wood should be touched when boastful words are uttered must be taken into account. The bone object of unknown use (p. 354, fig. 152) may be conjectured to be a shuttle (cf. the spindle whorls and loom weights found). The connexion with Bosnia in the bronze age should probably be understood to have been maintained by sea along the coast (p. 427), a view confirmed by the distribution of the fibula and Type II sword (pp. 430–1). T. NICKLIN.

Hellenistic Athens; an Historical Essay. By WILLIAM SCOTT FERGUSON. (London: Macmillan, 1911.)

THE aim of the author in this work has been to write the history of Athens from the death of Alexander the Great to the capture of the city by Sulla in 86 B.C. It is a bold undertaking from more points of view than one; for not only is the help to be obtained from previous writers fragmentary, uneven, and very often in need of criticism and correction, but in addition the story to be told suffers from the most deadly of all taints—it is dull. Mr. Ferguson has made a gallant effort to overcome the latter difficulty, and if he has not been able to obtain success, he has at any rate deserved it; nor can anything more be accomplished for the political history of Athens during this period. The inevitable consequence is that Mr. Ferguson's book suffers in part from the same defect as his subject. It is almost impossible to read steadily through the chapters which narrate the dreary history of the relations between Athens and the Macedonian princes, for despite the wealth of detail with which the author's learning has invested them, they remain ruthlessly uninteresting. But it must not be thought that the book itself is dull as a whole. Wherever Mr. Ferguson's subject permits him—wherever, that is to say, he is concerned with Athenian life and not with Athenian foreign politics—he charms and instructs his reader in exemplary fashion. From this point of view two sections of the work may be selected for special praise. One is the chapter dealing with Athens under the rule of Demetrius of Phalerum; the other is that entitled 'Athens and Delos'. In the former we have a masterly picture of Athenian life so far as it may be inferred from the Comic Fragments and the *Characters* of Theophrastus, made vivid and intelligible by interesting analogies from Christian ages; while at the same time the author does not overlook the fact that these sources are far from giving us a correct view of the ordinary private life of the average citizen. I may quote as applicable here a remark made by Boissier:

Les bonnes gens qui vont écouter aujourd'hui avec tant de plaisir les comédies en renom ne se doutent guère que la postérité les jugera d'après les pièces qu'ils applaudissent, qu'on établira doctement dans quelques siècles qu'il n'y avait chez nous ni financier honnête, ni femme vertueuse, ni ménages unis, parce qu'il a plu à nos auteurs dramatiques de ne représenter jamais que des escroqueries et des adultères.[1]

Mr. Ferguson is here, of course, on beaten ground, and his merit is simply that he has retold skilfully an oft-told tale. The chapter on Athens and Delos is quite a different matter. It treats of the history of Delos during its occupation and administration by Athens from the year 166 B.C., and for this Mr. Ferguson has been forced to rely upon his own discernment and learning, which are fortunately equal to the task. The sources are mainly epigraphical; and in this connexion the author might have used much harsher language than he does (p. 348, n. 4):

We are not yet able to continue these investigations [into fluctuations of values] beyond 166 B.C., though the materials have been in the hands of M. Homolle for a quarter of a century. Hence all that remains is to quote his generalizations.

[1] *La Religion romaine d'Auguste aux Antonins*, ii. 154.

As Mr. Ferguson is the chief living authority on this period, it would be dangerous to question any of his inferences from the evidence available, without the most elaborate consideration. But it may, perhaps, be said that some at least of these inferences are made with a boldness which the evidence hardly warrants, the author being seduced by the burning desire of every good American to 'make a story'. As regards style, the book is frankly written in the United States dialect of English, which does indeed preserve words that we have given up. Thus, Mr. Ferguson's opening line is: 'In Greece liberal institutions were acclimated,' &c. The last instance of *acclimate* quoted by *The Oxford English Dictionary* from an English writer (excluding journalists) belongs to 1856—and the writer was Charles Lever, an Irishman. Misprints are remarkably few, and so are wrong references, though the book contains thousands, made to every kind of publication; but there is one remarkable mistake which runs all through it: Kock, the editor of the Comic Fragments, is invariably called Koch. W. A. GOLIGHER.

The Religious Experience of the Roman People from the Earliest Times to the Age of Augustus. By W. WARDE FOWLER, M.A. (London: Macmillan, 1911.)

IT is needless to enlarge on the value which this book possesses for the student of Roman religion, and for that matter of religion in general; for in spite of all that has been said of the formalism and commercial spirit of the worship paid by the Roman to his gods, there can be no doubt that he was stirred by the truly religious impulse which leads primitive man to seek for the means of putting himself in right relation to the dimly conceived and deeply feared powers of surrounding nature. No one can bring greater gifts of sympathy and insight to the elucidation of the many obscurities which, from the nature of our record, beset the history of Roman religion than Mr. Warde Fowler; patiently he disentangles the ravelled skein of half-understood ritual and wholly confused tradition, and his clew seldom fails him. But the historian will also find that the book brings grist to his mill. The political importance of the *ius divinum* and its rules makes any fresh light thrown upon the story of its growth valuable to the student of the Roman constitution; and although Mr. Warde Fowler has no conjecture to offer as to the origin of the *pontifices* and their title, he has decided views, which are well worthy of consideration, about the nature of their activities. The gradual change in their functions is very clearly explained in chapter xii, and the view that the famous list of *indigitamenta* was compiled by them at an advanced date in the history of the republic is convincingly put (though not for the first time) by Mr. Fowler; we must remind him, by the way, that the great plebeian *pontifex maximus* was not *Titus* but *Tiberius* Coruncanius (p. 281).

The chief question upon which the study of Roman religion might be expected to throw some fresh light is that of the supposed mixture of races in Rome. The theory that patricians and plebeians were distinct in race, though not new, is 'in the air' at the present time. Professor

Ridgeway's tract and the laboured essay of Binder, to which Mr. Fowler draws attention, both start from the same assumption, although each raises a different fabric of hypothesis upon somewhat slender foundations. Mr. Fowler, in his earlier chapters, preserves a sceptical attitude; on p. 289 he goes so far as to call Binder's hypothesis 'improbable'; but on p. 393 he tells us that 'the conviction is steadily gaining ground that in early Rome we have to recognize the existence of two races', and furnishes what seems to him 'a really valid argument' in favour of the theory. This he sees in the double festival of the dead in the Calendar of Numa— the cheerful and orderly Parentalia in February and the grotesque and primitive Lemuria in May. The latter, he suggests, not only represents an older stratum of thought, but belongs to a more primitive race, from whom, as he believed, certain other barbarous ceremonies, such as those of the Lupercalia, were borrowed by the compilers of the patrician calendar. But is the argument conclusive? The study of the beliefs and practices of such peoples as the Greeks and Romans (to name no others) who have but recently emerged from the condition in which uncivilized man remains to this day seems to show that rudiments of savage custom remain long after they have ceased to be consistent with the newer and higher beliefs; to assume the presence of a subject race in all such cases is gratuitous. The purificatory processes of *februatio* and *lustratio* are very properly and clearly distinguished by Mr. Fowler; they imply quite different views of the nature of pollution, but that is simply because they belong to different strata in the development of Roman belief. So, too, it may be with the double festival of the dead. The *flamen dialis*, again, was hedged about with taboos for which we have to seek parallels amongst primitive peoples: yet Mr. Fowler does not suggest that he was the priest of an earlier stock, but only that he represents the 'medicine-making' king of the Latins themselves, brought to Rome from Alba because he was 'too precious to be left behind'.

There is little to criticize in the details of Mr. Fowler's work. He is less familiar with the archaeological material than with the literary record, and might have made larger use of such sources. Helbig's work, for example, seems to have escaped his notice, e.g. on the cult of the Dioscuri. Again, the temple of Castor or (to be strictly accurate) of 'the Castores', as the Romans called the Twin Brethren, was in all probability restored for the last time by Trajan or Hadrian and not in 7 B.C. Some of the references in the notes should be corrected. The same article is cited from the *Classical Review* and *Classical Quarterly* on successive pages (p. 450 f.). On p. 65 we are referred to Appendix D, where Appendix II is meant.
H. STUART JONES.

A History of English Law. By W. S. HOLDSWORTH, All Souls Reader in English Law in the University of Oxford. Vols. i–iii. (London: Methuen, 1903, 1909.)

DR. HOLDSWORTH is succeeding admirably in the accomplishment of his great task. The first three volumes of his history of English law are scholarly, enlightening, and entertaining. The author essays to write a systematic account of the long story of English legal development from the earliest times down to our own day ; and no other work of our own generation purports to cover the same vast field as that embraced in Dr. Holdsworth's plan. The printed materials at the disposal of the legal historian are, however, fairly abundant, and the unprinted materials are indeed more than abundant. Many works and essays on special subjects or special periods have been recently published, and the workers of the Selden Society and other scholars have been giving us trustworthy editions of a good many original sources. It is time, therefore, that some capable scholar should collect and consolidate the results of recent researches. But Dr. Holdsworth does much more than present the results of other men's toil. He combines with those results the gleanings of his own diligent and scholarly work upon the original sources themselves ; and if it be remarked that no scholar could adequately write of the fourteenth and fifteenth centuries with nearly all the Year Books in their present untrustworthy editions, the reply must be that to have waited for the editing of all the Year Books in the accurate fashion of Mr. Pike and the late Professor Maitland would have postponed the writing of any history of those centuries for many years to come. Dr. Holdsworth was right to proceed at once with the help of the best materials now available, and future scholars will agree that his work with reference to those centuries is singularly cautious and sound.

Volume i, which it must be remembered was published in 1903, is devoted to a history of the courts from the age of William I down to present times ; and although the Anglo-Saxon system of judicature is thus given no separate treatment, there are nevertheless occasional references to it throughout the account of the later development. We know of no better statement of the origin and growth of the English courts than that contained in this volume ; and in view of the fact that English law is largely case-law, it seems fitting that the history of the courts should precede the history of the law itself.

The subject-matter of the second and third volumes is divided into two books, the first dealing with the Anglo-Saxon period and the second with the period from the Norman Conquest to the end of the fifteenth century. In each book the writer first discusses the sources and general development, and then proceeds to a consideration of the legal rules themselves. Even though this scheme of arrangement necessarily results in a certain amount of overlapping and in repetitions, it nevertheless seems a thoroughly sound method of setting forth the development. As worked out in Dr. Holdsworth's masterly way this method certainly enables the reader to obtain a firmer grasp of the whole development, both in outlines and in details, than he usually obtains from works of legal history constructed upon other lines. His method is essentially the same as that followed by Pollock and Maitland, with such admirable results, in their history of English law down to the time of Edward I. In its main features it is very like the methods of arrangement adopted by Brunner and other continental legal historians. Dr. Holdsworth has done well to give the Anglo-Saxon period a proper and dignified place by itself, devoting to it over a hundred pages. Too often has pre-Conquest law been accorded only scanty and incidental treatment in historical productions. The Anglo-Saxon age is, however, worthy of separate and systematic treatment; and we believe, indeed, that only when it is fully and carefully studied as a distinct epoch will the legal development in later periods be seen in proper light and clear perspective. Much of the Anglo-Saxon law survived the Conquest and contributed to the growth of local, ecclesiastical, and common law in Norman and later ages. The debt of the common law to the Anglo-Saxons is recognized by Dr. Holdsworth at the very beginning of his second volume, where he says :

> We hold that we cannot date the beginnings of the common law much earlier than the first half of the twelfth century. But though we do not see the definite beginnings of the common law much before that date it is nevertheless necessary to go back behind the Norman Conquest for the origin of many of its rules. These rules of the Saxon period were, it is true, administered and shaped by Norman lawyers; and, if we are to understand the rules themselves, we must go back to the Saxon period. Without some knowledge of that period we cannot understand the law of the twelfth and thirteenth centuries (ii. 1–2).

It will be well for future historians of English law, whose studies will be immensely furthered by the completion of Professor Liebermann's monumental work on the Anglo-Saxon laws, to follow Dr. Holdsworth's example.

In this section Dr. Holdsworth does not seem to us quite to recognize the full significance of contract. He defines contract in its modern sense as 'the agreement of wills embodied in mutual promises directed towards some one subject', and then maintains that ' there is practically no doctrine of contract in Anglo-Saxon law ' (ii. 72). Certainly the modern notion of the simple contract is not to be found in Anglo-Saxon times. The contracts of early Germanic societies are 'real' and 'formal'. This is freely admitted by Dr. Holdsworth (ii. 73); but we believe it is not quite in accordance with historic fact to hold that in the period before the Conquest contract is 'but an insignificant appurtenance to the law of property', and that 'we have but a few scattered hints which must be eked out with the help of continental analogies' (ii. 72, 73). Contrary to Dr. Holdsworth's view, shared by other scholars, we hold that contract—chiefly the formal contract—played an independent and important part in Anglo-Saxon life and law, and that extant sources furnish abundant evidence of this. Originally the formal promise was used for a few special purposes, such as the buying off of the feud and the engagement to marry; but it gradually became usual for persons to bind themselves formally, for instance, by the delivery of a chattel of trifling value or by oath, for any purpose whatsoever.[1] A second feature of Dr. Holdsworth's account of the Anglo-Saxon age which calls for notice is his care in marking off minor periods and in his consequent recognition of the legal significance of the Danish invasions. Professor Vinogradoff, in his *English Society in the Eleventh Century* (pp. 4–11, 478), directed attention to the Scandinavian element in English law before the Conquest, holding that 'there is a distinct stream of Scandinavian

[1] See the present reviewer's article on 'The Formal Contract of Early English Law', in the *Columbia Law Review*, x. 608–17.

principles and practice running through this pre-conquestual legal lore', though not forgetting to remind us that ' the differences between English and Scandinavian arrangements turn out to be differences in degree and period, not in the essence of institutions'.

In the author's second book, on the medieval common law, we observe the same attention paid to minor periods. In the years from the Norman Conquest to Magna Carta we are taught to look for ' the beginnings of the common law'. The reign of Henry III is viewed as the period of 'the progress of the common law'. In Edward I's time there is 'the settlement of the sphere of the common law'. In the fourteenth and fifteenth centuries we see 'the working and development of the common law'. Dr. Holdsworth sets forth, lucidly and with emphasis on salient characteristics, the environment in which the common law took root, sprang up, and flourished. Our notice is directed to the existing body of Anglo-Saxon law, the incoming of Norman law and institutions, the influence of Roman and canon law, the growth of royal power, the rise of parliament, the establishment of common law courts, the institution of a legal profession, the growth of a mass of sources of the law and of a legal literature. In his account of the rules of law themselves, the land law, crimes and torts, contracts, persons, succession to chattels, procedure and pleading are all treated in a careful, detailed, and illuminating manner. In the appendix the reader will find specimens of original writs from the register, early conveyances, wills, and one or two other interesting texts. The first and second parts of the second book supplement each other. The story of the general development is amplified and enriched by the detailed account of definite rules of law. Only by reading both parts can one expect to obtain the breadth of view and the exact knowledge necessary to a proper understanding of the medieval law in its entirety; and surely the attentive and thoughtful reader will conclude his perusal of the second book with the firm conviction that the study of English medieval law is the study of much more than the technicalities of rules and of courts. The reader will come to see indeed that the history of England's legal past is largely, in Dr. Holdsworth's hands, the history of social progress and of the ideas developed in the course of social progress—ideas that concern the ecclesiastic, the statesman, and the philosopher, as well as the scholarly lawyer.

It is to be regretted that the author's account of crime and tort contains but two or three scattered references to conspiracy (ii. 309, 382 ; iii. 313–14), for this subject is one of considerable importance. If, as we think, Dr. Holdsworth means to hold that the criminal offence of conspiracy was created by legislation of Edward I,[2] his view receives the support of the late Mr. Justice Wright and of certain other authorities. But there is much to be said for the opinion lately expressed by Mr. James Wallace Bryan in his *Development of the English Law of Conspiracy*, that criminal conspiracy had a prior existence at the common law.[3] It is a pity, too, that the author has only touched upon a subject of the greatest

[2] See iii. 313–14.
[3] See the present reviewer's comments on Mr. Bryan's book, *ante*, xxv. (1910), 146–7.

interest, namely, the early development of equitable procedure and equitable principles in the common-law and local courts *prior* to the beginning of the chancellor's equity.[4] That here is a fertile field for original investigation is evidenced by Dr. Holdsworth's comments and by additional knowledge possessed by scholars in regard to this first stage in the development of equity. The king's court—the court of the common law itself—had already developed a procedure very like the equity of redemption and the decree of foreclosure of the later equity courts. The king's court early enforced the specific performance of contracts, and so too did the medieval local and ecclesiastical courts.

Of particular interest is the author's treatment of the incorporate person.[5] Apparently the author takes the view that the fiction theory of foreign lawyers was adopted by the courts and became naturalized in English law. Since the appearance of the work under review Sir Frederick Pollock has presented a strong argument in favour of the opposite view that no English court ever officially or semi-officially adopted the fiction theory.[6] Dr. Holdsworth rarely makes use of the sources of Teutonic law on the continent to explain and elucidate legal development in England. His work would perhaps have been strengthened in places by a fuller comparison of English with continental development. But his subject is, after all, English law, and his native sources are, in general, ample or more than ample for his purposes. As a history of English law down to the beginning of the sixteenth century the volumes before us are accurate, informing, and inspiring. They constitute a highly valuable contribution to legal and historical science.   HAROLD D. HAZELTINE.

Life of the Black Prince. By the Herald of Sir John Chandos. Edited with Linguistic and Historical Notes by MILDRED K. POPE and ELEANOR C. LODGE. (Oxford : Clarendon Press, 1910.)

A CRITICAL edition of Chandos Herald's *Life of the Black Prince* has long been needed. H. O. Coxe's edition, though a careful reproduction of the unique manuscript in Worcester College, suffers both from the inaccessibility which it shares with all the limited editions of the Roxburghe Club, and from the fact that the state of the manuscript rendered some sort of critical treatment necessary, if the sense of every passage was to be established. Of the other edition by Francisque Michel, which most workers have been compelled to use, the less that is said the better. All students of fourteenth-century history, and fourteenth-century French, will therefore feel grateful to Miss Pope and Miss Lodge for the immense toil which they have lavished in giving us an edition which is both accessible and trustworthy. It is conceived on a large scale. A 'linguistic introduction' of nearly fifty pages, followed by an 'historical introduction' of about six, prepares us to expect that the main strength of the editors has been thrown on the philological rather than the historical side of the text. Few historians on this side of the Channel are competent to criticize

[4] See, e. g., ii. 248-9, 321, 502-7 ; iii. 177.   [5] See ii. 322-37 ; iii. 362-76.
[6] See his essay in the *Festschrift für Gierke*, 1911, pp. 105-23 ; reprinted in the *Law Quarterly Review* for April 1911, pp. 219-35.

the elaborate study of the language of the poem which is here given, though they may be permitted to express their admiration for the precision, clearness, and breadth of the editors' scholarship. One reflection must, however, be permitted. However strong may be the cumulative evidence which is adduced to prove from his dialect that the writer of the poem was a compatriot of Froissart's and a native of Hainault, it seems rather a rash policy almost to rewrite the poem on this assumption, and to base the elaborate study of the language, not on the only available ancient text, but upon this modern and admittedly hypothetical reconstruction of it. In accordance with this plan the text of this edition is presented in two parallel columns. On the left hand we have a reproduction of the Worcester College manuscript, and on the right hand of each page is a normalization of it, in which, we are told, ' the suppression of recognized Anglo-French traits has been combined with a restoration of such Hainault traits as are supported by the manuscript.' No doubt the result is easier to read than is the reproduction of the crabbed Worcester manuscript, and even more certainly the success of the attempt is a remarkable testimony to the linguistic skill of the editors. It must, however, be permitted to doubt whether such a reconstruction has much historical value.

One's doubts become confirmed since the study of pp. xxix–xxxi of the introduction hardly seem to indicate that the editors rightly appreciate the full part played by the French tongue as an English vernacular language of the later fourteenth century. To them, French written in the England of Edward III must either be a ' technical or courier-like jargon ', the tongue of Langtoft or Bozon, or ' the painfully acquired accomplishment of late childhood or youth ', the language of Gower's *Mirour de l'Omme*. Such a view may not seem unreasonable to students who have concentrated their attention on the literary remains of fourteenth-century English-French. It becomes, however, almost inconceivable to those who have turned over, however superficially, the immense mass of writs, accounts, letters, and other documents, which forces them to conclude that French was an ordinary vernacular language of the English court down to the end of the fourteenth century, and that the barons and knights, who fought the battles of Edward III against the chivalry of John and Charles V, were to a large extent able to express themselves in French with almost the fluency and naturalness of their enemies. In short, the ruling and fighting classes in England spoke French, neither because they were forced to learn it by the exigencies of foreign travel, nor because they had painfully acquired it at school, but because it was a natural home-tongue of their class, and when not that, at least the cosmopolitan tongue of all western chivalry. We shall never conceive aright the social conditions of fourteenth-century England if we do not realize that the London of Edward III was, as between French and English, almost as bilingual as is twentieth-century Antwerp or Ghent between French and Flemish. This being so, it is unnecessary to suppose that because the biographer of an English hero wrote decent French we have to find for him a continental birthplace. It is even permissible to imagine that the followers of the son or husband of Queen Philippa may have acquired

Hainault tricks of speech without necessarily importing them directly from Valenciennes.

These general historic doubts are urged with all respect, and without the least wish to traverse the philological arguments of the learned editors on the part of a critic who has no claim whatever to be a philologist. One may venture to think, however, that the truth of the matter is most likely to be attained by studying the more literary Anglo-French prose of the fourteenth century on the lines so successfully followed by Maitland in his examination of the language of the Year-Books. Maitland has suggested that the contemporary law French, most easily and most frequently criticized by the modern as a corrupt jargon, was the natural, vivid, and expressive medium of generations of French-speaking, French-thinking lawyers. Would it not be better to approach from an insular, rather than from a continental point of view, a poem written for Englishmen, on the exploits of an English hero, and by a writer who was certainly an Englishman by adoption, and who may, we still believe, have been an Englishman by birth? We all have great respect for the school of Paris, but is not its present point of view the outcome of modern French conditions? The school of Valenciennes is allowed its rights as a tolerated 'provincial' speech. Is it not the historian's duty to put in a similar plea for toleration for the school of Stratford-atte-Bow? Correctness, therefore, for a text like Chandos Herald's should, in Maitland's phrase, be 'an Anglo-French correctness'. If the fourteenth-century English knight chose to call himself 'chivaler', what right has his modern editor to make him call himself a 'chevalier'? Would not the method of the editors of this book be in a sense a justification for an editor of Burns in turning the Scottish poet's vernacular lyrics into the speech in which Burns wrote his most insipid experiments in the conventional poetic language of his day?

Let me hasten to say that the normalized version of Chandos Herald, whether necessary or not, is at least absolutely innocuous. The student has side by side with it the real text to make out as best he can, and that is after all the root of the matter. This has been most carefully printed, with an exactness which records every abbreviation, and must have involved great labour. The editors give no facsimile, and a reviewer, who has not seen the manuscript, can only compare the relevant portion of their text with the short facsimile given by Michel. The austerest critic of these forty lines can only object that 'et' on lines 440 and 451 are differently printed, though expressed by the same character in the manuscript, and that the 'tresparfite' of line 452 should, if photographic accuracy be insisted on, have its s printed above the line. Those of us who hold that it is enough for an editor to set forth in extended print what he believes the author wrote will have absolutely no fault to find at all. One may venture, however, to think that the manuscript is one of rare distinctness if the n's and u's, and their like, can be clearly differentiated from each other. It is hard, then, to see why such readings as 'Reuant' for 'Renaut' (line 571), 'dantoire' for 'daucoire' (line 751), 'Ginane' for 'Guiane' (p. 46), should have been adopted, when it is surely more certain that they are wrong than that the manuscript really distinguishes forms of letters so easy to be confused ? Besides the two texts, the editors have printed an English prose translation, which is, in the light of the recognized difficulties of the text, an exceedingly valuable feature of this edition. A comparison between it and the version printed by Michel shows a very substantial advance in scholarship and coherence. A certain element of guesswork there must clearly be in any English rendering of the Worcester manuscript, and we have no reason to complain that the translators have embodied their conjectures in it, even when we wonder whether all of them are quite necessary. Punctilious in most matters, the editors sometimes allow themselves considerable latitude. It does no great harm that they occasionally shorten the English by leaving out formal phrases, put in more for rhyme than reason ; but it is hard to see why the important headlines are, in no case, translated. Also, if the last two sections of the poem, lines 4189–4280, were worth printing, it is curious that they were not worth translating or normalizing. However, on all problems that count we have in this English version a far surer guide to the meaning of Chandos Herald than has previously been available.

I have already referred to the meagreness of the historical introduction. It puts some of the chief problems clearly enough, but does not help us much further forward in solving them. The most interesting point made in it is the fact that the Amiens manuscript of Froissart is much nearer the account of the Spanish campaign written by the Herald than are the other versions. The historical notes, which follow critical notes on the text, suffer to a less extent than the introduction from excessive brevity, but it cannot be said that the authors make much effort to discuss in detail the leading moot points. Thus we are not helped to settle the very difficult question of the substantial accuracy of the Herald's account of the battle of Poitiers, and no attempt is made to determine whether or not the Herald's story is compatible or incompatible with that of Geoffrey le Baker. The most helpful notes are those dealing with the Spanish campaign, and this is as it should be, since for the whole Nájera expedition the Herald is a chief original authority. In the majority of cases, however, the historical commentary limits itself to the elucidation of details. Perhaps it would be unreasonable to expect editors to go beyond this. It is unfortunate, however, that there is some evidence of carelessness in a few small points, notably in citation of references. Very often (as on p. 186, n. 3) references are given to the page, but not to the volume of a work. The absence of any historical bibliography to correspond with the excellent linguistic bibliography adds unnecessarily to the reader's trouble. He is not always sure which edition of a book is referred to, and it requires some research to find out that the references to the *Foedera* are all to the Hague edition. What edition of Jean le Bel is used we do not know : it is certainly not the recent edition by Viard and Déprez, and it is not clear that it is the edition of Polain, since that is only in two volumes, and on p. 182, n. 6, a vol. iii of Jean le Bel is referred to. It is curious that Buchon's Froissart should ever be quoted. Some of the more recondite references are too vague to be of any use, as for instance the reference to ' Queen's Remembrancer Rolls ' on p. 180, while ' Record Office, Ancient

Correspondence, Box X' (p. 185) is not a reference that can be checked from the official list of 'Ancient Correspondence of the Chancery and Exchequer'.

Despite such occasional lapses, the historical notes deserve cordial praise for many a short and unostentatious but useful and precise elucidation of the text. As an instance, I may refer to the evidence collected that Amerigo of Pavia, though no captain of Calais, was an important personage, certainly not the mere captain of one of the towers of Calais. We are told also that Amerigo was suffered to remain at Calais after his apparent treason in January 1350. A more extensive use of the *Foedera* would have shown that he and his brother were prominent enough to be included, as one of the English king's allies, in the truce concluded six months later. And had our editors made more use of the Calendars of Patent Rolls, they might have lighted on the very significant grant to Amerigo of the large annuity of £160 for life, dated 1 February 1350, which is a conclusive evidence that the Lombard adventurer, far from betraying his trust to the king, simply fooled the French into believing that he was willing to open the gates of Calais to them, and so gave Edward III a well-used opportunity for displaying his personal prowess.

After the historical notes comes a very careful glossary, though one would have been glad to see added to it a few more words, as for example 'bacheler', which is somewhat too persistently translated as 'esquire'. In conclusion comes the index of proper names, which is also useful, especially as short biographical notes are appended. Some of the details in the notes may perhaps require reconsideration for a second edition.

In dealing with a work of erudition it is easy to take the good for granted, and to find fault with what one does not approve of. If in the present notice the tendency has been rather too much in that direction, let it be understood that my criticisms are largely of mere details, and that we all of us make a reasonable proportion of such slips. Most of my more fundamental criticism is based on a difference of point of view, which is after all a matter of opinion. For the rest, I should like to repeat my appreciation of this very useful, painstaking, and scholarly edition, and to congratulate the editors on having successfully supplied a real want in our historical literature.   T. F. TOUT.

Vie de Charles d'Orléans. Par PIERRE CHAMPION. (Paris: Champion, 1911.)

IT is a large and handsome volume which M. Champion has devoted to one of the most unfortunate French princes and eminent French poets of the fifteenth century. A life of Charles of Orleans must take account both of the entanglements and disappointments which he experienced in public affairs, and of the relief and recreation which he sought in the pursuit of literature. M. Champion has found the main theme of his book in the career rather than in the work of his hero. But the poetry of Charles of Orleans was so large a part of his life that much space is of necessity devoted to his writings and to the light which they throw on his career. The result is instructive; but the writings of the poet had no direct bearing on the career of the prince and politician, and there is no occasion here to discuss this aspect of M. Champion's book. The life of Charles of Orleans was broken by his long captivity in England. If the negotiations for his ransom gave him his greatest political importance, he had lost the best years of his life. The murder of his father and the quarrel with Burgundy forced him into politics at an early age. Still, he was little more than a boy when he was taken prisoner at Agincourt. When he returned to France twenty-five years afterwards he was a middle-aged man, and did not possess the experience, if he had possessed the ability, to play such a part in public affairs as his rank might have warranted. It is thus only in a limited way that a biography of Charles of Orleans can be a history of his time. On the other hand, a prince of the fifteenth century lived in the full daylight, and there is abundant material for the study of an attractive personality. M. Champion has made good use of his opportunity. His pages reflect in minute detail the social life of the French court, the anxieties and tribulations of the captive, and the recreations and pursuits with which he solaced his old age. The wealth of detail is sometimes overwhelming, as when several pages are devoted to a list of the prince's benefactions. Such instances are, however, exceptional.

M. Champion has the faculty to extract the human interest from a document, and has woven the material which he has thus obtained into a narrative which is full of picturesque detail and charm. It is chiefly from documents, for the most part unpublished, that he has been able to finish so completely the picture of a man whom we should otherwise know only through a few episodes and through his own writings. The most useful of M. Champion's sources are the collections made during the Revolution by Baron de Joursanvault, who rescued many precious archives from destruction. Joursanvault's collections were dispersed in 1838 ; part found their way to the British Museum, part to the Bibliothèque Nationale, and part to the Phillipps collection or elsewhere. From the Joursanvault collection the Comte de Laborde derived many of the documents in his history of the dukes of Burgundy. M. Champion has not limited his researches, but has also ransacked the public archives in Paris and London, and French municipal and departmental archives, and even the archives of Milan and Asti, for information on the connexion of Charles of Orleans with the Italian lordship and claims on Milan which he inherited from his mother. The result is admirable, and the value of the work is increased by the scrupulous care with which the authorities are cited. M. Champion is not always so successful in his use of other material. There are some traces of a lack of familiar knowledge in details relating to England. It is extraordinary to find the ' mammet of Scotland ' (the pseudo-Richard II) identified with Margaret, the future wife of Louis XI (p. 171). Henry V's helmet at Westminster is not the one which he wore at Agincourt (p. 157). Henry V was a patron, not the persecutor, of Celestins and Brigittines (p. 135). Pontefract is not in the *north* of Yorkshire (p. 167). The account of events in 1411–12 leaves something to be desired, and might have been improved by the use of other English authorities than Walsingham. Thomas Elmham is quoted several times as 'Elham', both for the genuine *Liber Metricus* and the spurious *Vita*. These are, however, minor defects which we mention only by way of correction. The volume ends with an elaborate itinerary, which fills nearly fifty pages, and a copious index. There are a number of illustrations beautifully reproduced from illuminated manuscripts.

C. L. KINGSFORD.

Savonarola nach den Aufzeichnungen des Florentiners Piero Parenti. Von JOSEPH SCHNITZER. (*Quellen und Forschungen zur Geschichte Savonarolas, IV.* Leipzig: Duncker & Humblot, 1910.)

THIS is the most important contribution to Savonarolist literature that has been made for some years. Parenti's diary has been used by all writers on this period from Ammirato and Pitti down to Ranke, Villari, and Gherardi, but for the first time the text is now printed of all portions that bear upon Savonarola. This completeness is particularly essential in Parenti's case, because his attitude towards Savonarola gradually changed, and thus from arbitrarily selected extracts it would be impossible to gather his earlier or more mature opinions. Our only regret is that Dr. Schnitzer, having given so much, is prevented by the limits of his series from giving more. The fate of Savonarola is by no means the only interesting episode of the republican experiment at Florence, and a complete edition of Parenti would be most welcome. As it is, the volume closes with Savonarola's death, though a few isolated passages, chiefly relating to revivalist preachers, carry the story down to 1517, a year before the author's death. Passages which do not bear upon Savonarola are omitted, but Dr. Schnitzer takes a liberal view of the relationship of general history to the Dominican's biography.

The main source utilized is the original manuscript of the diary, but the gap in this from April 1496 to April 1497 is fortunately filled by a sixteenth-century copy. The admirable introduction comprises a full account of Parenti and his family, bearing especially on his close relationship to the Strozzi, a summary of his account of Savonarola, and an invaluable criticism of his trustworthiness as an authority, and of the reasons for his change from ardent admiration for Savonarola to pronounced hostility. Parenti has the advantage of writing as a full-grown man, highly educated, of undoubted position in the city, with friends or relations in either camp. Of his two rival authorities, Cerretani and Guicciardini, neither is so strictly contemporary. The latter, however, was of a particularly impressionable age, between fifteen and sixteen, at the time of Savonarola's death, and wrote his youthful work, the *Storia Fiorentina*, only a few years later, while his father from first to last played a more prominent part than Parenti himself, and was notorious for his moderation.

Parenti's early enthusiasm for Savonarola was natural enough. A Strozzi on his mother's side, he might tolerate the genial despotism of Lorenzo de' Medici, but rejoiced in the fall of the bearish and incompetent Piero. A republican of the classical, humanistic type, he saw in Savonarola's political reforms the prospect of an ideal state wherein merit alone was the passport to office. He welcomed the purification of public morals, and, if this was rather from ethical than spiritual motives, he had no great respect for the papacy and its claims. But by degrees the illusion vanished. Dr. Schnitzer gives as the primary reason Parenti's indignation at Savonarola's intervention in favour of the partisans of the Medici, which saved them from proscription. The text hardly seems to bear this out, except in the case of Ser Giovanni delle Riformagioni, an unpopular Medicean agent whom Parenti represents as owing his escape to liberal benefactions to S. Marco. He recognizes that the ablest Mediceans necessarily worked their way back to power, because they alone had administrative experience. Full weight is, however, given to his dislike for Savonarola's pro-French policy, and this would appear to have been the determining cause for Parenti's change of attitude. If he did not dream with Macchiavelli of Italian unity, he at least longed for an Italy rid of barbarians. As a man of business he knew that prosperity could only return with the recovery of Pisa, and that depended upon union with the Italian league. And so at length he breaks out against Savonarola and his Francophil preaching as being the ruin of Italy. Other causes doubtless contributed. The families with whom he was most closely allied, the Strozzi, the Nerli, and the Morelli, were among the leaders of the aristocratic opposition, and, though he had dissociated himself from this aristocratic ring on the constitutional question, he could in foreign policy meet them on common ground. His church, moreover, was Santa Croce, and here the Franciscans never ceased to denounce their Dominican rival. To the humanist and man of business their more practical point of view must in the long run appeal rather than Savonarola's mystical and prophetic utterances, especially when his prophecies ceased to find fulfilment. The decisive moment was, however, when Valori, after long hesitation, definitely put himself at the head of the Savonarolist party. Henceforth the republic meant government by faction, and to the victors went the spoils. The chief interest, indeed, of the diary is that of a study in Florentine faction, and that is why a continuation of the volume until the fall of the republic would have been so welcome. Parenti was not so much moved as other writers by the annoying raids of Savonarola's troop of children, nor yet by the papal threats of interdict. To Savonarola himself, indeed, he rarely shows personal hostility ; the worst that can be said, is that he was not spiritual enough to understand him. But the system must go, and this was impossible without his death. It is noticeable that, when the new Eight (the Committee of Justice) was appointed with an express view to Savonarola's condemnation, Parenti was a member.

In the text all the incidents of the four fateful years find illustration. Parenti points out that after the failure of the ordeal by fire the Signoria was reluctant to take active measures against Savonarola himself ; it diverted the attack from S. Marco to Valori's palace, and was only forced by public pressure to arrest the preacher, and then would willingly have allowed the case ' to run into the sand '. But the opposite faction could now control the official government, which all Savonarola's reforms had rather weakened than strengthened ; nothing, indeed, could be less like the Venetian constitution, upon which model the Florentine republic had been avowedly built up. One of Parenti's merits, as indeed of Guicciardini's, is to give lists of the leading adherents of the several factions.

Thus it is interesting to find that among prominent Mediceans who were confined in the Palazzo Pubblico when Piero de' Medici made his feeble movement against the Porta Romana, were not only the future life-gonfalonier Piero Soderini, the darling of the liberal party, but the choicest spirits among the later patriotic and progressive leaders, Luca Albizzi and Alamanno and Jacopo Salviati. It is hard to resist the conclusion that the Mediceans had ruled and were restored to power because they alone were capable of wielding it. It was ominous that as early as February 1497 the peasantry who had flocked into Florence for the municipal doles raised the cry of *Palle! Palle!* under the very windows of the Signoria. Even Parenti ultimately submitted, and, as Dr. Schnitzer suggests, he may well have thought of his Strozzi grandmother's saying, *Chi sta co' Medici sempre ha fatto bene.*

E. ARMSTRONG.

A History of French Architecture from the reign of Charles VIII till the death of Mazarin. By REGINALD BLOMFIELD, A.R.A., M.A. 2 vols. (London : Bell, 1911.)

The Architecture of the Renaissance in France, 1495–1830. By W. H. WARD, M.A. 2 vols. (London : Batsford, 1911.)

THESE two books appeared almost simultaneously; they do not, however, conflict, but rather complement one another, and together they form an ample record of a phase of architecture probably more thorough than any other works which we have. Not only to architects, but surely also to all historians who would understand modern France, these volumes will be of great service. It is a commonplace that architecture is the mirror of history, but nowhere is it more perfectly true than of the period dealt with in these volumes. Professor Blomfield's handsome book covers a shorter time than Mr. Ward's does, and therefore the treatment is more spacious, there is more room for general considerations and for particular criticism, and as far as possible the account is gathered round the names of the great architects as they succeeded one another. The illustrations are excellent; many of the 178 plates are from the author's own drawings. Slight as some of these drawings are—or possibly because they are so slight—they make admirable foils to the reproductions of old prints. The study of Mansart's ceiling at Blois (plate clv) is a masterly piece of swift draughtsmanship. Mansart, it may be remarked, is Professor Blomfield's hero ; of the staircase at Blois he writes that it alone would justify Mansart's reputation as ' the finest domestic architect of the world '. The text is clear and fresh, and often most energetic ; thus on the Pitti palace, which Ruskin had praised, we have the remark :

> On the whole, it is about the most brutal design for a palace front ever perpetrated, and its only possible justification might be that Luca Pitti, who built it, needed a fortress for himself and his ruffians.

In his work, which contains 528 pages and 465 illustrations, large and small, Mr. Ward gives an admirably full account of the architecture of France, from the time when Gothic architecture began to change under the influence of Italian ideals, until the end of the restored monarchy. The text is close packed with facts, the illustrations—which are mostly photographic—are well selected to elucidate the text, and there is a remarkably full bibliography and an exhaustive index. Mr. Ward has made himself a specialist on the architecture of France in the period covered by his work, and his results may be accepted with confidence.

It is interesting to find in the works illustrated in these books the sources for many English designs. Thus the Luxembourg palace, with its Court of Honour screened from the street by a cloister-walk with a cupola above the central entrance, must have been the prototype of Montague House, Bloomsbury, and of Queen's College, Oxford. Professor Blomfield speaks of some spires built by Lemercier 'which anticipate in general treatment what Wren was to do in the City churches'. Wren honourably acknowledged our architectural debt to France: we copied their works at all times, he says, 'imitating them even when we were at war with them.'
W. R. LETHABY.

Die Anfänge Karls V. Von ANDREAS WALTHER. (Leipzig: Duncker & Humblot, 1911.)

DR. ANDREAS WALTHER has the courage to select perhaps the most difficult period in Burgundian history for his elaborate studies. His former book, *Die burgundischen Zentralbehörden unter Maximilian I. und Karl V.*, which, by an unfortunate accident, was not here reviewed, traced the evolution of the central administration down to the time when the differentiated councils appear under the Spanish domination as the Three Collaterals, familiar to readers of the revolt in the Netherlands. This process, in itself distinct from that of France, was complicated by the greater vitality of provincial institutions, such as the Court of Holland, and, above all, by the exotic experiments of Charles the Bold and Maximilian. Wherever Maximilian appears, he creates difficulty, and it is to him that Dr. Walther now returns, for, though he remains in the background, his inconsequent actions tangle the threads of Burgundian policy until the death of Ferdinand the Catholic at least.

As the first book was exclusively constitutional, so is this pre-eminently personal. The author shows that the interest of this period consists in the relation of the government to the great nobles, who had neither sunk to the position of a court nobility, confined to ceremonial offices, nor had retained their feudal isolation. They were now alike powerful in their provinces and in the ducal councils. The institution of the Golden Fleece had given them a peculiar prominence, almost forming, as it did, a council of state with wide powers of criticism and remonstrance. An account, therefore, of the principal families is a necessary introduction to the history of these years, and this gradually narrows itself down to the personality of Guillaume de Croy, lord of Chièvres, who until his death dominated Charles V's court, and who is the hero of Dr. Walther's story. From the treaty of Arras (1435) onward three groups of noble families seem fairly constant in their relation to the two poles of Burgundian policy, the friendship of France or of England, and this is determined in great measure by provincial commercial interests. The nobility of Flanders and Hainault, headed by the house of Croy, leans towards France, and demands protection against the English woollen trade, whereas that of North Brabant and the later Dutch provinces is in favour of free trade and friendship with England. To this party belong the houses of Berghes and Egmont. It finds an ally in an old military, feudal section, headed by the house of Luxemburg, and lying near Calais and the later English conquest of Tournai, which had never given up its sympathy for England. A somewhat neutral, purely personal position was held by Henry of Nassau, not himself a Netherlander, but the richest landholder in the provinces.

Parallel to this valuable analysis Dr. Walther adds one of the chief Castilian families, which after Isabella's death stood in much the same relation to Ferdinand as did the Netherland groups to Maximilian. As is well known, on Philip's second visit to Spain civil war was with difficulty avoided. When his death left his supporters at Ferdinand's mercy, many of them took refuge in the Netherlands, and formed a natural alliance with the party of Chièvres, whose French proclivities they shared. Their attitude towards Maximilian and Margaret varied with the fluctuations of hostility and friendship between Ferdinand and the Habsburgs. To complete his ground plan the author adds a useful chapter on the peculiar importance of Franche-Comté, as furnishing the jurists and diplomatists who almost monopolized the administration under Margaret's regency and during Charles V's reign. This is ascribed to the fact that this province was the centre of the study of Roman law, and to its geographical position, which gave it a curiously international character. To this must be added the industry and brains of the Burgundians, who were to the Netherlands as later the Scots to England, and were consequently unpopular. A later chapter shows that in their own province the jurists did not have it all their own way, for the feudal nobility offered stout resistance to their centralizing tendencies, and finally defeated their ablest champion, the great Gattinara, himself, indeed, a Piedmontese.

When, after Philip's death, Maximilian appointed Margaret as his representative in the Netherlands, he gave her as counsellors members of the three chief families, Croy, Luxemburg, and Berghes. He weakened her authority by withholding the full title and powers as regent until 1509, and then, as if to thwart her, he promoted Chièvres to the office of first chamberlain and governor of Charles. Hitherto the leading jurists had long been Burgundians, but now both the chancellorship and presidency of the council were held by Jean le Sauvage, a Fleming of the party of Chièvres. All Margaret's traditions were anti-French; her personal desire was for an Anglo-Spanish alliance. A clash, therefore, with Chièvres was sooner or later inevitable, especially as Charles gave his whole reverence and affection to his governor. Netherland nobles naturally began to form a party round the young duke, and this assumed the appearance of a nationalist opposition to an alien regency. The party was reinforced by the Castilian refugees, and it was over them that the first open trial of strength took place.

Maximilian, by joining the Holy League in April 1513, was reconciled to Ferdinand, who persuaded the Netherland government to arrest their leader, Juan Manuel. Their Burgundian allies prepared for resistance, the Golden Fleece protested, and the government prosecution broke down. This was only one of many failures. From want of troops and money Margaret had been unable to continue the ruinous Gueldrian war; her generals resigned, even the bureaucrats began to desert her. Just as she seemed to have revived the old Burgundian-Anglo-Spanish alliance, Ferdinand, who cared mainly to secure his conquest of Navarre, made his peace with France. Owing to misunderstandings in the recent war there was coolness between the pro-English Burgundian party and their allies. The final blow was the marriage of Mary Tudor to Louis XII. By the middle of 1514 Margaret's cause was clearly hopeless, and on 7 January 1515, somewhat to her surprise, the declaration of Charles's majority brought her regency to its close.

In his enthusiasm for Chièvres Dr. Walther seems a little less than fair to Margaret. It was she, after all, who, surrendering her prejudices, negotiated the league of Cambrai, in order to give the provinces relief on the side of Guelders. It was no easy task to persuade Maximilian, who was bent rather on a French campaign, and still less easy to reconcile Ferdinand, who in the war of 1508 had favoured Venice. She, too, brought England into line by the betrothal of Charles and Mary Tudor. It is true that she soon repented, and strove to detach Maximilian from Louis XII, but for this the rapid French successes against Venice were sufficient reason. When Maximilian resisted or delayed the appointment of a separate household for Charles, Margaret settled the matter on her own responsibility, somewhat to her own disadvantage, and greatly to her father's displeasure. The author always speaks of Chièvres and his following as the nationalist party, but that of Berghes was equally national, and perhaps the future was rather with it. Protection for the southern provinces and free trade for the northern may be regarded as programmes equally reasonable. Margaret's difficulties should be duly weighed. The unpopular Gueldrian war was the main cause of her failure, but the quarrel began before her birth, and was only ended by Charles V long after her death. Chièvres would have married the irrepressible duke of Guelders to one of Charles's sisters, but this would only have been a palliative, and future history was to prove that the absorption of Guelders was necessary to the Netherlands, however unjust its original annexation. Margaret, after all, was ruling for Maximilian, and must consider the welfare of the dynasty, and not only of the Netherlands. If Maximilian had loyally supported her, she might possibly have succeeded, but no reliance could be placed upon him. At one moment she is complaining of his *lettres rudes*, at another she dockets his instructions with the words, *De ce que l'Empereur veult charger Madame d'avoir esté toujours de contraire opinion à la sienne.* There is no reason to think that she would have opposed the declaration of Charles's majority; she resented only that it had been prepared by her government and her father behind her back. Nor did she sulk; she is described as looking fresher and prettier than ever, which is incompatible with sulks. By the close of the following year she was reconciled to

Chièvres, and, though she was somewhat shelved, as soon as a difficult international task reappeared in the election to the empire, it was to Margaret's diplomatic experience that recourse was had.

Defence of Margaret is no depreciation of Chièvres. He had fought her with much skill and not unfairly, and when at the head of the new government he used his power with moderation. At first, indeed, he formed a close cabinet by excluding his opponents from all important deliberations, but feeling that this was provoking general resentment, he based his government upon the moderates of both parties, coming to terms even with his rival Berghes. Though he naturally made immediate peace with France, he followed this up by English treaties. Dr. Walther enters into an elaborate defence of Chièvres against his Spanish critics, showing that their ideal of central government, and their very humanistic culture, were antagonistic to the old-world, quasi-feudal traditions of Chièvres. He was blamed for allowing a year and a half to pass after Ferdinand's death before Charles was allowed to visit Spain. Dr. Walther makes good his case that this was none too much time for making a definite peace with France for persuading Maximilian to give up his long-drawn hostilities against Venice, to extract money from England for the voyage, and to reconcile all parties within the Netherlands. The Castilian malcontents had expected a monopoly of office under the new régime. But Charles was now king of Aragon also, and Chièvres gave employment to several of Ferdinand's confidants, though generally not in the political but in the diplomatic service, for which they possessed an admirable training. Criticism of Chièvres has usually been directed not against his Burgundian but against his Spanish policy. Dr. Walther agrees with Baumgarten in regarding the treaty of Noyon as a mere blind to secure Charles's safe conveyance to Spain: Chièvres told the English ambassador that when once in Spain he would no longer speak on his knees, but upright. The Spaniards, however, knowing that its provisions accorded with the minister's previous policy, were naturally affronted. It is difficult to defend the tactless behaviour of Charles's advisers on his Spanish visit, and impossible to excuse the elevation of the boy cardinal of Croy to the see of Toledo. This does not, however, form part of the present volume.

The concluding chapter contains a useful collection of contemporary and contradictory opinions on the personality of Charles, and admirably put is the contrast between the character and life-work of Chièvres and his successor Gattinara. Chièvres had taught Charles that work is a king's duty; he had impressed upon him the conservatism, the seriousness, perhaps even the romanticism, of the old order; his steady, tranquil temperament had moulded the boy's character. He had brought him to the threshold of the empire, but it was not for him to pass it. To give the wider outlook, the more progressive policy, were the tasks of Gattinara, the humanist, the international statesman, familiar with all courts, passionate in his ideal of the empire of which his young master was the symbol, and brooking no opposition from the unpractical survivals of the feudal past.

E. ARMSTRONG.

Johannes Sichardus und die von ihm benutzten Bibliotheken und Handschriften. Von PAUL LEHMANN. (*Quellen und Untersuchungen zur lateinischen Philologie des Mittelalters*, iv. 1. München: Beck, 1911.)

THE publication of the present work is a gratifying proof that the valuable series to which it belongs has not ceased with the third volume. The author, one of the foremost pupils of the late Dr. Traube, has already contributed to the same series a monograph on Franciscus Modius, which was most favourably noticed in these pages (xxiii. 787 f., 1908). The promise of the early volume is more than fulfilled in this, where a similar topic is essayed. Sichardus had a remarkably successful career in the publication of first (or early) editions of various classical and theological works, and, in view of the appalling loss of manuscripts used in the preparation of such editions, the publication of scientific works like the present is imperative. All the more is this the case that modern editors too often assume there is nothing of value in the earliest printed editions that has not descended to their modern successors, whereas the fact is otherwise. The work is divided into two parts, the first and shorter dealing with the life of Sichardus and presenting the text of twenty-three of his letters. The second part, which is a consummate model of lucid arrangement, contains a list of Sichardus's publications, followed by a general account of his journeys and investigations, and then by a detailed account of the manuscripts he used and of the medieval libraries in which he found them. Admirable indexes conclude the work.

The reader will be impressed not only by the qualities already named, but by the easy command which Dr. Lehmann possesses of the most recondite books and articles, ancient and modern, which are in any way associated with his subject. It is no light task merely to master the relations of the Basle group of scholars in the first third of the sixteenth century, but in this sphere, too, he moves about with perfect ease. The many new facts concerning the medieval libraries of Germany, which are communicated to us, will not surprise those who know that Dr. Lehmann has been for some time engaged in the preparation of a new critical and comprehensive edition of all the surviving medieval catalogues of these libraries. His expert knowledge has enabled him to provide us with many *opera supererogatoria*, which are far from constituting the least important part of the book. The identification of surviving manuscripts belonging to the old German libraries is one of the most fascinating, if one of the most saddening, of his achievements. No student of medieval libraries can afford to neglect this section, and the book as a whole will be most useful to all editors of Latin texts.

A few notes may be given, if only to show with what care and pleasure the book has been read. P. 32, l. 29, read probably *reprehenderet*; p. 39, &c., I miss a reference to the fact that Dom Morin published the catalogue of the Gorze library in the *Revue Bénédictine* for 1905; p. 41, letter 23, l. 3, perhaps read *assessorum*; p. 48, 'Quesnel' is more usual than 'Quesnell'; p. 57, l. 7 from foot, for ' 1881 ' read ' 1891 '; p. 62, only the first volume of Radermacher's *Quintilian* has appeared, and for ' Lehnerdt ' read ' Lehnert '; p. 66, the edition of Frontinus's book on Roman aqueducts by Lanciani might have been mentioned; p. 70, l. 3, read *sumere* (?); p. 75, n. 5, read *exemplum*; p. 84, l. 4 from foot, a misprint; p. 120, l. 13, read *uera* (?); p. 130, n. 2, it would be better to refer to the second edition of Mommsen's *Solinus* (Berlin, 1895), p. xlix; p. 132, n. 2, add references to Merrill's and Kukula's editions, &c., of the Younger Pliny; p. 135, l. 10 from foot, a misprint; p. 139, l. 11, ought not xi to be ix?; p. 144, l. 5 from foot, read *Liuore* (?); p. 151, n. 3, read 'Troussures'; p. 156, l. 6 from foot, read *profanas*; p. 157, ll. 8 f., Dr. Lehmann has overlooked Hilberg's Vienna edition of Jerome's *Epistles*, published in May 1910; p. 168, n. 2, a misprint; p. 170, l. 7, and in index, read 'Rylands'; p. 182, n. 1, surely '1529' should be read for '1528'; p. 184 f., Dr. Lehmann appears to have overlooked Bergman's investigation of the manuscripts of Prudentius in the Vienna *Sitzungsberichte* for 1908; p. 190, where Chifflet's reference (1681) to 'S. Maximini Treuerensis codex peruetustus' of Bede might be added, n. 6 is misnumbered 5; p. 195, l. 1 read *commendabiles*, l. 5 read *scriptorum*; p. 203, l. 19, read *Carolum* (?); p. 204, perhaps add a reference to Clark's *Ammianus*, vol. i (1910); p. 207, Dr. Lehmann might have mentioned also the edition of Cassiodorus's *Institutio* announced to appear in Teubner's *Bibliotheca*; p. 209, l. 7, read *inchoatam* (?); p. 213, l. 7 from foot, read 'Mopsuestia'; p. 214, l. 2 from foot, read *Religiosissimi*; p. 219, a reference to Rose's edition (Leipzig, 1894) of Theodore Priscian might have been in place; p. 221, a reference might have been given to Sirmond's later discovery of these commentaries on St. Paul by Victorinus in a Belgian (Herenthals) manuscript; p. 221, l. 14, read *minimam*. ALEX. SOUTER.

Accounts of the Lord High Treasurer of Scotland. Edited by Sir JAMES BALFOUR PAUL, LL.D., Lord Lyon King of Arms. Vol. ix: 1546–51. (Edinburgh: H.M. General Register House, 1911.)

THIS is the eighth volume of treasurer's accounts which has been published under the capable editorship of Sir James Balfour Paul. Like its immediate predecessor, it suffers to some extent by the fact that it belongs to a period when the sovereign of Scotland was a minor. The picturesque and romantic interest attaching to the movements of James IV and James V, of which the editor made so good a use, is lacking in the documents which refer to the doings of the Regent Arran. He and his family occur often enough on the 'discharge' or expenditure side of the ledger; they occupy eight columns of the index, and we are told the sums expended upon his eldest son's nightgown, upon the lining of his younger son's 'brekis', and upon the trousseau of his eldest daughter. 'Armosene' was brought from the island of Ormuz for the regent's tunic; his napkins were of 'camrage' from Cambray; his present to the nurse when he became a godfather was paid by the state; a 'bair hat of felt' was purchased 'to make ane welwote hat' for him, the felt costing five shillings and the velvet three pounds fifteen shillings. There is thus plenty of incidental material for social and economic history in the volume, and the editor has solved most of the problems of this kind. The most interesting explanation (for which he acknowledges indebtedness to Dr. George Macdonald and Dr. Joseph

Anderson) is a payment to an officer who went to Haddington ' to discharge the taking of the bagcheik grottis ', i.e. to prohibit the circulation of the English coins with which Lord Grey, the English commander at Haddington, would attempt to purchase necessaries. ' Bagcheek ' is a not inappropriate term for the full-faced effigy of Henry VIII.

The importance of the volume for political history lies in the light it throws on the details of Anglo-Scottish warfare; the siege of the castle of St. Andrews, the ultimately successful attacks upon the English garrisons at Broughty Ferry and Haddington, and the battle of Pinkie. The Scottish preparations can be reconstructed from these pages, and the delay in the capture of the fortresses is partly explained by such an entry as a payment for the carriage to St. Andrews of sixty stones of lead from the roof of the great hall of the abbey of Holyrood. There is a reference to the fiery cross before Somerset's invasion, but, as the entry refers to the carriage of ' letters with the fyre croce ', Sir James Paul is doubtless right in regarding it as a figurative expression. We have some information in the accounts about the ineffective Scottish artillery at Pinkie and the safe removal of some of it after the battle, and there is a recorded payment for carts ' to helpe to erd the deid folkes be the space of twa dayes '. The records also throw light on the assistance given by France to the Scots, and, possibly on the unpopularity of the French in Scotland : ' Memorandum. That the France men promisit to haf payit this money ... and nevir payit ane d thairof.' The St. Andrews bakers, too, had to be paid for bread furnished to the French at the siege of Broughty, ' for quhilk the Franchemen wald mak na payment.' The editor's introduction provides a masterly survey of the contents of the volume, and the index is beyond reproach.   ROBERT S. RAIT.

Ostfrieslands Handel und Schiffahrt im 16. Jahrhundert. Von Dr. BERNHARD HAGEDORN. (*Abhandlungen zur Verkehrs- und Seegeschichte*, Bd. iii. Berlin : Curtius, 1910.)

THE trade and shipping of Emden, the leading port of East Friesland, rose from a condition of comparative insignificance during the struggle between Spain and France in the middle of the sixteenth century. Before the peace of Cateau-Cambrésis it had outpaced its old rival Groningen, and was abreast with such Dutch ports of the second rank as Enkhuizen and Hoorn. During the seven years' war of the Baltic states (1563–70) Emden came to take a leading part in the trade through the Sound. The outbreak of the Dutch war of liberation occasioned a still more rapid development. On the one hand Emden afforded the nearest refuge for the crowds of Calvinist emigrants, whilst on the other hand it took over as the nearest neutral port the largest part of the carrying trade temporarily lost by Holland, and furnished the most convenient dépôt for the transshipment of supplies to the region of the war. By 1569 Emden could boast a larger carrying trade than any other port in Europe (in 1570 the shipping in the ports of East Friesland exceeded that of the whole of England), and this pre-eminence, in spite of considerable decline after 1573, it maintained for thirty years.

A development so extraordinary gives Emden an undeniable claim for separate consideration in the excellent series of handbooks, promoted by the Hansischer Geschichtsverein, on the history of commerce and navigation. It has found a worthy historian in Dr. Hagedorn, who combines a close acquaintance with the local archives with a scholarly control of the wider literature that surrounds the subject, and who possesses, to a degree rarely found in so learned a writer, the gift of clear and lively narrative. In the first of his four sections Dr. Hagedorn describes the economic conditions prevailing in East Friesland at the beginning of the sixteenth century; its dependence on foreign supplies of grain and timber and beer; its export trade in cattle and dairy produce; its industries of brick-making, linen-weaving, and fishing; its trading relations with the neighbouring Oldenburg and Westphalia, with Amsterdam, Hamburg, and Bremen, and with Scandinavia. The second section is devoted to the development of the port of Emden during the first half of the sixteenth century. This period has two opposite aspects—a struggle of a distinctively medieval character to assert the staple-rights of Emden over the trade up and down the river Ems against the rival port of Groningen, and the achievement by Emden of a share in the larger carrying trade which supplied northern Europe with French salt and furnished Portugal with corn from the Baltic. The effects of the international complications of the sixties on the trade of Emden are dealt with in the third section, which is mainly occupied with the protestant immigration and with the experimental settlement of the Merchant Adventurers during the tariff dispute between England and the Netherlands. The fourth and much the longest section of the book describes the culmination of Emden's prosperity during the operations of the 'Sea Beggars' who made their head-quarters in the neighbourhood. The naval situation in the years 1568–76 is one of such extraordinary interest, and Dr. Hagedorn has found so much new and valuable evidence concerning it in the Emden records, that he has altered the original plan of his work so as to give a full and admirable description of it. But the book's unity of design suffers by the change, and the foreign student of economic history, who has not ready access to the *Hansische Geschichtsblätter*, to which Dr. Hagedorn has relegated his statistical and technical account of the commerce of Emden, will lose by it.[1]

The English student will especially miss the account of the later relations of the Merchant Adventurers with Emden. But this ought not to diminish his gratitude for the excellent account of the settlement in 1564 and of the three-cornered conflict of England, the Hanse, and the Netherlands that led to it. By no means the least of the debts that will be owed to the Dutch and German and Belgian scholars by the English historian of the Merchant Adventurers when he or she takes up the tardy pen will be due to Dr. Hagedorn for these chapters. But it may be hoped that that historian will not accept without question the neo-mercantilist implications that underlie the writings of most German and some English

[1] Since this review was printed we are glad to see that the objection in the text has been forestalled by the continuation of Dr. Hagedorn's account of Emden in another volume of the series which has appeared recently.

scholars dealing with this period :—the assumption that the economic future of England and of Germany was a stake won and lost in the game of sixteenth-century diplomacy, that the rigid and unscrupulous monopoly of the Merchant Adventurers, aided by the *konsequente Politik* of Gresham and Burghley and supported by the alternate effrontery and sinuosity of Elizabeth, laid the foundations of the commercial and industrial supremacy of Great Britain, and that if the Hanseatic League had combined at the critical moment to show a firm front to the aggressor the whole course of subsequent history might have been different. The real factors of English economic development were far beyond the knowledge and control of Gresham and Burghley; and not even the statesmanship of a Bismarck could have restored the vitality of the Hanse in the sixteenth century.
GEORGE UNWIN.

Histoire de Belgique. Par H. PIRENNE. iv: La Révolution politique et religieuse; Le Règne d'Albert et d'Isabelle; Le Régime espagnol jusqu'à la Paix de Munster. (Bruxelles: Lamartin, 1911.)

THE fourth volume of M. Pirenne's history of Belgium covers the most critical period in the evolution of that country, the eighty years between Alva's arrival in the Netherlands and their definite separation into two states in 1648. The story has naturally been an attractive subject to the Dutch and their protestant sympathizers; but for the southern provinces it was a tragedy with little relief, and M. Pirenne has had few precursors in the field of Belgian history from the death of Alexander Farnese to the conclusion of the Thirty Years' War.

The ultimate causes of the separation have been generally traced to either race or religion, and M. Pirenne is a stanch advocate of the latter theory.

Ce serait [he writes, p. 136] une erreur complète que de chercher les motifs de ce revirement dans la différence de mœurs et de langage qui distinguait l'une de l'autre la population romaine et la population flamande.... Ce n'est point à une lutte de races, c'est à une lutte confessionnelle que va nous faire assister la défection des provinces wallonnes, ou, pour mieux dire, de la majorité des provinces wallonnes. Elles n'abandonnent leurs compatriotes que pour sauvegarder leur foi catholique contre le calvinisme triomphant.

M. Pirenne might have quoted in support of this view a letter to the English government written in January 1578/9, ' the war which is about to begin will be a war for religion '; and it is clear that the majority of the Walloons preferred catholicism with Spain to independence with the Dutch. But would they have made the choice they did had they been Dutch, or the Dutch Walloons? Calvinistic violence at Ghent and elsewhere doubtless alienated thousands of catholics, but may not the decisive factor have been a fear lest the Dutch should prove as domineering in other spheres of action as they were in the religious, a suspicion that an independence shared with the Dutch would be no independence at all, but a partnership in which Walloon trade and industry as well as Walloon religion would be at the mercy of the more stubborn and enterprising members of the firm ? Surely the economic importance of the sea was already differentiating the seafaring Dutch from the land-loving Walloons before the Walloons were faced in 1578 and the following years with the dilemma of choosing between subordination to Calvinistic sea-dogs and subjection to catholic Spain.

However that may be, the issue was the result of many complex causes, and the Walloons themselves in 1578 were not consciously sacrificing their autonomy to their faith. They fondly hoped that they could preserve them both, and that Spain would protect their religion without demanding their independence as the price of its protection. Many of the hardiest or most schismatic Walloons had embraced Calvinism and migrated to Holland and Zealand, and the more submissive remainder were incapable of self-defence. Alexander Farnese was allowed to recall the Spanish troops, the Walloon forces were reduced to insignificance, and the reconciled provinces gradually relapsed into a subjection from which they had only been raised by the support of their stronger compatriots. Their states-general made feeble efforts in 1600 and 1632 to escape the atrophy imposed by Spanish kings, who in the words of Philip IV held that states-general were 'pernicious at all times and in all monarchical countries without exception'; but after 1632 they did not meet again till 1788. The provincial states, indeed, survived in Belgium as in France; and the retention of its *joyeuse entrée* by Brabant gave it an opportunity in the revolution of that year. But the particularism of these provincial states was perhaps in Belgium, as in France, an obstacle rather than a help to the development of national representation.

Belgium, however, was not even permitted a despotic government of its own. Philip II's devolution of sovereignty upon Albert and Isabella was a mockery, the hollowness of which became more and more apparent; political authority was wielded by Spanish generals or by Spanish secretaries of state, nominated at Madrid, irresponsible to the states-general, and irremovable by the nominal rulers of Belgium. The Belgians, like the English under Philip and Mary, were not permitted to trade with the Spanish Indies; it was in vain that the states-general in 1632 anticipated the Emperor Charles VI with the demand for the formation of an Ostend East India Company; and finally Belgium was made to pay the price for the treaty of Münster by the permanent closing of the Scheldt and the ruin of Antwerp.

Privé de la libre disposition de lui-même [writes M. Pirenne, p. 288] il ne sera plus qu'un corps sans âme, qu'une matière à traités, qu'une barrière, qu'un champ de bataille . . . les provinces n'ont échappé à l'hérésie qu'au prix de la ruine.

Catholicism, indeed, gave the court at Brussels its *éclat* in the first half of the seventeenth century. Encouraged by the piety of Albert and Isabella, Belgium became the *pied-à-terre* of the religious orders in northern Europe, and in particular of the Jesuits, who almost monopolized Belgian education, literature, and culture. But again, it was at the price of Belgian nationality; the Walloon language was sacrificed to Latin, and lost its chance of becoming the vehicle for a national literature. Belgian art was glorified in Rubens; but Rubens embodies the counter-reformation rather than Belgian nationality: he founded no school and left no tradition in his native country.

It would be partially true, but not quite fair, to say that M. Pirenne belongs to the school of Lamprecht and J. R. Green rather than to that of Ranke and Gardiner. He writes with a graphic pen, but he has no love for 'drum and trumpet' history ; and his account of the wars which fill so much of these eighty years is the barest summary of events. He is something of a psychologist and also of an economist, and his surveys of intellectual and economic conditions are among the best parts of his book. His impartiality is admirable : at least we have not been able to discover from this volume his personal *parti pris*. It goes without saying that in a general history of Belgium from the earliest times, planned on a scale of six or seven moderate volumes, details have to be suppressed, and economy practised in the resort to original sources. Confronted with this necessity, M. Pirenne has somewhat rigidly restricted himself to domestic materials. Belgium, it is true, had no foreign policy during this period ; but foreign archives contain a mass of information on Belgian domestic politics, and we are a little surprised to find no reference to the English *Foreign Calendar* or the Spanish *Documentos Inéditos*. We do not, however, imagine that these sources would have materially modified many of M. Pirenne's conclusions, though his view of the negotiations between Elizabeth and Anjou might have been among them. M. Pirenne is perhaps a little emphatic on the cardinal-archduke's mediocrity as a general : did not Henry IV say that one of the three things which were true but would never be believed was that Albert was a good general ? And need we attribute to Charles V and Philip II the conventional characteristic of a desire for 'domination universelle' (p. 4) ? But these trifles do not obscure the facts that M. Pirenne is writing a very good general history of Belgium, and that historical students were very much in need of such a book. A. F. POLLARD.

Archives du Musée Teyler. Série II, vol. xii. Deuxième Partie : *Correspondance inédite de Robert Dudley, Comte de Leycester, et de François et Jean Hotman.* Publiée par P. J. BLOK. (Haarlem : Loosjes, 1911.)

THE link between these three collections of documents preserved in the Teyler Museum at Haarlem consists in the circumstance that Jean, the son of François Hotman, was secretary to Leicester ; and Professor Blok's laborious investigations have enabled him to give a detailed history of the letters down to their acquisition by the Teyler Museum. The first part, as he points out, may be regarded as a supplement to the Leicester Correspondence published in 1844 by the Camden Society, and the other two as supplements to the *Hotomannorum Epistolae* published at Amsterdam in 1700 ; but a number of letters from the two Hotmans, including some thirty in the British Museum, still remain unpublished.

The value of the correspondence varies, but some of it is of great importance. Among the letters to Leicester we note several from the notorious Master of Gray, a letter from Henry of Navarre giving an account of the battle of Coutras, and a long one from La Noue. Gray tells how in the autumn of 1586 he was sent to England by James VI 'chiefly for two causis. The one that in tryell of his mother or rather in punising of hir, that His Majesteis honour be respectit, both for naturall obligation as also for the strict amitie now betvene him and the Queens Majestie. The second point is that hir fact sumever be not preiudiciable to His Majestie in the title he pretendith to have throv hir by blood to ye croun efter the Queen Majesteis deceis.' James affected to be anxious to save his mother's life; 'yit,' says Gray, 'I think he could verie veil content him self, if maiters ver commingly [? cunningly] handelit and he not acquent vithe them.' Professor Blok naturally finds some difficulty with Gray's spelling and calligraphy; and for 'deleynis (?)' (p. 145) we should read 'deleyings', for 'the English Majestie' (p. 146) 'the Kynges Majestie', for 'woolde be lost' (p. 148) 'woolde be loth', for 'yff he be fame' (p. 149) 'yff he be faine', for 'nòn' (p. 153) 'now'. Some slips in the text are not quite so excusable. The reference to a 'Cotton' (p. 119) should not be annotated 'probablement Sir Robert Cotton, le célèbre antiquaire'; for Robert was then but twelve years old, and the reference is doubtless to Thomas Cotton who occurs in the *Foreign Calendar*. The comment on Ruy Lopez, 'évidemment un Portugais appartenant à la suite de Don Antonio,' (p. 152) is a little naïve. The Edward Stafford, whose letter is printed, pp. 148-9, was not 'Lord Stafford'. 'Pécausse' (p. 118) is surely not a pseudonym for Marchaumont, but a corruption of his real name, Pierre Clausse de Marchaumont, and the letters (xv-xvi), which on the strength of Hotman's endorsement are assigned to November 1582, belong, we think, to November 1581; even Burghley's endorsements are not always to be trusted, and we are unaware of the reasons for which Professor Blok says that 1582 'est la seule année qui convient ici'. He cites the *Dictionary of National Biography* as the authority for his note on Everard Digby (p. 156), but it does not justify his statement that Digby was 'fellow of Lady Margaret at Oxford'.

Among the correspondence of François Hotman the most interesting letters are those from Duplessis-Mornay, which show how Hotman wrote and modified his *De Jure Regni Galliae* under the official inspiration and correction of Henry of Navarre and his advisers. The letter from Henry dated 'Leitoure' (p. 217) should surely be dated 'Lectoure'. Jean Hotman's correspondence is also mainly of literary interest; one (cix) gives some fresh details about Henry Constable, the poet; and the last in the volume is addressed to Isaac Casaubon and refers to the Arminian controversy. A note might have been added on p. 248 identifying 'mon amy Wetston' with George Whetstone; the 'monsieur Marten' (p. 254), who is described as 'inconnu', was probably Martin Marprelate; and 'ce prince', whose conduct in reopening religious difficulties Duplessis deplores in 1605 (p. 273), was almost certainly not Henry IV, as Professor Blok thinks, but James I. A. F. POLLARD.

La Marine militaire de la France sous les règnes de Louis XIII et de Louis XIV. Tome I: Richelieu, Mazarin, 1624-61. Par G. LACOUR-GAYET. (Paris: Champion, 1911.)

IN a comparison of the services rendered towards the French navy by Richelieu and Colbert respectively, the merit of the former, we are told, 'est moins dans des institutions qu'il ne fit qu'ébaucher que dans la vision très nette qu'il eut du rôle maritime de la France'. He opened French eyes to new perspectives and showed 'le monde de la mer avec ses horizons illimités'. The clue to his practical maritime policy will be found in the following precept taken from the *Testament politique*: 'Jamais un grand État ne doit être en état de recevoir une injure sans pouvoir en prendre revanche.' A development of naval strength was necessary from the beginning of his ministry, not only on general grounds, but also to meet the exigencies of the Spanish war and the Huguenot revolt, and for the furtherance of colonial enterprise and the deliverance of the coasts from the ravages of the Algerian pirates. The moment was favourable to his plans, the sea seemed open to any one who could take possession of it, the maritime ambitions of both Spaniards and Turks had been effectively checked, and the navies of England and Holland were still more or less undeveloped. Richelieu realized the potentialities of France as a maritime power, and pointed out some of her natural advantages to the Assembly of Notables in December 1626 :

nous avons les grands bois et le fer pour la construction des vaisseaux, les toiles et les chanvres pour les voiles et cordages, dont nous fournissons toutes les provinces voisines. Nous avons les matelots et mariniers en abondance, qui, pour n'être pas employés par nous, vont servir nos voisins. Nous avons les meilleurs ports de l'Europe, et nous tenons la clef de toutes les navigations de l'Est à l'Ouest, et du Sud au Nord. Les galères d'Espagne ou d'Italie sont obligées de passer à la vue et sous la couleuvrine des îles de Provence, les vaisseaux qui vont d'Espagne dans les mers du nord passent le ras Saint-Mahé à la miséricorde de nos canons.

The miserable condition of the marine was, however, amply demonstrated in the reports made at the instigation of Richelieu, 1629–33, as the outcome of inquiries entrusted to d'Infreville and Séguiran. The ports were in ruins, there was no proper defensive organization of the coasts, the merchants were victimized by the exactions of local seigneurs or by the piracies of the corsairs, the 'marine de guerre' was reduced to a few scattered and unseaworthy vessels. The first step in naval reorganization was the substitution of absolute centralization for the anarchical arrangement of marine commands which had hitherto been maintained. In March 1627 the office of admiral was suppressed, and Richelieu was instituted 'grand maître, chef et surintendant général de la navigation et commerce de France'. Under the presidency of the Conseil de Marine, instituted in 1624, a regular administrative system was formulated for the navy. Ship-building rapidly increased, and new arsenals and dockyards were erected, the four great military establishments instituted by Richelieu being Havre, Brest, Brouage, and Toulon. In 1624 the annual expense of the marine was 800,000 livres; in 1642, the year of the cardinal's death, it stood at 4,300,000 livres, to which must be added at least another two millions for extraordinary operations at the ports.

In September 1642 the fleet comprised sixty-five vessels and twenty-two galleys. Richelieu had centralized naval administration, restored order on the coasts, projected a reorganization of maritime services, and established the principle that 'la puissance en armes requiert non seulement que le roi soit fort sur la terre, mais aussi qu'il soit puissant sur la mer'. Owing to the disorders of the Fronde, and the neglect of Mazarin,

Richelieu's principles were in abeyance till they were revived by Colbert. M. Lacour-Gayet defends Mazarin against the charge of indifference in naval matters, but in view of the rapidly diminishing sums spent on the navy during his ministry, and contemporary evidence as to size and efficiency, he confesses to a difference ' entre la passion ardente et féconde de Richelieu et l'attention un peu superficielle de son successeur '. The account given of the English and Dutch fleets forms an interesting parallel to Captain Mahan's comparison of the naval policies of their governments and that of France during the same period. The English alliance, as expressed in the treaty of Paris (1657), is condemned as contrary to the maritime interests of France. An unflattering picture of the rise of English ' impérialisme ' is also presented as a ' titre sonore et magique qui a suscité chez un peuple de marchands l'amour de la gloire militaire '. Cromwell is referred to as 'le fondateur de l'impérialisme . . . à qui l'Angleterre a pardonné à peu près son hypocrisie et sa tyrannie en échange de la grandeur de sa politique étrangère et de l'énergie avec laquelle il lança son pays à la conquête des mers '.

During the course of maritime operations in the middle of the seventeenth century the following developments are noted : the growing importance of navies as factors in the strength of states, the increasing number of war-vessels of a specialized character, a preference for flank and cannon attack over the old-fashioned galley charge and ' boarding ' tactics which were reserved for actions with the corsairs, the former methods leading to the institution of the ' ligne de file ' and to the group formation of warships with their attendant fire-ships. The functions of these ' brûlots ' can be illustrated by the use to which they were put by Sourdis at the battle of Guttari, 22 August 1638, or by Vendôme in the action off the Ile de Ré, 9 August 1652, where they are compared to the torpedo tactics employed by Admiral Togo at the battle of Tsou-Shima.

M. Lacour-Gayet has already published two books on the French navy under Louis XV and Louis XVI respectively. This new volume is similarly based on lectures given before naval lieutenants at the École Supérieure de Marine, and though thus written for a specific purpose, strewn with practical counsels and analogies, it compares favourably in point of general historical interest, except for the regrettable absence of maps and plans, with M. de La Roncière's *Histoire de la Marine française*, part of the fourth volume of which, by the way, covers the same period. M. Lacour-Gayet, we think, exaggerates the importance of the French marine in the first half of the seventeenth century. What justification, judging from practical and durable results, has he, for example, for the following remark (p. 204) : ' La reconnaissance du pays doit mettre sur le même rang les soldats de Condé et de Turenne, les marins de Brézé et du chevalier Paul ' ? In numbers the French fleet was generally inferior to that of England or Holland, and the tonnage of individual vessels was comparatively small. At no time, in fact, during this period can France be said to have exercised a real ' empire de la mer '.   CONSTANTIA MAXWELL.

The University of Cambridge. Vol. iii: From the Election of Buckingham to the Chancellorship in 1626 to the Decline of the Platonist Movement. By JAMES BASS MULLINGER, M.A. (Cambridge: University Press, 1911.)

IN his third volume Mr. Mullinger brings down the history of the university of Cambridge to the time of the Restoration, or, as he prefers to call it, from an event of greater importance in the republic of letters, the time of the decline of the Platonist movement. Like its predecessors it displays a knowledge at once extensive and profound, and a constant realization of the connexion between the life of the university and the course of events in England as a whole and in the world at large. We may sometimes, indeed, be inclined to think that the author's interest in this connexion has occasionally carried him away. Thus, having had pointed out to us the influence of Cambridge—and particularly of the great Cambridge tutor Joseph Mede's system of interpreting prophecy—on the puritan exiles in America, we cross the ocean with them and do not return for forty pages. Still, the foundation in the transatlantic Cambridge of the great college which eventually came to bear the name of Harvard of Emmanuel may perhaps be reckoned not the least glorious event in the history of the mother-university, and therefore fit to be dwelt upon here; but it is more difficult not to feel that the account of Descartes, important as was his influence on the Cambridge thinkers of the next generation, is disproportionately long. These are criticisms to which only the work of one whom in the best sense ' reading maketh a full man ' could give occasion, yet it cannot be denied that one sometimes feels the discursiveness of the book injurious to its effect. Thus, while Mr. Mullinger makes of the Platonist movement, as we have seen, an epoch in the history of the university, he nowhere quite succeeds in bringing it before his readers as a single movement with a unified character of its own.

It would be a miracle if in a work so full of the most various information Mr. Mullinger had never made a slip; and here and there a statement needs correction. ' The College ' at Manchester, mentioned in the petition of 1642 for the founding of a university in that town (p. 205), is certainly not ' Hugh Oldham's Grammar School ', but the building described in Whatton's *History of Manchester School and Chetham's Hospital*, p. 176, as having been, until the dissolution of the collegiate church under Edward VI, the residence of the warden and fellows, and as afterwards conveyed to the family of the earls of Derby. At the time of the petition it belonged to James, Lord Strange, to whose intentions respecting it the document itself refers: and soon after this date it was taken over by the new foundation of Humphrey Chetham. From the note on p. 285, concerning the use' of parish churches by Cambridge colleges, one would not gather that such use was the regular practice in earlier days; and one misses a reference to the chapter on ' The Chapel ' in Willis and Clark's *Architectural History*, though that work is actually quoted in the same note. On p. 433 Mr. Mullinger says that ' the lineaments ' of Cromwell's ' countenance appeared in the representation of the Leviathan on the title-page ' of Hobbes's book. This is to me quite a new suggestion: I had always imagined the face to be intended for Charles II's, and with its moustache and short beard it certainly resembles this far more than the smooth-shaven Oliver's. Had it been like the latter, surely contemporary critics like Wallis, who scented flattery of Cromwell in the doctrine of the text, would have mentioned the fact as decisive; but they do not seem to have done so. Further, the appearance of the picture in the copy of the book presented by Hobbes to Charles at Paris, now in the British Museum, seems to settle the point against Mr. Mullinger. We hear on p. 577 of Tuckney's professorship, and on p. 611 of Cudworth's; but we are not told what chairs they held till we come to p. 599 for Tuckney and to p. 659 for Cudworth. With respect to Cudworth, one is surely not left (as p. 612 would suggest) to a conjecture of Tulloch's as to the immediate incentive to his undertaking a work on *Eternal and Immutable Morality*. He expressly tells us that he had Hobbes in view. And it is not easy to see why his theory of the eucharist is called (p. 613) ' purely Platonic '.

An Oxford man's eye is struck by the mention of a *President* (instead of a *Warden*) of Merton on p. 347, and of *St. Aldgate's* (instead of *St. Aldate's*) Church on p. 580; and a Magdalen man's by the reference to the hymn *Te O Deum colimus* (instead of *Te Deum Patrem colimus*) on p. 520. This hymn, by the way, is not ' still daily sung in the hall of Magdalen ', but only once or twice a year, on gaudy days. The expression ' senior student of Christ Church ' is used on p. 321 of Jasper Mayne in a way that suggests that the ' senior students ' were then a distinct order. But they only became so under the ordinance of 1858. Prior to that date, all, senior and junior alike, were called ' students ', while by the statutes of 1881 the seniors alone are ' students ', the juniors being called ' scholars '. There is a misprint of *Cambridge* for *Cromwell* on p. 47.

This notice is belated; but the delay has enabled us to congratulate Mr. Mullinger on the well-deserved honour which his university has just bestowed upon her historiographer. C. C. J. WEBB.

The Great Civil War in Lancashire, 1642-51. By ERNEST BROXAP, M.A. (Publications of the University of Manchester. Historical Series. No. 10. Manchester: University Press, 1910.)

No separate history of the civil war in Lancashire has previously seen the light, although, as Mr. Broxap undertakes to show, the local conflict has a strong claim to special study. It was a real struggle, complete as an incident in itself, yet having a vital bearing on the final fate of king and parliament. Isolated from their neighbours by natural boundaries and, within those boundaries, so equally divided as to make the result long uncertain, the natives of the county fought out a fierce contest almost unaided by alien forces, and thereby decided in no small measure the issue of the greater war beyond. In 1643 Lancashire was the key to the situation, and could the royalists then have retained it the war would certainly have been much prolonged and might have had a different ending. Its loss at a time when royalism prevailed in all other quarters altered the balance of the scale and cut off the royalist north from the base at Oxford with fatal results to that cause. In Lancashire, as in the country at large,

the puritans were a minority, but they triumphed there, as they did elsewhere, by reason of superior discipline, concentration, and ability. In principles, party divisions, and general details the local contest exemplifies in miniature the national struggle of which it made a part; even between the royalist earl of Derby and his master, Charles I, a curious parallel may be drawn. But though the general history of the war serves occasionally to elucidate the course of local affairs, Mr. Broxap is never guilty of unnecessary digressions. Throughout he adheres strictly to his chosen subject, of which he gives an account minute, lucid, and impartial. The greater part of the book deals, of course, with the events of the first civil war, beginning with the preliminary petitions, levies, and skirmishes, showing the gradual conquest of the whole county from the puritan base at Manchester, a process only temporarily checked by Rupert's meteoric invasion of 1643, and concluding with the surrender of Lathom House in December 1645. The two last chapters relate the part of Lancashire in the second civil war and Derby's gallant but futile attempt to raise the county for Charles II in 1651, and the book closes with Derby's execution (15 October 1651). The incidents of the war, the personalities of the leaders, and the social, economic, and topographical conditions of the district are carefully described with much interesting detail, and an exhaustive list of authorities evidences diligent and critical research. These authorities are primarily the publications of the local antiquarian societies, supplemented by the public records and the *Reports of the Historical MSS. Commission*, with other works, contemporary and modern, too numerous for indication here. The text is illustrated with frequent notes and references, a map of the county forms the frontispiece, and there are besides six plans of towns, campaigns, and battles. The whole is a sound and scholarly piece of work, which comes with a peculiar fitness from the Manchester University Press.
EVA SCOTT.

The Life of Edward Earl of Clarendon. By Sir HENRY CRAIK, K.C.B., LL.D. 2 vols. (London : Smith, Elder & Co., 1911.)

So much work has been done within recent years upon the history of the times in which Lord Clarendon lived that it would probably be difficult to find much new material bearing upon his life. Sir Henry Craik, at all events, does not profess to have discovered any. His object in this biography is rather to offer what is to some extent a new interpretation of Clarendon's life and place in history, and to redress the injustice with which, in his opinion, the lord chancellor has on the whole been treated by posterity. This injustice he attributes in the first place to the Whig historians of the last century who, in their endeavours to vindicate ' the unassailable rectitude of those who stood out as the assertors of popular rights against the Crown in the seventeenth century ', have contributed to a view wholly unfair to the royalist cause and to its adherents. Later writers have magnified the crime by veiling their hostility under a specious semblance of impartiality, which ' always contrives, in dealing with particular incidents, to find opportunity for depreciating the mental calibre, if not the moral character, of the adherents of the King '. We are warned, therefore, to expect a presentation of the facts more favourable to the royalists and to Hyde than that which is commonly allowed; but while we may sympathize with Sir Henry's desire to set matters in a truer perspective and to do justice to the character of a really great man, we may question whether he has not overstated the royalist case and ignored those limitations without which Hyde would have been scarcely human.

Hyde's chief service to the royalist cause, from the time that he definitely attached himself to it until his departure from England with the prince of Wales, was performed in his capacity of author of many of the state papers and publications issued either in answer to the addresses of the parliament or with the object of influencing public opinion, and it may be agreed that the part which he took in moulding the policy of the royalists, or at least in giving expression to it, has not been sufficiently recognized. Not the least important of these productions was the Declaration published in answer to the Grand Remonstrance. Sir Henry quarrels with S. R. Gardiner because, while he alludes to a shorter reply sent to the parliament by the king, he passes over the more exhaustive 'declaration' in silence. He adduces this as an instance of Gardiner's 'overmastering desire to belittle Hyde's part in the history of his time', but the criticism is hardly warranted, for the two answers were quite distinct and were not issued at the same time or for the same purpose. The abstract given by Hyde[1] is an abstract of the king's reply, and not as Sir Henry states, of the published 'declaration', which is described and epitomized later.[2] Hyde's share in the royalist counsels at this time was undoubtedly an important one, but though he had sufficient political insight to enable him in after years to criticize the manner in which the king's interests were defended, we have no reason to suppose that he possessed that essential grasp of the situation that could have averted the disaster of the war. It is indeed rather remarkable, considering his earlier relations with them, that he was not better able to understand the parliamentary leaders or the principles which underlay their action. During the greater part of the time which Hyde spent in exile with the court of Charles II, his share in politics, as Sir Henry admits, was necessarily limited, and even in the restricted sphere in which he could exercise his influence he was not always able to make it prevail. His own mission to Spain was, as he had probably anticipated, a failure, and the king's attempt to regain his throne with the help of the Scots was undertaken in opposition to his wishes. The Restoration, when it came, came as the result of causes which the exiled court had done little to establish.

The period which succeeds, on the other hand, is in many ways the most interesting in Clarendon's life, and the most instructive for the purpose of an estimate of his qualities as a statesman. His administration cannot, of course, be judged by its immediate results, for he was hampered and thwarted in every direction by the corruption of the court and the machinations of his personal enemies, but, in spite of these disturbing forces, it is possible to form some opinion of the policy which he set before himself, and of the relation in which it stood to the tendencies of the time.

[1] *History of the Rebellion*, bk. iv, sect. 82-4.   [2] Bk. iv. sect. 168-72.

Roughly stated, that policy was the restoration in church and state of all the essential conditions which had existed prior to the war, and it is because he was prepared to disregard so completely the significance of the intervening years, that Clarendon did not make good his claim to be considered in the first rank of statesmen. So much may safely be allowed without falling into the mistake, which Sir Henry rightly deprecates, of introducing ' the political ideas of a later day '. It is to be regretted that Sir Henry has not dealt very fully with this aspect of the question, and that he has given greater prominence to the influence of Clarendon's personal relations. In his use of Clarendon's *Life* of himself as a source of information for this period, Sir Henry appears to us to have made the mistake of regarding an account, written in exile several years afterwards, as necessarily representing the writer's attitude of mind at the time the events described took place. The book ends somewhat abruptly, and the last seven years of Clarendon's life, as well as the literary activities to which they were devoted, are passed over rapidly, and with less attention than they deserve.

The picture of Hyde given in this latest biography is the work of a warm admirer; but if Sir Henry is generous in praise he can also be vigorous in denunciation. For him Cromwell is ' a consummate actor' who deliberately played a double game with Charles I and the parliament; the elder Vane, one ' whose character showed no consistent trait except that of undeviating treachery '; Monk, a dullard whose ' sphinx-like attitude ' in the crucial time preceding the Restoration ' proceeded more from inability to discern the line of least resistance than from conscious dissimulation '. In some cases, no doubt, the interpretation of known facts must be a matter of opinion, but Sir Henry's verdicts are not invariably justified by the evidence. The book, however, has considerable merits. The narrative is vivid, and the main interest is never obscured by an undue attention to the historical setting. That the subject is approached from a definite point of view, rather than from a position of studied impartiality, will be to some a recommendation, and if Sir Henry succeeds in reviving an interest in a man unjustly forgotten he will have achieved a worthy purpose. G. B. TATHAM.

Revolutionary Ireland and its Settlement. By the Rev. R. H. MURRAY. With an introduction by J. P. MAHAFFY. (London: Macmillan, 1911.)

DR. MURRAY's title hardly explains with sufficient definiteness the purpose of his book. It begins with a description of the state of Ireland at the time of the revolution of 1688 and of the rule of James II in Ireland: this is followed by an account of the reconquest of Ireland by William III and his generals; the concluding chapters deal with the settlement after the war, the development of the penal laws, the restrictions on Irish trade, the disputes as to the authority of the Irish parliament, &c., and carry the story down to the reign of Queen Anne. About two-thirds of the book, therefore, deal with subjects treated at some length in Macaulay's history, but the politics of the ten or twelve years which follow the treaty of Limerick have hitherto never been adequately treated by any

English or Irish writer. Dr. Murray's book is therefore an indispensable addition to the library of any student of Irish history. His point of view differs from that of previous writers. He has endeavoured to show the extent to which the course of affairs in Ireland was influenced by international politics and by the European schemes of Louis XIV. This is very fully brought out in chapters i and vii—perhaps a little overstated here and there; but it needed making plain, and is generally altogether forgotten by nationalist historians. Finally, the sobriety and fairness with which questions which still excite the strongest political feeling are discussed in Dr. Murray's pages demand unstinted recognition.

In the earlier part of his book Dr. Murray corrects and amplifies in many places the narrative of Lord Macaulay. It is over fifty years since Macaulay wrote, and in the interim much new material for the history of the period has been printed by Gilbert, Ranke, and others. The Domestic State Papers of the reign of William III have been calendared down to 1695, and the contents of many private collections have been made accessible by the reports of the Historical Manuscripts Commission. Dr. Murray has used all these sources and also searched the unpublished state papers in the Record Office, the Clarke and King MSS. in Trinity College library, the Southwell MSS. in the British Museum, and the Archives des Affaires Étrangères in Paris. In short, his researches have been both wide and thorough, and he has succeeded in throwing fresh light on all sides of his subject. One little collection of letters appears to have been overlooked, namely the correspondence between Richard Hamilton, Melfort, and Tyrconnel during the siege of Derry, which is printed in the *Eighth Report of the Historical MSS. Commission*, pp. 493–7.

Dr. Murray's account of the relief of Derry is too much influenced by the famous passage in which Macaulay describes that event. He follows Macaulay in saying that the *Mountjoy* broke the boom by its impact, and that the *Phoenix* passed through the breach the *Mountjoy* had made. Macaulay omits all mention of the fact that the boom was cut by a man-of-war's boat, and that this cutting enabled the two merchantmen to pass through it. There are many references to this fact in contemporary accounts. One of them is even quoted by Dr. Murray in a footnote to p. 108, but he does not appreciate the bearing of the fact on the narrative given in his text. Similarly, to follow Macaulay in describing the battle of Newtown-Butler as a victory of 'two thousand amateur soldiers over six thousand professionals' is scarcely justifiable. The Jacobite forces had no claim to be called 'regular troops'; but were for the most part an ill-drilled and undisciplined collection of peasants (cf. pp. 55, 62, 83, 93, 150). Schomberg's army in 1689 consisted of newly raised regiments little superior if at all to those arrayed under the banner of James II. If he had brought with him to Ireland ten or twelve thousand veteran soldiers, as Cromwell did, it is safe to assume that his strategy would have been bolder. There is an interesting story about Schomberg told in Ailesbury's Memoirs (pp. 252–3), which explains his reasons for not fighting, and though Ailesbury is no very trustworthy authority he got it from a good source. Dr. Murray, who frequently quotes the papers of George Clarke, has not noticed that Clarke's autobiography, which is printed in the *Report on the Manuscripts of Mr. Leyborne-Popham*, contains some important details about William's campaign in Ireland. To Clarke Schomberg complained of William's reticence and lack of confidence, thus confirming the statement made by Dr. Murray on the authority of Schomberg's biographer. Clarke was present at the battle of the Boyne, which he describes, and was one of the negotiators of the treaty of Limerick, of which he gives a rather fuller account than the memorandum Dr. Murray quotes[1]. There are three subjects treated in the latter part of Dr. Murray's book in dealing with which he should have made some reference to the manuscripts of the house of lords, namely the question of appeals from the Irish house of lords, the suppression of the Irish woollen trade, and the dispute about the disposal of the forfeited lands. On all these points these manuscripts contain a considerable amount of information. The new series of these papers, of which four volumes have been published, begins in 1693. On pp. 319, 321 Dr. Murray refers to the third of these volumes, but describes it wrongly as being part of the *Fourteenth Report of the Historical MSS. Commission*, though since 1900 the house of lords has published its papers independently.

These minor errors and omissions are noted for the sake of a possible second edition. A more serious defect is a tendency to repetition, and a lack of clearness in some portions of the book, especially in the latter part of it. A number of interesting passages from King, Molyneux, Maxwell Cox, and other writers in favour of a union between Ireland and England are quoted, but the addresses of the lords and commons of Ireland in its favour are but vaguely referred to. In 1703 the lords addressed Queen Anne in favour of 'a more comprehensive and entire union' with England, while the commons asked for relief 'by restoring them a full enjoyment of their constitution, or by promoting a more strict and firm union with her majesty's subjects of England'. In 1707 the commons, in congratulating the queen on the completion of the union with Scotland, prayed that God might put into her heart 'to add greater strength and lustre to your crown by a yet more comprehensive union'. The work done by Mr. Froude to elucidate the history of Ireland during the reign of Queen Anne deserves more recognition than Dr. Murray is inclined to give it, and the remark on one of his errors, in a footnote to p. 363, is not in good taste.
C. H. FIRTH.

Henry Fox, First Lord Holland. By T. W. RIKER. 2 vols. (Oxford: Clarendon Press, 1911.)

MR. RIKER'S work, as the author himself modestly admits, can hardly rank as a final biography of Henry Fox, for it gives little about Fox's private life which is not to be found in Sir George Trevelyan's *Early History of Charles James Fox*, and even concerning his political life it is not exhaustive. The want of further information about the private life is probably no great loss, for it is difficult to believe that there is much of importance to add to Sir George's brilliant sketch, supplemented by the

[1] *MSS. of Mr. Leyborne-Popham*, p. 280.

details to be found in the *Life and Letters of Lady Sarah Lennox* and in Princess Marie Lichtenstein's *Holland House*; about some parts of Fox's political life, on the other hand, there are obvious gaps in Mr. Riker's book. He has hardly touched the evidence of Fox's work contained in the dispatches and other papers preserved in the Record Office, and it is quite conceivable that more light could be thrown on his activity as secretary at war and during his term of office in George III's reign, where again Mr. Riker has been content to rely on Sir George Trevelyan. The importance of the work lies in those chapters, forming the bulk of the two volumes, which deal with the three years from the death of Pelham in March 1754 to the formation of Pitt's second ministry in June 1757. For this period Mr. Riker has exhaustively studied the original material in the British Museum, where he has quarried deeply in the rich mine of the Newcastle and Hardwicke papers.

This period is vexatiously important in the lives of both Pitt and Fox. It is one of petty intrigues and bewildering negotiations in which, though the fate of the country seemed to hang in the balance, there is little evidence that much thought was taken save of the claims of rival politicians, mostly of second-rate importance, to places and emoluments. But petty though they were, a knowledge of these obscure manœuvrings is essential to a full comprehension of the circumstances which produced the man that England needed, and indeed of the great rivalry between Pitt and Fox which developed their character and manifested one as a statesman, the other as a politician ready to tire of the struggle as soon as his own interests seemed likely to suffer. By his conscientious presentment of the documents, and the lucid narrative he extracts from the garrulous verbosity of Newcastle or the stilted hypocrisy of other office-seekers, Mr. Riker has rendered a notable service to the history of the period. For, whatever one may feel about some of his judgements, he is so fair in giving the evidence that any reader is free to form his own conclusions on the facts. It is true that Mr. Riker's researches have been to a certain extent forestalled by Torrens in his too-little-known *History of Cabinets*; but he has worked independently, has discovered or at any rate made use of fresh material, and above all has given ample references, which are rather deficient in Torrens's work. This wealth of citation is not the least useful part of Mr. Riker's labours, for it facilitates access to the original on any point which the author has not thought it necessary to elaborate for his special purpose. Indeed, it may safely be said that Mr. Riker's labours have made it unnecessary for any future student to wade through the thirty or forty vast volumes relating to these three important years in the Hardwicke and Newcastle correspondence. Nor is it only for these British Museum manuscripts that Mr. Riker's work is valuable. He has studied and made good use of the pamphlets, caricatures, and newspapers of the period, and has especially brought out the historical value of the ably written series of denunciations of Pitt and Newcastle in the *Test* newspaper.

In most of his judgements Mr. Riker is eminently sane and fair. We may be especially grateful for the fact that he is not led into the temptation of so many biographers to make a hero of his subject simply because his attention is principally concentrated upon him. Fox is left by him very much as Sir George Trevelyan left him, a cynic, as a rule good-humoured, but when he was crossed apt to be cruel and malicious ; and an excellent business man with good judgement but little persistence in face of difficulties. The writer also brings out very effectively a point already noticed by Lord Rosebery, that had Fox either had the courage to stand by Pitt in 1755, or in 1756 to abide by the responsibility he had undertaken as secretary of state, he might well have kept the lead he had over his rival. But such patriotic stanchness was not in the man. Newcastle is no mystery, and Mr. Riker says all that can be said for him ; and as for Hardwicke, a sadly overrated politician, he has hit him off exactly. On Pitt he is less satisfactory. He has evidently not studied his career except so far as the generally prejudiced correspondence of Newcastle, Fox, and Hardwicke allows him, and he follows implicitly and sometimes even explicitly the unfavourable judgement on him expressed, no doubt for the same reason, by Torrens. 'A mortified egotist,' applied to Pitt, is a ludicrous phrase to anybody who understands anything of eighteenth-century history, and even Mr. Riker, like Torrens before him, when it comes to pointing the difference between him and his rival, is bound to admit the orator's underlying patriotism and his generous enthusiasm.

One important instance of critical acumen in these volumes should be specially noted to Mr. Riker's credit. Writers, among others Lord Rosebery, have been puzzled as to the date of Fox's accession to Newcastle's cabinet owing to the misdating of the correspondence between him and Pitt in the *Chatham Papers*, i. 124–37. Mr. Riker, observing that in the case of seven of the eight letters the date [25 April 1755] is printed in square brackets, deduces that these dates are merely an hypothesis of the editors, and is confirmed in that belief by his discovery of another copy of one of these letters dated December 1754. He therefore dates the whole correspondence in December 1754. It is a pity that he did not seek for actual proof of his theory by consulting the original letters in the Chatham MSS. (Bundle 1) at the Record Office. He would there have seen that all the dates were inserted in a later handwriting, while the eighth letter, boldly dated 26 April 1755 without any square brackets, on p. 132 of the *Chatham Papers*, has no date at all in the original. However, his deduction is quite correct, and he has thereby removed a considerable difficulty as to the real reason for Pitt's sudden revulsion of feeling against Fox in April 1756 immediately, as it formerly appeared, after he had encouraged him to join Newcastle. Now it is clear that it was not because Fox joined the cabinet, but because in doing so he agreed to betray Pitt, and that Pitt only heard of the last stipulation in April.

BASIL WILLIAMS.

Lives of the Hanoverian Queens of England. By ALICE DRAYTON GREEN-WOOD. Vol. ii. (London : Bell, 1911.)

IN the first volume of this work, which appeared two years ago[1], Miss Greenwood sketched the careers of the wives of the first two Hanoverian kings ; and in the present volume the consorts of George III, George IV, and

[1] See *ante*, xxv. 365 ff.

William IV are similarly treated. We now possess a continuous biographical study of the Hanoverian queens of England, and it is unlikely that Miss Greenwood's readers will deny that she possesses many of the essential qualities of the successful biographer. To write history proper she does not undertake to do; and those who go to this volume for a detailed account of the latter half of the eighteenth century and the early part of the nineteenth will meet the disappointment that they deserve. Politics, both external and internal, are touched upon no more than is necessary for purposes of lucidity; and this self-imposed limitation adds not a little both to the agreeable character and to the value of the book. Nor is it only the mode of presentation that is worthy of commendation. Miss Greenwood displays a thorough and scholarly acquaintance with the main authorities of the period; and though the hypercritical might take objection to one or two of the anecdotes gleaned from rather gossipy writers such as Walpole and Wraxall, it will generally be allowed that in the use of her materials she displays both skill and judgement. And this is no small praise when applied to an author dealing with an age abounding with writers who thought more of being amusing than of telling the truth, and who, when they turned their attention to the court, were inclined to be vivid at the expense of their accuracy.

Yet, pleasant and agreeable reading as this volume is, it would be an exaggeration to describe it as a notable addition to our existing knowledge. More than half of it is taken up by a biography of Charlotte Sophia, the wife of George III; and, interesting though this is, it contains little that is new. This is hardly surprising, seeing that Madame d'Arblay has given us a picture for all time of the inner life of George III's court. But though Miss Greenwood's account of Queen Charlotte does not possess the charm of novelty, it would be absurd to deny it very real and substantial value. By a careful study of the many memoirs and letters of the period, Miss Greenwood has been able to put in a brief and comprehensive form all the available information about the queen's life; and those who read her account will discover how agreeably free she is from the defects of hero-worship and special pleading. Full justice is indeed done to the many admirable virtues of the wife of George III, to her devotion to her husband, her unobtrusive benevolence, and her conspicuous courage in the face of many difficulties and even dangers; but her many and great deficiencies are by no means overlooked.

Queen Charlotte's endorsement of the all-sufficiency of convention, of an arbitrary difference of standard for different sexes and classes, her deliberate blindness to some of the main realities of life, have, not without reason, caused her to be remembered as a striking example of the harm which may be done by a good woman;

and severe though the judgement be, it is supported by ample proof. In one brought up in the stifling atmosphere of a petty German court it may be possible to pardon a ludicrous insistence upon the narrowest etiquette; but it is hard to forgive the queen, who was a truly virtuous woman, and generally sought to encourage virtue in others, for her cruel behaviour towards the unhappy wife of her eldest son, and for the public encouragement which she gave to Lady Jersey, that same son's acknowledged mistress.

It is obvious that Miss Greenwood has little affection for Sophia Charlotte; and her treatment of Caroline, the wife of George IV, and of Adelaide, the wife of William IV, is far more sympathetic. It is in dealing with these last two queens that Miss Greenwood appears at her best, and praise can unreservedly be given to this part of her work. A most careful and critical inquiry is instituted into the rather sordid life of George IV's unfortunate wife; the evidence brought against her is carefully weighed and considered, and she is pronounced guiltless of the crime of which it was necessary to convict her if a divorce was to be granted. Nor is such a verdict the result of special pleading; and impartial inquirers will hardly be likely to dispute Miss Greenwood's conclusions. No one has ever denied that Caroline was foolish and thoughtless, and much of her conduct is difficult of explanation save on the hypothesis that she was the victim of insanity; but however great the stress that is laid upon culpable perversity and lack of all decorum, it remains true that the more serious charge of infidelity is, to say the least, not proven. Insulted by a worthless husband, separated from her daughter, and made the cat's-paw of contending political factions, Caroline, a silly and unstable woman at the best, proved unequal to the arduous trials which fate called upon her to suffer; and if she was not the heroine of a romance, she was at least the victim of a tragedy.

The biography of Queen Adelaide, the wife of William IV, is far pleasanter and happier reading; and inasmuch as for most people that queen is a very dim and shadowy personality, a debt of gratitude is owing to Miss Greenwood for the care and skill which she has expended upon this part of her work. The task which Queen Adelaide successfully performed was the reformation of an elderly rake into a respectable old gentleman, and she accomplished it by the exercise of unfailing tact and genuine affection. It is easy to talk of 'poor dear Queen Adelaide', and to say that 'she never did anything that history is aware of save hold her tongue and help the poor'; but such a remark is based upon a very superficial view of history, and Miss Greenwood has conclusively shown that it was well for England that the king who was to rule the country during the troubled thirties possessed a wife who rose to the full responsibility of her station, and never passed beyond it.

In conclusion it may be said that this volume is fully equal to its predecessor. The same high standard of accuracy is maintained; and if it be a blunder to assert that it was George III, and not George Grenville, who refused to buy the fields adjacent to the queen's house, the mistake is hardly serious. D. A. WINSTANLEY.

The First American Civil War. First Period, 1775–8. By the Rev. HENRY BELCHER. 2 vols. (London: Macmillan, 1911.)

MR. BELCHER, in these energetically written and somewhat discursive volumes, aims at bringing before his readers the social rather than the military side of the revolutionary war in America. The characteristics of colonial life, the leaders of the 'patriot' party, the sufferings of the loyalists, and the composition of the militant forces on both sides are his principal subjects, though he also gives a spirited account of the more important events of the war down to the convention of Saratoga. The causes of colonial discontent are stated with fairness. While it is true that the reckless issue of paper money in pre-revolutionary times was closely connected with impatience of taxation, it was also an expedient for meeting the inadequate supply of bullion. This inadequacy, which was a drawback to commercial progress, made the measures taken to check illicit trading peculiarly annoying, because they tended to deprive the Americans of the coin received from the French and Spanish colonies. Smuggling, which could not be prevented by ordinary means, was met by writs of assistance, which are said here to have 'most seriously violated the first principles of British constitutional liberty'. Certainly they were an abridgement of liberty, but liberty must be subject to law, for otherwise one man's liberty might become injurious to another, and a liberty which is lawless is not constitutional. These writs were perfectly legal in England, and were based upon statute. If, as Otis contended, and we are told 'that no candid mind can fail to admit the cogency of his reasoning', the writs were in themselves unlawful, then an act of parliament was void, which is probably more than Mr. Belcher would allow.

He insists too frequently on the darker aspects of American life, on the brutal ill-usage of the loyalists by mobs too often encouraged by men of good position, on the cruelties inflicted on slaves, and on the delight which the border men took in shooting Indians at sight. There is much to be commended in the contempt he pours upon the empty professions of loyalty to the crown made by men engaged in every act of rebellion short of actual war, and in his outspoken condemnation of the disgraceful exultation displayed by Fox and his friends at the misfortunes of the British arms. The Howes, both Sir William and Viscount Howe, who, by the way, is often called here Lord Richard Howe, are rather harshly treated, and we are reminded too often of General Howe's relations with Mrs. Loring. In spite of contemporary suggestions, it is not 'presumable' that General Howe, in consequence of some understanding with the opposition at home, deliberately jeopardized the king's sovereignty in America by declining to press the enemy. With all his faults, he was a man of honour. Mr. Belcher relies much on the opinions of loyalists, who were naturally impatient of any slackness in the conduct of the war and were apt to impute it to the worst motives. On the other hand, he acquits Howe of all responsibility for the failure of Burgoyne's expedition, which he attributes to 'Germaine's meddling and Burgoyne's defective judgement'. His volumes contain many appropriate illustrations, some of them well-executed plans of battles and campaigns.   W. HUNT.

Letters and Papers of Charles, Lord Barham. Edited by Sir JOHN KNOX LAUGHTON. Vol. iii. (Printed for the Navy Records Society, 1911.)

WITH this volume Sir John Laughton brings to an end his valuable edition of Lord Barham's correspondence. Like its predecessors it contains much that is interesting, though it is rather disappointing to find in it no new light on the battle of Trafalgar, save that it gives us a plan representing the beginning of the action in which the British fleet is attacking in two lines ahead. This plan, which is certified by the French captain Magendie, though agreeing in general disposition with that reproduced from the *Naval Chronicle* by Mr. Newbolt in his *Year of Trafalgar*, differs from it 'in several not unimportant particulars'. The earlier and smaller part of the papers before us belongs to the period between Middleton's resignation as senior naval lord in 1795 and his appointment as first lord of the admiralty in the spring of 1805. In one he recounts his work as comptroller in getting ships fit for service during the American war, and specially in coppering their bottoms. From this paper it may be inferred that his anxiety for the return of Sandwich to office in 1789 was due to the support that he had previously received from the earl; and a remark as to Pitt's liberal grants to the navy during the early years of his administration is also noteworthy. A memorandum of Lord Melville dated 5 March 1805 has some suggestions as to the best means of increasing and regulating the supply of seamen, then a matter of the first importance, and shows that the writer had learnt one of the chief lessons of the mutinies of 1797, the necessity of doing more to promote the comfort of the prime seamen, from whom the petty and warrant officers were selected. Middleton, who was nearly seventy-nine when his cousin Melville resigned office in consequence of the vote of the house of commons of 9 April 1805, had no wish to become first lord, but he was anxious for a peerage, and Pitt induced him to accept his offer by gratifying his wish.

When Barham entered on his new office Napoleon was still threatening invasion from Boulogne, and Sir John Laughton takes opportunity to observe that the theory advanced by that distinguished historian, Colonel Desbrière, that he did not seriously intend to invade England, is untenable, and, further, that his preparations caused our admirals no anxiety, and that at the admiralty the protection of trade was held to be a more pressing need than attempts to thwart an invasion which the most experienced naval officers considered impossible. Lord Keith, who held command in the North Sea and kept watch for any attempt from the Texel and for privateers, held that the French troops could not be embarked in less than six tides. His letters complain bitterly of the way in which his action was hampered by the detachment of frigates to serve under Sir Sidney Smith, who, with Congreve, described by Keith as 'wholly wrapt up in rockets', and others, was making experiments in the hope of destroying the Boulogne flotilla with the help of some new invention. Barham heartily agreed with Keith, but the government would have it so, and both alike found Sir Sidney troublesome. Barham was eager for a policy of attack; 'defensive operations,' he writes, 'with such a force as we have collected on shore must end in bankruptcy.' Activity was immediately necessary, and offensive action not far off. The escape of the Rochefort squadron is explained by the temporary withdrawal of Graves from the blockade in order to get water. Villeneuve sailed out from Toulon, joined the Spaniards under Gravina, and sailed to the West Indies, intending on his return to act with the Brest fleet, drive our ships from the Channel, and escort the invading army to England. Nelson put matters on a different footing in the West Indies from that which Napoleon planned, and it became of the first moment to catch the combined fleet on its return. This led to Sir Robert Calder's action off Cadiz, illustrated by some of these letters: it is impossible to read them without feeling that Calder had hard measure dealt him, and acquiescing in Sir John Laughton's approval of Mr. Corbett's sagacious remark to the effect that had his trial taken place before Trafalgar set up a new standard of conduct, the result would probably have been different. The fact that the order to Cornwallis to send Calder to cruise off Cape Finisterre was signed by the board effectually disposes of the story that Barham dispatched it on his own responsibility and while he was dressing, though, as Sir John Laughton remarks, the brief memorandum of 9 July, which is printed here, may represent the result of his thoughts 'whilst shaving', and have been written at once.

While Trafalgar destroyed all hope of success against our fleets, it was followed by various attempts to injure our trade, and the two squadrons commanded respectively by Willaumez and Leissègues, which sailed from Brest in December, were a serious menace to it. A letter from Barham to Collingwood referring to Sir John Duckworth's chase of Willaumez expresses his disapproval of 'gentlemen under command' acting as Duckworth did, without orders from his commander-in-chief. Before Duckworth returned home he was able to report that he had completely destroyed the squadron under Leissègues off Saint-Domingo, a victory, which Sir John Laughton shows, has been disparaged unduly owing to the fact that it was won by seven ships against five, an unscientific way of estimating comparative strength. When Barham received the news of this victory he had already resigned office, and he wrote to Duckworth that 'notwithstanding the city of London are thanking his Majesty for changing his ministers, men of reflection will at least own we have been fortunate', adding that a list of the enemy's ships destroyed and captured during the last ten months 'would be as good a picture as could be drawn of our diligence'. To the naval glories of those months Barham had largely contributed by his foresight and energy. The documents which record his life's work could not have found a more capable editor than Sir John Laughton.   W. HUNT.

Naples sous Joseph Bonaparte, 1806–8. By JACQUES RAMBAUD. (Paris: Plon, [1911].)

WHEN Napoleon bestowed the crown of Naples on his eldest brother, he not only conferred on the latter the highest award he then had at his disposal, but he also gave him a signal proof of the confidence he reposed in him. The Neapolitan kingdom was at that juncture of supreme importance in the Napoleonic system, for steam navigation had not yet come into being, and southern Italy and Sicily were still the keys to the Mediterranean and the stepping-stones to the east. The promotion of Joseph was looked upon by Napoleon, not in the light of the creation of an independent monarchy, but merely as the establishment in southern Italy of an agent of the empire, who should be the visible embodiment of the military occupation of the kingdom. This conception of his duties and his position was, however, repugnant to Joseph, whose ambition it was to rule as an Italian sovereign and not as a French general; and to win the affection of his subjects rather than to reduce them to submission. It was this policy which led him to endeavour to identify himself with Neapolitan ideas in spite of violent opposition from Napoleon; and his reign, though ephemeral and overshadowed by the picturesque and dramatic elements which characterized that of his successor Joachim Murat, nevertheless marks an epoch in the history of Naples. Joseph was, it is true, in some respects a failure. His easy-going and luxury-loving temperament rendered him unfitted for the arduous task of cleaning out the Augean stable which the fugitive Bourbons had abandoned to him. His instincts were democratic, and he was nonplussed by the active hostility displayed by the Neapolitan proletariat towards his benevolent projects. In spite of this he was, however, able to introduce many valuable and long over-due reforms, such as the abolition of feudalism, and he achieved this in spite of the fact that he was seriously handicapped by the chaotic state of his dominions, due to civil war, and to the constant attacks of the British navy and the British garrison in Sicily. Moreover, the Neapolitan treasury was in a bankrupt condition, which involved the imposition of excessive taxation followed by the inevitable penalty of unpopularity. In some respects, notably in dealing with ecclesiastical affairs, he acted somewhat indiscreetly; but at all events enough was achieved to render his reign memorable and deserving of the detailed treatment which is accorded to it in M. Rambaud's scholarly monograph. The learned author has made very full use of all available sources of information, including a considerable mass of papers in private custody; and this volume, which follows a well-planned scheme, may rightly claim to be regarded as the standard work on the subject. A special tribute should be paid to M. Rambaud's impartiality. It is gratifying to note that he is free from those Anglophobe tendencies which have—perhaps not unnaturally—obscured the judgement of many recent French writers who have dealt with the period of the Napoleonic wars.   H. C. GUTTERIDGE.

History of the Peninsular War. By CHARLES OMAN. Vol. iv. (Oxford: Clarendon Press, 1911.)

THIS volume covers the year 1811, the middle period in the seven years' war in the Peninsula and the south of France. It opens with Masséna's retreat from Portugal after the failure of his attempt to drive the English into the sea. From that time forward Wellington was engaged on the problem how to carry the war into Spain, and the French fought on the defensive. Yet the total of the French forces in the Peninsula rose to 368,000 in the autumn, while the Anglo-Portuguese army numbered only 90,000 (one-fourth of them sick). The Spanish armies were weak and ineffectual, but their partidas were ubiquitous and enterprising; and owing to British command of the sea, insurrection could be rekindled wherever it had been stamped out. The jealousies of the French marshals prevented the available resources from being turned to the best account, and a commander-in-chief was the one thing needful. As Napoleon had written in 1808, 'à la guerre les hommes ne sont rien, c'est un homme qui est tout.' But, as Professor Oman shows, there were strong reasons against his going back to Spain himself, and he would not give full powers to any one else. He tried to direct operations from Paris, and sent instructions that were impracticable based on reports that were out of date. There was the further difficulty, peculiar to Spain, that if large armies were brought together they could not be fed for any length of time.

The British government did not make the most of the opportunities offered by the situation in Spain. Before Masséna's invasion of Portugal they were scared by croakers who predicted disaster, and they warned Wellington that he would be more readily excused for bringing the army away too soon than for staying too long. In February 1811, when Masséna had failed, they informed Wellington, 'it is absolutely impossible to continue our exertions upon the present scale in the Peninsula for any considerable length of time'; yet it proved possible to make much greater exertions in subsequent years. Mr. Oman tries to justify the Perceval administration, and blames Wellington for 'querulous and captious language' in the winter of 1810–11. No doubt there were extenuating circumstances, and no doubt Napier has used unduly strong language; but the fact remains that in the time of trial ministers were faint-hearted, and Wellington had the additional burden thrown upon him of keeping up their courage. At one time he dared not ask for reinforcements lest the reply should be an order to embark. Nor was he fortunate at this time in his lieutenants, except Hill. Spencer, the second in command, was not a man to lean upon; William Stewart was a compound of diffidence and impetuosity; and Beresford, a good organizer and disciplinarian, was not equal to the command of an army in the field. Mr. Oman holds that Napier's severe comments on him were inspired by personal animosity, and does his best to defend Beresford's conduct at Albuera. He concludes, however, that 'though there were excuses and explanations to be found for each one of his individual acts, yet the general effect of his leadership had not been happy'.

Mr. Oman devotes thirty pages to the battle of Albuera, and his account of it is admirable in its fullness, fairness, and lucidity. There is no attempt to vie with Napier in word-painting, but it is shown that the rhetoric of his famous battle-piece is sometimes misleading. Mr. Oman has succeeded in giving what Napier was unable to give, a detailed statement of the strength of units in Beresford's army. This makes the British and the Portuguese troops each of them over 10,000 (officers and men). Lord Londonderry, who as adjutant-general ought to have been well informed, gave the strength of the British as 7,500. The difference seriously affects the percentage of loss. Napier spoke of 1,800 unwounded men, 'the remnant of 6,000 unconquerable British soldiers'; but the total of the 2nd and 4th divisions is given by Mr. Oman as 7,640, and their loss as 3,933; rather more than one half. A novel feature in Mr. Oman's narrative calls for examination. According to the version hitherto accepted, the two divisions of Girard's corps were held in check by Hoghton's brigade of the 2nd division, but were gradually overpowering it, when Cole (at Hardinge's instance) brought up the Fusilier brigade and struck the left flank of the French columns. At the same time the other flank of Girard's corps was threatened by Abercrombie's brigade. In Hardinge's words: 'While Hoghton's brigade held the hill, Myers and Abercrombie passed the flanks on the right and left, and made a simultaneous attack on the enemy, who began to waver and then went off to the rear.' Mr. Oman says that when Cole was seen to be advancing the nine battalions of Werlé's reserve were sent forward diagonally to protect Girard's flank, and that was the force with which the Fusiliers came into collision. He resolves the battle at this stage into two separate encounters—the 4th division with Werlé, the two brigades of the 2nd division with Girard. In each encounter the French were defeated, and simultaneously 'the fugitives of the 5th corps mingled with those from Werlé's brigade, and all passed the Chicapierna brook in one vast horde'. It would be interesting to know on what evidence this theory of the battle rests. It gives two brigades of the 2nd division the glory of having routed the 5th corps unaided. Napier brought the French reserve into play only after the 5th corps had given way. Lapène, a French artillery officer who was present, says that the reserve was brought up to support Girard, whose troops were falling back in a confused mass; it made a stand for some time, but Werlé was killed, and after losing heavily it retired in better order than the 5th corps.

The battles of Barrosa and Fuentes de Oñoro are excellently described. In the latter case the exploit of Norman Ramsay is reduced to its true proportions, which are still considerable. In the account of the sieges of Badajoz Mr. Oman is rather too severe on the British engineers, and does not make allowance for the disadvantage at which they were placed by the want of trained sappers and miners. The choice of San Christobal as the point of attack is not indefensible. But it must be owned the narrative of Suchet's capture of Tarragona is likely to leave the reader with the impression that 'they manage these things better in France.' The investigation of the Spanish losses at Tarragona (given in a footnote on p. 504) is a good example of the pains which Mr. Oman invariably takes to arrive at the facts. E. M. LLOYD.

Histoire du Royaume des Pays-Bas et de la Révolution Belge de 1830. Par FRANS VAN KALKEN. (Bruxelles : Lebègue, 1911.)

PROFESSOR VAN KALKEN truly points out how the memory of the Belgian rising of 1830 has been softened by the later growth of mutual understanding and of common interests between the Netherlands and Belgium. The Dutch are now Belgium's third best customers ; the Belgians are the second best customers of the Dutch. Of foreign residents in Holland nearly a quarter are Belgian ; of foreign residents in Belgium more than a third are Dutch. The time has therefore arrived for historians, however national in their sympathies, to write dispassionately of the events that severed the two peoples eighty years ago.

The book before us gives a clear and readable account of Belgian history from 1814 to 1831, and explains how the passive indifference of the people to accept William I as their sovereign in 1814 was slowly transformed into burning resentment by 1830. The king was no intentional tyrant ; he was, in fact, virtuous and economical, but he was obstinate, self-centred, and Dutch. The writer considers his alienation of the catholics by attempting to capture the control of clerical education in 1825 as having given the first impetus to the separatist movement. In 1827 he yielded to the church party, but meanwhile an energetic liberal party, led by clever journalists and orators, had entered the field against him, irritated by his disregard for Belgian sentiment. The French revolution of July 1830 inspired both these antagonistic elements to make common cause. The two most striking features in the author's story of the actual rising are the accidental origin of the first outbreak at Brussels, and the king's extraordinary slowness and incapacity in trying to stem the tide of rebellion. It started as a wholly unorganized orgy of window-breaking and shop-lifting on the part of a mob of young men; their excesses forced the bourgeoisie to take steps to restore order in the absence of government troops, and it was the bourgeoisie who really guided the country to independence. The underlying cause of the rising was not so much the king's insistence on enforcing unpopular taxes, as his impolitic determination to unify and 'Hollandize' the administration of the Low Countries. The population of Belgium was over three and a half millions, that of the Netherlands barely two, but the whole system of civil, judicial, and military organization was concentrated in the northern community, in whose eyes Belgium was but a territorial acquisition. Even parliament, though it sat alternatively at Brussels and the Hague, was composed of Dutch representatives to the extent of half its personnel, and the use of the Dutch language was insisted on in all courts of law and public offices. So one-sided a policy was bound to provoke national hostility in Belgium.

Professor van Kalken's most suggestive pages are those which argue that the king's dream of amalgamating the two peoples was inevitably bound to fail. This view is not so much based on the previous historical cleavage between the two, as on their intrinsic differences of race, religion, customs, language, and mental bias. The one chance of successfully working the dynastic arrangement of 1814, for which neither people was ever really anxious, was some such dual sovereignty as that of Austria-Hungary. Absorption of the one state by the other was essentially impossible. The English reader will be glad to find that in this particular instance, for once, Palmerston's foreign policy was as effective as it was spirited. The author regards him as 'the father of Belgium' by reason of his decisive influence in securing the recognition of Belgian nationality by the powers. He was also largely responsible for ending the 'ten days' campaign' undertaken by the Dutch by way of reprisal in 1831, and for the selection of Leopold of Saxe-Coburg as king of the Belgians.

Some thirty portraits of leaders of the day add to the value of the book.   GERALD B. HERTZ.

Oesterreichs innere Geschichte von 1848 bis 1907. Von RICHARD CHARMATZ. 2 vols. (Leipzig: Teubner, 1909.)

HERR CHARMATZ, whose volume of essays on Austrian politics [1] attracted considerable attention, has earned the gratitude of students by this

[1] *Deutsch-Oesterreichische Politik*, Leipzig, 1907.

admirable textbook. As the title indicates, the foreign policy of the Austro-Hungarian monarchy is touched upon only in so far as it influenced the course of internal politics in Cisleithania. But perhaps in no European country has this influence been so pronounced as in modern Austria. It is only necessary to point out that the gradual triumph of constitutional over absolutist government between 1860 and 1867 was the direct result of the disastrous Italian campaign of 1859 ; that the compromise of 1867 was in great part due to the defeat of Königgrätz ; and that the dual system would have given way to federalism in 1870 but for the victories of Germany. The author gives a brief clue to the interconnexion of internal and external affairs ; but his main task is to unravel the tangled thread of constitutional and parliamentary progress in Austria. The first volume falls into two main divisions. The first deals with the revolution of 1848, the short-lived constitutional experiment of Kremsier and the *oktroyirte Verfassung* of March 1849 ; the long period of reaction associated with the name of Alexander Bach ; the vacillating policy which ended with the Austro-Hungarian Ausgleich of 1867, and its complement the ' December Constitution ' for Austria. The second section treats of the first eleven years of the dual system, the period during which the policy of abstention adopted by the Czech leaders enabled the German Liberal party to dominate Austrian parliamentary life and to leave their stamp upon Austrian institutions. Herr Charmatz describes this ' golden age ' of the Reichsrat with genuine impartiality. He is by no means blind to the shortcomings of the old-fashioned German Liberal school, and does not hesitate to criticize Herbst and Giskra and other leaders, just as, earlier in the book, he frankly admits Schmerling's lack of respect for parliamentary forms and his hostility to freedom of the press. On the other hand, he does full justice to men who, with all their limitations and despite their narrow outlook in racial and international questions, unquestionably set themselves a high standard in public life and made the modernization of Austria their foremost aim. The corruption which raised its head for a short time under the liberal régime, and which Herr Charmatz treats with perfect frankness, cannot fairly be regarded as touching the core of Austrian public life. It coincided with an era of overgrowth and over-speculation, and the great financial *Krach* of 1873—which led somewhat unfairly to the rise of anti-Semitic feeling—certainly roused public opinion to action. If the general standard of parliamentary life tended to deteriorate under the ' Iron Ring ' of Count Taaffe, and during the stormy decade which his resignation ushered in, this was not due to any grave moral defects, but to the unsound, because essentially unreal, basis upon which the franchise rested, and to the racial rivalries which prompted the dominant parties to perpetuate an electoral system that set logic and reason at defiance.

The second volume carries the narrative from the fall of Prince Adolf Auersperg in 1878 till the introduction of universal suffrage in 1907. From the moment when the Czechs renounced their barren policy of abstention and decided to enter the Reichsrat the German majority of Auersperg was doomed. For fourteen years Count Taaffe dominated Austrian politics, by the aid of his so-called ' Iron Ring ' of clerical, feudal, and Slav deputies. His position was strengthened by a partial extension of the franchise in 1882, by which the political centre of gravity was transferred from the liberal *grande bourgeoisie* to the clerical *petite bourgeoisie*, to *der kleine Mann*, who was later on to form the backbone of the Christian socialist party in Austria. Taaffe's famous policy of *Fortwursteln* or 'scraping along'—the phrase was his own invention—grew yearly more difficult, and in 1893 he sought to strengthen his position by fresh electoral reform. Its disapproval by an oligarchic parliament led to his fall, and the coalition which succeeded him introduced a reform which retained most of the evils of oligarchy without securing any of the advantages which democracy could offer. The next decade (1896–1906) is too closely connected with current politics for discussion in these pages. Suffice it to point out that throughout the period preceding the year 1896 Herr Charmatz never allows racial prejudices to influence his narrative, and that the remainder of the book, though written from the distinctively German-Austrian point of view, is far from assigning all the blame to one side, and is not unworthy of an historical writer whose sympathies lie rather with the broad imperial than with any narrow racial outlook upon Austrian affairs. On the other hand, he makes no secret of his anti-clerical views, whenever ecclesiastical or educational matters are under discussion. But here again it is wellnigh impossible for any educated Austrian, even if he be an historian, to avoid taking sides in such burning questions as the Concordat, the marriage laws, or the Roman church's control of education.

One of the happiest features of the book is the author's gift of characterization; in a few terse phrases he brings out the character, motives, and aims of the more prominent politicians who figure in his pages. But he is certainly very far outside the mark when he draws a comparison between the fanatical if gifted Georg von Schönerer and Edmund Burke (ii. 30). With this exception his estimate of Schönerer and of Dr. Karl Lueger is especially instructive; but his theory that Christian socialism owed its triumphs to the strong personality of Lueger and not to its own merits is a dangerous half-truth, and is hardly consistent with his recognition of the fact that Lueger succeeded where Schönerer failed, mainly because the one exploited and the other ignored the decisive influence exercised in Austria by the dynasty and the church.

His criticism of Bohemian *Staatsrecht* as 'an elastic expression which comprises everything and nothing' is indeed only too accurate. But it is impossible to follow with approval the strange remark—all the stranger in so careful a student of parliamentary procedure—that 'constitutional questions are questions of power (*Machtfragen*), as Lassalle has already demonstrated with all possible clearness. He who has the power to break through old forms and to create new ones need not resort to legal protestations; for him it is superfluous to appeal to such a quarter'. Such an assertion goes much too far beyond the somewhat contemptuous but not unmerited reference to Czech political 'romanticism, which combats the course of history by mere paper remonstrances'. On the whole, however, his compressed summary of racial troubles gives the foreign reader some clue to the rivalries and aspirations of German, Slav, and Latin in Cisleithania, though he might have done well to indicate the close bearing of economic questions upon these rivalries. His interpretation, though it does not contain the whole truth, is absolutely true so far as it goes. In the words of Herr Charmatz's favourite hero, Adolf Fischhof, 'Austria is no accidental conglomeration, but a necessary political entity,' which, 'in order to secure its existence, must be the promoter of a high ethical idea.'

R. W. SETON-WATSON.

Camden Miscellany. Vol. xii. Camden Third Series, vol. xviii. (London: Royal Historical Society, 1910.)

THIS volume contains four interesting pieces. The first is a careful edition, by Mr. C. L. Kingsford, of Two London Chronicles, from the Collections of John Stow in the British Museum. The former of these runs from 1523 to 1555 (its year commencing with the election of the lord mayor, 29 October), the latter from 1547 to 1564. The second piece is the Life of Sir John Digby (1605-45) by a contemporary author, Edward Walsingham, now printed for the first time, by M. Georges Bernard. Sir John Digby, whose fame has been overshadowed by that of his elder brother Kenelm, was a typical roman catholic cavalier, loyal, brave, stubborn, and generous, loved by his dependants and soldiers, respected by his enemies. At the age of fourteen he was sent to Flanders to be educated, and four years later went to Italy. After this he served under the earl of Lindsey at sea, and then under the earl of Arundel against the Scots. During the Civil War he was active in his native districts, Buckinghamshire and Oxfordshire. His greatest exploit was the stubborn defence of Grafton House, near Towcester, with less than 200 men against several thousand of the enemy under Skippon. Prince Rupert failed to bring his promised relief, and Digby was forced to surrender. He was imprisoned in the Tower, and was exchanged for Colonel Buttler just before the royalist victory at Lostwithiel. He was appointed major-general of the army in the west, and was severely wounded in the arm at the siege of Taunton. He died on 16 July 1645 at Bridgewater, a few days before its capture by Fairfax. Walsingham concludes his work with a short character of Sir John, and some indifferent verse on him and other royalist leaders. The third piece, edited by Mr. H. E. Malden, is a diary kept by Adam Wheeler, drum to the Wilts militia, from 16 June to 9 July 1685. The regiment was present at Sedgemoor on 6 July, though not under fire, and as the prisoners passed on their way to Weston Church, Wheeler wrote down their number and description on his drumhead.

The last piece is also the most valuable. It consists of a collection of documents, dating from 1596 to 1622 and 1820, which relate to common rights at Cottenham and at Stretham in Cambridgeshire, edited, with an introduction, by Archdeacon Cunningham. During the sixteenth century the enclosure of commons or waste lands surrounding villages caused much complaint and suffering. This was especially so in the districts round the Fens, where the land was almost useless for tillage, but excellent for pasture. There are records of disputes over pasture rights at Cottenham before 1596, but the agreement of forty-seven articles, between Sir William Hinde of Madingley, lord of the manor, and 130 inhabitants, signed on

20 November in that year, despite attempts in the next century to upset it, regulated the management of the common waste until the final enclosure in 1842—a remarkable instance of the stability of manorial government. A tithe schedule of 1622 shows that the produce of the manor consisted of cattle, sheep, pigs, hay, apples, pears, damsons, and plums. In 1820 tithe was taken of cattle, sheep, pigs, foals, goslings, pigeons, eggs, hemp, and honey. The case of Stretham was in some ways parallel to that of Cottenham; but instead of one masterly agreement we find records of constant quarrels between Sir Miles Sandys, lord of the manor, and his tenants, which resulted in a series of orders and by-laws from 1607 to 1622. The tithe was a further cause of dispute. The management of the waste of a manor was as important as the tillage of the common fields, for no system of small holdings can be successfully worked without extensive rights of common. Hence the interest of these papers, which deal with a department of manorial economy for the study of which the printed materials are not abundant. J. E. W. WALLIS.

Short Notices

THE second part of Dr. Gisbert Brom's *Archivalia in Italië belangrijk voor de geschiedenis van Nederland* (The Hague: Nijhoff, 1911) is concerned with the Vatican library, the contents of which are dealt with as the Vatican archives were treated in the preceding part (see *ante*, vol. xxv. 390 f.). The eight groups of manuscripts which Dr. Brom has examined, Vatican, Palatine, Urbino, Reginae, Ottoboni, Capponi, Barberini, and Museo Borgiano, are each given a section of the volume headed by a succinct account of their several histories. The small number of items, only 399 as against 2,650 dealt with in part i, has made it possible to print a good many of the more interesting documents, and extracts from many others, at length. As before, they throw some light on English history at points where it touches Dutch, and may be useful as supplementing the series of transcripts made for the Public Record Office. Not unexpectedly, the largest number of items comes from the great Barberini library, a considerable portion of which might well, like the Borghese papers, have been made a part of the Vatican archives. Perhaps the most interesting is an account, presumably by an Italian spy in the French service, of the secret negotiations between England, France, and Holland in 1672. The description of the unhappy Henrietta of Orleans by an English gentleman, the 'Cavalier Denodai', is worth quoting : ' vivace d'ingegno, disinvolta nel parlare, soave ne' tratti, gratiosa ne' gesti, maestosa ne' portamenti, vaga nel passeggio, vermiglia nel volto, negra negli occhi, mediocre in statura, grande nell' animo, e generosa ne' pensieri.' C. J.

Mr. E. A. Savage's compendious volume on *Old English Libraries* (London: Methuen, 1911) well deserves its place in the series of ' The Antiquary's Books'. It makes no attempt to be monumental and exhaustive ; with discoveries yet being made in every direction the time for such a work is not come. Nor does it lay claim to first-hand research. Its purpose is to give a popular account of what is known about libraries in England, during the age of manuscripts—their size and distribution, the books they contained, and their founders. With this aim the authors— one of whom, Mr. J. Hutt, fell ill during the progress of the work—have searched far and wide among learned books and periodicals, and have brought together much material from scattered sources. From the number of those cited it would seem that little can have escaped them amongst the fleeting shades of periodical literature. The libraries of England are divided into three groups, according as they belonged to monasteries, cathedral and other churches, or universities and colleges. A great deal of information is brought together and arranged under these headings, and there are chapters on the making of books, the book trade, and private collections so far as they can be traced. In a

concluding chapter Mr. Savage discusses the general contents of medieval libraries, and gives reasons for concluding that they were less dull than commonly appears. The illustrations are numerous and well chosen. The most permanent part of the book is contained in three appendixes. The first is a collection of prices recorded for books and their materials; it fills fifteen pages, and the sources carefully given show how widely the author has cast his nets. The second is a list of classics found in various medieval libraries. The third enumerates medieval libraries and collections of books; twenty-five pages being required, though the notices can only be brief. The present volume does not aim to give a history of learning in England during the middle ages: but a great deal may be derived from it on this subject, and it will prove a very useful handbook.
P. S. A.

The Rev. William Cole, antiquary and topographer of Cambridge, the writer of the Cole MSS., lived from 1714 to 1782, and amassed an immense series of notes and memoranda. Mr. G. J. Gray's *Index to the Contents of the Cole Manuscripts in the British Museum* (Cambridge : Bowes & Bowes, 1912) is accordingly a real boon to students of Cambridge and Cambridgeshire history, and is of interest to a much wider circle. Its production as an act of *pietas* to Cambridge must have been as pleasant to Mr. Gray as it is welcome to others. A key to the contents of Cole's topographical and miscellaneous volumes doubles their value, and the methods of a trained indexer like Mr. Gray trebles it. The chief articles which will interest readers of general tastes are Bells, Bletchley (where Cole was rector), Dr. Zachary Grey, London, Drs. Lort and Moss, Oxford, Seals, Horace Walpole, and Browne Willis; and few counties are unrepresented. The introduction says all that is needed about the manuscripts themselves, and about the known portraits of Cole, one of which is reproduced as a frontispiece.
F. M.

The *Transactions of the Royal Historical Society* for 1911 (3rd series, vol. v) include an important paper entitled 'Respublica Christiana', in which Dr. Neville Figgis maintains that 'in the middle ages church and state in the sense of two competing societies did not exist', and traces the influence of the notion of the unity of the Christian society upon later political theory and practice. Mr. H. E. Malden writes on 'The Possession of Cardigan Priory by Chertsey Abbey', and examines the forgeries made to support the claim of Gloucester abbey (cf. *ante*, xx. 616 f., 1905). Dr. J. H. Wylie contributes 'Notes on the Agincourt Roll', and shows, with an elaborate appendix of documentary extracts, how defective the materials are for its reconstruction. Miss O. J. Dunlop illustrates 'Some Aspects of early English Apprenticeship'. Professor Firth contributes a spirited paper on 'The Ballad History of the Reign of James I'. The Rev. C. E. Pike describes, unfortunately without references to authorities, 'The Intrigue to deprive the Earl of Essex [Arthur Capel] of the Lord Lieutenancy of Ireland'; and Miss M. Lane writes on 'The Relations between England and the Northern Powers, 1689-97'.
A.

The *Transactions of the Baptist Historical Society* have now completed their eighth number and their second year. A good deal of space is taken up with reprints of the proceedings of small local churches, which are of value as typical, and with antiquarian matter; there is also the inevitable revival of dead controversies and pamphlets. But there is much of historical value. It is startling to learn that the whole number of baptist congregations that have been enumerated up to 1660 is only 115 of General and 131 of Particular Baptists. If baptists were so rare, must not the total number of unofficial congregations in England under the Commonwealth have been much smaller than we commonly suppose? There is a careful account by Dr. Thirtle of Peter Chamberlen, physician and sabbatarian, who has considerable space in the *Dictionary of National Biography*. Dr. Whitley tells of several baptists who were ejected on St. Bartholomew's Day; and we learn that Newcomen, the inventor of steam-engines, was a baptist. The *Transactions* give equal attention to both branches of the baptist body, and are instructive and interesting in many ways. E. W. W.

The appearance of a second edition of Professor Rudolf Kittel's *Die alttestamentliche Wissenschaft* (Leipzig: Quelle & Meyer, 1912) is an indication that this useful book, already noticed in these pages (*ante*, xxv. 808, 1910), supplies a want. Professor Kittel has added several new illustrations, a number of footnotes, and some paragraphs (pp. 58–64, 135, 141 f., 144, 145 f., 245 f.) on the excavations at Samaria, the patriarchal figures, composite writings, and other points. S. A. C.

In the *Second Interim Report on the Roman Forts at Castleshaw* (Manchester: University Press, 1911) Mr. F. A. Bruton gives further information about the Roman fort of Castleshaw, which is planted almost exactly over the Stanedge railway tunnel between Manchester and Huddersfield. Its excavation was begun in 1907 and continued in 1908: the results of 1908 are now described. The account is carefully written and well illustrated, but the uncovering of the fort is still incomplete, and the historical results are therefore still somewhat indefinite. It would seem that the place was first established about A.D. 75, probably—though Mr. Bruton does not actually say this—at the time when Cerialis conquered a part of the Brigantes; it might, of course, have been occupied earlier, since the Romans probably reached Chester soon after A.D. 50, but of such early occupation no convincing proof has yet emerged. It was an earth-walled fort, and its arrangement suggests an area for temporary occupation with a smaller citadel inside which probably held a tiny permanent guard. It seems to have been abandoned not long after A.D. 120, and there its history ends. B.

The history of the imperial towns of southern Italy from the fall of the exarchate till the time when they were all absorbed by the Norman kingdom might well form the subject of a volume, in which we should read how the dukes of Naples first became for all practical purposes independent of the emperor, and then the rulers of Amalfi and Gaeta in the same way ceased to obey the Neapolitan dukes, while all the time these little states by their adroit policy, and by the fact that they alone possessed a naval power, were able to defy Pope, Lombard, Frank, and Saracen. The documents which are our best authority for the internal history of these states have, however, only recently been edited, and we must therefore for the present be content with monographs, of which *Gaeta im frühen Mittelalter (8. bis 12. Jahrhundert), Beiträge zur Geschichte der Stadt,* by Fräulein Margarete Merores (Gotha : Perthes, 1911), is an admirable example. Literary sources for the history of Gaeta hardly exist ; and the authoress, a pupil of Professor Hartmann, therefore bases her study almost entirely upon the invaluable documents contained in the Codex Cajetanus. After a history of Gaeta during the period covered by her work, she describes the character and development of the constitution, and then discusses the position held by the town of Gaeta, which, as she is able to show, was in the latter part of the period almost independent of the duke, and even made treaties on its own account, and the book ends with a similar account of the other portions of the duchy and the semi-independent counties which sprang out of it. The most interesting side of the subject is the constitutional history, that is, the method by which an independent city-state grew out of the centralized despotism of the later empire ; but, though the author has given us an excellent study of the constitution of Gaeta, as the documents reveal it, she treats it too much as a thing of itself, and makes little attempt to show how the institutions arose or to connect them with those of other cities. For instance, she tells us that the *comites* were the landowners (p. 88), but does not suggest any explanation of the steps by which the title came to have this meaning. Dr. E. Meyer's *Italienische Verfassungsgeschichte,* which must now be considered the first authority on these matters, is never mentioned in the book, and his theory that the municipal constitutions of the empire maintained an uninterrupted existence through the dark ages is entirely neglected. The documentary evidence is used with accuracy and ability; but the statement that the death of John the patrician broke the last bond that united Gaeta to the empire (p. 25) is at least misleading, since the emperor's name is mentioned in the Codex as late as 955, and we do not understand the meaning of the strange assertion that one of the *hypati* bore 'the imperial title' (p. 9). E. W. B.

The aim of Dr. D. Pesl in *Das Erbbaurecht, geschichtlich und wirtschaftlich dargestellt* (Leipzig : Duncker & Humblot, 1910) is chiefly to assist in solving the housing problem in present-day Germany. As an introduction to the consideration of the economic situation in Germany, and as a basis for his legislative proposals, the author traces the history of leasing land in all the principal countries of Europe. This historical sketch, beginning with the *superficies* of Roman law and the *Erbbaurecht* of the German middle ages, is interesting ; but its brevity—the whole sketch occupies only fifty pages—renders it of little real value to the historical scholar specially concerned with the subject. Those familiar with the history of the English leasehold will be interested in the author's statement (pp. 7-8) that the Roman *superficies* was originally only a personal obligation as between the parties themselves, and did not become a true proprietary interest in land until the praetor gave the necessary protective actions. Similarly, the English lease for years was originally looked upon as merely a personal covenant between the lessor and lessee, and did not acquire the rank of an estate in the land until the possession of the lessee was fully protected by writ. In the author's remarks on the English lease (pp. 48–57) he has drawn attention to the interesting fact that England is exceptional in the prominence which it still gives to this form of landholding, whereas in all other European countries similar interests in land have either disappeared altogether or become very insignificant in modern times. In England Dr. Peal's interest is confined, for his present purposes, to the building lease (p. 51). H. D. H.

In his *Essai sur les Origines et la Fondation du Duché de Normandie* (Paris: Champion, 1911) M. Prentout has given a useful sketch of the history of Normandy from the earliest times to the close of the tenth century. The paucity of evidence for the Roman and Frankish periods inevitably produces in the narrative a certain disproportion, which is increased by the rather detailed treatment of certain much discussed but somewhat special problems, such as the Saxon settlements in the Bessin and the origin of Rollo. The chapter on the Saxons traverses the ground which the author has gone over in a recent number of the *Revue Historique* (July, 1911) under the title *Littus Saxonicum, Saxones Bajocassini, Otlinga Saxonia*; the examination of the texts and place-names tends towards a negative conclusion, which, while admitting the fact of Saxon colonization, denies that it produced permanent and ascertainable results. With respect to the origin of Rollo, M. Prentout, originally a follower of Professor Steenstrup, was led first to abandon the theory that Rollo was a Dane and then, after temporary refuge in agnosticism, to accept the view that he was probably a Norwegian. Perhaps the middle ground was the safest; it is easier to demolish the Danish view, or any other founded upon the authority of Dudo of St. Quentin, than it is to find confirmation for the version of the Norse saga, and after all the really significant fact is that the settlers of Normandy comprised representatives of both peoples. In any case it is well to have a new discussion of the question by one who will not be suspected of national prejudice. M. Prentout is quite right in challenging Professor Steenstrup's easy acceptance of Lair's optimism respecting the value of Dudo, whose *De Moribus et Gestis* is here called (p. 149) 'pas une œuvre historique, mais une épopée et un écrit politique'; certainly the students to whom this volume of lectures was originally addressed need to be warned at the outset against Dudo's work. In a period where the available material is so scanty and for the most part so untrustworthy it would have been well, for pedagogical reasons at least, to bring out more clearly the importance of the charter of Charles the Simple which shows Rollo and his followers established on the Eure *pro tutela regni* in 918. With reference to the chronology of the events of 911, there is a curious slip on p. 194 by which *in sabbato* is rendered 'on Sunday'; but as this is counterbalanced by an error of a day in the calculation, the author's argument remains unaffected. Doubtless the printer should bear the responsibility (p. 127) for placing Wace under Henry I. C. H. H.

The scale of Mr. Alfred Harvey's work on *The Castles and Walled Towns of England* (London: Methuen, 1911) precludes its author from describing more than a limited number of typical examples of medieval castles. He traces the evolution of the English castle from the rectangular keep through the shell keep and circular keep to the keepless castle and finally the concentric castle of Edwardian times, and gives examples of each. His instances are well chosen and described in detail, though too rarely accompanied by plans, without which any architectural account, however explicit, must give a confused impression to any reader who is not already familiar with the building under discussion. The blame for this probably attaches less to the author than to the limitations imposed upon all popular handbooks; and it should be remembered that photographs are both cheaper to reproduce and are more attractive in themselves than ground-plans. Mr. Harvey is naturally much influenced by Mr. G. T. Clark's treatment of the same subject, and is inclined, in spite of recent research, to follow him in regarding the motte and bailey type of castle as of Saxon origin. The arguments for and against Mr. Clark's theory are set out at pp. 54–9. An attempt is made to give in an appendix a list of all known castles in England and Wales. If the book comes to be corrected for a second edition, the appendix should be very thoroughly revised; since, at a moderate estimate, about a quarter of the names given in it are misspelt or are given in obsolete forms. Thus in Northumberland alone we have Bunaden for Burradon, Hennell for Clennell, Highfarland for Heiferlaw, Whelping Kirk for Kirkwhelpington, and so forth. The most original and best executed portion of the book is contained in the sixty pages dealing with walled towns. Here Mr. Harvey gives short notes of all English towns that possess or are known to have possessed fortifications. The subject is one that might have been given a volume to itself, but Mr. Harvey's notes are well worth having, even in their present brief form. It cannot be said that they attain accuracy on every point, e.g. the statement at p. 235 that the town walls of Newcastle were not carried along the river-bank is incorrect. One of the finest examples of our walled towns—Berwick-upon-Tweed—is omitted from the list, presumably because it is regarded as being in Scotland.   H. H. E. C.

In the first part of his *Studien über Otto von Freising*, which appeared in the *Neues Archiv der Gesellschaft für ältere Deutsche Geschichtskunde*, xxxvii. 1, Dr. Adolf Hofmeister, after treating of Otto's family and surroundings, gives an admirable account of the conditions of his life as a student in France. He begins by describing the schools of Rheims and Paris just before Otto's time, and then goes through the list of his contemporaries as students. Finally, he considers those of his teachers who had most influence upon him as shown in his writings. The notes and references are remarkably complete, and add to the value of an uncommonly interesting study.   R. L. P.

Every student will be grateful to the syndics of the Cambridge University Press for printing *The Royal Charters of the City of Lincoln*, transcribed and translated with an introduction by Dr. Walter de Gray Birch

(1911), but sorry for them that it contains so many errors. The earliest charter is an original of Henry II; the latest is of 1696. One of the most interesting is of December 1546, in which Henry VIII takes upon himself the office of a bishop and grants to Lincoln the appropriation of three rectories and ordains vicarages. Besides charters, the editor prints letters patent of Henry VI and two French deeds of the reign of Edward II concerning the wool trade. An English translation of all the deeds is given at the foot of the page, but it is so bald that it will be of no value to those who have no Latin. What will they understand by 'we have granted them quittance of murder' (instead of 'to be quit of fines for murder')? Moreover, the translator can have had no idea what the charters really mean: thus *si aliquis emerit terram ... de burgagio Lincolie* is rendered 'if any one shall have bought land of the Burgage of Lincoln' (p. 2). On the next two pages there is a storm of blunders. The phrase *si quis a recto defecit* is translated 'if any one shall have failed in the right'; *terras et tenuras et vadia sua et debita sua omnimoda iuste habeant quicunque eis debeat* is translated 'that their lands and tenures and *wages* and all manner of their debts be held justly whoever owes them anything'. The charter ends *reddendo per annum novies viginti libras numero de Lincolnia cum omnibus pertinentiis*: the editor is unaware that this was the fee-farm that had always been paid (p. xiv) and declares that it was a new payment, made 'in return for these truly valuable concessions', and his translation is amazing—'yielding yearly nine score pounds of Lincoln tale with all the appurtenances;' he does not notice that *de Lincolnia* goes with *reddendo*, and that *numero* means that the money would not have to be assayed. In the glossary (p. 297) under 'numerus de Lincolnia' he discusses whether there was 'any special numeration or method of counting used in Lincoln', and suggests *nummo* for *numero* because there was a mint at Lincoln; and in the introduction (p. xiv) he renders the words 'nine score pounds of Lincoln money'. On p. 49 he has misunderstood *absque eo quod.* On p. xxxiii there is some perverse learning. Henry IV granted a fair at Lincoln on the feast of the burial of St. Hugh; the date, 17 November, is given in any calendar, even the calendar of the Prayer Book; but the editor fixes on 29 June, the day of the boy Hugh, whom the Jews were supposed to have crucified. On p. 96 *aliqui ad gerendum huiusmodi officium dignius minime haberentur* is rendered 'some would be chosen to bear such office who were not worthy', and two lines later *de remedio summe oportuno providere*, 'at this most opportune moment to provide a remedy;' again, on p. 76 *colligere non possunt in communitatis depressionem*, 'cannot collect *on account of* the depression of the commonalty.' The charter of Henry II is described as relating to 'the method of collecting the fee-farm' (p. xiii), but the charter does not mention this matter at all. Another charter of Henry II says that no foreign merchants are to stay in Lincoln to dye their cloth or sell it by retail (*ad taleam*), except those that are in the guild and contribute to the payments of the town (*qui sunt in gilda et ad omnes consuetudines ville*). The editor's summary is 'this charter requires *the actual presence* of the merchant who dyed or retailed his cloths in Lincoln, and *confirms the customs*'; in the glossary *vendere ad taleam* is explained to mean 'sell by tally, not by weight'. When was cloth sold by weight? In 1301 Edward I granted the citizens to be exempt from murage, pavage, pontage, wharfage, stallage, and terrage throughout the realm; no doubt terrage and stallage mean 'pitching pence', but the editor's version is that the citizens were to be 'exempt from *dues on crops*'. Of a charter of Henry III (p. xvii) we are told ' a new provision is that of the erection of a Merchant Guild '; but the merchant guild is mentioned in all the charters from the beginning, and the first charter of Henry II says that it existed in the time of Edward the Confessor. In 1447 the king gave permission to the mayor and commonalty to acquire land in mortmain; the editor's remark (p. xxxvii) is that if Lincoln had been a corporate body, this licence would have been unnecessary. What does he mean? It would be easy to make this list of errors twice as long. The misprints are not many: p. xxi, l. 1, *heart* should be *hurt*; p. 4, l. 6, *terre et tenure* should be *terras et tenuras* as on p. 10; p. 96, l. 13, *quod* should be inserted before *absit*; p. 96, l. 16, *aportuno* for *oportuno*; pp. 131 and 132, *ob olim* should be *ab olim*; probably *devenerunt* on p. 160 should be *devenerint*. C.

The Pontifical of Magdalen College, edited by the Rev. H. A. Wilson (London: Henry Bradshaw Society, 1910), is a valuable piece of work, as the editor's name would naturally bespeak. His more thorough study of the manuscript has thrown further light on its history, and it is clear that at some date it was somehow connected with Hereford, since the names of three members of the Sparry family of Woolhope in that county are scribbled in its margins. The editor found that these names could not be verified in the Woolhope registers, and we hear that Mr. John Amphlett, of Clent Cottage, Stourbridge, who is interested in the family, is unable to identify them. The name, however, occurs repeatedly in the Franciscan Registers of Birmingham,[1] and it is natural to suspect that the signatories may not have been Anglicans. Shakespeares, we may note, occur in these Franciscan Registers, and a Sparry marriage took place at Snitterfield, the parish of the Ardens. The vicar of Woolhope might have mentioned that there were Sparrys in the neighbourhood if not in his parish as late as 1890. Six of the family were matriculated at Oxford about the time the Pontifical came to the Magdalen library. The editor holds, and with reason, that the Pontifical, originating at Canterbury, found its way to the church of the Black Friars at Hereford before 1448. It is possible perhaps to guess that it was William Courtenay (1342?–96), successively occupant of the Hereford, London, and Canterbury sees, through whom the transference of the book took place, the more so as he was the only bishop of Hereford for at least three centuries who was translated to Canterbury, and we find him associated (e.g. in 1382) with the Black Friars. If this be sound, probably we may argue also that Simon Langham gave the Trinity College, Cambridge, MS. (B) to Ely, for his will[2] specifies gifts to Langham and Ely churches. Other-

[1] Phillimore's *Warwickshire Registers*, vols. ii, iii, iv.
[2] *Dict. of Nat. Biogr.* xxxii. 100.

wise Thomas Arundel (archbishop 1396-1414) might be suggested. All
these three prelates, it may be observed, were diocesans when Richard II
and his consort were crowned ; and the coronation order, studied in the
light of the notes supplied by the editor, seems to support the view
that the book might have been discarded in favour of a later work
about the date we have suggested, for about 1315 the *Liber regalis*
seems to have come into use. One or two features of interest may be
noticed. The original text, like the modern Anglican, had no rubric (p. 177,
n. 15) as to what next should be done after a child was baptized. In
the form for ordaining priests, if we understand aright, there is an interesting survival from the conception found in the *Didache* that the members
of the church form as it were one loaf. The bishop blesses the ordinands in
the form ' Deus . . . munus tuę benedictionis infunde : ut . . . purum et
immaculatum ministerii sui donum custodiant et per obsequium plebis tuę
panem et vinum in corpus et sanguinem filii tui immaculata benedictione
transforment : et inviolabili karitate in virum perfectum in mensuram
ętatis plenitudinis Christi . . . spiritu sancto pleni appareant '. But this
and other interesting points of liturgical development belong rather to
the theologian. The symbol † seems to be unexplained. D.

La Vie paroissiale en France au XIIIᵉ Siècle, by Madame Olga Dobiache-
Rojdestvensky (Paris : Picard, 1911), is based upon considerable research.
The author has examined forty-five sets of synodical statutes, sixteen sets
of statutes promulgated by bishops otherwise than in synod, and seven
records of proceedings at visitations, episcopal or archidiaconal. Most
of this material is unprinted, and her general account of the contents,
fortified by ample extracts at the foot of the page, is of real value. She
duly notes the amount of repetition that is found in the canons, and
points out the common origin in the third and fourth Lateran Councils
or in old compilations such as Theodore and Bede. But the more important part is the picture of clerical life drawn from local canons and
diocesan records. Proportion would have been better preserved had the
writer's horizon been wider, and her instances used to illustrate fuller
generalizations than can be derived from one class of documents. But
even for France her reading has been narrow, and though she cites some
German literature, no English writer is mentioned. On some topics,
such as neglect of clerical duty, quarrels over procurations and tithes, and
abuses in regard to wills, her illustrations are ample, and confirm our
information as to the customs of the century elsewhere ; but her evidence
as to the general continuance of clerical marriage is more important.
The share of the parish clergy in the suppression of heresy in southern
France is an interesting point. Subjects on which a more general survey
would have modified the author's severity are advowsons and the vacation
of benefices through death. The obliquity of patrons and presentees
cannot be inferred from episcopal denunciations, which are merely moves
in the long conflict over patronage ; and any one who has had to do with
the dilapidations of an English living will understand, and allow for, the
irritation of the thirteenth century. Indeed, as we should have expected,
the facts in France are very like those in England. This useful book would

have been better if a certain tone of superiority, and even of hostility, had been absent. E. W. W.

The second volume of the British Society of Franciscan Studies, entitled *Fratris Iohannis Pecham quondam Archiepiscopi Cantuariensis Tractatus tres de Paupertate* (Aberdeen: University Press, 1910), contains three treatises now printed for the first time: (1) selections from Pecham's *Tractatus Pauperis or De Paupertate Evangelica*, edited by Mr. A. G. Little; (2) his *Tractatus contra Fratrem Robertum Kilwardby*, edited by Professor Felice Tocco; and (3) a poetical *Defensio Fratrum Mendicantium*, edited by Mr. C. L. Kingsford. Each writing has an illuminating introduction by its editor The publication of these treatises contributes a valuable addition to our knowledge of the great controversy between the mendicants and the secular clergy in the thirteenth century, and of the relations between the two great mendicant orders *inter se*. The sympathies of most modern readers will be curiously divided. When Pecham is defending his order against the mere abuse of worldly opponents, most of us will feel that he has much to say for himself, if it is clear enough that the reality fell further behind the ideal than he is willing to admit. When he attempts to defend the position that the wealth of which they enjoyed so ample a command was not really property because they enjoyed merely the *usus* and not the *dominium* of it, we must marvel that well-meaning men can have been imposed upon by such transparent sophisms. The treatise against Kilwardby will surprise many readers by showing how much difference already, *c*. 1270, there was on this subject between the two nominally mendicant orders, a difference which already prepared the way for the time when the Dominican Inquisitors were devoting their chief energies to the persecution of the Spiritual Franciscans. Here we cannot but acknowledge that the advantage in the matter of reasonableness and good sense lies on the side of the Dominican; but perhaps the strongest impression that is left on one's mind by the treatise is astonishment at the fact that so little of the spirit of St. Francis remains even in the man who is nominally defending his ideas. E.

The *Tractatus contra Kilwardby* is also printed in Professor Tocco's *La Quistione della Povertà nel Secolo xiv secondo nuovi Documenti* (Naples: Perrella, 1910). The rest of this work is devoted to the documents bearing on the same subject, most of it being occupied by the opinions given by the various cardinals and others in answer to the queries of John XXII with regard to the doctrine of the Spiritual Franciscans that Christ had no *dominium* in anything, and that the highest degree of perfection required a similar abnegation. The reader will be surprised at the number of opinions and shades of difference which were possible upon the subject, and will note with interest that a few of the cardinals seem to have been sufficiently in advance of their age to hold that the theory was absurd, but that there was no reason why it should be treated and persecuted as heretical. The contents of the documents are admirably summarized and exhibited in their historical setting by Professor Tocco.
F.

Part xxvii of the publications of the Canterbury and York Society (London, 1911) contains the few remaining entries in Stephen of Gravesend's register, covering the years 1333 to 1338. These take up the first ten pages, while the other 150 which complete the volume are occupied by appendices. The first of these is both important and interesting—a list of institutions and collations to benefices within the diocese from 1321 to 1338, with the name of the person presented and of the patron. Another useful appendix is the fifth, which puts together an itinerary of the bishops of London from 1306 to 1337, as far as is possible from the registers. For most years, of course, if the itinerary were to be anything like complete, this source would need to be largely supplemented by others. H. J.

In the second volume of his *Calendar of Patent Rolls, Henry V* (London: H.M. Stationery Office, 1911) Mr. R. C. Fowler completes the reign. Military preparations, and provision for the equipment and maintenance of the army in France are prominent, and contain a variety of useful details. There are several interesting entries with regard to ships and shipbuilding, which illustrate the attention paid by Henry V to the development of the navy. As regards home affairs, there are numerous references to Oldcastle's lands; one of Henry's first acts after his return to England in 1421 was to direct inquiry to be made on a petition of Joan Cobham as to lands which she claimed to be hers of right and not liable to forfeiture (p. 322). Of greater interest is a pardon to John Prest, vicar of Chesterton, in Warwickshire, for having received Oldcastle at Chesterton in August 1415 (p. 372). Of other personal references the most noteworthy are two to John Malvern, the physician (pp. 30, 438), and to Friar John Randolph (Queen Joanna's confessor), who is described as late of the house of Friars Minor at Shrewsbury (p. 271). Of a different character is a commission for the arrest of ' one assuming the name of Frer Tuk and other evildoers of his retinue who have committed divers murders, &c.', in Surrey and Sussex (p. 84); this early illustration of the Robin Hood legend had not escaped Stow (*Annales*, p. 352). A series of documents attested in France between 1417 and 1420 (pp. 331-4) illustrate the king's movements during those years. Another series is of interest for Henry's English progress in 1421; he was at Leicester on 19 to 27 March, at York on 4 and 5 April, at Howden on 8 and 11 April, and at Lincoln and Newark on 15 April (pp. 370-2). A lengthy document (pp. 183-95) deals with the settlement of disputes between the bishop of Ely and the monks of his cathedral church as to their respective rights and tenures. An inspeximus and confirmation to the priory of St. Bartholomew, Smithfield, gives five new charters of the twelfth century (pp. 239-45). We may notice a few errors and oversights in names. Richard Beauchamp, earl of Worcester, seems to be confused on p. 400 with his namesake, the earl of Warwick, under whom this entry is indexed. Humby (Hambye) in Normandy (p. 411), and Montreu Fauteyon (p. 435), i. e. Montereau-faut-Yonne, are not identified. St. Weneppa, Cornwall (p. 359) is no doubt Gwennap. C. L. K.

A pamphlet by Dr. Johannes Sieber entitled *Zur Geschichte des Reichsmatrikelwesens im ausgehenden Mittelalter* (*Leipziger Historische Abhandlungen*, No. 24 (Leipzig: Quelle & Meyer, 1910) sketches the development of the taxation of the German states in the form of matricular contributions, the only one ever practised in the older empire and still an important one in the present. It was a compromise between the feudal levy of military contingents (the commutation of which into money, though started in 1487, was deprecated as late as 1521) and the vain attempts at the direct taxation of property for the benefit of the federation. The great wealth of materials relevant to this question, which is chiefly contained in printed and unprinted records of the diets, illustrates the capricious character of the imperial administration. In the parliamentary experience of a century, when the diet was at times held almost yearly, no standards and rules of assessment were able to unite upon themselves the contending forces of the government and the different elements in the federated states, although there appears to have been a hitherto unappreciated tradition already during the last period from the matricula of Constance, 1507, onwards (cf. p. 19). And the gross mistakes the chancery used to commit in the identification of the assessed states merely prove to what an incredible extent also the yield of the taxation was left to chance. The most prominent general feature in the mass of detailed information collected by Dr. Sieber is the slow process of the formation of the larger states by the swallowing up of the lesser ecclesiastical and secular territories. The economic resources of the larger towns, which enabled them to resist this movement as a pretty solid corporation of immediate members of the empire, subjected them on the other hand from the outset to disproportionate assessments. C. B.

A leading type of imperial town is depicted by Dr. Raimund Steinert in his essay on *Das Territorium der Reichsstadt Mühlhausen*, i. (*Forschungen zur Erwerbung, Verwaltung und Verfassung der Mühlhäuser Dörfer*, No. 23 of the same collection). That the specialization of political power represented by the territorial economy of this and so many other cities of central Germany was a result of the decline of their commercial and industrial activity may be argued from the fact (p. 34) that the corporation, being in reality a small aristocracy of landlords, exploited the surrounding agrarian population both as an exclusive source of victuals and raw produce and as an equally exclusive market for their own trades. Compared to this indirect dependence it is true that the direct pressure of 'public' services and taxes does not appear to have weighed heavily on the subject villages, no doubt owing to the valuable rights and powers of self-government which markedly distinguished them from the contemporary constitution of the estates of the nobility. Later on, indeed, the rulers had recourse to an excise which came very near extortion, and destroyed their character long before their mediatization by Prussia in 1802. In analysing the details of this administrative system Dr. Steinert seems on the whole to underrate the consistent tendency of class rule so unmistakable, e. g., in the differentiation of citizen and peasant assessment to the *Geschoss* (pp. 39–45). The problem of the attitude of the Mühlhausen villages in the peasants' rising of 1525 (p. 89) is hardly to be got over by satirical remarks on Zimmermann's *Fabeleien*. The statement that the village of Sollstedt, the only noble estate in the territory, was the only one 'uf der Beschedigungk des Adels mit gewest', proves nothing.   C. B.

In her preface to her life of *Mary Tudor, Queen of France* (London: Methuen, 1911) Miss Mary Croom Brown refers to 'the present incorrigible habit of valuing personality above ceremony'. The epithet is perhaps ironical; at any rate there is much less personality than ceremony in the life of Henry VIII's younger sister, who hardly appears above the surface except in 1514–16, during which she married first Louis XII to suit English policy, and secondly Charles Brandon, duke of Suffolk, to suit herself. The latter romantic episode is told at length by Miss Croom Brown from original sources; but her unpublished materials are drawn for the most part from the wardrobe accounts, and deal mainly with Mary's clothes. The political chapters introduced to explain Mary's marriage with Louis XII are hardly so happy. To say that Ferdinand 'did nothing' in 1511 while the English expedition lay cooped up at Passages (p. 38) is a misleading method of expressing the fact that he used it as a screen from the French, behind which he proceeded to conquer Spanish Navarre. Nor is it correct to represent the action of the English government from 1509 to 1511 as Henry VIII's personal policy. In details, too, Miss Croom Brown will mislead her readers out of deference to her original authorities. No doubt Poynings's name was generally spelt Ponynges (p. 34), but Miss Croom Brown's readers would not without help identify him with the famous lord-deputy of Ireland. Wolsey's secretary, too, was not *Sir* Richard Pace (p. 232), but Dr. Richard Pace, afterwards dean of St. Paul's; and the battle of 'Novarro' (p. 47) is more familiar under another spelling. The statement (p. 110) that 'in spite of Dr. Brewer' it was Anne and not Mary Boleyn who accompanied the queen to France in 1514 is far too categorical; the balance of evidence has shifted back, since Friedmann wrote, in Brewer's favour. There is little to tell of Mary's life after 1516, but Miss Croom Brown might have let us know the date of her death: the latest year mentioned in the text is 1528–9, and we are then told that 'she died on Midsummer's Day, says Hall; on June 26, says the Heralds' College'. Of course a student could discover that the year was 1533, but we doubt if this volume is designed for students. It might also have been worth while stating that Mary's only son, who, as Miss Croom Brown says, 'might have been king of England,' died on 1 March 1534. There are a number of illustrations, most of which, however, have been reproduced before.   A. F. P.

The January number of the *Revue Historique* contains an article by Madame Inna Lubimenko on *Les Marchands anglais en Russie au XVIᵉ Siècle*, for the purpose of which the author has had the advantage of being able to draw upon Russian authorities inaccessible to most English students, though one of them, it seems (Tolstoi, *The First Forty Years of Intercourse between England and Russia*), was published in 1875 in Russian and English, and another (by Klutchevsky) is, we believe, in process of translation. Although vol. ii of Dr. W. R. Scott's recent work on the Joint Stock Companies contains a much fuller account of the commercial activities of the Russia Company which the writer had not, apparently, the opportunity of consulting, her article is still of distinct interest and value to English readers, and emphasizes the value of the English contribution to Russian civilization.   G. U.

In *The History of the Great Moghuls*, vol. ii (Calcutta : Thacker, Spink & Co., 1911), Mr. Pringle Kennedy continues his narrative from the death of Akbar to the sack of Delhi by Nadir Shah in 1739, winding up with a brief epilogue on subsequent events and a few reflections on the lessons to be learnt from the history of India under her Moghul rulers. In a modest preface the author describes his aim as being merely to furnish ' the man in the street ' with a little more knowledge than he already possesses on the subject ; and this being so, detailed criticism would be out of place. The book is admittedly a compilation from well-known authorities ; it is written in an easy, not to say slipshod, style, and contains some fairly obvious inaccuracies.   G.

In his Ford Lectures, delivered at Oxford in 1910 on *Anglo-Dutch Rivalry during the first half of the Seventeenth Century* (Oxford : Clarendon Press, 1911), the Rev. George Edmundson has singled out a very marked and interesting epoch of history. The competition of powers for the succession to the medieval agents of European commerce, Germany and the southern peninsulas, even if one leaves on one side the secondary parts taken by France and Sweden, is so vast a subject both with regard to geographical area and political action that it becomes as unavoidable as it is difficult to concentrate research and narrative round some fixed point of view. As such a point Mr. Edmundson has not inappropriately chosen the diplomatic intercourse between England and Holland. The main subjects on which the economic interests of the two nations first clashed, the questions of the herring and whale fisheries in the North Sea, the English cloth and the Indian spice trade, are very well brought out, though the chief contrast of later times, that of west Indian colonization, does not seem to have been then much noticed in politics. The disadvantage to which England was subjected almost along the whole line by possessory titles of its rival appears to have been greatly increased by the unwise policy of the first two Stuarts, whose ineffective ambition is strangely set off against the consistent and well-directed pertinacity of the Dutch aristocracy. The diplomacy of men like the Oldenbarnevelts, Jacob Cats, and Aerssen van Sommelsdijk, while outwardly yielding to the arrogance of the kings, succeeded in evading James I's fishery order of 1609 for more than a generation and at the same time upholding their own new regulations about the import of English cloth against the protests of the growing English industry. It was not until the rebellion and the commonwealth that England was for the first time able to make good the pretensions of the deposed dynasty. In an appendix Mr. Edmundson has brought together his larger notes, among which are useful little monographs, for instance, on the Merchant Adventurers and on the British troops in Dutch service.   C. B.

The anonymous author of *The First Duke and Duchess of Newcastle-upon-Tyne* (London : Longmans, 1910) forestalls criticism by the statement that he 'does not labour under the delusion that he has written a book'. His aim has been a mere compilation of passages bearing on the lives and characters of his hero and heroine, and the result of this industry, excellently bound, printed, and illustrated, will doubtless afford pleasure and interest to the general reader. Its historical value is negligible, but it possesses at least one merit not always found in works of this class : the numerous quotations have been selected at first-hand, and all references are duly given. Moreover, while the compilation is avowedly based on Clarendon's *History* and the Duchess of Newcastle's *Life* of her husband, it is not confined to extracts from these well-worn sources. The *Reports of the Historical MSS. Commission*, the *Calendars of Domestic State Papers*, and other collections and contemporary works have been pressed into the service. The whole is linked together by comments discursive, conversational, and occasionally inaccurate. The position of Newcastle as excepted from pardon by parliament (p. 162) was by no means unique ; he had in that misfortune many companions among the royalist leaders, including Prince Rupert himself. Rupert was not twenty-two, but nearly twenty-five in July 1644 (p. 140). It was the elder George, Lord Goring, created earl of Norwich, November 1644, who aspired to the governorship of the prince of Wales, not his son the cavalry general (p. 76). The famous 'Bess of Hardwick' is scarcely recognizable under the name of 'Margaret' (p. 3). And it seems a pity to spoil Wotton's aphorism regarding ambassadors by a transposition of words : the contemporary translation approved by Wotton, 'sent to lie abroad,' contains a double-entendre lacking in 'sent abroad to lie' (p. 8).   E. S.

The *Catalogue of Tracts of the Civil War and Commonwealth Period relating to Wales and the Borders*, printed at the private printing press of the library, contains the titles and descriptions of 264 tracts to be found in the National Library of Wales. It is arranged on the lines of the catalogue of the Thomason Tracts, and although the collection is by no means a complete one, the catalogue will be a useful guide to the contemporary publications relating to Wales. It includes, besides the tracts dealing with the war and with political affairs, a certain number of pieces written by or about Welshmen and a few satirical tracts. The full title, the date of issue, and the sizes are given, and there is a short introduction and a good index. The catalogue is interleaved, and contains a scale of metric and English measurements.   G. B. T.

Miss Lucy Sealy states the object of her book, *Champions of the Crown* (London : Methuen, 1911), as twofold—an analysis of the motives and ideals that led men of very various disposition and circumstance to embrace the royal cause in the Great Civil War, and a vindication of the cavaliers in general as men of honest, earnest purpose who, no less than their opponents, took up arms 'upon conscience of religion and law '. To this end she offers ten short sketches of prominent royalist leaders, nobles, statesmen, country gentlemen, and professional soldiers, born and bred in different districts and of widely divergent character and outlook. The plan of these sketches, which deal chiefly with the conduct of the war, involves inevitable repetition, and though they are well illustrated and pleasantly written, they add nothing to the knowledge of the historical student. They follow well-beaten paths and are largely drawn from well-known sources, such as Clarendon and Lloyd. Certain other quotations have a rather second-hand aspect, but no references are given. There are a number of small inaccuracies, of which the most notable occurs on p. 81, where the seizure of the king by the army in December 1648 is confused with the earlier seizure at Holmby by Cornet Joyce in June 1647. The message quoted on p. 196 was not addressed to Prince Charles, but to the duke of York; Prince Rupert owed his sobriquet of 'le Diable' to his own family, not to his foes (p. 155); his marriage certificate exists, though its legality has not been fully established (p. 200), and a frequent mention of Langdale (p. 56) may be found in the annals of the exiled court. E. S.

Professor Firth has brought out a revised edition of his Ford Lectures of 1900–1 on *Cromwell's Army* (London: Methuen, 1912), which we reviewed in January 1903 (xviii. 169 f.). The new features of the book are a preface giving references to the recent literature of the subject and a series of capital illustrations. H.

In his *Histoire des Princes de Condé au XVIIIe Siècle* (Paris: Plon, 1911) General de Piépape has given a useful account of Henri Jules, Louis III, and the duke of Bourbon-Condé. The title of the volume is not quite accurate, for the period dealt with is from 1643 to 1743. The attitude of the author to his subject is unlike that of the majority of biographers. For the three princes, notably the last, General de Piépape expresses profound contempt. As soldiers and as rulers in Burgundy and Chantilly capable work was done by Henri Jules and Louis III. As public men they rendered service to their country not entirely unworthy of the great name they bore, but their private life was immoral to a high degree. The author gives us an account of the ceremonial employed at the opening of the *Pays d'états* of Burgundy in 1697, whereas we wished to hear about its doings. The parts played by the intendant, the captains, and the sergeants in the state entry are not of much interest; on the other hand, we should have been glad to hear more about the 'gratuitous gift' and the manner of arranging the incidence of it. Finot, the physician, makes it clear that Henri Jules was as mad as he was debauched. His mother could scarcely read or write, but he was a cultured man. The last prince was more odious than either of his predecessors. Monsieur le Duc, as he was styled, was of brutal mind and manners, the slave of his mistress the Marquise de Prie, who was the pensioner of Walpole. For about three years Fleury allowed him to act as first minister, and in 1726 the duke and the mistress were exiled. The book furnishes us with an acute insight into society in France, and enables us to see that the policy of Louis XIV left his nobility helpless and powerless when the Revolution came. R. H. M.

The last instalment of the *Calendar of the Court Minutes of the East India Company, 1644–9*, by Miss E. B. Sainsbury, with an introduction and notes by Mr. W. Foster (Oxford : Clarendon Press, 1912), finds and leaves the Company at the point of disruption. Its treatment by the king and his courtiers had not been such as to encourage loyalty. At the same time its claim to a monopoly depended upon a royal grant ; and unless similar privileges could be obtained by a parliamentary ordinance, its position was merely precarious. Its old enemy, William Courteen, met with financial failure ; but a new competitor arose in the person of one Maurice Thomson, with whom the East India Company had finally to join forces. Thomson was preoccupied with the idea of founding a colony on the little island of Assada, to the north-east of Madagascar, a not very hopeful enterprise.[1] With the help of Mr. Foster's notes it is possible to understand the complicated transactions of the joint stocks and of the first and second general voyages. When we consider the background of war and lawlessness our wonder is that the trade went on as smoothly as it did. In 1645 the master of one of the ships sailed home on a privateering venture on behalf of the king. ' He came with the shipp, &c., safe into Bristoll and there made awaie with what was found in the shipp, yet that was not an end of his villanie, but others also suffered much from his depradations and robberies in those parts.' Although the events of the volume do not often take us into the general political history of the time, on economic and antiquarian grounds it is none the less valuable.

H. E. E.

In his lucid account of *Religious Liberty under Charles II and James II* (Cambridge : University Press, 1911) Mr. Russell Smith has done a careful piece of work. The Clarendon Code, the Test Acts, the Exclusion Bills do not suggest that the age in which these measures were passed was a tolerant one. In spite, however, of this legislation the author draws attention to the opinion of thoughtful men of the same period, and he has not much difficulty in showing that a definite theory of religious liberty was asserted by the nonconformists, the national theologians, and the whigs. The contemporary accusation that nonconformists were seditious Mr. Russell Smith dismisses too lightly. As a matter of fact they were not seditious, but as a matter of opinion they were deemed to be so. The essence of Roman catholicism was supposed to be a belief in the deposing power, and from this point of view Roman catholics and dissenters were identified. Many annotations could easily be given in proof of this statement. For instance, in Leslie's *The Rehearsal* it is solemnly declared, ' The Puritans were mere tools to the Jesuits (as they are to this day), from whom they learned the deposing doctrine, and to set up the private spirit against the Holy Scriptures, and all the authority of the Church.' It is evident that so long as dissenters were looked upon as disloyal, so much the more remote were the prospects of their toleration. Mr. Russell Smith discusses with much insight the position of John Locke, and explains the two exceptions in his system of religious liberty. Locke refused to tolerate Roman

[1] See above, pp. 239–50.

catholicism and Mahometanism, and he also refused to tolerate atheism. The grounds of the first exception are obvious, for the religious views of adherents of these bodies were such that they were not capable of becoming citizens in the true sense of the term. The grounds of the second exception, as Mr. Russell Smith points out, are much less easy to justify.

R. H. M.

Dr. C. Brauns's *Kurhessische Gewerbepolitik im 17. und 18. Jahrhundert (Staats- und sozialwissenschaftliche Forschungen*, No. 156. Leipzig : Duncker & Humblot, 1911) is occupied with a country which from its small size and industrial backwardness furnished peculiar conditions, difficulties as well as advantages, making the course of industrial reform there different from most German states. On the one hand, both characteristics made it dependent for progress on the concurrence of the surrounding (and, as imperial towns, mostly rather conservative) territories of central Germany. On the other, the growth of capitalism had as yet neither reinforced the companies of artisans nor urged the labour question and the social conflict to that degree which so materially complicated the industrial policy of the leading German states. Under these circumstances the Hessian government succeeded not only in establishing, side by side with the imperial legislation on the subject, that of its own general *Zunftordnungen* of 1693 and 1730, but also in slowly reducing the privileges of the individual companies, and at last even their most persistent customary law, to a system compounded of the beneficial sides of free and incorporated trade. To return to this level after the French interregnum of 1807–14 was, if not necessitated by the example of all Germany with the exception of Prussia, at least not prompted by the reactionary spirit recently denounced by Bovensiepen in his book on *Die Kurhessische Gewerbepolitik 1816–67*.

C. B.

The second volume of *The Correspondence of Jonathan Swift, D.D.*, edited by Mr. F. Elrington Ball (London : Bell, 1911), like the preceding volume, is very well annotated. Practically nothing is left unexplained. The volume covers the period from January 1713 to the end of August 1717, that is to say, it contains the letters printed in volume xviii of Scott's edition of Swift (pp. 20–298). In addition to these it includes many new letters to or from Swift. Some of these letters are taken from the correspondence with Knightley Chetwode, printed by Dr. Birkbeck Hill in 1899, which are now printed from a different and a better manuscript than that used by Dr. Hill. Chetwode's letters to the dean are also added. Other additions are letters from Swift to Dr. Walls, the originals of which are in the possession of Mr. John Murray, and a good deal of new material has been obtained from the King MSS. The new letters throw more light on Swift's life after his return to Ireland than on the period when he played an important part in English politics, so that they are of more value to the biographer than the historian. In January 1715 Erasmus Lewis warned Swift to hide his papers, and possibly the necessity of taking precautions led to the destruction of some letters of political interest (p. 267). His correspondence with his friends in England was examined by the Irish government in the hope of discovering political secrets (p. 421). It is evident that the dean himself was exceedingly careful what he wrote and also told his friends not to write to him on political topics (pp. 277, 423). This makes passages such as the criticism on the famous 'Report from the Committee of Secrecy' on the Utrecht negotiations of greater interest. 'I do not believe or see,' says Swift, ' one word is offered to prove their old slander of bringing in the Pretender. The treason lies wholly in making the peace' (p. 285). In one of the appendices Mr. Ball prints Bolingbroke's application to Shrewsbury on behalf of Swift for the post of historiographer royal. He recommended Swift as successor to Rymer, on the ground that he was 'fitter than any man in the Queen's dominions . . . for writing a complete history of our own country ' (p. 419). Mrs. Masham's influence was also employed in Swift's favour (pp. 174, 184). It was given to Thomas Madox, whom Swift angrily describes as ' a worthless rogue that nobody knows ', and Mr. Ball dismisses in a footnote as an antiquary of the dryasdust type (pp. 188, 196, 210). The queen's advisers deserve great credit for preferring the man who was really qualified for the post to the distinguished pamphleteer. C. H. F.

M. Paul Duchaine in his *La Franc-Maçonnerie Belge au XVIII° Siècle* (Bruxelles : P. van Fleteren, 1911) has given us a careful account of Belgian freemasonry in the eighteenth century. His book is based on documents preserved by the lodges, and he has collected a great mass of information which he places before us clearly. The first part of his book treats of freemasonry in the Low Countries from 1721 to 1780, and the second of its general history from 1780 to 1798. Though the volume makes a special appeal to members of the craft, still it possesses interest for a wider public. It sheds light upon the workings of the secret associations of the eighteenth century, and these have an intimate connexion with the French Revolution. Moreover, the author has much to say upon the policy of Joseph II and the causes of its failure. He thinks that the philosopher-statesman did not understand the masonic spirit, which he supposed to be akin to that of the religious orders, and in this manner he accounts for his change from the favourable attitude he had assumed in 1785. This lack of insight is characteristic, and goes far to explain the non-success of Joseph II.
R. H. M.

In *New Jersey as a Royal Province, 1738 to 1776* (Columbia University Studies in History, Economics, and Public Law, xli) Dr. E. J. Fisher attempts to outline the political history of the province, and to show the part taken by New Jersey in the third and fourth intercolonial wars, and in the preliminaries of the revolution. The previous history has been dealt with by Dr. Tanner ; otherwise there seems no special significance in the date 1738, which merely marks the time when New Jersey was given a separate governor, not the time (1702) when it became a royal province. The political history of the province was singularly uneventful and dull, and Dr. Fisher's manner of treating it does not add to its liveliness. The part taken by New Jersey, both in the French wars and in the events which preceded the revolution, was of little importance; so that not much is added on this side to our knowledge of the general history. Dr. Fisher seems to have made careful use of the *New Jersey Archives*, but his monograph will mainly appeal to those interested in the details of its provincial history. To the general student the chapter on 'The Proprietary System and the Land Troubles' will perhaps be found the most interesting.

H. E. E.

Colonel St. Paul of Ewart, Soldier and Diplomat, edited by Mr. George G. Butler (2 vols.; London : The St. Catherine Press, 1911), contains in two bulky volumes St. Paul's diplomatic correspondence, prefaced by a sketch of his life. A career so honourable as his could scarcely have had a more unfortunate beginning. While a student at Gray's Inn he killed an acquaintance in a duel of which there were no witnesses, was declared guilty of murder by a coroner's jury, fled the country, was outlawed, and lost his paternal inheritance. He entered the Austrian army as a captain, and served with distinction during the Seven Years' War, became a colonel of cavalry and a count of the empire. The journal which he kept during the war is, we are interested to hear, about to be published by the Cambridge University Press. After obtaining a pardon from the crown through the good offices of Lord Sandwich, he was employed as secretary of legation in Lord Stormont's embassy to the French court from 1772 to 1776, and as minister plenipotentiary during the last months of his official residence in Paris : Stormont was often absent in England, and during his absences the secretary had charge of the affairs of the embassy. St. Paul's diplomatic correspondence, though not of first-rate importance, illustrates various questions and disputes between the two courts, as the determination of the British government to order a fleet to sail to the Baltic if the French sent ships to help the Swedes in case they were attacked by Russia, and difficulties which arose regarding the French works at Dunkirk, trading rights in Senegal, and the French garrison and fortifications at Chandernagore. This last was no trifling matter, for in 1773 the duke d'Aiguillon proposed in the council a plan for attacking the British in Bengal in alliance with the Moghul emperor. While St. Paul was minister he was chiefly occupied in negotiations connected with the quarrel between Spain and Portugal, finally arranged in 1777 by the treaty of San Ildefonso, and in trying to detect the proceedings of American agents. He sent home many notices of court intrigues and official rivalries, of the anxiety of Queen Marie Antoinette for the restoration of Choiseul, and of her more successful efforts to obtain d'Aiguillon's banishment from court. As usual, some heterogeneous business came to the embassy : St. Paul was requested to buy ' eight ells of black and white gauze ' to trim a dress for Lady Ailesbury, and to get two young ladies out of religious houses ; one of them, Miss Rose Plunket, was the heroine of a curious story which was the subject of much diplomatic discussion and correspondence.

W. H.

In *Colonial Opposition to Imperial Authority during the French and Indian War* (*California University Publications in History*, i. 1, Berkeley, 1911) Dr. E. J. McCormack shows by a careful study of the records in the case of each of the American colonies that the constitutional doctrines, asserted after the passage of the stamp act, were already familiar at the time of the French war. 'Unity of action was practically the only new element. Their doctrines, theories, and arguments were the same; the policy of England, not that of the colonies, had changed.' Much of the evidence here adduced will be fairly familiar to students of the period, but its cumulative effect when drawn from each colony in turn is great. H. E. E.

In the *Proceedings of the Massachusetts Historical Society*, October 1911, are printed some letters from the Record Office relating to the subject of prisoners in the war of independence. The following, written by Franklin after the capitulation of Yorktown, is characteristic:

I enclose our last *Gazette* by which you will see that Gen. Burgoyne has now a companion in misfortune. This world is full of changes and of chances. War in particular abounds with them. The present I think has done mischief enough. When will your rulers be of the same opinion? I am with others empower'd to treat of peace, and for the sake of humanity I heartily wish it; but I draw near to the end of life, and hardly expect that in my time there will be any use made of our Commission.

In the same number there is an equally characteristic sentence from a letter of T. Paine (1 October 1800) in the Jefferson MSS., which was struck out by Jefferson and is thus not printed in Conway's *Life*:

That you might keep your eye on brother Adams whose talent was to blunder and offend. His fractious, untractable disposition has justified this opinion of him. Like his secretary Timothy (Pickering) he mistakes arrogance for greatness and sullenness for wisdom. Were you in Europe, you would feel afflicted as I do for the degradation of the American character. The silent hypocrisy of Washington (for I venture my opinion) gave the first stab to the fame of America, and the entire nothingness of Adams has deepened the wound.

H. E. E.

We are glad to welcome the first number of the *Revue des Études Napoléoniennes* (Paris: Alcan, 1912), which appeared in January under the capable direction of M. Édouard Driault. First numbers are proverbially good, and this is no exception to the rule. The editor summarizes the history of Napoleonic studies since Napoleon, M. Masson writes on the count of Montholon before St. Helena, M. René Schneider on the art of Canova and imperial France, while M. Roger Lévy supplies a useful account of the recent literature relating to the internal history of the first empire. The new quarterly is pleasantly printed, and is uniform in size and appearance with a *livraison* of Lavisse's *Histoire de France*. The editor has secured the promise of support from leading Napoleonic scholars all over Europe, and if he can get such men as M. Masson or Dr. Fournier to supply regular, or even intermittent, contributions he will establish its reputation beyond cavil. At present the danger would seem to be the very natural one, namely, that the most zealous contributors are the most undiscriminating admirers, so that to some eyes the Review might appear in the light of a Bonapartist manifesto. Needless to say this is not M. Driault's intention. *Sine Ira et Studio* is to be the motto of an enterprise which is to embrace the highly controversial history both of the first and of the second empire.　　　　　　　　　　　　　　H. A. L. F.

A valuable supplement to the correspondence of Napoleon was published by Professor Adam Skalkowski in 1910, but in a Polish periodical, the *Kwartalnik Historyczny*, which is not well known to western scholars. It has since, however, been made generally accessible under the title *En Marge de la Correspondance de Napoléon I* (Paris: Grasset, 1911), and is the most important addition to the published collections of imperial letters since the appearance of Brotonne's volume in 1898. All the pieces concern the Poles, or rather the Polish contingent, in the Grande Armée; but there is one document which also throws a most interesting light upon Napoleon. This is a report of Napoleon's address to the Polish officers on 28 October 1813, just after the battle of Leipzig, printed from the original autograph of John Skrzynecki, then a colonel in the army of the duchy of Warsaw. The whole speech, with the interruptions of the Poles and the rejoinders of the emperor, is wonderfully vivid and lifelike, and looks as if it were taken down verbatim. The emperor employs all his powers of cajolery to persuade the Poles to follow his fortunes, and is brilliantly successful. 'Il faut aller en France, messieurs les Polonais. Je suis le seul sur lequel vous pouvez compter.' As the emperor concluded thus there were cries of 'Vive l'Empereur'. Napoleon took off his hat and saluted. The spell was perfect. The air rang with shouts of 'Vive l'Empereur, notre unique espérance, notre unique providence'. The whole passage should be read, for there are very few pieces of recorded Napoleonic conversation better or more characteristic than this admirable scene.　　　　　　　　　　　　　　　　　　　　　　　　H. A. L. F.

In *Napoleon's Brothers* (London: Methuen [1910]) Mr. A. Hilliard Atteridge has essayed the somewhat difficult task of separating them from the general narrative of the rise and fall of the empire. His aim has been to trace the course of events from the point of view of the four brothers, and not to treat them as mere satellites of the emperor. Incidentally he also defends them from charges of incapacity and disloyalty which have been made against them by M. Frédéric Masson and others. The conclusion at which he arrives is that their history is 'at best the story of a failure'; but he attributes this to the fact that Napoleon refused to take his brothers seriously, and looked upon them not as ruling monarchs, but rather as governors of provinces, whom he could control and move about from country to country in the same manner as his marshals and generals. It is not necessary, however, either to blame Napoleon for the failures of his brothers, or to find the brothers guilty of bringing about the downfall of Napoleon. It is true enough that Napoleon's despotic temperament and dictatorial methods placed very great obstacles in the way of his royal brothers, but it is also clear that none of them—with the possible exception of Lucien—possessed the qualities which were essential to success in the extremely arduous and delicate positions to which they were called. Louis and Jerome were throughout a source of continual annoyance and expense to Napoleon; Joseph and Lucien, on the other hand, were frequently of great assistance to him, and it is highly probable that on some occasions—notably the *coup d'état* of Brumaire—they saved the situation for him. The story of Napoleon's brothers is an exceedingly fascinating one, and Mr. Atteridge is to be congratulated on presenting it to the English-speaking public in an eminently readable form. The book contains a few mistakes of a minor character. Thus the term used to describe a Carbonaro lodge was *vendita* and not *venta* as stated at p. 480. By an obvious slip of the pen the seventeenth century is transformed into the sixteenth at p. 281. Otherwise the volume under review appears to be accurate as well as interesting.　　　　　　　　　　　　　　　　　　　　　　　H. C. G.

The Library of Congress has published a *Calendar of the Papers of Martin van Buren* (Washington, 1910). The state papers, correspondence, &c., here calendared were collected by Van Buren as current files, or in his later life as material for his *Autobiography*. There are many gaps due to the carelessness with which he kept his papers.　　　H. E. E.

M. Pierre Albin has produced an admirable French version of Professor A. von Ruville's extremely able narrative of the part played by Bavaria and, incidentally, by the other south-western German states in the process of the refoundation of the German empire in 1870 (*La Restauration de l'Empire allemand ; le Rôle de la Bavière*. Paris : Alcan, 1911). This translation is introduced by a short essay from the pen of M. Joseph Reinach, of which the interest is political rather than historical. All readers of the memoirs of Prince Chlodwig Hohenlohe will be glad to continue their study of Bavarian politics at the hand of an authority so competent as Professor von Ruville, whose bibliography alone might secure a welcome to his volume. His general account of the political intentions and procedure of Count Bray seems to us alike full and fair, and he is perfectly justified in arguing that the failure of this minister to settle the future of Germany after his own fashion by no means proves him to have been a mere narrow-minded particularist. German historians are apt to forget that at one time more than a single way of achieving German unity seemed possible. On the other hand, the study of the action (as well as the inaction) of King Lewis II will not fail to secure attention, though there may be a touch of exaggeration in the significance attached to the king's declaration in his speech from the throne of 17 January 1870, that he had pledged his royal word to carry out the treaty of alliance. For, if this was a separate and secret promise on the part of King Lewis, how can the king of Prussia's declaration, on 14 February following, that the German princes had mutually engaged their word, be analogous to, or an echo of, his brother of Bavaria's reference to his own personal promise ? It is not quite clear whether this episode of Lewis II's 'royal word', of which the echo is to be found in the same monarch's personal intervention in the crucial question of the offer of the imperial crown, is directly connected by Professor von Ruville with the secondary, but at the same time the most striking, portion of the plan of his volume. This is his endeavour to solve the problem of Bavaria's ultimate acceptance of the Prussian scheme for effecting the new German unity. Professor von Ruville's method, which he complains was very imperfectly appreciated by English critics when applied by him in the case of the elder Pitt and the large legacy inherited by him, is fully expounded by the author in the present work. The task of the historian inquiring into a hitherto obscure passage or problem of history is to find the missing piece of a broken ring which will exactly—or, if not exactly, at all events up to a certain point—fit the part of the circle already in our hands, and the discovery of which will thus restore, or approximately restore, the original ring. In Professor von Ruville's present research, of which the crucial difficulty lies in the hitherto unexplained, or insufficiently explained, action of Bavaria—and of Bray in particular—towards Bismarck's plan of union ultimately accepted by her, the missing part of the ring consists in the fact of the possession by Bismarck of secret information as to earlier dealings between Napoleon III and his most confidential advisers on the one hand, and the Bavarian and neighbouring cabinets on the other. That such information was contained in the large quantity of papers removed by Rouher, the ' vice-emperor ', to his country-house at Cerçay and after seizure by the Prussians transferred into Bismarck's hands, is not an original conjecture of Professor von Ruville; but he has set himself, with extraordinary ingenuity, to convert conjecture into actual or virtual certainty. How far he has succeeded (for there can be no question of an absolutely complete result) it would be futile to seek to show without a detailed examination. A. W. W.

Before 1891 the question which forms the subject of Mr. H. P. Fairchild's *Greek Immigration to the United States* (Yale : University Press, 1911) did not exist; since then, however, it has become an important factor in the social history of contemporary Greece, and a serious problem for statesmen. The author traces its origin from the depression of the currant trade and the rise in prices, and describes its effects upon Greece and the United States. He has collected much information, but he is apt to consider as specialities of Greek emigration phenomena common to other southern lands, and is harsh in his judgements. There is more than ' one ' monastery ' at Meteora '; M. Koromelâs has for some time ceased to be Greek representative at Washington; and M. Kalopothákes is dead. The bibliography is ill-assorted and inadequate. W. M.

The Full Recognition of Japan (London : Frowde, 1911) is the not very happy title which Mr. Robert P. Porter has chosen for his valuable account of Japanese progress in recent times. The chapters in which he has sketched Japanese history are not of great importance, but the mass of information collected in his surveys of Japanese trade, industry, finance, and railways is striking, and should be of much value to politicians and statisticians. Some portions of the book have already appeared in *The Times*, but the surveys to which we refer have not. Mr. Porter writes with the ease of the experienced journalist on many other aspects of Japan, ranging from its agriculture to its amusements, and his book will be useful to travellers. G. B. H.

M. Gabriel Hanotaux's delightful little book, *La Fleur des Histoires Françaises* (Paris: Hachette, 1911), may be recommended to all lovers of graceful things. It does not profess to be systematic or exhaustive or useful for examinations. It is sparing of dates and often rebellious against a strict chronological arrangement. Its design is to give to the children of the French people the sentiment of their national history, to tell them about their own country, its soil, its waters, its skies, its men, and with what special qualities of soul and spirit the nation has declared itself in recorded time. And though we have some doubt whether a book, so learned and yet so dainty, is specially calculated to appeal to the young—unless indeed the youth of France is quite exceptional for its precocity—M. Hanotaux does certainly, with great brilliance and incisiveness and in a very small compass, achieve the object which he has in view. He gives us the feeling of French history. He touches upon geography and climate, law and politics, science and literature, architecture, painting, and battles. The people of France he depicts as undergoing a series of phases ' according to logical necessities subordinate to laws of nature and experience '. Thus in the seventeenth century we have the classic, in the eighteenth the philosophic age. Then comes the revolution when the dominant tendencies are political and juridical, which in turn is followed first by the heroic-lyric period and finally by the age of science and realism. What is the next logical necessity ? M. Hanotaux does not tell us. In the course of ' a nonchalant promenade through the flowery gardens of France ' we cannot expect to be told everything. The surprising thing is the polished literary artifice whereby our accomplished guide is enabled at once to tell us so little and so much.

H. A. L. F.

Admirers of the diplomatic work of the late *Léopold Delisle*, and all students of diplomatic were such, will find pleasure in the essay by Mr. R. L. Poole which is published in the fifth volume of the Proceedings of the British Academy (London: Frowde). The author writes first a brief memoir of Delisle, and then turns to discuss some of his most important contributions to diplomatic, especially his monograph on the Acts of Innocent III and his unfinished labours upon the Norman Acts of Henry II.

F. M. P.

The first volume of Professor L. Oppenheim's treatise on *International Law* (' Peace '), which we reviewed in 1907 (xxii. 388 f.), has appeared in a second and revised edition (London: Longmans, 1912).   I.

In a volume of *Kleine Historische Schriften* (Munich: Oldenbourg, 1911) Professor Max Lenz has collected what he believes to be the more popular of his smaller works. One who (as in the essay on Janssen) knows so well how to characterize the deep-rooted party conceptions of modern German historiography might perhaps not object to being himself called an enthusiastic representative of the spirit of Prussian protestantism so prominent in the new empire. This is shown in his exposition of Luther's politics and of Bismarck's religion, as well as in the other monographs which treat of his two favourite subjects, the reformation and nineteenth-century Prussia. By foreign readers, therefore, the few studies relating to other subjects will be found most valuable. That on Napoleon I and Prussia is quite a model of insight into the necessities of a career obscured by the nationalist prejudices of all Europe. Likewise the account of the German revolution of 1848 contains a remarkably fair estimate of some facts that are seldom acknowledged, such as the opportunist policy of the 'idealist' moderates. The skilful reconstruction, in 'König Wilhelm und Bismarck in Gastein, 1863,' of the events preceding Prussia's separation from the Frankfort congress, ought indeed to act as an appeal to governments in general not to withhold from research the records of diplomatic negotiations which passed at the time and expressed themselves in the contents of the newspaper press. C. B.

In *The Counties of England, their Story and Antiquities* (London: Allen, 1912) a great opportunity has been missed. The two volumes are handsomely printed and well illustrated, but their contents for the most part insult the reader's intelligence. The editor, the Rev. P. H. Ditchfield, has written the largest and the worst part of the work. In a florid and slipshod style he retails the old errors and falsehoods that we had hoped were finally exorcized by the Victoria History. The Roman period allows him the fullest scope : Boadicea fights her battle at King's Cross, and the author knows more than any historian has dared to assert since the days of Monkbarns. King Vortigern appears, without a whisper of doubt ; and 'Ingulph' is cited at length (though not by Mr. Ditchfield) for the history of Lincolnshire. As a specimen of the editor's inaccuracy we may cite his assertion that the battle of Shrewsbury was fought within sight of the walls of Chester ; and we are not more surprised to learn of the conversion of George Fox by Margaret Fell than of the 'political integrity' of Lord Brougham. If he borrows the Bedfordshire jingle about the Burgoyne property from the old *Gentleman's Magazine,* he ought not to say that John of Gaunt 'granted the estate to their ancestor by these simple rhymes', without any warning to his more innocent readers that he is jesting. Of several counties, however, really sound and instructive accounts are given, notably of Surrey, which is by Mr. H. E. Malden, and of Northamptonshire, Essex, Middlesex, and Hampshire, though Mr. Jeans, the author of the last, has almost confined himself to the city of Winchester. Such writers cannot be proud of the company in which they find themselves. J.

Cheshire in the *Oxford County Histories* (Clarendon Press, 1911) is one of the best books of the kind that has appeared. It covers its ground systematically and clearly from geological times to electric trams ; and it may be sound pedagogy that the writer, Mr. C. E. Kelsey, should use the second person throughout in addressing his readers. A schoolmaster must lay down the law, and it is pardonable that Mr. Kelsey should assert much more about the Romans than he could prove ; but he ought to have made it clear that the Britain which the Romans left was a Christian country. And he ought to have mentioned the survival of Celtic names, Liscard and Landican, in the hundred of Wirral, whether or no he commented upon them. The architecture is well done, and the accompanying pictures, many from the author's sketches, are excellent. The constitutional history of the county is also treated admirably; but the notorious raids into Staffordshire are not explained by saying that the offenders 'were safe in Cheshire, for the county was governed directly by the king, and did not yet send representatives to Parliament'. The encouragement to crime was that felony outside Cheshire did not involve the forfeiture of property within it. Mr. Kelsey makes valiant efforts to be impartial, but his own sympathies are obviously such as are often associated with Manchester, and some of his views will not find universal welcome. There are some actual mistakes, e. g. about Bishop Cartwright and about what happened in Derby in 1745. And every Birkenhead boy knows that the *Alabama* was no blockade-runner, and never visited England or America after her escape from the Mersey. K.

The Sussex Coast, by Mr. Ian C. Hannah, illustrated by Miss Edith B. Hannah (London: Unwin, 1912), is a good example of its class, for the author judiciously avoids getting beyond his depth. His knowledge is not profound, and he often misses points of interest, but he never talks nonsense, as many writers do whose business is to comment on pictures. He is well acquainted with the places, and with the more accessible sources of information. If he had more general knowledge he would not be surprised at finding Commonwealth ministers called 'priests' by the quakers. The drawings are pretty, and the book would have been better had there been more of them and fewer photographs. It will be a pleasant, if cumbrous, guide to a charming district, and has the great merit of omitting no church or desecrated chapel, however small, within its area. The architectural notes are full and clear. L.

The King's Book of Quebec, a handsome two-volume souvenir of the tercentenary celebrations in 1908, derives a less ephemeral distinction from an account of the 'Historical Background' by the Dominion archivist, Dr. Doughty, though this scarcely comes beyond 1763. The object is stated to be twofold, ' to unite more closely Canadians of French and of British descent; and to create a public opinion in favour of preserving the Battlefields of Quebec in a manner worthy of their traditions.' In a prefatory note Earl Grey speaks of ' the claim of Canada on the gratitude of India' in connexion with the exchange of Louisbourg for Madras; but surely the empire's creditor in 1748 was the colony of Massachusetts Bay, and the debt has been long since cancelled. J. M.

CORRECTION IN THE JANUARY NUMBER.

P. 103 n. 17. The editorial addition in brackets, which related to a reading found in the unrevised proof, was left standing by inadvertence, and ought to be cancelled.

THE ENGLISH HISTORICAL REVIEW

NO. CVII.—JULY 1912 *

Normandy under Geoffrey Plantagenet

THE conquest of Normandy by Geoffrey of Anjou raises an interesting question for students of Norman history, since by establishing between the two countries a personal union which was to last sixty years it opened the way to Angevin influence in the affairs of the duchy and to the possible modification of Norman institutions in accordance with Angevin practice. The problem of the nature and extent of this influence presents itself in its simplest form during Geoffrey's own reign of six years, not only because the new duke was, unlike his successors, exclusively the product of Angevin training and tradition, but also because under him the Norman and Angevin lands led a life of their own, distinct from that of the larger empire of which they afterwards formed a part. Unfortunately the available information is meagre, especially with reference to the preliminary elements in the problem, for we know but little of conditions in Normandy under Henry I, and no special study has yet been made of Anjou under Fulk of Jerusalem and his son.[1] In general it appears that the state which Fulk the Red and his descendants hammered out on the borders of the Loire was smaller and more compact than the duchy to the northward, and the government of its rulers was more direct and personal, so that its administrative needs were simpler, and seem to have been met without the creation of a fiscal and judicial system like the Norman and without any such fixity of documentary form or rigour of official procedure as are discernible in Normandy by the beginning of

---
[1] For the eleventh century there is an admirable study by L. Halphen, *Le Comté d'Anjou au XIe Siècle* (Paris, 1906). For the twelfth, a certain amount of useful material is contained in Beautemps-Beaupré, *Coutumes et Institutions de l'Anjou et du Maine*, part ii, 1 (Paris, 1890); see also Powicke, *The Angevin Administration of Normandy*, ante, xxi. 625–49, especially 648 f., xxii. 15–42. For Normandy see my article on *The Administration of Normandy under Henry I*, ante, xxiv. 209–31.

* All rights reserved.

the twelfth century. In point of organization there is no ground for considering the Angevin government to have been in advance of the Norman, nor, unless it be in the more immediate control of affairs by the count, is there inherent reason for expecting it to have had the marked effects upon Norman policy which are sometimes ascribed to it. Statements on these matters are, however, premature until more is known of the state of Anjou during this period, but it is possible in the meantime to bring together the Norman evidence for Geoffrey's reign and consider it with reference to the persistence of older institutions as well as to possible innovations. For such a study the death of Henry I forms the natural point of departure.

In Normandy, as in England, the reign of Stephen seems to have had a merely negative importance. After Henry's death the Norman barons invited Theobald of Blois to rule over them, but the news of his brother's accession in England decided them to accept the lord of whom their English fiefs were held. Stephen took the title of duke of the Normans, and had it engraved on his seal, but he used it rarely, even in Norman documents,[2] and never exercised an effective government over the whole of the duchy. The great strongholds of the southern border, Argentan, Exmes, and Domfront, had been promptly handed over to the empress by a loyal *vicomte*, as had also the castles of the count of Ponthieu, notably Séez and Alençon, which were restored to Count William in return for his support of the Angevin party. From this basis, after a short truce, Geoffrey and his followers carried their ravages westward into the vale of Mortain and the Cotentin, and northward as far as Lisieux, while the party of Stephen waited in vain for the arrival of its leader.[3] It was not till March 1137 that the king, accompanied by the queen, the bishops of Winchester, Lincoln, and Carlisle, and his chancellor, Roger,[4] arrived at La Hougue and proceeded by way of Bayeux [5]

---

[2] Delisle, *Recueil des Actes de Henri II*, introduction, p. 115 f.

[3] Ordericus Vitalis, ed. Le Prévost, v. 56-78; Robert of Torigni, ed. Delisle, i. 199 f., 205; John of Marmoutier, in Marchegay, *Chroniques des Comtes d'Anjou*, p. 294; William of Malmesbury, *Historia Novella*, p. 538; Henry of Huntingdon, p. 260.

[4] See their attestations in Delisle, pp. 117-19, nos. 2-8, 10. For Alexander of Lincoln, see Henry of Huntingdon, p. 260, and two notifications issued in his favour by Stephen at Rouen and preserved in the Registrum Antiquissimum of Lincoln Cathedral, nos. 180, 194, a reference which I owe to the kindness of Mr. H. W. C. Davis. The king was accompanied as far as Portsmouth by Roger of Salisbury and several other members of the *curia* who do not seem to have crossed: *Calendar of Charter Rolls*, iii. 338. On Stephen's sojourn in Normandy see Rössler, *Kaiserin Mathilde*, pp. 185-93; Ramsay, *Foundations of England*, ii. 359-64.

[5] His presence at Bayeux is shown by a charter for Montebourg (Delisle, *Henri II*, p. 117, no. 1; Robert of Torigni, i. 206), which is dated 1136, and must accordingly have been issued between Stephen's arrival in Normandy, in the third week of March, and Easter (11 April 1137). Other points in Stephen's itinerary which appear from

to the valley of the Seine. Although he was well received by the Normans, who had been embittered by the excesses of the Angevin soldiery, and was recognized by the French king, Stephen's presence was not sufficient to bring peace to the country. Geoffrey was able to lead an attack on Caen and force money from Norman monasteries as the price of safety for their lands, and after an abortive attempt at an expedition against Argentan, Stephen was forced, early in July, to purchase a truce by the annual payment of two thousand marks.

Through this parching summer and until his return to England early in December Normandy enjoyed whatever of order its duke was able to give it. Certain robber barons were coerced into obedience[6] and the forms of administration were maintained; but Stephen's own partisans were obliged to admit that he was a weak ruler.[7] His strongest support seems to have come from the Norman church: the archbishop of Rouen and four of his suffragans had hastened to his court in England early in 1136; Archdeacon Arnulf of Séez was his chief envoy to Rome in the same year;[8] and most of the Norman prelates continued to adhere to him with a loyalty which was to cost them dear at the hands of his successor. It is not surprising that of the score of Stephen's charters which relate to Normandy[9] two confirm

the charters but are not mentioned in the chroniclers are Falaise (Round, *Calendar*, no. 611), Lyons-la-Forêt (*ibid.* no. 1404), Rouen (*ibid.* no. 1055; Gurney, *Record of the House of Gournay*, i. 108; *Calendar of Charter Rolls*, iii. 374; *infra*, n. 9).

[6] Ordericus, v. 81–91; Robert of Torigni, i. 206 f. On the date of Stephen's return see also Gervase of Canterbury, i. 101; John of Worcester, ed. Weaver, p. 45; Henry of Huntingdon, p. 260.

[7] 'Normannia . . . totam efficaci gubernatore provinciam carere mesta videbat': Ordericus, v. 91.

[8] Round, *Geoffrey de Mandeville*, pp. 252 f., 260, 262 f. On the attitude of the Norman clergy cf. *Actus Pontificum Cenomannis*, ed. Busson and Ledru (Le Mans, 1902), p. 446.

[9] Delisle, *Henri II*, pp. 117–20, nos. 1–13 (no. 1 is printed without the witnesses in *Gallia Christiana*, xi, instr. 238; no. 7 is in part in *Neustria Pia*, p. 778, and is indicated, probably erroneously, in the *Inventaire Sommaire* as having been in the Archives of the Eure, H. 592); Round, *Calendar*, nos. 9, 239, 291–6, 427, 570, 611, 800, 802, 1055, 1404. Also a charter for Beaubec issued at Rouen (Archives of the Seine-Inférieure, G. 851, f. 57'; printed from a vidimus of Charles VI in Gurney, *Record of the House of Gournay*, i. 108); a writ for Bec, printed below, p. 420; a charter for Bec given at Marlborough (MS. Lat. 13905 of the Bibliothèque Nationale, f. 21'); another addressed to his officers of Wissant and Boulogne and given at Rouen (ibid. f. 86); a charter for the cordwainers of Rouen (La Roque, *Histoire de la Maison d'Harcourt*, iii. 149, where it is wrongly attributed to William I); and an agreement in his presence at Rouen in 1137 between the canons of St. Évroul and the monks of Notre-Dame de Mortain, notified by Richard, bishop of Avranches (MS. 292, f. 309', of the Library of Caen, from the original; MS. Lat. 5411, part ii, p. 409; Collection Moreau, lvii. 126; MS. Fr. 4900, f. 70; all in the Bibliothèque Nationale). Of these nos. 11–13 in Delisle and nos. 9, 295, 296, 427, 800, 802 in Round were issued in England, leaving fifteen documents issued in Normandy, if we include the charter for Fontevrault (Delisle, no. 10; Round, no. 1055). To these may be added three others given at Rouen for establishments outside of Normandy, namely one for Boulogne (*Calendar of Charter Rolls*, iii. 374) and the two for Lincoln mentioned above, n. 4.

the bishops in their privileges [10] and most of the others concern the religious establishments of upper Normandy. Both in form and in substance these documents follow closely the charters of Henry I and assume the maintenance of his administrative system, with its justices, *vicomtes*, and subordinate officers. They also show that the ducal revenues were kept at farm, at least in eastern Normandy [11]—indeed, a fiscal roll of 1136 is said to have once existed [12]—and that the Norman treasurer, Robert of Évreux, continued in office.[13] It is, however, noteworthy that only one order to a Norman official has survived, and while it refers to an earlier writ on the same subject, it is perhaps significant that this previous command has not been obeyed : [14]

(1) S. rex Angl[orum] Ing[eranno] de Wasc[olio] salutem. Scias quoniam vehementer miror de hoc quod non fecisti preceptum meum de terra monachorum de Becco de Turfrévilla de elemosina Willelmi Pevrell[i]. Quare tibi precipio quod facias in pace et iuste et quiete terram illam tenere sicut melius tenuerunt die qua rex Henricus fuit vivus et mortuus, ita quod non requiras aliquam novam consuetudinem de hominibus in terra illa residentibus. Teste comite de Mell[ento] apud Pont[em] Ald[omari].

At his departure Stephen left the government of Normandy in the hands of certain justiciars, among whom we have the names of only Roger the *vicomte*, who met his death shortly afterwards in the effort to maintain order in the Cotentin, and William of Roumare,[15] who is mentioned as justiciar in a Rouen document of 18 December 1138.[16] Beyond this point no regular administration of the duchy can be traced, and even in the castles and towns which continued to recognize Stephen his authority must have become merely nominal after the outbreak of the civil war drew the leaders of his party across the sea.[17] William of

[10] Delisle, nos. 5, 11 ; Round, nos. 9, 291.   [11] Round, nos. 292 f., 570.
[12] It is mentioned in 1790 : *Mémoires des Antiquaires de Normandie*, xvi, p. xxx.
[13] *Ante*, xxiv. 224 f.
[14] Fragment of cartulary of Bec in the Archives of the Eure, H. 91, f. 35. Probably issued in June, when Stephen was at Pontaudemer (Ordericus, v. 85 ; cf. Delisle, no. 8).
[15] Ordericus, v. 91 f., 105 ; Delisle, *Histoire de S. Sauveur-le-Vicomte*, p. 28 f.
[16] Printed *ante*, xxiv. 212 ; Valin, *Le Duc de Normandie et sa Cour*, p. 260.
[17] The charter of Stephen as count of Mortain, purporting to have been issued at Mortain 'in aula comitis' in 1139 (*Gallia Christiana*, xi. 478), is false, at least so far as the date is concerned, for Stephen spent that year in England, and the bishop of Avranches was then Richard, not Herbert, whose seal was attached to the accompanying charter (MS. Lat. 5441, ii. 416). Charters of Stephen as count of Mortain are known for Bec (Round, no. 378) ; for St. Étienne (Deville, *Analyse d'un ancien Cartulaire de l'Abbaye de S. Étienne de Caen*, p. 18) ; for the Dames Blanches of Mortain (Stapleton, *Magni Rotuli*, i, p. lxv) ; for Savigny (cartulary in Archives of the Manche, no. 211) ; and for the nuns of Moutons, in the style of the Anglo-Norman writ, as follows : 'St. comes Bolonie et Mortonii Stephano vicecomiti omnibusque suis baronibus atque servientibus salutem. Mando et precipio vobis ut omnes res dominarum sancte Marie de Mustoñ, scilicet in terra et in vaccis et in aliis bestiis, in pace et quiete dimittatis, easque et quidquid ad eas pertinet honorifice custodiatis et

Ypres and Richard de Luci, who were fighting for him in Normandy in 1138, joined him in England at the close of the year, Galeran of Meulan and his brother the earl of Leicester were with him in 1139, and William of Roumare went over to the empress in 1140.[18] Left to itself, the country quickly fell back into the disorder and bloodshed from which it had never really emerged during Stephen's nine months' sojourn. The descriptions of the Norman anarchy lack something of the realism with which William of Newburgh and the Peterborough chronicler depict conditions on the other side of the Channel, but the account in Ordericus is vivid enough, both in its general summary and its concrete examples, and its venerable author saw no hope of better days when he brought his work to its noble close in 1141.[19]

Yet this same year proved the turning-point in the re-establishment of ducal authority.[20] Secure in the possession of Argentan

manuteneatis. Tibi autem, Stephane, firmiter precipio ne de aliqua causa implacites eas nisi per me et coram me, quia sunt in mea custodia illisque deffendo ne placitent sine me. Istis testibus: Hamfredo dapifero et Addam de Balnayo et Hamfredo de Camersyo [or camerario]' (copies, based on a vidimus of 1310, in Archives of the Manche, fonds de Moutons).

[18] Ordericus, v. 108, 115, 125 ; Round, *Geoffrey de Mandeville*, pp. 46, 55 ; Ramsay, *Foundations of England*, ii. 396 ; *ante*, xxv. 116.

[19] Ordericus, v. 57–77, 79 f., 89–91, 104–9, 114–17, 130 f., 133. One of the regions which suffered most severely was the Avranchin, where the account of Ordericus (v. 89) and Robert of Torigni (ii. 234) is supplemented by an original notice from the archives of Mont-St.-Michel (Archives of the Manche, H. 14997 ; MS. Avranches 210, f. 80ᵛ): Certain men of the Mount 'post mortem enim carissimi domini nostri Henrici regis in abbatem dominum suum et contra totius villę salutem nequiter cum pluribus huiusce mali consciis conspirationem fecerunt. Quo comperto a pluribus abbas consilio fidelium suorum eos convenit et super tot et tantis malis conquestus eos alloquitur, quibus negantibus et obtestantibus iterum fidelitatem tam suę salutis quam totius villę iuraverunt. Qui iterum in proditione illa vehementer grassati hominibus alterius regionis ad tantum facinus patrandum adheserunt, iterum allocuti et tercio sacramentis adstricti funditus in malitia sua perseveraverunt. Ad ultimum congregata curia ad dies plurimos constitutos omne iudicium subterfugerunt et sic malitia eorum comperta omnibus patuit. Quo comperto liberales ipsius villę et ipsius provintię proceres super ignominia tanta confusi eos omnino exterminaverunt et sacramento affirmaverunt extunc illos non recepturos nec cum eis deinceps habitaturos. ... [Rogerius camerarius] post mortem regis Anglie sacramentum irritum fecit Britanniam cum omni suppellectili petiit, unde multa mala, non solum per se verum etiam dux factus inimicorum qui tunc temporis nimia aviditate Normanniam infestabant, terre et hominibus ecclesie irrogavit.' It will be noted that in this document there is no trace of ducal authority after Henry's death, and the barons take matters into their own hands.

[20] On Geoffrey's recovery of Normandy see Miss Norgate, *Angevin Kings*, i. 338–42, and the authorities there cited. That, as Miss Norgate says, ' the story of this campaign, as told by the historians of the time, is little more than a list of the places taken, put together evidently at random,' is true only of William of Malmesbury, who lacked local knowledge. The succession of events in Robert of Torigni and John of Marmoutier is intelligible and consistent, and of the additional places mentioned by William of Malmesbury, Bastembourg and Trevières were apparently the result of special expeditions from Caen and Bayeux, while the others—Briquessart, Villers, Plessis, Vire—lay in the direction of Mortain, though not ' up the left bank of the Orne '.

and the adjoining *vicomtés*, and controlling Caen and Bayeux through his alliance with Robert of Gloucester, Geoffrey of Anjou in 1141 won Lisieux, Falaise, and the country as far as the Seine, and the following year gave him not only the outstanding places in the Bessin, but the county of Mortain, the Avranchin, and the Cotentin.[21] By the beginning of 1144 he was in a position to proclaim his peace throughout the land [22] and to enforce the submission of the city of Rouen, followed three months later by the surrender of its tower. Although the castle of Arques held out until the summer of the following year, the barons of the duchy had already made their peace with the new duke, who had won over their leader, the count of Meulan, as early as 1141; and even the Norman church, which had received Stephen's nephew as abbot of Fécamp in 1140 and his chancellor as bishop of Bayeux in 1142, was driven to acknowledge the king's defeat. John of Lisieux, the justiciar of Henry I, submitted to Geoffrey just before his death in 1141; the bishop of Avranches led the procession which welcomed the Angevin army to his city in the following year; and even the archbishop of Rouen, *maximus regis propugnator* at the outbreak of the civil war in England, who dated his documents by Stephen's reign as late as 1143, was doubtless present when Geoffrey was received into his cathedral upon the city's surrender, and thenceforth recognized him as ruler of the duchy.[23] Although he had been so styled by his partisans some time before,[24] Geoffrey did not

[21] The chroniclers say nothing of the Channel Islands, although modern writers upon the islands say that Geoffrey sent a certain Raoul de Valmont there to establish the duke's authority and ascertain his rights. It would be interesting to know the origin of this statement. See Dupont, *Histoire du Cotentin et de ses Îles* (Caen, 1870), i. 354–7; Tupper, *History of Guernsey* (Guernsey, 1876), p. 76; Pégot-Ogier, *Histoire des Îles de la Manche* (Paris, 1881), pp. 133 f.

[22] 'Postquam precepi in Epipphania Domini quod terra esset in pace:' *Livre noir de Bayeux*, ed. Bourrienne, no. 25. No year is given, but the most probable date is 1144, when Geoffrey crossed the Seine at Hilarymas and received the submission of Rouen 19 or 20 January. The completion of the conquest as far as the Seine in 1143 is confirmed by a charter of that year given 'Andegavis civitate in anno quo annuente Deo et sancta matre eius partem Normannie que est citra Sequanam adquisivimus': Chifflet, *Histoire de l'Abbaye de Tournus*, preuves, p. 424.

[23] Böhmer, *Kirche und Staat in England und in der Normandie*, p. 313 f. Hugh still recognizes Stephen in a document of 1143 in *Gallia Christiana*, xi, instr. 23, but acknowledges Geoffrey in charters of 1145 (Pommeraye, *Histoire de S. Ouen*, p. 425; Laffleur de Kermaingant, *Cartulaire de l'Abbaye de S. Michel du Tréport*, p. 31; Métais, *Cartulaire de la Trinité de Vendôme*, ii. 331; Collection Moreau, in the Bibliothèque Nationale, lxi. 188, 206). So Arnulf of Lisieux dates a charter for Fécamp by Stephen's reign in 1142 (Archives of the Seine-Inférieure, fonds de Fécamp), but attests a charter which recognizes Geoffrey in September 1143 (see the next note), and is soon busy securing the favour of the new prince (*Epistolae*, no. 2). That Geoffrey had been able to put pressure upon the Norman church appears from the instance of the treasurer of Lisieux, who was kept out of his church of Mesnil-Odon 'propter ducatus divisionem': letters of Bishop John in MS. Lat. 5296, f. 68.

[24] Charter of William, count of Ponthieu for Vignats, 19 September 1143, witnessed

assume the ducal title until the acquisition of Rouen gave him full control of his new dominions and justified his prompt recognition by the king of France.[25]

Geoffrey's reign as duke of Normandy extends from 1144 to early in 1150, when he handed the duchy over to his son Henry, the heir of Matilda and of Henry I.[26] This transfer, accomplished when the young duke was in his seventeenth year, shows plainly that the count of Anjou had won and held Normandy for his son and not for himself, and earlier evidence points to the same conclusion. Besides the few weeks which may have intervened between his return and his assumption of the ducal title in 1150, Henry was on the Norman side of the Channel from the end of 1146 to the spring of 1149,[27] enjoying the instruction of the most famous Norman scholar of the time, William of Conches, who prepared for his use a choice selection of maxims of the gentile philosophers;[28] yet even at this tender age his name was used to give sanction to ducal acts. A charter for Bec[29] and one for

by the bishops of Séez, Lisieux, and Coutances and three abbots: *Gallia Christiana*, xi, instr. 162. On the other hand Geoffrey is called count in a charter of Reginald of St. Valéry issued some time before the capture of Dieppe: Round, *Calendar*, no. 1057; Fréville, *Histoire du Commerce de Rouen*, ii. 9.

[26] On the assumption of the ducal title, see Delisle, *Henri II*, p. 135 f.; and cf. the date of no. 728 in Round's *Calendar*. According to Robert of Torigni and the annals of Mont-St.-Michel (ed. Delisle, i. 234, ii. 234), Geoffrey became duke upon the surrender of the tower of Rouen (23 April 1144), but a charter of Ulger, bishop of Angers (Delisle, *Henri II*, p. 135), places 29 June 1145 in the first year of his reign. Lucius II addresses him 16 May 1144 as count of Anjou merely: *Livre noir de Bayeux*, no. 206.

[26] Against the annals of St. Aubin (Halphen, *Recueil d'Annales angevines*, p. 12), which give 1149, and Miss Norgate's argument for 1148 (*Angevin Kings*, i. 369, 377; *Dictionary of National Biography*, s.v. 'Henry II'), the date of 1150 seems to me clearly established from Gervase of Canterbury (i. 142), Robert of Torigni (i. 253), and the annals of Caen (*Historiens de France*, xii. 780) and of St. Évroul (Orderious, v. 162), and especially from the regnal years in certain of Henry's charters. Gervase gives January as the month of Henry's return to Normandy, and two charters for Savigny, given in the eighth year of his reign as duke and issued before the beginning of April 1157, show that he must have become duke before the end of March (Delisle, pp. 122, 231, 279 f., 515, nos. 30, 30 a). A charter of Archbishop Hugh (La Roque, *Histoire de la Maison d'Harcourt*, iii. 45) is dated 1150 'principante in Normannia duce Henrico'. On the other hand Geoffrey omits the title of duke in a charter of 28 October 1150 (*Liber albus Cenomannensis*, no. 6; cf. Delisle, p. 138) and in a notification addressed to the archbishop of Rouen at Montreuil, evidently in 1150-1 (*infra*, n. 90).

[27] On the dates of Henry's crossings see Round, *Geoffrey de Mandeville*, pp. 405-10.

[28] William's *Dragmaticon* is dedicated to Geoffrey as duke of Normandy and count of Anjou in an introduction which praises his care for the education of the young princes (R. L. Poole, *Illustrations of the History of Medieval Thought*, pp. 347 f.); and his treatise on moral philosophy, *De honesto et utili*, is dedicated to Henry before the assumption of the ducal title. See this work, attributed to Hildebert of Le Mans, in Migne, clxxi. 1007-56; and, on its authorship, Hauréau, in *Notices et Extraits des MSS.*, xxxiii. i. 257-63. Curiously enough, it was used by Giraldus Cambrensis in writing the *De Principis Instructione*, where Henry II serves as a terrible example.

[29] 'Non lateat vos nec quenquam presentium sive futurorum me consilio H. filii mei et baronum meorum concessisse quod ecclesia sancte Marie de Becco et monachi illius ecclesie habeant omnes consuetudines et quietudines et libertates quas habebant

St. Wandrille[30] are issued by Geoffrey with the advice and consent of his son Henry; another confirmation for Bec[31] and one for Fécamp[32] are issued by the two jointly; while a document of 1147 for St. Ouen, attested by Geoffrey's chancellor, Richard of Bohun, is given by *Henricus ducis Normannorum et comitis Andegavie filius* and addressed to his officers of Normandy.[33] We should also expect to find the empress taking an active part in Norman affairs; but her absence in England from 1139 to 1148[34] removed her from any share in the events of these critical years on the Continent, nor has any trace been found of her participation in her husband's administration after her return. The lack of documents which can be specifically referred to these two years is, however, probably accidental, for we have a grant of land at Argentan to one of her followers before her departure for England,[35] and several charters, issued in her own name or conjointly with her son, which show her activity in the years immediately following his accession.[36]

The sources of information for the study of Geoffrey's government of Normandy are remarkably scanty and fragmentary. The narrative writers fail us entirely, for Ordericus stops before the conquest is completed, and Robert of Torigni and John of Marmoutier give us nothing beyond an enumeration of campaigns.

in tempore H. regis. Quapropter ego precipio ut omnes res eiusdem ecclesie sint quiete et libere in terra et in aqua et in plano et in nemore per totam Normanniam ab omni consuetudine et vexatione, sicut erant in tempore Henrici regis' (Extract by Dom Jouvelin Thibault, in MS. Lat. 13905, f. 85ᵛ.)

[30] Round, no. 170; Delisle, *Henri II*, p. 508, no. 9*.

[31] 'Geofroy duc de Normandie et d'Anjou, Henri 2ᵈ son fils, confirment et declarent que monachi de Becco et omnes res eorum sunt quiete de theloneo et passagio et pontagio et de omni consuetudine, sicut a retroactis temporibus fuerunt apud Archas et apud Diepam:' MS. Lat. 13905, f. 85ᵛ.

[32] Delisle, p. 508, no. 6*, and facsimile no. 1.

[33] *Neustria pia*, p. 15; La Roque, *Histoire de la Maison d'Harcourt*, iv, suppl., p. 10; Delisle, p. 508, no. 3*. Delisle queries the date, but we know that Henry was solemnly received at Bec on Ascension Day, 1147 (Robert of Torigni, i. 243). Henry likewise makes a grant to the nuns of Almenesches as son of Duke Geoffrey: Delisle, *Cartulaire normand*, no. 5.

[34] Delisle, *Henri II*, p. 140, and the older Norman writers give 1147 as the year of her return, which took place 'ante Quadragisimam'. There is some uncertainty because of the confusion of chronology—which is, however, less than has been supposed (see Round, *Geoffrey de Mandeville*, pp. 405-10)—in Gervase of Canterbury, but as he (i. 133) places Matilda's return after the death of Robert of Gloucester (31 October 1147) and just before the council of Rheims (21 March 1148), it would seem to fall in 1148. Rössler, *Kaiserin Mathilde*, pp. 410-12, assumes 1147, but his book has no value for Matilda's later years.

[35] Original in MS. Lat. 10083, f. 3, analysed in *Mémoires des Antiquaires de Normandie*, viii. 388; Delisle, *Henri II*, p. 141, no. 4; Round, no. 591. As this charter is given at Argentan and witnessed by Matilda's brother Reginald, who attests as earl of Cornwall after 1141 (Round, *Geoffrey de Mandeville*, pp. 68, 271), it must be anterior to her departure in 1139.

[36] Delisle, *Henri II*, pp. 126, 141-3, nos. 5-13. See also her charters for Silly, Round, *Calendar*, nos. 679 f., 683.

We are perforce restricted to the charters, among which those of the duke himself, about forty in number, are so fundamental as to call at the outset for somewhat special examination. The following list includes such Norman charters of Geoffrey as I have been able to find, arranged, since few of them are dated, in the alphabetical order of the places for whose benefit they were issued :

Almenesches. Delisle, *Cartulaire normand*, no. 4, and p. 273.

Bayeux ; probably 1145-7. Eight charters and writs of Geoffrey : *Antiquus Cartularius Ecclesiae Baiocensis* (*Livre noir*), ed. Bourrienne, nos. 16-19, 24, 25, 39, 100 (1147). Also four reports addressed to him by his justices : nos. 43, 44, 89, 90. These are all, except no. 100, attributed to Henry II in the edition (see, however, the corrections at the end of the second volume), but in the cartulary the initial G appears in every case on the margin. See *American Historical Review*, viii. 618 ; Delisle, *Henri II*, 137 f., 511, nos. 42*, 43*, where the last two are wrongly attributed to Henry II. No. 17 is also in the *Livre rouge* (Bibliothèque Nationale, MS. Lat. n. a. 1828, no. 401), of which there is a poor edition by Anquetil (Bayeux, 1909).

Bec. Extracts from two charters, printed above, pp. 423, 424, nn. 29, 31.

Bec, priory of Notre-Dame-du-Pré ; 27 March 1149, at Bec. Original, printed below, no. 2.

Bec, priory of St. Imer ; 1147, at Saumur. MS. Lat. n. a. 2097, p. 9 ; Collection Lenoir at Semilly, LXXII. ii. 169. *Cartulaires de S. Ymer et de Briquebec*, ed. Bréard (Paris, 1908), p. 7 ; Round, *Calendar*, no. 360 ; Delisle, no. 3* A.

Cluny ; before 1147, as it is attested by Hugh, archbishop of Tours. Bruel, *Chartes de Cluni*, v. 447 ; cf. Duckett, *Charters and Records of Cluni*, ii. 78. In Martène and Durand, *Thesaurus Anecdotorum*, i. 383, it is attributed to a duke R.

Coutances ; at Saint-Lô. Cartulary, now in Archives of the Manche, p. 350, no. 285. Printed in *American Historical Review*, viii. 630 ; cf. Delisle, *Cartulaire normand*, no. 162 ; *Henri II*, no. 17* A. Ascribed to Henry II by Round, no. 960.

Évreux ; at Rouen. Printed below, no. 6.

Fécamp ; (1) at Rouen. Original, misplaced, in Archives of the Seine-Inférieure ; modern copies in MS. Lat. n. a. 1245, ff. 122-3 ; MS. Rouen, 1210, f. 17.[37] (2) with his son Henry ; at Rouen. Original, in the same archives. Delisle, *Henri II*, no. 6*, with facsimile ; Round, no. 126, omitting most of the witnesses.

Lessay ; at Saumur. Original, printed below, no. 3.

Lisieux, St. Désir, and the Knights of the Hospital ; 1147, after

[37] 'Gaufredus dux Normannorum et comes Andegavorum omnibus hominibus Fiscanni salutem. Sciatis me vidisse cartam ecclesie Fiscanni que testatur ecclesie Fiscanni portus maris de Stigas usque ad Leregant. Ideo mando vobis et prohibeo quod vos non intromittatis de aliqua re que ad portus istos veniat vel sit, nisi per manum Henrici abbatis vel servientium suorum, quia in ipsis nichil habeo. Teste Raginaldo de Sancto Walerico apud Rothomagum.'

Easter ('in Pascha precedenti'), at Mirebeau. Modern copies in Archives of the Calvados. Extract in Grente and Havard, *Villedieu-les-Poëles* (Paris, 1899), p. 6; Round, no. 576, where it is dated at Easter and the witnesses are omitted; *Mémoires des Antiquaires de Normandie*, xiv. 382 (translation).

Montebourg; (1) at Argentan. Printed below, no. 4. (2) at Lisieux. Printed below, no. 5.

Mortemer; 11 October 1147, at Rouen. La Roque, *Histoire de la Maison d'Harcourt*, iii. 152, iv. 1396, 1636, suppl., p. 8; *Neustria pia*, p. 779. Analysed in *Bulletin des Antiquaires de Normandie*, xiii. 115; Round, no. 1405; cf. *Historiens de France*, xiv. 511.[38]

Préaux; 1149, at Rouen. Notice of transaction in *curia* sitting at Geoffrey's order. Archives of the Eure, H. 7, no. 453. Printed in Valin, *Le Duc de Normandie et sa Cour* (Paris, 1910), p. 265.

Rouen, cathedral chapter; at Rouen. Archives of the Seine-Inférieure, G. 7, p. 793. Printed in Valin, *loc. cit.*, p. 266 (where the undeciphered word is *scilicet*). The initial is left blank in the cartulary, so that the author may be either Geoffrey or Henry II. Delisle, no. 37*, ascribes it to Henry, but gives no reason. Geoffrey's authorship seems to me likely from the phrase 'tempore H. regis Anglie', for in such cases (e.g. *Livre noir de Bayeux*, nos. 27, 28, 32; *Neustria pia*, p. 15) Henry II adds 'avi mei'.

Rouen, town; probably in 1144 and doubtless at Rouen. Incorporated in Henry II's charter: Chéruel, *Histoire de Rouen*, i. 241; Round, no. 109.

Rouen, gild of cordwainers; at Rouen. Vidimus of 1267 in MS. Lat. 9067, f. 155^v; and MS. Rouen 2192, f. 189. Printed from vidimus of 1371 (Archives Nationales, JJ. 102, no. 317) in *Ordonnances des Rois*, v. 416; translated in Chéruel, *Rouen*, i, p. cxiv.

Rouen, Henry the Marshal, the duke's serjeant; probably before 1147, at Rouen. Printed below, no. 13.

Rouen, leper-house of Mont-aux-Malades; (1) at Rouen. Original, printed below, no. 12. (2) Charter notifying the reception of the palmers of Rouen into confraternity: translation in Langlois, *Histoire du Prieuré du Mont-aux-Malades-lès-Rouen* (Rouen, 1851), p. 4.

Rouen, St. Amand; at Lisieux. Printed below, no. 7.

Rouen, St. Ouen. 'Gaufredus dux Normannorum et comes Andegavorum confirmat donationem c[omitis] Walterii Giffardi. Testibus Roberto de Novoburgo, Widone de Sabluel.' MS. Lat. 5423, f. 232^v.

St. André-en-Gouffern; at Argentan. Printed below, no. 10.

St. Évroul; probably in 1144. Printed below, no. 8.

St. Wandrille; (1) at Rouen. Printed below, p. 438, n. 97. (2) at Argentan. Cartulary in Archives of the Seine-Inférieure, T. i. 7; Coppies des Chartes, ibid., iv. 1998; MS. Lat. 17132, f. 37; Collection Moreau, lxi. 107; MS. Rouen 394, f. 2; Collection Lenoir at Semilly, lxxiii. 347. *Neustria pia*, p. 176 (extract); Round, no. 170.

---

[38] The epact in this charter is of 1148, showing that it was calculated from 1 September, as in a charter of Geoffrey in the *Cartulaire de S. Laud d'Angers*, ed. Planchenault, p. 66.

Savigny; (1) at Argentan. Original, Archives Nationales, L. 969; cartulary in Archives of the Manche, no. 408; Round, no. 812. (2) At Argentan. Original, printed below, no. 11. (3) At Montreuil; 1150–1. Original, printed below, p. 437, n. 90.

Séez, St. Martin. Printed below, no. 9.

For a reign of six years this is a respectable number of documents, if we take into account the relatively small body of Norman charters which has survived from the first half of the twelfth century; and their geographical distribution is significant. All the episcopal sees are represented with the exception of Lisieux, whose archives are an almost total loss; and the monasteries of the list are scattered throughout the duchy, from the ancient establishments in the region of the Seine to Montebourg, Lessay, and Savigny on the west. All this bears evidence of an effective rule of the whole land. At the same time it is noteworthy that, if we except the charter for the town of Rouen, which was granted under special circumstances, there are among them all no general enumerations and confirmations of lands and privileges such as are found under Henry I and in still greater number under Henry II.[39] What we have instead is specific grants, letters of protection, declarations of freedom from toll, and orders to the duke's officers to hold inquests, make payments, and maintain rights. The writs bulk large in proportion to the charters. This cannot be mere accident, for the detailed confirmations which are so numerous under Henry II rarely mention his father,[40] but hark back constantly to the conditions of his grandfather's time. We get distinctly the impression of a reign which restores rather than creates, and administers rather than ordains, of a regency rather than a permanent government.

Considered from the diplomatic point of view, Geoffrey's charters show variety, but they also show something of the regularity and definiteness of form which come only from an organized chancery. That Normandy had the advantage of such a system under Henry I is of course well known, but we cannot speak with equal certainty of conditions in contemporary Anjou. Down to the close of the eleventh century the counts of Anjou, like the kings of France, had not entirely differentiated their chancery from their chapel, the same man appearing at one time as chaplain and at another as chancellor; nor had they

[39] An apparent exception, the long charter for Bayeux (*Livre noir*, no. 39), is merely a statement of the results of inquests held to determine the ancient rights of the see. The difference from the policy of other dukes may be seen even in the case of Stephen by comparing his detailed confirmation for Montebourg (*Gallia Christiana*, xi, instr. 238) with the charters of Geoffrey for the same abbey printed below, nos. 4, 5.

[40] Later references to Geoffrey's official acts are rare. See *infra*, nn. 89, 91, 121; Round, no. 1296; and the grant to Aunay cited in a bull of Eugene III (*Bulletin des Antiquaires de Normandie*, xix. 256).

developed a regular set of forms for their official acts. Until 1109 at least, the only period which has been carefully studied, almost all of their documents were drawn up by the monasteries in whose favour they were issued,[41] and the evidence of style would indicate that this custom persisted in large measure under Fulk of Jerusalem and even under his son. Geoffrey's Angevin charters have something of the variety, the prolixity, and the narrative form which belong to the monastic notice rather than to the charter proper, and which are in sharp contrast with the brevity and fixity which the Anglo-Norman charter, and especially the writ, has attained before the close of the Conqueror's reign.

Still, mention is found from time to time of the chaplain or notary who composed the document, and especially of Thomas of Loches, the historian of the counts of Anjou, whose attestation appears as early as 1133 and continues as chaplain or chancellor throughout the reign.[42] Thomas also accompanied Geoffrey on his Norman expeditions, for his signature as chancellor appears in documents issued at Argentan, Lisieux, and Rouen, and he witnesses as chaplain a charter given at Bec in 1149.[43] Curiously enough, this last document bears likewise the name of the duke's other chancellor, Richard of Bohun. Dean of Bayeux since the days of Henry I, Richard bought the chancellorship from Geoffrey by pledging the income of his deanery for an amount which he had much difficulty in paying and which subsequently brought him into trouble with his bishop and with the pope; and in 1151 he was rewarded with the bishopric of Coutances.[44] Nine of Geoffrey's charters and writs bear his attestation,[45] and

[41] Halphen, *Le Comté d'Anjou*, pp. 192 f., 237. For the confusion of chancellor and chaplain under the Capetians see Prou, *Recueil des Actes de Philippe I*, pp. liv-lvi.
[42] On Thomas see Mabille's introduction to the *Chroniques des Comtes d'Anjou* pp. xiv-xxv ; Beautemps-Beaupré, *Coutumes*, II. i. 220-2.
[43] *Infra*, nos. 2, 4-7. Thomas is mentioned in a writ of the empress for Cherbourg (Delisle, *Henri II*, no. 84* ; Round, no. 938) in a way that suggests (particularly if we conjecture *tenuerunt* in the missing portion) that Geoffrey may have given him some part of the considerable possessions of Roger of Salisbury (cf. Round, no. 909) in the Cotentin.
[44] 'Postmodum vero venientis ad nos venerabilis fratris nostri Philippi Baiocensis episcopi suggestione accepimus quod antedictus frater noster pecuniam illam, non pro ecclesie Baiocensis utilitate aut sui honesta necessitate suscepit, sed ut cancellariam sibi nobilis memorie Gaufridi quondam Andegavensis comitis compararet, et cum in capitulo Baiocensi se infra biennium soluturum eandem pecuniam promisisset, licet multum post decanatum habuerit, debitum tamen ipsum, ut promiserat, nequaquam exsolvit' (*Livre noir*, no. 185). As Richard continued to hold the deanery, not only for two years but 'multum post', he evidently became chancellor not long after Geoffrey's conquest of the duchy. He had been dean under Bishop Richard Fitz-Samson (*ibid.* no. 480), who died in 1133, and is mentioned with this title in several Bayeux documents : ibid. nos. 60, 100 (1147), 103 (1146), 106, 207 (1146), 291. On the date of his elevation to the bishopric see Robert of Torigni, i. 257 and note.
[45] *Livre noir*, nos. 17, 19, 39 ; Round, nos. 126 (= Delisle, 6*, with facsimile), 170, 960, 1405 ; *infra*, nos. 2, 3. To these should be added the charter of Henry in *Neustria pia*, p. 15.

as one of these is dated at Saumur,[46] it is plain that he followed the duke beyond the confines of Normandy. No chronological separation between the charters of Richard and Thomas seems possible : the Bayeux writs attested by Richard belong to the early years of the reign ; two of the others fall in 1147[47] and one in 1149 ;[48] and he appears as chancellor in six documents issued by Henry II.[49] Probably the explanation is that Richard was chancellor in Normandy and Thomas chaplain, as in the charter for Bec, but that in Richard's absence Thomas possessed the title as well as the functions of chancellor, which he had exercised in Anjou as early as 1142.[50]

Richard's work can be tested in two originals, issued at places as far apart as Bec and Saumur, but written by the same scribe [51] and showing such resemblances in their formulae that the first, excellently preserved with its seal, may safely be used to supply some of the gaps in the mutilated text of the second. These are :

(2) G. dux Norm[annorum] & comes And[egavorum] H. archiepiscopo & omnibus episcopis comitibus baronibus iusticiis Norm[annie] & omnibus suis fidelibus salutem. Notum sit vobis atque omnibus tam presentibus quam futuris quod ego dedi & concessi monachis sanctę Marie de Becco tres prebendas de Buris, ea conditione quod post quam illę fuerint liberatę a tribus presentibus clericis, scilicet Ivone Hugone atque Alexandro, monachi sanctę Marię de Prato illas perpetuo libere & quiete possideant. Huius rei sunt testes : Ric[ardus] cancell[arius], Gaufr[edus] Roth[omagensis] decanus, Tomas capellanus, Robertus de Novoburgo & alii quam plures. Hoc autem concessum est anno ab incarnatione domini .M.C.XLIX. in pascha instanti die dominica de ramis palmarum in Beccensi capitulo.[52]

(3) G. dux Norm[annorum] et comes And[egavorum] H. archiepiscopo & omnibus ep[iscopis comitibus] baronibus iusticiis & omnibus suis servientibus salutem. [Notum sit vobis] atque omnibus hominibus tam presentibus quam futuris quod ego concessi donationem quam

[46] *Infra*, no. 3.   [47] Round, no. 1405 ; *Neustria pia*, p. 15.
[48] *Infra*, no. 2.   [49] Delisle, *Henri II*, p. 88 n.
[50] *Cartulaire de l'Abbaye du Ronceray*, ed. Marchegay, p. 244 (*Archives d'Anjou*, iii).
[51] That Richard was not himself the scribe is seen from the recurrence of the same hand in the notice printed below (p. 437, n. 90), issued by Geoffrey as count of Anjou at Montreuil-Bellay in 1150-1, in which Richard is not mentioned.
[52] Sealed original in Archives of the Seine-Inférieure. Cf. Demay, *Inventaire des Sceaux de la Normandie*, no. 20. The phrase ' in pascha instanti ' seems at first sight to indicate that the style of Easter was here used, which would give the date 9 April 1150. This is, however, inconsistent with the fact that Henry had by this time become duke (*supra*, n. 26), and we should need stronger evidence to establish so striking a variation from the practice of beginning the year at Christmas or 1 January, which prevailed in both Normandy and Anjou (Delisle, *Henri II*, p. 230 ; Halphen, *Le Comté d'Anjou*, pp. 237-9). Evidently the phrase has no reference to the beginning of the year, as is likewise true of ' in pascha precedenti ' in the charters of 1147 in *Neustria pia*, pp. 15, 779, in the latter of which, dated 11 October, the reference to Easter could have no significance under any system of reckoning. The Bec charter belongs accordingly to 27 March 1149.

Willelmus de Aureavalle fecit ecclesię sanctę Trinitatis de Exaquio, videlicet de molendino de sancta Oportuna quod predictę ecclesię dedit cum omnibus consuetudinibus & molta & omnibus rebus que ad illud molendinum pertinebant & de parte illa quam in ecclesia sancte Oportune habebat [ecclesie] Exaquii dedit sicut carta illius testatur. & ut hec dona[tio et concessio] perpetuo fiat sigilli mei testimonio illam confirmari
      [T]estes autem inde sunt Ric[ardus] cancellarius, Willelmus de Vernone,   Engelg[erus] de Boh[one], Alexander de Boh[one], Robertus de Montef[orti,]   de sancto Iohanne, Rualocus de Saeio, Iosl[inus] de Tyr[onibus] Pi[ppino de Tyronibus] Willelmo de [Sai ?] Adam de Sotewast. Apud Salmuram.[53]

No originals have been discovered from the hand of the chancellor Thomas, but we can follow him with some confidence in certain early copies. Let us begin with two charters in the cartulary of Montebourg :[54]

(4) Ego Goffr[edus] dux Norm[annorum] et comes And[egavorum] relatione multorum cognoscens audiendo et audiens cognoscendo quoniam H. rex predecessor meus abbatiam Montisburgi sancte Marie tanquam propriam capellam nimio dilexit amore diligendo custodivit augmentavit nobilitavit, similiter abbatiam eamdem in mea custodia et in tuitione capio et quicquid ille contulit vel concessit in bosco et in plano et in omnibus consuetudinibus et in omnibus modis unde habent monachi cartas et brevia prefate abbatie diligenter annuo. Insuper illi addo do et concedo in perpetuam elemosinam perpetuo iure habendam pro salute mea et filiorum meorum necnon et predicti regis omniumque predecessorum meorum illam terram que est in suo aisimento inter suam terram et forestam usque ad rivulum sicut oritur et descendit de veteri fonte et ipsum rivulum cum alveo concedo ita ut rivulus fosseatus sit firma divisa inter eos et forestam, cum constet quia redditus nichil inde foreste minuitur sed melius clauditur munitur atque defenditur.

Testibus Thoma cancell[ario], Alex[andro] de Boh[one], Ric[ardo] de Haia, Ric[ardo] de Wauvilla, W[illelmo] Avenel, Olivier de Albiniaco, Gisleb[erto] archid[iacono], Rob[erto] de Valoniis, Rob[erto] Bordel, Unfr[edo] de Bosevill[a] et aliis multis, apud Argent[omum].

(5) Ego Gaufridus comes Andegavis (sic) et dux Normannorum cunctis baronibus meis vicecomitibus ministris et omnibus hominibus meis salutem. Sciatis quod habeo in mea propria custodia abbatiam de Monteburgo omnes monachos et omnes res ad eos pertinentes tanquam meam propriam elemosinam sicut habuit rex Henricus antecessor meus, et concedo abbatie et ipsis monachis quicquid concessit eis predictus rex in omnibus rebus et omnibus consuetudinibus et unde habent ipsius regis cartas et brevia, et ut habeant omnes consuetudines suas in forestis meis liberas et quietas et focum in Monteburgo, et ut sint quieti a theloneo et consuetudine ubicunque vendant vel emant vel conducant aliquid quod homines eorum possint affidare esse proprium ecclesie et monachorum, et

---

[53] Original, with *double queue*, but no trace of seal, in Archives of the Manche, H. 7771. Printed in proof-sheets of *Inventaire Sommaire* ; Delisle, *Henri II*, p. 509, no. 17* B.

[54] MS. Lat. 10087, nos. 35, 36.

omnes donationes baronum quas dederunt vel dederint ipsi ecclesie. Precipio igitur vobis ut abbatiam et quicquid ad eam pertinet manuteneatis et defendatis et regatis sicut meam propriam elemosinam ne pro penuria recti inde clamorem audiam.

T[estibus] Will[elmo] de Vernon, Alex[andro] de Bohun, Pag[ano] de Claris Vallibus, Th[oma] cancellario, Rob[erto] de Curc[eio], apud Luxovium. + Preterea concedo eidem abbatie coram supradictis testibus illam terram que est inter suam terram et forestam usque ad rivum et ipsum rivum sicut descendit de veteri fonte et quoddam warlocum quod est in altera parte.

The first of these uses a comparatively untechnical phraseology, and has something of the more literary flavour of the Angevin charter. The second, from its substance evidently posterior, is full of the legal terminology of the charters of Henry I on which it is based,[55] and culminates with the characteristically Norman clause, *ne pro penuria recti inde clamorem audiam.*[56] Such repetitions of the language of earlier charters for the same establishment are perfectly natural, and are familiar to all students of diplomatic.[57] When, however, we find Thomas adopting the brevity and precision of the Anglo-Norman writ, as well as its typical phrases, we see how thoroughly Norman an institution the chancery of Geoffrey has become.

The first of the following relates to the see of Évreux,[58] the second to the nuns of St. Amand : [59]

(6) G. dux Normann[orum] et comes And[egavorum] G[uidoni] de Sablol[io] et Will[elmo] Lovello atque prepositis et ballivis suis de Vernolio et de Nonancort salutem et dilectionem. Mando atque vobis precipio quod episcopo Ebroicensi reddatis omnes decimas suas de Vernol[io] et de Nonancort sicut eas umquam melius habuit in tempore H. regis et sicut carta eius garentizat, ita quod eas habeat prout tempus ierit ad voluntatem suam et de tempore transacto quicquid ei debetur absque dilatione reddatis. Insuper etiam vobis precipio ne quid inde amittat neque pro refactura molendinorum neque pro augmentatione reddite supradictarum villarum. De pace vero fracta mando vobis quod ei inde quicquid habere debuerit plenarie reddi faciatis, scilicet .ix. libras sicut carta H. regis garantizat.

---

[55] *Ante,* xxiv. 220 f. ; Delisle, *Cartulaire normand,* no. 737.

[56] *Ante,* xxvi. 446 f. Can we see Thomas's hand in a writ of Geoffrey in 1146, mentioned in a notice from La Trinité de Vendôme (*Cartulaire,* ii. 343), where we have 'ne amplius super hoc clamorem audiret ' ?

[57] An excellent illustration is furnished by the charter of Geoffrey and Henry for Fécamp (Delisle, *Henri II,* p. 508, no. 6*, with facsimile), which reproduces the language of the early grants of immunity : ' absque ulla inquietatione vel imminutione secularis vel iuditiarie potestatis.' See *American Historical Review,* xiv. 459.

[58] Archives of the Eure, G. 122, no. 204, G. 123, no. 196, printed in Le Prévost, *Mémoires et Notes pour servir à l'Histoire du Département de l'Eure* (Évreux, 1862–9), ii. 488. For the charter of Henry I see *Très Ancien Coutumier,* ed. Tardif, p. 65 ; Round, *Calendar,* no. 290.

[59] Copy by Gaignières in MS. Lat. 17031, p. 137.

Tibi etiam, Willelme Lovel, precipio quod iusticiam ei facias de Gilleberto nummario (?). Teste Thoma cancellario apud Rothomagum.

(7) G. dux Normann[orum] et comes And[egavorum] R. de sancto Walerico et ministris suis de Archis salutem. Precipio quod habere faciatis S. Amando decimam suam de forestis de Awi et de Alihermont in denariis frumento et avena sicut eam melius habuit tempore Henrici regis, quia nolo ut elemosina in ea minuatur. Teste Toma cancellario apud Lux[ovias].

The triumph of the traditions of the Anglo-Norman chancery can also be seen in documents in which no chancellor is mentioned. The following, which probably belongs to the early part of 1144, is a good example of a brevity which is literary rather than legal in its phraseology : [60]

(8) Notum sit omnibus tam futuris quam presentibus quod ego Gaufridus Andegavorum comes, Fulconis bone memorie Iherusalem regis filius, monachis sancti Ebrulfi res eorum universas ita habendas et possidendas libere et quiete concedo et affirmo, sicut habebant temporis regis Hainrici antecessoris mei. Et omnibus communiter ne predictos monachos de rebus suis in causam mittant precipio, insuper illis ne cum aliquo inde placitentur prohibeo, et amicis meis ubicunque fuerint, sicut me diligunt, ut eos manuteneant et ab omnibus defendant cum summa diligentia submoneo et rogo.

The next is similar, though Geoffrey is now duke : [61]

(9) Goffridus dux Normannorum et comes Andegavensium omnibus dapiferis et prepositis villicis et servientibus suis salutem. De his que pertinent ad proprium victum et vestitum monachorum sancti Martini de Sagio et serviens eorundem monachorum proprium esse eorum affiducare poterit, nullum inde capiatis teloneum aut pedagium aut consuetudinem aliquam minimam vel magnam. Quod si feceritis meum incurretis odium et cum sexaginta solidis reddetis.

In the following charter the same matter is thrown into the legal language of Henry I's time ; indeed, except for the insertion of *sicut mee res proprie*, it reproduces exactly the terms of a writ of Henry for the same monastery : [62]

(10) G. dux Norm[annorum] comes And[egavorum] baronibus et omnibus vic[ecomitibu]s et ministris tocius Anglie et Normannie et portuum

[60] Cartulary of St. Évroul, MS. Lat. 11056, no. 681 ; Round, *Calendar*, no. 637. In the absence of place and witnesses this charter presents some curious features. Geoffrey speaks as successor of Henry I, yet he has not taken the ducal title. The news of Fulk's death, which occurred 10 November 1143 (Röhricht, *Geschichte des Königreichs Jerusalem*, p. 229), could hardly have reached his son before the capitulation of Rouen, where Geoffrey remained until his assumption of the ducal title ; yet a charter issued at Rouen in such an alien style is rather surprising.

[61] Copy from *Livre rouge* of Séez, in MS. Fr. 18953, pp. 37, 222.

[62] Cartulary of S. André-en-Gouffern, in Archives of the Calvados, f. 22, no. 90; no. 72 is the writ of Henry I. Note that Geoffrey has even let *Anglie* stand. This type of writ is familiar in England ; see, for example, J. Armitage Robinson, *Gilbert Crispin*, p. 150, no. 34. For a quite different Angevin form see *Cartulaire de Tiron*, i. 63.

maris salutem. Precipio quod totum corrodium et omnes res monachorum
de abbatia de Vinaz quas servientes eorum affidare poterint pertinere suo
dominico victui et vestitui sint in pace et quiete de theloneo et passagio
et omnibus consuetudinibus sicut mee res proprie. Et super hoc prohibeo
quod nullus eos disturbet iniuste super .x. libras forisfacture. Testibus
comite de Pontevio et Alexandro de Bohun et Roberto de Noburg' (sic),
apud Argentomum.

The following is parallel, but contains a further provision : [63]

(11) G. dux Normannorum et comes Andegav[orum] omnibus baronibus et fidelibus suis et ministris totius Normannie et Cenomannie et portuum maris salutem. Precipio quod totum corredium abbatis de Savign[eio] et monachorum suorum et abbatum qui sunt de obediencia Savign[eii] et omnes res quas ministri sui affidare poterunt esse suas sint quiete de theloneo et passagio et omni consuetudine ubicunque venerint, et prohibeo ne ullus eos super hac re disturbet super decem libras forisfacture. Precipio etiam quod monachi Savigneii totam terram suam et homines et omnes res suas in firma pace teneant et non inde placitent, quia terra et omnes res eorum in mea custodia et defensione sunt et nolo quod aliquis eis inde contumeliam faciat neque de aliqua re eos inquietare presumat.

Teste (sic) Guidone de Sabl[olio] et Alexandro de Bohun, apud Argentomagum.

Another writ of a well-known type is : [64]

(12) G. dux Norm[annorum] et comes And[egavorum] vicec[omitibus] Roth[omagensibus] salutem. Precipio quod tradatis leprosis Roth[omagensibus] xl. solidos Roth[omagensium] singulis mensibus sicut rex H. eis dedit et carta eius testatur.

T[este] Rob[erto] de Novo burgo, apud Rothomagum.

Further illustration is unnecessary. We recognize not only the sobriety, conciseness, and clearness which Delisle notes as the characteristics of the Anglo-Norman chancery,[65] but also its regular terminology, such as the address, the *nisi feceris* clause,[66] *sicut umquam melius habuit, ne inde amplius clamorem audiam*, and the ten pounds' penalty for infringement.[67] In all essential

---

[63] Copy of 1237 under seal of William, bishop of Avranches, in Archives of the Manche, fonds de Savigny.

[64] Original, with fragment of *simple queue*, in Archives Nationales, K 23, 15³². Printed in Delisle, *Henri II*, p. 136; Langlois, *Histoire du Prieuré du Mont-aux-Malades-lès-Rouen*, p. 397; calendared in Tardif, *Monuments Historiques*, no. 516.

[65] *Henri II*, pp. 240–6.   [66] *Livre noir*, no. 24.

[67] A further indication of Norman influence is seen in Geoffrey's second seal, where he takes the title of ' dux Normannorum ' and carries still further the imitation of the Norman type which his father had begun. Only one original of this seal is known to exist, attached to a charter for Bec, printed above (no. 2), and described by Demay, *Inventaire des Sceaux de la Normandie*, no. 20; but there are also certain drawings (Delisle, *Henri II*, p. 138 f.). On the introduction of the Norman type into Anjou, see Manteyer, *Le Sceau-matrice du Comte d'Anjou Foulques le Jeune*, in *Mémoires des Antiquaires de France*, lx. 305–38.

matters Geoffrey's ducal chancery was a Norman institution, and, what is more important, it was an instrument for maintaining the rights which his predecessors had granted and the administration through which they had governed.

Since few of Geoffrey's charters are dated, it is impossible to construct an itinerary or form any estimate of the distribution of his time between Normandy and Anjou. He visited Normandy every year of his reign as duke,[68] but, apart from his sojourns at Rouen and Argentan and an occasional military expedition, the only places at which he can be traced are Bayeux, Bec, Lisieux, and Saint-Lô. By far the greater number of his charters are issued from Rouen, which seems to have acquired new importance as the capital of the duchy. Geoffrey rebuilt the tower and the bridge over the Seine,[69] and after Rouen became the abode of the empress in 1148,[70] a local poet did not hesitate to compare to imperial Rome the ancient and noble city which resembled it so closely in name [71] and claimed Julius Caesar for its founder.[72] To Geoffrey Rouen owed a detailed and comprehensive charter, the earliest of the city's surviving muniments,[73] which restored to the citizens the privileges which they had enjoyed under Henry I, safeguarded particularly their jurisdictional and fiscal immunities, confirmed the gild organization, as represented in

[68] In 1145 he is at Arques and Rouen (Robert of Torigni, i. 237, 239); in 1146 at Rouen (*ibid.* i. 242) and Courcy-sur-Dive (charter for Cormery given ' in presentiam meam apud Curciacum super Divam in exercitu meo . . . anno domini millesimo centesimo quadragesimo sexto regnante Ludovico rege Francorum qui tunc crucem assumpserat' : Bibliothèque Nationale, Collection Housseau, v. no. 1718); in 1147 at Argentan (*Livre noir*, no. 100) and 11 October at Rouen (Round, no. 1405); in 1148 at Fauguernon, near Lisieux (Robert of Torigni, i. 247); 27 March 1149 at Bec (*supra*, no. 2).

[69] Robert of Torigni, i. 239, 242, 368. Cf. Deville, *Recherches sur l'ancien Pont de Rouen*, in *Précis des Travaux de l'Académie de Rouen*, 1831, pp. 171–3.

[70] *Supra*, n. 34. Most of Matilda's Norman charters are dated at Rouen or Le Pré : Delisle, *Henri II*, p. 142 f., nos. 6–13 ; Round, nos. 263, 679 f., 683.

[71]
Rothoma nobilis, urbs antiqua, potens, speciosa,
Gens Normanna sibi te preposuit dominari ;
Imperialis honorificentia te super ornat ;
Tu Rome similis tam nomine quam probitate,
Rothoma, si mediam removes, et Roma vocaris.
Viribus acta tuis devicta Britannia servit ;
Et tumor Anglicus et Scottus algidus et Galo sevus
Munia protensis manibus tibi debita solvunt.
Sub duce Gaufredo cadit hostis et arma quiescunt,
Nominis ore sui Gaufredus gaudia fert dux ;
Rothoma letaris sub tanto principe felix.

The remaining nine lines are a eulogy of King Roger of Sicily : MS. Fr. 2623, f. 114ʳ, printed in Richard, *Notice sur l'ancienne Bibliothèque des Échevins de Rouen* (Rouen, 1845), p. 37. ' Imperialis honorificentia ' is, of course, an allusion to the coming of the empress.

[72] Ordericus, ii. 324, where its size and prosperity are also spoken of.

[73] Chéruel, *Histoire de Rouen*, i. 241 ; Round, *Calendar*, no. 109. Cf. Giry, *Établissements de Rouen*, i. 25–7.

the merchant and cordwainers' gilds,[74] and guaranteed the rights of Rouen merchants in England and their monopoly of the commerce of the Seine and the Irish trade of Normandy. Naturally Rouen had no rival in political or commercial importance, nor can much trace of municipal life be discovered elsewhere in the duchy during this reign. Verneuil and Nonancourt on the southern border seem to have continued something of the prosperity which they owed to the fostering care of Henry I,[75] but it is perhaps significant that Geoffrey's charters make no mention of Caen or of its religious establishments, and the fortunes of both Caen and Dieppe waited upon the re-establishment of close relations with England under his son.[76] Charters and chroniclers are also silent in Geoffrey's reign respecting another phase of local life, namely castle-building, which had been a traditional practice of the Angevin counts at home and played a prominent part in the Norman policy of Henry I and Henry II.[77]

On his visits to Normandy Geoffrey was often accompanied by Angevin barons, such as the seneschal Joslin of Tours and his brother Pippin, Geoffrey de Cleers, and Pain of Clairvaux; but he had also an important Norman following. His most frequent attendants were the seneschal Reginald of St. Valéry, Robert de Neufbourg, Robert de Courcy, William de Vernon, Guy de Sablé, Alexander and Enjuger de Bohun, Osbert de Cailli, Richard de la Haie, and Enguerran de Wascœuil. The attestations of the great men of the duchy, such as the counts of Meulan, Roumare, and Ponthieu, appear more rarely, while the subscriptions of the bishops occur only in occasional documents dated at Rouen,[78] where they doubtless attended the more formal meetings of the court, although they played no regular part in the ducal administration. The appearance of Norman barons with Geoffrey in Anjou [79] likewise goes to show that there was no mechanical

---

[74] The privileges of the cordwainers are contained in a special charter: *Ordonnances des Rois*, v. 416; *supra*, p. 426. See the similar charters of Henry I, Stephen, and Henry II in La Roque, *Histoire de la Maison d'Harcourt*, iii. 149 (cf. Round, no. 107), where the charter of Stephen, found in his name in MS. Lat. 9067, f. 155, is wrongly attributed to William the Conqueror.

[75] See Henry's charter to Verneuil in *Ordonnances des Rois*, iv. 638; and the documents mentioning these towns in Le Prévost, *Eure*, ii. 476 f., 488, iii. 345, 347; Round, nos. 282 f., 287, 292 f. For Geoffrey's reign see *supra*, p. 431; and Ordericus, v. 132, where the *conventus* of Verneuil in 1141 is estimated at 13,000 men.

[76] For Dieppe under Geoffrey see below, n. 97; and Round, nos. 109, 170, 1057 f. The growth of the town under Henry II is seen in the various grants of houses to the king's officers preserved in the *Coutumier de Dieppe* (Archives of the Seine-Inférieure, G. 851): Delisle, *Henri II*, nos. 82, 258, 517, 521, 527.

[77] For a full discussion of the Norman castles of the twelfth century see Professor Powicke's forthcoming book on *The Loss of Normandy*.

[78] *Livre noir*, nos. 17, 19; Round, no. 126; Delisle, no. 6*; *infra*, p. 442, no. 13.

[79] *Supra*, p. 430; *Cartulaire de S. Ymer*, p. 7; Round, no. 1058.

separation between his two groups of followers; but the regular officers of government were quite distinct in Normandy from those in his other possessions,[80] in which indeed there does not seem to have been entire unity of organization.[81]

It was in this nucleus of administrative officers that the breach of continuity created by time and civil war between the *curia* of Henry I and that of his son-in-law was most serious, yet it is significant that the new recruits came from Normandy and not from Anjou. The change was most marked on the ecclesiastical side, for Henry's justiciar, John of Lisieux, had died in 1141, and Archbishop Hugh and the bishop of Coutances were the only prelates who survived from Henry's time. The bishops had taken Stephen's part; Philip of Bayeux, the most experienced of them in public affairs, had even been his chancellor; and it was not to be expected that Geoffrey would turn to them for confidential advice or place one of them at the head of his administration. Under these circumstances the suppression of the justiciarship was natural, particularly as no such office existed in Anjou. The principal seneschal of Henry I, Robert de la Haie, was also dead,[82] and his son Richard had held Cherbourg for Stephen;[83] so that this dignity fell to a new man, Reginald of St. Valéry,[84] under whom it seems to have gained something of the relatively greater importance which, in the absence of a justiciar, it had come to possess in Anjou.[85] We hear very little of the other seneschals, although Robert de Courcy, *dapifer* under Henry I, has the same title in one of Geoffrey's charters;[86] and while I have not found the title applied to him before Henry II's reign, I believe that Robert de Neufbourg, whose

[80] What has been said above (pp. 428 f.) of the chancellors can hardly be considered an exception to this statement.

[81] Note the mention of Hugh and Geoffrey de Cleers as seneschals besides Joslin of Tours in Marchegay, *Chroniques des Églises d'Anjou*, p. 88 (cf. the documents cited in Delisle, *Henri II*, p. 387 f.); and also the special officers for Maine who appear in a charter given at Le Mans in 1146 (*Bibliothèque de l'École des Chartes*, xxxvi. 433).

[82] On his place under Henry I, see *ante*, xxiv. 218. He disappears after Henry's time.

[83] John of Marmoutier, pp. 299–301. If, as John says, Richard was carried off by pirates, he would seem to have returned to Normandy, where he holds an important position under Geoffrey and Henry II. There may, of course, have been two barons of this name; the seneschal (*infra*, n. 88) was a son-in-law of William de Vernon (Stapleton, *Rotuli Scaccarii*, i, p. cxlv).

[84] On Reginald see Delisle, *Henri II*, p. 421.

[85] On the seneschal in Anjou see Beautemps-Beaupré, *Coutumes*, II. i, cc. 8, 10; and cf. Powicke, *ante*, xxi. 649.

[86] *Livre noir*, no. 19. Robert de Courcy, who was in Normandy in 1138, when he befriended Geoffrey (Ordericus, v. 109), in 1141 (Tardif, *Très Ancien Coutumier de Normandie*, p. 117; cf. Round, *Calendar*, no. 1198), and in 1145 (*Bibliothèque de l'École des Chartes*, xxi. 127, 131), may not be identical with the Robert de Courcy who as *dapifer* attests charters of the empress in 1141 and 1142 (Round, *Geoffrey de Mandeville*, pp. 170, 183). The Courcy genealogy needs clearing up; see Tardif, *loc. cit.*; Delisle, *Henri II*, p. 440.

signature regularly precedes that of Robert de Courcy in the charters,[87] must also have been *dapifer* under Geoffrey before he became chief seneschal under Henry II. The same title may have been restored to Richard de la Haie, who uses it in 1152.[88]

Of actual meetings of the *curia* we have few notices, and these are concerned entirely with its judicial decisions. It was in Geoffrey's court that Philip of Bayeux established his rights over Ducy and Louvières [89] and released to the abbey of Savigny his claim to land in Escures;[90] here also the abbot of Fécamp won control of the port against the townsmen,[91] and the canons of Rouen established their privileges in the forest of Aliermont.[92] In these instances the duke appears to have been himself present;[93]

[87] *Livre noir*, no. 39; Round, *Calendar*, nos. 170, 960; *Neustria pia*, p. 15; cf. Round, no. 126; and the charter for Bec, *supra*, p. 429. Robert de Neufbourg was one of the early partisans of Geoffrey: Ordericus, v. 68. On his position under Henry II see Delisle, pp. 445-7.

[88] See his charters in the Archives of the Manche, H. 4622, 5230; and cf. H. 692. Stapleton, i, p. xxxiv n., says he was *dapifer* under Geoffrey, but cites no evidence.

[89] 'Quas in curia nobilis memorie Gaufridi quondam Normannie ducis per iudicium obtinuisti': *Livre noir*, no. 156.

[90] 'H. Dei gratia Rothomagensi archiepiscopo totique capitulo Rothomagensis ecclesie G. Andeg[avorum] comes salutem et dilectionem. Notum sit vobis atque omnibus hominibus tam presentibus quam futuris quod Philipus Baiocensis episcopus in pace dimisit et quietam clamavit terram de Escuris quam ipse adversum monachos Saviniacenses calumpniabatur et quam monachi in tempore regis H. et duorum Baiocensium episcoporum predecessorum eius libere et quiete tenuerant. Illam autem terram dimisit eis quietam et liberam ipse Ph. Baiocensis episcopus in presentia Guillelmi Cenomannensis episcopi et mea aput Cenomannos, presente Raginaldo de Sancto Walerico et Guidone de Sabl[eio] et Gofferio de Brueria atque plurimis aliis. Quare vobis mando ac vos diligenter deprecor ut si Baiocensis episcopus vel aliquis alius super hoc reclamare aut terram calumpniari presumeret, monachi prefati vestram protectionem atque adiutorium inde haberent. Testibus Gaufredo de Claris Vallibus et Guillelmo de Botevilla et magistro Hugone decano Sancti Martini, apud Mosterol[ium]' (original, with *double queue*, in Archives Nationales, L. 969; Cartulary of Savigny, in Archives of the Manche, no. 201; Round, no. 809, where the place and witnesses are omitted and Geoffrey's title is arbitrarily altered by the insertion of 'duke of the Normans'). For the date see above, p. 423 n. 26. Another account of the transaction, showing that Hugh de Cleers was also among those present, is given in the following letter of William, bishop of Le Mans: 'H. Dei gratia Rotomagensis ecclesie archiepiscopo totique eiusdem ecclesie capitulo G. eadem gratia humilis Cenomannensis episcopus per bona temporalia immarcescibilis vite coronam feliciter attingere. Discretioni vestre notum fieri volumus quod Philippus Baiocensis ecclesie episcopus terram de Escuris, quam abbati et monachis de Savinneio calumpniabatur et quam predictus abbas et monachi solute et quiete in tempore duorum episcoporum predecessorum suorum et Henrici regis tenuerant, in presentia nostra et domini Gofredi Normannorum ducis et Andegavorum comitis et Guidonis de Sabloŏ et Raginaldi de Sancto Galerico et Goferii de Brueria et Hugonis de Cleriis et aliorum multorum in pace dimisit. Hoc ideo vobis scripsimus quod si prefatus episcopus vel aliquis alius erga ecclesiam Savinneii insurrexerit, prescripte ecclesie, sicut decet sanctos, ius suum defendatis' (original in MS. Lat. 9215, Savigny, no. 1; cartulary, no. 202; omitted by Célier, in his *Catalogue des Actes des Évêques du Mans*, Paris, 1910).

[91] 'Sicut eum disrationaverunt in curia patris mei et postea in curia mea:' charter of Henry II, Delisle, no. 85; Round, no. 132.

[92] Valin, *Le Duc de Normandie*, p. 266; cf. *supra*, p. 426.

[93] Pleas 'ante ducem Normannie' are mentioned in the charter to Rouen (Round,

but the *curia* at Rouen, which effected a compromise between the abbot of Préaux and Enguerran de Wascœuil, was composed of *iudices, baillivi,* and *proceres* under the presidency of Reginald of St. Valéry as *dapifer Normannie*.[94] Possibly Angevin precedents may have done something to develop the seneschal's importance on such occasions, but as an itinerant justice he is in no way distinguished from his associates. As under Henry I,[95] the judicial authority of the duke seems to have been exercised chiefly by travelling justices who acted under his writs. Such officers are constantly found in the inquests held on behalf of the bishop of Bayeux, specific mention being made of Reginald of St. Valéry, Robert de Neufbourg, Robert de Courcy, William de Vernon, Richard de la Haie, Gui de Sablé, Enjuger de Bohun, and Galeran, count of Meulan.[96] Certain of these reappear in the same capacity in other parts of Normandy: Robert de Neufbourg and William de Vernon at Arques and Dieppe;[97] Gui de Sablé, this time with William Lovel, at Verneuil and Nonancourt.[98] In the Cotentin we read of an inquest held at the duke's assize (*in assisia mea*) at Valognes; no justice is mentioned, but four who are otherwise known to have exercised such functions witness the charter of Geoffrey which declares the result.[99] Evidently the system extended throughout the duchy; evidently also the justices were chosen from the principal lay members of the *curia*, without recourse to the clergy.

The problem of chief interest in connexion with Geoffrey's justices is their administration of the sworn inquest in the determination of disputes concerning land, a question which need not here be treated at length, as I have had occasion to discuss it with some fullness elsewhere.[100] The evidence comes for the

no. 109). In the eulogy of Geoffrey by Étienne de Rouen his justice is especially praised: *Chroniques des Comtes d'Anjou*, p. 313; Howlett, *Chronicles of Stephen*, ii. 772.   [94] Valin, p. 265.   [95] *Ante,* xxiv. 213–22.

[96] *Livre noir,* nos. 17, 19, 24, 25, 39, 43, 44, 89, 90.

[97] 'G. dux Norm[annorum] et comes And[egavorum] Willelmo de Vernon et Rob[erto] de Novoburgo iusticiis suis salutem. Mando vobis et precipio quod vos faciatis habere plenarie et recte et integre abbati sancti Wandreg[iaili] amico nostro familiari et conventui illius ecclesie decimas redditum meorum de Archis de Deppa et de toto vicecomitatu Archarum sicut ecclesia illa melius in tempore Henrici regis habuit et septimanas suas de redditu Rothomagi secundum cursum et ordinem septimanarum sicut unquam liberius et plenius habuit. Et si quis eos super hoc inquietare vel disturbare voluerit, plenariam eis inde iusticiam faciatis, ne clamorem inde ulterius habeam. Teste Willelmo comite de Rolmare apud Rothomagum' (copy in library of Rouen, MS. 394, f. 2). Reginald of St. Valéry was also concerned with Dieppe, where he held the revenues of the port: Round, nos. 1057–8.

[98] *Supra,* p. 431, no. 6. In the region of Argentan Fulk d'Aunou and Robert de Neuville seem to have been justices: Delisle, *Cartulaire normand,* no. 4, p. 273.

[99] William de Vernon, Enjuger de Bohun, Robert de Neufbourg, and Robert de Courcy: *American Historical Review,* viii. 630 (1903).

[100] *The Early Norman Jury,* in the *American Historical Review,* viii. 613–40. Certain of the texts are discussed by Valin, *Le Duc de Normandie et sa Cour*, pp. 208–18,

most part from the cartulary of Bayeux and is connected with the active efforts of the bishop, Philip d'Harcourt, for the recovery of his property in the years immediately following the Angevin conquest. For his benefit Geoffrey provided for a general recognition of the demesne, fiefs, and other rights of the see, and added special writs to individual justices with reference to particular estates and feudal holdings. The facts were determined by the oath of lawful men of the vicinage, and each of the justices in charge made a written return to the duke, four such returns having survived as detailed evidence of the procedure employed. The sworn recognition was also used under Geoffrey to determine the rights of the bishop of Coutances over Tourlaville [101] and those of the chapter of Rouen in the forest of Aliermont; [102] and its diffusion is further shown by the practice of submitting the question of a champion's professionalism to the oath of ten citizens of Rouen selected by the duke's justice,[103] and by a case in the baronial court of the count of Meulan where the parties put themselves on the verdict of eight lawful knights.[104]

Brunner has inferred from the phrase *secundum assisiam meam* in two of the Bayeux writs, attributed by him to Henry II but now known to be Geoffrey's, that their author promulgated a general ordinance introducing the recognition into Normandy; but no trace of such an ordinance has been found, and even if it be assumed that the word assize is here used in the sense of a legislative act, there is no reason for supposing that it affected others than the bishop of Bayeux. Possibly the assize in question may be found in a writ which provides that 'if a dispute shall arise between the bishop and any of his men concerning any tenement, it shall by the oath of lawful men of the vicinage be recognized who was seized of the land in Bishop Odo's time' [105]—an important extension of this mode of trial, since it confers a general privilege applicable to a whole class of cases and looks in the direction of the regular application of the inquest to possessory actions. This and the other instances cited indicate that Geoffrey's reign was a period of importance in the development of the jury in civil matters, but they do not show that the recognition was then introduced or that it was affected by the practice in Anjou,[106] where it appears to have been

who, however, overlooks Brunner's discussion and mine and ascribes the Bayeux documents to Henry II. See also Bourrienne, in *Revue Catholique de Normandie*, xix. 170–2, 266–71, 295–301 (1909); and Brunner, *Geschichte der englischen Rechtsquellen*, p. 65 (1909).   [101] *American Historical Review*, viii. 630.

[102] Valin, p. 266. On the attribution to Geoffrey see above, p. 426.

[103] Round, no. 109.

[104] Valin, pp. 201, 264. Cf. *American Historical Review*, viii. 636–8.

[105] *Livre noir*, no. 16.

[106] As is suggested by Prentout, *La Normandie* (Paris, 1910), p. 57; and by Powicke, *ante*, xxii. 15.

in a more rudimentary stage. Here again Geoffrey seems to have been a follower of Henry I. It is true that no writs prescribing this method of trial have come down from the reigns of Geoffrey's Norman predecessors, but we know that Henry, in 1133, commanded a comprehensive inquest, 'on the oath of ancient men who knew the facts,' respecting the possessions of the bishop of Bayeux, and a portion of the returns, together with the names of the jurors, has been preserved. This was the precedent which Lucius II and Eugene III urged upon Geoffrey in behalf of Bishop Philip, and in following it the duke expressly states that he is walking in the footsteps of Henry I.[107] Whatever he may have done for the establishment of the procedure by recognition was in the nature of extension, not of origination.

Next to the justices, who may be considered as both central and local officers, came the *vicomtes*, who had since the eleventh century been the principal agents of local administration, charged with the general oversight of the *vicomté*, and particularly with the collection of the duke's revenues and the payment of the farm at which their district was let.[108] These fiscal arrangements, which also covered the parallel but inferior jurisdiction of the *prévôts*, show remarkable fixity from the time of William the Conqueror to that of Henry II,[109] and it is not surprising that Geoffrey sought to re-establish and maintain them, especially since his resources had been diminished by the extensive grants from the ducal demesne which he had been obliged to make as the price of the barons' support.[110] He is careful that the bishop of Évreux shall have his tenths from the farm of Verneuil and Nonancourt,[111] the nuns of St. Amand their tithes in the forests of Awi and Aliermont,[112] the monks of St. Wandrille their ancient rights in his rents at Arques and Dieppe, in the proceeds of the fair at Caen, and in the toll of Rouen, Exmes, Falaise, and Argentan.[113] We have the actual writ ordering the *vicomte* of Rouen to

---

[107] 'Vestigiis regis Henrici inherentes qui hoc idem iuramento antiquorum hominum fecerat recognosci.... Iuramentum quod rex Henricus fieri fecerat ratum esse volentes, iuramento eorundem qui tempore regis Henrici iuraverunt et aliorum recognosci fecimus iura, possessiones, consuetudines, libertates quas ecclesia Baiocensis tempore Odonis episcopi habuerat et habere debebat.' *Livre noir*, no. 39. For the letters of the popes see also nos. 157, 206.

[108] Stapleton, *Rotuli Scaccarii*, i, pp. xxxiv–vi, lxi; Delisle, in *Bibliothèque de l'École des Chartes*, x. 264 f.; *Henri II*, pp. 212–8; *American Historical Review*, xiv. 468–70.

[109] *American Historical Review*, xiv. 465–7; *ante*, xxiv. 223; xxvi. 328.

[110] Robert of Torigni, i. 267.

[111] *Supra*, p. 431, no. 6.   [112] *Supra*, p. 432, no. 7.

[113] *Supra*, p. 438 n. 97; Round, *Calendar*, no. 170. Another example of the continuity of the fiscal system is seen in the empress's grant to St. André-en-Gouffern (1151–4) of 46s. 6d., which had been paid annually to the *vicomte* of Argentan for the *gravaria* of Montgaroult: Round, no. 593; Delisle, *Henri II*, p. 142, no. 10.

pay the lepers of the city the forty shillings monthly which King Henry had given them,[114] and the charter to the citizens of Rouen shows the duke's officers collecting the tolls and customs- and wine-dues which are mentioned in the documents of his predecessors.[115]

While, however, the *vicomtes* and *prévôts* continued to account to the exchequer 'for the issues of their more ancient jurisdictions', the Angevin dukes superimposed upon the local government of Normandy the new area of the *bailliage*.[116] It is not likely that under Geoffrey this new unit acquired any such importance as it possesses in the military returns of 1172, yet the name *bailia*, probably in the more general sense of an officer's district, occurs first in his reign,[117] and the *baillivi* make their appearance in his charters, where, however, the term, like the more common *ministri*, may have been applied collectively to all below the rank of *vicomte*.[118] We meet also with the duke's constable at Cherbourg,[119] the wardens of his forest of Argentan,[120] his goldsmith at Arques,[121] and his moneyer at Verneuil or Nonancourt,[122] as well as a group of *servientes*—a loose term which in one instance describes those who exercise the duke's authority on the lands of the bishop of Bayeux,[123] and in another denotes the serjeants of Rouen whose offices the charter of the city promises to restore.[124] One hereditary serjeanty of this sort, that of Henry the Marshal in Rouen and its

---

[114] *Supra*, p. 433, no. 12. Compare the charters of the empress and Henry for Beaulieu : Delisle, p. 126.

[115] Round, no. 109. On the dues collected at Rouen under the Norman dukes see Charles de Beaurepaire, *La Vicomté de l'Eau de Rouen* (Paris, 1856), pp. 2, 18–20, 40–52.

[116] Stapleton, i, pp. xxxiii f.; *Bibliothèque de l'École des Chartes*, x. 259 f.; Powicke, *ante*, xxii. 22 f.; and, more fully, in his *Loss of Normandy*.

[117] *Livre noir*, no. 24. Cf. no. 40, issued shortly after Geoffrey's death; and Stapleton, i, p. xxxiv.

[118] *Livre noir*, no. 15; *Neustria pia*, p. 15; Valin, *Le Duc de Normandie*, p. 265; *supra*, nos. 5, 10, 11. Cf. Delisle, *Henri II*, pp. 207, 219.

[119] Delisle, pp. 142 f., 409, 513, no. 84*. This is a writ of the empress, probably issued between 1151 and 1154; but the constable in question, Osbert de la Heuse, was a companion of Geoffrey (John of Marmoutier, p. 231), and had doubtless been placed by him in charge of Cherbourg.

[120] Delisle, *Cartulaire normand*, no. 4.

[121] Charter of Henry II granting 'Waltero cambiatori aurifabro et heredibus suis totam terram Roberti cambiatoris patris sui sitam apud Archas quietam et liberam et totum cambium et totam aurifabricaturam toscius castellarie Archarum et tocius Deppe ... preterea ... omnes consuetudines et quittancias et libertates quas pater meus G. comes Andegavorum dedit et concessit Roberto patri suo et carta confirmavit'. Archives of the Seine-Inférieure, G. 851, f. 55ᵛ; MS. Lat. 9209, Rouen, no. 2; Delisle, *Henri II*, no. 527.

[122] *Supra*, no. 6, where I read 'Gisleberto nummario' instead of Le Prévost's 'mimenario'.

[123] *Livre noir*, no. 16. The general meaning is also found in nos. 3 and 9, *supra*.

[124] Round, no. 109, where the 'proprium marescallum civitatis' is also mentioned.

banlieue, is known in its curious privileges from the document, preserved in a corrupt form, by which Geoffrey conferred it : [125]

(13) G. dux Normenn[orum] et comes Andeg[avorum] . . archiepiscopo Rothomagensi et omnibus episcopis Normennie et comitibus[126] et iusticiis suis salutem. Noveritis quod ego dedi et concessi Henrico le Mareschal servienti meo sergenteriam de bagnileuca Rothomagensi sicut se proportat de feodo de Pratellis et de feodo de Cailliaco, et dedi eidem Henrico et suis heredibus sergenteriam de Cailliaco sicut se proportat in longum et in latum et sicut extendit de feodo de Cailliaco et de feudo de Pratellis et de feodo de Feritate usque ad partes de Gournayo, et omnia alia ad placitum spate pertinencia, tenenda et habenda dicto Henrico le Mareschal et suis heredibus bene et in pace servientium (*sic*) faciendo. Et volo et concedo quod dictus Henricus le Mareschal et eius heredes habeant omnes robas tallatas omniaque superlectillia et omnia vasa nisi fuerint argentea et aurata, et carnes baconum nisi bacones fuerint integri, et dolium nisi plenum sit vini, videlicet eorum et earum que membra sua forefacient, et de domibus que cremabuntur forefactura que eidem Henricus et eius heredes habeant tantum quantum poterunt sursum percutere de moura [127] spate sue si eques fuerint ignem deffendendo. Volo etiam et concedo quod eidem Henricus et eius heredes habeant suum hardere et suum edificare in foresta mea de Tisone et pasturagia ab omnibus libera et quieta. Et quia volo quod omnia et singula predicta dicto Henrico et eius heredibus rata et stabilia in perpetuum teneantur, hanc presentem cartam munimine sigilli mei confirmavi.

Testibus Hugone Rothomagensi archiepiscopo, Ern[ulfo] Luxoviensi episcopo, Philippo Baiocensi episcopo, Galerano comite Mellendi, Reginaldo de sancto Walerico, Rogero de Claris vallis (*sic*), Gaufredo de Cleres, apud Rothomagum.

Respecting Geoffrey's policy toward the Norman church, there is little to add to what Professor Böhmer has said on the subject.[128] On three occasions during his reign the effort was made to exercise freedom of election in place of the practice of ducal appointment which had prevailed under Henry I and even under Stephen ; but while in each case Geoffrey ended by accepting the candidate so chosen, he asserted his authority with a vigour which left his real control undiminished. He held the property of the see against Arnulf of Lisieux for two years and three months, and restored it then only after the exaction of a heavy payment ; Gerard of Séez, elected under questionable

---

[125] Archives Nationales, JJ. 72, no. 191, based on a vidimus of Philip V in 1318. The charter is probably anterior to 1147, as it is witnessed by the count of Meulan. Interesting serjeanties connected with Rouen under Henry I and Henry II are those of Odo Malpalu the pantler (Delisle, *Cartulaire normand*, no. 14 ; Round, *Calendar*, no. 1280; *ante*, xxiv. 228 ; Round, *The King's Serjeants*, pp. 199–201) ; and Baldricus filius Gileberti (Delisle, *Cartulaire*, no. 13). See also the grant to Roland d'Oissel : Delisle, no. 2 ; Round, no. 1278. [126] MS. *communibus*.
[127] i. e. the blade : Old French *moure, meure* (Godefroy).
[128] *Kirche und Staat in England und in der Normandie*, pp. 310–25.

circumstances about the beginning of 1144, suffered at the hands of Geoffrey's followers acts of violence which were subsequently compared to the murder of Becket,[129] and was not reconciled to the duke until Easter 1147; the abbot whom monks and pope set over the monastery of Mont-Saint-Michel was compelled to purchase his peace with the duke at a price which left his house under a heavy burden of debt.[130] Contests such as these, as well as the long adherence of the prelates to Stephen's cause, make it plain why the bishops play so little part in the secular affairs of the duchy during Geoffrey's reign, the only notable exception being the use of Arnulf of Lisieux as intermediary in the difficulties of 1150 with Louis VII.[131] Apart, however, from the energetic assertion of his claims during vacancies, when he doubtless did much to earn St. Bernard's characterization of *malleus bonorum, oppressor pacis et libertatis ecclesie*,[132] Geoffrey can hardly be accused of injustice in his dealings with the Norman church. If the case of Bayeux may be taken as an example, we find him placing the full machinery of judicial administration at the bishop's disposal for the recovery of rights and property which had been lost during the anarchy and earlier,[133] and it is significant, in contrast with conditions in Anjou,[134] that no complaints of Geoffrey's exactions in Normandy meet us at the outset of the succeeding reign. It was in accord with the tendencies of the age that the Norman church should in Geoffrey's time be drawn into closer relations with Rome and with the rest of northern France, but it is noteworthy that he did not permit Eugene III or his legates to enter his dominions;[135] and, with due allowance for the inevitable growth of curial influence and of solidarity within the church in this period, it would seem that the ducal prerogative was handed on unimpaired to his successor.

[129] Giraldus Cambrensis, viii. 301.
[130] Annals of Mont-Saint-Michel, in Labbe, *Nova Bibliotheca Manuscriptorum*, i. 352.
[131] *Historiens de France*, xv. 521; *Œuvres de Suger*, ed. Lecoy de la Marche, p. 267.
[132] *Epistolae*, no. 348, in Migne, clxxxii. 553. So Peter of Cluny says, 'totius ecclesie Dei que in partibus illis est hostis comes Andegavorum audiatur:' *Historiens de France*, xv. 637.
[133] *American Historical Review*, viii. 620 ff.; *Revue Catholique de Normandie*, xix. 167–72, 266–72, 295–301. Observe also the enforcement of the fine of £9 for breach of the bishop's peace: *supra*, p. 431, no. 6.
[134] See the charters of Henry II for St. Florent and Fontevrault, in Delisle, nos. 24*–26*.
[135] 'Certus erat se Romanam ecclesiam offendisse, quod nec domnum papam nec aliquem legatum passus erat ingredi terram suam:' *Historia Pontificalis*, in *Monumenta Germ. Hist., Scriptores*, xx. 531. Böhmer overlooks this passage. The mission of the legates Alberic and Imarus, upon which he bases his statement that legatine authority was freely exercised in Normandy, belongs to 1144 and hence can hardly be considered typical: *Gallia Christiana*, xi. instr., 80; *Livre noir*, no. 58; *Historiens de France*, xv. 696 f.

So far as this investigation furnishes an answer to the question with which we started, it is that in his administration of Normandy Geoffrey continued the institutions and the policy of Henry I. The judicial and fiscal system and the organs of local government remain as before, with no trace of Angevin admixture. The personnel of the *curia* undergoes some change, and the seneschal perhaps acquires somewhat greater importance; but if the justiciar disappears, it is only to re-emerge under Henry II, and the department which stands in the most intimate relation to the new ruler, the chancery, is normanized even to its smallest phrases. Where, as in the case of the sworn inquest, some development appears probable, it roots in the practice of Henry I's reign and follows no discoverable Angevin precedents, nor do we find in Normandy that direct and personal rule which is so characteristic of the government of the counts of Anjou. All the evidence goes to show that Geoffrey observed for himself the policy which at the close of his life he laid down for his son, that of avoiding the transfer of customs or institutions from one part of his dominions to another.[136] How far this advice was followed by Henry II is a problem which must be reserved for future study.

CHARLES H. HASKINS.

[136] 'Terre vero sue et genti spiritu presago in posterum previdens, Henrico heredi suo interdixit ne Normannie vel Anglie consuetudines in consulatus sui terram, vel e converso, varie vicissitudinis altercatione permutaret:' John of Marmoutier, p. 292.

The Reigning Princes of Galilee

OF the various states constituted by the crusaders in Syria at the end of the eleventh century the kingdom of Jerusalem comprised all the conquests south of the river Adonis (Nahr Ibrahim), and was divided into four greater and a fluctuating number of smaller baronies. Of the former Jaffa and Sidon were on the coast, while that of Montreal, in the Oultrejourdain, and Galilee guarded the inland frontier towards Arabia and Damascus respectively. Jaffa was often held by the king, and before the disruption of the kingdom at Hattin was regarded as the proper fief for the heir apparent or presumptive of the crown. Sidon enjoyed the continuous succession of a single dynasty, while Oultrejourdain and Galilee were ruled by some of the most celebrated fighting men among the Latins. In attempting to enumerate the princes of Galilee and their families the historian is to a certain extent hampered by the fact that the 'Lignages d'Outremer', which may perhaps be called the 'Burke' of the Latin kingdom, is at fault in its record of Galilee. The account can be supplemented from charters, from the records of other families, and from modern research, but still it can never be as ample and detailed as could be wished.

The principality was first given to Tancred towards the end of 1099, but it is difficult to establish the exact date when he became prince. He may have raided Tiberias and taken it during the period between the surrender of Nablus, about 27 July,[1] and his arrival at Ramleh on 7 August;[2] or he may have conquered his fief at the end of August, when there was a large assembly of crusaders at Cayphas (Haifa).[3] It is improbable that the conquest could have taken place between 15 October and 15 December 1099, as the whole strength of the Latins was then occupied in the siege of Arsuf.[4] At any rate, when Bohemond and Baldwin du Bourg left Jericho on 5 January 1100, they returned north by way of Tiberias, which would have been unlikely had it still been a hostile city.[5] In May 1100 Tancred was well enough established in his new dominions to be able to leave them in order to join with his overlord, Godfrey de Bouillon, in the successful raid

[1] Hagenmeyer, *Chronologie du Royaume de Jérusalem*, 410.
[2] *Ibid.* 417.   [3] *Ibid.* 427.   [4] *Ibid.* 431, 435.   [5] *Ibid.* 442.

against Damascus.[6] He returned before the end of the month, but hurried to Jaffa on hearing of Godfrey's illness.[7] He left Jaffa on 17 July in joint command, with the Patriarch Daimbert, of the army against Acre,[8] but on hearing of Godfrey's death he besieged Cayphas instead.[9]

Godfrey had promised the lordship of Cayphas, so soon as that town should be taken, to one of his own knights, Waldemar Carpinel.[10] On Godfrey's death, however, Tancred, who was disappointed in not being chosen as his successor, seems to have had the idea of forming a large and independent dominion for himself at the expense of the crown. In pursuit of this, being supported by the patriarch,[11] he seized Cayphas on its surrender,[12] and added the territory to his fief of Galilee. He even tried to seize Jerusalem itself by a *coup de main*, but Baldwin, the king-elect, who was coming south[13] to take up the government, got wind of his intentions and hurriedly sent Hugh of Falkenberg and Robert, bishop of Ramleh,[14] to hold it against Tancred, who had already attacked the city, but failed, on 25 October 1100.[15] Tancred thereupon went to Jaffa, but had no greater success there.[16] Waldemar sued for his promised fief before the high court at the session held from December 1100 to January 1101, and won his case.[17] The new king's tact prevented an actual outbreak of hostilities, and after two interviews, one at the ford over the Nahr el Audje near Jaffa, on 22 February 1101,[18] the other at Cayphas, on 8 March following, persuaded Tancred to accept the ruling of the high court and surrender Cayphas to Waldemar Carpinel.[19]

Tancred also took advantage of the offer of the regency of Antioch, which had been made to him, to hand over Galilee to the king on the condition of being allowed to resume that fief after an interval of at least fifteen months. He then proceeded [20] to administer Antioch during the captivity of his uncle, Bohemond I, who had been taken prisoner together with Tancred's nephew,

[6] Hagenmeyer, *Chronologie du Royaume de Jérusalem*, 459.
[7] *Ibid.* 469.   [8] *Ibid.* 481.   [9] *Ibid.* 488.
[10] Albert of Aix, *Historia*, vii. 27, in Migne, clxvi.
[11] Hagenmeyer, *Chron.* 491.
[12] The siege began on 25 July, and the town was taken on 20 August 1100: *ibid.* 489, 496.
[13] *Ibid.* 503.   [14] *Ibid.* 512.   [15] *Ibid.* 509.
[16] *Ibid.* 511.   [17] *Ibid.* 526.   [18] *Ibid.* 534.
[19] *Ibid.* 540. Waldemar Carpinel, who had been lord of St. Abraham before he was seised of Cayphas (Röhricht, *Geschichte des Königreichs Jerusalem*, 57), was killed in the battle between Ramleh and Ascalon, 7 September, and was buried in the church of the Holy Sepulchre, 16 September. He is reported to have appeared in a vision to Hugh, archbishop of Lyons, next night (Hagenmeyer, *Chronologie du Royaume de Jérusalem*, 618). It seems that he was succeeded in Cayphas by Rohart, who was also lord of St. Abraham (Ducange-Rey).
[20] Hagenmeyer, *Chron.* 542.

Richard of Principato, on 15 August 1100, near Melitene, by Gumushtakin ibn Danishmend.[21] The kingdom was thus rid of its most dangerous vassal. But it was only for a short time, for when the Patriarch Daimbert, who had been Tancred's guest at Antioch since March[22] 1102, went south in the September of that year to reclaim his see (from which he had been absent, under a cloud, since 20 September 1101[23]), he was accompanied by Baldwin du Bourg and Tancred. They arrived at Arsuf on 25 September, and after an unsuccessful expedition against Ascalon went to Jaffa. Here, on 4 October, the king recognized Daimbert as patriarch subject to the final decision of the papal legate, Cardinal Robert. Four days later, however, that decision was given at a council held at Jerusalem, and Daimbert was deposed from his charge.[24] He died on 16 June 1107.[25] After this blow to his policy Tancred returned north.

On 9 March 1101 the king invested Hugh of Falkenberg with the principality of Galilee. He was seneschal of the kingdom, and next year was on his way south to join the king when the disaster of Ramleh took place on 17 May 1102.[26] Hugh came up with eighty knights, and on arriving at Arsuf, 19 May,[27] found the king, whom he accompanied to Jaffa two days later and assisted in the defeat of the Egyptians at the battle of Jaffa, on 27 May.[28] Hugh was in Jerusalem during 1104,[29] and was again with the king at another battle of Ramleh, on 27 August 1105;[30] he attended the council of the barons held at that town early in 1106,[31] and in the spring of the same year built the castle of Toron, now Tibnin.[32] This was to guard the northern march of the principality against Tyre, which was still in the hands of the Saracens.[33] Hugh was killed in action in the Hauran, on August 1106, by Tugtakin of Damascus, and his brother Gerard died of his wounds eight days later at Nazareth.[34] Hugh left two daughters, but they were so young that their claims to the fief were overlooked in the interests of the general safety of the kingdom, and in September 1106 the king invested his kinsman, Gervais of Bazoches,[35] with the

[21] Ibid. 495. [22] Ibid. 633.
[23] Ibid. 619. [24] Ibid. 645-53, 656.
[25] Röhricht, Geschichte des Königreichs Jerusalem, 70.
[26] Hagenmeyer, Chron. 645. [27] Ibid. 650. [28] Ibid. 652, 656.
[29] Röhricht, Regesta Regni Hierosolymitani, 43.
[30] W. B. Stevenson, The Crusaders in the East, 47.
[31] Röhricht, Geschichte des Königreichs Jerusalem, 60.
[32] William of Tyre, Historia, xi. 5, in Migne, cci.
[33] Tyre was taken on 17 July 1124.
[34] Röhricht, Geschichte des Königreichs Jerusalem, 61.
[35] Prioux, Bull. de la Soc. Arch. de Soissons, xix. 1865, 351-71. Gervais was son of Miles de Châtillon, lord of Bazoches in Picardy, who died c. 1080 (cf. Schlumberger, Renaud de Châtillon, 3, note on possible relationship between Gervais and Reginald of Châtillon). Gervais probably went on the crusade in the train of Hugh of Vermandois in 1096. He had two brothers, one Hugh, who succeeded his father,

principality. Gervais's reign was of short duration, as he was taken prisoner by the forces of Damascus under Tugtakin in May 1108. His captor, apparently presuming on the relationship of his prisoner with the king of Jerusalem, demanded the unheard-of ransom of Acre, Cayphas, and Tiberias for his release. Baldwin I offered 30,000 gold bezants and the exchange of five hundred Saracen prisoners, but could promise no more. Tugtakin declined this as insufficient, and gave Gervais the alternative of the Quran or the sword. The prince refused to apostatize and was thereupon beheaded. The Atabeg had his skull mounted as a drinking-cup.[36]

This brought the vacant principality into the king's hand, and a difficulty at once arises. In a charter of the abbey of Val Josaphat of the year 1109 a certain 'Willelmus Tyberiadentium princeps' appears.[37] Röhricht, in a note,[38] suggests 'de Buris', but this would clash with another charter[39] wherein 'Balduini II regni anno III Willelmi de Buris anno I' are mentioned as coinciding for the date. The third year of Baldwin II was from 14 April 1120 until 13 April 1121, consequently William de Bures cannot have been prince in 1109. Now it is stated that in August 1108 the king, being at the time in the midst of preparations for the siege of Sidon, sent William, the son of Robert, duke of Normandy, in command of 200 horse and 500 foot to raid across Jordan.[40] The enterprise was wholly successful, and William brought a quantity of captives and plunder to Jerusalem. The force under William's command was large for those days, and more than the king would be likely to detach from his main array now gathering for the campaign against Sidon, particularly if it were to be placed under the command of a comparatively obscure knight. In these circumstances it is reasonable to suppose that it was this William who was invested with Galilee (under the conditions laid down by Tancred in 1102), and that his 700 men represent his levy [41] as prince, together,

---

the other Gaucher, prior of St. Gemme in the diocese of Soissons. Ibn el Athir, in *Recueil des Historiens des Croisades, Historiens Orientaux*, i. 268 calls him ' son to the king's sister '; in this case either Gerberge or Ida de Bouillon must have married Miles. Guibert de Nogent (quoted by Prioux) says that the fief was taken from Gervais by the king, who almost immediately restored it as the result of a feat of arms on the part of the prince. This seems unlikely, unless Gervais were only administrator in the king's name, and not actual prince; but this is not borne out by Röhricht, *Regesta*, 293, where he ranks as equal with Hugh I.

[36] Ibn el Athir, in *Recueil, Historiens Orientaux*, i. 268 f. ; Röhricht, *Geschichte des Königreichs Jerusalem*, 73.

[37] *Revue de l'Orient Latin*, vii. 114–15.

[38] Röhricht, *Regesta*, additamentum, 56 a.

[39] *Ibid.* 97. [40] Albert of Aix, *Historia*, x. 47.

[41] It is difficult to know exactly what the feudal levy of the principality was at this time, as there is no contemporary record, both Ibelin (*Familles*) and Sanudo being later in date. The early principality included territories which subsequently became

perhaps, with some small assistance from the king. At any rate that would supply a prince of the name of William in time to sign the charter above mentioned. Further, when Tancred and Baldwin du Bourg[42] joined the king before Tripolis in April 1109, it was arranged that Tancred should recover Galilee and the overlordship of Cayphas,[43] giving up in exchange all claim to Edessa. The Latins took Tripolis on 12 July 1109,[44] and William became possessed of house property therein.[45] Shortly after the fall of Tripolis Tancred captured Tortosa (Antartus), and gave it to William.[46] Tortosa was an important place in a rich district, and a port, and it may well have been granted to William as compensation for the loss of Galilee. William is last heard of as lord of Tortosa in the muster-roll of the vassals of Antioch, when Tancred took the field against Aleppo in September 1111.[47]

It is uncertain whether Tancred went to Tiberias on the occasion of resuming the principality, and, as he was fully occupied with the affairs of Antioch, it does not seem that he revisited his southern dominions before he died, on 12 December 1112.[48] In consequence, it is more than probable that the king had a certain

---

detached from it, and the prince was overlord of Cayphas and Bessan, both of which are reckoned by Ibelin under other fiefs. The prince himself owed 100 knights, the fief of Toron 18, that of Bessan 15, that of Cayphas 17, and the archbishop of Nazareth 6— in all 146 knights. The city of Tiberias owed 200 men-at-arms, the bishop of Tiberias 100, the archbishop of Nazareth 150, the abbot of Mount Tabor 100, the lord of Cayphas 50, and the lord of Gerin 25—in all 625 men-at-arms. All these were owed to the king, but it is probable that in emergencies part at least were placed at the disposal of the prince, more particularly when he was constable or marshal of the kingdom, or when, as was often the case, the king was present in Galilee. Ibelin and Sanudo do not agree as to the identity of all these figures, and it is unlikely that the figures even refer to the same period, as it is more than doubtful that when Acre (which appears elsewhere in the lists) was important enough to supply under various headings 80 knights and no less than 700 men-at-arms the principality of Galilee could continue to supply its quota of 40 knights from the territories beyond Jordan. Moreover, many of the headings under Acre suggest that at the time referred to in the lists Acre was already the capital, i.e. after 1191, at which time Jerusalem could certainly not supply 500 men-at-arms, and the principality was practically non-existent.

[42] Baldwin du Bourg had been released by Jawali in August 1108, and after fighting Tancred, who had been administering Edessa, 18 September, he was defeated near Turbessel and fled to Tulupe, but ultimately recovered his county of Edessa: Stevenson, *The Crusaders in the East*, 85 notes.

[43] Albert of Aix, *Historia*, xi. 12.

[44] Ibn el Athir, in *Recueil, Historiens Orientaux*, i. 274 ; Röhricht, *Geschichte des Königreichs Jerusalem*, 81.

[45] Röhricht, *Regesta*, 620.

[46] A. H. 503, i. e. 31 July 1109 to 19 July 1110. Valenie, north of Tortosa, surrendered about 22 July 1109, thus cutting off that town from the north: Stevenson, 86.

[47] Albert of Aix, *Historia*, xi. 40. William was a natural son of Robert of Normandy, born c. 1078-9, probably at Gerberoi, on the Norman border. He took the cross after Tenchebray (2 September 1106): *Dictionary of National Biography*, art. 'Robert, Duke of Normandy'. In 1108 'Willelmus filius comitis' signs a royal charter : Röhricht, *Regesta*, 52. Albert, xi. 40, calls him ' Wilhelmus filius comitis Nortmanorum '. [48] Stevenson, 94, n. 3.

amount of control over the fortunes of the principality during this period. Certainly he was at the head of an army at Tiberias in the beginning of 1111 [49] and again in June 1113, when he was severely defeated by Maudud of Damascus.[50] It is probable that it was at this time that the principality was given to Joscelyn of Courtenay, a fighting man of repute in the north who had been lord of Turbessel (Tell bashir) until recently, when, owing to a quarrel with his overlord, Baldwin du Bourg, count of Edessa, he had been deprived of that fief.[51]

Joscelyn attested a royal charter as prince in 1115,[52] and himself granted a manor to the abbey of Val Josaphat in February 1119 [53] as 'Goscelinus princeps Galilaeae'. In May 1118 [54] Tiberias was ravaged by the Saracens, probably owing to Joscelyn's absence with the king on the raid into Egypt. Tugtakin and his forces retired about the end of July, and immediately Joscelyn raided the Hauran. He reached Bosra and wasted the country; he retook the castle of Hubais, and defeated the Damascenes under Buri.[55] Next year he repeated the raid with a small force, but having unwisely divided it was severely handled by the Beni Khalid on 30 March 1119.[56] Later in the year Joscelyn seems to have made an unsuccessful attempt upon Ascalon, and afterwards went north by way of Tripolis [57] to join in the campaign against Aleppo. In August,[58] after the battle of Danith, King Baldwin II invested Joscelyn with his own former county of Edessa.[59] Joscelyn thereupon relinquished Galilee into the king's hands. During the later years of his administration, since June 1115,[60] a certain knight, William de Bures, a Norman, witnessed his charters. This man may have been in Palestine as early as 1101,[61] and seems to have been wealthy, since he and his wife Agnes granted the manors of Jeraz and Soesme to the abbey of Val Josaphat in 1115.[62] Apparently this wife died, and he married Eschiva I, daughter of Hugh of Falkenberg, the real heiress of the fief, as Tancred had no children and Joscelyn had voluntarily relinquished it.

William de Bures first appears as prince, William II, in 1120.[63]

[49] Stevenson, 60; Albert of Aix, *Historia*, xi. 36.　　[50] Stevenson, 63.
[51] *Ibid.* 96; William of Tyre, *Historia*, xi. 22. Joscelyn was younger son of Joscelyn I of Courtenay by Elizabeth of Montlhery, sister of Melisende, countess of Rethel, who was mother of Baldwin du Bourg. He became lord of Turbessel c. 1101–2, and was taken prisoner with his cousin and overlord Baldwin in May 1104 (Ibn el Athir, in *Recueil, Historiens Orientaux*, i. 222; Röhricht, *Geschichte des Königreichs Jerusalem*, 50). He was released in August 1108.
[52] Röhricht, *Regesta*, 79.　　[53] *Ibid.* 87.　　[54] Stevenson, 66–7.
[55] Ibn el Athir, in *Recueil, Historiens Orientaux*, i. 315; Stevenson, 67, n. 3.
[56] Albert of Aix, *Historia*, xii. 31; Röhricht, *Geschichte des Königreichs Jerusalem*, 129.
[57] Stevenson, 67; Fulcherius Carnotensis, *Historia*, iii. 2, in Migne, clv.
[58] Stevenson, 105, n. 4.　　[59] *Ibid.* 106, n. 2.
[60] Röhricht, *Regesta*, 79.　　[61] *Ibid.* addit. 36 a.
[62] Röhricht, *Regesta*, 80.　　[63] *Ibid.* 91.

By his first wife, Agnes, he had a son, Geoffrey, who stayed behind in Normandy. He also had a brother, Godfrey, who was killed on Joscelyn's ill-fated expedition into the Hauran in March 1119, and a sister who married Ralph de Ysis, and had three sons, Ralph, Simon, and William; of these William was a monk of the abbey of Val Josaphat,[64] Simon a canon of the Holy Sepulchre,[65] and Ralph, who was a layman in 1132, may have become a canon of Mount Sion.[66] By his second wife William II was childless.

William II was a capable prince, as he was acknowledged to be by his contemporaries. He was constable of the kingdom 1123–41,[67] and was elected regent by the high court, and acted in that capacity during the latter part of the captivity of King Baldwin II, from 15 June to 29 August 1124.[68] He was present, and possibly, as regent and constable of the kingdom, commanded at the successful siege of Tyre, from 15 February to 7 July 1124.[69] He attended the king at Acre in May 1105,[70] but left him during the end of the northern campaign of 1125–6, being apparently detached to guard Jaffa and the south, where he is found in January 1126,[71] some time before the king's return from the Hauran. Later in the year, however, he rejoined the court at Jerusalem.[72] In October 1128,[73] William II, accompanied by Guy Brisebarre, lord of Baruth (Beirut),[74] was sent on an embassy to Fulk, count of Anjou, to ask him to marry Melisende, King Baldwin's only child, and heiress of the kingdom. He returned in April 1129, having been successful in his mission, and shortly afterwards went to Tiberias.[75] In the autumn of 1136 William was with Fulk, now king of Jerusalem, at Naples,[76] and next year accompanied him on the campaign against Zanki of Aleppo, who was attacking the border fortress of Mons Ferrandus in Tripolis. The king attempted to raise the siege, but was surprised on the march through the broken country in that district, and defeated. Raymond of Tripolis was captured, but the king and his people reached the castle, which lies on an isolated hill, and there they in their turn were besieged.[77] The approach of

[64] Röhricht, *Regesta*, 131.   [65] *Ibid.* 142.   [66] *Ibid.* 174.
[67] *Ibid.* 102; Albert of Aix, *Historia*, xii. 21.
[68] Stevenson, 114; Fulcherius Carnotensis, *Historia*, iii. 22. King Baldwin was captured by Nur ed daula Balak, nephew of Ilgazi of Aleppo, near Karkar, 18 April 1123 (Stevenson, 109, n. 3). He was released by Timurtash, Ilgazi's son, 29 August 1124. His ransom had been settled on 24 June 1124 as the surrender of Ezaz (Stevenson, 111, n. 5) and 80,000 bezants (Röhricht, *Geschichte des Königreichs Jerusalem*, 171, n. 1). On 6 September the king dishonourably declined to be bound by his promise and refused to pay the ransom.
[69] Fulcherius Carnotensis, *Historia*, iii. 28.   [70] Röhricht, *Regesta*, 105.
[71] *Ibid.* 112–13.   [72] *Ibid.* 115.
[73] Röhricht, *Geschichte des Königreichs Jerusalem*, 185.
[74] Guy was brother of Walter I and father of Walter II. He was lord of Baruth from about 1127 to June 1153.   [75] Röhricht, *Regesta*, 127, 131.
[76] *Ibid.* 164.   [77] Ibn el Athir, in *Recueil, Historiens Orientaux*, i. 481.

Raymond of Antioch, however, induced Zanki to allow the garrison, who did not know that help was at hand, to march out with the honours of war and retire, together with the prisoners recently taken by the Saracens, into Tripolis. This was before 19 August 1137.[78] In April 1140 William II received King Fulk at Tiberias, where there was a great gathering of the Latins. The king moved against Zanki in the Hauran, and after the enemy had retired (25 May) the Latins, in alliance with the Damascenes, took Banias, at the source of the Jordan, after a short siege in June 1140.[79] William II is last heard of in February 1141, when he witnessed a charter at the king's palace in Naples.[80] The exact date of his death is uncertain, but his nephew Elinard, who may perhaps be the same as the Helias who witnessed a charter in 1126 as 'heres feudi',[81] was already prince in 1142. He was Godfrey's son, and married Ermengarde d'Ibelin.[82] Elinard went with Philip of Naples under Manasses d'Hierges, constable of the kingdom, to help Joscelyn II of Edessa. But the expedition was too late to prevent the capture of that city by Zanki,[83] December 1144 to January 1145. Elinard was present at the great council of war held by the Emperor Conrad III near Acre, on 24 June 1148,[84] and after the ignominious retreat from Damascus in the following August the prince of Galilee was suspected of having taken a bribe from the Saracens to use his influence against continuing the siege. One historian says that the 50,000 bezants which he is supposed to have taken were spurious.[85]

Elinard de Bures died leaving one daughter, afterwards Eschiva II, but she was too young to be married. After the death of Elinard, who last appears in August 1148, no evidence is available until 22 June 1150,[86] when one Simon appears as prince of Galilee. Du Cange suggests that he married Ermengarde d'Ibelin, widow of Elinard, and administered the fief on behalf of his infant step-daughter.[87] Simon may perhaps have been the brother of William Tirell, marshal of Antioch, who witnessed as such in February 1149 and again in January 1167,[88] or Simon de Châtillon, who was a vassal of the barony of Caesarea, 1145–6.[89] If this be so he may have been a relation of Gervais de Bazoches, who was of the Châtillon family,[90] and have been given the fief

---

[78] Stevenson, 138. [79] William of Tyre, xv. 9–10 ; Stevenson, 145.
[80] Röhricht, Regesta, 201. [81] Ibid. 115.
[82] She was daughter of Balian I, third lord of Ramleh (d. c. 1154), and step-daughter of Manasses d'Hierges. Her mother was daughter of Baldwin, second lord of Ramleh and Mirabel. Her brother, Balian II, married the widow of King Amaury I.
[83] Ibn el Athir, in Recueil, Historiens Orientaux, i. 448 ; Röhricht, Geschichte des Königreichs Jerusalem, 236. [84] Röhricht, Regesta, 250.
[85] Röhricht, Geschichte des Königreichs Jerusalem, 255 ; Abul Faraj, 342.
[86] Röhricht, Regesta, 258. [87] Du Cange-Rey, Les Familles d'Outremer, 447.
[88] Röhricht, Regesta, 253, 428. [89] Ibid. 237, 243.
[90] See above, p. 447 n. 35.

in virtue of this kinship. It is also possible that he was Simon de Ysis, nephew of William II, who was a canon of the Holy Sepulchre. This last supposition would not fit in with du Cange's suggestion that he married the widowed Ermengarde. Simon was prince undoubtedly until 20 April 1154,[91] and as such was present at the siege of Ascalon, from January to August 1153.[92] Simon signs as Tiberiadensis, but after Guilelmus Tiberiadensis, in a charter of Baldwin III given at Acre 30 July 1154; and later in the same year Ermengarde, viscountess of Tiberias, grants land to the church of St. Lazarus with the consent of William, prince of Galilee.[93] This William III was Elinard's younger brother, who now appears to take over the fief on behalf of his niece, perhaps after an absence in the west or on return from captivity among the Saracens. 'W de Buris' grants land to the Hospital in Tiberias, on 28 October 1153,[94] by a charter which is witnessed by many of the chief men of the principality, but he does not style himself prince. But on 20 April of next year Simon still signs as Tiberiadensis with precedence over Philip of Naples, which seems to show that he signs as prince and not as a baron of the principality. Possibly William's claim to rule the fief for his niece was still before the high court. William III married Mary, sister of Walter III, lord of Baruth,[95] who had himself married Agnes of Falkenberg, daughter of Hugh I. William had an only daughter, Eschiva, who married Hugh II, lord of Puy.[96]

Soon after September 1158[97] William III either died or else handed over the principality to his niece, Eschiva II, as in March 1159[98] Walter of St. Omer was already husband of the princess and in her right prince of Galilee. He witnessed a charter on the thirteenth of that month describing himself as 'nunc dominus Tyberiadensis', from which it may be implied that at that date he was but newly raised to the dignity. Walter of Falkenberg, castellan of St. Omer 1145-57, was son of William II, castellan of St. Omer 1097-1126 and again 1128-43. It is more than likely that he was nephew of Hugh I of Falkenberg, prince of Galilee, who is called of St. Omer,[99] and had a brother Gerard, who died at Nazareth in August 1106.[100] Walter had

[91] Röhricht, *Regesta*, 291.   [92] William of Tyre, xvii. 21.
[93] Röhricht, *Regesta*, 293, 294.   [94] *Ibid*. 283.
[95] Walter III was son of Walter II, who died *post* March 1164. He was lord of Baruth 1165-6, lord of Blanchegarde 1166 to October 1179, and lord of Montreal May 1168 in right of his second wife, Helen de Milly. By his first wife he had a son and four daughters. Mary, the widowed princess of Galilee, married Gerard de Ham, constable of Tripolis June 1199 to October 1217.

[96] Hugh II was son of Hugh I, constable of Tripolis 1161-3, and grandson of Walter the Penniless. He was lord of Puy October 1177-84, and by this marriage had one daughter, Mary, who was twice married.   [97] Röhricht, *Regesta*, 332.
[98] *Ibid*. 336.   [99] *Annales*, in *Archives de l'Orient Latin*, ii. 430.
[100] Röhricht, *Geschichte des Königreichs Jerusalem*, 61.

brothers, Gerard and Hugh.[101] If this relationship be established it at once explains why Walter of St. Omer was given the hand of Eschiva II, heiress of Galilee, instead of some local baron. Eschiva II was daughter of Elinard, who was nephew by marriage to Eschiva I, daughter of Hugh I. But the disparity of age may not have been great. William II de Bures, husband of Eschiva I, had a son Geoffrey, who was born in Normandy and never came to Palestine. William's brother Godfrey, who was killed in 1119, was father of Elinard, who may well have been born at the beginning of the century. At any rate he was of full age in 1142, as no regency in his name is recorded for the principality, and he is found commanding his levy on an important expedition. He was probably of age in 1126, when he and his brother sign a charter as 'heredes feudi', and had two cousins old enough to be priests.[102] He was probably of the same generation as his aunt by marriage, Eschiva I; consequently his daughter, Eschiva II, was in fact only one generation junior to Walter. It may be assumed that she was born about 1143, as she was still under age in September 1158 and married in March 1159. It is not unreasonable to suppose that Walter was born about 1116, seeing that his third brother was old enough to be a priest in 1142. This would make him forty-three at the time of his marriage, which took place on the occasion of his second pilgrimage to the Holy Land.[103]

There is record of five of Walter's children by this marriage: Hugh II, William, Ralph, Odo, and Eschiva. Of these Hugh and Ralph succeeded their parents, William is heard of no more after 1192,[104] Eschiva married Eimery Rivet, seneschal of Cyprus (November 1197 to November 1210),[105] and Odo became constable of Tripolis in January 1194 and retained the office until August 1196.[106] After this he went with his brothers to Armenia, where he is found in December 1199.[107] There he passed into the service of King Levon II and was given the lordship of Gogulat. In April 1216 [108] he was with Prince Raymond Rupin at Antioch, and is last heard of in July 1218 [109] at the court of Queen Alice of Cyprus. He left a daughter, Eschiva, who married Eimery Rivet, grandson of that other Eimery Rivet who had married her aunt. In 1261 she disputed the title to the principality with her cousin, Eschiva III, daughter of Ralph. There were in all no less than six different ladies, daughters of the three reigning houses of the principality, all of whom were called Eschiva, three of them being princesses in their own right.

[101] Giry, in *Bibl. de l'École des Chartes*, 1874, 335–45.
[102] Röhricht, *Regesta*, 142.   [103] Giry, *ubi supra*.
[104] Röhricht, *Regesta*, 707.   [105] *Ibid.* 738, 846.   [106] *Ibid.* 718, 731.
[107] Potthast, i. 909.   [108] Röhricht, *Regesta*, 886.   [109] *Ibid.* 912.

Walter had accompanied Dietrich, count of Flanders, on the second visit of the latter to Palestine. He was probably present at the siege of Damascus in July 1148, and served under the king as his paid man at the siege of Ascalon from January to August 1153.[110] He was with him at the siege of Blahasent (Bel hasem), a Saracen robber-castle in the hill-country above Sidon, on 16 March 1160,[111] and in Jerusalem at the end of November in the same year.[112] Next year he was one of a great gathering of prelates and barons which met the king at Nazareth on 31 July 1161,[113] after which he attended him at Acre on 21 November 1161, during what was his last visit there.[114] He was with the king's successor, Amaury I, at Ascalon on 15 July 1164,[115] and it is more than probable that he served through the second Egyptian campaign undertaken by that monarch from July to October 1164. Next year he returned by way of Jerusalem, where he was on 7 April 1165,[116] to Tiberias at the end of that month.[117] He was with the court at Acre in April 1166 and May 1168,[118] and again at Jerusalem in August.[119] In October 1168 Walter accompanied the king from Jerusalem, 11 October,[120] to Ascalon, 20 October,[121] and probably was with him during the third Egyptian campaign, from October 1168 to January 1169. In September 1169 [122] the prince of Galilee was again with the court at Acre, and had apparently returned to his principality by 1170.[123]

Walter died before the king in 1174, for his widow, the Princess Eschiva II, in a charter dated 'Amalrico I rege',[124] makes arrangements for masses to be said for the repose of the soul of her husband. The fact that her eldest son, Hugh, was still a minor, although of intelligent age,[125] made it essential for Eschiva II to choose another consort. Raymond III, the celebrated count of Tripolis, had just been released from his ten years' captivity among the Saracens,[126] and was now selected, either by the princess or by the high court, to administer the fief. Raymond, who was one of the ablest and best of the Syrian Latins, appears to have married about September 1174, and a month later was elected regent of Jerusalem by the king and the high court. He remained in Jerusalem until 13 December 1174,[127] when he went north to Tripolis to

[110] William of Tyre, xvii. 21.   [111] Röhricht, *Regesta*, 344.
[112] *Ibid.* 355.   [113] *Ibid.* 366.
[114] *Ibid.* 368. Baldwin III died at Beirut, 10 February 1162: Stevenson, *The Crusaders in the East*, 184, n. 4.
[115] Röhricht, *Regesta*, 400.   [116] *Ibid.* 413.   [117] *Ibid.* 414.
[118] *Ibid.* addit. 422 a; Röhricht, *Regesta*, 449.   [119] *Ibid.* 450.
[120] *Ibid.* 452.   [121] *Ibid.* 453.   [122] *Ibid.* 467.
[123] *Ibid.* 479.   [124] *Ibid.* 522.   [125] *Ibid.* 447.
[126] He had been taken prisoner at Harim, 10 August 1164, by Nur ed din of Aleppo, and was released before May 1174.   [127] Röhricht, *Regesta*.

send help against Saladin to Es salih of Aleppo, but, failing to conduct a vigorous campaign, made peace in May 1175.[128] In the August of next year Raymond was engaged with Reginald of Châtillon in a raid on the Bika.[129] In November, William of Montferrat, who had been invited to marry Sibyl, the heiress presumptive of the kingdom, arrived, and Raymond laid down the regency in his favour. After this he returned to Tripolis, whence he engaged in the northern campaign, 20 November 1177,[130] joining with Bohemond III of Antioch in the attack on Harim. This siege, however, had to be raised at the end of March 1178, on the arrival of reinforcements from Aleppo.[131] In the spring of 1179 Raymond raided the Turkomans, and joined the king at Chastellet in February.[132] In April, Baldwin IV ravaged the district of Banias and was defeated by Izz ed din, Saladin's nephew, on 10 April 1179.[133] He retired on Tiberias, where Raymond was awaiting him,[134] and remained there until May. Raymond and his two eldest step-sons accompanied the king when he marched up past Toron to Marj uyun, where Saladin defeated them disastrously on 10 June.[135] After this, Raymond, who had with difficulty escaped with the king, retired to Tripolis, where he stayed until he rejoined the king at Jerusalem in Lent 1180 to arrange for peace with Saladin for the kingdom at Easter, 20 April, a policy which Raymond adopted for his county in June.[136]

On the death of William of Montferrat, count of Jaffa, Raymond was greatly opposed to the marriage of his widow to Guy of Lusignan, who had only his good looks to recommend him as a suitor. His opposition was overruled, and he fell into such disfavour that the king, persuaded by the Lusignan faction, actually forbade the prince to return from Tripolis to Galilee in the spring of 1182.[137] A sort of reconciliation was, however, patched up, and the prince of Galilee joined the king on his mismanaged attack on Saladin's caravan and its convoy in the Oultrejourdain in the following June.[138] This exposed Galilee to the Saracens, who at once raided the principality under Izz ed din. Raymond hurried north with the Latin army to Galilee, where there was much fighting during the summer. In February 1183 a great council of the barons was held at Jerusalem at which Raymond was almost certainly present;[139] in March he was in Acre,[140] and when Guy of Lusignan, the count of Jaffa,

---

[128] William of Tyre, xxi. 8.
[129] Beha ed din, in *Recueil, Historiens Orientaux*, iii. 63.
[130] William of Tyre, xxi. 20.
[131] Beha ed din, in *Recueil, Historiens Orientaux*, iii. 64.
[132] Röhricht, *Regesta*, 572.   [133] William of Tyre, xxi. 27.
[134] Röhricht, *Regesta*, 582.   [135] Stevenson, 221 notes.
[136] William of Tyre, xxii. 1.   [137] *Ibid.* 9.   [138] *Ibid.* 15.
[139] Röhricht, *Regesta*, 622.   [140] *Ibid.* 624.

became regent for King Baldwin IV in August, Raymond joined him with his levy at Sepphoris. The Latin army was of unusual size,[141] but the party quarrels of its leaders destroyed all chances of success, and the regent was unable to achieve anything of note. By remaining on the defensive, however, he compelled Saladin, whose army was suffering from lack of supplies, to retire in October without a decisive action.[142] Next month the king dismissed Guy from the regency and resumed control of affairs. In December he set out on his last expedition, having as chief of his staff Raymond, who seems to have been responsible for the strategy of the campaign.[143] The Latins successfully engaged Saladin in the Oultrejourdain, thereby raising the siege of Kerak, which had lasted less than a month.[144]

After this the king and Guy of Lusignan quarrelled openly, and the latter refused to admit him into his city of Ascalon.[145] The king withdrew to Jaffa and thence to Acre, where he called a council of the barons in January 1184, and appointed Raymond to be regent for himself and his nephew, Baldwin the Boy, who had already been crowned on 20 November of the previous year.[146] The regency was to last ten years. In the summer the Saracens again came up against Kerak in the Oultrejourdain on 13 August, and Raymond had to take steps for its relief. This was done on 3 September, but at the cost of exposing Galilee and Naples to a hostile raid which lasted a week.[147] In March 1185 King Baldwin the Leper died, and was succeeded by King Baldwin the Boy with Raymond as regent, but on the death of the little king in August 1186 Guy of Lusignan, as husband of Sibyl, the heiress of the kingdom, seized the throne, in spite of the declaration of the high court in January 1184. Guy's cause was upheld by the patriarch and the grand masters, all of whom were likely to gain from the presence of a weak king upon the throne, and Raymond was deserted. He withdrew to Tiberias, where he remained until the fatal campaign of the next year. When his advice had been neglected and the king had lost all hope of safety, Raymond with his stepsons cut a way through the Saracens and fled to Tyre; thence he retired to Tripolis, where he died childless at the end of September 1187.[148] He was succeeded in the principality by his step-son, Hugh II.

The Falkenberg was a fighting stock, and Hugh II and his

---

[141] William of Tyre, xxii. 27, 1,300 knights and 15,000 infantry.
[142] William of Tyre, xxii. 27.
[143] Röhricht, *Geschichte des Königreichs Jerusalem*, 409.
[144] Beha ed din, in *Recueil, Historiens Orientaux*, iii. 77.
[145] Röhricht, *Geschichte des Königreichs Jerusalem*, 409.   [146] *Ibid.* 416.
[147] Beha ed din, in *Recueil, Historiens Orientaux*, iii. 82.
[148] Röhricht, *Regesta*, 662.

brothers were true to type. The two eldest boys distinguished themselves at the battle of Ascalon, 25 October 1177,[149] and saw service again next year, when Hugh was taken prisoner by Saladin after the disaster of Marj uyun on 10 June 1179. Ransomed in September 1181, Hugh was again in the field against Saladin in July 1182, and in August was with his step-father in Acre.[150] The date of his marriage is unknown, but his wife was Margaret of Ibelin, daughter of Balian II, lord of Ibelin, Naples, and Ramleh, and sister of John of Ibelin, the 'Vieux Sire de Baruth' of the next forty years. It must have been a difficult position for Hugh, a young man with a taste for war, eldest son of a princess *suo iure*, and step-son of a famous warrior who was administering his hereditary fief on his behalf. Hugh was well over fifteen, the age at which the assizes of Jerusalem allowed a boy to escape from the tutelage of his minority, but it appears that he did not succeed as heir of his grandfather until after Raymond's death. It is possible that when Raymond became regent of the kingdom for the second time in 1184 he may have allowed Hugh at least to administer the principality. There is no actual charter granted by Hugh as such, but his high precedence among the barons of the kingdom when witnessing royal charters appears to indicate that he was more than heir apparent at the time. He was at Acre on 16 May 1186,[151] when he signs third among the barons. Hugh and his three brothers served with their step-father at the fatal battle of Hattin, 3 July 1187, and with him cut their way through the Moslem army before the fires were lit which choked what was left of the Latin forces into surrender with their smoke and heat. During and after this disastrous battle the Princess Eschiva II reappears, holding the castle of Tiberias, the town having been already taken. On Sunday, 5 July 1187, it became known that there was no hope left for the Christians. The princess then capitulated upon terms and was allowed to retire freely from her castle.

The fugitives reached Tyre, where they bade farewell to their step-father, and on 13 July they were joined by Conrad of Montferrat with a shipload of crusaders from the west. Gaining heart, some sort of a defence was arranged, and scattered Franks and stragglers who had escaped from the almost universal ruin came in, and under Conrad the shattered kingdom found its rallying-point in Tyre. It would appear that Hugh II was second in command under Conrad, who may be considered as regent of the kingdom in Tyre. In October Hugh witnesses first among the barons,[152] and in November, when the siege was set, distinguished himself greatly in the defence. In the great assault on the city, on 31 December, Hugh and his brother Odo themselves

[149] Röhricht, *Geschichte des Königreichs Jerusalem*, 378.   [150] Röhricht, *Regesta*, 617.
[151] *Ibid.* 643.   [152] Röhricht, *Regesta*, 665–6.

held the breach and beat back the stormers.[153] This repulse led to the abandonment of the siege by Saladin on 2 January 1188.[154] Shortly after the end of the siege, at some date not specified, Hugh II led an expedition from Tyre which raided Arsuf, captured the place, and released fifty Christian prisoners. It happened that the emir who had captured King Guy at the battle of Hattin was governor of the place, and he, together with some 500 of his men, was taken prisoner. No attempt was made to hold the town, but in July this emir was exchanged against William, marquess of Montferrat, father of Conrad, and grandfather of Baldwin the Boy, who also had been taken after Hattin.[155] After this exploit Hugh II took part in the siege of Acre, where he is found on 19 November 1189.[156] From the evidence of charters it is possible to gather that he continued there until 7 May 1191,[157] and probably was present at the surrender on 12 July.[158] Hugh II was entrusted by King Richard with the command of the rearguard on the successful march to Jaffa, from 25 August to 10 September,[159] during which took place the curious marching battle of Arsuf on 7 September.

When King Conrad died, on 28 April 1192, after a reign of three weeks,[160] Hugh became the trusted adviser of Count Henry of Champagne, who succeeded to the power and the wife, but not the title, of the king of Jerusalem. He was with him in Jaffa in January 1193,[161] and went to Acre the next month.[162] On 5 January 1194 Hugh's brother Ralph first appears as seneschal of the kingdom, in succession to Joscelyn de Courtenay, Prince Joscelyn's grandson, who seems to have resigned the office.[163] Both brothers appear to have been in either Tyre or Acre until the end of Richard's truce in 1196. On Henry's death, 10 September 1197,[164] Hugh II was anxious that his brother Ralph should be chosen as his successor on the throne and in the affections of thrice-widowed Isabella I, the queen of Jerusalem. With the view of making this candidature more acceptable to the high court, the prince voluntarily abdicated from his claims to Galilee in favour of Ralph. The other suitor for the queen's hand was the king of Cyprus, Amaury of Lusignan, brother to King Guy now dead, and the high court rightly decided that it was more to the advantage of the continental kingdom that it should be united with the island monarchy, rather than

[153] Röhricht, *Geschichte des Königreichs Jerusalem*, 470, n. 1.
[154] *Ibid.* n. 9.
[155] Röhricht, *Regesta*, 683.
[156] Stevenson, 269, n. 4.
[157] Beha ed din, in *Recueil, Historiens Orientaux*, iii. 297.
[158] Röhricht, *Regesta*, 709.
[159] *Ibid.* 710, 716.
[160] *Ibid.* 438, n. 6.
[161] *Ibid.* 705.
[162] *Ibid.* 275–6 nn.
[163] *Ibid.* 717.
[164] Röhricht, *Geschichte des Königreichs Jerusalem*, 671, n. 3.

be entrusted to the sword of a prince who had but a handful of territory left to him.

The new king was unfavourable to the Falkenberg brothers, and even accused Ralph of trying to murder him in 1198. It would appear that there was not much in the charge, as the king never brought the accused to trial, but banished him from the realm at eight days' notice.[165] The whole family seems to have gone north after this, and Ralph married Agnes, daughter of Reginald, who had been lord of Sidon and Beaufort,[166] but now had to content himself with the dominion of the little town of Sarepta; her mother, however, was an Ibelin, Héloïse, sister of the 'Vieux Sire'. They went up into Armenia in 1199, and when the Latins attacked Constantinople in 1204 Ralph and his brother Hugh left Syria before 20 May of that year.[167] Hugh died in Romania soon after this, and his widow, Margaret of Ibelin, married Walter III, lord of Caesarea. Ralph returned to Syria after the death of King Amaury, April 1205, and took part with Reynard of Nephin in his quarrel with Bohemond IV of Antioch and Tripolis in 1206. Next year, 27 July 1207,[168] Ralph reappears at Acre as seneschal of the kingdom, in which capacity he was present at the coronation of King John of Brienne,[169] on 3 October 1210. He was with the court in July 1211[170] and in January and August 1217,[171] but was absent from the great gathering of kings and princes, prelates, and barons, which took place in the October of that year. The prince of Galilee accompanied King John into Egypt, and served through the Damietta campaign, from August 1218 to March 1220.[172] He is last heard of at Acre in May of this last year.

Ralph left one daughter, who married Odo of Montbéliard, who was constable of the kingdom and son of Walter of Montbéliard, a former constable of the kingdom and regent of Cyprus.[173] Odo, in right of his wife, became entitled to what remained of the principality, but this was not reconquered until after the treaties of February 1229 and June 1240. Odo was grandson of King Amaury, the former rival of Ralph, by his first marriage, and was one of the most important men in the kingdom. But he was important rather as constable, as regent, as a royal kinsman, than as prince of Galilee; and it is unnecessary to detail his exploits, which belong to the story of the kingdom at large and not to that

[165] Du Cange-Rey, *Les Familles d'Outremer*, 456.
[166] Reginald was fourth lord of Sidon 1171–87, second lord of Beaufort 1171–92, first lord of Sarepta 1193–1200. He died before 1204.
[167] Röhricht, *Geschichte des Königreichs Jerusalem*, 693.
[168] Röhricht, *Regesta*, 821.
[169] Röhricht, *Geschichte des Königreichs Jerusalem*, 701, n. 2.
[170] Röhricht, *Regesta*, 853.
[171] *Ibid.* 892, 898.   [172] *Ibid.* 930.
[173] Regent of Cyprus 1205–10.

of the vanished principality. Let it suffice to record that Odo was regent of the kingdom January 1223 to July 1227, again from April 1228 to September 1228, lieutenant-regent from February 1236 to April 1243, and co-regent with Balian I of Ibelin, lord of Baruth, and Philip de Montfort, lord of Tyre, from April 1243 to June 1243. He recovered Tiberias in June 1240, and is last heard of in Acre on 11 September 1244.[174] Eschiva III, his widow, enjoyed the principality but little longer; Tiberias itself was lost finally to Fakhr ed din at the head of an Egyptian army, 16 June 1247.[175] Some portions of the fief were left, and in 1261 Eschiva, daughter of Odo of Falkenberg, lord of Gogulat, claimed the principality from Eschiva III, as being daughter of an elder brother to Ralph. This may have been true, but Odo had never been prince, while Hugh II had given the fief to Ralph for an express purpose, and had never reclaimed it. Besides, Odo should have disputed the title with Ralph in 1197, not left it for his daughter to raise the claim nearly seventy years later.

Eschiva III, the last sovereign princess, died after February 1265,[176] leaving two daughters, Simone and Mary, who both married into the Ibelin family. Simone, being within the prohibited degrees with her husband, Philip of Ibelin, constable of Cyprus, had a dispensation from Pope Innocent IV to marry,[177] and so brought the title of Galilee into that family. But no one held the principality again.

H. PIRIE-GORDON.

[174] Röhricht, *Regesta*, 1123.
[175] The principality had been raided in July 1244 by Kharismians: Stevenson, *The Crusaders in the East*, 323–4 nn.
[176] Röhricht, *Regesta*, addit. 1336 a.   [177] Bull of 13 August 1253.

The First Version of Hardyng's Chronicle

WHEN Sir Henry Ellis published his edition of John Hardyng's Chronicle, now just a hundred years ago, he followed for the most part the printed version of Richard Grafton, collating it with the copy in the Harleian MS. 661. He did not, however, overlook the fact that the first manuscript in point of time, and perhaps the most curious of all, is the Lansdowne MS. 204.[1] But since the text is 'altogether so different from the other copies as not to admit of a collation' Ellis contented himself with making some considerable extracts for his preface, and did not stop to consider the relation of this, the oldest and fullest version of the chronicle, to the later copies. Hardyng's Chronicle is not a work of the first importance, but what value it possesses turns largely on the personal view of the author. A just estimate of that view can only be formed by comparing the Lansdowne copy, which was written for Henry VI with a Lancastrian bias, with the later copies, which are continued to the reign of Edward IV and have been modified to suit the altered circumstances of the time. The failure of Ellis to deal fully with the Lansdowne MS. has robbed his edition of the virtue of finality. It is therefore not unimportant to devote some space to an account of Hardyng's Chronicle in its earliest form.

Since the quality of the work depends so much on the character and career of the author, I must begin with a brief sketch of John Hardyng's life. This is the more necessary because the account given by Ellis, and followed by subsequent biographers, contains various errors and omissions, which if not serious in themselves are of importance for their bearing on the composition of his chronicle. Hardyng tells us that he was 'brought up from twelve years of age in Sir Henry Percy's house to the battle of Shrewsbury, where I was with him armed of twenty-five years of age, as I had been afore at Homildon, Cocklaw, and divers other raids and fields'.[2] Thus Hardyng was born in 1378 and entered the service of Percy in 1390. The battle of Homildon or Humbledon was fought on 14 September 1402, and the siege

---
[1] Preface, p. xiv. Ellis describes it as Lansdowne 200, but the correct number is as given above.　　　[2] Ed. Ellis, p. 351.

of Cocklaw took place in the following spring. These therefore can hardly have been his first essays in arms. But he has told us nothing more of his early career; he was, however, clearly in the confidence of his patrons; for he knew Hotspur's intent and had it written,[3] and had heard the earl of Northumberland relate how Henry IV had proposed before the deposition of Richard II to put forward a forged chronicle pretending that Edmund Crouchback was the elder brother of Edward I,[4] and how John of Gaunt had previously devised this chronicle in order to support his claim to be recognized as heir to the crown.[5]

After the battle of Shrewsbury Hardyng entered the service of Sir Robert Umfraville, a Northumbrian knight of distinction, grandson of Gilbert, earl of Angus, and uncle of Gilbert Umfraville, who was to win renown as titular earl of Kyme in Lincolnshire. Umfraville made Hardyng warden of Warkworth Castle, and kept him in his service till his death more than thirty years later. Under his master Hardyng made the campaign of Agincourt, of which he embodied a valuable account in Latin prose in the later editions of his work; but this account is not, as Ellis seems to have supposed, a personal journal of Hardyng's own composition; it is derived in the main from the *Gesta Henrici Quinti* of Thomas Elmham, though with some small additions relating to the Umfravilles;[6] its chief interest consists in the fact that it is perhaps the only instance in the fifteenth century of the use of Elmham's prose narrative. From his use of 'us' and 'our' in the account of Bedford's expedition to Harfleur in 1416 it would seem that Hardyng was present there.[7] In 1417 Robert Umfraville was employed on the Scottish marches, and the precision of Hardyng's narrative of 'The Foul Raid' of the Scots in that year suggests that he himself was engaged in his master's company.[8]

During the early years of Henry V Hardyng was at court with Umfraville. He tells that he had seen the muniment in support of the Yorkist claims to Spain and Portugal,

> Which your uncle to my lord Umfrevill
> At London shewed, which I red that while.[9]

Probably he thus came under the king's notice, and was by him entrusted with a mission to Scotland to spy out the prospects of an invasion of that country, and to collect evidence on the English claim to sovereignty.[10] This would seem to have been

[3] Ed. Ellis, p. 351.　　[4] *Ibid.* p. 353.　　[5] *Ibid.* p. 354.
[6] *Ibid.* pp. 389–91; cf. *Gesta Henrici Quinti* (Engl. Hist. Soc.), pp. 13–58.
[7] *Chron.*, ed. Ellis, p. 377.
[8] *Ibid.* pp. 380–2.　　[9] *Ibid.* p. 21.
[10] Lansdowne MS. 204, f. 3. Extracts from this manuscript will be published in the next number of this Review.

in the early part of 1418; for Hardyng states that he spent three years and a half on that mission, and writing in 1457 alleges that he had kept certain documents, which he obtained in Scotland, for six and thirty years. Hardyng must have been back in England in the summer of 1421, if it is true, as he says, that he was present at that time when Henry V put an end to the private warfare of two knights.[11] However, that incident may have belonged to an earlier date, and in any case it was probably not till a year later that Hardyng delivered the first-fruits of his mission to the king at the Bois de Vincennes, where Henry V resided for a few days in May 1422. Hardyng alleges that the king rewarded him with a promise of the manor of Geddington in Northamptonshire, but that after Henry's death he was defrauded of it by Henry Beaufort, who gave it away in dower to the queen.[12] Nevertheless Hardyng, who was already pursuing his historical studies, seems to have profited by the patronage of Beaufort, at whose instance he obtained daily instruction in Justin's Epitome of Trogus Pompeius from Julyus Caesarine, auditor of the Pope Martin's Chamber. This we learn from a rubric in the Lansdowne MS.,[13] which Ellis interpreted to indicate that Hardyng had visited Rome in 1424. More probably Hardyng obtained his instruction in England, where Julius de Caesarinis was present as a papal envoy in 1426 and 1427.[14]

Some years later Hardyng would seem to have paid a second visit to Scotland on a similar errand to that of the first. One of the documents which he afterwards produced in support of his claims for reward was a safe-conduct granted by James I of Scotland on 10 March 1434, in which the king offered to pay him a thousand marks in return for the surrender of his 'Evidences'.[15] Though the document is a forgery, it may be sufficient evidence that Hardyng visited Scotland at this time. At all events, he made his professed honesty in rejecting the bribe an additional excuse for seeking from Henry VI his promised reward. Hardyng relates that he delivered a second

[11] *Chron.*, ed. Ellis, p. 383. The story clearly relates to the same incident as that in a late version of the *Brut* (p. 595), where, however, it is attributed to the first year of the reign. [12] *Chron.*, ed. Ellis, pp. 292-3.

[13] f. 5. Hardyng there recites amongst his authorities: 'As the grete cronycler Trogus Pompeyus in his book of Storyes of alle the worlde hath wryten: the whiche Book hys disciple Justynus hathe drawe into xliiij books that bene at Rome in the kepynge of the pope, all compiled agayn in til oon, so that The Stories of alle the worlde in it may be clerelyche sene: the whiche Julyus Caesaryne, auditour of the pope Martynes Chaumbre the Fyfte, in his seuent yer gafe the maker of this book John Hardyng dayly instruccion and discripcion in at instance and writyng of the Cardinal of Wynchestre.'

[14] *Calendar of Papal Registers*, vii. 16, 34, 36.

[15] Palgrave, *Documents and Records relating to Scotland*, p. 376.

instalment of documents to Henry VI at Easthampstead.[16] This is true; for on 16 July 1440, at Easthampstead, the king made a grant

for life to John Hardyng of the county of Lincoln of the 10*l* a year, which the farmer or occupier of the manor or preceptory of Wyloughton pays the King for the fee farm of the same ; in completion of the promise of the King's father of such reward to the said John for obtaining at great risk from the King's enemies of Scotland certain evidences concerning the King's overlordship of Scotland, which evidences have now been handed to the King.

There was some error in the first grant, but Hardyng's interest was secured to him by later letters in the following December.[17]

Hardyng's patron, Robert Umfraville, who died in 1436, had some time previously granted him the post of constable of the castle of Kyme in Lincolnshire. Accordingly he is described as John Hardyng of Kyme in 1434,[18] and again in 1457.[19] In his later years at Kyme Hardyng seems to have busied himself with the compilation of his chronicle ; for the Lansdowne version bears evidence of having been in part at least composed between 1440 and 1450. Hardyng was not, however, content with Wyloughton, the value of which was so much less than the £40 a year which he alleged had been promised him in Geddington. So in 1451 he sent in a petition for this better manor. According to his own account he actually obtained letters of privy seal granting his desire. But the chancellor, ' that Cardinal was of York,' would not suffer that he had such warison, and rather than let him have Geddington would let the king forgo his sovereignty of Scotland.[20] John Kemp was made chancellor on 31 January 1450, and was translated from York to Canterbury early in 1452 : so the petition must have been made in 1450 or 1451. Hardyng speaks of the incident as having happened six years ago,[21] which in its turn fixes the time of writing to 1456 or 1457. This agrees with other known facts. For it seems to have been in 1457 that Hardyng, having completed his Chronicle, presented it to the king with a final petition for his promised reward. On 15 November of that year the earl of Shrewsbury, as treasurer, executed an indenture with Hardyng acknowledging the delivery of six documents relating to the Scottish overlordship,[22] and three days later Hardyng was rewarded with a grant of £20 by the hands of the sheriff of Lincolnshire.[23] This was in consideration of his having acquired,

---

[16] Lansdowne MS. 204, f. 3.
[17] *Calendar of Patent Rolls*, Henry VI, iii. 431, 484, 490.   [18] *Ibid.* ii. 382.
[19] Palgrave, *Documents*, p. 377.   [20] Lansdowne MS. 204, ff. 4, 223.
[21] *Ibid.* f. 4.   [22] Palgrave, *Documents*, pp. 377–8.
[23] *Calendar of Patent Rolls*, Henry VI, vi. 393.

not without peril of his body and grave expenses, certain evidences touching the king's overlordship of Scotland ; which he delivered to the king notwithstanding that James, late king of Scotland, offered him a thousand marks therefor.

Hardyng's reward does not seem to have fitted his own estimate of his merits. He began almost at once to prepare a fresh version of his Chronicle for a new patron. The proem of this later version is addressed to Richard, duke of York,[24]

> And eke to please the good feminitie
> Of my lady your wife dame Cecily.

Clearly this was written before Richard of York was slain at Wakefield in December 1460. In the earlier version the proem would seem to be somewhat later in date than the main text. In the later copies the reverse is the case, for the narrative is brought down to May 1464.[25] Actually it was written somewhat later, for Hardyng begs in excuse of his book [26]

> Please it also unto your royaltie
> The queen may have a verie intellecte
> Of your eldres of great antiquitie,
> And of England, of which she is electe
> Sovereign lady.

Since the marriage of Edward IV to Elizabeth Woodville was not made public till Michaelmas 1464, Hardyng cannot have finished his rewriting of the chronicle till near the close of the year. Yet some part of his final text must have been written earlier, since he speaks of Henry VI and his wife and son as being still in Scotland, and in the same place states that it was sixty-three years since Edward's kin were divorced of the royalty.[27] Probably a copy was prepared and presented to Edward IV at Leicester in May 1463. Even in his address to Richard of York [28] Hardyng describes himself as ' me that am this time an aged wight '. He was then already over eighty years of age, and probably he did not long survive the completion of his Chronicle in its latest shape.

The last half of Hardyng's life was occupied with his researches for the evidences of the overlordship of Scotland, and the grievances which sprang therefrom. His writing of his Chronicle may almost be called incidental, since its purpose was clearly to press home to one patron or another the policy of Scottish conquest, which had become an obsession with him, and also his own claim to reward for his services in that behalf. The documents which he produced in support of his argument therefore call for immediate consideration, both for their essential

[24] *Chron.*, ed. Ellis, p. 23.   [25] *Ibid.* p. 408.
[26] *Ibid.* p. 421.   [27] *Ibid.* p. 410.   [28] *Ibid.* p. 15.

bearing on his Chronicle, and for the light which they throw on his credibility as an historian.

The indenture between the earl of Shrewsbury and Hardyng recites the delivery of six documents : [29]

1. Letters patent of David II acknowledging that he held Scotland of Edward III.

2. Letters of the same to the like effect.

3. Letters patent by which the earls, barons, and magnates of Scotland declare their performance of homage to the king of Scots, saving their allegiance to the English crown.

4. A declaration by David Strabolgi, earl of Athol, that he had not been guilty of treason in becoming the liege man of Edward III.

5. A similar declaration by John Grame, earl of Menteth.

6. Indenture of truce between Edward III and David II on 12 April 1352, in which Edward takes the title of sovereign lord of Scotland.

In his Chronicle he recites the delivery of other documents. To Henry V at Bois de Vincennes in 1422 : [30]

7. The submission of Florence of Holland and other competitors for the crown of Scotland to Edward I.

8. The instrument placing the castles of Scotland in Edward's custody.

9. The release which King Edward II made to Robert Bruce at Dunbar.

Presumably to Henry VI at Easthampstead in 1440: [31]

10. Homage of Malcolm Canmore to Edward the Confessor.

11. Homage of Duncan to William Rufus. (This was one of the documents which Hardyng alleged that James I wished to purchase.)

12. Homage of David I to Henry II and the Empress Maud.

13. Charter of David Bruce, exemplifying a charter of Alexander I, and acknowledging his homage to Edward III, king of England and overlord of Scotland.

14. Letters patent of Robert II saving the homage due to Edward, king of England and overlord of Scotland.

15. Release which King Edward III made in his tender age to Robert of Scotland. To these must be added :

16. The safe-conduct of James I offering Hardyng a thousand marks in return for the evidences, which document was clearly produced at Easthampstead. No. 7 was also reproduced on the same occasion.[32] Nos. 9 and 15 were again delivered to Edward IV at Leicester, probably in May 1463.[33]

[29] Palgrave, *Documents*, pp. 377-8.
[30] *Chron.*, ed. Ellis, pp. 293, 305 ; Lansdowne MS. 204, ff. 130, 168ᵛ.
[31] *Chron.*, ed. Ellis, pp. 239, 240, 247, 317 ; Lansdowne MS. 204, ff. 3, 138-9, 145.
[32] Lansdowne MS. 204, f. 168ᵛ.   [33] *Chron.*, ed. Ellis, p. 317.

Of these documents nos. 1, 2, 3, 6, 10, 13, 14, and 16 are still preserved in the Record Office;[34] whilst nos. 4, 5, 9, 11, 12, and 15 are no longer extant. Three other documents (a charter of David Bruce, 21 March 1352; letters patent of Robert II exemplifying the charter of Alexander I; and letters of Robert II exemplifying no. 1), which come clearly from the same source, are, however, still preserved. Sir Francis Palgrave showed that the whole series are forgeries; the seals, where they exist, are either of dubious authenticity or palpably false. 'The language, the expressions, the dates, the general tenor—all bespeak the forgery. The writing is in a character not properly belonging to any age or times.'[35] The documents numbered 7 and 8 were presumably genuine copies, which Hardyng may have recovered. Possibly he added his forgeries to increase the volume and importance of his services. The very circumstances of the manner in which he doled out his discoveries by instalments would be of itself suspicious. Ellis suggested that Hardyng might himself have been imposed on.[36] It is more likely, as Palgrave argued, that Hardyng was himself the forger. 'He was a diligent antiquary, and the style of the forgeries is just such as would result from an individual possessing archaeological knowledge, and yet using it according to the uncritical character of his age.'[37] If the documents afford a certain evidence for Hardyng's knowledge and antiquarian skill, they inevitably throw some discredit on his trustworthiness as an historian. They are not used merely to illustrate the Chronicle; rather might it be said that the Chronicle was composed to defend them. Hardyng's purpose in writing was manifestly to urge his claims to reward in return for the forged documents. The references to the Scottish overlordship appear throughout the whole Chronicle as occasion offers, and are coupled with notices of his delivery of the documents and of his disappointed hopes. The principal copies of the Chronicle were presented successively to Henry VI and Edward IV with a prayer for recognition of his services, and a long argument of the English rights in Scotland and the advantage that might come from their enforcement.

The manner in which Hardyng's collection of documents found its way to the Record Office deserves brief notice. A memorandum, dated 19 November 1451, relates the delivery to the treasury of two round boxes under the seal of Lord Cromwell, the treasurer, containing documents unknown to the said treasurer but relating to the 'Relaxacio regni Scocie'. Afterwards they were placed with two other square wooden

[34] Printed by Palgrave, *Documents*, pp. 367–76.
[35] Palgrave, *Documents*, p. ccxvi.
[36] Preface, p. ix.
[37] Palgrave, *Documents*, p. ccxxiii.

boxes in 'the great chest in which parchment is kept over the Receipt and marked *Scocia Hardyng*'.[38] These other boxes contained the documents delivered under the indenture of 1457; the round boxes presumably contained the documents delivered at Easthampstead in 1440, which had perhaps been taken out of the treasury for the information of Cardinal Kemp at the time of Hardyng's petition for reward in 1451.[39] It is possible that there may be a reference to Hardyng's collection in the declaration of Henry VIII of 'how the Scots practised to steal out of our treasurie diverse of these instruments, which neverthelesse were afterwards recovered again'.[40]

I can now turn to my proper subject, the Chronicle of John Hardyng in its original form. As already pointed out, we have clear evidence for its completion and presentation to Henry VI in 1457. The only copy is the Lansdowne MS. 204, which was probably the actual volume presented to the king:

> Thus now newly made for Rememorance,
> Which no man hath in the world but only ye.[41]

It is a large and handsome folio of 230 leaves. The Chronicle proper begins on f. 5. At the end the 'figure' of Scotland, with copies of the letters of Edward I and the barons of England to Boniface VIII in defence of the English claims in Scotland, fill nearly eight pages. Six stanzas are written on each page. Thus we get a total of approximately 2670[42] stanzas for the main Chronicle; the dedication and proem add another 22. The later version is much shorter: the Harley MS. 661 has 190 leaves with five stanzas on a page; there are, however, some blanks, together with considerable prose passages interpolated in the text, so that the total number of stanzas, including the dedication, is under 1800. With this latter number the other manuscripts of the later version agree.[43] The printed text as given by Ellis

---

[38] Palgrave, *Antient Kalendars and Inventories*, ii. 225, 234–5; *Documents*, pp. cxcvi–viii.

[39] See p. 465, above.   [40] Holinshed, *Hist. Scotland: Chronicles*, v. 524.

[41] Lansdowne MS. 204, f. 2. The text of this and other passages will appear in the next number of the Review.

[42] In a few instances there are five or seven stanzas to the page.

[43] There are two manuscripts in the Bodleian Library: Selden B. 10, in which the chronicle fills ff. 5–183; and Ashmole 34, which has ff. 177; in each case there are five stanzas to the page, but with some gaps. In the former the chronicle is followed by a map of Scotland, with the Latin and English prose additions. In the latter both map and prose additions are wanting. In the Selden MS. on f. 198ᵛ appears the coat of arms of Henry Percy, fifth earl of Northumberland, who succeeded in 1489 and died in 1527, viz. Quarterly of five: i Percy and Lucy quarterly, ii Percy ancient, iii Poynings, iv Fitz Payne, v. Bryan; with his supporters, a boar and unicorn, motto 'Esperance in Dieu', and monogram (see Doyle, *Baronage*, ii. 654). A fifth manuscript, Egerton 1992 in the British Museum, also represents the later version; it is imperfect, stopping short on f. 169 at 'Wherfore good lord now gird you with your swerde' (Ellis, p. 414); another leaf is missing between f. 168 and f. 169 (*ibid.* pp. 407–9,

is a little longer, thanks to the fuller account of Scotland. In the history of the fifteenth century the part which is common to both versions contains 185 stanzas in the Harley MS., as against 206 in the Lansdowne MS. Here, as even in the earlier portion, there are nevertheless some considerable passages which were added in the later version. Further, the Harley MS., like other copies of the same version, contains forty new stanzas for the later years of the reign of Henry VI and the first three years of Edward IV.

From this it will appear that the greater fullness of the Lansdowne MS. is most marked in the earlier part of the Chronicle. But here, where the author of necessity reproduces the material of older writers with little colouring of his own, except for the references to the Scottish overlordship and to the exploits of ancestors of his patrons the Umfravilles, the Chronicle is of least interest. It has not, therefore, seemed worth while to attempt any minute comparison of the two versions. For the most part, what I have to say will in consequence be confined to the later history from 1399 onwards. But first I will begin with the dedication and proem.

The Harley MS. and its kindred copies have a proem of forty-one stanzas [44] in the form of an explanatory dedication addressed to Richard of York. This, as above noted, must have been composed some years before the final completion of the chronicle. In the Lansdowne MS. there is a formal dedication in four stanzas, with an explanatory proem of eighteen stanzas. The pages which contain them are much less carefully written than the main text, and were no doubt an addition made by the author when his volume was ready for presentation to the king. Hardyng begins his dedication by stating that he had written for the king, for the queen's consolation, and for the prince to have cognizance of his realm. To these three royal personages he presents his book,

> To been evermore within your governance
> For soveraynte and your inheritance
> Of Scotland hool.[45]

It is obvious that this must have been written after the birth of Prince Edward in 1453.

The proem is addressed to the king, and describes the author's grievance and how he had been robbed of his reward for his mission to Scotland undertaken at the command of Henry V.

And Alnewike castell' to 'evil and folie'); it does not contain the prose additions. The Harley MS. is the best copy of the later version. In both the Bodleian MSS. some lines are left blank; presumably they were later copies.

[44] The first eleven are missing in the Harley MS.
[45] Lansdowne MS. 204, f. 2ᵛ.

Hardyng reminds Henry VI of how he had at great peril obtained the evidences, and delivered them to him at Easthampstead. An injury to the manuscript has destroyed part of three stanzas; but the loss is of little importance, since they are nearly identical in substance with a passage at the close of the work.[46] Hardyng goes on to state that six years before he had petitioned the king for reward, and obtained letters of privy seal granting him Geddington. But the king's purpose was defeated by the chancellor, Cardinal Kemp, and since his purse would not suffice to sue to all the council,

> So went I home without any avail.

Such injustice would have been impossible under the king's father. For six-and-thirty years Hardyng had kept the evidences of Scotland

> In trust ye would of your abundant grace
> Your Father's promise so favour in this case.

The evidences had cost him 450 marks, and therefore he begs the king 'me to reward as pleaseth your excellence'.[47] From this we see that the proem was written six years after Kemp's chancellorship, and thirty-six years after the conclusion of Hardyng's first mission to Scotland. Both these data agree with 1457 as the time when this proem was written.

I now pass on to that part of the Chronicle which relates to the Lancastrian period from 1399 onwards, and may be presumed to depend in some degree on Hardyng's own knowledge. The reign of Henry IV is described in the Lansdowne MS.[48] on much the same lines as in the later version, and is for the most part derived from similar sources; there are, however, very considerable textual variations and some noteworthy omissions or additions. The first five stanzas correspond in matter to the first six of the printed text, but are quite different in form. The Lansdowne MS. then has a stanza on the reversal of the condemnation of Thomas of Gloucester. With this exception the resemblance of matter and variation of form continue to the death and burial of Richard II, where seven lines are quoted in the margin as from Gower's Chronicle of Richard II;[49] this

---

[46] Lansdowne MS. f. 3 and f. 223. [47] Ibid. f. 4.
[48] Ibid. ff. 203-9; eighty-two stanzas.
[49] Cronica Tripertita ap. Works of John Gower, ii. 342-3, ed. G. C. Macaulay. Since Hardyng's quotation differs from both of the texts given by Mr. Macaulay I print it here:

> O speculum mundi, quod debet in aure refundi,
> Ex quo prouisum sapiens acuat sibi visum;
> Cum male viuentes deus odit in orbe regentes:
> Est qui peccator, non esse potest dominator;
> Ricardo teste, finis probat hoc manifeste:

quotation was omitted in the later version. Robert Umfraville's fight at Redeswyre, and the invasion of Scotland, are similarly described. In the account of the beginning of the Welsh war some noteworthy variations of detail appear. The war is described as due to 'little cause that might have been content'. Mortimer could find no grace with the king, so was forced to appeal to Percy. Lord Grey of Ruthin was so impoverished by his ransom 'that no power he had to war or strife'; this was worthy, since it was his withholding of Glendower's rights that led to all the trouble. The battle of Homildon and the events which led up to the rebellion of the Percys are described with some small additions; two stanzas are given to the exploits of Robert Umfraville at Homildon, where he took prisoner the earl of Angus. The battle of Shrewsbury is described at much greater length than in the later version, though with nothing particularly novel. The reference to the surrender of Northumberland at Baginton [50] does not appear. The account of Scrope's rebellion is fuller: it is stated that the Lord John and the Earl of Westmorland had meant to stay at Durham and not to fight, but were counselled by Umfraville to take the field and march on York, 'for of the North they need no more to dread'; this statement deserves credence since Hardyng was then in Umfraville's service and was probably present. According to the Lansdowne MS. Umfraville afterwards gave similar bold advice to the king, when a false rumour was spread of trouble in Wales :

> Go to your foe that next you is certain
> And get the North, then work ye not in vain.

The narrative of events in Northumberland is somewhat superior; it shows that Dr. Wylie [51] was right in his correction of a curious corruption in the printed text, 'And Prendergast ran on the see also,' [52] by reading :

> Rande of the See and Richard Aske to sayne,
> Robert also of Prendregest no doute.

There is something more on the last days of the earl of Northumberland.

The capture of James of Scotland is described in a stanza

> Sic diffinita fecit Regia sors stabilita,
> Regis vt est vita, cronica stabit ita.

Vt patet in metris dicti Iohannis Gower in cronica sua tempore Ricardi Regis predicti.

Stow (*Summary*, fo. 145, ed. 1566) quotes the lines as given by Hardyng, and adds a translation into English verse; he attributes them to the *Vox Clamantis*; his translation appears also in his *Annales*, p. 325, ed. 1633.

[10] Ed. Ellis, p. 362.
[51] *Henry IV*, ii. 261. The reference is to Ranulph del See, lord of Barmston.
[15] Ed. Ellis, p. 363.

which is nearly identical with the one in the later version;[53] this is the first instance of the kind in this part of the chronicle. The account of Gilbert Umfraville's first feats of arms is much fuller. The history of Robert Umfraville's exploits at sea is given somewhat differently; but the story of him as Robin Mendmarket at Peebles is curiously absent.[54] We then come to the account of the French expedition of 1411, where the description of the dispute between the prince of Wales and his father is perhaps the most valuable new passage in this part of the Lansdowne MS.[55] The account of the fighting in France is, on the other hand, less complete than that in the later version. The concluding stanzas for the reign of Henry IV are nearly identical in both versions; but it is instructive that the Lansdowne MS. does not contain the last stanza,[56] which is somewhat depreciatory in its criticism of the king.

The first few stanzas of the Lansdowne MS. for the reign of Henry V are very similar to those in the later version; but the references to the king's change from 'his old condition', and to the home-coming of Clarence, do not appear. When it reaches the French expedition of 1415 the Lansdowne MS. is much less full, except for a list of the French prisoners of Agincourt, which is supplemented by a Latin note in the margin. The visit of Sigismund to England is described briefly, and the list of his companions does not appear. From this point onwards the two versions are textually very different. In the Lansdowne MS. the account of Bedford's relief of Harfleur is shorter; that of 'The Foul Raid' in 1417 is, on the other hand, rather better; there is a little fresh detail on the exploits of Gilbert Umfraville. In the account of Baugé the two versions show much variation and supplement one another; but the later one is on the whole the better.[57] In the final chapters for Henry V the Lansdowne MS. includes two stanzas on the birth of Henry VI, and has a much longer passage in praise of Henry V, contrasting the good order which he kept with the riots and default of justice which prevailed at the time when Hardyng wrote. This passage is one of the most noteworthy in the older version. In it the writer appeals to the king to enforce his authority against those who disturbed his peace:

And at the least ye may send them over the sea
To keep your right in France and Normandy.

This seems to indicate that the time of writing was before the

[53] Ed. Ellis, p. 364.   [54] Ibid. pp. 366, 367.
[55] Quoted in *First English Life of Henry V*, pp. xxii, xxiii.
[56] Ed. Ellis, p. 371.
[57] The proper history of the reign is given in seventy-nine stanzas on ff. 209-16; the Maker's Lamentation follows on ff. 216-17.

loss of Rouen in 1449. These stanzas, together with some other
subsequent passages of a like character, afford a valuable illustration of the state of England at the close of the first half of the
fifteenth century.

In the reign of Henry VI the two versions show a greater
divergence of purpose than they have done hitherto. The earlier
one is also marked by much confusion of chronology, which is
for the most part corrected in the later one. The Lansdowne
MS.[58] begins by recording Henry's accession when he was 'not
three quarters old', and Humphrey of Gloucester's desire to have
supreme authority, which was not allowed by the council.
Thomas Beaufort was the king's keeper in his tender age, and
after his death the earl of Warwick succeeded him in that office.
Bedford ruled France as regent, and was worthily supported
by the earls of Salisbury and Suffolk. In his seventh year
Henry was crowned at Paris, and afterwards at Westminster,
the Lord Cromwell acting as chamberlain at both ceremonies.
Bedford defeated the French and Scots at Verneuil, where
Salisbury and Suffolk again distinguished themselves. Afterwards Salisbury died at Orleans. Bedford ruled well as regent,
his marriage with Burgundy's sister having strengthened the
alliance; after his first wife's death Bedford married the daughter
of the count of St. Pol, but did not long survive. Then Warwick
was regent, and after him Burgundy. Later Sir John Ratcliff
was besieged by Burgundy at Calais, but was reinforced by
Edmund, count of Mortain, and the Lord Camoys. When Duke
Humphrey came to the rescue Burgundy trumped up and fled
away. Humphrey then raided Picardy and came home with
great honour. About the same time James of Scotland besieged
Roxburgh in vain. Who ever saw two such hosts forsake their
siege with such humiliation? Never were two princes so forsworn
as were the king of Scotland and the duke of Burgundy. Of
their fate all should take heed:

> The tone murdered at home in Scotland so,
> The tother wode or elles wytlesse is.

Then the earls of Stafford and Huntingdon successively ruled
Normandy, and afterwards Richard of York maintained it well
during seven years. By this time the king was at his full age,
and ruling well his realm and baronage.

At this point the proper narrative of the Lansdowne MS.
ends; there is indeed no real consecutive history later than
1437. Even to that point the only salient facts recorded are the
coronations, the battle of Verneuil, and the siege of Calais;
it is important to note this against the place where the sources

[58] ff. 217-20; thirty-four stanzas.

from which Hardyng derived his history come up for consideration. It will be obvious how confused the chronology is; the history is described above in the order in which Hardyng relates it. Suffolk is spoken of with praise, which points to this version having been composed before his downfall in 1450. The references to Salisbury and Warwick, though favourable, are slight. Such reference as there is to Henry VI himself is complimentary. This contrasts in a somewhat remarkable manner with the later version. The chronology is then for the most part corrected. The references to Suffolk are less favourable. The praise of Salisbury is amplified, and the marriage of his daughter to Richard Neville, father of the king-maker, is recorded. The earl of Warwick is commended even more warmly than before. But of Henry VI it is said :

> He could little within his heart conceive,
> The good from evil he could uneth perceive.[59]

Warwick is alleged to have sought his discharge from his office with the king out of weariness with his 'symplesse'.[60] The account of the siege of Calais is much shorter; the creditable part played by Edmund Beaufort is slurred over, and even Duke Humphrey is depreciated as having done little 'to count a manly man'.[61] The erroneous placing of the governments of the earls of Stafford and Huntingdon in Normandy is repeated. The notice of York's rule is supplemented by a reference to his official banishment to Ireland; this may perhaps be taken to indicate that this portion of the earlier version was written before 1447; the later version was of course written more than ten years later.

In the Lansdowne MS. the main narrative is followed by three chapters which did not reappear in the later version. The first consists of twenty-nine stanzas in praise of Robert Umfraville, some extracts from which were printed by Sir Henry Ellis in his introduction.[62] The example of Umfraville, as one who was no rioter, but a true justice of peace in his country, is made the occasion for an exhortation to the king to rule most specially for the common profit of his realm : 'in every shire with jakkes and salades clean Misrule doth rise'; the poor were oppressed, and there was no justice of peace who dared to resist the evil. The king is adjured to withstand the rioters and maintainers, or his monarchy would be ruined ; since the growth of maintenance was the destruction of all law :

> Consider als in this symple tretyse,
> How Kynges kept neyther law ne pese
> Went sone away in many divers wyse.

Peace, law, and good governance were the foundation of a strong

[59] Ed. Ellis, p. 394.   [60] Ibid. p. 396.   [61] Ibid.   [62] pp. ix–xi.

monarchy. Only a realm so united could preserve its right in France or Scotland. This brings Hardyng back in the next chapter [63] to his old theme of his own grievances; to the story of his mission to obtain the evidences of Scotland; and of how his endeavour to obtain his promised reward of Geddington had been frustrated. Some part of this was repeated in similar language in the proem.

The Lansdowne MS. closes with a long chapter [64] describing how the king might most easily conquer Scotland; with the route to be taken and the distances from town to town; it is illustrated by a 'figure' or map of the land. The stanzas contained in this chapter were given by Grafton, and are printed in Ellis's edition; they do not appear in the Harley MS., which, however, contains an itinerary with three descriptive stanzas.[65] The two versions present some textual variation, and the Lansdowne MS. has frequently better readings than those in the printed text.[66] The coloured 'figure' or map of Scotland,[67] with its quaint drawings of towns and castles, is superior to that in the Selden MS., and is much more curious and interesting than the neat diagram of the Harley MS.[68]

The source whence Hardyng drew his material is a matter of some little interest for other details of literary history. In a marginal note in the Lansdowne MS. at the beginning of the reign of Henry IV, Hardyng states that he wrote of what he had heard, seen, and witnessed, as appears more clearly in Master Norham's Chronicle. Similar notes are given at the beginning of the reigns of Henry V and Henry VI.[69] Ellis, whilst stating that he could find no mention of Norham elsewhere, notes that his name appears in John Stow's list of authors in his *Summary of English Chronicles*.[70] Whether Stow had any real knowledge

---

[63] Lansdowne MS. 204, ff. 222, 223.
[64] *Ibid.* ff. 223ʳ–6ᵛ. [65] See Ellis, pp. 414–20.
[66] e.g. ed. Ellis, p. 423, l. 27, 'Doun in Menteth,' and l. 29, 'From Doun in Menteth,' instead of 'the downe of Menteth', and 'then from the downe'; p. 424, l. 22, 'at Seynt Margaret Hope' instead of 'Seynt Margaret I hope'.
[67] On ff. 226ᵛ and 227ʳ.
[68] Ellis (Introduction, p. xiv) calls the map in the Lansdowne MS. 'much ruder' than those in the later manuscripts. I cannot agree. The map from the Selden MS. is engraved in Gough's *British Topography*, ii. 579.
[69] I give these three notes in full:

Nota quod totam cronicam istius Henrici Regis compilator huius libri audiuit, vidit, et interfuit. Et vt patet clarius in quadam cronica Magistri Norham doctoris Theologie.

Nota quod cronica istius Regis Henrici patet in quadam cronica Magistri Norham doctoris in theologia, et secundum quod compilator huius libri vidit et audiuit.

Nota quod cronica istius Henrici Regis in isto libro contenta patet in dicta cronica Magistri Norham, et secundum hoc quod compilator huius libri vidit et concepit.   [70] Ed. 1566, 'Norham Chronicler.'

of Norham's Chronicle may be doubted, for when he twice refers to it in the margin of his text he does so as 'John Hardyng following M. Norham, doctor of divinitie'.[71] Of these references one is to the creation of Henry of Monmouth as prince of Wales, the other is to the siege of Harfleur. In neither instance is there any evidence of more than commonplace information, or any reason to suppose that Hardyng was specially indebted to Norham. As a matter of fact, nearly all the passages in the Chronicle proper, which are of peculiar interest, are ones which we may most fairly attribute to Hardyng's own knowledge of what he had heard and seen ; that is to say, the passages descriptive of the exploits of his own patrons the Percys and Umfravilles. The passages of this character are, as might reasonably be expected, fuller and more numerous in the older version ; on the other hand, in addition to some variation in passages common to both versions, the later version contains one noteworthy passage which had not appeared in the earlier one.[72] It is natural that this material of Hardyng's own should be fullest under Henry IV, diminish under Henry V, and disappear altogether under Henry VI ; but some references to Ralph, Lord Cromwell, under the latter reign may possibly be due to Hardyng's association with Kyme and Lincolnshire. The change in the form of the three notes as to Norham's Chronicle would appear to indicate that whilst Hardyng's indebtedness to that work was continuous, his own contributions not only diminished in quantity but were less and less the outcome of his personal knowledge and observation.

If the argument of the last paragraph is accepted, it will be natural to conjecture that Norham's Chronicle was a meagre history for 1399 to 1437, which Hardyng expanded in places from his own knowledge. There is nothing in the kernel of Hardyng's own Chronicle to suggest that its original was a work of any particular value. The fact that it seems to have closed with the death of James I of Scotland in 1437 affords a possible clue to its identity. It was at this date that one version of the *Brut* or English Chronicle was completed. This version survives, possibly in an abbreviated form, as the earlier part of the *English Chronicle* edited in 1856 for the Camden Society by the late Rev. J. S. Davies. The English original was very soon afterwards translated into a Latin abbreviation, of which numerous somewhat divergent copies are extant. With these versions of the *Brut* Hardyng's chronicle agrees in the main for the deposition and death of Richard II, the accession of Henry IV, and the rebellion of the lords in 1400. Other points of resemblance for the reign of Henry IV are Grey of Ruthin's share in causing

[71] *Ibid.* ff. 144, 152. [72] See p. 473 above.

Glendower's revolt, and the events of 1411 and 1412. Nearly the whole of the rest of this reign, as recorded by Hardyng, relates to the career of the Percys and exploits of the Umfravilles. Under the reign of Henry V Hardyng agrees with the Latin *Brut* in dating the king's accession by the feast of St. Cuthbert. In the following years there is nothing very marked; but the accounts of the burial of Richard II, of Oldcastle's rebellion, and of the dukedoms conferred on the king's brothers may well be derived from a version of the *Brut*. In the account of the campaign of 1415 the Lansdowne MS. is too meagre to afford any sure evidence; but the lists of the slain and prisoners at Agincourt probably come from the common source. Hardyng may, as noted before, have described the relief of Harfleur in 1416 from personal knowledge, but he may also have used the common account. In the history of the later French campaigns Hardyng's Chronicle resembles the Latin *Brut* in its lists of captured towns, and of the lords and knights who served at the siege of Melun. The more interesting passages which deal with the parts played by Robert Umfraville on the Scottish border and by Gilbert Umfraville at Baugé were probably composed by Hardyng from his own material. The derivation of some other matter, and especially that for the years 1421 and 1422, is less clear; but Hardyng may here write from his own knowledge, since he was present in France during part of the time.

In his meagre history of 1422 to 1437 Hardyng's Chronicle resembles the Latin *Brut* and Davies's Chronicle in dwelling chiefly on the little king's two coronations, the battle of Verneuil, the sieges of Calais and Roxburgh, and the double treachery of Philip of Burgundy and James of Scotland, and in ending with the murder of James in 1437.[73] The similarity is too well marked to leave much room for doubt that Hardyng had made use of the *Brut* either in its English or Latin form.

From this it would appear that the main thread of Hardyng's whole history from 1399 to 1437 was derived, whether directly or through an intermediary, from some version of the *Brut*. Of the rest of his narrative the more important parts are those which we may almost certainly attribute to his personal knowledge. This leaves little of original quality for the Chronicle of Master Norham; I would therefore hazard the conjecture that this Chronicle was no more than a copy of the Latin version of the *Brut*, and that Norham had no greater connexion with it than that of ownership.

There are certain passages the sources of which call for some

---

[73] *English Chronicle*, ed. Davies, pp. 53–6; there is a marked break in this chronicle at 1437; the next event recorded belongs to 1440. For the Latin *Brut* (1422–37) see Gairdner, *Three Fifteenth-Century Chronicles*, pp. 164–6.

further comment. The memorial verses on Henry IV include a speech attributed to the dying king which resembles those given by Capgrave, Elmham, and John Streche;[74] its contents were probably a matter of common report. The praise of Henry V[75] is probably of Hardyng's own composition, coloured by his sentiments at the time of writing some five-and-twenty years afterwards. The stanzas on the successive governors of Normandy, which with their confused chronology appear in both versions immediately after the death of James of Scotland, are likely to be a muddled reminiscence of Hardyng's own. Greater interest, however, attaches to the long passages with which the earlier version ends. In these we have certainly Hardyng's best and most original work. Foremost are the stanzas commemorative of Robert Umfraville. These were given in part by Ellis in his Introduction. But they well deserve to be printed in full, not only for the simple pathos of Hardyng's picture of his old master :

> Truly he was a Jewel for a King
> In wise counsayle and knightly deeds of war :

but also for the fact that, perhaps through his personal interest in his theme, the writer was warmed into something more approaching to poetry than the common doggerel of his usual paraphrase. Hardyng wrote his praise of Umfraville from his heart, but, as before noted, he turned it into an occasion for pointing the moral of the decay and disorder of the time at which he wrote. Here again we come into touch with the writer's own personality, and in consequence we again get something of real value. Had this lamentation been an addition of the later Yorkist version, it might have been discounted as at least coloured by partisan bias ; but coming as it does in the form of a special address to Henry VI it must be accepted as a faithful picture. The somewhat similar lament and exhortation which appears in the stanzas in praise of Henry V was, from its reference to Normandy, clearly written before 1449. The later passage, with its denunciation of the misrule and riot in every shire, was probably composed some years afterwards, perhaps after the first battle of St. Albans in 1455, and may have reference to the widespread and continued disturbances which followed on the outbreak of the Wars of the Roses.

It is clear that the writing of Hardyng's original version was spread over a considerable period ; for this indeed its enormous length would be a sufficient excuse. The actual narrative ends

[74] Ed. Ellis, p. 370 ; Capgrave, *De Illustribus Henricis*, pp. 110–11 ; Elmham, ap. Wright, *Political Songs*, ii. 120. For Streche see *First English Life of Henry V*, p. xxviii.
[75] Lansdowne MS. 204. ff. 215–16.

with 1437, and the work of composition probably began only a few years later. Its progress was far advanced whilst Suffolk was still in power; hence the favourable tone of its references to the unpopular minister. The finishing touches were given when disorder had become rampant, but whilst Henry VI was still the acknowledged king and source of favour; hence he is treated with kindly reverence. Hardyng had scarcely obtained his long-sought reward in return for the first version of his Chronicle before he set to work to rewrite it in quite another spirit. The extraordinary contrast which is thus presented is little to the author's credit. His change of attitude was too quick, and his motive too obvious. As a consequence, no reliance can be placed on the writer as a judge of other men. As an historian he has for the most part no claim to be considered an original authority, except in the isolated passages in which he wrote from his own knowledge, or in those in which incidentally he throws light on the state of England at a time that was not germane to his proper subject. The latter are the more valuable for their appearance only in the earlier version. Their omission is no doubt to be explained by the fact that their form, as part of eulogies of or addresses to Lancastrian kings, made them unsuitable for Hardyng's later purpose when he was revising his Chronicle for presentation to the Yorkist sovereign. When he completed his final version in 1463 the new king's kin had been divorced of all the royalty for sixty-three years. So the writer was anxious to show that Henry IV obtained the crown

> Not for desert nor yet for any wit
> Or might of himself.[76]

With this intention he no doubt inserted his account in prose of the relations of the Percys with Henry IV, and of the alleged scheme to manufacture an hereditary title for the new dynasty by pretending that Edmund Crouchback was the elder brother of Edward I.[77] The insertion of lines depreciating Henry IV, the curtailing of the praise of Henry V, and the change in the references to Henry VI followed naturally. For the omission of the long passage on Robert Umfraville it is difficult to find any reason except the desire for brevity. In this respect the whole Chronicle underwent drastic revision, though it is curious that in the process the author should have sacrificed much that would seem to have been of most interest to himself.

In spite of the extensive changes in the phraseology of his later version Hardyng added only a little new matter. For the period from 1399 to 1437 he seems to have used for the most part

[76] Ed. Ellis, pp. 409, 410.   [77] *Ibid.* pp. 351–4.

the same sources as before, but sometimes abbreviating and sometimes amplifying passages which related to the Percys and the Umfravilles. In his general history the two most noteworthy additions are the list of Sigismund's companions in 1416, and the story of how Henry V made two knights cease from private war.[78] The former clearly comes from the same source as the list in the Cleopatra Chronicle of London [79]; possibly it may have been given in some lost version of the *Brut*, for Tito Livio [80] also made use of it. For the latter a parallel exists in a similar story in the unique copy of the *Brut* [81] in Lambeth MS. 84, which, though not written till 1479, no doubt reproduces earlier material. Probably in the interval between the composition of his two versions Hardyng may have obtained access to another copy of the *Brut* than the one which he had followed in the first instance. It may be that he then realized the real character of Norham's Chronicle; at all events the references to that work disappear. I have already noted that the prose account of Agincourt in the later version seems to be derived from the *Gesta Henrici Quinti* of Thomas Elmham.[81*] The stanzas which Hardyng added to bring his chronicle down to 1464 do not contain anything which might not have been written from common knowledge; the most valuable part is the final chapter, which deals with events in the north in 1461–4.[82] Hardyng, writing in retirement, was perhaps not in touch with Yorkist sentiment; his chilly reference to the downfall of Humphrey of Gloucester and his condemnation of Suffolk's murder [83] are in conflict with the opinion which became popular after the accession of Edward IV. The stanzas advocating the assertion of English claims in Scotland underwent some modification to suit the altered circumstances. That he urged the wisdom of treating Henry VI and his family with generosity is so much to his credit.

Hardyng's Chronicle was first printed by Richard Grafton in 1543. As is well known, Grafton produced two separate editions in the same year, though the difference between them is mainly one of typography. Nearly thirty years afterwards the true character of Hardyng's work became one of the main topics in the dispute between Grafton and John Stow. That dispute is of some interest for the light which it throws on the history of the manuscripts. Grafton had used a copy of the later version, and Stow commented on his text thus: 'John Hardyng exhibited a Chronicle of England, with a Mappe or description of Scotland, to King Henry the Sixt, which Chronicle doth almost altogether differ from that which

[78] *Ibid.* pp. 376, 383.   [79] *Chronicles of London*, p. 124.
[80] *Vita Henrici*, p. 23.   [81] *Brut*, ed. Brie, p. 595.   [81*] Above, p. 463.
[82] Ed. Ellis, pp. 406, 407.   [83] *Ibid.* pp. 400, 401.

under his name was imprinted by Ri. Grafton.' Grafton took this to be a charge of falsification against himself, and represented Stow to have said that 'a Chronicle of Harding's, which he hath doth much differ from the Chronicle which under the said Harding's name was printed by me'. Stow retorted: 'I say not that I have such a Chronicle of J. Harding.'[84] This was in 1572–3. But in spite of Stow's denial of ownership, it seems abundantly clear that when Stow wrote he had access to the Lansdowne MS. For not only is Stow's first-quoted statement an obvious description of that copy, but he had also made use of it for his *Summary* of 1566. This is shown by his citation of 'Norham Chronicler', and by his quotation of the peculiar version of Gower's lines as given in that copy.[85] It is curious that at a later date Stow owned the Harley MS., which was afterwards acquired by Sir Simonds D'Ewes, who purchased much of Stow's library, and so passed into the Harleian collection. The Lansdowne MS. apparently at one time belonged to Sir Robert Cotton, who was also a purchaser of Stow's manuscripts; this, however, is no proof that Stow had owned the Lansdowne MS., even though his denial of ownership was somewhat disingenuous. Stow also took Grafton to task for bragging that he had a Chronicle of Hardyng written in the Latin tongue. Stow apparently did not believe this to be true. It is, however, possible that Grafton may have seen more than one copy of the Chronicle, and that when he spoke of a Latin Chronicle he referred to the Latin prose passages which appear in the Harley MS. but are not given in his own edition. Grafton's printed text is in substantial agreement with the later version, though he gives in full the stanzas descriptive of Scotland, which in the extant manuscripts of that version appear only in an abbreviated form. From this circumstance and from the frequent variation of readings it would seem that he had used a copy which differed from any of those which have survived.[86]

C. L. KINGSFORD.

[84] *Survey of London*, i, pp. lxxviii, lxxix.   [85] See p. 471 n. 49, above.

Northern Affairs in 1724

ALLIED with Prussia under his treaty of Charlottenburg and successful in dissuading France from concluding a separate alliance with Russia,[1] George I at the beginning of the year 1724 had reason to be satisfied with his position in northern Europe. But the satisfaction was seriously disturbed towards the end of March by news of a treaty concluded between Russia and Sweden on 22 February (o.s.),[2] which, though in its main clauses inoffensive, carried a sting in its tail. A secret article, which was not kept secret, obliged the parties to employ their strongest offices at the Danish and other courts to obtain for the duke of Holstein-Gottorp restitution of his share of Sleswick, and, if they failed, to take counsel with the other powers interested, and particularly with the emperor, how this dispute might be ended satisfactorily and the danger to the peace of the north arising from it be removed.

The treaty was the result of Peter the Great's threats of the previous summer, combined with the refusal of George I, under the restraint of his British government, to render Sweden help against him.[3] At first the Swedes had required that Great Britain should be a party, and to that end had tendered their mediation for a reconciliation between George I and Peter the Great; they had in view, in fact, a quadruple alliance between Russia, Sweden, Great Britain, and France. On George's part, in reply, was demanded as an indispensable preliminary a declaration on Peter's part that he was ready to forget the past, and it was stated that the only matter really requiring accommodation was the expulsion of Michael Bestuzhev from London in 1720, an incident for whose cause it was the king of England's right to claim satisfaction, but which he was willing to consign to oblivion.[4] This same Bestuzhev was now the tsar's minister

[1] *Ante*, xxvi. 305-7 and xxvii. 71-6.
[2] Dumont, VIII. ii. 76. A copy in the original German—the language, says resident Jackson, 'now used in all transactions between these two Nations'—with his dispatch of 15 April (o.s.), Record Office, Sweden 33; translations (various), with those of Finch and Jackson of March and April, *ibid.* 33, 34.
[3] *Ante*, xxvii. 61, 67.
[4] Townshend to Finch, from Hanover, 26 August 1723, Record Office, Foreign Entry Book 155 and Regencies 4.

in Sweden, and he was believed to be anxious to forward the reconciliation, in order that he might return to London. William Finch had written on the subject from Stockholm :—

I shall by this acquaint your Lordship that the King of Sweden is informed of the project of an alliance with the Czar and is not displeased with it, but on the contrary very well inclined to it, provided the King be included as a principal party. I do not perceive that the King [of Sweden] has been forced into this project by the Holstein faction, or that His Majesty and the Secret Committee came into it for any other reason than to keep the Czar quiet and themselves free from apprehension of being invaded, which they believe they shall do by such an alliance, provided the King be included as a principal party.

Recounting conversations with Count Horn, whom he was specially instructed to consult and for whose eye very complimentary dispatches were written in French, Finch stated that Bestuzhev had spoken of a reconciliation, so he learnt, in terms which he could not have used without permission, and that Horn undertook to procure an address from the riksdag to the king, praying that no alliance should be made without inclusion of the king of England.[5] Townshend replied that this was entirely approved,[6] and that, if friendship with the tsar were re-established, the king would rather see Bestuzhev back in England than any other minister, he being personally most agreeable.[7]

But the negotiations did not proceed as was desired. To summarize the dispatches briefly, it was found that the Swedish plenipotentiaries appointed to treat with Bestuzhev were instructed only to offer their master's mediation, not to make the inclusion of the king of England in the treaty a preliminary condition. Thereupon Count Horn was informed through Finch that George I did not consider his differences with the tsar of sufficient weight to merit mediation, and Finch himself was told privately :

It is impossible the King should think of consenting to entrust any of his affairs in the hands of the Swedes ; their Government is so weak and divided, and the Czar has so great an influence among them, that they could not but be the worst Mediators we could pick out, if we wanted any.[8]

[5] Finch, 28 August (o.s.), Record Office, Sweden 32, and further to like effect 11 September (o.s.).
[6] 'His Majesty wou'd have you leave no stone unturned to carry the point of the Address. . . . Such an Address would be both honourable and advantageous to His Majesty, and must mortify the Czar in a very tender part, to see that after all the noise he has made, and the alarms he has given, he is so farr from keeping the Kingdom of Sweden in awe, that they will prescribe their own terms in case he is desirous of making an alliance with them.'
[7] Townshend to Finch, 23 September, Record Office, Foreign Entry Book 155.
[8] The same, 26 October.

And though later Finch wrote of assurance that in a counter-project handed in to Bestuzhev there was nothing in the least disagreeable to King George, who would always be distinguished as the prince most friendly to Sweden, even though, for its repose and tranquillity, steps must be taken to satisfy the tsar's doubts, yet at the end of the year he had to report that, having learnt from their minister at Hanover that their mediation would not be accepted, the Swedes were disposed to obstruct a reconciliation in any other way.[9] He was instructed in reply to let the Swedish ministers know that the king of England would not take the 'least step that is derogatory to his honour to bring about a reconciliation with the Czar'.[10] And so the negotiations dropped, and the separate treaty was proceeded with.

That the duke of Holstein-Gottorp should have Sleswick back the Swedes naturally desired. But against Peter the Great's demand, that he should be declared successor to the throne, they stood out. Bestuzhev, advancing the proposition, was answered that, while the affection of the nation towards the duke might support his hopes, if he conducted himself well, the present form of government must be maintained and full liberty of election must be preserved. And when he and Bassewitz, the duke's minister, presented a formal memorial on the subject, ministers, says Finch, were not a little pleased to have in their hands a document directly contravening the treaty of Nystad ; their intention, indeed, would seem to have been from the first not to grant the demand, but only to get it put forward.[11] And so in the secret article there was no mention of the succession, but only of the restitution of Sleswick.

The powers who felt themselves immediately threatened were Denmark and Prussia. But they did not combine for their defence ; each had separate recourse to George I. The Danes, indeed, could wish to be supported by the master of so fine an army and so well-filled a treasury, and Prussia, as Holm shows, in spite of dissension on certain questions, for instance on those of the Sound tolls and of East Friesland, was on the whole more friendly to Denmark than opposed to her.[12] But Frederick William I was not prepared to make an alliance particularly offensive to Peter the Great and which promised no advantage to himself. With Sleswick, as shown below, he refused to be concerned.

Hated both in Sweden and in Russia,[13] the Danes had watched

[9] Finch, 27 November and 19 December (o.s.), Record Office, Sweden 32.
[10] Townshend to Finch, 10 January (o.s.) 1724.
[11] Finch, 19 October (o.s.) 1723.
[12] See Holm, *Danmark-Norges Historie, 1720–1814*, i. 125 f.
[13] Holm (i. 77) cites Westphalen on the tsaritsa Catherine's hatred of everything that was Danish, and remarks that the tsar's principal confidants, Yaguzhinsky and

with anxiety Bestuzhev's negotiations, and had continued to press for treaties of alliance with George I. When at the end of 1723 Lord Glenorchy returned from a visit to Hanover, surprise was expressed that he did not bring proposals with him. He had to report that Admiral Gabel was urging his advice for alliance with the tsar instead,[14] and he expressed the fear that it would be hard to keep the king of Denmark in his present good disposition unless something were done to reassure him, for he seemed resolved to secure himself in one way or the other, rather than be obliged every year to equip a fleet.[15] But receiving no light he was reduced to plead that the multiplicity of business at the opening of parliament prevented attention being given to other affairs. When he said that his master's help could always be depended upon, if wanted, ' the Grand Chancellier replied that he was very well satisfied of the good intentions of his Majesty, but that it would have a much greater effect if confirm'd by a Treaty,' and he noted ' a great desire of entring into stricter measures with his Majesty '.[16]

When there came to Copenhagen in March not only the news of the Russo-Swedish treaty but also reports that the Swedes were arming and that all the men-of-war at Carlskrona were being got ready to join the Russian fleet equipping at Cronslot and Reval, sixteen or eighteen of the line and six frigates, the Danish envoy at Stockholm was recalled and appeal was again made to George I. But while Townshend admitted to Finch at Stockholm that the secret article, with its ' strong intimations of further more effectual measures ' to be taken for the recovery of Sleswick than the mere exercise of good offices, must make the Danes believe that war upon them was intended,[17] yet he was careful to minimize the danger at Copenhagen, and it was only suggested to Glenorchy that, if the Danes had any offers to make for removing the difficulties which had hitherto stood in the way of a treaty, they should send some one with them to London.[18] For in the first place there was no thought in England of sending men-of-war

Osterman, were of like mind. A principal cause of offence, Westphalen observed, was the refusal to match the crown prince of Denmark with the tsarevna Anne.

[14] ' The Grand Chancellier tells me that M^r. Gabel takes advantage of this Treaty's not having gone on as easily as the King expected, to endeavour to perswade him to enter into measures with the Czar, telling him he may see what he is to expect from England.'

[15] Glenorchy, 28 December 1723, Record Office, Denmark 46.

[16] The same, 26 February 1724, *ibid.* 47.

[17] Townshend to Finch, 24 March (o.s.), and similarly to Scott at Berlin, Record Office, Foreign Entry Books 155, 53.

[18] To Glenorchy, 20 March (o.s.), *ibid.* 5. The king ' wonders that it should be expected at Copenhagen that your Lord^p should receive instructions to conclude that business there, when it has stuck for this great while chiefly upon two points, the one relating to the trade of his Majesty's subjects, and the other to the reciprocal obligations of the treaty ' (the naval succour, that is, cf. *ante,* xxvii. 61, 62).

to the Sound, and secondly heed had to be taken of French jealousy of an alliance between Great Britain and Denmark. The duke of Newcastle, who had now succeeded Lord Carteret as secretary of state for the southern province, instructed Horatio Walpole at Paris :

the King's engagements with that Crown having been entered into jointly with France, Mons[r] de Morville might be assured that His Ma[ty] was not about entring into further engagements with that Court, but would deferr all thoughts of that kind, at least for some time till He saw how the Czar would act with regard to Him.

And though he would like to concert an answer to be made to the king of Denmark, if necessary, in view of his 'daily instances', yet he 'in this as in everything else would do nothing but in concert with the Court of France'. He was glad to know that Morville thought that some expedient might be found to satisfy both the king of Denmark and the duke of Holstein-Gottorp.[19] Later, when there was a report at Paris that Denmark had acceded to the treaty of Charlottenburg, Horatio Walpole gave assurance that the king was not capable of allowing such a thing after his repeated promises, and after having deferred alliance with Denmark 'purely out of regard to the instances of the French court'.[20]

Turning to Prussia, we find that power not only on the worst of terms with Sweden,[21] but also increasingly mistrustful of Russia, largely in consequence of the non-execution of the late Courland marriage-treaty. At the beginning of the year Frederick William I could still call the tsar his 'waarer und bester', his 'bester und sicherster' friend, assuring him that the objects of the treaty of Charlottenburg were entirely peaceful and not in the least opposed to his interest—he could not take it ill that Prussia should seek to strengthen her position by the renewal of

[19] 6 April (o.s.), British Museum, Add. MS. 32738.
[20] H. Walpole to Newcastle, 21 June, *ibid.* 32739.
[21] Diplomatic relations between Prussia and Sweden had been broken off in consequence of the arrest of the Swedish envoy, Count Posse, in November 1723, for debt. At the end of January 1724 Posse left Berlin without taking leave. Also there were disputes of considerable acerbity touching trade at Wolgast and the non-fulfilment by Prussia of her obligations to Pomeranian landowners under the treaty of 1720. The gravity of the Posse affair is shown by an expression of James Scott : 'S'il arrive que les Russes et les Suédois prennent ensemble des mesures contraires à la tranquillité du nord, Je croy que l'affaire du Comte Posse en sera regardé comme la cause prochaine' (15 January 1724, Record Office, Prussia 17). George I refused to interfere in these disputes because, in Townshend's words, 'the King has by experience seen that remonstrances made by his Minister [at Berlin] make but little impression and have no good effect' (to Finch, 8 February (o.s.), *ibid.*, Foreign Entry Book 155). And, says Finch of the Swedes : 'They talk very much of the King of Prussia's ill usage of them, and give hints, that this would not have happed, if something had not been concerted between the King, the King of Prussia, and the King of Denmark, when His Majesty was at Berlin ;' a thing which he denied positively (19 December (o.s.) 1723, *ibid.*, Sweden 32).

her ancient treaties with Great Britain—and asserting that there was nothing on foot with the imperial court but the ' punctation ' concluded with Count Flemming [22] and efforts for a reconciliation. But at the same time suspicious inquiries were made of Mardefeld at St. Petersburg about the ships equipping at Reval and about Prince Kurakin's return to Paris, a fresh evidence, it was said, of an alliance impending between France and Russia. France, Mardefeld was told, with her far-reaching and dangerous views, was in no way to be trusted, and no doubt the growing might of Prussia was a ' Stachel im Auge ' to her as well as to Austria. And his attention was called to the reports of an alliance between Russia and Sweden, a measure of which the tsar was thought, indeed, to be incapable, but which was dangerous alike to Prussia, England, and Denmark.[23]

When the proximate conclusion of the treaty was known Mardefeld was informed that it was believed to have in view the recovery of the former possessions of Sweden in Germany, and urgent instructions were sent him, and again a month later, to get a copy communicated.[24] Then on 1 April Wallenrodt in London was ordered to ascertain the views of the British government on the subject. He in reply reported Townshend to say in strict confidence that it was not doubted that the treaty was directed against Denmark, now the prey of a thousand anxieties about it, nor that if Denmark were overcome by Sweden the latter would go further. Therefore the king of England would like to know what measures the king of Prussia would propose ; he could not advise a Prussian guarantee of Sleswick to Denmark, for the French and English guarantees already given were sufficient, but only that measures should be taken to submit the affair to negotiation. Denmark was very anxious to make alliance with Great Britain, but nothing would be done in that until the king of Prussia's views were known.[25] In answer Frederick William discussed the dangers of the situation at length, and emphasized their reality,[26] but meanwhile Wallenrodt

[22] *Ante*, xxvii. 58.
[23] Rescripts to Mardefeld, 1 January to 19 February, Staatsarchiv, Berlin. In the last-named we have further : ' So lange der Tzaar lebet, halten Wir Uns genugsam versichert, dass Wir, in keiner Occasion, es mag dieselbe beschaffen seyn wie sie will, von demselben nichts, als eine sincere Freundschaft, und alles gute, Uns zu promittiren haben ; kommen aber künfftig andere Zeiten, so wird sich auch Rath dabey finden.'
[24] Rescripts of 26 February and 21 and 28 March, *ibid.*
[25] Wallenrodt, 14 April, *ibid.* Later, however, Colonel Du Bourgay, Scott's successor at Berlin, was directed to insinuate unofficially how proper a Prussian guarantee of Sleswick, as solicited by the Danish envoy, General Lövenorn, would be. But he was forbidden to support the request openly, because the king of Prussia would certainly require some advantage from Denmark in return, and the king of England would not risk his credit by being involved in the demand (Townshend to Du Bourgay, 21 July (o.s.), Record Office, Foreign Entry Book 53).
[26] Rescript to Wallenrodt, 25 April, Staatsarchiv, Berlin.

was writing that he and Townshend agreed that the Swedish armaments reported were but a gasconade, the latter reaffirming his master's desire to do anything that was necessary in concert with the king of Prussia, but asserting his own disinclination to take precipitate action in so serious a matter before receiving further light.[27]

Frederick William declined to share the optimism expressed. He was genuinely alarmed at the reports of arming in Sweden and Russia, as his rescripts to Mardefeld show,[28] and he was still oppressed by the fear of an alliance between Russia and France, even ascribing to French underhand intrigue the present developments.[29] Now he desired that a joint Prussian and Hanoverian corps should at once take the field, ready to oppose in arms the apprehended Swedish invasion. And he transmitted further advices of new Russian naval preparations, suggesting that France might act by offering her mediation between Russia, Sweden, and Denmark. Austria also, he thought, had a hand in the matter, but the king of England and himself, he said, were strong enough to hold their own, though they must be ready to act, if necessary, and must prevent France from taking sides with Sweden and the tsar.[30]

But now reports came from Sweden of a reassuring character, for instance, of statements by Count Horn ' that the true and sincere intention of the Swedish government is to keep at peace with all the world ', and that the secret article, to which Sweden was obliged to consent, should be looked upon only as words.[31] And so Wallenrodt now wrote that Townshend did not expect any enterprise on the part of the Swedes this year, and that while the assembling of an army corps was assented to, if matters became serious, it was thought to be paying too great a compliment to them to show any disquietude as yet.[32] And Chambrier,

[27] Wallenrodt, 18 and 25 April, and further 5 May, *ibid.*
[28] 25 April to 20 May, *ibid.*
[29] ' Das schlimmste bey diesem gantzen Werck ist dieses, dass die Crohn Frankreich, ohne allem Zweiffel, mit unter der decke lieget, und an allen diesen Nordischen Affairen in faveur des Tzaaren, der Crohn Schweden, und des Hertzogs von Holstein, viel theil nimbt, in dem Abschau, dadurch sich eine solche bande im Norden zu formiren, deren Sie sich zu ihrem interesse, bey den künfftigen Conjuncturen, gebrauchen, und wodurch Sie Uns, und vielleicht auch die force des Chur-Hauses Braunschweig, im Reich, alle mahl in échec halten könne ' (to Wallenrodt, 11 April, *ibid.*). Townshend assured Wallenrodt that France had no hand in the affair and only desired the preservation of peace.
[30] Rescripts to Wallenrodt, 2 and 6 May, and similarly again 16 May, *ibid.*
[31] Finch, 15 April (o.s.), Record Office, Sweden 34.
[32] 16 and 19 May, Staatsarchiv, Berlin. Wallenrodt expressed the wish that the Swedes would undertake something, for it would give Prussia the opportunity of annexing the rest of Swedish Pomerania, seeing that the Swedes were now in favour neither in England, nor, as he noted from utterances of his French colleague Chavigny, in France.

the Prussian minister at Paris, reported a like belief there, 'non obstant le désir, que la Cour de Vienne pourroit en avoir, à fin de brouiller de nouveau les affaires dans le Nord.' It was thought, he said, that the tsar's object in insisting on the secret article was to give a touch of the spur to England, in order to hasten on the reconciliation which he so much desired, as France did also, 'parcequ'Elle ne souhaittoit point d'avoir d'autres Alliez en Allemagne, que V^{re} M^{té}, le Roy d'Angleterre, et le Tzaar, que ce seroit la plus magnifique Alliance, que la France pourroit avoir.'[33]

It seems strange to us that such real alarm of invasion should have prevailed. Power of offence on the part of Sweden was barely existent, and the bulk of Peter the Great's forces were engaged in the Caspian provinces or on the Turkish frontier. Of the 118,000 regulars, with two or three times the number of Kalmucks, Cossacks, and Tartars, which Campredon reckoned him to command, only 33,000 regulars were in the Baltic provinces.[34] But eyes were directed southwards as well as to the north and east, in consequence of the special mention of the emperor in the secret article.[35] St. Saphorin was reporting frequent conferences of the Russian and Swedish residents at Vienna with the arch-enemy of Great Britain and Prussia, Vice-Chancellor Schönborn, and himself and the French envoy treated with contemptuous neglect,[36] and it was believed that the emperor intended to accept the invitation given and to take up the cause of the duke of Holstein-Gottorp seriously.

The relations of George I with Austria were more strained than ever. The court of Vienna would yield no point on the contentions of the south, attacks on protestant constitutional

[33] 23 May, *ibid.*

[34] Campredon, 9 February, *Sbornik* of the Imperial Russian Historical Society, lii. 159.

[35] A year and a half later Stephen Poyntz, envoy at Stockholm, sounded Count Horn on the reasons for the mention. They were strange, he said, and he forwarded them for curiosity; but the final one was that 'the Czar would have it so', and so many material alterations had been necessary that the Swedes were glad to let the compliment to the emperor stand (25 August (o.s.) 1725, Record Office, Sweden 38).

[36] St. Saphorin on 8 February (at great length) and 25 March, Record Office, Germany (Empire) 52. He wrote in his vexation : ' Que faire, my Lord, avec des gens, lesquells s'ils pensent, ce qu'ils font très foiblement, pensent pour se former des illusions, qui sont plus divisés entr'eux qu'ils ne l'ayent jamais été, et qui ont un Maître qui se laisse toujours dévoyer de ses sentiments pour adopter ceux que le dernier qui luy parle luy propose. Et comme le procédé qu'ils ont eu envers Monsr: Du Bourg et moy en ne nous communiquant point le projet qu'ils avoient envoyé en France leur a en quelque manière réussi, ils prennent le soin le plus attentif de nous dévoyer de tout.' As partly the cause of this neglect he complained of boastings on the part of the Hanoverian envoy, Count Huldenberg, that the long-pending negotiation for the investiture of Bremen and Verden was now confided to him: ' je ne me suis que trop apperçu, que depuis lors on me regardoit icy comme n'y signifiant presque plus rien.'

rights in Germany continued, the investiture of Bremen and Verden was still withheld, and a further quarrel had arisen on the subject of the Ostend Company. On the side of Charles VI his ambassador, Count Conrad Starhemberg, had presented in October 1723 a long list of complaints, ranging from King George's attitude towards the religious disputes, alleged aspiration on his part to predominance in the empire, and his opposition to the Ostend Company, down to personal offence given to the count in the matter of customs, excise, and carriage of letters.[37] And fuel had been added to the fire by the treaty of Charlottenburg.

Prussia was in like case, in spite of the formal resumption of diplomatic intercourse. Frederick William I persisted in acts of insubordination, as they were regarded at Vienna; and in his military power Charles VI saw the principal obstacle to his own aims at autocracy in the empire : as Droysen puts it, he had to capture the Prussian position first and humble that prince who aspired to be independent.[38] On the other side, while Frederick William always expressed the greatest veneration for the emperor personally, his quick temper was continually being roused by decrees of the Aulic council against him, which he attributed to Austrian ill-will.[39] The part taken by Saxony in these affairs of the empire—for instance, the issue of imperial commissions to Augustus II to make execution in Tecklenburg and in East Friesland—made matters worse. The king of Poland was the man whom Frederick William most hated; his frontier lay but thirty miles from Berlin, and he was working against him even on the very tender point of the succession to Juliers and Berg.[40] On the Saxon side the activity and impudence of Prussian recruiting officers [41] brought from Augustus the threat of raising

[37] See Townshend to Starhemberg, Hanover, 5 October 1723, Record Office, Foreign Entry Book 222.

[38] *Geschichte der preussischen Politik*, iv. ii. 367.

[39] See the letters of Frederick William to his friend General Seckendorf, employed in mediating between him and the court of Vienna, and the latter's reports in Förster's *Friedrich Wilhelm I, König von Preussen*, iii. 243, and Urkundenbuch ii. On 26 January Prince Eugene had written to Seckendorf that it was hardly possible to be well with the king of Prussia if he continued ' in seiner bisherigen ausserordentlichen Betragniss und beständigen Anstösslichkeiten ' (*ibid.* p. 6).

[40] See Scott's dispatches of 25 April and 6 May, Record Office, Prussia 17, and Droysen, pp. 356-7. St. Saphorin wrote on 6 May : ' Il y a déjà longtêms que j'ay marqué à Vôtre Excellence que les Catholiques de l'Empire n'omettent rien pour empêcher que le Roy de Prusse ne puisse remplir les vues qu'on luy attribue sur les Pais de Bérgue et de Juliers, après le mort de l'Electeur Palatine ' (Record Office, Germany, Empire, 52). Erdmannsdörffer observes that Frederick William I was as much preoccupied during his life by this ambition as was Charles VI by the Pragmatic Sanction (*Deutsche Geschichte*, ii. 404).

[41] See Pöllnitz, *Mémoires pour servir à l'Histoire des quatre derniers Souverains de la Maison de Brandebourg Royale de Prusse*, ii. 139-46. Erdmannsdörffer (ii. 507) writes of the ' brutalen Gewaltsamkeiten und listigen Kniffen ' of the officers. Not less indignation was roused in Hanover and other countries than in Saxony, and in

the 'cartel', a thing which might mean serious loss to the Prussian army by desertion.[42] On this head Frederick William sought to calm the court of Dresden; he sent a cordial invitation to Count Flemming to come to Berlin for friendly conferences again. But an interview, which took place, only resulted in further misunderstanding.[43] In addition, belief in hostile intentions on the part of the emperor and the king of Poland had lately been strengthened by the report of the formation of a catholic league which should dispose of a force of 60,000 men [44]—a paper array, and not one which could intimidate Prussia with her full treasury, her own larger army ready for the field, her well-stored magazines and modernized fortresses. But Frederick William did not want war unless he was forced into it.

To Austria the natural counterpoise was France, and George I now sought to obtain from the French government the same support in the north which it was faithfully rendering in the south. With this object, while at Copenhagen and Berlin, as we have seen, the cue was to allay the alarm aroused by the Russo-Swedish treaty, in order that Great Britain might not be committed to the expense of armaments, at Paris the danger was magnified. Not, care was taken to affirm, that the king of England stood in any fear of the tsar; the prosperous state of his affairs at home and the treaties made with Prussia and solicited by Denmark rendered him easy on that head; but precautions must be taken for the

Denmark a Prussian lieutenant caught would probably have been hanged, but that it was desired to exchange him for the murderer Pretorius, who had taken refuge in Prussia. Pretorius was eventually exchanged for twelve giant recruits (Scott, 22 February; Glenorchy, 19 February, 19 September, 28 October: Record Office, Prussia 17, Denmark 47).

[42] Thus Scott on 8 April: if the court of Dresden made further demands, 'Je vois qu'icy on sera porté à soupçonner qu'elle est instiguée à cela par la cour de Vienne, qui regarde peut-être la levée du cartel entre la cour de Saxe et celle-cy comme un moyen seur et plausible pour faire diminuer le nombre des troupes prussiennes, et pour préparer le chemin pour l'exécution de ces desseins que sa Majesté Impériale, à ce que bien des gens croyent, médite en faveur de la catholicité ou pour étendre son autorité dans l'empire.'

[43] Scott, 20 to 30 May. The interview took place at Luckau on the Saxon frontier between Flemming, travelling to Aix-la-Chapelle, and the Prussian ministers Ilgen and Katsch. Flemming affronted Ilgen by carrying off Katsch to discuss a private matter apart, and an open quarrel was with difficulty averted. Scott says: 'Après s'être chamaillés un peu sur les affaires de Tecklenburg et d'Ostfrise, comme aussi sur les prétentions de sa Majesté polonaise sur les Duchez de Juliers et Berg, ils se sont séparez sans venir à aucune résolution, et fort peu contens Je croy les uns des autres.' Further negotiations took place when Flemming came to Berlin late in July, and though Scott's successor, Du Bourgay, sent word that all differences were 'as good as adjusted' with him, this was by no means the case. In January 1725 the questions of East Friesland and of the cartel had become acute, and Du Bourgay then wrote that, if Flemming did no more good on a coming visit than on the last, he had better stay away (13 January 1725, Record Office, Prussia 18).

[44] Droysen, p. 357. The news was forwarded to London from Berlin with an expression of the desire that the British court should dissuade France from joining it (Wallenrodt, 16 May, Staatsarchiv, Berlin).

general interest of Europe and particularly for the negotiations at Cambray, 'which any diversion by new disturbances in the North at this juncture would certainly give the House of Austria an opportunity of defeating.'[45] Arguing the matter with the French secretary for foreign affairs, the Count de Morville, Horatio Walpole persuaded him, he says, to represent to the Swedish minister, Baron Gedda, 'in friendly but in very strong terms . . . the great jealousy and umbrage' which the secret article of the treaty must give to the northern powers, and its violation of that made between Sweden and Denmark in 1720 and guaranteed by Great Britain and France. Gedda, Walpole goes on, disclaimed having seen the treaty, but protested that it was defensive only and harmless.[46] According to Finch, Gedda reported home that Morville had particularly inveighed against the special mention of the emperor and the omission of any reference to the king of France, in spite of what the latter had done for Sweden ; and ministers, said Finch, were seriously disquieted, some divining the pressure put upon Morville by Walpole.[47]

What was decided upon was to endeavour to obtain the accession of France, and incidentally that of Holland,[48] to the treaty of Charlottenburg. Walpole, opening the proposal privately to Fleury, with whom he had established very confidential relations,[49] found him greatly in favour of it. But Morville opposed, alone almost, so Fleury stated, among the members of the council. At an interview with Morville Walpole set forth that, should the tsar 'contrary to all expectations return suddenly to Petersburgh with his peace with the Turks in his

[45] See Newcastle's dispatches of April, British Museum, Add. MS. 32738.
[46] To Newcastle, 3 May, ibid.
[47] Finch, 13 May and 3 June (o.s.), Record Office, Sweden 34.
[48] The Dutch were being urged to increase their military forces with a view to impressing the court of Vienna : see, for instance, a long letter from Townshend of 25 February (o.s.) to his friend Van Goslinga, Record Office, Holland 280, a volume of very interesting correspondence of Townshend with various Dutch statesmen.
[49] Fleury's position was stated by Horatio Walpole in September as follows. The duke of Bourbon and Morville concerted the management of foreign affairs before they were discussed in the council, and were able to send secret orders of themselves to foreign courts; but they would venture on nothing very material without the privity of the bishop of Fréjus (Fleury), so long as he maintained his influence over the young king ; he, however, was a very temperate man, and did not seek to encroach upon their authority, only 'to speak his mind with strength and freedom upon matters of consequence as they came before him' (to Newcastle, 26 September, British Museum, Add. MS. 32740). Previously Walpole had written of Fleury's discoursing to him 'a series of as good reasoning and judgement and with as great a compass relating to the whole system of Europe as I ever heard. . . . Although his proceedings are calm and soft, yet his way of thinking is strong and vigorous' (31 May, Add. MS. 32739). And Lord Peterborough, who came to Paris in August to urge enterprises against Austria of his own spirited conception, named him as 'the ablest man concerned in publick affairs' (9 September, ibid. 32740).

pocket ',[50] and should force the free passage of the Sound or otherwise disturb the tranquillity of the north, then he was afraid he should be 'considered in England as having been amused with fair and dilatory assurances instead of settling something solid and essential that might have warded and prevented the mischief'. Some method, he urged, should be concerted 'for being in a readiness to act upon the first alarm, and I endeavoured by this means to draw from him, without mentioning it myself, his sentiments about France's entring into the Alliance concluded between his Majesty and the King of Prussia'. Morville, however, maintained that there was little cause for alarm, and objected the danger of giving offence at Vienna and so breaking up the congress of Cambray. Fleury, on the other hand, 'assured me that his sentiments concurred entirely with mine, and that as he had the same way of thinking as I had with regard to the Emperour, so he had spoke to the same effect at the Council,' and had proposed that 'preliminaries or heads' should be drawn up and signed.[51]

Newcastle now informed Walpole of expressions used by Count Rottembourg at Cambray to the British plenipotentiaries, Lords Polwarth and Whitworth, in favour of what was proposed, not only 'for the preservation of the peace of the North and for the securing of those acquisitions of which His Ma^{ty} is now so rightfully possest in those parts', but also as likely to further the alliance in negotiation with Russia ; in fine, to make all the northern powers court the king's friendship. To the Dutch Newcastle thought that the first proposals should come from France, with the promise to support their opposition to the Ostend Company and to have that question brought forward at Cambray ; the king, he said, would use his utmost endeavours to persuade them to comply. Yet, he concluded, if it should appear that what Rottembourg said came chiefly from himself, 'and is not much relisht where you are,' the matter must not be pressed, lest the impression should be given that the king was looking to his own advantage.[52] Walpole replied that he believed that Rottembourg's utterances 'arose purely from his own true judgment with relation to the North ',[53] and that Morville was strongly opposed to raising the question of the Ostend Company

[50] A prospect not at all well looked upon by George I. He thought, Newcastle had written, that France had been too hasty in promoting the peace before the tsar was reconciled to him and had renounced all views of troubling the north, at least for the present. And he had wanted instructions to be sent to the marquis de Bonac at Constantinople 'to put such rubbs in the way' as should delay the negotiation (to H. Walpole, 6 April (o.s.), Add. MS. 32738).

[51] H. Walpole to Newcastle, 17 May, *ibid.*   [52] 7 May (o.s.), *ibid.*

[53] 'Being very conversant and intelligent in those affairs ; as also from his sincere disposition and desire that France should act in concert with His Majesty for preserving the tranquillity there.'

at Cambray and still 'very cool and backward in taking the least step towards the treaty with Prussia, untill we have a final resolution from the Czar relating to a reconciliation with His Majesty '.[54]

The negotiations went on till August, Fleury consistently supporting Walpole's contentions, or professing to do so, and Morville maintaining the danger of a rupture at Cambray on the one hand, and of angering the tsar, before his real intentions were known, on the other. Walpole argued on the contrary that

it was plain to me that if the Czar out of pure caprice, or with no good design was resolved to keep at a distance with his Majesty, the only means to bring him to a better temper, or to prevent his fomenting any troubles, would be the accession of France to the treaty with Prussia.

He summed up: 'Upon the whole ... there is a general good intention here to act in concert with his Majesty with regard to the affairs of the North as well as of the South;' and as to the present proposal Fleury was for it, Morville against, and the duke of Bourbon 'extremely doubtfull and divided in his opinion '.[55] He was ordered in reply to cease from further instances and to await the issue of the negotiations with Peter the Great.[56] Yet on 1 September Wallenrodt could report Townshend's opinion that, once the difficulties arising from the Quadruple Alliance—that is, the negotiations at Cambray—were settled, he would be able to persuade the French government to accede to the treaty of Charlottenburg and give a guarantee on the known point.[57]

Frederick William of Prussia was now invited to accede to the Russo-Swedish treaty, and apparently would have liked to do so, were it made worth his while. But no advantage, Mardefeld was told, was to be hoped for from acceptance; his master preferred to keep his hands free in regard to northern affairs, and nothing would persuade the king of England to revoke his guarantee of Sleswick to Denmark. Yet he must not decline the invitation absolutely, but thank the tsar, and say that the matter was under consideration.[58] The offer and its rejection were duly imparted to George I by Wallenrodt, and pleasure was expressed in reply. It was impossible, he was told, to find an equivalent for Sleswick excepting at the hands of Denmark,

[54] 24 May, *ibid*.
[55] To Newcastle, 17 July and 9 August, Add. MS. 32739.
[56] Townshend to H. Walpole, 3 August (o.s.), Add. MS. 32740.
[57] Staatsarchiv, Berlin. Townshend still expected a successful outcome at Cambray, writing to Du Bourgay at Berlin that the main principles of settlement were agreed upon (14 August (o.s.), Record Office, Prussia 18). The 'bekandter punct' was, presumably, the succession to Juliers and Berg.
[58] Rescript to Mardefeld, 22 August, Staatsarchiv, Berlin. For Frederick William's statement of his principle, to enter into no treaty from which he did not derive considerable advantage, see *ante*, xxvii. 54 n.

and so the question must be postponed until there was opportunity for its solution. But the king was entirely of the king of Prussia's opinion that, in view of the duke of Holstein-Gottorp's expectation of the crown of Sweden, it would not be good for him to be too strong on the German side of the Baltic.[59]

George's position in regard to Sleswick was that he would neither force the king of Denmark to find an equivalent, nor contribute to compensation himself. On the latter point he protested strongly against the Danish assertion, that under his treaty of 1715 he had agreed to pay the half of any such compensation ; and this attitude, though its justice is difficult to understand, was consistently maintained during the ensuing years.[60] On the former, when complaint was made by the Danish minister at Paris of utterances on the subject by Campredon at St. Petersburg, his contention that France had no right to support the tsar in such a demand was strongly backed from London, it being pointed out that no such condition attached to the British and French guarantees given in 1720. Newcastle wrote emphatically : 'neither France nor England have any right to impose or even so much as recommend to Denmark their giving an equivalent for Sleswick,' to do so might stir up at Copenhagen a dangerous enmity to both crowns.'[61]

On the Prussian side Mardefeld had been ordered at the beginning of the year to have no converse with Westphalen on Holstein affairs, for what had passed on the subject formerly was well remembered.[62] Solov'ev says that Frederick William

[59] Wallenrodt, 15 September, Staatsarchiv, Berlin.

[60] Compare the author's *George I and the Northern War*, pp. 70, 72. The assertion now made was that the claim was only 'founded upon a declaration made, as the words of it lead you to think, at the time of the ratification of the treaty 1715. But the King never heard any mention made of it, till the year 1720, when the K. of Denmark mention'd it to Ld Polwarth as a separate article to the effect and in the manner above mention'd. If such a declaration was given, it was not only without H. Ma^{ty}'s privity or previous order, but it was neither transmitted to him, at the same time with the ratifications of the s^d treaty, nor at any time since, neither has the King yet ever seen any thing of it but a pretended copy without any date and signed by nobody' (Townshend to H. Walpole, 10 August (o.s.) 1724, British Museum, Add. MS. 32740). The article does not appear in the counterpart of the treaty of 26 June 1715 between Denmark and Hanover preserved in the Staatsarchiv at Hanover, because it was not signed till 16 July, when the king of Denmark refused to ratify the treaty without it. At the Record Office (Treaty Papers 4) is a copy of it in German as signed by Baron Eltz in the camp before Stralsund on 16 July and ratified by George I in London on 28 July. He must have forgotten this, and of course his British ministers had nothing to do with the matter, the treaty of 1715 only concerning Hanover. For the contentions on the subject in 1728 see British Museum, Add. MS. 32755, f. 563 f., where copies of the treaty are misdated 26 July.

[61] To H. Walpole, 21 August (o.s.), Add. MS. 32740.

[62] Rescript to Mardefeld, 1 January 1724, Staatsarchiv, Berlin. It was remarked : 'Ob aber, und was der Königliche Dänische Hoff aus Tractaten, die Er, Seiner Seits, selbst nicht gehalten, sondern dehnen Er directo zuwieder gehandelt, praetendiren könne, das wird sich zu seiner Zeit zeigen.'

declared to the Russian ambassador at Berlin that he would never oppose the succession of the duke of Holstein-Gottorp in Sweden, and that he favoured the restitution of Sleswick to him, though he would not act in that matter excepting in good company;[63] and it is not in dissonance with this that we find orders sent to Mardefeld in June to make the Holstein ministers understand that their master's prospects depended upon a reconciliation between the tsar and the king of England.[64] In Scott's version, as Cnyphausen informed him, Mardefeld was instructed to declare that the king of Prussia would not run counter to the British and French guarantees of Sleswick to Denmark, and that the duke had best apply himself to promote the said reconciliation, which accomplished, it might not be difficult to persuade the Danes to find him a proper equivalent.[65]

France also refused to accede to the Russo-Swedish treaty. When Gedda, after putting off the requests of Prince Kurakin to join with him in soliciting the accession, received formal orders to desire it, Morville, so Walpole says, desired the matter to be deferred until a conclusion had been come to with Russia, and affirmed that no engagements would be entered into separately from the king of England.[66]

In the meantime the British court had been seriously alarmed by reports of the king of Sweden's desire to abdicate. It was feared that the consequence would be the accession of the duke of Holstein-Gottorp and the complete subjection of Sweden to the tsar, who would then be able to attack Great Britain from its ports. The abdication, Townshend wrote, would be 'of fatal consequence' to the king's affairs at the present juncture, nor could it be believed that the king of Sweden was willing to act so mean a part, and one so injurious to his honour and interest. Finch was ordered to make inquiry—strictly private, lest the king and his ministers should 'by dismal representations of their wants and necessitys' magnify their distress, in the hope of extracting unreasonable conditions—about the strength of the royal party and of the so-called 'Patriots', and what ground

[63] *Istoria Rossy*, book xviii, ch. 2.
[64] Rescripts of 3 and 6 June, Staatsarchiv, Berlin.
[65] Scott, 6 June, Record Office, Prussia 17. Campredon pressed the same advice on the duke, as instructed, but says: 'Il est convenu de cette vérité avec moi, mais comme il est entièrement dévoué à la cour de Vienne, et qu'il est certain, que cette dernière le fortifie dans l'opiniâtreté de ne jamais consentir à la cession du Sleswig, on ne peut nullement compter sur les paroles du duc de Holstein, très mal disposé d'ailleurs pour la France et pour l'Angleterre. Mais comme il est sous la tutelle du Czar, il faudra bien, qu'il en passe par tout ce que ce Prince voudra, et je ne puis pas croire, nonobstant tout ce que dessus, que le Czar veuille courir la chance d'une guerre pour ses intérêts' (26 May, *Sbornik*, lii. 224).
[66] H. Walpole to Townshend, 30 August and 22 September, British Museum, Add. MS. 32740; confirmed by Morville to Campredon, 7 September, *Sbornik*, lii. 284.

the Holstein faction had gained since the treaty of February.[67] And Horatio Walpole was instructed to sound the court of France on the matter, emphasizing the danger and intimating that, were the blow to fall 'at this juncture when neither the Duke nor the Czar are come to any terms of agreement with His Majesty', the last-named might be obliged 'to withdraw his attention from the affairs of the South in order to guard his own affairs from the confusion and disaster that will threaten them', and so be unable to give to France the aid she might desire, in case the negotiations at Cambray fell through. He should show the French ministers, Newcastle went on, a copy of Townshend's dispatch of 22 June (o.s.), 'concerning the King's sentiments of the affairs both in the South and North,' in order to let them see ' upon what conditions alone they may expect that assistance from the King, which perhaps they may stand so much in need of '.[68]

Finch's reply was reassuring ; the king's enemies, he said, were few in number, and the constitutionalists could never enjoy so much power under any other ruler : the reports, he thought, were purposely set on foot in order to obtain financial assistance.[69] And Walpole, having busied himself with obtaining from Gedda an exact account of the disposition of each Swedish senator, advised, as the result, that the neutrals, whose leader was Count Horn, might be influenced by favours shown to themselves or their families ; that those opposed to the king might be bought, if only he had money ; and that the army, clergy, and populace were thoroughly well disposed towards him. To Gedda's hint of the propriety of a supply of money he was well enough advised to turn a deaf ear.[70]

These accounts, however, were distrusted, and rightly, as it soon appeared. It was determined to transfer Finch to the Hague and to send to Stockholm in his place Townshend's immediate subordinate at the foreign office, Stephen Poyntz,

[67] Townshend to Finch, 6 July (o.s.), Record Office, Foreign Entry Book 155.
[68] Newcastle to H. Walpole, enclosing a copy of the dispatch to Finch, 13 July (o.s.), British Museum, Add. MS. 32739. The proviso was added : ' After you have done this, the King would have you forbear for some time pressing them more upon these subjects, lest they should think that He stands so much in need of their assistance to reconcile him to the Czar, that they may impose any terms upon him, in order to gain it, or that His Maj[ty]'s affairs are upon such a foot, that without it they would be exposed to the utmost difficulty and hazard.'
[69] To Townshend, 27 July (o.s.), Record Office, Sweden 34.
[70] H. Walpole to Newcastle, 2 August, British Museum, Add. MS. 32739. Gedda's list showed six senators for the king, six neutral, of whom two were inclined towards him, and seven for the duke, a very imaginative estimate. In another dispatch, of 19 August, Walpole set forth Gedda's arguments for a subsidy from France, and his belief that ' they will do nothing in it here, but as they shall find his Majesty disposed to do ' ; he himself thinking the reason for refusal to be the fear of disobliging the tsar.

in whom confidence could be placed.[71] He was instructed to apply himself 'with particular care and attention' to discover the party inclinations of the several senators; 'especially to cultivate a strict friendship and intimacy with Count Horn;' to be 'very well with' the Hessian envoy, General Diemar, who was so much in the king's confidence; and particularly to watch Bestuzhev,

and give constant and exact accounts of what you shall discover relating to the views and designs of the Muscovite Court, it being of the greatest importance to Our service to be well informed of all the Czar is carrying on in Sweden, that We may be the better enabled to prevent any new disturbances breaking out in the North.

In private instructions, set out in extended detail, Horn was stated to be 'the man of the greatest capacity and integrity at that Court, the best disposed towards Us and Our nation', and what Poyntz was to say and how conduct himself towards him was exactly prescribed. Whereas, it was stated, 'the main end' of sending him to Stockholm was 'to prevent the success of any attempt the Czar may make this summer for placing the Duke of Holstein on the throne of Sweden,' if his inquiries should result in finding that a sum of fifty or a hundred thousand pounds would enable the kingdom to be put in a proper state of defence, he might let it be known that such a sum could be found, in case only of an actual attempt on the part of the tsar and upon condition that he himself should direct the disbursement of the money. And further he was authorized to expend in case of absolute necessity £15,000, or £20,000 at most, in 'gratifications' to the senators, but very cautiously and 'by different and distant payments', in order to keep them in a greater dependence. And, as Count Horn was 'strongly inclined' to favour the duke's succession, 'and as we have no reason to be against the said Duke, but what arises from his relation to, and dependence upon the Czar,' Poyntz might let it be known that, were the latter dead, or the duke out of his influence, all friendly offices could be rendered to him; but he must do this very cautiously, lest the king should come to know of it. The instances, which the king and Diemar were sure to make immediately for a supply of money, must be repelled,

---

[71] As correctly published in the *Lettres historiques*, lxvi. 214, there was required ' un Ministre affidé, qui soit capable de manier avec dextérité une affaire si délicate'. Finch could not be summarily recalled, as had been Sir Luke Schaub, that other of Carteret's men, from Paris, on account of the great influence of his family; and as the post at the Hague was higher, though now of little consequence, Newcastle was able to represent the transfer to be a mark of the king's esteem (to H. Walpole, 20 July (o.s.), British Museum, Add. MS. 32739).

but 'in so soft and gentle a manner, as not to drive them into an absolute despair as to this particular'.[72]

Poyntz reached Gothenburg on 2 October, and, as expected, was immediately approached on the king's behalf for money 'for counter-bribing the Czar'.[73] Into his elaborate expositions of the state of parties and of individual inclinations it would be out of place to enter.[74] He stated the real contest to be not between Hessian or Holsteiner for the throne, nor between adherence to Great Britain or to Russia, but whether the crown should govern or the senate. In their 'implacable jealousy' of the king, suspected of aiming at recovering the lost prerogatives of the crown, all, he said, seemed 'to look with an evil eye on any Foreign Power from whom they think he may receive the least personal support', and therefore were disposed 'to run blindfold into the interests of the Czar and the Duke of Holstein, though in their hearts they are afraid of them both'. Two or three senators at most were for the king, and, if he retained the crown, it would be principally through the jealousies and divisions of parties. As to his financial embarrassments, not only had he no money of his own, but was £28,000 in debt to General Diemar. But the British government was less disposed to send help now than ever. In January, discussing the question at length, Townshend expressed the concern of George I at the condition of Sweden and of its king, but also his conviction that the disorders arose from causes which no foreign power could remove; he blamed especially the weakness shown by Frederick I during his reign, as causing him to forfeit all confidence at home and deterring any one abroad from helping him.[75]

We must now turn to the work of reconciliation between George I and Peter the Great. The ceaseless endeavours of Campredon at St. Petersburg were still defeated by the refusal of either to yield on the questions of Mecklenburg and Holstein, although on those directly affecting Great Britain there was a disposition to agree. That George was desirous at least of giving no further offence to Peter is indicated by a special instruction to Colonel Du Bourgay, who was appointed in May to replace James Scott at Berlin,[76] to converse with Count Golovkin there as freely as

[72] Instructions to Poyntz, open and private, 7 September (o.s.), Record Office, Sweden 35. The above is but a very brief indication of the contents of the twenty-four clauses of this lengthy document.

[73] By the king's private secretary, Törne, a long private interview with whom Poyntz, still at Gothenburg, recounts on 30 September (o.s.). He reached Stockholm on 19 October.

[74] Record Office, Sweden 35. One of them, of 4 November (o.s.), covers fifty-one pages of manuscript, rivalling the essays of St. Saphorin.

[75] 12 January (o.s.) 1725, *ibid.*

[76] Scott's recall had been requested in a rescript to Wallenrodt of 21 December 1723 (Staatsarchiv, Berlin), on the ground that he could not be trusted to work with

with the other foreign ministers, and without entering into excuses for or vindication of what was past to hear his offers and report.[77] Frederick William of Prussia, as has been noticed, was anxious for the reconciliation, partly from the natural desire that the two powers, to whom he most looked for support, should be at one, partly from his old fear of a separate alliance between Russia and France. And if one were to be made between Great Britain, France, and Russia, he wished to be included in it. Thus Chambrier, in reply to his dispatch of 23 May cited above, was instructed that nothing could be more desirable than such a quadruple alliance, and that the king of Prussia hoped to succeed in his efforts for the reconciliation, could Campredon be ordered to act in concert with Mardefeld.[78] Further dispatches from Chambrier were encouraging; they set forth Morville's sympathy with the aim expressed and his consent to send Campredon the desired orders.[79] To which his master replied in his pleasure: 'Je seconderois, autant qu'il me sera possible, les intentions de la Cour de France, non seulement dans cette affaire, mais aussy dans toutes les autres qui se pourroient jamais présenter.'[80]

Yet in London there was doubt in regard to the real intentions of the Prussian court. Du Bourgay was instructed:

We think fit more particularly to recommend to your care the hindring his Majesty from entring into any engagements with the Czar without consulting us beforehand.... Whenever you shall discover any transaction of such a nature going on, you should not contradict the King in what he is doing, but skilfully disswade his Majesty from proceeding too farr without making a confidence of his views that way to Us; by shewing him how sincerely earnest We are to advance his true interests; how great an affection We have for him, and how much it is for the real service and advantage of his affairs to preserve inviolably the strict union of counsells and designs, which was so happily settled between us by the late allyance.

For his behaviour at the Prussian court Du Bourgay was recommended to apply himself particularly to obtain the good opinion and confidence of the queen of Prussia, George's daughter, to cultivate intimacy with her servants, and of the king's ministers

sincerity for a good understanding between Great Britain and Prussia. Apparently his relations with the Polish court, to which he had formerly been accredited, made him suspect. In choosing Du Bourgay respect seems to have been had to the small estimation in which Frederick William held civilians. Others proposed, says Wallenrodt, were Lord Scarborough and General Wade, but Du Bourgay was preferred to please the duke of Argyll (4 August, *ibid.*).

[77] Townshend to Du Bourgay, 11 May (o.s.), Record Office, Foreign Entry Book 53. The order had reference to the trouble between Finch and Bestuzhev at Stockholm (below, p. 504 n. 95).

[78] Rescript to Chambrier, 3 June, Staatsarchiv, Berlin.

[79] 27 June and 1 July, *ibid.*   [80] Rescript of 22 July, *ibid.*

especially with Ilgen and Cnyphausen, 'and in a more particular manner to transact Our affairs by their means and through their hands.' He was also 'to be very well' with General Grumbkow, who could be of great use to him and was so disposed to be, having broken with the prince of Anhalt 'and being thereby become ready to embrace measures more expedient for Our service'. But in this he must be very circumspect, in order not to give offence to the others, and with the prince of Anhalt and his party civil but not intimate.[81]

Du Bourgay arrived at Berlin on 4 July. A fortnight later, he says, the king, who had just returned from Wusterhausen, 'did me the honour to entertain me upon the methods he thought the most effectual to reconcile our Court and the Czar.' But after that other subjects held the field. Thus on 12 August: 'there is nothing talk'd of now relating to the affairs of the north,' attention being wholly devoted to the prospects of the congress of Cambray. Should a rupture between Spain and Austria take place, he was asked, what would be the king of England's attitude? To which he replied, as best he could, evasively.[82] Complaints, too, against Hanover embarrassed him, the more annoying because they were well founded.[83]

About the middle of August very encouraging advices were received from Mardefeld and transmitted to Chambrier and Wallenrodt.[84] But there was still distrust. Townshend, Wallenrodt reported, while desiring him to thank the king of Prussia and stating that the king of England's views upon a reconciliation were well known to the tsar, yet believed that the Russian utterances were only intended to amuse.[85] And mystery still attached to Prussian engagements with Russia.[86] To clear matters up the

[81] Private and additional instructions, 11 May (o.s.), Record Office, Prussia 18. The two ministers named had all along been the principal adversaries of George I at the Prussian court. Full particulars of their quarrel are given in *Die Briefe König Friedrich Wilhelms I. an den Fürsten Leopold zu Anhalt-Dessau*, text and introduction.

[82] 'The King of Prussia's desire for a rupture in hopes to make an advantage is beyond what can be imagined.'

[83] Du Bourgay, 22 July to 15 August, Record Office, Prussia 18.

[84] Rescripts of 14 and 15 August, Staatsarchiv, Berlin. In the latter: 'Haben Wir die Nachricht von dem Russischen Hoffe, dass der Tzaar, jetzo, sehr portiret sey, das vorige gute Vernehmen mit dem Könige in Engeland zu retabliren.'

[85] Wallenrodt, 1 September, *ibid.*

[86] 'Since the conclusion of the Czar's peace with the Turks, his Prussian Majesty having appear'd to be under some great uneasiness and anxiety, the Queen was pleas'd to let me know, that she believed it proceeded from some former engagement, that his Prussian Majesty had contrary to his interest unwarily entre'd into with the Czar, who chalenged newly the performance of it, which his Prussian Majesty would gladly shifft off.' This, Du Bourgay went on, was in accordance with the behaviour of Cnyphausen and Grumbkow, and no doubt the tsar was advised by the prince of Anhalt through his creature Mardefeld. Grumbkow, he said, had not so far responded to his advances, but he was certainly at utter variance with the prince, with whom none of the ministers seemed to side.

queen of Prussia counselled Du Bourgay to invite the king to dinner at the first opportunity (he was again away at Wusterhausen), and in the meantime 'to use all the art and labour I can to get a good footing in Messieurs Ilgen's and Cniphausen's favour and confidence as the most effectual means to enable me to answer the Queen's desire '.[87] Shortly he was able to send word of orders going to Mardefeld to do all he could to further the reconciliation.[88]

And now surprising and pleasurable news had been received at Paris from Campredon. From conferences with Osterman and Chancellor Golovkin he drew the conclusion that the tsar desired a reconciliation, would waive his personal 'griefs', and would consent to receive a British minister, if the king of England would promise to work for a settlement in Mecklenburg and withdraw his troops thence and make understood his willingness to join with France and Russia in compensating the duke of Holstein-Gottorp for his loss of Sleswick.[89] On these points Morville had already written that George I was not absolutely inflexible.[90] Next Campredon reported an interview with Peter the Great himself on the day that he received the instrument of his peace with Turkey, obtained for him mainly by the efforts of the French ambassador at Constantinople. Seizing the opportunity to speak of his own negotiation, Campredon was answered that orders would at once be given which would satisfy him.[91] On receipt of which news Morville wrote :

Vous avez plus fait en un moment de conversation avec le Czar lui-même, que vous n'auriez pu faire en plusieurs conférences avec ses ministres ; aussi faut-il dire, que le succès de l'affaire vous sera dû principalement.[92]

In Sweden also the ministers communicated to Finch and Colonel Bassewitz, the Hanoverian minister, overtures from Bestuzhev, with an expression of belief that the tsar might now be prevailed upon to give the simple declaration which George I required, that all past incidents should be forgotten. And now as always, Finch wrote, the king of Sweden expressed himself desirous of serving his majesty to the best of his ability.[93] But when these dispatches reached London Swedish mediation was even less acceptable than formerly, for the news from Campredon had anticipated them. A memorandum given to Count de Broglie with copies of them, recalling its former rejection

[87] Du Bourgay, 30 August, Record Office, Prussia 18.
[88] The same, 5 September.
[89] Campredon, 22 July, *Sbornik*, lii. 256 f. [90] 11 August, *ibid.* p. 276.
[91] Campredon, 1 August, cited by Vandal, *Louis XV et Élisabeth de Russie*, pp. 72, 73.
[92] 31 August, *Sbornik*, lii. 283.
[93] Bassewitz, 12 August; Finch, 19 and 26 August and 2 September, all old style, Record Office, Sweden 34.

out of consideration for France with the result that the treaty of February had been concluded, informed him that, while the present turn of affairs created great surprise, the king did not propose to avail himself of the Swedish offers, that he was still resolved to be reconciled with the tsar only through the mediation of France, and that the only answer to be given, one which it was hoped would soon be possible, was that that mediation had already been successful.[94] However, expressions of satisfaction were returned to Stockholm, Finch being instructed to render thanks for the kind offices employed and to use all civility towards Bestuzhev, giving him the same reason as before for not visiting him,[95] but assuring him of the king's readiness to receive him as minister once more, so soon as the reconciliation should be effected.[96] This, however, was but poor consolation for the rebuff administered, and both the Swedes and Bestuzhev were greatly mortified.[97]

Campredon's advices having been received in London, Horatio Walpole was enabled to notify the French government that George I

consented to the reconciliation and alliance in the manner proposed by the Czar himself, with such an explanation only relating to the admission of the Dukes of Holstein and Mecklenburg as was necessary to make things plainly understood to preserve the honour and faith of the two Crowns.[98]

Later he sent word that it was not expected that a British ambassador should be sent to Russia before the tsar's acceptance of the proposed treaty was known, so that he would have nothing to do but to sign it on arrival ; ' so that the conclusion of this

[94] 'Sa Majesté espère avec la dernière confiance ... qu'après toutes les concessions qu'Elle a faites, le Roy très-Chrétien la mettra en état de donner la seule réponce solide et convenable, à savoir de donner à entendre à la Suède que sa réconciliation avec le Czar est conclue par la médiation de sa Majesté très-Chrétienne. La Cour de Suède ne pourra que se réjouir de voir une si bonne œuvre amenée à sa conclusion, et applaudir à l'interposition dont le Roy mon Maître s'est servi pour cet effet. Et cet évènement ne pourra manquer d'avoir des conséquences très-heureuses tant par rapport aux affaires du Nord qu'à celles du Sud, et de nous débarasser de toutes les difficultés qui pourroient retarder le succès des négociations de Cambray ' (unsigned draft, 21 September (o.s.), Record Office, Foreign Ministers 4).

[95] Finch declined to exchange visits with Bestuzhev until an affront given by the latter to Colonel Bassewitz was atoned for.

[96] Townshend to Finch, 22 September and 9 October (o.s.), Record Office, Foreign Entry Book 155.

[97] Thus Poyntz on 28 October (o.s.): 'Thô Count Horn and Secretary Höpken had art enough to conceal their resentment, yet I believe they are heartily piqued at the neglect shewn them by the Czar as well as Britain, in this affair of a reconciliation, and I am well informed, that they have already sent positive orders to their minister at Paris, to insist on being admitted to a share in finishing it.' And a week later : Bestuzhev also was greatly mortified at having no hand in the affair. (Record Office, Sweden 35.)

[98] H. Walpole, 19 September, British Museum, Add. MS. 32740.

tedious and difficult negotiation seems to have taken a lucky turn.' Also that the intimation of the king's willingness to recognize the tsar's title of emperor and to receive Bestuzhev back in England, as soon as the treaty should be finished, had given great pleasure.[99] It was decided to draw up a formal treaty to be submitted to St. Petersburg. When the draft had been presented in London Newcastle wrote of the king's satisfaction, especially with the articles concerning the two dukes, and ordered Walpole to express to the French ministers in the strongest manner his sense of obligation, though with the observation that he accepted the terms purely out of regard to France. The dispatch concluded with congratulation 'upon this great work's being brought so near a conclusion, which His Ma[ty] cannot but look upon to be as good as finished', and with the desire that particular thanks should be rendered to Fleury.[100]

The draft treaty was for a defensive alliance between France, Great Britain, and Russia, but provided for the accession of ' tous les rois, princes et états, qui seront mûs du même zèle pour le bien de la chrétienté '. Specified for mutual guarantee were the treaties of Utrecht and Baden, of the Hague and London (the Triple and Quadruple Alliances), those concluded by Sweden in 1719–20 with Hanover, Great Britain, and Prussia, and that of Nystad. The tsar's title of emperor was recognized, with the proviso that no new prerogatives or pre-eminence should accrue to him thereby. Other clauses provided for mutual succour, for liberty of commerce, and so on; the term was fixed at fifteen years; and Sweden and Prussia were specially named as powers whose accession was desirable. The separate and secret articles were three in number. The first stipulated full liberty of election to the crown of Poland by the republic, the second engaged the kings of France and England to use their best offices in favour of the duke of Mecklenburg-Schwerin, out of regard to the tsar, and the third obliged them to do their best to procure for the duke of Holstein-Gottorp, to whom the tsar destined one of his daughters to wife, a proper indemnity for Sleswick, though without derogating from the guarantees which they had given to Denmark.

With the draft went to St. Petersburg dispatches from Louis XV and from Morville discussing the articles in detail, and new full powers for Campredon, in which the tsar was recognized as emperor. Morville wrote:

Je suis persuadé, qu'il ne naîtra aucun obstacle au succès de la négociation, et que les premières nouvelles, que l'on reçevra de vous, seront la certitude de la signature de l'alliance.[101]

[99] The same, 3 and 6 October, *ibid.*
[100] Newcastle to H. Walpole, 26 September (o.s.), *ibid.*
[101] The whole under date 16 October, *Sbornik*, lii. 295–321. Morville promised the

Horatio Walpole for his part expressed himself

very sensible of the influence that this great work, when it comes to be publickly known, will have upon the affairs of Europe, and what an éclat it will give for his Majesty's honour and interest both at home and abroad.[102]

And Townshend wrote to Poyntz :

As the scene of affairs is intirely changed with relation to the Czar since you left this place, the K. having all the reason in the world to think his reconciliation with that prince as good as concluded, you will not enter into any of the particular private instructions given you till you hear further from me, but will content your self with carrying your self as easily and civilly as you can to everybody, without giving any person or party any occasion of offence.[103]

The progress of the affair was well looked upon at Berlin. When Wallenrodt expressed himself unable to understand the haughty attitude outwardly maintained by the British court towards the tsar, while he was certain that at heart it would gladly be reconciled with him, he was answered that he need not trouble himself thereat, the king of Prussia being quite contented that the affair was in such good train, even though he had no hand in it, and thinking that an alliance between Great Britain, France, and Russia, which he himself would gladly join, would excite great attention throughout Europe.[104] In further dispatches, after reporting the attention given to the affair by the Austrian and Saxon envoys in London and the sending of the draft treaty to Russia, Wallenrodt opined that France could not have succeeded so far, had she not been so instrumental in procuring for the tsar his peace with Turkey ; that her success would influence the congress of Cambray and bring the emperor [105] to reason ; that she desired no war, having abandoned her former principle of conquest ; and that the accomplishment of the negotiation would have good results for Prussia, as a guarantee for Juliers and Berg could be obtained : in fact, the new alliance might be regarded as founded on the treaty of Charlottenburg. But the Hanoverian ministers, he said, disposed to a good understanding with the emperor and jealous of Prussia, viewed the proceedings malevolently, and Bernstorff in particular, since he would no longer be able to play the master

immediate dispatch of 40,000 crowns for gratifications to persons at court, and did not doubt that George I would pay the 80,000 already arranged for.

[102] 14 October, British Museum, Add. MS. 32741.
[103] 9 October (o.s.), Record Office, Sweden 35.
[104] Wallenrodt, 26 September, and rescript to him of 10 October, Staatsarchiv, Berlin. Mardefeld on 24 October was ordered again to press the said alliance with the tsar and his ministers (ibid.).
[105] 'Welcher sich gleichsam von allen Ecken belagert siehet.

in Mecklenburg. And the king appeared still to be in doubt of the tsar's sincerity.[106] He was instructed in reply to watch carefully what went on, in order that Prussia might not be behindhand in guarding her own interests, and to deny absolutely and at every opportunity that Prussia had any engagements with any one, particularly with the tsar, excepting in regard to the Courland marriage-treaty, wherein Russian aid had been enlisted in order to defeat Polish intrigue ; any assertion to the contrary was the false invention of the Austrian and Polish courts. And since to accede to the treaty subsequently would bring but little advantage, he must try to get Prussia included in it as a principal party. Chambrier was ordered to say to Morville :

que j'étois véritablement charmé de le voir dans de si bons sentiments par rapport à une étroite liaison entre la France, l'Angleterre, le Tzaar et moy. Que j'y répondrois de mon côté avec toute la sincérité imaginable, et contribuerois tout ce qui dépendroit de moy, pour un si grand ouvrage.[107]

These instructions were sent in full belief that the alliance would be made. Du Bourgay had written on 21 October : ' I am now positively assured by the ministers here, that the reconciliation between our Court, and the Czar, is concluded,' on the tsar's part with great cheerfulness and good resolve for the future.[108] And later :

Whilst I was in his Majesties closet, he sent for Count Golowkin, and desired we should embrace and congratulate each other in his presence, on the happy reconciliation of our Courts, which we did accordingly very heartily. On which his prussian Majesty expressed both in his countenance and words, all the joy and satisfaction imaginable. Among other things his Majesty said, that the Protestant interest might now truly be sayd to be free from any insults of its adversaries, and that he could declare with pleasure, he had contributed all in his power to this good work, which he had at heart for these two years past.[109]

Public report attributed the supposed success to the king of Prussia's influence with the tsar, and even declared that at this interview the ratification of the treaty was actually presented by the British envoy.[110]

Of course all this roused the greatest disquietude at Copenhagen. Du Bourgay on 5 September had cited Lövenörn's

[106] Wallenrodt, 24 October to 14 November, *ibid*.
[107] Rescripts to Wallenrodt, 31 October and 28 November, and to Chambrier, 14 November, *ibid*.
[108] ' As he is assured, that it is the onely method, to gain credit and influence in the affairs of Europe : especialy in his intended treaties of commerce with France and Spain ' (Record Office, Prussia 18).
[109] The same, 7 November.
[110] *Lettres historiques*, lxvi. 519 ; Wich from Hamburg 16 and 22 November, Record Office, Hamburg 41.

expression of fear that Denmark would have to pay. Shortly afterwards Frederick IV made fresh advances to Russia, personally drawing up instructions to Westphalen at St. Petersburg to endeavour to establish a good understanding with the tsar and with the duke of Holstein-Gottorp. He offered the duke Oldenburg and the right to redeem Delmenhorst, mortgaged to Hanover, in return for the cession of his share of Holstein to Denmark, in case he succeeded to the throne of Sweden. And he undertook to recognize the tsar's imperial title, if he would give up his claim to exemption from the Sound tolls. To help the negotiation, Westphalen was empowered to offer to Campredon and to Bassewitz, the duke's minister, a real ' reconnaissance '.[111] But nothing came of this, and Danish fears increased. Wich at Hamburg bears witness to this, saying that the Danish minister at Paris had been ordered to find out what he could.[112] And Glenorchy wrote on 2 December :

I find the Court is alarm'd at the reconciliation between his Majesty and the Czar, and tho the Ministers have never spoken to me on that subject, I know that the Grand Chancelier has said it would be to the prejudice of Denmark.[113]

Townshend advised him on 12 January (o.s.) 1725 :

Monsr. de Söhlenthal is very uneasy here and continually teizing me about the business of His Ma^{ty}'s reconciliation with the Czar, and thô I have told him fairly how careful His Maj^{ty} has been of his engagements with his Master, . . . yet I find he is still incredulous. . . . His Majesty has been so sollicitous in the progress of this affair to preserve and secure the guaranty given to the king of Denmark both by himself and France, that he thinks it the best thing that can happen for the advantage of that Kingdom that the reconciliation should go on and succeed in the method it is put.[114]

But it was not succeeding. Sanguine as were the hopes expressed, they were doomed to disappointment. Only after receipt of the draft treaty could Campredon obtain an interview with the Russian ministers even to discuss preliminaries. In interpreting as he did Peter the Great's outburst of confidence in July he must have been mistaken, for immediately afterwards Peter informed Prince Boris Kurakin, now once more accredited to Paris,[115] that the reply to his exposition of French policy (of 13 March [116]) must be deferred until it was seen whether there

[111] Holm, pp. 85–7.
[112] 6 October, Record Office, Hamburg 41. The minister in question, Wederkop, was Wich's brother-in-law.
[113] Record Office, Denmark 47.   [114] Record Office, Foreign Entry Book 5.
[115] He had returned thither at the beginning of January, and later received formal credentials of date 13 February (o.s.), *Kurakin Archives*, ii. 158.
[116] *Ibid.* iii. 243, cf. *ante*, xxvi. 308.

was not some change of view at the French court, for written obligations would not be entered into with England.[117] In any case Peter's attention was almost wholly taken up by his domestic affairs, particularly by the Mons scandal, which so gravely affected him, while the illness which was soon to prove fatal was increasing upon him. Moreover, the clauses concerning his two client dukes were not to his content, and he had lately received a fresh rebuff to his great ambition, to marry his daughter Elizabeth into the royal house of France.

In the first week of December took place the betrothal of the duke of Holstein-Gottorp to the eldest tsarevna Anne, and Campredon had word of a secret treaty attaching thereto, which guaranteed to the duke the succession in Sweden, promised either to recover for him his lost estates or to indemnify him by others yielding an equal revenue, and engaged the succession in Russia for whichever of his sons should be most fit.[118] And though on 16 December he could still write, after an interview with Count Tolstoi, ' Je ne désespère point . . . que la négociation n'ait un heureux succès,' he had next to report that excuses were still made, and on 9 January Osterman's definite statement that, while the tsar still wished to ally himself with France, he would only admit the king of England subsequently, nor form alliance with him previously to a reconciliation. He concluded : ' il est certain que le Czar ne se serait point porté aux avances, qu'il a faites, touchant sa réconciliation, s'il n'y avait pas trouvé son avantage, le seul motif, qui le détermine.'[119]

Meanwhile Morville could not bring himself to believe the truth of Campredon's accounts,[120] and Horatio Walpole consoled himself by writing : ' I must own I do not like the appearances of this affair at present, . . . but at all events we may depend upon it, that this Court will not enter into any alliance with the Czar exclusive of us.'[121] Yet Du Bourgay learnt at Berlin that ' I might depend the treaty was in so great forwardness that it would soone be perfected, in the manner the french would have it, and to the King's entire satisfaction ',[122] and even at the

[117] *Ibid.* i. 34.   [118] Campredon, 1 and 9 December, *Sbornik*, lii. 348, 357.
[119] *Ibid.* pp. 366, 378, 385.
[120] ' Je ne puis pas croire, qu'après que le Czar a consenté à admettre un ambassadeur d'Angleterre, qu'il a obtenu du roi de la Grande-Bretagne l'admission du Sr Bestougeff et sur les interêts des ducs de Holstein et de Mecklembourg une stipulation aussi étendue, que les engagements antérieures du roi d'Angleterre ont pu lui promettre, il veuille se retracter, renoncer à tant d'avantages différents et compromettre le nom du roi. . . . Éclaircissez, s'il vous plait, ce mystère et mettez-moi en état de savoir, sur quoi l'on peut compter, lorsque l'on voit une variation si marquée au moment, qu'on a lieu d'espérer une fin prochaine, qui en effet n'est suspendue par rien de la part du roi et du roi d'Angleterre ' (Morville to Campredon, 7 December, *Sbornik*, lii. 355).
[121] 26 December, British Museum, Add. MS. 32741.
[122] 6 January 1725, Record Office, Prussia 18.

end of January Walpole reported Morville to say that 'he did not find, by anything that Mr. Campredon had wrote, the least reason to apprehend that this affair would miscarry', and the duke of Bourbon to think that 'the dilatoriness of the Czar' was rather due to preoccupation by his domestic concerns 'than out of any backwardness or aversion to the thing itself'.[123]

On 1 February Bourbon expressed to Campredon his extreme impatience to know the truth, seeing that it was necessary to take, one way or another, steps to secure the tranquillity of the north.[124] Seven days later Peter the Great died. His widow and successor was credited with a hatred of Hanover even greater than his[125] and with a special affection for the duke of Holstein-Gottorp. And so, on receipt of the news of her successful usurpation, Campredon, on request from London, was ordered to suspend negotiations until he should be further instructed.

Nor did greater success attend another consequence of the new situation created in September, the resumption of negotiations for the accession of France to the treaty of Charlottenburg. Morville, his chief objection being removed, was now found to favour the proposal, but Fleury, strangely, to oppose it.[126] To meet his objections, presumably, the idea of a simple accession was given up and a new treaty was drafted, modelled on that of Charlottenburg but containing alterations suited to France becoming a party.[127] There was a strong desire at Paris, Walpole wrote, for taking Prussia 'into a strict union', but it was thought that the article regarding Juliers and Berg would prove a stumbling-block in the way of the accession of the Dutch.[128] Newcastle,

[123] 27 and 30 January, British Museum, Add. MS. 32742.

[124] *Sbornik*, lii. 416.

[125] 'La Czarine ayant été personnellement traitée avec peu d'égards, lorsqu'elle passa par l'électorat de Hanovre, elle aura conservé contre le roi de la Grande-Bretagne un mécontentement plus difficile à surmonter, que n'avoit été celui du Czar, dont l'éloignement était contrebalancé par des projets et des vues, que la Czarine ne serait peut-être pas en volonté, ni en pouvoir, de poursuivre' (Bourbon to Campredon, 8 March, *ibid.* 451).

[126] H. Walpole, 4 November, Add. MS. 32741. He could only conjecture Fleury's motives, suggesting that, as a bigoted catholic, he might object to Juliers and Berg falling into the hands of a protestant power. To the duke of Bourbon, who sided with Morville, he ascribed the possible hope of acquiring, as the price of his assent, the sovereignty of Neuchâtel. Later (24 February 1725) he retracted his conjecture about Fleury: 'I must do him this justice to say, that in the many conferences I have had with him, he has often made this distinction, of being a thorough Roman Catholick, and for supporting that religion in the highest degree in France, and at the same time a good Protestant in the alliances to be made by this Crown abroad' (Add. MS. 32742).

[127] For instance, 'the omitting to mention the protestant religion in the preamble, and the inserting of the necessary clauses with relation to the cases in which His Majesty and the King of Prussia as Princes of the Empire are, or are not to pay their contingent, should a war happen between the Empire and France.'

[128] H. Walpole, 14 November, Add. MS. 32741. He had previously suggested (4 November) that the Dutch might be satisfied by an agreement on the Orange succession and by obtaining the upper quarter of Guelders and the Elector Palatine's seignory of 'Raveteyn' (Ravenstein).

for his part, intimated the king's pleasure at seeing a disposition on the part of France to come into the treaty, while not thinking it so necessary as formerly ; on the very delicate question of the succession to Juliers and Berg he was loth to enter into further engagements, and did not think that the king of Prussia would have cause to be disobliged if Walpole answered, if approached on the subject in form, that it was not considered advisable at this juncture to alter their nature ; only he must beware of giving any explanations which might not be very agreeable to the king of Prussia.[129] The draft having been presented by Count de Broglie in London, Newcastle wrote that George I entirely approved of it, and only desired the insertion among the treaties to be guaranteed of that of 1720 between Great Britain and Sweden, to which, though objected to in the case of the proposed Russian treaty, ' as containing some engagements which, thô at an end, might have been disagreeable ' to the tsar, there was no such objection in this case.[130] And he desired Walpole to express to the duke of Bourbon and the other French ministers

in the strongest manner the sense His Maj^ty has of this new mark of their zeal for strengthening and improving the union and harmony between the two Crowns, by France's becoming a party to a treaty of such importance to the preservation of the publick tranquillity both in the North and South.[131]

The negotiations went on during the winter, but not with the easy course expected, Prussia advancing demands reasonable enough from her point of view but from the other inadmissible. They were suspended when at the beginning of March 1725 news arrived not only of the death of Peter the Great but also of the secret work which Ripperdà was doing at Vienna, on behalf of Spain, behind the backs of the mediators at Cambray. How Great Britain, France, and Prussia eventually entered into alliance under a political situation greatly altered belongs to the story of the treaty of Hanover of the following September.

J. F. CHANCE.

[129] Newcastle to H. Walpole, 2 November (o.s.), *ibid*.
[130] To meet the difficulty of the reference to the protestant religion in this treaty, it was proposed to add to the mention of it the words, ' Sa Majesté Très Chrétienne se remettant en tout ce qui regarde la Religion au Traité de Westphalie.'
[131] Newcastle to H. Walpole, 12 November (o.s.), *ibid*.

Notes and Documents

The Danes at Thorney Island in 893

IN describing the great campaign of 893 against the Danes, Æthelweard remarks that the invading army, after suffering defeat at Farnham, fled across the Thames, and was thereafter besieged by the king's son Edward in an island named Thorney. The passage in which these events are recorded is written obscurely, but its general sense is clear :

Sed post induuntur et Occidentales Anglos, fit in occursu minacibus stridens agmine denso Fearnhamme loco: nec mora, contra insiliunt facta iuventus armis irrepti sultant liberati rite clitonis adventu, veluti suetam advectæ post prædam pastoris suffultu pascua bidentes: vulneratur ibi tyrannus, iuvantum Suualidas turmas transpellunt fluvium Temesæ ad partes Boreæ. Interea tenentur obsessi Dani in Thornige insula pali. Subsidium clitoni praebuit rex Æthered, Lundonia scilicet ab urbe profectus.[1]

The corresponding passage in the *Chronicle*[2] states that the island on which the Danes fell back lay in the river Colne.[3] The name of the island is not given in the *Chronicle* narrative, and its position has not yet been identified. It has apparently escaped the notice of historians[4] that a hamlet called Thorney[5] stands on the right, or Buckinghamshire, bank of the Colne, some six miles above its junction with the Thames. The Colne flows to the Thames in several channels, which intersect here and there to form islands; and the preservation of the local name Thorney by Æthelweard entitles us to conclude that the Danish army was besieged at some point in the broken course of the river near to the modern hamlet. It is probable that Thorney was always a small place, and it is rarely mentioned in medieval documents, but land there was conveyed in 1454 by a charter preserved in the Harleian collection.[6] The islands of the lower Colne are crossed by the main line of the Great Western Railway immediately below West Drayton station, and Thorney

---

[1] *Mon. Hist. Brit.*, p. 518.   [2] *Sub anno* 894.

[3] 'Hie flugon ofer Temese buton ælcum forda þa up be Colne on anne iggað.'

[4] This may be inferred from the comments of Mr. Plummer, *Life and Times of Alfred the Great*, 114, and from the absence of any definite identification in the recent histories of the period by Dr. Hodgkin and Professor Oman.

[5] In the parish of Iver in Buckinghamshire.

[6] Harl. Chart. 57 D 51, cited in the Index Locorum to the charters and rolls in the British Museum.

stands a short distance to the south of the line. The survival of this name affords another proof that the additions made by Æthelweard to the information supplied by the *Chronicle* deserve serious consideration. F. M. STENTON.

The Making of the New Forest

IT may be useful to compare with Domesday the interesting suggestion, made by the late Mr. F. H. M. Parker in the January number,[1] that the lands added to the forest were originally wasted in 1085 as a protection against a Danish invasion and only added to the forest when waste. Florence and the other chroniclers say that the destruction of villages and churches to enlarge the forest was punished by the death in the forest of both William Rufus and his elder brother Richard.[2] This implies that Richard's death was after the clearances, and that must have been true, for the time of Richard's death would be well known, and it would not help the story about William Rufus to support it by a story about Richard which every one, at least in Hampshire, would know to be false. Now, as William Rufus was old enough in 1079 to fight at Gerberoi, Richard must have been born 1055–61. He was killed before he was old enough to be a knight, i.e. (to judge by his brother Henry, born 1068, ' dubbed to rider ' 1086) before he was eighteen, some years, therefore, before 1085. This is confirmed by an entry in Domesday which seems to treat his death as some years before 1086, and he is not mentioned, as his brothers are, in connexion with the events of 1079.[3] The clearances would appear, therefore, to have been made 1071–7.[4] It might perhaps be said that, though there were some evictions before Richard's death, the mass of them belonged to 1085. But that would not agree well with the general tone of the forest entries in Domesday, which seem to treat the state of things in the spring of 1086 as everywhere well settled and established, not as partly the result of recent clearances made only six or seven months before the survey.

Moreover, Domesday shows that, except for the inclusion in the forest of their woodland and such arable as lay within it, the villages in this district within two miles of the south coast and all up the Avon were as flourishing in the spring of 1086 as

[1] *Ante*, p. 35.
[2] Florence, *a.* 1100 ; Contin. of William of Jumièges, viii. 9 ; Orderic, x. 13 (781 A).
[3] Saxon Chronicle (E), 1079, 1086 ; Orderic, v. 11 (573 c), iv. 20 (545 D) ; D.B. 141 a–b, ' in Teuuinge A. holds of Peter (de Valonges) 5½ hides. . . . But king W. gave this manor for the soul of his son Richard to A. and his mother. . . . Now Peter claims it as given him by the king.'
[4] D.B. 51 a : ' Walchelinus episcopus (Winton, 1070–98) habuit in Falelie 1 hid. 3 virg. . . . valuit 50s., modo est in foresta.'

in 1065, e.g. on the coast Hordle is valued in 1086 at £5 + £3 'in the forest' against £8 in 1065; Milton at £1 + £1 against £2; Winkton at £5½ + £4½ against £10; Christchurch (Thuinam) at £10 + £12½ against £19.[5] Nor is there in 1086 any trace of wasting on the east side of Southampton Water, where '*valet et valuit* £n' is the rule.[6] On the Avon we have e.g. in 1086 Avon £5 + £5 'in the forest' against £10 in 1065; Ringwood £8½ + £7¼ against £16; Ibsley £3 + £1 against £4; Ellingham £3¼ + £3¼ against £7.[7] The value of what is 'in the forest' seems to represent mainly pannage, i.e. rent-swine at 9*d*. to 12*d*. apiece,[8] but sometimes it covered also holdings lying within the woodland. On the other hand, from the villages which in 1086 were entirely 'in the forest', between the Avon and Southampton Water, practically all the inhabitants and their ploughs had been swept away. In all the villages in the main forest there were left in 1086 only three or four ploughlands worth less than £3 against some 150 worth £121 in 1065.[9] The contrast with the coast villages and the Avon villages is very strong, yet for protection against invasion the villages next the coast would not be less wasted than those further inland. Even if we could suppose that the coast villages were left untouched to oppose the enemy's landing, while those further inland were entirely wasted to hinder his advance, still that would not explain the exemption of the Avon villages, lying immediately to the west of the villages taken entirely 'into the forest' and entirely wasted. Nor would it agree very well with the chronicle, which speaks of wasting 'the land along the sea'—*abutan* seems to mean, not 'near', but 'round', i.e. 'along' the sea. The Domesday evidence therefore does not favour any wasting of this district in 1085.

Even if we could suppose that the whole value given to that part of the villages on the coast and the Avon which in 1086 was 'in the forest' was exclusive of pannage and all of it represents holdings lying within or near the woodland, which is certainly not the case, still the rest of the holdings in each village were worth as much in 1086 as in 1065. If there was any military 'wasting' here in 1085, it could not have wasted the holdings in the woodland only, or on one side of a village and not on the other side—it would be distributed pretty evenly. As at least a large part of each village on the coast and the Avon shows in 1086 no trace of 'wasting', any 'wasting' there can have been here in 1085 must have been comparatively slight or

[5] D.B. 51 a 2, 51 b 2, 48 a 2, 38–9. The Chronicle does not say how much of the coast was wasted in 1085, or which part of it.
[6] Alverstoke, 41 b 1; Stubington, 45 a 1; Brownwich, 40 b 2; Hound (Hune) 45 a 2.   [7] D.B. 46 a 1, 39 a 1, 46 a 1, 50 a 2.
[8] See Durley and Milton, 50 b 2; Ashley, 51 b 2; Ringwood, 39 a 1.
[9] See *ante*, xvi. 430, 434 (1901).

temporary, extending at most to the year's crop, and cannot have extended to the eviction of the inhabitants. Even, therefore, if the chief additions to the forest had come after some military 'wasting' in 1085, the eviction of the inhabitants from the villages taken entirely into the forest must still have been due, not to that military wasting, but, as the chroniclers say, to the villages being taken into the forest.   F. H. BARING.

NOTE

As we are dealing with Domesday values it may be worth adding, with reference to Mr. G. J. Turner's paper in the April number,[10] that Domesday entirely supports a crossing of the Thames by some part of the Conqueror's army, large or small, much nearer to London than Wallingford. We find signs of damage in 1066 on the south bank of the river at Mortlake, valued in 1065 at £32, then at £10, and then again at £38 in 1086, and at Combe, Malden, Molesey (3), Ditton (2), and Walton (2), together valued at £45, £26, £44. On the opposite bank we have Hampton valued at £39, £20, £40, Feltham and Bedfont (2) together £20, £8, £13, Stanwell and Harmondsworth £59, £26, £47, and Hayes £40, £12, £30. Domesday seems to point to a crossing at Hampton, where there was a good ford,[11] rather than at Brentford—there are 'aits' at both —but which has the better claim is not of much importance.

Henry Symeonis

IT has often been quoted as an example of the persistence of university customs that down to 1827 every member of the university of Oxford was required, before admission to the degree of bachelor of arts, to swear that he would not lecture nor attend lectures at Stamford, *tanquam in universitate, studio, vel collegio generali*,[1] although the secession to that town of the northern party in Oxford ended in 1335. It is also well known that down to the same year in the nineteenth century all bachelors before inception made oath that they would never consent to the reconciliation of Henry Symeonis; but it has never been established who Henry Symeonis was. The terms of the statute are,

Singuli eciam bachilarii quum responderint in vesperiis fidem prebeant quod nunquam consencient in reconciliacionem Henrici Symeonis nec statum bachilarii iterum assument.[2]

[10] *Ante*, p. 216 f.
[11] *Ante*, xxii. 726; Drayton, *Polyolbion*, xvii. 26-31; Fea, *King Monmouth*, 314. This ford, connecting the damage at Molesey and Hampton, was not known to the writer in 1898. The rest of the army seems to have started by the old Roman road to Chichester and marched to Guildford through Cuddington near Ewell, Ashstead, Leatherhead, Gomshall, and Albury, together valued £51, £29, £55.
[1] Laudian Code, tit. ix, sect. vi, § 1. The oath is found in the Junior Proctor's Book (Arch. Univ. Oxon., Reg. C. fo. 2 b); it also appears as an insertion in the Senior Proctor's Book (Reg. B. fo. 37).   [2] Reg. C. fo. 20 [olim 14].

Brian Twyne, in his *Antiquitatis Academiae Oxoniensis Apologia*, § 342 (p. 376, Oxford, 1608), connected the two declarations mentioned in the passage quoted, and speaks of the

iuramentis Magistrorum de non resumendis (non dico Henrici Simeonis gradibus quem in artibus Oxoniae Regentem imperante Ioanne, ut apud exteros in monasterium cooptaretur, baccalaureum se finxisse ferunt) lectionibus alibi in hoc regno, quàm hic Oxoniae et Cantabrigiae.

But the statute does not say that the reconciliation of Henry Simeon and the resumption by a master of a bachelor's degree have reference to the same class of offence. The last clause may be epexegetic, but it cannot be proved to be so unless we have evidence as to what Henry Simeon actually did. Twyne's interpretation is embodied in the Laudian Code of Statutes,[3] in which the form of oath is prefaced by the words *de non resumendo Gradum Simeonis*; but this is no proof that it is correct. A few years later it was admitted that the meaning was a matter of conjecture. In a convocation held on 13 June 1651 it was proposed by the delegacy for the reform of the statutes that the oath ' de non resumendo gradum Simeonis ' should cease :

Causa est quod cum ante secula aliquot ex causa nobis vel incognita vel incerta ortum habuerit, vtcunque pro eorum temporum ratione rationabili tanti tamen non videtur ut posteri omnes in eandem sub vinculo Iuramenti astringantur.[4]

But the recommendation does not appear to have been approved.[5]

There was in Oxford one Henry, son of Symeon, who is mentioned in the pipe roll of 1177[6] and appears as a witness to a charter in the last decade of the twelfth century;[7] he was perhaps one of the reeves of the town in the time of John,[8] and was alive in 1226.[9] He had a son, Henry son of Henry son of Simeon, who appears in 1225.[10] In the next generation ' son of Simeon ' or ' fitz Simeon ' or perhaps ' Simmonds ', seems to have become a surname. On 22 May 1242 Henry son of Henry son of Simeon and Robert Oweyn made fine with the king for £80 in respite of the outlawry which should have been proclaimed against them *pro morte scolarium Oxoñ*, so that they might stay at Northampton or further north, but not approach nearer Oxford until the king's return from Aquitaine.[11] The king was back in

[3] Tit. vii, sect. i, § 6, cf. § 15.   [4] Reg. T, p. 142, in the University Archives.
[5] Anthony Wood, who records this decision, assigns it in error to 13 January, i. e. 1651/2 : *Life*, i. 173, ed. A. Clark, 1891.
[6] *Roll of 23 Henry II*, p. 16, 1905. For this and several other references I am indebted to the kindness of my friend the Rev. H. E. Salter.
[7] *Eynsham Cartulary*, ed. Salter, 1907, i. 129, no. 172 ; Wood, *City of Oxford*, ed. Clark, ii. 534, 1890.
[8] *Ibid.* iii. 4, 1899.   [9] *Rotuli Litterarum Clausarum*, ii. 151, 1844.
[10] *Patent Roll*, 9 Henry III, m. 1 (p. 556, 1901).
[11] *Excerpta e Rotulis Finium*, i. (1835) 379.

England in the autumn, and in the following spring Henry Simeonis seems to have been again in Oxford.[12] In 1245 Henry III granted to the friars minor an island which he had bought from Henry son of Henry Simeon.[13] Many years later many of the Oxford scholars seceded to Northampton: on 12 March 1264, the king suspended the university during the session of his council at Oxford,[14] and on the 25th he issued letters patent reciting that, whereas he had ordered

that if it should appear . . . that the chancellor and university would be content that Henry son of Henry Simeonis, who withdrew for the death of a man, would return to Oxford and stay there, so that the university should not retire from the said town on account of his staying there; then they should permit him to return without impediment and have the king's peace; the king . . . has pardoned the said Henry the said death, on condition that he stand his trial if any will proceed against him, and has granted that he may return and dwell there so long as he be of good behaviour and that the university do not withdraw from the town on account of his return and the death of the said Henry.[15]

From this it appears that Henry son of Henry Simeonis was charged with homicide, and that his alleged crime was a cause of the secession of the university to Northampton. When it returned to Oxford, the king was a prisoner and the country was in the hands of his enemies.[16] It was not to be expected that the scholars would pay attention to the order of 25 March requiring them to permit Henry the son of Henry Simeonis to come back peaceably to Oxford. Naturally they resumed their former attitude of hostility to him: they would never consent to his reconciliation. This, it seems to me, was the origin of the oath, which was maintained until 1827.   REGINALD L. POOLE.

Copyhold Tenure at Felsted, Essex

THE manor of Felsted in Essex, that is, the chief manor of that parish, which had its manor-house, 'the Bury,' close by the church, belonged in 1576 to Robert, second Baron Rich of Leeze. In that year he caused an exhaustive survey to be made of it by Edward Worsely, gentleman, as well by walking the bounds of the manor as by the evidence, taken on oath, of a manorial jury of fifteen and of other tenants. The greater portion of this record is still extant, in an excellent eighteenth-century transcript, undoubtedly made, for professional purposes, under the direction of a steward of the manor. This manuscript is the property

[12] *Red Book of the Exchequer*, p. 1076, 1896.
[13] 22 April a. 29, *Calendar of Patent Rolls*, 1232–47, p. 451, 1906.
[14] *Cal. of Patent Rolls*, 1258–66, p. 307, 1910.   [15] *Ibid.* p. 309.
[16] The order for the return is dated 30 May (*ibid.* p. 320).

of Alfred Hills, Esquire, of Braintree and Booking; consists of 156 folio pages, of close and neat writing, thirty-eight to forty lines to a page, with some unfolioed leaves; and contains the boundaries of every freehold and copyhold of the manor, with a statement of the manorial customs. The concluding portion of the original survey, which dealt with the demesne-lands, is not known to be extant. The customs of this manor are of especial interest, as showing copyhold tenure in its nearest approach to freehold.

Felsted Manor had been conferred, at the dissolution of the monasteries, on Sir Richard Rich, afterwards (1547) Baron Rich of Leeze (Morant's *Essex*, ii. 416). Since about 1415 it had been the property of the abbess and nuns of Sion in Middlesex, of Henry V's foundation. The Crown had acquired it on the seizure, by Edward III, of the lands of alien priories. Originally, by grant of William I, it had belonged to the Norman nunnery of Holy Trinity, Caen. The fact of long ownership by a foreign nunnery no doubt explains the anomalies found among its customs.

Its law of succession was not that recognized by the law of England:

The custome of the mannor is that the eldest son of every customary tenant within the mannor is next heir unto his father or other ancestors; and, for default of such issue male, then the eldest daughter shall be only heir. And allbeit there be three or four daughters more, yet she only (being eldest) shall be heire of such customary lands, and not to hold the same in coparcenary with the rest according to the course of the common law (p. 149).

Its tenants enjoyed to the full the large immunities granted by the Crown to the estates of religious ladies. They claimed, among many other exemptions from duties to the Crown, to be free from

(a) the suite of the county sheriff's turne, and hundred; (b) all things that belong to the office of the clerke of the king's market; (c) all aids to be given to the sheriffe; (d) all payments towards the expence of choosing knights of the shire; (e) that noe sheriff shall arrest any tenent, by writt, precept, or other processe, within the county where they are resident, although they be without the bounds of the mannor, but that Lord Rich may remand them to the mannor to receive execucion there; (f) that the perveyor of the king's household shall not take any of the goods and chattells of Lord Rich or any of his tenents or residents for the use of his majestie's household; and (g) that it shall be lawfull to resist all his majestie's officers whatsoever who shall goe about to doe anything contrary to the customes aforesaid, and to make rescues as the case shall require (p. 147 A). Also there belongeth to the mannor an especiall priviledge or libertie that no tenaunte whatsoever belonging to this mannor can or ought to be arrested at any time or times within the towne of Braintree [i.e. the natural market-town of the manor] for or upon any debt or trespas, except for felonie murder or treason (p. 151).

The long-continued foreign ownership, in early times, similarly accounts for the emancipation of the tenants from most of the obligations imposed on copyhold land in England. The Norman nunnery escaped frequent trouble and legal expenses by accepting fixed dues in place of variable dues, and even by surrendering ordinary manorial claims. A list of such exemptions follows.

(i) Copyhold land elsewhere was subject to entrance-fine on each change of tenant. The amount of this fine was fixed by bargain, on each occasion, between the steward (acting for the lord of the manor) and the new tenant. At Felsted the entrance-fine was a 'fine certain', i.e. fixed, at the rate of 10s. for the yardland, 5s. for the half-yardland, and 2s. 6d. for the quarter-yardland.

Every customary tenant of one yard-land there, after every alienacion, exchange, or death, shall yeild to the Lord of the mannor for the fine of his yardland, of certainty, tenn shillings (p. 147).

Where the copyhold was ancient, but not of the nature of a yardland, or a determinate fraction of the yardland, the entrance-fine was one year's quit-rent, exactly as 'relief' was paid on admission to freehold.

Every customary tenant, commonly called an ancient customary tenant, of the manor, after every alienacion, exchange, or death, shall yeild to the Lord of the fine for his land the value of one year's rent of assize, and not above (p. 147).

Where the copyhold was a tenure created by the custom called 'undersettling', presently to be noticed, the entrance-fine was assessed by the acreage.

Every tenant customary, commonly called an undersetling tenant after every alienacion exchange or death, shall yeild to the Lord for the fine of his lands, for every acre thereof two pence and not above (p. 147).

Some copyholds were recognized to be enclosures from the 'waste', i.e. common-land of the manor, or grants on copyhold conditions of demesne-land. Such of them as were long prior to the survey were allowed the benefit of the custom, and paid only one year's quit-rent as entrance-fine. The more recent of them the steward wished to subject to ordinary copyhold fine 'arbitrable at the Lord's will' (p. 148).

(ii) Copyholders were almost everywhere strictly bound to keep their buildings in repair. Even if the buildings were no longer required, leave had to be obtained, and a fee paid to the manor, for taking them down. From this Felsted tenants were quite exempt.

They may suffer their customary tenements and buildings to the same belonging, either to fall into utter ruine and decay, or else to sell away the timber thereof so decayed at their like liberties and pleasures, without any danger of forfeiture of their estates, because (as they alledge) they hold their tenements and lands by the tenure of ancient demesne (p. 148).

(iii) In ordinary copyholds timber growing on the land belonged to the manor, and to fell any of it the copyholder had to obtain leave and pay fees and agreed-upon share of profits. At Felsted the copyholder had absolute right to all timber on his land.

Customary tenants have and may from time to time not only fell all woods, underwoods, and trees, as well meete for timber as otherwise, of what kind soever they be, growing and being in and upon their severall Copyhold lands, and the same to carry away and sell at their own liberties and pleasures, without any impeachment of wast, or any other forfeiture made whatsoever (p. 148).

(iv) Ordinary copyholds were held under a general threat of forfeiture for any breach of manorial custom. At Felsted the conditions of forfeiture were very narrowly defined, and the practical effect of forfeiture reduced to a minimum.

Moreover (as they say) there is no maner of forfeiture incident to their estates, except only for denyall of their annuall rents, services, or suite of court to the Lord's Court Baron from three weekes to three weekes upon lawful summons.

If the Lord shall at any time take any such advantage of forfeiture of their estates, and thereupon is awarded a seisure upon the lands to the Lord's use, neverthelesse their custome is that the Lord is, at the next court after, upon the tenant's petition, to regrant the same lands unto such tenant soe offending in as large and ample manner as he did hold the lands before the forfeiture, and that thereupon the tenant ought to pay unto the Lord one yeare's rent of assise, for and in name of a fine, and not above (p. 149).

(v) An ordinary copyholder could not let any part of his land for more than one year, without leave asked and paid for. Nor could he sell any part, except by complete surrender into the hands of the lord, who then (in theory) made a new grant of it to the purchaser. At Felsted binding leases for terms of three years were granted by copyholders at their own free will; and portions of such copyholds as were yardlands, or fractions of original yardlands, were freely sold by copyholders, according to the custom called 'undersettling', subject to an annual quit-rent to the copyhold, and suit of court to the manor.

Every customary tenant may from time to time sell and lett the customary tenancies, without license of the Lord, to any person or persons whatsoever for and during the terme of three yeares (p. 149).

Any customary tenant, being a yardland, halfeyardland or quarteryardland tenant, may at any time surrender into the Lord's hands any part or parcell of his customary lands to the use and behooffe of any other person whatsoever, to have and to hold such part or parcell of land (soe surrendred) to the use of him to whom the surrender is made, and to his heires for ever, reserving to the vendor and his heires for ever an annuall rent to be paid yearly to his customary tenement and lands by him and his heires unto whose use the surrender was made; and every such tenant thereupon is called a tenant of undersetling (p. 150).

(vi) The only impost on copyhold land in Felsted manor which was not also borne by freehold was the heriot, and even this was limited to the yardland and fraction of yardland holdings, and could be claimed of most of those only if the holding were in the tenant's own actual occupation, and not mortgaged or leased.

Every of the yardland, halfeyardland, and quarteryardland tenents of the mannor, are to yeild an heriot, vizt. his best beast, to the Lord for their lands at the tyme of their death, only if soe be that any such tenent or tenents doe dye seised of such estate (p. 147).

But ancient customary tenants, undersettling tenants, copyholders of waste or formerly demesne-land are

clearly discharged from time to time from yeilding or paying any heriot or heriotts whatsoever (p. 147).

The reservation just mentioned did not apply to five of the half-yardlands,

the severall tenants whereof, by force of the custome of the manor, doe yeild to the Lord, at the time of their deaths, a severall heriott, viz. his or their best beast, without [the qualification] 'that any such tenant or tenants die seised of any such customary lands (yea or nay)', as is before expressed (p. 150).

(vii) There were, however, some copyholds which continued subject to an old burden, reminiscent of their original serf condition.

Certain customary tenants, commonly called the tenants of the Swinwick-hold, are bound from time to time, at their own proper costs and charges, to repair and maintaine, as often as need shall require, the Lord's hoggs-cote or swine-house, scituate lying and being near to the scite of the mannor (commonly called Felsted-bury), in and by all manner of sufficient reparacions (p. 150).

Among the unfolioed sheets in the manuscript are notes of the statements of tenants of the manor made, 1567, to 'Mr. Cordall' (brother of Sir William Cordell, master of the rolls 1557–81), acting as commissioner for the second Lord Rich on his succeeding to the estate. They then set out their privileges very curtly and incisively :

For our wood and timber, by our Custome, we may doe what we will.

For our houses of our coppie-holds wee may take them down and doe with them what we will.

For our customarie lands our fine is a yeare's rent (what we pay the Lord by the year).

For our halfeyardland (xxx. acres is halfe a yard) the fine to the Lord is v*s*.

For a licence to let our lands above three years (our custom is) iiii*d*. a year so many years as we will have it. Our custom is to let it for three years without a lycense.

The lord of the manor was also rector of the parish. The troublesome tithe of hay, which in other parishes led to much litigation, was here commuted for a charge of so much per acre yearly from sixty-seven specified patches of meadow. The richer meadow-land by the streams paid 4*d*. an acre; the poorer upland meadow only half that rate.

Our customs is, for River mead, iiii*d*. an acre; for Land mead, ii*d*. an acre for tythe.

A. CLARK.

The Names of Zermatt

IT may interest some readers of this Review to have a short account of the history of the names that have been borne by this celebrated Alpine village. It must first of all be stated that in reality this village has never had but a single name, though that has assumed two forms, one being Romance and the other German, so that one translates, as it were, the other—Praborgne or Zermatt—each of these forms, however, being spelt in many divers fashions. The German form does not appear till 1495 on a map, or 1544 in a text, but naturally may have been employed on the spot long before, since, as usual, local information is lacking on such a point. The reason of this sudden change—the two streams flowing henceforth together, though not absorbing each other—is not known with certainty. But very probably it may be assigned to an alteration in the language (and therefore naturally of the race also) of the inhabitants of the village—a Romance-speaking folk would then have been gradually replaced by a German-speaking colony. It is well known, as a matter of fact, that in the Upper Vallais such changes have been known. In the case of Zermatt there are still extant certain traces (quite apart from the name of the village itself) which seem to show that originally it was inhabited by a Romance-speaking race—so the names of ' Aroleit ', close to Zermatt, of ' Randa, ' and of ' Chouson ' (later Teutonized into ' Gasen '—the village is now called St. Niklaus, from the dedication of its church)—in fact the name ' Chouson ' occurs in 1218 already,[1] some sixty years before the earliest known documentary

[1] Gremaud, *Documents relatifs à l'Histoire du Vallais*, i. 205.

mention (1280) of 'Pratobornum', and later many times (its church of St. Nicholas in 1272) earlier than 1280. It is known that a similar phenomenon certainly appears in the neighbouring valley of Saas, in the upper portion of which an Italian-speaking colony, which in the thirteenth century came over from the Val Anzasca, has gradually become Teutonized, though many local names still show their Italian origin (and not their Arabic or Saracen origin, as I once believed long ago for a short time). In the case of Zermatt the German name would gradually become that commonly used in the German-speaking Upper Vallais, while the Romance form would linger on in the Romance-speaking region (the Aosta valley) to the south of the Vallais. This theory seems to explain most of the facts that we find, though not all of them, since in such cases there is always a certain amount of overlapping, linguistic changes being naturally spread over a long period.

It will be practically most convenient to trace the history of the earlier Romance form before considering the later Teutonic dress of the name. But it should be borne in mind that both have just the same meaning—the meadows ('prés' or 'Matten') closing the end of the valley—the name thus signifying 'the village on the meadows'. Possibly this points to some very remote time when the head of the Zermatt valley consisted simply of summer pastures, used by the permanently inhabited villages lower down the valley. But C. M. Engelhardt in 1852[1] is perhaps right in interpreting the Romance name as meaning 'meadows which are situated at the end of a blind alley' ('prés bornés'), in other words, inaccessible save through the valley below them. However, the real original meaning of the name concerns us less than the forms in which it appears in history.

I. THE ROMANCE FORM (PRABORGNE) DOWN TO 1775

In the middle ages the matter is perfectly simple (save for a single mention of the German name 'Matt' on Conrad Türst's map of 1495–7). During the whole period 'Pratobornum' is the Latinized form which is all but universal. It first occurs (so far as I know) in a deed, dated 27 October 1280, executed at 'Pratobornum', to which 'Waltherus, curatus de Pratoborno' is one of the witnesses, and which relates to the sale of a field at 'Finellen' and a house, with a cheese hut, also situated there. The Latin text (the original document itself is preserved among the archives of the parish church at Zermatt) is given in Pfarrer Ruden's history of Zermatt.[2] Oddly enough it does not appear in Abbé Gremaud's great collection of *Documents relatifs à l'Histoire du Vallais* (8 vols., extending down to 1457). But this

[1] *Das Monte-Rosa- und Matterhorn-Gebirg*, p. 171.
[2] *Familien-Statistik der löblichen Pfarrei von Zermatt*, Ingenbohl, 1869, pp. 100–1 n.

collection does contain many other deeds in which the name
'Pratobornum' (sometimes divided into two words and in 1285
and 1318 taking the form of 'Pra Borno') does occur—1285,[4]
1291,[5] 1318,[6] 1324,[7] 1334,[8] 1357,[9] 1362,[10] 1368,[11] 1398,[12] 1414,[13]
1428,[14] 1449,[15] and 1450.[16] Besides these Latin forms at least
two French forms have found their way into Latin deeds—
'Praborny' in 1350 [17] and 'Pratoburnoz' in 1364,[18] which very
likely represent the local Romance form. In 1368 we hear
also of 'Prato Broni',[19] which is probably a simple mistake,
but has been used to prove that the name of the stream in the
Zermatt valley was once 'Borgne' ('Borny' or 'Bornie' in
many original documents from 1239 to 1448—see Gremaud,
passim), as in the case of that in the Hérens valley (the importance
of this view will appear later on). We should also mention the
form 'Praborgne', which is found in a French version of the
1285 document,[20] but is pretty certainly very modern. Rather
later we find the form 'Pratobornum' in the official document
of 1517, in which the St. Théodule Pass is mentioned. But though
Pfarrer Ruden summarizes many interesting charters of the
sixteenth and seventeenth centuries relating to Zermatt, he
unluckily does not give the original text, or even the form of the
name of the village which is found therein. I can therefore
offer no fresh instance of the Romance name till 1584, when on
Septala's map of the duchy of Milan (in the great atlas of Abraham
Ortelius) we find 'Impraborna', placed at the head of the
'Val de Praborna' (we shall see presently that this form was
later wrongly transferred to the head of the Hérens valley).
Another great leap brings us to 1694, when P. A. Arnod, a high
Aostan official, describing the passes round the Aosta valley,
has occasion to mention our village under the names of 'Praborna'
and 'Praz borna'.[21] A further great leap brings us to G. S.
Gruner's important work of 1760,[22] wherein he speaks of 'Paraborque, the highest village of the Viescherthal', though on his map
of the same date he marks 'In Matt', but, as de Saussure pointed
out in 1796,[23] Gruner certainly means to refer to our village. With
1777 begins a new phase of the history of the Romance form
of the name we are studying, as thenceforth it is commonly used
in conjunction with the Teutonic form. Before 1775, however,

[4] ii. 579.   [5] ii. 426, 428–9.   [6] iii. 291.   [7] iii. 470.
[8] iv. 81.   [9] v. 163.   [10] v. 214, 219.   [11] v. 346.
[12] vi. 459.   [13] vii. 130.   [14] vii. 534.   [15] viii. 402.
[16] viii. 454.   [17] iv. 557.   [18] v. 262.   [19] v. 345.
[20] ii. 330.
[21] See the text in my *Josias Simler et les Origines de l'Alpinisme jusqu'en 1600*,
Grenoble, 1904, pp. 308* and 325*.
[22] *Die Eisgebirge des Schweizerlandes*, i. 230.
[23] *Voyages dans les Alpes*, iv. 421 n.

I have not been able to find any certain cases of the Romance form beyond those enumerated above.

But there are two sets of maps (no *texts* commit this blunder) which mark the Romance form otherwise than at the head of the Zermatt valley.

One set includes 6 maps which inscribe 'Praborne' at the head of the *Sesia* valley, that is, pushed far up into the Monte Rosa chain—1680 and 1765 editions of Tommaso Borgonio's great map of Savoy, two maps of Savoy by Hubert Jaillot, dated 1690 and 1707, a map of 1751 of the Dauphiné, &c., dated 1751, by R. J. Jullien, and finally one of the Alps published in 1801 in the *Mémoires Militaires* of Bourcet, but certainly made before 1775. In four of the six cases (not 1680 or 1765) a *second* village of the same name (under the form of Praberna, or Proberna in 1751) is also marked at the head of the *Hérens* valley.

Our second set of maps includes those (dated before 1775) which (besides these four) indicate the Romance name at the head of the *Hérens* valley. But this second set must be subdivided, for (under *a*) 15 maps mark that form in that position, as well as the German form 'Matt' or 'Matten' in the right position, at the head of the Zermatt valley, while another subdivision (*b*), 10 in number, marks only the Romance name, but in the wrong position, at the head of the Hérens valley.

Now either both or the former only of these two series of maps (25 in all) may simply misplace the name. Yet in either case another theory is possible, which, from the historical point of view, is much more interesting (for the following details see Pfarrer Ruden's *History*, pp. 144-7). There is a tradition that in former days intercourse between Zermatt and the head of the Hérens valley was much easier than now, the Col d'Hérens then offering but slight difficulties. In particular, a number of Zermatt families are said to have settled in the upper Hérens valley, where (among the archives of St. Martin, the original parish church of the whole Hérens valley) divers Zermatt family names occur as early as 1358 (Julen) and 1359 (Fabri), and many others in the fifteenth and sixteenth centuries. Further, a separate Zermatt colony established itself in 1443 in the hamlet of Villa, just south-east of and above Evolena. Whatever its origin it seems certain that a German-speaking colony did really once exist at the head of the Hérens valley, for an extant document (in the St. Martin archives), dated 25 June, 1455, is a direction by the reigning Bishop of Sion that the parish priest of St. Martin should have an assistant priest, skilled in the German tongue, who was to live in the region above Evolena, if the priest of that village was unwilling to perform this duty.[24] This singular order is said by Ruden to rest on a written request made by the Zermatters, and dated 14 April, 1364. Unluckily these most interesting documents seem to have escaped the attention of the Abbé Gremaud. But such a colony would explain the placing of the Romance form of the name of our village at the head of the Hérens valley, even though it only appears there from 1589 onwards.

Another point of connexion between Zermatt and the Hérens valley

[24] The very curious Latin text is printed by Ruden, p. 145, n.: 'quod parochus s. Martini debeat habere unum capellanum idoneum et sufficientem, qui sciat linguam theotonicam in ecclesiâ, qui autem habeat suam moram in interiori de Evolenaz, simodo curatus ibidem facere nolet.'

may have been the annual pilgrimage to be accomplished by the priest of Zermatt and eight of his parishioners from Zermatt to Sion, there to pray in three churches to which stated offerings were to be made. The route taken on this journey is not fixed, but Pfarrer Ruden is of opinion that it lay over the Col d'Hérens. However that may be, the pilgrimage was commuted on 20 May 1666 into an annual procession to the nearer Täsch, this change being made by the reigning Bishop of Sion on the petition of the Zermatters, who urged the great difficulties encountered on the way to Sion. It was agreed in 1666 that the dues annually owed to the three churches of Sion should be retained (2 pounds for each church); but in 1816 this annual payment was redeemed on payment of a lump sum down, 120 pounds, this being done in 1816 in the days of Pfarrer Gottsponer, the host of the earlier visitors to Zermatt (curé of Zermatt from 1812 to 1839).

So much for the possible explanations of the position of the Romance name of our village on these 25 maps.

Here is a list of these 25 maps:

a. Fifteen giving both forms: 1589 (Mercator's map of Alpine Lombardy), 1594 (Metellus, Vallais), 1616 (Guler, W. Raetia), 1643 (Boisseau, Switzerland), 1644 (Du Val, Vallais), 1648 (Jansson, Switzerland), 1657–8 (Blaeuw, Switzerland), 1700 (Walk, Switzerland), 1703 and 1704 (Jaillot, both Switzerland), c. 1710 (Visscher, Switzerland), 1730 (Seuter, Switzerland), 1732 (Homann, Switzerland), 1740 (Lotter, Switzerland) and 1746 (Tillemon, Switzerland). I know of no later maps of this class with the Romance form in this curious position.

b. Ten giving only the Romance form: 1622 (Hondius, Savoy), 1642 (Boisseau, Savoy), 1648 (Jansson, Savoy), 1657–8 (Blaeuw, Savoy), 1686 (Cantelli da Vignola, Switzerland), 1703 (N. de Fer, Switzerland), 1714, 1730, and 1764 (the general Swiss map of the earlier editions of the *Délices de la Suisse*, which is also given in those of 1776, 1778, and 1804), and 1723 (Scheuchzer, Switzerland, in his great work). (We have noted above that one map, that of Septala, 1584, places the name *rightly*.)

Now we must go on to examine the exact forms assumed by this name on these 25 maps (dated before 1775). Here we find an almost bewildering variety, which can be best classified under three main heads, with subdivisions.

    i. IMPRABORNO or IMPRABORNA.

       (1) Impraborno—1589, 1622, 1642, 1648 (Savoy), and 1657–8 (Savoy).

       (2) Impraborna—1616, 1643, 1644, and 1657–8 (Switzerland). (The Impraberna of 1700 is probably a slip.)

       (3) Impraborn—1594 and 1648 (Switzerland).

    ii. INPRABERNA (second letter 'n')—c. 1710, 1714, 1723, 1730 (2 maps), 1732, 1740, 1746, and 1764 (with 1776, 1778, and 1804). Two variants are—1686 (Inn Prabera) and 1703, de Fer (Inn Prabern).

    iii. PRABERNA—1703–4 (both Jaillot).

To this list of 25 variants we must add those found on the 4 maps of the first set of six, which show a village at the head of the Hérens valley, as well as one at the head of the Sesia valley: 1690 and 1707 (Jaillot) and 1801 (Bourcet, really made before 1775) have 'Praberna', while 1751 (Jullien) has 'Proberna' (probably a mere slip).

It seems impossible to arrive at any generalization as to these various forms. We may note, however, the historical fact that the prefix 'Im' occurs on all the *earlier* maps, but is replaced by 'Inn' in 1686 and 1703 (de Fer), though this soon (1710) gives way to 'In'. The six cases without any prefix seem to be guesses at the truth.

II. THE GERMAN FORM (MATT, MATTEN, OR ZERMATT) DOWN TO 1775

Under this head matters are rather simpler, while in all cases the name (under whatever form it may appear) is rightly placed at the head of the Zermatt valley. First as to the forms under which it is given. Here again we find three main heads, each with several variants.

A. MATT (the oldest German form of all).

> *Texts*—1544 (Stumpf's Diary of his journey through the Vallais made in that year),[25] 1548 (Stumpf[26]), 1714,[27] 1730,[28] and 1764[29] (*Délices de la Suisse*, as well as the later editions of 1776, 1778, and 1804), 1768 (J. C. Fäsi[30]), and 1770 (J. C. Fuesslin[31]). In 1723 Scheuchzer (p. 303) has 'Mattia Vallis'.
>
> *Maps*—1495–7 (Türst, Switzerland), 1548 (Stumpf's special map of the Vallais, p. 338), 1768 (Walser, Vallais), and 1769 (Grasset, Switzerland).

The variant 'Matta' may be classed either with A or with B. It is found in 1574 in Simler's text,[32] and on the maps of Guler, 1616 (W. Raetia), of Du Val in 1644 (Vallais), and of Walk in 1700 (Switzerland). In 1760 Gruner's map of Switzerland marks, under no. 145, 'In Matt'.

B. MATTEN (the form most frequently found before 1775, but, as far as I know, on maps only).

> *Maps* (all of Switzerland unless otherwise stated)—1538 (Tschudi, most probably, for, though no copy of this first edition is known, this form appears on the second edition, 1560), 1555 (Salamanca), 1584 (Ortelius), 1589 (Mercator, Alpine Lombardy), 1594 (Metellus), 1643 (Boisseau), c. 1645 (Du Val, Savoy), 1648 (Jansson), 1657–8 (Blaeuw), 1690 (Jaillot and Danckerts, both Savoy), c. 1695 (Danckerts,

---

[25] Not printed till 1884 in the *Quellen zur Schweizer Geschichte*, vi. 256.
[26] p. 346.   [27] p. 716.   [28] *Ibid.* iv. 183.   [29] *Ibid.* iv. 174.
[30] *Staats- und Erdbeschreibung der schweizerischen Eidgenossschaft*, iv. 297.
[31] Similar title, iii. 321.
[32] *Vallesia*, p. 18. Scheuchzer, in 1723, copying Simler, does not reproduce this particular form.

a different Savoy map), c. 1700 (de Wit, Savoy), 1703, 1704, and 1707 (Jaillot, the two former Switzerland, the third Savoy), c. 1710 (two different maps by Visscher, one of Switzerland, and the other of the Upper Rhine), 1730 (Seuter), 1732 (Homann), 1740 (Lotter), 1746 (Tillemon), 1751 (Jullien), and Bourcet's (published in 1801 but made before 1775). On Jansson's map of Switzerland the name is spelt rightly, but on that of the Vallais (same date and maker) it is spelt 'Mattn', probably by a simple slip. Borgonio's map (1772 edition by Stagnoni) has 'Mathen'.

C. ZERMATT (slowly but surely coming to the front).

Text—1571 or 1579 (certain regulations as to the common lands or 'Allmend' of the village). A. Heusler[33] gives the German text, with date 1571 and spelling 'Zermatt', while Ruden, p. 137, mentions the regulations, with the date 1579, but unluckily no name for the village. No doubt other early local documents also have the name, but this is the only one I know. That of 1571, therefore (in which the name occurs twice), is the earliest occurrence of the name as yet known.

Maps—1682 (Lambien's remarkable map of the Vallais[34]), 1712 (Scheuchzer's big four-sheet map of Switzerland), 1715 and 1730 (G. de l'Isle, two maps of Switzerland), 1730 (special map of west Switzerland in the *Délices de la Suisse*, iv, opposite p. 166—it is found also in the 1778 edition, but in none of the others), 1748 (Dheulland, Savoy, &c., here oddly placed to the north of 'Dasch' or Täsch), 1751 (Homann, Switzerland), 1756 (Robert de Vaugondy, Switzerland), 1760 (Rouvier, Switzerland), and 1762 (Rizzi Zannoni, Switzerland).

In 1768 Walser's map of the Vallais offers us the variant 'Zur Matt', coupling it with 'Matt'; it is followed in 1775 by Jäger's map of Switzerland, which spells 'Zurmat', and in 1791 by Albrecht's maps (nos. 417 and 418) of the East and West Vallais, that write 'Zur Matt'—in each case the name 'Matt' is also given. In 1791 Albrecht's general map (no. 416) of the Vallais and in 1798 Mallet's map of Switzerland give 'Zur Matt' *alone*. I know of no other cases of the adoption of this spelling and division of the name.

III. THE ROMANCE AND THE GERMAN FORMS USED SIDE BY SIDE

As far as I know this first occurs in 1777, which, roughly speaking, is the date of the visit of the first travellers to our village. We have seen above under I that the thirty-one (25+6)

---

[33] *Rechtsquellen d. Cantons Wallis*, Basel, 1890, pp. 374–5.
[34] Reproduced in the *S.A.C.Jahrbuch*, xl, opposite p. 264.

maps which give the Romance or (and) the German forms apply them, rightly or wrongly, to two distinct villages. In 1760 Gruner, indeed, employs both forms for our village, the Romance in his text and the German on his map, while under II I pointed out that Walser's Vallais map of 1768 marks two forms of the German name. But from 1777 onwards both Romance and German forms are employed, in texts or on maps, of one and the same village—that at the head of the Zermatt valley.

The number of the *Journal de Paris* for 23 May 1777 [35] speaks of 'une Vallée nommée *Praborgne*, en allemand *Zermatt*' (a phrase which from the context seems to be based on an actual visit), while in 1796 H. B. de Saussure, narrating his experiences of 1789 and 1792,[36] having quoted Gruner's phrase of 1760, writes, 'le village qu'il nomme *Paraborque* est celui que les Allemands nomment *Zer-Matt* et les Italiens *Praborn*'—the Romance form therefore, according to this author, was not then used *locally*, but only in Italy. In 1805 the second edition (the first edition, 1793, has nothing on the subject) of Ebel's *Guidebook*[37] says that our village was called '*Matt*, also *Zer Matt*, *Zur Matt*, and *Praborgne*', thus collecting all the names known for it; in the French translation of 1818 [38] we read, besides the three forms of the German name, the words 'en françois *Praborgne*', here 'français' is probably a general term for Romance, as the native language of the valley of Aosta is of course a kind of French. But in Daniel Wall's English translation (1818) of Ebel we hear simply [39] of 'the village of *Zermatt* (otherwise *Praborgne*),' though in the longer description [40] the Romance form only is used. In 1824 the map attached to Baron L. von Welden's book, *Der Monte-Rosa*, is the first map to give '*Zermatt* or *Praborgne*', and this example is followed by those of Wörl (1835), of Keller (1836 edition), and of Engelhardt (1840, 1850, and 1856). In 1833 an original English text (for 'Wall' is simply a translation) first writes, 'Zermatt, better known on the Piemontese (*sic*) side by the name of Praborgne.'[41] A few years later Brockedon again writes in the first edition (1838) of *Murray's Handbook for Switzerland*, &c., (p. 248), 'the village of Zermatt is known on the Italian side of the mountain as Praborgne,' and this information is confirmed in 1843 by Principal Forbes,[42] though in 1841 the first edition of Joanne's *Suisse* (p. 617) limits the use of the word, writing '*Zermatt*, que les habitants du val Tornanches (*sic*)

---

[35] See the phrase reprinted by me in the *Alpine Journal*, xxiii. 288.
[36] *Voyages dans les Alpes*, iv. 421, n.
[37] iv. 207.   [38] iii. 147, 620.   [39] p. 463.   [40] p. 384.
[41] W. Brockedon's *Excursions in the Alps*, p. 223. It is very odd that Archdeacon W. Coxe, otherwise so copious as to Swiss matters, never mentions—1779, &c.—our village either on his map or in his text.
[42] *Travels through the Alps of Savoy*, p. 311.

nomment *Praborgne*'. But the maps of later date than 1775, with the few exceptions noted above, prefer the single form 'Zermatt'.

It only remains for me to gather up a few crumbs of information, illustrating what may be called the transition period from 1775 to about 1820. The latest mention of 'Inpraberna', referring to a village at the head of the Hérens valley, is found on the *general* Swiss map of the 1804 edition of the *Délices de la Suisse* (which is simply an inheritance from the earlier editions from 1714 onwards), though the *special* map of west Switzerland (given in the 1730 and 1778 editions only) has 'Zermatt', while the text of all the six editions (1714 to 1804) names 'Matt' only. The *shorter* German form 'Matt' lingers on for some time after 1777 on the maps of Keller (1818), of Raymond and Jomini (both 1820), and of Sidney Hall (1828—the latest case on a map of which I know); it last occurs in 1842 in the *text* of A. Schott.[43] It is also last used, jointly with 'Zur Matt', on the maps of Jäger (1775) and of Albrecht (1791). But the *longer* German form 'Matten' has a still shorter life, for after 1777 I have found but one instance—and that spelt 'Matter'—on the general map (1827) attached to the official work entitled *Opérations Géodésiques pour la Mesure d'un Arc du Parallèle Moyen*. The quaint form 'Zur Matt' occurs for the last time on a map on Mallet's Swiss map of 1798, and for the only time in a text in 1835.[44] Otherwise 'Zermatt' is more and more triumphant all along the line. The text of Wall (1818) is the latest which has 'Praborgne' only, later texts always combining that name with Zermatt. An early post-1777 *text* which gives 'Zermatt' in some form is that of M. T. Bourrit, 1781,[45] which has 'Zermatten', like Abraham Thomas in 1795,[46] though he has the variant 'Tzermatten'[47], like Murith in 1803.[48] H. B. de Saussure (1796) prefers 'Zer-Matt',[49] Schiner in 1812[50] 'Zermat'—the very latest variant of 'Zermatt'. In 1820 P. C. Bridel[51] has 'Zermatt ou Praborgne' in his text, but 'Zer Matt' on his map annexed. Among the early post-1777 *maps* which give 'Zermatt' only are those of the 1778 edition of the *Délices de la Suisse*, Buache (1780), Zatta (1781), Laurie and Whittle (1798), Weiss (1798), and Bacler d'Albe (1799).

W. A. B. COOLIDGE.

[43] *Die Deutschen Colonien in Piemont*, pp. 29 and 39.
[44] M. Viridet's *Passage du Roth-horn*, p. 6.
[45] *Description des Alpes Pennines et Rhétiennes*, i. 115.
[46] See the reprint in the *Alpine Journal*, xxiii. 301, 302.
[47] *Ibid.* p. 303.   [48] *Ibid.* pp. 351–2.   [49] iv. 382–3, 420.
[50] *Description du Département du Simplon*, p. 271.
[51] *Essai Statistique sur le Canton de Vallais*, p. 110.

Reviews of Books

The Economic Principles of Confucius and his School. By CHEN HUAN-CHANG, Ph.D. (*Columbia University Studies in History, Economics, and Public Law*, nos. 112, 113. New York, 1911.)

THIS is a book which few men could have written, requiring as it does on the part of its author an intimate familiarity with the philosophical and historical literature of China, combined with a knowledge of the principles of political economy as recognized by European students. Mr. Chen, who evidently was well equipped for his work, has produced a great mass of valuable information. He is indeed too fond of building up a theory on some isolated statement which is too weak to carry the weight of the structure. Also, there are many passages in the Chinese classics, as to the meaning of which the great critics through all the intervening centuries have never been able to come to an agreement, and many historical and literary points the truth of which is similarly disputed; but Mr. Chen, having made up his mind one way or another, draws most important conclusions from his interpretation of these passages and facts, without letting the reader know that there is any doubt as to the correctness of the premises. He is an ardent Confucianist. He holds that Confucius was 'the founder of a religion', and carefully explains away the sage's own description of himself as 'a transmitter, not an originator, believing in and loving the ancients'. His whole book is much coloured by his feeling and belief on this point.

The reader will probably be most interested by the historical part of the work, the descriptions of the social life of the past with its duties and pleasures, and the narrative of the action of the government through successive ages in economic matters of all kinds. Here we are often confronted by a difficulty, past which the author generally fails to guide us. The Chinese statesmen of the last two thousand years have certainly been at least nominally Confucianists. But often their measures did not coincide with the views expressed by Confucius himself. Are such measures to be looked upon as developments or as infringements of Confucian principles ? For instance, Confucius was a free-trader and much more than a free-trader. He disapproved, Mr. Chen tells us, of all taxes but two, namely a land tax and a *corvée* of a few days' personal service each year. But there is hardly a conceivable tax that has not been imposed in China at some period or other since his day, external and internal customs duties, excise on many articles, income tax, poll tax, taxes on shipping, passengers, buildings, carriages, women's dowries, and what not.

Were these taxes right or wrong from a Confucianist point of view? We cannot say. The land tax was certainly the main impost of ancient China, and 10 per cent. of the produce was looked upon as the proper amount, to increase which was a great crime. It is interesting to note that Mencius, the greatest of the wise men who came after Confucius, disapproved not only of its being increased but also of its being reduced. To a statesman who boasted of levying only 5 per cent., he replied that this misplaced leniency would necessarily starve the government service. One gathers from this book that both in earlier and later times there were many statesmen and writers, who, though extremely unsystematic, were not wanting in either sound sense or economic knowledge. What could have been more apt than the remark, uttered nearly a thousand years ago, that when paper money was made on account of the heaviness of copper coins, it was a convenience, but when made because of the scarcity of coin, it was really an evil?

Mr. Chen is not easy to follow on the doctrine of *laisser faire*, about which the Confucianists appear to have differed in their opinions. But it is plain, at any rate, that the rulers of China have constantly practised state socialism, if that be the proper term for interference in the affairs of the people for the people's good. Of all measures of this class the most important is that known as 'equalizing the price of grain'. The main features of the scheme are that, whenever the price of grain falls below a certain level, stocks of it should be purchased by the state, to be resold when the price has risen again. The scheme has changed its name and has undergone modifications at various periods, has been at times neglected and at times enforced; but it was in existence long before Confucius was born, and has come down in some form or other to modern times. Mr. Chen holds that it 'has done immeasurable good to China' in the past, but that to-day, though it 'exists not only in name but in fact, it is not of great importance'. But as one never hears or reads anything about it at the present time, one may be pardoned for thinking that it must now be much more a name than a fact. Grain is not the only article in which the state has traded for the benefit of the people. In medieval times several attempts were made to treat commodities of all kinds in a similar way. The state became a kind of universal middleman, and purchased goods of every description whenever their price had fallen below a certain standard. But these attempts, as might be expected, were all failures and all short lived. One alone achieved a momentary success, which was due to the ability of its originator and the enthusiasm with which he was able to inspire his subordinates. Among minor measures for the assistance of the poor, one may mention loans of grain to farmers for the period between seed-time and harvest, gifts of grain in years of dearth, state pawnshops, and loans to those who had nothing to pledge, but could produce three guarantors. This last soon failed; for, when both the borrower and his backers had nothing, the government was unable to exact payment. As may be seen from what has been said, the reader will find in this book a great deal more than the dry bones of political economy.

T. L. BULLOCK.

The Greek Commonwealth; Politics and Economics in Fifth-Century Athens.
By ALFRED E. ZIMMERN. (Oxford: Clarendon Press, 1911.)

MR. ZIMMERN's object, as stated in his preface, is 'to make clear what Fifth-Century Athens was really like'. Whether the Athens of Pericles was in any sense the typical Greek commonwealth may be doubted, but, however that may be, Mr. Zimmern has produced an interesting and indeed a remarkable book. He has a vivid imagination, a singularly fresh and novel outlook, and an attractive style, which if somewhat journalistic yet often rises to eloquence. He is well acquainted both with the original authorities and the latest and most recondite modern research, and he is intensely interested in modern political and social problems.

The book is artistically divided into three parts: first we are given a section on the geography of the Mediterranean area and its influence on Greek life and character—a section full of ingenuity and insight. The author has made the best use of his travels in Greece, and seems to have found room for the whole of classical literature in the pocket which most travellers reserve for Baedeker. Part ii treats of the development of the Greek state from the earliest times to its culmination in the Athens of Pericles, and a translation of the Funeral Speech is appropriately appended as a climax. In this section Mr. Zimmern follows pretty closely the lines of Eduard Meyer's *Geschichte des Altertums*, but with a far greater wealth of illustration both ancient and modern. We note with surprise that the Delphic Oracle has resumed the place in which Curtius enthroned it, and in the chapter on law it is curious to find Draco summarily dismissed with six words when *I.G.A.* 112 is translated in full. The treatment of the rise of magistracies is characteristic of the whole section. We are not troubled with life-archons or decennial archons or the opening chapters of the 'Αθηναίων πολιτεία. ' Negligimus ista et nimis antiqua ac stulta ducimus.' A passage of Hesiod and the Herodotean parable of Deioces are much more satisfactory authorities. Part iii traces the development of trade and commerce as part ii traced that of politics, and a chapter on the Peloponnesian war forms an epilogue to the book. This section is of special interest as being the first presentation in an English dress of the labours of foreign scholars such as Guiraud and Francotte. Though obviously attracted by the economic side of history, Mr. Zimmern is too good an historian to commit the error, into which some have recently fallen, of making economics the measure of all things. He discusses the arts and crafts of Athens, slavery, population, foreign trade, sea power, and finance, and lays every ancient Greek and modern German writer under contribution. It is impossible to praise too highly the industry which has massed together so many authorities and the vivacious and attractive way in which the results are presented, but equally impossible not to feel that very little solid knowledge of ancient economics is attainable at present. The section as a whole, and especially the statistics, must after all be pronounced highly conjectural. In dealing with finance Mr. Zimmern follows Cavaignac perhaps more closely than is wise: the statement that ' the reserve funds of the goddess and of the Empire had been united by 440 ' (p. 404) is surely too precarious to appear in the text. In regard to slavery Eduard Meyer's views are largely adopted. Slavery was not the foundation of Greek life : slaves were 'fellow workers' trained by persuasion rather than compulsion, paid the same wages as free workmen, homogeneous with the free in character and spirit. We think that too much weight is allowed here to the *ex parte* statements of the pseudo-Xenophontic treatise, and the treatment of the slaves at Laurium scarcely accords with such a view. Mr. Zimmern devotes a chapter to the slaves at Laurium, but does not succeed in explaining the discrepancy. The admirable chapter on sea power deserves special mention.

A book of this kind, which seems to aim at the general reader and produces its effect by broad and vivid colouring, cannot be expected to show rigorous accuracy in detail, and we are inclined to be indulgent to slips and over-statements. But here the numerous footnotes make it difficult for Mr. Zimmern to claim such indulgence. Many of his statements need justifying notes, and many, we fear, no note could justify. Thus we are told on p. 137 that Solon threw open the nine archonships to all but the poorest class of citizens ; p. 144 that the first-class members of Phratriai were known as γεννῆται, the others as ὁμογάλακτες or ὀργεῶνες ; p. 142 that the Naucraries each supplied one sailor to each unit of the fleet ; p. 148 that the four Ionic tribes and all their associations disappeared for ever after Cleisthenes ; p. 151 that the demes were an entirely new creation ; p. 168 that the strategi were elected out of the whole body of the people ; p. 168 that civil cases in cities of the Delian League were heard at Athens if they involved a sum of more than ten drachmae. This last statement, incredible in itself, is derived from an unfortunate note in Meyer, who refers to the well-known decree about Hestiaia (*C.I.A.* i. 29 and iv. 12) ; but Hestiaia was a cleruchy, and we cannot extend its arrangements to allied cities. These examples are by no means exceptional, and we cannot help thinking that had Mr. Zimmern devoted to the explanation of such statements the space in his notes now encumbered by digressions, he would have improved his book.

This brings us to the most salient peculiarity of the book, its audacious modernity. The most modern terminology is used whenever possible ; the two Xenophontic treatises are consistently referred to as ' Old Oligarch ' and ' Ways and Means ' ; the popular assemblies become ' Parliaments ', the πρυτάνεις τῶν ναυκράρων a ' General Purposes Committee ', the κατωνακοφόροι ' Woolly Bears ', the ἐπίσκοποι of the Athenian empire ' Imperial Bishops '. How Mr. Zimmern could quote Polyb. ii. 15 and resist *en pension* and *à la carte* we cannot understand. Modern writers and modern parallels are quoted with bewildering profusion : in the index of modern authors we find some strange bedfellows—Busolt and Charles Booth, Wilamowitz, Wilhelm and H. G. Wells, Pauly-Wissowa and *Punch*, share compartments. But the entries under the letter G are even more characteristic of the book and deserve quotation in full : ' Gallio, Gardens, Gaza, Geishas, General Purposes Committee, Gibraltar, Giotto's Campanile, Gipsies, Goats and Goat pasture, Gorillas, Gortyn, Laws of, Gramophones.' ' Nihil humani alienum ' Mr. Zimmern may say with truth, but we have sometimes felt in reading his book that it is overloaded with such things, and that the digressions of which he goes in search confuse rather than elucidate the issue. We have here in fact a new kind of Greek history: hitherto the Greek has been to us a somewhat remote and statuesque figure: we have certainly never attempted any familiarities with him. But Mr. Zimmern brings him down from his pedestal and establishes the most free-and-easy relations with him. He shows us the everyday Athenian, the ' man in the street ' haggling in his shop hard by the Agora, toiling in his smithy or tannery or stone-cutter's yard, his house without drains, his bed without sheets or springs, his rooms as hot or as cold as the open air, only draughtier, his meals that began and ended with pudding. We have to ' think away railways and telegraphs and gasworks and tea and advertisements and bananas '. No man is a hero to his own valet, and we are even allowed to enter the Greek bedroom and note the absence of any washing arrangements. This sort of writing might seem to historians of an older school irreverent and undignified, but it is certainly entertaining and suggestive. Mr. Zimmern has succeeded in saying a surprising number of things that have not been said or thought of before, and has said them well. Students will find his book most stimulating, though they should be on the look-out for places where the ground is less solid than it seems, while the most jaded teacher of Greek history will read it with unabated interest and infinite refreshment from cover to cover. H. J. CUNNINGHAM.

The Amazing Emperor Heliogabalus. By J. STUART HAY. With Introduction by Professor J. B. Bury. (London: Macmillan, 1911.)

PROFESSOR BURY writes in his introduction that Mr. Hay ' has done history a service in making Elagabalus the subject of a serious and systematic study '. We do not know if he had read the book in manuscript or proof before writing these words, but we are very sure that it does not reach the standard which he would himself set for a ' systematic study ' of so remarkable though so brief a reign; nor are the views of Professor Bury easy to reconcile with those of Mr. Stuart Hay. Neither, indeed, has much that is complimentary to say of Christianity. Professor Bury ' suspects that, if the religion which was founded by Paul of Tarsus had, " by the dispensation of Providence," disappeared, giving place to one of those homogeneous oriental faiths which are now dead, we should be to-day very much where we were ', and is at any rate sure that ' the Christians were not conspicuous as a sect of extraordinary virtue ', and that ' the notion that the poor Greeks and Romans were sunk in wickedness and vice is a legend propagated in the interest of ecclesiastical history '. This is hardly the impression which one derives from reading Mr. Hay's glowing descriptions of the ' wonderful and beautiful age, full of colour, full of the joy of living ', when ' the Roman world sinned and sparkled ', being filled with the ' spirit of philosophic paganism, a spirit whose morality does not consist in improper thoughts about other people, but in a mind set free from terror of the Gods '. Indeed, the chief object of Mr. Hay seems to have been to draw a picture, as highly coloured as possible, of the most typical figure of the society in which Gannys and Comazon and Hierocles and Zoticus played prominent parts. In Heliogabalus, he writes, 'the glow of the purple reached its apogee;' and it is rather as a word-painter than as an historical critic that he merits attention. He professes himself 'deeply indebted to Mr. Walter Pater, Mr. J. A. Symonds, and Mr. E. E. Saltus for many a *tournure de phrase*'. We confess that the last-named writer was unknown to us; nor do the extracts from his 'vivid and beautiful studies on the Roman Empire and her customs' contained in Mr. Hay's book strike us as worthy to be placed in the same rank with the prose of Pater and Symonds. Still, we like them better than Mr. Hay's own 'journalese'.

As a piece of historical research we cannot speak very highly of Mr. Hay's study. One who writes of 'the Collegio (*sic*) Fratrum Arvalium' is hardly likely to prove an adept in the manipulation of inscriptions. If it be true that Severus Alexander was promoted from the rank of Caesar to that of Augustus before the death of Elagabalus, the fact shows how untrustworthy and incomplete our literary record is, and for that reason deserves examination. But the statement (p. 146) that 'on no coin does Alexander appear with the imperial insignia (the laurel wreath) before the month of March 222, though the titles which he received at his adoption—Augustus, Imperator, and Caesar—are frequently used before that date, because Antoninus never had the least objection to other people using titles, so long as he kept the power' needs a great deal of explanation. Mr. Hay has, however, done good service in examining and furnishing corrected readings of certain coin-legends upon the insecure foundation of which theories had been built regarding the renewals of the emperor's *tribunicia potestas*. The most important thesis of the book (could it be established) is that Elagabalus made a genuine attempt at religious reform—a thesis apparently commended to our favourable consideration by Professor Bury, who writes that 'after Mr. Hay's investigation it will be recognized that this emperor made, according to his lights, a perfectly sincere attempt to benefit mankind'. The scheme of the boy-priest, it would seem, was to amalgamate all the other cults under the supremacy of the emperor and thus check 'the disintegrating tendency of the mystical and independent monotheisms'.

Had Elagabalus lived (writes Mr. Hay); had the beauty and impressiveness of his Semitic ritual made its way; had time been given for men to grasp his idea of one vast beneficent, divine power, with the Empire of whose central authority men might escape from the thousand and one petty marauders of the spirit world, they might have been attracted to the worship of life and light instead of enmeshed by the seductive force of obscure and impossible dogmas, tempted by the bait of an elusive socialism and a problematical futurity.

Here we have a reference to Mr. Hay's *bête noire*, Christianity. We doubt whether the painted boy, who caused the gods of ancient Rome to bow before his fetish, had any such conceptions of the godhead. Mr. Hay speaks more truly in the following words: 'Antoninus thought to make his God great by means of a pompous show. He succeeded in presenting him as a low comedian in the last act of a puerile melodrama.' So thought Rome, and the *damnatio memoriae* which befell the emperor overtook the fetish also. And Rome was right. H. STUART JONES.

S. KRAUSS. *Talmudische Archäologie.* 2 vols. (Leipzig: Fock, 1910, 1911.)

THE archaeological material buried in the Babylonian and Jerusalem Talmuds has more than a merely Jewish interest. It concerns, indeed, mainly the life of the two divisions of the Jews, those living in Mesopotamia and those of Syria, in the early centuries of the Christian era, but it is also invaluable to the student of the New Testament, with which an important part of the literature is contemporary. Moreover, since the east, if not unchanging, at any rate changes with difficulty, many of the customs and objects of daily life described in the Talmud may be taken as representing Jewish life in Old Testament times, at least as far back as the Exile. The subject has been treated before, for instance by Hamburger, Zunz, and Löw, to mention only a few names, but Hamburger's *Real-Encyclopädie* is disappointing, while Zunz and Löw deal (admirably) only with special departments of the subject. Consequently scholars have been obliged to note down for themselves, in the course of their reading, the passages bearing on particular points in which they were interested. In the present work Dr. Krauss has done this for us by making a systematic analysis of everything in the Talmud relating to what the Germans call *Realien*. The difficult task of dealing with so large a mass of literature, and of disentangling the facts from obscure and often hardly intelligible statements, could only have been undertaken by a scholar thoroughly versed in the language and spirit of Jewish tradition, as Dr. Krauss has long been known to be. It generally happens that when any one has immersed himself in the subject, his mind becomes so much infected with the Talmudic method (or lack of it) that his work is almost as difficult to use as the original documents. Hamburger's *Encyclopädie* is a case in point. Dr. Krauss has successfully escaped this infection. Though, as professor at the Israelitisch-theologische Lehranstalt at Vienna, he has been mainly engaged with the subjects of Jewish tradition, he is also at home with western methods and western interests. The result is a book clear, precise, well arranged and well expressed, for which we have nothing but praise. The text is intended to be readable as a continuous description for scholars generally : the notes and references are put together in the second half of each volume, for the use of specialists. The notes not only contain discussions of the Talmudic passages, but also cite other Rabbinical and Syriac literature, classical authors, recently published papyri (e. g. those of Tebtunis and Elephantine) and Babylonian documents from the code of Ḥammurapi onwards. The learned author is thus well abreast of modern scholarship, and has neglected nothing which can throw light on the details of his subject. He further illustrates it by observations made in the course of his own travels in Egypt and Palestine, and by pictures of objects obtained in various excavations. His quotations of parallel Greek and Latin terms will make the work useful to classical students, who may be surprised to find how many of such terms have been adopted into the language of the Talmud, showing the extent to which the Jews, about the time of Christ, were influenced by Hellenistic and Roman culture. The work thus throws considerable light on the life of a Roman province, and even on its language, under the empire. An excellent instance is the account of baths and bathing in vol. i, pp. 209–32.

The first volume deals with dwellings and buildings, furniture and domestic pursuits (food, &c.), clothing and adornments, washing, medicine; the second with family life (mourning, slaves, animals), agriculture, industries (weaving, pottery, &c.), trade (travelling, weights and measures, time). Each chapter is preceded by a good bibliography, and is subdivided into a number of sections, so that particular points are not hard to find. The sixty-four illustrations are not always very satisfactory, and are generally not described fully enough to show their relevancy to the text. There is at present no index, or list of abbreviations. The preface does not show whether the work ends with vol. ii, so that perhaps we may yet hope for an index volume, which would greatly add to the usefulness of the book. In the immense mass of details collected in the notes it is inevitable that some points should be open to criticism. In vol. i, p. 272, n. 50, the usual account of the origin of σκηνή may not be very satisfactory, but it can hardly be derived from the Semitic root *ikn*. In vol. i. 281, n. 117, Petrie's *Researches in Sinai* might have been quoted rather than the German translation of Palmer, and the account of the legendary *Shamir* is rather inconclusive. There is no need to suppose that it was either a diamond drill or a stone hammer. In vol. i. 81 the Semitic *kad* may be the original of κάδος, but surely neither has anything to do with the Arabic *ḳâdûs*, which is a common word, not peculiar to Gaza, as suggested in the note. Vol. i. 493, 599, 'mixed pickels' are not customarily served as a hors-d'œuvre in England. There are several slips, in English quotations especially, as *iquite* (i. 433, 129) for *ignite*; *key-stonetter* (i. 301, 257, where it might have been mentioned that *ardîkal* occurs in the Elephantine papyri, so that the derivation from Assyrian *arad êkal* is very probable); Herford's book is quoted as *The Christianity in the Talmud* (i. 508, 715, and often); other misprints are *ahnlich* (i. 493, 599) for *ähnlich*; *acqua* (i. 432, 119) for *aqua*. Vol. ii. 504, 769, the reading *kebhes* in the Elephantine papyri is now quite abandoned in favour of *krš*, and the parallel with *kesiṭa* and LXX ἀμνῶν must therefore be given up. But these are unimportant details and do not lessen the value of the book, which does credit to the author and to the Gesellschaft zur Förderung der Wissenschaft des Judentums, under whose auspices it is published.   A. COWLEY.

The Cambridge Medieval History. Vol. I. *The Christian Roman Empire and the Foundation of the Teutonic Kingdoms.* (Cambridge: University Press, 1911.)

THOUGH all students of history must regret the fact that the name of Professor Bury appears only on the title-page of this work, the editing has fallen into capable hands, and the general result may be described as a great success. The system pursued is that by which, as the preface puts it, 'in every chapter a specialist sums up recent research upon the subject.' The advantages and disadvantages of this method of writing history by a committee of experts are so obvious that it is hardly worth while to dwell upon them. Against the loss of the consistent and unifying conception of a single mind may be set the claims of modern specialization and the undeniable satisfaction of reading the *ipsissima verba* of one who is a recognized authority in his subject. Here the dangers of inconsistency and contradiction have been successfully avoided. In one matter, however, that of repetitions, we cannot but think that rather more severe editing would have saved space which must always be valuable in a work of this kind. The battle of Hadrianople was a striking event, though, perhaps, ultimately not more important than the battle of Cannae, to which it is compared. But three descriptions of it, by three separate writers, within fifty pages, seem superfluous. Nor is this an isolated example. The events of the reign of Theodosius I are narrated by Mr. Norman Baynes in chapter viii, but a number of them (e. g. the massacre of Thessalonica and the battle of the Frigidus) are repeated by Dr. Schmidt in chapter ix, the subject of which is 'The Teutonic Migrations'. In the same way the story of the rise of Odovacar in 476 is told by Mr. Barker in chapter xiv, and repeated immediately after with slight variations by Professor Dumoulin.

The twenty-one chapters of the volume fall into two classes. In the first place there are the historical narratives, for which Professor Gwatkin, one of the editors, and nine other writers are responsible. We are not told, by the way, whether the contributions of foreign scholars (Dr. Bang's chapter on the Teutons and Professor Pfister's on the Franks deserve special notice) are translations. If so, they are remarkably well done. These excellent narratives afford little occasion for criticism, and we can only mention a few points that have occurred to us. In the first chapter 'Donatist' is frequently used without any explanation of the origin of the name, though this may be found elsewhere in the book, but not any definite account of the bishop himself. When we come to the fifth century we miss any attempt to explain and insist on the importance of Ravenna, and, we may add, of the other subordinate capitals such as Milan and Trier, or even Rome, the re-fortification of which at the beginning of the fifth century is barely mentioned (p. 264). We note that Dr. Schmidt (chapter xi) describes the story of the invitation of the Vandals into Africa by Bonifacius as 'a fable', 'invented to veil the real reason,' which was the collapse of the Roman administration. Dr. Hodgkin and Professor Bury have argued with some success on behalf of the authenticity of the traditional accounts of the relations of Aetius and Bonifacius, and in his well-written chapter (xiv) Mr. Barker agrees as to the fact, though he points out that the contemporary, Prosper Tiro, says that both Bonifacius and his opponent appealed to the Vandals. We almost wonder that he has not applied to it his interesting but, perhaps, rather fanciful theory of the influence of the later romances on history, for 'the fifth century was the age of the erotic novel' (p. 398).

Professor Dumoulin's remark, that the one authority which emerged victorious from the struggles which followed Theodoric's failure to found an Italian kingdom was the Papacy, suggests to us that, with the exception of a few words by Mr. Barker (p. 395), sufficient emphasis is not laid on the fact that the centre of political gravity in this age was predominantly in the Eastern Empire—a result to which the abandonment of Rome as the governmental capital must have contributed. The same writer calls attention to the renewed importance of the Roman senate and consulate in the fifth century,—an instance of the vitality of institutions with a great history, even under adverse conditions, provided that their deep roots be not cut. By the way, in his description of the costume of the consul (derived, apparently, from Cassiodorus, *Variae* VI. i. 6), we are told that 'a spreading cloak hung from his shoulders' (p. 445), which is hardly the impression one would have gained from the well-known representations on the ivory diptychs. Possibly something has gone wrong in the translation.[1] M. Dumoulin cannot believe that a third part of the land of Italy was really given to the Gothic followers of Theodoric: it was only the *ager publicus*, the state lands, of which a third was assigned to the barbarians (p. 447). This theory does not appear to us to agree with the evidence, vague as much of it is. The point of the well-known passage in Cassiodorus is that Romans and Goths were neighbours all over Italy, and in that sense shared the same lands;[2] and the system seems to have been analogous to that of the settlement of the Visigoths in Aquitaine, where we are told that, on the principle of the Roman quartering of troops, the Roman landowners were obliged to give up two-thirds of their land to the conquerors (p. 287), so that here the *tertiae* belonged to the original owners and not to the intruders as in Italy. This difference would be due to the relatively larger numbers of the Visigoths as compared with the Ostrogoths, and will take away something of the force of the objection that Theodoric's soldiers were not sufficiently numerous to occupy a third part of the land in Italy.

Undoubtedly the most important sections of the book are the eleven chapters which treat of general subjects outside the scope of historical narrative. Several of these have been entrusted to authorities of the first rank. Thus Professor Reid deals with the constitution of the reformed empire, Professor Gwatkin with Arianism, Professor Haverfield with Roman Britain, Professor Vinogradoff with the social and economic conditions of the age. Other names, too, such as those of Mr. C. H. Turner, Dom Butler, and Professor Lethaby, suggest high qualifications to write on church organization, monasticism, and Christian art respectively. Some of these chapters deserve a more complete treatment than is possible in the pages of this Review, and here it is obvious that we must be content with very brief notices. Professor Reid's account of the reorganization of the empire supplies a much needed summary of the administrative and military system developed under Diocletian and his successors. The chapter is a masterpiece of compression combined with lucid exposition, and has just that certainty of touch which inspires confidence in the reader. There is little or no room here for criticism. Two things strike us as being of special value : the comparison of the old with the new provincial administration, and the account of 'the greatest military reform introduced by the new monarchy '—' the construction of a mobile army ' which replaced, and more than replaced, the Praetorian Cohorts. By the way, to talk of the Praetorian Guard in the time of Julian,

[1] The words of Cassiodorus are : 'Pinge vastos humeros vario colore palmatae.'
[2] *Var.* II. xvi. 5 : 'Istis praediorum communio causam videtur praestitisse concordiae.'

as Dr. Lindsay does (p. 104), seems to be an anachronism. Another section looked forward to with great interest is Professor Haverfield's sketch of Roman Britain. It is only fourteen pages long, but here again we feel the touch of a master hand. With that ease which comes of profound knowledge of the evidence, and an almost excessive scrupulosity not to go beyond it, he describes the geographical conditions, the story of the conquest, the army of occupation, the extent and character of Roman civilization, the systems of communication by land and sea (why is Ermine street not mentioned among the roads ?), and, finally, what is known about the downfall of Roman power and influence. Professor Haverfield's section is supplemented by Mr. Beck's excellent story of the Saxon Conquest. We may notice in passing one of those slight discrepancies which inevitably occur in a work of this kind. To Professor Haverfield the 'Saxon Shore' of the *Notitia Dignitatum* is a system of coast defence so called from the assailants. Mr. Beck suggests, though he does not commit himself to, the view that it may have derived its name from Saxon settlers as early as the fourth century.

Professor Vinogradoff's chapter on the social and economic conditions is full of striking views and interesting facts presented with extraordinary freshness. His answer to that fundamental question, Why did civilization decline under the empire ? may be summed up in the word 'degeneration'. The extension of Roman culture led to its corruption and, in some cases, its suppression by the inferior standards of imperfectly assimilated populations. But it is well pointed out that the fourth and fifth centuries presented features of renovation as well as of decline. Slavery as known to the ancient world disappeared, and the moral authority of the Christian church enabled it to exercise influence both in the social and the economic sphere.

A good deal of space is devoted to the history of religion ; on the one hand the conflict between Paganism and Christianity, and on the other the internal development of Christianity itself. Dr. Lindsay's striking chapter on 'The Triumph of Christianity' gives a sketch of the new paganism which was the real rival of Christianity, and there is much to the point in the Rev. H. F. Stewart's account of the 'Thoughts and Ideas of the Period'. We would suggest with all deference that Dr. Lindsay writes rather too exclusively from the standpoint of victorious Christianity. At times we almost seem to detect the tone of the pulpit. If it be true that early Christianity taught that 'everything that made man's life wider, deeper, fuller, . . . could be taken up into and become part of the Christian life' (p. 96), we can only say that it is unfortunate that the results for culture were so poor. We cannot forget that other aspect of the case, stated, perhaps with exaggeration, by Mark Pattison when he described the triumph of the church as, to the humanist, 'the saddest moment in history' (*Memoirs*, p. 96). This is a vast subject, and we must content ourselves with referring to two points of view (we do not say that they are the only points of view) which we rather miss in these discussions. One is the idea, so forcibly stated of late by M. Cumont,[3] that Christianity won its way in a world which already agreed with it in certain fundamental

[3] *Les Religions Orientales dans le Paganisme Romain*, 2nd ed., preface.

conceptions. As M. Anatole France has put it : ' Le christianisme ne put se substituer au paganisme qu'au moment où le paganisme vint à lui ressembler et où il vint à ressembler au paganisme.'[4] The other is the fact that while neo-paganism and the oriental cults went down before the superior force of Christianity, the real vitality of paganism is to be found in the rural worships of the powers of nature—that religion of the country folk of which we hear so little, but which so long maintained itself in one form or another, and can hardly be said to be quite extinct to-day.

Professor Gwatkin's chapter on Arianism is everything that we should expect from such an authority. Miss Gardner has also been successful in making interesting reading of an unattractive subject—the religious controversies of the fifth century, Nestorianism and the rest. If we must make a criticism it is that, while the *Henoticon* and other documents are fully described or quoted from, there is no account of the contents of Pope Leo's *Tome*. The important subject of monasticism has been assigned to the well-known specialist, Dom Butler, who has produced a compact and well-written chapter. He has, perhaps, rather ignored the darker side of the Egyptian monks of the fifth century ; but though a professed Benedictine can hardly be free from some prejudice, he has given an impartial account of eastern monachism, and we have never seen better stated the debt of western civilization to his order when, at a critical time, its monasteries ' became object-lessons in disciplined and well-ordered life, in organized work, in all the arts of peace, that could not but impress powerfully the minds of the surrounding barbarians, and bring home to them ideals of peace and order and work, no less than of religion '.

A portion of the book to which many will turn with interest is Mr. Turner's chapter on the organization of the church. Very high praise has been bestowed upon it by a great authority, who has described its treatment as classical and its conclusions as inevitable. It will be interesting to see what other scholars have to say about it, for this is eminently a subject for specialists. Like Professor Harnack, though from a rather different point of view, Mr. Turner is a strong ' episcopalian '. For him the original and essential elements of a Christian community are ' a bishop and his people ' ; and the history of church organization is simply the process of differentiation of functions by which a hierarchy of clergy was developed to meet the needs of more complex conditions. That all this is presented with skill and knowledge of a very high order goes without saying. That it takes the form of statement rather than of discussion is, perhaps, inevitable ; but we feel suspicious that, at times, there is a tendency to evade or glide over difficulties. No doubt Mr. Turner is right in saying that the higher ministry of the earliest times was not local but ' apostolic '. But when we ask ' how the supreme powers of the general ministry were made to devolve on an individual who belonged to the local ministry ', we are told that the problem is outside our investigation, and ' we have only to recognize the result '. Yet that question is fundamental to Mr. Turner's theory—a theory based, apparently, on the

[4] *Sur la Pierre Blanche*, p. 177.

statements of Theodore of Mopsuestia (p. 156) which Harnack does not accept as historical.[5] And again, we do not feel that the account of the *sacerdotium*, its origin and development, is perfectly clear or consistent. The latter part of the chapter is occupied with very valuable sections on the councils, the relations of 'the three great sees', and the origins of church law. The treatment of the creeds is almost too short to be quite satisfactory. We should have thought, for instance, in view of the amount of modern discussion, that more might have been said about the Apostles' Creed. And in describing how the original Nicene Creed was superseded by that of Constantinople it might have been well to explain how they differed. The text of the Nicene Creed is, however, given in full by Professor Gwatkin in his chapter on Arianism.

One chapter is of a peculiar character: as the preface confesses, it contains 'very little history'. This is 'The Asiatic Background', by Dr. Peisker of Graz, which is intended to introduce us to the Huns and other central Asian invaders of Europe. It provides quite the most fascinating reading in the book, and treats, sometimes at length, such a wide range of subjects as the soil and climate of central Asia, the manner of life and religious beliefs of the Turkomans, the virtues of 'kumiz', and the origin of domestic animals (accepting without reserve Hahn's theory of enclosures for sacrificial purposes, in spite of the serious objections to it). The last ten pages are history (after all, we are told nothing about the origin of the Huns), ending with a description of the effects of nomadism on eastern Europe, where it has 'transformed and radically corrupted the race, spirit, and character of countless millions for incalculable ages to come'. Were it not all so good, we might ask whether, from a business point of view, fifty pages are not too much to spend on the introductory part. Space must always be a consideration in a volume of this kind, and there were already subjects which might demand fuller treatment. The Roman and Barbarian codes of law are only mentioned incidentally; very little is said about the literature of the period; and there are serious omissions in the field of art. Frankly, in spite of many good points, we find Professor Lethaby's chapter rather disappointing. Possibly his instructions may be partly to blame for this, for the heading is 'Early Christian Art'. Fortunately, even in the fourth and fifth centuries, there is a good deal of art, and especially architecture, which is not religious; and we cannot accept as adequate any account of the age which entirely omits to notice those stupendous achievements in building, of such far-reaching influence—the Baths of Diocletian and the Basilica of Constantine. Some of the statements about Constantine's churches at Jerusalem are open to criticism. The 'hemisphere' described by Eusebius, which was clearly the apse of the 'Martyrium' basilica, becomes 'the dome-building over the tomb', which was really in a separate church, the rotunda known as the 'Anastasis'. Of the three buildings in Rome which we are told belong to the Constantinian age, the Lateran Baptistery preserves at the most the plan of Constantine's structure; S. Costanza no doubt belongs to the Constantinian age, the only question being whether, instead of being so late as 354 (as here suggested), it be not the work of the emperor

[5] *Mission and Expansion of Christianity* (2nd ed.), ii. 445 *seqq.*

himself; S. Agnese, as we see it, belongs entirely to a later age. The only Constantinian building which survived till our times—the apse of the Lateran Basilica, is not mentioned. There is a good account of the Catacomb paintings, but only abnormal specimens of Christian sarcophagi are described; and among the minor arts, to which a good deal of space is devoted, the finest of the ivories—the archangel in the British Museum—is omitted.

The volume concludes with bibliographies extending over some eighty pages. So far as we can judge they are of varying value. We are not told whether they are the work of the special writers, or of the editors, or of both; so that we do not know who is responsible for such an entry as 'Herodotus. Ed. Blakesley, J. W. London. 1854' (p. 660). Some of them (e. g. those on church organization and art) strike us as curiously meagre in their list of modern works, but this is not a common fault. We may remark that a new and almost re-written edition of Harnack's *Mission and Expansion of Christianity* appeared as long ago as 1908. Some of the maps are valuable and interesting, but, if it was worth while to provide them in a separate case, they might have been on a more adequate scale. The book has been printed with great care. We have noticed only one error of importance—*Campus Martii* (p. 419).

G. McN. RUSHFORTH.

The Early Norman Castles of the British Isles. By E. S. ARMITAGE. (London: Murray, 1912.)

THE appearance of this work affords a convenient opportunity for reviewing the remarkable reaction from those theories of Mr. G. T. Clark, which were formerly accepted without question, but which are now completely discredited in the eyes of competent students. The subject of early castles is of direct interest to historians, not only for its bearing on Norman rule, but also in connexion with the origin of the borough; it further affords a striking illustration of the risk that historians incur by accepting the theories of a specialist without investigating their truth. That Mr. Clark's authority on castles was once unquestioned and supreme is shown by passages cited in my *Geoffrey de Mandeville* (1892), where I began by challenging his views on the meaning of *castellum* as applied to Newcastle, Rochester, and Arques. Two years later, in an article on 'English Castles',[1] I went further and assailed his fundamental theory, that the castles of the 'moated mound' type were all pre-Norman, by showing that the Normans undoubtedly constructed castles of this type, not only here, but in Ireland, that his own conclusions on their origin were confused and contradictory, and that they led one into grave difficulties. It is certainly a strange fact that Freeman, who saw clearly enough that the Normans introduced a new type of stronghold, was prevented, by the supposed necessity of accepting Mr. Clark's dogmas, from arriving at the right conclusion, and had to postulate as the castles of the Conquest ' the stern square tower . . . massive square keeps '.[2]

[1] *Quarterly Review*, July 1894.
[2] See my paper on 'The Castles of the Conquest' in *Archaeologia*, lviii, 1902.

Mrs. Armitage, as the readers of this Review may remember,[3] has laboured for years on the subject of this book, and has spared no pains to make her study as exhaustive and as accurate as possible. She claims as the result to have proved the theory that the moated mounds, 'the motte-castles, in the British Isles are, in every case, of Norman origin.' She adds, however, that she 'does not claim to have originated this theory', as the contention originated with me, and that she has only carried it ' a stage further and shown that the private castle did not exist at all in Britain until it was brought here by the Normans'. Now this betrays a confusion of thought which occurs throughout the book. What the writer really means is that the ' *motte*-castle ' was first brought here by the Normans—which she was the first to assert without reserve—but she treats these strongholds as essentially 'private' castles. Indeed, on p. 8, she defines them, at the outset, as 'the private fortified residences of great landowners', while a whole chapter is devoted to 'the origin of private castles', by which she means 'the motte-and-bailey castle' (p. 72). Now the well-known 'motte-and-bailey' castles, which the Conqueror raised at York to overawe the capital of the north, are duly assigned to him by her and are sufficient to dispose of the axiom that castles of this type were, of necessity, 'private.'

The fact is that, as she explains, Mrs. Armitage approached the subject from an independent point of view. What, in my opinion, led Mr. Clark astray was the phrase that a *burh* was *getimbrod*. Knowing that the mound castle had a timber stockade round its summit, he must have jumped at the conclusion that the *burh* was a mound. Freeman, Green, Sir James Ramsay, and Professor Oman[4] adopted this view without hesitation, and even Maitland saw, as they did, Edward the Elder and his sister raising 'mounds' for 'burgs'.[5] This is the view that Mrs. Armitage set herself especially to combat; the *burh*, she insists, was not a mound; it was 'a borough', 'a fortified town'. Unfortunately, she was led (she admits) to this conclusion ' by examining the Anglo-Saxon illustrated manuscripts in the British Museum', and the illustration which she reproduces, and which anticipates the conventional design on a borough seal, shows the danger of drawing conclusions from such vague evidence. Moreover, she herself speaks in one place of ' the word *burh*, which almost certainly referred to a vallum or wall', &c. (p. 243), and in another of ' the *burh* or enclosing bank' (p. 174). It is, however, her conception of the *burh* as a fortified town 'to shelter all the folk' that has led her to define the 'motte and bailey' as a 'private' castle. Its essence was that it was Norman; it was not of necessity 'private'.

One must not dwell too long upon the *burh* of Edward and Æthelflæd, in spite of its alleged bearing on the origin of the English town; but Mrs. Armitage seems too fond of assumption, she speaks of 'the thirty boroughs built (*sic*) by Ethelfleda and Edward', but Colchester, Towcester, and Nottingham were only repaired. Of Eddisbury the author has to admit that 'no town or village has ever grown out of it', and at Witham,

---
[3] See *ante*, xix. 209, 417 (1904), xx. 711 (1905).
[4] *Art of War in the Middle Ages*, i. 517.
[5] *Domesday Book and Beyond*, p. 186.

of which the evidence is very important, the area within the earthwork appears to have never been inhabited. The deliberate founding of 'fortified towns' is an unproved hypothesis; what the *burh* seems to have meant, under these rulers, was a fortified enclosure, which may sometimes have been intended only, like those on the Roman wall, for an armed camp. The moated and palisaded mound appears to have been the novelty introduced by Norman settlers on the eve of the Conquest; but it was not the only type of early Norman stronghold. The great 'tower' keeps of London and of Colchester were raised before the close of the eleventh century, and my view that their distinctive design indicates a common origin appears to be now accepted. The age of early 'tower' keeps has been so often exaggerated that one hesitates to accept the extant, though ruined, tower of Langeais as the actual work of Fulk Nerra in 994 (pp. 72, 353). Mrs. Armitage contrasts it with those of London and of Colchester, 'built', she writes with curious looseness, 'some seventy or eighty years later' (i.e. 1064–74). They are both, of course, later than this.

Considerably more than half the book consists of a detailed catalogue of the 'motte-castles' in England, Wales, Scotland, and Ireland, of which the English portion appeared, in a less complete form, in the pages of this Review.[6] Mr. George Neilson[7] and Mr. Goddard Orpen,[8] who have respectively done such valuable work on the mound-castles of Scotland and of Ireland, have assisted Mrs. Armitage for those countries, and the careful ground-plans to scale by Mr. Duncan Montgomerie, which must have entailed great labour, are a most useful feature of the work. The book should prove invaluable to writers on local topography who have to deal with a mound-castle, and who may not have studied the subject. One may venture to express regret that in what should have proved a definitive work there is too large a proportion of contradiction and error. The text tells us (p. 4) that on the summit of the mound was 'a small court, ... in rare cases as large as half an acre', while facing this statement there is a plan of Hedingham as a 'typical motte-castle' with a court nearly 300 feet by 400 feet on the alleged 'motte'. Moreover, we are told that at Old Sarum 'the area of the top of the motte is about 1¾ acres ... not larger than that of several other important castles'. Of the *burh* we read (p. 7) that the inner enclosure was sometimes large, '6 acres in the case of Witham;' yet on pp. 29, 39, we learn that 'the area of the inner enclosure was 9¼ acres'. Under 'Bourne' the author has confused the Lincolnshire Bourne of Oger the Breton[9] with the Cambridgeshire Bourn of Picot the sheriff,[10] and has applied the evidence relating to the latter to the castle existing at the former.[11]

In view of the importance of Winchester under the Norman kings, the author's novel theory that its *aula* or *domus regis* was no other than the castle (pp. 233–5) strikes me as a grave heresy. In *Geoffrey de Mandeville* I proved, from the Hyde cartulary,[12] that the 'palacium Regis cum aula

[6] See above, n. 3. [7] *Scottish Review*, October 1898.
[8] *Ante*, xxi, xxii. [9] D. B. i. 364 b. [10] D. B. i. 200.
[11] *Liber Memorandorum de Bernewelle*, p. 40.
[12] Published since as *New Minster and Hyde Abbey* (Hampshire Record Soc.), p. 1.

sua' was built by the Conqueror and burnt in the siege (1141). There is nothing more 'highly improbable' in the Norman kings having at Winchester both 'a palace and a castle' than there is in their having at their other capital Westminster palace and hall as well as the tower of London. The author has overlooked my paper on *The Origin of Belvoir Castle*,[13] and has consequently missed (p. 103) the important Domesday entry (i. 234) on Bottesford, which she calls 'Bottesdene'; 'Hastings Castle stood;' she writes, in 'the manor of Bexley' (by which she means Bexhill), but Domesday does not say so. Mr. Clark is charged with postulating a mound 'with his usual confidence' (p. 39), but Mrs. Armitage herself seems too ready to do so at Carlisle (p. 123) and Chepstow (p. 125).[14] My own suggestion that the 'Robert's castle' mentioned in the chronicle was at Clavering, Essex, where Robert Fitz-Wymarc was a man of power, has been twice explained by me;[15] but I am here (p. 192) made to suggest 'Canfield', with which Robert had nothing to do. So also the author claims to have arrived at my own conclusion as to Ewias Castle,[16] though it was the essence of that conclusion that Osbern Pentecost was *not* the ' son of Richard Scrob '. More serious, however, is the author's eagerness to detect the existence of a *motte* in every Norman castle, although they were not always present, while in some cases, as at Hedingham, the tower (like that of Rochester) stands on a platform rather than a *motte*. But this, of course, does not affect that rejection of Mr. Clark's theories which is the main contention. J. H. ROUND.

Päpstliche Wahlkapitulationen ; ein Beitrag zur Entwickelungsgeschichte des Kardinalats. Von JEAN LULVÈS. (Rom : Loescher, 1909.)
Die Machtbestrebungen des Kardinalats bis zur Aufstellung der ersten päpstlichen Wahlkapitulationen. Von JEAN LULVÈS. (Rom: Loescher, 1910.)

THESE two interesting and important lectures—forerunners of a larger work—are significant contributions to papal history. The later publication is the earlier in its historical setting; it traces the growth of the cardinalate from a purely local office associated with public worship to that of papal advisership. The eleventh century with its development of papal power gave an impetus to the growth of the college; the increase of consistories—Alexander III held them daily, Innocent III three times a week—and the use of formulae such as *de patrum nostrorum consilio* show the growing importance of the college, which has many analogies, Byzantine, ecclesiastical, and secular. Constitutionally the cardinals appear as representing the Ecclesia at large as well as being a purely Roman chapter: they might be the advisers of the pope, but they were also significantly the guardians of a rival doctrine which was certain to come into conflict with papal power; and yet their power in the first place

---

[13] *Ante*, xxii. 508.
[14] Mrs. Armitage now withdraws a *motte* she thought she had detected at Pontefract (*ante*, xix. 418 f., 1904). Excavation has disposed of the alleged *motte* at Pevensey, but she still detects one at Hastings.
[15] *The Castles of the Conquest*, p. 16 ; *Victoria County History, Essex*, i. 345.
[16] *Feudal England*, pp. 323-4.

grew with that of the pope. In this twofold relation to the papacy lies the explanation of much of the history of the college. They not only represented synods when these were not held, but on the secular side they inherited the jurisdiction of the *iudices palatini*.

The writer discusses the current use and exact meaning of the phrase *de patrum nostrorum consilio*. Much depended upon the personality of the pope; Boniface VIII, we are told, exacted their consent, and a diplomatic pope could easily play off factions against each other. It was convenient for opponents of the papacy, such as Frederick II, to emphasize the power of the college as a convenient and constitutional check upon the pope. An index to the varying relations of pope and cardinals is seen in the concessions given or promised (not always the same thing), which to begin with were mainly financial. The pontificate of Boniface VIII is an epoch in these relations, which are expounded in literature from both sides. But Boniface's claims made no lasting impression, and after the reign of Benedict XI even a powerful pope like John XXII was dependent upon the college; his very extension of papal jurisdiction and finance brought him into close touch with new interests everywhere, national and otherwise; for the working out of his plans he came to depend upon his cardinal helpers even if their advice was often only a form. In the following period French statesmen made use of the cardinals, and the dream of Frederick II—to control the pope by a majority of cardinals—was realized by France. The college also made its financial footing more certain, and thus we come to the first election capitulation—that of Innocent VI in 1352. But six months later, by the bull *Sollicitudo*, the pope released the cardinals and himself from their oath on the ground that the capitulation was inconsistent with the papal *plenitudo potestatis*. But the analogy with similar capitulations in cathedral chapters (forbidden as these, in spite of their frequency, had been by papal authority) was not suggested. Thus the cardinals gained no golden bull for themselves, as the imperial electors had done under analogous circumstances.

The second pamphlet deals with the capitulations themselves. During the troubled periods of the councils it was inexpedient to lessen in any way the papal power. In 1431 Eugenius III had to promise the confirmation by a bull of the agreement made by the cardinals in conclave with reference to the council. But there was no attempt to carry it out, and so the cardinals again failed to establish their definite control. The councils and the need of the crusade put off further attempts, but the advance upon the claims made in 1352 and 1431 should be noted. The nepotism of Calixtus III and his oppression of the cardinals made the college determined to safeguard their interests, and thus the election of Pius II in 1458 was marked by a new and more stringent capitulation. The support of the cardinals was secured (the monthly allowances, *piatti cardinalizj*, now appear), the need of their consent to new nominations of cardinals was decreed; once a year the college was to review the papal observance of the capitulation and enforce it if necessary by a triple admonition. But Pius II was able to ignore it; he insisted (as at Mantua) on his *plenitudo potestatis*, and he disregarded (as in the cases of Jouffroy and d'Albret, 1461) the wishes of the college about new nominations. The death of

Pius was followed by a capitulation made so stringent that it would have reduced the new pope, Paul II (1464), to a mere president of a governing board. But Paul modified the capitulation; experts comfortably assured him his oath did not bind him. In succeeding elections some important differences appear, and here M. Lulvès is able from his researches to add much to our knowledge. A hurried review cannot do justice either to the matter or to his presentation of it; the history of the capitulations (Paul III had no election capitulation) shows us not only the varying powers of pope and cardinals, but (as in the 'regenerated' capitulation of Julius III) the growth of a genuine wish for reform. The constitutional history of the papal government is often put too much on one side, and its theory as discussed in pamphlets and treatises of the day insufficiently studied. Thus special importance belongs to the capitulations, significant and sensitive as they were to variations of temperature, and our gratitude is due to M. Lulvès for his able and interesting elucidation of their history.
J. P. WHITNEY.

Studien aus der Florentiner Wirthschaftsgeschichte: Band II. Das Florentiner Zunftwesen vom vierzehnten bis zum sechzehnten Jahrhundert. Von ALFRED DOREN. (Stuttgart: Cotta, 1908.)

THE claims of Florence to take precedence over all other distinctively medieval cities seem to be meeting with fitting recognition from the scientific historians of Germany. The second volume of Davidsohn's great work[1], which has recently unfolded in masterly fashion the political history of Florence down to the days of Dante, is admirably supplemented by this second volume of Dr. Doren's, which completes his survey of the industrial and commercial organization of the republic in the two following centuries. In some respects Dr. Doren's work—the fruit of many years' devotion to the subject—must be regarded as the most important contribution that has yet been made to gild history, not merely because of the supreme degree of interest which the gilds of Florence in themselves possess, nor even because of the exhaustive research that has been spent upon them, but mainly on account of the insight which has been achieved into the complex organic structure of medieval urban civilization.

The essential body of Dr. Doren's work sets out from the definite establishment of the gild régime in Florence in 1289-93. Before this time the records of the gilds themselves are comparatively scanty, and the interesting discussion of the much-controverted references in other records, which occupies a long introductory chapter, has been, as the author himself anticipated, mainly superseded by Davidsohn's ample and authoritative treatment of the constitutional development of Florence during the thirteenth century. It was in the course of that development that three groups of gilds, representing more or less distinct sections of the *bourgeoisie*, emerged successively upon the political arena, and at its close the twenty-one gilds comprised in the three groups collectively dominate the arena and furnish the central framework of the Florentine constitution. The process through which this result is achieved was not peculiar to

[1] See *ante*, vol. xxvi. 371.

Florence. Its main features are to be found in the history of many of the leading cities of Europe, e.g. in Strassburg, Basle, and London, during the thirteenth century. The conflict of two dynastic factions is partly reinforced, partly confused, by the divergent class interests of two sections of feudal society; and this situation is further complicated by the rising importance of a growing civic population, which, whilst it has a strong potential unity of interest as against feudal anarchy, exhibits a wider divergence of class interests than feudalism itself. The endless permutations and combinations on this basis which diversify the political life of the larger cities in the thirteenth century facilitated not only the social intermixture by which caste was softened into class, but also the ready adaptation and transmission of social institutions through which the power of self-organization permeated the ever-widening circles of civic society.

The incorporation of gild structure in the civic constitution was a widespread, and indeed—in one form or another—almost universal feature of urban development in the middle ages. We are still very much in the dark as to how it came about and with what results; and the chief merit of Dr. Doren's book is that it casts a flood of light upon a leading case. It provides ample illustrations of the curious twofold relation of the Florentine state to the gilds, which served on the one hand as the instruments of its administrative authority and acted on the other as the powerful organs of the expanding and fluctuating social forces that controlled it. In this connexion chapter iv on ' Die Organe des zünftlerischen Willens', and more especially the section on the election of the consuls of the gilds, is of primary importance. The government of a gild was in the hands of a prior and a college of from three to a dozen consuls, who were assisted by an executive council, and must consult, in important matters, a general assembly. But the main weight of the administration lay upon the shoulders of the consuls, who corresponded closely to the wardens of a London livery company. (It is interesting, by the way, to find Dr. Doren entertaining the suggestion that in the consuls of trade gilds might be found the long-sought missing link with the Roman municipality.) For thirty years after the gilds had become organs of the constitution, the election of their consuls continued to be regulated by each gild separately, and the variety of electoral methods expressed a divergence in the social and economic character of the gilds. But the adoption of the lot in the choice of priors and other officers of the republic in 1323 was followed in 1328 by its application to the elections of the consuls of gilds, which thus fell under the uniform regulation and control of the civic authorities. This change, according to Dr. Doren, opened a way for the intrusion of party violence and corruption into the gilds, and the solemn formalities and safeguards of the lot did not prevent its wholesale manipulation, especially during the later struggles of the Albizzi and the Medici, by all parties in turn.

Closely related to this subject in their bearing on the interaction of society and the state are the questions of the civil and criminal jurisdiction exercised by the gild (chapters vi and vii), of its relations to individual members (chapter ii), of its internal social and economic structure (chapter iii), and of its relations with other gilds. The republic, like all cities with a gild constitution, was in effect a federation of self-governing communities whose rival interests and ambitions were backed by different and constantly varying degrees of social and economic influence. Most of the greater gilds, e. g. the *Calimala*, the *Arte di Lana*, the gilds of exchangers and notaries, represented the corporate solidarity of unified commercial, industrial, or professional interests, whilst many of the lesser gilds were fortuitous amalgamations of unrelated small trades drawn together by the need of social and political co-operation. Hence the *Zunftzwang*—the sanction of the state enforcing the gilds regulations—was from the first very unequally distributed. The greater gilds, which had been powerful organizations long before they entered the constitution, had acquired prescriptive rights of civil and even in some cases of criminal jurisdiction—the *Arte di Lana* had a private police of its own with knightly officers,—whilst a small trade was much more dependent on the intervention of the state and could only invoke it through the demand of one of the lesser gilds, of which perhaps it was a subordinate and ill-assorted member. It should be added that at Florence, as elsewhere, the autonomy granted to other trades was withheld from the victualling and building trades in the interests of the consumers.

Under these circumstances it is clear that the degree of power exercised by each of the gilds would depend on the degree of solidarity secured by its internal structure between the varied and continually shifting elements which it represented. In this respect each gild was faced with a different problem. The great wool gild, for example, was a ' vertical combination ' strong in its unity as an integrated and capitalized industry, but weakened by the labour problems which led to the *Ciompi* rising. Other gilds were ' horizontal amalgamations' of small traders. The *Por. S. Maria*, or mercers' gild, will serve as an example of an intermediate class. It consisted at first of the silk manufacturers and the retailers of cloth. With these in the first half of the fourteenth century were incorporated the goldsmiths and a number of inferior crafts such as the coverlet makers and the mattress makers, the members of which held a secondary rank in the gild, paying a smaller entrance fee and enjoying only restricted rights. Later on, however, as capital came to be applied to all these industries, the larger merchants and employers connected with them were placed on a level with the cloth dealers and silk manufacturers and formed a third section of the ruling body, whilst the lower ranks of the gild were occupied by the smaller masters and shopkeepers of all the trades and by the workers who had no active share in the organization. The play of economic forces, which was thus continually remoulding the structure of the gilds and shifting the balance of power between them, was further complicated by the expansion of Florentine rule over the *contado* and over other cities. The woollen manufacture came to depend very largely upon a widely scattered class of country workers whose interests were safeguarded by no political rights; and the ordinary traders and craftsmen in the suburbs, the territory, and the subject cities were brought under the control of the metropolitan gilds in a degree that varied with the conditions of each trade.

Of the technical aspects of gild regulation Dr. Doren gives a full account, as also of the conditions of entrance to the gilds, of their powers of legislation, of their military functions, their activities in administering religious and charitable foundations, and above all of their highly developed finance, in which, he considers, more than in any other feature, the gilds of Florence were distinguished from those of German cities. His account of the *Mercanzia*, which from acting as a kind of intermediary between the gilds and the state became during the fifteenth century a definite part of the state machinery, is of special interest and value. Along with so many merits the book has two defects: it has no index and its style occasionally recalls that of Immanuel Kant. GEORGE UNWIN.

Les Comtes de Savoie et les Rois de France pendant la Guerre de Cent Ans (1329–91). Par JEAN CORDEY. (Bibliothèque de l'École des Hautes Études, fasc. 189. Paris: Champion, 1911.)

THIS book contains a careful and scholarly, though not very animated, study of the relations between France and Savoy during the reigns of Counts Aimon (1329–43), Amadeus VI (1343–83), and Amadeus VII (1383–91). These relations are conceived in so wide a sense that the work is a substantial contribution to Savoyard history during all this period. M. Cordey has succeeded in discovering many new and precise details relevant to his theme, the most important of which come from the rich archives of Turin, and especially from the accounts of the financial Camera of Savoy there preserved. The whole work is a useful supplement to the general accounts of the early stages of the Hundred Years' War, and contains a side of the subject very scantily illustrated even in works so detailed as M. Delachenal's *Histoire de Charles V*. Though the counts of Savoy were nearly always on the side of the Valois, their jealousy of French advance, especially after the establishment of the future Charles V as the first French dauphin of Vienne, led to occasional approaches towards a good understanding with England. The result of this twofold process was that Savoy nearly always played a distinctive, if minor, part of its own at nearly every stage of that struggle. Nobles of Savoy, notably Godemard du Fay and Le Galois de la Baume, took a prominent part in the earliest phases of the fighting both in the Netherlands and in Gascony. Count Aimon himself was present in 1339 in the campaign of Buironfosse, and in 1340 in the campaign of the Tournaisis. Before taking part in these operations Aimon had to resist the attempts of Edward III and Lewis of Bavaria to win him over to the other side. He also made it a scruple of conscience to obtain from Philip VI a declaration that the vague homage which the counts of Savoy had paid to England since the days of Henry III did not preclude him from honourably bearing arms against the English monarch.

During the minority of Aimon's successor, Amadeus VI, the famous 'comte vert', Savoy showed a stronger disposition to listen to English offers. M. Cordey publishes some very interesting particulars of an English embassy to Savoy in 1345, and of a proposal to unite the two ruling families by marriage. In particular he prints an entirely unknown letter under Edward III's privy seal, preserved in the Turin archives, in which the English king lays down the conditions of such an alliance. He might have added from the *Calendar of Patent Rolls*, 1343–5, p. 450, that the prior of Lewes referred to in the letter was John de Jancourt, and that the king took advantage of his attending a chapter of his order at Cluny to send him on to Chambéry on this mission. Nothing came of it at the moment, and in 1346 Louis of Vaud, the count's kinsman, led a strong Savoyard contingent which joined Philip VI just too late to take part in the battle of Crecy, while Le Galois de la Baume continued to distinguish himself in the opposition to the English power in Languedoc. In 1351–2, however, Amadeus, already of full age, negotiated with Edward III for his marriage with the king's daughter, Isabella. Once more, however, French influence prevailed and the marriage of Amadeus with Bonne of Bourbon was followed by the renewal of active hostilities between England and Savoy, and preceded by the treaty of Paris which settled the long-standing differences between Savoy and Dauphiny. Under these circumstances we may hesitate to agree with M. Cordey that English noblemen helped Amadeus in his conquest of Faucigny in 1355. The evidence from the Turin archives quoted to prove this does, however, establish a hitherto unknown visit of so great a personality as Sir John Chandos to Chambéry, apparently in the early part of that year (p. 141). Anyhow, in the autumn of 1355 Amadeus in person led his troops to defend Picardy from the assaults of Edward III, drawing wages to the amount of more than 13,000 florins for very modest services (p. 152). The 'green count' was, however, more and more occupied in his judicious aggressions in his own neighbourhood, and less disposed to give either chivalrous or well-paid help to the French king.

After the treaty of Calais—M. Cordey should not call the treaty of October 1360 'the treaty of Brètigny' (p. 155)—we have no unfriendly relations between England and Savoy mentioned for a long time. M. Cordey prints from the Turin archives a letter of the Black Prince of 1365 ordering his men to do no damage to the lands of his 'dear cousin' of Savoy because of the great courtesy the count had shown to 'all our people passing through his lordships' (p. 330). A conspicuous example of such courtesy came in three years from the occasion of the marriage of Lionel of Antwerp with Violante Visconti, whose mother was the sister of Amadeus. Amadeus had already in April 1368 participated in the reception given to Lionel at Paris, and M. Cordey gives curious details of the shopping of the Savoyard prince on the occasion of his visit to the great city (p. 184). Amadeus afterwards royally entertained Lionel at Chambéry and accompanied him over the Mont Cenis as far as Milan. Despite all this Amadeus VI was again on the French side when war broke out again, and narrowly escaped taking part in the battle of Roosebeke. His son, Amadeus VII, the 'comte rouge', sent troops to resist Bishop Despenser's Flemish 'crusade'. This brief summary of Anglo-Savoyard relations may suffice to show the detailed character of M. Cordey's work, of which they are of course but a mere side issue. There is an excellent index, and a very valuable appendix of original documents.

T. F. TOUT.

La Crise Religieuse du XVe Siècle. Le Pape et le Concile (1418–50). Par NoËL VALOIS, Membre de l'Institut. 2 vols. (Paris: Picard, 1909.)

IT is needless to say more of this important work, in a notice too long delayed, than that it is by M. Noël Valois, and is just what we should expect from him. The narrative flows on as if there were no notes filled with criticisms and rearrangements of evidence; the notes tell their own story almost without the text, and yet the two fit in most exactly. The author has an absolute control of the sources, and yet the details are never allowed to obtrude themselves. The work is thus a model of literary art and of historical exactness. In reading it one is tempted to wonder why the period has so often appeared not only difficult but dull. M. Valois makes it appear quite easy, and he never suffers it to be dull.

A few points clearly made may be indicated here. Martin V did not ratify *all* the decrees of the council of Constance, either in his bull *Inter cunctas* of 22 February 1418 condemning Wyclif or in his declaration of 22 April 1418 upon Falkenberg and the Polish appeal; he dealt merely with isolated points. On the other hand, it is equally clear that the council did not seek confirmation for its decrees. The struggle between conciliar and papal supremacy remained therefore where it was, and remained for future settlement. The pope was prepared to call councils at the dates fixed for their meeting. But the place was a difficulty; he hesitated about the place fixed, Pavia, and as few came there, and an epidemic prevailed, Siena was chosen. Then the negotiations with the Siennese citizens are traced, resulting in their safe-conduct to the pope, which would have subjected the council to him. The muster here was not strong; the pope probably did intend to come in person, but the intrigues of Alfonso of Aragon and the endeavours of the French 'nation' for reform raised difficulties for him. Basel was named as the next place of meeting, and then the council, which never showed any signs of life, was dissolved. The papal policy was only occasional, and guided by circumstances; there was as little of greatness in it as there was in the debates of the council itself, but the small changes which moulded it are well and clearly traced. Martin V must bear the responsibility for the dissolution, but that responsibility is in any case small. 'The care of His church was left in the hands of God,' a pious reflexion which was as real as most other things at Siena.

Before Martin V died he had done much for the papacy, at Rome itself and elsewhere; he had even made a beginning with reform. But the question of pope against council, or (a solution better than anything else) their co-operation, still remained open. Little delays and small expedients, even excuses that had some reality, only put off the evil day. The election of Eugenius IV in 1431, 'self-opinionated like all Venetians,' was marked by an election capitulation which begins a new series. The cardinals were anxious as a college to have a full share in the papal government, and this each cardinal promised to give if elected in the matter of a council; the majority of the sacred college was to fix the place and time of its assembly. M. Valois rightly sees here the real distrust of the council by the cardinals. Then the state of Bohemia, which made Cesarini disinclined to take the responsibility of president, affected others besides the great cardinal. Thus matters moved towards the dissolution on 18 December 1431. But the council, which denied the pope's right to dissolve it, went on sitting. The sketch of the gradual change by which Eugenius was led to approve of the council's continuance (14 February 1433) is one of the most interesting parts of the work. 'The victory of the council' in 1433 follows—a result brought about largely by the growing hostility of the cardinals to Eugenius and the growing support given by the states of Europe to the council, now more largely attended; the strong and independent part played by Cesarini stands out. Two minor points may be mentioned to illustrate the thorough method of the author: the interesting identification of the unhappy Prior Thomas executed in 1431 in the Colonna plot (p. 107), and the discussion of the so-called bull of 13 September 1433, which was really a paper by Antonio di Roselli (pp. 252-60). The years 1434-5 form a truce between pope and council, but by their close an understanding between pope and council is impossible. By this time Cardinal Aleman is numbered among the enemies of the pope, and his career, so ably sketched of late by Dr. Pérouse, is interesting and significant.

Political causes helped the pope, and the council broke up into cliques. Union with the Greek church—a matter dearer to the pope than to the council—caused difficulty, especially as to the place for the council of reunion. The council broke out into disorder, which even showed itself at Constantinople. Aleman came forward as the leader of the extreme anti-papalists, and Cesarini lost his hold upon them. Before the pope transferred the council to Ferrara it had been already seen plainly that the council could only prove ineffective: the cardinals did not wish for a reform, and the fathers could not bring it about. The triumph of Eugenius was slowly prepared, and its causes, political and diplomatic, are described with great skill. Rapidly follow the deposition of Eugenius IV by the council under Aleman on 25 June 1439; the papal union with the Greek church, temporary but a diplomatic success; the constitution *Moyses* of 4 September on the authority of councils, repeating an old argument of Torquemada's against the decrees of Constance on the point; the election of Felix V, the new antipope, after the council had vindicated themselves against the definitions of the constitution *Moyses*; a set discussion at Florence in which Cesarini was appointed to defend, Torquemada to attack the supremacy of general councils; the definition of the relative rights of pope and council by the bull *Etsi non dubitemus* (20 April 1441). Thus the general principle had at length emerged, but its emergence was due more to accident and trifles than to definite action on strong lines. In the later reconciliation with the empire, due so much to the ability of the papal representatives and especially of Aeneas Sylvius, the diplomatic caution of the pope was to be noted; he could not wholly escape reviewing the decrees of Basel or even of Constance, but by a secret act declared that being too ill to examine duly the German demands he annulled any concessions he had made which were against either the doctrine of the church or the authority and rights of the holy see. The expedient was peculiar, but the illness was real, and after having received on 7 February 1447 the homage of the German ambassadors the pope died on the 23rd. In his last discourse to the cardinals he found comfort in the love shown to him by God in the many chastisements He had sent him: 'he had not known,' says Aeneas Sylvius, 'a single day of tranquillity in all his reign.' It was easy for his successor, Nicholas V, to formulate the triumph which Eugenius had really gained, and the year of jubilee signalized it. But the exact authority of councils was settled more by practice than by theory; even the decree *Frequens* ordering their regular assembly could be disregarded now, although Eugenius had so painfully kept it in the letter. Advocates of the conciliar theory —which the ineffectiveness of the councils themselves had discredited —remained; but the papal theory, formulated afresh by its advocates even if not defined by the popes, really held the field, and events seemed to have given it a new vitality. J. P. WHITNEY.

The first English Life of King Henry the Fifth. Edited by C. L. KINGSFORD. (Oxford: Clarendon Press, 1911.)

THE rediscovery in the Bodleian library of the long-lost 'Translator of Titus Livius' quoted by Stow and other Elizabethans and used by Hearne a century later, but successfully concealed by a wrong entry in Bernard's Catalogue, shows that such finds need not be despaired of even in the most unlikely places. Lest a reflexion may seem to be cast upon the present staff of the Bodleian we hasten to add that in this case the recovery was due to Mr. Madan. In identifying the *Life of Henry V* in Bodley MS. 966 with the missing work Mr. Kingsford must have had (though he does not say so) one of the most pleasurable thrills that relieve the scholar's labours, and he has edited it with even more than his usual patient care. This labour is expended upon no mere literary curiosity, for the anonymous translation of Titus Livius's semi-official biography of Henry V has great interest both for the historian of that king's career and for the student of English literature. From the citations and descriptions of the sixteenth-century writers it was already known to be a good deal more than an English version of Livius, the author having incorporated in it material from memoirs of Henry V's life compiled by his contemporary the fourth earl of Ormonde, or at least working up his reminiscences. What gives special importance to its rediscovery is that Stow and Holinshed are now seen to have far from exhausted the matter it contains which is drawn from this lost source. It was Ormonde's stories of Henry's life as prince which specially attracted the Elizabethan historians, but even in the case of these it is no small gain to have them in their oldest extant form. Moreover, owing to Stow's imperfect method of indicating his sources we are only now in a position to state with certainty that such a story as that of the riotous Prince Henry lying in wait for and robbing his own receivers was told by his contemporary Ormonde and not invented, as Mr. Solly-Flood maintained, eighty years after Henry's death, by Fabyan, the London chronicler. It is impossible to escape from Mr. Kingsford's conclusion that the legend of Henry's dissolute youth, though exaggerated by contemporary ecclesiastical prejudice and still more by the Elizabethan dramatists, has some foundation in fact. These stories would, however, not have excited such general interest had they not been taken up by Shakespeare and his predecessors, and the long and valuable section of the editor's introduction, in which their use of them is analysed, requires no justification. But the work of the translator has a literary interest quite independent of the material it furnished for the Elizabethan drama. Written, as internal evidence shows, in 1513, while More was still engaged upon his English history of Richard III—hitherto considered the first of its kind—and Polydore Vergil upon a Latin history of England on a non-annalistic plan, the *Life of Henry V* modestly disputes the priority of each in the new line he struck out. Without making any excessive claims for his author, Mr. Kingsford, with justice, asserts his right to a place among the creators of English prose and among historians as contradistinguished from chroniclers. JAMES TAIT.

L'ancienne Faculté de Théologie de Louvain au premier Siècle de son Existence (1432–1540). Par H. DE JONGH. (Louvain: Bureaux de la Revue d'Histoire Ecclésiastique, 1911.)

OF the university of Louvain no adequate history has yet been written, though numerous treatises and essays exist which deal with various aspects of its life. The way, however, for a comprehensive work upon it is now being prepared by the publication of the university records; and the present book contributes a valuable study of its most important faculty during its early days. Like many other universities founded in the fifteenth century Louvain began in 1425 without a faculty of theology; the influence of the theologians of Paris being strong enough to persuade a succession of popes not to create any rivals to their dominant school, which on the whole had shown loyalty to Rome. But in 1432 the new university succeeded in convincing Eugenius IV that such a faculty might prove a valued bulwark to orthodoxy in the Netherlands; and this hope was fully justified. When the time came, the Louvain theologians stood firmly against Luther, and drove Erasmus away to Basel; and their phalanx availed really to defend the faith. Until now they have not received their due of praise. For the critical period of the struggle with the humanists and the reformers the chief source is the letters of Erasmus and his satellites, who made no attempt to see, or at any rate to represent fairly, their opponents' point of view. They vilified the theologians with unchastened abuse, heaping a Pelion of scandal upon an Ossa of ridicule to overwhelm their unfortunate victims; and they were remarkably successful, at least as regards posterity. To this tainted source have come many writers, who seeing with Erasmus's eyes have found much to blame in the theologians of Louvain. Professor De Jongh has set himself to redress the balance; and if his natural sympathies have prevented him from quite attaining the impartiality he seeks, none will be disposed to quarrel with him on that score.

The fact is that at the period of the Reformation the theological faculty at Louvain was composed of a body of highly respectable doctors, whose conservative principles were shocked by the ideas of progress newly set afloat. The situation is one that recurs at all periods; and if modern disputants are more restrained in their language, the bitterness of the perennial struggle is hardly less keen. It was high time that the credit of the theologians should be restored; by showing them, if not as perfect, at least as intelligent and reasonable beings. Professor De Jongh opens with an admirable account of his sources; and throughout the book he is exceedingly strong in bibliography. He then sketches the growth of the faculty during the fifteenth century—its courses and regulations, the character of the teaching and the powers that it had of self-protection. Before dealing with the actual struggle over reform he gives biographical accounts of the more prominent theologians in the university: and the concluding chapter has many interesting episodes—especially one on the relations between the faculty and Busleiden's newly founded *Collegium trilingue*. It was this latter or the personal fame of Vives, rather than that of the faculty, which drew over to Louvain students from the new humanist colleges in England—from St. John's at Cambridge in 1522, from Corpus Christi in Oxford two years later.

At the end of the book are ninety pages of documents, mostly printed for the first time: acts of the faculty, of the university and of its deputies, which are of great value. A few rectifications may be made. On p. 147 the letter of the archbishop of Mainz to Erasmus should be dated 13 September 1517; on p. 174 the newly-found letter of Erasmus is addressed to John De Hondt, canon of Courtray, 20 April 1526, and deals with Charles, not William, of Croy; on p. 195 as early as 1517 Erasmus was claiming Briard's whole-hearted approbation (app. 183 in the Leiden edition of Erasmus's *Epistolae*). P. S. ALLEN.

ALBERT WADDINGTON, *Histoire de Prusse.* Tome I. *Des Origines à la Mort du Grand Électeur* (1688). (Paris: Plon, 1911.)

M. ALBERT WADDINGTON has produced a substantial first instalment of what promises to be a work of enduring value, and one which will enhance the distinction of a name already of high repute in modern French historiography. The materials for Brandenburg-Prussian history to the death of the Great Elector are unusually ample; and it would be difficult to indicate any other section of modern history which has been explored with so devoted a zeal and expounded with so satisfying a fullness by scholars and writers of the same calibre. The labours of political historians such as Ranke, Droysen, and Treitschke have of late been supplemented by economic and ecclesiastical researches on the part of Schmoller, Max Lehmann, and others, which allow of a reconstruction singularly complete of systems and methods of government of which in this instance it is of primary importance to arrive at a fundamental understanding. But neither these circumstances, nor the fact that Philippson's in most respects adequate monograph, which does justice *inter alia* to the far-sighted, novel, and colonial projects of Frederick William, has for some years been in our hands, renders a volume like M. Waddington's superfluous. Indeed, they can but make a book at once comprehensive in scope and careful of detail all the more welcome, if it proves equal to the demands of the task courageously undertaken by its author. So far as he has at present proceeded, he may be without hesitation judged to have proved not unequal to the match. The lucidity of his narrative as well as its coherence after it ceases to be bipartite (of the origins of the westernmost portion of the monarchy a less cursory account might perhaps be desiderated) deserve high praise, as do the quickness of insight and breadth of judgement which it constantly exhibits.

The history of what ultimately grew into the Prussian state is more than that of any modern monarchy the history of its dynasty; and though M. Waddington is not at pains to elaborate the characters which he draws of a long series of margraves and electors, he differentiates them with sufficient sureness of touch to leave on the reader a distinct impression of their several personalities. In the first elector, Frederick I, he rightly refuses to see an apostle according to Droysen, or a prince who so much as 'acclimatized' himself in the newly acquired lands where lay the future of his house, but he shows him to have, like a true Hohenzollern, had a full sense of his responsibility before God as his true Lord and Master. He is not overawed by the surviving Renascence *agnomen* of Albert Achilles into ignoring the qualities which obtained for him the second 'addition' of the name Ulysses; while he regards that of John Cicero, the first Brandenburg Hohenzollern proper and a strong wielder of his police authority, as absurdly misplaced. He points out with great distinctness the weak sides in the character of the first duke of Prussia, but recognizes in the love of learning which marked the patron of Crotus Rubeanus and the founder of the university of Königsberg the redeeming feature of an otherwise far from glorious reign. While making no hero of the elector George William, he shows how overwhelming was the pressure of difficulties and troubles which, whether he gave way before it or resisted it, his electorate as well as he lacked the strength for meeting. Thus in George William's son and successor he reaches the chief figure of his narrative, so far as it is carried in the present volume, and presents to us, with abundant but not excessive detail, the portrait of a prince whose actions were as full of sinuosity as his character was true to its main and determining lines. The key to that character, as M. Waddington rightly perceives, is to be found in its unshaken and unshakeable religiosity, which inspired a firm belief in the end to be reached and in the duty of neglecting no means of drawing nearer to it. That this end was not merely the satisfaction of an ambitious desire for self-aggrandizement is conspicuously shown by Frederick William's action in the matter of the Polish crown, for which he was at one time found ready to renounce anything and everything—even the independence of ducal Prussia, which had hitherto been the cardinal point of his policy—save always his protestant faith. Even to the electoral prince (as he became after the death of his more interesting elder brother) who was ultimately to become King Frederick I of Prussia, M. Waddington renders more justice than he has received at the hands of many previous critics—from his wife downwards. 'Of a rather dry and cold character, and accessible to vanity, he redeemed these defects by serious moral qualities and a laborious diligence.' To his insight into character and well-sustained balance of judgement M. Waddington adds on occasion a pleasant descriptive touch which shows that the woods and waters of the sandy Mark, as well as the more mysterious outlines of the Prussian coastlands, together with the charming variety of Franconian scenery, have faithfully impressed themselves upon the historian. His incidental criticism of the *faux air de vieux neuf* in the restoration of the ancestral castle of the Hohenzollern dynasty was perhaps hardly called for where it occurs; but there is undoubtedly a great deal too much of this sort of thing in the New Germany. I must, however, express my regret that M. Waddington, if he thought an introduction necessary to his *History* as a whole, should not have provided a more suitable portico for so satisfactory an edifice; though I decline to comment upon the phrases and ' flouts ' with which he has interspersed it; to examine his '*plutôt*' perfunctory analysis of the Prussian character as evidenced by the unimaginativeness of Berlin culture and the ingrained respect of the people for the ' hierarchy '; or to dwell upon the closing passage of this preliminary flourish.

The value of M. Waddington's continuous survey of Brandenburg-Prussian history may be illustrated by indicating how one or two of its most notable features are, of course under varying conditions, recognizable in almost every stage of the narrative. The relations between the Brandenburg electors and the house of Austria on the imperial throne can never be too closely kept in view by the historical student who is willing in considering the problem of which the knot has only been cut— and cut in no thoroughly satisfactory way—in our own times, to go back beyond the Silesian wars and even the Schwiebus intrigue. Already the latter half of the sixteenth century had brought home to the Brandenburg electors the nature of ' the thanks ' to be looked for ' from the house of Austria' for a loyalty which, whether wholly disinterested or not, had been consistent even in the trying times of the Schmalkaldic war and the Augsburg *Interim*. Notwithstanding imperial promises, expectations, the fulfilment of which might have anticipated the ultimate destiny of Schleswig-Holstein by two centuries, and, though less decisively, have altered the balance of territorial power between the Guelphs and the Hohenzollerns, had been thrown to the winds in the reigns of Joachim I and of Joachim II respectively, and the attitude of Rudolf II towards the question of the admission to the diet of John George's son, the administrator of Magdeburg, was in substance as unyielding as that of his predecessors had in others matters been fruitless. It was not till the death of Rudolf II and the accession of Matthias that in the more critical question of the Rhenish duchies John Sigismund could venture on ignoring the Saxon claims which had the imperial countenance. It was only a year or two earlier—in 1609—that the imperial vice-chancellor, Strahlenberg, had declared that the power of Brandenburg must be broken while it was still in process of formation. With the outbreak of the Thirty Years' War the opportunity for carrying out this policy seemed to have vanished; but, before that struggle had ended, the unfortunate George William had entered into the last and only enduring phase of his chequered policy—into that of entire subservience to the imperial house. It was not till, in the last decade of the great war, Frederick William succeeded to his half-ruined inheritance, that the house of Austria began to realize that its faithful vassal and ally could place the interests of his own state above all other considerations. From the moment in which this had been perceived to be the case, the goodwill of Brandenburg had become to the emperor an object of solicitation, and the Great Elector's lifelong game of balance had begun. It was the French diplomatist d'Avaux who was first charged with the elector's interests at Münster, and for the settlement of the Brandenburg 'satisfaction' in the peace of Westphalia, imperfect as it was, no item of 'thanks' was due to the imperial house.

Apart from questions of foreign policy, little consideration was shown by the imperial government for Frederick William's plans and schemes; even the modest reforms by which he sought to remedy the time-honoured abuses of the guild system, though approved by the diet, were knocked on the head by the emperor. Yet the Great Elector undoubtedly cherished a sincere regard for the emperor as such, and the open expression which he gave to the feeling of national German patriotism is one of the most signal proofs that this sentiment was not, as is sometimes supposed, wholly extinguished by the Thirty Years' War and the peace of Westphalia. Nor can it be said that in home affairs he was at any time opposed to the emperor's wishes or an antagonist of his traditional authority. Though an ardent protestant, he was always fair to his catholic subjects; and his share in the movement of the so-called 'Extendists' (the princes who sought to extend the financial powers in their several states supposed to be secured to them by an article of a recess of the diet of 1654) was directed against the claims of their estates rather than against those of the emperor, albeit he could hardly be expected to look with sympathy upon these endeavours. It would take me too far to examine the significance of the Great Elector's entry into the *Rheinbund* at the comparatively late date of November 1665; but M. Waddington is assuredly right in minimizing the importance of this step, the effect of which, he says, was to paralyse the action of the league. And, indeed, the name given to the league should not mislead us into regarding it as either established or carried on essentially in the interests of France. The final phase in the relations between the Great Elector and the house of Austria was not, as might have been expected from any less cool-headed politician, the equivocal action of the latter which, after a campaign which Pensionary Fagel compared to the wanderings of the children of Israel in the desert, practically forced the elector into concluding the separate peace of Vossem, the most humiliating transaction of his political life. It was not till after the final disillusionment which obliged him to agree to the peace of St. Germain in 1679—a sorry end to the great successes against Sweden which form the basis of his popular fame—that he completely changed what M. Waddington happily calls his 'orientation' and turned from Austria to France. And even this change was not absolutely final. The last four years of the Great Elector's life brought him, after much oscillation, to a defensive alliance with the Emperor Leopold, and when, physically unlike his former self, but mentally and morally not less *tenax propositi*, he died in 1688, he was one in purpose with William III of Orange, and resolved upon a rupture—though it might not be an immediate rupture—with the author of the revocation of the edict of Nantes.

When we turn to the relations between the Brandenburg rulers and their estates—relations which go back to the days of the Ascanian margraves and almost reach a stage of anarchy in the unhappy reign of George William,—we may find a parallel to the ascendancy of the Brandenburg estates in that of the Prussian in the days of the first duke ; but in this instance the historical evolution of relations, which continued to trouble the Great Elector during many years of his rule, had been different and cannot be understood without a review of the whole history of the German Order, whose rule had really succumbed to the revolt of the Lizards and its consequences. That history M. Waddington has retold, if not with the picturesqueness and *verve* of Treitschke, at least with signal clearness and fairness.

In the tolerant policy of the Hohenzollern historians have long detected one of the causes of the greatness and prosperity of the state founded and sustained in a large measure by their sagacity and high courage—so much so that any aberration from the principle of this policy seems to the student an incongruity in Prussian history. M. Waddington has well shown that this policy was promoted by the cautiousness with which the Reformation was accomplished in Brandenburg, and, still more notably by the adoption of the Calvinistic form of protestantism by John Sigismund, without the application to his Lutheran subjects of the *cuius regio eius est religio* principle—which in Prussia (where as late as 1617 the diet excluded all but catholics and Lutherans from offices) would almost have undone the union. It is known how the toleration which had been established as a principle of government in Brandenburg opened the electorate to a stream of foreign, especially French, immigration of inestimable value to the progress and prosperity of the country, and how the seal was set upon this twice-blessed policy by the consistent declaration of it, even in the face of Louis XIV, by the Great Elector. We may or may not agree with M. Waddington that the Berliners owe their reputation for repartee to the immigration of French Huguenots ; but he has not said a word too much in his statement of the lofty motives which actuated the Great Elector in sowing with generous hands the seed from which in almost every department of life—administration both civil and military, trade and industry, science and art, education and thought—his children's children and their subjects were to reap untold benefits. It should never be forgotten that though of the two universities in his state one (Königsberg) was Lutheran and the other (Duisburg) Calvinist, he proclaims the principle that no academical professor was responsible for his teaching to either synod or council. His sympathy was not wanting to the broad-minded efforts of John Ducie, though in those of the bishop of Tina (Spinola) he may have suspected an intention which annoyed him. Englishmen, at least, will not grudge a tribute to the magnanimous ambition which fired Frederick William and which found expression in this as well as in other aspects of his rule and policy, that he should be true to his responsibility as ' the head of all evangelically reformed potentates in Europe '. The claim might or might not be tenable ; but there was at least one European sovereign who was unlikely to dispute it, and that sovereign sat in the place formerly occupied by Oliver Cromwell.   A. W. WARD.

Pio II e la Politica Italiana nella Lotta contro i Malatesti (1457–63). Da GIOVANNI SORANZO. (Padova: Drucker, 1911.)

THE detailed study of a single short phase of Italian history makes possible that concentration on the political relationships between the various states which more general works must neglect. With praiseworthy determination Signor Soranzo has denied himself any excursions into contemporary history not directly relating to the subject in hand. He writes strictly of the struggle between the Malatesti and Pius II. The inevitable result is a book which few save professed students will read, but one which is a real contribution to the history of fifteenth-century Italy. Throughout these five hundred closely packed pages the style is monotonous and the criticism weak. There is a serious attempt to present the true facts so far as they are ascertainable, and the work is admirably supplied with references. Archives have been ransacked, and some of the more important documents are printed in an appendix, but save for a few pages by way of introduction there is not enough criticism of the value of the authorities cited. Moreover, there is no full list of authorities and no index, not even a list of chapters and their contents: there are no headings to the pages, few dates, nothing to help the reader to find what he wants.

Signor Soranzo has been so much overwhelmed by the mass of material which he has collected that he has failed to give continuity to his study. His chapters are too few and his facts too closely packed for any clear realization of the course of events. Clarity of presentation is above all necessary in writing at such length on so short a period, but this we do not find, thanks largely to the exaggerated self-restraint of the author. Only once (p. 230) does he so far forget himself as to give his judgement on Sigismondo Malatesta's character, so that the narrative remains a narrative and nothing more. The figures who move across the stage are always figures and not human beings, and this at a time when human characteristics played such an important part in the moulding of history. Yet in spite of the deliberate and disappointing reserve of the author, some figures do thrust themselves forward. There is Piccinnino, the *irrequieto condottiere* equally feared by friend and foe, the terror of his various employers and in some ways the dictator of Italian politics. On the other hand stands Francesco Sforza, the *condottiere* become duke, whose skill at sitting on the fence made him the wonder of all Italy. Unlike so many who practise this art, he seems to have succeeded in pacifying all parties and in alienating few, and his influence in the particular struggle under review, both over the pope and the Malatesta, was curiously great. Yet a third type of *condottiere* is to be found in Federico d'Urbino, the gallant and chivalrous foe of Sigismondo Malatesta, the mercenary who did not forget that he was a gentleman and who knew when to exercise the virtue of clemency. Above all stand out the two leaders in the drama, Sigismondo Malatesta and Pius II. The former would surely have repaid a more reasoned character study than we get in this work. A typical Italian of the Renaissance period, he was a strange mixture of qualities—on the one side a philosopher devoted to art and learning, on the other accused, and with much truth, of all kinds of vice; on the one side a man of undoubted courage and perseverance, on the other a cruel monster and bloodthirsty tyrant. Even more complex but perhaps less typical of his age was the man who tried to sink the characteristics of Aeneas Sylvius Piccolomini in the rôle of Pope Pius II. In the present work two points are emphasized, his implacable and obstinate animosity against Sigismondo and his quixotic but quite genuine desire to revive the crusades. On the whole we find him revealed in his less pleasant aspect—his nepotism, his violent temper, his fierce resentment of all injuries, his satisfaction in trampling a foe down to the very dust. There are, however, pleasanter sides of his character, and it would have been well at least to indicate them in a work which bears his name on its title-page. Still, if we do not find adequate characterization in Signor Soranzo's book, we get the material which may be used for such a purpose. He has done excellent work in revealing the endless intrigues of the various Italian states with each other, and the future historian of Italy during this period will here find much assistance in elucidating the more obscure aspects of his subject. K. H. VICKERS.

Jakob Fugger der Reiche: Studien und Quellen, I. Von MAX JANSEN. (Leipzig: Duncker & Humblot, 1910.)

JAKOB FUGGER, who was probably the most influential financier that ever lived, may be cited in contradiction of the superstition that clergymen make bad men of business. He was already a canon when, owing to the early death of four of his six elder brothers, he was called upon to abandon orders for commerce. It is true that he was only nineteen, for he was born in March 1459, and in 1479 was sent to watch over the Venetian branch of the family business. He early took the leading part in the mineral department, and after the death of George in 1506 and of Ulrich in 1510 he had sole control of the firm, though his nephews had their share of the profits. Nothing is known of Jakob's education, and little can be gathered from Dr. Jansen's book of his personality, not so much indeed as can be gleaned from a page of the journal of the Apulian-chaplain Antonio de Beatis, who was invited by him to the magnificent house at Augsburg, of which the old merchant was justly vain. The one touch of purely personal interest relates to his dying hours, when Ferdinand of Austria, entering Augsburg in state on 19 December 1525, ordered his drums and trumpets to cease playing as he reached the house, 'for he had heard that he was sick to death, and wished to cause him no annoyance; so he marched by with all his people without a sound.' If personal details are lacking, there is here an abundance of information on the growth of the Fugger fortunes. Dr. Jansen's book is divided into five main heads, dealing with the entrance of Jakob into the firm, its general trade and expansion, its operations in Tyrol and in Hungary, and Jakob's relation to *hohe Politik*. This is perhaps the most convenient arrangement, but it leads to repetition especially in the chapters on the metal trade in Tyrol and on Jakob's importance in the policy of Maximilian and Charles V. In Tyrol the repeated loans to Sigismund and Maximilian secured for the Fugger the lion's share of the silver and later the copper trade. The loans were repaid by assignment of the silver from the rich mines of Schwaz and Innsbruck at a fixed price, which was 25 per cent. or 30 per cent. below the market value. So long as the Habsburgs stood by their bargains, as indeed they loyally did, save for a moment's wavering in 1502, the security was unimpeachable and the profits enviable. In vain the Tyrolese Estates, the government, and the smelters entreated Maximilian to break the Fugger toils. The emperor knew that loans from such a firm were more trustworthy than the paper profits which the memorial set forth. In 1522 Jakob Fugger himself undertook smelting, which resulted in a large increase in the output.

The chapter on Hungary is more interesting than that on Tyrol, because here Jakob Fugger was engaged as principal and not middleman. He entered into partnership with Johann Thurzo, who had obtained from the crown and the bishop of Fünfkirchen a concession of old waterlogged copper workings in north-western Hungary. We hear of the introduction of capital for new plant, the operation by which silver was separated from the copper, and above all of the routes through Pomerania and the Baltic or through central Germany to the Netherlands, or southwards to Venice. This is an excellent lesson in German geography of the sixteenth century. The Venetian trade after a time fell off owing to the jealousy of the Tyrolese government, which wanted an exclusive market, but that with the Netherlands reached enormous proportions. When the Fuggers obtained control of the Swedish copper also, they had practically established a monopoly. Yet the Thurzo-Fugger syndicate was never in quite smooth water. At one moment there was a strike of the miners for higher pay. The discontent in the town of Neusohl, the company's head-quarters, was chronic, for the company imported all its own supplies and brewed its own beer, and this truck system was popular with the miners who got, as part of their wages, better articles at a lower price. The tradesmen of Neusohl suffered, and their government complained of the company's interference with the civic courts. The great storm of 1525 was due to a court revolution, engineered by the Woiwode Zapolya and the Hungarian gentry, which overthrew the well-bribed patrons of the syndicate. It was in the main a nationalist movement against Thurzo the Pole and Fugger the German. The weak King Lewis was prevailed upon to seize the syndicate's property, and to imprison and persecute its local agents. The whilom strikers, however, rose for their masters, and the commissioner sent to the mines was in peril of his life. Jakob Fugger was a fighter, and he soon found backers. The king of Poland, the dukes of Bavaria, the Suabian League, the council of regency, the Archduke Ferdinand, and the emperor himself forced the king of Hungary to his knees. Charles V wrote that if Jakob Fugger brought his complaint before the empire, the emperor would set the whole empire in motion against the king. Jakob, now on his death-bed, proudly refused any terms of restitution, unless his honour was entirely satisfied.

The general trade of the Fugger firm is more familiar than its dealings in metal. They traded in cloth, silk, and furs, in spices and citrus fruits, in arms and ammunition. Their loans were frequently partly paid in cloth, which was passed on by way of wages to soldiers or even to envoys, as Gattinara's letters prove. Maximilian wanted all the cloth to be red, but the Fuggers insisted that he must take a fair share of less popular colours. They invested money in the Portuguese fleet which with such fateful consequences sailed from Lisbon, not indeed for Calcutta as the author states, but for Calicut, even now the home of the choicest spices. Curiosities sometimes fell in the merchants' way. Thus the Fuggers picked up from the Swiss the girdle taken from Charles the Bold's body at Nancy, and sold it to Maximilian. Their banking business comprised exchange, deposits, transport of precious metals, the collection of indulgence money, and papal tributes. As with the Medici, much money was placed in their hands for investment, and upon this they usually paid interest at a fixed rate of 7 per cent. They established an efficient postal service, supplementing or supplanting the official system of Taxis, and their early information of important events was of great service to their patrons, and doubtless to their own speculations.

Of course Jakob Fugger was generally unpopular. The knights who went in silk attire and consumed unlimited mulled drinks thought a profit of 175 per cent. on spices usurious. *Wucherisch* and *fuggerisch* became synonyms. The literature of the Knights' War and the Peasants' War echoes with diatribes against the monopolists who tempted the simpler classes with eastern luxuries to their ruin. The Hanse towns as a rule resented the attempt of the Fuggers to capture the trade of Novgorod, and their contribution to the growing prosperity of Antwerp. Yet if Lübeck plundered their ships, Dantzig and Hamburg welcomed their caravans of copper, while Venice granted neutrality for their goods in the Cambrai War. The excellent Duke George of Saxony enjoyed Jakob's hospitality, and in return sent a cask of wine to be drunk with his *Hausfrau* in all joy and health. The relations of Jakob to Maximilian cover every phase of the emperor's reign, from the rescue of Tyrol from Bavarian designs to the negotiations for Charles's election as king of the Romans during his grandfather's lifetime, but they are especially close during the Venetian War (1509–16). Charles, as is well known, owed his election mainly to Jakob, who was fully aware of the fact. The firm financed the purchase of Württemberg from the Suabian League, and rendered signal service in the first French war. Charles, with a sense of favours to come, was not ungrateful. The diet of 1522 inveighed against the monopolies of the great companies, and wished to dissolve all firms which had over 50,000 gulden of capital, and to cover the frontiers with a ring of custom-houses, imposing tolls on imported merchandise. The council of regency pressed this policy upon the emperor, who was now in Spain. But Charles threw cold water upon the scheme, and one of the most interesting documents here printed is a letter of 1525 to the effect that any measure against monopolies should not apply to trade in metals, which was best confined to single or at most to a few hands.

Nearly one-third of the volume consists of illustrative documents arranged according to the sections of the subject, but the bulk of them relate to the family partnerships and to Jakob Fugger's extremely elaborate will.
E. ARMSTRONG.

Österreichische Staatsverträge: Fürstentum Siebenbürgen (1526–1690). Bearbeitet von RODERICH GOOSS. (*Veröffentlichungen der Kommission für Neuere Geschichte Österreichs*, IX.) (Wien, 1911.)

THE publications of the Kommission für Neuere Geschichte Österreichs are known to the English student especially through their third volume, which contains the Anglo-Austrian treaties from 1526 to 1748 (edited by Professor Pribram in 1907 [1]). The present volume deals with a subject which lies apart from general European history, but is all the more important as illustrating the development of the dual monarchy itself. The relations between the principality of Transylvania and the imperial house of Austria began in 1526, when the crown of Hungary, vacant by the death of King Louis II, in the battle of Mohacs, was contested between Ferdinand of Habsburg and John Szapolyai, voivode of Transylvania. International relations came to an end in, or soon after, 1690 through the death of Michael Apafi I, practically the last prince of Transylvania, which was thenceforth a province of the Austrian monarchy. These two dates fix the period to which the present collection of treaties between Austria and Transylvania is naturally limited. A truce concluded in 1527 between King Ferdinand I and John Szapolyai is the first and a commercial agreement of 1690 between Austria and Transylvania the last document in this handsome volume.

The difficult position of the principality, wedged in as it was between the Habsburg and the Ottoman empires, accounts for the turbulent and warlike character of its history. By far the greater part of the documents relate to treaties of truce, peace or alliance, and military arrangements of various descriptions; forty-four out of the ninety-four treaties in this volume are armistices concluded between Transylvanian and imperial authorities. This, of course, gives the whole collection a rather monotonous character. A good many of these treaties, however, are of interest not only for the history of the contracting parties, but also for that of the Turco-Austrian wars of the sixteenth and seventeenth centuries. Nearly all the important ones, it is true, are already known; but in most cases either the texts were not accurately printed before this, or the ratifications and other supplementary documents were omitted. As far as possible the editor, in preparing the texts, has gone back to the original documents, and only in cases where these are no longer attainable has he followed the best transmitted text, adding in footnotes variant readings of material importance. In some instances also drafts of treaties have been included. The treatment of the texts and the whole technique of the edition show a good scholarly training. The language of the treaties is as a rule Latin, in a few instances Hungarian. In many cases the editor has been obliged to confine himself merely to a statement when and where a certain treaty was concluded, and to infer its purport from other sources, without being able to reproduce the text itself. A great advantage of the editorial system adopted lies in the introductory remarks placed at the beginning of every text, which include summaries of the documents. Some of these introductions, which are well written and always to the point, extend to

[1] *Ante*, xxv. 335 ff.

articles of considerable length. Put together they form a complete history of the relations between Austria and Transylvania, with sidelights on the affairs of the neighbouring countries. It has by no means been an easy task to write such a history. Though large materials have been already collected in the *Monumenta comitialia regni Transsylvaniae*, these throw but little light on the diplomatic transactions which are the subject of the present introductions. The author has had, therefore, to draw on archives far more than on printed literature. Some inconsistency with regard to the spelling of Austrian and Hungarian proper names might have been avoided ; but no one who knows the puzzling variety of forms under which names in that period usually appear will blame the author severely for this. Dr. Gooss has accomplished his task in a way which does every credit to the Kommission, under whose auspices the edition is published.   A. O. MEYER.

Lollardy and the Reformation in England; An Historical Survey. By JAMES GAIRDNER, C.B., LL.D., D.Litt. Vol. iii. (London : Macmillan, 1911.)

THIS third volume brings with it a touching memorial of the writer's fidelity to historic truth in the shape of a long list of errata and corrections in the preceding volumes ; a few of them are more than corrections, and show that the author, unlike lesser scholars, is almost more than willing to confess mistakes. In the preface some matters are touched upon which we are here forced to avoid, but through the questions raised by Dr. Gairdner it is well for us to see two things. The first thing is that he goes straight to the study of questions that matter most and are with us still, and the second thing is his intense belief in our own likeness to men of the past. Many people who share Mr. Gairdner's intense devotion to truth are so apt to treat characters and ages in history as mere specimens. Mr. Gairdner's method has its own dangers, but at any rate he avoids this special danger.

In this volume the beginnings of the reign of Edward VI are amply treated ; the relations of Paget with Gardiner (correcting S. R. Maitland's Essay xvi) are described as at the stage where Paget's due gratitude was passing into political dislike although hardly into personal enmity (p. 14) ; then the objection raised by Wriothesley—but not pressed— to the protector's appointment (p. 19) is significant, but the original authority for this Mr. Gairdner says he does not know. It is curious to note that when Henry II of France suggested the admission of a papal envoy into England the official reply was, first, that Henry VIII had charged the council to make no change in religion and government, and secondly, that exemption from papal power was the devout wish of the English people. Perhaps we should not lay too much stress on these official statements. There is an interesting quotation from Gardiner at this time : ' Many commonwealths have continued without the Bishop of Rome's jurisdiction ; but without true religion, and with such opinions as Germany maintained no estate hath continued.' Here is an intermediate phase in Gardiner's change. On p. 57 (and note) there is an interesting reference to a speech of John Rogers, first published by Colonel Chester in 1861, which shows that only pressure from the protector and Cranmer induced the higher clergy to support clerical marriage. A little later (pp. 73 f.) is a discussion of Cranmer's mental history in regard to the eucharist; Mr. Gairdner seems inclined to think he was at this time a Lutheran, but the suggestion (p. 78) ' he was considering the German view, whether it could possibly be upheld ', may be a little nearer the truth. The discussion by Professor Pollard in his life of Cranmer may be compared with what is said here. A question is raised as to the date of Calvin's letter to the protector, 22 October (1548 or 1549), and it is certainly odd that the difficulty of dating Calvin's letters to his English friends is also in other cases great. Calvin's European position is well described, but we hardly think justice is done to the really fine and conscientious character of Charles V. A note (p. 163) on Paul IV and reform, on the other hand, unduly praises the pope's reforming zeal, and ascribes his failure rather to the naughty world, the methods of which he adopted, than to himself. But surely his original zeal for reform had now become a suspicion of anything novel; his experiences had led him to value repression as a means of preventing error, and so he came after all to forsake the larger hopes of his youth. Again, on p. 220, we should feel a little doubtful if Dudley did recognize his own unfitness to organize ' a new religion ', and that thus Cranmer was ' the real author of the theology which it was now sought to enforce '. It is not easy to impress upon politicians a sense of their own limitations, and Dudley was neither reticent nor over-conscientious. Of Hooper's early life (p. 260 f.) we have one of those sketches which were so welcome in the earlier volumes and form a very valuable part of the work.

Mr. Gairdner's instinct and knowledge—quickened by the fear of having in an earlier work misled inquirers—makes him give constant details of the Commission of 32 on Canon Law. By references to pp. 47–8, 177, 337, 363, 319–20 n., and 383–4, the student may get much guidance on a very intricate and interesting subject. And it may be suggested that the matter of ecclesiastical law was even then not approached with a conviction of the absolute separateness of church and state as sources of law. Whatever a medieval lawyer found to his hand he took and was ready to use ; principles might have different origins, but they were all available for use in a common field ; hence it was not such an absolutely new departure as is sometimes thought when the validity of existing canon law (always *minus* papal authority) was left side by side with the restrictions of the law of the state. To a medieval canon lawyer in former days those restrictions would have had not binding force, which we must not seek for in medieval legal thought and action, but some presumption in their favour.

Mr. Gairdner speaks in his preface of the long struggle by which even in matters of morality the Reformation in the end came out victorious. That there was such a process is a consideration not to be forgotten, but its existence is sometimes put aside by those who look only at one age by itself. Revolutions make their appeal to ages to come. Mr. Gairdner does not profess to have written an exhaustive history of the reign of

Edward VI, but for some parts of it and some aspects of it he has written a very full account. It may be allowed that Lollardy originally was merely discontent with current religion, but to use the term Lollardy of late religious movements does need (as Mr. Gairdner, to judge from his introduction, seems to feel) some apology. His note (p. vii) on the substitution for it of the expression ' New Learning ' is very interesting, but the only advantage of carrying on the term ' Lollard ' is to emphasize something Mr. Gairdner is not here concerned with—the assertion (or the possibility) that Lollardy was not a temporary product due to Wyclif, but an inevitable appearance of religious discontent due to general causes. There seems little gain from the extension of the term; if we do extend it we have to apply it to many people and some thinkers very unlike one to another. But there is so much of interest and importance in Mr. Gairdner's book that we should hardly complain of the thread upon which he has strung his valuable pages. J. P. WHITNEY.

The Early English Dissenters in the Light of Recent Research (1550–1641). By CHAMPLIN BURRAGE. 2 vols. (Cambridge: University Press, 1912.)

THE history of early English dissent is still in the stage in which early church history was before the *Mémoires pour servir à l'Histoire Ecclésiastique* of Tillemont. It needs a reasoned discussion of an accumulating mass of evidences on which there may rest some future history of nonconformity. Such work is not attractive to the general reader, but it is fascinating to the student: and, further, it is both essential and lasting as no ordinary historical work is. Tillemont has survived a number of church historians who have used his labours, and will probably survive more still. The work that Mr. Burrage is doing is work of this sort, the accumulation of evidence from many quarters, and a close discussion of its bearing on uncertain or disputed points of the history of English dissent. He has therefore followed up his previous discussions, reprints, and monographs with two thick volumes, one containing documents, and the other a set of ' Mémoires pour servir '. They will be of first-rate importance henceforward to all students in this field. A number of hoary blunders are revealed and corrected; a number of gaps are filled; and, in the process, the writer shows judgement, discrimination, and a dispassionateness which is no doubt helped by American aloofness from ancient quarrels, and is perhaps more than one could demand of an English writer. Mr. Burrage defines in his preface the nature of his book: it ' is not intended as an exhaustive history of English Dissent during even the period treated '; the author is supplying gaps and correcting errors : ' accordingly some subjects, that ought at least to be mentioned in a complete history, will scarcely be referred to here.' In order to make more plain the points which he wishes to bring out, he gives in his introduction a list of sixty-four propositions concerning which he has a new witness to bear. The device is convenient; though it is one that might easily be abused, and treated (as is not the case here) after the manner of the prospectus of a patent medicine. Certainly it tends to make the reviewer's task lighter, or to tempt him to be content with the summary. It will be found, however, that a close perusal of the book justifies Mr. Burrage in his sixty-four claims; it reveals the width and care of his inquiries, that have brought forward so much fresh light, as well as the soundness of his judgement which has led him to reverse many an accepted verdict.

Much is based on rare or unique volumes; and in such cases it is difficult to test the quality of the writer's scholarship. But a great deal of the first volume depends on documents printed in full in the second; and in such cases it is easy to see that he has handled the materials skilfully and faithfully. It is possible that he has shown rather less care in dealing with better-known sources than with his own novelties. For example, the account of affairs drawn from the familiar *Brieff discours off the troubles begonne at Franckford* is not so clear as one might wish; and no distinction is made between the early doings of 1554, which occupy the first half of the *Discours*, and the episodes of 1557, which occupy the second half and are divided from the earlier by a fresh heading or title. One might quarrel a little with the transcription (ii. 132) of the facsimile given to face p. 120 of vol. i. Also it seems a pity to distribute the facsimiles evenly through the book without reference to the passages to which they belong. Some of the documents are not entirely new, e.g. the Latin letters of Parkhurst from which extracts are printed (ii. 7) are both given in full (in a translation) in Gorham's *Gleanings*, 477, 493; Whitgift's letter about Bancroft (partly printed at i. 132) is given in full in Usher's *Reconstruction of the English Church*, ii. 366-9. A few small misprints may also be noted for future correction: i. 41, 45, David Wilkins, not Davide; i. 83 and ii. 12, 341, the vicar-general's name was Huicke or Huick, not Hinck. But such things are small as compared with the great services rendered by these two volumes.

It is always difficult in the case of conventicles to know whether those who frequent them do so as a matter of convenience or of principle. Do they withdraw from the churches because they dislike their habits of worship and the like, or because they fundamentally disagree? Are they nonconformists, in short, or separatists? The tendency of many writers hitherto has been to find separatism in every conventicle. Mr. Burrage is more cautious. In many cases where others find the beginnings of modern separatism he finds only non-conforming puritan churchmanship. The Plumbers' Hall congregation of 1567 is claimed for the latter, though Richard Fitz's church of the same date is claimed as separatist. These judgements seem sound; and the second is proved to be so by the text of the covenant of Fitz's 'Privy Church', which is printed in full and given in facsimile as well. Similarly the rise of the English baptists is not here connected with any early congregations of the sixteenth century, nor with the foreign anabaptists of that date. They are traced only to John Smyth and his inauguration of a rebaptizing English church in 1608 at Amsterdam; though it is shown that already before 1600 some seceders from Johnson's Brownist church had anticipated him and his congregation in a self-baptism followed by a rebaptism of the believers. More revolutionary still is the author's contention as to the origin of independency: for he takes it to be, not the direct outcome or continuation of Brownism or Barrowism, but a development from a congregational form of non-separatist puritanism, which owes its shape mainly to Henry Jacob in the first decade of the seventeenth century. There can be little doubt that in strict genealogy this is true. Puritanism under James and Charles became something very different from what it had been under Elizabeth. The opposition between puritanism and separatism broke down, while at the same time the puritans more and more sat loosely to their churchmanship. Without being separatist or renouncing the communion of the English church, they tended in the direction either of the old presbyterian or the new congregational church polity. And when the pressure of royal and episcopal coercion was removed, they came out in the familiar form of the presbyterians and the independents of the days of the rebellion ; and moreover they stood forth in large numbers, beside which the small companies of sectaries were quite insignificant.

While valuing thus highly the ' Mémoires pour servir ' which Mr. Burrage has given us, we hope that he will not stay in this stage, as Tillemont did, but go on (and in his much more restricted area it should be possible) to give us a full history of the whole subject. W. H. FRERE.

Inventaire des Archives Farnésiennes de Naples au point de vue de l'Histoire des Pays-Bas catholiques. Par ALFRED CAUCHIE et LÉON VAN DER ESSEN. (Bruxelles : Kiessling, 1911.)

THIS volume is the outcome of one of those ' missions scientifiques ' which have become so regular and so admirable a part of continental historical labours, but are so sadly lacking in British enterprise ; and MM. Cauchie and van der Essen have found in the Farnese archives at Naples a rich vein of almost unworked historical ore. M. Gachard, indeed, among his many services to Belgian scholarship, had made a cursory survey of these archives, but his pioneer work failed to indicate the extent or the value of these materials. They consist for the most part of the private and official correspondence of members of the Farnese family, notably Margaret of Parma, her husband, Ottavio Farnese, and her famous son, Alexander. Philip II, on Alexander's death, made strenuous efforts to get possession of these papers, which contained much that he wished to bury in oblivion ; his efforts were partially successful, and we are glad to learn that M. Lonchay is working at Simancas on the documents which found their way thither. But Alexander's secretary, Cosimo Masi, more attached to the Farnese than to Philip II, managed to convey the bulk of the correspondence to Parma, where it remained until Don Carlos, who had succeeded to Parma as Elizabeth Farnese's son on the death of the last Farnese duke in 1731, conquered Naples in 1734 and took with him to his new capital much of the family archives. Those which remained at Parma are to be the subject of a separate report : this volume deals only with Naples, but its authors have reached the conclusion that, so far as the Netherlands are concerned, the Naples documents are far more important than those at Parma.

The contents of the five hundred files of papers marked ' Fiandra ' in the Farnese archives at Naples relate of course mainly to the affairs of the Low Countries ; and MM. Cauchie and van der Essen have only been able to give a brief descriptive catalogue of so bulky a collection, supplemented by an introduction of 226 pages calling attention to the main features of its historical importance. The documents are not calendared, and curiosity is stimulated rather than satisfied by the brevity of these indications. It is clear that the collection, if published in full or calendared, would present a very different view of affairs from that contained in official correspondence, though it does not follow that that view would be the truer one. The editors give an illustration on pp. lxxiii–iv. Alexander, in an official dispatch, justifies the massacre of the garrison of Sichem by the Spanish troops, on the ground that the garrison consisted of soldiers liberated on parole after their capture at Gembloux ; but in a ciphered letter to his mother he complains that Don John had imposed these rigorous orders upon him to prejudice his popularity and prevent his rivalry for favour. The correspondence, indeed, is full of Farnese grievances against Philip II and his other agents ; but it obviously contains most valuable materials for the history of the Netherlands during this period, and materials less abundant and less original for their history in the seventeenth and first quarter of the eighteenth century.

It is only incidentally that English affairs occur, but a reference to them will indicate the extent and the value of this source of English history. There are, for instance, the correspondence of Quadra with Margaret, of Mendoza with Alexander Farnese (pp. 23–5, 344–5), the keys of Margaret's and Alexander's cipher correspondence with Parsons, Hugh Owen, and other Jesuits and conspirators (p. 60), letters from Allen, Father Garnet, Bruce (of whose treachery the editors do not seem to be aware), numerous *avvisi* from London, and an account by Ascanio Ciuffarino of his mission from Alexander to Elizabeth in 1585—a mission which is not mentioned by Froude and is represented by a single reference in the *Spanish Calendar* ; and later on we have some letters from the famous earl of Peterborough. Altogether there is enough material for British history to justify attention from the British School at Rome, if ever that school could be developed into an institution for historical as well as archaeological research. Or perhaps the Record Office, which has already calendared documents in Rome and in north Italian archives, might extend its operations as far as Naples.   A. F. POLLARD.

Tangier, England's last Atlantic Outpost, 1661–84. By E. M. G. ROUTH. (London : Murray, 1912.)

MISS ROUTH'S *Tangier* is a careful and interesting monograph which will be of much service to historians of the reign of Charles the Second. Hitherto the best account of the English occupation of this place has been the first volume of Lieut.-Colonel John Davis's *History of the Second Queen's, now the Royal West Surrey Regiment*, published in 1887. Colonel Davis confined himself mainly to the military history of the occupation ; Miss Routh adds chapters on the trade, the civil government, and the social life of Tangier. She also gives a much fuller and more accurate account of the various native potentates against whom the different governors of the English garrison had to struggle, and of the negotiations with them which from time to time took place. The purely military history is well told, though more briefly. Some documents are printed in full by Colonel Davis which are merely summarized or extracted from by Miss Routh, therefore the older book retains its value. Miss Routh, however, has consulted many authorities not used by her predecessor, so that even on military points her book often contains new information. In both books Hollar's etchings are reproduced: Miss Routh adds about half a dozen not in the older book. She also gives four very interesting drawings by Thomas Phillips: the two views on pp. 264, 266, showing Tangier from the west before and after the demolition of the fortifications, are specially remarkable. On the other hand Colonel Davis's book contains photographs of three paintings by Stoop, in the museum of the earl of Dartmouth, which Miss Routh does not reproduce. But the plans and views she does give make the topography of Tangier perfectly plain.

Much the best governor of Tangier seems to have been its second, Lord Teviot, who was killed in an ambuscade by the Moors on 3 May 1664. There is a curious broadside in the Luttrell Collection (i. 132) which has escaped Miss Routh's notice: 'Death's envious Triumph, a brief memorial of the loss of the incomparable Andrew . . . Earl of Teviot.' It contains besides verses on Teviot 'a card of the town of Tangier according to the exactest delineation'. The curious and interesting monument of Sir Palmer Fairborne, referred to on p. 196, is engraved in Dart's *History of Westminster Abbey* (ii. 87); it is a pity that it was not included amongst the illustrations, for his name is inseparably associated with the successful repulse of the Moors in the great siege. The last governor of the town was Colonel Percy Kirke. Kirke's letters, says Miss Routh, 'seem almost to belie his reputation. He appears to have been not indifferent to the welfare of his men, and made many humane and sensible suggestions for improving their condition and increasing the efficiency of the garrison.' Judging from the figures given in Miss Routh's appendix the cost of maintaining the garrison of Tangier varied from £53,000 to £70,000 per annum, while the building of the mole cost £340,000. From first to last it must have cost the government of Charles II not less than a million and a half. Charles II cannot be fairly blamed for its evacuation: the refusal of the Parliament to provide money to maintain it, unless he passed the Exclusion Bill, made its abandonment inevitable.

A few minor errors may be noted. On p. 10 read 'Sir Richard' not 'Sir John' Stayner. The note on p. 30 does not give the history of the various councils which managed the colonies quite clearly: the best account of them is to be found in *British Committees, Commissions, and Councils of Trade and Plantations, 1622–75*, by Professor C. M. Andrews, in series xxvi of the Johns Hopkins University Studies in Historical and Political Science. In the first chapter Miss Routh might with advantage have treated the relations of England and Portugal before the marriage of Charles II rather more fully. The policy of assisting the Portuguese to maintain their independence against Spain had been adopted long before the restoration of Charles II.

C. H. FIRTH.

Le Comte F.-C. de Mercy-Argenteau. Par le COMTE DE PIMODAN. (Paris: Plon, 1911.)

THE future ambassador came of the families of Argenteau and Mercy which had long been settled in the Low Countries. He was born at Liége in 1727. Little is known of his youth except that, for some reason that has never come to light, he was confined by his father's orders on a family estate in Hungary. This time of solitude somewhat embittered a nature formerly gay and precocious; but in or about 1750 he was allowed to travel, and to study law and history at Paris. There he became attached to the Austrian embassy as one of the chevaliers in attendance on Kaunitz, by whose favour he gained an entry to the diplomatic career. Kaunitz described him as altogether wanting in genius, but kind-hearted, industrious, and full of zeal. He returned with his patron to Vienna early in 1753, and in the following year was named plenipotentiary to the court of Turin, remaining there until the year 1761. Unfortunately, the references in this volume to his stay at the Sardinian capital are extremely brief. An account of his quarrel with a French colleague, and his taste for perfumes, which that court detested, make up nearly all that is told of these seven years. Transferred to St. Petersburg in 1761, Mercy, or Argenteau as he preferred to call himself, moved amidst the exciting events of the end of the Seven Years' War. The death of Elizabeth, the accession, dethronement, and murder of Peter III (wrongly called 'Paul III' on p. 33), and the accession of Catharine II, are merely mentioned; and the rôle played by Argenteau is not even hinted at. Almost equally brief is the notice of his attitude towards the Polish troubles of 1764, which nearly concerned Austria. The Comte de Pimodan disclaims the intention of writing a history of Argenteau, but even a slight biography like the present should have explained the import of these topics. Further, the question should be faced, if not solved, whether Argenteau did not displace Starhemberg at the Paris embassy in order to push on more vigorously Maria Theresa's favourite project of marrying Marie Antoinette to the dauphin of France.

Transferred to Paris in 1766, Argenteau sought to carry out the political aims of Maria Theresa. In the spring of the year 1769, after the death of Marie Leszczynska, projects of a marriage alliance for Louis XV occupied his attention; but, as is well known, the du Barry thwarted them. The author admits that Argenteau subordinated his feelings as a man to his duties as Austrian ambassador in all the advice which he tendered to Marie Antoinette. The story is well known, and this volume adds very little to our knowledge of it. His opposition to Vergennes in various episodes of the early part of the reign of Louis XVI is described, but, again, without the detail which is necessary to a due understanding of the Dutch and Turkish disputes of the years 1783-7. On pp. 230-2 there is no notice of the serious diplomatic check sustained by France in the Dutch affair of 1787, and of the increase of unpopularity of the queen and of the Austrian alliance which resulted from it. Similarly, the part played by Argenteau in arranging for the flight of the royal family to the eastern frontier at midsummer 1791 is but faintly outlined; and the story of his last days in

London in August 1794, during a final effort to bring England and Austria to a closer union, is very briefly dismissed. The evidence in the *Dropmore Papers* (ii. 617, 624–6) shows that that mission may have been, and probably was, one more device of the Austrian chancellor, Thugut, to postpone a definite decision, while Austria evacuated the Netherlands and turned her forces towards Poland. Such at least was the belief of the British ministers and of Lord Spencer and Mr. Thomas Grenville, whom they had dispatched to Vienna in the hope of concerting more vigorous measures. George III and Lord Grenville deemed Argenteau's conduct dilatory; but that of course may have resulted from the weakness caused by the disease which carried him off on 25 August 1794. By far the best chapters of the book are those which deal with the French Revolution, especially when the life of the queen was in danger. The appendixes show that disputes arose between Ferson and Argenteau; also that the latter strongly disapproved the policy of threatening France adopted more or less openly at and after the declaration of Pillnitz. It is to be wished that the author could have treated the years 1761–89 as fully as the last period of this interesting career. J. HOLLAND ROSE.

The Constitutional History of England since the Accession of George III.
By the Right Hon. Sir THOMAS ERSKINE MAY. Edited and continued to 1911 by FRANCIS HOLLAND. 3 vols. (London: Longmans, 1912.)

MR. HOLLAND possesses qualifications, some of which are natural and some accidental, for the task of continuing Erskine May's *Constitutional History*. Engaged, we believe, in that service of the house of commons in which Erskine May had a distinguished career, he has enjoyed exceptional opportunities for observing the constitutional changes of recent times, and has had good reasons for cultivating a judicial attitude towards them. At the same time, loyalty to the house he serves induces him to look with a favourable eye on its progress at the expense of the other house, and to feel a decently veiled sympathy with constitutional alterations similar to that which Erskine May avowed with the developments he described. Mr. Holland finds it possible to distribute criticism with a fairly impartial and not too lavish hand; but we do not imagine we do him any injustice in remarking that his selection of the parliament act of 1911 as the climax of his story and his handling of the subject-matter indicate a distinct preference for the liberal over the conservative point of view. If that is not the case, we can congratulate him on the success with which he has imitated successive Speakers whose rulings have, if anything, favoured the party to which they did not belong.

Mr. Holland, too, has followed in the style as well as in the spirit of Erskine May; and he has felt bound as a continuator to adopt the plan laid down by his predecessor. It has its defects as well as its merits; and it may be doubted whether constitutional history should not be written in an analytical form rather than in that of a narrative. Bishop Stubbs's plan of alternating such chapters is one of the best features of his book, and narrative lends itself to political better than to constitutional history. Some of Mr. Holland's chapters, notably those on 'Party' and on 'The Home Rule Movement,' are hardly distinguishable from ordinary political history. The home rule movement has not yet affected the framework of the constitution—unless we regard the Irish local government act as its effect; and the space given to party warfare might, perhaps, have been better occupied by other things. We miss, for instance, any comprehensive survey of the tendency from under-government to over-government which has marked so strongly the last fifty years, and has changed the British constitution from a negative agent for preventing what was thought to be wrong into a positive agent for producing what is thought to be right. We should have liked some exposition of the constitutional expedients by which sovereignty, almost abolished by 'the rights of man' in the eighteenth century, has in these latter days been rehabilitated as 'la volonté générale' and galvanized into unprecedented activity; some elucidation of the principles upon which the right to express this general will is distributed, presumably according to their intelligence, between the most enlightened central government, less enlightened counties, and least enlightened parishes and districts; some estimate of the extent to which government has really been centralized or decentralized; and some account of the methods by which bureaucracy controls or serves the state. Mr. Holland's volume is, we think, too conventional; it gives exactly the version of history which an intelligent reader of the daily press would give. Yet the reasons commonly alleged for political action are merely conventional reasons. Cabinets seldom reveal their real motives; no doubt their reasons are those of all sensible men, but what these are they, perhaps like sensible men, never tell. Almost certainly they are more interesting and more profound than the public versions of them which have to be accommodated to the public taste.

For this conventionality, however, Erskine May rather than Mr. Holland is responsible. Questions of this character were not discussed in the original work, and we cannot expect to find them in its continuation. Apart from a remark that there is a great deal of repetition in Mr. Holland's volume, we must limit our criticism to one or two of his arguments and to a few slips which should be corrected in view of the number of editions likely to be required of a standard work. From the alleged fact that ministries never failed to win general elections, Mr. Holland repeatedly deduces the conclusion, as Erskine May had done before, that the Crown controlled these elections down to 1830 (pp. 17, 87-8, 270). We doubt the premiss: if the Crown could always get a majority, what was the motive of the septennial act of 1716 ? and how do we explain Walpole's fall almost immediately after the general election of 1741 ? or the elder Pitt's fall so soon after that of 1761 ? Moreover, the rule, which Mr. Holland discerns in eighteenth-century general elections, is truer of the last twenty years. An existing ministry has not been defeated at a general election since 1892; is that because the Crown has controlled the elections ? We doubt whether it did so in the eighteenth century. Men voted then for persons rather than for parties; and they did not expect to decide the fate of ministries. Sometimes, no doubt, policies affected votes; but ministries and parties were not then wedded to policies. Now it appears that cabinets and parliaments respond to public opinion without waiting for its expression at a general election.

His anxiety to prove this point leads Mr. Holland into errors of fact: he writes (p. 22) ' from 1867 until 1910 every general election, except the abnormal one of 1900 . . . has *resulted* in a change of government '. This interpretation of the general election of 1885 might be disputed, but there is no disputing the facts that Lord Salisbury was in office at the dissolution of 1895 and secured a majority of 152, and that Sir Henry Campbell-Bannerman was in office at the dissolution of January 1906 and secured a majority of 354. It is curious, too, that Mr. Holland should give 105 as the number of Irish members (pp. 40, 73, 171); the number which was fixed at 100 by the union was increased to 105 in 1832, but subsequently reduced to 103 through the disfranchisement of two boroughs for corruption. Lord Rosebery's campaign against the house of lords in 1895 began before and not after his resignation (p. 45); nor was he a ' former Prime Minister ', as Mr. Holland states (p. 254), when he was elected first chairman of the London County Council. The ' National Schools ' (p. 131) were not the schools under the control of the school boards, but those belonging to the National Society. The governors of the states of the Australian Commonwealth are not ' Lieutenant-Governors ' (p. 317), while those of the provinces of Canada are. Ireland was in 1885, and is still, a part of the United Kingdom, a phrase which Mr. Holland on p. 55 restricts to England, Scotland, and Wales; nor is it quite correct to describe the progressives as ' the Liberal party ' in the London County Council (p. 255). He must enjoy a singular detachment from poor law agitations to be able to state (p. 250) that with very few exceptions their administrative obligations were not imposed upon the justices of the peace until the nineteenth century. Mr. Holland will pardon this attention to minutiae. He has dealt with a difficult subject in a highly competent fashion; his powers of political reflexion and interpretation are not, we think, inferior to Erskine May's; and the drawbacks to his volume are due less to him than to the original scheme which he has undertaken to complete. A. F. POLLARD.

George III and Charles Fox. The Concluding Part of the American Revolution. By Sir GEORGE O. TREVELYAN, O.M. Vol. i. (London: Longmans, 1912.)

American Colonial Government, 1696–1765; A Study of the British Board of Trade. By O. M. DICKERSON. (Cleveland, Ohio: The Arthur Clark Co., 1912.)

THESE books are placed side by side, not because they cover the same ground, but because they represent the opposite poles, or rather the equator and the pole, in their methods of dealing with history. Of Sir George Trevelyan's general treatment of the American Revolution it is difficult to say much which is new. The late Mr. J. A. Doyle, in the pages of this Review (xiv. 596–604, 1899, and xix. 367–73, 1904), seems to have spoken the final word, and subsequent reviewers can only say ditto to Mr. Burke. The cynical may note with amusement that, in spite of Sir George's respect for the men of the Revolution, he is not prepared to bore himself or his readers in their company ; and so hardly sixty pages of the present volume are concerned with the doings in America. On the very first page we find the old note of exaggeration. Great Britain is described as having put forward all her strength and yet been vanquished by the Americans. The truth, surely, was that nothing can atone for bad generalship ; and that the generalship on the British side had, time after time, let go the fruits of victory. Nor was the final issue even in 1778 as certain as it is represented by Sir George Trevelyan. In October of that year Washington expressed a doubt whether the Americans could carry on the war much longer, unless radical financial reform was effected.

Those who have followed the story of the difficult coming to birth, in 1789, of the United States as a nation will note with astonishment the following passage. The revolutionary government

was destined to have its own troubles and difficulties as long as the war lasted ; but they were troubles and difficulties of a nature to which the most firmly settled and long-established monarchies have always been liable during a period of national emergency. There were wrangles and intrigues in Congress, just as there was quarrelling between Whigs and Tories at Westminster. There were outbreaks of turbulence in Washington's army, just as there was a mutiny at the Nore. . . . The American Treasury flooded the country with issues of worthless paper, just as Frederic the Great had debased the silver coinage of Prussia. . . . But these are internal maladies, of which a nation does not die ; and the United States were now to all intents and purposes a self-contained and independent nation.

' Self-contained and independent ' when there was no common tariff ; when there was no central government, that could enforce its commands on individual citizens, and when the local concerns of the several states were of infinitely greater interest to them than was the good of the common weal.

Sir George Trevelyan quotes with apparent approval the charge against Lord George Germain that he omitted, or forgot, to communicate to General Howe Burgoyne's instructions. It is now clear from the publication by the Historical Manuscripts Commission of the Knox Papers that Howe was informed of the proposed expedition and of the need for co-operation, though not in such a manner as to absolve Germain from blame.

It is not only with regard to America that we detect this note of exaggeration. It was facts, not Fox, which converted the house of commons to a recognition of the necessity of peace ; and, though Sir George knows much more about Fox than is known by any of his readers, the picture given of the young tory reprobate, suddenly finding conversion, strikes one as a little overdrawn. As a work of art the book may suffer from its dual subject ; but it deals with material of which the author is certain to make the most. It fortunately happens that, on the most dramatic themes dealt with, there can be no two opinions. Sir George Trevelyan himself (and what praise could be higher ?) has never give us more vigorous, moving writing than the chapters in which he tells of Keppel and Palliser, and of Benedict Arnold and André. The story how the gallant whig admiral consented, at the request of the king, to take command of the weakened channel fleet ; how the battle of Ushant came to nothing through the neglect of the tory Palliser to co-operate ; how Palliser sought to cover his own disgrace by bringing charges against his superior ; how the court martial ended in the triumphant acquittal of Keppel, and how the whole nation rejoiced over his justification—all this is told by Sir George in a manner that no one, save his uncle, could have equalled. Yet more impressive is the last chapter in the volume which deals with the traitor Arnold and André, the blameless spy, rightly hanged, yet no less rightly the object of pity and of sympathy. He must be a thankless reader indeed who, fresh from such writing, condemns the picturesque in history.

Of a very different character is Mr. Dickerson's careful book; yet if the aim of the historian be to widen the area of knowledge it is of greater importance than is the more brilliant volume. Hitherto the knowledge of the eighteenth-century board of trade has been generally derived from Pownall's *Administration of the Colonies*, an interesting book, which suffers from its complete neglect of the historical method. It is a mystery why a book, first published in 1764, should have omitted to point out that from 1751 onwards for ten years the board of trade, through its president, possessed those powers which he urged should be given it. Mr. Dickerson's volume, along with the volumes of the acts of the privy council and their illuminating introductions, enable one to understand the colonial administration of the eighteenth century in a manner which was in the past impossible. The subject is dealt with under the separate heads of the organization and personnel of the board of trade; its relations to other departments; its difficulties; its imperialistic (why the last two syllables ?) policy; its treatment of colonial legislation and of boundaries, trade, defence, and Indian affairs. Some of these subjects have been dealt with in other books, approached from a different point of view, e.g. the question of obtaining for the governors a permanent salary; but the chapter on the treatment of colonial legislation by the home authorities seems largely to break new ground. The

method of repeal [we are told] could not be called arbitrary, for it had thrown around it, at every point, all the forms of legal procedure. No law could be disallowed except after an opportunity had been given all parties concerned to oppose such action. The Board really gave to every person concerned due process of law; each party had his day in court; and, after the Board had acted, it was always possible to carry the case to the committee [of the Privy Council], when a judicial review of the action of the Board could be had. In fact it was very similar to a system of repeals by the action of a Superior Court. It is no exaggeration to say that our Supreme Court declares state laws unconstitutional with even less ceremony than the Board used in disallowing colonial Acts. . . . The control exercised by the Board over legislation was no doubt often irritating to the colonists, just as the invalidation of laws by the courts is irritating to both state and nation, at times, in the United States. Some of the restrictions imposed by the Board were evaded by means of temporary laws, but the importance of these has probably been overrated, as they could be successful only to a limited extent. . . . Taken all together, the royal veto proved a pretty effective check upon even the Charter Colonies, as witness the action of Massachusetts with regard to its bankruptcy law. . . . Probably no other part of the administrative machinery worked so effectively as did the control of colonial legislation, especially when one considers the common willingness of the provincial governors to evade their Instructions and permit forbidden practices.

The final conclusion reached is that

The Board was no better and certainly but little worse than other parts of the British Government, and periods of inefficiency in the one are contemporary with similar periods in the other. In each case the cause of bad government must be sought in the personality of the men who were responsible for the conditions. . . . The Board of Trade was not ignorant of the political tendency within the colonies, nor slow to recognize the practically unworkable character of the imperial arrangements for governing them. With unerring foresight it picked out the most vital defect in the Constitution, and sought to remedy it by securing in each of the royal and proprietary provinces a fixed civil list. . . . No doubt principles of government, worked out under the administration of the Board of Trade, have influenced later administration in many ways. The Indian policy of the Board by its very example persisted for many years, at least so far as its main features are concerned. And it is a significant fact that when the New American Government acquired territories, that is colonies, of its own, it did not place the governors, judges, or territorial officers at the mercy of a local legislature, nor were unlimited financial powers conferred upon such legislatures, and all laws were subjected to a review and possible veto by the central government.

From these quotations and from the general result of Mr. Dickerson's investigations we may recognize the value of Burke's statement that 'the Board of Trade was reproduced in a job' and was 'the only instance of a public body, which has never degenerated, but to this hour preserves all the health and vigour of its primitive institution'. In fact it is books of this kind, now happily becoming common among the new school of American historians, that afford the antidote to the teaching of the Bancroft school, in which Sir George Trevelyan is content to dwell. But unfortunately for every reader of *American Colonial Government* there will be a hundred for *The American Revolution*. *Populus vult decipi et decipiatur* ; and it makes no difference, except in the way of aggravation, that the deceiver should be a laborious, as well as brilliant, author, who would sooner cut off his right hand than put down on paper anything he did not conscientiously believe to be the truth. H. E. EGERTON.

William Pitt and the Great War. By J. HOLLAND ROSE, D.Litt. (London : Bell, 1911.)

THE part of the career of the younger Pitt which Dr. Rose tackles in this volume involves such a number of threads and issues that one hardly wonders that up to the present there should have been so few attempts to deal with it exhaustively, or that when a writer has come forward with the requisite knowledge of the period and enthusiasm for his subject he should have only achieved a rather partial success. The book is a most valuable contribution to the study of the period and throws a great deal of new light on doubtful and disputed points, but Dr. Rose's treatment of the naval and military questions involved does not carry conviction, and to that extent the book falls short of success. Much as he knows about the period he nowhere shows that grasp of the principles of strategy, that understanding of the relations between naval force and military power, which is required to appreciate properly the problem before Pitt and the adequacy— or the reverse—of the measures he adopted to solve it. The diplomacy of the period Dr. Rose unravels with masterly skill : he lays bare the intrigues of Thugut, Godoy, and Haugwitz, the vagaries of Paul and Alexander I, the vacillation and greed of Frederick William II and his son, the hesitation and weakness of Francis Joseph ; he brings out admirably the connexion between the affairs of Poland and the collapse of the First Coalition, and shows how French aggressions were far more responsible than was 'Pitt's gold' for the succession of wars in which Europe was plunged, how patriotic, consistent, and honourable Pitt's policy really was; and if he is at times a little disposed to exaggerate Pitt's work and to claim for him even more than his due share in the ultimate overthrow of Napoleon, it is a pardonable error in a biographer.

Among the important points on which Dr. Rose does seem to have given a final verdict one may mention in the first place his refutation of the charge that Pitt plunged England into an avoidable war in January 1793. In the face of great provocation Pitt and his foreign minister, Grenville, clung to non-intervention and neutrality as long as it was possible, perhaps longer than was wise. Indeed, 'by remaining neutral while the French overran Belgium, Pitt was favouring the French more than any British statesman had done since the time of James II' (p. 48). As late as October 1792 Pitt was ready to recognize the republic and be friendly to it if only it would abstain from the acts of aggression and from the revolutionary propagandism which in the end brought about the rupture between England and France (p. 100). Dr. Rose is able to show most convincingly that it was the famous decrees of 16 and 19 November and of 15 December, not the execution of Louis XVI, which made a continuation of peace impossible (p. 91). And it may be added that Dr. Rose has no fanatical hostility to the Revolution and its principles. Far from it, he is disposed to make excuses for the French and even to blame Pitt where blame is hardly justified. Even if Pitt had favoured the Royalist cause it would be ridiculous to hold him therefore responsible for the war (p. 47); and to talk reprovingly about 'unconciliatory manners' (p. 101) and 'insular and innate austerity' (p. 114) as if they had had a serious share in causing the war is absurd, as it is also to speak of Pitt's precautionary measures, feeble as they were, as precipitating the conflict they were designed to avert (p. 77). Really a peaceful settlement was quite out of the question at the end of 1792. Dr. Rose's account answers his own criticisms of Pitt: the French meant war and nothing short of abject surrender to their pretensions could have averted hostilities. Their professions that they were not going to attack Holland were insincere and merely intended to delude us (p. 107). Jemmapes had raised visions of easy conquest which had excited the cupidity of France.

It is one of the merits of the thoroughness with which Dr. Rose has gone into every episode that one can sometimes refute his conclusions from the evidence he himself produces. He is continually criticizing the measures adopted by Pitt for checking the spread of republican and revolutionary principles in England and girding at 'repressive legislation', arguing that Pitt ought to have 'taken the nation into his confidence', to have 'trusted and armed the people', and 'embattled it as a whole' (whatever that may mean: it apparently does not mean the only step which could have proved efficacious, enforcing universal liability to military service). One has only to read Dr. Rose's seventh chapter, 'The British Jacobins,' to see that the danger was one to be treated seriously. Efforts were being made to spread sedition among the troops; there were grounds for believing that the mutiny at the Nore was fomented by political disaffection on shore (p. 316) even if definite proof was not forthcoming; the actions of the London Corresponding Society in 1798 amounted to nothing short of treason (pp. 349-50). And, as Dr. Rose shows, in 1793-4 discontent was widespread, and the fact that the 'repressive' legislation which Pitt introduced was successful in checking sedition is no proof that sedition did not exist or that this legislation was unnecessary. Chauvelin's intrigues with the English malcontents were not a thing to be treated lightly, and it is folly to talk about 'frothy talk' being best 'treated with quiet contempt' (p. 115) when it is encouraging enemies outside and causing them to believe that they have only to attack to be generally welcomed. One can be wise after the event and see that the disaffected were but a small minority, but when Dr. Rose talks vaguely about a law-abiding majority holding in check the Jacobinical minority it is a little difficult to see how this is to be done except by the action of the organized forces of the state. After all, the French Revolution itself was the work of a minority who carried the majority a great deal further than it wished to go, because the minority knew what it was seeking and the majority did not, and only wanted not to be left dangerously far behind.

On the question of Ireland Dr. Rose is able to show the absurdity of the accusation that Pitt and Camden fomented the '98 rebellion in order to push on the Union (p. 391). He is brief but clear on Fitzwilliam, whose indiscretion, if it was no worse, for Pitt had most certainly not given him a free hand (p. 341), was responsible for much of the trouble that followed. Pitt's attitude towards the question of the Irish Catholics is sympathetically and fairly treated. A man with a less high standard of honour would not have resigned, as Pitt did, because he found he could not fulfil a promise which was not much more than implicit (p. 446). Pitt's difficulties and hesitations about resuming office in 1803-4 are shown to have been due to his strictness in keeping his pledge to Addington, a pledge he would have been fully justified in breaking in the existing emergency, and from which Addington ought to have released him long before he did.

Pitt's efforts to arrive at an honourable peace in 1797 are commended, and the failure is shown to have been caused by the triumph of the extreme party in France on 18 Fructidor. But Dr. Rose condemns Pitt's rejection of Napoleon's overtures in 1799 (p. 304). We hardly follow his reasoning. One would have expected the biographer of Napoleon to have realized what sort of use Napoleon would have made of peace. As he himself says, 'the prospects of the campaign were not unfavourable.' Indeed, had Pitt's conception of the way in which England could best assist her allies and at the same time attain her own object been a little sounder, it is quite probable that Marengo would never have placed Napoleon firmly in power. But Dr. Rose never as much as alludes to the chance which England missed in Italy in the spring of 1800 for want of troops, who were available had Pitt known how to use them, to follow up our naval successes.

This brings one to the weakest point in the book, the handling of the strategic questions. Dr. Rose glides not unskilfully over the thin ice of Pitt's failure to do anything in the way of providing the country with an efficient military system before the war or during it, and by not discussing at any length the various measures adopted he avoids having to expose their futility. He does not seem to realize that unpreparedness for war is the most costly folly a nation can commit; that 'the dauntless spirit of Britons' is a poor thing to rely on when it is a mere fluid sentiment, untrained and unorganized; that if we had been prepared for war in 1793 all the crushing taxation, at which he girds as if it were possible to have security without paying for it, might have been avoided. He admits that the expedition to Flanders was determined on political not military grounds (p. 267), and ascribes the credit for our success in Egypt to Pitt without a word about the culpable carelessness with which Abercromby was sent with 15,000 men to attack a force which turned out to be twice his strength and twice what ministers expected. He is completely at sea when he seeks to justify Pitt's military measures by representing them as a revival of Chatham's, as he shows by the extraordinary statement that Chatham gave 'comparatively little military aid to Frederick II' (p. 219). Has he ever heard of Minden? But here again he supplies his own refutation. One could not want a severer condemnation of Pitt's policy than the quotation on p. 219 from Colonel Graham, or than the admission that the chief aims of Pitt and Dundas were to harry the coast of France and secure Hayti.

It is true that Dr. Rose explains that intervention in St. Domingo looked a promising venture (pp. 219–29), but he quite fails to meet Mr. Fortescue's criticisms of the waste of men in the West Indies, a quarter in which success, however great, could not be definite. The enemy had to be struck in a vital spot, not on the extremities, and this Dr. Rose never seems to grasp. Our naval successes were inconclusive in themselves, they needed following up. That the intervention of Spain in 1796 was really very important Dr. Rose does show (p. 241 f.). It is true that the Franco-Spanish alliance caused us to evacuate Corsica and the Mediterranean and so opened the way for Napoleon's expedition to Egypt, that it also contributed to our lack of success in the West Indies, but Dr. Rose displays the limitations of his understanding of strategy when he talks about Spain's position threatening the coast of Ireland (p. 244), just as when he draws a gloomy picture of the disasters which would have befallen us had Napoleon made for Ireland instead of for Egypt in 1798 (p. 364). He does not seem to have realized that thirteen French battleships encumbered with the protection of a vast fleet of transports would have had a singularly poor chance of getting out of the Mediterranean when Jervis was lying off Cadiz with a fleet superior not only in efficiency but in numbers. A similar statement, which makes one think Dr. Rose has overlooked the difference between the probable and the possible in war, is that on p. 493 about the cruisers and gunboats off the Kentish coast being quite able to destroy Napoleon's flotilla. Of course they were, had it come unescorted, but if the French fleet had gained the mastery of the Channel our cruisers and gunboats would not have had much influence over the further operations.

C. T. ATKINSON.

L'Église de Paris et la Révolution. Par P. PISANI. Tome iv, 1799-1802. (Paris: Picard, 1911.)

THE Abbé Pisani has now completed his detailed history of the church of Paris during the French Revolution, and he has earned the congratulations of scholars upon the accomplishment of a task involving several years' patient labour. The volume before us displays to the reader the record of a period of hope and joy to the Christians of France, when the overthrow of the directory and the rule of Bonaparte inaugurated a new policy of friendship with Rome and health to the wounded conscience of France. The book falls into two distinct parts: there is the historical account of the negotiations which led to the great ceremony in Notre-Dame on Easter Day, 1802, together with the history of the police methods employed in Paris to prejudice the well-meaning efforts of the government; and secondly, the abbé gives us, in accordance with his usual plan, some short sketches of the clergy who were appointed under the concordat to the churches of Paris. So when we close the book, we leave the church in Paris fully equipped for the work before it.

The history of the concordat has been worked over during the last few years with a frequency which exempts the Abbé Pisani from any blame if he does not add substantially to our knowledge on this matter. Where, however, he does make a contribution to learning is in his detailed work on the police reports prior to the signature of the concordat, and in his study of the rules laid down by Cardinal Caprara and his advisers with regard to the readmission of married clergy into the fold and the regularization of marriages contracted within the bonds of kindred and affinity during the Revolution. Very wisely it was decided that discipline in these matters should be strict: married clergy who had lost or put away their wives were but gradually admitted to rehabilitation, and in the case of irregular marriages, the practice appears to have been far less accommodating than that of the Roman curia in cases which have come before it. The study of the new clergy is naturally of less interest to those who are not acquainted with the church of Paris and are not attached to it by the intimate bonds of M. Pisani, but it will remain a valuable work of reference for his successors in the study of French ecclesiastical history. We may note in passing that the clergy of the church under the concordat, both non-juring and constitutional, gave an admirable example how to sink differences, radical though they were, and unite in work which was for the good of the city in which they lived. The shameful story how Bernier succeeded in inducing Caprara to give institution to the new constitutional bishops is told without any glozing by M. Pisani, whose judgement on the constitutional clergy, with its oblique reproaches on Bernier, is worth quoting:

Dans leur lutte acharnée contre le Légat, ils font preuve d'une diabolique obstination; mais ils l'ont toujours attaqué en face; s'ils se sont souvent trompés, ils n'ont jamais menti; ils ont atrocement diffamé leurs adversaires, ils ont répandu contre eux d'abominables calomnies, mais ce qui apparaissait calomnie aux esprits clairvoyants et impartiaux était pour eux la stricte vérité, vérité étrangement déformée par leurs rancunes et par leur vaniteuse infatuation (p. 284).

It is a pleasure to find an ultramontane clergyman in these days bearing a tribute to the sincerity of the constitutional clergy, whose chief crime, in an Englishman's eyes, seems to have been a whole-hearted acceptance of a well-intentioned attempt to correct abuses, carried out so ill-advisedly as to be the standing monument of the legislative folly of the constituent assembly.
L. G. WICKHAM LEGG.

La Politique Extérieure du Premier Consul. Par ÉDOUARD DRIAULT. (Paris: Alcan, 1910.)
Austerlitz, la Fin du Saint-Empire. Par ÉDOUARD DRIAULT. (Paris: Alcan, 1912.)

M. ÉDOUARD DRIAULT has now brought his work upon Napoleon and Europe to the brink of the Jena campaign; and upon the present scale of a volume for every three years of history, the book, when completed, should extend to five volumes. One is tempted to ask whether it was wise of M. Driault to embark upon an undertaking which in scope and character so closely recalls M. Sorel's masterpiece, for it is no disparagement to M. Driault, one of the most competent of living Napoleonic scholars, to observe that his work, good and trustworthy as it is, falls far short of *L'Europe et la Révolution Française* as an effort of scientific and imaginative reconstruction. M. Driault could doubtless answer that if his canvas is less variously and richly tinted, it has certain qualities of its own, notably a very close and first-hand study of diplomatic material, and that it is founded upon a view of the relations of Napoleon and Europe different from, and indeed opposed to, the doctrine held by M. Sorel. It is sufficient to say that M. Driault dissents, and in our judgement wisely, from the view that the wars of Napoleon were essentially defensive in character. The strong point of M. Driault as an historian of these times consists in his remarkable familiarity with the Paris archives, and in particular with the rich collection of diplomatic correspondence which may be read (in circumstances of extreme physical comfort) at the Quai d'Orsay. He uses, as of course any student of the period must, the imperial correspondence as the substructure of his history, but there is not a chapter in the two volumes before us which does not receive additional illumination from the dispatches of Talleyrand or else from the reports of the French agents at foreign courts. These reports vary of course in value. Some of them are excellent, notably the letters of Alquier from Naples and Bacher from Regensburg; and in any case it will be useful to have at hand so many accessible and well-chosen extracts from a literature which, though frequently consulted before, has never, we think, been exhibited so fully as in these two volumes from M. Driault's pen. It would have demanded a good deal more time than M. Driault has allowed himself over these volumes, to make even a partial search in the depositories of Germany, Italy, and England. M. Driault does not emulate the catholicity of Dr. Alfred Stern. He confines himself to Paris. For England he relies on Dr. Rose, for Prussia on Bailleu, for Italy on the published papers of Melzi d'Eril and the like. The angle of observation is throughout the French foreign office.

In other words, M. Driault's treatment is strictly political and diplomatic. He provides neither maps, nor battle pieces, nor elaborate analysis of character, the object being to represent just that part of Napoleon's action upon Europe which can be enclosed in treaties and political correspondence, and to leave the remainder for the drum-and-trumpet historian and the philosopher of progress. These limitations given and accepted, we have little but praise for M. Driault's sincere and unpretentious workmanship. The account of the destruction of the holy Roman empire, for instance, strikes us as specially clear and adequate ; so, too, the story of the difficulties which surrounded the birth of the Third Coalition. It is also satisfactory to note that M. Driault has not lost the power of criticizing Napoleon. Indeed, a very good test might be proposed to discriminate those who are qualified from those who are not qualified to act as sound guides to Napoleonic history. Do they or do they not believe that Napoleon was sincere in his professions of peace ? If they follow M. Driault, who describes the famous letter of 2 January 1803 to George III as a 'coup de sonde diplomatique', they are treading in the right way. But we are not certain about another proposition which we meet in this book casting doubt upon the reality of Napoleon's intention to invade England on the ground that he would have risked everything and could not, even had he taken London, have made much use of his conquest, for when did Napoleon listen to the counsels of prudence, and how, upon the assumption of a feint, are we to explain the tenor of certain St. Helena conversations ? And in connexion with 'the insupportable tyranny' exercised by England on the seas, it is perhaps worth remembering that France exercised an even more rigorous tyranny till 1744, and only adopted the Prussian doctrine that free ships make free goods in 1778 for the purpose of damaging England in the American war. The whole subject is admirably summarized in Lecky's *History of England*, v. 65-7.   H. A. L. FISHER.

ALBERT CASSAGNE, *La Vie politique de François de Chateaubriand ; Consulat, Empire, Première Restauration*. (Paris : Plon, 1911.)

THE work of M. Cassagne supplies fresh evidence of the recent growth of interest in Chateaubriand, and, when completed, will form the most important contribution to the interpretation of his life and thought since Sainte-Beuve published his brilliant and malicious volumes half a century ago. Though the title confines the scope of the book to his political career, the preface discounts the effect of the limitation by declaring that he was in essence a man of action and a poet by accident. The accident has become in the eyes of posterity the essential, partly owing to his incomparable style, partly to a conspiracy among hostile politicians to disparage his aptitudes and achievements. In reality he belongs to the race of La Rochefoucauld and Retz. 'His character, tastes, ambitions, heredity urged him towards action, not incidentally at certain periods, but continuously from youth to old age.' Literature was an instrument, a consolation, a pastime, not a career. *René* reflected the mood of a moment, not the temperament of a lifetime. Unlike Lamartine and Victor Hugo, the man of action in Chateaubriand explains the poet, and even his most purely literary productions only become fully intelligible in the light of his political ideas and ambitions. The author's apprehension that his thesis may appear highly paradoxical is scarcely justified. At any rate no attentive reader of the *Mémoires d'Outre-Tombe* will be greatly surprised. That marvellous work, whose studied misrepresentations of detail are frequently exposed in these pages, reveals the devouring ambition of the writer to play a part in great affairs. The novelty of the present volume lies less in its general conception of Chateaubriand than in the patient application of the political master-key to his most celebrated books. The work opens with a sketch of the unfinished *Essay on Revolutions*, written in poverty and exile, and breathing a sombre scepticism. Soon after its appearance he made the acquaintance of Fontanes and the royalist group which was waiting for the collapse of the Revolution. 'In those days,' declared Chateaubriand later, 'it was only possible to reach politics through literature.' He therefore resolved to compose the manifesto of the clerical and reactionary party. M. Cassagne throughout refuses to take his professions of religion very seriously, and shows that the *Génie du Christianisme*, contrary to the testimony of the *Mémoires*, was sketched while he was a freethinker and held back till the suitable moment for publication arrived with the concordat. This famous book led, as it was intended to lead, to public employment; but his nomination as secretary to the embassy at Rome brought little satisfaction. He had aspired to be the virtual chief, but Fesch kept him steadily in the background.

So far the portrait is the reverse of flattering. Chateaubriand is presented as a skilful self-seeker, determined to make his way to place and power. But the nobler qualities of the man now begin to appear. His resignation on the death of the Duc d'Enghien, though less heroic than the *Mémoires* suggest, was none the less a courageous act, which Fontanes and his other friends were too selfish to imitate. M. Cassagne traces the echoes of the crisis in *Les Martyrs*, where Napoleon figures as Diocletian and the terrible Fouché as Hierocles. Still bolder was the famous article in the *Mercure* in 1807. 'When the world trembles before the tyrant the historian appears, charged with the vengeance of the peoples. It is in vain that Nero prospers, for Tacitus is already born.' M. Cassagne is fully justified in pronouncing this resounding protest one of the finest episodes of his life. But neither the ruler nor the writer, who frankly recognized each other's genius, desired a final breach. The atmosphere of the *Itinéraire* was conciliatory, associating the memories of St. Louis in Egypt with those of Napoleon. When the Austrian marriage strengthened the emperor's desire for royalist support he secured Chateaubriand's election to the academy; and M. Cassagne discusses, without deciding, whether he accepted money from the government to pay his debts. But Chateaubriand never became a Bonapartist, and when the downfall was at hand he launched his thunderbolt, *Bonaparte et les Bourbons*. M. Cassagne's verdict on that famous pamphlet, more favourable than that of many judges, pronounces it both a continuation of the *Génie du Christianisme* and a contribution to the philosophy of the Holy Alliance. Of even higher merit, though of far less influence, were the *Réflexions Politiques*, written on the eve of the return from Elba, described by the author as embodying the wisest and most liberal thought of its time. While it was the task of Benjamin Constant to instruct the nation in representative government, it was the more arduous endeavour of Chateaubriand to commend it to the noblesse.

The effect of this volume will be to raise the reputation of one of the greatest figures of modern France. Not even his most devoted admirers can accept the flawless patriot of the *Mémoires*; and M. Cassagne claims nothing more than that he compares favourably with many of his celebrated contemporaries as one of the few who held their heads erect in a servile age. Before his reading of this complex personality can be unreservedly adopted we must wait for the volume which will carry the narrative through the Restoration and the monarchy of July; but the first instalment establishes a strong prima facie case.
G. P. GOOCH.

Archaeologia Aeliana (Society of Antiquaries of Newcastle-upon-Tyne). Edited by R. BLAIR. Third Series, volume vii. (Newcastle-upon-Tyne, 1911.)

OF the eight numbers in this volume the first six are of less general interest than the other two; but they all show sound work and contain many points worth attention. The Dean of Lichfield discusses the curious careers of two Durham clergymen at the time of the great rebellion. The secretary of the Surtees Society records some deeds from Burton Agnes. The assessment of hearth or chimney tax at Newcastle in 1665 illustrates the nature of that impost and furnishes a full directory of the householders. Dr. Dendy describes a phase of the struggle between the merchant and craft gilds of Newcastle in 1515, which may yet have some lessons for modern times. 'Ilderton and the Ildertons' is an admirable specimen of exact methods in genealogy; it shows within what limitations a family can claim a 'Norman' pedigree. There is also a discussion of the three Middleton villages which are mentioned in the paper on the Ildertons. In the seventh part the excavators of Corstopitum report on their labours in July—October 1910. All who have seen the western wing of the supposed 'forum', discovered earlier, will read with interest their description of its eastern side, though they are careful not to dogmatize (p. 164) either on the purposes or on the masonry of these remarkable buildings. Their map of the settlement is being gradually filled up; but there was not much of importance in the sites to the east of the 'forum'. Professor Haverfield adds notes on the smaller objects, including some good *fibulae*, which are well illustrated; Mr. Craster catalogues the coins, and draws a few inferences. But the most elaborate contribution is the dissertation by Professor Meek and Mr. Gray on the animal remains unearthed from 1906 to 1910; the array of tabulated figures is rather appalling to a mere antiquarian, but it is not wasted labour if it really enables the investigators to state 'with greater confidence than has hitherto been attempted the nature of the domesticated animals of the Roman period in Britain as represented at Corstopitum and the relationship of these to the domesticated animals of the present day'.

The last paper (pp. 268–360) is the first instalment of Dr. Greenwell's 'Catalogue of the Seals at Durham' (i.e. those in the treasury and in his own collection), collated and annotated by Mr. C. Hunter Blair. This part contains the seals of private persons in A to D. There are 820 entries, a few of which are double: and they are illustrated by nine good collotype plates, on which 138 seals are figured. The seals are systematically described and referred to their charters; naturally most of them belong to Durham ecclesiastics, or to the families of the Palatinate, such as Balliol, Blakiston, Bowes, Burdon, Claxton, Conyers, Dalton, &c. But there are numerous examples of French and Italian seals; several of the great barons are represented, and there are a few from Oxford and other places in the south. The papers on Corstopitum will have to be rearranged and rewritten when the excavations are completed; but this great catalogue of seals will only require combination of sections. We must, however, call the attention of the annotator to one point; by an unlucky accident, probably some rearrangement of the items on the plates, nearly ten per cent. of the references from the catalogue to those plates have been made erroneous.   H. E. D. BLAKISTON.

Short Notices

DR. BERTHOLD BRETHOLZ's *Lateinische Paläographie*, of which a second edition has appeared (Leipzig: Teubner, 1912), forms part of a series of manuals intended for students of German history, and edited under the title of *Grundriss der Geschichtswissenschaft* by Professor Aloys Meister. Dr. Bretholz's treatise was published in 1906 together with similar contributions on *Diplomatik* by R. Thommen and *Chronologie* by Hermann Grotefend. The utility of his work is sufficiently shown by the fact that it now reappears in a separate form, a concession to the needs of palaeographers as distinguished from students of history which should be much appreciated by them. So far as the text is concerned the new edition is substantially a reprint of the previous one. The notes, however, in which the special value of the manual resides, have been very considerably modified and enlarged. They contain references to the very latest monographs, and the reader may be assured that he is supplied with the most advanced results arrived at by palaeographical experts. It is impossible to speak too highly of these notes, in which every one who is interested in palaeography or textual criticism will find much that is new. As Dr. Bretholz's work was not noticed in the pages of this Review when it first appeared, it may be worth while to say that the general plan and arrangement resembles that adopted in various previous works, e.g. the well-known manual of Sir E. Maunde Thompson. The writer first describes the materials used, the form of manuscripts, medieval libraries, and archives. He then treats early scripts found in inscriptions and in specimens of old Roman cursive, the development of capital, uncial, and half-uncial script from the third to the eighth century, the Irish and Anglo-Saxon hands, the various national hands founded on the old cursive, the introduction and diffusion of the Caroline minuscule, and the so-called 'Gothic' hand which succeeded it. There are also appendixes on contraction, *notae Tironianae*, numerals, the division of words, punctuation, and critical marks. The work is a model of compression, and not a word is wasted. There is certainly no treatise on palaeography which contains so much information in so small a space.   A. C. C.

In 1904, in the twenty-fourth volume of the *Abhandlungen der k. Bayerischen Akademie der Wissenschaften* (*philosophisch-philologische und historische Klasse*), Ludwig Traube announced his extremely interesting discovery of the sources from which the emperor Henry II obtained the nucleus of his library at Bamberg. Four of these manuscripts bore evidence of having belonged to John Scottus (Erigena), from whom they passed in turn to Gerbert and Otto III. Of Traube's special address on John Scottus, delivered in 1905, only brief notes are preserved. They have now been published by his pupil, Dr. E. K. Rand, of Harvard University, as

Paläographische Forschungen, v, in the *Abhandlungen*, xxvi. 1 (1912), with twelve plates of facsimiles from manuscripts at Rheims, Laon, and Paris, as well as Bamberg, from which it is possible to trace the two or three successive redactions of the *De Divisione Naturae* with the help of the autograph corrections and insertions of the author. Dr. Rand has added a lucid commentary on the plates, and points out that Floss's edition represents one of the latest revisions of the work, while Gale's, of 1681, represents in parts one of the earliest. We wish there were any hope that the first two parts of the *Paläographische Forschungen* which were promised in 1904 might even now see the light.

Traube's masterly treatise on the *Textgeschichte der Regula S. Benedicti* appeared in the same *Abhandlungen*, xxi. 3, in 1898, and we commented on its high importance at the time (*ante*, xiii. 611). It has recently been re-edited in vol. xxv. 2 (1910) by Dr. H. Plenkers, who furnishes some useful notes and gives a summary of the discussions raised by the publication of what he rightly describes as Traube's 'classical' work.

In view of these discussions it is satisfactory to notice that Dom Cuthbert Butler, who long argued against Traube's conclusions, has now been led to accept them in all but one, and that not a vital, point. In his well-printed edition of *Sancti Benedicti Regula Monachorum* (Freiburg: Herder, 1912) he maintains that the evidence does not prove St. Benedict's autograph manuscript to have been preserved at Monte Cassino in the eighth century (pp. xix, xx), but he adopts Traube's view that the text of the Rule which was widely distributed in the seventh and eighth centuries is the interpolated text, and that the pure text is that derived from a copy which was obtained from Monte Cassino by Charles the Great in 787 and which is represented by several manuscripts of the ninth century. Dom Butler notices (p. 128), what Traube had overlooked, that the scribe of the Tegernsee MS. had both texts before him, though this was duly pointed out by E. Wölfflin in his edition of *Benedicti Regula Monachorum*, 1895, p. vii. The learned notes are of great value for the comparative study of monastic Rules.   R. L. P.

In the *Byzantinische Zeitschrift*, xx. 3, 4, we notice an account by Paul Maas of the *Doctrina Iacobi nuper baptizati*, an early Greek text of the age of Heraclius, recently discovered by N. Bonwetsch and important for the history of Judaism. There is also a musical study of the hymns of Casia (842–67) by H. J. W. Tillyard, who transcribes many of them in modern notation.

Vol. xxi. 1, 2 contains an article by K. Praechter on the relations of neo-Platonism to Christianity, in which he reviews the teaching of Hierocles and Nemesius. Professor Bury collects data for the reconstruction of the Great Palace of Constantine at Byzantium. H. Schreiber discusses the oldest form of the Byzantine Belisarius saga. J. Maspero writes on *foederati* and *stratiotae* in the army of the sixth century. N. H. Baynes examines the date of the Avar surprise of Constantinople and fixes it to 617. N. A. Beês has a paper on the *ius primae noctis* among the Byzantines, and J. H. Mordtmann on the capitulation of Constantinople in 1453.
   M.

The *Historische Vierteljahrschrift* for August 1911 contains an important article by Professor Felix Saloman upon the French official publication 'Les Origines diplomatiques de la Guerre de 1870-1'. Of the articles in this and other numbers for 1911 several discuss matters of general interest in the constitutional history of medieval Germany: Professor Hermann Bloch on 'Die Kaiserwahl im kanonischen Recht' (April), Professor Hans Schreuer on the election and coronation of Conrad II in 1024 (August), and Professor Ludwig Riess's diplomatic study upon the significance of the phrases 'data' and 'actum' in the acts of the Emperor Henry II, may be noticed.   N.

Professor E. G. Sihler's *Annals of Caesar* (New York: Stechert, 1911) is a reproduction of lectures originally delivered for the benefit 'chiefly of instructors in American high schools' (p. 177), and should be judged accordingly. It is annalistic in form throughout, and the narrative is supported by copious references to the authorities; but there is not much discussion of broad constitutional issues—one would find it difficult to obtain a very clear idea of the controversy between Caesar and the senate from Professor Sihler. The author is a pronounced anti-Caesarian, and his attacks on Mommsen and Froude defeat their own ends by their intemperance of expression. Professor Sihler quotes a previous utterance of his own which may serve to illustrate the style which he affects: 'As for the "*World-spirit*" called in to sanctify the conquests of the great captain, that *World-spirit*, unfortunately, like flea or locust, hopped soon away and lighted on the brawny chest of Antony, or the languorous eyelashes of Cleopatra. What a pity!' Amongst ancient authorities, Professor Sihler selects Dion Cassius for commendation, ascribing to him 'a pen and purpose more personally acute, let me say, than the transcriptions of Appian or the psychological and moralizing electivism of Plutarch'. By a curious slip which remains uncorrected it is stated on two successive pages (34, 35) that Caesar was consul in 58 B.C.
   H. S. J.

The *Reign of the Emperor Probus* was not of the first importance, and our authorities for the period are meagre and untrustworthy; Mr. J. H. E. Crees hardly goes too far, in the study published under the title given above (University of London Press, 1911), when he says that 'the dearth of all reliable information must be taken as a fundamental principle at the outset of all investigations of the period'. He leaves matters pretty much as he found them: for the chronology which he suggests is mere guesswork, and Lépaulle's study of the coinage of the reign is not superseded. We find no mention of the remarkable use of secret mint-marks making up the name AEQVITI(us), which has some unexplained connexion with the title *Equitius Probus* given to the emperor in the *Epitome de Caesaribus*. Much space is taken up with a recital of the views held by various critics regarding the composition of the *Historia Augusta*; but the forged documents contained therein are allowed more weight than they can justly claim. 'Cyzicum' is a spelling found twice.   H. S. J.

In *Armoricains et Bretons* (Paris: Champion, 1912), a pamphlet of 132 large closely printed pages, M. Albert Travers makes a vigorous attack on the view advocated by the late M. A. de la Borderie, and after him by M. Loth, that the Bretons are the descendants of emigrants from Britain who came over in the fifth and succeeding centuries. It is evident that the author's interest in the question is far from being purely scientific. He declaims loudly against the ignominious supposition that the Bretons had for their ancestors the cowards who abandoned their native land to the invader instead of dying in its defence; and he complains that the prevalence of M. de la Borderie's doctrine has had a mischievous influence in inducing the Bretons to regard themselves as a separate race from the French, and therefore as absolved from the obligations of national patriotism. All this appeal to prejudice adds nothing to the value of his arguments, and may even prevent them from receiving the consideration which they deserve. M. Travers is certainly wrong in denying the conclusion of Celtic philologists that the Breton language is not the descendant of the Armorican dialect of Gaulish, but an importation from Britain. He informs us in his preface that he has endeavoured to demonstrate the identity of Breton and Gaulish in two former pamphlets, which were roughly handled by M. Loth. In this book he wisely refrains from linguistic argument, though he tenaciously adheres to his conclusion. He would have done better if he had taken the ground that the insular origin of Breton does not prove that the immigrants who brought it to Armorica outnumbered the native inhabitants, and therefore does not warrant the conclusion that the existing Bretons are *mainly* of British descent. Ignorance of philology does not disqualify an otherwise competent student from fruitfully discussing such questions as the extent of the migrations from Britain to Armorica, the abundance or scantiness of the population of that region in early times, and the more or less general supersession of the native language by Latin. M. Travers has given assiduous if far from unbiased study to the documentary evidence bearing on these questions, and he has no lack of dialectical cleverness. Amid a great deal of sophistry and empty rhetoric, the book contains some arguments which at least deserve to be carefully weighed. O.

In *Sidelights on Teutonic History during the Migration Period* (Cambridge: University Press, 1911) Miss M. G. Clarke presents the results of 'an attempt to discover the amount of historical truth underlying the allusions to persons and events in the Old English heroic poems'. This investigation has been carried out methodically and with considerable fullness, dealing first with the three great nations mentioned in the Beowulf (the Geats, Danes, and Swedes) and their chief heroes, and then with other personages like Offa, Finn, Hilde, Wêland, Waldere, and Ermanric. Those who have not made a special study of the heroic age of the Teutonic peoples will find much useful information in Miss Clarke's work, and even to the scholar its collection of data will not be unwelcome, although its usefulness would have been greatly increased by a full index. In spite of the conscientious spirit in which Miss Clarke has obviously carried out her researches, there are indications all through the work that she has not attained to complete mastery of all the subjects connected with her study. On the Scandinavian side, which naturally comes into considerable prominence, there are many minor inaccuracies in the forms of words, inconsistencies in spelling and accentuation, and occasional errors of statement or translation. In one place (p. 191) the mistranslation of a passage from *Skáldskaparmál* raises the suspicion that Miss Clarke has not clearly remembered the object with which that treatise was written. Similar errors in other departments of the work are less prominent, although they are occasionally to be found. Miss Clarke is also not exempt from the tendency, too common in works of this kind, to propose new and hypothetical versions of a story in place of those given in the original sources, and to combine two different accounts in one statement in a way that might easily create a wrong impression. Some points of which discussion might have been expected are not touched upon, e.g. although there is a special chapter on Finn, the question of where he ruled is entirely omitted, nor indeed is the reader told anything about the geographical relations of the Frisians to the other peoples. In spite of its merits, the book as a whole leaves an impression that a longer and more intimate acquaintance with the various aspects of the subject would have been likely to give a surer touch, and yield more definite results, than have actually been attained. W. A. C.

Professor Luigi Schiaparelli has so completely made the study of the Italian chancery of the ninth and tenth centuries his own that we are grateful to him for the edition of *I Diplomi Italiani di Lodovico III e di Rodolfo II* in the series of *Fonti per la Storia d'Italia*, published by the Istituto Storico Italiano (Rome, 1910). The documents unfortunately are few and mainly of local interest, but the editor has done all that could be done from a diplomatic, an historical, and a bibliographical point of view to make the texts serviceable to students. His systematic treatise on the diplomatic of the period must be sought in the *Bullettino dell' Istituto Storico Italiano*, xxix, xxx. We may perhaps regret that the plan of the publication forbade the inclusion of Lewis and Rodulf's documents issued in Burgundy. P.

The aim of Mr. Robert S. Rait in his *Scotland*, a volume in the series of 'The Making of the Nations' (London: Black, 1911), is to trace the stages of national development in those periods of Scottish history where the outlines are most marked and the evidences most abundant. Three critical periods in the national story take up a large portion of the book: the anglicization of the country under Malcolm Canmore and his immediate successors, the struggle for national unity during the war of independence, and the prolonged religious conflict at the Reformation, out of which emerged, after many vicissitudes, modern Scotland. The intervening stages have been filled up with connecting narrative, which, though in many ways subordinate, lend a distinct value to the whole. This new presentation of the making of Scotland will be welcomed as a genuine attempt to give a comprehensive survey of the forces which moulded the development of the nation from the earliest centuries to a comparatively recent period, but little is said of the constitutional and administrative aspects of its growth. The sense of proportion in allotting space to stated periods according to their importance has probably prevented a thorough examination of the causes which contributed to the Anglo-Norman civilization of the kingdom. The decision is to be regretted, as a veil of obscurity hangs over the period in most histories. The tumultuous period of the Bruces, with the gradual concentration of national energies towards unity, has received adequate and instructive exposition. In his discussion of the Reformation and its sequel the author appears at his best, threading his way with consummate impartiality through the tangled wilderness of Scottish ecclesiastical controversy. It may perhaps not be ungracious to note that the priory of Scone was not filled by King Alexander ' with English monks ' (p. 21), but with English canons, a very different thing; that it is not consistent to speak of ' the De Morevilles ' (p. 28) when the author writes regularly of the Balliols and Bruces; and that the battle of Solway Moss in 1542 did not take place in Scotland (map, p. 285) or on the Debatable Land (p. 137), but in England, south of the Esk, where the land was never debatable, a bit of recorded history as old as Roger Ascham. The illustrations are numerous and well chosen. J. W.

La Clameur de Haro dans le Droit Normand, by M. H. Pissard, is the first of a series of *études* published in the new 'Bibliothèque d'Histoire du Droit Normand' (Caen: Jouan, 1911). It is an exceedingly careful and penetrating study of the development in Norman law of the legal processes to which the cry of *haro* gave rise. M. Pissard shows how the dukes added to the pleas of the sword the cases of the unnecessary cry, and of neglect to heed it, and analyses the way in which the cry was introduced into and acquired its main importance in the procedure of civil cases. Its extension to cases of dispossession gave still further protection than that given by the twelfth-century possessory assizes. M. Pissard furnishes a careful analysis of the elaborate legal procedure to which the cry might give rise, and explains the way in which, by a natural process, the pleadings on the cry and on the less important criminal cases were merged together to the profit of the common law. More should have been said upon the difference between Norman and English treatment of the aggressor caught in the act; and we venture to think that M. Pissard has adopted rather too lightly the juridical treatment by M. Valin and M. Perrot of the development of ducal justice. But his essay is a valuable contribution to Norman history.
F. M. P.

Le Parage Normand (Caen: Jouan, 1911), by Professor R. Génestal, belongs to the same series as the essay of M. Pissard. In a tract of less than fifty pages M. Génestal analyses the nature and working of tenure by parage in Normandy during the thirteenth century. Confining himself to the text of the custumals and judgements of the exchequer, the author dissects his subject with admirable precision, and after reading him, the present writer must plead guilty to some loose writing in an earlier number of this Review (xxi. 38). M. Génestal shows that what he terms general parage existed till the fifteenth century, and was hardly affected by the ordinance issued by Philip Augustus in 1209 : it covered all tenures of more than one impartible tenement except that of baronies ; the unity of the family holding was maintained by the distribution of separate fiefs to the sons of the deceased under the headship of the eldest son, who was responsible for the service of all. If the eldest took the homage of the younger sons, tenure by parage ceased, and was replaced by ordinary subinfeudation ; yet even here the unity of the family was recognized, for while lands held in parage reverted to the eldest son, those held by homage were, in case of death, divided among the remaining younger brothers. General parage, then, was a very definite as well as widespread form of tenure ; it regulated the succession to holdings which contained more than one impartible fief, and reconciled the Norman principle of family succession with Henry II's legislation against the partibility of the knight's fee. It must be distinguished from particular parage, or the division of partible lands, i.e. the lands not affected by local customs of impartibility or by Henry II's legislation, among males subject to the elder. Female succession introduced particular parage into impartible lands. Rather unfortunately, M. Génestal confines his attention to the developed system of the thirteenth century ; and has thus overlooked the early reference to parage in a document edited by Professor Haskins in this Review (xxii. 647). This reference makes it necessary to modify the clear-cut theory on the Angevin origin of parage, which the author adopts from M. Guilhiermoz.

F. M. P.

M. Louis Halphen has edited a new edition of the late Achille Luchaire's work, *Les Communes françaises à l'époque des Capétiens directs* (Paris : Hachette, 1911). Published in 1890, Luchaire's study is still indispensable to the study of the medieval communes, and it is not necessary for us to do more than call attention to this edition. M. Halphen has made a few alterations in the text, and suppressed two or three passages of doubtful validity. In a brief introduction he has summarized some of the results of recent literature, especially of M. Pirenne's work, and has indicated the more important contributions to the subject. M. Halphen might, we think, have referred at greater length to the German controversies upon the origin of the self-governing city, and should have called attention to the value of English and American studies upon towns which, though not strictly communes, present many analogies to the commune. No reference is made to Miss Bateson or Professor Gross. In other respects we have nothing but praise for the editorial work.

F. M. P.

The volume of the *Calendar of the Patent Rolls, Henry III, 1258-1266* (London : H.M. Stationery Office, 1910), begins a few days after the king proclaimed his adhesion to the Provisions of Oxford and ends at Kenilworth a few days after the publication of the Dictum. It thus includes the whole period of government by oligarchy and of the ensuing civil war ; and it bears fresh testimony to the remarkable skill shown by Rymer and his editors in selecting the most important documents for the *Foedera*. The well-known writ addressed to Adam of Newmarket on 4 June 1264, which orders the appointment of a guardian of the peace for Lincolnshire and the summons of four knights of the shire to parliament, appears in this volume only in a general description, 'Appointment of keepers of the peace in various counties, named, and mandate to them to send four knights elected from each county to London' (p. 360). On the other hand the terms of the mise of Lewes, which have hitherto been known only from the accounts of chroniclers and the text of which has been supposed to be lost, are here (p. 370 f.) presented in a very full summary. There is also the record of the order in council, March 1264, limiting the conditions on which Archbishop Boniface was allowed to return to England (p. 413). Sometimes (e.g. pp. 406, 419, 550) we have corrections of the *Foedera*. It is interesting to notice the constant changes made in the custody of castles. References to the disputes between the king and Simon de Montfort in 1261 will be found on pp. 136, 145, 162. As illustrations of complicated financial transactions we may cite pp. 66, 71, 223, and with regard to the future king Edward I the grant on p. 233 may be compared with that on p. 263. John of Kirkby is mentioned as early as November 1263 (p. 299), and in September 1264 as a king's clerk (p. 349). On p. 140 is an order for a levy of 2*d*. on each merchant ship putting into the port of Winchelsea for the maintenance of a light. The arrangement for the feeding of a hundred thousand (*sic*) poor at Westminster at the feast of St. Edward (p. 282) is remarkable. The king's new seal is mentioned apparently under 24 December 1259 (p. 112), but the old seal was not broken until 17 October 1260 (p. 97). These Calendars are now drawn up on so methodical a system that there is a risk of the interests of historical students who are not familiar with the technicalities of documents being sacrificed. Thus we find 'simple protection' (p. 45), 'protection with clause' (*ibid.*), 'protection with clause *rogamus*' (*ibid.*), 'protection with clause *volumus*' (p. 63), 'protection with clause, except the four pleas' (p. 218), 'simple protection without clauses' (p. 347). It would be well to give a brief table of these forms in the preface to each volume. So again, a safe-conduct 'without the clause *Ita tamen*, &c.' (p. 575) might deserve explanation. On p. 235 the king crossed from not 'to Dover' (see p. 226). On p. 257 1,000*l*. should be 1000 marks, and on p. 354 Mapeldertoop is a misprint for Mapeldertorp. In the index we miss any entry of Amaury de Montfort, who needs at least three references. Q.

Dr. Paul Joachimsen's *Geschichtsauffassung und Geschichtschreibung in Deutschland unter dem Einfluss des Humanismus*, i (Leipzig: Teubner, 1910) is a very useful and interesting attempt to show the change in the outlook upon history and the writing of it caused by the Renaissance. There is a change in the outlook as we pass from the annalistic, traditional chronicle, modelled upon preceding histories of the world, to the more literary work, often inspired by love of country, of town, or dynasty, marked by pretensions to style, and by a more critical use of authorities or disregard of tradition. The change is one common to all countries; Switzerland gives us very good examples of it, but in our own country the change is perhaps less striking than elsewhere. Dr. Joachimsen first lays down the problem, and then discusses the beginners, Charles IV and his influence, Valla and Aeneas Sylvius. His third chapter brings before us the Scholastic Humanists among whom are Trithemius and Jacob Wimpfeling; his fourth the Humanist world-chronicles, German writers and their Italian predecessors; in the fifth he deals with the critics Erasmus, Hutten, Celtes, the new material, and Beatus Rhenanus; and in the sixth gives the history of the plan for a 'Germania Illustrata', bringing all the new wealth of material into the service of a cultivated but enthusiastic patriotism, and in this connexion saying much of Willibald Pirckheimer and Nuremberg. The last chapter is centred round the brilliant if wayward court of Maximilian with its zeal for new investigations and its authorities such as Konrad Peutinger. The writer covers a large ground and with much skill steers a wise course between the over-burdening with fact to which some medieval writers fell victims, and the yielding too easily to generalizations which misled some Renaissance writers. Among the details that illustrate the main theme we may instance as specially good and interesting the analysis of Vincent of Beauvais and Martin of Troppau among early writers, the account of Valla, an instructive comparison between Aeneas Sylvius and Thomas Ebendorfer, the full account of Nauklerus, and the apt contrast between him and Trithemius. Such special studies of historic material for a particular time are useful to others besides younger students. It is difficult to make them pleasant reading, but the writer has succeeded in this. It is still more difficult to combine adequate knowledge and a sound judgement, but here again he has succeeded. J. P. W.

M. G. Pérouse introduces his appreciation of *Georges Chastellain* (Paris: Champion, 1910) by the inevitable comparison with Commynes, much to the advantage of the former. There is more breadth, he thinks, in Chastellain's views, for he looks at facts by the light of general principles, which are the synthesis of all the moral and political ideas elaborated throughout the middle age, which speaks through him and recounts its own death, passing judgement on the authors and causes thereof. Commynes' plan he considers mean : he did not and could not dream of being the historian of the birth of the modern age; he is limited to his own experience, or rather to the example and precepts of his master. He concludes that Commynes has been the more popular because Chastellain was defending political principles which all statesmen were renouncing, and an ideal of a fatherland which at the moment of his death was vanishing: Chastellain left literary disciples, but no heir to his thought. It is, however, possible that these very principles which attract M. Pérouse may repel the general reader, who may easily mistake principles for platitudes. Personality is unquestionably the charm of the Memoirs of Commynes. The tragedy of Chastellain was the detachment of the Burgundian feudal state from the greater France, which he regarded as his moral and intellectual fatherland. M. Pérouse admirably points out how this Fleming was essentially French, in Chastellain's own words, not English but French, not Italian nor Spaniard but French, a Frenchman and the historian of two Frenchmen, the one king, the other duke : he is a type of the literature of northern France, both in prose and verse an important link in the French literary chain. And yet Chastellain had to follow and defend his feudal lord, who was really breaking up the greatest monarchy on earth. His Chronicle, his pamphlets and his poems are all in their essence the apologia of Burgundian policy. The Chronicle was, indeed, a set piece composed with this end in view during his literary retirement as official historian. The pamphlets are compared by M. Pérouse to journalistic articles thrown off in the heat of the conflict, bringing Chastellain's principles to bear upon the particular grievance of the moment. From the historical point of view the poems, or most of them, are but pamphlets in verse. Poems and pamphlets, once perfervid, are now cold, but M. Pérouse's enthusiasm will cause the reader to study the Chronicle with heightened pleasure and understanding. E. A.

For his study on *Die Finanzen Albrechts des Beherzten* (*Leipziger Historische Abhandlungen*, no. 26. Leipzig: Quelle & Meyer, 1911) Dr. Alexander Puff has used for the first time an entirely unique source of financial history, viz. the general registers, preserved in the archives of Dresden, of the revenue and expenditure in one of the larger territorial states of Germany at the period of the development of their central administration. As they extend over nearly ten years (1488–97), the contents of these budgets of the duchy of Saxony may be fairly taken to reveal averages of real significance, and the form of statistical tables into which Dr. Puff has brought most of them are therefore particularly useful. Moreover, his introductory recapitulation of the history of Saxon finances especially from 1469, and his glances forward into the reign of Duke Albert's son and successor, George, help to control the statistics by a genetic treatment. Although the finances of the duchy are naturally still based to a great extent (that of a third on the average, p. 128) upon the agricultural production of the ducal domain, it is just the imperfect state of its movable resources which very intimately connects it with the private economy of the territorial and extra-territorial towns. While the former appear not only as the chief objects of the growing ordinary and extraordinary taxation, but (p. 173 f.) as the customary brokers and guarantors of the loans necessitated mostly by Duke Albert's military enterprises against Hungary and the Netherlands, the latter's money market was required to supply the immediate wants of public and court expenditure. The administration of the most important financial boards, such as those of the ducal silver monopoly and above all the central *Rentkammer* at Leipzig, was powerfully influenced by the employment in the chief posts of prominent citizen capitalists, the supervision of the Dresden officials being merely nominal. Jakob Blasbalg, to whom the first lasting arrangement of the Saxon budget is due, did not cease as *Rentmeister* of the duke to keep his shop at Leipzig, and his successor, Georg von Wiedebach, no doubt belonged to the same class, as he married his predecessor's strenuous widow, who had herself occupied her husband's place for some time after his death. A photograph of Wiedebach's portrait by Lucas Cranach is a fitting frontispiece to this most instructive treatise. C. B.

M. E. Rodocanachi's sumptuous volume on *Rome au temps de Jules II et de Léon X* (Paris: Hachette, 1912), with its wealth of illustrations, is not a mere picture-book, as might be thought at first sight, but contains a vast amount of systematic information, largely derived from original sources, about the life and manners of Rome in the first quarter of the sixteenth century. Herein, as with the author's previous work, lies its strength and value. Indeed, the accumulation of instances is sometimes almost overdone, and becomes monotonous. Topics connected with art and archaeology are less successfully treated. 'Acheropictos' (i.e. acheiropoietos) can hardly be the correct designation of the sacred picture of the Sancta Sanctorum (p. 304), and we notice that in plate 61 the word has become 'Achérotype'. But the book is a storehouse of facts, though there is little attempt to combine them in an artistic picture. G. McN. R.

Herr Ernst Daenell, who is preparing a history of the United States for German readers, has presented them in *Die Spanier in Nordamerika von 1513–1824* (Munich: Oldenbourg, 1911) with a clear and succinct account of the achievements of the Spaniards in North America (outside Mexico) from 1513 to 1824. The period from 1783 to 1824 is treated very briefly, as the author hopes to deal with it more fully in the second volume of his history mentioned above. The main theme of this volume would appear to be the struggle between Spain, France, Russia, and England, for the territory now forming the United States. Expeditions and voyages of mere discovery are passed over in a summary manner. More attention is paid to the pushing out of advanced outposts from land already held. The author's conclusions are, in the main, sound, and the result of very considerable study. Writing in the United States, he is familiar with the most important local monographs, as well as with those published in Europe. The most interesting portion of the work is probably that in which he traces the history of Spanish North America in the eighteenth century, giving an effective picture of the influence of the ideas prevalent in Spain on the development of the Spanish possessions in America. He relies perhaps too much on French sources, omitting, however, those in Ternaux-Compans, and also the Mexican collections. A few slips are noticeable, as, for example, Kretschmar (p. 39) for Kretschmer. Herr Daenell is evidently unfamiliar with F. Weber's *Beiträge zur Charakteristik der älteren Geschichtsschreiber über Spanisch-Amerika*,[1] as well as with the late Professor E. G. Bourne's edition of the sources of De Soto's expedition. No mention is made of the late Mr. Woodbury Lowery's second volume on *The Spanish Settlements in Florida, 1562–74*. For identifying events in the West Indies described in Spanish sources Herr Daenell would have found the third volume of La Roncière's *Histoire de la Marine française* of value. H. P. B.

M. Paul Courteault's edition of the *Commentaires de Blaise de Monluc*, of which the first volume (1521–53) has appeared in the *Collection de Textes pour servir à l'Étude et à l'Enseignement de l'Histoire* (Paris: Picard, 1911), is unquestionably an improvement upon that of the Baron Alphonse de Ruble (1864–7), much as that excelled its more immediate predecessors. M. Courteault has followed more closely the original editor of Florimond

[1] *Ante*, xxvi. 838–9.

de Raemond, correcting only obvious errors, filling up accidental *lacunae*, and restoring from the two existing manuscripts passages which the first editor suppressed from prudential motives. The reason for not making a fuller use of the manuscripts is that they are anterior to June 1571, while Monluc constantly retouched his original, hasty composition until his death. The identification of the names of places and persons, often a difficult task in Monluc, is now far more complete. The materials utilized by M. Courteault for his *Blaise de Monluc, Historien* are the chief source for the notes, but, ample as these were, they have been supplemented by yet more recent publications, especially the *Mémoires de Martin et Guillaume de Bellay*. E. A.

Dr. Philipp Hermann Stoeckius, in his *Forschungen zur Lebensordnung der Gesellschaft Jesu im 16. Jahrhundert* (München : Beck, 1910), has made skilful and diligent use of the many collections of letters and other materials which have been lately edited. The first part (*Ordenshörige und Externe*) deals with the control of the externs, in their two divisions, those who were being trained for the priesthood and the 'pensioners'. It became an accepted principle that between these classes and the members of the society there should be complete separation of life. The spiritual discipline and training laid down for members necessitated this. The view often taken of the society makes their free mixing in the world too large a feature of their life ; the training demanded something very different. Dr. Stoeckius follows out the working of this principle of separation and shows its effect. The immense care shown in regulation of details explains the success of the society. Everywhere, at Paris, Rome, Dillingen, local circumstances were considered, while leading principles were never lost sight of. Changes between successive officers come before us also : Oliverus Manareus (who, as on pp. 18 and 44, is sometimes denoted by his Latin and sometimes by his ordinary name) was less strict in Germany than Natalis ; after successive visitations regulations were altered, and these changes are here described in detail. The second part (*Das gesellschaftliche Leben im Ordenshause*) deals with a larger subject. For the work of the society a separate dwelling was needed, but it was sometimes difficult to provide. Very interesting is the narrative of what took place at Cologne (p. 15 f.), and the attack made there upon these founders of a new sect, as they were called ; the house was visited by the town authorities and had to be given up for a time. Canisius had remained behind to nurse a sick brother, and in the end was able to take a new house larger than the old one. Among other details of much interest are the policy followed with regard to festivities and invitations, the control of novices, recreation, the language of ordinary conversation (at first Latin, and then afterwards, with a view to gaining local influence, the language of the country) : for the purpose of the society itself Latin would be most useful ; for missionary equipment (as in Germany) the vernacular was more valuable : St. Ignatius himself (1 January 1556) commanded the change. Throughout the book Dr. Stoeckius illustrates from special colleges ; the importance of that at Messina (p. 166) as a model—pointed out by Father Meyer in his *Der Ursprung des jesuitischen Schulwesens* (1904) as here referred to—is recognized, although we get more light upon the separation of members and externs from Coimbra. The special value of these studies lies in their illustration of conflicting principles. The method of training made the new society seem akin to monastic orders; its work of education and its general mission to the world marked it off as distinct from them. The conflict between these two aspects appears in papal attempts to regulate the society; here we see it in the internal history of the society. The close observation of details by the directors of the general policy, and their reduction to general principles are also to be noted. J. P. W.

In his *History of Witchcraft in England from 1558 to 1718* (Washington: American Historical Association, 1911) Dr. W. Notestein has done honest journeyman's work in a humdrum way. His book serves a useful purpose in calling attention to an important side of English life in the past. The year 1558 is selected for the opening of the narrative because then a noteworthy statute against witchcraft was passed, and the year 1718 marks the close, for Francis Hutchinson published at that time his *Historical Essay on Witchcraft*. Beginning at so late a date the author is gravely hampered in his understanding of the witch controversy, since he necessarily omits to treat of the belief of primitive people in the 'wise woman', and of her disappearance before the new polytheism of warrior spirits. With the advent of Christianity the old rites and superstitions gradually became coloured with rabbinical conceptions of the devil's hierarchy and with the neoplatonic doctrine of demons and intermediary powers. These ideas of demonology became widespread, and the author carefully traces the influence of continental conceptions upon English. Puritanism cannot be held completely responsible for the horrors Dr. Notestein describes; men of other creeds were as firmly convinced of the existence of witches as the Puritans. There is a detailed account, with ample references, of the trials of unfortunate men and women, and from the lists it is evident that the number executed was small. Of course the fact that many lived in dread of being apprehended is one that must not be neglected. The author subjects the important treatises on his subject, e.g. Reginald Scot's *Discoverie*, to an accurate and lucid analysis. To the present generation Joseph Glanvill is best known through the mention of him by Matthew Arnold, to whom his *Vanity of Dogmatizing* supplied the material for *The Scholar-Gipsy*. Another work of his furnished Addison with the story on which he based his ill-starred play *The Drummer; or, The Haunted House*. Glanvill, moreover, anticipated Hume's theory of causation; and there is an anticipation of the electric telegraph in the striking prevision that 'to confer at the Indies by sympathetic contrivances may be as natural to future times as to us is a literary correspondence'. From Glanvill, too, Charles Reade borrowed the phrase, 'The devil is dead.'
R. H. M.

M. Henri Hauser has reprinted in the *Revue Historique*, cviii and cix, 1911-12 (and separately), the *Acta Tumultuum Gallicanorum*, an anonymous catholic account of the three first wars of religion. This pamphlet is found only in the collection named *Illustria ecclesiae Catholicae trophoea*, printed at Munich by Adam Berg in 1573, and dedicated to Ernest of

Bavaria, administrator of the bishopric of Freising. Only three copies of this book are known, and M. Hauser has used that belonging to the Cambridge University Library. The *Acta* was addressed to certain German lords, and was doubtless intended as a set-off against the more common Huguenot publications composed for German consumption. The heretics had captured the press, and the interest of this recital is enhanced by the rarity of catholic polemics in the early stages of the civil wars. M. Hauser gives strong reasons for suspecting the author to be the Jesuit stalwart, Emond Auger of Toulouse. He was, at all events, a Guisard extremist having nothing but praise for Alva and nothing but blame for Catherine, while he reprobates the ' prudence ' of Anne de Montmorency, and quotes gossip to the discredit of his son François. The author was evidently in Paris before and during Condé's attack on Saint-Denis, and vividly describes the nervous tension of the capital. He was later an eyewitness, as was Emond Auger, of the campaign of Jarnac and Moncontour, but his account of the latter interesting battle, in which Coligny was thoroughly outmanœuvred, shows him to possess no soldierly knowledge of tactics. This more detailed section of the work ends with a bare notice of the peace of Saint-Germain, while the earlier portion runs from 1555 to the peace of Longjumeau. Between the two intervenes a wholesale catholic martyrology, attributing the regulation atrocities of all ages to the Huguenot soldiery. The details are not generally at first hand, but are mainly borrowed from Claude de Sainctes. The pamphlet is well worth reading, not for its accuracy, but for its atmosphere. E. A.

Although the greater portion of Mr. C. Warren's careful and learned *History of the American Bar* (Cambridge : University Press, 1912) belongs to the domain of law rather than of history, its account of the legal conditions in the various colonies during the seventeenth and eighteenth centuries is of interest to others besides lawyers. The only complaint that can be made of the volume is that it is perhaps too closely packed with names. H. E. E.

The Ejected of 1662 in Cumberland and Westmorland (Manchester : University Press, 1911) is a much more considerable contribution to the ecclesiastical history of the seventeenth century than the title suggests. Primarily no doubt Mr. B. Nightingale's work is concerned with the nonconformist ministers who were deprived of their livings by the Act of Uniformity, but his researches have in fact led him much further afield, and he has been able to give the names, with, in most cases, some biographical notice, of all or nearly all the clergymen who held livings in these two counties during the century. Nor is the interest of the book solely local and biographical. Mr. Nightingale has made an exhaustive study of the manuscript records of the period, and has collected an enormous mass of information illustrating the effect of the Puritan régime and the Restoration upon the church life of the country. Cumberland and Westmorland are hardly typical counties, of course, but it is only by the study of local conditions that a just view of the whole can be obtained, and it is to be hoped that others will be found to undertake a similar work for other districts. In the introduction Mr. Nightingale gives an outline of the course of events, as they affected the position of the nonconformists, from the Restoration to the withdrawal of the Declaration of Indulgence in 1676, in the course of which he develops an interesting theory as to the basis of the king's ecclesiastical policy. He rejects the common view that it was conceived in the interests of the Roman catholics, and finds its true explanation in Charles's character as the ' great opportunist of his day '. The Declaration of Indulgence, Mr. Nightingale holds, was ' an honest attempt to put an end to the twelve years' sad experience of repressive legislation '. G. B. T.

Mr. Charles ffoulkes's reprint of Gaya's *Traité des Armes*, *1678* (Oxford : Clarendon Press, 1911), leaves nothing to be desired as regards elegance of *format*, and our wish to give it a cordial welcome is only cooled by Lord Dillon's curiously guarded preface, which frankly tells us that the setting exceeds the stone in value. The editor's introduction is rather descriptive than critical. We wish he had not called the historian of the battle of Agincourt ' Sir Harris Nicholas ', and it is hard to admire Gaya for quoting Olivier de la Marche for some details of medieval usage on the ground that ' the writers of the seventeenth century seem to have preferred to draw their information from classical authors '. But Gaya's book is interesting and very fairly instructive. R.

Cambridge under Queen Anne was a work prepared and mainly printed by the late Professor John E. B. Mayor, whose memory is cherished by all scholars, more than forty years ago. The first part of it, containing the *Life of Ambrose Bonwicke*, was separated from the rest of the book and published in 1870. The remainder was privately circulated, and the preface to the *Life of Bonwicke* promised that a few copies should be issued for general circulation. It is not certain whether this intention was carried out, but all that was printed became well known and highly valued in a select circle. The whole has now been issued by the Cambridge Antiquarian Society (Cambridge : Deighton, Bell & Co., 1911), with a preface by Dr. Montague R. James. It includes the *Life of Bonwicke* (but not Mr. Mayor's preface of 1870) and translations of the diaries of Francis Burman and Zacharias Conrad von Uffenbach. It is not made clear whether the book is reprinted or not. The pages of Uffenbach agree with those cited by Dr. Macray in his *Annals of the Bodleian Library* (second edition) in 1890 ; but though the Bonwicke part follows the published book line for line, the notes have been repaged. The notes to the diaries are a storehouse of erudition, primarily bibliographical but also a great deal more, such as perhaps Mr. Mayor alone could have produced : see, for example, the notes on Benjamin Whichcote (pp. 297-306), on Bentley (pp. 421-36), and on William Bedwell (pp. 438-44). After writing a note of forty-four pages on Edmund Castell, the editor seems to have desisted from writing more, and about half of Uffenbach's text remains unannotated. But those who wish to know what can be known of the learning and the learned world of the beginning of the eighteenth century will be thankful for so much as they are given in the present volume. S.

In his essay on *The Trade of the East India Company from 1709 to 1813* (Cambridge: University Press, 1912) Mr. F. P. Robinson has brought together in a compact shape the chief incidents and stages, with the salient characteristics, of that inevitable process of development by which the most famous of English trading companies was transformed, unwillingly · rather than *proprio motu*, from a commercial corporation into a political power. He has collected and examined his material with pains and judgement, and the arrangement he has adopted is appropriate and clear. There is perhaps not much that is new to be added now to this important chapter of economic history; nor is an academic exercise the place where we should expect revolutionary opinions. That the story should be accurately told with the help of the best authorities, that the required emphasis of outstanding facts should neither be exaggerated nor misplaced, and that the underlying motives prompting to, or restraining from, significant acts should not remain undiscovered, are considerable merits in such an essay; and to these our author has abundantly made good his claim. He has also supplied some fresh details and contrived to impart a sustaining interest to the narrative; and in many respects, as he shows, the early history of the East India Company was typical. An apparent omission, to which we would draw his notice, is the absence from the list of authorities furnished in his appendix of any reference to Dr. W. R. Scott's recent treatise on Joint Stock Companies: and, although Dr. Scott's account ends with 1720, and Mr. Robinson starts with 1709, some allusion to so important a book would seem to be demanded, if the bibliography is to be regarded as complete.   L. L. P.

Captain W. V. Anson, R.N., was evidently moved by a pious duty in writing the life of the great admiral, whose name he bears (*The Life of Lord Anson*. London: Murray, 1912); but his success is unequal to his intention. Most of the book is compounded out of well-known textbooks on Anson and his period, to which are added a few unpublished letters from the Record Office and the British Museum. But the text-books are ill-digested, and Captain Anson's narrative of historical events is by no means clear, while the original correspondence loses much of its value by the absence of references and sometimes by what appears to be unintelligent copying (e.g. p. 136). The book abounds in mistakes or misprints: for example, the duke of Newcastle became secretary of state in 1723 not 1727, the duke of Bedford not the duke of Richmond became first lord of the admiralty in 1744, Egremont not Egmont succeeded Pitt as secretary of state. But in spite of its errors the book has the real merit of drawing attention to Lord Anson's great and somewhat forgotten services to the English navy. His administrative capacity, his noble fight against corruption and red tape, and his determination to enforce a better discipline and a high standard of naval ability and courage are well indicated. But the best part of the book, as might be expected from a sailor, is the spirited account of Anson's great voyage round the world. This is illustrated by a good map, and there are several interesting pictures of ships of the period.   B. W.

Herr Reinhold Koser has extracted from the forthcoming edition (the fourth) of his *Life of Frederick the Great* ' those chapters which have a special biographical interest ' and linked them together into a very readable popular life (*Friedrich der Grosse. Volksausgabe.* Stuttgart: J. G. Cotta, 1911) issued in connexion with the centenary of Frederick's birth, 24 January 1912. Diplomatic, military, and administrative details are omitted or condensed; but the condensation is well done and the central biographical problem, the play of circumstance on Frederick's personality, is excellently handled. J. H. C.

The small sovereign principality of Montbéliard was one of the largest of those territories whose princes, enjoying rights in the neighbouring country of France, found themselves despoiled by the decrees of August 1789. Duke Frederick Eugene of Württemberg, who succeeded his brother to the ducal throne of that country in 1795, was the last and best of the princes of Montbéliard. A benevolent despot of the most attractive type, he seems to have modelled his court and policy on that of the kindly Stanislaus Leszczynski at Nancy. But in 1789 evil days came upon him; the summer and autumn of that year were full of alarums and excursions, and he had to beg for a garrison from Belfort to protect him from the Jacquerie. Necker's scheme of a 25 per cent. income tax, to which he was ordered to subscribe, did not diminish his difficulties, for as a sovereign he refused to do so, though he entered his name on the list for the *don patriotique*. This was likely to prejudice his popularity; though as a matter of fact it did not do so seriously. The principality was ruined by the economic policy of France, the new tariff of which completely isolated Montbéliard from the rest of the world; it found the export of its caps, for which it was renowned, seriously impeded, while on the pretext that the law of France forbade the exportation of corn, no grain could enter Montbéliard from the surrounding country. The nerves of the duchess broke down under these circumstances, and the duke followed her to her refuge at Bâle, and gradually withdrew his belongings from his houses; the last item to be moved being an *importante batterie de cuisine*. After 10 August the end was not long in coming. Two successive raids of the French carried away all the munitions of the principality, and in October 1793, Renaud de Saintes, a deputy on mission, entered Montbéliard, suppressed the Regency council, and set up in the square a guillotine, the emblem of the new government. All this is told with much charm and some spice of humour in *La Fin d'un Régime* (Paris: Champion, 1911) by M. Léon Sahler, who has discovered, and printed at the end of the book, the diary of the Comte du Lau, who was governor of Belfort under Rochambeau in 1789. It extends over two critical months, August and September 1789, and contains interesting minutiae about the history of the surrounding country during that exciting time. L. G. W. L.

Le Socialisme Français de 1789 à 1848, by MM. Georges and Hubert Bourgin (Paris: Hachette, 1912), raises the question of the value of *L'Histoire par les Contemporains*, the title of the series to which it belongs.

The student who knows the story in outline is grateful for extracts from some of the less-known 'socialistic' pamphleteers of the revolutionary age, though he may regret that stretching of the term which makes it include almost every utterance of passionate sympathy for the poor, such as Barère's advocacy of old-age pensions for ploughmen. But the extracts all need a full commentary. And when we come to Saint-Simon and Fourier, particularly Fourier, the feeling is irresistible that five pages of 'second-hand' analysis of the notions of that diffuse thinker would be of far more value to the beginner, for whom presumably this little book is mainly intended, than the five pages of extracts here offered. The section dealing with Saint-Simon and Fourier is followed by some valuable extracts from the writings of socialistic republicans in the thirties, and the final section covers Cabet, Proudhon, Louis Blanc, and the makers of '48. Marx and Engels' 'Communist Manifesto' (condensed) is the appropriate tail-piece to what is on the whole a useful collection. J. H. C.

The Hon. J. W. Fortescue displays his powers of trenchant criticism in his *British Statesmen of the Great War, 1793–1814* (Oxford: Clarendon Press, 1911). Polemics have not often figured so prominently in the Ford Lectures, and the lecturer obviously had not the space in which to supply proofs for his many disputable assertions. Some of them are familiar already to readers of *The History of the British Army*, namely, the foresight of George III in regard to the American War, and the follies of Pitt and Dundas during the Great War. But here, while the invective is embittered, the evidence is much slighter. Burke is lauded as an angel of light for inveighing against the war policy of Pitt and Dundas; but the lecturer severely censures his conduct on Indian affairs, especially with regard to Warren Hastings, and he even states (p. 157) that in office 'he would have been guilty of flagrant, shameless, and continuous jobs', because he was an Irishman. Sidney Smith and Home Popham figure as 'brilliant impostors', cunning at deceiving ministers 'with facts, figures, and pledges, one and all of them fallacious'. Similarly the French royalists regularly deputed by the constituted local assemblies of Hayti and Martinique for British help are dismissed as greedy and unscrupulous adventurers. The information supporting these denunciations is not always sound. In blaming the Pitt cabinet for its conduct in the early months of the war, the author leaves out of count the fact that Great Britain was bound by treaty to succour Holland; and that this fact, and the plans earlier formed by Austria and Prussia, determined the character of the campaign of 1793. He also writes as though Dunkirk was all along the British objective; whereas the first to suggest the siege of Dunkirk were, not Pitt and Dundas, but Lord Auckland at the Hague and George III himself at the end of March, and for reasons which are clearly insufficient (see *Dropmore Papers*, ii. 386, 387). Mr. Fortescue also states that La Vendée would even then have been a promising sphere of British operations: but the rising there was not formidable until far into the spring of 1793; further, the Vendéans and Bretons had no assured position on the coast; and the correspondence of ministers shows that the difficulty of communication with them was insuperable even in November 1793.

Mr. Fortescue also charges Pitt with neglecting the navy, an accusation refuted by the *Journals of Sir T. Byam Martin* (iii. 380 *seq.*), where Middleton (afterwards Lord Barham) ascribes the recovery of the navy mainly to Pitt. On home affairs these lectures are sometimes untrustworthy. The brief reference to the Pitt-Fitzwilliam dispute is strangely favourable to the whigs, whose rapacity is elsewhere derided; and the censure on Pitt for leaving the arrangements at Dublin vague falls to the ground in view of Grenville's account of the conference of ministers in which Fitzwilliam's conduct was clearly prescribed (see *Dropmore Papers*, iii. 35-8). Similarly the censures lavished on Pitt for pressing on the union and yet leaving out the question of catholic emancipation display little knowledge of the facts of the case. If space permitted, it would be possible to point out the bias operating against Canning and in favour of Perceval and Castlereagh. The best part of the lectures is that dealing with the personality and correspondence of Windham.   T.

Mr. A. Hilliard Atteridge's *Joachim Murat* (London : Methuen, 1911) is an interesting and readable biography of that ambiguous soldier of fortune. Napoleon's verdict, ' You are a good soldier on the field of battle, but elsewhere you have neither energy nor character,' is hardly belied by Mr. Atteridge's story. There are occasional slips of some importance (as on p. 169), and the ice episode at Austerlitz reappears in its glory, but in the main the popular character of the book has been arrived at without prejudice to its scholarship. The illustrations are very good.   G. B. H.

In his two volumes on *The Eve of the Catholic Emancipation* (London : Longmans, 1911) Monsignor Bernard Ward gives a continuation of his work on *The Dawn of the Catholic Revival in England*, which ended in 1803. They bring the history of the Roman catholic church in England down to 1820, the year of Grattan's death, when emancipation seemed as far off as ever, and the catholic board had decided to discontinue for a while their annual petition to parliament. As in his earlier book, whenever the support of an original authority seemed advisable, Monsignor Ward has gone to the best sources, in this case to the records of propaganda as well as to episcopal archives at home, and has treated his facts with judicial fairness and literary skill. A briefer narrative omitting some details of a more or less personal kind would have been more interesting and equally useful, but the reader of these volumes will at least have the satisfaction of knowing that, along with other matters, they give an exhaustive account of the various disputes between the English Roman catholics during the period under review. The author has not undertaken a complete history of catholic emancipation ; that, as he points out in his preface, can only be written from an Irish point of view; he has written of the part which English catholics took in it, and of the affairs of their church generally. The English catholics, a small body, but important as including many persons of high social standing and as being in touch with the government, were not generally averse from assenting to ' securities ', such as the veto, the *exequatur*, or some special oath. Here the champion of the unconditional policy was Milner, who was for many years the agent of the Irish bishops, and his quarrels with the catholic board and their secretary, Charles Butler, and with his fellow vicars apostolic fill a large part of these volumes. The policy of Rome was necessarily affected by the fortunes of the pope. During the exile of Pius VII and the Roman cardinals the administration of the church was in the hands of the secretary of propaganda, Monsignor Quarantotti, whose rescript of 1813 was in favour of the acceptance of 'securities'; on the return of the pope, however, the matter was declared to be under the consideration of the cardinals; when he was again forced to flee he took shelter in Genoa, then garrisoned by British troops, and the 'Genoese letter' expressed the result of an agreement with Castlereagh. Among the affairs of the church other than emancipation which are recorded here are the Blanchardist schism, which arose from the condemnation of the concordat by a party among the French refugees, the institution of the catholic Bible society, a step due to the action of the catholic board, and the contributions made by catholics to literature. In this connexion students of history will read with pleasure some notices of Lingard, against whose *History* Milner in vain tried to excite the authorities at Rome and the Irish bishops. Monsignor Ward devotes some pages to a miracle worked at Holywell, which, he may be reminded, is in Flintshire, not in Cheshire. Whether the legend of St. Winefrid's martyrdom is credible or not, there is not a shred of historical evidence for the saint's existence; the cure of her namesake seems well attested, and was of the same kind as some which from time to time take place at Lourdes. There is a useful chronological index of events at the end of each volume, and both are furnished with many portraits and other illustrations. W. H.

Those who take up the book of the Vicomte du Motey, *Un Héros de la Grande Armée* (Paris: Picard, 1911), in the hope of meeting with the adventures of a Marbot will be disappointed. The subject of this volume, Jean Gaspard Hulot, seems to have been an excellent officer and saw a good deal of service; but it was not of a showy kind, and he did not gain the cross of the legion of honour till after the fall of Napoleon. He came of an Ardennes family several members of which rose to distinction, but luck was against him. He was an artillery officer, and was chiefly employed with artificers of that arm, in arsenals or in the rear of the army. In the campaign of 1805 he was with Augereau in the Tyrol. He served under Marmont in Dalmatia, and joined Junot at Lisbon in the beginning of 1808. When the Spanish insurrection broke out he was at Oporto, and was made prisoner with the other French officers there. He spent seven months on a hulk in the harbour of Corunna, and his journal contains interesting details of what he witnessed there, the landing of Baird's force and the embarkation of Moore's army. He shared the fortunes of Soult's army when it was driven out of Oporto, and helped to destroy the guns, but was invalided to France soon afterwards. He survived the hardships of the Russian campaign of 1812, though losing nearly all his men and two of his toes. He wrote later :

Lorsque les vivres commencèrent à arriver de la Prusse, un grand nombre de militaires ou d'employés de l'armée périrent, plutôt pour avoir bu sans modération de l'eau-de-vie que par l'insupportable rigueur de l'atmosphère ou le manque de nourriture ; tandis que quelques onces de pain de seigle ou de biscuit, par jour, ont suffi, pendant les plus mauvais moments de cette longue retraite, à la plupart de ceux qui se sont abstenus de cette liqueur, ou n'en ont bu que rarement et très peu.

He took part in the campaign of 1813 in Germany, and at the end of it he was made *chef de bataillon*, and was charged with the artillery defence of Thionville. After the Restoration he took part in the invasion of Spain in 1823, and was wounded before Pampeluna. He was afterwards sent to Martinique, where he married ; and on his return to France in 1830, finding he was denied promotion, he retired. He was only fifty years of age, but his health was broken by what he had gone through. He lived till 1854, happy with his wife and children and occupied with science and moral reflexions. It can hardly be said that this career called for a biography of over 500 pages, or that the letters quoted are in any way remarkable. Still, the sterling character of Gaspard Hulot, and the affection which bound together the members of his family, make the picture a pleasant one, while it helps us to realize the life of the minor actors in the Napoleonic drama. E. M. LL.

Dr. E. F. Henderson's *Blücher and the Uprising of Prussia against Napoleon*, 1806-15 (New York : Putnam, 1911) gives a vivid picture of Marshal ' Vorwärts '. If at times he magnifies him, and exaggerates the part he played in bringing about the downfall of Napoleon, other passages correct the false impression. A good summary of Blücher's strong and weak points is given on p. 115. In his outline of the war of liberation Dr. Henderson has made use of German works by Friederich, Janson, Lettow-Vorbeck, and others, but not, we think, of the most recent publications, such as that of Pflugk-Harttung. His narrative is clear and animated, giving enough and not too much as a setting for his hero. He misrepresents Castlereagh's attitude when he speaks of him as urging peace with Napoleon as speedily as possible, in the latter part of February 1814. His account of the Waterloo campaign seems to be drawn too exclusively from German sources, and must in fact be described as a Prussian version. He puts forward the charges made against Wellington in connexion with the battle of Ligny, without presenting the case in reply to those charges. He pronounces Wellington to have been wrong in claiming that he made ' the attack which produced the final result ' at Waterloo ; it was Zieten, he says, who made that attack. He speaks slightingly of Houssaye as ' puny ' in comparison with the German historians, but he would have found in Houssaye a well-considered judgement on the point :

Il y eut dans la retraite de l'armée française trois mouvements bien distincts, dont le premier et le troisième sont dûs aux Anglais seuls. D'abord l'échec de la moyenne garde entraîna le fléchissement de plus des deux tiers de la ligne française. Ensuite l'irruption des Prussiens provoqua la panique et le désordre à la droite (corps de d'Erlon). Enfin la marche en avant de Wellington précipita la déroute à la gauche (corps de Reille et débris de la cavalerie).

When Dr. Henderson says that there has been no previous English biography of Blücher, original or translated, he has overlooked a substantial volume of 429 pages published in 1815, *The Life and Campaigns of*

Field Marshal Prince Blucher, by J. E. Marston: it claimed to be in part translated from Gneisenau, who had written an account of the campaign of 1813.
U.

Those who have read Mr. Justin H. Smith's *Our Struggle for the Fourteenth Colony* are aware that, in spite of a fantastic style, the author is untiring in his efforts to obtain the best first-hand evidence. In *The Annexation of Texas* (New York: The Baker and Taylor Company, 1911) the style is more chastened, Mr. Smith quaintly remarking that in the earlier book he had adopted a vivid and rather highly coloured style so as to impart in some degree a sense of the agitation and enthusiasm of the time, whilst the arguments of the present volume require to be made known as clearly and unobtrusively as possible. But in other respects *The Annexation of Texas* abundantly makes good the promise of its predecessor. Mr. Smith has burrowed deeply in the diplomatic papers, American, Texan, Mexican, British, and French, of the time, and good use is made of the proceeding of congress and of newspapers. He has, however, an annoying habit of paraphrasing documents in his own words, instead of giving the *ipsissima verba* in inverted commas; but, as he approaches his subject without bias, there is no reason to question the fidelity of his reproductions. From the evidence here brought forward certain conclusions seem clearly established. It was the interest of the United States to absorb its southern neighbour, which, under conceivable circumstances, might have become a source of no little danger. The policy of annexation suffered from falling into the cauldron of party politics. It was at first identified with President Tyler, whom neither whigs nor democrats would recognize, and it only prevailed when taken up by the successful democrats. There was a strong feeling for independence amongst the governing men of Texas; though the majority of the rank and file of the people, themselves emigrants from the United States, were favourable to the policy of union. Great Britain and France were ready by all means short of war to prevent the acquisition of Texas by the United States. England was urged by two main motives, the desire to restrict the area within which negro slavery prevailed, and the desire to benefit her commerce. Louis Philippe was mainly actuated by the wish to co-operate with England; but French public opinion was hostile to such co-operation, and Great Britain, in any case, had no intention to act alone. Upon the whole the effect of Mr. Smith's investigations is to put the conduct of the United States in a more favourable light than has been the prevailing impression. 'For a variety of reasons,' he writes, 'chiefly natural prejudices, an equally natural want of information, and the fact that certain gifted opponents of annexation enjoyed great prestige in quarters where much attention has been paid to historical writing, some inaccurate views regarding the matter have unavoidably prevailed.'
H. E. E.

Mrs. Hamilton King has issued, and Mr. G. M. Trevelyan has appropriately edited, an interesting little volume of *Letters and Recollections of Mazzini* (London: Longmans, 1912). The author of *The Disciples* is 'perhaps the last English survivor of those who knew' Mazzini, though in Italy the present mayor of Rome is generally regarded as the depositary of the Mazzinian tradition. Mrs. King's devotion to Italy and to the great Italian apostle, originally due to the perusal of Gladstone's translation of Farini's book on *The Roman State*, led her to write to Mazzini in 1862; and her correspondence with him, prohibited by her relatives in May 1863 but renewed on the eve of her marriage later in that year, led to her meeting him for the first time in January 1864 and to their subsequent friendship. From these letters and from some of Madame Venturi, included in the volume, we have an intimate picture of the famous conspirator. Besides his well-known views on the future of his own country, Mazzini's correspondence contains prophetic opinions on the Balkan Slavs. It is curious to find him urging as early as 1863 study of 'the Nationalities of the East of Europe', because '*there*, after Italy, is the seat of mighty changes and events'—a forecast amply realized twelve years later. But the Italian war against Austria in 1866 did not 'give the signal . . . to the whole of the Southern Slavonians'; the effect of the exclusion of Austria from Italy was rather to make the former ruler of Venetia a south Slavonic power; nor have the Slavs yet 'regenerated' Europe. From Madame Roselli, in whose house at Pisa he died, the author had an account of his death, with his Christian ending. By a slip the date of the battle of Mentana is wrongly given (pp. 65–6); every one who has visited that picturesque town of the Roman Campagna will remember that one of its streets is called after the fatal day—November 3. It is to be feared that his subsequent career as a politician removed Nicotera from the category of 'saints' (p. 11). W. M.

The *Proceedings of the Massachusetts Historical Society*, November 1911, contain a vigorous statement of the Trent affair by Mr. C. F. Adams. The contention is that, even if the arrest of the southern envoys was justifiable according to 'English principles' and 'English practice', such principles and practices were not recognized elsewhere; least of all in the United States.[1] An interesting collection of letters is appended to the paper. In the December number of the same publication Mr. C. F. Adams's brother, Mr. Brooks Adams, deals, in a very different spirit, with a later phase of Anglo-American relations, 'The Seizure of the Laird Rams.' The paper is a bitter indictment of the Palmerston-Russell ministry, and of its treatment of the American question. Mr. Brooks Adams certainly makes out a strong case against British statesmen and judges, supported by no little evidence. He writes, however, in a tone of exaggeration: thus, 'After Waterloo England became the heart of modern civilization, the centre of the world's economic system, and as such she wielded, until February 1864, a supremacy which was, in substance, unquestioned. On that night she abdicated, and her supremacy has never returned.' (The ministry obtained a majority on a motion, in effect, censuring them for having, later in the day, yielded to the pressure of the American govern-

[1] The paper appears in a briefer form in the *American Historical Review* for last April (xvii. 3).

ment with regard to the Laird Rams.) After this we are not surprised to learn that

> For just one hundred years prior to the election of Abraham Lincoln to the Presidency, the aristocratic principle in England had been striving to subdue the democratic principles in America, and to that end had fought two wars, from which democracy had escaped, as it were, by miracle. In large part democracy in America had been saved by means of a union with a slave-holding oligarchy, a union which would have been impossible under pressure less severe. Suddenly the bond, designed to fuse these discordant elements into a single organism, burst asunder, and in 1861, the North found herself hemmed in between the slave-holding and the British aristocracies, which were natural allies. To conquer the South, even the South unaided by England, strained the North to the limit of endurance. . . . Therefore she had to confide the defence of her Atlantic coast, facing England, to her diplomats, for other defenders she had none. Desperate as the situation seemed at first to the two statesmen (Seward and Adams) they presently perceived one path to safety. They might be able to bring the disfranchised and discontented classes of Great Britain to support the North. . . . Finally the aristocracy, unable to consolidate its forces, capitulated. The vote of the Commons on February 24, 1864, marks an epoch in civilization.

H. E. E.

Professor Ernst Marx's *Bismarck und die Hohenzollernkandidatur* (Stuttgart: Metzler, 1911) supports the highly probable conclusion that, in furthering the proposal of placing a Hohenzollern prince on the Spanish throne, Bismarck was mainly actuated by the desire to be assured of a considerable military force opposed to France being in arms on the further side of the Pyrenees; while the notion that an immediate provocation of France formed part of his scheme, or indeed that he was looking forward to the speedy outbreak of war, must be definitively abandoned. The documentary evidence required for a complete treatment of the episode (including its beginnings, which Dr. Marx practically pretermits) is indeed fuller than it was in Sybel's days; but the existing material (including Gramont's ingenuous narrative) is handled with skill in the present pamphlet, though here and there with much boldness. Thus Bismarck's celebrated letter—first published in 1876, but not until a more recent date noticed as of importance for the controversy on the whole subject—which suggested a way for avoiding, or at least mitigating, French excitement on the acceptance of the proposal, is concluded by Marx to have been dated as late as 21 June, and to have been addressed not to Bucher, but to Salazar, the active intermediary in the matter of the candidature, and formerly secretary to the Spanish embassy in Berlin.

A. W. W.

The fifth volume of the collection of dispatches published for the French Foreign Office by Justus Ficker (Paris, 1912), under the title *Les Origines Diplomatiques de la Guerre de 1870–1*, has just made its appearance. It extends from 6 November 1864 to 27 February 1865, and is mainly, though not exclusively, concerned with the penultimate phase of the Schleswig-Holstein question—the last phase, that of the annexation of the duchies to Prussia, drawing nearer and nearer on the face, as it were, of the correspondence between M. Drouyn de Lhuys and the agents of French diplomacy. The lesser factors in the problem are the compensation—if any—to be demanded by or given to Austria; the efforts, almost heroically futile, of Beust, not altogether well seconded by von der Pfordten, and actually opposed by Platen, to give effect to the widespread preference for the Augustenburg claims; and, finally, the proposal, urged persistently but ineffectively by France, for the retrocession of the northern districts of Schleswig. But they are all overtopped by the steady progress of Bismarck's policy towards its consummation. Much valuable historical material is accumulated in this volume—not only in the sagacious diagnoses of Benedetti and the frank *aperçus* of Gramont; but, carefully and elaborately edited as the volume is, it is without an index of its own, specially desirable where no summary is supplied of those dispatches, or portions of dispatches, which are printed at length.   A. W. W.

European scholars are beginning to estimate the value of Georgian studies in numerous branches of knowledge. The ecclesiastical, biblical, and liturgical manuscripts of the Iberian church are now found to supply important materials for the early history of Christendom. The vague suppositions that modern Georgian furnishes a key for the decipherment of Sumerian and other cuneiform languages are now on the point of becoming scientifically justified. The fragments of ancient law still surviving in the customs of the peoples of the Caucasus, to which Professor M. Kovalevskii drew attention in his *Zakon i Obychai na Kavkazië*, are being systematically investigated. In the field of history, also, native students have organized themselves into a Georgian Historical and Ethnographical Society at Tiflis and have attracted collaborators ready to bestow time, money, and gifts of documents. The directing force of the society and its most indefatigable worker is Mr. E. S. T'haqaishvili, who has won distinction by his bibliographical work, especially by his monumental and scholarly *Catalogue of the Manuscripts of the Georgian Literary Society in Tiflis*. A prominent place among his works is occupied by the three large volumes of materials for Georgian history entitled *Sakart'hvelos Sidzveleni E. T'haqaishvilis redaktorobith* and published by the Georgian Society of History and Ethnography (Tiflis, 1899–1910). He has now carefully edited and printed 1,527 documents ranging in date from A.D. 1027 to the early part of the nineteenth century and, as he says in his preface to vol. iii (issued in French, as well as Georgian, for the convenience of western students), 'touching every point of Georgian life.' For example, there are royal letters patent defining the privileges of certain noble families, charters to monasteries, inventories of property, documents relating to taxation, military organization, offices of state, judicial procedure. Not a few of the papers contain interesting narratives of events, e.g. concerning the travels in Persia of Kings T'heimuraz II and Erecle II and the distinguished part taken by the latter in Nadir Shah's expedition to India. There are a large number of royal letters, and in many of them the events connected with the entry of the Russians into Georgia and their political action are presented in a much more intelligible form than we find in any books hitherto published. The *Akty* of the Archaeographical Commission, despite their bulky proportions and splendid appearance, leave much that is unexplained in the history of Transcaucasia in the early years of the nine-

teenth century, and it is possible that the records contained therein have
been over-edited by zealous officials; a comparison of them with Mr.
T'haqaishvili's book will help the historian of the future to gain a clear
idea of the difficult period of the establishment of Russian supremacy, and
the student of the immediately preceding half-century (1768–1801) dealt
with in Professor A. A. Tsagareli's *Gramoty* (in Georgian and Russian) will
have much fresh material placed at his disposal. In fact, we are here
presented with a mass of records which not only add greatly to our
knowledge of the internal history of Transcaucasia from the beginning of
the eleventh century down to our own days, but throw much light on the
affairs of Persia, the eastern empire, and Turkey.   O. W.

M. E. Angot's *Mélanges d'Histoire* (Paris: Paul, 1911) contain four
light but agreeable studies of curiously varied subjects. The author
writes with equal ease on 'Louis XVII' in the Temple, on the private
correspondence of some members of the Prussian royal house in the
dark days after Jena, on Franks and Bulgarians at the beginning of the
thirteenth century, and on the four daughters of Raymond-Berenger IV
of Provence, who all became queens. The last, which is the most substantial of the papers here bound together, tells the ordinary facts about
these ladies pleasantly, but its scholarship leaves much to be desired.   V.

Under the title of *Männer und Zeiten* (Leipzig: Quelle & Meyer, 1911)
Professor Erich Marcks has collected some two dozen addresses and
sketches of the last twenty-five years, almost all of which have already
appeared in print. The author declares that he has in mind not only
professional students of history but still more the general public. Both
classes will find much to their taste in these delightful and eloquent
volumes. Though ranging over a wide field they claim to possess a certain
unity, the first dealing mainly with the past, the second with the era of
unification. Among the most valuable portions of the former are the
lecture on Coligny and the detailed examination of his attitude towards
the murder of Guise in 1563. As the *Life of Coligny* has never progressed
beyond the first volume, published twenty years ago, it is interesting to
possess the judgement of his biographer on the later chapters of his career.
The seizure of Strassburg by Louis XIV is a skilfully handled controversial theme. The larger part of both volumes is devoted to the history
of Prussia. *The Kingdom of the Hohenzollerns*, written in 1901 for the bicentenary of the monarchy, is a truly admirable survey of the building of
the Prussian state and of the work of its chief architects. The second
volume is dominated by the personality of Bismarck, on whom the professor
is the greatest living authority. The sketch of the visit to Friedrichsruh
in 1893 adds but little to the familiar picture of the hibernating bear,
but reveals the enthusiasm of young Germany for the fallen hero. The
address on William I summarizes the views expressed in the author's classical
biography of the monarch. More interesting are the studies of Roon and
the Grand Duke Frederick of Baden, the former more conservative, the
latter more liberal than the Iron Chancellor with whom they co-operated
for so many years. The closing addresses deal with the evolution of

European diplomacy, that on England and Germany since the Reformation having appeared in English dress in 1900. Dr. Marcks is a convinced imperialist, and it is regrettable to detect in certain passages the suspicion that Great Britain is in some degree hostile to the legitimate development of the German nation. One of the most attractive features of these volumes is the group of sketches of the ' political historians ', above all Sybel and Treitschke, who helped to make as well as record the unification of Germany.

G. P. G.

A course of lectures on *Germany in the Nineteenth Century*, delivered before popular audiences in Manchester last year by Dr. Holland Rose, Professor Herford, Professor Gonner, and Dr. Sadler, has been published by the Manchester University Press with a preface by Viscount Haldane and some oddly unequal footnotes. The conception of the course was admirable, and parts at any rate merit the perpetuation of print, but much of it does not call for criticism in this Review. Dr. Rose's lecture on the political history is, one must say, just a lecture. If a reference was really needed for the statement that the population of the empire has grown in forty years from 41,000,000 to 65,000,000, it might have been to some more primary statistical authority than the *Cambridge Modern History*. Professor Gonner's account of the economic history shows the arrangement that marks a good lecture, and only once that condensed reference to an imperfectly explained topic that marks a bad one. There is more freshness, however, in Dr. Sadler's comparison of the courses of German and English educational progress. But the most striking contribution is Professor Herford's long essay — obviously expanded and altered since delivery—on the intellectual and literary history. There must be few English scholars who could have cast so wide a net and brought in so much that is essential and distinctive. It is not a survey of ' literature ' in the narrow sense, but ranges from Wolf to Wundt and from Savigny to Lamprecht. Apart from a few ugly and unnecessary words—' novelistic ', ' mentality ', ' nuance '—and an occasional odd appreciation or stilted sentence, it never slips from an exceptionally high level of learning, criticism, and exposition.   J. H. C.

Mr. Cyrus F. Wicker's *Neutralization* (London: Frowde, 1911) is the first treatise in the English language to deal with the bearing of international law upon the imposition of a condition of permanent neutrality on lands and waterways. In the first seventy-two pages of the book the author investigates permanent neutrality, and sets forth with clearness and legal acumen an analysis of neutrality, a summary of all the existing treaties effecting neutralization, and a short but suggestive sketch of the consequences of neutralization. In his opinion, ' the points of greatest difficulty in the future will most probably arise in determining the commercial relations between neutralized states or colonies and other countries.' He believes that a neutralized state ought to enjoy an unfettered discretion in adjusting its trade relations with its neighbours. The last chapter, on the United States and Neutralization, appeared originally in the *Atlantic Monthly*. It is written with greater literary freedom than the rest of the book, and includes recommendations which lie outside the sphere of this Review. G. B. H.

The series of prettily printed little books which have been appearing under the title of the *Cambridge Manuals of Literature and Science* from the University Press cannot be dealt with here; but we may mention the titles of a few of them which within their limits are of historical interest. Mr. A. Hamilton Thompson's two volumes on *The Ground Plan of the English Parish Church* (1911) and on *The Historical Growth of the English Parish Church* (1911) have an independent value. *Life in the Medieval University*, by Mr. R. S. Rait (1912), gives a competent and attractive survey, and in other ranges we may mention *The Troubadours* by Mr. H. J. Chaytor (1912), and *Methodism* by Dr. H. B. Workman (1912). W.

The Statesman's Year-Book for 1912 (London: Macmillan) appears again under the editorship of Dr. J. Scott Keltie, and bears evidence of careful revision. The introductory tables are, as usual, interesting, and it would be ungracious to call attention to a rare misprint in so large a collection of figures. Among the maps are one showing the recent rearrangement of the north-east provinces of India, and three marking boundaries fixed or claimed in Africa. X

Miss Margaret Mahler's *Chirk Castle and Chirkland* (London: Bell, 1912) gives a slight account of the castle and marcher lordship of Chirk in Denbighshire. From being an English royal castle under Henry II and John, Chirk came, in the thirteenth century, into Welsh hands, but was forfeited to the Crown in 1281. Held successively by the Mortimers, Arundels, and Beauforts, Chirk was frequently forfeited, and, as the result of these circumstances, various ministers' accounts for Chirk in the fourteenth and fifteenth centuries are to be found in the Public Record Office. These are here translated. During the greater part of the sixteenth century Chirk Castle was Crown property, but in 1595 it was bought by Sir Thomas Myddelton, father of the Sir Thomas Myddelton who sided with the parliament in the civil wars. The authoress gives extracts from the Chirk Castle accounts of the early seventeenth century which have been privately printed by Mr. W. M. Myddelton, and also documents from the state papers and in private possession bearing upon the part played by Chirk in the civil wars. The castle is Edwardian, but no architectural description is given of it. H. H. E. C.

The Township Booke of Halliwell (Chetham Society, new series, no. 69, 1910), edited by Mr. Archibald Sparke, covers the years 1640–1762. Opening with a list of the tenants of the earl of Derby, to whom the land of the township, then part of the parish of Deane in Lancashire, belonged, the volume is mainly taken up with the accounts of the constable and, later, the accounts of the overseers of the poor. After 1738 the offices of constable, churchwarden, and overseer were served by one man, and the accounts are united and given in more detail. Very occasionally there are entries of some resolution of the township, e.g. concerning the payment of tithe (p. 52), the change of date for the election of village officers from Christmas Day, as 'inconvenient', to the day following (p. 62), protests against what was considered unfair burdening of the village in the matter of poor relief (pp. 64, 69). Mr. and Mrs. Webb's account of the working of local institutions in this period (*English Local Government, Parish and County*, bk. i) receives some slight confirmation from this record. The offices of constable and churchwarden were served by ' houserowe ' : there was a fixed rotation of houses which had to provide the officers, either the owners or other inhabitants of the village. The accounts detail the normal expenditure of a township at that period—bridge and road building and repair, care of the church and the school-house, assessments for taxes, relief of the poor, and so forth. The only entries of other than purely local interest refer to the years of the civil war. The levies of men and money on the village for the parliamentary forces are duly recorded. The township paid for horsemen ' attending the army under Sir Thomas Fairfax to relieve Nantwich ' in 1643, and sent victuals to the garrison in Manchester in the same year. In the following year it sent horsemen and victuals for the siege of Liverpool by the parliamentarians, and victuals for the siege of Lathom House. In 1648 it had ten soldiers quartered on it, but after that date the record is almost barren of items of general historical interest—as indeed one would expect from its nature. R. F.

The volume of *Testamenta Leodiensia, 1539 to 1546*, issued by the Thoresby Society (1911), contains the text of more than 260 wills of people belonging to Leeds and its neighbourhood. The testators are chiefly farmers, but there are also several priests, some clothiers or weavers (in 1543 one bequeaths ' a lomme, a pare of sheres, and a pare of tenters ', p. 95), and smiths (in 1544 one bequeaths part of his implements to his servant, p. 104). The bequests are mainly of household stuff, of wearing apparel, of farm implements, and especially of live-stock. They contain a variety of remarkable words, which will furnish out a striking glossary. Unhappily, the copyists of the wills are plainly not equally competent, and in several words it is doubtful whether the original is correctly given. There is no verb, to ' wit ' or to ' witto ', meaning to bequeath ; the copyist must have misread ' will ', written with a colligation-stroke. The proverbial ' silver spoon ' occurs frequently, e. g. 1538, ' to everie childe of his a syluer spoyne ' (p. 2). The citizen-soldier is represented by bequests : 1539, ' to Thomas my sonne my bowe, my quyver, and my shaftes ' (p. 2) ; 1541, ' vnto . . . my sone my swerde and buckler, jake and sallet, with all my other fensible aray.' The wills are short documents, following a traditional form, and probably drafted by the parish priest. A testator recites his faith and gives directions as to place and manner of his burial, for services and pious works for the good of his soul, for payment of church dues, especially of a mortuary, according to a recent act of parliament. The confession of faith generally includes ' St. Mary and all the Saints in heaven', but towards the end of the volume there are several instances of a protestant formula, ' Almighte God, my redemer,' without mention of ' the blessed company of heaven '. The place of burial is most frequently the church, and often a special place in the church is fixed on. Latterly, the churchyard becomes not uncommon, with preference occasionally expressed for the south side of it (e.g. 1541, a priest, p. 55). The church porch is also selected (a widow of Wakefield, 1543, p. 101). Favourite forms of pious works are distribution of bread or pence to the poor, donations to repair of highways, contributions to the church-lights, or the bestowal of some cherished garment or piece of linen to church use (1543, 'my best towell to our Ladie altar,' p. 102). After dealing with his church duties, a testator proceeds to dispose of his goods in legacies, and residuary legacies. Here the wills are brief and simple. There are few instances of entail or reversionary provisions; property is usually left to unfettered judgement of executors, for prompt and final partition.

A. C.

The Lincoln Record Society, which was founded in 1910, begins its publications with *Lincolnshire Church Notes by Gervase Holles* (Lincoln: Morton, 1911). Holles, who was born in 1607, aimed at writing a history of Lincolnshire, and for that purpose copied the inscriptions and coats of arms from windows and sepulchral monuments in 290 of the churches of Lincolnshire between the years 1634 and 1642. As he was expert at heraldry and accurate, his work is unusually valuable, and now that more than half of what he saw exists no longer, every Lincolnshire antiquary has recourse to him repeatedly. No volume could be more fit as a commencement of the Lincoln Record Society. Many of the coats of arms were identified by Holles, but the present editor, the Rev. R. E. G. Cole, has been able to make some additions. The original is Harl. MS. 6829, a fine manuscript with 1900 coloured coats of arms, and it is unfortunate that this volume has been prepared not from the original but from a transcript in Lincolnshire, which has introduced some errors of which Holles is innocent. Thus on p. 181, ' Penses qd.' is in Holles ' Penses que ', which makes sense; p. 14, the writ of the earl of Chester should of course be ' Quare volo et precipio ', not ' Quia volo '; p. 8, it need hardly be said that Alexander III did not write ' quum quidem ', and Holles gives correctly ' quoniam igitur '; p. 22, ' in loco ' should be ' in loco eorum '; p. 23, ' conceperunt ' should be ' concesserunt '. In these cases Holles is not to blame, but there are some obvious mistakes on his part which might have been pointed out; such as ' deforcientes ' for ' deforciantes ' repeatedly; and on p. 7 the papal letter makes no sense, and for ' accepimus quod enim ' we must read ' accepimus quod cum '; on p. 21 he gives ' tenebant ' where ' tenebunt ' is required. There are some misprints that have been overlooked; *clameam* for *clameum*; *omne* for *omni*; *Iohanni* (p. 28) for *Iohanne*, and others. Also the dating of the deeds is unsatisfactory: thus on p. 22 a fine levied ' in the quindene of St. Michael, 20 Hen. III ', i.e. October 1236, is assigned by the editor vaguely to 1235-6; and in the same way with a fine on p. 21. These are small points comparatively, and do not touch that which is the most important part of the volume, viz. the monumental inscriptions and the accounts of the coats of arms. There is a good index.

H. E. S.

In his *Norfolk Families*, part i (Norwich: Printed for subscribers, 1911), Mr. Walter Rye sets an excellent pattern to antiquaries of other counties. He supplies a critical list of families who have owned land in the county, from the thirteenth century to present date, with an exact statement of their coats of arms, the source of these arms, and the dates of assumption of them. His censures on fictitious pedigrees and spurious heraldry are terse and caustic. Incidentally, many matters of county interest come in : e.g. the Norfolk connexion of Chaucer (p. 100), of Dean Colet (p. 111), of Robinson Crusoe (p. 135), and boycotting (p. 65). This, the first of five projected parts, contains names A to C.

A. C.

It is pleasant to find that the migration of Dr. Armitage Robinson from Westminster to Wells—in other and more pluralistic days the illustrious Busby was a prebendary of both churches at once—has not put an end to his studies in the history of the former foundation ; and to welcome a very full account from his pen of *The Abbot's House at Westminster* (Cambridge : University Press, 1911), of which the present deanery forms a part. It is needless to say that the task which the dean has set himself is admirably performed ; and the story of Westminster is so closely bound up with that of England that many who have not, like the writer of this notice, a peculiar piety towards the Close of St. Peter, will find much matter of no little interest in the book before us. The dean shows how the lodgings of the twelfth-century abbots, still embedded in the southern portion of the existing deanery, developed into the great fourteenth-century house designed by that magnificent builder and (as we learn from p. 10) keen sportsman, Abbot Litlyngton, and let by Abbot Esteney under the name of Cheynegates to Edward IV's widowed queen, who had twice taken sanctuary there during the Wars of the Roses ; and he goes on to trace the subsequent fortunes of this mansion as abbot's house, as bishop's palace (during the ten years in which Westminster was an episcopal see), and as the residence successively of the Lords Wentworth, of Feckenham, the abbot of Mary's restored monastery, and since his time (except for the interval from 1650 to 1659) of the successive heads of Queen Elizabeth's collegiate foundation, still happily in being. During the interval just mentioned it was occupied by Bradshaw the regicide, as the tenant of the governors whom parliament set in the place of the dean and chapter to control ' the School and Almshouses of the late Colledge '. There are added to the main body of the book a number of interesting ' illustrative documents ', extending from the fourteenth to the eighteenth century ; and several excellent plans. Might it be suggested that readers not very familiar with the locality would probably have been glad to have the points of the compass indicated both in the large folding-map and in Mr. Gladwyn Turbutt's plan of the first floor ? One would also have liked notes on Vaughan's House (p. 57) and ' the Screen by the Clock ' (p. 78). Was ' the Chapel now behind the Screen ' in the last-quoted extract the Islip Chapel in the presbytery ? On p. 59 the dean says ' Lady Hoby must have been a friend of Dean Goodman '. The friendship is of course readily explained by Goodman's long and intimate connexion with her brother-in-law, Cecil, afterwards the great Lord Burghley.

C. C. J. W.

In his *History of the Castle of York* (London : Elliot Stock, 1911) Mr. T. P. Cooper gives a supplement to his monograph on the walls of York (*The City of York; the Story of its Walls, Bars, and Castles*). The subject is well deserving of treatment, since it has no independent literature of its own other than Twyford and Griffiths's *Records of York Castle*, and this last-named work deals principally with the modern prison. Yet from its erection by William I down to 1684, when Clifford's Tower was burnt, the castle remained a fortress of the first rank, the scene of the well-known massacre of the Jews under Richard I and of two great councils held by Edward II, a prison, the seat of a royal mint, and the meeting-place for the county court and the assizes. All these aspects of its history, as well as the castle mills and the free chapel of St. George, are here briefly but adequately described. Mr. Cooper has worked largely on the calendars of patent rolls and close rolls, and though the series of chancery inquisitions and exchequer accounts might have provided him with additional material, the documents he has collected are well arranged. The history of the castle as a prison is given in detail, but is of less general interest. The work is well illustrated by numerous reproductions of early views of the castle, including three interesting drawings by Francis Place, but it lacks a satisfactory plan of the castle which might show its medieval arrangement. A report on the nature of the mound on which the keep stands, as revealed by trenching and boring undertaken in 1902, is printed at pp. 200–7. H. H. E. C.

In the series of *Les Régions de la France* undertaken by the *Revue de Synthèse historique*, the number treating of *La Normandie* (Paris : Cerf, 1910) has fallen to the lot of M. Prentout, who occupies at the university of Caen the chair of local history which forms an excellent feature of French provincial universities. He here gives a sketch of the development of historical studies in Normandy, and a review, by periods and topics, of what has been done and what remains to do in the field of Norman history, economic, social, and literary, as well as political and constitutional. The enumeration of the publications in each field is detailed and careful, so that the volume offers the best topical bibliography of Norman history at present available. At the close *desiderata* are briefly considered : for the Anglo-Norman period attention is called particularly to the need of a collection of charters, a feudal geography of the duchy, special studies of towns and monasteries, especially in their economic aspects, and a more thorough treatment of characteristic legal and political institutions. It is a satisfaction to note that some progress has been made in these directions in the time since M. Prentout's pages were written. The Law Faculty of Caen has inaugurated its series of studies and texts in Norman law ; M. Legras has produced an admirable example of a municipal monograph in his *Bourgage de Caen* ; and the Société de l'Histoire de Normandie has arranged to supplement other undertakings of the same sort by issuing the charters of the early dukes under the highly competent editorship of M. Ferdinand Lot. C. H. H.

M. Étienne Dupont's *Le Mont-Saint-Michel inconnu* (Paris : Perrin, 1912) is an agreeable little book, designed to give intelligent visitors to the Mount more information than they can find in the usual guides. It deals with the manuscripts which are now preserved at Avranches, the pilgrimages and hostelries, with Mont-Saint-Michel as a prison, and with certain curious incidents in the history of the abbey. M. Dupont belongs to a coterie of *michelien* scholars of Avranches who take themselves very seriously, and to the general student of monastic history his book will have most value as a reflexion of the academic tradition which has gathered about the place since the days of Dom Huynes and Dom Le Roy. But, as his previous books show, he is well acquainted with the manuscripts and literature of Mont Saint-Michel, and the most learned might glean something from the pleasant trivialities of this volume. F. M. P.

Mr. H. F. Reeve, who has lived many years in the country, has written an imposing book on *The Gambia* (London : Smith, Elder & Co., 1912). The historical portion of the volume is perhaps the least satisfactory. Mr. Reeve, as a hard-working official, has every reason to claim 'the indulgence of those who wield the facile pen and the purple pencil', and a plain story would receive a respectful welcome ; but some patience is needed with an author who, when he has to mention Mr. Chamberlain, finds it necessary to describe him as 'that bright particular star ... in our political firmament, whose mission it was to teach, and by whose intuition and luminous guidance the bulk of the British nation has been taught to think imperially and to regard our colonial possessions as gems in the imperial diadem, adding both to the lustre thereof and to the solidarity of the British Empire'. It is, moreover, a little startling to read of the treaty of Paris, 1814, which ended the war of independence with our American colonies and also with France. Mr. Reeve, as a local official who has been brought into personal relations with the native tribes, may very reasonably resent any apparent betrayal of their interests in west Africa ; but it is surely an exaggeration to suggest that if Great Britain, with interests in east, central, and south Africa, as well as in most other portions of the globe, be willing to effect a deal with France regarding west Africa, it is therefore a proof of decadence. It should be added that the author is thoroughly interested in his subject, and has made a careful study of whatever material he could command. H. E. E.

Professor E. R. Turner must be congratulated on the thorough character of his work, *The Negro in Pennsylvania*, 1639–1861 (Washington : American Historical Association, 1911) ; no less than 3,000 printed volumes, more than 10,000 pamphlets, and some 50,000 pages of manuscript having been consulted in its preparation. It cannot truthfully be said that the conclusions reached are startlingly novel. We knew already that, thanks to its German, as well as Quaker, population, Pennsylvania took the lead in the opposition to negro slavery; that the position of the slave there was very different from what it was in the south, and that the Pennsylvanian abolitionists represented, upon the whole, the more moderate section, as against the New England anti-slavery stalwarts. It is curious to note the strong dislike of the negro that grew up *pari passu* with opposition to negro slavery, and the uncertainty which existed on the question whether or not the negroes possessed a vote as freemen under the constitution of 1790. The better opinion appears to have been that they did not; in spite of having voted for many years in the country districts unchallenged. In any case the question was set at rest for the time by the amendment to the constitution of 1838, which declared that only white freemen could vote. The position of Pennsylvania upon the borders of Maryland made it the special resort of fugitive slaves, and in consequence the centre of the agitation over the difficult question of their treatment. H. E. E.

California under Spain and Mexico, 1535–1847, by Mr. Irving Berdine Richman (Boston: Houghton, Mifflin & Co., 1911), is a disappointing volume. In spite of a subject full of interest, which offers many opportunities for lively reading, this book is both dry and dull. The author has never thoroughly mastered his material, which indeed overwhelms him. He deserves credit for his two years' investigations in America and for receiving transcripts from European archives, but his results are presented in such an unconnected, monotonous manner as to be unpalatable. The book is provided with nearly 150 pages of notes and references, with plenty of maps, and with a good index—everything indeed except a clear and readable style. In addition to being over-fond of out-of-the-way terms, such as 'involvement' (p. 107), 'concernments' (p. 143), &c., the author at times uses incorrect expressions, such as 'mal-inclined' (p. 220), 'river margin' (pp. 100 and 134), 'met a fall from his horse' (p. 199), 'secularization was given pause' (p. 244), &c. The following paragraph offers an example of the style of this volume:

> Hurt by the projected *Custodia*; hurt by the enforced toleration of Indian *alcaldes* and *regidores*; hurt by fear of the *Reglamento*; hurt by need of interposing at Mexico and Arispe defense against charges of insubordination; and hurt, lastly, by the presence, aggressive and unsavory, of the pueblos, there yet remained to State Sacerdotal a consolation. The missions of Santa Bárbara and La Purísima Concepcion—desired by Serra and planned by Neve, but suspended in their founding by the refusal of the College of San Fernando to assign to them Padres—both at length were to be erected (p. 153).

Facts are dragged into the narrative by the heels whether or not they are of importance and bear on the subject. Should any of them have been previously unrecorded, this is announced in such terms as 'event hitherto unchronicled' (p. 103), 'documents here first used' (pp. 203 and 322). Proper names abound in such profusion that they are bewildering. In Appendix D there is a detailed list of the Spanish founders of San Francisco. H. P. B.

THE ENGLISH HISTORICAL REVIEW

NO. CVIII.—OCTOBER 1912 *

The Tribal Hidage

THE ancient territorial list which Maitland named the 'Tribal Hidage' is known in two slightly differing forms, which may for convenience be designated the 'English' and the 'Latin', from the circumstance that one form is in English throughout while the other has been partially translated into Latin. The only 'English' text now known was discovered by Dr. Birch in the Harleian MS. 3271, fo. 6 *b*, and printed by him in full,[1] but the names and figures had been published by Spelman in 1626 in his *Glossarium* (s.v. Hide), from what he calls a *veterrima scheda* (perhaps a loose leaf or gathering) in the possession of Francis Tatum.[2] The volume in which Dr. Birch found it is occupied mainly with grammatical treatises, but some miscellaneous pieces are entered, in several hands, all of much the same period. The 'Tribal Hidage' fills up what had been a blank page near the beginning.[3] In the same or a like writing at the end of the book are chronological notes, ending with the statement that it was 6,132 years from the Creation; that Easter would fall on 2 April; that it was a leap year and the fifteenth indiction. These conditions are satisfied by the year 1032. In the 'Hidage' the numbers are written out at length; the whole has been corrected by another and perhaps somewhat later hand. Thus *hund* has been added in *Herefinna* (twelf *hund* hyda) and in the final total (twa *hund* thusend), and some words have been corrected;[4] while to *Fœrpinga* has been added the marginal note—'Is in Middel Englū Færpinga'. This text and some later ones are collected in the *Cartularium Saxonicum*, i. 414–16.

[1] *Brit. Arch. Assoc. Journal*, 1884, p. 29; whence printed in Earle's *Land Charters*, p. 458. Cf. Maitland, *Domesday Book and Beyond*, pp. 506 ff.
[2] *Archaeologus*, p. 353. In later editions Tatum is changed to Tantum.
[3] At the foot of the page are some notes of the characteristics of different nations, ending with 'Ira Bryttanorum, stultitia Saxonum vel Anglorum, libido Iberniorum'.
[4] In the fourth place *ti elf* has been made *tpelf*, and in the sixth *syi an*, *syfan*.

VOL. XXVII.—NO. CVIII.   S s

* All rights reserved.

THE VERSIONS COMPARED

'English' Form		'Latin' Form	
Myrcna landes is	30,000 hyda	(M)yrcheneland est de	30[000][c] hid'
Wocen sætna	7,000	Porcensetene	7,000 ,,
Westerna	7,000	Yesterne eac	7,000 ,,
Pec sætna	1,200	Þechsetena	600 ,,
Elmed sætna	600	Elmethsetena	600 ,,
Lindes farona mid Hæth feld land [a]	7,000	Lindesfarere Midheðfelda	7,000 ,,
Suth Gyrwa	600	Suðgyrpa	6,000[d] ,,
North Gyrwa	600	Norðgyrya	6,000[d] ,,
East Wixna	300	Estpyxna	300 ,,
West Wixna	600	[missing][e]	
Spalda	600	Syalda	600 ,,
Wigesta	900	Þygesta	800 ,,
Herefinna	1,200	Herfinna	602 ,,
Sweord ora	300	Speodora	300 ,,
Gifla	300	Gyfla	300 ,,
Hicca	300	Hicca	300 ,,
Wiht gara	600	Pythgare	600 ,,
Nox gaga	5,000	Hexgaga	5,000 ,,
Oht gaga	2,000	Ochtgaga	2,000 ,,
	66,100 [a]		
Hwinca	7,000	Hinca	7[000][c] ,,
Ciltern sætna	4,000	Cylternesetene	4,000 ,,
Hendrica	3,500 [b]	Hendrica	3,000 ,,
Unecungga	1,200	Ynetunga	1,200 ,,
Aro sætna	600	Ærotena	600 ,,
Færpinga	300	Ferpynga	300 ,,
Bilmiga	600	Bilmiliga	600 ,,
Widerigga	600	Þyderinga	eac sya
East Willa	600	East pella	600 hid'
West Willa	600	Þest pella	eac sya
East Engle	30,000	East Engla	30,000 hid'
East Sexena	7,000	East Sexa	7,000 ,,
Cantwarena	15,000	Cantparena	15,000 ,,
Suth Sexena	7,000	Suðsexa	100,000 ,,
West Sexena	100,000		
	242,700 [a]		[200,700] [c]

[a] Spelman omits the phrase 'mid Hæth feld land' and the totals, but these omissions may have been intentional. There are some small variations in spelling also.

[b] Spelman gives 3,000, in agreement with the 'Latin' texts.

[c] In two cases the transcriber or translator has omitted the line over the numeral which would make it thousands; and in the total he has transposed it, reading "cc. h' et dcc. h'" instead of "cc. h' et dcc. h'".

[d] This vi. instead of dc. is probably a slip in translation, but it points to a single original for the 'Latin' form.

[e] In the Hargrave MS. alone of the 'Latin' texts is there an entry answering to West Wixna. That manuscript reads 'Herstina 600'; but this may be merely a mistake for 'Herfinna' entered here by anticipation and correctly in its own place. Still, it is worthy of a note.

The 'Latin' form, as found in the Red Book of the Exchequer (King's Remembrancer's Miscellaneous Books, 2, fo. 296, about 1230), is printed above. It bears obvious marks of being translated from an English original in which the numbers were written out in words (as in the manuscript above described) instead of in the Roman numerals usual in the 'Latin' form. The other copies are in Hargrave MS. 313, fo. 15 b, copied about 1250 from the 'Red Book';[5] Oriel College MS. 46, and Corpus Christi College, Cambridge, MS. 70[6]—both about a century later; and Claudius D. ii, fo. 1 b, a fifteenth-century copy.[7] The obvious differences are due to the inability of later scribes to distinguish between the old letters y, p, and p; the initials in Ynetunga and Hexgaga appear to be mistakes for U and N. It is, therefore, safer to adhere to the 'English' text in the spelling,[8] for it was written while the older alphabet was still in full use.

After the first entry of 30,000 hides is added the sentence *Thær mon ærest Myrcna hæt* in the 'English' text and *Ab eo loco ubi primum Mircheneland*[9] *nominatur* in the 'Latin'. Though probably an interpolation, it was earlier than the separation of the two forms, and it will be noticed that the Latin is not an exact translation of the English, which may here be defective. The meaning is not quite clear: if historical, it seems to be an assertion that the Mercians at first took their name from the country which nevertheless was called the 'Mercians' land'; if geographical, it may be expanded into 'Beginning from that district which is the first to be called Mercia', viz. the *Wocen sætas*, and so on, the word *ærest* being understood as 'first' or nearest with respect to the commentator's point of view.

A marked difference between the two forms is seen in the totals. The 'English' form has a total at *Oht gaga* and another at the end; of these the former is correct if each separate hidage is to be regarded as independent, but the latter is not. The 'Latin' form has a total only at the end, and falls far short of the sum of the separate items, but is nearly correct if the total down to *Oht gaga* is regarded as 30,000. This seems to prove that the list is composed of two portions; the 'English' compiler

[5] Hall, *Red Book of Exchequer*, introd., l. In the 'Red Book' the rubricator has overlooked the initial *M*, and the Hargrave MS. omits it also.

[6] This copy has been extensively corrected by erasure, &c. The thousands have been carefully marked, e.g. the x̄x̄x̄ at the beginning, instead of xxx as in all the other 'Latin' copies.

[7] Printed in *Liber Albus* (Rolls Series), iii. 626. The manuscript is interesting as having numerous initials decorated with the Cotton and Bruce arms and alliances.

[8] The forms of the names have been retained, though they are genitives plural, because the nominatives are not certainly known.

[9] The termination *land* seems to be derived from the *hæt* of the 'English' text, which word is nevertheless translated by *nominatur*.

or editor showed that he understood the division by making a special addition for the first part, while the 'Latin' editor regarded the whole of the first portion as a detailed statement of the components of the Mercian 30,000 hides, and so he made no needless summation at *Oht gaga*, contenting himself with a final total which can be explained at once. The 'English' total may be a mistaken attempt to amend an older one. The point here touched is of the first importance for the explanation of the 'Hidage'. It is obvious that if all the items from *Wocen sætna* down to *Oht gaga* can be regarded as details of the initial 30,000 hides, a vast amount of useless speculation will be saved; for these obscure details can be reserved for a special inquiry, and in any case must be sought within the limits of the Mercian kingdom as it existed when the table was originally compiled.

The next important difference between the two forms is in their endings. A hidage of 100,000 is absurd for the South Saxons and grossly excessive for the West Saxons, compared even with the East Angles. While the 'English' form is certainly right in giving 7,000 hides to the South Saxons, being corroborated by Bede,[10] it is as clearly wrong in its subsequent detail. Probably the original ended thus : *Suth Sexena 7,000. 100,000* ; without any explanation at all of the final figures. Then either by corruption of the copies, or by mistaken emendations, the two forms which have come down to us took their rise.

Another difference may be noted. While the 'English' editor regarded all the Mercian details as independent and thus made 30,000 into 66,100, he was more cautious or better informed as to the second part of the table and gives a final total of 242,700 instead of 244,100. As he could add correctly, the inference is that he regarded some of the hidages in this second part as details of the larger ones, and therefore omitted them in adding. The 'Latin' editor, on the other hand, regarded all as independent, being not so well informed here as in the earlier part of the table. Both of these divergent attempts at summation must belong to a time when the true meaning of the 'Hidage' had been forgotten ; and therefore the original compilation must be thrown back a long way beyond the beginning of the eleventh century when the earliest extant copy was written. In one respect this may have been an advantage, for the copyists, not understanding it, would transcribe the ancient document as exactly as they could.

In the figures there are three other divergences which must be considered. (1) The 'English' form gives the Peak-dwellers 1,200 hides as against 600 in the 'Latin' one. (2) It gives *Herefinna* 1,200 hides against 602.[11] (3) It gives 3,500 hides

[10] *Hist. Eccl.* iv. 13.   [11] ' dc. v ' in the Hargrave MS. for ' dc. ij '.

to *Hendrica* against 3,000. For this last difference a solution is offered below ; in the other cases it seems possible that an original ' six hundred hides. ii.'—meaning twice 600 hides—was read erroneously as 600 hides in one case and 602 hides in the other.

As to the place of compilation there can be little doubt. An enumeration of English districts which begins with Mercia can only be of Mercian authorship, just as a school geography which begins with ' the British Isles ' has its origin marked upon it. It is here that the ' Hidage ' becomes an historical document of importance. Scarcely anything is known of the early Mercian kingdom or kingdoms. The English conquest and settlement of Central England are unrecorded by tradition [12]—as, indeed, are those of the eastern counties, though perhaps for other reasons—and so a mere list of tribal districts is welcome, and all the more if these districts can be defined with any degree of accuracy. Bede states [13] that the Mercians were divided by the Trent into two great bodies, the North Mercians with 7,000 hides (or families) and the South Mercians with 5,000 hides. He cannot be writing of the conditions of his own time, when Mercia was the dominant kingdom, but must be recording some tradition of the settlement of the midlands in the time of Peada, son of Penda. The rest of the country was parted among numerous smaller tribes, and their union seems to be due to the great Penda, probably king of the South Mercians,[14] who by his conquests on all sides raised the central kingdom to a position of supremacy, which it held from his overthrow of Oswald in 642 till his own defeat and death in 655. After a brief eclipse Mercia recovered under Wulfhere, and retained the leading place till the rise of Wessex in the ninth century. It had no ' sacred prophet ', like Bede in Northumbria and Alfred in Wessex, to record its story ; but its political importance is of the first rank in the formation of a united England, and its dialect has become the English language in spite of the literary importance of its northern and southern neighbours.

The date of the ' Tribal Hidage ', assigning, as it does, 30,000 hides to Mercia against Bede's 12,000, cannot be earlier than Penda's time. Again, assuming that the first part gives the details of those 30,000 hides, its date cannot be later than Wulfhere ; for among those details appear the 600 hides of the

[12] All that Henry of Huntingdon (ed. T. Arnold, p. 48) can tell is that ' many came over from Germany and occupied East Anglia and Merce, but were not under one king '. He gives no names.
[13] *Hist. Eccl.* iii. 24.
[14] During the brief tyranny of Oswy, Peada was allowed to have the rule of the South Mercians. This was probably because it was his father's hereditary right ; the son would succeed to that, but not to the conquests of Penda.

people of Wight, and it is on record that in 661 Wulfhere laid the island waste and in 678 gave it [15] to the newly converted king of the South Saxons. From that time it has no record of any Mercian connexion. In 686 it was conquered by the West Saxons. A more precise date may be suggested, for there is an obvious connexion between the 'thirty legions' of Penda's army at Winwæd [16] and the 30,000 hides of the Mercians. May not this table have been compiled in 655 [17] with a view to the assembling of the army defeated by Oswy ? If so, it would account for the absence of any reference to Northumbria such as might be expected in a Mercian table of a later age.[18]

Three other remarks may be made here. First, the compiler had an accurate mind geographically speaking. Where the districts he mentions are certainly known they are arranged in proper order. Thus the East Angles are followed by the East Saxons, Kentishmen, and South Saxons without any confusion; the districts of the Peak, Elmet, Lindsey with Hatfield, and the Gyrwa country also come in regular sequence. Hence in more obscure cases it may be assumed that there is some ascertainable topographical grouping. The second point is that the Mercian hidage recorded in Domesday Book very closely agrees with the 30,000 hides of our table; it may be urged that if the total, then the details should agree. How this can be worked out is shown in the sequel,[19] but we do not claim that no other or better way can be found, having regard to ancient and well-established boundaries, such as those of dioceses, counties, and hundreds, and any references to political association that have survived. The third point is that place-names afford practically no assistance in this inquiry. The tribal name *Gifla*, for example, has possible traces as far apart as Somerset and Bedfordshire; but even should any or all of these be established, the position of the 300 hides assigned to the tribe would not be settled, because each and all of the place-names might represent nothing more than isolated settlements by straggling detachments from the main body. So also *Spalda* appears in several place-names, but the tribal district cannot be determined by them. On the other hand, it is noteworthy that the *Gyrwas*, whose position is known, have left no

[15] Bede, *Hist. Eccl.* iv. 13, Wight and the province of the Meonwaras. It may be assumed that it was under the immediate rule of Wulfhere from 661 to 678; whether or not Penda had previously held it is matter for speculation only.

[16] Bede, *Hist. Eccl.* iii. 24.

[17] Mr. Corbett, in his essay on the 'Hidage', advocated a somewhat earlier date; see *Trans. of the Royal Hist. Soc.*, New Series, xiv. 207. His explanation of the document is radically different from that here put forward.

[18] In view of its absence from the 'Hidage' it is interesting to notice that Northumbria as a whole has not been included in England.

[19] A preliminary attempt, founded on Maitland's figures, was printed in *Notes and Queries*, 11th series, ii. 212.

traces—at least, no obvious traces—in the names of the region they inhabited. Consequently it is on relative position, on hidage, and on traces of early association that the present argument mainly rests; and for early association the ecclesiastical divisions may afford evidence as important as the secular ones.

The two other early hidages extant have some bearing on the matter. The total of the 'Burghal Hidage' agrees very closely with the record of Domesday Book for the southern counties concerned—27,170 against 27,621—showing that the hidages recorded in 1086 were those already established about 900;[20] and the same conclusion may be applicable to other counties.[21]

The 'County Hidage' names thirteen midland counties with the number of hides in each. In seven cases this number agrees with Domesday Book, in two others it is somewhat in excess, while in the remaining four it is double or more. These cases are Cambridgeshire 2,500 against 1,230, Northamptonshire 3,200 against 1,360, Shropshire 2,400 against 1,380, and Cheshire 1,200 against 500. In the first of these it seems possible that Hertford was included with Cambridge, for these counties together had twenty-five (or twenty-six) hundreds and a recorded hidage of 2,360 (or 2,460). In Northamptonshire it seems clear that there had been a reduction before the Domesday survey was made, and in this article the Geld Roll, which gives 2,673½ hides for the county (including part of Rutland), has been treated as the old hidage;[22] but it still falls short of the 3,200 named in the 'County Hidage'. Cheshire, like Cambridgeshire, may be accounted for by the inclusion of neighbouring districts, such as Derbyshire or South Lancashire, but this explanation will not serve for Shropshire, which affords the critical test. According to Domesday Book there were in Shropshire (excluding Shrewsbury with its 100 hides) fourteen hundreds assessed at 1,380 hides—figures which have a normal appearance; but there was apparently[23] 'land for 2,550 ploughs', or rather more than the 2,400 hides of the 'County Hidage'. The figures in this document may therefore indicate that an attempt had been made to raise the assessment of the county. In Cheshire also there was 'land for 1,000 ploughs', or but little short of the 1,200 hides required. On the other hand, it may be argued that the figures in the 'County Hidage' are those of the counties when they were first formed,

[20] See an attempt to arrange the details in *Notes and Queries*, 11th series, iv. 2.
[21] The exceptional cases of Northampton and Nottingham are mentioned in the text.
[22] See F. H. Baring, *ante*, xvii. 495.
[23] The details are not given in every case.

and that the figures of Domesday Book, when they disagree, in all cases show later reductions or readjustments ; but one would expect border counties like Cheshire and Shropshire to have been rated very lightly to begin with. Seeing that Staffordshire was assessed at 500 hides, the hidages in 1086 for the more western counties seem fair.

MERCIA

If we may judge from the ' Tribal Hidage ', the Mercia of 660 was a confederation of some seventeen or eighteen independent communities, each with king, underking, or alderman, which had been gathered round the central power by kinship or self-interest or conquest. In its small way, except for the cities, it resembled medieval Germany. But amalgamation under the Mercian kings must have proceeded rapidly, for not only are the smaller tribal names otherwise unknown to history, but before the end of the seventh century the whole appears to have been reduced to four or five main groups with which the bishoprics of Lichfield, Leicester, Lindsey, and Worcester were associated.

The list opens with *Wocen sætas, 7,000 hides*. *Wocen*, therefore, is a territorial name. The ' Latin ' texts suggest that the true spelling is *Worcen*. In a charter of Burghred, king of Mercia, dated in 855, it is stated that the ' pagans ' were then in *Wreocensetun*,[24] but there is nothing in the charter itself (a Worcester one) to identify the district, and nothing is known of any Danish invasion in that year. A century later ' in provincia Wrocensetna ' defined the position of lands in Shropshire round the Wrekin.[25] But it is difficult to assume the identity of *Worcen* with the Wrekin, because in any official statement it is natural, almost inevitable, to begin with the central or dominant district, which in the case of Mercia was probably the present Leicestershire.[26] The components of the 7,000 hides are suggested below in the section about the *Nox gaga* and *Oht gaga*.

The *Westerna* will then be the tribes to the west of the central people—in this case those known to us as Hwiccii, Hecana, &c., their position being that of the dioceses of Worcester and Hereford. The West Saxons fought with Penda at Cirencester in 628, and the treaty which followed is supposed to have handed the whole region over to him. The inhabitants may not have been West Saxon by race, so that they could join readily with the Mercians, and there is no trace later that they desired to separate.

---

[24] Birch, *Cart. Sax.* ii. 89.   [25] *Ibid.* iii. 355, 650.
[26] Penda's defeat of Oswald at Oswestry may be a sign that he was specially interested in Shropshire. In Leicestershire are the river Wreak and the village Wartnaby (D. B. ' Worcnodebie ').

The Domesday Book hidage of the two dioceses falls much below the 7,000 :

Worcester	Gloucestershire	. . .	2,388 [27]
	Worcestershire	. . .	1,189 [27]
	Warwickshire (part)	. .	610 [28]
			4,187
Hereford	Herefordshire	. . .	1,324 [27]
	Shropshire (part) .	. .	749
			2,073
			6,260

There is thus a defect of about 750 hides. If the 'County Hidage' figures be accepted for Shropshire, it is obvious that most or all of it will be made up at once ; but if not, then it may be suggested that the north-west part of Wiltshire was at one time in the hands of the Hwiccii.[29]

The *Pec sætas* have 1,200 hides allotted to them. The Peak is central for Derbyshire and Cheshire, and in Derbyshire there were nearly 700 carucates, which with 500 hides in Cheshire make up the total. Both counties were in the Mercian diocese of Lichfield, in spite of the inclusion of Derbyshire in the Danelagh, which might reasonably have caused a separation.[30] The earliest English connexion with Cheshire is Ethelfrith's famous victory at Chester in 613, which was probably the final effort of his conquests in this direction. He would descend from Northumbria by the Ribble Valley and South Lancashire, which by history [31] and tradition [32] was Northumbrian until 923 ; but he may then or earlier have overrun what is now Derbyshire. The same hundred name, Hamestan, occurs in the north-east of Cheshire and the adjacent north-west of Derbyshire. Thus the entry in the 'Tribal Hidage' may mean that there was a small Northumbrian district (ruled from the Peak) which fell under Mercian sway after the defeat of Edwin or of Oswald and remained ever afterwards closely united with the Mercian kingdom. The 'County Hidage' figure for Cheshire may be a reminiscence of the 1,200 hides of the Peak-dwellers, and (as already suggested) may show an intention on the part of the king to raise the old county assessment to that figure.

[27] These figures are taken from Maitland, *Domesday Book and Beyond*, pp. 400, 401.
[28] B. Walker in *The Antiquary*, 1903, p. 183.
[29] The hundreds of Malmesbury and Chippenham contain about 600 hides. An outlying part of Gloucestershire is upon the eastern edge of the former.
[30] For the later importance of the Peak see F. M. Stenton, *Types of Manorial Structure in the North Danelaw*, p. 72.
[31] Anglo-Saxon Chronicle, a. 798.
[32] Medieval verses state that King Oswald had a great love for Winwick.

The situation of *Elmed* is known by the distinguishing affixes of Barwick-in-Elmet and Sherburn-in-Elmet still in use for two places between Leeds and Selby. It was the name of a British kingdom which retained its independence till Edwin of Northumbria seized it; after his overthrow, or Oswald's, it would probably acquiesce in a union with Mercia. According to Domesday Book there were 326 carucates in Skyrack wapentake and 246½ in Barkston—together 570, or only 30 short of the hidage attributed to Elmet in our list. The southern boundary of the country may be assumed to have been the Aire; this is not only a hundred boundary, but also the limit of the deanery of York, and it is possible that this deanery was formed by York and the Ainsty united with Elmet. Its northern boundary is the Nidd, which is also the archdeaconry boundary, for in this part of Yorkshire the ridings and archdeaconries have different limits. That the Nidd was the boundary of Northumbria in 705 seems certain from the story of St. Wilfrid, for it was there that the synod was held at which the final peace was made, when he was allowed to return to his Northumbrian bishopric.[33] Ripon, to the north, was in Northumbria.

In the next district there can be no difficulty in identifying the names given with Lindsey[34] in Lincolnshire and Hatfield in the West Riding of Yorkshire. That the West Riding on the whole was Mercian is shown by its dialect. Thus Elmet, left untouched by the great king Ethelfrith, seems to have been for a time a 'buffer state' between Northumbria and Mercia. With so large a hidage as 7,000 it is clear that the 'dwellers in Lindsey' must have had wide rule outside the district from which they took their name; 'Hatfield' may then have included all the West Riding south of the Aire, and the northern end of Nottinghamshire.[35] That part of Yorkshire contains 1,300 carucates;[36] Lindsey and Kesteven about 3,900,[37] and Nottinghamshire only 567[38]—less than 6,000 in all. In this last county there is some reason to suspect a considerable reduction in the assessment for geld.[39] There was 'land for 1,166 ploughs', and if this be taken as showing the older rating, the total will rise to 6,400 carucates. The remainder may have been found in Rutland and the Framland wapentake of Leicestershire. Those who maintain that the 'County Hidage' records the primitive

---

[33] Bede, *Hist. Eccl.* v. 19.
[34] The bishop was styled 'episcopus Lindisfarorum'.
[35] The phrase 'Cuckney upon Hatfield' occurs; Thoroton, *Nottinghamshire*, iii. 372. Hatfield Grange, close by, preserves the name. The Hatfield division of Bassetlaw appears as 'Hatfield in the wapentake of Bassetlaw' in a roll of 1544; Lay Subsidies, 159/160.
[36] Mr. W. Farrer's figures.
[37] Maitland, *l.c.*
[38] Maitland, *l.c.*
[39] Stenton, *op. cit.* p. 48.

assessment of Cheshire will supply the defect from Derbyshire.[40] The total is probably identical with the 7,000 hides which Bede ascribes to the North Mercians. He states that the Trent separated the North and South Mercians, and this is true if Nottinghamshire and Leicestershire be taken as the typical counties of the two peoples. The people of Lindsey were Mercians and extremely hostile to Northumbrian rule, as is shown by their angry objection to St. Oswald's relics staying among them.

According to Bede[41] the country of the Gyrvii included Peterborough. He relates also[42] that Tonbert, the first husband of St. Etheldreda, was early in the seventh century prince (not king) of the South Gyrvii. The 'Tribal Hidage' places the South before the North Gyrwa, indicating either some political ascendancy or the origin of the compiler of the 'Hidage'. Bede may have used the adjective merely to distinguish these midland people from his own Gyrvienses around Jarrow, not in the sense of the 'Hidage'. Thomas of Ely states that Tonbert gave Ely to his wife as her dower, to which she returned after separating from her second husband. Ely, therefore, was in Tonbert's principality. Bede says it had 600 hides, and these may correspond with the 600 hides of the North Gyrwa in the 'Hidage'; but Etheldreda's dower was perhaps a third part of it, viz. the 200 hides contained in Ely proper (80) and Chesterton (120). This latter hundred is so obviously artificial[43] that it is not out of reason to suggest an assignment of dower as the origin of it; while the phrase 'two hundreds of Ely' later used of the Isle of Ely may be a tradition of the time when Ely, in the narrower sense, did contain 200 hides, i.e. before Chesterton became a distinct hundred. The rest of the North Gyrwa hidage might then be drawn from North Stow hundred in Cambridgeshire (112 hides) and Holland in Lincolnshire (about 280 carucates).

The South Gyrwa 600 hides may be identical with that district of eight 'hundreds' in the south of the county which had some sort of political unity at the end of the tenth century; for about 975 it is recorded[44] that at a great public assembly at Whittlesford the men of those hundreds met to hear evidence and decide in a dispute concerning land at Swaffham and 'Berlea'; Alfric of Wickham was one of the witnesses. Unfortunately the

---

[40] That is, 500 carucates might be taken from Derbyshire, leaving 200 in the Peak district to be added to the 'land for 1,000 ploughs in Cheshire' and complete the 1,200 hides of the 'County Hidage'. This makes the formation of county and diocese difficult.

[41] *Hist. Eccl.* iv. 6.   [42] *Ibid.* iv. 19.

[43] It consists of three separate and well-defined parts: Chesterton, 30 hides; Histon, Westwick, and Cottenham, 60 hides; Dry Drayton and Childerley, 30 hides.

[44] *Liber Eliensis*, ii. 34.

names of the hundreds are not given ; but it is natural to suggest that they were Whittlesford (80 hides), Chilford (54), Radfield (70), Staine (50), and Flendish (46) on the east side—300 hides in all ; and Wetherley (80), Triplow (90), and Armingford (100) on the west—270 hides.[45] The total is thus very near the 600 hides of the South Gyrwa.

Respecting the next following districts of the 'Hidage' some suggestions may be offered, though with hesitation. So far as the figures are concerned *East Wixna 300* corresponds best with the Cambridge hundred of Longstow (100 hides) joined with Toseland (215) in Huntingdonshire ; this ignores the conjunction of Longstow and Papworth hundreds to form an ecclesiastical deanery,[46] while it emphasizes the importance of the Cambridge-St. Neot's road as an ancient tribal boundary. *West Wixna 600* may then be the north-eastern half of Bedfordshire, viz. Biggleswade 100 hides, ' Weneslai ' 50, Wixamtree 110, Barford 105, Stoden 100, Wiley 104, and ' Buchelai ' 52—621 hides in all.[47] Here Wixamtree may preserve the tribal name.[48] *Spalda 600* will be the remaining part of Huntingdonshire—Leightonstone with Kimbolton 200, Normancross 180, and Hurstingstone 150 [49]— together with the hundred of Papworth (96) in Cambridgeshire,[50] making in all 626 hides. Here Spaldwick (D. B. 'Spaldewic') may show a trace of the old tribal name ; in 1086 the place was included, non-naturally, in Hurstingstone, but soon afterwards it was in Leightonstone.

The next tribal district, *Wigesta*, has 900 hides in the ' English ' version but 800 in the ' Latin ' one. Now the north-eastern end of Northamptonshire (including part of what is now Rutland) had a district of 805 hides divided into hundreds as follows : ' Wicesley ' (Rutland), 160 hides ; Willybrook, Polebrook, Navisford, and Huxlow, 62 each ; Navesland (two), 160 ; Higham, 150 ; Corby, 47 ; Stoke, 40. These correspond (except as to Wicesley) with the deaneries of Oundle, Higham, and Weldon. The chief place therein is Oundle, and the ' Eight Hundreds ' of Oundle

[45] This is the total of the *Inquisitio Com. Cant.* ; that of Domesday Book itself is 285.

[46] The best alternative seems to be to join Hurstingstone (without Spaldwick) with Longstow and Papworth, making 327 hides. The remainder of Huntingdonshire (with Spaldwick) will be 614 hides.

[47] F. H. Baring, *Domesday Tables.*

[48] The older forms—Wichestanstou (D. B.) and Wyxconestre (Hundred Rolls)— agree better with *Wigesta* ; the part of Bedfordshire south of the Ouse contains almost exactly 900 hides.

[49] Another 50 hides belonged to the borough of Huntingdon, but the borough hidages have been left out of consideration as obviously later than the ' Tribal Hidage '.

[50] Two hundreds in Cambridgeshire (Radfield and Cheveley) have not been reckoned because they are beyond the Devil's Dyke and in the diocese of Norwich ; they must, therefore, have been East Anglian at the date of the ' Hidage '. The difficulty is to account for their inclusion in Cambridgeshire.

formed an established district in 963, when it was confirmed to Peterborough.[51] No names or boundaries are recorded;[52] but whatever its meaning may have been then, it is legitimate to suggest that the phrase preserves the tradition of a time when a district of 800 hides was subject to the lord of Oundle, thus forming a parallel to the 'two hundreds' of Ely. When in 1329 the abbot of Peterborough was required to name the 'eight hundreds' he claimed in virtue of that confirmation, he said they were the vill of Peterborough, the hundreds of Nassaburgh, Polebrook, Navesford, Huxlow, North Navesland, South Navesland, and the hundred of the vill of Thingden.[53] Thus the old number was maintained, but it is obvious that the first and last are artificial; indeed, Thingden or Finedon (in Huxlow) is not otherwise known as a hundred, and the lordship at the Conquest did not belong to the abbey but to the Crown.[54] At the Dissolution the hundreds pertaining to the abbey were Nassaburgh, Polebrook, Huxlow, and Navesford. The inclusion of Nassaburgh (Nasso, 108½ hides) with the Oundle group named at the beginning of this paragraph would raise the hidage to over 900, and thus account for the figures in the 'English' form. The 'Latin' form would then show the extent of the lordship of Oundle after Peterborough had been cut off from it to make an almost independent state and before Oundle had been granted to the abbey.

The whole of the compact district of 3,600 hides just surveyed was perhaps the Gyrvian principality of Tonbert, corresponding with the country of the South Angles mentioned in the history of St. Botolph. The places chiefly associated with this saint are Botolph Bridge near Peterborough and Boston; both within the bounds. The Middle Angles, properly so called, would in that case occupy the country to the south-west, in the north of Buckinghamshire and Oxfordshire, being 'middle' between the other Angles and the West Saxons. Peada was alderman of the Middle Angles in his father's lifetime, but king of the South Mercians afterwards. Bede makes a distinction between the 'Mercians' and the 'Middle Angles', but all these terms were confused later.[55] The Gyrwa were in origin and sympathy East Anglian. This is known as well from incidental references as from the express statement of Bede. Thus Thomas, second

[51] Anglo-Saxon Chronicle.
[52] Bounds of some Peterborough lands at Oundle are printed in Birch, *Cart. Sax.* iii. 368, but do not appear to have any connexion with the 'Eight Hundreds'.
[53] *Placita de quo Warranto*, p. 553.
[54] The members of Thingden were in the hundreds of Navesland, Huxlow, Higham, Rothwell, Orlingbury, and the otherwise unknown 'Geritone'—27 hides in all.
[55] In Florence of Worcester (ed. Thorpe, p. 242) 'South Angles' is used of the people round Dorchester. The phrase also meant all the Angles south of the Humber, i.e. in the whole of Mercia. Henry of Huntingdon says that Mercia was called Middle England.

bishop of the East Angles, was a Gyrvian; in the story of St. Botolph (c. 650) the king of the East Angles appears as overlord of the South Angles; and when (c. 670) the Abbot Ceolfrid wished to learn something of Botolph's foundations, he visited the East Angles.[56] Their inclusion within the Mercian confederation may have been due to conquest by Penda in 635,[57] or his later ravaging of East Anglia in 654. The group as a whole points to invasion by the Ouse and Nen, the immigrants meeting the main stream of the Mercians, coming south from the Trent valley, about Kettering, and perhaps also the advance-guard of the West Saxons about Bedford.

As to the *Herefinna*, with the large district of 1,200 hides, nothing whatever is known. From their position in the table it can only be surmised that they occupied part of Buckinghamshire and Oxfordshire,[58] and belonged to the Middle Angles above mentioned. They became Christian in 653 by the efforts of Diuma. It is possible that Finmere (Finemere) in Oxfordshire may indicate a place on the tribal boundary.

The small areas of 300 hides which occur in Central England in this early document appear again in 1008, when the lord of 300 hides was ordered to supply a ship for the fleet.[59]

Of the Mercian 30,000 hides the details given account for all but 900. These may have embraced the 600 hides in south-west Bedfordshire not reckoned above, together with 300 hides in Hertfordshire or else the district of 300 hides round Banbury. This district, however, may be the *Sweord ora 300* which follows *Herefinna*. Otherwise these figures may refer to the Winchester district.[60] There is no record of the capture of Winchester by West Saxons or Mercians, and it seems possible that in 655, if the 'Hidage' is of that date, the city was still the centre of a little British principality,[61] in which case it would not be included in this document at all.

The next details, *Gifla 300, Hicca 300*, and *Wiht gara 600*, may from the last named be presumed to form the 1,200 hides which Bede[62] ascribes to the island of Wight. Unfortunately the hidage for the Jutish portion of Hampshire cannot be calculated

---

[56] Earle and Plummer, *Two Saxon Chron.* ii. 24.

[57] Bede, *Hist. Eccl.* iii. 18.

[58] In Buckingham the Ashendon (335) and Buckingham (330), or north-western quarter; in Oxford the hundreds of Ploughley (269) and Bullingdon (210): in all, 1,144 hides.

[59] In the Peterborough version of the Anglo-Saxon Chronicle. There are various readings, for which see Mr. Plummer's note, *Two Saxon Chron.* ii. 185. Reference is there made to a Worcester charter of 964, 'not wholly genuine,' in which three hundreds are stated to be a 'scypfyllith or scypsocne': Birch, *Cart. Sax.* iii. 380.

[60] There are the Swere river in North Oxfordshire and Swarraton near Winchester as possible clues.

[61] *Vict. County Hist., Hampshire*, i. 384, 391.   [62] *Hist. Eccl.* iv. 16.

exactly, but from what is recorded it is clear that 1,200 hides is very near the total. Hence *Gifla* may be those otherwise known as Meonwara; *Hicca*, the people round Southampton; and *Wiht gara*, those of the island itself with the closely associated New Forest district.[63]

Then the first or Mercian part of the table closes with the mysterious entries: *Nox gaga, 5,000 hides*; *Oht gaga, 2,000 hides*. As the total of 30,000 is practically made up without them, they may refer to subdivisions of one of the large districts of 7,000 hides each, recorded at the head of the list, more probably the first. Bede's statement that the South Mercians had 5,000 hides appears to be contradicted by the 7,000 hides assigned to the *Wocen sœtas* in the 'Hidage'—for these must be the South Mercians, if there is force in the argument that the central and dominant tribe takes first place in any orderly enumeration. But if they were subdivided into two well-known sections of 5,000 and 2,000 hides, then Bede's statement is at once reconciled with the 'Hidage'. His South Mercians will be recognized as the *Nox gaga* division of the *Wocen sœtas*, i.e. the main or original part; while the *Oht gaga* will be either emigrants or colonists who had conquered and settled lands outside or else 'foreigners' of these lands who had been incorporated with the central tribe. The diocesan division between Lichfield and Lincoln probably went back to the partition of Mercia into dioceses in 679.[64] The hitherto uncounted part of Mercia in the latter diocese includes Leicestershire (say 2,500 carucates [65]), the greater part of Northamptonshire (1,760 hides), and the north-eastern corner of Buckinghamshire (710 hides), with possibly part of Bedfordshire, should it be found that the deficiency in the men of Lindsey's hidage must be made up from Leicestershire. The 2,000 hides of the *Oht gaga* are almost made up from the hidage of the parts of the diocese of Lichfield not already accounted for, viz. Staffordshire, 500 hides;[66] part of Warwickshire, 704;[67] and part of Shropshire, 632 (without Shrewsbury).[68] The 7,000 hides of the Westerns, as shown above, seem to divide in similar fashion. It is probable, therefore, that the otherwise unknown *Nox gaga*

[63] See *Notes and Queries*, 11th series, iv. 482–4, and Mr. R. A. Smith's article in the *Vict. Hist. of Hampshire*, i. 373. There are possible traces of *Gifla* and *Hicca* in adjacent districts of Bedfordshire and Hertfordshire—Northhill (Givele), Southhill, Yilldon and Ivel; Hitchin and Hiz. Should these names indicate the tribal districts, then 600 hides of the people of Wight will be part of the 'unrecorded' 900.

[64] The later diocese of Lincoln was then in three—Lindsey, Leicester, and Dorchester; but the last named did not prove permanent. There does not seem any evidence of the time when the Mercian districts of Nottingham and the West Riding were added to the diocese of York; perhaps it was after the Danish conquest: see *Vict. County Hist., Nottinghamshire*, ii. 38.   [65] Maitland, *l. c.*
[66] Eyton's figures.   [67] Walker, *ubi supra*.
[68] If the 'County Hidage' be used, the Shropshire figures will be 1,233.

and *Oht gaga* are not tribal names at all, but descriptive ; and the problem becomes one for the philologist.[69] If the view here advocated be true, the formation of the diocese of Lichfield was extremely simple, viz. from the two ancient districts of the ' Pec-dwellers ' and *Oht gaga*, with South Lancashire added after its annexation to Mercia in 923.

THE WEST SAXONS

The West Saxons, if their traditions as recorded in the Chronicle may be trusted, invaded and conquered their part of England from landings on the Hampshire coast. Either the traditions have become intermixed or else the Jutes, who took possession of the Isle of Wight and the southern part of Hampshire, were part of the invading host. The course of conquest is marked by a few place-names and dates : 495–534, Hampshire and Wight ; 552, Salisbury ; 556, Barbury ; 568, battle with men of Kent ; 571, Eynsham, Bensington, Aylesbury, Lenborough ; 577, Gloucester, Cirencester, Bath.[70] Later battles are named, but the places are not always well identified ; but the general effect is an advance north and north-east into Gloucestershire, Surrey, and Oxfordshire and Buckinghamshire. On the eastern edge of their dominions they came into contact with the East Saxons, a battle being fought between the two nations about 620, when two sons of King Sebert were killed.[71] The rise of Mercia checked further advance. The people of Gloucestershire became Mercian under Penda in 628 ; and he was able to drive the West Saxon king from his throne for a few years. It would be natural, therefore, in a Mercian table of that time to place the West Saxons next after the dominant people : they were in process of absorption.

Of the two entries in the ' Tribal Hidage ', *Hwinca 7,000* and *Ciltern sœtas 4,000*, the former are not known by that name, but the latter, the dwellers in the Chilterns, were probably West Saxon in Penda's time and for a century later,[72] till Offa took Bensington in 777. When in 636 the West Saxon king became a Christian, he gave Dorchester, at the north-western edge of the

---

[69] It has been suggested that they are corruptions of Noxinga and Ohtinga, on which see Mr. W. H. Stevenson's remarks, *ante*, iv. 355. For another attempt to solve the difficulty see *Notes and Queries*, 10th series, ix. 384.

[70] These statements appear to show that by about 570 the West Saxons had fully colonized their districts south of the Thames, and were then compelled to make advances east, north, and north-west.

[71] Henry of Huntingdon, p. 57.

[72] See *Vict. County Hist., Buckinghamshire*, i. 196. The 'Chiltern Hundreds' in Oxfordshire (see below, p. 642, n. 80) retained a kind of solidarity down to the end of the thirteenth century. The 'Chiltern Hundreds' in Buckinghamshire are united by a nominal stewardship under the Crown to the present time.

Chiltern country, to be the seat of Birinus, the missionary bishop who had baptized him. It seems certain, from the position of these names at the head of the second part of the table and from one of them being West Saxon, that the other (*Hwinca*) was West Saxon also. This is confirmed by the story that King Cenwalh on his restoration to the kingdom in 648 gave 3,000 hides [73] of land by Ashdown to his kinsman Cuthred; while William of Malmesbury changes this into the statement that Cenwalh 'conferred nearly the third of his kingdom' on his nephew, which is accurate enough if the West Saxon kingdom then had 11,000 hides.[74] There seems to have been a double kingship among the West Saxons, and this accords with the double naming in the ' Hidage '. Penda could scarcely have driven Cenwalh from his kingdom without invading and partially conquering Wessex, but the extent of his acquisitions is not recorded. If the date we have assigned to the ' Tribal Hidage ' be correct, then it is not going too far to assume that in the next names on the list we have the West Saxon districts which he overran and considered more or less his own even after he had allowed Cenwalh to return to his kingdom. In that case, when Wulfhere in 661 overran the country as far as Ashdown, and also ravaged the Isle of Wight, he was repeating his father's exploit.

It is probable [75] that *Hendrica* (3,500 hides in the ' English ', 3,000 in the ' Latin ' form) includes *Unecungga* (1,200 hides,[76] the Wantage district in North Berkshire), *Aro sœtas*[77] and *Fœrpinga*[78] (600 and 300 hides)—perhaps in Oxfordshire to the west of the Cherwell—and *Bilmiga* and *Widerigga* (600 hides each),[79] which

---

[73] The word 'hides' is omitted in the oldest copy of the Chronicle, but seems necessary.

[74] How this historian knew about the 'third part' is unexplained; probably he relied upon some local tradition. If the interpretation in the text be correct, Cenwalh gave about a third of each division, viz. 2,100 hides out of the Hwinca 7,000 and 1,200 out of the Chiltern 4,000.

[75] See *Notes and Queries*, 11th series, iv. 482.

[76] The hundreds approximately corresponding with the rural deanery of Abingdon are: Wantage 239 hides, Sutton 123, Marcham 141, 'Wifol' 144, Shrivenham 71, 'Hilleslau' 140, Ganfield 185, Blewbury 127, and Hormer 110; a total of 1,280 hides, These figures are from Mr. Baring's *Domesday Tables*.

[77] *Aro* should be the name of a district or dominant place (like *Pec*); but the only name of the kind in the locality suggested is Harrowden, on the wrong side of the Thames.

[78] *Aro* is perhaps the district along the Thames and Cherwell, now the hundreds of Bampton (206) and Wootton (406), containing a little over 600 hides. *Fœrpinga* may be Chadlington Hundred, with 292 hides recorded. Possibly it was the 'Feppingum' in Middle England where Diuma, the missionary bishop, died. Charlbury is associated with a St. Dionia, supposed to be the same: Stanton, *Menology*, p. 742. It would not affect the general argument should it be found that either *Bilmiga* or *Widerigga* must be interchanged with *Aro*.

[79] Following the deanery boundaries, with one exception (Bucklebury), the centre and east of Berkshire thus divides: Newbury—Lambourn 73, Kintbury 133, Eagle 96,

were perhaps the remaining or eastern part of Berkshire; then *East* and *West Willa* (600 hides each) would be in North Hampshire around Basingstoke and Wallop respectively. The Hundred Rolls and Domesday Book show that groups of six 'hundreds' remained attached to these places at a later time, suggesting, in accordance with the argument already advanced, that political districts of 600 hides each had once been governed from them as centres. Yet the whole of the north end of Hampshire must have been united under one ruler at an early time, for the ancient 'farm of one day' was shared by three places there—Basingstoke, Kingsclere, and Hurstbourne Tarrant. According to the Anglo-Saxon Chronicle Hampshire was a distinct principality or administrative district in 755; a century later (860) Hampshire and Berkshire were acting together, under their respective aldermen, for the defence of Winchester. The identifications here suggested mark the parts of Wessex through which an invading Mercian army would pass on its way to the south coast and the Isle of Wight, the goal certainly reached by Wulfhere and probably by Penda before him. Then the phrase 'as far as Ashdown' in the Chronicle under 661 will mean 'as far *west* as Ashdown', showing that the West Saxons in Wiltshire were left alone for that time, though Wulfhere attacked them later.

The following are the hidages suggested for *Hwinca* 7,000:

In Wiltshire (part) and Dorset	4,900
In Berkshire (*Unecungga*, or Wantage)	1,200
In Oxfordshire (*Aro sœtas* and *Fœrpinga*)	900
	7,000

and for *Ciltern sœtas* 4,000:

In Oxfordshire (the former Chiltern Hundreds,[80] with Dorchester and Thame)	800
In Buckinghamshire (the three hundreds of Aylesbury and the Chiltern Hundreds)	800
In Berkshire	1,200
In Hampshire	1,200
	4,000

The recorded hidage of the Aylesbury and Chiltern groups in Buckinghamshire amounts to 750;[81] the other 50 hides may

---

Roeberg 128, Nachedorne 103, Thatcham 74, a total of 607; Reading and Wallingford—Bray 93, Rippleamere 60, Charlton 145, Reading 153, Healesford 117, Bucklebury 47, a total of 615.

[80] According to the *Hundred Rolls* (ii. 43) the king had held the four and a half hundreds of 'Ciltrie' until Henry III gave them to the earl of Cornwall. In another place (ii. 751) the names of the hundreds are given—Lewknor, Pirton, Langtree, Benefield, and Ewelme (half)—being those still in use.

[81] Baring, *Domesday Tables*.

have been drawn from some adjacent hundred in the county or from Tring in Hertfordshire. It is recorded in Domesday Book that before the Conquest eight hundreds ' in the circuit of Aylesbury ' had paid a church scot to Aylesbury church.[82] The names are not recorded, but whatever the ' circuit ' may have become in its later history, it is in accordance with what has been said above about Ely and the *Wigesta* to suggest that in early times a district of 800 hides had been subject to Aylesbury politically.[83]

In support of the *Hwinca* grouping may be adduced the Abingdon tradition that the abbey was founded by a King Cissa who was ruler of Wiltshire and the greater part of Berkshire, having his capital at Bedwin and bishopric at Malmesbury[84] (? Ramsbury). The abbey was also, curiously enough, said to be in the south of Oxfordshire ; a statement which has some sort of basis in the grouping above.[85] Again, the Abingdon tradition also records that after Offa had seized upon Bensington in 777 (or 779) he ravaged all Berkshire, not only the part south of the Ridge Way, but also that north of it.[86] This distinctly suggests that Berkshire was under two rulers, the Ridge Way being the division. The union of Berkshire with the diocese of Salisbury is easily explained also if it be allowed that the northern and more important end had always been closely allied politically with Wiltshire and drew the east with it, when the two parts were united in one shire. It seems possible that Berkshire was never in the diocese of Winchester, so that the partition of this diocese would not affect it. The diocese of Ramsbury (or Salisbury) was entirely West Saxon ; Winchester was composite—Jutes in the south, perhaps British in the centre, West Saxon in the north, and the men of Surrey in the north-east. There is the obvious difficulty to be met that the recorded hidage of Wiltshire (4,050)[87] and Dorset (2,321)[88] is greatly in excess of the 4,900 required ; but it may reasonably be urged that so early as 650

[82] *Vict. County Hist., Buckinghamshire*, i. 223, 233 ; Morley Davies in *Home Counties Mag.* vi. 136.

[83] There may also have been eight instead of six hundreds in the south of the county, ' detached parts' of hundreds having been originally independent. Aylesbury, according to the story of St. Edburga and her sister, had a monastery early in the seventh century. A little later the church of Buckingham is said to have received the relics of St. Rumbold.

[84] *Abingdon Chron.* (ed. J. Stevenson), ii. 268.

[85] Possibly Hormere Hundred, in which Abingdon stands, belonged to the Wootton district north of the Thames. In that case the Wantage district would have almost exactly 1,200 hides, but Wootton would have 700 instead of 600 hides.

[86] According to the *Abingdon Chron.* i. 14 ; Offa subdued all the West Saxon king's land ' ab oppido Walingfordie in australi parte ab Ichenilde strete usque ad Esseburiam, et in aquilonali parte usque ad Tamisiam '. As Ashbury is on the north side of the Ridge Way the second ' usque ad ' cannot be intended to balance the first.

[87] Maitland. The figures of the Exon Domesday are about 100 less.

[88] Eyton (not including the boroughs).

the hidage of these counties, supposing them to have been entirely in West Saxon hands,[89] may have been estimated at a lower rate than in the ninth century, when this kingdom had grown immensely in numbers and importance. It has also been suggested above that part of the present Wiltshire may have been in earlier days in the hands of the Hwiccii.[90]

With regard to Buckinghamshire it will be noticed that the southern half is here assigned to the Chiltern-dwellers, the north-western quarter to the Herefinna, and the north-eastern to the main body of the Mercians. In the ' Burghal Hidage ' to Buckingham and ' Sceaftelege ' were assigned 1,500 hides, or about three-fourths of the hidage of the county. Possibly it was the north-eastern quarter (or third) which was omitted, on account of its occupation by the Danes.

On the suppositions made, the country now formed into Oxfordshire had a complex history. At first West Saxon—if the *Herefinna* were part of that confederation—it had become divided by 650 into three parts. The *Herefinna* having allied themselves with Mercia, the Middle Angles had gained access to the Thames at Oxford, while west of the Cherwell the *Hwinca* branch of the West Saxons still held most of the land, and south of the Thame the Chiltern-dwelling branch of the same people were secure. The Mercians continued to gain ground. The removal of the West Saxon bishopric to Winchester, and the establishment of a Mercian one at Dorchester—even for a time only—indicates an advance. The battle at Burford in 752 shows that the West Saxons still held that corner of the present shire, but it may mean also that at that side of the Cherwell they had lost all except Bampton Hundred. As already stated, the Chiltern hundreds seem to have remained West Saxon without disturbance until 777. There is no record of the formation of the county, but the 2,400 hides assigned in the ' Burghal Hidage ' for the defence of Oxford and Wallingford may be identified as the hidage of Oxfordshire, so that the county had been organized by about the year 900.

East Angles

In one respect this is the most difficult part of the ' Tribal Hidage ', for though the district is known, the 30,000 hides assigned to it seem excessive. They allow an average area of less than 80 statute acres to each hide. The country was perhaps

---

[89] Cenwalh's battle at Bradford-on-Avon in 652 may mean that his kingdom had not till then extended over West Wiltshire.

[90] See above, p. 633. The north-west quarter of Wiltshire contains about 1,200 hides: Malmesbury and Chippenham (as above) 604, and Bradford, Melksham, Whorwelton, and Swanborough 636. The omission of these would make the Hwinca hidage numerically almost exact.

the most ancient of the Anglian settlements, so that the explanation may lie in the supposition not only that its population was great, but that it had become an 'industrial' population to a considerable extent, having trades as well as agriculture and important fisheries to depend upon.

EAST SAXONS

The East Saxon kingdom, according to the later boundaries of the diocese of London, contained the counties of Essex (D.B. 2,650 hides),[91] Middlesex (880),[92] and the southern and eastern fringe of Hertfordshire. At the date of the 'Hidage' the Mercian annexation of the last-named county may not have taken place to any great extent, but it is clear that some reduction of assessment was made. Assuming one of 40 per cent. the 7,000 hides of the East Saxons would be reduced to 4,200, so that Hertfordshire would have to supply about 600. Its total hidage in 1086 was 1,108. Mr. Rickword has ingeniously arranged the Essex assessments to show 70 hundreds, each reduced from 100 to 40 hides,[93] but his conclusions are invalidated by the omission of the East Saxon lands in Middlesex and Hertford. If the reduction above suggested were that effected, three of his hundreds would go to two of the original ones, making the primitive assessment of Essex about 4,400 hides and that of Middlesex about 1,500.

KENT

According to Bede[94] there were 300 hides in Thanet, which contains about 26,000 acres. In Kent and Surrey together there are about 1,480,000 acres, which on the above scale would allow 17,000 hides for the two counties. Thus, while remembering that the woodland of Kent and the heaths of Surrey were anciently extensive, the 15,000 hides of the Kentish men is not excessive if the two later counties were at the time of the 'Hidage' under one rule.[95] There is nothing improbable in the supposition, and it is to some extent borne out by the tradition that Chertsey Abbey, in the north-west of Surrey, was founded by Egbert, king of Kent. Before 675, however, Surrey had an underking of its own, who was subject to the Mercian king. Soon afterwards, in 686, the West Saxons ravaged Kent, and when one of their princes had been burned there, the outrage was, in 694, compounded for by a fine of 30,000 shillings,[96] or two for each hide.

[91] Maitland, p. 400.
[92] Baring, *Domesday Tables.*
[93] *Trans. Essex Archaeol. Soc.* xi, part 3.
[94] *Hist. Eccl.* i. 25.
[95] Mr. Corbett in his essay joined Surrey with Kent.
[96] There is confusion over this sum in the different texts of the Chronicle, but all give 30.

SOUTH SAXONS

As already stated, the 'Tribal Hidage' agrees with Bede's statement as to the ancient reckoning of the hides or families of this kingdom. The hidage in Domesday Book is 3,474, or about half the ancient one.

THE TOTALS

The 'Latin' total of 200,700 hides is thus formed:

Mercians	30,000
Hwinca and *Ciltern sœtas*	11,000
Hendrica	3,000
Unecungga to *Widerigga*	3,300
E. and W. *Willa*	1,200
East Angles	30,000
East Saxons	7,000
Men of Kent	15,000
South Saxons	100,000
	200,500

The doubtful figure is the 3,000 hides of *Hendrica*, where the 'English' form gives 3,500; possibly the original was 3,300 (being the total of the subsequent group), in which case the 'Latin' total should be 200,800,[97] or 100 hides more than that recorded. The 'English' total also is attainable if 3,300 be read instead of 3,500; thus

Total to *Oht gaga*, as given		66,100
Hwinca and *Ciltern sœtas*		11,000
Hendrica (amended)		3,300
Unecungga to *Widerigga*		3,300
E. and W. *Willa*	1,200	
East Angles		30,000
East Saxons		7,000
Men of Kent		15,000
South Saxons		7,000
West Saxons		100,000
		242,700

Some district of 1,200 hides must have been omitted to obtain this total, but possibly the compiler intended to omit *Unecungga* not *East* and *West Willa*.

[97] In two copies—Claudius D. ii and Corpus Christi College, Cambridge, 70 (but only as altered, not *prima manu*)—the total is written 200,800.

BERNICIA
York
DEIRA
Elmet
Hatfield land
Lindsey
Peak-dwellers
MERCIA
Wocen-dwellers
Leicester
Gyrwas
EAST ANGLES
Worcester
Westerns
EAST SAXONS
London
MEN OF KENT
SOUTH SAXONS

It may, therefore, in conclusion be suggested that the 'Tribal Hidage' should be arranged as follows:

		hides			hides	hides
The Mercians have	. . .	30,000	*Hwinca* have	. .	7,000	
[including]	hides		Chiltern-dwellers	.	4,000	
Wocen-dwellers	. 7,000					11,000
Western men	. . 7,000		[including]			
Peak-dwellers	. . 1,200		*Hendrica*	. .	3,300	
Elmet-dwellers	. 600		[viz.]	hides		
Men of Lindsey with Hatfield-land	} 7,000		Wantagers *Aro*-dwellers *Færpinga* *Bilmiga* *Widerigga*	1,200 600 . 300 . . 600 . 600		
	hides					
South Gyrwa	600					
North Gyrwa	600				—	
East Wixna	300				3,300	
West Wixna	600		*East Willa*	. 600		
Spalda . .	600		*West Willa*	. 600		
Wigesta .	900				1,200	
		3,600	East Angles	. . . .	30,000	
Herefinna . .	. 1,200		East Saxons	. . . .	7,000	
Sweord ora	. . 300		Men of Kent	. . . .	15,000	
[Unrecorded	. . 900]		South Saxons	. . . .	7,000	
Gifla . .	300				100,000	
Hicca . .	300					
Men of Wight	600					
		1,200				
		30,000				
Nox gaga	5,000					
Oht gaga	2,000					

There is nothing new or revolutionary in this solution of the problem afforded by the 'Tribal Hidage'; but if it be accepted, clear and definite areas will be substituted for vague approximations, and some advance will have been made in the conception of the formation of the Mercian kingdom and then of the later counties.
J. BROWNBILL.

The Battle of Sandwich and Eustace the Monk

THE battle of Sandwich, 24 August 1217, followed so closely upon the fair of Lincoln, 20 May 1217, that the careful analysis of authorities made some years ago by Professor Tout for the Lincoln contest is, in point of time, almost equally good for the other event.[1] His discussion of the battle of Lincoln

[1] *Ante*, xviii, 1903, 240–4. But since the two engagements had for the most part different participants and took place in widely different localities, the evaluation of authorities for the battle of Sandwich presents some variations that require notice. The 'History of William the Marshal' is still of the highest value. The twofold account of the battle given in the poem led the editor, M. Paul Meyer, to infer that the minstrel had drawn upon two recitals which he had not been able to blend, a circumstance that gives us increased confidence in the trustworthiness of the poem as furnishing legitimate historical material (*Histoire de Guillaume le Maréchal*, iii. 243, n. 3). Roger of Wendover has for our purpose a smaller importance (*Chronica sive Flores Historiarum*, ed. H. O. Coxe). Matthew Paris, who in the case of Lincoln added little to Wendover, has for us a distinct independent value (*Chronica Maiora*, ed. H. R. Luard). His supposed intimate acquaintance with Hubert de Burgh (*ibid.* iii, preface, xiv and n. 2) would account for the chronicler's open partisanship for him, and also for what appears to be his private information about the battle of Sandwich in which the justiciar bore such a prominent part. Paris, in fact, offers two versions of the battle, one from Wendover with slight emendations, the other entirely his own and very laudatory of Hubert. We derive the impression from reading Paris's second version that he is describing that portion of the battle in which Hubert took a personal part and which he would have most liked to have remembered. The Annals of Dunstaple (*Annales Monastici*, ed. Luard, iii. 50) are of comparatively little importance. The brief account by the canon of Barnwell contained in the *Memoriale Fratris Walteri de Coventria* (ed. Stubbs, ii. 238–9) throws light particularly upon the notorious leader of the French reinforcements, Eustace the Monk. The valuable *Histoire des Ducs de Normandie et des Rois d'Angleterre*, which has little upon Lincoln, is quite full upon Sandwich; as we might reasonably expect, having regard to the fact that the author was of the entourage of William, earl of Albemarle, who was at Sandwich at the time of the battle (cf. Tout, *ante*, xviii. 242 and n. 9). The contemporaneous account of the Annals of Waverley (*Annales Monastici*, ii. 287–8), while rather brief, accords in important particulars with the *Histoire des Ducs de Normandie* just mentioned. Ralph of Coggeshall, in Essex, has a brief but independent and suggestive account of important corroborative value (*Chronicon Anglicanum*, ed. J. Stevenson, pp. 185–6). The account of William le Breton, chaplain of King Philip, gives an excellent glimpse of the tactics of the fight (Guillelmus Armoricus, *De Gestis Philippi Augusti*, in Bouquet, *Recueil*, xvii. 62–116); but the Chronicle of Rouen (*Ex Chronico Rotomagensi*, *ibid.* xviii. 357–62) adds little. From the *Chronica de Mailros* (ed. J. Stevenson) we get details of the numbers of the captives and the names of the great lords. This informa-

itself likewise furnishes an excellent introduction to the battle of Sandwich. Before proceeding directly to the consideration of that topic, however, we may well trace with some care the circumstances of the career of Eustace the Monk, who as Louis's admiral had seemed endowed with diabolical ingenuity in working havoc among his former friends the English.[2] The points of his biography which we shall narrate go far, in our opinion, to indicate the bravery, the readiness of resource, and the other qualities requisite for success in the rough work that fell to the lot of a Channel 'master-pirate'[3] of those days. To such a career as this the sanguinary battle of Sandwich brought a fitting close.

The birthplace of Eustace[4] was not far from Boulogne, the Romance tells us at 'Cors';[5] and there is a document of 1243 relating to the neighbouring abbey of Samer which mentions a 'Guillaume le Moine, seigneur de Course', thus apparently bearing out the tradition of such a family in that vicinity.[6] That Eustace came from near there is not open to doubt,

---

tion, coming by way of Warden, has a certain relationship to that of the *Histoire des Ducs* (see the *Dictionary of National Biography*, reprint of 1908, s. v. Falkes de Breauté). Of the modern writers we should mention particularly M. Charles Petit-Dutaillis, whose valuable study of the life of Louis VIII (*Étude sur la Vie et le Règne de Louis VIII, 1187–1226*) appeared in 1894; and M. Paul Meyer, whose third volume of the edition of *L'Histoire de Guillaume le Maréchal* containing his scholarly notes appeared in 1901. Both of these authors were under a certain disadvantage owing to the fact that the Patent Rolls for 1216–25 were not published until 1901. The account of Sir James H. Ramsay (*Dawn of the Constitution*, 1908, pp. 12–13), though brief, is excellent; and the treatment by Mr. G. J. Turner of *The Minority of Henry III* (*Transactions of the Royal Historical Society*, New Series, xviii, 1904, 245–95) is of special value.

[2] The *Histoire des Ducs de Normandie* supplies a brief account of his early life and other details for the period of Louis's invasion. The Romance of Eustace (*Wistasse le Moine*, ed. Foerster and Trost, Halle, 1891; this is based upon Michel's edition, London, 1834), written between 1223 and 1284, though rather depreciated by M. Petit-Dutaillis (*Louis VIII*, pp. 168, n. 1, 98–9; cf. his biography of Eustace in *La Grande Encyclopédie*, xvi. 855), may be safely treated—with due allowances for poetic licence—as legitimate source material. The editors of the Romance have collected much source material for explanation of the poem (cf. the biographical note by Meyer, *Guillaume le Maréchal*, iii. 242, n. 3). Of further assistance is the study of this poem made by M. Malo (*Revue du Nord, Conférence faite à Boulogne-sur-Mer le 12 Mars 1898*; our references are to the *Extrait*).

[3] Matthew Paris, *Chronica Maiora*, iii. 29, 'piratarum magister'.

[4] This is the accepted English form of the name. The *Histoire des Ducs de Normandie* gives the contemporary form 'Wistasses'; the poem uses the forms 'Wistace', 'Wistasce', 'Wistasse', 'Wistase'. The Latin chroniclers ordinarily write 'Eustachius', which in Silgrave (*Chronicon*, Caxton Society, 1849, p. 101) and *Chronique de Douvres* (*Collection de Documents Inédits, Rapports au Ministre*, 1839, iii, *Rapport de M. Francisque Michel*, p. 44, n. 2) becomes 'Stacius'. M. Michel points out (*ibid.*) that the form 'Buske' found in the *Rot. Misae* (*Rot. de Liberate ac de Misis*, 1844, p. 115) is another variation. M. Michel preferred 'Eustache'. 'Eustachium cognomine Matthaeum' in the Chronicle of Lanercost is evidently a mistaken emendation of the copy 'Eustachium Monachum' (cf. Michel, *Roman d'Eustache*, preface, xxxvi, n.; and *Chronica de Mailros*, p. 128).

[5] ll. 304–5. Probably Courset, about twelve miles distant from Boulogne: cf. Malo, p. 11.   [6] Malo, *ibid.*

as many subsequent events of his career will show.[7] The Romance points out circumstantially that his father was 'Bauduïns Buskes', a peer of Boulogne;[8] in the *Histoire des Ducs de Normandie* he is called 'i. chevaliers de Boulenois';[9] William le Breton refers to him as 'miles'.[10] In his early life, the Romance recounts, he visited Toledo, where he studied the black art so successfully that no one in France was his equal.[11] We appear to have no other authority for this journey, which is announced in the first few lines of the poem as a necessary introduction to the droll adventures the poet attributes to his hero. Whether the poet is the author of this tradition or simply took it as he found it is uncertain.[12] Later generations believed it thoroughly, and it may have grown up, as in the instance of the Romance, to account for his incredible exploits. The author of the *Histoire des Ducs de Normandie* wrote in Eustace's own day : 'No one would believe the marvels he accomplished, nor those which happened to him many times.'[13]

We next find him as a monk in the abbey of Samer,[14] having for this the direct evidence of the Romance[15] and such corroborative evidence as that of the Anonymous Chronicle of Laon, which speaks of Eustace 'from a black monk becoming a demoniac';[16] of Ralph Coggeshall, who calls him 'Eustace, formerly a monk';[17] and especially that of Matthew Paris, who states the circumstances under which Eustace had put aside his habit and renounced his order.[18] The Romance tells us that Eustace left the abbey to demand justice from the count of

---

[7] The supposed counter-statement that he was a Fleming is in no sense a contradiction. It goes back to Lefebvre, who in his *Histoire de Calais* (Paris, 1766), i. 633, n. *a* (quoted by Michel, *Roman*, p. vi ; Foerster and Trost, *Wistasse*, viii and n. 2), quotes *Hist. Nav. d'Anglet.* tom. i, p. 59, ex notis, which proves to be by Thomas Lediard (cf. Lefebvre, p. 513, n. 2). Lediard in the English original (*The Naval History of England*, 1066-1734, London, 1735, i. 28, n. *c*) plainly follows Matthew Paris, one of his references. So the whole tradition goes back to Paris, who wrote (*Chronica Maiora*, iii. 29) : 'Erat autem ille natione Flandrensis.' In the thirteenth century the term Fleming was often applied to the Boulogne country. See Michel's note in *Histoire des Ducs de Normandie*, introd. ii, and compare the usage of that narrative.

[8] ll. 305 ff.   [9] p. 167.

[10] *De Gestis Philippi Augusti*, in Bouquet, *Recueil*, xvii. 111 B.

[11] ll. 6 ff.

[12] Cf. Malo, p. 11.   [13] p. 167.

[14] Samer, eight miles south-east of Boulogne, is a shortened form of St. Vulmer. It was an old Benedictine abbey (*Gallia Christiana*, x, Paris, 1751, col. 1593-8).

[15] ll. 3-5.

[16] *Chronicon Anonymi Laudunensis Canonici*, in Bouquet, *Recueil*, xviii. 719 D ; cf. Trivet, *Annales*, 201.

[17] *Chronicon Anglicanum*, p. 185.

[18] Paris relates that he desired to secure the inheritance which had fallen to him because of his brothers' decease without children (*Chronica Maiora*, iii. 29). But we afterwards meet with mention of the brothers of Eustace (e. g. in the treaty of peace, 11 September 1217 ; Rymer, *Foedera*, i, ed. 1727, p. 221, c. 10).

Boulogne against the murderer of his father. The appeal of battle went against the champion of Eustace.[19]

After this he went into the service of Count Renaut of Boulogne in the capacity of seneschal.[20] According to the Romance, Eustace's old enemy, Hainfrois de Hersinghen, who had slain the father, at length accused the son to the count of Boulogne to such good purpose that the count summoned him to deliver up his charge. Eustace appealed to a court of his peers, but at length took fright and fled. Thereupon the count seized his property and burned his fields; Eustace in return swearing that this wrong should cost the count 'ten thousand marks'.[21] With his subsequent exploits of revenge while living as an outlaw in the forest of the Boulonnais, interesting as they may be to the poet of the Romance,[22] we need not concern ourselves, except to note that his enmity against the count is too well attested to doubt. The writer of the *Histoire des Ducs de Normandie* relates that Eustace had warred much with the count of Boulogne; so much so that in consequence of the count going over to the king of France he went over to the king of England.[23]

Eustace's career under John began as early as 1205.[24] Various writs from 1205 to 1208[25] would indicate that during those years he was generally abroad on the king's service, possibly in the Channel Islands, to which John dispatched five galleys and three large ships in the spring of 1206.[26] The Romance states that John sent him 'with thirty galleys' to capture the islands, and describes the raid by which Eustace executed his commission.[27] According to the *Histoire des Ducs de Normandie* Eustace had done so well that John granted him the islands.[28] For a number of years after this Eustace was in good standing with the English king.[29] During

[19] *Wistasse*, ll. 319–70. Michel holds that the defeat of the innocent party substantiates the truth of the account (*Roman*, p. 94).
[20] *Wistasse*, ll. 371 ff. Lambert d'Ardres, under 1203, describes Eustace acting as seneschal (*Historia Comitum Ghisnensium*, in Bouquet, *Recueil*, xviii. 587–8). This is the first date for his biography that we possess
[21] *Wistasse*, ll. 375 ff. Cf. Malo, p. 14. [22] *Wistasse*, ll. 399–1879.
[23] p. 167. We also find an oath taken by the count of Boulogne to abjure Eustace and certain others, and if possible to hand them over to King Philip (L. Delisle, *Catalogue des Actes de Philippe-Auguste*, Paris, 1856, no. 1245, app. pp. 516–17). This agreement is dated by the editor as 'towards 1210' (*ibid.* 546). If this dating is correct the agreement is to the point here only as indicating the count's hostility. As to Eustace's fear of Philip, compare *Wistasse*, l. 1741.
[24] At length, thus the Romance, the Monk was taken into the service of King John and evidently gave his daughter as hostage; later on Eustace complained to Prince Louis that John had slain, burned, and disfigured her (*ibid.* ll. 1880 ff., also ll. 2226–7). Cf. *Rot. Litt. Pat.* i, part i, 144 a.
[25] *Rot. Litt. Claus.* i. 57 a; *Rot. Litt. Pat.* i, part i, 65 a; 81 a.
[26] *Rot. Litt. Claus.* i. 69 a.
[27] *Wistasse*, ll. 1910 ff. [28] p. 167.
[29] *Rot. Misae*, in Hardy, *Rot. de Liberate*, 113, 119, 123, 127, 165, 232; *Rot. Litt. Claus.* i. 126; cf. 248 b.

this period, and before he had to flee from England, he may have made the raid described in the Romance upon the territory guarded by Cadoc, the master of the famous castle of Gaillon on the Seine above Rouen. The Romance terms Cadoc 'le senescal de Normendie', and relates how Eustace came to Harfleur at the mouth of the Seine, and after penetrating inland as far as Pont-Audemer met Cadoc, and returned to his ships. Cadoc thought to pursue him to Boulogne, but Eustace went west to Barfleur. Finally Cadoc overtook him with a fleet, but suffered a loss of five boats and withdrew.[30]

On his return to England after this exploit, the poet relates, Eustace secured permission of King John to build a 'palais' in London. 'Eustace finished the palace which was very rich and well built.'[31] However it may be with the London house, to which there seems to be no other reference, there is little doubt that his home port, when in England, was Winchelsea. For this we have first the evidence of the Romance, where 'Winchelsea' is given as his battle-cry in the Islands.[32] Again, the account in the *Histoire des Ducs de Normandie*, on the occasion of Louis's distress in Winchelsea in the early part of 1217, represents Eustace as coming to Louis and giving the following advice: 'Sire, if you would have prepared a certain very fine galley which is in this town and which I know well, for it was indeed mine, you would be able with it greatly to restrain their ships.'[33] Finally, in the account of the death of Eustace, as given in *Guillaume le Maréchal*, his executioner is named as Stephen of Winchelsea, who seemed to know him well;[34] who is further identified in the *Histoire des Ducs de Normandie* as 'Stephen Trabbe, who had long been with him'.[35]

This nearly concludes the sum of what we know directly of Eustace's career under King John.[36] He was in England when

[30] *Wistasse*, ll. 1952–2132. For Cadoc, see S. Bougenot, in *La Grande Encyclopédie*, viii. 702. Cf. Delisle, *Recueil de Jugements de l'Échiquier de Normandie au XIII⁴ Siècle*, notes to nos. 49, 137.   [31] *Wistasse*, ll. 2134–57.
[32] *Ibid.* l. 1931. Cf. Meyer, *Guillaume le Maréchal*, iii. 220, n. 2.
[33] p. 185.   [34] l. 17439.   [35] p. 202.
[36] Some light is thrown upon the career of Eustace under John in connexion with that of his countryman and friend, Geoffrey de Lucy. Cf. *Rot. Litt. Pat.* i, part i, 9, 75, 143; *Rot. Litt. Claus.* i. 46, 70, 126, 230, 235 b, 236 b, 237 b, 239 b, 241, 268 b, 277 b, 280, 288 b, 295, 322 b, 326 b, 350 b, 626 b, &c.; also Annals of Dunstaple, *Annales Monastici*, iii. 46. Upon comparing the data for Eustace and Geoffrey, we find that the latter had evidently preceded Eustace to England, and was posted at Winchelsea in August 1205 at about the time of the arrival of Eustace, our first notice of Eustace being in November of that year. Then from May 1206 we find Eustace apparently out of England much of the time, presumably in the Islands; Geoffrey, too, after May 1206, was also in the Islands at least intermittently until November 1212, when he left for Poitou. As early as November 1214 Eustace had gone over to Louis, followed by Geoffrey between July and October 1215. We may fairly conclude that the two had been working harmoniously together for most of the time while Eustace was with King John.

the count of Boulogne came to John after breaking with the king of France. 'Then the Monk wished to return, when he saw Renaut de Boulogne,' but the king had the seaports guarded to prevent his departure.[37] A passage from the Annals of Dunstaple, under 1211 (really 1212), explains this further:

> ... There came ... the count of Boulogne. And the king of France took all the ships of England which came to his land; and therefore the king of England took many towns of the Cinque Ports. And then Eustace the pirate, called the Monk, fled from us to the king of France with five galleys because the count of Boulogne laid snares for him.[38]

The Romance gives a humorous detailed account of Eustace's escape from England in disguise and his unexpected appearance before Louis,[39] which in the light of the specific statement in the Annals of Dunstaple, given above, that he left England with five galleys, we are compelled to ignore. The fact that he was ostensibly in the service of Louis, however, and not of Philip, is clear. Philip was particular to explain that point to Gualo the legate when the latter applied for a safe-conduct in 1216: 'Through our land I will willingly furnish you safe-conduct; but if by chance you should fall into the hands of Eustace the Monk or of the other men of Louis who guard the sea-routes, do not impute it to me if any harm comes to you.'[40] Walter of Coventry attributes a degree of activity on the part of Eustace when under Louis equal to that which he displayed when in John's service.[41]

The Romance intimates that until the period of Louis's English invasion he was more particularly engaged in the Channel Islands.[42] The Annals of Dunstaple speak of their capture after Louis's invasion. That they were in the possession of Eustace at the time of his death we know from the terms of peace finally entered into between Henry III and Louis in 1217, for by the treaty Louis agreed to send letters to Eustace's brothers in the islands, directing them to surrender them to the English. The treaty also leads us to infer the high degree of independence Eustace had enjoyed there from the elaborate arrangements it contains for ensuring obedience to its terms.

The aid afforded Louis by Eustace in his English campaigns was considerable, indeed almost essential. In 1215 he had

[37] *Wistasse*, ll. 2158 ff.
[38] *Annales Monastici*, iii. 34. Eustace was present when the count's arrangements with John were completed, in May 1212 (Rymer, *Foedera*, i. 158), and as we have seen above (n. 29) he was in favour with the king so late as October of that year. So Eustace must have gone over to Louis sometime between that month and 4 November 1214; for under the latter date the records show that the English had taken prisoners some of Eustace's men (*Rot. Litt. Claus.* i. 175 b, 177, 262 b; *Rot. Litt. Pat.* i, part i, 126, 130 b, 133 b).   [39] *Wistasse*, ll. 2164 ff.
[40] Wendover, *Flores Historiarum*, iii. 367; cf. Petit-Dutaillis, *Louis VIII*, p. 94.
[41] *Memoriale*, ii. 238–9.   [42] *Wistasse*, ll. 2250-1.

made a beginning by carrying machines of war from the French to the English barons, landing them at Folkestone greatly to John's annoyance.[43] When Louis sailed from Calais in person Eustace had prepared his fleet, which amounted, according to the chroniclers, to seven or eight hundred ships,[44] a total which, even if reduced considerably, affords no mean indication of his ability and of his resources at the time. It was largely owing to the strenuous efforts of Eustace that Louis survived the Winchelsea campaign at the beginning of 1217.[45] We may assume that Eustace saw him safely home from this, and was waiting for him when Louis was prepared to recross the Channel to England once more. Finally, we come to the battle of Sandwich, on 24 August, which the biographer of the marshal gleefully called Eustace's feast-day, the day on which thereafter his death would be celebrated.[46]

The disastrous Lincoln campaign, if not decisively affecting the position of the French in England,[47] was at least a severe blow to their prospects. Louis, who received the news on Thursday, 25 May 1217, while conducting the siege of Dover,[48] felt obliged to remove to London and send to France for aid. The decision to abandon the siege of Dover, the reduction of which was of the greatest importance and had been most carefully prepared for,[49] is in itself eloquent testimony of the straits to which the French were reduced. On the other hand, when the royalists disbanded after the Lincoln campaign, the confident appointment of Chertsey on the Thames, only twenty-two miles out of London,[50] as the rendezvous, is a sufficient indication of their high hopes.

The appeal for aid directed to Philip and to Louis's wife, the Lady Blanche of Castile, met with peculiar diplomatic difficulties. The well-known opposition of the papacy to the invasion of England had required from the beginning that it should pass as the private enterprise of Louis.[51] At the beginning

---

[43] Coggeshall, *Chronicon Anglicanum*, p. 172; *Rot. Litt. Pat.* i, part i, 155 b; cf. Petit-Dutaillis, *Louis VIII*, p. 69, and n. 3.

[44] Wendover, iii. 367–8; *Histoire des Ducs de Normandie*, p. 166–7.

[45] *Histoire des Ducs de Normandie*, p. 182–7; cf. *Chronica de Mailros*, p. 130.

[46] *Guillaume le Maréchal*, ii, ll. 17161–2, 17456; iii. 243, n. 1.

[47] Cf. Petit-Dutaillis, *Louis VIII*, p. 154. For the progress of the war down to the engagement at Sandwich see Turner, *Transactions of the Royal Historical Society*, New Series, xviii, 1904, 258–66.

[48] *Histoire des Ducs de Normandie*, 195. Cf. Meyer, *Guillaume le Maréchal*, iii, 241, n. 1.

[49] See Professor Tout's remarks upon the new siege-engine, the trébuchet, *ante*, xviii. 263–5.

[50] *Guillaume le Maréchal*, ii, l. 17061; iii. 240, and n. 4. Cf. the marshal's itinerary, *ibid.* p. cliii.   [51] Wendover, iii. 363–7.

of the year the situation had become still more delicate owing to the reconciliation of Philip and Honorius III.[52] The scene portrayed by the 'Ménestrel de Reims', wherein the king first refuses to aid his son and then slyly offers his daughter-in-law as much of his treasure as she cares to take, to do with what she will, explains the spirit of the compromise that Philip effected with himself.[53] Wendover states the case exactly when he says : 'Since the King feared to bear aid to his excommunicate son, having often been censured by the Pope for complicity with him, he imposed the whole of the work upon the wife of Louis.'[54] Under the energetic leadership of the Lady Blanche the preparation of the fleet went rapidly forward. Calais was the point of concentration,[55] where 'she toiled very hard to make his people pass over to rescue their lord '.[56]

In the meantime affairs in England had been practically at a standstill,[57] but by 13 August threatening news from the Channel must have been received such as to demand the personal attention of the earl marshal. He was at Reading on 14 August, at Farnham on the 15th and 16th, at Lewes on the 17th, and at Romney on the 19th. As the marshal's biographer puts it, he was greatly perplexed upon hearing of the extensive preparations that were going forward at Calais, and promptly made his way to the coast to make the necessary counter-preparations.[58] The coast had not been left unguarded, however, for as early as 20 January the veteran counsellor, warrior, and seaman, Philip d'Aubigny, had been given charge of all the southern coast. His commission was addressed to all in Kent, Surrey, Sussex, and Hampshire, including the Weald, the Cinque Ports, and all maritime parts of Hampshire.[59] When Louis, in February, had gone on his expedition to Winchelsea and burned the town, the inhabitants, we read in the *Histoire des Ducs de Normandie*, entered their ships and went to Rye 'to Philip d'Aubigny, who was there with a great plenty of ships well fitted and well armed, as one whose business it was to guard the sea

[52] Cf. M. Petit-Dutaillis, *Louis VIII*, p. 162.
[53] *Récits d'un Ménestrel de Reims* (ed. N. de Wailly), 157-8 ; cf. pp. ix, x, lxi.
[54] *Flores Historiarum*, iv. 27-8.
[55] Cf. *Guillaume le Maréchal*, ii, ll. 17108-24.
[56] *Histoire des Ducs de Normandie*, pp. 198, 200 ; cf. M. Petit-Dutaillis, *Louis VIII*, p. 164, n. 1.
[57] The marshal remained at Lincoln until 25 May, when he returned to Oxford. June was employed in the vain endeavour to bring about a peace. When these efforts were plainly futile, the marshal, who had remained near, appears to have gone for a fortnight to the west. He was back at Oxford, 20-4 July ; and by 7 August was again there and passed the week at that place. Cf. *Rot. Litt. Claus.* i. 336.
[58] *Patent Rolls*, 1216-25, 64-8.
[59] *Patent Rolls*, 25. For Aubigny, cf. *Rot. Litt. Claus.* i. 91, 126 b, 164, 226 b, 230 b ; *Patent Rolls*, 88, 281 b, 282 b ; Wendover, iv. 1, 75 ; *Guillaume le Maréchal*, ii, ll. 15336-9 ; iii. 214, n. 3 ; *Histoire des Ducs de Normandie*, p. 207.

for the king'.[60] Again, we are told by the same authority that while Louis was besieging Dover in that spring, on the very day that he settled down to the siege, 12 May, forty of his ships came before Dover, but owing to a storm all but five were driven back to Calais. On Monday the 15th they set out for Dover again, but Philip d'Aubigny and Nicholas Haringos [61] came from before Romney with quite four score ships, of which twenty were great ships well equipped for fighting. Louis's people seeing them, and having only small ships, did not dare attack, but attempted to retreat to Calais. Twenty-seven of the French ships, having come too far to retreat, were forced to fight, with the result that eight were captured by the English while the nineteen escaped in great confusion. The soldiers and sailors, we are told, were soon all slain, and the knights were cast into prison in the holds of the ships, where they were badly treated. The English then cast anchor before the town to prevent food and reinforcements from reaching Louis while conducting his siege.[62]

On Thursday, 25 May, the news of Lincoln came to Louis at Dover; on Monday, the 29th, six score sail were seen approaching. When the English saw them,

they raised their sails and went to meet them on the high sea. Wistasses de Noeville and the others who were in the ships began to give chase: they pursued the English vigorously but could not overtake them. And when they saw they could not catch them they turned back and sailed for Dover. But when the English saw them turn, they also came about and fell upon the rear of the fleet, capturing eight ships, the rest arriving together at Dover.[63]

The feint of fleeing and returning to attack the rear is of interest as helping to explain the tactics of the subsequent battle of Sandwich.

Returning now to the preparations made by the marshal for the reception of the approaching expedition, we find that he evidently passed from Lewes on 17 August to Romney on the 19th. This supports the narrative of the *Histoire de Guillaume le Maréchal*, in which we are told that he summoned the mariners of the Cinque Ports. They complained vigorously of ill-treatment at the hands of King John both in regard to their losses and the serfage to which he had reduced them. The marshal, however, promised them recompense for their losses from the vessels they should capture, and also restoration of their franchises in addition to the gift of great wealth, if only

[60] p. 183; *Guillaume le Maréchal*, ii, ll. 15782 ff.; and iii. 220–1.
[61] For Nicholas Harangod', see *Rot. Litt. Claus.* i. 229, 233 b, 242 b.
[62] *Histoire des Ducs de Normandie*, pp. 192–3.
[63] *Ibid.* p. 196. Roger of Wendover is wrong in supposing that Aubigny joined the levy that took part in the battle of Lincoln (iv. 19; cf. 28).

they would go out and fight the French with spirit. He prevailed so well upon them that they betook themselves straightway to Sandwich and overhauled their ships for action. The rigging was carefully seen to, as well as 'good anchors and strong cables for anchoring before the ports'.[64] We understand by this account that the marshal put new life into Aubigny's fleet and strengthened it in every way possible. The brave old earl was with difficulty restrained from embarking with the fleet, but the danger of leaving the realm without its chief defender was too great to permit the risk of his death or capture.

The *Histoire des Ducs de Normandie* now presents another preliminary engagement which *Guillaume le Maréchal* seems to corroborate. While Blanche was preparing her reinforcements at Calais, the English, so we are informed, often came before the harbour to attack them.[65]

One day fully three hundred came there: and when the French saw them come, they armed and entered into their ships, and went to meet the ships of the English, which were at that time rather lightly manned. So the English were discomfited and the French captured quite seven score and the others were scattered among the various havens of England.

The first recital of *Guillaume le Maréchal* apparently refers to this occasion. It tells us (we translate freely) that,

when the English saw the great fleet of the French approaching, they went to meet them in combat, though since they were without leadership they greatly feared the French. In their despair they [at length ?] abandoned their ships with the sails set and took to their boats.[66]

On the other hand, the French had their share of misfortunes, for ' One night the French came before Dover where they were at anchor ; and on the morrow when they thought to proceed to the mouth of the Thames a storm arose with a rough sea and drove them back upon Boulogne and Flanders and caused them great distress '.[67]

Finally, on St. Bartholomew's day, Thursday, 24 August, the French fleet was once more ready to sail : ' the day was fine and clear and they could look far out at sea.'[68] It was descried

[64] *Guillaume le Maréchal*, ii, ll. 17167–233.
[65] *Histoire des Ducs de Normandie*, p. 198. Is this the explanation of the anchors and cables, that the English might keep the French shut up in Calais as John had attempted to do in 1216 ? Cf. *ibid.* p. 167–8 ; and Petit-Dutaillis, *Louis VIII*, p. 100.
[66] *Guillaume le Maréchal*, ii, ll. 17234 ff. ; cf. 17347–50, and *Chronica de Mailros*, p. 128.
[67] *Histoire des Ducs de Normandie*, p. 198 ff. The accounts of the two French narrators may possibly, however, not refer to the same discomfiture.
[68] *Guillaume le Maréchal*, ii, ll. 17281 ff.

issuing from Calais 'sailing toward the mouth of the Thames'.[69] 'So dense was the fleet and in such good order that it was like a pitched battle. In advance proceeded the ship of Eustace the Monk, who was its guide and master.'[70] This ship was 'the great ship of Bayonne' which contained 'the treasure of the king'.[71] The editor of *Guillaume le Maréchal*, M. Meyer, understands by this a reference to King Philip's treasure destined for Louis.[72] It also carried a trébuchet and a number of choice horses for Louis, so that with the burden of its crew and fighting men, together with their supplies, it was altogether too heavily laden. In fact it was so deep in the water that its deck was almost awash.[73] The ship carried the leaders of the expedition. First among them was Robert de Courtenay, the French queen's uncle.[74] From his order given to Eustace at the critical point of the engagement we may gather that he was in real command of the expedition; and the *Histoire des Ducs de Normandie* accords him a certain precedence.[75] Ralph de la Tourniele is then mentioned by this authority next after Eustace; so too in *Guillaume le Maréchal*.[76] Next in order is the famous William des Barres the younger, whose own brilliant reputation is usually by error merged in that of his equally famous father.[77] Among the others was Nevelos de Canle, son of the bailiff of Arras. In all, there were thirty-six knights in this ship.[78] 'In the second ship manned with knights was Mikius de Harnes,' whom we may regard as being in command.[79] In the third ship, presumably as leader, was the châtelain of Saint-Omer, William V.[80] The fourth ship was that of the mayor of Boulogne, in which there was a great number of knights.[81]

It is hardly worth while to attempt to fix closely the total number of knights in these four ships. The author of the *Histoire des Ducs de Normandie* states the number in the leading

[69] *Histoire des Ducs de Normandie*, 200 ff. Cf. Wendover, iv. 28: The fleet had been entrusted to Eustace, 'to lead it under safe-conduct to the city of London. . . . They had a strong wind at their backs which drove them vigorously towards England.'

[70] *Guillaume le Maréchal*, ii, ll. 17286 ff.   [71] *Ibid.* ii, ll. 17366–8.

[72] *Ibid.* iii. 245.   [73] *Ibid.* ii, ll. 17387–96.

[74] *Histoire des Ducs de Normandie*, p. 202; cf. 166, 172. Cf. also Petit-Dutaillis, *Louis VIII*, p. 336 and n. 3; and Appendix no. 5, 445.

[75] *Ibid.* pp. 200–1.

[76] *Ibid.* p. 201. *Guillaume le Maréchal*, ii, l. 17147; iii. 242, n. 2.

[77] Vide *Guillaume le Maréchal*, iii. 32, n. 1. The father was at Bouvines, the son at Muret. These personages are confused in Oman's *Art of War in the Middle Ages*, p. 470, and in Tout's *Political History of England, 1216–1377*, p. 11. The *Histoire des Ducs de Normandie*, p. 201, calls him: 'Li jouenes fils Guillaume des Bares'; in the Worcester Annals, *Annales Monastici*, iv. 409, it is 'W. de Barre, iuvenis'.

[78] *Histoire des Ducs de Normandie*, p. 201.

[79] Cf. *ibid.* pp. 166, 169, 198, 201.   [80] Cf. *ibid. passim.*

[81] *Ibid.* pp. 160, 184, 201; *Guillaume le Maréchal*, ii, l. 17374; cf. iii. 246, n. 1.

ship as thirty-six; but this ship was apparently an unusually large one, and the leaders would have the finest company with them. 'A great mass of knights,' however, entered the fourth; so that between one hundred and one hundred and twenty-five knights would probably offer a fair approximation.[82] In addition to these four there were six other great ships, well fitted out and prepared for fighting, given over to the men-at-arms.[83] The rest of the fleet consisted of small boats, containing equipment and merchandise, which brought the total up to some fourscore.[84]

We are fortunate in having somewhat definite particulars of the English leaders. In the absence of the marshal from the fleet,[85] Hubert de Burgh, who had throughout the war been defending Dover, took precedence as commander, doubtless by virtue of his office as justiciar. Paris specifically states that 'there were given to his command about sixteen ships well fitted out, besides attendant small boats to the number of twenty'; a statement which we see no reason to dispute. As to his particular ship and ship's company, the same author tells us that he took, probably from the garrison at Dover castle, two knights in particular, Henry de Trubleville and Richard Suard, with certain others few in number; furthermore, that he entered the best ship with a few skilled seamen from the Cinque Ports.[86] Next in order of importance was Richard Fitz-John,[87] whose parentage is given by the author of the *Histoire des Ducs de Normandie*. He was nephew to the earl of Warren, being the son of the earl's sister and King John, 'so he was both his son and cousin'.[88] After the description of Hubert's embarkation in

[82] *Histoire des Ducs de Normandie*, p. 198; but cf. *Chronica de Mailros*, p. 128, and Wendover, iv. 28.

[83] *Histoire des Ducs de Normandie*, pp. 200, 201. Cf. Wendover, iv. 28: 'cum multa armatorum manu.' The *Chronica de Mailros*, p. 128, include among the captives 146 'servientes equitum'.

[84] *Histoire des Ducs de Normandie*, p. 200. So also Wendover, iv. 28: 'naves quater viginti.' Paris's addition to the account of Wendover is worthless. *Chronica Maiora*, iii. 26: 'magnas, et plures de minoribus et galeis armatis.' Coggeshall, *Chronicon Anglicanum*, p. 185, a strictly contemporary authority of high value for this period (cf. Pauli, *Geschichte von England*, iii. 880), contents himself with sixty ships. The Worcester Annals, *Annales Monastici*, iv. 408, give sixty. *Guillaume le Maréchal*, l. 17294, states that there were 'bien treis cenz nez en lor estorie'.

[85] *Guillaume le Maréchal*, ll. 17197–210, 17251–61, 17295–301.

[86] *Chronica Maiora*, iii. 29. For special information as to Hubert de Burgh, see Turner, *Transactions of the Royal Historical Society*, New Series, xviii (1904), 246 ff. For Turberville, see the *Dictionary of National Biography*; also *Rot. Litt. Claus.* i, index. For Richard Suard, see *Patent Rolls*, 1216–25, 282, 283, 284, 300.

[87] M Petit-Dutaillis confuses him with Richard of Cornwall, the younger brother of Henry III, who would at that time have been only about eight years of age: *Louis VIII*, 168, n. 1.

[88] In Wendover, iv. 29–30, he is called 'filius regis nothus'; cf. *Guillaume le Maréchal*, l. 17308, and *Histoire des Ducs de Normandie*, 201, and especially 200, where his parentage is given.

Guillaume le Maréchal we are told next about Richard.[89] Into another ship, as the context shows, 'there went aboard with a fine troop Sir Richard the King's son'.[90] We have reason to believe that this 'fine troop' was furnished by his uncle the earl of Warren, who, we are informed, 'did not embark but fitted out a ship with knights and men-at-arms where his banners were'.[91]

With the exception of the ship that carried the men-at-arms of the marshal, whom we shall mention presently, 'they who had the other ships fitted them out as best they could.'[92] There were eighteen large ships, according to the *Histoire des Ducs de Normandie*,[93] and a number of galleys and fishing boats.[94] Paris, as we have seen, in his independent version gives the number of large boats as 'about sixteen'; of small, twenty. Wendover states that with galleys and other ships the number of the English did not exceed forty.[95] The author of *Guillaume le Maréchal* says simply: 'our people had only a few ships.' Earlier in the poem he states that the marshal had twenty-two ships great and small.[96] Of the large boats, in addition to those commanded by Hubert de Burgh and Richard Fitz-John, one especially stands out both by reason of its size and its crew. This is the 'cog', an unusually large ship for the times. It was lightly laden, and so stood high out of the water. Even the smaller ships of those days, of as low as twenty tons burden, were built with high bow and stern, fitted when need be with 'castles' fore and aft. The 'cog'—a term which had come to be applied to a particularly large ship—would have these characteristics developed to a high degree; and we know that in John's day some especially large ships had been built.[97] Although these ships of John had been dissipated in the great storm of 18 May 1216, just before Louis's first crossing, we find a writ of 8 June which informs us that there were great ships of Rye and Winchelsea which the king's official was to maintain.[98] It was at Rye, we remember, that Philip d'Aubigny 'had a great plenty of ships well fitted and well armed'. We may feel satisfied that the great ships at

[89] Cf. Annals of Waverley, *Annales Monastici*, ii. 288.
[90] ll. 17307-8.
[91] *Histoire des Ducs de Normandie*, 201. The poet of *Guillaume le Maréchal* says that Richard's ship was the first to attack Eustace (ll. 17377-80), and the author of the *Histoire des Ducs de Normandie* states that the ship which first attacked Eustace contained the people of the earl of Warren (201). But cf. M. Petit-Dutaillis, *Louis VIII*, 167.
[92] *Guillaume le Maréchal*, ll. 17311-12. As to the poverty of the royal treasury at this period, see Turner, *ubi supra*, 285-6.
[93] So too the Annals of Waverley, *Annales Monastici*, ii. 288. [94] p. 201.
[95] *Flores Historiarum*, iv. 28. [96] ll. 17352, 17214.
[97] *Histoire des Ducs de Normandie*, 130, 134, 135.
[98] *Rot. Litt. Claus.* a. 1216, 274 b.

Sandwich were the remainder of these which had so far survived the exigencies of the war.

The commander of these ships, including the cog, would, under ordinary circumstances, have still been Philip d'Aubigny, but on this occasion Hubert de Burgh and Richard Fitz-John seem to have had precedence; or perhaps Hubert alone outranked him, and Richard held an independent command of one ship, just as in the battle of Muret William des Barres, the younger, had held an independent command in front of the first troop of horse.[99] Of the troops that were on the cog sufficient information has come down to us to give grounds for supposing that it was manned by the marshal's men-at-arms, who, we are told by the marshal's own biographer, had been sent aboard the day before.[100]

A few words remain to be said concerning the composition and character of the remainder of the fleet. Some of the larger ships may, like the cog and the earl of Salisbury's great ship of a previous day, have been given or entrusted by the king to various individuals with the implied condition of war service. The rest of the ships, with perhaps here and there an exception, probably came, as we have seen, from the Cinque Ports, whose duty it was to furnish a navy when called upon.[101] In addition to the sailing ships there were galleys, of which the Ports were accustomed to have some, and also the king.[102] Wendover states that at the battle there were galleys armed with iron prows for ramming their adversaries,[103] and the affair of Richard I with the ship from Beirut, in June 1191, shows how deadly these galleys could be, when properly led, against even the largest ships.[104]

If we now proceed to summarize the respective advantages enjoyed by the two sides in the combat, we find the following conditions. The French had the advantage in respect to the wind, the choice of the day, the number of their ships, the number of their knights, and possibly the number of their men-at-arms. They had the redoubtable Eustace for their pilot, and apparently excellent leadership. On the other hand their ships, and especially that of Eustace, were encumbered with cargo, they were much weaker in large vessels, and were obliged to make for a certain objective—London. Furthermore, they had the defect

[99] Oman, *Art of War*, 453. As to Philip's presence, see *Guillaume le Maréchal*, l. 17270 ; and Wendover, iv. 29.

[100] From the presence on the cog of two men who were in the marshal's troop, namely, Ranulf Paganus and Theobald Blund, we may safely conclude that the troops aboard the cog were his: *Guillaume le Maréchal*, ll. 17309–10, 17405, 17406, 17425 ; *Rot. Litt. Claus.* i. 317 *b*, cf. 382 *b*, &c.; also *Patent Rolls*, 1216–25, 168.

[101] Cf. *Patent Rolls*, 1216–25, 89, 370–3, &c. The question of their quota is discussed in Burrows, *Cinque Ports*, 85 ff.

[102] *Ibid.* 87 ; cf. *Patent Rolls*, 1216–25, 71.

[103] *Flores Historiarum*, iv. 29.

[104] *Itinerarium Regis Ricardi*, in *Chronicles, &c., of Richard* (ed. Stubbs), i. 208.

of over-confidence, as the narrative will show, while the English were fully aware of the desperate nature of their enterprise and felt that little less than a miracle could enable them to stop the French fleet.

True to their custom followed in previous engagements, as in the fight off Dover on 29 May, the English sought to get to the windward of the French.[105] Hubert sailed out in advance of the others and made a feint of attacking, but so sailed outside the French line as to refuse combat. We may consider the rest of the English as advancing in column to follow his lead.[106] On their part the French, who were proceeding in ranks in close order toward the Thames, 'and had come much of the distance,'[107] 'toward the Isle of Thanet,'[108] upon seeing the English come out of the harbour, misapprehended them. Mindful of their recent success over the English, they clewed up their sails with the intention of capturing this little force of fishing vessels—as they supposed without the efficient leadership of knights, 'only foot'—' to pay their expenses '.[109] That this misapprehension of the English fleet is not merely the fanciful interpretation of the poet of *Guillaume le Maréchal* is made clear by other accounts. William le Breton, chaplain of King Philip, tells us that ' while they were on the high sea they descried a few ships coming slowly from England; whereupon Robert de Courtenay caused the ship which he was in to be directed toward them, thinking it would be easy to capture them '.[110] Evidently the French had little idea of a serious engagement, and the touch of the marshal's biographer wherein he depicts the French as shouting in a spirit of bravado when they saw that Hubert apparently sought to avoid them is true to the situation.[111] We may notice here that Eustace, according to Paris, would have let them go ; but that it was Robert de Courtenay, according to William le Breton, who gave the fatal order to attack. The result was disastrous. The ship of Eustace veering struck that ship of the English column, probably the second, which contained Richard Fitz-John.[112] We hear no more of Hubert de Burgh until the close

[105] The best account of the battle is perhaps that given in the *Dictionary of National Biography*, under Hubert de Burgh, by Dr. W. Hunt and Sir J. K. Laughton, 1886 (cf. Meyer in *Guillaume le Maréchal*, iii. 245, n. 1); but they used neither the *Histoire des Ducs* nor *Guillaume le Maréchal*, which was not published until 1894.

[106] *Guillaume le Maréchal*, ll. 17354 ff. Matthew Paris, *Chronica Maiora*, iii. 29 : 'Perrexerunt igitur audacter, obliquando tamen dracenam, id est *loof*, acsi vellent adire Calesiam.'

[107] Wendover, iv. 28.   [108] *Histoire des Ducs de Normandie*, 201.

[109] *Guillaume le Maréchal*, ll. 17332–52 ; cf. Matthew Paris, *Chronica Maiora*, iii. 29.

[110] *De Gestis Philippi Augusti*, in Bouquet, *Recueil*, xvii. 111 A.

[111] *Guillaume le Maréchal*, l. 17360 : ' Lors escrient : " La hart ! la hart ! " '

[112] *Ibid.* ll. 17376 ff.

of the engagement; evidently he passed beyond the French lines and fell upon the rear according to the original plan. The statement of tactics by Paris may be given at this point as applicable to Hubert's ship: ' But when the English found that they had gained the wind, tacking about with the wind now favourable to themselves, they rushed eagerly upon the enemy.' [113] After the battle Hubert brought in two ships which he had captured.[114]

Eustace and Richard fell upon each other fiercely, but the conflict was wholly indecisive until the next ships in the English column began to come up one after another. Three thus arrived and began to attack Eustace upon all sides.[115] We may well believe that the rest of the French fleet was puzzled to know what to do. Arrayed in rank in close order, with a strong wind blowing them on their course, it would have been extremely difficult so to manœuvre to the left flank as to attack the English column effectively. Moreover, we may doubt if they fully realized the seriousness of the predicament of their admiral's ship until too late. It seems idle to blame the rest of the French, as William le Breton does: ' But the other ships of his fellows did not follow him (Courtenay). Alone, therefore, that ship having joined combat with four English ships was in a brief time overcome and captured.' [116] When the cog came up, its company had the distinct advantage of the superior height which enabled them to use their missile weapons most effectively. The *Histoire des Ducs de Normandie* states that they cast stones.[117] They also had vessels of lime, which, when thrown down upon the deck of the enemy's ship, blinded the crew. This manœuvre is spoken of with emphasis not only by the writer of *Guillaume le Maréchal* [118] and by Wendover,[119] but also in the Romance of Eustace. After describing the valour of the French, who defended themselves so well that the English could not board, the Romance goes on to relate that the English ' began to throw finely pulverized lime in great pots upon the deck, so that a great cloud arose. Then the French could no longer defend themselves for their eyes were full of powder; and since they were before the wind it caused them torment. Into the ship of Eustace the English leaped, and very badly did they misuse the French.' [120] Similarly, after the lime had taken effect, the marshal's historian tells us of the boarding of the ship; but with greater detail, as we should expect from one interested, not only in a great battle, but especially in the deeds of the marshal's own men. He relates, in brief,

[113] *Chronica Maiora*, iii. 29
[115] *Histoire des Ducs de Normandie*, 201.
[116] Bouquet, *Recueil*, xvii. 111 B.
[117] pp. 201-2.
[119] *Flores Historiarum*, iv. 29.
[114] *Guillaume le Maréchal*, ll. 17505-9.
[118] ll. 17400-4.
[120] *Wistasse*, ll. 2289-99.

that Ranulf Paganus leaped from the cog upon the ship among the leading knights, scattering them by his fall and taking Raoul de la Tournelle prisoner. After him leaped Theobald Blund, who aided him vigorously; and then came the rest of the company, who pressed the enemy sorely, finally capturing the ship. 'Gladly would they have killed the thirty-two knights, who would not have escaped had the English knights permitted their execution; but with great difficulty they restrained them.'[121]

With Eustace, however, the case was different. When the ship was captured, the English instituted a search for him, and he was at length discovered down in the hold (Matthew Paris says in the bilge-water) by 'Richard Sorale and Wudecoc'.[122] Then Eustace offered a large sum of money for a ransom, ten thousand marks, as the writer of *Guillaume le Maréchal* puts it; 'but it could not be.'[123] His additional offer (so Wendover) to serve the king of the English faithfully thereafter, if actually made, would have been only a reminder of his previous injuries. It was Stephen Trabe (or Crave), one of the mariners, 'who had long been with him,' that executed him, so the *Histoire des Ducs de Normandie* tells us;[124] or as the poem of *Guillaume le Maréchal* narrates it:[125] 'There was one there named Stephen of Winchelsea, who recalled to him the hardships which he had caused them both upon land and sea and who gave him the choice of having his head cut off either upon the trébuchet or upon the rail of the ship. Then he cut off his head.'[126] The head was subsequently fixed upon a lance and borne to Canterbury and about the country for a spectacle.[127] The Romance concludes with the sentiment: 'Nor can one live long who is intent always upon doing evil.'[128]

The capture of the leading ship was the turning-point of the battle, for the English then were encouraged to attack, and the French began a retreat which did not cease until the remnant of their fleet regained Calais. The English appear to have used all the methods of attack known to them. Wendover states that they rammed some of the ships;[129] Paris, in addition, that they grappled them and cut the rigging so that the sails fell

[121] *Guillaume le Maréchal*, ll. 17405–62.
[122] Wendover, iv. 29; Matthew Paris, *Chronica Maiora*, iii. 27, 29.
[123] ii, ll. 17436–7; iii. 247; Wendover, iv. 29. [124] p. 202.
[125] We quote the brief paraphrase by Meyer, iii. 247; cf. ii, ll. 17436–56.
[126] Stephen Crabbe (Trabe, or Crave, or Crabbe), as we have seen above, was an historic character. Cf. *Rot. Litt. Claus.* i. 193; ii. 44, 45 b, 68, 162; *Patent Rolls*, 1216–25, 96; *ibid.* 1225–32, 10, 11, 14, 44.
[127] *Histoire des Ducs de Normandie*, 202; *Chronicon Anonymi Laudunensis Canonici*, in Bouquet, *Recueil*, xviii. 719 D (cf. Trivet, *Annales*, 201).
[128] *Wistasse*, ll. 2304–5. [129] *Flores Historiarum*, iv. 29.

upon the crews.[130] Wendover vaingloriously adds that the French were not used to naval fighting, while the English, who were very skilful at that, employed missiles, lances, and swords. As the English promptly slew the crews of all the ships they captured, with the exception of from one to three for each ship, many chose rather to leap into the sea as a preferable mode of meeting death.[131] In *Guillaume le Maréchal* the slaughter is represented as so great that the writer had been told that of those slain, apart from the number of those that drowned themselves, there were four thousand, but for this number he took no responsibility. Nine of the ten large ships got safely back to Calais.[132] The Annals of Waverley state that only fifteen altogether escaped.[133] M. Petit-Dutaillis draws the conclusion that nearly all the French ships were taken or destroyed.[134]

As to the number of ships captured, not to consider what were sunk, we have little knowledge save the slight indications afforded by the statement that Hubert de Burgh captured two.[135] As he was the first out of the harbour, and got to windward of the French, and had one of the best ships, we should suppose him to have taken the largest number. Perhaps a score or two would be a safe estimate. That there was an appreciable number of captured ships is made evident in the marshal's writ of 1 September, wherein he summoned to the Thames the whole navy of the Cinque Ports ' as well that part lately won, as the rest '.[136]

From the fact that few of the common folk were spared, the number of prisoners must have been relatively small. Both Coggeshall's statement that 'many were taken with the other ships and led captive ', and the statement of the Melrose chronicler—of 145 knights, 146 horsemen, 33 balistarii, and 333 footmen—are manifestly incorrect.[137] Most of the captives, or a very large percentage of them, were knights. Of these we know that all in the ship of Eustace, with the exception of Eustace himself, were spared. We do not know that any others were captured, and in *Guillaume le Maréchal* the same number of captive knights is given, thirty-two, as it mentions of knights taken in Eustace's ship.[138] Who these were the marshal's biographer does not state further than we have noticed above with reference

[130] *Chronica Maiora*, iii. 29.
[131] *Guillaume le Maréchal*, ll. 17473 ff. ; *Flores Historiarum*, iv. 29.
[132] *Histoire des Ducs de Normandie*, 202.
[133] *Annales Monastici*, ii. 288.   [134] *Louis VIII*, 167.
[135] *Guillaume le Maréchal*, l. 17507.
[136] *Patent Rolls*, 1216-25, 89 : ' Veniatis cum toto navigio vestro, tam nuper lucrato quam alio.'
[137] *Chronicon Anglicanum*, 185 ; *Chronica de Mailros*, 128 (cf. *Chronicon de Lanercost*, 24).   [138] ll. 17458, 17572.

to that ship's company. The Annals of Waverley report that 'ten magnates with many nobles of France were captured'.[139] In the *Histoire des Ducs de Normandie* four are named: Robert de Courtenay, William des Barris, Raoul de la Tourniele, and Nevelos d'Arras;[140] in the Melrose chronicle, besides these four, eight additional names are given.[141] These knights were at once taken to Sandwich and put into safekeeping, thence to be conducted to Dover and entrusted to the care of Hubert de Burgh. In a few days Robert de Courtenay was given leave to go to London to advise with Louis about the peace, which was concluded on 11 September.[142] The spoils taken were considerable. On the next day after the battle the marshal, in a grateful message to the barons of the Cinque Ports, appointed two of them 'to see that all your people, who lately despoiled our enemies upon the sea, shall have thence what they ought to have'.[143] The detailed description of the booty in *Guillaume le Maréchal* is very life-like.[144]

The victory led to immediate peace, and completed the ruin of the cause of Louis, already disastrously affected by the battle of Lincoln. The English, both of that and later generations, however, were impressed most of all with its importance as bringing to a close the career of Eustace the Monk. To them his overthrow and death was such an unlooked-for stroke of good fortune that it could be explained only as a special interposition of God. Accordingly round the historical occurrences connected with the battle of Sandwich and the life of Eustace grew up legends which vividly reflect the deep impression made by these events upon the English.

Walter of Hemingburgh, who died after 1313, followed by Knighton, who died about 1366, gives an account under 1217 of a certain tyrant of Spain, surnamed Monachus, who, after gathering much booty and subjugating many places, longed for the conquest of England, particularly upon hearing that it was ruled by a child. When he was still far off the coast, with a large fleet and an enormous equipment, the sailors of

[139] *Annales Monastici*, ii. 287–8.   [140] p. 202.
[141] *Chronica de Mailros*, 128; cf. the Annals of Worcester, *Annales Monastici*, iv. 409.
[142] *Guillaume le Maréchal*, ll. 17569–76; *Histoire des Ducs de Normandie*, 202.
[143] *Patent Rolls*, 1216–25, 88.
[144] We may quote in part the abbreviated paraphrase of the editor: 'After the battle our people returned to land bringing their booty which was very considerable. Sir Hubert had taken two ships. Some ships had made so great gain that the sailors distributed the cash in full porringers. The marshal ordered that the division should be made in a fashion to give entire satisfaction to the sailors. Then he decided that with the part reserved they should found a hospital in honour of Saint Bartholomew who on that day had given them the victory. The sailors carried out his orders and founded the famous establishment where are harboured and entertained God's poor:' iii. 247–8; for the text, ii, ll. 17501–68.

the ports learned of his approach and feared him by reason of the great evil that was reported of him. They said: 'If he lands he will devastate everything, for the country is not prepared and the king is distant. So we will take our life in our hands and meet him at sea; valour is not all, and aid will come to us from on high.' A volunteer was instructed to climb the mast of the tyrant's ship and cut down the sail with an axe so as to deprive the fleet of the guidance of its leading ship. God gave the enemy into their hands, and after many were drowned and killed they returned with joy bearing great booty. So the youthful king was saved.[145]

In this narrative one notices especially the entire absence of any mention of Louis: the central figure is Eustace, who is overcome only with divine assistance. A still more startling variation appears in another chronicle of about the same date, c. 1313, the *Polistorie de Jean de Cantorbéry*.[146] In this account we are told that in the year 1217, on the day of Saint Bartholomew the Apostle, there came toward Sandwich with a great fleet a monk named Eustace, accompanied with many great lords who hoped to possess the land, and with that idea brought their wives and even children in the cradle. They trusted rather to their leader's knowledge of magic than to their own might. Upon their entering the harbour of Sandwich their numerous ships could all be seen except that of the leader, which was invisible. The people of Sandwich despaired of resistance except by God's help, and to that intent prayed to Him that out of love for Saint Bartholomew, whose day it was, He would save them. They also vowed a chapel with a perpetual chantry in honour of the saint if he would secure the victory for them. ' At that time there was in the town a man named Stephen Crabbe who had previously been very intimate with the monk surnamed Eustace.' Out of love for Stephen, Eustace had taught him much magic. Crabbe heard the lamentations, and said to the chiefs of the commune that he would give his life to save the city the disgrace of allowing Eustace to enter England at that port. Stephen accordingly embarked in a vessel, and leaped aboard that of Eustace. Then he cut off Eustace's head, and at once every one could see the ship clearly which heretofore had been invisible. Stephen was killed. A great tempest blew off shore, harming no one on land, but causing the hostile ships to founder. Saint Bartholomew appeared in the air to the inhabitants at the time and assured them that they had nothing to fear.

---

[145] Hemingburgh, *Chronicon* (ed. H. C. Hamilton), i. 260–1; Knighton, *Chronicon* (ed. J. R. Lumby), i. 205–6.

[146] Cf. T. Duffus Hardy, *Descriptive Catalogue*, iii. 350–1; Meyer, *Guillaume le Maréchal*, iii. 247, 1; Petit-Dutaillis, *Louis VIII*, 168–9. This part is quoted in *Wistasse*, pp. xvii–xix.

The portion of the story which describes the plan of the lords to settle in England, for which purpose they had brought their wives and even their infants, and also the foundering of their fleet from the force of a great tempest, is simply a confusion in the legend of the battle of Sandwich with the attempted arrival of Hugh de Bove's party in England in the year 1215, so graphically described, even to the cradles, by Roger of Wendover.[147] Hugh de Bove had, moreover, been an old partner in deeds of daring with Eustace, being included in the number of proscribed persons whom the count of Boulogne had sworn to attempt to deliver to King Philip.[148] The substitution of Eustace for Hugh, and the confusion of the storm and the battle, explain much of the legend.

The rest of the account deals with Eustace's skill in magic, his death at the hands of Stephen Crabbe, and the religious element of divine aid and the appearance of Saint Bartholomew. The belief in the magic skill of Eustace was probably existent in his own day, and undoubtedly so by the time of the composition of the Romance of Eustace. Crabbe's true share in the death of Eustace we have previously considered; and this account is a natural variation with the addition of the magical element. The emphasis upon the miraculous element is explicable by a reference to the next paragraph of the text which now remains to be considered. It is entitled 'Concerning the Hospital of St. Bartholomew Founded Near Sandwich', and is as follows:

After the people of Sandwich had thus secured the victory over Eustace and their enemies, they bought, at the expense of the commune, a site not far from the town and had built there a chapel dedicated to St. Bartholomew. They erected houses near by for the aged of both sexes of the town who might chance to fall into poverty, and they bought some lands and rents for the hospital to support for ever the aged poor who should dwell there, and to support devoutly the chantry. Moreover they ordained among themselves, that every year on the day of St. Bartholomew the commune should meet in the city of Sandwich and make a solemn procession to the aforesaid hospital with tapers in their hands.

The reader will recall the contemporary extract given above from *Guillaume le Maréchal*, where is recorded the determination of the marshal to found such a hospital from the remainder of the spoils, and also the obedience of the sailors to this wish. Even the marshal believed that Saint Bartholomew had secured them the victory.[149] So the legend stands out not only as an evidence of the faith of after generations in the miraculous aid at the battle of Sandwich, but as a record of the belief most sincerely

[147] *Flores Historiarum*, iii. 332–3; cf. *Chronica de Mailros*, 119–20.
[148] See p. 652, n. 23.
[149] Page 667, n. 144 above; compare also especially ii, ll. 17527–40, and iii. 248, n. 2.

held by contemporaries. The Hospital of Saint Bartholomew, concerning the circumstances of whose foundation there can be no doubt, still exists in its original location, faithfully performing the functions assigned to it almost seven centuries ago. Its custumal, dating from 1301, agrees in important particulars with the account given above from the *Polistorie*.[150] The hospital itself stands a silent witness of the faith of its founders and of the deep impression made upon them by the signal victory.

HENRY LEWIN CANNON.

[150] The custumal is to be found in William Boys, *Collections for an History of Sandwich in Kent* (Canterbury, 1792); the date is discussed on p. v. The seal of the hospital, attached to a deed of 1225, mentioned in Boys, 114, can no longer be found 'in the archives of the cathedral church of Canterbury', but the seal of 1317 is extant.

German Opinion of the Divorce of Henry VIII

THE divorce of Henry VIII and Catharine of Aragon has long been regarded as one of the turning-points in English history. Shakespeare and Thomas Gray, in attributing to Anne Boleyn the introduction of Lutheran ideas into England, did but express the view which until comparatively recent times has generally obtained. Although far less weight than formerly is now attributed to the personal action of the king, yet the connexion of the divorce with the Reformation is still sufficiently obvious to make the study of this curious affair, with its strange mixture of private and public considerations, of conscience, policy, and lust, instructive in the highest degree. So much minute research has been devoted to the subject during the past generation, that it may seem singular that one side of it, namely the connexion with it of the leading theologians of Germany, has been almost entirely overlooked. The fullest account of the negotiations with these men, and of their attitude, is still to be found in Bishop Burnet's *History*, written two centuries ago, but owing to the publication since then of many new materials this account is no longer adequate. In a previous paper I narrated the story of Luther's attitude towards the divorce;[1] in the present one I propose to do the same for some of Luther's contemporaries. The study casts light on both English and German history; it shows that Henry's government was far more persistent than is usually supposed in getting from the protestants a favourable opinion which might serve as a basis for alliance, and at the same time brings out the interesting ideas of the reformers on the questions of divorce and polygamy.

Erasmus was one of the first on whom the coming event cast its shadow. He had been presented to Henry, when the latter was a mere boy, in 1499;[2] ten years later he had hailed his accession to the throne with joy,[3] and during his long stay in

[1] *Ante*, xxv. 656 f.
[2] P. S. Allen, *Opus Epistolarum Erasmi* (Oxford, 1906), i. 239.
[3] *Ibid.* pp. 449 f. Erasmus left Italy for England on the expectation of receiving promotion from Henry, anticipated by Warham and Mountjoy.

England from 1509–14 he had been graciously received at court, and had, indeed, made so favourable an impression on Queen Catharine that she asked him to give her lessons, a duty from which he begged to be excused.[4] In 1514 it was first rumoured that Henry intended to obtain a divorce,[5] but the birth of the Princess Mary (1516), by giving the king hope of further issue, postponed the execution of the plan for many years. In view of later events it does not seem unreasonable to assume that the queen continued to be anxious about her position, and that, in the endeavour to strengthen it, she requested two eminent authorities, Erasmus and another Burgundian subject of her nephew Charles V, to write on the topic of marriage. Vives published his work, *De Femina Christiana*,[6] dedicated to Catharine, in 1523, but said little about divorce. In the following year accordingly, the queen, through her chamberlain, Lord Mountjoy, asked Erasmus to write her a book on marriage. Erasmus complied, and published in 1526 *The Institution of Christian Matrimony*,[7] in which he so thoroughly examines the question of divorce as to make us suspect that his opinion was particularly solicited on this point. After remarking how inauspicious the dissolution of marriage has been considered even by those nations which allow it, and expatiating on the solemn and binding character of the contract,[8] the writer proceeds to consider the impediments, some of which suffice to render any union void, some of which can break a marriage contract, but not one which has been consummated.[9] Union with a brother's widow is expressly stated to be an insufficient cause for nullification,[10] and the value of a papal dispensation is considered, with the conclusion that it is valid in some cases but not in all. In general

[4] *Ibid.* p. 569. [5] *Calendar of State Papers, Venetian*, 1509–19, no. 479.

[6] Vivis *Opera* (Valentia, 1798), vol. vi. We do not know that Vives was requested to write this work by the queen, but the example of Erasmus and the fact that Vives was later accused of giving Catharine advice on the divorce make us suspect it: *Letters and Papers of Henry VIII*, iv. ii. 4990, November 1528. Martin Hume, *The Wives of Henry VIII*, p. 142, says that the queen applied to Vives and Erasmus, but his references are all wrong, as well as his conclusion: ' *Epistles* in stilted Latin *was* all she got from either.' In 1531 the imperial ambassador at London, Eustache Chapuys, made several efforts to secure an opinion favourable to the queen from Cornelius Agrippa of Nettesheim. Agrippae *Opera* (Lugduni, *s.a.*), ii. 973 f., 989, 996. The conjecture of A. Prost (*Agrippa de Nettesheim*, 1881, ii. 262) that Henry VIII approached Agrippa in 1529 for an opinion is untenable. The scholar declined to write on the subject.

[7] *Matrimonii Christiani Institutio, Opera* (Leyden, 1703), v. 613 f. Erasmus appears to have known Vives's work, which he followed in advising that girls be forbidden to read romances. In the dedicatory epistle to the queen, 15 July 1526 (*Epistolae*, London, 1642, xxix. 40), he says that he promised the work to Mountjoy more than two years before. On the other hand, in a letter to Piso, 9 September 1526 (*ibid.* xxi. 65), he says the queen had asked for the book a year ago. See also his letter to Beda, 10 June 1525, *ibid.* xix. 91.

[8] *Opera*, v. 618 f.   [9] *Ibid.* 633 f.   [10] *Ibid.* 639.

the writer may be said to take a well-balanced view, inclining slightly to the side of his patroness. The queen was too much preoccupied to acknowledge the work at once, but after a gentle reminder from him [11] she directed Mountjoy to write expressing her pleasure and thanks [12] and sending a gift.[13]

By this time the plan for a divorce was well known. Erasmus received information of the rumoured separation of ' Jupiter and Juno ' from John Crucius Berganus, who visited England in 1527, but did not think it safe to write until he had reached Louvain in the following January.[14] On 2 September Erasmus wrote to his friend Vives at London : ' Far be it from me to mix in the affair of Jupiter and Juno, especially as I know little about it. But I should prefer that he should take two Junos rather than put away one.' [15] In thus declaring a preference for bigamy to divorce Erasmus expressed an opinion which, strange as it may seem to us, was very widespread at this time. Henry himself at one time suggested it as a possibility.[16] The pope had recently allowed the king of Castile to take two wives.[17] Clement VII at one time proposed this solution of the difficulty to the English ambassador.[18] The distinguished catholic theologian Cajetan judged that polygamy was not against natural law, and was not forbidden in the Bible, and that the pope might grant dispensation for it to avoid a greater evil.[19] Luther, too, had already in his *Babylonian Captivity of the Church* affirmed that bigamy was a lesser evil than divorce,[20] and in his reply to this work Henry VIII (or his assistants) did not contradict the assertion.[21] Sir Thomas More, however, was shocked by it, and severely censured it in his *Responsio ad Lutherum*, published under the pseudonym of William Ross.[22] Erasmus knew both the *Babylonian Captivity* and More's reply (though he was not aware that this was by his friend). He was repelled by the violence of both parties, and thought that if anything the Englishman was in this respect the worse.[23]

[11] 1 March 1528, *Epistolae*, xix. 69.
[12] 1 May (1528), Förstemann-Günther, *Briefe an Desiderius Erasmus* (1904), no. 66, wrongly dated 1527.
[13] 2 September 1528, *Epistolae*, xx. 87.
[14] Enthoven, *Briefe an Desiderius Erasmus* (1906), no. 12, wrongly placed in 1522. The true date, 28 January 1528, is given by Vocht, *Englische Studien*, 1909, p. 386.
[15] *Epistolae*, xx. 87. Vives replied on 1 October, ' Iupiter et Iuno utinam aliquando litent non priscae illi Veneri sed Christo verticordio ' : *Opera*, vii. 192.
[16] Pollard, *Henry VIII* (London, 1905), p. 206.
[17] *Calendar of State Papers, Spanish*, ii. 379. [18] Pollard, p. 207.
[19] W. W. Rockwell, *Die Doppelehe des Landgrafen Philipp von Hessen* (Marburg, 1904), pp. 304 f.
[20] In 1520 : *Luthers Werke* (Weimar), vi. 559.
[21] *Ante*, xxv. 659. [22] *Mori Opera* (1689), p. 145.
[23] Erasmi *Opera* (1703), x. 1652. Erasmus says that those who write against Luther are ' apud Anglos Rex ipse, Iohannes Episcopus Roffensis, et tertius quidam

When, in 1529, Henry found he could not get the desired dispensation from the pope, he began to collect the opinions of universities and learned men to support him in summarily repudiating Catharine. It is not certain that he applied to Erasmus, but one of the latter's epistles, to his intimate friend Boniface Amorbach, written early in 1530, certainly makes it appear that this was the case.[24] Erasmus tells his friend that the king says he had not taken Catharine from love, and that he (Erasmus) advises him to marry his daughter to a noble and make her son his heir. Yet he asks whether, as so much bloodshed would result from a disputed succession, a dispensation might not be given, though this would be hard on the queen. Amorbach replied on 28 February 1530[25] that the question involved was one for jurists, and that the pope had power of dispensation for divorce only in extreme cases. It was not certain that a second marriage would produce an heir. Amorbach adds: 'If I were a Lutheran I should add that a new wife might be taken without putting away the old one, for polygamy was practised by the patriarchs and Luther teaches that it is not forbidden by the New Testament.'[26]

About a year later Erasmus's opinion was solicited by the party opposed to Henry, two nobles from the imperial court acting as agents. Apparently he tried to avoid giving them a direct answer, and thus a rumour arose that he was favourable to the divorce.[27] His position was indeed a delicate one. His horror of war, and his belief that a disputed succession would be followed by this calamity, naturally led him to regard a second marriage as desirable; at the same time as a subject of the emperor he felt unwilling to take a decided part against his sovereign's aunt.[28] We thus find his expressions on the subject somewhat contradictory. To Damian a Goes he gave the impression that he was against the divorce;[29] to another friend he wrote that he thought the king justified in it as he had obtained the approval of so many doctors.[30] To a third he wrote in November 1533, that he had heard the king had taken back the queen, and,

tam amarulentus ut ipsi Luthero possit medium unguem ostendere'. This can only refer to More, who was indeed every whit as violent as Luther. There is nothing worse in all Luther's works than the passage in More's *Responsio* found in his *Opera*, p. 38.

[24] Erasmi *Epistolae ad Bon. Amerbachium* (Basle, 1779), no. 11.

[25] Burckhardt-Biedermann, *Bon. Amerbach und die Reformation* (Basle, 1894), pp. 238 f.

[26] Luther's *Commentary on Genesis* (1523), *Werke* (Weimar), xiv. 250 f., 171.

[27] Damian a Goes to Erasmus, 20 June 1533, Förstemann-Günther, *op. cit.* no. 188; Erasmi *Epistolae*, xxvii. 19.

[28] Burnet says that Erasmus was secretly in favour of the divorce, but would not appear in it for fear of the emperor: *History of the Reformation*, ed. Pocock (Oxford, 1865), i. 160.

[29] Förstemann-Günther, *op. cit.* no. 188.

[30] To Viglius Zuichemus, 14 May 1533, Erasmi *Opera*, iii, appendix, ep. 372.

though he could not believe it, he hoped it was true.[31] His policy was evidently to keep as far as possible friends with all parties; when Anne Boleyn's star was in the ascendant Erasmus dedicated several works to her father, Lord Rochford.[32] The terrible history of the year 1535, with the execution of More and Fisher, changed Erasmus's feelings in the matter. In a poem attributed to him, written before he had heard of the death of Queen Catharine,[33] but first published afterwards, Henry is severely arraigned for tyranny and lust, and bidden to cast out his harlot and take back his legitimate wife. If these words are authentic, as is probably the case, they give us the last opinion of Erasmus on the repudiation of Catharine.[34] It is highly characteristic of the Dutch humanist that he approached the question almost entirely from the practical point of view. While in the *Institutio Matrimonii* he carefully examines the theological arguments in general, when the specific case is put before him the considerations which move him are, first, to avoid a civil war, and then to spare the feelings of all parties as much as possible, particularly those of the queen.

It is strikingly different with the other German theologians to whom Henry applied. They, though showing the influence of political, and especially of propagandist motives, are chiefly concerned to ground their decisions on a careful study of the Bible and the canon law. Henry began soliciting their opinions in 1531, and entrusted the business to several agents. One of them, William Paget, was accredited to Philip, landgrave of Hesse, with whom he had a conference at Rothenburg in September 1531.[35] Paget promised his master's support to the German protestants against the emperor, and particularly requested the advice of Philip's divines on the divorce. He so much impressed the landgrave that the latter wrote to Luther urging him for political reasons to give the answer that the king desired,[36] and at the same time submitted the proposition to his new university at Marburg. Their answer, dated on 12 October 1531, was forwarded to Henry, whose name, however, is not mentioned in the document. The rector and professors, with an independence surprising in view of their later obsequiousness in Philip's own

[31] To Olaus, secretary of Queen Mary of Hungary, *Monumenta Hungariae historica, Diplomataria*, xxv (Budapest, 1875), p. 424.
[32] The *Catechismus, Opera*, v. 1133 f., and the *Enarratio triplex in Psalmum XXII*, ibid. 1294 f. Several letters that passed between them are extant.
[33] On 6 January 1536. Chapuys wrote to Erasmus a full account of the queen's decease on 1 February 1536, Enthoven, *op. cit.* no. 145.
[34] *Incomparabilis . . . D. Erasmi . . . in sanctissimorum martyrum Rofensis Episcopi ac Th. Mori . . . Heroicum Carmen.* Mense Septembre, MDXXXVI. (Colophon) Hagenau.
[35] F. Küch, *Politisches Archiv des Landgrafen Philipp von Hessen* (Leipzig, 1911), ii. 452.
[36] *Ante*, xxv. 665.

case, advised against divorce, and said nothing about bigamy.[37] Thomas Cranmer, who was ambassador to the emperor at Ratisbon in 1532, also busied himself to collect opinions on the divorce. He induced Andrew Osiander, a very prominent Lutheran pastor at Nuremberg whom he visited and whose niece he married, to declare in favour of the king. Osiander had previously stated that he considered union with a brother's widow lawful;[38] but now he changed his opinion on this point, and wrote a book, *De incestuoso Matrimonio*, which was suppressed by the Nuremberg town council out of respect to the emperor.[39]

But Henry's principal agent in Germany was Simon Grynaeus, a learned Greek scholar, who had taught at Heidelberg from 1524 to 1529 and had then been called by Oecolampadius to Basle with some idea of filling the vacancy caused by Erasmus's recent removal to Freiburg.[40] In the early summer of 1531 he made a journey to London to consult some manuscripts, taking with him introductions from Erasmus to some of his friends, apparently including More and Tunstall.[41] Though the impression he made on these persons, owing to his warm defence of Zwingli, was far from favourable, they brought him to the notice of the king, who caused him to meet three or four doctors to argue the question of the divorce, and requested him, armed with their reasons, to collect the judgements of his leading countrymen on the subject, and at the same time gave him a sum of money for his services.[42] Immediately after his consultation with the doctors he returned to the continent, and arrived by 12 June at Ghent, where he had an interview with Vives[43] who had already written in favour of the king.[44] Coming to Basle shortly afterwards he at once set about his task.

He apparently did not write to Luther (who was approached from another quarter), perhaps thinking that his quarrel with

[37] Marburg Archives, England, 1531–45, under date, kindly communicated to me by my friend Professor W. W. Rockwell. It may be interesting to note here that Tindale's *Practice of Prelates; whether the King's Grace may be separated from the Queen*, 1530, purporting to be printed by Hans Luft at Marburg, was not really printed at Marburg at all. Mr. Robert Steele, in a recent article in *The Library* (April 1911), thinks that the 'Marburg' books of Hans Luft were printed at Antwerp. But there is evidence that three of them at least were printed at Cologne: see my article in the (New York) *Nation*, 16 May 1912.

[38] In 1528: G. Kawerau, *De Digamia Episcoporum* (Kiel, 1889), p. 51.

[39] W. Möller, *A. Osiander*, pp. 154 f.; Pocock, *Records of the Reformation*, ii. 483 f.; W. W. Rockwell, *op. cit.* p. 220.

[40] *Realencyklopädie für protestantische Theologie* (3rd edition), vii. 218. I am not aware that Erasmus ever taught at the university of Basle.

[41] Erasmi *Opera*, iii, appendix, ep. 374.

[42] Chapuys to Charles V, 6 June 1531, *Letters and Papers*, v, no. 287; cf. *Calendar of Spanish Papers*, 1531–3, ii. 177.

[43] Vives to Erasmus: Vivis *Opera*, vii. 194.

[44] Vives to Henry VIII, Bruges, 13 January 1531, *ibid.* p. 134.

Henry would render him disinclined to interfere in the matter. He applied instead to Melanchthon in July,[45] and asked for an opinion which was drawn up by the latter with great care on 23 August.[46] The Wittenberg professor begins by investigating the nature of the commands given by God in the Bible, some of them being laws of nature, which may never be transgressed under any circumstances, and some of them merely positive commands which have been either abrogated by the new dispensation or may be dispensed with for good cause by the church. The marriage with a brother's widow is clearly, he holds, of the second class, whereas divorce, save for adultery, belongs to the former. The English king is therefore unable to repudiate his wife, and Melanchthon thinks that he would naturally prefer not to do so simply to spare her and their daughter the consequent disgrace. He then considers the public welfare and the necessity of securing the succession. His method of finding a solution for this problem, consistent with his former propositions, would be, to one who was not in some degree prepared for it, equally ingenious and startling : ' It may be done without any peril to the conscience or reputation of any one by polygamy.' He hastens to add that he would not concede this to every one, but as the examples of the patriarchs show that it was not forbidden by the law of nature, he thinks it may be practised in certain circumstances. It is impossible to be sure whether this document ever reached London.[47] The Saxons, however, entertained some expectation that Henry would follow the advice to take a second wife.[48]

The plan did not recommend itself to the English king, who sent several other embassies to Wittenberg to get a positive approval of the divorce. The most important of these missions was that of Edward Fox, bishop of Hereford, and Nicholas Heath, archdeacon of Stafford, who arrived at Wittenberg in December 1535, and negotiated with the reformers for four months.[49] On the way they stopped in November at Strassburg, where they discussed the divorce with Bucer, though without any definite

[45] *Corpus Reformatorum*, ii. 515.
[46] Two forms of this document are extant, *Corpus Reformatorum*, ii. 520 f. and *Theologische Studien und Kritiken*, lviii (1885), 728 f. (from a manuscript copy by Bugenhagen). I have investigated the letters and works of the Wittenbergers Bugenhagen and Jonas without finding anything relative to the divorce.
[47] It is not mentioned by Grynaeus among the other letters he sent, nor by Burnet, who had before him manuscripts of letters which had reached England. It is also surprising to note that in a letter of Melanchthon to Grynaeus, August 1531 (*Corpus Reformatorum*, ii. 530 f.), no allusion is made to it or to the question in general. On the other hand it may have been taken to Henry by Barnes.
[48] George Spalatin, the chaplain of Frederick the Wise, wrote to Hans von Dolzig in February 1532, that it was still doubtful whether Henry would do so : *Zeitschrift für Kirchengeschichte*, xix. 499.   [49] *Ante*, xxv. 668.

result, as the latter stated it to be the only point of controversy left between them.[50] The English divines were commissioned to treat 'as well in the king's great cause of matrimony as in other causes pertaining to the wealth of this realm'.[51] They discharged their task with thoroughness; the progress of their disputations on the theological points is in great part known to us,[52] as well as the result, a series of articles which had some direct influence on the formation of English theology.[53] Here again the divorce proved the hardest problem for solution. The opinion of the Wittenbergers, drafted by Melanchthon, shows some modification of their previous views, which was apparently due not so much to the arguments of the Englishmen as to those of Osiander.[54] The Saxons have now [55] come to believe that the union with a brother's widow is forbidden by divine law, but as they think divorce is also forbidden by it they beg the king to allow them to express no decision on so intricate a case. That the real opinion of the theologians was still against the validity of the marriage of Anne Boleyn may be gathered from a letter of John Frederick, elector of Saxony, dated 9 August 1536, in which that marriage is condemned and is stated to be the reason why alliance with England is impossible.[56]

In the meantime Grynaeus had solicited, obtained, and forwarded to London the opinions of a number of the Swiss and South German reformers. Zwingli's opinion was given on 17 August 1531 [57] in a long letter. After full discussion of the pertinent biblical texts, he concludes that marriage with a brother's widow is forbidden by divine law, from which no pope can dispense, that therefore the king's marriage is null and void, and that the queen should be honourably put away. After seeing the contrary judgements of some of the other reformers he reasserted his own decision in a second letter of 1 September.[58] His opinion of polygamy is sufficiently shown by the fact that a citizen of Zürich was beheaded for this crime, doubtless with

[50] T. Schiess, *Briefwechsel der Blaurer* (1908, 1909), i. 760, ii. 823.
[51] Cromwell to Cranmer, 5 January 1535: R. B. Merriman, *Life and Letters of Thomas Cromwell*, i. 372.
[52] P. Drews, *Disputationen Dr. Martin Luthers* (Göttingen, 1895). The English embassy is stated to have been present at the debate on private masses, 29 January 1536, p. 69; and it is probable that they were also present at the debate on justification, 14 January, p. 33, and perhaps at others.
[53] First published by Professor G. Mentz under the title *Die Wittenberger Artikel von 1536*, Leipzig, 1905; cf. J. Gairdner, *Lollardy and the Reformation*, ii. 316 f.
[54] Rockwell, *op. cit.* 220.
[55] *Corpus Reformatorum*, ii. 527, wrongly placed under the year 1531; the mention of Fox and Heath gives the true date, 1536 to which it was assigned by Seckendorf, following Burnet.
[56] G. Mentz, *Johann Friedrich*, iii. 354 (Jena, 1909).
[57] His letter is not now in print. Burnet summarizes it, *op. cit.* i. 160 f.
[58] Burnet, *l. c.*

Zwingli's approval, on 30 April 1527.[59] Grynaeus was pleased with his answer.[60] Oecolampadius agreed with Zwingli, by whom he was apparently influenced. On 18 July he wrote to Bucer asking him to forward the documents in the case.[61] On 13 August he sent a full account of the affair to Zwingli, requesting his advice.[62] He stated that as Henry had been deceived by the pope and badly treated by Luther he was now turning to them, and he hoped that for political reasons such an answer as the king wished might be given him, though he would not do anything wrong. He enlarged on the king's sufferings of conscience and the decisions of the universities, and quoted the Old Testament passages in his favour. A week afterwards he had received his friend's answer and replied that he agreed exactly with it, and hoped that Bucer and Capito, though they were conceited in their own ideas, would accept it.[63] He blamed them severely for suggesting bigamy as a possible solution, adding: 'God forbid that in this we should obey Mohammed rather than Christ.' He accordingly stated his conclusion, to the effect that the marriage was null, in two letters to Grynaeus.[64] With Zwingli and Oecolampadius sided Paul Phrygio.[65]

The group of reformers of Strassburg, Wolfgang Capito,[66] Martin Bucer, Kaspar Hedio,[67] and Matthew Zell,[68] were of an opinion more nearly approaching that of the Wittenbergers, namely that divorce was a worse evil than marriage with a brother's widow, and that the most practical solution of the problem would be polygamy. Bucer was at great pains to form an opinion, getting all the documents and advice in the case

[59] E. Egli, *Aktensammlung zur Zürcher Reformation*, 1879, no. 1174. Again in May 1533 (after Zwingli's death) a man thought better to plead guilty to adultery than to bigamy, *ibid.* no. 1941.

[60] Zwingli's *Werke*, ed. Schuler und Schulthess, viii. 635.

[61] Oecolampadii et Zwinglii *Epistolarum libri quatuor*, Basle, 1536, p. 94.

[62] Zwingli's *Werke*, ed. Schuler und Schulthess, viii. 631.

[63] Zwingli's *Werke*, viii. 634.

[64] Burnet, *l. c.*, dates these letters 10 and 31 August, but the facts given above would suggest that the first letter was of a later date.

[65] Burnet, *l. c.* Phrygio's real name was Seidenstecker; he was born at Constance and after his conversion to the reformed church, about 1524, occupied various positions as pastor and professor at Schlettstadt, Basle, and Tübingen, until his death in 1543: Baum, *Capito und Butzer* (1860), p. 268. His death is mentioned in a letter from Hedio to Myconius, 25 September 1543, printed in K. und W. Krafft, *Briefe und Documente aus der Reformationszeit*, p. 92.

[66] Baum, *Capito und Butzer*, gives the lives of these reformers, but says nothing of their connexion with this case, or of that of Bucer with the landgrave's bigamy. His strongly protestant bias probably led him to avoid mention of unedifying facts which he must have known. The same must be said of Bishop Burnet, who merely mentions that Bucer was of 'another opinion', though without saying what it was.

[67] See his life in the *Realencyklopädie für protestantische Theologie*, s.v.

[68] F. Unselt, *Mathieu Zell, le premier Réformateur de Strasbourg*, 1854.

possible, and even writing to Melanchthon.[69] He was particularly anxious to ascertain the king's motives ; he asked for a description of the king and of Anne Boleyn from Grynaeus, and wished to know whether they had yet any children ;[70] and he wrote to one of his most intimate friends that some said that the king was moved by scruples of conscience, but others that he was only tired of his present wife and in love with the girl he wanted to marry.[71] He was so much exercised by the fear that a breach with the Swiss would result from his persisting in his first opinion, that he finally decided to send in no official statement whatever, and informed Zwingli that he would do nothing to oppose his view of the case.[72] In 1534 we find him blaming Henry for his marriage with Anne.[73] The other Strassburg divines were less pliant ; Hedio slightly modified his opinion, but Capito and Zell refused to change theirs,[74] and three years later Capito wrote a book on the subject, dedicated to the king, who sent him in return one hundred and twenty crowns.

Grynaeus copied in a book all the letters he had collected, and sent them with a summary to Henry VIII.[75] There is no extant account of their reception, but it is probable that their influence was felt in several ways. The opinion of Zwingli, Oecolampadius, and Phrygio, that his first marriage was null, was exactly what Henry wanted, and may have led him to look more favourably on the Reformation, while at the same time it made the names of those men odious to Sir Thomas More.[76] The alternative of bigamy met with no acceptance in Henry's mind, as it did later in that of Philip of Hesse. The reason for this is to be found neither in Henry's superior morality, nor in the opposition of

[69] See Melanchthon's answer, 8 November 1531, *Corpus Reformatorum*, ii. 552.

[70] *Original Letters*, Parker Society (Cambridge, 1846–7), ep. cclv.

[71] Schiess, *Briefwechsel der Blaurer*, i. 268; cf. 278.

[72] Zwingli's *Werke*, ed. Schuler und Schulthess, viii. 644. On Bucer's opinion, see *ibid.* 635. That Bucer sent in no statement to Grynaeus may be inferred by the absence of his name in the list of letters given by Grynaeus, *Original Letters, loc. cit.*, and by the assertion of Burnet, *l. c.*

[73] Schiess, *op. cit.* p. 460.

[74] *Original Letters, l. c.* The book was *Responsio de missa, matrimonio et iure magistratus in religione*. D. Wolfgango Capitone autore. Strassburg, 1537. The dedicatory epistle is dated 9 March. A second edition, revised by the author, appeared in 1540. The honorarium is mentioned in T. W. Röhrich, *Geschichte der Reformation im Elsass*, 1832, ii. 171.

[75] *Original Letters*, no. cclvii, dated conjecturally 10 September 1531.

[76] 'Zwingle and Frere Husgen' (Oecolampadius being the Greek for Hausschein) are often mentioned with detestation by More, though he does not refer to this episode. Burnet states that there was a letter from Calvin on the subject. This is certainly a mistake, as Calvin was only twenty-two at the time and there is no such letter extant. In various places in his works he condemns polygamy (*Corpus Reformatorum*, li. 51, lv. 666 f.), and especially for kings (*ibid.* xxxviii, part ii, 257 f. (1538), lv. 474 f. (1555)). He also speaks severely of Henry VIII (*ibid.* lxx. 208, lxxi. 134).

men like More and Cranmer,[77] but chiefly in the different situation of the two princes. Philip of Hesse already had heirs and did not desire to supplant them. His one motive was the reconciliation of a libertine passion with the scruples of a sensitive, if abnormal, conscience. His second marriage was only, in fact, as Bucer put it,[78] ' a holy, useful remedy for lust,' though unfortunately an ineffective one.[79] Henry's principal motive was to secure the succession; and whatever may have been considered the biblical doctrine of marriage, it was clear that in civil law polygamy was a crime, and that, being without precedent, the children of such a marriage would undoubtedly have been considered illegitimate.

PRESERVED SMITH.

[77] *Cranmer's Works*, ed. Parker Society, ii. 25 f., 329; Pollard, *Cranmer*, 121. On More, see above, p. 673.
[78] Rockwell, *op. cit.* p. 277.   [79] H. Grisar, *Luther* (1911), ii. 427 f.

Inner and Outer Cabinet and Privy Council, 1679-1783

THE true history of policy in the eighteenth century can never be written without a correct understanding of the machinery of the central executive. The working of this machinery is still somewhat of a mystery, though much light has of late been thrown upon the constitution of committees and of the privy council in the early part of the reign of Charles II. This problem will be here treated mainly in the period from William III to George II, based on the evidence from the materials at the Record Office, in the Privy Council Office, and in the British Museum.

THE KING'S RELATIONS TO THE EXECUTIVE

It is evident that the reign of William III forms a decisive turning-point in the development of the executive. The old theory of government appears to have been that the king directed the executive on the advice of his council. The theory of Clarendon was that the king was constitutionally bound to abide by the advice of his privy council.[1] But, as experience showed, this theory was difficult of realization. The king, as supreme executive officer, held that he should control his own council; no Stuart ever willingly submitted to its sway, and each employed different expedients to evade it. They refused to summon the privy council as a whole, or they formed different committees of the council and thereby divided the councillors. Moreover—and herein lies an important point—the king had unquestionably the power of taking executive measures, either on the advice of a single minister or of a few secret councillors.[2] So long as this power might be put into practice the restraint exercised by the privy

---

[1] See Mr. E. I. Carlyle's article, *ante*, xxvii. 251 *seqq*.

[2] Even as late as the 2 October 1761 this doctrine could still be asserted by Lord Granville, who said in the cabinet to Pitt, 'He [Pitt] knew very well that the King might take a foreign measure with his Secretary of State only, but that if the King referred the matter to the Council, the opinion of the majority of the Council was the measure': British Museum, Additional MS. 32929, fo. 18, quoted by Winstanley, *ante*, xvii. (1902) 691.

council could be but slight. Charles II was unwilling to surrender the power, and, though a determined effort was made in 1679 to subject him to the privy council, James II used the same secret powers to emancipate himself from its control. It was natural that, under William III, there should be a renewed attempt to regain power for the council, or at least for some representative part of it. All Englishmen saw that the executive acts of a foreigner needed control. William's taste and temper were often arbitrary, but he was willing to make some concession, and to allow committees of the privy council to deal with matters of routine and with internal affairs. He even went further and maintained a sort of cabinet council throughout his reign. But he remained extremely jealous of the ministers as a whole exercising any control in foreign affairs. In reality he was his own secretary of state, and Somers was forced to affix the great seal to treaties in blank at the dictation of his imperious master. In taking this step William undoubtedly went too far, and the impeachment of Somers was a sharp lesson both to prince and to minister. The result was that the hostile critics in the commons inserted a provision in the act of settlement binding ministers to sign acts of which they approved, and thus forcing each minister to be individually responsible for his advice.[3] This provision was repealed in 1705 as unworkable in practice. The sovereign still therefore remained master of the situation. He could take measures on the advice and with the signature of a single minister. He could choose and dismiss his own ministers, he could set one minister against another, and in the last resort could overrule his whole council in all executive measures. The theory and traces of the practice remained to the end of the reign of George II. But in reality the sovereign found it first convenient, and then necessary, to submit to the dictation of his ministers, not as embodied in the form of a privy council, not usually even as embodied in the outer cabinet council, but as seen in the inner cabinet or *conciliabulum*. The men who formed this last body were the real governors of England in the first two Hanoverian reigns.

The decline of the power of the sovereign can perhaps best be traced by sketching the decline of the privy council, in the development of the outer cabinet, and of the *conciliabulum*. It will be seen that each body developed out of the failure of its predecessor; under Charles II the privy council is

---

[3] 'All Matters and Things relating to the well governing of this Kingdom which are properly cognizable in the Privy Council by the Laws and Customs of this Realm shall be transacted there and all Resolutions taken thereupon shall be signed by such of the Privy Council as shall advise and consent to the same.' (Repealed by 4 & 5 Anne, c. 20, § 27.)

still attempting to govern; under James II and William III the cabinet supersedes it; under Anne and the first two Georges the cabinet becomes formal and makes way for the committee or *conciliabulum*.

THE PRIVY COUNCIL

Both the beginning and the end of the reign of Charles II exhibit some real attempt to govern with the privy council as an effective organ of the state. The history of the first failure, largely due to the increase of numbers,[4] is admirably summed up by Charles himself when, on 21 April 1679, he resolved to try a second experiment in reorganizing the council on Temple's lines, and addressed his existing privy council as follows :[5]

His Ma^{ty} gives You all thanks for Your Service to Him here, and for all the Good Advices You have given him, wch might have been more frequent, If the great Number of this Councill had not made it unfit for the Secrecy & dispatch that are necessary in many great Affaires. This forced Him to use a smaller Number of you in a forreigne Committee, and sometimes the Advices of some few among them (upon such occasions) for many yeares past. Hee is sorry for the ill success He has found in this Course, and sensible of the ill posture of affaires from that, and, some unhappy accidents wch have raised great jealousyes and dissatisfaction among His Good Subjects & thereby left the Crowne & Government in a Condition too weake for those Dangers we have reason to feare both at home & abroad.

These His Ma^{ty} hopes may be yet prevented by a Course of wise & steady Councells for the future. . . . To this End Hee hath resolved to lay aside the Use he may have hitherto made of any Single Ministry or private advices, or forreigne Committees for the general direction of His affaires, and to constitute such a Privy Councell, as may not only by its Number be fit for the Consultation and Digestion of all business both Domestique & forreigne but also by the choise of them out of the Severall parts this State is composed of, may be the best informed in the true Constitutions of it, And thereby the most able to Councell him in all the Affaires and Interests of this Crowne & Nation, And by the Constant advice of such a Councell, His Ma^{ty} is resolved hereafter to govern His Kingdomes, together with the frequent Use of his great Councill of Parliament, wch he takes to be the true ancient Constitution of this State & Government.

Now for the greater dignity of this Councill His Ma^{ty} resolves their Constant Number shall be limited to that of Thirty, and for their greater authority there shall be fifteeen of His chief Officers, who shall be Privy Councellours by their places, and for the other fifteen Hee will choose

---

[4] In the Privy Council Register, Charles II, vol. i, 1 June 1662, the list of the privy council is thirty-six; in vol. xi, April 1673, it is fifty-one; in vol. xii, 1675, it is fifty. The numbers are approximate, as several names appear to have been added at later dates.

[5] Privy Council Register, Charles II, xv, 21 April 1679, 1.

ten out of the Severall Ranks of the Nobility, and five Commoners of the Realme, whose knowne Abilityes Interest & Esteeme in the Nation, shall render them without any suspition of either mistakeing or betraying the true Interests of the Kingdome and consequently of advising Him ill.

In the first place therefore and to take care of the Church His Ma^{ty} will have the Archbishop of Canterbury, and Bishop of London for the time being ; and to Informe Him well in what concernes the Lawes, the Lord Chancellour, and one of the Lord Chief Justices : for the Navy & Stores (wherein consists the chiefe strength and safety of this Kingdom) the Admirall & Master of the Ordnance : For the Treasury the Treasurer & Chancellour of the Exchequer (or, whenever any of these charges are in Commission, then the first Com^r to serve in their roome), the rest of the fifteen shall be the Lord Privy Seale, the M^r of the Horse, Lord`Steward, and Lord Chamberlain of His Household, the Groome of the Stole, and the two Secretaryes of State. And these shall be all the Offices of his Kingdome, to wch the Dignity of a Privy Councellor shall be annexed. The other (15) His Ma^{ty} has resolved, and hopes he has not chosen ill. His Ma^{ty} intends besides to have such Princes of His Blood as he shall at any time call to this Board, being here in Court, a President of the Councill whenever he shall find it necessary, and the Secretary of Scotland, when any suit shall be here. But these, being uncertain, Hee reckons not of the constant number of thirty wch shall never be exceeded.

. . . His Ma^{ty} was also pleased to declare that he would have all his affairs here debated freely, of what kind soever they were and therefore absolutely [in] secrecy.

His Ma^{ty} was also pleased to declare that he would communicate this alteration of the Councill unto both Houses of Parliament in a few words.[6]

The purpose of Charles is quite clear, he wished to confine the numbers of the privy council within due bounds, and to make it a working and effective body. Shaftesbury's opposition caused the scheme to fail, but until the end of his reign Charles never allowed the council to exceed thirty-five.[7] That the privy council remained something of a check on the king, even after the disgrace of Shaftesbury in October 1679, is clear from a letter of Leoline Jenkins on 5 October 1681.[8] On his accession in 1685 the arbitrary James at once made an end of these powers of the privy council, and effectively prevented it from becoming a real check on his government by raising its numbers to forty-nine.[9] Under William III the privy council included over sixty members, and was already too large for purposes of effective debate and control. Still, it was the only formal and legal executive council

---

[6] *Parl. Hist.* iv. 1122–3. The declaration, as given in the text, is from the Privy Council Register, Charles II, xv. 1. Cf. Temple, *Works* (ed. 1814), ii. 71 ; T. P. Courtenay, *Life of Sir W. Temple* (ed. 1836), ii. 34, 77 ; and Anson, *Law and Custom of the Constitution*, ed. 1907, II. i. 83.

[7] The Privy Council Register, Charles II, vol. xvi, June 1680, gives thirty-five ; vol. xvii, June 1683, thirty-four.   [8] See appendix, document iii, to be published hereafter.

[9] List in Privy Council Register, James II, vol. i, 18 February 1684/5.

and, as such, was not negligible. Halifax records on 14 February 1689: he (William) 'had a wrong notion of a Privy Councell; thought the Gov^t was to reside there.'[10] He was soon undeceived, but Southwell, the clerk to the council, records an effective debate in the privy council as late as 2 April 1695.[11] It appears, however, that steps were taken to stop such possibilities in future.

Under Anne, the formal character of the privy council increases. The number of the formal council rises to eighty, that of the actual attendants sinks below thirty. Even at the acceptance of the peace of Utrecht only twenty-eight councillors attended, almost all of them being the partisans of the ministry. It was only just before Anne's death that the privy council was roused to a last manifestation of its power. The Privy Council Register shows that, when the news of Anne's dangerous illness was made known, a meeting of twenty-three privy councillors assembled. Of these, two were the dukes of Argyll and Somerset, who are reported to have broken in upon the meeting unsummoned, pleading the greatness of the crisis and their rank as privy councillors. This account, based on the unproved contemporary rumour, would seem to show that the intruding dukes appeared at a cabinet of *conciliabulum*.[12] There is, however, no evidence of this fact, whilst the Privy Council Register shows that a privy council was held. Again there is no evidence that the two dukes were irregularly summoned. The duke of Argyll had attended council as late as 13 March and 8 May 1714,[13] and the duke of Somerset, whose duchess was at Anne's bedside, may have been summoned at her direct command; at any rate, the decisive measures which secured the Hanoverian succession were taken in the privy council, as appears from the Register.

Her Majesty having this morning at ten of the clock been taken dangerously ill, Their Lord^{ps} mett in the Council Chamber and considering the present exigency of affairs were unanimously of an opinion that she would constitute the Duke of Shrewsbury Lord Treasurer. . . . Whereupon the Ld Chancellor, the Ld Privy Seal, the Ld Steward and the Ld Visco^t Bolingbroke at the request of the Board having waited upon Her Maj^{ty}

[10] Miss Foxcroft's *Life of Halifax* (1898), ii. 204. Cf. Southwell's Rules and Observations, 'Powers of the Council Board,' Brit. Mus., Add. MS. 34349. Southwell notes one curious little instance of the decline of the privy council under James II: 'The Clerk of the Parliament did allways bring the Acts of Parliament to be read in Councill before the K[ing] came to the House to pass them: but this was left off in K[ing] James 2^d time. The Privy Councill were glad hereof, because it might not seem to lie on them, the advising not to pass any Bill.'

[11] Brit. Mus. Add. MS. 35107 (cf. entry in Privy Council Register, William III, iv. 364.)

[12] So Blauvelt, *Development of Cabinet Government*, New York, 1902, p. 119, and all other writers, whether secondary or contemporary.

[13] Privy Council Register, Anne, vi. 346-59,

to acquaint Her therewith, the Duke of Shrewsbury was forthwith commanded to attend Her Majesty, and returned to the Board after having received from Her Majesty's hand the staff of Lord High Treasurer of Great Britain,

and he thereupon proceeded to assure the Hanoverian succession.[14] The privy council had vindicated its powers, but for the last time. Once or twice, under the first two Georges, it exercised powers other than formal or legal ones.[15] Generally, Lord Peterborough's witty epigram that 'The Privy Council were thought to know everything and knew nothing',[16] though not altogether true under Anne, is substantially correct under the first two Georges. The decline in the power of the privy council coincides with the waning of the power of the king.

THE STANDING AND TEMPORARY COMMITTEES OF THE PRIVY COUNCIL

One obvious reason of the decline of the powers of the privy council was that so many of its functions were handled by committees, standing or temporary, special or secret. These are to be found even under the Tudors, and were, to some extent, systematized under Charles I and II.[17] Under James II we learn that

His Majesty was pleased to order that the several Standing Committees appointed in his late Majesty's time be revived and that their Lordships do meet about all matters referred to them as they did before His Majesty's demise.[18]

Under William III their existence continued, though it is harder to trace it. The standing committees other than the ordinary

---

[14] Privy Council Register, Anne, vol. vi. A larger council of thirty-eight, including the whig lords, met later.

[15] Granville questioned the validity of a commercial treaty at privy council (30 January, 1752); Lord Melcombe's *Diary*, ed. 1834, p. 130. On 28 February, 1754, Hardwicke addressed the judges in privy council, the king present: Brit. Mus., Add. MS. 35870, fo. 241. [16] *Parl. Hist.* vi. 974.

[17] Cf. Carlyle, *ante*, xxvii. 251-2 *seqq.*; see also List of Standing Committees in Privy Council Register, Charles I, i, xv. 4–5, which gives the list for 1679, for Intelligence 9, for Tangier 13, for Ireland 10, for Trade and Plantations 22 (also for Jersey and Guernsey). Standing Committees continued under Anne and the first two Georges; e.g. Privy Council Register, Anne, vi. 357-65, mentions Committees on the Church, for Plantations, and for Scotland: see also Grant and Munro, *Acts of the Privy Council Colonial Series*, vol. iii, pp. vii–viii. It appears that the different Standing Committees, since they often included many of the same members, were not very clearly marked off from one another. The phrase 'Committee of the whole Council' is sometimes used, e.g. Privy Council Register, Anne, vi. 357-9, but it seems to have no special implication. There are several instances in which the Plantations Committee under George II afterwards sat as a formal privy council, without adding to its numbers. On the whole question see Torrens' *History of Cabinets* (1894), ii. 162.

[18] Privy Council Register, James II, i. 17, 20 February 1685.

ones, which were recognized under Charles II, were those for foreign affairs and for intelligence. Of the powers and position of these last two bodies, this is not the place to speak. It is enough to say that they differed markedly from the other standing committees, which prepared and digested business for subsequent decision by the king at a more secret council. Certain councillors appear to have been ' added to all Committees ',[19] and these would probably form that nucleus of advisers whom we may describe as the cabinet council. The important point is that between the larger privy council and the smaller conclave, whether cabinet or *conciliabulum*, there existed a number of large standing committees, which did the preliminary work in digesting the business of the various departments of the state, but which, as such, had no share in the general control of the government or policy.[20]

THE CABINET COUNCIL OR OUTER CABINET

Under Charles II the terms cabinet council and councillor seem sometimes to imply a secret knot of a few irresponsible advisers, sometimes a more recognized body. In the *Lives of the Norths* we read

the Cabinet Council, which at first was but in the nature of a private conversation, comes to be a formal Council, and had the direction of most transactions of the Government, foreign and domestic.[21]

If a uniform control was to be secured, the too great size of the privy council, and the large numbers of committees, permanent and temporary, rendered a small central body most desirable, yet the reliance of Charles and James upon individual councillors tended to neutralize the power of any such collective body.

---

[19] e.g. Lord Godolphin, 20 November 1690, Privy Council Register, William III, ii. 56. See also Privy Council Register, Charles II, xv. 5, 23 April 1679, where it is ordered that the lord chancellor and president ' who wth the two Secretaryes may be present at all Committees as often as they see fit '. This last rule may be part of a special arrangement for the scheme of Temple's council.

[20] The lords commissioners of trade or board of trade must not be confused with the standing committee of council for trade and plantations. The former included some men who were not privy councillors, and it was obliged by the law of 1696 to report to parliament when necessary; the latter, the standing committee, consisted only of privy councillors and frequently overruled the board of trade's recommendations: Grant and Munro, *Acts of the Privy Council, Colonial Series*, vol. iii, pp. vii–viii, *et passim*. The earlier relation (1622–75) is described by C. M. Andrews, *British Committees, Commissions, and Councils of Trade and Plantations* (1622–75), Johns Hopkins Studies, Series xxvi, Baltimore, 1908.

[21] *Lives of the Norths* (ed. 1826), ii. 51. There is added the rather interesting remark, ' the Spaniards have peculiar Councils, called Juntos, assigned to each great branch of a royal power, which prevents such sub-emergent Councils as these '. Incidentally this observation shows that in England the ' Standing Committees ' never had much power.

We hear before 1679 of a foreign committee, and after it of a committee of intelligence, both of which seem sometimes to have been loosely described as the cabinet council. They are sharply differentiated from the 'Standing Committees', in that their function is one of general decision as to policy. Diplomacy appears to have been the sphere of the foreign committee, while affairs both domestic and external come before the committee of intelligence. In 1679 Temple's scheme of a council was tried, and was used by Shaftesbury to control the king, first by the council as a whole, and then by its central organ the committee of intelligence.[22] This attempt is clear from the wording of the appointment of the committee of intelligence, 'For the opening and considering all advices as well foreign as Domestique and to meet where and as often as they should see fit'.[23] If this project had been realized there would have been little difference between the committee of intelligence and the modern cabinet. The attempt, however, broke down; Charles dismissed Shaftesbury, and in future directed his own privy council and cabinet.[24]

Under James II we get references to a cabinet distinct from the privy council, and it is on the whole probable that this body resembled the former committee of intelligence in its powers of general control.[25] Under William III the cabinet certainly developed, but its existence and composition seem to have entirely depended on the discretion of the king. Thus in 1690 he left Mary as his vicegerent, with a council of nine to assist her, which she calls a cabinet council.[26] But in 1694 when William went abroad he left injunctions

There was to be no Cabinet Council, but Lords should be summoned, sometimes one, sometimes another, as they should be judged most proper

---

[22] Privy Council Register, Charles II, vol. xv. The committee of intelligence was constituted on 22 April 1679, and numbered nine. Its quorum was any three, a secretary of state always being one. See p. 29, 12 May, where a rule is made that no ambassadors or other foreign ministers were to have audience of his majesty without sending a memorial to one of the secretaries as to the business of which they proposed to speak.

[23] Privy Council Register, Charles II, xv. 5. There are minutes of the committee of intelligence in Add. MS. 15643 *passim*. During 1679, however, the privy council met regularly and with a good average of attendance, so that the committee was never entirely dominant.

[24] Add. MS. 32520, fo. 253. In the *Lives of the Norths*, ii. 53, 62, 'the Cabinett' in 1684 is reckoned at seven or eight (Radnor, North, Halifax, Conway, Jenkins, Rochester, Ormond, and Godolphin). In ii. 102 a distinction is drawn between cabinet and foreign committee.

[25] Add. MS. 34350, Southwell's Notes, app. 29 March 1694. 'In King James' time in 1686 . . . both being summoned to attend the Cabinett Council.' Cf. also Add. MS. 34512, 21 Sept./1 Oct., 1688, Van Citters' Dispatch: 'Resolutions— taken by James in his Privy Counsil of this evening. . . . The moment H.M. left the great Counsel he entered the Cabinet with some Lords,' where he took an important decision in foreign policy.

[26] R. Doebner, *Memoirs of Mary*, Leipzig, 1886, pp. 27–9.

for the business they were to advise about; only some whose employments belonged to the Crown made it necessary they should not be excluded.[27]

Before the end of his reign the cabinet council seems to have become fairly established, and under Anne it became a recognized and permanent institution, of which the form at least endured until 1783.

The cabinet council consisted of those privy councillors whom the king chose to summon to his secret deliberations, but there gradually and naturally arose the custom of limiting and assigning cabinet rank to certain great offices. Even in 1694, when William would have no cabinet council, he allowed certain great officials to meet in secret consultation. Sunderland in 1701 reckoned ten as the right number for the cabinet, and all these were to be great officials.[28] In 1711 the cabinet consisted of twelve, and included all the officials named by Sunderland.[29] In 1724-5 the number had risen to sixteen,[30] and in 1740 the number appears to have been the same.[31] In 1757 we read of nineteen,[32] in 1761 of twenty-one, and in 1765 of sixteen.[33] It is clear that, as the years pass by, this body has become too large for the efficient transaction of business. It is, in fact, being superseded by a species of interior cabinet, known as the committee or *conciliabulum*, but it still retains a formal authority, and a legal or quasi-legal position.

There is every reason to suppose that during most of the eighteenth century ministers thought that the outer cabinet had a legal or at least a quasi-legal position. The privy council was, of course, in an unassailably legal position. The inner or secret *conciliabulum* could hardly be known to the law, but the outer cabinet might have some legal pretension. It met regularly,

[27] Shrewsbury to the king, 11/21 May 1694. The king in reply (22 May/1 June) reckons the great officers of the Crown who should attend as the lord keeper, the lord president, the lord privy seal, and the two secretaries of state, but denies that this meeting would be a cabinet council : Coxe's *Shrewsbury*, ed. 1821, pp. 34, 38.

[28] Sunderland to Somers, November 1701 : *Hardwicke State Papers*, ii. 461. His suggestions are practically those of Charles II in 1679. Blauvelt, p. 84, asserts that there is no evidence that this cabinet ever met, but the testimony is sufficient under Anne, and overwhelming under the first two Georges (see below).

[29] *Hist. MSS. Comm.*, Rep. xv, app. 4, *Portland MSS.*, iv. 669, 22 March 1711.

[30] See State Papers, Dom., Various, vol. i.

[31] Hervey, *Memoirs of George II*, iii. (1884) 358-9. In Coxe's *Pelham* (ed. 1829), i. 478, we find that the number actually present at a division in the cabinet in 1744 was thirteen, and in 1745 at another division it was fourteen. Torrens, *History of Cabinets*, ii. 49, reckons the cabinet at fourteen in 1745. Of the 178 cabinet meetings I have found in State Papers, Dom., Entry Books and Various, from 1729-41 the largest attendance of ministers is seventeen ; of seventy-one between 1741-58, Mr. Winstanley, *ante*, xvii. 680, finds the largest attendance to be fourteen ; cf. *infra*, n. 56.

[32] Brit. Mus., Add. MS. 32997, 18 May 1757.

[33] Add. MS. 32999, 5 November 1761 ; Add. MS. 33001, 1765.

and apparently at the command of the king. It drew up formal minutes, especially in dealing with foreign affairs, and forwarded these minutes to the king.[34] It is mentioned in more or less formal documents; on at least one occasion a petition of merchants was made publicly to the 'Lords of the Cabinet Council'.[35] Moreover the king, long after the Hanover succession, could be, and sometimes was, present at the cabinet, a fact which appears to have imparted to it a more or less formal character.[36]

The question of the legality or otherwise of a body such as the cabinet, i.e. a committee of the privy council recognized by the king, came up for full debate in 1753. On that occasion the appointment by the king of a committee of the privy council to try some persons suspected of Jacobitism was called in question, and deemed illegal by some opposition peers. Lord Hardwicke, than whom there was no greater or more learned constitutional authority, replied by the assertion that the cabinet was legal.

The term Cabinet Council, said to be borrowed from France, was no novelty. ... It was to be found in the Journals of Parliament. That the Duke of Devonshire being added by His Majesty's particular order on this occasion was not unprecedented. That it had been called by our ancestors, sometimes the Cabinet for foreign affairs, sometimes the Cabinet for private. How they corresponded as a Council in Queen Elizabeth's time might be seen in Forbes's State Papers.

The duke of Bedford answered in the modern style.

Denied it being the Council; it was only a private Meeting of certain Lords. Were they a Committee of Council? ... If they were, the President of the Council should have presided—but here was no President, no forms, no essence, no authority of Council.[37]

Hardwicke's assertion of legality was supported by Bath

[34] Mr. D. A. Winstanley, *George III and his first Cabinet, ante,* xvii. 679–80, gives valuable lists of cabinet councils and shows clearly the distinction between the outer cabinet and the secret committee. Formal minutes are to be found everywhere in the Record Office, State Papers, Dom., Various; unofficial minutes of some cabinet meetings in 1740 are in Hervey, *Mem.,* iii. 360–77.

[35] Petition of West India merchants on Spanish depredations 'heard before the Lords of the Cabinet Council on the 15th October 1737'. See my article on the 'War of Jenkins' Ear', *Trans. of the Royal Hist. Soc.,* 3rd series, iii, 1909, 209. The severely formal instructions of George I to his son, as guardian of the realm in his absence (16 July 1716), mentioned the cabinet: 'Vous ne placerez personne sans ma direction express dans le conseil du Cabinet ni dans le conseil privé:' Brit. Mus. Add. MS. 34523, fo. 377.

[36] See below, pp. 693–4 for instances of the king's presence at outer cabinets after the Hanoverian succession.

[37] 22 March 1753. Lord Orford (Horace Walpole) *Memoirs, Works* (ed. 1822), vii. 272–3 *seqq.* Cf. Coxe's *Pelham,* ii. 258 *seqq.*; there is a very brief reference in *Parl. Hist.* xiv. 1294–7. There had been a previous debate in 1711 (12 January) *Parl. Hist.* vi. 970–81, in which the legality of the cabinet was by no means so emphatically affirmed.

Y y 2

(Pulteney) with evidence from Queen Anne's reign,[38] but it is difficult to answer Bedford's criticism that, as the president of the council did not preside, the committee could not be a legal one. Moreover, this examination is not on the records of the privy council,[39] though Hardwicke's minutes of the outer cabinet record it. None the less it appears that the assertion of the legality of the outer cabinet was sincerely made by the ministers. The supervision exercised by the king, the need of obtaining his consent to admission to the outer cabinet, the formality of its meetings and minutes, all gave it a semi-legal character. Some half-century afterwards the legality of the cabinet was again in question, when in 1806 the ministry of all the talents was attacked by the opposition for including the lord chief justice in the cabinet. Fox met the attack by saying that the lord chief justice was a privy councillor, and that the cabinet was wholly unknown to the law, laying down, in fact, the strict modern doctrine that it is a private and wholly unofficial meeting of certain privy councillors.[40] The explanation of this startling change of front is not, in fact, very difficult. After 1783 the outer or large semi-legal cabinet was abolished altogether and was succeeded by the inner or secret committee, the *conciliabulum*, and known in modern times as the cabinet.[41] This latter body certainly has no pretensions to legality, and it is the difference between it and the upper cabinet which explains the difference between the doctrine of Fox and of Hardwicke.

THE PRESENCE OF THE KING IN THE OUTER CABINET

Anne presided constantly at the cabinet, and possibly in one instance also at the *conciliabulum*, though this instance may be regarded as doubtful.[42] It looks rather as if the *conciliabulum*

---

[38] Coxe's *Pelham*, ii. 262–3. Pulteney refers to the judicial examination to which he was subjected under Anne; another such is recorded in the minutes of the privy council, Privy Council Register, Anne, vi, app. 14 March 1714.

[39] 12 February 1753. See Hardwicke's notes, Brit. Mus., Add. MSS. 35870, ff. 226–9.

[40] It appears that Auckland suggested this defence. Auckland to Grenville 10 February 1806, *Hist. MSS. Comm., Fortescue MSS., Dropmore Papers*, viii. 26. The doctrine was traversed by Canning on the modern ground that the cabinet was known to the public from the newspapers; see my *Life of Canning* (1905), p. 99, and *Parl. Deb.*, vi. 254–342. Fox wrongly asserted (p. 308): 'It is the first instance that I have ever heard of such a thing as a Cabinet Council becoming a subject of debate in this House.' In the lords it certainly was a subject of debate in 1711 and 1753, and it was a subject of debate in the commons in 1692. *Parl. Hist.* v. 733 *seqq.*, and *supra*, p. 691, n. 37.

[41] *Parl. Deb.* vi. 312, app. 1806. Fox distinguishes between meetings of the cabinet: they are sometimes 'For affording members an opportunity of consulting with each other . . . but with no intention of communicating result to His Majesty. . . . On other occasions the Cabinet Council meets to advise His Majesty in person.' This distinction practically existed between the *conciliabulum* and the outer cabinet before 1783.

[42] Nottingham to Colonel Gibson: 'I have laid your letter of the 15th before the

originated in a desire on the part of the ministers to meet and discuss important business in private, without the necessity of summoning the sovereign.[43] When the sovereign became German it was absolutely necessary for ministers to formulate their own foreign policy independently of the king. He could not be denied access to the cabinet council, if he wished it, but it was possible to prevent his attending a more secret and irresponsible committee. Whatever the explanation, no instance of the king's attendance at the *conciliabulum* can be produced after the Hanoverian succession, though there are several of his attendance at the outer cabinet. George I, indeed, apparently because of his ignorance of English, appeared very seldom at the cabinet,[44] but in his father's absence in Germany in 1716 the Prince of Wales attended with great regularity. Thus Methuen writes to Stanhope, on 13 July 1716: 'There was a (Privy) Council called yesterday morning where his Royal Highness patent' (as guardian of the realm) 'was read, after which he sat almost three hours with the Cabinet Council.'[45] George II's queen also appears to have attended the cabinet as regent in 1729.[46] On 6 December 1745 formal minutes record a meeting of fourteen, with the endorsement 'the King present'.[47] There are at least two other instances, in 1756 and 1758, in which George II may have attended the cabinet,[48] but Waldegrave says it was 'unusual for the King himself to be present at such consultations'.[49]

Queen at the Committee.' State Papers, Dom., Entry Book, vol. civ, 17 December 1703. Cf. *ibid.* vol. cv, 29 April 1704. The expressions 'Committee' and 'Committee of Council' are undoubtedly used at times to describe the outer cabinet. At the same time, as Lord Morley (*Walpole*, p. 145) points out, a distinction can also at times be drawn between the cabinet and the committee (i.e. *conciliabulum*); cf. Bolingbroke, *Correspondence* (1798), ii. 69.

[43] Most writers assert that the king was never present at the committee, e.g. Leadam, *Political History of England* (1909), ix. 231. Cf. Bonet, 24 December 1714/ 4 January 1715: 'Je veux parler du Comité du Conseil du Cabinet, composé des principaux officiers qui s'assemblent en *l'absence du Roi*.' Professor Wolfgang Michael quotes this dispatch in *Englische Geschichte im XVIII. Jahrhundert* (1896), i. 440 n.; but he erroneously argues that the committee and the cabinet were identical.

[44] Coxe, *Walpole*, i. 71 n., mentions, on the doubtful authority of Townshend's grandson, an instance in 1715; another is given in a letter of Townshend to Stanhope (see Blauvelt, p. 179).

[45] State Papers, Dom., Entry Books, colxvii, p. 2, and cf. pp. 21, 23, 31, 41, 63, 100, 102, for other instances of the prince's presence at the cabinet.

[46] State Papers, Dom., Various, vol. i, contains a paper endorsed in Newcastle's hand, 'Summons for a Cabinet Council to all that are in town, to attend her majesty tomorrow, 9th June 1729.' The same volume contains a list of seventeen ministers and the queen (11 June 1735), but this may be a privy council.

[47] State Papers, Dom., Various, vol. v, 6 December 1745. It is worth noting that on the same day there was a meeting of the smaller body of ten ministers, at which the king was not present.

[48] One instance is in Brit. Mus., Add. MS. 32997, fo. 372, 23 February 1758; for the other see next note.

[49] Waldegrave, *Memoirs*, ed. 1821, p. 66, gives an instance in 1756. The evidence is, in neither case, decisive.

George III on at least two occasions, in 1779 and 1781, attended ministerial meetings which appear to have been cabinet councils.[50] We may doubt, however, whether vital importance is to be attached to the presence or absence of the king at the cabinet, in view of the fact that he either did not or could not attend the committee or *conciliabulum*. The real power he wielded was the power of appealing to the cabinet to outvote the *conciliabulum*, a power not always or often used, but a really dangerous and alarming one. Consequently, if ministers wished to avoid his control altogether, the way was to abolish the outer cabinet, and keep only the *conciliabulum*, and this is what Fox and North did in 1783.

POWERS OF THE OUTER CABINET COUNCIL

The powers of the cabinet varied considerably from time to time. Under William, and to some extent under Anne, it had an effective share in the government, but the increase in its numbers caused it to be superseded by the *conciliabulum*, which rose to power in the days of Walpole and Newcastle. The process resembles the pulling out of the sections of a telescope, which sections correspond to the attempts of the ministers to control the king. First the ministers tried to observe the king's policy through a folded telescope—the privy council. Then they pull out a section from within the privy council and name it the outer cabinet. Last, as their sight again fails, they pull out a third section, and name it the *conciliabulum*. Through that section the policy of the king becomes at last clear.

THE COMMITTEE, INNER CABINET, OR CONCILIABULUM

It is our contention that from Anne onwards the outer cabinet was an intermediary body between the large formal privy council and the small, effective, secret and central committee. This *conciliabulum* or committee is hard to discover because it is extremely easy to confuse it, either with the standing committees, or with committees appointed *ad hoc*.[51] From all these it differs profoundly in several important particulars :

(a) It was probably not regarded as legal or quasi-legal, because it is seldom mentioned in formal documents.

[50] *Hist. MSS. Comm. Reports on Manuscripts in Various Collections*, vi. 260–1, 272 (manuscripts of Captain H. V. Knox), 1909. Cf. another instance as late as 1806, Anson, I. ii. 105–6 and notes.

[51] This confusion has affected many writers, e.g. Morley, *Walpole*, p. 145–6; Michael, *Englische Geschichte im XVIII. Jahrhundert*, i. 440–1 n., traverses Lord Morley's statement, but identifies the cabinet with the committee of council. F. Salamon, *Geschichte des letzten Ministeriums Königin Annas*, Gotha (1894), p. 356 n., makes a similar mistake.

(b) It was not a body merely for routine or preliminary digestion of business.

(c) It was a central committee, which enabled the inner ring of ministers to exercise a general control of all policy.

The committee's procedure under Anne is well illustrated in the discussion of peace negotiations from 1709 onwards. The main measures were settled in the committee, afterwards laid before the large outer cabinet, and when formal ratification was required, before the privy council.[52] But even under Anne the real control appears to have lain in the committee.[53] Henceforward it had a continued existence, and its general control over foreign policy is well illustrated in the third year of George I.

The fifth [September 1716] the Lords of the Committee met and the answer to M. d'Iberville was formed and settled by the Lords. The next day being Thursday, it was laid before the Prince [guardian of the realm in the absence of George I] and read to the Cabinet Council, where it was approved by H.R.H., and we have this day sent it to M. d'Iberville.[54]

Under Walpole the difference between the outer cabinet and the secret committee or *conciliabulum* increases, and the former declines rapidly in power. This fact appears in 1737, when a message of rebuke from George II to the Prince of Wales was submitted to the outer cabinet, 'who attempted to discuss it, but Sir Robert [Walpole] said the Cabinet Council was summoned by the King, not to give advice whether these orders should be sent, but on the proper mode of executing them '.[55] Obviously

[52] On the distinction between the foreign committee and the cabinet, which appears under Charles II in 1684, see *Lives of the Norths*, iii. 102 ; but this is more difficult to trace under James and William. Under Anne, a letter of Nottingham to the lord keeper, 6 July 1702, shows that the committee drew up the queen's speech ' Preparatory to the Meeting of the Great Council ' : State Papers, Dom., Entry Book, vol. civ. For its control of foreign policy see Cowper's *Diary*, 1709, p. 41 ; Bolingbroke, *Correspondence*, iv. 294, 302, &c. Morley, *Walpole*, p. 146, and Blauvelt, p. 126, and Salamon, p. 356 n., make this committee disappear after Anne's death ; but this is inaccurate, see below. Sir W. Anson, II. i. 94–5, is dubious but suggestive.

[53] See J. S. Corbett, ' Queen Anne's Defence Committee ', *Monthly Review*, 1904, p. 505, and also his *England in the Seven Years' War*, 1907, i. 33.

[54] Methuen to Stanhope, 8 September 1716, State Papers, Dom., Entry Book, cclxvii. 41. Cf. 17 April 1755, where a foreign dispatch is discussed before the committee, six in number, who draw up a minute that they are 'humbly of opinion that that extract should be laid on Monday next before the Lords of the Cabinet Council '. (Brit. Mus., Add. MS. 32996, fo. 77.) Townshend's letter to the king of 11/22 November 1716, Coxe's *Walpole*, ii. 129, shows the committee as a chief power in foreign policy. The nomenclature is very confusing ; sometimes we hear of the outer and of the effective cabinets, sometimes the outer cabinet is called the committee, and the inner a cabinet, whilst both are occasionally described as the lords of the council. None the less the real distinction can nearly always be drawn.

[55] Hervey, *Memoirs*, iii. 236. Yorke speaks of divisions in the cabinet as unusual, but records an important one in 1744 ; see Coxe's *Pelham*, i. 478. Mr. Winstanley, to whose assistance in this article I owe much, has called my attention to an important

the secret committee is gaining power at the expense of the outer cabinet.[56] In 1748 there is no minute of the meeting of cabinet ministers which contains more than five names, so that for most of the year England seems to have been governed by the *conciliabulum*, and by a very small *conciliabulum*.[57]

COMPOSITION OF THE CONCILIABULUM

The secret committee appears first to have been very limited in numbers.[58] It was five under Anne, six in 1755,[59] and apparently the same in the early part of 1757. On 13 March 1757 Newcastle wrote : 'The *Conciliabulum*, that silly term, is to be the Duke of Bedford, the Duke of Devonshire, Lord Halifax and the Secretaries of State, my Lord President you see, is excluded.'[60] This would make five, but eventually between 1757 and 1761 the *conciliabulum* seems to have numbered six or even more members. Custom limited membership to certain great offices,[61] yet the numbers seem gradually to have increased.[62] In Shelburne's

---

extract from Hardwicke in 1739 showing the power (or lack of power) of the cabinet, Brit. Mus., Add. MS. 32692, fo. 538. He deprecates its being informed of two proposed expeditions against Spain: 'I have always been told that it was not the custom to bring matters which require such absolute secrecy before such a number of persons.'

[56] Evidence of this abounds: see Torrens, *History of Cabinets*, i. 375. Broken lists in State Papers, Dom., Various, &c., show from 1729–41, 178 cabinet meetings—93 of 9 ministers or more (i. e. probably the outer cabinet); 85 of 8 ministers or less (i. e. probably the *conciliabulum*). Between 1741 and 1758 Mr. Winstanley, *ante*, xvii. 680, reckons 71 cabinet councils, 17 of which were attended by 9 ministers or more, i. e. outer cabinet meetings; 36 by 8 ministers or less, i. e. probably meetings of *conciliabulum*; 17 by 5 ministers or less, i. e. certainly the *conciliabulum*.

[57] Under Anne it is called the secret committee, and seems to have contained only five real members (including Marlborough, who was often absent). Certain others who appear there, such as the members of the admiral's council, Peterborough, or the Dutch admiral, were apparently summoned only to give special or technical information. The Finch-Hatton Papers in the British Museum contain the minutes; see Corbett, *Monthly Review* (1904), p. 505–6.

[58] Winstanley, *ante*, xvii. 680.

[59] Minute of the committee, 17 April 1755, Add. MS. 32996, fo. 77.

[60] Newcastle to Hardwicke, Add. MS. 35416, fo. 181. Horace Walpole, *Lord Orford's Works*, ed. 1822, viii. 265–6, says that Lord Mansfield was added in December 1757; but Add. MS. 32997, fo. 207, gives ten names of the 'Committee of the Cabinet to meet on business': possibly, as it was a coalition ministry, the number of the *conciliabulum* had to be increased.

[61] Miss Bateson, *Newcastle's Narrative of Changes in the Ministry*, 1765–7 (1898), p. 7 : The duke of Cumberland asked why Newcastle should not be privy seal. 'Lord Northumberland replied, . . . the King wished to have him of the *Conciliabulum*, where all business of consequence was first settled; which the Privy Seal was not.'

[62] Hardwicke to Newcastle, Add. MS. 32929, fo. 143: 'Those Meetings' [of the *Conciliabulum*] 'understood to be of persons entrusted by the King in his most secret affairs, were now made up of as many persons as a whole Cabinet Council ought to consist of, and perhaps more, and I hoped he would narrow them.' Cf. Grafton, in Donne, *Correspondence of George III and North*, ed. 1867, i. 75–6.

ministry of 1782-3, the cabinet numbered eleven, but a *conciliabulum* certainly existed.[63] On his fall, a *conciliabulum* seems to have been proposed by the duke of Portland to the duke of Richmond for the Fox-North ministry of 1783, but the project dropped, as the whole ministry consisted only of seven or eight.[64] From that time forward there is no trace of a distinction drawn between cabinet and *conciliabulum*, and that secret or political committee assumes the modern and familiar form of an unauthorized caucus of chief ministers.

RELATION OF THE CONCILIABULUM TO THE OUTER CABINET
(1755-83)

Though, as has been seen under Walpole, the *conciliabulum* was unquestionably the more powerful, the outer cabinet had occasionally to be consulted on occasions of great importance, as the ratification of treaties and declaration of peace or war. As it included in its ranks permanent and non-party officials who were often simply the king's servants—the archbishop of Canterbury, and the groom of the stole, &c.—there was always a possibility that a close division in the committee might be reversed on appeal to the cabinet as a whole. This fact sometimes gave the king considerable power, and always caused Newcastle considerable alarm.[65] When George III sought to grasp power he began by putting Bute in the cabinet, and afterwards elevated

[63] Brit. Mus., Add. MS. 34523, fo. 370, 4 January 1783: 'The D(uke) of R(ichmond) . . . cannot continue a member of the Cabinet when after the Terms had been settled at a meeting L⁴ Grantham had been authorised to offer Tobago instead of Dominica by a more intimate consultation'. Cf. FitzMaurice, *Life of Lansdowne*, iii. 229. Shelburne told Bentham, *Works*, ix. 218, there were three kinds of cabinet ministers: (1) Those without the circulation of foreign dispatches, i.e. the outer cabinet; (2) those with it, i.e. the *conciliabulum*; and (3) those with the post office, i.e. with the privilege of opening letters in the post.

[64] Add. MS. 34523, 25 February 1783, Copies of Letters of the duke of Richmond to the bishop of Exeter. He mentions ' the efficient offices' as the treasury, secretaryships, admiralty, and commander-in-chief. The whole cabinet eventually numbered seven or eight. It is uncertain whether Northington was included in this cabinet or not; see Buckingham, *Courts and Cabinets of George III*, ed. 1853, i. 255 *seqq*.

[65] Thus in 1746 Pelham and Newcastle insist that Bath shall be 'out of the Cabinet Council': Coxe, *Pelham*, i. 295. On 18 May 1757, Add. MS. 32997, Newcastle desires 'That the King should give the Lords of the Cabinet Council to understand that he expects his administration, as now settled, shall be thoroughly supported by them.' Cf. *ibid.*, Newcastle's memorandum of business with the chancellor, 22 March 1758: 'The King's discourse about the part he was determined to take. . . . He would have the King of Prussia's demands laid before a Cabinet Council. . . . Opinion of the Cabinet Council (must it be taken?) . . . The King (to persuade him) to avoid the Cabinet Council.' Cf. Winstanley, *Personal and Party Government*, pp. 85, 134-5, 175, for instances in 1762-3 when the outer cabinet was employed with effect. In view of these examples and the singular doings of 1765-6 (*Newcastle's Narrative*, p. 5), it cannot be held that Burke's denunciation of the 'double Cabinet system' in *Thoughts on the Present Discontents* (1770) was wholly fantastic.

him to the *conciliabulum*.⁶⁶ There can be no doubt that the manœuvres of summoning the cabinet to outvote the *conciliabulum* caused considerable alarm to ministers on more than one occasion in George III's reign, and it is probably not an accident that Fox and North's coalition, which aimed at destroying the king's power, began by abolishing the outer cabinet altogether. Still, though on rare occasions the outer cabinet might prove formidable, the *conciliabulum* was undoubtedly the real governing power. Newcastle summoned Fox to it as 'the private meetings of the King's servants that he may not only be informed of the measures taken ' [as at the cabinet to which he was already called], 'but assist with his opinion in the forming of them '.⁶⁷ Hardwicke said it consisted of the persons 'entrusted by the King in his most secret affairs '. There is no doubt that it was already before 1783 the real effective cabinet; after that date it was the only body possessing either the name or the authority of a real executive council.

My attempt has been throughout to describe the form of the outer cabinet, and to distinguish it from the *conciliabulum* and the privy council. It would need another article to relate and connect the changes of form to the shiftings of the balance of political power, and to the development of the modern principles of cabinet government. A few indications may be given here. The reigns of Charles II and James II were occupied by a struggle of parliament to control the king through the privy council, but the use of secret committees evaded that control. The attempt failed and, under William III, the ministers still continued to debate secretly in cabinet or secret committee, as the king dictated. The commons made a determined effort again to make ministers responsible for advice given, first by the impeachment of Somers, and second by a clause in the Act of Settlement. The impeachment failed, the clause was repealed, and under Anne the privy council has its last flicker of real power, the outer cabinet its first assured status. Under Walpole the *conciliabulum* grows in power, and the commons cease to be jealous, because the ministers are agreeable to the majority in that house. There still, however, remains a difficulty, because the outer cabinet still includes royal servants as well as parliamentary ministers, and is therefore at times invoked by the king to defeat the *conciliabulum*. With the struggle between the king and his ministers under George III this royal power becomes dangerous,

---

⁶⁶ Winstanley, *ante*, xvii. 681. The consent of the king was always necessary to admit members into either *conciliabulum* or cabinet.

⁶⁷ Newcastle to Fox, 19 September 1755, Brit. Mus., Add. MS. 32996. Cf. *supra*, p. 696, n. 56.

and Fox and North therefore take the opportunity in 1783 to identify the two bodies, and form a true homogeneous parliamentary and formally illegal cabinet of the modern type.

It is in 1783 that we find the true starting-point of the modern cabinet system, which Lord Morley has so admirably described.[68] Before that date it cannot be said with certainty that any of the distinguishing modern cabinet principles were recognized as binding. The unity and solidarity of the cabinet could not be conspicuous when formal minutes sent to the king recorded the dissent of one minister from the collective advice,[69] or when ministers assailed the measures of their colleagues, as Pitt did in 1755. The collective resignation of ministers came as an agreeable surprise to Newcastle in 1746,[70] and did not establish a precedent that was universally followed. In the same way, though Walpole, by resigning in 1741, did homage to the principle that the existence of the cabinet depends on its preserving a majority in the commons, Lord North declined to accept that principle on several occasions in 1780–2. The fact is that these principles were developed from expediency and necessity, and it was only the prolonged struggles of king against ministers which forced their recognition in 1783. That recognition was most emphatically shown in that year by the abolition of the double cabinet, and Fox and Pitt continued the practice and thus established the essential principle of cabinet solidarity. It is for that reason that they, far more than any other eighteenth-century ministers, are the real authors of the modern cabinet system.   H. W. V. TEMPERLEY.

[68] Morley's *Walpole*, c. vii. Compare also Anson, II. i. 176 *seqq.*
[69] In a minute of 18 April 1739, when the draft treaty with Spain was read before a cabinet of fourteen, the duke of Argyll was recorded as dissenting.
[70] Brit. Mus., Add. MS. 32706, Newcastle to Chesterfield, 18 February 1746 : 'It was soon evident that the Resignations would have been almost universal, tho' without any Concert or any Endeavour used, of any Kind, for that purpose.'

Burke, Windham, and Pitt

Part I

THE acquisition by the British Museum of a considerable portion of Windham's correspondence during the revolutionary period enables us to gauge more accurately his relations to Burke and to the Pitt administration which he joined in July 1794. But these letters also throw new light on certain episodes in the careers of Burke and Pitt. Along with documents in the Chatham manuscripts, now preserved in the Public Record Office, they add materially to the information concerning the motives and actions of the three statesmen in the revolutionary period. The letters reveal characteristic differences. Those of Burke, though often clouded by passion, are instinct with intellectual power and sparkle with felicities of expression. Those of Pitt throw a clear light on the topics at issue and conceal the personality of the writer. No correspondent, not even Chatham himself, possessed more completely the gift of enshrouding his own figure; and these letters do not help us to lift the veil. The correspondence of Windham in these years possesses a more personal interest, especially as showing the influence of Burke on a character by no means antipathetic to the principles of 1789. As he is the least known of the three men, he deserves a short initial notice.

At that time William Windham was thirty-eight years of age, thus being the junior of Burke by twenty-two years, and the senior of Pitt by nine years. At Eton and Oxford he was the contemporary of Fox, with whom his relations were very cordial. He also studied mathematics and philosophy at Glasgow, and the love of these pursuits never left him. In his morbidly introspective diary time is referred to as wasted which was not devoted to them or to linguistic studies. He derived many of his gifts from his father, an officer in the army, distinguished by a chivalrous character and a love of languages. The son was to be almost a knight-errant. Whether at his family seat of Felbrigg, near Cromer, or in parliament, or during his numerous tours, he sustained with dignity the character of a cultured and warm-hearted gentleman. Yet there was something wanting in Windham. Restlessness and self-examination impaired alike his health and his capacity for decision and action. His studies, as he was painfully aware, led to no definite results ; and in the political arena his critical aloofness weakened powers of eloquence and enthusiasm which should have carried him to the highest rank. He served as chief secretary for Ireland in the Fox-North ministry of 1783, but sickness or disgust led to his withdrawal ; and though, as member for Norwich in and after 1784, he endeared himself to his constituents and to the house of commons, he figured more as a freelance, tilting against the Pitt cabinet, than as a convinced and consistent whig. The first events of the French Revolution did not awaken in him the antagonistic zeal which at once strained to the utmost the faculties of Burke. Windham was in France during the *Jacquerie* of the late summer of 1789 ; he visited the national assembly at Versailles during the exciting debates on agrarian topics and the rights of man ; but his diary is that of an ordinary traveller in times of calm, though varied by strangely introspective musings. In truth, he needed a more determined and persistent nature to arouse in him a feeling of resentment at the barbarities of that time. This influence he found in Burke.

Writing to Windham on 27 September ·1789 Burke congratulates him on his return from ' the land of liberty ' and thanks him for his information on French affairs. He continues :

That they [the French] should settle their constitution without much struggle, on paper, I can easily believe ; because at present the interests of the Crown have no party, certainly no armed party, to support them ; but I have great doubt whether any form of government they can establish will procure obedience, especially obedience in the article of taxation. In the destruction of the revenue-constitution they find no difficulties ; but with what to supply them is the *opus*. . . . It does not appear to me that the national assembly have one jot more power than the king.

With remarkable insight Burke, even at this stage, detected the weakness of the democratic movement in France. Its champions showed far less ability in construction than zeal in destruction ; and their fatal inability to restore order suggested to Burke the well-known passage in the *Reflections on the Revolution in France*, in which he foretold the advent of the Directory and Bonaparte. A strain of pessimism is essential to the mental equipment of a prophet ; and certainly Burke, whom Windham describes as ' decried, persecuted, and proscribed, not being much valued even by his own party, and by half the nation considered as little better than an ingenious madman ', had the characteristics and the experiences that befit a seer. On this occasion he at once gained belief. As Windham foretold, that greatest of pamphlets turned the stream of public opinion throughout Europe against the national assembly. Wilberforce refers to a discussion at Wimbledon on Burke's *Reflections*, in which Lord Chatham, Pitt, and he approved the book, while Grenville and Ryder differed. The entry in his diary is so brief as to be scarcely conclusive ; but it seems probable that Burke's arguments and the continued confusion in France had told on Pitt, leading him to modify the hopeful forecast on French affairs which startled parliament on the 9th of February previous.

> The present convulsions of France must, sooner or later, terminate in general harmony and regular order. . . . Whenever the situation of France shall become restored, it will prove freedom rightly understood, freedom resulting from good order and good government ; and, thus circumstanced, France will stand forth as one of the most brilliant powers in Europe.

The prophecy is conditioned by the phrases 'sooner or later', 'whenever', &c., and 'thus circumstanced' ; but, even so, it is a striking proof of the optimism which was the glory of Pitt as a man, but not seldom his weakness as a statesman.

Unfortunately, neither Burke nor Pitt knew France well. Accordingly, their attitude towards the Revolution was the outcome of instinct and of a general acquaintance with the course of political convulsions rather than of knowledge of the problems besetting her people. Burke, failing to understand their difficulties, launched into unmeasured invectives ; Pitt, hopefully believing in the advent of a settlement *à l'Anglaise*, failed to realize the depth and passion of the revolutionary sentiment, which turned against him after the outbreak of war in 1793. The philosopher saw in that event a struggle to the death between two irreconcilable principles ; the statesman deemed it a collision of interests due to the high-handed treatment of our Dutch allies by the French republic. In a sense both were right. The *casus belli*, the opening of the Scheldt to navigation by all nations, in defiance of Dutch claims, was a case of natural rights against treaty rights ; but material interests as well as the clash of principles brought about the dispute. Danton might challenge the kings to mortal conflict by hurling down the head of Louis XVI as gage of battle ; but behind him were men intent on garnering the spoils of the Netherlands and the Rhineland. The declaration of war by France against Great Britain and Holland on 1 February 1793 brought to an acuter phase the struggle between democracy and monarchy already raging ; but it also marked the beginning of another round in the secular conflict between France and England for supremacy in the Netherlands. Pitt, as a diplomatist, may have underrated the fighting value of the ideals of democracy :

Burke, raging at the intrusion of the Scheldt affair into the arena of his holy war, certainly overlooked the importance of the political and commercial issues involved ; and his call to the allies, especially Austria and Prussia, to forgo all claim to indemnity at the expense of France was a counsel of perfection utterly at variance with the statecraft of that age. We can now see that his advice was instinct with foresight. Only by forswearing all thought of material gains could the monarchical hosts be kept together. But all who knew the courts of Vienna and Berlin saw the futility of that advice. While Burke summoned Europe to a crusade, Thugut and Haugwitz were intent on outwitting one another in the allotting of the spoils. This was but natural. Regarding France as the aggressor owing to her declaration of war against Austria in April 1792, they determined to make her pay the expenses of the war, and she could pay only in land. Burke did not fully know the extent of their schemes, and, idealist as he was, refused to take into account the pressing financial needs of the two German states. Pitt, as a practical statesman, saw the reasonableness of their claims to compensation.

In estimating the differences of judgement that separated him sharply from Burke, we must further remember that he was not in a position to dictate the course of action of Austria and Prussia. In February 1793 Great Britain was involved in a conflict which had raged for ten months, and whose diplomatic issues had already been decided at Vienna and Berlin. Burke's invectives against Pitt for allowing the dictates of statecraft to override the claims of monarchy were based on the assumption that Great Britain could act as arbitress. This was not so. Not since the Lancastrian period had she been able to attack France on land without the help of allies. The imperious need of economy after the disasters of the American war necessarily left her unprepared for a great conflict ; and, when the challenge came unexpectedly early in 1793, she entered the arena as a military power of the second rank, and therefore unable to regulate the policy of her German allies. Finally, a cardinal maxim of British policy bade Pitt second the aim of Austria to secure a better frontier for her Belgic provinces. Some of her statesmen, notably Thugut, questioned the wisdom of holding those distant and troublesome domains ; and probably the emperor, Francis II, looked on them as little better than a valuable asset for bargaining, unless he secured a strong frontier in French Flanders. Every consideration of sound policy, as then understood, bade Pitt establish Austria firmly in the Belgic lands ; and the accomplishment of this desirable end implied the acquisition of Lille and Valenciennes.

Thus, the characteristics of Pitt and Burke, no less than their differences in position and in diplomatic knowledge, led them to take very different points of view. For Pitt the aim of the struggle was to keep France within bounds and to restore the balance of power; for Burke it was to stamp out Jacobinism and restore the French Bourbons. This he termed making war on the Jacobins, not on France, though by this time the two terms had become closely intertwined. They became indissoluble when the allies, after the conferences of their plenipotentiaries at Antwerp in April 1793, issued a declaration which implied a resolve to seek territorial indemnities at the expense of France. Therefore, while admirers of Burke must admit that his knowledge of the situation was inferior to his monarchical zeal and his philosophic insight, yet they may warmly commend his appeals to the allies to separate, not to unite, the Jacobinical cause with that of France; and the neglect of them led to that hardening of the national resistance, which even short-sighted politicians might have foreseen.

The energy of the Jacobins, the unexpected weakness of Austria, and the perfidious apathy of Prussia, soon paralysed the campaign in Flanders; and the progress of sedition in these islands added further reasons why all friends of monarchy should form a working union. Burke and Windham seem to have had no hand in the abortive proposals for the accession of the old whigs to the ministerial ranks in the summer of 1792. The diary of Windham at that time gives an impression of nonchalance on French affairs; but the horrors of that autumn and the aggressions of the Jacobins served to draw him nearer to Pitt. Acting with Lords Loughborough and Malmesbury, he sought to induce the duke of Portland to break away from Fox and openly support the government. Constitutional indecision or fondness for Fox kept the duke tongue-tied; whereupon the whig subalterns privately assured ministers of their support in all matters tending to preserve order at home and treaty rights abroad. This occasion called forth the first letter from Pitt to Windham.

On 24 November 1792 Pitt invited Windham and Burke to an interview on that evening at Lord Grenville's house in St. James's Square. He added that, even if Burke were not in town, he (Pitt) desired to see Windham, 'as, besides the subject of their last conversation, he wishes to mention to him some particulars which have been stated to him respecting Norwich and its neighbourhood'. Norwich was a stronghold of the new radical clubs; but the chief topic for discussion must have been the hoped-for union of the Portland whigs with the government. Though Burke was not present, the interview between Pitt and Windham took place; and Malmesbury afterwards noted that

Windham favoured a friendly separation from, not a rupture with, Fox. Neither event occurred; but evidently Pitt hoped much from the decided royalism of the squire of Felbrigg, and wrote to him thus in view of Fox's notice of motion for peace with France on 17 June :

Downing Street, Friday, June 14, 1793.

Mr Pitt presents his compliments to Mr Windham, and wishes much if Mr Windham will give him leave to have some conversation with him before Monday on the subject of the motion of which Mr Fox has given notice for that day. It would also be a great satisfaction to MrPitt to have an opportunity, if it is not disagreeable to Mr Windham, of stating confidentially to him some circumstances arising out of the present state of politics, and which Mr Pitt rather wishes to communicate personally to himself than thro' any other channel. It is hardly necessary to add that, if Mr Windham has the goodness to comply with Mr Pitt's wishes in this respect, any thing which may pass will not transpire any where, without Mr Windham's particular permission. Mr Pitt will be at leisure any hour either to-morrow or Sunday, at which Mr Windham could find it convenient to call in Downing Street.[1]

The first extant letter of Windham to Pitt, dated 11 October 1793, deals at the outset with the intended proposals through Mr. Hippisley for friendlier relations with the Vatican, so that England may become 'the protector of the Italian States, and (odd as the idea may seem) the supporter of the Papal Power'. He then refers as follows to the appointment of Sir Gilbert Elliot (afterwards first earl of Minto) to the post of civil commissioner at Toulon during the British occupation of that place, also to the British reverse at Dunkirk :

... As the opportunity is presented to me, I cannot help offering my congratulations on the late successes at Toulon, as also on the choice of the person, about to be sent out there to conduct our political concerns in that very new and critical situation. I really doubt whether in the compass of the three kingdoms a person could be found so furnished at all points, with the powers and properties, necessary for that very delicate service. I rejoice accordingly not a little at Sir G. E[lliot] having undertaken it. On the same principle and with the same views, I am perfectly well pleased to remain myself in the situation, in which I have acted hitherto, and in which it appears to me, in the present state of things, that my support of the same cause, is likely to be most effectual.

On the affairs of our armies in the north I wish I had the same congratulations to offer. From the moment that I had reason to believe (I know not how truly), that the plan of our operations in that quarter did not carry with it the full approbation of the best military judgements on the spot, I must confess I was full of alarms. I hope our success at the other side of France as well as in the expedition [for the West Indies] now fitting out will serve to cover and heal this wound; and keep the

[1] Add. MS. 37844, fo. 7.

publick opinion right on the subject of the war; which is the point in which error and failure is most to be apprehended. You have received from Norwich probably an account of a seditious paper, which made its appearance immediately on the miscarriage at Dunkirk, but which drooped and died away, on the news of the success of Toulon; so little true is it, that the progress of arms has no influence on that of opinions.[2]

Pitt's reply breathes his usual hopefulness. It minimizes the 'check' at Dunkirk, expresses the belief that the expected success of Coburg in reducing Maubeuge would end the resisting power of France in the north, while the south was raised from Toulon as base :

Hollwood, Sunday, Octr 13th 1793.

I received yesterday the favor of your obliging letter enclosing several papers from Mr Hippisley, the substance of which I had before learnt in some measure, but less fully, from the lord chancellor. Allow me to return you my thanks for the communication, and at the same time to beg your permission to retain the papers for a few days, in order to examine them more at leisure than I have yet been able to do. I partake thoroughly in your sentiments both with respect to Toulon, and to the person with whom the political concerns arising out of the possession of that place are entrusted. This event seems to me to furnish a better opening than could have presented itself in any other way for the facilitating the restoration of regular government in France and for terminating the war satisfactorily, perhaps speedily. In Sir Gilbert Elliot's hands, I am sure every advantage will be improved to the utmost. I need not say how happy I should have been if your concurrence of opinion on the great questions now depending, had led you also to take an active share in conducting the affairs of government. At least however I have the satisfaction of knowing from experience how much the public may benefit by your exertions even in your present situation. The check before Dunkirk is certainly much to be regretted. But unless any impression should be produced by it at home to impede the vigor of future operations, the mischief will I trust be little felt in the general scale of the war. We expect in a few days important accounts from Maubeuge. Success in that quarter would in a great measure relieve us from any further anxiety on the side of the Netherlands, and lead to further vigorous measures, either before the end of the campaign, or very early in the next. I have inquired about the paper transmitted from Norwich which I understand was immediately referred to the attorney-general.[3]

Very different was the judgement of Burke. In a letter to Windham, written before the news of the Austrian failures at Wattignies and Maubeuge, he deplores the moves in that direction as no less fatal than that against Dunkirk or the West Indies. Indeed, the whole plan of the war had been wrong, arising as it did from the false political principles on which it is formed. . . . No victory, however great, can reconcile my mind to this business of Maubeuge, no

[2] Add. MS. 37844, fo. 11. [3] Add. MS. 37844, fo. 13.

more than it could to that of Dunkirk, where indeed victory was in a manner impossible. But the fault is not wholly in our ministry : the whole body of the allies is concerned in it. Things can never be brought to a decision, in the way they proceed in, by any victory or victories.

Burke, it should be remembered, desired the allies publicly to abjure all thought of conquest and annexation, to appeal to the French people as against the Jacobin faction dominant at Paris, and to encourage the French royalists everywhere, especially in La Vendée (Poitou, as he calls it). In a letter of 1 November to Windham, he calls the execution of Marie Antoinette an act of unequalled cruelty, and adds the significant words—' O poor Poitou '. The occupation of Toulon and the fomenting of a royalist rising in Provence surely ought to have earned his approval ; but some time early in November he wrote to Windham criticizing the British declaration destined for Toulon, which affirmed that that fortress was held in trust for the French Crown and that Great Britain disclaimed all intention of retaining any conquests that her troops might make on the continent of Europe :

. . . I agree with you that the proclamation is well drawn, perhaps too well drawn, as it shows too much art. I admit that it seems more than anything else that has yet appeared to depart from the unfortunate plan of making war against France, and to direct it where it ought to be directed, to the relief of the oppressed, and to the destruction of Jacobinism. I wish, however, that nothing had been said about indemnity. It is a thing unheard of in this stage of a war ; and, as in fact, we have no pledge whatever in our hands but Toulon, it looks as if we meant to keep that place and the ships in its harbour for that indemnity, though surrendered to our faith upon very different terms. This previous demand of indemnity, which has a sort of appearance (even so much as perhaps to hazard the whole effect of the declaration) of fairness, is yet so very loose and general that I scarce know what it is that we and the allied courts may not claim under it. The worst of the matter is that the only object which we have hitherto pursued is the previous security of this indemnification.

The thing, however, that perfectly sickens me in this declaration is its total disagreement with everything we have done, or (so far as I see) that we are going to do now. We promise protection and assistance to those who shall endeavour the restoration of monarchy in that country. Yet, though Poitou is in a manner at our door, and they have for eight months carried on a war on the principles we have pointed out, not a man, not a ship, not an article of stores has been yet sent to these brave unfortunate people. All the force we can spare was destined for our indemnity ; and, when now released (I do not know with what prudence) from the Flemish service, it is intended again to go to the West Indies. No talk, nor no thought of giving the least of the succour we stand engaged for, and which common justice and common policy ought to have induced us to send, though we were under no positive engagement at all. This, joined with our refusing to recognize that monarchy in those who have the right to exercise its authority, is a defeasance to our declaration which nothing but a total change of conduct can cancel. [He added that, owing to the insensate conduct of the late whig party, he would refrain from public censure on the Pitt administration. The French princes had received the news of the execution of Marie Antoinette callously.]

As usual, Burke was unfair to the government. Valenciennes and two lesser fortresses in Flanders were in our possession; and France, being the aggressor in a struggle which was then going against her, might fairly be called on to pay an indemnity. But Burke's royalism had been inflamed by the arrival of a letter from the Comte d'Artois (the future Charles X), then resident at Hamm near Hamburg, which bade him use his influence to induce the British ministers actively to assist the royalists of the west of France. The count set forth eloquently his desire to join them and his fear that the authorities at Whitehall were throwing obstacles in his way. He enclosed the appeal of the younger Larochejaquelin and other Vendéan chiefs begging for his presence.[4] These letters infuriated Burke. Becoming the mouthpiece of the French princes, he saw little more than their side in what was a many-sided problem. Pitt could not neglect the interests of Austria, Prussia, and Holland. Still less could he turn a deaf ear to the appeals of our West India planters for protection against the revolutionary schemes emanating from the Jacobins of Hayti, which threatened a general rising of the slaves; and, as the planters of Hayti sent an official offer to place that wealthy colony in his hands, he was surely justified in sending out an expedition. Besides, Burke's charge of neglect of the French royalists was incorrect, as will appear from the following letter of Pitt to the earl of Moira, commanding a force in the Solent destined for the coast of Brittany :[5]

(Private.)   Downing Street, Nov. 25, 1793.

Your lordship will receive by this messenger a copy of an account received this day from Jersey, and some very important papers from the chiefs of the royalist army, which put us much more in possession than we have hitherto been, of their situation and of their intended operations. The reports brought by M. Bertin of the events of last week may probably prove in some degree true, but are not precise or authentic enough to be much relied upon; and, the letter from the royalist commanders being of so distant a date as the 10th, no very certain conclusions can be drawn from it for any present purpose. But on the whole it is, I think, satisfactory to see that the royalist army is actually in greater force than could have been imagined, and that the assistance which your lordship will be enabled to give them (if the communication can be opened)

[4] Burke, *Corresp.* iii. 166–77.   [5] Chatham MS. 102.

goes beyond not only their expectation but their demand. The points which they seem to have in view on the sea coast are, as your lordship will perceive, numerous. I take for granted that your lordship will arrange with Admiral Macbride the means of ascertaining as soon as possible after your arrival at the islands, whether they have succeeded in getting possession of any of them. If they should not be in actual possession, probably the knowledge of your being so near them will lead to their making great efforts to secure any place that you point out, especially if you find that you can either assist or countenance their attempt or speedily support them if they succeed. We shall not fail to attend to the supply of the articles of which the royalists state themselves to be most in need, and to apprize your lordship what steps we can take, beyond those which you are already informed of, for that purpose. . . . I am aware that it can only be by the result of the last information on the spot that your opinion or decision ought to be regulated.

Another letter of about the same date, probably from Dundas to Lord Moira, stated that the news from the council of the Christian and royal army held at Dol on the 10th instant had on that day arrived through the medium of Lord Balcarres. Moira is directed, immediately on his arrival at Guernsey, to open communications with that council and to inform it that supplies of flour are being prepared for the succour of the royalists, as that is what they most require. Clearly, then, government had endeavoured to help the Bretons, but the difficulty of opening communications with them on that coast, where the republicans controlled most of the landing-places, was very great.[6] Obviously the north of Brittany offered better opportunities than the coast of La Vendée, where the succouring convoys would have to pass Brest and L'Orient at a time when the Union Jack did not wave supreme at sea. Civilians could not understand the complexity of the problem of helping the bands which roamed through Brittany and Poitou ; but the letter just quoted brings it into clear light, and reveals one of the causes which doomed to failure the hopes of Burke and the later plans of Windham and Pitt.

But another cause of failure remains to be noted. The Comte de Provence, who had assumed the title of regent for the little Louis XVII, was much disliked by the constitutional wing of the royalist party, which detested *les purs* and their head, the Comte d'Artois. These, on their side, looked on the supporters of the constitution of 1791 as scarcely less objectionable than the Jacobins. Yet, amidst the horrors of the reign of terror, France began to regret that constitution ; and it was clear that only under its aegis could large masses be rallied, except in the fanatical west. This was one among several reasons why Pitt and the foreign secretary, Lord Grenville, strongly objected to the

[6] See too *Dropmore Papers*, ii. 454, 464, 469, 476.

arrival of the Comte de Provence or the Comte d'Artois at Toulon. Their presence, besides hampering the allied commanders, would increase the friction among the inhabitants. Nevertheless, Burke, who early in December went with Windham to have a conference with Pitt, prevailed on his friend to set forth the views of the French princes, as he did in the following letter to Pitt : [7]

Hill St., Monday evg., Dec. 16, 1793.

Sir, the only point on which it is material that I should trouble you is that which relates to the communication with the [French] princes. On this too, I would only wish to state such facts as I have happened to hear, without repeating opinions with which you are already acquainted. The princes, I understand, are full of jealousy of the conference, which, they conceive, is to precede any recognition of their title. Their jealousy turns principally on the following points,—a fear lest the purpose of this country should be to limit their authority, with a view to keeping France hereafter in a feeble and depressed state. A fear lest the ideas of the constitutionalists should be suffered to prevail too much in any settlement proposed, particularly since the terms adopted in the capitulation of Toulon. A fear lest views of indemnification should extend too far, and sacrifices be required of them inconsistent with their duty and character. A general apprehension growing out of all the former that the cabinet here is not in earnest in wishing to see them, for the present, at the head of the royalist party, but would rather that the cause should, to a certain degree, be carried on without their assistance. These, as I recollect, were the principal heads of uneasiness, which, whether reasonable or not, may be considered as very excusable in their most anxious situation. The danger is that, in their present state of ferment, and called upon in particular as the Comte d'Artois conceives himself to be, he should be led to take some rash step, and, without consulting anything but the feelings of the moment, should throw himself upon the coast of Brittany in the first vessel that he could procure to convey him. Nobody could perhaps much blame the proceeding ; yet every one would have reason to lament it. The person from whom I principally hear this, and who, though placed in a situation inferior to that of the Duc d'Harcourt, is still much in the princes' counsels, is persuaded that they are perfectly disposed to be tractable, and would be quieted by any general assurance relative to the above points conveyed to them by a person in whose sincerity they could confide. He seems to think that, could they be set at ease on those points, no other difficulty would remain. . . .

Windham's informant (probably the Comte de Sérent) little knew the intractable nature of the Comte d'Artois. But this whole question was ended for the present by Bonaparte's brilliant recapture of Toulon on 17 December. That event and the failure of the allies to hold the lines of Weissenburg in the north of Alsace produced general consternation. Even before the arrival of those

[7] Chatham MS. 190.

doleful tidings Windham informed Mrs. Crewe of his resolve to join any party that would openly and relentlessly war against ' the whole Jacobin faction '. Early in 1794 Burke and he sought to induce the Portland whigs to give a more decided support to the ministry. Pitt also on 16 January submitted to Windham the draft of the king's speech, to be delivered on 21 January, with the result that a meeting of representative whigs at the duke's residence, Burlington House, resolved on a loyal adhesion to Pitt—so Windham informed him by a note late on that night. To that occasion we may probably assign the following undated letter of Burke : [8]

[Endorsed, 1794.] Tuesday morning.

Everything went off at Burlington House as well as possible. The meeting was not very numerous, not exceeding, as I guess, thirty. But some who were absent are not ill inclined. The mountain was suffered to attract too many, who are inclined, I believe, to return, but who do not know their way back. The duke of P[ortland] opened the business extremely well and with the utmost possible clearness and decision. He put the principle of the war upon the proper foundation ; and, having stated the necessity of persevering in its support in a very forcible light, he recommended that no collateral considerations should divert their minds and attentions from it ; that therefore they should resist to their utmost all inquiries into miscarriage as tending to destroy the confidence necessary to the ministers at this time with regard to home support ; but, as, what he considered of far greater importance, tending to prejudice the whole of our government with regard to foreign powers. I never remember him to have opened any business, at any time, with so strong and decided a declaration of his own opinions, his way in general being to state the case and to wish the company to take it into consideration.

In consequence of Portland's decided lead Fox was left with few supporters ; and most of these drifted away in the course of the session. George Byng later on had occasion to mention the story that the Foxites usually went off to Brooks's in a hackney-coach. 'That is a calumny (he said) ; we filled two coaches.' Treason trials, volunteering, and plans for retrieving the failures of 1793 filled up the spring of 1794 ; and, as is well known, the Portland whigs joined the cabinet early in July, the duke becoming secretary of state for home affairs and the colonies, while Dundas took the seals of state for the newly constituted war department with Windham as colleague. Into the disputes caused by these accessions of the ' Old Whigs ', especially that which centred around the viceroyalty, it is not proposed to enter. Burke threw himself into them with his usual vehemence ; but his four letters to Windham, of 16-28 October 1794, published in *Windham's Diary*, show that he was not acquainted with

[8] Chatham MS. 118.

the ministerial side of the case; and his later assertion that Earl Fitzwilliam went with a free hand to Dublin is disproved by the important memorandum in which Grenville described a conference of Pitt and himself with the new ministers.[9]

Before adverting to the important mission undertaken by Windham in his ministerial capacity to the head-quarters of the duke of York in Flanders, we will notice a matter of personal interest affecting Burke. His services to the state had been long and meritorious, though marred occasionally by eccentricities and outbursts of temper which probably account for his never attaining cabinet rank. Of late he had helped indirectly to bring about the accession of the Portland whigs; for, while disclaiming any direct part in the negotiations, he informed Windham that he had spared no pains ' to produce the dispositions which led to it '. Further, his succour to the distressed French exiles had strained his scanty resources to the breaking-point. All this was made known to Pitt by some friend, probably Windham; and the prime minister seems to have suggested the writing of a memorandum detailing his services. The original is in the Chatham MSS., no. 118. As it has been published in the *Stanhope Miscellanies* a précis must suffice here :

Burke understands that Pitt is so obliging as to think that his public services during thirty years may be recommended to H. M.'s gracious consideration. Burke has never solicited, or suggested, a reward; he has done nothing beyond his strict duty. But, if he may compare his services with those of certain contemporaries, he will refer to his arduous duties before and during the ministry of Lord Rockingham, at the conclusion of which it was generally expected that some provision would be made for him. On the other hand the services of Colonel Barré and Dunning, though no more conspicuous, were rewarded by annual pensions of £3,000 and £4,000 respectively, the latter gentleman gaining also a peerage. Burke's reform of the pay office has led to important savings of public money; and in general his work for the state has been far greater than that of Barré and Dunning, who were amply rewarded twelve years ago. Many others whose careers have been shorter and less arduous than Burke's have secured full recognition and pecuniary rewards, Lord Auckland being a prominent instance.—' Mr. Burke does not conceive that whatever H. M. may be graciously pleased to do for Mr. Burke in the present temper of the public mind would be more unpopular or ill received in the nation than what has been done for any of these gentlemen.'

Probably Pitt desired to make use of this memorandum in order to overcome the dislike with which George III regarded the champion of the American colonists and of economical reform. It is inconceivable that services so splendid as those of Burke should hitherto have failed to secure recognition, had not the

[9] *Dropmore Papers*, iii. 36–8.

king continued to nurse feelings of resentment. Burke, as we have seen, compared his career with those of two men who had early gained peerages ; and his desire to gain a title for his beloved estate at Beaconsfield is proved by the following new letter of his son Richard to Windham. The sentences in the middle, which are omitted, refer to the wish of the writer that, as matters stand, he would (if he could put aside the thought of his mother) prefer that no reward whatever should be accorded, though that would involve the sale of the Beaconsfield estate :

June 14, 1794.

I am much obliged to you for your communications of government with regard to my father, which, as far as the pecuniary consideration goes, are fully adequate to my wishes. But I cannot help expressing my surprise that there should be anything like a demur with regard to the peerage. It is not that I lay much stress on what Sir Gilbert Elliot conveyed to me from the ministers on that subject. I think his pretensions stand upon grounds much stronger than any promises, actual or implied. The terms used to Sir Gilbert Elliot might have been general, tho' he seemed to attach a particular sense to them. They were certainly, however, not such as to imply that the ministers had very mean ideas with regard to my father, and I did not conceive that what was considered as a debt due from the country, and due to the opinion of Europe at large, could be less than the peerage. However, it is for the ministers to judge what they will do or not do. It is a matter absolutely in their own breasts. It would be as ridiculous for my father at this time of day to haggle about the recompense for his services, as it would have been absurd in the ministers to chaffer with him about the price before those services were rendered, services which, if the effects of them could have been foreseen, or could have been bargained for (if he was a man capable of bargaining) I do not believe any rewards the country has to bestow would have been thought too much. But in the retrospect things have a different appearance, especially when impressions are no longer fresh and when the man is going off the stage and can be of use no further. It is therefore not unnatural that difficulties should be made. . . . As matters stand, however, some sacrifice of dignity must be made to ease ; and, tho' I think he might expect an *otium cum dignitate*, and that the peerage is not more than his due, and (if I may say) the specific reward of his services, yet, if the ministers think otherwise, and think that services like his can be paid in money, as far as my vote goes I shall advise him to submit, and I see nothing else for him to do, but to take what is given him with thankfulness and with as good grace as he can. I cannot think that the ministers have sufficiently considered, or that it can be their intention, that what they do should lose so much of its grace and effect with regard to the public by what they withhold ; or that they have reflected what will be thought when it comes to be known that this was an object to my father and that it was refused on any grounds whatever. If they do not give it to him, for God's sake, for what kind of services is it reserved, unless it is determined that it should never be given to civil service or only follow in the common line of official promotion ? And who do they mean to make peers in the future ?[10]

The letter serves to refute the statements of Earl Stanhope in his *Life of Pitt* and Burke's biographer, Prior, that Burke would have been raised to the peerage but for the death of his son Richard, which occurred on 2 August 1794. On the contrary, the last months of Richard Burke were embittered by the knowledge that that honour was not to be conferred on one whom he loved as his father and revered as one of the greatest men known to history. Either the death of the son, or some carelessness on the part of Dundas or Pitt, caused a delay painful to the friends of Burke, who were aware of the critical state of his finances. This appears from the following letter of Windham to Pitt. The final paragraph, which refers to the topic of a peerage, is omitted.

[Endorsed. Aug. 13, 1794.]

Dear Sir,

Let me recall to your recollection the business of Mr. Burke, in case it should not have been mentioned to you by Mr. Dundas, with whom I had a good deal of conversation about it the other day at Wimbledon. At all events the pecuniary part of it should be settled before the king's departure [for Weymouth]; and the only footing on which it could be well settled would be in my opinion for the £1,200 a year to be given immediately; a sum to be promised from parliament for the lives of Mr. and Mrs. Burke and the survivor; and another sum for a term of years such as he may dispose at a price sufficient to pay his debts. The debts are supposed to be under £25,000, and the income of Beaconsfield to be near £500. I cannot but think this income that ought to be secured to him should be in all £3,000. . . .

W. WINDHAM.

At last, on 30 August, Pitt wrote to Burke informing him of the intention of the king to apply to parliament in the following session for the bestowal of ' an annuity more proportioned to His Majesty's sense of your public merit than any which His Majesty can at present grant '. In the meantime an annuity of £1,200 a year ('the largest sum which His Majesty is entitled to fix ') was conferred. Burke's reply to Pitt is missing; but its tenor may be judged from the following letter of the king to Pitt :

Weymouth, September 5, 1794.

I have received Mr. Pitt's note enclosing the letter he has received from Mr. Burke. Misfortunes are the great softeners of the human mind, and has (*sic*) in the instance of this distressed man made him owne what his warmth of temper would not have allowed in other circumstances, namely, that he may have erred. One quality I take him to be very susceptible of, that is, gratitude, which I think covers many failings,

[10] Add. MS. 37843.

and makes me therefore happy at being able to relieve him. His chusing the pension to be settled on his wife I thoroughly approve of, and it will with the better grace enable the other pension to be settled on him.

For some reason far from easy to fathom, Pitt did not apply to parliament for the further pension, but granted from the civil list an annuity of £2,500 which was found to be available. Earl Stanhope suggests that this course averted the possibility of an angry debate. But would Fox, Grey, or Sheridan have dared to dispute the propriety of granting pensions to Burke? If any question had been raised, would it not have been as to their inadequacy? Surely the occasion was such as to elicit an almost unanimous assent. Sympathy with sorrow, and admiration of the transcendent genius which had shone forth during thirty years, would have lifted the house of commons above the low levels of faction, and breathed into members something of the public spirit which they united to honour. Burke's second letter to Pitt, of date 28 October, deserves quotation in full:

Beaconsfield, October 28, 1795.

Dear Sir,

When you first did me the honour to signifye to me the king's gracious intentions in my favour, I took the liberty of charging you with my most dutiful and grateful acknowledgments to his majesty for that inestimable mark of his royal condescension and goodness. The act is now completed. I beg you, Sir, once more to lay me at his majesty's feet to express the lively gratitude with which I am penetrated on this occasion. They will come best thro' that servant who has so generously seconded and forwarded his royal beneficence, and who has conducted his majesty's general affairs with a degree of ability, spirit, and zeal, the lustre of which no circumstances of fortune can tarnish. These great qualities, which have enabled you to struggle with so many difficulties, supply the most rational ground of hope, that providence will make use of them under his majesty's wise and auspicious direction to give a glorious termination to this necessary, this politick, and (what can be surely added, but which cannot be too often thought on) this moral war.

I look on this provision for the repose of my age to be partly in consideration of my feeble but well intended efforts in that cause. If I were capable of exertion, my labours to my latest breath would be in the same way. But, being no longer capable of any exertion, my prayers will be that my royal benefactor may long reign in the enjoyment of a victorious peace, the fruit of his magnanimity and perseverance. I trust it will be such as to fix all just and temperate government on as firm a basis as the condition of human affairs will permit us to look for; and, in the overthrow of the corrupters and destroyers of mankind, will for ever discourage the principles and maxims which have called for his resolute exertions in favour of his people and of all people.

I have the honour, &c.,

EDM. BURKE.

The phraseology of this letter rings hollow when compared with the feelings poignantly expressed in his letters of 20 and 28 October to Windham. There he describes his state of mind as near to complete despair. The last blow had been the failure of his hopes respecting the Irish viceroyalty; but on all sides he saw ruin approaching :

I am very miserable [he wrote] tossed by public upon private grief and by private upon public. Oh! have pity on yourselves! and may the God whose counsels are so mysterious in the moral world (even more than in the natural) guide you through all these labyrinths. Do not despair! If you do, work in despair.

The causes of his despondency must be set forth in another article.

J. HOLLAND ROSE.

Notes and Documents

A Report on the Penenden Trial

THE trial of Penenden Heath, where Archbishop Lanfranc litigated in 1072 for the possessions and rights of his church against Bishop Odo of Bayeux, the Conqueror's brother, is ' perhaps the best reported trial of the reign ',[1] famous not only as a specimen of a lawsuit before a county court in the beginning of the Anglo-Norman times,[2] mentioned also in the Domesday Book,[3] but famous also as illustrating the political intentions of the Conqueror.[4] The text of the record has so far been known from two copies, viz. the *Textus Roffensis* (fo. 109) in the cathedral library of Rochester, compiled about 1125 in Rochester partly from a Canterbury source [5], and the Cotton MS. Vespasian A. xxii (fo. 120) in the British Museum, no doubt also of Rochester origin,[6] and has been printed several times since Selden [7] and Wharton.[8]

[1] Stubbs, *Constitutional History of England*, 6th edition, i. 300.

[2] Cf. Stubbs, *l. c.* ; Pollock and Maitland, *History of the English Law*, 2nd edition, i. 93.

[3] Domesday Book, I, fo. 5^v; L. B. Larking, *The Domesday Book of Kent*, London, 1869, p. 21.   [4] Cf. Freeman, *Norman Conquest of England*, iv. 364–8.

[5] Cf. Hearne, *Textus Roffensis*, Oxford, 1720, p. 140 (c. 84); F. Liebermann, *Notes on the Textus Roffensis* in *Archaeologia Cantiana*, xxiii, 1898, pp. 94–112, and *Die Gesetze der Angelsachsen*, i, 1903, pp. xxvi seqq.

[6] Cf. *Catalogue of the Manuscripts in the Cottonian Library*, 1802, p. 437.

[7] Selden, *Eadmeri Historiae Novorum Libri VI*, London, 1623, pp. 197–200 (perhaps from the Cotton MS.). Selden's text has been reprinted by Gabriel Gerberon, *Sancti Anselmi Opera nec non Eadmeri Historia Novorum*, 2nd edition, Paris, 1721, appendix, p. 127 ; by Migne, *Patrologia Latina*, clix, Paris, 1854, col. 543–5 ; by Larking, *l. c.*, appendix, pp. 16*, 17*, who has collated it with the Cotton MS., and by M. M. Bigelow, *Placita Anglo-Normannica*, London, 1879, pp. 5–9, where the last sentence is left out.

[8] H. Wharton, *Anglia sacra*, i, London, 1691, pp. 334–6, from the *Textus Roffensis*. The same text has been published by David Wilkins, *Concilia Magnae Britanniae et Hiberniae*, i, London, 1737, pp. 323, 324. Neglecting *lectiones variae* of minor importance, I mention only that the text of Wharton and Wilkins is much shorter than Selden's in the middle part of the document containing the enumeration of the vindicated possessions; the passages *scilicet Ratulfe, Sandwic—in Sutfolchia Frachenham* and *Stokes vero—antiquitus fuerunt* of Selden's text, which certainly hail from Rochester, are wanting in Wharton and Wilkins, and are perhaps a later addition. David Wilkins, *Leges Anglo-Saxonicae*, London, 1721, pp. 293–5, has a mixed text, apparently based on the shorter, but interpolated from the longer copy. I have not myself seen the *Textus Roffensis* or the Cotton MS.

The accounts of Eadmer[9] and Gervase of Canterbury[10] are of no value, based as they are on the judicial record itself and compressing its contents into a few words; nor do the Latin acts of Lanfranc in a manuscript of the Saxon Annals[11] furnish any new fact excepting the year of the litigation, whereas no date appears in the printed text of the record. It cannot have been composed immediately after the trial; the introductory tale and the very first words,

Tempore magni regis Willelmi, qui Anglicum regnum armis conquisivit et suis ditionibus subiugavit, contigit . . . Et quia illis diebus in comitatu illo quisquam non erat, qui tantae fortitudinis viro resistere posset,

seem to suggest that at least the introduction was written after the death of William I.

There exists, however, a third, fragmentary copy, not yet printed, to my knowledge, which, if I am not mistaken, preserves the original text of the introduction. The MS. *Cartae Antiquae* A. 42, in the library of the dean and chapter of Canterbury, is a large roll of the thirteenth century; it contains short lives of the popes, and of the archbishops of Canterbury down to the tenth century, which have been ascribed to 'a contemporary admirer of St. Dunstan'.[12] As the sources of the history of the popes are very scanty in that age, I have had, in preparing the continuation of Mommsen's edition of the *Liber Pontificalis*, to examine this manuscript.[13] It was a disappointment: the text is a late compilation, made some centuries after Dunstan, although it contains a few extracts of the *Liber Pontificalis* closely connected with the English manuscripts of that biographical collection which I have discussed in the second section of my *Mitteilungen aus Englischen Bibliotheken*.[14] A part of the back of the roll, originally left blank, has been filled afterwards with additions of other scribes of the thirteenth century.[15] There is in the upper part a list of charters given to Christ Church, Canterbury, especially by Alexander III and his successors, which some day may prove useful, when to the *Italia*, *Germania*, and *Gallia*

[9] *Eadmeri Historia novorum*, ed. M. Rule, p. 17.
[10] *Gervasii Actus pontificum*, Works, ed. W. Stubbs, ii. 369.
[11] Earle and Plummer, *Two of the Saxon Chronicles parallel*, i. 289. Walter de Gray Birch, *Domesday Book*, London, 1887, pp. 293–6, has printed from the Cotton MS., Augustus, ii. 36, a text that seemed to him to be a 'minute of the points moved by Lanfranc'; but I doubt that it refers to the Penenden suit.
[12] J. B. Sheppard, in the *Fifth Report of the Royal Commission on Historical Manuscripts*, 1876, p. 462; cf. F. Liebermann, in the *Neues Archiv der Gesellschaft für ältere deutsche Geschichtskunde*, iv. 622.
[13] I have to thank the Rev. E. Moore, D.D., and the Rev. C. E. Woodruff, of Canterbury, for their great kindness shown to me.
[14] *Neues Archiv*, xxxv. 1910, pp. 331–431.   [15] Cf. Sheppard, *l. c.*

pontificia of Kehr's *Regesta pontificum Romanorum* an *Anglia pontificia* is joined. Then on the last membrane of the roll the fragmentary text on Penenden Heath has been added. I propose very soon to give a short account of the compilation on the history of the popes in the *Neues Archiv*, where I have published the report referred to on manuscripts of a related kind ; but I have thought it better to present the text of the Penenden trial, as yet only mentioned shortly by Dr. Sheppard,[16] in a periodical more accessible to students of English history. The text has no heading, nor has the initial letter been filled in. I have expanded the abbreviations.

Anno[17] ab incarnacione domini nostri Iesu Christi MLXXII, pontificatus domini Alexandri pape undecimo, regni vero Guillelmi regis sexto, presidente Lanfranco archiepiscopo ecclesie Cantuariensi pontificatus sui anno secundo, ex precepto predicti regis ad instanciam archiepiscopi iussum est totum comitatum absque mora considere et comitatus omnes Francigenas et precipue Anglos in antiquis legibus et consuetudinibus peritos convenire ad diracionandum libertates et consuetudines, quas ecclesia Christi in terras proprias habet atque in regias terras habere debeat. Qui cum convenirent apud Pynindenne, omnes consederunt, et quoniam multa placita de diraciocinacionibus terrarum et verba de consuetudinibus[18] legum inter archiepiscopum et Odonem Baiocensem[19] episcopum, qui multas terras de archiepiscopatu sibi usurpaverat, ibi surrexerunt[20] et etiam inter consuetudines regales et archiepiscopales, que prima die expediri non potuerunt, ea causa totus comitatus per tres dies ibi fuit detentus. In hiis tribus diebus diracionavit ibi Lanfrancus plures terras, quas homines ipsius episcopi tenuerunt, scilicet Detlinges, Estoce, Prestuna, Danintona ; super Hugonem de Monteforti Horcinges et Broc, super Radulphum de Curva Spina LX solidatas de pastura in Grean. Omnes istas terras diracionavit ita liberas atque quietas, ut nullus homo in toto regno esset, qui inde aliquid calumpniaretur. In eodem siquidem placito non solum istas prenominatas terras, sed et omnes consuetudines ecclesie sue et libertates renovavit et renovatas ibi diracionavit, scilicet soca and saca, tol, team, flymena-fyrmthe, grytbrece, forestal, haimfare, infangenepeof, cum omnibus aliis consuetudinibus paribus istis vel minoribus istis, in terris et in aquis, in silvis, in viis et in pratis et in omnibus rebus et locis, scilicet infra civitatem et extra, infra burgam[21] et extra. Et ab omnibus sapientibus, qui affuerunt, fuit ibi diracionatum atque iudicatum a

Thus abruptly the copy ends, though there would have been room for more. It is of little value as to the trial itself ; it has nothing not contained in the other copies except the beginning, nor have I burdened my reproduction with their various readings, which belong rather to a definitive edition, when a successor of Haddan and Stubbs arises in the future. The Canterbury MS. agrees almost entirely with the shorter of the printed texts

[16] *Ubi supra.*   [17] MS. nno.   [18] MS. *consuedinibus.*
[19] MS. *Baionencem* altered into *Baiocencem.*   [20] MS. *surexerunt.*   [21] So MS.

as given by Wharton and Wilkins [22] and differs accordingly from Selden's larger text; but it is distinguished from both by the first lines. The long historical introduction is here missing, and replaced by a few chronological notes, which confirm the year 1072 established after some hesitation and errors of former authors by Plummer from the Lanfranc acts mentioned before,[23] and the form of the date points to the conclusion that we have here a kind of official Canterbury record of the litigation. There are very few similar reports of that age, and it would be hard to write a diplomatic dissertation on such documents; [24] but we have one record of the same year akin to our text, viz. the *Constitutio Windlesorensis* of 1072, relative to the famous controversy of Lanfranc and Thomas of York over the primacy of Canterbury and presenting the results of a trial in a similar way. The *Constitutio* begins with the words : [25]

Anno ab incarnatione domini nostri Iesu Christi millesimo septuagesimo secundo, pontificatus autem domni Alexandri papae undecimo, regni vero Wilelmi gloriosi regis Anglorum et ducis Northmannorum sexto, ex praecepto eiusdem Alexandri papae, annuente eodem rege, in praesentia ipsius et episcoporum atque abbatum ventilata est causa. . . .

A comparison of the two documents settles the priority of our new text of the Penenden record, in spite of its being fragmentary and impaired by some blunders. Later years have had to supply the previous history of the litigation, as it appears in the texts brought to light before. W. LEVISON.

Studies in Magna Carta

I. *Waynagium* and *Contenementum*

NOT a few of the difficulties encountered and the mistakes made in interpreting documents written in medieval Latin are due simply to the failure of their interpreters to observe, or at least to keep in mind, that the terms used are often nothing but French words with a Latin ending. Even the exegesis of what Pitt called the 'Bible of the English Constitution' has suffered from this oversight. Despite centuries of comment the exact

---

[22] Cf. above, p. 717, n. 8.   [23] Cf. Earle and Plummer, *l. c.* ii. 315.
[24] Compare the short mention of narratives of law-suits by H. Hall, *Studies in English Official Historical Documents*, 1908, p. 311.
[25] Wilkins, *Concilia*, i. 324; Eadmer, ed. Rule, p. 252; J. B. Sheppard, *Literae Cantuarienses* (Rolls Series, lxxxv), iii, 1889, p. 351; *Palaeographical Society* (First Series), iii, pl. 170; H. Boehmer, *Die Fälschungen Erzbischof Lanfranks von Canterbury* (in Bonwetsch and Seeberg's *Studien zur Geschichte der Theologie und der Kirche*, viii. 1), Leipzig, 1902, p. 167.

meaning of certain words and phrases in Magna Carta is not well understood, and in some respects the latest interpretation is considerably less accurate than that offered two hundred years ago. This is certainly the case with the well-known clause 20 of 1215 limiting royal amercements :

> Liber homo non amercietur pro parvo delicto, nisi secundum modum delicti ; et pro magno delicto amercietur secundum magnitudinem delicti, salvo contenemento suo ; et mercator eodem modo, salva mercandisa sua ; et villanus eodem modo amercietur salvo waynagio suo, si inciderint in misericordiam nostram ; et nulla predictarum misericordiarum ponatur, nisi per sacramentum proborum hominum de visneto.

Postponing for the moment discussion of the much-disputed expression *contenementum*, let us see what meaning is attached to the *waynagium* which is saved to the villein. One naturally turns first to Mr. McKechnie's elaborate commentary. *Waynagium* is here translated *wainage*, which is explained as the villein's ' plough and its accoutrements, including possibly the oxen '.[1] For this interpretation he may quote high authority of this and the last generation. Professor Maitland translated *waynagium* by ' instruments of husbandry ',[2] and Professor Vinogradoff, accepting this view, identifies the instruments in question with the villein's ' plough and plough-team '.[3] Bishop Stubbs does not seem to commit himself to a definite translation either in the *Constitutional History* or in the *Select Charters*, for the two meanings given to the term in the glossary of the latter work can hardly have been regarded by him as applicable to the passage before us. The modern explanation of *waynagium* was already current in the eighteenth century when Giles Jacob, in his *New Law Dictionary*, first published in 1729, insisted that the word meant no more than the plough-tackle or implements of husbandry, in which he seems afterwards to include the beasts of the plough.[4]

Before coming to a decision on the adequacy of this definition it will be convenient to dispose of one which has obtained less currency and which rests upon a false etymology. It was Sir Edward Coke, so far as we know, who first defined *waynage* as ' the contenement of a villein ; or *the furniture of his cart or wain* '.[5] This interpretation, though it reappeared in the later and less authoritative section of Spelman's *Glossarium*,[6] did not find much support, but it was revived, perhaps unconsciously, by Sir Travers Twiss in the index to the second volume of his

---

[1] *Magna Carta* (1905), p. 343.
[2] *Hist. of Engl. Law*, i. 416. The *New English Dictionary*, s. v. *Gainage*, says that this meaning is ' probably ' the correct one.
[3] *Villainage in England*, pp. 74–5.
[4] Ed. J. Morgan (10th edition), 1782, s. v. *Gainage*. [5] 2 Inst. 28.
[6] Published by Dugdale after Spelman's death.

edition of Bracton, where *waynagium* in clause 20 of Magna Carta is glossed ' *waggonage* of villeins '. More recently the editor of a volume of local records has fallen into the same error in translating a passage from the *Testa de Nevill* : [7] ' Ricardus prepositus tenet duas bovatas pro wanagio et namiis domini regis custodiendis.' This is Englished : ' Richard the reeve holds two bovates by the service of keeping the king's *waggon-teams* and distresses.' [8] It need hardly be said that there is no connexion whatever between the Old English word *wain* and *waynagium*, which is merely the French *gagnage* with a Latin ending. Jacob was well aware of this in 1729, but with a stupidity which goes far to justify his inclusion in the *Dunciad* he introduces into his definition, as a gloss on *gagnage*, the words *plaustri apparatus*, thus convicting himself either of taking *plaustrum* to mean a plough or of not having shaken himself free from Coke's erroneous definition.

The ordinary interpretation of *waynage*, which renders it by ' implements of husbandry ' or some equivalent phrase, is not so far removed from the real sense as that which has just been discussed. There is reason, however, to believe that it is too concrete, and fails to reproduce the exact shade of meaning which the original conveys. In Old French *gagnage* may mean (1) profit, gain ; (2) tillage ; (3) crop ; (4) land under tillage ; (5) grain ; but Godefroy gives no instance of its use in the sense of ' implements of husbandry '. It is not at all likely that Anglo-Norman by the beginning of the thirteenth century had already developed a new meaning for the word which never came into use abroad. In the other passages in which *waynagium* (or *gagnage*) occurs about that date in England it is easily brought under one or other of the meanings illustrated by Godefroy. This is the case in the fifth clause of Magna Carta itself, which requires a guardian to restore to an heir, when he comes of age, all his land ' instauratam de carrucis et *waynagiis* secundum quod tempus *waynagii* exiget et exitus terrae rationabiliter poterunt sustinere '. Mr. McKechnie sees that ' tempus waynagii ' can only mean season of husbandry or tillage ; but though the *waynagia* with which the land was to be stocked are here expressly distinguished from ploughs, which according to him form the chief objects covered by the term in clause 20, he still translates it ' implements of husbandry '.[9] It is far more probable that the word is used here in the sense of ' crops ' (Godefroy's third meaning) or of ' lands under cultivation ' (Godefroy's fourth sense), and that the passage should be compared with the requirement in modern leases that the outgoing tenant shall leave the land in as good condition as he received it.

[7] p. 403.   [8] *Lancashire Inquests* (Lanc. and Chesh. Record Soc.), i. 26.
[9] *Op. cit.* p. 247.

In writs of 1232 and 1237 for the collection of a fortieth and a thirtieth respectively 'equi deputati (assignati) *ad wainagium*' are contrasted with 'equi *carettarii*',[10] in which cases *wainagium* is clearly used in Godefroy's second sense, viz. tillage. It is in this sense that the word first occurs in the *Domesday of St. Paul's*, drawn up in 1222,[11] but it is also found there with the meaning of 'land under cultivation' (Godefroy's fourth sense).[12] It is employed in a way rather more difficult to interpret in another passage:[13] 'Item dicunt [iuratores de Barling] quod manerium emendatum per W[alterum de Barling] firmario (*sic*) in domibus et wainagiis in L sol'.' It seems likely that what is meant is increase in crops rather than increase of the cultivated area, which would doubtless have been expressed by *essartis*. In any case there is no reason to suppose that 'implements of husbandry' are in question.[14] The *Dite de Hosebondrie* of Walter de Henley and another thirteenth-century treatise edited with it by Miss Lamond[15] yield only the sense of 'tillage', but it is worth notice that in one case ploughs and *gagnages* are carefully distinguished.[16]

More direct light is thrown upon the use of the term under scrutiny in clause 20 of Magna Carta by the famous passage in which Bracton asserts the (highly theoretical) right of villeins to an action against their lords for bringing about their economic ruin.[17] Professor Vinogradoff translates the important words of the clause as follows: 'Should the lord go so far as to take away the villein's very *waynage*, i.e. plough and plough-team, the villein has an action.' But this is to give to *waynage* a meaning which, as we have seen, is not found in any clear case in thirteenth-century documents. Dr. Vinogradoff's interpretation seems to be coloured by the turn of phrase in a qualifying clause, stigmatized by him as a later interpolation, which limits the privilege to villeins on ancient demesne,[18] and ascribes to every other lord the power '*auferre* a villano waynagium suum et omnia bona sua'.

[10] Stubbs, *Select Charters*, pp. 360, 366.
[11] Ed. Hale, Camden Soc., p. 1: 'MANERIUM DE KADENET. *Wainnagium* potest fieri cum duabus carucis viii capitum.' Cf. p. 59.
[12] *Ibid.* p. 28: 'In dominio tam de *wainagio veteri* quam de novo essarto DC et lxvii acre terre arabilis.' Archdeacon Hale translates 'land anciently ploughed'. Cf. *Cockersand Chartulary*, Chetham Soc., New Ser., xl. 362.
[13] *Domesday of St. Paul's*, p. 63.
[14] Though this would probably have been Hale's interpretation, for he accepts it in both clauses of Magna Carta (preface, p. lxv).
[15] *Walter of Henley's Husbandry*, &c., ed. E. Lamond (1890), pp. 2, 10, 22, 92.
[16] 'Le baillif deit suruer les charues, les gaignages,' &c. (p. 92).
[17] 'Si eos destruant, quod salvum non possit eis esse waynagium suum:' Bracton, fo. 6, quoted by Vinogradoff, *Villainage in England*, p. 74.
[18] Exactly reversing the distinction of Magna Carta, in which the restriction upon royal amercement was closely limited to seigniorial villeins by the insertion of the words 'alterius quam noster' in the reissue of 1217.

The actual clause 20 of Magna Carta is made the basis of an interesting if theoretical legal distinction between villeinage and serfdom by the author of that imaginative treatise the *Mirror of Justice*. In the clause in question, he says, it is granted ' que villein ne soit mie cy grievement amercie que sa *gaigneur* ne soit a luy salve, car de serf ne fait il my mention pur ceo que ils ount rien propre que perdrent. Et de villeins sont leurs *gaignures* appelle Villenages.' [19] Reference to Godefroy shows that *gaigneure* was used synonymously with *gagnage* in the sense of 'tillage', and if the last sentence in the extract from the *Mirror* given above can be trusted, it was, again like *gagnage*, used in the further sense of 'land under cultivation'.

The Statute of Westminster I (1275), which in its sixth clause re-enacted clause 20 of Magna Carta, also contained a provision [20] that if a distress was impounded in a castle or fortress, the said fortress or castle was to be destroyed and the complainant was to receive from the offender double the amount of the damage done to his cattle or by the disturbance of his tillage (' de son gaingnage disturbe ').[21]

It is obvious that a villein's tillage would be made difficult if not impossible supposing his plough and plough-oxen were taken from him either temporarily in the form of a distress or permanently in the form of a royal amercement. But we have found no evidence that *gagnage* (*waynagium*) could mean these implements of husbandry, while the passage just quoted from the Statute of Westminster strongly supports the interpretation of *waynagium* in clause 20 of Magna Carta as ' tillage '. The expression ' saving his tillage ', i.e. without disabling the villein from carrying on the agriculture which was his livelihood, gives a good sense and casts protection over more than the mere ' implements of husbandry '. For the economic ruin of the villein could in many cases be brought about as effectually by impounding his seed-corn or his growing crops as by depriving him of his plough or plough-team.

The recognized senses of the French word *gagnage* and the probabilities of the case both speak with no uncertain sound for a broader and less concrete interpretation of the term *waynagium* in the clause of Magna Carta under discussion than has hitherto been put upon it. We are not, however, limited to this line of proof. For if it can be shown that the other two classes whom this clause protects against arbitrary amercement, the *liberi homines* and the merchants, are given this protection in general terms rather than by the exemption of particular articles,

---

[19] p. 169 quoted by Vinogradoff, *op. cit.* p. 419.
[20] c. 17, *Statutes at Large*, i. 31.
[21] *Gaingnage* is translated ' tulthe ' in MS. Tr. 1.

the evidence of analogy will be all in favour of an equally general protection in the case of the villeins.

The interpretation of the *contenementum* which Magna Carta (and the common law already in Glanvill's time) saved to the *liber homo* has, it is true, followed a not dissimilar course to that of *waynagium*. There has been a strong tendency, largely under the influence of the term *tenementum*, to ascribe to it the sense of a particular estate, a freehold. The learned Spelman, indeed, in his *Glossarium Archaeologicum*, the first part of which appeared in 1626, wrote with perfect correctness : ' Contenementum est aestimatio et conditionis forma, qua quis in republica subsistit. His *Countenance* a *con* et *teneo*. Sic *manutenementum*, *Maintenance* a *manu* et *teneo*.' Jacob, however, while putting the first sentence of this explanation at the beginning of his account of the term, immediately proceeds to twist it into something different :

But [he says] *Contenementum* is more properly that which is necessary for the support and maintenance of men, agreeable to their several qualities or states of life ; and seems to be freehold land which lieth to a man's tenement or dwelling house, that is in his own occupation.

For which rendering he appeals to clause 20 of Magna Carta and to Glanvill. The origin of this perversion of the real meaning of the term in those passages may probably be traced to Coke's definition in his *Institutes*, published eight years after Spelman's *Glossary* : ' Contenementum signifieth his Countenance *which he hath together with and by reason of his freehold*.'[22] Coke was evidently influenced by *tenementum*, but it was left for later writers to complete the confusion. The authors of the *History of English Law* in a very reticent passage content themselves with a note that ' the origin and exact meaning of the term *contenement* seem to be very obscure ', and a reference to the *New English Dictionary*. But the wording of their brief summary of clause 20, ' that the knight's contenement, the merchant's merchandise, the villein's wainage should *escape*,' does not suggest that they understood the salvoes in the general sense for which we are arguing.[23]

Mr. McKechnie is less cautious, and goes even further than Jacob in identifying *contenementum* with *tenementum*. After referring to ' the many laboured and unsatisfactory explanations from the days of Sir Edward Coke to our own ', he continues :

There seems to be no real obscurity, however, since it is clearly a compound of 'tenement'—a word well known as an exact term of feudal conveyancing—and the prefix ' con '. A ' tenement ' is precisely what

[22] 2 Inst. 28.
[23] *Hist. of Engl. Law*, ii. 515. Incidentally it may be noted that *liber homo* was a wider term than knight.

a freeman might be expected to have, namely, a freehold estate of his own. The 'con' merely intensifies the meaning, emphasizing the closeness of the connection between the freeman and his land. Any other tenements he had might be taken away, without inflicting extreme hardship; but to take from him his 'contenement'—his ancestral lands—would leave him poor indeed.[24]

This is a good illustration of that speculative etymology for which the laws of word-formation do not exist. It should be needless to state that *contenement* is not a compound of *tenement* but is derived from *contenir*, while *tenement* comes from the simple verb *tenir*. In fact we may at least agree with Mr. McKechnie in failing to see such obscurity in its origin as even the editors of the *New English Dictionary* seem to find. The meaning which he ascribes to it is, however, inadmissible. It is true that Godefroy gives a single instance of its use as a synonym for *tenement*.[25] But its root sense, with which this has no very obvious connexion, was the same as that of the still living word *contenance*, i. e. capacity, content ('mesure de ce qu'un réceptacle peut tenir'), whence it got the meaning of social capacity, position. That the freeman's *contenement* of Magna Carta was his status or position in the social scale would therefore be the natural assumption even if we had not evidence, in a passage to be quoted later, that *contenance* was sometimes substituted for *contenement* in this connexion.[26] The conclusion can be clinched by proof that *contenement* could not here bear the meaning of freehold. It was not in the interest of the state itself that the *liber homo* should be so heavily amerced as to be incapable of keeping up his position. Hence the common law confirmed by Magna Carta prohibited such ruinous amercements. But it did not expressly protect a man's freehold, for that was not directly in danger. The idea that the freeholder's land could be taken from him as an amercement betrays a complete misconception of the nature of that form of punishment. It was applicable only to offences which fell short of felony, and in its widest extension was a forfeiture of all chattels, though exemptions were early introduced.[27] Thus the *Très Ancien Coutumier* of Normandy excepts in the case of a knight his arms, destrier, palfrey, and rouncey, his ploughs and beasts of the plough, his seed-corn and victuals enough for a year.[28]

It seems clear, then, that in Magna Carta *contenementum* must have its common sense of position, standing, and not its

[24] *Op. cit.* p. 345.

[25] 'Item ont en tous leurs *contenements* toute justice et seigneurie—Denombr. des baill. d'Amiens' (Arch., P. 137, fo. 109ᵛ).

[26] See below, p. 727. Glanvill's phrase 'saving his *honourable* contenement' (*De Legibus Angliae*, ix. 11) becomes much more intelligible on the interpretation adopted in the text. [27] *Hist. of Engl. Law*, ii. 514. [28] *Ibid.* p. 515.

rare meaning of tenement, freehold. The saving of the merchant's merchandise may appear at first sight to disprove the suggestion made above that we have to do in this clause with general salvoes and not with things expressly excepted from amercement. Mr. McKechnie translates this portion of the clause as follows : 'and a merchant in the same way saving his wares.'[29] But though merchandise is now almost exclusively used in this sense it has not even yet entirely lost its original meaning of trade, commerce, and in this sense, we take it, the word is employed in Magna Carta. The meaning is not that the goods with which a merchant traded were entirely exempt from forfeiture if he were amerced and failed to pay the sum fixed, but that the amercement was not to be so heavy as to render him incapable of carrying on his trade. One has only to turn to the *Select Cases Concerning the Law Merchant*, edited by the late Professor Gross,[30] to dispel the idea that any special sacredness attached to the goods of merchants. Instances occur on almost every page of their being distrained by them, while they were sometimes taken in pledge for payment of an amercement where a personal security was not forthcoming.

In the light of the facts given above the clause under discussion may be translated thus :

A freeman shall not be amerced for a slight offence except in proportion to the degree of the offence, and for a grave offence he shall be amerced in proportion to the gravity of his offence, yet saving always his position ; and a merchant in the same way, saving his trade ; and a villein shall be amerced in the same way, saving his tillage—if they have fallen into our mercy, &c.

It is only fair to add, however, that at least one passage may be found which seems to militate to some extent against the view which we have been advocating. The passage in question occurs in a guide to the keeping of a Court of View of Frankpledge composed about 1342, in the description of the proceedings of an imaginary court of Weston in 1340 :

Orre serrunt esluz iii taxours e serrount deux frankes e deux bondes e serrount jurez quils deverent lealment taxer chescun homme solonc le trepas, save a gentil home sa countennance de son hostiel ten' (*sic*), a marchaunt sa marchandise, a terre tenaunt sa carue et sa charette.[31]

Professor Maitland translated the concluding words, not altogether satisfactorily, as follows : 'saving to a gentleman the contenement of his house, to a merchant his merchandise, to a land-tenant his plough and his cart.'

The evidence offered by this passage is somewhat conflicting, for while it supports the more abstract interpretation of *con-*

[29] *Op. cit.* p. 334.   [30] Published by the Selden Society.
[31] *The Court Baron*, ed. Maitland (Selden Society), p. 101.

tenementum it seems to confirm the most concrete meaning that has been put upon *waynagium*. In view of its late date, however, we ought not perhaps to attach much importance to it in elucidating a clause of Magna Carta, especially as it is not part of the actual record of a real court but occurs in a description of a typical court invented by the author to illustrate his rules. In any case since the small holder's plough and cart were property not easily concealed upon which hands could be laid at any time of the year, it would be natural enough that by the fourteenth century their exemption should be specified in place of the more comprehensive but vaguer *salvo waynagio suo*.

JAMES TAIT.

A Papal Visitation of Bury St. Edmunds and Westminster in 1234

IN 1232 Gregory IX ordered a general visitation of monasteries 'throughout the world'.[1] On 9 June he sent a mandate to the abbot of the Cistercian house of Boxley, the abbot of the Premonstratensian house of Bayham and the precentor of Christ Church, Canterbury, to visit those monasteries in the province of Canterbury which were exempt from episcopal visitation.[2] In the mandate he stated that he was informed that certain of these monasteries were disfigured in spiritual things and grievously impoverished in temporal things, and that the monks and nuns appropriated and retained the goods of their monasteries, and bartered them for profit and usury, and thus brought monastic discipline into contempt. He empowered the visitors to introduce reforms and to draw up statutes without any appeal to himself, and to excommunicate all who opposed them. The visitors proceeded to use their powers, and met with strong opposition from the abbots and convents of St. Augustine's, Canterbury, Westminster, and Bury St. Edmunds; as the result of a costly appeal at Rome they obtained other visitors.[3] The bishop and prior of Ely were received at Westminster on 25 January 1234; the abbot of Waltham and the priors of Sempringham and of Holy Trinity, London, at Bury St. Edmunds in July 1234. A copy of the statutes which were framed by the visitors for these two houses is contained in the Cotton MS. Julius D. II, ff. 157–61, a manuscript of a miscellaneous character, which formerly belonged to St. Augustine's, Canterbury, and was compiled mainly in the thirteenth century. The statutes of the visitors closely resemble the statutes which had been drawn

---

[1] Matthew Paris, *Chronica Maiora* (ed. Luard), iii. 234.
[2] *Ibid.* 238.　　　[3] *Ibid.* 239, *Cal. of Papal Letters*, i. 133.

up and accepted by the general chapter of Benedictine abbots at Northampton in 1225,[4] and which follow them in this manuscript. They do not substantiate the very serious charges in the mandate of Gregory IX. Yet it is clear that there was some laxity of discipline and administration and considerable extravagance in both houses, and Westminster was in debt; building was always a heavy charge on the finances of a monastery, and the lady chapel, which had been begun in 1220 and was built mainly at the cost of the abbey, was not complete in 1234.[5]

ROSE GRAHAM.

STATUTES FOR THE MONASTERY OF BURY ST. EDMUNDS

In nomine sancte et individue Trinitatis et gloriose Virginis Marie et beati regis et martiris Edmundi monasterii istius patroni, nos H[enricus] abbas de Waltham, Th[omas] de Simplingeham, et R[icardus] sancte Trinitatis Londonie priores, a summo pontifice G[regorio] nono dati uisitatores,[6] anno domini MCC°xxxiiij° ad hoc monasterium sancti Edmundi die dominica proxima post translationem sancti Thome martiris ad officium uisitandi exequendum personaliter accessimus, et a uenerabili uiro H[enrico] abbate eiusdem monasterii et eiusdem loci conuentu honorifice suscepti, in crastino capitulum intrauimus, et mandato domini pape ad nos directo sollempniter recitato cum debita reuerencia et deuocione ad predictum officium exequendum sine omni contradictione fuimus admissi. Officii igitur nostri executioni diligenter insistentes, a singulis sub interminacione anathematis inquisiuimus tam super statu ecclesie quam personaliter rei ueritatem. Cognito uero eiusdem monasterii statu, auctoritate apostolica ea que subscripta sunt duximus instituenda[7].

In primis statuimus ut abbas diligens sit in omnibus, sed primo et precipue circa curam subditorum tamquam in districto examine de eorum animabus rationem redditurus, quia iuxta regulam ad abbatem pertinet quicquid delinquitur a subiectis; eo etiam moderamine discrecionis uersus subiectos suos se habeat, ne aut in correptione modum excedens nimiam exerceat austeritatem aut correptionem omittendo nimia remissione eorum correptionem negligere uideatur, caute tam in uerbis quam in sentenciis proferendis, uicium declinans precipitationis. Volumus etiam ut libertates et possessiones sui monasterii pro posse suo teneat[8], et ut alienata sic studeat reuocare ne de cetero aliqua sine conuentus sui assensu presumat alienare, familiam habeat moderatam et bene compositam, et superfluitatem tam in uecturis quam in personis studeat resecare, patrimonium Crucifixi sibi commissum ita discrete et fideliter disponat ut tamquam fidelis dispensator et prudens remunerari a Domino eternaliter mereatur; et ut melius officium suum exequi possit, districte precipimus ut monachi sibi subditi tamquam patri et pastori reuerentiam debitam impendant et in

---

[4] Reynerus, *Apostolatus Benedictinorum in Anglia*, appendix 94–7.
[5] Lethaby, *Westminster Abbey and the King's Craftsmen*, 107.
[6] MS. *uisitatoris*. The MS. is very carelessly written, and I am much indebted to the Editor for his kind help in emending the text.
[7] MS. *instatuenda*. [8] MS. *teneatur*.

hiis que secundum [legem] Domini et regulam[a] sancti Benedicti sunt deuote et regulariter obediant, honorem et eius dignitatem et potestatem tam in spiritualibus quam in temporalibus; indulgentias sedis apostolice sibi commissas et a nobis inspectas et omnia alia rite saluanda tam circa personam ipsius quam circa ecclesiam sibi commissam interius et exterius salua, illibata, et intacta uolumus permanere.

Preterea statuta domini R. abbatis de Wardona et collegarum suorum qui ab Innocentio papa ad hoc monasterium directi sunt uisitatores [10] et statuta generalis capituli huius ordinis auctoritate eiusdem Innocentii in Anglia celebrati faciat dominus abbas huius domus in martilogio scribere et bis in anno coram conuentu legere, scilicet [11] in crastino sancti Iohannis Baptiste, et ea que sibi continentur faciat obseruare, salua ordinatione nostra facta de ieiunio et dieta.

Item, cum confessio mater sit et nutrix deuotionis et religionis et potissima debellatrix dissolutionis, abbas ter in anno si personaliter possit ad audiendas confessiones in claustro et in capitulo paratum se exhibeat, scilicet contra Natalem, contra inicium Quadragesime, et contra Pentecosten: quod si personaliter hiis temporibus confessionibus audiendis non possit interesse, ille qui loco eius preest uices eius studeat, saluis cotidianis confessionibus et privatis de delictis cotidianis faciendis; prouideat etiam abbas ut non solum priori, subpriori, et tercio priori sed [12] et aliis uiris discretis tribus uel quatuor potestatem confessionum audiendarum committat qui uices eius in hoc officio supplere secundum Dominum sciant, uelint, et ualeant.

Vt in choro melius et sollemnius diuinum fiat obsequium, prouidimus ut omnes obedientiarii in quantum rationabiliter possunt nitantur matutinis et uesperis et maiori misse interesse nisi certa impediantur [13] necessitate; minores uero obedientiarii aliis intersint regularibus horis nisi impediantur officiis sue administrationis: et ut hoc melius obseruetur prior et subprior et alii custodes ordinis prout res exigit de nocte et de die ita satagant diuino obsequio personaliter interesse ut, uisis et cognitis defectibus absentium, in capitulo possint ea securius et liberius emendare. Claustrales uero qui nec [seruitium] reddunt nec alios in claustro docent inter horas celebrent, et obedientiarii qui dormitorium sine speciali licencia egredi possunt sic tempestiue missas suas cantent, ut claustrales cantare cum surrexerint non impediantur. Dum hore etiam regulares dicuntur et misse in conuentu celebrantur, in locutorio loquendi et alibi diuertendi sine euidenti necessitate licencie non concedantur. Discipline etiam secundum consuetudinem huius domus a certis personis ad hoc deputatis in statutis locis capiantur.

In claustro et in omnibus aliis locis et temporibus ad hoc deputatis silentium antiquo more huius domus obseruetur et transgressores silentii ex consuetudine grauissime puniantur. Et ne quies claustralis meditationis conturbetur precipimus ut hostia locutorii et celarii per extrinsecos

---

[a] MS. *et regulam et.*

[10] In 1214, *Memorials of St. Edmund's Abbey* (ed. Arnold), ii. 72, where the abbot of Wardon's initial is given as 'H', pp. 69, 71.

[11] Probably 'in crastino Epiphanie et', as in the Westminster Statutes below, p. 737, should be supplied.

[12] MS. *et sed.* [13] MS. *impediant.*

custodes ordinis interius bene obseruentur, ut transitus et discursus secularium presente conuentu a claustro arceantur: quod si autenticas personas per claustrum coram conuentu oporteat transire per aliquem monachum ducantur mature et pacifice.

In claustro etiam nouicii ita discrete tractentur et custodiantur ut ea que ad monastice professionis [regulam] pertinent efficaciter addiscant[14] nec a custodia libere dimittantur donec ea que pertinent ad ordinis obseruanciam sciant: secretis capituli non intersint antequam professionem faciant, nec sine certa necessitate cum aliquo seculari colloquium habeant, nec ad ordinem sacerdotis promoueantur, nec si sacerdotes fuerint ad maius altare celebrare permittantur donec ea que secundum monasterii consuetudinem de ecclesiastico seruitio corde tenus scire tenentur pro posse suo plene et integre reddiderint. Cum uero abbas uiderit expedire, professionem secundum quod continetur in regula faciant, sed professione facta propter hoc seruitium reddere et ordinem addiscere non omittant preterea quia secundum euuangelicam ueritatem arguuntur a Domino mandata Dei transgredientes et suam iusticiam statuere volentes.[15] Hoc inter alia diligentius addiscant nouicii, ut nunquam propter nouas introductas consuetudines paruipendant uel contempnant regulam uel regule iussiones. Nullus etiam nouicius officio forinseco occupetur nec sine magna necessitate et utilitate foris alicubi mittatur, nisi prius per triennium uel ad minus per biennium in claustro uixisse laudabiliter comprobetur. Communes locutiones, que in claustro aliquando fieri permittuntur de scripturis sint et edificacione et de ordinis obseruatione, et in quantum fieri potest in audientia custodum ordinis fiant. Cum uero de contraria fuerit materia per custodem ordinis celerrime finiantur. Omnes etiam serrure claustri, preter illas que concesse sunt illis qui in capitulo loquuntur uerbum Dei, secundum antiquam consuetudinem huius domus de cetero ammoueantur. Mulieres non ducantur per claustrum nec ad refectorium nec ad infirmariam nec in uestiarium : nec etiam intrent uiride hostium nisi fuerint nobiles matrone uel bone mulieres, matres uel sorores et cognate monachorum, quibus honor debetur, de quibus nullum malum suspicatur; et hoc fiat per custodes ordinis uel licentias eorum.

In refectorio apponenda sine diminutione apponantur et de omnibus appositis omnes relique tam cibi quam potus per elemosinarium integre pauperibus erogentur. Prohibemus etiam sub pena grauissime discipline ne aliquis de cibi appositis foras presumat aliquid mittere, excepto solo presidente et hostilario, si necesse habeat pro aliquo hospite aliquid foris deferre; et quia periculosum est de patrimonio Crucifixi aliquid in malos usus expendere et superfluos, uolumus ut panis et potus de cellario solito more in refectorio deferatur, set quod conuentui non apponitur uel in necessarios usus fratrum non expenditur secundum disposicionem prelati uel cellario restituatur uel ad profectum domus conuertatur, salua pauperum debita portione. Hoc idem obseruetur de pitantiis uini et ceruisie in refectorium delatis et de redditibus ad officium refectorii assignatis ut si quid ibi fuerit residuum in utilitatem domus cedat et profectum. Dum seruitores comedunt nullus per mensas uagando uel stando inordinate se ingerat uel sine certa necessitate ibi bibat uel aliquem secularem ad

[14] MS. *officaciter addiscantur.*   [15] Cf. Rom. x. 3.

bibendum inducat; post prandium uero seruitorum usque ad uesperas et post completorium qui in refectorio necessitatem habuerint bibere sic desolutionem caueant et honestatem regularem custodiant ut in potatione teneant moderantiam et freno silentii non laxent habenam. Post completorium etiam tempestiue satagant cubare cum matutinis sobrie presunt interesse. Ignobiles persone a prandio conuentus penitus excludantur nec alie persone sine euidente necessitate uel utilitate domus ibi passim admittantur, famuli quoque refectorii honesti sint et maturi nec numero superflui nec apparatu incompositi[16]. De communi uictum et stipendia percipiant ne eos de elemosina uiuere et fraudem facere oporteat. Omnes etiam more debito communiter obseruent horas prandendi et bibendi, et commedentes similiter exeant uel ad gratias uel ad claustrum uel ad dormitorium uel ad obedientias suas si fuerint necessarie nisi remanserint cum presidente, et hoc ex eius nutu uel mandato et pro rationabili necessitate. Nulli etiam liceat post gratias iterum in refectorium redire uel in infirmariam ire ut hic uel ibi se habeant inordinate. Quia sic post cenam intendere debent quieti spirituali ita hora meridiane intendere debent quieti corporali. Certa iusta et ciphus certus per refectorarium coram singulis apponantur nec aliquis de alterius iusta uel cypho presumat bibere sine certa ratione. Omnes etiam ciste refectorii cum doliis ammoueantur preter seruras subelemosinarii et refectorarii. Omnes etiam de eodem potu in refectorio bibant.

Fratres in [in]firmaria commorantes, exceptis stacionariis et hiis qui in lectis decubant, in una mensa reficiant, et non solum a turpibus et uanis sed etiam a superfluis et uanis sermonibus abstineant. De cellario et coquina per infirmarium uel alium ad hoc assignatum, secundum quod necessitas uniuscuiusque infirmi poposcerit, iuxta facultatem domus singulis prompte et benigne necessaria subministrentur, ut ita omnis occasio cibum uel potum foris querendi uel alia necessaria mendicandi omnibus auferatur. Infirmarius etiam sic eis prouideat de redditu sibi assignato in emplastris et speciebus, unguentis, medicinis, et aliis necessariis, ne murmur oriatur pro defectu sue subtractionis. Seculares persone omnino per infirmarium ab infirmaria arceantur, nisi pro[17] aliqua necessitate de licencia prelati uel illius qui preest ordini ibi introduci permittentur. Hoc autem summopere caueatur ne alicui seculari ibi commedere cum monachis concedatur. Obedienciarii quoque uel alii, cum in infirmaria commorantur, sine licencia superioris seruientes suos ibi non introducant nec lautiores cibos et potus sibi preparari uel mitti procurent. Quod si forte missi fuerint fratribus eos indigentibus fraterne communicent; seruientes etiam infirmarie honesti sint et benigni, et seruire infirmis prompti et apti, qui nec uillam frequentare nec in ipsa nocte habeant pernoctare; prouideatur etiam ne superflui ibi sint famuli, et ut de communi sicut seruientes refectorii uictum et stipendia percipiant, et ne elemosinam in suum uictum male consumant; prohibeantur etiam rumores seculares in infirmaria deferre et secreta que inter fratres audierint extra publicare. Nullus etiam monachus in infirmaria moram faciens preter solum infirmarium missam celebret uel cum conuentu manducet, nisi abbas aliter ordinet uel dispenset pro aliqua necessitate uel utilitate. Infirmi etiam qui

[16] MS. *incomposita*.   [17] MS. *per*.

in [in]firmaria aliquo tempore iacuerint, quam cito conualuerint manifeste, statim redeant ad conuentum non exspectato die ueneris uel spacio quindene.

Item, sicut Leo papa dicit, si[18] necessitas non est nullo modo sanctorum patrum statuta uiolentur ; ubi uero necessitas fuerit ad utilitatem ecclesie qui potestatem habet ea disponet, ex necessitate enim fit mutatio legis, precipimus ut in hoc monasterio dieta et ieiunium obseruentur prout in regula sancti Benedicti continetur, salua pro loco et tempore pia consideratione circa iuniores et senes debiles et infirmos, et salua prelati circa se ipsum et suos subditos discreta et rationabili dispensacione, causis et personis, locis et temporibus pie et fideliter consideratis et examinatis. Volumus etiam ut portantibus pondus diei et estus abbas, si presens fuerit uel in eius absencia prior, quo ad refectiones carnium aliasque necessarias[19] recreaciones pia secundum regulam consideratione pro sua discrecione cum opus fuerit sufficienter et honeste de communi faciant procurari, non habita personarum accepcione set pensata communiter indigentia singulorum, quod quidem in cella [in]firmorum tantummodo fieri decreuimus, ita tamen quod isti recreati simul intersint completorio conuentus, nulla deinceps, sicut regula precipit, egrediendi et loquendi licenciam habituri, set cum conuentu similiter cubent nisi certa et assignata necessitate impediantur. Excipimus autem eos qui in regula pro suis officiis excipiuntur. Item quia morose sessiones et confabulationes[20] post completorium multa mala et pericula mittunt in religione, precipimus ut tempestiue in quantum possunt cubent, quicunque post completorium foris remanserint pro sua administratione uel alia necessitate.

Item in dormitorio lecti monachorum ita sint ordinati quod dormientes in lectis palam possint uideri, sicut statuitur in capitulo generali. Vestimenta uero et calciamenta monachorum et coopertoria ita sint ordinata sicut in prefato capitulo[21] statuitur, et ea que predictis capitulis contraria sunt per abbatem et priorem sine dilacione ammoueantur.

Item sicut prouidimus in claustro et refectorio de serruris ammouendis, ita uolumus ut omnes tam in ecclesia quam in aliis locis careant clausuris et serruris nisi quibus competit eas habere ex suis officiis.

Item hospitalitas huius domus, sicut actenus obseruata est, de cetero melius et honorabilius secundum facultates loci obseruetur, et prata et omnes exitus horreorum uille Sancti Edmundi una cum incremento decimarum de Midehale excepto dominico totaliter feno et prebende hospitum assignentur.[22]

Item decreuimus ut hospitale Sancti Saluatoris alicui monacho discreto et morigerato committatur, qui bona temporalia discrete dispenset exterius et animas infirmorum edificare uelit et sciat interius. Nec de cetero aliquis perpetuo remansurus est nisi per abbatem ibidem admittatur, et quia periculosum[23] est uiris cum mulieribus in tali loco commanere, mortuis mulieribus qui ibi nunc sunt, nulla ab isto die uel deinceps mulier recipiatur.

Item uolumus ut omnes certi redditus huius monasterii in tribus rotulis

---

[18] MS. *die nisi* for *dicit si*. Cf. Decr. Gratiani i. dist. xiv. 2.
[19] MS. *necessitas*.   [20] MS. *confamulationes*.
[21] Reynerus, *op. cit.* 96.   [22] MS. *assignetur*.   [23] MS. *periculosus*.

scribantur, quorum unus scilicet in custodia abbatis, alter in custodia procuratorum, tercia in tesauraria perpetuo deponatur.

Preterea uolumus ut omnes et singuli monachi qui in uilla fuerint intersint celebrationi capituli, nisi infirmitas uel alia manifesta necessitas et communis utilitas eos[24] impediat. Qui alium uoluerit clamare illud faciat cum caritate et clamatus clamorem suscipiat cum deuocione. Nullus etiam alium defendere presumat, set arbitrio presidentis penam infligendam relinquat, qui absque[25] acceptione personarum penam infligat culpe respondentem; et quia ea que in capitulo tractantur sub sigillo confessionis debent celari, prouideant sibi singuli et uniuersi ne per aliquem eorum contingat secreta capituli reuelari. Detegentes uero secreta capituli et alios inordinate defendentes regulari subiaceant discipline.

Preterea uolumus ut nullus claustralis intret commune locutorium cum seculari colloquium habiturus ante primam uel post uesperas nisi in casu manifeste necessitatis. Nullus etiam monachus habeat colloquium cum muliere cognata uel extranea in locis non debitis,[26] uidelicet ad uiride hostium uel ad crucem, nec in aliis locis priuatis et solitariis, nec temporibus indebitis, sicut prandii uel cene uel hore meridiane uel tempore potus assignato.[27] Interdicimus etiam monachis frequentia et familiaria colloquia cum monialibus huic monasterio uicinis [uel] cum mulieribus reclusis ut ita tollatur materia omnis suspicionis. Nullus etiam monachus infra cepta cimiterie loquatur cum muliere absque monacho teste.

Preterea statuimus ut status maneriorum et redituum et bonorum ad celer[ar]iam spectantium in quatuor partes secundum fidelem estimacionem in quantum fieri possibile est diuidatur, et singulis partibus anni sua porcio tribuatur ne una pars anni [deficiat]. Status uero maneriorum firmariorum per estimacionem similiter diuidatur et temporibus firmarum faciendarum assignetur. De balliuis quolibet et bedellis omnibus sufficiens cautio capiatur, cum iuramento quod prudenter et fideliter continue et diligenter seruient et de modo et de ordine, numero, et quantitate omnium receptorum et expensarum fideliter et integre respondebunt tempore rationum et quociens requisiti fuerint ab abbate et conuentu. Et ut omnia premissa melius obseruentur, uolumus ut per xv dies ante festum Sancti Petri ad uincula sciatur status omnium maneriorum †tactus† celerarie qualiter annus futurus anno preterito possit continuari, et ab illo tempore usque ad festum Sancti Michaelis de dictis maneriis nichil capiatur nec aliquo modo distrahatur, nisi quantum necessarium fuerit ad sustentacionem conuentus et maneriorum. Et hec omnia fiant per celerarium et alios per abbatem et saniores capituli ad hoc destinatos. Et [ut] celerarius melius et liberius possit exequi officium suum, uolumus ut omnes empciones cibariorum et aliarum rerum ad celerariam spectantium cum eius auxilio et consensu fiant si domi fuerit, cum autem absens fuerit ei exprimentur cum reddierit. Prohibemus etiam ne subcellerarius uel refectorarius uel hostiliarius uel aliquis alius preter abbatem et priorem contra suam uoluntatem uel ordinationem de hiis que spectant ad celerariam aliquid distrahere uel attemptare presumat.

Item nullus obedienciarius sine scientia abbatis et conuentus mutuum aliquid v marcas excedens accipiat. Item nullus monachus depositum

[24] MS. *eum.*   [25] MS. *quidem.*   [26] MS. *debetis.*   [27] MS. *assignati.*

alicuius noti uel extranei recipiat sine licentia prelati nec ipse prelatus hoc faciat sine trium uel quatuor fratrum testimonio. Nullus etiam monachus extra abbatiam in aliquo manerio solus commoretur, nec aliquis, nisi commendabilis utilitas uel urgens necessitas exegerit, ante uicesimum annum in monachum recipiatur.

Nullus etiam monachus dare uel accipere presumat aliquid nisi superioris auctoritate uel licencia, nec aliquis monachus aliquid proprium penes se habeat, sub pena Lateranensis concilii proprietariis[28] infligenda;[29] in quo concilio cautum est ut uiuentes a communione altaris ammoueantur, et qui in extremo cum peculio inuenti fuerint nec pro eis oblatio fiat nec cum fratribus sepeliantur. Sub pena excommunicacionis tam obedienciariis quam aliis precipimus ne bona conuentus sibi commissa distrahant aut consumant, set ea in utilitates conuentus integre et fideliter expendant. Nullus etiam ammotus ab obediencia sua ammotus uel ab una ad aliam translatus penes se aliquid de sua obediencia retineat, set totum integre et fideliter quicquid de prima obediencia habuerit in sua ammotione et translatione utilitati fratrum restituat, et ut penitus pestis proprietatis extirpetur, uolumus ut secundum statuta abbatis de Wardone et sociorum eius omnes principales obedientiarii huius ecclesie, scilicet sacrista, celerarius, camerarius, elemosinarius, infirmarius, pitanciarius, reuestiarius, et maneriorum custodes monachos[30] habeant sanos[31] et testes omni suspicione carentes et conscios de omnibus receptis et expensis, et tam sacrista quam celerarius coram abbate et priore et aliis octo monachis per discrecionem abbatis et prioris ad hoc de conuentu electis quater in anno reddant compotum de receptis et expensis et maneriorum instauramentis eorum sociis et testibus ad hoc officium conuocandis. Ceteri autem obedienciarii bis in anno reddant compotum de suis obedienciis, retentis rotulis receptarum et expensarum omnium usque in finem anni, ut de statu meliorationis uel deteriorationis monasterii de anno in annum possit conuentui liquere. Omnes etiam proprietarii uel fraudem de bonis huius domus facientes, fures et conspiratores, incendiarii et falso crimen fratribus imponentes et Sodomite, sicut in generali capitulo[32] statutum est, feria ij[a] prime ebdomade quadragesime in capitulo publice et cum sollempnitate excommunicentur.

De minutis sic uolumus, quod spacium minuendi et numerus minuendorum ut[33] consuetum et usitatum obseruentur, addentes ut non detur licencia minuendi nisi semel in qualibet septimana quadragesime et in septimana quinque festiuitatum sollempnium; in aliis uero septimanis per annum bis, salua pia consideratione prelatorum circa egros et minutione manifeste indigentes. Volumus etiam ut omnes minuti similiter horas dicant, similiter eant, similiter commedant et bibant aut in refectorio aut alias ex prelati dispensacione, et similiter compleant; ut ille qui primum scrutinium facit inueniat eos in capitulo ad completorium; et ut amputetur omnis occasio murmurandi pro defectu recreacionis, per consensum et ordinationem domini H. abbatis prouidimus quod de noua Bertune iuxta middehale sumantur x libre annuatim per manus sacriste ad Pascha et ad

[28] MS. *proprietaris.*
[30] MS. *manchos.*
[32] Reynerus, *op. cit.* 97.
[29] Cf. Mansi, *Concilia*, xxii. 1047. 1051.
[31] MS. *sonos.*
[33] MS. *et.*

festum Sancti Michaelis celerario soluende ad recreationem secundo minutionis die.

Item Elemosinarius omnem elemosinam prouenientem de cibis et potibus tam de infirmaria quam refectorio [34] per se uel per subelemosinarium uel per fidelem et honestum ministrum colligat et recipiat, et idem de elemosina et fragmentis abbatis et prioris et hospitum faciat, nec inde famulos suos ad orrea pascat ; set taliter et integre in clericos et scolares, reclusas et liberaciones assisas et in pauperes mendicantes exspendat. Hoc idem faciat de omnibus exitibus et prouentibus orreorum et decimarum ad obedienciam suam assignatarum deductis necessariis expensis et stipendiis suorum famulorum necessariorum.

Item omnes seruientes, tam de celeraria quam de sacristaria uel camera uel hostilaria uel infirmaria uel elemosinaria uel refectorio seu uel aliis obedienciis, in propriis personis deseruiant singuli de suis officiis et uiuant de suis terris, correcdiis, et stipendiis ; quod si noluerint abbas terras et corredia eorum aliis assignet qui in propriis personis uelint et ualeant deseruire et de rebus sibi assignatis uiuere. Omnis autem superfluitas garcionum, qui sunt quasi uicarii seruientium, tam in ecclesia quam in coquina tam in infirmaria quam in hostilaria, tam in refectorio quam in stabulo et aliis locis amputetur ; similiter etiam superfluitas equorum ammoueatur.

Item, ut nemora conventus illesa custodiantur, uolumus ut nichil grossum excepto subbosco ab eis capiatur sine assensu abbatis et conventus; et ad profectum domus uolumus quod numerus et precium tocius stauri ad conuentum pertinentis, cuiuscumque fuerit obediencie, singulis annis semel in anno coram abbate et conuentu in capitulo palam exprimatur.

Item uolumus ut omnes uagaciones inutiles monachorum per prouinciam inhibeantur, et quia [in] uia commessaciones et pernoctationes a tribus leucis prope villam penitus interdicantur et maxime penes maneria conuentus cuiuscumque fuerit obediencie, precipimus etiam ut nec sine iusta causa nec sine euidenti utilitate licencia equitandi de cetero monachis concedatur. Quod si alicubi ex licencia proficisci debuerint, prouideat ille qui licentiam dedit ut honestam societatem, uecturas et apparatus sufficientes, et expensas de communi percipiant, et die sibi a prelato prefixo modis omnibus redeant, nisi iusta causa et manifesta eos ulteriorem moram facere compellat. Nullus etiam claustralis capam pluuialem uel sellam uel alia ad equitaturam pertinentia penes se retineat, nec aliquis obedienciarius equum in stabulo teneat, nisi eum pro administratione sui officii equum habere oporteat.

Item uolumus ut honestas circa altaria in omnibus apparatibus seruetur ad altaria pertinentibus, et circa istud prior et sacrista sint solliciti.

Item, sicut inuenimus in aduentu nostro de pixide, uolumus ut ita remaneat sub tribus clauibus, et cum aliquid, utilitate domus poscente, de dicta pixide sumendum fuerit, per uisum abbatis, prioris, et subprioris, et aliorum ad hoc uocatorum sumatur et in utilitatem domus expendatur.

Item parentes monachorum ad domum istam diuertentes honorificentius solito admittantur, et uberius procurentur maxime parentes claustralium.

Omnia autem hec premissa auctoritate apostolica obseruari precipimus,

[34] MS. *refectorario.*

non intendentes in aliquo beati Benedicti regule et huius ecclesie priuilegiis derogare. Precipimus etiam in uirtute obedientie ut abbas, uel prior si abbas presens non fuerit, faciat legi et exponi diligenter hoc scriptum in capitulo bis in anno, uidelicet prima die lune Quadragesime et in crastino assumptionis beate Virginis. Abbas autem quantum ad ipsum pertinet hec omnia diligenter obseruet et ab aliis omnibus faciat obseruari, alioquin de manibus ipsius in extremo examine requirat sanguinem eorum Deus ultionum. Hec uero omnia ordinauimus, ad presens retenta nobis potestate interpretandi, relaxandi, corrigendi, et etiam rebelles compellendi, et alia faciendi, quantum de iure possumus iuxta formam apostolici mandati.

Statutes for Westminster

In nomine Patris et Filii et Spiritus sancti Amen. Commisso nobis H[ugoni] Dei gratia Eliensis episcopo, R[adulpho] eiusdem priori, et W[illelmo] priori Norwicensi a sede apostolica uisitacionis officio in monasterio Westmonasterii, nos episcopus et prior Heliensis, tercio collega nostro legitime excusato, VII Kal. Februarii anno pontificatus domini Gregorii pape noni VII° ad dictum monasterium personaliter accedentes causa exequendi mandatum apostolicum, ab abbate et conuentu eiusdem loci reuerenter et deuote admissi fuimus. Et intrantes capitulum monasterii mandato apostolico, solempniter ibi recitato et prestito a singulis iuramento de ueritate dicenda tam super statu ecclesie quam personarum, de hiis diligenter inquisiuimus. Et cognito eiusdem monasterii statu auctoritate apostolica subscripta duximus statuenda.

In primis igitur statuimus ut abbas, magis studens amari quam timeri, saluti animarum subditorum suorum diligenter inuigilet, eo moderamine discrecionis adhibito ne aut modus correctionis excedendo nimiam excedat austeritatem aut correptionem omittendo nimia remissione earum correptionem negligere uideatur; statuimus ut subditi [35] ipsius, eidem tanquam patri et pastori reuerenciam impendentes et honorem, ei secundum regulam studeant obedire.

Item ut abbas familiam habeat moderatam et bene compositam, et superfluitatem tam in personis quam euectionibus resecare studeat.

Item ut abbas ad confessiones audiendas et penitencias iniungendas se facilem et benignum [prestet] et cetera que ad officium suum pertinent diligenter exequatur, et potissime libertates et possessiones omnes sui monasterii pro posse suo tueatur, reuocet alienata nec de cetero aliqua sine sui conuentus assensu alienare presumat.

Item statuta capituli generalis bis in anno legantur in capitulo, in crastino scilicet Epiphanie et in crastino S. Iohannis Baptiste. Et abbas ea inuiolabiliter faciat obseruari. Hoc excepto quod districte precipimus ne aliquibus pateat facultas uescendi carnibus nisi debilibus et egrotis et recreacione indigentibus, et hoc non attemptent nisi licentia superioris prius petita et optenta in infirmaria maiori et minori, reseruata nobis potestate in posterum aliter ordinandi in hoc articulo omnia [que] uiderimus expedire; et cum fuerint recreati, similiter omnes compleant cum conuentu, nullam deinceps, sicut regula precipit, egrediendi et loquendi

[35] MS. *subdati*.

licenciam habituri, exceptis hiis qui in regula pro suis officiis excipiuntur, ita quod [si] post [36] completorium propter administrationes suas et alias certas causas foris emanserint, statuimus quod ita cubent tempestiue quod ad matutinas sobrius ualeant interesse.

Item fratres infirmi in infirmaria existentes in una mensa similiter reficiantur preter in lectis decubantes exclusis omnibus personis extraneis secularibus, et seruientes habeant necessarios maturos et honestos, et reliquie fideliter colligantur et per elemosinarium pauperibus erogantur. Similiter idem fiat de reliquiis refectorii, excepto ab hac necessitate presidente. Talis autem sit infirmarius qui fratrum compatiatur necessitatibus, singulis diebus infirmos uisitando, eisdem in crastino secundum facultates suas competenter subueniendo.

Item reliquie tam refectorii quam infirmarie [37] fideliter colligantur et per elemosinarium erogantur, excepto ab hac necessitate presidente in refectorio.

Euagaciones monachorum penitus interdicimus, nec aliquis abbate existente domi egrediatur nisi de eius licencia, preter obedienciarios quibus rerum temporalium administratio fuerit commissa. Si qui autem claustrales uel obedientiarii ab abbate uel eo absente a priore pro utilitate ecclesie et alia iusta causa licenciam egrediendi optinuerint, eisdem in honesta societate uecturis, apparatu, et expensis sufficientibus prouideatur, certo tempore eis prefigendo infra quod reuertantur, nisi iusta [38] de causa et rationabili moram compellantur facere ulteriorem.

Hospitalitatem procuret abbas solito uberiorem, et per celerarium suum hospitibus nec non seruientibus religiosorum secundum facultatem suam honorifice faciat prouideri, et ut uiri religiosi tam albi quam nigri solito honestius recipiantur de consensu abbatis uol[tas][39] in quibus uina sua solebant reponi ad eorum receptionem assignauimus in eo statu perpetuo remansuras.

De [40] hoc quod dictum monasterium inuenimus ere alienato honeratum, prouidemus quod iuste in refectorio usque ad triennium rescindantur, ita tamen quod potus absque certa mensura fratribus sufficienter ministretur, et ad liberacionem dicti monasterii prouentus de Bamflet pitanciarie deputati assignamus, per prouisionem conuentus usque ad dictum terminum in pecuniam redigendos et in debitorum solucionem conuertendos, precipientes sub pena excommunicacionis, ut solutis debitis conuentus status eius pristinus quo ad omnia que nunc occasione debitorum subtrahuntur plene redintegretur.

Item inhibemus ne de cetero abbas sine conuentu nec conuentus sine abbate per sigillum capituli bona monasterii mutuum contrahendo clam et palam obliget, sed sigillum capituli sub fideli custodia et quatuor seris custodiatur, de quibus claustralis ab abbate deputatus clauem custodiat scrinii interioris. Tres uero claues scrinii exterioris prior et subprior et precentor custodiant, sicut actenus consueuerunt. Preterea inhibemus ne aliquid ecclesiarum beneficium seu redditus annuus uel corredium [41] saluis antiquis ministris sine communi consilio abito conferatur.

Precipimus etiam ut omnes certi redditus monasterii tam de porcione

[36] MS. *prius.*   [37] MS. *in firmaria.*   [38] MS. *iusta sit.*
[39] MS. *uol.*   [40] MS. *Do.*   [41] MS. *corridium.*

abbatis quam conuentus in tribus rotulis redigantur, quorum unus in custodia abbatis, alter in custodia procuratorum, tercius in tesauraria perpetuo deponatur.

Item laici ignobiles et alii in absentia abbatis ad prandium in refectorio passim non admittantur nisi prouidente utilitate aut necessitate.

Item uolumus ut nulli ordinis custodi aliqua obedientia exterior committatur per quam officium spirituale exequi impediatur.

Item singularitatem in refectorio prohibemus; etiam si alicui claustrali uel obedientiario aliquid fuerit in refectorio appositum preter ea que conuentui communiter apponuntur, illud presidenti mittatur ab ipso pro uoluntate sua percipiendum.

Item non tractetur in capitulo nisi de hiis que ad salutem pertinent animarum, et ad magnam ecclesie utilitatem. Extrinseca autem negocia per discretiores de capitulo extra capitulum tractentur et in capitulo recitentur.

Item prohibemus ne camerarius deinceps denarios pro uestimentis det, sed temporibus statutis det noua et recipiat uetera secundum institutionem regule.

De proprietariis, conspiratoribus, furibus, et crimen fratribus falso imponentibus obseruetur quod in statutis generalis capituli continetur, scilicet quod semel in anno excommunicentur prima die quadragesime.

Nullus amotus simpliciter de obedientia uel ab una translatus ad aliam penes se aliquid retineat, set si quid penes se de prima obediencia retinuerit communitati fratrum restituat.

Computationes reddantur ab obedienciariis fideliter ad minus semel in anno uel quod prouisum fuerit ab abbate et discretioribus domus.

Parentes monachorum et amici ad eos uenientes ab abbate in mensa sua exhibeantur, uel in uilla in hospitio ipsorum a celerario abbatis sibi necessaria recipiantur, ne aliqua nacta occasione elemosina minuatur.

Item discursum per claustrum et per infirmariam uersus cameram prioris tam monachis quam aliis fieri firmiter prohibemus ne tranquillitas claustralium turbetur.

Item firmiter iniungimus camerario quod prouideat ne seruientes sui[42] aut a monachis quorum uestimenta preparant inuitis aliquod pro labore suo exigant[43]; et si quis fuerit in hoc deprehensus amoueatur.

Item districte precipimus sub pena excommunicacionis ut omnes prouentus ad elemosinariam pertinentes pauperibus erogantur. Supradicta ad presens ordinauimus uolentes ea uim[44] statutorum habere, abbati, priori, et aliis ordinis custodibus sub pena excommunicacionis iniungentes ut ea pro possibilitate sua obseruent et ab aliis faciant arcius obseruari, retenta nobis potestate corrigendi, mutandi, interpretandi, et alia faciendi, sicut forma mandati apostolici permittat. Supramissis adiicimus statuentes firmiter [ut compositio][45] inter abbatem et conuentum super bonorum suorum separacione confecta in omnibus articulis obseruetur preter quam de hospitalitate de qua aliter ordinatum est, nisi papa aliter duxerit ordinandum.

[42] Omission in MS.   [43] MS. *exigent.*   [44] MS. *in.*
[45] For the composition made between Abbot Richard of Berking and the convent in 1225 see the Cotton MS., Faustina A III, fo. 225, and *Victoria County History of London,* i. 448.

Extracts from the First Version of Hardyng's Chronicle

As promised in the last number of this Review, the three most distinctive passages of the version of Hardyng's Chronicle, which the author finished and presented to Henry VI in 1457, are now given in full from the only copy in the Lansdowne MS. 204. They are (i) The Introduction, (ii) The Praise of King Henry V, and (iii) The Conclusion celebrating the fame of Robert Umfraville, and exhorting Henry VI to keep peace and law and reward the writer. As explained on pp. 470–6 above, these passages give something of Hardyng's autobiography, and have a special interest for their picture of the state of England at the time when he wrote. To the description of Umfraville as the accomplished knight should be added Hardyng's account of the training of a young lord, which is quoted by Ellis, on p. i of the preface to his edition, from f. 12 of the same manuscript. C. L. KINGSFORD.

I. INTRODUCTION

[DEDICATION]

O Souerayne lorde, be it to your plesance
This book to take of my symplicite,
Thus now newly made for Rememorance,
Whiche no man hath in worlde bot oonly ye;
Whiche I compiled vnto your Rialte,
And to the Queenes hertes consolacion
To know thestate of youre domynacion;

And for the Prynce to haue playne conyshance
Of this Region, in what nobilite
It hath been kept alway of gret pushance
With baronage and lordes of dignyte;
The whiche alway God graunte that ye and he
May so kepe forth vndyr your gouernance
To Goddes plesir withouten variance.

Thus to yow thre Rials in vnyte
This book with hert and lowly obeishance
I present now with al benygnyte
To been euermore within your gouernance,
For soueraynte and your inherytance
Of Scotlond hool, whiche shulde your Reule obaye
As Souereyn lorde, fro whiche thay prowdly straye.

Wythin thre yer thair grete Rebellion
Ye myght oppresse and vttirly restrayne,
And haue it all in youre possession,
And to obaye your myght make thaym full fayne,
As Kynge Edward the first with hungir and payne
Thaym conquerde hool to his subieccion
To byde for euer vndir his hole proteccion.

[PROEM]

Who hath an hurte and will it nought diskure
And to his leche can nought his sore complayne,
In wo euermore withouten any cure
All helples forth he muste comporte his payne;
And who his own erande forgatte to seyne,
As alle thise wise men say alway and wote,
Men calle a Fool or elles an Idyote.

Wherfore to yow, as prynce most excellent,
I me compleyne, as reson techeth me,
That youre Fadir gafe me in commaundement
In Scotlonde ryde for his Regalyte
To seke his ryght thar for his souereynte,
And euydence to gette and to espy
Appurtenant vnto his monarchy.

Whiche euydence by labour and processe
Thre yere and halfe amonge the enmyte,
On lyfes peryle, maymed in grete distresse,
With costages grete as was necessite,
I boughte and gatte of grete auctorite;
Of whiche I gafe vnto your excellence
At Esthamstede[1] parte of that euydence.

I gafe yow ther a lettre of Rialte,
By whiche ten men claymyng the croune
Of Scotlond than boonde thaym by thaire agre
The iuggement to bide and constitucion
Of kynge Edward with longshankes by surnoun,
Whiche of thaym shulde of Scotlond been the kynge
Vndir thaire seels hys souereynte expressynge.

I gafe yow als other two patentes rial,
By whiche Dauid and Robert ye Scotes Kynges
Boonde thaym and al thaire haires in general
To holde Scotlond of Kyng Edward, expressynge
His soueraynte by clere and playn writynge
Vndre thaire seels to bide perpetualy,
As playnly is in thaym made memory.

I gafe yow als the Relees, that Edwarde
The thrid to Kyng Robert of Scotlond made
In tendre age; whiche whill it was in warde
Of Vmfreuile was dreynt in oyl and defade,
Sex woukes ligging in it, as it abade;
Bot noght forthy it may hurte yow right noght,
For it is all agayn youre hieghnesse wroght.

[1] In July 1440; see pp. 464–5, 467, above.

[In] the lettres is graunt Yorkes primacy[2]
[Thru]gh all Scotlonde and to hys successours
[To ha]ue and vse aboue the prelacy
[As dyd] afore of olde hys predecessours
[And also t]he hows of Durham of honours
[And C]uthbertes ryght with all the liberte
[Thrugh al]l Scotlonde withoute difficulte.[3]

[Also that p]rynce of grete magnificence,
[Your Fadir] so gafe me in commaundement
[Scotlond to] spy with alkyns diligence,
[How that it] myght bene hostayde thrugh and brent
[. . . . .] wele to his wille and intent,
[Whatkyns p]assage were for ane hoste to ryde,
[What toures a]nde touns stode on the este see syde,

[Wher tha]t hys flete myght londe and with hym mete
[With hys] vitayle, gunnes and ordenance
[Hys host to] fresshe, and lygge in all quyete
[From stor]mes grete and wethyrs variance.
[Whiche] all I dydde and putte in remembrance
[At hys] biddynge and riall commaundement,
[Bot was] nought rewarded aftyr his intent.

Whiche remembrance now to youre sapience
Vpon the ende of this boke in figure
Illumynde is for your intelligence,
Declared hool by wrytynge and lettrure,
How lyghte wer now vnto your hiegh nature
For to conquer by rial assistence,
And kepe it euer vndir your hiegh regence.

Now seth that prynce is gone, of excellence,
In whom my helpe and makynge shulde haue bene,
I vouche it sauf, wyth all benyvolence,
On yow, gode lorde, hys sonne and hayre that bene,
For to none other my complaynte can I mene;
So lynyall of his generacioun
Ye bene discent by very demonstracioun.

For other none will fauour his promyse,
Ne none that wylle ought forther myne intente,
Bot if it lyke vnto your owne avyse,
Alle oonly of your rial Regymente

---

[2] The defect of these stanzas is due to a corner of the leaf on which they are written having been torn away. The words in brackets are restored in part from a comparison with the parallel passage on p. 751, below.

[3] This refers to the forged letters of David Bruce exemplifying a charter of Alexander of Scotland, in which the English overlordship is acknowledged, and the rights of York and Durham are reserved: Palgrave, *Documents*, pp. cciv-v, 368-9.

To comforte now withoute impedymente
Your pore subgite, maymed in his seruyse,
Withoute rewarde or lyfelode any wyse.

Sex yer now go I pursewed to your grace;
And vndirnethe your lettres secretary,
And Priuy Seel that longeth in that cace,
Ye graunted me to haue perpetualy
The maner hool of Gedyngton truely
To me and to myne hayres in heritage,
With membres hool and other all auauntage.

Bot so was sette your noble chaunceller,
He wolde nought suffre I had such waryson,
That cardinal was of York withouten per;
That wolde noght parte with londe ne yit with ton,
Bot rather wolde, er I had Gedyngton,
Ye shulde forgo your ryall soueraynte
Of Scotlonde, whiche long to your rialte.

Your patent couthe I haue in nokyns wyse,
Bot if I sewed to alle youre grete counsayle,
To whiche my purs no lengar myght suffyse:
So wente I home withoute any auayle;
Thus sette he me all bakhalfe on the tayle:
And alle your grace fro me he dyd repelle,
Your lettres bothe fro me he dyd cancelle.

Bot vndirnethe your Fadir's magnificence
He durste nought so haue lette hys righte fall doun
Ne layde asyde so riall euydence
Appertenant vnto hys rial croun,
Who sonner wolde suche thre as Gedyngton
Hafe youe than so forgone that euydence
By whiche the Scottes obey shulde hys regence.

For whiche Kynge Iames vnto my waryson
A thousonde marke me highte of Englisshe golde;
Whiche I forsoke in myne oppynyon,
As natyfe birth and alkyns reson wolde;
Sex and thretty yer I haue it kepte and holde
In truste ye wolde of youre haboundant grace
Your Fadirs promyse so fauoure in thys cace.

Whiche euydence in this afore comprised,
With other mo whiche I shal to yow take,
Four hundre marke and fifty ful assised
Cost me treuly for youre Fadir sake,
With incurable mayme that maketh me wake.
Wherfore plese it of youre magnificence
Me to rewarde as pleseth youre excellence.

II. The Praise of King Henry V

The compleynt and lamentacion of the maker of thys for the Kynges deth, w^t commendacion of his gouernance.

  O gode lorde god, why lete thou so sone passe
  This noble prynce, that in all Cristente
  Had than no pere in no londe more ne lesse;
  So excellent was his fortunyte
  In florisshyng age of all fresh Iuuente:
  That myght haue lete hym leue to gretter age
  Tyll he had hole reioysed his herytage

  Of Fraunce, all hole Guyen and Normandy,
  Whiche thre wer his of olde inheritaunce,
  And Angoy eke of full olde auncetry,
  As Cronyclers haue made remembraunce;
  For he was sette with myghty grete puisaunce
  To conquere than the londe of all Surry,[a]
  That ys the londe of byheest proprely.

  To whiche he than, and eke the Emperour,
  Accorded wer withoute colusion
  To Criste, goddes sonne, to gyfe thair hole labour
  Fro tyme that thay myght make an vnyon
  Betwyx Englonde and Fraunce by gode reson,
  With helpe of other londes that wolde assent
  To that vyage and conquest excellent.

  O gode lorde god, that knew his hertes intent,
  That was so sette for soules remyssion
  To thyne honour by his attendement
  To conuerte so that londe of promyssion;
  Or elles it sette by Cristes hole permyssion
  With Cristen folke, fayling thair conuersion
  For thair foly and thayr peruersion.

  O verry lorde, that arte omnipotent,
  What hath Englonde so felly the offende,
  This noble prynce, peerlesse of Regyment,
  To Rauysshe so fro vs withouten ende ?
  O lorde, who shall Englond now defende ?
  Seth he is gone that was our hiegh Iustyse
  For whom none durste his neyghbor than supprise.

  Aboue all thynge he kept the lawe and pese
  Thurgh all Englonde, that none insurreccion
  Ne no riotes than wer withouten lese,
  Ne neyghbours werre in fawte of his correccion:
  Bot pesybly vndyr his proteccion
  Compleyntes of wrongs alway in generall
  Refourmed were so vndyr his yerde egall.

[a] Syria.

Whan he in Fraunce dayly was conuersaunt
His shadow so abowmbred all Englonde
That pese and lawe wer kept contynuant
In his absence full wele thrugh all the londe:
And elles, as I can sayne and vndyrstonde,
His power had bene lyte to conquerr Fraunce
.Nor other Reme that wer wele lasse perchaunce.[5]

The pese at home and law so wele conserued
Wer rote and hede of all his grete conqueste,
Whiche exilde bene away and foule ouerterued
In so ferr forthe that north and south and weste
And este also is now full lytill reste,
Bot day and nyght in euery shire thurgh out
With salades bright and iakkes make grete route.

O souereyne lorde, take hede of this meschefe,
That regnyth now in londe so generaly;
Such Ryottours sende after by your brefe
And prison so the partyse opynly,
And raunson thaym; els is no remedy:
And seurte take of thaym, afore ye cese,
With thayr neyghbours forthward to bere the pese,

Enrolled in your courte of Chauncelry,
Thar to abyde for alway of recorde:
For your Iustyse of pese darr noght reply
Suche tyrauntes that perteyne to any lorde,
For parseners thay bene of suche discorde;
Or els thay ere the comon Barectours
Or of suche folyse the pryuy manteynours.

Or els thay bene so symple of estate
The malefesours by law to Iustyfy:
Or els thay bene with fe so alterate
That thay darr noght agayn suche Tyrany
By thayre office, so do no remedy;
Iustyse of pese thay bene, as I deme can,
As now on days men call the blacke oxe swan.

Bot, O gode lorde, by ye the chefe Iustyse
Of pese thurgh oute your londe as for a yer
Withoute fauour or grace to excersyse
Your offyce wele after your hiegh power,
And ye shall wyn heuyn to your mede full clere,
And Rychesse also of fynes for thayr outrage,
That suche riote do make ouer your homage.

[5] This and the previous stanza appear with but slight variation in the later version Ellis, p. 388.

And at the leeste ye may sende hem ouer se
To kepe your right in Fraunce and Normandy :
Thayr hiegh corage to spende and Iolyte
In sauyng of your noble Regaly ;
For better is ther thair manly vyctory,
Than her eche day with grete malyuolence
Make neyghbours werre with myghty violence.

Men chastyse ofte grete courours by hakenayse,
And writhe the wande while it is yonge and grene ;
Therfore whare so er any such affrayse
For both partyse sende, forth to come, I mene,
To your presence riall what so er ye bene,
And putte thaym in suche reule and gouernaunce,
Than men shall drede youre wytte and gouernaunce.

III. The Conclusion

⁶ How the maker of this commendeth his maystir syr Robert Vmfreuile, and by exemple of his gude Reule to enforme the Kynge to kepe the publike profite of his Reme and with pees and lawe.

In this mene tyme syr Robert Vmframuyle,[7]
That was my lorde distilde by kynde nature,
Thurgh besy age, right as I can compile,
To suche waykenesse he might no more endure,
Bot fell so in his graue and sepulture
Thrugh cruell deth that wyll forbere no wyght,
Whom so afore that neuer man conquer myght.

Thof my body here be a symple wyght
Abydynge at the wyll omnipotent,
My herte with hym shalbe bothe day and nyght
To pray for hym with all my hole intent.
A beter lorde I trow God neuer yit sent
Into the north of all gode sapience,
Ne so helply with knyghtly diligence.

Ne contekour he was in his Cuntre,
Nor neuer drewe swerde ne knyfe to Englyshman,
Ne Riotour, ner neuer made assemble
Agayn neyghbour that any man tell kan.
The Comonte he halpe and neuer ouer ran ;
A trew Iustyse of pese in his Cuntre
He was alway withouten partyalte.

A beter knyght was neuer in that Cuntre
To kepe the trewes whils that it dyd endure ;
With costage grete eche wouke in sertaynte
Days of redresse to euery creature,

⁶ In the margin are illuminated the Umfraville arms : gules, a cinquefoil, the field powdered with crosslets paty, or.

⁷ Robert Umfraville died on 29 January 1436.

To Scottes he helde, and Englyssh also full sure;
Who so complaynde of ought it was refourmed,
So godelyly to pese he hym conformed.

In so ferr forth his Iugementes wer approued
That Scottes feel byyonde the Scottysshe see
Thar own Iugges forsoke as hole reproued,
And by assent to Berwyke came I se;
And bonde thaym thar to stonde to his decre,
And plesed were with all his iugymentes,
So right wyse was his reule and Regymentes.

With Couetyse he was neuer yit infecte,
Nor key of lok kepte neuer in his possession
Iewell ne golde, so was he hole protecte
With gentyll herte by his discression.
Comon profyte withoute oppression
Was his labour and all his diligence
In pese and werr with hole benyvolence.

Bot noght forthy whan enmyse gafe vp pese,
And it away with werre had hole exilde,
As lyon fell he putte hym forth in prese,
The werre maynteynde and kepte hym vnreuylde.
What so men gat couetyse noght hym fylde,
The wynners had it all withoute surpryse;
For whiche the folke wer glad to his seruyse,

And with hym rode away euer at his wyll,
So hole he had thayr hertes to hym inclyned;
What so he wolde the londe assent hym tyll,
His language so thair hertes medycyned,
So benygne was and trewe it vndyrmyned
Thair hertes hole to loue hym at thair myght,
And go with hym whar as he went to fight.

Of the Garter full eght and thretty yere
He was a knyght electe for worthihode,
Whan his lyfelode exceded noght all clere
An hundreth marke to leue vpon in dede,
Bot oonly of the werres thurgh his manhede;
Yit helde he than a countenaunce and estate
With hym that was a baron nomynate.

His seruantes wolde he noght rebuke ne chide,
Bot softely say to hym in pryuyte
All his defaute and as his preest it hide;
And whan thay stale his gode that he dyd se,
He wolde it layne fro his other maynee,
And noght repreue hym more in any wyse,
So was he kynde withouten couetyse.

An hardyer knyght was neuer none gatte ne bore,
For at my dome he was neuer yit aferde;
Nor wyser knyght for to deuyse afore
The fetes of werre, with whiche he had conquerde
His foose full ofte and made thaym many auerde;
Nor frear knyght of herte was none I gesse,
So he want noght he count by no rychesse.

A clenner knyght of his leuynge was none
In all degre withouten vice detecte,
And as of treuth he myght be sette allone;
His worde so sadde was wele and euer protecte,
With variance yit that it was neuer infecte;
In so ferre forthe his fose had delectacion
Mor in his worde than neyghbours obligacion.

Of sapyence and verry gentylnesse,
Of lyberall herte and knyghtly gouernaunce,
Of hardyment, of treuth and grete gladnesse,
Of honest myrth withoute any greuaunce,
Of gentyll bourdes and knyghtly daliaunce
He hath no make: I darr right wele auowe;
Now is he gone, I may not glose hym nowe.

His vertuse dygne so hole were and plenere,
That thay hym made so excellent in all,
That fortune satte hym on hir whele so clere
At his deuyse and wolde neuer latte hym fall;
Ne his honoure she suffred neuer appall,
Bot euer hir whele tyll hym she dyd apply
That of his fose he had ay vyctory.

And yit he faught vndyr his own banere,
And what also vndyrnethe his penon,
Eghtene tymes agayne the Kynges fose clere
In socour of the Kynges Region,
And nothyng for his own opynyon,
Bot in defence of all the comonte
Marchyng so with the Scottes in his contre.

How the Kynge shulde Reule moste specialy the comon profyte of his Reme with pese and lawe aftir syr Robert Vmfreuile.

Treuly he was a Iewell for a Kynge
In wyse counsayle and knyghtly dede of werre;
For comon profyte aboue all other thynge
He helped, euer was nothyng to hym derre,
In werr and pese comon profyte he dyd preferre,
For that poynt passed neuer out of his mynde,
Which poynt he sayde shulde longe a Kynge of kynde.

Wharfore to yow, moste souereyn prynce and lorde,
It fytteth wele that poynte to execute,
The comon wele and verry hool concorde,
That none ouer ronne your comons ne rebute,
And kepe your lawe as it is constytute,
And chastyse hem that market dassehers bene
In euery shire that now of new er sene;

In euery shire with Iakkes and Salades clene
Myssereule doth ryse and maketh neyghbours werre;
The wayker gothe benethe, as ofte ys sene,
The myghtyest his quarell wyll preferre,
That pore mennes cause er putte on bakke full ferr;
Whiche thrugh the pese and law wele conserued
Myght bene amende, and thanke of God deserued.

Thay kyll your men alway by one and one,
And who say ought he shall be bette doutlesse;
For in your Reme Iustyse of pese bene none
That darr ought now the contekours oppresse;
Suche sekenesse now hath take thaym and accesse,
Thay wyll noght wytte of Ryot ne debate,
So comon is it now in eche estate.

Bot this I drede full sore withouten gabbe
Of such riottes shall ryse amore mescheue,
And thrugh the sores vnheled wyll brede a skabbe
So grete that may noght bene restreynt in breue;
Wharfore gode lorde, iff ye wyll gyffe me leue,
I wolde say this vnto your excellence,
[8] Withstonde the first mysreule and violence.

Wythstonde, gode lorde, begynnyng of debate,
And chastyse well also the Ryotours
That in eche shire bene now consociate
Agayne youre pese, and all thair mayntenours;
For treuly els wyll fall the fayrest flours.
Of your coroune and noble monarchy,
Whiche God defende and kepe thrugh his mercy.

Who prayeth yow for any contekoure,
Whether he be Duke, Erle, or other estate,
Blame him as for the verry mayntenoure
Of suche mysreule contecte and eke debate:
Whiche elles your lawe woulde chastyse and abate,
If mayntenours wolde suffre it haue the course
That playntyffs myght to lawe haue thayre recourse,

[8] In margin: Principiis obsta ne deterius contingat.

The lawe is lyke vnto a Walshmannes hose,
To eche mannes legge that shapen is and mete;
So mayntenours subuerte it and transpose,
Thurgh myght it is full low layde vndyr fete,
And mayntnanse vp in stede of law complete;
All, if lawe wolde, thynge wer by right reuersed,
For mayntenours it may noght bene rehersed.

Consyder nowe, moste gracious souereyn lorde,
In this tretyse how long your auncetry
In welthe and hele regned of hiegh recorde,
That keped pese and law contynuly:
And thynke thay ere of all your monarchy
The fayrest floures and hieghest of empryse
And sounest wyll your foreyn foos suppryse.

Consyder als in this symple tretyse,
How kynges kept nayther law ne pese
Went sone away in many dyuers wyse
Withouten thanke of God at thayr decese,
And noght were dred within ner out no lese,
Bot in defaute of pese and law conserued.
Distroyed wer, right as thay had deserued.

Consyder als, most souereyn lorde and prynce,
In these Cronycles that hath bene redde or seyne
Was neuer no prynce of Bretayns hole prouynce
So yonge as ye wer wan ye gan to reyne;
And thenkes hym that was so your wardeyne,
Aboue all thynges that is omnipotent,
That keped yow whils ye wer innocent.

Consyder als, he [9] that the dyademe
Of Remes two, of Englond and of Fraunce,
Vpon your hede bene sette, as dyd wele seme,
In tendre age suffred withoute distaunce
Thurgh pese and lawe and all gode gouernaunce
Whiche if ye kepe, ye shall haue vyctory,
Shall none gayn stonde your noble monarchy.

Consyder als, moste souereyn erthly lorde,
Of Frenssh ne Scottes ye gette neuer to your pay
Any trety of trews and gode concorde,
Bot iff it be oonly vndyr your Baner ay;
Whiche may neuer bene by reson any way
Bot iff your Reme stonde hole in vnyte
Conserued wele in pese and equyte;

* Read how.

Than may ye wele and saufly with baner
Ryde into Fraunce or Scotlonde for your right,
Whils your rereward in Englond stondyth clere;
With you hauyng gode power for to fight
Vndyr your baner, the enmyse will yow hight
Better trety within a lytill date
Than in foure yere to youre embassiate.

How the maker of this boke compleyneth his greuance and sore to the Kynge touchant the Euydence of the souereynte of Scotlonde, that he gefe to the Kyng and noght rewarded as the Kynges wille was.

O souereyn lorde, to yow now wyll I mene
Myne owne erande that greueth me full sore.
Your noble Fadyr, most famouse as was sene,
To me, his pore liege subgyt, that was bore
Iohn Hardyng so, promysed for euer more
Fourty pounde by yere of londe assised
Whare that it myght by reson ben deuysed,

To holde for ay to me and to myne hayres
For feute fre of all maner seruyse
In fe symple to thaym and to thayres:
So thought he wele that it wolde me suffyse
For my labour amonges his enmyse
And costage grete with sore corporall mayme,
Whiche I may neuer recouer ne reclayme.

For to enquere and seke his Euydence
Of his riall lordship and souereynte
Of Scotlond, which longe to his excellence
Of auncyen tyme ande longe antiquyte;
And vndyr that that prynce of dignyte,
Your Fadyr, so gafe me in commaundement
Scotlonde to spye than after his extent;

How that it myght bene hostayed and distroyed,
Whatkyns passage wer for an hoste to ryde.
Thrugh out that londe, with whiche thay myght ben noyed:
And what tounes stode vpon the Este se syde,
Whare that his flete myght mete hym and abyde
With his vytayll and all his artelry
His hoste to fressh in eche coste by and by.

Whose charges so I labourde bysyly,
And wrote it all to his intelligence,
And drew it eke to byde in memory,
Lyke as he bad me of his sapience,
And as me thought was moste expedyence
For his noblay to haue that londe conquerde,
With grete costage I spyed it and enquerde.

Of whiche Cuntrey a fygure now depaynte
To your noblesse right as my wytte suffyse
I haue her drawe, whils that this boke remaynte
To byde with yow and with your hayres wyse,
By whiche ye may it hostay and supprise,
And conquerr it as your priorite,
Or by concorde reioyse your souerente.

For whiche lyfelode I pursewed to your grace,
And vndyr neth your lettres secretary
And pryuy sele that longed in that case
Ye grauntid me to haue perpetualy
The maner hole of Gedyngton trewly
To me and to myne heyres in heritage
With membres hole and all other auauntage.

Bot so was sette your noble Chaunceller,
He wolde noght suffre I had suche warison
By counsayll of your trusty Tresorer,
That wolde not parte with londe ne yit with ton,
Bot rather wolde er I had Gedyngton
That ye shulde lese your riall soueraynte
Of Scotlonde, whiche longe to your Rialte.

Youre patent couth I haue in nokyns wyse,
Bot iff I serued to all youre wyse counsayle,
To whiche my purse than myght nothing suffyse :
Wharfore I yede than home withoute avayle.
Thus sette thay me all bakkhalf on the tayle,
And all your grace thay dyd for me repelle,
Youre lettres bothe thay dyd fro me cancelle.

Bot vndyrneth your Fadyrs magnificence
Thay durst noght so haue lette his right fall doune
Ne layde on syde so riall euydence
Appurtenaunt vnto his riall croune :
For whiche Kyng James vnto my warison
A thousonde marke me hight of Englisshe golde,
Deliuerde thaym than to hym iff I wolde.

O noble prynce and moste souereyn lorde,
Meruell yow noght thof I thus sore compleyne,
Seth my makyng stode in his mysericorde,
That now is dede and all my truste in veyne ;
And no wyght wyll for me ought to yow seyne ;
Youre offycers vnfauours his promyse,
That som tyme wolde haue plesed hym in all wyse.

[In the following chapter Hardynge describes

How the Kynge may moste esely conquere Scotlonde, with a figure of the londe and the myles fro towne to towne, and whare his flete may vpon euery ooste mete hym, begynnynge on the Este coste of Scotlond at Berwyk on Twede ; and how he may charge the wardeyns of Marche to do with lesse costages if he will abide at home.[10]

At the end (fo. 226ᵛ) he gives the two stanzas following, as an Envoy: with slight alteration they reappear in the later version at the beginning of the Excusacion to Edward IV.[11]]

> Off thys mater I haue sayde myne intente,
> Like as I couthe espy and thare inquyre ;
> Whiche if it may yow plese and wele contente
> Myne herte reioyeth to comforte youre desyre,
> And of youre grace euer more I yow requyre
> For to consider my losse in this matere,
> My mayme also that neuer more may be clere.

> Besechyng euer vnto your Rialte
> To take in thonke this boke and my seruyse,
> Thus newly made of my symplicite :
> Amonges makers that neuer was holden wyse ;
> Bot yit I wolde in that I couthe deuyse
> To your estate Rial do some plesance,
> To whiche I lakke nought elles but suffishance.

The Anglo-French Peace Negotiations of 1806

IN the Napoleon *Correspondance* (no. 10604) there is printed a draft treaty with the emperor's notes on it. The text of the draft was not in the French archives, but was obtained from the British foreign office records. M. Coquelle in his *Napoléon et l'Angleterre*, published in 1904, regarded it as a document presented by Lord Yarmouth, conveying the offers of the British government ; and he blamed the emperor for not accepting such favourable terms. It was pointed out, however, in this Review (xx. 817) that several of the clauses were inconsistent with such a supposition, and that the draft seemed to have been prepared in the French foreign office.

The eighth volume of the *Dropmore Papers*, which has been published this year, throws some fresh light on the document. On 1 August, when Fox was too ill to attend to business, Lord Grenville (who was acting for him) wrote to the king :

> Mr. Goddard, who was the bearer of Lord Yarmouth's dispatch, has brought with him the enclosed notes of a project which Monsieur Talleyrand

[10] Cf. *Chron.*, ed. Ellis, pp. 423-9 ; see p. 476, above.
[11] *Chron.*, ed. Ellis, p. 420.

and General Clarke read to Lord Yarmouth, but which Lord Yarmouth refused to accept or to transmit officially. These notes were taken by Mr. Goddard at the desire of Monsieur Talleyrand and Lord Yarmouth, and in their presence, but it was understood that they were not to be considered as official communications. Your majesty will perceive that they are wholly inadmissible, differing hardly at all from the terms stated in Lord Yarmouth's last dispatch (p. 252).

The dispatch here referred to had caused Grenville to send Yarmouth, on 28 July, explicit and positive directions not to commit the government without instructions. It had been decided before this to send Lord Lauderdale to Paris to take part in the peace negotiations, and his private letters to Grenville after his arrival there led to Yarmouth's immediate recall. On 2 August Grenville sent to the king a narrative drawn up by Goddard ' of the circumstances attending the notes of the project which he brought over' (p. 254). It was returned to Grenville next day, but is not printed in the *Dropmore Papers*. It is much to be wished that some one would clear up the tangled web of these peace negotiations. They occupy eighty-five pages in' the *Annual Register* for 1806, but comparison with the originals in the Record Office shows that large omissions were made in the papers presented to parliament.   E. M. LLOYD.

Reviews of Books

OTTO SEECK. *Geschichte des Untergangs der antiken Welt.* Band iv. (Berlin: Siemenroth, 1911.)

THE fourth volume of this fascinating book begins with the years preceding the death of Constantine and continues (scarcely interrupted by a chapter on rhetoric) until the end of the reign of Jovian. Every student of the history of the Roman empire in the fourth century is bound to read this volume, and it would thus be idle to attempt to describe its contents. We must almost entirely confine ourselves to suggesting a few criticisms. The least satisfactory part of Professor Seeck's work is his treatment of the history of the eastern provinces of the empire. Save for the hymns against Julian the Apostate, translated by Bickell in the *Zeitschrift für katholische Theologie*, there appears to be no reference to the works of Ephraim the Syrian, and in particular neither Bickell's edition of the Carmina Nisibena nor the ancient life of Ephraim is cited. Again, no use has been made of the Acta of the Persian martyrs published by Assemani, despite Nöldeke's hint of their importance as a supplement to the account of Ammianus Marcellinus,[1] nor of G. Hoffmann's *Auszüge aus syrischen Akten persischer Märtyrer* (1886), while it is disappointing to find that the name of Faustus of Byzantium does not once occur in the supplement of notes.[2]

Perhaps Dr. Seeck's most novel theory is that Constantine, shortly before his death, had formed the intention of annexing the Persian empire—in fact 'dass er die Grossmacht des Ostens zu einer Sekundogenitur des Kaisertums machen wollte'. Hannibalianus was to be 'king of kings', and the entire civilized world was to be united under the same religion, under the same royal house (pp. 7, 25, 97). This view is based on a passage in the Anonymus Valesii, 6. 35, which, it is claimed, alone gives the correct style of the new monarch: 'Annibalianum data ei Constantiniana filia sua regem regum et Ponticarum gentium constituit.' Now if this were really so, it was a most amazing conception; the empire never

[1] Th. Nöldeke, *Geschichte der Perser und Araber zur Zeit der Sassaniden*, Leyden, 1879, p. 59, n. 1.

[2] Further, full use has hardly been made of the fragments of Philostorgius preserved in the Vita S. Artemii; cf. P. Batiffol, *Fragmente der Kirchengeschichte des Philostorgius*, in the *Römische Quartalschrift*, iii. (1889) 252-89. The historical material presented by the Acta of the Persian martyrs I have endeavoured to collect and hope to publish shortly, while the historical matter to be gleaned from Ephraim's work will be similarly treated in a separate study.

again contemplated such a step. Even at the moment of Persia's deepest humiliation Heraclius might add βασιλεύς to the imperial title,[3] but further than that he would not go. The explanation is in fact untenable. Ammianus, 14. 1. 2, speaks of Hannibalianus only as rex, while—and this is surely conclusive—the extant coins have merely FL. ANNIBALIANO REGI.[4] My own view, based on the history of Faustus of Byzantium, that Hannibalianus was created king of Armenia, was recently set forth in this Review.[5] To that account should be added the fact that Julian[6] could write of the time (A.D. 332) when Constantine left Gaul and moved to the east, ἐπὶ τὴν ἐτέραν ἤπειρον μετιὼν τοῖς Παρθναίων καὶ Μήδων ἔθνεσιν ἀντετάχθης μόνος. ὑποτυφομένου δὲ ἤδη τοῦ πολέμου καὶ οὐκ εἰς μακρὰν μέλλοντος ἀναρριπίζεσθαι κτλ. The stress laid upon the word μόνος is important; Hannibalian had not yet been created rex, but trouble with Persia was soon to follow.[7] Further, Dr. Seeck places the embassy from Persia to the court at Constantinople mentioned by Libanius[8] towards the end of the year 336 and distinguishes it from that referred to in Rufus Festus[9] and Eusebius,[10] which was in the capital in the Easter week of 337. These embassies are, I think, one and the same. The purpose of the former, according to Dr. Seeck (p. 24, l. 23), was to demand back the lost Persian provinces, i.e. the provinces which had been ceded to the empire by the peace of 297. The words of Libanius,[11] however, are πέμπει (sc. Sapor) πρεσβείαν ὑπὲρ τῶν ὅρων ἀμφισβητήσουσαν ἵν' εἰ μὲν παραχωρήσαιμεν τῆς χώρας, ἀκμητὶ κεκρατηκὼς εἴη, εἰ δὲ μηδαμῶς εἴξαιμεν, ἀφορμὴν ταύτην τοῦ πολέμου προστήσαιτο—i.e. would the Romans evacuate Armenia which they had occupied?—if not, a Roman Armenia was too great a menace and Persia would go to war. Constantine accepted the challenge, but death overtook him at Nicomedia.

Dr. Seeck states (p. 28, l. 2) that none of the heirs of Constantine were with him when he died, and that Constantius arrived only in time to convey the corpse to Constantinople. Julian,[12] however, positively asserts that Constantius was present at the death-bed: τῷ μόνος ἐκ πάντων τῶν ἐκείνου παίδων ζῶντος μὲν ἔτι καὶ πειζομένου τῇ νόσῳ πρὸς αὐτὸν ὁρμῆσαι, τελευτήσαντος δέ κτλ. and Dr. Seeck only gets the sense required for his view by inserting a negative in the account of Zonaras[13]—a proceeding which appears to be without justification. The battle of Singara is dated 'with certainty'[14] to the year 348. The chronological question is

[3] Cf. L. Bréhier, *L'Origine des Titres impériaux à Byzance*, in *Byz. Zeitschr.* xv (1906) 161–78; J. B. Bury, *The Constitution of the Later Roman Empire* (Cambridge, 1910), pp. 19–20.
[4] Cf. Cohen, *Description historique*, etc. (éd. 2, Paris, 1888), vii. 363–4.
[5] *Rome and Armenia in the Fourth Century*, ante, xxv (1910) 625–43.
[6] p. 15, l. 12, ed. Hertlein.
[7] It is unnecessary, I think, to conclude with Dr. Seeck (p. 388) that there is here a chronological confusion in Julian's account.
[8] *Orat.* lix, §§ 71–2, ed. Förster, iv. 243, l. 12 seqq.   [9] *Brev.* 26.
[10] *Vita Constantini*, iv. 57 (title).   [11] *Op. cit.* p. 243, l. 17.
[12] p. 19, l. 16.
[13] iii, ed. Büttner-Wobst, p. 24, l. 14: ὃν ὁ υἱὸς Κωνσταντίος ἐξ 'Αντιοχείας παραγενόμενος . . . ἔτι ζῶντα εὑρὼν ἐκήδευσε μεγαλοπρεπῶς. Dr. Seeck inserts οὐκ before ἔτι (p. 390).
[14] p. 93, l. 2; 'Das Jahr ist durch die Chronik von Cp. sicher beglaubigt,' p. 424.

perplexing, but Professor Bury's arguments for the earlier date (the summer of 344) can hardly be thus lightly dismissed.[15] Had Dr. Seeck consulted the *Carmina Nisibena* of Ephraim, he would have been able to state as a fact what he hazarded as a conjecture in 1900, viz. that Constantius was present at the second siege of Nisibis in 346,[16] and he would not have repeated in his present volume [17] the chronological error of allowing the bishop Jacobus to encourage the besieged with word and deed during the third siege. The worthy pastor was long since dead and buried, though his body was regarded by the inhabitants as the palladium of their city. Further, Dr. Seeck's explanation (p. 365, l. 27) of a passage in the second hymn of Ephraim against Julian, in which the poet appears to state that Nisibis was not evacuated under the terms of Jovian's peace, is opposed to the evidence alike of Ammianus, of the *Vita Ephraimi*, and of the Acta of the Persian martyrs.[18] In his brilliant, though unduly severe, character sketch of Constantius, Dr. Seeck speaks (p. 35, l. 14) of the emperor's passion for husbanding the lives of his soldiers and for taking no risks which could possibly be avoided. For this trait he refers to Ammianus, 19. 3. 2 and 21. 13. 3; but an even more interesting passage occurs in Julian's second oration (p. 93, l. 15), where Alexander is contrasted unfavourably with Constantius. The former ἀπέβαλε πολλοὺς Μακεδόνας . . . ὁ δὲ ἡμέτερος ἄρχων καὶ στρατηγὸς οὐδὲ χιλίαρχον ἀποβαλὼν ἢ λοχαγόν τινα, ἀλλ' οὐδὲ ὁπλίτην τῶν ἐκ καταλόγου, καθαρὰν καὶ ἄδακρυν περιεποιήσατο τὴν νίκην. It was a clever stroke of the youthful panegyrist.

Dr. Seeck dates the birth of Julian towards the end of the year 331. But he does not refer to the oracle given in the *Anthologia Palatina*, xiv. 148, ed. F. Dübner, which is described as χρησμὸς δοθεὶς Ἰουλιανῷ τῷ ἀποστάτῃ ὅτε τὴν γενέθλιον ἡμέραν ἐπιτελῶν ἑαυτοῦ διῆγεν περὶ Κτησιφῶντα ἀγῶνας ἱππικοὺς θεώμενος.[19] That is to say, that Julian's birthday fell in May—June, and therefore, as Neumann concluded, in the year 332.[20] But there is a more serious question in regard to the whole chronology of Julian's youth. For this, Dr. Seeck argues (p. 457), the certain point of departure is the raising of Gallus to the position of Caesar on 15 March 351, since both brothers had previously to this time spent six years—a round number in Dr. Seeck's view, say five and a half

[15] Bury, *The Date of the Battle of Singara*, in *Byz. Zeitschr.* v. (1896) 302–5.

[16] Cf. Pauly-Wissowa, *Real-Encykl.* iv. 1 (1900), s.v. Constantius, col. 1060 med. ' Vielleicht wurde die Stadt durch das Heer des C. entsetzt, da dieser im Sommer zu Edessa, d. h. auf der grossen Strasse, die nach Nisibis führte, nachweisbar ist (Athan. apol. c. Ar. 51)'.

[17] p. 95, and *Real-Encykl.*, ibid. col. 1,064, l. 11.

[18] Cf. *Zeitschrift für katholische Theol.*, ii. 2 (1878) 346 ; and see p. 755, n. 2 *supra*.

[19] This tends to confirm the account of the games celebrated at Ctesiphon which has been questioned by e. g. Reinhardt, *Der Perserkrieg des Kaisers Julian*, in *X. Jahresbericht des Herzoglichen Friedrichs-Realgymnasiums und der Vorschule des Fridericianum für das Schuljahr 1891-2*, Dessau, 1892, p. 28, n. 4. The oracle is also found in Suidas (*s. v.* Ἰουλιανός, p. 1012. 5, ed. Bernhardy) with the note ἔστι δὲ καὶ ὁ χρησμὸς ὁ δοθεὶς αὐτῷ ὅτε περὶ Κτησιφῶντα διῆγε.

[20] Cf. C. Radinger, *Das Geburtsdatum des Kaisers Julian Apostata*, in *Philologus*, 50 (1891) 761 ; K. J. Neumann, *Das Geburtsjahr Kaiser Julians*, *ibid.* pp. 761–2.

years—at Fundus Macelli. Arguing back from this date he obtains the following scheme :

<blockquote>
Julian's birth at Constantinople.
Early in 338. Murder of his father and removal to Nicomedia.
About 342. He moves to Constantinople, where he begins his studies.
344. Returns to Nicomedia, and
345. Is banished to Fundus Macelli.
</blockquote>

Now in the first place it would appear very difficult to accept Dr. Seeck's view, in which he follows Weissenborn,[21] that Julian and his brother only left Fundus Macelli when Gallus was created Caesar. In this connexion there is an important passage in Julian's letter to the Athenians, p. 350, l. 11, which may be translated as follows :

<blockquote>
From Fundus Macelli I was, though with difficulty, freed by good fortune through the help of the gods; but my brother was by ill fortune <i>kept a close prisoner</i> (καθείρχθη), <i>if ever there was one, at the court</i>. For if he did appear wild and intractable in character this was increased through his being brought up amongst the mountains. But the person who in my judgement should bear the blame is he who forced upon us this upbringing : from the effects of this I was kept pure and unharmed by the grace of the gods through philosophy : but no one gave him such an opportunity. He went straight from life in the country to the court, and no sooner had Constantius placed the purple robe upon his shoulders than he began to regard him with suspicion and never ceased so to do until he had destroyed him utterly.
</blockquote>

According to this account Gallus was kept under close surveillance at court, presumably following the movements of Constantius, and thus must have left Macellum considerably earlier than the year 351.

There are other objections to Dr. Seeck's chronology. According to his scheme Julian returned to Constantinople at about the age of ten years, and was only between twelve and thirteen when he resumed his studies in Nicomedia. Yet when he was still in Constantinople Libanius could speak of him as ἤδη πρόσηβος,[22] while on his departure from Constantinople Eubolius had made the child swear ' many great oaths '[23] that he would not attend Libanius's lectures. Yet such was the passion of this disinherited twelve-year-old boy to hear the great rhetorician that he secured notes of the lectures πορθμεῖα τινα τῶν καθ' ἡμέραν λεγομένων δωρεαῖς μεγάλαις κτησάμενος:[24] and though a πρόσηβος at the age of ten, when he left Nicomedia for Macellum at the age of thirteen and a half he was then, in his own words, only κομιδῇ μειράκιον.[25] The fact would seem to be that Gallus must have left Macellum about 347-8.[26] Julian was therefore torn from his teachers in Nicomedia in 341-2 when he was ten years old (κομιδῇ μειράκιον); when released with Gallus in 347-8 he went to Constantinople—his birthplace. Here Libanius saw him, and says of himself that noting Julian's success in study (he was now sixteen, πρόσηβος) ἤλγουν οὐ σπείρων αὐτὸς εἰς τὴν τοιαύτην ψυχήν.[27] Libanius had probably moved to Nicomedia in 344,[28] but Nicomedia is not Antioch, and he could very

---

[21] Ersch and Gruber, p. 224 b.
[22] Förster, ii. 242, l. 5.   [23] Ibid. l. 18.
[24] Ibid. p. 243, l. 7.   [25] p. 350, l. 1.
[26] It must be as early as this to allow for Julian's reaching Nicomedia (after his visit to Constantinople) while Libanius was still in Nicomedia. Libanius left, it appears, late in 349 or early in 350.   [27] Op. cit. p. 241, l. 17.
[28] So Seeck, after Sievers, Das Leben des Libanius, p. 53.

easily have visited the capital during Julian's stay there. Fearing the popularity of Julian, Constantius withdraws him from Constantinople [29] and sends him to Nicomedia παιδεύεσθαι δὲ δίδωσιν ἐξουσίαν.[30] It is now, when Julian as a youth between sixteen and seventeen is given leave to pursue his studies, that Eubolius takes from him an oath that he will not visit Libanius, who had by this time [31] taken up his residence at Nicomedia. The oath and the μεγάλαι δωρεαί are in these circumstances comprehensible, which they are not on Dr. Seeck's chronology.

One of the most interesting questions in Julian's life is that of the ideals which he set before himself. Dr. Seeck, while recognizing the influence of Marcus Aurelius, denies [32] that the emperor also took Alexander the Great for his model, and cites in support of his view the unfavourable judgements on Alexander which are found in Julian's works. In this, I think, Dr. Seeck has forgotten what he himself has excellently explained in his chapter on rhetoric. Writers of Julian's time do not always express personal views: they are influenced by a tradition, and the rhetorical tradition was in the main hostile to Alexander.[33] Now it has been recognized that Julian drew much material from the works (especially the περὶ βασιλείας) of Dio of Prusa, and it seems at least probable that many of Julian's references unfavourable to Alexander may be traced to the influence of Dio and the rhetoricians.[34] In fact, as philosopher and ruler Marcus Aurelius was Julian's model; his exemplar as general and conqueror was Alexander. Thus the latter's generosity (p. 54, l. 8), his love for Homer (p. 494, l. 9, cf. Ammianus, 16. 5. 4), his nobility (p. 123, l. 18, p. 263, l. 1), and especially his conquests over Persia (p. 20, l. 20, p. 274, l. 17, and the paeans, p. 137 and p. 147) are all celebrated.[35] In the light of the confession of the intimate letter to Themistius (p. 328, l. 7) καί μοι πάλαι μὲν οἰομένῳ πρός τε τὸν Ἀλέξανδρον καὶ τὸν Μάρκον καὶ εἴ τις ἄλλος γέγονεν ἀρετῇ διαφέρων εἶναι τὴν ἅμιλλαν κτλ. two passages from the *Vita S. Artemii* to which Dr. Seeck does not refer are of particular interest. The first describes Julian's journey in 362 from Constantinople to Antioch : [36] Ἄρας οὖν ἐκ τῆς Κπόλεως σὺν παντὶ τῷ στρατῷ τὴν ἐπὶ τῆς Συρίας ἐποιεῖτο

[29] *Op. cit.* p. 242, l. 7.   [30] *Ibid.*, l. 12.

[31] ἤδη, *ibid.*, l. 14 (as against Seeck, p. 458). need mean no more than this.

[32] Seeck, p. 472; contrast J. Geffcken, *Kaiser Julianus und die Streitschriften seiner Gegner*, in *Neue Jahrbücher für das klass. Altertum*, xxi. 164.

[33] Cf. W. Hoffmann, *Das literarische Portrait Alexanders des Grossen im griechischen und römischen Altertum*, Leipz. hist. *Abhandlungen*, viii (1907) 45 ; and see C. Neumann, *Griechische Geschichtschreiber und Geschichtsquellen im zwölften Jahrhundert* (Leipzig, 1888), 5599.

[34] With Alexander's greed for fame, Jul. 324, l. 23, cf. Dio περὶ βασ. iv. 4; with Alexander's intolerance of his father, Jul. 51, l. 21, cf. Dio περὶ βασ. i. 16, and περὶ τυχ. (2) lxiv. 20; with Julian's taunt as to Alexander's murders, 575, l. 13 (cf. 425, l. 16), compare the last-mentioned passage in Dio, while the τρυφή of Alexander, Jul. 333, l. 3, had long been a rhetorical commonplace. For the judgements of the early rhetoricians cf. Franz Weber, *Alexander der Grosse im Urteil der Griechen und Römer* (Leipzig, 1909), and see J. R. Asmus, *Julian und Dio Chrysostomos, Beilage zum Jahresbericht des Grossherzoglichen Gymnasiums zu Tauberbischofsheim*, 1895, 20 seqq.

[35] Alexander is under the protection of Heracles, pp. 406, 431, l. 1. Cf. περὶ βασ. iv. 70. Compare Hoffmann's judgement (p. 87): 'Alexander gilt nur etwas wenn's in den Krieg geht; sobald der Januskopf Julians das Philosophenantlitz zeigt, sieht er Alexander nicht mehr.'   [36] P. Batiffol, *op. cit.*, p. 274.

ὁδόν·, διελθὼν τοίνυν ἅπασαν τὴν Φρυγίαν καὶ πρὸς τὴν ἐσχάτην αὐτῆς πόλιν τὸ καλούμενον Ἰκόνιον καταντήσας, ἐξέκλινε τὴν Ἰσαυρίαν καταλιπὼν καὶ τὸν λεγόμενον ταῦρον ὑπεραναβάς, ἦλθεν ἐπὶ τὰς πόλεις τῆς Κιλικίας, καὶ τῷ σταθμῷ προσπελάσας τῷ ἐν Ἰσσῷ αὐτοῦ κατασκηνοῖ, τὸν ἐκ Μακεδονίας Ἀλέξανδρον μιμησάμενος· αὐτόθι γὰρ κἀκεῖνος ἐν Ἰσσῷ τὸν πρὸς Δαρεῖον τῶν Περσῶν βασιλέα συνεκρότησε πόλεμον, καὶ τοῦτον νικήσας ἐπίσημον τὸν τόπον εἰργάσατο. Ἐκεῖθεν τὸν Ἰσσικὸν κόλπον διαπεράσας, ἦλθεν ἐν Ταρσοῖ τῇ πόλει, κἀκεῖθεν εἰς Ἀντιόχειαν κτλ. Julian went right out of his way to visit the spot where the Hellenic hero had defeated the foe which he himself was now preparing to attack.[37] The other passage is as follows :[38] τὴν Κτησιφῶντα πόλιν καταλαβὼν ἐδόκει μέγα τι διαπραξάμενος ἔργον ἐφ' ἕτερα μεταβαίνειν κρείττονα ... ἔρωτα γὰρ διαβολικὸν τῆς εἰδωλομανίας ἐγκτησάμενος καὶ ἐλπίσας διὰ μὲν τῶν ἀθέων θεῶν αὐτοῦ πολυχρόνιον τὴν βασιλείαν ἕξειν καὶ νέον γενέσθαι Ἀλέξανδρον, περιγενέσθαι δὲ καὶ τῶν Περσῶν κτλ. The evidence in fact points, I think, to a conclusion contrary to that of Dr. Seeck.

One more remark out of the many which suggest themselves : Dr. Seeck adopts the view that towards the extreme end of his reign Julian issued a law forbidding the Christians not only to teach in but even to attend the public schools. This he feels bound to do by reason of the quotations from this law given by the church historians and by Gregory of Nazianzus. He does not, however, note Gregory's statement :[39] ταῦτα μὲν ὁ σοφὸς ἡμῖν βασιλεύς τε καὶ νομοθέτης ὥσπερ ἵνα μηδὲν αὐτοῦ τῆς τυραννίδος ἄμοιρον ᾖ καὶ προκηρύξῃ τὴν ἀλογίαν ἐν ἀρχῇ τῆς ἑαυτοῦ βασιλείας τυραννεύσας πρὸ τῶν ἄλλων τοὺς λόγους. What is the meaning of this ? Is it simply a mistake ? Dr. Seeck's judgements on character and motive open up a wide field for discussion, but this is no place for such a debate. The new volume of the *Geschichte des Untergangs der antiken Welt* is a book to read and re-read more than once.[40]   NORMAN H. BAYNES.

Christianity in Early Britain. By the late HUGH WILLIAMS, M.A., D.D. (Oxford : Clarendon Press, 1912.)

THIS book is an expansion of a lecture delivered under the Davies Lecture Trust in a Welsh Calvinistic Methodist chapel at Birkenhead in June 1905, and the delay in its appearance was caused by the long illness and death of the author, who was only able to correct the first proofs. It therefore suffers under the disadvantages of not having been finally prepared for press by the author himself, and of having been published without reference

[37] With this compare Julian at Arbela, Libanius, ii. 349, l. 9 *seqq.*, and note Julian's ambition to march to Hyrcania and the rivers of India, *ibid.* 350, l. 5. See also ii. 213, l. 10 Ἀλεξάνδρου τοῦ φίλου τε αὐτῷ καὶ οὐκ ἰόντος καθεύδειν κτλ.

[38] With this compare the remarkable passage in Socrates, *Hist.* iii. 21 πεπιστευκὼς δὲ μαντείαις τισίν, ἃς αὐτῷ συμπαρὼν ὁ φιλόσοφος Μάξιμος ὑπετίθετο, καὶ ὀνειροπολήσας τὴν Ἀλεξάνδρου τοῦ Μακεδόνος δόξαν λαβεῖν ἢ καὶ μᾶλλον ὑπερβαίνειν τὰς ἱκεσίας Περσῶν ἀπεκρούσατο· καὶ ἐνόμιζε κατὰ τὴν Πυθαγόρου καὶ Πλάτωνος δόξαν ἐκ μετενσωματώσεως τὴν Ἀλεξάνδρου ἔχειν ψυχήν, μᾶλλον δὲ αὐτὸς εἶναι Ἀλέξανδρος ἐν ἑτέρῳ σώματι. Αὕτη ἡ οἴησις αὐτὸν ἐξηπάτησε καὶ παρεσκεύασε τότε τὴν ἱκεσίαν τοῦ Πέρσου μὴ παραδέξασθαι.

[39] Migne, *Patrol. Gr.* xxxv, Or. iv, c. 6, p. 537 A.

[40] I have noticed very few misprints, e. g. pp. 49, l. 16; 72, l. 20; 387, l. 11; 398, l. 25.

to works which appeared after he laid down the pen. If, for instance, Dr. Williams had seen Professor Oman's *England before the Norman Conquest*, the short account of the English occupation in ch. 20 would no doubt have taken a different form. Nevertheless the work is a scholarly production which will be heartily welcomed by all who are interested in the subject with which it deals, the history of Christianity in Britain (by which Dr. Williams seems to mean the country inhabited by Welsh, the other races of Britain being only incidentally mentioned) down to the end of the Easter controversy about 800. On this subject we have a mass of legend and fable, but very little authentic information, and it has been the fashion on one side to accept Welsh tradition and hagiographical legend, and even the falsifications of Geoffrey of Monmouth, without serious criticism, and on the other to pass over the whole as undeserving of attention. It is therefore a great thing to find a competent scholar with the necessary knowledge of Welsh who has taken the trouble to go through the authorities for the whole of this period and make a genuine attempt to sift the false from the true. It seems hardly credible that it should be necessary to devote a whole chapter to demolishing Geoffrey, but such is the persistence of falsehood based upon patriotism or religious prejudice that the labour cannot be said to have been wasted. It would of course be impossible to write anything like a continuous narrative where information is so scanty, and for a large portion of the work the author has merely taken certain celebrated names and told us all that can be discovered about them. Accordingly, from no fault of his, the composition often presents a disjointed appearance, and the conclusions are sometimes lame, or even, as in the case of the personality of Arthur, scarcely intelligible ; but, if the book could have received the author's finishing touches, some of these defects might have been remedied.

Of British Christianity before the departure of the Romans we may almost be said to know nothing, and the chapters which Dr. Williams has devoted to it are in large measure a general history of Christianity in the empire, or at least in the west, rather than of British Christianity in particular. Especially the chapter on the Faith of Nicaea seems almost entirely superfluous, and, as the subject lies outside the author's province, it is perhaps the least satisfactory in the book. It was of course the Homoeusians, not the Homoeans, who inclined towards the Nicenes (p. 159), and I cannot see how the opinion of Sulpicius Severus quoted on p. 162 shows 'ascetic ideals'. But even in these early chapters the author appears at his best in his critical discussion of the martyrdom of St. Alban (pp. 106, 109); and the account of little-known natives of Britain in cc. 13 and 15 (Dr. Williams successfully vindicates the British origin of Pelagius) is of considerable interest.

When we think of the circumstances under which the book was published, the number of points to which objection can be taken must seem extraordinary few. I do not know what is meant by 'Lucan in the dozen or fewer lines of his preserved' (p. 47), the whole of Lucan's poem being extant, and it is strange to describe Gregory of Tours as a Frank (p. 277). Again, the opinion of Professor Bury quoted on p. 206 may be right or wrong, but I cannot see that Dr. Williams's argument is an answer to it.

'Trajan' (p. 342) must be a slip for 'Hadrian', and 'Constantius' (p. 98) for 'Caesarea', while the name Caelestius should not have been written 'Coelestius' (pp. 203, 204, 207), especially as Caelestine is correctly given. 'Sulpitius' (p. 33) and 'Huntington' (p. 332) are no doubt misprints. E. W. BROOKS.

A History of the Eastern Roman Empire from the Fall of Irene to the Accession of Basil I (A.D. 802–67). By J. B. BURY. (London: Macmillan, 1912.)

IT is twenty-three years since the appearance of Professor Bury's *History of the Later Roman Empire from Arcadius to Irene*, and he has now followed it up by a continuation extending to the death of Michael III and covering what he describes as the Amorian period, though this name strictly applies only to the last forty-seven years. The termination of the preceding work was determined by the fact that it nearly coincides with the coronation of Charles the Great, with which an eastern as opposed to a western empire may be supposed to have begun; but the date does not in fact mark any important epoch in eastern history, and a more satisfactory division would have been 813, where the Chronicle of Theophanes ceases and there was a lull in the long war with the Arabs. The present work, therefore, really consists of two unequal portions, in one of which we have a detailed, though prejudiced, contemporary authority to guide us, while in the other we are, at least as far as secular events are concerned, more in the dark than in any other period of Byzantine history. In spite, however, of this lack of authorities the work is on a much larger scale than the earlier, for a whole volume is occupied by the events of sixty-five years, while in the *History of the Later Roman Empire* 407 years were comprised in two volumes. It is indeed possible that the very obscurity of the period necessitates greater length, since more discussion is required, especially as Professor Bury is able to use Syriac, Arabic, and Bulgarian sources which have only recently been made accessible, and his knowledge of Slavonic literature enables him to deal with the northern neighbours of the empire in a more scientific fashion than has ever been attempted before, at least in Western Europe. But besides the difference of scale the volume differs in plan also from the earlier work, for instead of the chronological order there adopted, domestic affairs are related first, and foreign affairs follow, as in Gibbon. This plan has its advantages, but it also causes considerable inconvenience, since some events are necessarily related twice, and the first time in a shortened form which is hardly intelligible without reference to a later chapter, as in the case of the reign of Michael I, where the Bulgarian war is inextricably connected with the affairs of the court. Perhaps the plan of the book may be held responsible for a certain unevenness in the composition. For instance, a detailed narrative of the Arab war of Nicephorus is described as useless and tedious, and in this section little attempt is made to solve chronological and topographical problems on which Professor Bury's opinion would have been welcome, while the Arab war of Theophilus is discussed at considerable length in an appendix, where, by means of the new light thrown upon the subject by the publication of Michael the Syrian, Professor

Bury is able to fix the chronology of the campaigns with what may almost be described as certainty. My own supposition, however, that Manuel fled during the reign of Michael II is treated with greater respect than it deserves, for since the publication of Michael it is untenable, and the difficulty about the embassy of John may perhaps be removed by supposing that, though the ostensible object was to announce the emperor's accession, it was not in fact sent till two years later. As we have no information about similar embassies, we cannot say if such delay was unusual.

The Amorians were unfortunately succeeded by a dynasty who set themselves to belittle their exploits; and, as the period covered by this volume falls between the great eras of the Isaurians and the Macedonians, it has been the custom to regard it as one of decadence, and in particular, because Michael III was a worthless voluptuary, the government during his reign has been treated as one of negligence and incapacity, in oblivion of the fact that for ten years the control of affairs was in the hands of his able and vigorous uncle. It is one of the chief merits of this volume that it does full justice to the Amorians, and especially to Bardas, though, if Professor Bury had paid more attention to Sicilian affairs (another much condensed section), he might have found support for his opinion there also. To the account of the Bulgarians I have already referred, and another portion of the book to which I should like to call special attention is the chapter on Photius and Ignatius. Previous writers have either written to support one side or the other, or been unable to free themselves from the mist in which the subject has been enveloped by their predecessors; and it is to Professor Bury's credit that he has explained the true causes of the quarrel and set forth the merits and weaknesses of either party as no one has before done. Unfortunately the limits of his period compel him to leave the story half told. It is, however, to be regretted that in dealing with theological affairs he sometimes adopts the style of Gibbon, and that similarly in another chapter he speaks of a converted Bulgarian as 'changing his superstition'. Such expressions may cause offence and add nothing to history. Professor Bury will not allow any but a political or ecclesiastical object to the missions of the period; and, as far as the statesmen and patriarchs are concerned, his position can hardly be disputed; but it is another thing to be told that the Slavonic apostles wished only to extend the influence of the eastern church and empire. If this were so, it is hard to understand how after the fall of Photius they sought papal support and Methodius maintained the papal connexion till his death. To me it seems much more likely that the apostles desired simply the conversion of the heathen, and for this end were willing to work with either pope or patriarch.

Professor Bury often surprises us by the vast extent of his reading and the keenness of his intuition, but there are places in which even he can be found nodding. For instance, he is much puzzled by the statement that Leo V was of Armenian and Assyrian birth, and that his progenitors slew their parents and fled to Armenia—the meaning of which is that he was a member of one of the two Armenian families (Gnuni and Artsruni) which claimed descent from the sons of Sennacherib. I have seen in some Armenian writer the name of the family to which he belonged, but cannot now recover the reference. This is a trifle, but it is a serious matter that, though he points out the prime importance of the Chronicle of Michael for eastern affairs, he has in relating the conquest of Crete wholly neglected it. Michael describes the movements of Abdallah at considerable length, and places the expulsion of the Andalusians from Alexandria in December 827 (transl. p. 60), from which it follows that we must date the occupation of Crete in 828, not with Professor Bury in 825. The account of their relations with the authorities in Egypt is also quite different from that which Professor Bury derives from the Spanish encyclopaedist Al Humaida (not ' Humandi ', as he writes it).

In any large historical work, especially one dealing with so difficult a period as this, there must be many points on which the author's conclusions will be challenged. For my part, I am unable to believe that Photius was born ' not much later than 800 '. If so, he was seventy-eight at the Greek eighth synod, eighty-five at his second deposition, when he was playing an active part in politics, and at least ninety at his death, even if we do not with Professor Bury make him live to 897 ; yet the sources give no indication of great age. The reason given is that according to his own statement he was anathematized by an Iconoclast synod, and no such synod later than 815 is known. But would a synod really anathematize a boy of fourteen ? If he was nephew of Tarasius, he is not likely to have been much younger; but πατρόθειος should, on the analogy of ἀδελφόπαις, mean not ' paternal uncle ' but ' father's uncle '. It is odd that in another place also (p. 459) Professor Bury has involved himself in a chronological difficulty through what seems to be a misunderstanding of a word of relationship, for the usual meaning of ἐξάδελφος in Byzantine Greek is not ' nephew ' but ' cousin '. I cannot, however, believe that the Basil here mentioned is not the emperor ; if the *rector* were intended, the expression would surely be τοῦ αὐτοῦ Βασιλείου. Moreover, while it was natural that Basil's own kinsmen should support him, it would be strange to find three members of another family among his accomplices. While upon the subject of translation, I may refer to another word which I understand differently from Professor Bury. Simeon says that Theodora objected to Eudocia Ingerina on account of ἀναίδεια, which Professor Bury renders ' impudence ', inferring that she was a woman of spirit, whom Theodora feared as a rival influence. But, as Basil's wife, Eudocia showed no signs of strong character, and the word seems more naturally to mean ' immodesty ' and imply that she was already Michael's mistress. But, whatever the meaning, the passage is a serious objection to the theory that Simeon drew from a chronicle written under Basil or Leo.

Professor Bury, following Finlay, holds that the civil war of 821–4 was a chief cause of the disappearance of the small proprietors in Asia Minor; but the perpetual insecurity caused by the Arab raids would surely be much more effectual than a four years' war, and indeed the financial system described on p. 214 would alone suffice to bring about the result. I cannot also but think that desire to rescue the Amorians from undeserved opprobrium has sometimes caused the author to overstate his case. It is scarcely justifiable to speak of the charge against Bardas as mere rumour, for one can hardly believe that Ignatius would have run his head against the wall over the matter unless the fact had been open and manifest. This consideration perhaps explains his silence with regard to Basil's crimes, which Professor Bury finds so inconsistent (p. 188); for Basil's guilt was never admitted. Again, he says that the life of Theophilus was so exemplary that even the hostile chroniclers could only rake up one story against it, and this characterization of Theophilus may be correct; but the argument, which Professor Bury used in his earlier work also (ii. 304, 367), seems to me fallacious, the fact being that simple unchastity was regarded in much the same light as attendance at theatres, as a thing which in monks or clergymen was a gross offence, but in other men theoretically reprehensible, but in fact not worth noticing: nor does this story convey the impression of having been raked up to discredit Theophilus. If silence on this point is proof of innocence we shall have strange results.

I conclude with a few minor points. It is surely misleading to render λογοθέτης τοῦ δρόμου ' Logothete of the Course ', for no one knows better than Professor Bury that δρόμος is the post; on p. 194 it seems to be implied that the papal patrimonies in Calabria and the papal jurisdiction in Calabria were the same thing; on p. 10 the appointment of Bardanes as μονοστράτηγός is mentioned as if it were an innovation, though Heraclius held the same position under Tiberius III (Theoph., A.M. 6190); the assumed identity of Babek's general Nasr with the Syrian freebooter (p. 253, n. 4) seems most unlikely; the mention of a ' governor of Tunis ' (p. 244) reads like an anachronism; the name Gabala or Jabala should not be written ' Jaballah '; on p. 93 ' Constantius ' should be ' Constantine ', and at 141, l. 26 ' Theodora ' should be ' Theoctiste '. It is more important that Professor Bury states (pp. 152, 430) that the iconoclastic controversy permanently removed statues from the churches. This assertion is often made; but it would be more satisfactory if evidence for the use of statues in eastern churches before the iconoclastic period were given.   E. W. BROOKS.

Cartulaires de l'Abbaye de Molesme, 916–1250. Publiés avec une Introduction diplomatique, historique et géographique par JACQUES LAURENT. Tome II: Texte et Index. (Collection de Documents publiés avec le Concours de la Commission des Antiquités de la Côte-d'Or.) (Paris: Picard, 1911.)

THE editor of this volume gives the text of the first and an epitome of the second cartulary of Molesme. The first cartulary was compiled about 1142, but received some additions in the years 1142–70 and others in the thirteenth century. The object of the compilers was to form a register of title-deeds. Excluding the additions of a miscellaneous character at the end of the volume, this cartulary contains 272 documents. Many of these are valuable for the local history of Champagne and Burgundy, or for the light which they throw upon the law and institutions of the French kingdom. The second cartulary, planned as a supplement and a continuation to the first, was compiled about 1250, and contains 761 documents. To have printed it *in extenso* would have been too costly. M. Laurent, therefore, contents himself with analysing the majority of the documents, only giving the full texts of those which he considers exceptionally interesting. We regret that he has not been able to reproduce all documents belonging to the period covered by the first cartulary. But, as nearly three hundred pages of this volume are devoted to the second cartulary, we cannot fairly complain of an economy which was doubtless forced upon him. He has spared no pains to make this volume useful. There is a full index of persons and places; previous editions and existing manuscripts of every document are duly noted; and there are many footnotes. These cartularies are not unknown to French historians. They were used by M. d'Arbois de Jubainville; and more recently many extracts have been printed by MM. Ernest Petit and Émile Socard. But the bibliographies of M. Laurent show that many of the documents here printed or summarized have neither been edited nor used.

One problem, however, must be faced before the first cartulary, which is for several reasons the more important, can be accepted as a veracious source. Was the copyist fairly accurate and honest in the reproduction of the originals which he had before him? A small number of these originals still exists, and M. Laurent has duly collated them with the cartulary. In some cases the result is reassuring; nos. 143, 222, and 244 are faithful copies of extant originals. Elsewhere, however, the divergence is serious enough to necessitate the printing of the two texts in parallel columns. M. Laurent, it seems to us, has approached the problem of the variations in a spirit of excessive optimism. He makes a practice of assuming that, where the cartulary differs from a known original, the copyist was following another original (now lost) relating to the same transaction. It is a simpler explanation of the facts to suppose that the copyist felt free to paraphrase the document before him, and that he occasionally omitted passages, either through inadvertence or because he regarded them as superfluous for the purpose of legal evidence. There are many verbal differences between the cartulary and the originals; there are serious omissions in the cartulary; but the compiler is not in the habit of interpolating. Herein he differs from the scribe of the second cartulary, who appears at times to commit, or to endorse, a fraudulent interpolation. In support of this view we may cite one or two instances. No. 20 (p. 29) of the first cartulary is a case of deliberate omission; the scribe only reproduces so much of the original as relates to the chapel of St. Vaubourg; and he paraphrases freely, converting a charter, written in the first person, into a memorandum written in the third. The rest of the original is not needed for his purpose, because he gives elsewhere a sufficient title-deed, from the same seigneur, for the properties in question (no. 240). In no. 26 (p. 36) the cartulary omits three passages of the original; the first and second are concessions of valuable privileges, while the third (containing a threat of anathema and a dating clause) has no practical import. In no. 28 (p. 40), where the cartulary must be compared with two originals differing *inter se*, the most material peculiarity of the cartulary is that it omits all mention of certain chapels which, according to both originals, formed part of the grant. The one case in which we feel inclined to admit the existence of a lost original different from that which we possess is no. 217 (p. 198). Here the cartulary gives a conventional preamble, which is wanting in the extant original. The cartulary says that the grant was made at the instance of Bishop Robert of Langres, while the original names the successor of Robert; the list of witnesses in the original begins with Hugh, count of Champagne, who does not appear in the copy of the cartulary. Here it is plain that we are dealing with two different records of the same grant; but M. Laurent thinks that both the so-called original and the document of the cartulary may have been drawn up some years after the event. It would, perhaps, have been worth his while to scrutinize more closely all the originals which he has printed. One or two of them contain passages which look like interpolations, and in the case of no. 28 one is inclined to condemn the second 'original' on internal evidence.

Many of the topics which the cartularies illustrate have been discussed by the editor in his volume of prolegomena.[1] Thus he has given (i. 138) a complete list of the documents relating to crusaders and their benefactions. As might be expected from the geographical situation of Molesme, the number of such documents is exceptionally large. Among the more notable crusaders mentioned in the cartularies are Odo I of Burgundy, William II of Nevers, Hugh of Champagne, William III of Nevers, and William I of Sancerre. The earliest references belong to the closing years of the eleventh century; the last is dated 1218. The transactions of the crusaders with the abbey are not uninstructive. In several cases a seigneur obtains from Molesme the necessary funds for the *iter Hierosolimitanum*. One sells his allod to the monks for £27 of the money of Molesme; after his return he is enraged to find that his younger brother, dying childless, had given to the monks another part of the paternal inheritance; but finally he compounds his claim for £10 (ii. 222). Two brothers, who had founded the priory of Crisenon and granted it to Molesme, start for Jerusalem about the year 1100; the monks of Molesme give to one of them a mule and to the other the sum of thirty shillings (ii. 84). But they fail to perform their vow at that time: when the younger of them at last sets forth he obtains funds from the abbot on the security of allodial property at Crisenon, granting the income of the land during his absence to the monks of Crisenon; then, a little later, to provide for the health of his soul, he conceded that the land so mortgaged should pass absolutely to the monks at his death, and that security for his debt, if still unpaid, should be given to them elsewhere (ii. 64). Another makes a similar bargain in a slightly different form: he pledges an estate for £16 with the condition that either he or his brother, on returning from Jerusalem and repaying the money, may hold the estate for life, after which it shall pass absolutely to Molesme (ii. 229). The seigneur of Maligny, being stricken by grievous infirmity, makes a grant of lands to the abbey on the sole condition that, should he afterwards start for Jerusalem, the monks shall give him a suitable sum, to be fixed at their discretion (ii. 114). It is worth noticing that these transactions date from the early years of the crusading movement, that the seigneurs who strike such bargains are comparatively insignificant, and the lands in question of small extent. We are not led to the conclusion that religious houses battened extensively upon the needs of crusaders; or that the crusades

[1] See *ante*, xxiv. 125.

made land a drug in the market. But it is clear that the crusades created
a new demand for ready money, and that prosperous houses such as
Molesme benefited from the movement owing to their possession of spare
capital. In other ways also they reaped advantages. The ordinary
crusader provided for his spiritual weal by making some small donation
on the eve of departure; a good instance is the grant of one serf by
Odo I of Burgundy, 'ut in suis orationibus apud Deum sui memoriam
facerent, quatinus eius votum et iter, quo Iherusalem tendebat, in bonum
dirigeret' (ii. 143). Others remit their claims against the monks (ii. 483).
Others, again, make amends for past outrages; a count of Nevers 'de
incendio quod in villa Molismensi fecerat' (ii. 42); a smaller man for the
serfs whom he had carried off by force (ii. 379).

Passing from such abnormal benefactions to those of a more usual
character, we find that the commonest subject of a grant to Molesme is
a private church, or some part of its lands and rights. Glebes and tithes
and fees and offerings were the most considerable sources of the great
revenues which Molesme had acquired by the middle of the twelfth century.
The documents which record these gifts would have been invaluable
to Professor Imbart de la Tour, the most recent historian of the rural
parish. He was chiefly concerned with the legal position of the lay proprietors;
and nowhere is this so clearly explained as in the charters by
which they surrender their rights to religious houses such as Molesme.
We obtain, in the first place, a complete list of the valuable rights which
they possessed, of the temporalties and spiritualties belonging to a parish
church. It is a long and interesting inventory. The charters conveying
the whole interest in such a church give only the briefest analysis:

ecclesia cum decimis et oblationibus, atrio et terra altaris et censualibus ad altare
pertinentibus (ii. 37).
ecclesia cum omnibus appenditiis suis : omnes videlicet decimationes, oblationes
quoque et sepulturas, silvam etiam et terram et aquarum decursus, cuncta
scilicet ad ipsam ecclesiam pertinentia (ii. 41).

But when we turn to the grants of part-owners, or to documents which
define the rights of the priest as opposed to those of the patron, we are
almost overwhelmed with details. No form of profitable estate was more
complex, or lent itself more easily to subdivision among heirs and feoffees.
There is first of all the sacred edifice *ecclesia ipsa*, in which the different
altars might belong to different persons; already between the years 1080
and 1090 we see the founder of a new parish church at Nancy assigning the
parish altar (*altare principale*) to the monks of Molesme 'ita liberum ut
nullus in eo aliquid haberet preter monachos' (ii. 73). This grant might
naturally be supposed to include the *terra altaris* which regularly figures
among the possessions of a parish church; but the *terra altaris* is separately
specified by the benefactor, and only one-half of it is assigned to the
monks. The tithes again, though in a sense they belong to the altar,
are granted separately; it is quite usual to find that the *ecclesia*, the
decimatio, the *terra que ad ecclesiam pertinet* are distinguished in a grant
(e.g. ii. 57, 97). A further complication is introduced by the existence
of the parish priest. For he has a customary endowment (*presbiteratus*)
the constituents of which vary from place to place, but which is treated

as an integral whole, a separate estate. The priest has some of the fees and oblations pertaining to the altar; he may have land as well, 'feodum quod pertinet ad presbiteratum' (ii. 71); he will certainly have a house (ii. 80). None of this property is included in a grant of the altar or of the land of the altar (ii. 73). Finally, we have to notice the rights connected with the body of the church, and with the *atrium* or forecourt. In several cases the lay proprietor reckons among his sources of profit the 'censum archarum que in ipsa essent ecclesia' (ii. 152, 234); according to Ducange a rent exacted from the merchants who bought and sold in the church, though it seems possible that the *archae* were simply strong-boxes for safe custody. The *atrium* is consecrated ground, a necessary adjunct of every parish church in the neighbourhood of Molesme, commonly used as a cemetery, and so sacred that it ought not to be in possession of a layman (ii. 127, 227). But it is often held separately from the church, and in various ways is a source of revenue. The *sepulturae* do not go with the *atrium* (they are distinguished, for instance, in a grant of the church of Nailly, ii. 68); but the land comprised in the *atrium* is let at a high rent to peasants and others for their houses (ii. 75); and the holder of the *atrium* has the justice over those who live in it (ii. 65, 96, &c.). Sometimes the holder builds for himself a house within the *atrium* (ii. 71, 238); and in one case at least the *atrium* seems to be used as arable land (ii. 54).

So much for the sources of revenue. In the period covered by the first cartulary of Molesme they are seldom found united in a single hand. The parish priest has but a contemptible part of them. Much is held allodially by the representatives of the original founders, 'antiqui fideles ... qui ipsam ecclesiam in proprio alodio fundaverunt' (ii. 67). The tithe and the consecrated land, to say nothing of the *terra altaris*, belong to the lord of the manor in absolute ownership (ii. 47). Consequently he may grant them away as a fief; and much property pertaining to parish churches is held in feudal tenure. We find the endowment of the priest thus treated; in one place it is called *feodum presbiterale* (ii. 103); in another, *iunioratus* (ii. 35). We find a layman holding a church in fee from the bishop of Langres, and apparently holding it by military service (ii. 141–2). Tithes, the *presbiteratus, quicquid pertinet ad altare*, the *atrium*, the *oblationes, sepultura, baptisterium*—all appear in the hands of lay vassals (ii. 96, 211, 217).

It is not surprising that the reformers of the Hildebrandine period should have attacked these scandalous cases of misappropriation. On the whole we must be surprised at the forbearance which they manifested in devising remedies. Historically these endowments belonged to the parish priest. If they had become larger than was needful for his maintenance the bishop was the person entitled to the superfluous revenues, since the parish had been created at the expense of the bishop. But the cartularies of Molesme show us that the bishops of Langres and Troyes and Châlons were always ready to accept, as a satisfactory compromise, a grant by a lay proprietor of the church, or of his interest in the church, to a deserving religious community. M. Laurent explains the policy of the bishops by assuming that they hoped in this way to achieve 'la restauration de chaque église paroissiale dans ses droits ... la reconstitution lente des patrimoines paroissiaux ' (ii. 131-2). In a sense this is true. The abbots of Molesme, when once they had acquired any species of right in a parish church, spared no efforts to secure the remainder of the endowment. As a last resource they were prepared to buy up the layman's interest (ii. 243). More often they found that one benefaction led naturally to another : it was in this way that they gathered together from different hands the property of the church of Saint-Moré (ii. 66, 71, 132); in the case of the church of Merrey, the count of Brienne, to whom the church had originally belonged, was induced to take the first step by surrendering the few rights which still remained to him, and by signifying that he would sanction any grants of restitution which his vassals might be induced to make ; a number of them followed his lead (ii. 96). But the result of such transactions was not to enrich the parish priest. At Merrey, for example, a priory was founded ; and this was a not infrequent outcome of such acquisitions. If there was no such new foundation, the monks of Molesme appropriated to their own use all that the seigneurs had resigned.

The bishops were content that this should happen. Their main consideration was that ecclesiastical endowments were being emancipated from lay ownership : ' protestamur maximum nefas esse bona ecclesiastica in manu laicorum, maxime militum, devenire ' (ii. 141). They also secured a further advantage, in that they were able to reassert and re-define their relation to the parish priest. In 1114 William of Champeaux confirms to Molesme the churches which they have acquired in his diocese of Châlons ; but he stipulates that the priests appointed shall be suitable persons and shall be presented to the bishop of Châlons to be invested with their cures (ii. 180). There is no attempt to dictate the use which shall be made of the endowments ; unless it be a general stipulation that the purposes named by the benefactors shall be observed (ii. 182). The one case in which the bishop interferes with the abbey's administration of a benefice is when the vested interests of the parish priest are attacked. Deservedly or undeservedly, religious houses were supposed to treat their priests badly. A bishop of Troyes, himself granting a parish church, makes a significant reservation : ' quoniam aliquot monachi maletractant suos presbyteros, icciroo presbiteratum illius ecclesie retinui in episcopi dominio, ne forte aliqua violentia minuatur sibi aliquid de suo beneficio ' (ii. 142). From time to time a priest appeals to the bishop, on the ground that dues which should be his are taken by the abbey. The bishop in one case confines himself to an investigation of the local custom, without inquiring whether the customary endowment is adequate (ii. 35). In another, after long litigation, he imposes what he regards as an equitable settlement—an equal division of oblations, testamentary gifts, and fiefs pertaining to the altar (ii. 484); but as the litigation had been prolonged it may be taken for granted that the facts in dispute were obscure. What seems clear from these cases is that, if the parish priest seldom benefited materially by the change of patron, a religious house was not allowed to exploit the presbyteral endowment. The ill-paid curé, rendering to Molesme an exact account of the fees earned by his services—' baptisterium, benedictionem perarum, visitationes infirmorum, missas pro defunctis, oblationes nuptiarum et purificationum, confessiones' (ii. 35)—was a survival from the period of seigneurial ownership.

We hope enough has been said to show the great importance of these cartularies. Many other lines of investigation are suggested by the editorial introduction. Others suggest themselves even to a cursory reader. It is evident, for instance, that there is much to be learned about the seigneurial jurisdictions of Molesme. M. Laurent deserves our cordial thanks for placing such a valuable storehouse of documents at the service of medieval students. H. W. C. DAVIS.

A History of Preston in Amounderness. By H. W. CLEMESHA. (University of Manchester Publications, no. lxvii, 1912.)

ALTHOUGH of more purely local interest than other volumes in the Historical Series of the Manchester University publications, Mr. Clemesha's *History of Preston* is a careful and readable piece of work. The writer has had various materials to hand in Lingard's *Preston Charters*, Abram's *Preston Guild Rolls*, Hewitson's *Preston Court Leet Records*, and Smith's *Records of Preston Parish Church*. There are also three monographs on the history of Preston already in existence, the work of Messrs. Hardwick, Fishwick, and Hewitson. Preston cannot, therefore, be said to lack historians; nor has there been any want of enterprise in publishing its local archives.

Preston occurs in Domesday Book at the head of the townships of Amounderness. Sixty-one townships are there said to 'belong to' it, a phrase that has been variously interpreted. 'The probable explanation,' says Mr. Clemesha, ' seems to be that they belonged to Preston in a tenurial and not a fiscal way ; that, in short, they were grouped together, because they were held of the lord of the manor of Preston.' The phrase may, however, it is submitted, point to a pre-feudal bond of connexion, and as chief town of a hundred Preston may have formed the centre of an administrative district in pre-conquest times, and have possessed a burghal character before it received (probably by grant from Roger of Poitou) the borough customs that it borrowed from the ordinances of Breteuil. The fact that Preston was the place of meeting of the sheriff's county court as well as of the hundred court of Amounderness accords with the supposition that Preston was a centre of administration and jurisdiction long before Roger of Poitou became possessed of it.

The earliest recorded charter granted to Preston was given to the town by Henry I, but has not survived. Nothing can be learnt either from the charter whereby Henry II granted to the men of Preston the privileges of Newcastle-under-Lyme, since the charter granted to Newcastle-under-Lyme is also wanting. There is, however, preserved in the municipal archives a custumal of the early fourteenth century, which has been printed by Miss Bateson in this Review (xv. 496 *seqq*.). Another valuable town document is the orders made at the gild merchant of 1328. The first article of the custumal sets out that the men of Preston ' may have a gild merchant with hanse and other customs and liberties belonging to that gild '. The gild merchant is, needless to say, theoretically distinct from the governing body of the borough ; yet neither the orders of 1328 nor those made at the next recorded gild merchant in 1397 give any trace of the existence of a gild merchant as a separate organization or semi-corporate body, nor does the Preston gild appear to have possessed any other officials than the officers of the borough. Mr. Clemesha is probably correct in his conclusion :

> The explanation may possibly be, that in Preston the trade privileges and rights of trade legislation which were contained in a grant of a gild merchant, with or without hanse, such as were conferred upon the burgesses of Preston, were not, as in other towns, exercised by a separate body formed to deal with them and called a gild merchant, but were the function of the mayor and the capital or principal burgesses.

The chief business of the gild merchant in later times was the admission of burgesses, and these were admitted either as in-burgesses or out-burgesses, the former being the persons who were resident in the town. The distinction between in-burgesses and out-burgesses plays an important part in the history of Preston. In the reign of Henry VIII, Sir Richard Hoghton, a neighbouring landowner and the principal of the out-burgesses, endeavoured to obtain control of the election of the mayor as well as of the borough members of parliament. Hoghton's action was found to be contrary to certain articles drawn up for the good rule of the town, forbidding out-burgesses to meddle in the mayoral election. The right of election of members of parliament for the borough was claimed by, and seems to have been exercised by, the corporation to the exclusion of all other burgesses, whether resident or non-resident, but was disputed on the occasion of the election of 1661. The report of the committee for privileges and elections, adopted by the house of commons, had unexpected and far-reaching results. It declared that, 'the question being, whether the mayor and twenty-four burgesses had only voices, or the inhabitants at large, the committee was of the opinion that all the inhabitants had voices in the election '.

In 1768 an ingenious whig vicar of the parish, dissatisfied at the return of the two tory candidates, instigated an election petition. The foundation of the petitioners' case was the vague drafting of the resolution of 1661, and the fact that, whereas the parliamentary franchise had in practice been restricted to inhabitant in-burgesses, a literal construction of the resolution of 1661 threw it open to all inhabitants. The house of commons gave its verdict in favour of the petitioners, with the result that manhood suffrage was thereby established for the borough of Preston. The reform bill of 1832 acted as a disfranchising measure. Previously to this and to the municipal corporation act of 1835 Preston combined a democratic parliamentary franchise with an oligarchic municipal constitution. The mayor was in theory elected by an electoral board of twenty-four (who are to be distinguished from the twenty-four who formed the town council), but, from the reign of Queen Elizabeth, the practice was to nominate as mayor the senior alderman.

In dealing with the part played by Preston in the civil war, Mr. Clemesha has followed Mr. Broxap's monograph on *The Civil War in Lancashire*, published in the same series. He gives careful accounts of the two battles of Preston (1648 and 1715). For the state of Preston at the close of the seventeenth century he has utilized Kuerden's *Brief Description of the*

Burrough and Town of Preston and its Government and Guild, written shortly after 1682, and three local diaries, covering the years 1683–90, of which one, namely that of Edward Fleetwood, is as yet unpublished. The municipal and political history of Preston in the nineteenth century is also given at length. The treatment of the medieval history of the town is, perhaps, rather scanty, but, as a study in town government, Mr. Clemesha's work deserves every commendation.   H. H. E. CRASTER.

Charters of the Borough of Southampton. Edited by H. W. GIDDEN. Two vols. (Publications of the Southampton Record Society. Southampton, 1909–10.)

THE charters of Southampton form an instructive series, both for the comparative study of municipal institutions and as illustrating the various devices by which a paternal government might foster the trade or relieve the financial necessities of a favoured town. These two volumes are very welcome, although the editor's work leaves something to be desired in method and in accuracy. He has printed a number of inspeximuses, when it would have been the natural and reasonable course to re-arrange in chronological order the charters which they contain. His method involves the printing of duplicate versions of several charters, whereas he should have formed one critical text of each by collating the versions. Neither his transcriptions nor his translations are impeccable. They contain slips which may mislead the inexperienced student, and which suggest that Mr. Gidden is insufficiently acquainted with the idiom of chancery Latin.

The municipal development of Southampton starts with the formation of a gild-merchant, which, as we learn from a charter of Henry II (i. 10, 26), was in existence before 1135. Already in the reign of Henry II the burgesses held Southampton and Portsmouth in farm from the Crown. But of a borough constitution the charters tell us nothing before the reign of Henry III. Southampton was ruled by a mayor in 1217, and did not appreciate the privilege; in 1249 Henry III conceded the abolition of the office. In 1256 he granted to the burgesses the right of dealing directly with the exchequer through their bailiffs, and of electing their own coroners *ad attachiamenta placitorum coronae*; he endowed the borough court with exclusive jurisdiction over their tenements and chattels within the borough; he also gave the return of writs and promised that no writs save those of right, of novel disseisin, and of dower, should run in Southampton (i. 14, 30). A distinct advance is made in the charter of Henry IV (1401). This recognizes the existence of the mayor, who sits with the bailiffs in the gildhall to hear all pleas, real or personal or mixed, arising within the borough. It grants to the burgesses the privileges of infangthief, outfangthief, view of frankpledge, *catalla felonum*, and fines for transgressions. It mentions the four aldermen, who are joined with the mayor and four elected representatives of the community, to act as justices of the peace for the purposes of the statute of labourers (i. 40). The first charter of incorporation was granted by Henry VI in 1445. It provides that the burgesses are to be ' una communitas perpetua, corporata in re et nomine, per nomen Maioris,

Ballivorum, et Burgensium villae illius '. The mayor and bailiffs are to be annually elected, and must be sufficiently skilled in the law to be capable of pleading in all suits before the royal judges. The grant of a staple is added; and the burgesses are ordered to elect annually a mayor of the staple and constables (i. 54). Two years later the king granted that Southampton and Portsmouth should be *unus integer comitatus corporatus*, with an elected sheriff wielding all the powers that belong to other sheriffs in other counties (i. 70). In 1461, in a charter of Edward IV, we come across the recorder; *quidam iuris peritus* is to sit as a *custos pacis* with the mayor, aldermen, and four other burgesses, to do justice under the assizes of watch and ward, the statutes of labourers and those directed against liveries and Lollards (i. 106). From this date to the reign of Charles I the charters give no evidence of constitutional growth, but in 1640 the recorder is mentioned by his title. The charter of that year also recognizes the existence of the common council, sanctions the creation of a court of orphans, and provides for the election of a town clerk 'to do all things which pertain to the office of town clerk in any other borough' (ii. 76). Obviously the charters do not give us a complete account of constitutional growth. But they supply a rough outline, the details of which must be filled in from the other records of the town. H. W. C. DAVIS.

Livre de la Conqueste de la Princée de l'Amorée. Chronique de Morée (1204–1305). Publiée pour la Société de l'Histoire de France par JEAN LONGNON. (Paris: Renouard, 1911.)

ALEXANDRE BUCHON. *Voyage dans l'Eubée, les Îles Ioniennes et les Cyclades en 1841.* Publié pour la première fois avec une notice biographique et bibliographique par JEAN LONGNON. Préface de MAURICE BARRÈS. (Paris: Émile-Paul, 1911.)

THE editor of these two volumes, both connected with the name of Buchon, has rendered a conspicuous service to medieval Greek history. Not only has he given us a critical edition of the French version of the *Chronicle of the Morea*, last published by Buchon in 1845, but he has exhumed from the Bibliothèque Nationale that part of the French scholar's journal of travel in Greece which refers to the islands. Hitherto Buchon's journey through insular Hellas was known only in a few articles, published in the rare *Revue de Paris* and *Revue Indépendante* during 1842–4, and limited to a part of Euboia and some of the Cyclades.

In a long introduction to the text of the *Chronicle* M. Longnon examines the theories as to its date and authorship advanced by his predecessors. He then puts forward the strange hypothesis that 'the original of the *Chronicle* was written in Italian and probably in the Venetian dialect' (p. lxxvi). From this lost Venetian original were compiled, according to him, the French, Greek, Italian, and Aragonese versions, which we still possess. To the present writer the historical and philological evidence adduced for an Italian original appears inadequate. Here and there, as in the date of the accession of Guillaume de Villehardouin (pp. viii, lxxxviii), the editor has not kept abreast of recent research in the Vatican archives. But his edition is scholarly and the map useful.

Thus the student now has modern reprints of both the Greek[1] and the French versions.

Buchon's travels possess a double interest—for the light which they throw on the history of Frankish Greece, and for their sketches of the modern kingdom in the last years of absolute monarchy and of the Ionian islands under the commissionerships of Sir Howard Douglas and Mackenzie. The entirely new portions of the narrative (pp. 45-149, 220-47) accordingly contain much of value to students of both periods. English readers will peruse with pleasure the account of Mr. Noel's property at Achmet Aga; they will be less gratified by the criticisms, often just, of the British protectorate in the Ionian islands, where Buchon met such celebrities as Mustoxidi and Mercati, the respective historians of Corfù and Zante; Mackenzie, the newly-arrived lord high commissioner; and Viaro Capo d'Istria, eldest brother of the murdered president and lately accused of complicity in the so-called 'phil-orthodox' conspiracy. The French visitor paid tribute to the material progress of the islands, but observed that the British, with the exception of Lord Guilford, had done little for education; and he foresaw the union with Greece. In Euboia and the Cyclades he studied the remains of the medieval Italian rule, and copied down extracts from the manuscript history of Naxos by Father Lichtle, whom he erroneously calls 'Riechter', and who is mentioned by Pasch von Krienen in 1773 as superior of the Jesuits in that island. These extracts are given in an appendix; but a study of the whole manuscript from Hopf's papers at Berlin has convinced the present writer that the historical part is largely based upon Sauger and Lebeau. This valuable diary of travel contains a few other errors. The date '1361' (p. xxxviii) is an obvious slip; by 'Zaccaria' (p. 37) is meant Licario; '1863' is thrice erroneously given as the date of the Ionian union with Greece (pp. 78 n. 4, 142, 146); De Bosset was the name of the officer connected with the cession of Parga; Epeiros not 'Acarnanie' (pp. 130, 146) lies opposite Corfù; Marco Sanudo was not 'second' duke of Naxos (p. 166), nor was Barbarossa the pirate living in '1390' (p. 167). We are thrice wrongly told that the Turks took Andros 'in 1596' (pp. 215, 228, 231). Much, of course, has been published on the medieval history of Greece since Buchon travelled there; but his work will always be useful, and the sketch of his life and the preface by the author of that charming book, *Le Voyage de Sparte*, give additional importance to this delightful volume.   WILLIAM MILLER.

Histoire des Corporations d'Arts et Métiers des Ville et Comté de Montbéliard et des Seigneuries en dépendant. Par LÉON NARDIN et JULIAN MAUVEAUX. 2 vols. (Paris: Champion, 1910.)

As the town and *comté* of Montbéliard, which lie at the southern end of the Vosges, passed to the house of Würtemberg in 1397 and did not become part of France till 1793, and as the earliest document referred to is dated 1430, all the phases of corporate life described in this book arose under German influences. This is further indicated by the

[1] Cf. *ante*, xix. 573.

gradual substitution of the term *Schomffe* or *Chomffe* (*Zunft*) for *mestier*, and by the fact that one of the leading motives for the revision of trade ordinances was to secure the recognition of the town's journeymen as qualified craftsmen in the cities of the Rhine. The sets of ordinances on which the work is based, and a full selection of which is presented in the second volume, represent four distinct periods of corporate development, the earliest being due to the autonomous activity of the gilds in the fifteenth century, and the rest being embodied in three groups of ducal charters granted respectively in the last decade of the fifteenth century, in the last half of the sixteenth century, and in the middle decades of the eighteenth century.

The range of corporate life thus covered is wide for a small town of 3,000 inhabitants. Exclusive of the company of doctors, apothecaries, and surgeons, with its subordinate detachment of *sages-femmes*, and of the company of *archers*, *arbalétriers*, *coulevriniers*, *arquebusiers*, and *mousquetaires*, there were twenty-four corporations of traders, many of them representing groups of two or more occupations. The mercers' company occupied the foremost place, and laid claim as usual to a monopoly of the retail trade in all imported goods. It included from the first (1491) the grocers, goldsmiths, silversmiths, and jewellers; and it absorbed in the course of the sixteenth and seventeenth centuries the cappers (*bonnetiers*), the hatters, the drapers, the pewterers, the dyers, the corders, the tailors, and the whitetawyers (*chamoiseurs*), most of which trades had possessed or belonged to independent organizations. The cause of this tendency was the growth of the trading function in the crafts. The craftsmen were becoming shopkeepers and needed the shelter of the mercers' privilege. Each craft retained its separate ordinances after the amalgamation, and was nominally confined to its own branch of the retail trade in foreign goods. But in course of time the general merchants who had formed the original nucleus of the mercers' gild found that they were being ousted from the control of the amalgamation by the craftsmen they had admitted, and at the same time losing their monopoly of the general trade. Hence in 1724 they procured a separation and were reestablished on the original basis, including only the mercers, grocers, goldsmiths, and jewellers. Next year the cappers and drapers also seceded from the amalgamation and obtained a charter of their own; and this example was followed by the dyers in 1741 and the whitetawyers in 1754, leaving the hatters in almost solitary possession of the shell of the earlier amalgamation.

Of the gilds that early acquired charters independently of the mercers three represented victualling crafts, the butchers (1499), the fishers (1513), and the bakers (1562), whilst three others represented amalgamations of the crafts working in stone and clay (masons, tilers, potters, &c., 1573), the metal-workers (1573), and the workers in wood (1580). These amalgamations were founded to protect the handicraft interest of groups of related trades in deliberate opposition to the merely trading interest of the mercers; but that the trading interest was becoming dominant in them also is clear from an ordinance common to the wood-workers and the metalworkers, allowing a member, on payment of special dues, to deal in the products of all the group of crafts to which he belonged, though he might only work at one craft himself. The coopers and the cabinetmakers set up corporations of their own in the middle of the eighteenth century. The company of *marchands de la grand'verge* deserves special notice. It included dealers in all kinds of live stock and provisions, in fish, butter, and cheese, whether townsmen or countrymen. The derivation of its title from the staff of the cattle-driver is unconvincing. It is much more likely to have reference to some feudal jurisdiction under which the market was first organized. The *filandriers et crampiers* were pedlars who supplied the country folk with chandlery, pipes, and tobacco, and collected in exchange, along with butter and eggs, the yarn spun by peasants' wives. Their company was therefore united in the seventeenth century to that of the weavers, whose manufacture of fustians and druggets and printed cottons furnished the town with its chief export trade in the eighteenth century and gave employment to the country round. The manufacture of caps and hosiery and of gloves, organized on the domestic system by the *bonnetiers* and glovers of the town, constituted the only other considerable industrial interests of the *comté*. All these trades depended partly for their labour supply, and still more for their market, on the neighbouring French provinces, so that the deliberate pressure of hostile tariffs furnished a strong motive for acquiescence in annexation in 1793.

In regard to the internal economy of the gilds, whilst there is nothing entirely new, there is much valuable confirmation and illustration of existing knowledge. The pre-Reformation charters enforce the religious customs as well as the trade rules of the gilds; and the later ordinances reveal the existence in many crafts of separately organized bodies of journeymen, in most cases under the supervision of the masters, but in one case (shoemakers, of course) acting independently. The moment of transition in gild structure is illustrated by a set of rules drawn up amongst the locksmiths and gunsmiths in 1565, which elaborately prescribe the method of bringing a newly arrived journeyman into contact with an employer. No one who compares this arrangement with that of the London blacksmiths in 1434, cited by Professor Ashley, and reflects that both these bodies of smiths belonged to the fraternity of St. Eloi, will fail to be struck with the continuity of gild traditions. The unity of the book does not appear to have suffered from the fact that it is the product of collaboration between the local archivist and a *lauréat de l'Institut*, and, perhaps in consequence of this method, it is admirably balanced between the interests of the local archaeologist and genealogist and the interests of the social historian. A reference here and there to the wider literature of the subject, e. g. to M. de Lespinasse's *Métiers de Paris* or Professor E. Gothein's *Wirthschaftsgeschichte des Schwarzwaldes*, might have added value to an excellent work. GEORGE UNWIN.

Ye Solace of Pilgrimes. By JOHN CAPGRAVE. Edited by C. A. MILLS, with an introductory note by the Rev. H. M. BANNISTER. (London: Frowde, 1911.)

THIS book is an important addition to the literature of the medieval topography of Rome, and Mr. Mills has earned the gratitude of students by transcribing and editing the manuscript (in the Bodleian) to which attention had only recently been called. It may be described as a guide-book for English pilgrims at Rome, compiled about 1450; and it consists of (1) an account of ancient Rome derived from the *Mirabilia* in one of its later forms, and a description (2) of the ' Station ' basilicas and churches, and (3) of churches not included in the former category. The third part is imperfect. In the course of editing the work the interesting discovery (first, apparently, suggested by Sir G. Warner) was made that it was the lost description of Rome by the Augustinian friar of King's Lynn, John Capgrave; and Mr. Bannister has shown in his admirable introductory note that this is probably one of three autograph manuscripts which can be ascribed to him. The information contained in the text is copious even in the part derived from the *Mirabilia*, and still more so in the description of the churches, for Capgrave was evidently a diligent compiler and inquirer. With one of those personal touches which are not uncommon in the book he expresses his regret at being unable to explain the name of one church, 'for the dwelleres ar wroth a non if men ask ony questiones' (p. 161). It must be admitted that facts of direct archaeological or historical importance are rare, and the main interest of the book is that of a record of what was said and believed about Rome in the later middle ages. Capgrave occasionally shows the germs of a critical spirit, but as a rule he is a typical child of his age in believing what he is told, and adding edifying comments of his own. One of the most curious and characteristic occurs in the account of Santa Maria Trastevere with its traditional wells of oil, the emblem of divine mercy : ' This is our byleue that soules in hell haue lasse peyne than the be worthi' (p. 112). Occasionally we have vivid touches of description. Thus, of San Vitale he says : ' A ful desolate place it is and al in ruine as there be many moo '—an extraordinary contrast to its situation to-day in the Via Nazionale. Among the rare and curious legends recorded we may mention that of St. Peter escaping from prison and hiding in a recess of the wall of S. Pudenziana, where he was invisible to his pursuers till pointed out by an angel—a story which Capgrave feels requires some explanation, for one miracle nullifies the other.

The editor is so modest about his own capacities, and has, under the circumstances, performed his task so well, that it would be ungracious to criticize him too minutely. The text appears to be carefully transcribed, though there are places in which we should have liked to be reassured by a 'sic' that the reading printed is actually that of the manuscript. To give one instance, it is incredible that the author can have written 'Aue marie stella' for 'maris' in quoting the familiar vesper hymn (p. 169). The question of writing a commentary on a work of this kind is not an easy one. The material is so abundant that there is a danger of the notes becoming too lengthy. Mr. F. M. Nichols's edition of the *Mirabilia* (*The Marvels of Rome*, London, 1889) is a masterpiece of compression, and may well serve as a model in its way. Several of Mr. Mills's notes are useful and valuable, but many points of difficulty or interest are left unexplained, while, on the other hand, superfluous or irrelevant matter is introduced. We refer to such notes as those giving the modern history of St. Peter's and other churches (pp. 61, 83, &c.), or the life of the Empress Helena (p. 126). A few of the less obvious Middle English words which occur are annotated, but more are left without explanation, and we see no reference to Mr. Stratmann's *Dictionary*. When Capgrave says that the Pantheon was surmounted by the ' coproun ' now in front of St. Peter's —meaning, obviously, the pine-cone—a note suggests ' copper ' as the interpretation, though ' copir ' occurs elsewhere in the book. We have only to look in Stratmann to find ' coperun, the ornament on the lid of a vessel '. Mr. Mills has made good use of the best books relating to Roman topography and hagiology ; otherwise his apparatus is not very adequate. Moreri's *Dictionary*, for instance, is obsolete for bibliographical purposes. G. McN. RUSHFORTH.

Der Untergang des Ordensstaates Preussen und die Entstehung der preussischen Königswürde. Aus den Quellen dargestellt von Dr. J. VOTA. (Mainz : Kirchheim, 1911.)

AMID the interminable lines of colourless German monographs it is almost refreshing to come across so full-blooded an historical polemic as this arraignment of the Hohenzollerns by an author, presumably a member of the German Centre, who has been constrained, against his will he tells us, to conceal his identity under the pseudonym of ' Dr. Vota '. He makes no secret of his catholic convictions, but claims exemption from religious and territorial particularism, and discovers *die wahre vaterländische Gesinnung* in the conscientious maintenance of natural and positive law (*Recht*). There is, according to the author, a bond of unity between Prussia and the Reformation, but it is a bond of force and fraud. Albert of Brandenburg, grand master of the Teutonic Order, had brought himself, by his arbitrary government and by his reckless and unprovoked attacks on his suzerain, Sigismund of Poland, to extremities ; he was deeply in debt and defenceless. He found salvation in the Lutheran Reformation, the essence of which was *der Wiedereintritt des heidnischen Staatsgedankens in das Christentum*, the surrender of church to state, and sacrilege ; Lutheran doctrine was *ein Freibrief gegen das siebente Gebot*. Hence Albert's historical importance; before any Elector of Saxony, before Philip of Hesse, Gustavus Vasa, or Henry VIII, Albert gave a practical demonstration of the real meaning of the Reformation by secularizing the Teutonic Order in Prussia and converting it into an hereditary fief of Poland. In order to achieve his purpose he had to terrorize the knights, hoodwink the papacy, and betray the empire. The ban was proclaimed against him, but Charles V's difficulties with his protestant subjects, the Turks, and Christian enemies prevented its execution. Even after Mühlberg he dared not risk the breach with Sigismund which would have followed an attack upon his vassal. Sigismund's son had, moreover, married Ferdinand's daughter ; further marriage alliances were contracted by Albert with the families of the king of Denmark, the duke of Brunswick, and the elector of Brandenburg ; and in 1561 his secularizing example was followed by the Order in Livonia. Its remaining branch in Germany continued its vain protests till Napoleon put an end to its existence ; but the Hohenzollerns in Prussia flourished like the bay-tree. Albert's line, indeed, died with his son in 1618; but East Prussia fell to the electoral house of Brandenburg, and the Great Elector by unscrupulous dealings with Sweden, Poland, and the empire secured the independence of his fief, while his son Frederick I achieved the ducal and then the royal dignity.

Dr. Vota's ponderous tome of six hundred closely printed pages is for the most part not an exposition of the causes of the fall of the Teutonic Order, but an exposure of the delinquencies of its grand master, Albert, who provided an exhibition of *Realpolitik*, the cynicism and efficiency of which have not been surpassed by any later monarch or minister of the house of Hohenzollern. It is an historical treatise, but it is not history. We hear little or nothing of the real causes of the ruin of the Order. It had secularized itself to a large extent before Albert's day; each of its three provinces, the Livonian, the Prussian, and the German had claimed a practical autonomy; each knight treated his commandery as an independent fief; the conversion of the Baltic lands to Christianity deprived it of its *raison d'être*, and the union of Poland and Lithuania raised up a powerful foe. Even the loss of Prussia failed to galvanize its decaying spirit, and it declined the offers of emperors to transplant it into Hungary where it might have recovered its prestige by resuming its function of defending Christendom against the Turks. These worldly considerations are alien from Dr. Vota's mind; the only thing that satisfies his moral sense is the imperial ban against the Hohenzollern. He comforts himself with the fact that, although it was never executed, it was never withdrawn; it stands as a moral protest against the forces of evil. But even that ban was launched against Albert, not on the ground of his Lutheranism, but of his treason to the empire in transferring his homage to Poland. Nor, we may remind Dr. Vota, was it necessary to be a Lutheran in order to spoil the church: Henry VIII suppressed monasteries; Charles V himself secularized bishoprics, and his grandfather Ferdinand the Catholic had suppressed the Teutonic Order in Spain. The catholic Sigismund, too, had contemplated a similar step; and the main difference between him and Albert was apparently the Lutheran's greater promptitude, which was not a question of doctrine. A. F. POLLARD.

The Political History of England, 1547–1603. By A. F. POLLARD, M.A., Fellow of All Souls College, Oxford; Professor of English History in the University of London. (London: Longmans, 1910.)

IN the debates in the house of commons on the bishopric of St. Albans bill in 1875, Sir William Harcourt described the reign of Edward VI as 'the best days of the Church of England'. The distance between such a view and the result of a scientific study of the facts can be measured by this book. No one who sets out to tell the story of the second half of the Tudor period can escape, probably, the charge of prejudice, but Professor Pollard seems to have attained impartiality as nearly as is possible for mortal man. He is perfectly at home in the authorities, and he sets out the story without concealment and with no case to prove. Amid the sordid politics of the days of Edward VI, through the dreary reign of Mary, and among the tangled network of Elizabeth's policies he moves easily, sometimes a shade swiftly, yet with singular fairness. He has a gift of epigram which is displayed to advantage in summing up policies. Henry VIII's Scottish campaign of 1543 was ' an action for breach of promise, and not a conquest of Scotland' (p. 10). The Tudor policy in Ireland, 'in its efforts to extirpate Irish septs, created an Irish nation' (p. 439). In his judgements of character he exhibits the same happy gift. Somerset as Protector ' took his office seriously and himself too seriously' (p. 37). Northumberland was ' one of the most desperate political gamblers in English history' (p. 98), Gardiner ' was an Englishman first and a churchman afterwards' (p. 144), Mary was ' the most honest of Tudor rulers, she never consciously did what she thought to be wrong' (p. 174) ; less dignified though not less true is the *obiter dictum* on Elizabeth, ' like the ships of her navy, she owed much of her success to the nearness with which she could sail to the wind' (p. 179). Judgements as just and as terse as these can be found up and down the book: Cranmer was ' not noted for steadfast adherence to lost causes' (p. 41); Leicester's defection from the council's policy in 1585, ' was singular, except that he usually betrayed his friends' (p. 383, n. 1); and the picture of Sir Richard Grenville is excellent : ' a magnificent barbarian who hunted Red Indians for amusement, treated Spanish prisoners as slaves, and ate wineglasses out of bravado ; and his splendid bravery resulted in the loss of the only English warship taken in Elizabeth's reign' (p. 44). The verdict on Edward VI is, however, one of the most striking in the book:

From the fiery furnace of Mary's reign protestants looked back on Edward VI as a saint, and his reign was long regarded as the golden age of the protestant reformation. The gold is tarnished now, and the halo gone from Edward's head. That his abilities were above the average his journals and state papers show. . . . But . . . the wooden bigotry of his religious, and the obstinate absolutism of his political, views support the probability that the prolongation of his life and reign might ultimately have provoked an upheaval, in which the rejection of protestantism would have combined with reaction against despotism to undo the work of the Tudor monarchy (p. 79).

This needed saying, and it will be agreed that it is well said. Most admirable, too, is the account of the crisis of 1569. Nowhere can be found so acute an analysis of the parties and policies which were then struggling for mastery in Elizabeth's council as in the beginning of chapter xv in this book.

Throughout the greater part of the period the theological interest is dominant, and Mr. Pollard gives it its due place. He is confusing at times in his use of the word ' catholic ', as when he says that Mary ' made straight her successor's path by uprooting whatever desire Englishmen had for catholic faith' (p. 178). Elizabeth would have been greatly surprised— as witness her proclamation during the rebellion of 1569, to say nothing of the Book of Common Prayer—to know that she and her subjects did not hold ' the catholic faith ', and as a rule, when treating the Elizabethan settlement, Mr. Pollard is perfectly conscious of this and distinguishes Roman from other ' catholics '. But the *minutiae* of the theological and ceremonial controversies are not the author's strongest points : he does not apparently recognize that a ' vestment ' meant the chasuble with stole and maniple (which a glance at the printed sixteenth-century inventories would have shown), and he appears to hold that the Thirty-nine Articles formed after Elizabeth's days an integral part of the Prayer Book (e. g. pp. 25, 69). An uninstructed reader might perhaps suppose from the not infrequent references to the bishops as royal nominees that the appointment of bishops by the Crown was a result of the sixteenth-century Reformation, and once or twice Mr. Pollard writes (on p. 367) as if the right of the Crown to appoint implied that the bishops exercised merely a delegated royal jurisdiction. But he is too good a constitutional historian to have forgotten that episcopal appointments in England were practically (and, until the thirteenth century, nominally also) in the hands of the Crown, and the fact that Elizabeth appointed English bishops does not differentiate her from Alfred or Edward the Confessor or Henry I. Nor, again, is Mr. Pollard strictly accurate when he writes that the changes made in the Prayer Book of 1552 were 'uniformly in the protestant direction'. Broadly, of course, the book was revised in that interest, but the far more frequent recitation of the Athanasian Creed and the very definite statements in the baptismal office as to regeneration, dictated doubtless by the exigencies of the controversy with the anabaptists and the Arians, were certainly a stiffening of what he would call, we imagine (as on p. 212), 'antipapal catholicism'.

These small points are the more noticeable because Mr. Pollard has grasped fully the greater theological issues at stake. He describes the Elizabethan settlement candidly and fairly, and he handles the vexed question of the continuity of the post-reformation with pre-reformation church with complete understanding. 'The old order continued under somewhat changed conditions, and she [Elizabeth] no more established the English church than she did the English state' (p. 212). Again,

Her work is sometimes described in confusing terms, which seem to imply that she and her father established, started, or even founded the Church of England. But in truth the Tudors founded neither catholicism nor protestantism; and they only modified the outward fabric of ecclesiastical organization by substituting the monarchy for the papacy (p. 355).

And with a sure touch he lays his finger on the real controversy between the English church and the separatists who attacked episcopacy. 'There was an intimate connexion between catholic dogma and catholic organization; and ... an attack upon catholic dogma was bound sooner or later to lead to an attack on catholic forms of ecclesiastical government' (p. 359).

Mr. Pollard seems to lose his strict fairness when he deals with Bishop Gardiner. In the face of the facts it is hardly true to say without explanation that Gardiner was 'sent to the Tower in 1548 for refusing to obey the council's injunctions', and it is an error to say (p. 78) that Edward VI, like 'all Tudor sovereigns except Henry VII', was born at Greenwich, for his birth took place at Hampton Court. We wish that Mr. Pollard had given a reference for his statement that the see of Durham in 1553 'had been divided into two, Durham and Newcastle' (p. 119, n. 1), for no record of such a division remains; and in justice to Mary he might have recorded the provisions of her will for pensioning old soldiers—a direction entirely neglected by Elizabeth. These are small details, and the fact remains that Mr. Pollard has written a book which is quite indispensable to any serious student of the period. The appendix of twenty-three pages on authorities is of great value. The list of published and unpublished sources is a mine of information, and the criticism of J. A. Froude on p. 494 is the last and probably the fairest word on that most industrious historian. It is surprising to find no mention of Dr. Frere's monograph on 'The Marian Reaction' (Church Historical Society), based as it is on those comparatively untouched sources, the episcopal registers. Dom Birt's book on the Elizabethan Settlement is mentioned among the authorities without praise or blame, though one or two of its mistakes are corrected in the text, but it is odd to think of Dixon as an exponent of the ' high Anglican point of view ', all the more when his last two volumes were edited by Dr. Gee.

S. L. OLLARD.

The Life of James, First Duke of Ormonde, 1610–88. By LADY BURGH-CLERE. 2 vols. (London : Murray, 1912.)

LADY BURGHCLERE furnishes us with a clear and convincing estimate of the career of the first duke of Ormonde : in it everything of outstanding significance is skilfully disentangled from the vast mass of subsidiary clues to interpretation. One of the great merits of her two volumes is the discrimination and judgement invariably shown. The author never loses herself in details, nor forgets in following out their ramifications the object she has in view. The labour of research, though enormous, has not killed the freshness and interest of the book ; the dry bones of Irish history live. Her work has obviously cost immense labour, minute, exacting, and but faintly realizable by any one who has not gone through some similar process of investigation. Thomas Carte, in his preparations for his biography of Ormonde, surveyed the manuscript evidence with exceeding care. Unfortunately for his successor he divided the evidence, leaving the unimportant at Kilkenny Castle and bringing the important to England ; the latter forms the great Carte Collection in the Bodleian. From a careful perusal of the author's work it is at once evident that she has drawn upon the Bodleian manuscripts very largely. Indeed, she has used all the available evidence, throwing light upon all sides of her subject.

Of the man himself Lady Burghclere furnishes us with an able estimate, and gives a fascinating account of his home life. She sets before us his early life at Lambeth under the guardianship of Archbishop Abbot, his attachment to the church of Ireland, and his marriage to the Lady Elizabeth Preston, who was the sole heiress to the Desmond property ; the addition made to his estates by his marriage rendered Ormonde the wealthiest subject of the British Crown. On his first appearance in public life he had a sharp encounter with Strafford, and the imperious lord deputy formed a high estimate of the young man's abilities. This estimate he conveyed to Charles I, who consequently placed great confidence in Ormonde's loyalty. Indeed, it is not too much to say that personal devotion to the Stewarts was his predominant motive ; of this the author gives many proofs. Thrice he was viceroy of Ireland, and each time he was obliged to deal with matters of the gravest import. The rebellion of 1641, the Restoration settlement, and the popish plot were each sufficient to call into use all the powers of his mind.

Dr. S. R. Gardiner explored the Carte papers with that thoroughness we always associate with his work, and his history of the 1641 rebellion is authoritative. Since his time, however, the new series of the Ormonde papers, ably edited by the late C. Litton Falkiner and Dr. Elrington Ball, provide new material. Thus the letters of the Irish lords justices and privy council to the English government from the commencement of the Irish rebellion, in October 1641, to the appointment of Ormonde to be lord-lieutenant at the end of 1643, are now available for the first time in proper sequence. Of course these papers will cover the whole life to 1688, and a seventh volume is in the press. It is a pity that Lady Burghclere has not been able to use the completed series, but in a second edition doubtless she will be able to do so. She gives a careful analysis of the outbreak, and it is clear from her narrative that, as usual, land and religion were the two potent causes of it. The Ulster plantation of 1608 left many natives homeless, and they seized the opportunity of the civil war in England to regain their ancestral estates. Parsons and Borlase, the lords justices, had not striven sufficiently to gain the confidence of the Irish aristocracy, and the result was that they felt alienated. The author points out that the want of cohesion on the royalist side was as fatal as that on the side of the rebels. It is clear that the distrust of the gentry of the Pale was among the causes that made them the leaders of the opposition. Their position, if we except the matter of religion, was not unlike that of the men who won independence in 1782.

In his first viceroyalty and in his third Ormonde was compelled to consider the question of Roman catholic loyalty. In his own family there were many members of that faith, and he himself was of a tolerant nature. Indeed, this very tolerance was the cause of many of his difficulties during his third period of office, when the members of the Boyle family, Orrery, and Shaftesbury were urging him to take repressive measures. But as Lady Burghclere shows, there was no popish plot in Ireland, and the machinations of Titus Oates did not exist there. Nevertheless in the seventeenth-century men lived in perpetual fear of the allegiance which Roman catholics owed the pope. No doubt the colonists wanted to seize their estates, but the correspondence of their governors demonstrates that purely religious motives played little or no part in the policy of persecution. The dominant feeling of those days was that the gravest heresy of the Roman communion was the claim it put forth to hold a political supremacy over all princes and potentates. Its doctrines and practices were, in the eyes of an Englishman, but as dust in the balance compared with its claim to use the deposing power. For example, in 1662, the nuncio at Brussels, De Vecchis, had declared that a proposed address by the Roman catholic clergy of Ireland, stating their loyalty to the new sovereign, was a violation of the Roman catholic faith. Cardinal Barberini and Cardinal Rospigliosi concurred in this condemnation. In 1646 Cardinal Pamphili, the pope's secretary of state, had written to Rinuccini, the Nuncio in Ireland :

> The Holy See can never by any positive act approve of the civil allegiance of catholic subjects to a heretical prince. . . . It had been the constant and uninterrupted practice of the Holy See never to allow its ministers to make or consent to any public edict of catholic subjects for the defence of the crown and person of a heretical prince.

Such declarations prevented the viceroy from carrying out his views on toleration.

The fresh materials in the Ormonde papers do not add much to our understanding of the Restoration problems of revenue and land. Here the author unravels with much success the complications of the different items of national income, and we see that it was fairly adequate had not Charles II made unexpected grants to persons whom he favoured. On the land question Lady Burghclere has profited by the assistance of a master of the subject, Mr. R. Bagwell. The problem that lay before Ormonde was that of satisfying half a dozen claimants to each property, a problem that was obviously insoluble. The royalists had claims: so too had the Cromwellians, for they had received land for the money they had lent the state.

> If the adventurer and soldier must be satisfied to the extent of what they suppose intended them by the declaration (wrote the perplexed statesman), and if all that accepted and constantly adhered to the Peace of 1648 must be restored, as the same declaration seems also to intend, and was partly declared to be intended at the last debate, there must be new discoveries made of a new Ireland, for the old will not serve to satisfy their engagements. It remains then to determine which party must suffer in default of means to satisfy all; or whether both must be proportionably losers.

The working of the acts of settlement and explanation is then unfolded, but the cause of Ormonde's failure is apparent.

ROBERT H. MURRAY.

Correspondence of William Shirley, Governor of Massachusetts and Military Commander in America, 1731-60. Edited by C. H. LINCOLN, Ph.D. 2 vols. (New York: The Macmillan Co., 1912.)

THE same enlightened Society of the Colonial Dames of America, to whom we owe Miss Kimball's edition of Pitt's correspondence with the colonial governors, has enabled Dr. Lincoln to bring out the public letters of William Shirley. Some of these dispatches have been already printed elsewhere, and good use of them was made by Parkman; at the same time Shirley played for many years so prominent a part in the history of the American colonies that the publication of these volumes is most welcome.

Historians have seldom a good word for the first duke of Newcastle; but it may be counted to him for righteousness that his favour introduced to public life one of the most efficient, as well as popular, of colonial governors. (The series begins with an effusive letter of thanks for the duke's recommendation and closes with a gift to him of a turtle from the Bahamas.) The remarkable thing about Shirley was the manner in which he, a stranger from England with an eye to the loaves and fishes, succeeded in identifying himself with the interests of his adopted country, so that, when he was superseded, the men of Massachusetts felt it as a slur upon themselves. And yet, when he became governor of Massachusetts in 1741, the task before him was no easy one.

> I am sensible [he wrote] that I am now entering upon the government of a province where Col. Shute quitted the chair, and Mr. Burnett broke his heart, through the temper and opposition of the people ; and Mr. Belcher, in the midst of his countrymen, failed of carrying any one of those points for the Crown which might have been expected from him ; and that I enter upon it at a time when an empty treasury, an aversion in the House of Representatives to supply it, conformably to his Majesty's last instructions, a weak and ruinous condition of their fortifications, a bad spirit, raised throughout the country by the Land Bank scheme, . . . are what make up the present scene of affairs ;

and yet ' by the help of patience and moderation ' he managed ' to wade through ', so as to become the most popular governor in the history of Massachusetts as a royal government.

Nor was this popularity gained by any truckling to the people or surrender of the Crown's rights. Shirley was no democrat, and this is how he regarded the Boston system of local self-government. A riot had taken place in 1747, arising out of some cases of impressment, and Shirley comments :

> But what I think may be esteem'd the principal cause of the mobbish turn of this town is its constitution, by which the management of it is devolved upon the populace, assembled in their town meetings.

Again, called on by Governor Clinton to diagnose the political maladies of New York, he bluntly asserts

> that several late innovations have been introduced by the assembly into the government, and incroachments made upon his Majesty's prerogative, greatly tending to weaken his government, not only in the colony of New York but in his Majesty's other colonies in North America.

In the same spirit he criticized severely Franklin's Albany plan of union, on the ground that the prerogative was so much relaxed in it that it did not appear well calculated to strengthen the dependency of the colonies upon the Crown.

These things being so, it may be asked, how did Shirley contrive to remain on such good terms with the New England people ? The answer is to be found in the great moderation and good sense, which he throughout displayed. Consider his opinion on the question of a permanent salary.

> *If ever it is effected without the interposition of Parliament* . . . it must be done, not by dint of dispute when the people are upon their guard against it, but at some unexpected juncture when their settled affection for a governor may give the representatives courage to venture upon a short settlement at first, out of a personal regard to him, which might easily perhaps be followed with a settlement of it during his administration ; from which precedent it might be difficult for the province to recede upon the appointment of a new governor.

In all his opinions there is the same note of sanity. Thus he strongly urged, in 1746, that the most dangerous of the Acadians should at once be dealt with, and that measures should be taken to meet the danger from the Roman Catholic priests; by which means the final tragedy might have been avoided.

The general opinion of Shirley has been that he was a rather absurd barrister, who, on the strength of a lucky *coup* in the reduction of Louisbourg, henceforth panted for martial honours; but no one can read through these two large volumes, consisting mainly of his public dispatches, without arriving at the conclusion that his judgements concerning the military measures to be taken in the struggle with France were marked by singular prescience. In Dr. Lincoln's words, 'he discovered in the common weal the true basis of colonial loyalty, and sought to promote that end'. It was natural enough that, after Braddock's defeat, the home government should send out a professional soldier to be commander-in-chief in America; but it is none the less probable that an amateur, like Shirley, would have done at least as well as professionals of the type of Webb, Abercromby, and Loudoun. It is impossible to read without shame the brutal and blustering comments of Loudoun on Shirley's letters. He appeared to be astonished at his moderation in that he had not sent his predecessor, a perfectly honest and faithful public servant, home under arrest.

Shirley gives a striking picture of the difficulties under which a colonial governor worked.

Your grace, who have so long sustained so great a share of the lead of the most arduous affairs of the kingdom, may very possibly be surprised to hear me mention the business of a small government as burdensome and affecting my health; but if I could duly represent to your grace the fatigue which (after having procured the essential points for his Majesty's service ever since the present war, to be carried through a numerous assembly not used to such engagements as they have been led into lately) it has been necessary for me to undergo, in inspecting the execution of every part of the schemes, which have been concerted, for want of proper officers to execute the several orders of government under me, together with the various correspondences I have been obliged to maintain with the neighbouring governors, the camp and fleet before Louisbourg, and garrison at Annapolis royal ... the great variety of new incidents daily arising, and all difficulties centring in myself; and this over and above the care and protection of our own frontiers amidst continual alarms, and the ordinary business of the government ... your grace might easily conceive that such duty might make a deep impression upon firmer constitutions than mine.

The governor, in fact, stood alone; and the members of the executive council were far from sharing with him real responsibility.

Dr. Lincoln's editing is admirably done; the notes being brief but sufficient. Here and there a document printed elsewhere might have been omitted; and the present reviewer seems to remember in the Record Office a powerful argument by Shirley in favour of the retention of Louisbourg, which does not appear in these volumes. It is hardly fair to credit Shirley with 'the establishment of a sound currency system' in Massachusetts. Hutchinson, who was not given to boasting, claimed the work as his own; and there seems no reason to doubt the accuracy of his statement. In any case the fifteen years of Shirley's government reflected honour on himself and on the colony, into which he infused his own public spirit.

H. E. EGERTON.

Le Directoire et la Paix de l'Europe (1795–9). Par RAYMOND GUYOT. (Paris : Alcan, 1911.)

IN the introduction Dr. Guyot explains his chief aim in undertaking this work. It was to examine thoroughly the foreign policy of the Directory in order to ascertain the responsibility for the continuance of the war in the years 1796–9. The opposition of the views of Sybel and Sorel on this question is well known. While agreeing that the Directory pursued a warlike policy, the German historian denounced it as one of wholly unjustifiable aggression ; while the French historian saw in it the logical development of the historic traditions and political ideas of old and new France, Waterloo being a last effort to realize the aims formulated in 1794–6. Sorel's thesis has of late been combated in several quarters, notably in England ; but English writers have not yet been able to apply to the study of the French sources the minute examination of which the present volume is the outcome. Dr. Raymond has sifted all available evidence on this question, and he is free from bias. His introduction, spreading over thirty-seven closely printed pages, evinces both learning and critical acumen. The judgements on the French memoirs of the period are illuminating. Thus, he has examined the so-called Barras memoirs in order to distinguish, if possible, the original portions from those interpolated by Saint-Albin. The result is not reassuring. Further, a comparison of the notes added by M. Duruy to the edition of 1895–6, with the official procès-verbaux, revealed numerous mistakes ; and Dr. Guyot has therefore cited nothing from these memoirs which was not corroborated from more authentic sources. He also, as was inevitable, distrusts the memoirs of Larevellière-Lépeaux and of Carnot, besides dismissing those attributed to Bourrienne as historically valueless. In his citation of collections of documents, Dr. Guyot does full justice to the importance of the Dropmore Papers, the Wickham Correspondence, and other British sources. He blames Sorel for neglecting these sources, an omission which certainly impairs the authority of his work. Parts iv and v, which deal with the years 1794–1804, are admittedly inferior in thoroughness to the earlier volumes. Dr. Guyot also criticizes sharply Pallain's work *Le Ministère de Talleyrand sous le Directoire* ; but he generously acknowledges the merit of Sciout's four volumes. As happens with all bibliographies, some of the recent works are not named ; but, on the whole, this introduction provides perhaps the most complete and judicial assessment of the literature and documents of the period in question. Along with the *Cambridge Modern History* (vol. viii), to which Dr. Guyot accords high praise, and Dr. Luckwaldt's scholarly introduction to the volume of Hüffer's *Quellen*, entitled ' Der Frieden von Campoformio ', it furnishes an excellent groundwork for the study of the authorities of the period.

Dr. Guyot begins with a survey of the aims of the Directory. He calls attention to the effort to win over Prussia to active alliance by the negotiation entrusted to Caillard in the autumn of 1795. The Empire, Sweden, Denmark, Holland, Turkey, and even Poland, were to enter into a coalition with France so as to balance the recent treaties of England with Austria and Russia. Of course the scheme came to nought ; but it shows the ambitious ideas prevalent at Paris. Overtures were also made to some Italian states, notably Genoa. Meanwhile the British government (or rather Pitt alone, for Lord Grenville dissented almost *in toto*) sought to make overtures with a view to peace between December 1795 and March 1796. Utilizing the evidence which was printed in this Review for April 1903, Dr. Guyot maintains the sincerity of those overtures, which earlier writers had questioned. As is well known, the result was a curt refusal from Paris, which surprised both Pitt and his agent, Wickham. Dr. Guyot shows (p. 144) that Bonaparte's written assurance as to his ability to fight his way in Italy without financial support from the Directory probably hardened its tone. His victories seemed to Grenville *affreuses*, but they had the effect of cementing once more the Austro-British alliance which Pitt's pacific overtures had seriously strained. Chapters v and vi present an interesting account of the diplomatic situation resulting from the Italian campaign.

The evidence set forth in chapter viii shows conclusively the pacific attitude of Pitt in the winter of 1796-7 and the aggressive designs of the Directory. George III and Grenville saw in Lord Malmesbury's first mission merely a means of demonstrating the responsibility of the belligerents for the continuance of the war. But as to the sincerity of the government's desire to come to an accommodation, there can be no question. In a note on p. 278 Dr. Guyot assigns the recall of the British fleet from the Mediterranean to the month of September 1796. It did not leave that sea until two months later; but its departure was alleged by Austria as one of the reasons why she came to terms with France at Leoben. France was, in fact, in a position to exact severe terms both from Austria and Great Britain. Dr. Guyot calls the last section of chapter viii 'Victoire de Grenville'; but it is fairly certain that Pitt himself would not have acceded to the French demands. As is shown on p. 303, Grenville was to blame for not assuring the conditional and preliminary assent of Austria. The news of the death of Catharine II on 16 November 1796 seems to have strengthened the warlike resolves of the French Directory, which thwarted Malmesbury's first negotiation. All that Dr. Guyot urges against Pitt's conduct at this time is that, if he had ceded all that he was ready to cede ten months later, peace was possible (p. 304). But in the interval there had occurred three very serious events, the final overthrow of Austria, the bank crisis, and the mutinies at Spithead and the Nore. It was inevitable that he should lower his terms and that those of the Directory should rise. Armed with the Preliminaries of Tolentino and Leoben, the French government had very great advantages in the summer and autumn of 1797. Moreover, a revolt in Ireland then seemed imminent; and prominent men at Paris had pledged themselves not to sheathe the sword until the union of Ireland with Great Britain was severed.

Dr. Guyot had the advantage of consulting in manuscript form M. Ballot's work on Malmesbury's second negotiation, that at Lille, which we reviewed last year (xxvi. 604 f.); and he has also consulted other sources, notably the Chatham MSS., preserved at the Public Record Office. The result is the most authoritative account yet given of this transaction.

Points of interest in his narrative are Starhemberg's excuse for the *défaillance* of Leoben ; his endeavour to arrange an Austro-British defiance to France ; Pitt's refusal to countenance any such step ; the anger of Grenville at Austria's repudiation of her financial obligations ; the near approach to a rupture over the Portuguese negotiation ; the intervention at one point of Saint-Simon, the father of state socialism ; the underhand financial dealings which played so large a part in August and September 1797 ; and the effort of Spain to win back Nootka Sound and Jamaica, as well as Gibraltar. As to the final causes of the rupture, Dr. Guyot adds little or nothing to M. Ballot's narrative. He shows, however, that while Napoleon at St. Helena censured the actions of the Fructidorian Directory, they really played into his hands by opening out the career of conquest which brought him to power. No formal judgement is passed on Sorel's thesis ; but the facts, as here set forth, tell strongly against the inevitability of the claims of the Directory. Far from being the logical outcome of the events of 1793–5, they constituted a new departure, fraught with disastrous issues for France and Europe. No further light is here thrown on the fall of Venice or the directors' sudden renunciation of the plan of invasion of England (February 1798); but at several points in the later chapters valuable information is forthcoming. Thus, in chapter xiv it is shown that the French invasion of Switzerland was due, in part at least, to Bonaparte's desire to gain the control of the road through Canton Valais and over the Simplon, which he failed to secure in the spring of 1797. His responsibility, which he denied at St. Helena, is here once more conclusively established. Among the appendixes of this volume is a characteristic letter of Canning to Pitt, dated 1 October 1797, on the subject of the publication of an account of the Lille negotiation.

Dr. Guyot's work is marked by great erudition, sound judgement, and a conspicuous fairness of tone. He has not sustained a thesis, but he has broken new ground in nearly all portions of his wide field of research. We could, however, wish that at the end of each important chapter he had more fully summarized and passed judgement on the matters dealt with. On occasions like the failure of the Lille negotiation and the conclusion of the treaty of Campo Formio it is highly desirable to take a survey which illuminates the difficult path just traversed and throws light on the future. At certain points, mainly on subsidiary topics, Dr. Guyot's assertions are disputable. Thus, on p. 401, he states that the Anglo-French commercial treaty of 1786 provoked a terrible industrial crisis in France in and after 1788. But Levasseur and others have shown that many other causes, political, fiscal, and climatic, contributed to that crisis. It is also an exaggeration to say (p. 288) that Pitt left Malmesbury in ' une demi-disgrâce ' after an unsuccessful mission to Berlin in 1792. The mission could scarcely have succeeded ; and Malmesbury was soon afterwards employed in positions of great importance. The reference to the abandonment of the title ' roi d'Angleterre ' in 1797 (p. 400) is a mistake for ' roi de France '. In general English names and titles are correctly given ; but ' Sir Gilbert Elliott ' should be ' Elliot '.   J. HOLLAND ROSE.

Le Fils de la grande Catherine, Paul Ier, Empereur de Russie ; sa Vie, son Règne, et sa Mort, 1754–1801, d'après des documents nouveaux et en grande partie inédits. By K. WALISZEWSKI. Second edition. (Paris : Plon, 1912.)

M. WALISZEWSKI has added another volume, the ninth, to the already considerable number of monographs which he has devoted to the Russian imperial house. Beginning with Ivan the Terrible and including the whole of the seventeenth and eighteenth centuries, the series constitutes a history of modern Russia in general, with detailed and impartial accounts of the lives and characters of its rulers, their friends, satellites, generals, and diplomatists. The court, the relations of the various members of the imperial family with one another, and with other ruling houses, their dealings with the ambassadors of foreign countries in St. Petersburg, and the exploits of their own ambassadors abroad loomed so large and these few people controlled so much that the amount of space devoted to them is not surprising. The interest of the present volume lies chiefly in the excellent account it contains of the relations of Russia to the coalition and to the Directory during the reign of Paul, and in that of the campaigns of Suvorov in Switzerland and Italy. Paul himself was so unattractive a figure and his court so bereft of every amenity, that a history of it, however good, can only be tedious after the two wonderful volumes in which M. Waliszewski described the brilliant reign of the radiant Catharine. Overshadowed from his earliest youth by the cloud of the tragedy which had overwhelmed Peter III, and not absolutely certain as to his own parentage, Paul never felt anything but resentment against and jealousy of his mother and hatred of her favourite Alexis Orlov, who between them had caused his father to disappear. After this very unpromising beginning he had to exercise patience for forty years while his mother, in a series of successful adventures which astounded and terrified Europe, doubled the size of her empire, and built up, on foundations which were never secure but have stood the test of time, a reputation for herself and a credit for her country. Paul spent his time in drilling his troops, in drawing up schemes of reform which he thought were much better than those of his mother, and in trying to imitate Frederick the Great who was his ideal. He only succeeded in dressing a few regiments in uniforms which had been the fashion in Prussia fifty years before, and in arousing the suspicions of the empress and the hatred of his entourage. By the time he came to the throne he had not a single friend, even amongst the members of his own family. He found it so difficult to believe he was really emperor that for months the only thing he could do to convince himself of the fact was to issue streams of edicts, and confer rewards and decorations, or inflict fines and punishments, in showers, equally indiscriminately. The one thing he enjoyed was making people obey him, at the cost of his popularity and of his reputation for sanity. His sole object in legislation was to undo all his mother had done; his only idea in his distribution of punishments to destroy the fortunes which she had made ; his few generous impulses were the result of a desire to reward where his mother had chastised.

Paul was interested in nothing but the reform of his country, and he left it in worse chaos than he found. He was consumed with a passion for work and for making others work, but wasted all his time in unnecessary corrections of detail and in changing his mind. The only thing to be said for him is that he was often not fully responsible for what he did; at any rate his own courtiers and the whole of Europe thought him mad; but this very fact deprives his character of any interest which it might otherwise have. During his happily short reign commerce in Russia declined, literature and the arts languished, the peasants' lot became even worse than it had been before, and the only man who upheld his country's reputation abroad, Suvorov, earned only the ingratitude of his master. Paul was assassinated by his courtiers, unregretted by any one, and his son's at any rate passive complicity in the crime was quite excusable. M. Waliszewski has made the most of a very unattractive subject. Paul was never anything but morose and choleric, and his reign was uniformly dull and gloomy; but M. Waliszewski has relieved the history of both the one and the other with as much humour and anecdote as possible, and, thanks to his truly admirable style, the book is a pleasure to read. It is provided with an excellent index and bibliography, and all the necessary authorities are quoted.

NEVILL FORBES.

Pitt and Napoleon. By J. HOLLAND ROSE, Litt.D. (London: Bell, 1912.)
Geschichte des Europäischen Staatensystems im Zeitalter der Französischen Revolution und der Freiheitskriege. Von ADALBERT WAHL. (Munich: Oldenbourg, 1912.)

BOTH these works are useful additions to the vast mass of literature that has gathered round the memory of the years between 1789 and 1815. Dr. Wahl's book gives a compact and well-proportioned survey of European history during that crowded era. Dr. Rose's contains eleven essays and a number of original letters, and is a valuable supplement to his biographies of Napoleon and the younger Pitt. Special studies like these are naturally more apt than a general history to contain original matter. At least four of them break fresh ground and clear up questions that have long been left obscure. Nothing could exceed the skill and judgement with which Dr. Rose has investigated the problem, 'Was Pitt responsible for the Quiberon disaster?' He scatters to the winds the slanders with which Fox and Sheridan and many disappointed *émigrés* sought at the time to impugn Pitt's good faith, and shows that the true causes of the failure of his soundly conceived enterprise were the bad leadership and divided powers of the royalist commanders. The chapter on 'Pitt and Earl Fitzwilliam' may also be fairly claimed to say the last word on the events that led to the recall from Ireland in 1795 of that perverse and reckless whig magnate. 'Pitt and the Relief of the Poor' and 'British Rule in Corsica' are also interesting sketches, though of no striking historical importance. The spirited review of Marbot's memoirs that appeared in the *Cornhill Magazine* in 1906 was well worth reprinting.

Larger issues are dealt with in essays on Napoleon's intention to invade England, on 'The True Significance of Trafalgar', and on 'Napoleon's Conception of the Battle of Waterloo'. The first-named is adequate and convincing; Dr. Wahl's views (pp. 146-7) are substantially the same. Dr. Rose's estimate of the consequences of Trafalgar was first published seven years ago, and is singularly modest when compared with Dr. Wahl's. Dr. Rose ascribes Napoleon's downfall to the errors of his continental system, and the adoption of that system to his resolution after Trafalgar to effect by economic policy what he could not accomplish by invasion. To that extent only does he consider Trafalgar influential in relation to the fortunes of Europe. This view is no doubt confirmed by the modern discovery that England had stood in no real danger of invasion for some months before Trafalgar was fought, and by the remembrance that ten years of warfare intervened between that battle and Waterloo. Nevertheless, we may justly doubt whether Dr. Rose has fully expressed Trafalgar's 'true significance'. He has gauged its bearing on Napoleon's military career with his usual accuracy, but he has not concerned himself with its wider import. Dr. Wahl, on this point, is much more affected by Mahan and the school of naval historians. In a manner quite alien to the older German writers he describes Trafalgar as 'the most important and decisive battle of the whole age', and as being of much deeper significance in the world's history than the apparently greater conflict of Austerlitz (pp. 153-4). He recognizes that the victory, which secured to England the full fruits of maritime and colonial ascendancy, has a living influence on the political and economic conditions of to-day.

Dr. Rose discusses 'The Oratory of Pitt' in his opening chapter. It is difficult to-day to judge fairly the speeches of a generation whose canons of taste were so different to our own. Politics have become too practical in tone and temper to admit of the ornate and diffuse rhetoric that then delighted parliament. Pitt's capacity was thoroughly tested by the standard of his day, and he was deemed a past master of oratory when oratory was unfettered by the closure and unrelieved by the distractions of mass meetings in the country. Dr. Rose says that his speeches form 'the most perfect example of the union of grace and force, of stately rhetoric and convincing argument, fused in the white heat of patriotism'. There must be much truth in this opinion, and, if the truest test of the speaker is his power to persuade and convince, no British statesman ever approached the success which Pitt achieved in this respect. His speeches were invariably patriotic and hardly ever ambiguous. It must, however, be recognized that in black and white they fail to fascinate a modern reader. The reports of parliamentary debates are usually dull. We can enjoy Burke's speeches for their philosophical and literary excellence, and some of Disraeli's for their flashes of irony and insight. Oratory like Pitt's was of a different order. It must inevitably lead to disappointment if a reader turns from Dr. Rose's glowing eulogy to the *Orations on the War with France*, which were republished a few years ago in *Everyman's Library*. The correctness of the historian's estimate may be assumed upon contemporary evidence; it is less likely to be established by reading Pitt's recorded speeches.

Probably the most popular and useful of Dr. Rose's essays is his clear account of Waterloo. It is significant of the gradual 'crystallization' of the historical narrative of the battle that Dr. Wahl's version (pp. 252-3) is in agreement with that of the English author. Dr. Wahl's book is, indeed, marked throughout by wide information and a sense of perspective. He never treats the great war as a merely continental struggle. He does not ignore the far-reaching influence of the Peninsular campaigns. He lays stress on the predominant part played by Great Britain (pp. 34, 260). He gives a valuable account of the effects of the continental system on the well-being of the nations whom it concerned, and his account of the misery that it inflicted upon Russians and Germans is convincing. Not only did it lead to a great increase in the price of textiles and to the loss of sugar and coffee supplies, but also to the cessation of the English demand for continental food-stuffs and raw materials. The Hanse towns, and especially Hamburg, suffered terribly. Germany, Italy, and Switzerland were too much impoverished to buy the dear manufactures of France in place of English goods. A financial crisis in 1811, intensified by the loss of their Spanish and Russian markets, destroyed many of the young industries that Napoleon had tried to foster. Saxony, Lyons, Mühlhausen, and Ghent can, alone among continental communities, look back on the system as marking a step in their industrial development. It led to the desolation of the French ports. Politically, it lay at the very roots of the alienation of Russia and of the war of liberation. The reputation gained by Dr. Wahl in respect of his work on the antecedents of the French Revolution is well maintained in this short but ably planned history.   GERALD B. HERTZ.

Geschichte der freien Stadt Frankfurt a. M. (1814–66). Von RICHARD SCHWEMER. Band ii. (Frankfurt a. M.: Baer, 1912.)

THE second volume of Professor Schwemer's history of Frankfort under the confederation, though of little less than twice the size of the first one, brings the narrative down only to 1836, the date of the city's joining the long-contested Prussian Zollverein. Yet the author's treatment seems to us to have improved in clearness and breadth, and there is hardly a passage one would like to miss or see shortened. The truth is that his own researches for the first time fully illustrate the great importance which Frankfort had in the struggles for the economic regeneration of modern Germany. In spite of Nürnberg and Leipzig, it was the one independent city doing first-rate foreign trade in the interior of Germany, and the rise of industrial capital and a protected national production led by Prussia forced upon it even a more conspicuous, because a more active, part in German politics than it had played during the years of its political reconstruction. The chief new fact established by Professor Schwemer is that not Austria, as Treitschke believed, but Frankfort was the author of the Mitteldeutscher Handelsverein of 1828 between the sixteen states which engaged to stand aloof from the two customs federations of the north (Prussia and Hesse-Darmstadt) and the south (Bavaria and Württemberg), although of course the opposition also of industrial territories like the Saxonies went a long way to strengthen the conservative tendencies of the Bund and its president, who in his economic position was almost separated from the body of Germany. Accordingly, Frankfort was foremost to take resolute and logical steps towards the assertion of its commercial, and in the result of its political, independence. It ventured to arouse the national indignation by concluding in 1832 a commercial treaty with England, the chief feeder of its international market; it would but for the weakness of Austria have set in motion the jurisdiction of the diet to punish the elector of Hesse for his desertion from the Handelsverein to the Zollverein; and at least indirectly it called in the intervention of England and France as guarantors of the Vienna Act against the diet itself when subjected, during the riots of 1833, to an occupation by Austrian and Prussian troops.

The policy thus pursued by Frankfort was not less singular than the character and administration of the oligarchy of merchants by which it was upheld. The sham democracy of the new constitution scarcely allowed of resistance against the 'triumvirate' of the senators Thomas, Guaita, and Schmidt. Occasional opposition was either still more reactionary, such as that of the guilds which forced the repeal of the liberal trade laws in 1831, and that of the particularists whose protest against military protection by the confederation nearly drew federal 'execution' upon the city in 1834; or it was limited to small issues of local government, e.g. the gate fine or the 'Pragmatik' of the city officials, by the unfortunate ambiguity of a political situation then common to the smaller German states, where ultimate progress was certainly bound up with being ruled or absorbed by the most absolutist power. It must have been mainly this want of legal resources in a centre of German intellectual life which, together with the medieval slowness of police supervision, made the residence of the diet a focus of the German revolution of the thirties. On the other hand, there was only just growing up under the patrician class a broader one of smaller capitalists whose interest, partly represented by a consultative chamber of trade, slowly turned its attention from the traditional market of foreign goods and government loans to the distribution and production of domestic commodities. The bulk even of the industrial capital of Frankfort was still international, and if Stein lamented the death of Bethmann as a supporter of the Rhenish and Westphalian industry, Thomas could urge diplomatically that it was indispensable in the Dutch manufactures (pp. 735, 755). Ihm, the only man who from the beginning saw the necessity of being merged, even though under the control of Prussia, in a national economic system, had no party whatever, and was even deprived of his final triumph in negotiating at Berlin by the public distrust of the powerful neighbour whose unscrupulous pressure (e.g. in the closure of the Rhine till the Navigation Act of 1831, cf. pp. 59-71) cannot be denied.

In congratulating Professor Schwemer upon the continuance of his monumental work one may perhaps express a wish that, especially while one has to wait for an index of names, he should be a little more careful and explicit in his personal and other references to details in the diplomatic negotiations he explores with so great success. C. BRINKMANN.

Lord Durham's Report on the Affairs of British North America. Edited with an introduction by Sir C. P. LUCAS. 3 vols. (Oxford: Clarendon Press, 1912.)

LORD DURHAM'S celebrated report was first issued in folio in February 1839 by the British government, after its hands had been forced by the unauthorized publication of the greater portion of it in *The Times*, to which it had been communicated by that stormy petrel, Gibbon Wakefield. Between February and June five volumes of appendixes were issued, consisting chiefly of the reports of commissioners appointed by Durham, and of evidence taken by them. In the same year the report was reprinted in octavo in England and Canada, without the appendixes, but with the addition of the correspondence which had passed between Lord Durham and the colonial secretary, Lord Glenelg. In 1901 it was reprinted by Messrs. Methuen, but without the appendixes or correspondence. The present edition consists of an introduction, mainly historical, by Sir Charles Lucas; the report itself, with valuable notes by the editor; and a reprint of about one-third of the original appendixes, two or three letters from the correspondence, and a hitherto unpublished account of Lord Durham's mission, written in 1840 by Charles Buller, the ablest member of his staff, given recently by the present Lord Durham to the Canadian archives, and published by the courtesy of the keeper of the archives, Dr. A. G. Doughty. It is much to be regretted that it has been found impossible to publish the report and appendixes complete. It is true that the omitted portions consist of about 400 pages folio, but the whole publication could have been comprised within five volumes, and we should have possessed a definitive edition of a great work, which the present edition can in no way claim to be, much of what has been omitted being exceedingly valuable and interesting.

Of the editor's share in the work, the notes are numerous, accurate, and to the point. The introduction is scholarly, with many of the happy phrases and sentences which we expect from Sir Charles Lucas; his discussion of the constitutional importance of improvements in transportation is especially good. The general point of view is that of a moderate and fair-minded defender of the British government in general and of the colonial office in particular. It must be said, however, that Sir Charles often seems to miss the real gravamen of the charge brought by Lord Durham against his clients. He has no difficulty in showing that the British government was well-meaning and not unenlightened, the soldier-governors men of probity and honour, and the colonial assemblies, especially in Lower Canada, perverse and unreasonable. But he gives too little attention to Durham's description of the rise in both Upper and Lower Canada of an office-holding oligarchy, with traditions and prestige, strong enough for the most part to enforce its views on governor and colonial office alike. This oligarchy was social, political, and religious; it classed democracy and dissent alike as disloyal. It was not so much a political party as an office-holding clique, and often defeated the good intentions of its own more enlightened members, as when in Upper Canada it defeated Beverley Robinson's proposal to tax vacant land.

Though not a party, its members were bound together in opposition to democracy and to all other forms of Christianity except their own, which included at most a quarter of the young community in Upper Canada and Nova Scotia, and was extremely small in Lower Canada. To them was due the lack of municipal institutions in Upper Canada, which they throttled as undemocratic. Sir Charles Lucas lays the blame for the lack of education in Lower Canada at the doors of the French assembly, and gives the credit of the advances made in Upper Canada 'to Tory Lieutenant-Governors who had old-fashioned ideas as to Church and State, and to the members of the Family Compact' (i. 247). Really it was the attempt of the members of the church of England to control education in the interests of a minority, partly political and partly ecclesiastical, which rendered English education in Lower Canada a failure, and created a long-enduring grievance in the other provinces. Even such men as Beverley Robinson and Bishop Strachan—whose jobbery in the interests not indeed of himself but of his church Sir Charles unduly minimizes—were wholly out of touch with public opinion, and in the struggle against it grew more and more acrid and extreme. The worst foes of Canada were not the half-educated assemblies, but the grandees of the 'Family Compact' in the various provinces, and the charge against the colonial office and its soldier-governors is that for the most part they either encouraged the oligarchy or at least gave it a free hand. Sir Charles Lucas has proved the colonial office of a hundred years ago guiltless of tyranny; it is not so easy to acquit it of purblind acquiescence in an impossible state of affairs. W. L. GRANT.

Le Maréchal Canrobert. Par GERMAIN BAPST. Tome v. (Paris: Plon, 1911.)

THE battle of Rezonville (better known to English readers by its German name of Vionville–Mars-la-Tour) marked the crisis of the Franco-Prussian war. Had the French commander-in-chief displayed merely moderate ability in handling large bodies of troops he would have made good his retreat to the Meuse, and the Prussians would have had to face a fresh and more arduous campaign. Had he possessed any portion of the Napoleonic spirit he might have seized the initiative, and by attacking the enemy's forces in detail have thrown them upon the defensive. But he attained neither result. Tactically a drawn battle, Rezonville was strategically a Prussian victory, of which the fruits were the capitulation of Sedan and the fall of Metz. What was the cause of Bazaine's terrible failure? The chief interest of M. Bapst's book lies in the close study of that commander's military character. The analysis is merciless. The conclusion reached is that Bazaine, from the time that he assumed the chief command, virtually took for his motto, 'Those only make no mistakes who do nothing'. MacMahon had fought and had been defeated; to escape a similar fate Bazaine determined not to fight at all. Though the emperor had committed to him the task of withdrawing the army to Verdun, he had no intention of obeying orders, and hurried the emperor away that he might escape from his importunate questions. He meant to remain inactive until the emperor had got so far away as to lose all touch with the army, and then to return to Metz. He made no attempt to hurry up the 3rd corps from that fortress, because its absence was to serve as his excuse for returning thither. He found a battle forced upon him. He would defend himself, but he did not wish to win a victory; for then he would have had to rejoin the emperor at Verdun. Oppressed by a sense of his own incompetence to exercise high command he sought above all else to shift responsibility on to his subordinates. What he hated most of all was to be asked for definite orders. He was on bad terms with his chief of the staff (who would have best consulted his own dignity by resigning) and deliberately avoided all communication with him. So successful was he in his policy of isolation that during the crisis of the battle his staff could not find him, and it was proposed to transfer the command to Canrobert or Bourbaki. Yet at the same time 'he knew admirably well, when he appeared in the presence of his troops, how to conceal his incompetence and to impose upon them by the assumption of the rôle of a man of coolness and energy'. Two days earlier at the battle of Borny he had excited almost boundless admiration among them. He was excellent if he only had to handle a company, a battery, or even a regiment. So on that fateful day he let the battle take its own course and spent all his time in the skirmishing line.

The author has not made it clear why he has associated so prominently the name of Marshal Canrobert with this battle. Canrobert commanded the 6th corps, which with Frossard's 2nd corps bore the brunt of the fighting on 16 August. But his part was that of a subordinate only. He did not exercise any controlling influence over the battle as a whole, though he grasped the military situation far more clearly than his superior, and vainly pressed Bazaine to direct a great flanking movement against the Prussian left with the 3rd and 4th corps and the right of his own. Monsieur Bapst's main purpose has been, however, not to represent Canrobert as the hero of the day, but rather to depict Bazaine as 'the villain of the piece'. As a military study the book suffers from one grave defect. It entirely ignores the Prussian point of view, and the student, if he wishes to gain an accurate knowledge of the battle, must supplement it from other sources. W. B. WOOD.

Mission d'Ollone, 1906–9; Recherches sur les Musulmans Chinois. Par le Commandant D'OLLONE, Capitaine DE FLEURELLE, Capitaine LEPAGE, et Lieutenant DE BOYVE. (Paris: Leroux, 1911.)

THIS is a work of very high order from an intensive point of view, and Vicomte d'Ollone has proved once more how army and navy discipline can powerfully contribute to success in the organization and conduct of scientific travels. This particular volume, as its title indicates, deals specially with the extremely obscure and thorny question, 'When and how did the Mohammedans establish their religion in China; what have been the vicissitudes of Chinese Islam; and what are its prospects and condition at this moment?' But, apart from this specific question, to which this volume of 450 large pages is judiciously confined, the travels themselves should be carefully studied in conjunction with another volume, translated into English and recently published in England, entitled *In Forbidden China*, by Vicomte d'Ollone, which treats more fully of the geographical and ethnographical considerations involved. This second work, not specially concerning history, and therefore not strictly within the scope of this Review, is only mentioned here because both works contain practically the same inadequate maps to illustrate the gallant explorers' novel and dangerous routes: in a few instances even the photographic illustrations of persons and places are the same in both volumes. Considering that the author has discovered an error of sixty miles in the Upper Yellow River, together with definite facts about a mysterious 'Second Yellow River' or 'Little Yellow River', precisely in the region where Lamaism and Islam meet, and near where the head centre of Islam has always been and still is, we think it unfortunate that he has not been able to give us a detailed map showing distinctly the nature of his discoveries, which, both in the independent Lolo country of Yün Nan, at the sources of the River Min in Sz Ch'wan, and in the country of the Goloks or 'Wild' Tibetans, are of the utmost importance.

But to return to the questions immediately concerning the history of the Moslems; the following are the tentative results of M. d'Ollone's exhaustive and patient inquiries, made on the spot in the three provinces of Yün Nan, Sz Ch'wan, and Kan Suh respectively. There are fewer Chinese Mussulmans than is generally supposed to be the case: the latest systematic inquiry by a foreign specialist is that contained in the Rev. Marshall Broomhall's *Islam in China*, published by the China Inland Mission two years ago; the d'Ollone mission now places the total at nearer four millions than ten millions, or, say, at 1 per cent. of the population. Another provisional conclusion is that the amount of Arab blood, Turkish blood, and indeed any non-Chinese blood in the Chinese Mussulmans (as distinct from the Mussulmans of foreign blood living in the Turkestan portions of the Chinese empire) is exceedingly small, and also hard to trace. It would appear, too, that the *diffusion* of Islam in China—from the germs which have undoubtedly always existed there ever since the seventh century of our era, and from the special developments that took place in Kublai Khan's time (thirteenth century)—is of quite modern date, and is due not to propagation and proselytism so much as to the personal influence over local masses of a few powerful Chinese converts; and this apart from the fact that individual Chinese Mussulmans, like other Chinese, are given to the practice of buying children in times of famine, and of otherwise recruiting their Mussulman family interests by adopting 'heathen' children; in other words, solidarity of interest has had the effect of creating a kind of mutual protection society, which thus has political and 'dangerous' influence. M. d'Ollone insists (in both his books) over and over again, that the average Chinese, so far from being irreligious, is religious by nature, and is more especially inclined towards Islam, which clashes but little either with his own ancient basis of natural religion, or with the original or debased forms of adopted Taoism and Buddhism; hence, also, a certain irregular friendliness of Chinese Islam towards

Christianity. Islam in China has grown parochially, each community being self-contained, the *ahong* or clergy not being hierarchically appointed and independent, but elected and paid by the congregations, usually on the ground of their familiarity with Arabic or Persian, including sometimes even a good knowledge of foreign literature of the deeper kind. The most remarkable feature of Chinese Islam is that it has grown up entirely in ignorance (until quite recently) of the existence of either Caliph or Crescent. Another curious fact is that the *ahongs* and instructors are usually as ignorant of literary Chinese as the influential members of the congregations are ignorant of even elementary Arabic and Persian, not to say of Arabic and Persian literature; whilst the masses of the congregations are entirely ignorant spiritually, except in so far as they are kept in hand by the clergy and *literati* of their respective congregations. Very interesting accounts are given of the various schisms and the fierce inter-Islamic disputes and wars, of the 'tomb-worshippers' (possibly, we would suggest on our own account, connected with a sort of harking-back to ancestral worship), and of the introduction of competing Sophite and Shiite doctrines, and so on. Last comes an account of Abdul Hamid's attempts, apparently fostered by Germany, to acquire for the Caliphate a more real influence in China, and of the undoubtedly successful efforts of travelling Turkish emissaries.

It must be added, however, that the chief author is exceedingly conservative and prudent: all these provisional conclusions are subject to further and even more systematic inquiry all over China; in fact, extraordinary prudence and a determination to take no unnecessary chances is the chief trait in M. d'Ollone's character, alike as a traveller, a leader of men, a theorist, and a literary man. Possibly his anxiety to 'work up' his notes and observations more thoroughly may partly account for his having given us such miserable maps: he may be anxious to get things quite right before he commits himself to exact bearings on such a large scale as Mr. Colborne Baber gave us thirty years ago, when travelling over much of the same ground. Meanwhile he leaps at once into the first rank as an explorer, together with such men as Blakiston, Richthofen, Prjevalski, Chavannes, Pelliot, Younghusband, and Rockhill.

E. H. PARKER.

Short Notices

PROFESSOR EDUARD MEYER'S *Der Papyrusfund von Elephantine* (Leipzig: Hinrichs, 1912) is a serviceable presentment of the results that follow from the discovery of the Jewish colony existing at that place in the fifth century B.C. In some 130 pages the author tells the story of the finding of the papyri, sketches the popular religious development of the Hebrews, collects the evidence bearing on Jewish settlements in Egypt, pictures the general method of government followed by the Persians in their provinces, and directs attention to the ways in which these papyri confirm or correct the various theories as to the course of Hebrew history. He recognizes in the royal edicts cited in the canonical Ezra genuine documents, while he finds a widespread tendency (manifested in the transformations of the Achiqar proverbs and story) to imaginative embroidery of historical material, and this he joins most scholars of the time in extending to some of the later books of the Old Testament canon. He well illustrates the honesty of the popular worship of sacred pillars amongst Jahwe worshippers by citing the popular reverence in Christendom of the consecrated Host, the images of saints, and relics; and for the use of Bethel in Jewish proper names as a variant for Jahwe he compares the cult of the Sacred Heart as only a special form of devotion to our Lord, and not an apostasy from Him. Several passages in Herodotus and in the Old Testament receive illuminating illustration from these papyri, as Professor Meyer shows, and in his discussion of Achiqar he makes several shrewd suggestions for the restoration of the true text in Strabo, Diogenes Laertius, and a mosaic at Trèves. One suggestion may be hazarded, that Ostanes was the cousin, not the brother, of Hanani (pp. 72–3). Y.

The character and the object of Professor Carlo Pascal's book on *Le Credenze d' Oltretomba nelle Opere letterarie dell' Antichità classica* (2 vols. Catania: Battiato, 1912) are literary, not mythological, psychological, nor even historical. The author brings before us, in attractive though not very methodical sequence, a great many of the ideas, imaginations, and beliefs to be found in classical literature, from Homer down to Plutarch, concerning death, the underworld, and the fate of departed spirits. He makes use of the testimony as to ancient conceptions of the subject afforded by sepulchral inscriptions and by vase paintings, but these are used rather as illustrations of the literary material than as a principal source of information. Professor Pascal has studied and gives reference to a large number of modern works, archaeological and critical, on the various subjects handled. In some places he is bound to distinguish the various strands of popular belief combined in one classical writer, and in others he traces the influence of Orphic and of Pythagorean doctrine. But as his object is to describe rather than to investigate, he does not throw much light on the problems, ethnological and psychological, which encompass all discussion of mythological subjects. Though primarily concerned with pagan—one might say with Hellenic—ideas, the author refers to some Christian beliefs which are closely related to pagan tradition. Thus he brings together pagan and Christian expectations of a coming catastrophe and palingenesis. He might perhaps have made some reference here to late Jewish eschatology. It is, however, as a summary of the ancient literary appurtenances of post-mortem existence, the rulers and geographical features of the underworld, the appearances of the dead in dreams, the apotheosis of heroes, and the like, that the book is most likely to be useful. For this reason it is to be regretted that it has no index. A. G.

In *Greek Inscriptions from Sardes*, i. (extracted from the *American Journal of Archaeology*, xvi, 1912) Messrs. W. H. Buckler and D. M. Robinson begin, with commendable promptitude, to publish the texts which are being unearthed by the American excavations in the area of the temple of Artemis. As a first instalment they give us a highly important document of about 300 B.C. engraved on the inner wall of one of the temple chambers. It is a deed of mortgage in the form of a sale subject to redemption executed by Mnesimachus, probably an officer of Antigonus, who had borrowed money from the treasury of the goddess and, being unable to repay the loan on demand, conveys to her a large landed estate in the satrapy of Lydia which had been granted to him by Antigonus apparently before he assumed the royal title in 306 B.C. From the legal point of view the inscription has a unique interest as being both the oldest authentic specimen of a Greek mortgage and the only specimen hitherto discovered of this particular form of mortgage. But its chief importance lies in the new and very welcome light which it throws on agrarian conditions in the Hellenistic period—on the forms and conditions of land tenure, on the system of collecting the φόρος which we now learn was paid to the Crown in cash by the holders both of military fiefs (κλῆροι) and of crown land (χώρα βασιλική), and above all on the important part played in the economic life of the country by the great religious centres as owners, or holders, and managers of landed estates and as bankers lending money on security from their accumulated funds. The document corroborates Rostowzew's main conclusions in a striking way, and confirms some of his tentative suggestions, while supplying corrections on some points of detail. The editors are to be congratulated on having produced an excellent first edition with a very detailed commentary, which embodies suggestions contributed by Rostowzew, Mitteis, Ramsay, and other English scholars. Several points, however, remain obscure. The Greek text is in parts very loosely worded, and the exact interpretation must be left to further investigation based on fresh evidence. Thus it is far from clear what were the precise obligations of the peasant cultivators to their landlord. Apparently they paid dues both in money and in kind (besides contributing forced labour), but the exact conditions are obscure. The editors quote the Egyptian practice as a parallel: 'similarly the rent of Egyptian crown land consists in σιτική plus ἀργυρικὴ πρόσοδος' (p. 57). But it would appear that in Egypt these dues were not both paid in respect of the same kind of land. And the relation between the cash rental paid by the landlord to his royal overlord and that paid by the peasants to the landlord seems to us doubtful. In regard to the policy of the Macedonian kings towards the great temples, the editors express the view that all the temple estates were confiscated at the time of the conquest, but such an extreme policy is very improbable. Throughout the long section devoted to the proper names (pp. 28–52) there is naturally much that is highly conjectural. We notice slips on p. 42, where an article in the *Journal of Hellenic Studies*, vol. xvii, is attributed to the wrong author, and on p. 49, where Tanopolis in Phrygia is quoted from Hierocles as a parallel to the name Tandou, but clearly represents Tranopolis (Byzantine Tranoupolis), that is, Trajanopolis. J. G. C. A.

Mr. S. E. Stout has expended much labour in compiling his list of *The Governors of Moesia* (Princeton, New Jersey, 1911), and the materials which he has collected will be valuable to the historian of Rome's frontier policy on the Danube. Doubtful questions (of which there are not a few) are carefully handled, and the evidence is clearly and fully given. Mr. Stout perhaps goes too far in suggesting that the wording of the inscription which describes L. Funisulanus Vettonianus as 'leg. aug. pr. pr. provinc. Delmatiae, item provinc. Pannoniae, item Moesiae Super.' implies by the omission of the word *provincia* in the third case that the division of Moesia was a tentative measure. Such omissions are found in other inscriptions; that set up at Saepinum in honour of Neratius Priscus (*Corp. Inscr. Lat.* ix. 2455, cf. 2454) furnishes (if correctly restored) an interesting parallel. On p. 10 we miss a reference to the important, if tantalizing, inscription in honour of Flavius Sabinus, the brother of Vespasian (*Corp. Inscr. Lat.* vi. 31293). H. S. J.

Tabulae Fontium Traditionis Christianae, by Dr. J. Creusen, S.J. (Freiburg im Breisgau : Herder, 1911), is a conspectus on seven broad sheets of the literary history of Christendom from the beginning to the Council of Trent. For the early period the author has quoted the best recent writers, and where dates are doubtful he cites the decision of more than one authority. For later periods he does not name his guides ; the *Patrologia* has naturally served him well, and he gives the volumes in which each of his writers is contained. For the last 250 years the list is thin. Among mystics so important a figure as St. Bridget of Sweden is omitted, and the renaissance, except for one or two of its promoters who are entered as Platonists or Aristotelians, is ignored. The scheme of the work allows little more than the recording of names and dates under the headings of popes, councils, heresies, and writers eastern and western, who are roughly classified according to their topics. Such brevity may be misleading, but this compilation, made 'in usum scholarum', strikingly shows the width of the field of knowledge, and may be useful for reference. Z.

Dr. Nikolaus Müller deserves our sympathy for the unfortunate circumstances which have made it necessary for him to publish his account of *Die jüdische Katakombe am Monteverde zu Rom* (Leipzig : Fock, 1912) without completing the excavation which he had begun ; but the results already obtained were of sufficient importance to justify the publication. The inscriptions throw fresh light on the organization of the Jewish community in Rome, and deserve the careful attention of 'all students of the history of Judaism. It is to be hoped that the difficulties which attend the further exploration of the catacomb may shortly be removed.
H. S. J.

Mr. Wallis Johnson, in his *Byways of British Archaeology* (Cambridge : University Press, 1912), has not done justice to his wide reading and well-filled notebooks. He has put his most original and satisfactory articles at the end of his book. They deal with definite topics, the church-yard yew, the archaeology of the horse, and the use of oxen in agriculture, on which he has first-hand knowledge, scientific and antiquarian, to impart. Here his method is satisfactory ; we cannot say as much of his elaborate articles on ' Churches on pagan sites '. There is curious erudition, much of which is irrelevant, and an accumulation of second-hand and unsifted information. There is far too much of ' it is said ', ' it may possibly be ', and the like, which is the stranger since Mr. Johnson has many shrewd warnings against the guesses of other antiquaries. Unfortunately, his special knowledge is not balanced by an adequate general knowledge of history. When he is labouring to prove that church buildings were once largely used for secular purposes, he betrays ignorance of the fact that defamation and affiliation and testamentary matters belonged to the ecclesiastical forum. He discusses St. Michael without carrying him back to Monte Gargano, and omits Christian evidence, as in the Blickling Homilies, for the Teutonic frozen hell. Mr. Johnson is at his worst when he is scenting atavism in unlikely quarters, and finding survivals of paganism in such objects as the fox-heads nailed upon country doors. Such masks and pads, he ought to know, are simply memorials of a good run. If old women in the country use the grease of a church bell for their ailments, it is not superstition but a knowledge of the value of metallic ointments, discovered, like that of vegetable remedies, by ancient experiment. Mr. Johnson has, in fact, the faults as well as the merits of the old-fashioned antiquary. He has no criterion of authority, a term which he uses vaguely and constantly for writers and evidences both weighty and trivial, and he is apt to fall into errors in interpreting second-hand information. But he has collected a great mass of rare and perishing material, has told his story in an interesting manner, and furnished his book with pretty and instructive illustrations.
A.

Mrs. J. R. Green's volume, *The Old Irish World* (London : Macmillan, 1912), is a small collection of lectures and magazine articles ' having a connecting link in such evidences as they may contain of civilization in the old Irish world '. The first chapter is an impassioned plea for a more sympathetic treatment of the Gael in history, interspersed with strictures on other writers for their treatment of the subject. The most important essay is that on trade routes. A great effort is made to show that the road to Europe did not lie across England. 'The chief harbours of Ireland were those that swelled with the waves of the Atlantic Ocean,' and therefore 'her earliest traffic was through the perils of the Gaulish sea' (p. 64). Not only is this supposition not borne out by later experience, but we should imagine that the comparatively shallow inlets which dot the coasts bordering on St. George's Channel and the Irish Sea were more suited to the fragile bark of primitive times. 'As far back as we can see into the primitive darkness the inhabitants of the island were all in turn out on the great seas' (p. 65). To substantiate her vision Mrs. Green alludes to old myths, some extremely hazardous antiquarian speculations, and Irish annals relating to the third century B.C., all of which, even if accepted, would not prove the point. Problems, too, which have occupied eminent specialists without their reaching unanimity are decided off-hand by Mrs. Green. Thus according to her the first Goidelic invaders entered Ireland, not through Britain, but over-sea from Spain and Gaul (p. 66). Christianity and the art of writing and new forms of ornament first came across the Gaulish seas (p. 68). Ireland escaped the sword of Caesar, and henceforward she and Rome 'illustrated the free and peaceful union of two civilizations' (p. 69). It seems that modern scholarship is all wrong in smiling at the picture of the golden age of pagan Ireland drawn by Irish antiquaries of the seventeenth and eighteenth centuries. When we come to the period A.D. 500-1000 Mrs. Green's statements of Irish travelling, if not of trade, have no doubt a solid foundation of fact; but the work of Irish missionaries, to whom previous writers have done full justice, is magnified and extended until it is made to appear that Europe owed whatever learning and culture she possessed in the dark ages to Irish monks (pp. 72-3). No evidence, however, is adduced to show that in Ireland this learning ever extended beyond the precincts of a few monasteries, or that it survived the invasions of the Northmen so as to leave any permanent impress on the Irish race.

As examples of misstatements more easily brought to book, we may take the following. In an essay on Margaret, wife of Calvagh O'Connor Faly, Mrs. Green states: 'On that important trade route [of the Barrow] Thomas O'Connor Faly had founded a Franciscan monastery (1302) under the walls of Hugh de Lacy's fort [sic] at Castledermot' (p. 102). We are given two illustrations of the Franciscan abbey at Castledermot, and the O'Connors are again spoken of as having 'an establishment' in that town. But at the time mentioned the entire trade route of the Barrow was in the hands of Anglo-Normans, and what the O'Connors Faly had to do with Castledermot will puzzle students. The statement in Archdall's *Monasticon* is that 'Thomas, lord Offaly', founded the monastery in the year mentioned. By the silent introduction of the name O'Connor, and by ignoring the distinction between the Irish and the English Offaly, Mrs. Green has converted a Geraldine lord into a Gaelic chieftain. Again, Δοῦνον, latinized Dunum, in Irish *Dún*, happens to be a name on Ptolemy's map of Ireland. Mrs. Green without hesitation identifies it with the *dún* of Downpatrick (p. 131). Had she looked at her authority she would have found that Ptolemy's Dunum was far inland, in the south of

Ireland, nearly in the same latitude as Manapia, supposed to be Wexford. The chapter in which Dunum is mentioned is concerned with the recent apotheosis of the O'Neills in the castle of Ardglass. The place first comes into history as a fief of one of John de Courcy's vassals. In Anglo-Norman hands it soon became a flourishing trading-port, and it seems to have been continuously held by men loyal to England, even in the period of England's greatest weakness. Once, and once only, is the town said to have been burned by Irish raiders. There is no evidence that the castle was ever held or forcibly entered by an O'Neill, and it is best remembered for its successful resistance to capture during all the time of Hugh O'Neill's rebellion. It might well be regarded as a memorial of the tenacity with which those friendly to the English connexion have succeeded in retaining through the centuries their foothold in Ireland. All these essays are written with Mrs. Green's wonted fire, but somehow the flame does not always illuminate the facts. G. H. O.

In his *Der Karlsgraben* (Nürnberg: Korn, 1911) Dr. F. Beck has exhaustively discussed the origin and purpose of the so-called Fossa Carolina which cuts through the narrow water-parting between the watersheds of the Danube and the Rhine near Weissenburg in the Franconian Jura. After a summary of the sources and of the controversy on the subject, he has been able to show by dint of a topographical inquiry and excavations on the spot that the tradition is correct, and that the Fossa Carolina is really the canal with which Charlemagne vainly attempted to unite the two water-systems in 793. The rival theories, both as to the locality of Charlemagne's canal, and as to the real intent of the Fossa near Weissenburg, are conclusively disposed of. The account of the matter given by the *Annales Einhardi* appears to be accurate in all its details. Dr. Beck thinks that Charlemagne's main object was to facilitate the frequent journeys of the royal court between Aix-la-Chapelle and Ratisbon. But this seems unlikely to be more than a subordinate motive, in view of the magnitude of the work, and the Frankish kings' custom of subdividing their realm : there would not be the need for frequent journeys from Aix-la-Chapelle to Ratisbon after the partition which was to be expected on Charlemagne's death. Perhaps the general advantage in peace and war of a through-connexion by water from north to south, and a grandiose wish to perform a great work, are more probable reasons. Dr. Beck points out, incidentally, a curious slip in Spruner-Menke's Atlas by which the modern Ludwigs-Kanal is given as the Fossa Carolina.
C. W. P. O.

M. Philippe Lauer's *Robert Ier et Raoul de Bourgogne* (Paris: Champion, 1910) narrates the meagre annals of these two kings, leaders of the successful opposition to Charles the Simple. Robert has little other importance ; but Raoul made considerable endeavours to act as a genuine sovereign of the West Frankish realm. It is curious to see how the great vassals, who revolted against the attempts of Charles the Simple to rule, were yet obliged to choose a king who had far more material resources than the Carolingian. Perhaps they felt that they must have a leader with real power, and hoped that his elective kingship would lack the centralizing Carolingian tradition. In Francia only Herbert of Vermandois seems to have desired a mere figure-head for king. Raoul, from this point of view, was distinctly successful. He obtained general recognition : if, he lost Lorraine, he gained Vienne ; and, at the head of his confederates, rather than his vassals, he checked the Norman inroads into the heart of Francia. M. Lauer treats the tangled events of the reign with precision, and uses the latest research, although the value of his work is diminished by his omission to examine the genuineness of some of the royal charters. He is less prejudiced against Henry the Fowler than in his former book on Louis d'Outremer ; but his suggestion (p. 23, n. 2) that the cautious Henry did not support Herbert of the illegitimate Carolingian line of Vermandois as a candidate for the French throne, because of the latter's *droits éventuels* to the imperial crown, seems unlikely in view of Henry's general policy and Herbert's weakness. C. W. P. O.

The Origin of the English Constitution, by Professor George Burton Adams (New Haven, Connecticut : Yale University Press, 1912), contains a number of essays and studies intended to emphasize the importance of feudal ideas in shaping English institutions, and to prove that the beginnings of whatever is characteristic in the English constitution are to be found on this side of the year 1066. The general lines of his argument are simple. The Norman Conquest brought into England a ' political feudalism ', which must be carefully distinguished from the mere ' economic feudalism ' that had grown up under the English and Danish successors of Alfred the Great. And with feudalism came the Carolingian theory of absolutism. The constitutional development of the twelfth and thirteenth centuries is the product of a struggle between these two new forces. For by the English constitution we mean ' the machinery of a limited monarchy ; those devices by which an absolutism once existing in fact can be retained in form and theory, while the real government of the state is transformed into a democratic theory '. Magna Carta marks the first stage of development ; for it expresses the idea that Lex ought to be above Rex. The later stages are marked by the appearance of new institutions, of a coercive character, to enforce this principle. But the principle itself is feudal, and therefore the main features of the constitution are feudal in their origin. The argument rests upon an old-fashioned and misleading conception of the English constitution ; for Professor Adams is thinking not merely or mainly of Lancastrian parliamentarism. He appears to hold that what the United States and France have borrowed from this country is ' the machinery of a limited monarchy '. Furthermore, his view of the supreme importance of feudal theory as a formative force rests on the assumption that the growth and limitation of the central executive can be studied without reference to the history of law and local institutions. He admits the survival of Old English ideas in these two spheres ; but he does not seem to grasp the importance of the admission. He comes to a clear-cut result because he starts from a vicious abstraction. The book, however, is useful in more than one respect. It summarizes clearly enough the upshot of recent researches, particularly those of

Maitland and Vinogradoff, on Anglo-Saxon feudalism. It indicates the significance of the materials for Norman institutional history which Professor Haskins has collected. It emphasizes the feudal character of the best-known clauses in Magna Carta. And here and there we find a new point ably argued. For instance, Professor Adams collects evidence which appears to prove that the feudal lord could be sued in his own court (p. 95). He discusses the dictum of Glanvill that no man need answer for his free tenement without a writ from the king; he comes to the conclusion that Glanvill is not, as Maitland and Brunner have supposed, epitomizing a lost ordinance of Henry II, but is rather generalizing from his own experience of the practical operation of the writs of right (pp. 96–105). He also argues, less conclusively, that the stationary royal court which Henry II created in 1178 was the court of common pleas (pp. 136–43), his main argument being that the *clamores regni* which the new court was to hear were pleas between subject and subject. H. W. C. D.

It would be superfluous to add anything to the description which Mr. Frederic G. Bagshawe has himself given (p. 682) of his *History of the Royal Family of England* (Edinburgh: Sands, 2 vols.). 'I have endeavoured,' he writes, 'not to state, as a fact, anything about anybody which is not generally admitted to be true, or at all events is not to be found in one or other of the popular works of history which are not only in every library, but, and this is more to the purpose, in every *circulating* library in the kingdom.' A. F. P.

Gulielmus Neubrigensis, ein pragmatischer Geschichtsschreiber des zwölften Jahrhunderts (Bonn: Marcus & Weber, 1912), by Dr. Rudolf Jahncke, is the first part of *Jenaer Historische Arbeiten*. In it the author gives a minute and elaborate examination of the *Historia Rerum Anglicarum* of William of Newburgh, arriving at a conclusion very similar to that of Miss Norgate. Dr. Jahncke notes William's intention in writing for publicity as an historian through and through; the critical attitude with which he scrutinizes his authorities, and the scorn with which he rejects the Arthurian fables of Geoffrey of Monmouth; the width of his outlook and the freedom from medieval narrowness, which place him for historical capacity above all his contemporaries. If there is no great novelty in these conclusions, the fullness of the critical discussion on which they are based makes the work very useful for the historiography of the twelfth century. Dr. Jahncke rejects Mr. Salter's suggested identification of William of Newburgh with the William filius Elye, who is known to have been a canon of Newburgh (*ante*, xxii. 510–14). Apart from the difficulties of the genealogy, Dr. Jahncke holds that the historian's whole work is against the identification. Mr. Salter thought that the story of the miracle at Thame (*Historia*, i. 154) indicated that William had gone away before June 1183, when Walter of Coutances was consecrated bishop, and the prophet must have lost his reputation; against this Dr. Jahncke cites another passage (*ibid.* i. 236, 'sicque evacuata est prophetia,' &c.) which does not support this theory. Dr. Jahncke also dwells on passages which indicate William's dislike for women; but the story of Ramiro of Aragon, who did not return to his monastery till his daughter was of age to marry (*ibid.* i. 123–4), would rather help Mr. Salter. There is more force in the argument from the want of direct evidence, and from the absence of any other allusion to William's supposed secular career. But the strongest argument is William's own statement that he entered Newburgh as a child (*ibid.* i. 51, ' quae me in Christo a puero aluit '); it is difficult to reconcile this with an identification which supposes that he did not become a canon till he was nearly fifty years of age; William would probably have expressed himself differently if he had meant no more than that he was educated as a boy at the priory, to which he returned some thirty years later. C. L. K.

The Great Roll of the Pipe for the Twenty-ninth Year of the Reign of King Henry the Second, A.D. 1182–3 (published for the Pipe Roll Society: London, 1911), like its predecessors at once illustrates the general working of the machinery of government and reflects the special conditions of the year. Mr. Round supplies his customary introduction calling attention to points of general and special interest. He mentions the king's absence from England and the dispatch of treasure to him on the continent and at his direction to various parts of England. He is able to clear up some obscure points in connexion with the judicial circuits of the year and with the practice of the exchequer. The reader is reminded of the markedly feudal character of the period (too often obscured by an interest in the growth of centralization) by the very large revenue drawn from casual feudal incidents, such as the temporary enjoyment of lay and ecclesiastical fiefs. There are also the usual points of special or miscellaneous interest, and these Mr. Round has duly noted.

The Society has now very nearly completed the printing of these rolls for the capitally important reign of Henry II, and one had hoped to see such excellent service rewarded by an increased support which would have encouraged and enabled the Society to extend its activities. Unhappily this has been withheld, and as the range of volumes extends along one's shelves there has been no proportionate increase in the list of subscribers printed at the beginning of each volume. This is much to be regretted because with the organization and equipment at its disposal the Society might widen its programme to great advantage. There is much important work to be done ; for one thing the rate of publication of the pipe rolls might be increased from one to two volumes a year. This would be particularly useful since—as has frequently been pointed out—the peculiar value of these documents lies in the means which they furnish of tracing the fortunes of an institution over a long period. Then certain allied records might well be published or republished. The pipe roll of 31 Henry I, for example, is extremely scarce, and so is the Rotulus de Dominabus.[1] These, of course, are only suggestions, but whether they prove acceptable or not the fact remains that the Society has well deserved more general recognition and more substantial support than it has hitherto received. G. T. L.

[1] We are glad to understand that this latter suggestion has been forestalled by the committee of the Society, and that the Rotulus de Dominabus may be expected shortly.

In *Franciscan Essays*, by M. Paul Sabatier and others (Aberdeen: University Press, 1912), forming the first volume of the 'extra series' issued by the British Society of Franciscan Studies, M. Sabatier writes of the Originality of St. Francis, Father Cuthbert of his Poverty, and Father Paschal Robinson contributes a study of St. Clare. Perhaps the most interesting paper is Mr. Edmund Gardner's on Joachim of Flora. The difference between Joachim and later Joachism is well explained, and the disrepute of the sect is traced to the attempt made by Fra Gherardo of San Donnino and others to apply the term Everlasting Gospel to certain actual books composed by Joachim. Mr. Gardner also makes the interesting if dubious conjecture that the third *giro* of doctors mentioned by Dante in *Parad.* xiv. 67–75 may be an allusion to Joachim's doctrine. Dante's position in this matter has always been obscure. It is thought that his knowledge of Joachim may have been derived mainly from Ubertino da Casale's *Arbor Vitae Crucifixae*, yet the allusion to Ubertino in *Parad.* xii. 124 is, as Miss Evelyn Underhill says in her essay in this volume,'curt and unfavourable'. Dante may possibly have wished to vindicate the master as against his pupils, but it is doubtful if he possessed enough knowledge for such a purpose. Another interesting paper is Mr. Little's on Franciscans at Oxford. Mr. Little is here on familiar ground, but one is rather surprised that a scholar of his position should repeat the old error of attributing a certain *Compendium Scientiae* to Robert Grosseteste. Dr. Ludwig Baur edited this work in 1903 and showed that it was merely the two treatises, *De Divisione Philosophiae* and *De Unitate*, of the Spanish archdeacon Dominicus Gundissalinus. Some writers have made matters worse by confusing the *Compendium* with a *Summa* also attributed to Grosseteste, but Mr. Little does not appear to make this mistake. One hopes, too, that it is not an article of faith with the Society of Franciscan Studies to accept all Roger Bacon's statements. As regards the state of knowledge among his contemporaries, his assertions are often of no greater value than the similar assertions of his distinguished namesake in a later age. W. H. V. R.

A further important clue to the origins of the organized foreign commerce of England is furnished by M. Henri Obreen in tome lxxx of the *Bulletin de la Commission royale d'Histoire de Belgique* (1911) under the title *Une Charte brabançonne inédite de 1296 en faveur des Marchands anglais*. The legible remains of this document (which is preserved in the national archives at Brussels and is in French) exhibit a close correspondence to the terms of a Latin charter of 1305 printed in Mertens and Torfs' *Geschiedenis van Antwerpen* (1846), which M. Obreen reproduces in parallel columns. There can be little doubt that it is the charter referred to in the account of the rise of the merchant adventurers given in the Stowe MS. 303, ff. 99–108, and printed recently in Dr. Lingelbach's *Laws and Ordinances*, p. 198 ; and it may also probably be identified with the charter calendared in the inventory of the merchant adventurers' records made in 1547, which is preserved in the Sloane MS. 2103, f. 2, sect. 28, and is printed in Schanz's *Handelspolitik*, ii. 577 (the date there given of 1286 may easily be a slip for 1296, and the day and month are the same). The privileges granted to the English merchants, ' et alii quicumque eorum famuli et mercature,' are those later sought and obtained by the merchant adventurers. Yet M. Obreen is clearly justified in connecting the charter with the transfer of the staple by Edward I from Holland to Brabant in 1295–6 : and this strengthens the hypothesis that the staplers and the adventurers sprang from a common root. A similar conclusion was suggested by Dr. Cunningham's publication (*Growth of English Industry and Commerce*, i, appendix c. v) of an extract from the Staple Rolls, 1359, showing that the English merchants retained an organization at Bruges when the staple had been removed to England ; and this view has been recently adopted by a Dutch scholar, Mr. S. van Brakel, in an article on 'Die Entwickelung und Organisation der Merchant-Adventurers', which appeared in the *Vierteljahrschrift für Sozial- und Wirt-schaftsgeschichte*, 1907. G. U.

M. Arnold Fayen has completed his calendar of the letters of John XXII relating to Belgium (*Lettres de Jean XXII ; Textes et Analyses*, II. ii. 1330–4. Rome : Bretschneider, 1912), the earlier portions of which have already been noticed in this Review (xxiv. 190 : xxv. 610). The concluding section contains a short introduction, a subject-index, a collection of unregistered letters of John XXII, and of letters registered out of their proper place, and another of the letters of the antipope Nicholas V. The few unregistered letters, with one exception, would seem to have been issued in the course of judicial proceedings, and to be of a class not normally needing registration. The historical material for these last four years includes the letters relating to the abortive attempt to constitute a new see in the duchy of Brabant, and to the proposed crusade of 1336. Among minor matters of interest are two letters (3280 and 3318) showing how the pope paid for cloth bought in the Low Countries by an assignment of the annates levied in England. There are also confirmations and exemplifications of a number of privileges of the Carthusian order obtained by the priory of Notre-Dame-des-Prés. The subject-index reveals two cases of limitation of the dispensing power : in one (3259) the pope refuses to permit marriage under the canonical age, and in another (2619) he declines to recommend the conferring the degree of master, especially in theology, on persons who are not known to be duly qualified. A lively description of football (*pilota*) will be found in no. 2865. M. Fayen's methods have already been dealt with. It is to be regretted that he should expend a page of small type in a lively counter-attack on a reviewer who has also deserved well of John XXII. He has no need to defend his own procedure, which is admirably adapted to his task, but a less perfect system is at all events pardonable in work on a scale eighteen times as large. The slip *Worchester* for Worcester should be corrected in the index. C. J.

The second part of the *Registrum Johannis de Trillek, episcopi Herefordensis* (London : Canterbury and York Society, 1912) completes the register itself and ends with the usual lists of institutions to benefices and so forth. In the ordination lists no distinction has been made in the type used for printing general headings, *acoliti, diaconi, subdiaconi, presbiteri*, and sub-headings, *religiosi, seculares*. The effect is puzzling until the list is examined closely. Rather more information might have been given about persons presented to livings. A note explains that the recipient was a priest unless otherwise stated. There is no statement about John of Ercall, who was presented to the chapel of Caus Castle in 1346 (p. 373); yet an entry shows that he was not ordained subdeacon till 1353 (p. 595). The complete career of Roger Pagyn, made vicar of Clun in 1349 (p. 380), could have been noted : he became an acolyte at Whitsuntide, 1352 (p. 581), subdeacon in September (p. 584), deacon in December (p. 588), and priest in February 1353 (p. 594). A few more place-names might have been modernized in the index. Why not Bredwardine instead of Bredwardyn, Crickhowell for Crughowel, Rocester for Roucester, and Tattenhall for Tatunhulle ? H. J.

Die Hanse und England von Eduards III bis auf Heinrichs VIII Zeit was a well-chosen subject for one of the *Abhandlungen zur Verkehrs- und Seegeschichte* issued by the Hansische Geschichtsverein (Berlin : Curtius, 1911); and the lucid account of it given by Dr. Friedrich Schulz will be welcome to English students, few of whom can hope to keep abreast with the records and literature of Hanseatic history. As three-quarters of the book deals with pre-Tudor history to which Schanz only devoted ten pages, a much fuller account is given than was before accessible of the commercial relations between England and Germany during the fourteenth and fifteenth centuries. The dealings of Edward III with Hanseatic financiers (the extent of which has often been overrated) are somewhat cursorily handled, but an ample account is given from 1371 onwards of the struggle of the English mercantile interest with the league—of the endless diplomatic bickerings alternating with punitive piracy and actual warfare to which the treaties of 1388, 1409, 1437, and 1474 seem to have brought only brief intervals of truce. The facts are stated with great clearness and no perceptible bias ; but it is difficult for the writer or the reader to avoid exaggerating their importance. The primary significance of these diplomatic events for economic history is almost entirely a negative one. Their secondary significance will only appear when they are brought into connexion with a constructive account of the inward development of the countries concerned. The fluctuations of Richard II's policy in regard to the Hanse privileges will undoubtedly furnish a valuable clue to the English historian in tracing the divergence of industrial and commercial interests in London and its effects on civic policy. So, too, the careful account given by Dr. Schulz of the complicated diplomacy leading to the treaty of Utrecht (1474) will only realize its true purpose when it is used as a means of unravelling the complexity of the social, economic, political, and dynastic forces by the manipulation of which Edward IV was made king, dethroned, and restored. Of the two brief attempts at broad generalization made in the introductory and concluding sections, the latter is much the less satisfactory. It is, in fact, the mere repetition of a prevalent formula. The Hanse, it is said, failed for want of a powerful state to back it against the *zielbewussten und tatkräftigen nationalen*

Politik Englands. The explanation furnished in the introduction is far more illuminating. The privileged position of the Hanse in England, we are there told, which was maintained by the fiscal interest of the Crown combined with the interest of the main body of producers and consumers as expressed in parliament, was due to its superiority as an intermediary between east and west. That superiority, commercial and geographical, disappeared in the sixteenth century. As the world grew wider and the Hanse narrower, neither diplomacy nor force could have maintained the privileges. Dr. Schulz's most direct contribution to economic history is contained in his final chapter, which describes the organization of the various Hanse settlements in England and throws much new light on the constitution of the London *Kontor* and on its relation to the other settlements. The tendency of the *Kontor* towards exclusiveness and concentration was one of the causes of its decline. G. U.

In *Book of the Knowledge of all the Kingdoms, Lands, and Lordships that are in the World, and the Arms and Devices of each Land and Lordship* (London : Hakluyt Society, 2nd series, xxix, 1912) Sir Clements Markham has furnished a translation of the ' Libro del Conoscimiento de todos los Reynos ', &c., which was written by a Spanish Franciscan about the middle of the fourteenth century, and first edited by Señor Espada in 1877. The work was quoted for its account of Africa by Pierre Bontier and Jean le Verrier, the chaplains to Jean de Bethencourt, who wrote in 1404 ; but the complete text was long unknown. The writer, who relates that he was born in 1305, professes to have visited every part of the known world. ' This,' says Sir Clements Markham, ' cannot be conceded literally. But he was probably a great traveller.' His Spanish editor was also of opinion that he was not a mere compiler of tradition. Nevertheless the opinion of Professor Beazley (*Dawn of Modern Geography*, iii. 415) seems to be preferable, viz. that it was perhaps a description of an imaginary journey, compiled partly from a very detailed and valuable Portolano map, partly from genuine reports of travellers, and partly from other works. On reading it through one is struck at once by its inequality ; the writer was obviously familiar with the Spanish peninsula, and had good information about North Africa and the Atlantic islands. But one can hardly believe that he had been in the British Isles ; though he professes to have visited Scotland, the only places which he knows in England are Londres, Gunsa ' where are the general studies ', Antona (Southampton), Bristol, Artamua (Dartmouth), Premua (Plymouth), and Miraforda (Milford). For Gunsa the editor suggests in a foot-note Windsor (?), and in the index Winchelsea ; it must be either Oxford or Cambridge, but it is difficult to see how the corruption (perhaps a manuscript perversion of Oxonia) could have originated with any one who knew the towns by their English names. The other places are just those which would be familiar to Spanish merchants. From ' Irlanda ' the friar sailed in a ship bound for Spain, but arrived by way of the Shetlands in ' Ibernia ' ; this the editor suggests is a copyist's error for Iceland ; but when the friar tells us that there are no reptiles in this island one suspects that he has put in a second account of Ireland. Similarly Leon and Lucdevic (Lyons) appear close together as two towns on the Rhône. The friar had clearly some knowledge of the voyage of the Genoese Sorleone de Vivaldo to Magadoxo in 1315, and has excellent information about names in the Madeiras, Canaries, and Azores. However sceptical one may be about the range of his own travels, his 'Libro del Conoscimiento' is a valuable record of the extent of geographical knowledge in the middle of the fourteenth century, which it is most useful to have in an English dress. The difference of the flag of Majorca from that of Aragon proves in Sir Clements Markham's opinion (p. 25) that the friar wrote before 1375. But since the text gives the arms of France as three fleurs-de-lis of gold (p. 5) the date must be little, if at all, earlier. The actual emblazoning of the shields must be much later, for there the English king quarters 'France modern'. The arms assigned to African potentates are amusing. C. L. K.

Under the title of *Der deutsche Kaufmann in den Niederlanden* (Leipzig: Duncker & Humblot, 1911) the Hansische Geschichtsverein has published a series of studies by Dr. Rudolf Häpke which give the clearest and most succinct account yet attempted of the Hanseatic settlements in Bruges, Antwerp, and Amsterdam, and of the broader changes that have affected German trade in the Netherlands from the fourteenth to the eighteenth centuries. The first two chapters will serve as an excellent supplement to Dr. Häpke's *Brügges Entwickelung*. They describe with a vividness and precision based on close familiarity with the archives the conditions of international commerce in Bruges during the fifteenth century, the daily life of the German merchant, and his business and social relations with his Flemish host and with traders of other nations. The account of the transition to Antwerp is of great interest to English students. The decline of Bruges was due, amongst other causes, to the development of larger and freer forms of international trade than either Bruges or the Hanse towns were prepared to recognize. A proposal was even entertained in 1477 for erecting a staple that would have still further narrowed the channels of trade; and the formal transference of the *Kontor* to Antwerp was delayed half a century after the actual removal of the merchants and the trade by the unwillingness of the league to accept a less privileged position than they had previously enjoyed. In the meantime the *Kontor* lost its control over the merchants, and many of the more enterprising formed connexions with the Rhenish and South German capitalists whose operations dominated the money-market of the sixteenth century. The offer made by the government of Philip II to form an alliance with the Hanse towns against England provided the opportunity for the re-establishment of the control of the *Kontor* over the German trading community in Antwerp. The inception of this scheme by Dr. Heinrich Suderman must be connected with the breach between England and the Hanse in 1553-7, and its further development in 1562 with the breach between England and the Netherlands in 1563-4 ; just as the new Hansehaus at Antwerp in which the scheme was realized found its counterpart in Gresham's Exchange. Alva favoured the neutral commerce of the Hanse merchants, but the Spanish fury destroyed the hopes of the new establishment. In Amsterdam the North German traders learnt by necessity how to prosper in trade without the protection of a privileged status. Dr. Häpke's treatment shows not only learning but insight and unusual detachment.

G. U.

The second part of the fourth volume of the *Epistolario di Coluccio Salutati* (Fonti per la Storia d'Italia. Rome: Istituto Storico Italiano, 1911) is the coping-stone to Signor Francesco Novati's splendid monument of early renaissance learning. It has all the scholarly finish which has marked the preceding volumes, though it is necessarily a gathering up of fragments. In the opening section are printed letters from Salutati's correspondents, Petrarch, Pellegrino Zambecari, Giovanni Conversano, Innocent VII, Leonardo Bruni, Vergerio, and others. The most interesting is, perhaps, a long letter in Greek written at Constantinople by Chrysoloras, and dealing chiefly with Plutarch's *Lives*. The genealogical tables of the Salutati are copiously illustrated by documents, which include the naturalization of Coluccio as a citizen of Lucca and his election as chancellor by the Anziani, his election and re-election as chancellor of Florence and his oath of fidelity, his absolution from excommunication by Urban VI, his election as a member of the Art of Wool. Letters of Bruni, Poggio, and Vergerio lament his death, and these are followed by epitaphs and short biographies. Appendices deal with his portraits, his arms, and at great length with his property at Pescia, Stignano, and Buggiano. Incorruptible as he was, and meagre as was his fixed salary, the fees of the chancellor's office gave him a considerable income which he invested in land. Curiously enough he never owned a house in Florence, but rented one, as the author proves, in the little Piazza Peruzzi lying in the angle between the Borgo de' Greci and the Via de' Benci. The indexes cover the whole work, and one of peculiar value gives all the references to classical and medieval authors quoted by Salutati. Thanks to Signor Novati the student can now make intimate acquaintance with one of the most attractive characters in all Florentine history. Salutati may be said to have held much the same exalted position in the traditions of official life as did Sant' Antonino a little later in those of the church.

E. A.

Girolamo Savonarola, by Mr. E. L. S. Horsburgh (London: Methuen, 1911), is the fourth edition, revised and considerably enlarged, of the biography which the author published eleven years ago. It is described as the result of a renewed and far closer study of the documentary evidence on which our knowledge of Savonarola depends. That being so it is a pity that Mr. Horsburgh has given no account of the sources which he has used. Vague references to 'the researches of Gherardi' or to 'Villari, though he does not quote his authority', are not illuminating. If foot-notes were precluded, a brief section on the authorities would have added much to the usefulness of the work. However, the fact that it has gone through four editions in a comparatively short period must be accepted as evidence that this Life meets the needs of those for whom it is intended. It is pleasantly written, and gives an agreeable account of Savonarola's career and teaching. Apparently Mr. Horsburgh was not able to make use of Dr. Schnitzer's recent work, with the diary of Piero Parenti. There are some good illustrations.

C. L. K.

Abbot Gasquet has just published a neat little book entitled *Abbot Wallingford; an Inquiry into the Charges made against him and his Monks* (London: Sands, 1912). We can well understand the anxiety of Abbot Gasquet to redeem the credit of Abbot Wallingford and wipe off the imputations on the government of the abbey of St. Albans contained in Archbishop Morton's letter. But how is this to be done without imputing gross calumnies either to Archbishop Morton himself or to common report at the time which he thought credible? This was the question from the first, and with all Abbot Gasquet's care and thought upon the subject he leaves it quite unanswered. Moreover, when Abbot Gasquet himself showed that it was Wallingford, and no other abbot, against whom the charges were made, it was pointed out that they were all the more plausible as very bad stories were told of him before he became abbot in what is called Whethamstede's Register. It is true that Mr. Riley, the editor of this Register, followed by the author of the article on William Wallingford in the *Dictionary of National Biography*, treats the compiler of this book as a purely calumnious writer. But this judgement seems only to rest on a presumption that a man guilty of such things as fraud, lying, and perjury could not have become abbot; whereas there is some reason to fear, what the writer himself clearly indicates, that outside influences of this world really did affect sometimes the government of monasteries. On one point, however, I am anxious to do Abbot Gasquet justice, as some words of mine, perhaps rather carelessly chosen, have, he says, been interpreted as reflecting upon his candour. Nothing certainly was further from my intention. I always felt that the study of this case had been greatly advanced by Abbot Gasquet's inquiries about it at Rome, of which he permitted me to be the vehicle (*ante*, xxiv. 319 *seq.*). But referring to the matter in vol. iii of my *Lollardy and the Reformation*, after mentioning the final bull of 30 July 1490, I suggested that ' there must have been one more move upon the chessboard, of which Abbot Gasquet *does not seem* to have come upon any trace at Rome '. I did not in the least mean to insinuate that Abbot Gasquet would have concealed any matter at all relevant that had come under his observation. But in the vast stores of the Vatican there might have been something more. At all events something had to be accounted for; and I gave my reason: ' For the victory remained at last with St. Albans, which Wallingford succeeded by great efforts in preserving from the dreaded visitation.' This statement of mine, Abbot Gasquet says, ' is absolutely without foundation'. Well, he has quoted the foundation for it himself in a document which he considers to have been drawn up in 1490 with additions made after Wallingford's death in 1492. In this the convent say (p. 67), ' In the end this our best and most reverend father and most worthy Abbot obtained a just victory, and preserved intact and inviolate all our privileges, to our great honour and utility.' The victory, it will be seen, is simply the preservation of the privileges of the abbey. Not a word is said about the abbot's character having been vindicated, or even having been aspersed, though the whole question arose out of his alleged scandalous rule. What are we to think of this? It seems as if Abbot Wallingford never attempted to vindicate his own character against such abominable imputations. He vindicated the privileges of the abbey, and that was enough. Abbot Gasquet, indeed, finds what he calls ' a categorical denial of many of the evil reports ' in the obituary notice of Wallingford drawn up by Prior Ramridge. It scarcely deserves that name, even as regards the economical charges. But what are we to think of a monastery that meets insinuations against its abbot's management by such statements as, ' Oh, he paid off our debt completely ; he gave us that lovely and most costly altar screen ; ' and passes by unnoticed the most explicit charges of foul depravity ?

J. G.

Miss Hester Donaldson Jenkins has utilized her former experience as professor of history at Constantinople for a biography of *Ibrahim Pasha, Grand Vizir of Suleiman the Magnificent* (New York : Columbia University Press, 1911). Ibrahim's tenure of that office, as his biographer remarks, coincided with ' the first entrance of Turkey into the European concert '. Although he did not inspire the famous capitulations of 1535, which secured a predominant influence to France in the Levant, he was an active diplomatist ; from 1522 to 1536, the zenith of his career, he shared power with the sultan, while, as a general, he distinguished himself at the battle of Mohács. But the writer is not only his biographer, for considerable digressions are introduced to explain the Ottoman system of government. The work is based upon the best contemporary authorities, but the long list of misprints might be increased, especially in the Latin foot-notes. An error of political geography is committed (p. 18, n. 1) where Parga, the native place of Ibrahim, is described as ' on the coast of Greece '. That memorable village has been politically Turkish ever since the British government abandoned it in 1819. In the full bibliography (p. 122) *Reichthums* is an obvious mistake.

W. M.

Dr. Arthur Cushman McGiffert's *Martin Luther, the Man and his Work* (London : Unwin, 1911) was admirably adapted to a popular magazine in which it first appeared. It was impartial, mildly instructive, and fairly interesting. Moreover, in its reissue the book contains little misstatement ; having undergone, since its first publication, a thorough, and it must be confessed, a much-needed, revision. If, however, the scholar is led by the author's reputation in other lines to expect more than is here indicated he will be disappointed. Dr. McGiffert is able to add nothing new to previous research. He is also inclined to let generalities—more or less showy—do duty for concrete statements of fact. If he gives excellent summaries of the protestant principle of individual judgement (p. 144) or of Luther's historical significance (pp. 381 ff.), he frequently neglects definite and important events. The reformer's doctrine of justification by faith and his attitude towards the Bible are hardly mentioned ; his catechisms and hymns are hurried over with half a page. No subject is more interesting than that of Luther's development during his first years in the cloister, and there is none on which more has recently been discovered. On this subject Dr. McGiffert offers us next to nothing. The lately published *Commentary on Romans*, which casts so much light on Luther's monastic period, is indeed mentioned but there is no evidence of the writer's having read it. No fact in Luther's life is better attested than that he passed through some sort of a crisis when his life-message came to him, and few facts in his life are more important ; but of all this his latest biographer says not one word.										P. S.

M. Charles Bratli's *Philippe II, Roi d'Espagne* (Paris : Champion, 1912), to which M. Baguenault de Puchesse gives a guarded approval, consists for the most part of bibliographical information ; and from this point of view it is of real value to students of sixteenth-century history. The apology for Philip which makes up the 129 pages of M. Bratli's text is flimsier matter. It requires more substantial evidence and more substantial arguments than M. Bratli provides to convince us that the decadence of Spain was due to Charles V and the Flemings he imported, and that it was arrested for half a century by Philip II ; and proof of the bias of foreign and especially of protestant historians is no proof that Philip was a great or enlightened ruler.								A. F. P.

It was a happy thought to reproduce in facsimile *The First and Chief Groundes of Architecture*, by John Shute (London : *Country Life*, 1912), the earliest (1563) and the rarest English treatise on architecture. Shute appears to have been an artist rather than an architect by profession ; but he had studied in Italy when the renaissance was in its full flower, and his work was not without influence on English building, as Mr. Lawrence Weaver shows in the excellent introduction which collects all the facts known about him. Not the least of the charms of this beautiful volume is the stately English of Shute's writing.					B.

De Briefwisseling van Constantijn Huygens (1608–87), edited by Dr. J. A. Worp, i. (*Rijks Geschiedkundige Publicatiën*, xv, The Hague : Nijhoff, 1911), and *De Kroniek van Abel Eppens tho Equart*, edited with notes by Jonkheer J. A. Feith and Dr. H. Brugmans, I (*Werken uitgegeven door het Historisch Genootschap gevestigd te Utrecht*, Derde Serie, xxvii, Amsterdam : Müller, 1911) are sources of the same great period of Dutch history, but of entirely different character. The correspondence of the younger Huygens, the famous polyhistor and successor to his father as secretary to the council of state, never before collected in a complete edition, contains the documents of a life passed in the centre of high policy and amid the leading scientific and artistic culture of the time ; the Frisian chronicle of Eppens, a simple country gentleman of the Groningen Ommelanden and Calvinist refugee from the Spanish counter-reformation, now for the first time published from its manuscript, is the product of a mind which with a great veracity combined a decided party spirit and religious narrowness. Yet as historical authorities the two must not be classed according to the importance of their authors. The small amount of general information supplied by the Huygens correspondence has some time ago been taken account of by Groen van Prinsterer, whose *Archives de la Maison d'Orange-Nassau* contain what can be gathered from it respecting the history of this dynasty. Thus the chief interest of the new book, which is made very convenient by elaborate notes and indexes, lies rather in the direction of private and personal history, e.g. for the diplomatic intercourse between the States General and England in 1618-22 in which Huygens repeatedly took part; his letters to his parents are full of curious details, but official papers seem to be missing. His semi-official reports from the army to Princess Amalia of Solms do not begin until 1633, and the present volume ends with the following year. Abel Eppens's narrative has not only the advantage of a definite range, but the struggle between Spain and the United Provinces for the possession of Groningen, which forms the main subject of its third and largest part (1566–89), was one of the centres of the eighty years' war, and the protestant bias of the writer, while connecting every event with the religious contest, at least does not derogate to its international aspects. Its first-rate value has, already before the publication, been practically proved by the extensive use made of it in the second volume of Dr. B. Hagedorn's history of the trade and shipping of Emden, the place from which Eppens for ten years unrelentingly combated his apostate country. C. B.

There have been a number of good books recently on the literary relations of France and England. The ablest worker on the subject was Joseph Texte, and his work has been an incitement and a model to others. M. Charles Bastide's new book, *Anglais et Français du XVIIe siècle* (Paris : Alcan, 1912), is the latest, but it is not one of the best. He offers some details of the journey from Paris to London which are of interest, and he has something to say about the Huguenot theologians and journalists exiled in London. He has produced some facts about Pierre Coste, the friend and translator of Locke, and about Thémiseul de Saint-Hyacinthe, author of *Le Chef-d'œuvre d'un Inconnu* and translator of a part of *Robinson Crusoe*. But there is neither life nor learning in his feebly written and feebly reasoned book. His Huguenots are infinitely dull, and his knowledge of contemporary England unequal to the task of showing what share the exiles had in making it. He comments in his preface on the recent books on his subject : ' C'est, pour n'en citer que les principaux, en France les travaux de MM. Jusserand et Texte, en Amérique la thèse de M. Upham, en Angleterre les conférences de M. Sidney Lee.' It may always, of course, be disputed which are the principal works on any subject. We are inclined to believe that on this subject of the literary relations of France and England no list should be so short as to exclude the name of M. Louis Charlanne. G. S. G.

The Royal Fishery Companies of the Seventeenth Century (Glasgow : MacLehose, 1912) is one of the fruits of the historical research recently fostered at the Scottish universities by the grants of the Carnegie Trustees. The author, Mr. J. R. Elder, has entered a comparatively unoccupied field, and his otherwise excellent thesis suffers a little in consequence from a want of concentration. He would have gained very greatly in this respect if he could have had the help afforded by Dr. Scott's *Joint Stock Companies*, and by Mr. Edmundson's Ford Lectures on *Anglo-Dutch Rivalry*, the former of which appeared just before and the latter just after his thesis went to press. As it is he gives us many new and interesting details of one of the leading failures of Stuart mercantilism. The admirable use made of Pepys's comments on the later fishery schemes of which he was a governor ought to encourage others to labour in that neglected mine of materials for economic history ; and Mr. Elder's account of the earlier society of 1632 and its conflict with the earl of Seaforth and with the convention of burghs leads us to regret that he did not concentrate his attention upon this highly significant episode, for which he might have found further help in Mr. Mackenzie's *History of the Outer Hebrides*. Mr. Elder makes a common mistake in supposing that at the end of the seventeenth century the Dutch were ' comparatively speaking merely onlookers where once they had been supreme '. G. U.

The brief biography of *Cardinal de Retz*, by Mr. David Ogg (London: Methuen, 1912), has the merit of being the first English attempt to present a life of this paradoxical Frenchman, aptly described as ' a sixteenth-century Florentine living in seventeenth-century Paris '. The account is based mainly on a critical study of the *Memoirs*, the author being careful to point out the proclivities of De Retz to exaggerate his own political importance, and to conceal those facts which might have appeared to his detriment. His chief aim throughout the *Fronde* is shown to have been the acquirement of a cardinal's hat, and in fact we are told that the story of how he attained his ambition is the ' only single thread ' that serves to give unity to the movement. The pages devoted to De Retz's character and literary achievements are of special interest. C. E. M.

The most notable event in the latest volume of *The English Factories in India, 1637–41*, edited by Mr. W. Foster (Oxford : Clarendon Press, 1912), is the foundation of Madras, which has already been dealt with by Mr. Foster in *The Founding of Fort St. George*, 1902. But, as he observes, the picture obtains its proper setting by the information given regarding concurrent events at the other stations of the Company's factors. The general position during these years was considerably more favourable, the country having recovered from the famine. Goods were obtainable in abundance ; whilst the Company's expenses were lessened, mainly owing to the agreement with the Portuguese which had been arrived at by Methwold. The strong hand of the latter was removed ; but his successor, William Fremlin, proved conscientious and capable, although his dispatches home are duller reading than those of his predecessor. In December 1638 we find Andrew Cogan, writing from Surat, advising the abolition of the separate commands at Surat and Bantam, which led to jealousy and rivalry.

Are we sertayne [he wrote] of continuall peace with the Portugalls and Dutch ? Noe ; for the peace wee injoy by them is but for theire owne Ends. All which being duely considered, 'twer very requisitt that the makeing good a place were first put in practiz ; from which will arrise these bennefitts : you shal be ever seoond of the most part of your estate, and yf any affront offer'd be enabled to doo yourselves right.'

We have here a justification of the coming occupation of Madras. But the fairer outlook was darkened by the proceedings of Captain John

Weddel, the agent of the Courteen association, whose misdoings weakened the position of the company, and by the high-handed behaviour of the Dutch. In vain the English agents sought to

procure redresse against the Hollanders insolencies and affronts, which they now so frequently exhibit, to yor servants disheartning and our nations disgrace, that we are even become a by word to this people, who, in proportion to the knowledge they have of either, judge of and value accordingly their rising, our declining, fortunes.

The capture of Malacca by the Dutch in January 1641 did not add to the contentment of the English in the east. H. E. E.

T. H. Green's *Four Lectures on the Puritan Revolution* were originally printed in 1888 in the third volume of his collected works, and well deserve reprinting (London : Longmans, 1912). They bring out admirably the inner meaning of the movement described, by the aid of Cromwell's letters, Baxter's autobiography, and the pamphlets of Milton and Sir Henry Vane. Browning and Wordsworth are occasionally quoted to furnish illustrations (pp. 31, 53). The style is clear and eloquent, and there is no better introduction to the history of the times. It should be compared with Gardiner's small book on *The Puritan Revolution*, which in various ways supplements it. Green is inclined to over-estimate the importance of Vane, and his treatment of the Protectorate is hardly adequate. The editor, Mr. Kenneth Bell, might with advantage have added a few more notes. For instance, on p. 30 Green writes : ' The man who was to vindicate a higher reason for God's providence, and to be called an atheist for doing so, was still at Mr. van der Ende's school at Amsterdam.' Not every reader will know that Spinoza is meant. Some of the quotations, too, should have been verified. Milton is quoted on p. 67 as saying that when God has given the victory to a cause in the field of battle, 'then comes the task to those worthies which are the soul of that enterprise, to be sweat and laboured out amidst the throng and *noses* of vulgar and irrational men.' What Milton wrote was 'noises'. The misprint comes from Bohn's edition, which swarms with errors. C. H. F.

In his essay on *Colonel Thomas Blood, Crown-stealer* (London : Frowde, 1911), Professor Wilbur Cortez Abbott gives a pleasant and interesting account of a career which he describes as ' one of the most curious and extraordinary in English history '. At the outset he claims for his hero the dignity of a representative ' irreconcilable Puritan ', but such facts as he has been able to elucidate from the public records and other contemporary documents hardly bear out this contention. The name of adventurer or soldier of fortune better fits one who proved himself equally ' stout and bold ' in the service of Charles I and of Cromwell, plotted industriously against the restored monarchy, and eventually ended his days at court, the valued agent of the king's government. The records of Blood's life are scanty, his ceaseless but mole-like activities are traceable only by occasional upheavals (p. 53), and surmise has often to supply the lack of knowledge. But his most startling adventures, namely his attack on Ormond, his rescue of his fellow conspirator, John Mason, and his attempted theft of the regalia from the Tower, are here related with full detail, and some light is thrown incidentally on the manifold plots and intrigues that agitated the reign of Charles II. To the daring, resource, wit, and general unscrupulousness of the titular colonel ample justice is done, but the motives of his actions remain, as ever, shrouded in mystery; and though various conjectures are offered no conclusive explanation is found for the pardon and reward of a man convicted, on his own confession, of such notorious crimes. The book, of less than a hundred pages in all, concludes with a full list of authorities and a note on the existing portraits of its subject, one of which is reproduced as the frontispiece.　　　　　　　　　　　　　　　　　　　　　　　　　　E. S.

In his paper on *Die Besteuerung des Tabaks in Ansbach-Bayreuth und Bamberg-Würzburg im 18. Jahrhundert* (*Abhandlungen der philologisch-historischen Klasse der Königl. Sächsischen Gesellschaft der Wissenschaften*, xxix. 4, Leipzig : Teubner, 1911), Professor W. Stieda rather misstates his case in ascribing the failures of some 'enlightened despots' in this branch of fiscal exploitation to personal circumstances or the smallness of their territories. The contradictory justification of the tobacco tax as an impost on luxuries, and at the same time as a measure of state control over articles of consumption, could then no more than nowadays cover a crude attempt of cheating the consumers either jointly with, or over the heads of, the merchants. Even the mildest system of the three to be distinguished among Professor Stieda's materials, the Ansbach 'Konzessionsgeld' of 1741, a simple trade impost, did not outlast the century, and the tobacco monopolies, whether purely commercial as the earliest in Bayreuth (1701) or manufacturing as those granted by the prodigal bishops of Würzburg and Bamberg (1737–55 and again 1761–79), exhibit all the vices of a government's taking part in the speculative first steps of privileged capitalism.　　　　　　　　　　　　C. B.

Mr. J. A. Lovat-Fraser's little book, *John Stuart, Earl of Bute* (Cambridge: University Press, 1912), is an attempt to represent Bute as 'an interesting and almost pathetic figure'; it does not show cause for any alteration in the opinion which historians generally hold concerning him. Its value as a contribution to historical biography may be gauged by its omission to record George III's offer of the seals to Bute in the earliest days of the reign, or the earl's admission into the cabinet, and by its treatment of the representation to the king by Newcastle, Devonshire, and Hardwicke, in favour of Bute's appointment to office in March 1761, as a matter of some uncertainty, dependent only on the king's recollection many years later. That Bute was 'not anxious for ministerial position' is contrary to what we know from the Newcastle Papers; he was hoping to attain it, as soon as the opportune time came, as early as 18 January, when he employed or allowed that meddlesome intriguer Viri to broach the subject to Newcastle. Mr. Lovat-Fraser has apparently written his book without consulting any manuscript authorities.　　　　　　　　　　　　　　　　W. H.

The *Life of Prince Joseph Poniatowski*, by Professor Simon Askenazy, of which a notice appeared in this Review in October 1910 (pp. 787–8), has now been translated into German by Herr Julius Tenner (*Fürst*

Joseph Poniatowski, 1763-1813, Gotha : F. A. Perthes, 1912). This new edition is not only in a tongue more intelligible to western European readers, but it has useful brief summaries of the contents of the chapters, and is fuller and more correct in some matters of detail than the Polish original. The style is easy and agreeable, and the book deserves the attention of all students of the Napoleonic period, who will find in the supplementary notes (pp. 273-365) a great deal of hitherto unpublished material. O. W.

In *Souvenirs et Fragments*, tome iii (Paris: Picard, 1911), the Marquis de Bouillé (Louis-Joseph-Amour) describes the end of a not very eventful career. Formerly fighting for the *émigrés*, he in the early days of the Napoleonic empire regained his position in the French army and saw service in the Neapolitan campaign of 1806. He notes the special features of the siege of Gaëta, namely, the sapping up to the distance of eighty fathoms of the walls without firing a shot, a device which proved effective owing to the firmness of the troops and the skill of the engineers. On the other hand, his account of the battle of Maida is vague ; it gives no notion of the fierce fighting that went on at close quarters for a brief space. Also, to say (p. 28) that the British volleys brought down 1,500 Frenchmen is an exaggeration—as bad as that of Reynier in estimating the total British force at 13,000 men. Bouillé, however, rightly censures Reynier's fault in leaving a strong position to attack the enemy in one scarcely less strong ; and he does justice to the firmness of the defence. Bouillé was transferred to Spain in 1808. His account of Talavera is vitiated by his estimate of nearly 80,000 men for the allies and only 40,000 for the French. The account of the final British attacks which decided the day is also quite vague ; and though the criticisms on Jourdan and the French generals (pp. 251-4) are deserved, those on Wellesley suffer from the defect noted above and from the author's lack of clearness as to the details of the fighting. His final comment, that Talavera did not lead to much, loses sight of the fact that the Spaniards at Talavera, and their forces operating nominally in support of Wellesley, contributed little or no support at the crises which arose. Criticism which leaves out of count facts of prime importance is obviously of no value. The rout of the Spaniards by Soult at Ocaña is better described ; but the action of the French cavalry was so brilliant and decisive as to call for little description and no explanation. Bouillé's sight, which was impaired during the siege of Tarifa, vanished entirely towards the end of the campaign of 1812. On hearing of the occupation of Moscow by Napoleon, he foretold his ruin. But by that time Bouillé's views were sombre in the extreme. At the end of this volume he hints at the trials and hardships of his later years, to escape from which was partly his aim in dictating these memoirs. The fact explains their shadowiness at many points, and the acrid comments on several Frenchmen, notably General Sébastiani on pp. 413-18. Sébastiani did not owe his advancement merely to the fact that he was a Corsican. Napoleon never favoured his countrymen so far as to advance to high office one who was so incompetent, intriguing, and avaricious as is here represented. At several points notes are needed for correction of misstatements in the text; but the editor, M. P. L. de Kermaingant, has contributed a good preface, which serves as an introduction to the three volumes of the Bouillé memoirs now concluded.　　　　　　　　　　　　　　　　C.

Each fresh instalment of the *Dickson MSS.* (Royal Artillery Institution, Woolwich) provides convincing proof of their value. The latest part—chapter vii of series ' C '—covers the period from 1 July to 30 September 1813, and is mainly concerned with the siege and capture of San Sebastian, of which it gives many valuable details, including several plans and illustrations. The work of the Royal Artillery during the siege was certainly excellent, and Dickson's description of the way in which the guns fired over the heads of the stormers and beat down the fire of the defenders of the breach (p. 997) is specially noteworthy. There was good reason for the ' admiration and surprise of Sir Thomas Graham and Marshal Beresford and all who beheld it '. Of the fighting in the Pyrenees comparatively little is said, though the letters of Captain Cairnes, R.A., given on pp. 1014, 1032, and 1046, throw a little light on those operations. A notable thing is the very high praise Cairnes gives to Lord Dalhousie (cf. p. 1017), a divisional general of whom Napier says nothing that would lead one to expect the statement that 'our Peer (i.e. Dalhousie) is the man Lord W. is said to confide in ' (p. 1035). One may also add that Cairnes confirms the statement that the artillery played a decisive part in the French defeat at Vittoria (cf. p. 1016). Major Leslie has, as usual, edited the chapter with the greatest care and accuracy.　　　　　　　　　　　　　　　　C. T. A.

The period of French history (1814–48) covered by Professor Georges Weill's *La France sous la Monarchie constitutionnelle* (Paris : Alcan, 1912), though forming an interval of depression between two epochs of French military hegemony in Europe, was far from being for that country itself the age of mere material prosperity and moral inertia for which it is sometimes dismissed. Whether in literature or religion, in activity intellectual, industrial, or economic, few generations even in France have been more fertile in notable men and movements : and even where such movements partook of the nature of a backwater, rather than a forward-flowing current, there was at least no such stagnancy of thought as some have surmised from Lamartine's too familiar dictum, ' La France s'ennuie '. The revival of French catholicism, the birth of French romanticism, the common intellectual atmosphere which rendered both those movements possible ; the accomplishment of what was in effect for France a belated industrial revolution; most of all, perhaps, the economic and social theories in which a credulous generation sought crude remedies for hardships inflicted on the working classes in the process of this industrial transformation : all these, together with the several conditions of social life in Paris and the provinces during the period, deserve and receive at M. Weill's hands lucid and illuminating exposition ; an exposition to which his brief chapters on the actual political history of the three reigns form no more than a necessary introduction. The present edition is furnished, as its predecessor was not, with references to authorities; it contains also an index and a really serviceable bibliography.　　　　　　　　　　　　F. A. S.

The *Acte Additionnel aux Constitutions de l'Empire du 22 Avril 1815* has attracted perhaps less notice than any other part of Napoleon's legislation. M. Léon Radiguet, in his work on the subject (Paris : Marchal & Godde, 1911), has been fortunate in discovering a comparatively fresh theme, and has left little to be said by those who come after him. Strictly impartial he is not, for he is a frank Bonapartist who regards the Napoleonic system as better suited to French character and French history than any other. But he is laborious and generally accurate. He begins with analysing public opinion in France at the close of the empire. The soldiers, the workmen, and the peasants, he maintains, still clung to Napoleon with unabated fervour. But the middle and upper classes were alienated. Still vividly remembering the Revolution, they abhorred democracy as well as despotism, and once more turned for inspiration to England. A balanced constitutional monarchy in which wealth and education should have the casting vote was their ideal. Napoleon had not changed and he did not mean to repudiate his past. But at Paris almost all who surrounded him were imbued with the fashionable liberalism. He feared lest, if he leant on the people, he should become the creature of the Jacobins. He hoped by proclaiming himself a constitutional monarch to mitigate the hostility of Europe and strengthen the opposition in England. With visible reluctance, therefore, he lent himself to the movement for constitutional reform. M. Radiguet then traces in detail the genesis of the Acte Additionnel and the parts played by the imperial commission, by Benjamin Constant, and by Napoleon himself. He analyses and discusses at length the essential clauses of the instrument. As its name implies, it was not a complete constitution, but a somewhat incongruous appendix to the constitutions of the empire. It was a compromise between the mutually repugnant principles of the emperor and of the liberals. The liberals, for the most part, received it coldly ; the pure Bonapartists and Jacobins disliked it ; the royalists of course denounced it, and the bulk of the nation showed itself indifferent. Among Napoleon's advisers Carnot was the most averse to the Acte Additionnel. He declared that it would weaken the emperor in the impending struggle. On the other hand, Sismondi, a disinterested liberal, wrote strongly in defence of it, and believed Napoleon sincere in his concessions. M. Radiguet says truly that the working of the Acte Additionnel would have depended on the strength of the ruler. We may add that Napoleon was of all men the least likely to accept the restraint of any constitutional system. Looking back upon the Acte Additionnel and the charter in the light of history, we can see that the French liberals were really weak in numbers. They did not understand their countrymen as well as Napoleon did. Had Napoleon returned victorious, a new process of revision would almost certainly have restored personal government. F. C. M.

Good, 'popular' histories of recent events are not too plentiful. Mr. Oscar Browning's *History of the Modern World, 1815-1912* (London : Cassell, 1912) is not only well informed but full of life and spirit, and its descriptions of the wars of the last century are excellent reading. It is, however, rather proportioned by the personal interests of the author than by the relative importance of events, and the reader is given no help in the form of maps or bibliographies. It is a misfortune that the chapters dealing with English history are saturated by political partisanship. Mr. Browning's volumes are sufficiently sound and interesting to make this feature regrettable. G. B. H.

Few royal correspondences have equalled in the intimacy and closeness of their personal touch the *Briefwechsel zwischen König Johann von Sachsen und den Königen Friedrich Wilhelm IV und Wilhelm I von Preussen*, edited by Prince John George of Saxony, with the co-operation of Dr. Hubert Ermisch (Leipzig: Quelle & Meyer, 1911); and still fewer of them have possessed that indescribable charm which belongs to the confidences of equals assiduously trained in religious thought, in political philosophy, and in the art of literature. From this it may seem a descent to note that, in the case of Frederick William IV of Prussia, whose nature was far more exuberant than that of his friend and brother-in-law King John of Saxony, and of course very much more complex than was that of his own brother, the late Emperor William I, there was to be expected an amount of excellent fooling alien to most crowned letter-writers. His pen spares neither the gout of King George IV nor the 'Neronic' propensities of Duke Charles of Brunswick; it falls foul of the *Deutschkatholiken* and gibes at the ducal 'victor of Eckernförde'; and it brings perfectly to mind by a single touch the personality of a celebrated Greek Testament scholar: *il jase un peu beaucoup*. But it also has at its command a wealth of caressing affectionateness of speech, a sort of 'little language' of its own, which is singularly touching. The descendants of King John of Saxony have rightly judged that the portrait of their honoured ancestor would lose nothing either in truthfulness or in dignity by the human touch which it acquires from this living record of a lifelong friendship. Whatever may be the poetic qualities of King John's translation of Dante—and that they are worth argument is something—there can be no doubt whatever of its enduring merits as a historical study. But it is by no means as a man of letters or as a professor only that this sovereign of high moral sympathies and wide intellectual interests will live in the memory of a faithful people. His reign was not fortunate; and before it began he had been (something like the late Emperor William I when Prince of Prussia, though with even less reason) furiously unpopular, though he manfully took part in carrying out a parliamentary system of government; while his German policy was from first to last too frankly *Grossdeutsch* to suit the working of the needle of destiny. Thus, after suffering much obloquy in his earlier days, in his later he had nearly lost a kingdom. That such was not the case is hardly to be ascribed to his long and unselfish friendship with King Frederick William, with whose successor he was always on the most loyal as well as amicable terms, though in German politics they never marched abreast. Frederick William had, perhaps, often been more inclined to follow his advice than this correspondence may show; but it was by no means only in the direction of restraint that in the eventful years preceding his own accession to the throne King John advised his brother-in-law ; to whom no sounder counsel was ever tendered than that of never doing anything for the consistent execution of which he did not feel sufficient strength in himself and in the circumstances of the time. Frederick William IV, with all his noble and much underrated qualities, never attained to the consciousness either of himself or of his opportunities which is the beginning of successful action.　　A. W. W.

The new edition of Dr. Edwin Cannan's *History of Local Rates in England*, so far as the historical section is concerned, is a reprint with a few corrections and omissions of the original edition of 1896. That gave, and still gives, the only satisfactory narrative that we have of the local rate as an institution and ' why and how local taxation in England came to be confined to immovable property '. It was written from a particular point of view—that history in general, economic history in particular, ' a subject so dry not to say odious as local rates ' in a very eminent degree, should afford ' some moral, some lesson, or guidance '. Following out this doctrine, to which the first edition did not perfectly conform, three purely economic chapters are now added on The Local Ratepayer against the National Taxpayer, The Equity of Local Rates, and The Economy of Local Rates. Dr. Cannan made his 'dry not to say odious' subject uncommonly interesting, and his first-hand knowledge of the working of contemporary local government gives a precision to his handling and a value to his judgements that are often wanting in the conscientious economic history of writers inadequately provided with modern economic knowledge.　　J. H. C.

Mr. F. W. Hirst's new edition of Porter's *Progress of the Nation* (London : Methuen, 1912) is a most valuable storehouse of facts, mainly statistical, with regard to every aspect of the economic and social history of the United Kingdom since 1800. As Porter wrote his book in 1836, and no new edition has been published since 1851, the larger and more useful part of the present volume is due to the editor's own knowledge and diligence. It must be admitted that many of his tables are not carried sufficiently down to date to be of much service to practical politicians. Some close with the year 1903 ; others with 1905, 1906, and so forth. Few go further than 1909. In every case, however, the nineteenth century is dealt with to its termination, and the historian of that period in this country's history must be grateful for the collection of such diverse materials in handy form. It ranges from topics like wages, pauperism, crime, education, to most detailed surveys of every trade and industry. In chapters on the rising standard of comfort and on national expenditure and debt from 1850 to 1910, Mr. Hirst writes more as a publicist than as a statistician, and his opinions, already well known to readers of *The Economist*, will be studied with interest. Though the political conclusions to which the book point are plainly put, they hardly ever affect its judicious temper. Mr. Hirst's justification of coal exports (pp. 223 and 522) is very ingenious. The analytical index has been well compiled.　　G. B. H.

Two recent numbers of the Columbia University *Studies in History, Economics, and Public Law* are Miss Esther Lowenthal's *The Ricardian Socialists* (1911) and Dr. Louis Levine's *The Labour Movement in France* (1912). The former contains a full and careful analysis of the opinions of William Thompson, John Gray, Thomas Hodgskin, and John Francis Bray. Points in their teaching made familiar to students of the history of economic thought by Professor Foxwell in his preface to Menger's *Right to the Whole Produce of Labour*, or, in the case of Thompson, by Adolf Held in his *Soziale Geschichte Englands*, are elaborated, and a number of fresh points are brought out. Judging from the treatment of Thompson, whose main work runs to six hundred prolix pages, Miss Lowenthal may be thoroughly trusted as a summarist. The incidental comparisons of these socialistic thinkers with the classical economists on the one hand and Marx on the other are always useful and at times illuminating; but no special knowledge is shown of the age in which they lived, and the introductory chapter, called ' The Period ', contains in its four pages as many blunders, including the date 1842 for ' the repeal of the duties on corn '.

Dr. Levine has added a substantial volume to the short list of impartial studies of the French labour movement during the last twenty years. About a third of the book (69 pages) is devoted to events before 1892, rather less than a third to events since 1902. The more purely historical chapters at the beginning are based on a few well-known monographs. They are probably a necessary part of the book, but they add nothing to what is already known. The more important chapters deal with matters that have hardly yet become part of history—the Bourses du Travail, Syndicalism, the ' C.G.T.' and the theorists of the movement. Here there is a great deal of useful material and a conclusive refutation of the view popularized by Professor Sombart, that M. Georges Sorel and his disciples ' " created " the theory of revolutionary socialism ' which has gained support among the syndicates. In his narrative Dr. Levine gives more space to resolutions of congresses and less to the syndicates themselves, their daily work, and economic environment than one could wish. But this parliamentary history of the contemporary labour movement is valuable and is probably the only kind possible to a foreigner. Confidence in the absolute accuracy of the picture is somewhat weakened by several odd bits of translation from the French. The style of French parliamentary resolutions, with its abstract terminology, its ' considerings that ', and its ' passings to the order of the day ', is not easily rendered into English; but the renderings both of resolutions and of other matter are often unnecessarily literal, and sometimes suggest that the original was not perfectly understood. Dr. Levine tells us in one place that M. Sorel's ' main claim is " profundity ". The pages of his work bristle with the word *approfondir* ' (p. 147). Later we learn that Sorel has abandoned syndicalism and declared that he means ' to employ the remaining years of his life in the deepening (*approfondir*) of other questions which keenly interest the cultivated youth of France '. This suggests a misunderstanding of a very ordinary use of *approfondir*. But there is no reason to distrust Dr. Levine's general results or to under-estimate the value of a careful piece of work.

J. H. C.

To most readers the primary attraction of *Chawton Manor and its Owners*, by Messrs. William Austen Leigh and Montagu George Knight of Chawton (London: Smith, Elder & Co., 1911), will consist in the association of the place with Jane Austen. Her brother Edward was adopted by a distant kinsman, Thomas Knight, and succeeded him at Chawton. Here Jane settled with her mother and sister in 1809 in a small house in the village, and here she wrote the greater part of her books. But this by no means represents the real interest of the volume. Chawton Manor has only once changed hands by way of sale since the Norman Conquest. That was in 1578, and John Knight, the son of the purchaser, began to build the existing house a few years later. Though since that time the property has passed through several families, the old name and traditions have always been preserved. The history of such a house cannot fail to be interesting, the more so since each successive family has brought with it a store of new associations. The authors have done justice to their subject, and rendered good service in showing how much history may gather round a house which has never been the home of a man of the first distinction. Amongst the many documents which they quote, one of exceptional interest is Sir Christopher Lewkenor's long report of his gallant endeavour to hold Chichester for the king in December 1642 (pp. 99–113). Though Lewkenor himself was not connected with Chawton, his grandchildren succeeded to it. The charm of the book is much enhanced by the beautiful illustrations and reproductions of family portraits.

C. L. K.

Dr. Andrew Clark's *English Register of Godstow Nunnery* (London: Early English Text Society), the third and final part of which was published in 1911, is the most important addition to our knowledge of monastic life in England that has been made since Dr. Willis Clark issued the *Liber Memorandorum* of Barnwell. We do not find the avarice of a monastery at its worst candidly exposed as we do at Barnwell: a register of deeds cannot display motives and methods, and we have no right to assume that Benedictine nuns were as grasping as that particular body of Austin canons. But the process by which religious houses were enriched is admirably illustrated, as in the case of Wycombe, in Buckinghamshire, where the series of deeds relating to the tithe is very full; Dr. Clark, however, nowhere tells us with which Wycombe we are concerned. The causes which led to donations are often stated, and we can watch the process by which a house which never received any large grant steadily accumulated quite a comfortable property. There are many points of interest for general history. In 1346, on the eve of the black death, the parishioners of Bloxham were clearing their share of Wychwood Forest for cultivation; in 1284 a composition was made in which the wardship of lands, which in 1540 were worth £4 a year, was valued at a mark on each vacancy of the abbey. Dr. Clark has written a very full and interesting introduction to the *Register*, which contains a few disputable assertions. His definition of 'burgage' will not stand; free tenants often enough paid service as well as rent; his account of tithe of *novale* would have been improved had he consulted Schreiber's *Kurie und Kloster im zwölften Jahrhundert*, which, however, may have been published too late. It is a little doubtful whether a weekly dole of a half-quarter of meslin, claimed by the poor of Bloxham from Godstow, can be regarded as a church scot. It was a share of the rectorial tithe, which Henry II had granted to the abbey, and some explanation relevant to that fact is needed. Dr. Clark is interesting, if not quite convincing, on the inefficiency of the statute of mortmain; he regards *Quia emptores* as much more effective. But the points of interest in this learned edition of an important text are countless. The book is carefully printed (though *prebendinaverint* on p. lxxxiii should be *perhendinaverint*) and admirably indexed. D.

In the *Catalogue of Oxford Portraits* (Oxford : Clarendon Press, 1912) Mrs. R. L. Poole gives a large first instalment of a difficult and long-needed work. That Oxford is rich in portraits and busts has all along been plain to every visitor; but how rich in number, and how varied in interest, even long residents have never suspected. In the present volume no fewer than 770 examples are dealt with, and yet it confines itself to the official collections of the university, of the town hall, and the county hall, leaving the treasures of the colleges to succeeding volumes. Few great artists are represented, but there are excellent examples of many lesser men, and the list of known painters is increased by several names, especially of local artists. The portraits are by no means of exclusively Oxford interest. There was long a laudable ambition on the part of Oxford men to provide their university with pictures of men famous in history, scholarship, letters, and science. Thus Oxford comes to have striking likenesses of Frederick the Great, Napoleon, Cecil Lord Burghley, Martin Frobisher, Clive, Flora Macdonald, Erasmus, Casaubon, Chaucer, Gower, Samuel Butler, Sir Walter Scott, Shelley, D. G. Rossetti, Galilei, Réaumur. The most remarkable series of portraits, that of the musicians, is practically unknown even to Oxford residents, by reason of its being hung on the walls of the room sacred to the meetings of the council of the university. Here are thirty-nine portraits, ranging from Orlando Lassus (d. 1594) to Sir John Stainer (d. 1901). The description of every picture or bust includes a severely compressed but exact biographical notice of the subject, an accurate technical account of the painting, a critical examination of its provenance, and a statement of the way in which it came to Oxford. Each description is the result of careful study of the picture or bust and of university records and account-books. Photographic reproductions of eighty-one of the portraits are given. Some of them are rather repellent at first glance, but careful examination shows that even these are most exact in detail. Several are pleasing as mere photographs, as well as accurate in reminiscence of the original, the full-length of Sir Henry Savile, for instance, and Sir Joshua Reynolds's James Paine and his son. There is an excellent introduction, and three admirable indexes—of persons portrayed, of artists, and of former owners. A. C.

In giving to the public Blowfield's hitherto unknown *Survey of Oxford in 1772* (London : Frowde, 1912), with four contemporary plans of the eastern and northern approaches and of the central block of the city, equipped with a good index, the Rev. H. Salter has made a notable addition to the study of Oxford topography. The *Survey* not only provides a complete outline for a directory of the principal residents and tradespeople of eighteenth-century Oxford, which college account-books will go far towards filling up, but it gives the sorely needed link between modern and ancient Oxford. In 1772 the civic authorities, instead of placing their new market on one of the ample and convenient sites just outside their ancient precincts, and opening wider approaches at points where the damage to the circuit of the walls would have been slight, built over pleasant garden-grounds in the very heart of the town and swept away an old suburban church, a medieval bridge, two ancient city gates, and a network of quaint suburban lanes. The town was thus cruelly shorn of features which would have now rendered it the very gem of English cities. Blowfield's *Survey* was taken, street by street, house by house, before these violent changes. It thus gives us back the Oxford of Anthony Wood, and of the civil war, and goes far to explain the cartularies of the religious houses which formerly owned most tenements in the city and its suburbs. The editor's preface gives a clear account of the manuscript authorities, and of the questions which arise out of them. His identifications of streets and houses are marked by his habitual exactness of knowledge and terseness of statement. A. C.

Mr. J. T. Evans in his works on the church plate of Pembrokeshire, Carmarthenshire, and Gloucestershire has already proved himself an industrious and accomplished antiquary. That on *The Church Plate of Radnorshire* (Stow-on-the-Wold : Alden, 1910) is much more than a catalogue of church plate. The ample foot-notes give all sorts of miscellaneous information about charities, folklore, derivations of names, inscriptions, church furniture generally, and acts perpetrated under the name of 'restoration'. Thus under Llansanffraid Cwmtoyddwr the interesting inscription on the wrought-iron screen is duly recorded : ' Er gogoniant Daw ac er parchus goffadwriaeth am y diwedd[ar] David Oliver. . . .' The best folklore comes from Cascob. Some of it is not unfamiliar, such as keeping 'Good Friday-bread' as a protection against sundry evils. But people always sleeping with their feet towards the east is new to us. Mr. Evans's derivation of the name of his own parish of Stow-on-the-Wold (formerly 'Edward's Stow'), as the place where St. Edward's relics were *stowed* is, we venture to suggest, somewhat crudely expressed. 'Stow', a place, and 'stow', to put away, are no doubt etymologically connected, but the name surely meant St. Edward's place. The churches of Radnorshire cannot be said to possess sacramental plate of any great interest. There is nothing of medieval date and the post-Reformation work is ordinary. But it is sufficient. There are seven Elizabethan cups, of which the earliest are dated 1576, although the undated cup at Norton may be earlier. Mr. Evans notes the particulars in which these examples differ both in their decoration and their marks from contemporary work in Pembroke and Carmarthen, but defers inquiry into origins (only, we hope, until he has catalogued the nearer counties). It is, of course, common to find plate of this period with the maker's mark only, but one Radnor cup was assayed at London and one unmarked piece of later date (1624) is 'almost identical' in shape with a cup at All Hallows in Lombard Street. The history of the early plate has no doubt been made more difficult to unravel by most of the persons in one district having in recent times (under the influence of the archdeacon) remodelled their cups on would-be medieval lines. For the rest there is a rather early baluster-stem cup (1596) and two pieces of Cromwellian age. Our author is practical, and gives some good general hints to intending purchasers (p. xxi). The volume concludes with chantry certificates (2 Edward VI), some lists of bells, county families, and so forth, and 'an essay on the primitive saints of Radnorshire' by the Rev. A. W. Wade-Evans, prefaced by some account of the creation of the county by Henry VIII in 1536, and an index. E.

The first number of a new local archaeological periodical, *Annales d'Avignon et du Comtat-Venaissin*, 1ère année, no. 1, 1912, published quarterly by the Société des Recherches historiques de Vaucluse (Paris : Champion ; Avignon : Roumanille), will usefully supplement the series of large volumes issued by the same society, some of which have already been noticed in these pages. The first 'fascicule' contains a large number of short notices and documents. Perhaps the one most interesting outside the locality is a supplication from the municipal archives of Avignon which throws light on Du Guesclin's dealings with the city in 1368. There are some useful architectural photographs to the topographical notes. T. F. T.

M. René Gadave's work entitled *Les Documents sur l'Histoire de l'Université de Toulouse et spécialement de sa Faculté de Droit Civil et Canonique* (1229–1789) (Toulouse : Privat, 1910) is a catalogue of documents with references to the places where those which have been printed *in extenso* are to be found. To the 180 documents relating to the faculty of law printed by M. Fournier Dr. Gadave has been able to add references to 97 others. There is a long introduction dealing carefully and fully with the various libraries and manuscript collections from which the documents are derived and with the bibliography of the university—a university upon which much has been written, though there is no actual history of it in a separate form. The present work seems to be very well done.
H. R.

In *La Zélande, Étude Historio-Géographique* (Liège : Poncelet, 1911) M. Auguste Havenith has furnished a very useful account of the geographical and historical evolution of the province of Zealand. As he rightly observes, a study of the ancient geology and geography of the district is essential to an understanding of its history. The relations of land and water have here been changed again and again through the encroachments of the sea, and through the labours of the inhabitants. M. Havenith has traced out the process with much care, and though his book deals in the first place with local history, it has also a much wider interest. The shifting of the commercial mouth of the Scheldt has had from time to time a great influence on the prosperity and relative importance of the Flemish cities. It was only in the latter part of the middle ages that the West Scheldt, as it now exists, was formed, and became the principal mouth of the river. To have this shown is to explain how and why Ghent and Bruges have decayed from their former greatness. To the English student of medieval history it is of particular interest to have so clear a statement of the position of the Swyn, and of the old importance of Sluys. M. Havenith has brought his narrative down to the present time. A large map illustrates well the existing conditions and latest change. It would have been useful to have some smaller maps to show the older conditions. M. Havenith (p. 104) describes some ancient maps which have been useful in establishing his conclusion that Ghent had originally direct communication with the sea. C. L. K.

In *Historical Research, an Outline of Theory and Practice* (New York: Holt, 1911), Professor J. M. Vincent of Johns Hopkins University puts together the essential rudiments of historical method and source criticism on lines suggested by Bernheim. There is no doubt a public of beginners in historical investigation, especially in America, for which a readable and not unstimulating survey will be found useful. The doctrine expounded by the author is as a rule quite sound. It may, however, be permitted to doubt whether Mr. Vincent is not sometimes almost too general and indefinite for the requirements of the serious student, and whether, in the attempt to say something about everything, he has not treated his various sections in insufficient detail. To take one instance, how can it profit any man to be told that the ' color [of wax in seals] was sometimes a matter of privilege. In the fifteenth century red wax was permitted to favored persons by royal grant. Up to that time red had been retained exclusively for royal or imperial seals ' ? There are some curious mistakes, as for example on ' Sir William Wallace ' on p. 30, and on p. 126, where Froissart, a beneficed clerk, ' gained,' we are told, ' the rank of knighthood '. The reflexions on ' scholastic sophisms ' on p. 137 are not illuminating, and the ' Guacciadim ' of p. 140 is a weird misprint for Guicciardini. Medieval technique is not always strongly represented in the book, but there are some useful comments on traditional errors, forgeries, and legends. Some of the modern illustrations are distinctly happy, and the broad sweep from palaeolithic man to our own day is really valuable. T. F. T.

INDEX

TO

THE TWENTY-SEVENTH VOLUME

ARTICLES, NOTES, AND DOCUMENTS

ABACUS, The, and the king's curia: by Professor Haskins, 101

Anglo-French peace negotiations of 1806: by Colonel E. M. Lloyd, 753

BACON, Roger, The missing part of his *Opus Tertium*: by A. G. Little, 318

Balearic Islands, The, and France in 1840: by C. N. Scott, 330

Bernstorff, Struensee and the fall of: by W. F. Reddaway, 274

Burgundian notes, ii: Cisalpinus and Constantinus: by R. L. Poole, 299

Burke, Windham, and Pitt, i: by J. Holland Rose, 700

Bury St. Edmunds and Westminster, Papal visitation of, in 1234: by Miss R. Graham, 728

CABINET and privy council, Inner and outer [1679-1783]: by H. W. V. Temperley, 682

Castlereagh and the Spanish colonies: by C. K. Webster, 78

Chancellor and keeper of the seal under Henry III: by Miss L. B. Dibben, 39

Charlottenburg, The treaty of: by J. F. Chance, 52

Clarendon and the privy council [1660-7]: by E. I. Carlyle, 251

DIVORCE of Henry VIII, German opinion of the: by Preserved Smith, 671

EUSTACE the Monk and the battle of Sandwich: by H. L. Cannon, 649

Exeter Domesday, The: by the Hon. F. H. Baring, 309

Ezelo's Life of Hugh of Cluny: by Miss L. M. Smith, 96

FELSTED, Essex, Copyhold tenure at: by the Rev. A. Clark, 517

Forest laws, The, and the death of William Rufus: by the late F. H. M. Parker, 26

Fortescue, Sir John, in February 1461: by Miss C. L. Scofield, 321

France, Documents relating to the rupture with, in 1793: by J. Holland Rose, 117, 324

France and the Balearic Islands in 1840: by C. N. Scott, 330

GALILEE, The reigning princes of: by H. Pirie-Gordon, 445

HARDYNG'S *Chronicle*, The first version of: by C. L. Kingsford, 462, 740

Henry Symeonis: by R. L. Poole, 515

JERUSALEM, The restoration of the Cross at: by Norman H. Baynes, 287

Justices of the peace, The powers of: by C. G. Crump and C. Johnson, 226

MADAGASCAR, An English settlement in [1645-6]: by W. Foster, 239

Magna Carta, Studies in, i: Waynagium and Contenementum: by Professor J. Tait, 720

NEW Forest, The making of the: by the Hon. F. H. Baring, 513
Normandy under Geoffrey Plantagenet: by Professor Haskins, 417
Northern affairs in 1724: by J. F. Chance, 483

PENENDEN trial, A report on the: by W. Levison, 717
Philip Augustus and the archbishop of Rouen: by Professor Powicke, 106

SANDWICH, The battle of, and Eustace the Monk: by H. L. Cannon, 649
Struensee and the fall of Bernstorff: by W. F. Reddaway, 274

THORNEY Island, The Danes at, in 893: by Professor F. M. Stenton, 512
Tribal Hidage, The: by J. Brownbill, 625

WESTMINSTER and Bury St. Edmunds, Papal visitation of, in 1234: by Miss R. Graham, 728
William the Conqueror's march to London in 1066: by G. J. Turner, 209

YORKSHIRE surveys and other eleventh-century documents in the York Gospels: by W. H. Stevenson, 1

ZERMATT, The names of: by the Rev. W. A. B. Coolidge, 522

LIST OF REVIEWS OF BOOKS

ABBOT (W. C.) *Colonel Thomas Blood, crown-stealer*, 821

Acts and ordinances of the Interregnum [1649–60], ed. by C. H. Firth and R. S. Rait: by G. B. Tatham, 161

Acts of the privy council of England, colonial series, iv [1745–66], 197

Adams (G. B.) *The origin of the English constitution*, 807

Angot (E.) *Mélanges d'histoire*, 616

Angyal (D.) *Le traité de paix de Szeged avec les Turcs*, 191

Annales d'Avignon et du Comtat-Venaissin, i, 832

Anson (Sir W. R.) *Law and Custom of the constitution*, i., 4th ed., reissue, 204

Anson (W. V.) *The life of lord Anson*, 606

Archaeologia Aeliana, 3rd ser., vii: by the Rev. President of Trinity College, Oxford, 589

Armitage (Mrs. E.) *The early Norman castles of the British Isles*: by J. H. Round, 544

Askenazy (S.) *Fürst Joseph Poniatowski* [1763–1813] (Germ. tr.), 822

Atteridge (A. H.) *Joachim Murat*, 609
—— *Napoleon's brothers*, 4

BACON (Roger) *Compendium Studii Theologiae*, ed. by H. Rashdall: by W. H. V. Reade, 150

Bagshawe (F. G.) *History of the royal family of England*, 808

Bapst (G.) *Le maréchal Canrobert*, v: by W. B. Wood, 797

Baptist Historical Society Transactions, viii, 392

Barbagallo (C.) *Lo stato e l'istruzione pubblica nell' impero romano*, 182

Barham (Charles, lord) *Letters and papers*, ed. by Sir J. K. Laughton, iii: by the Rev. W. Hunt, 379

Bastide (C.) *Anglais et Français du XVII*e *siècle*, 819

Beck (F.) *Der Karlsgraben*, 806

Belcher (H.) *The first American Civil War*: by the Rev. W. Hunt, 378

Benedicti (Sancti) *Regula monachorum*: ed. by C. Butler, 592

Berr (H.) *La synthèse en histoire*, 181

Blok (P. J.) *Geschiedenis eener Hollandsche stad*: by Professor Unwin, 178

Blomfield (R.) *A history of French architecture from the reign of Charles VIII till the death of Mazarin*: by Professor Lethaby, 353

Bouillé (L. J. A., marquis de) *Souvenirs et fragments*, iii, 823

Bourgeois (E.) *La diplomatie secrète au XVIII*e *siècle; ses débuts*, iii: by E. Armstrong, 167

Bourgin (G. & H.) *Le socialisme français de 1789 à 1848*, 607

Bratli (C.) *Philippe II, roi d'Espagne*, 818

Brauns (C.) *Kurhessische Gewerbepolitik im 17. und 18. Jahrhundert*, 407

Bretholz (B.) *Lateinische Paläographie* (2nd ed.), 591

Brett (A. C. A.) *Charles II and his court*, 196

Brinkmann (C.) *Wustrau*, 207

Brissot (J. P.) *Mémoires* [1754–93], ed. by C. Perroud: by Professor Montague, 169

Brom (G.) *Archivalia in Italië belangrijk voor de geschiedenis van Nederland*, ii, 390

Brown (Mary Croom) *Mary Tudor, queen of England*, 402

Browning (O.) *History of the modern world* [1815–1912], 825

Broxap (H.) *The biography of Thomas Deacon the Manchester non-juror*, 196
—— *The great Civil War in Lancashire* [1642–51]: by Miss E. Scott, 369

Brummer (S. D.) *Political history of New York State during the period of the Civil War*, 202

Bruton (F. A.) *The Roman forts at Castleshaw, Second interim report*, 392

Buchon (A.) *Voyage dans l'Eubée, les Îles Ioniennes et les Cyclades en 1841*, ed. by J. Longnon: by W. Miller, 774

Buren, Martin van, Calendar of the papers of, 412

Burghclere (lady) *The life of James, first duke of Ormonde* [1610–88]: by the Rev. R. H. Murray, 783

Burrage (C.) *The early English dissenters* [1550–1641]: by the Rev. W. H. Frere, 570

Bury (J. B.) *A history of the eastern Roman empire from the fall of Irene to the accession of Basil I* [802–67]: by E. W. Brooks, 762
Butler (G. G.) *Colonel St. Paul of Ewart*, 409
Byzantinische Zeitschrift, xix, 3, 4–xxi, 1, 2, 184, 592

Calendar of the fine rolls, i [1272–1307], 188
Calendar of patent rolls, Henry III [1258–66], 597
—— Henry V, ii, 400
Calendar of treasury books, ed. by W. A. Shaw, ii–v [1667–79]: by Professor Firth, 163
Cambridge manuals of literature and science, 618
Cambridge medieval history, i: by G. McN. Rushforth, 538
Camden Miscellany, xii: by J. E. W. Wallis, 388
Cannan (E.) *History of local rates in England*, new ed., 827
Cans (A.) *L'organisation financière du clergé de France à l'époque de Louis XIV*, and *La contribution du clergé de France à l'impôt pendant la seconde moitié du règne de Louis XIV*, 194
Canz (O.) *Philipp Fontana, Erzbischof von Ravenna*, 186
Capgrave (J.) *Ye solace of pilgrimes*, ed. by C. A. Mills: by G. McN. Rushforth, 777
Caron (P.) *Paris pendant la Terreur*, i: by Professor Montague, 170
Cassagne (A.) *La vie politique de François de Chateaubriand*: by G. P. Gooch, 587
Catalogue of tracts of the Civil War and Commonwealth period relating to Wales and the Borders, 404
Catherine de Médicis, *Lettres*, x, suppl. [1537–87]: by E. Armstrong, 154
Cauchie (A.) & Essen (L. van der) *Inventaire des archives farnésiennes de Naples au point de vue de l'histoire des Pays-Bas catholiques*: by Professor Pollard, 572
Champion (P.) *Vie de Charles d'Orléans*: by C. L. Kingsford, 349
Chandos Herald's Life of the Black Prince, ed. by Mildred K. Pope and Eleanor C. Lodge: by Professor Tout, 345

Charmatz (R.) *Oesterreichs innere Geschichte von 1848 bis 1907*: by R. W. Seton-Watson, 385
Chroniken der Stadt Bamberg, ii, ed. by A. Chroust: by Professor Pollard, 153
Chuquet (A.) *Lettres de 1812*, and *Lettres de 1815*, 198
Clarke (M. G.) *Sidelights on Teutonic history during the migration period*, 594
Clemesha (H. W.) *A history of Preston in Amounderness*: by H. H. E. Craster, 771
Cobb (C. S.) *The rationale of ceremonial* [1540–3], 192
Cobham (C. D.) *The patriarchs of Constantinople*, 184
Cole MSS. in the British Museum, Index to the contents of, ed. by G. Gray, 391
Constant (M. G.) *Rapport sur une mission scientifique aux archives d'Autriche et d'Espagne*: by Professor Pollard, 157
Cooper (T. P.) *History of the castle of York*, 622
Cordey (J.) *Les comtes de Savoie et les rois de France* [1329–91]: by Professor Tout, 552
Craik (Sir H.) *Life of Edward earl of Clarendon*: by G. B. Tatham, 370
Crees (J. H. E.) *The reign of the emperor Probus*, 593
Creusen (J.) *Tabulae fontium traditionis Christianae*, 803

Daenell (E.) *Die Spanier in Nordamerika* [1513–1824], 601
De Boer (H. G.) *De Armada van 1689*, 193
De Jongh (H.) *L'ancienne faculté de théologie de Louvain* [1432–1540]: by P. S. Allen, 557
Dickerson (O. M.) *American colonial government* [1696–1765]: by Professor Egerton, 578
Ditchfield (P. H.) *The counties of England, their story and antiquities*, 415
Dobiache-Rojdestvensky (Madame O.) *La vie paroissiale en France au XIIIe siècle*, 398
Doren (A.) *Studien aus der Florentiner Wirthschaftsgeschichte*, ii: by Professor Unwin, 549
Dorien (K.) *Herzog Ernst II. von Koburg*, 203

Driault (E.) *La politique extérieure du Premier Consul, and Austerlitz, la fin du Saint-Empire*: by H. A. L. Fisher, 586

Dublin Parish Register Society Publications, 206

Duchaine (P.) *La franc-maçonnerie belge au XVIIIe siècle*, 408

Du Motey (vicomte) *Un héros de la grande armée*, 610

Dupont (E.) *Le Mont-Saint-Michel inconnu*, 622

Durham (earl of) *Report on the affairs of British North America*, ed. by Sir C. P. Lucas: by Professor Grant, 796

EDLER (F.) *The Dutch republic and the American Revolution*, 197

Edmundson (G.) *Anglo-Dutch rivalry during the first half of the seventeenth century*, 403

Elder (J. R.) *Royal fishery companies of the seventeenth century*, 819

Eppens tho Equart (Abel) *Kroniek*, 818

Evans (J. T.) *The church plate of Radnorshire*, 831

FAIRCHILD (H. P.) *Greek immigration to the United States*, 413

Fedorowicz (W. de) *1809; campagne de Pologne*, i: by C. T. Atkinson, 172

Ferguson (W. S.) *Hellenistic Athens*: by Professor Goligher, 339

Ficker (J.) *Les origines diplomatiques de la guerre de 1870-1*, v, 614

Firth (C. H.) *Cromwell's army*, revised ed., 405

Fisher (E. J.) *New Jersey as a royal province [1738-76]*, 408

Fleury (V.) *Le poète Georges Herwegh*, 201

Fortescue (J. W.) *British statesmen of the Great War [1793-1814]*, 608

Foster (W.) *The English factories in India [1637-41]*, 820

Fowler (W. W.) *The religious experience of the Roman people to the age of Augustus*: by H. Stuart Jones, 340

Franciscan essays, 810

Friedensburg (W.) *Cavour*: by W. Miller, 173

Fueter (E.) *Geschichte der neueren Historiographie*: by G. P. Gooch, 124

GADAVE (R.) *Les documents sur l'histoire de l'université de Toulouse et spécialement de sa faculté de droit civil et canonique [1229-1789]*, 832

Gairdner (J.) *Lollardy and the Reformation in England*, iii: by the Rev. Professor Whitney, 568

Gasquet (F. A.) *Abbot Wallingford; an inquiry into the charges made against him and his monks*, 816

Gaya, *Traité des armes*, ed. by C. ffoulkes, 605

Gemoll (M.) *Die Indogermanen im alten Orient*: by S. A. Cook, 336

Génestal (R.) *Le parage normand*, 596

Genève, *Registres du conseil de*, iii [1477-87], 191

Germany in the nineteenth century, 617

Godfrey (W. H.) *History of architecture in London*, 206

Godstow nunnery, English Register of, ed. by A. Clark, 829

Goes (de Gebroeders van der) *Briefwisseling*, ii [1659-73], 194

Göller (E.) *Die päpstliche Pönitentiarie*, ii. 1, 2, 190

Goldhardt (O.) *Die Gerichtsbarkeit in den Dörfern des mittelalterlichen Hennegaus*, 185

Gooss (R.) *Oesterreichische Staatsverträge; Fürstentum Siebenbürgen*: by Professor A. O. Meyer, 567

Gougaud (L.) *Les Chrétientés celtiques*, 185

Gravesend (Steph. de) *Registrum*, 400

Green (Mrs. J. R.) *The old Irish world*, 804

Green (T. H.) *Four lectures on the Puritan Revolution*, new ed., 821

Greenwood (Alice D.) *Lives of the Hanoverian queens of England*: by D. A. Winstanley, 376

Gubbins (J. H.) *The progress of Japan [1853-71]*: by F. V. Dickins, 175

Guyot (R.) *Le directoire et la paix de l'Europe [1795-9]*: by J. H. Rose, 788

HÄPKE (R.) *Der deutsche Kaufmann in den Niederlanden*, 814

Hagedorn (B.) *Ostfrieslands Handel und Schiffahrt im 16. Jahrhundert*: by Professor Unwin, 360

Halliwell, The township book of, 618

Hannah (I. C.) *The Sussex coast*, 416

Hanotaux (G.) *La fleur des histoires françaises*, 414

INDEX TO THE TWENTY-SEVENTH VOLUME

Hartmann (L. M.) *Geschichte Italiens im Mittelalter*, iii, 2 : by C. W. Previté Orton, 135
Harvey (A.) *The castles and walled towns of England*, 395
Hassall (A.) *Life of Napoleon*, 197
Hauser (H.) *Acta tumultuum Gallicanorum*, 603
Havenith (A.) *La Zélande*, 832
Hay (J. S.) *The amazing emperor Heliogabalus* : by H. Stuart Jones, 535
Henderson (E. F.) *Blücher and the uprising of Prussia against Napoleon* [1806–15], 611
Heywood (W.) *A history of Perugia* : by W. H. Woodward, 177
Historical Society, Transactions of the Royal, 3rd ser., v, 391
Historische Vierteljahrschrift, 1911, 593
Hofmeister (A.) *Studien über Otto von Freising*, 395
Holdsworth (W. S.) *A history of English law*, i–iii : by H. D. Hazeltine, 341
Holland (B.) *Life of Spencer Compton, eighth duke of Devonshire*, 204
Holles (Gervase) *Lincolnshire church notes*, 620
Holmes (T. R.) *Caesar's conquest of Gaul*, 2nd ed. : by H. Stuart Jones, 127
Horsburgh (E. L. S.) *Girolamo Savonarola*, 4th ed., 815
Huan-Chang (C.) *The economic principles of Confucius and his school* : by Professor Bullock, 531
Hugon (Cécile) *Social France in the seventeenth century*, 193
Huygens (Constantijn), *Briefwisseling*, ed. by J. A. Worp, i, 818

JAHNCKE (R.) *Gulielmus Neubrigensis*, 808
Jansen (M.) *Jakob Fugger der reiche*, i. : by E. Armstrong, 564
Jean XXII, *Lettres*, ed. by A. Fayen, ii, 2, 811
Jenkins (Hester D.) *Ibrahim pasha, grand vizir of Suleiman the Magnificent*, 817
Joachimsen (P.) *Geschichtsauffassung und Geschichtschreibung in Deutschland unter dem Einfluss des Humanismus*, i, 598
Johnson (W.) *Byways of British archaeology*, 804

Jorga (N.) *Breve storia dei Rumeni*, 183
—— *Les éléments originaux de l'ancienne civilisation roumaine*, 184

KALKEN (F. van) *Histoire du royaume des Pays-Bas et de la révolution Belge de 1830* : by G. B. Hertz, 384
Kelsey (C. E.) *Cheshire*, 415
Kennedy (P.) *History of the Great Moghuls*, ii, 403
Kern (F.) *Acta Imperii, Angliae et Franciae* [1267–1313], 187
Kimball (E.) *The public life of Joseph Dudley*, 196
King (Mrs. Hamilton) *Letters and recollections of Mazzini*, 613
Kingsford (C. L.) *The first English Life of King Henry the Fifth* : by Professor Tait, 556
Kittel (R.) *Die alttestamentliche Wissenschaft*, 2nd ed., 392
Koser (R.) *Friedrich der Grosse*, Volksausgabe, 607
Krauss (S.) *Talmudische Archäologie*, i, ii : by A. Cowley, 537

LACOUR-GAYET (G.) *La marine militaire de la France sous les règnes de Louis XIII et de Louis XIV*, i : by Miss C. Maxwell, 365
Lauer (P.) *Robert Ier et Raoul de Bourgogne*, 806
Lawrie (Sir A. C.) *Annals of Malcolm and William, kings of Scotland* [1153–1214] : by R. S. Rait, 142
Law tracts, Four thirteenth-century, ed. by G. E. Woodbine, 188
Legras (H.) *Le bourgage de Caen*, 622
Lehmann (P.) *Johannes Sichardus und die von ihm benutzten Bibliotheken und Handschriften* : by Professor Souter, 358
Lenz (M.) *Kleine historische Schriften*, 414
Leigh (W. A.) & Knight (M. G.) *Chawton Manor and its owners*, 829
Leodiensia, Testamenta [1539–46], 619
Leslie (major) *The Dickson MSS.*, Ser. C, 7, 824
Levine (L.) *The labour movement in France*, 828
Lowinski (J. S.) *L'évolution industrielle de la Belgique*, 200
Leycester, Robert Dudley, comte de, *Correspondance inédite de, et de François et Jean Hofman* : by Professor Pollard, 364
Lieblein (J.) *Recherches sur l'histoire et la civilisation de l'ancienne Égypte*, ii, 182

Lincoln, *Royal charters of the city of*, ed. by W. de G. Birch, 395
Lloyd (J. E.) *History of Wales to the Edwardian conquest*: by Professor Tout, 131
Lovat-Fraser (J. A.) *John Stuart, earl of Bute*, 822
Lowenthal (E.) *The Ricardian socialists*, 828
Lubimenko (Madame) *Les marchands anglais en Russie au XVI*ᵉ *siècle*, 402
Luchaire (A.) *Les communes françaises à l'époque des Capétiens directs*, ed. by L. Halphen, 597
Lulvès (J.) *Päpstliche Wahlkapitulationen and Die Machtbestrebungen des Kardinalats bis zur Aufstellung der ersten päpstlichen Wahlkapitulationen*: by the Rev. Professor Whitney, 547

McCormack (E. J.) *Colonial opposition to imperial authority during the French and Indian War*, 410
McGiffert (A. C.) *Martin Luther*, 817
Magdalen College, *The Pontifical of*, ed. by H. A. Wilson, 397
Mahler (Margaret) *Chirk castle and Chirkland*, 618
Marcks (E.) *Männer und Zeiten*, 616
Markham (Sir C.) *Early Spanish voyages to the Strait of Magellan*, 192
—— *The Book of the knowledge of all the kingdoms, lands, and lordships that are in the world*, 813
Marx (E.) *Bismarck und die Hohenzollernkandidatur*, 614
Massachusetts Historical Society, Proceedings of the, 410, 613
May (Sir T. E.) *Constitutional history of England*, edited and continued to 1911 by F. Holland: by Professor Pollard, 576
Mayor (J. E. B.) *Cambridge under queen Anne*, 605
Merores (Margarete) *Gaeta im frühen Mittelalter*, 392
Meyer (A. O.) *England und die katholische Kirche unter Elisabeth und den Stuarts*, i: by Professor Pollard, 159
Meyer (E.) *Der Papyrusfund von Elephantine*, 801
Mitra (S. M.) *Life and letters of Sir John Hall*, 199
Moffat (Mary M.) *Maria Theresa*, 197
Molesme, Cartulaires de l'abbaye de, ed. by J. Laurent, ii: by H. W. C. Davis, 765

Monluc (B. de) *Commentaires*, ed. by P. Courteault, 601
Morée, *Chronique de; Livre de la conqueste de la princée de l'Amorée* [1204–1305], ed. by J. Longnon: by W. Miller, 774
Müller (N.) *Die jüdische Katakombe am Monteverde zu Rom*, 804
Mullinger (J. B.) *The university of Cambridge*, iii: by C. C. J. Webb, 368
Murray (R. H.) *Revolutionary Ireland and its settlement*: by Professor Firth, 372

Napoléoniennes, Revue des études, i, 410
Nardin (L.) & Mauvaux (J.) *Histoire des corporations d'arts et métiers de Montbéliard*: by Professor Unwin, 775
Newcastle-upon-Tyne, The first duke and duchess of, 404
Nightingale (B.) *The ejected of 1662 in Cumberland and Westmorland*, 604
Notestein (W.) *History of witchcraft in England* [1558–1718], 603

O'Brien (H.) *Une charte brabançonne inédite de 1296 en faveur des marchands anglais*, 810
Ogg (D.) *Cardinal de Retz*, 820
Ollone, *Mission d'*, 1906–9; recherches sur les musulmans chinois: by Professor Parker, 798
Oman (C.) *History of the Peninsular War*, iv: by Colonel E. M. Lloyd, 382
Oppenheim (L.) *International Law*, i, 2nd ed., 414
Orpen (G. H.) *Ireland under the Normans* [1169–1216]: by Professor Tait, 144

Pascal (C.) *Le credenze d' oltretomba nelle opere letterarie dell' antichità classica*, 801
Pecham (Ioh.) *Tractatus tres de paupertate*, 399
Peet (T. E.) *The stone and bronze ages in Italy*: by the Rev. T. Nicklin, 337
Pérouse (G.) *Georges Chastellain*, 599
Peel (D.) *Das Erbbaurecht*, 393
Philip's New historical Atlas, 208
Piépape (général) *Histoire des princes de Condé au XVIII*ᵉ *siècle*, 405

INDEX TO THE TWENTY-SEVENTH VOLUME

Pimodan (comte de) *Le comte F.-C. de Mercy-Argenteau* : by J. H. Rose, 575

Pipe Roll, 29 Henry II, 809

Pirenne (H.) *Histoire de Belgique*, iv : by Professor Pollard, 362

Pisani (P.) *L'église de Paris et la Révolution*, iv : by L. G. Wickham Legg, 585

Pissard (H.) *La clameur de Haro dans le droit normand*, 596

Pollard (A. F.) *The political history of England* [1547-1603] : by the Rev. S. L. Ollard, 780

Poole (R. L.) *Léopold Delisle*, 414

Poole (Mrs. R. L.) *Catalogue of Oxford portraits*, i. 830

Porter (G. H.) *Ohio politics during the Civil War period*, 203

Porter (G. R.) *Progress of the nation*, ed. by F. W. Hirst, 827

Porter (R. P.) *The full recognition of Japan*, 413

Prentout (H.) *La Normandie*, 622

—— *Les origines et la fondation du duché de Normandie*, 394

Puff (A.) *Die Finanzen Albrechts des Beherzten*, 600

Quebec, *The king's book of*, 416

RADIGUET (L.) *L'acte additionnel aux constitutions de l'empire* [22 avr. 1815], 825

Rait (R. S.) *Scotland*, 595

Rambaud (J.) *Naples sous Joseph Bonaparte* [1806-8] : by H. C. Gutteridge, 381

Reeve (H. F.) *The Gambia*, 623

Richman (J. B.) *California under Spain and Mexico* [1535-1847], 624

Riker (T. W.) *Henry Fox, first lord Holland* : by B. Williams, 376

Robinson (F. H.) *The new history : essays illustrating the modern historical outlook*, 833

Robinson (F. P.) *The trade of the East India Company* [1709-1813], 606

Robinson (J. A.) *The abbot's house at Westminster*, 621

—— *Gilbert Crispin, abbot of Westminster* : by J. P. Gilson, 141

Rodocanachi (E.) *Rome au temps de Jules II et de Léon X*, 600

Rose (J. H.) *William Pitt and the Great War* : by C. T. Atkinson, 581

—— *Pitt and Napoleon* : by G. B. Hertz, 792

Rouergue, *Coutumes et privilèges du*, ed. by E. Baillaud and P. A. Verlaguet : by Miss E. C. Lodge, 147

Routh (Enid M. G.) *Tangier, England's last Atlantic outpost* [1661-84] : by Professor Firth, 573

Ruville (A. von) *La restauration de l'empire allemand ; le rôle de la Bavière* (French tr.), 412

Rye (W.) *Norfolk families*, i, 620

Sachsen Briefwechsel zwischen König Johann von, und den Königen Friedrich Wilhelm IV und Wilhelm I von Preussen, 826

Sahler (L.) *La fin d'un régime*, 607

Sainsbury (E. B.) *Calendar of court minutes of the East India Company* [1644-9], 406

Salter (H.) *Blowfield's survey of Oxford in 1772*, 830

Salutati (Coluccio) *Epistolario*, iv. 2, 815

Sandeman (G. A. C.) *Metternich*, 198

Sardes, *Greek inscriptions from*, ed. by W. H. Buckler and D. M. Robinson, i, 802

Savage (E. A.) *Old English libraries*, 390

Schaff (D.) *History of the Christian church*, v, 2, 189

Schiaparelli (L.) *I diplomi italiani di Lodovico III e di Rodolfo II*, 595

Schiffer (Zippora) *Markgraf Hubert Pallavicini*, 186

Schmidt (W.) *Die Partei Bethmann-Hollweg und die Reaktion in Preussen* [1850-8], 201

Schnitzer (J.) *Savonarola nach den Aufzeichnungen des Florentiners Piero Parenti* : by E. Armstrong, 351

Schulz (F.) *Die Hanse und England von Eduards III bis auf Heinrichs VIII Zeit*, 812

Schwemer (R.) *Geschichte der freien Stadt Frankfurt am Main* ,[1814-66], ii : by C. Brinkmann, 794

Scotland, *Accounts of the lord high treasurer of*, ed. by Sir J. B. Paul, ix : by R. S. Rait, 359

Sealy (Lucy) *Champions of the crown*, 404

Seeck (O.) *Geschichte des Untergangs der antiken Welt*, iv : by N. H. Baynes, 755

Seton-Watson (R. W.) *The southern Slav question and the Habsburg monarchy*, 204

Skalkowski (A.) *En marge de la correspondance de Napoléon I*, 411

Shirley (William) governor of Massachusetts and military commander in America, *Correspondence* [1731–60], ed. by C. H. Lincoln : by Professor Egerton, 785
Shute (John) *The first and chief grounds of architecture*, 818
Sieber (J.) *Zur Geschichte des Reichsmatrikelwesens*, 401
Sihler (E. G.) *Annals of Caesar*, 593
Smith (J. H.) *The annexation of Texas*, 612
Smith (R.) *Religious liberty under Charles II and James II*, 406
Soranzo (G.) *Pio II e la politica italiana nella lotta contro i Malatesti* : by K. H. Vickers, 563
Southampton, Charters of the borough of, ed. by H. W. Gidden : by H. W. C. Davis, 773
Staffordshire, Historical collections of (1911), 205
Statesman's year-book (1912), 618
Steinert (R.) *Das Territorium der Reichsstadt Mühlhausen*, i, 401
Stengel (E. E.) *Der Kaiser macht das Heer* : by H. W. C. Davis, 140
Stieda (W.) *Die Besteuerung des Tabaks in Ansbach-Bayreuth und Bamberg-Würzburg im 18. Jahrhundert*, 822
Stoeckius (P. H.) *Forschungen zur Lebensordnung der Gesellschaft Jesu im 16. Jahrhundert*, 602
Stout (S. E.) *The governors of Moesia*, 803
Swift (Jonathan) *Correspondence*, ed. by F. E. Ball, ii, 407

Tatham (G. B.) *Dr. John Walker and the 'Sufferings of the Clergy'*, 195
T'haqaishvili (E. S.) *Sakart'hvelos Sidzveleni*, 615
Tocco (F.) *La quistione della povertà nel secolo XIV*, 399
Tout (T. F.) *Flintshire, its history and its records*, 205
Town chronicles of England, Six, ed. by R. Flenley : by C. L. Kingsford, 151
Traube (L.) *Paläographische Forschungen*, v, and *Textgeschichte der Regula S. Benedicti*, 591
Travers (A.) *Armoricains et Bretons*, 594

Trevelyan (G. M.) *Garibaldi and the making of Italy* : by W. Miller, 173
Trevelyan (Sir G. O.) *George III and Charles Fox* : by Professor Egerton, 578
Trillek (Ioh. de) *Registrum*, 189, 811
Turner (E. R.) *The negro in Pennsylvania* [1639–1861], 623

Valin (L.) *Le duc de Normandie et sa cour* [912–1204] : by Professor Haskins, 138
Valois (N.) *La crise religieuse du XVe siècle* : by the Rev. Professor Whitney, 554
Vincent (J. M.) *Historical research*, 833
'Vota' (J.) *Der Untergang des Ordensstaates Preussen und die Entstehung der preussischen Königswürde* : by Professor Pollard, 779

Waddington (A.) *Histoire de Prusse*, i : by the Master of Peterhouse, Cambridge, 558
Waliszewski (K.) *Le fils de la grande Catherine, Paul Ier, empereur de Russie* : by N. Forbes, 791
Walther (A.) *Die Anfänge Karls V* : by E. Armstrong, 354
Ward (B.) *The eve of the catholic emancipation*, 609
Ward (J.) *The Roman era in Britain, and Romano-British buildings and earthworks*, 183
Ward (W. H.) *The architecture of the Renaissance in France* [1495–1830] : by Professor Lethaby, 353
Warren (C.) *History of the American bar*, 604
Weill (G.) *La France sous la monarchie constitutionnelle*, 824
Wicker (C. F.) *Neutralization*, 617
Williams (H.) *Christianity in early Britain* : by E. W. Brooks, 760
Woodward (Ida) *Five English consorts of foreign princes*, 192
Wroth (W.) *Catalogues of the coins of the Vandals, Ostrogoths, and Lombards* : by E. W. Brooks, 130

Yen (H. L.) *Survey of constitutional development in China*, 204

Zimmern (A. E.) *The Greek commonwealth* : by H. J. Cunningham, 533

LIST OF WRITERS

ALLEN, P. S., 557
Armstrong, Edward, 154, 167, 351, 354, 564
Atkinson, C. T., 172, 581

BARING, the Hon. F. H., 309, 513
Baynes, Norman H., 287, 755
Blakiston, the Rev. H. E. D., D.D., President of Trinity College, Oxford, 589
Brinkmann, C., 794
Brooks, E. W., 130, 760, 762
Brownbill, J., 625
Bullock, Professor T. L., 531

CANNON, Henry Lewin, 649
Carlyle, E. I., 251
Chance, J. F., 52, 483
Clark, Rev. Andrew, LL.D., 517
Cook, S. A., 336
Coolidge, the Rev. W. A. B., Ph.D., 522
Cowley, A., D.Litt., 537
Craster, H. H. E., 771
Crump, C. G., 226
Cunningham, H. J., 533

DAVIS, H. W. C., 140, 765, 773
Dibben, Miss L. B., 39
Dickins, F. Victor, C.B., 175

EGERTON, Professor H. E., 578, 785

FIRTH, Professor C. H., LL.D., Litt.D., 163, 372, 573
Fisher, H. A. L., 586
Forbes, Nevill, 791
Foster, W., 239
Frere, the Rev. W. H., D.D., 570

GILSON, J. P., 141
Goligher, Professor W. A., Litt.D., 339
Gooch, G. P., 124, 587
Graham, Miss Rose, 728
Grant, Professor W. L., 796
Gutteridge, H. C., 381

HASKINS, Professor C. H., 101, 138, 417
Hazeltine, Harold D., D.Jur., 345
Hertz, Gerald B., 384, 792
Hunt, the Rev. W., D.Litt., 378, 379

JOHNSON, C., 226
Jones, H. Stuart, 127, 340, 535

KINGSFORD, C. L., 151, 349, 462, 740

LEGG, L. G. Wickham, 585
Lethaby, Professor W. R., 353
Levison, Dr. W., 717
Little, A. G., 318
Lloyd, Colonel E. M., R.E., 382, 753
Lodge, Miss Eleanor C., 147

MAXWELL, Miss Constantia, 365
Meyer, Professor A. O., 567
Miller, William, 172, 774
Montague, Professor F. C., 169, 170
Murray, the Rev. Robert H., D.Litt., 783

NICKLIN, the Rev. T., 337

OLLARD, the Rev. Canon S. L., 780
Orton, C. W. Previté, 135

PARKER, Professor E. H., 798
Parker, the late F. H. M., 26
Pirie-Gordon, H., 445
Pollard, Professor A. F., Litt.D., 153, 157, 159, 362, 364, 572, 576, 779
Poole, Reginald L., LL.D., 299, 515
Powicke, Professor F. M., 106

RAIT, R. S., 142, 359
Reade, W. H. V., 150
Reddaway, W. F., 274
Rose, J. Holland, Litt.D., 117, 324, 573, 700, 788
Round, J. H., LL.D., 544
Rushforth, G. McN., 538, 777

SCOFIELD, Miss Cora L., 321
Scott, Charles N., 330
Scott, Miss Eva, 369
Seton-Watson, R. W., D.Litt., 385
Smith, Miss L. M., 96
Smith, Preserved, 671
Souter, Professor A., Litt.D., 358
Stenton, Professor F. M., 512
Stevenson, W. H., 1

TAIT, Professor James, 144, 556, 720
Tatham, G. B., 161, 370

Temperley, H. W. V., 682
Tout, Professor T. F., 131, 345, 553
Turner, G. J., 209

UNWIN, Professor George, 178, 360, 549, 775

VICKERS, K. H., 563

WALLIS, J. E. W., 388

Ward, A. W., LL.D., Litt.D., Master of Peterhouse, Cambridge, 558
Webb, C. C. J., 368
Webster, C. K., 78
Whitney, the Rev. Professor J. P., 547, 554, 568
Williams, Basil, 376
Winstanley, D. A., 376
Wood, W. B., 797
Woodward, W. H., 177

VOL. XXVII. No. 108, October, 1912

THE ENGLISH
HISTORICAL REVIEW

EDITED BY

REGINALD L. POOLE, M.A., LL.D.

KEEPER OF THE ARCHIVES OF THE UNIVERSITY OF OXFORD AND FELLOW OF MAGDALEN COLLEGE

CONTENTS

Articles   PAGE

The Tribal Hidage. By J. Brownbill 625
The Battle of Sandwich and Eustace the Monk. By Henry Lewin Cannon 649
German Opinion of the Divorce of Henry VIII. By Preserved Smith 671
Inner and Outer Cabinet and Privy Council, 1679–1783. By H. W. V. Temperley 682
Burke, Windham, and Pitt. By J. Holland Rose, Litt.D. . . 700

Notes and Documents

A Report on the Penenden Trial. By Dr. W. Levison . . . 717
Studies in Magna Carta. I. Waynagium and Contenementum. By Professor James Tait 720
A Papal Visitation of Bury St. Edmunds and Westminster in 1234. By Miss Rose Graham 728
Extracts from the First Version of Hardyng's Chronicle. By C. L. Kingsford 740
The Anglo-French Peace Negotiations of 1806. By Colonel E. M. Lloyd, R.E. 753

Reviews of Books (see List on next page) 755

Short Notices (see List on next page) 801

Index 834

TO BE CONTINUED QUARTERLY

LONGMANS, GREEN, AND CO.
39 PATERNOSTER ROW, LONDON
NEW YORK, BOMBAY, AND CALCUTTA

Price Five Shillings per number, or 22/- per year post free   *All Rights Reserved*

REVIEWS OF BOOKS

Seeck, *Geschichte des Untergangs der antiken Welt*, iv : by Norman H. Baynes . 755
Williams, *Christianity in Early Britain* : by E. W. Brooks 760
Bury, *A History of the Eastern Roman Empire* [802–67] : by E. W. Brooks . 762
Cartulaires de l'Abbaye de Molesme, ed. Laurent, ii : by H. W. C. Davis . 765
Clemesha, *A History of Preston in Amounderness* : by H. H. E. Craster . 771
Charters of the Borough of Southampton : by H. W. C. Davis . . . 773
Livre de la Conqueste de la Princée de l'Amorée, ed. J. Longnon : by William Miller . 774
Buchon, *Voyage dans l'Eubée* : by William Miller 774
Nardin & Mauveaux, *Histoire des Corporations d'Arts et Métiers de Montbéliard* : by Professor G. Unwin . . 775
John Capgrave, *Ye Solace of Pilgrimes*, ed. Mills : by G. McN. Rushforth . 777
Vota, *Der Untergang des Ordensstaates Preussen und die Entstehung der preussischen Königswürde* : by Professor A. F. Pollard, Litt.D. 779
Pollard, *Political History of England, 1547–1603* : by the Rev. Canon Ollard . 780
Lady Burghclere, *Life of James, First Duke of Ormonde* : by the Rev. R. H. Murray, Litt.D. 783
William Shirley, *Correspondence, 1731–60* : by Professor H. E. Egerton . 785
Guyot, *Le Directoire et la Paix de l'Europe* : by J. Holland Rose, Litt.D. . 788
Waliszewski, *Paul I*, Empereur de Russie*, 2nd ed. : by Nevill Forbes . 791
Rose, *Pitt and Napoleon* : by G. B. Hertz 792
Wahl, *Geschichte des Europäischen Staatensystems im Zeitalter der Französischen Revolution* : by G. B. Hertz . 792
Schwemer, *Geschichte der freien Stadt Frankfurt a. M.*, ii : by C. Brinkmann . 794
Lord Durham's Report on the Affairs of British North America, ed. Lucas : by Professor W. L. Grant . . 796
Bapst, *Le Maréchal Canrobert*, v : by W. B. Wood 797
Mission d'Ollone, 1906–9 : by Professor E. H. Parker 798

SHORT NOTICES

E. Meyer, *Der Papyrusfund von Elephantine* 801
Pascal, *Le Credenze d' Oltretomba nelle Opere letterarie dell' Antichità classica* . 801
Buckler & Robinson, *Greek Inscriptions from Sardes*, i 802
Stout, *The Governors of Moesia* . . 803
Creusen, *Tabulae Fontium Traditionis Christianae* 803
Müller, *Die jüdische Katakombe am Monteverde zu Rom* 804
Johnson, *Byways of British Archaeology* . 804
Mrs. J. R. Green, *The Old Irish World* . 804
Beck, *Der Karlsgraben* . . . 806
Lauer, *Robert I*er et Raoul de Bourgogne* . 806
Adams, *The Origin of the English Constitution* 807
Bagshawe, *History of the Royal Family of England* 808
Jahncke, *Gulielmus Neubrigensis* . . 808
The Great Roll of the Pipe for 1182–3 . 809
Franciscan Essays 810
Obreen, *Une Charte Brabançonne inédite de 1296* 810
Lettres de Jean XXII, ii. 2, ed. Fayen . 811
Registrum Iohannis de Trillek episcopi Herefordensis, ii 811
Schulz, *Die Hanse und England* . . 812
The Book of the Knowledge of all the Kingdoms in the World, tr. Markham . . 813
Häpke, *Der Deutsche Kaufmann in den Niederlanden* 814
Coluccio Salutati, *Epistolario di*, iv. 2 . 815
Horsburgh, *Girolamo Savonarola* (4th ed.) . 815
Gasquet, *Abbot Wallingford* . . 816
Jenkins, *Ibrahim Pasha* . . . 817
McGiffert, *Martin Luther* . . . 817
Bratli, *Philippe II* 818
John Shute, *The First and Chief Groundes of Architecture* 818
Constantijn Huygens, *Briefwisseling*, i . 818
Abel Eppens tho Equart, *Kroniek* . . 818
Bastide, *Anglais et Français du XVIIe siècle* 819
Elder, *The Royal Fishery Companies of the Seventeenth Century* . . . 819
Ogg, *Cardinal de Retz* . . . 820
Foster, *The English Factories in India, 1637–41* 820
Green, *Lectures on the Puritan Revolution* (new ed.) 821
Abbott, *Colonel Thomas Blood* . . 821
Stieda, *Die Besteuerung des Tabaks in Ansbach-Bayreuth und Bamberg-Würzburg* 822
Lovat-Fraser, *John Stuart, Earl of Bute* . 822
Askenazy, *Fürst Joseph Poniatowski* (Germ. tr.) 822
Marquis de Bouillé, *Souvenirs et Fragments*, iii 823
Leslie, *The Dickson MSS.*, C. vii. . 824
Weill, *La France sous la Monarchie constitutionnelle* 824
Radiguet, *Acte Additionnel aux Constitutions de l'Empire du 22 Avril 1815* . 825
Browning, *History of the Modern World, 1815–1912* 825
Briefwechsel zwischen König Johann von Sachsen und den Königen Friedrich Wilhelm IV und Wilhelm I von Preussen 826
Cannan, *History of Local Rates in England* (new ed.) 827
Porter, *Progress of the Nation* (new ed.) . 827
E. Lowenthal, *The Ricardian Socialists* . 828
Levine, *The Labour Movement in France* . 828
Austen Leigh & Knight, *Chawton Manor and its Owners* 829
Clark, *English Register of Godstow Nunnery* 829
Mrs. Poole, *Catalogue of Oxford Portraits*, i 830
Salter, *Blowfield's Survey of Oxford* . 830
Evans, *The Church Plate of Radnorshire* . 831
Annales d'Avignon et du Comtat-Venaissin, i. 1 832
Gadave, *Les Documents sur l'Histoire de l'Université de Toulouse* . . 832
Havenith, *La Zélande* . . . 832
Vincent, *Historical Research* . . 833

N.B.—The Editor's address is now The Museum House, Oxford.

THE GREAT ANNUAL SALE OF BOOKS

AT

The Times Book Club

Will COMMENCE on Thursday, October 10th, and Close on Thursday, October 31st, 1912

AN ENORMOUS NUMBER OF

Popular Books (English and Foreign)

both New and Secondhand, in all classes of literature

WILL BE OFFERED AT REDUCTIONS OF

33% to 80%

FROM THE PUBLISHED PRICES

Free Delivery within the United Kingdom of all parcels of Books selected from the Sale Catalogues

---

Bookbuyers should write at once for the Catalogues (Miscellaneous and Fiction) to ensure getting early copies, as orders will be dealt with in rotation.

The Times Book Club
376 to 384 OXFORD STREET, LONDON, W.
THE LARGEST BOOKSHOP IN THE WORLD

Messrs. BELL'S LIS

NEW BOOK BY DR. J. HOLLAND ROSE.

The Personality of Napoleon.

Being the Lowell Lectures delivered at Boston, February–March, 1
By J. HOLLAND ROSE, Litt.D., Reader in Modern History, The Un
sity of Cambridge. **6s. net.** (Ready Oct. 16.)

RECENT WORKS BY DR. ROSE.

The Life of William Pitt.
Vol. I. William Pitt and National Revival.
Vol. II. William Pitt and the Great War.

With Photogravure Plates. **16s. net each.**

'As thorough a piece of work as one can desire. . . . A fine piece of modern historical wr
in its research, its guise of evidence, and its neutrality. It is also a first-rate piece of controv
excellently distinguishing between the balance of witnesses when their statements are coml
and the acceptation of evidence from one witness or from another.'—Mr. HILAIRE BELL
The Academy.

Pitt and Napoleon: Essays and Letters Supplementa
to the 'Life of William Pitt'. **10s. 6d. net.**

'This book in reality forms the third volume of Dr. Holland Rose's "Life of Pitt." In it
and important light is thrown on many points which arise both in "William Pitt and Nati
Revival" and "William Pitt and the Great War". Taken together these three volumes ma
regarded as the standard biography of the patriotic statesman whose untiring exertions brou
about the Union between England and Ireland. . . . One of the most important historical w
which has appeared since the commencement of the present century.'—*Outlook.*

The Correspondence of Jonathan Swi

Edited by F. ELRINGTON BALL, Litt.D. With an Introduction by
Right Rev. the BISHOP OF OSSORY. To be completed in 6 vols., de
8vo. **10s. 6d. net each.**

Vol. IV. READY IMMEDIATELY. Vols. I, II, and III already published.

'One of the best annotated editions of any author that we know. The notes are a treasur
information on all points. . . . In short, we have here for the first time the promise of a comp
edition of Swift's Correspondence, both to and from, arranged in chronological order, pri
from the purest texts, and annotated with a learning and accuracy that cannot be surpassed.'
Athenaeum

A Chronicle of the Popes from St. Peter
Pius X. By A. E. McKILLIAM, M.A. **7s. 6d. net.**

'The author is deserving of praise for the thoroughness of his achievement. He has done w
he set out to do. All the great historians of the Papacy have been laid under contribution;
the work, including the index, is scholarly in detail. It is excellently printed.'—*Daily News*

'It is too much to expect that such a summary should be not only without bias, but also w
out mistakes; yet Mr. McKilliam has avoided both as far as human nature may.'—*Athenaeu*

G. BELL & SONS, Ltd., Portugal Street, Kingsway, London, W.C

HORACE HART, PRINTER TO THE UNIVERSITY OF OXFORD